AN AMERICAN DILEMMA

NOTE

The footnotes to Volume II appear immediately following page 1180 of the Text, and are folioed as in the original one-volume edition, as pages 1335 through 1439. The footnotes to Volume I appear in Volume I, also with the original pagination.

AN
AMERICAN
DILEMMA

The Negro Problem and Modern Democracy

Volume II

GUNNAR MYRDAL

WITH THE ASSISTANCE OF

RICHARD STERNER

AND

ARNOLD ROSE

HARPER TORCHBOOKS
Harper & Row, Publishers
New York, Evanston, and London

This study was made possible by funds granted by Carnegie Corporation of New York. That corporation is not, however, the author, owner, publisher, or proprietor of this publication, and is not to be understood as approving by virtue of its grant any of the statements made or views expressed therein.

AN AMERICAN DILEMMA: *Volume II*

First HARPER TORCHBOOK edition published in two volumes in 1969 by
Harper & Row, Publishers, Incorporated,
New York, N.Y. 10016.

LIBRARY OF CONGRESS CATALOG CARD NUMBER: 62-19706.

CONTENTS

Volume II

PART X.   THE NEGRO COMMUNITY

PART XI.   AN AMERICAN DILEMMA

LIST OF TABLES

Volume II

Part VI

JUSTICE

CHAPTER 24

INEQUALITY OF JUSTICE

1. DEMOCRACY AND JUSTICE

The American tradition of electing, rather than appointing, minor public officials[a] has its most serious features in regard to the judiciary branch of the government. Judges, prosecuting attorneys, minor court officials, sheriffs, the chiefs of police, and, in smaller communities, sometimes the entire police force,[1] are either elected for limited terms or are dependent for their offices upon political representatives of this uncertain tenure. In some places they can even be "recalled" during their terms of office, though this is comparatively rare.

The immediate dependence of court and police officials upon popular election—that is, upon local public opinion and political machines—instead of upon appointment strictly according to merit, and the uncertainty of tenure implied in this system naturally decreases the attractiveness of these important positions to many of the best persons who would otherwise be available. Professional standards are thus kept lower than those which could be attained under another system. The courts do not get the cream of the legal profession. The social prestige of judges in local courts is not as supreme as could be wished. Corruption and undue political influences are not absent even from the courtrooms. These facts themselves have the circular effect of keeping the best men from judicial positions.

But, apart from such general effects, the fact that the administration of justice is dependent upon the local voters is likely to imply discrimination against an unpopular minority group, particularly when this group is disfranchised as Negroes are in the South. The elected judge knows that sooner or later he must come back to the polls, and that a decision running counter to local opinion may cost him his position. He may be conscious of it or not, but this control of his future career must tend to increase his difficulties in keeping aloof from local prejudices and emotions. Of course, the judge's attitudes are also formed by conditions prevalent in his local community, but he has a degree of acquaintance with the law, and with public and legal opinion outside his community. This would tend to

[a] This tradition was referred to in Chapter 20, Section 2, as a main reason why the vote, or the lack of the vote, is of such paramount importance for the Negro people.

emancipate him from local opinion were it not for his direct dependence on it.[a]

The dependence of the judge on local prejudices strikes at the very root of orderly government. It results in the danger of breaking down the law in its primary function of protecting the minority against the majority, the individual against society, indeed, of democracy itself against the danger of its nullifying, in practice, the settled principles of law and impartiality of justice. This danger is higher in the problem regions where there is acute race friction and in rural areas where the population is small and provincial, and where personal contacts are direct. Under the same influences as the judges are the public prosecutors, the sheriffs, the chiefs of police and their subordinates. The American jury system, while it has many merits, is likely to strengthen this dependence of justice upon local popular opinion. If, as in the South, Negroes are kept out of jury service, the democratic safeguard of the jury system is easily turned into a means of minority subjugation.

The popular election of the officers of law and the jury system are expressions of the extreme democracy in the American handling of justice. It might, in spite of the dangers suggested, work excellently in a reasonably homogeneous, highly educated and public spirited community. It might also work fairly well anywhere for cases involving only parties belonging to a homogeneous majority group which controls the court. It causes, however, the gravest peril of injustice in all cases where the rights of persons belonging to a disfranchised group are involved, particularly if this group is discriminated against all around and by tradition held as a lower caste upon whose rights it has become customary to infringe. *The extreme democracy in the American system of justice turns out, thus, to be the greatest menace to legal democracy when it is based on restricted political participation and an ingrained tradition of caste suppression.* Such conditions occur in the South with respect to Negroes.

If there is a deficiency of legal protection for Negroes, white people will be tempted to deal unfairly with them in everyday affairs. They will be tempted to use irregular methods to safeguard what they feel to be their interests against Negroes. They will be inclined to use intimidation and even violence against Negroes if they can count on going unpunished. When such patterns become established, the law itself and its processes are brought into contempt, and a general feeling of uncertainty, arbitrariness and inequality will spread. Not only Negroes but other persons of weak social status will be the object of discrimination. "When an exception to the rule

---

[a] A shift from election to appointment of court and police officials would also be expected to increase efficiency, reduce corruption and raise the level of the persons appointed. This would tend to occur if appointments were made under the civil service system and generally even if the higher appointments were made directly by the governor of the state.

of justice is allowed the structure of the legal machinery is damaged, and may and does permit exceptions in cases which do not involve Negroes," observes Charles Johnson.[2] In the South there have been frequent occasions when the legal rights of poor white persons have been disregarded, and even when general lawlessness prevailed. When the frequency of law-breaking thus increases, it becomes necessary to apply stronger penalties than is necessary in an equitable system of justice. In all spheres of public life it will, of course, be found that legislation is relatively ineffective, and so the sociologists will be inclined to formulate a general societal law of "the futility of trying to suppress folkways by stateways." Lawlessness has then received the badge of scientific normalcy.

The Negroes, on their side, are hurt in their trust that the law is impartial, that the court and the police are their protection, and, indeed, that they belong to an orderly society which has set up this machinery for common security and welfare. They will not feel confidence in, and loyalty toward, a legal order which is entirely out of their control and which they sense to be inequitable and merely part of the system of caste suppression. Solidarity then develops easily in the Negro group, a solidarity against the law and the police. The arrested Negro often acquires the prestige of a victim, a martyr, or a hero, even when he is simply a criminal. It becomes part of race pride in the protective Negro community not to give up a fellow Negro who is hunted by the police. Negroes who collaborate with the police become looked upon as stool pigeons.

No one visiting Negro communities in the South can avoid observing the prevalence of these views. The situation is dynamic for several reasons. One is the growing urbanization and the increasing segregation of the Negro people. The old-time paternalistic and personal relationship between individuals of the two groups is on the decrease. Another factor is the improvement of Negro education which is continually making Negroes more aware of their anomalous status in the American legal order. A third factor, the importance of which is increasing in pace with the literacy of the Negro people, is the persistent hammering of the Negro press which, to a large extent, is devoted to giving publicity to the injustices and injuries suffered by Negroes. A fourth factor is unemployment, especially of young Negroes, with resulting insecurity and dissatisfaction.

Because of these changes, as Du Bois tells us, ". . . the Negro is coming *more and more* to look upon law and justice, not as protecting safeguards, but as sources of humiliation and oppression."[3] He expresses a common attitude among Southern Negroes when he continues: "The laws are made by men who have absolutely no motive for treating the black people with courtesy or consideration: . . . the accused law-breaker is tried, not by his peers, but too often by men who would rather punish ten innocent

Negroes than let one guilty one escape." To the present observer the situation looks far from peaceful and quiet, as white people in the South have tried to convince him. It has rather the appearance of a fateful race between, on the one hand, the above-mentioned tendencies which increase Negro mistrust, unrest, and asociality, and, on the other, the equally apparent tendency for the white group increasingly to be prepared to give the Negro personal security and equality before the law.

The literature is replete with statements that point to the Negro's restlessness and the need of giving him legal justice.[4] The representatives of the tradition of lawlessness do not write books even if they still, in many places, dominate practice.[a] We shall have to try to understand them in their historical setting from their actual behavior.

Having accepted the American Creed as our value premise in this study, we must also accept a corollary of this Creed for the purposes of this part, namely, that *Negroes are entitled to justice equally with all other people.* This principle has constitutional sanction and is held supreme in the legislation of all states in the Union. In this part we do not discuss inequalities *in law* or the results of the inequitable administration of the laws: all these material inequalities in legal status of the American Negro are dealt with in other parts of our inquiry. The subject of the discussion here is only the actual handling of justice, the manner in which inequalities in the enforcement of the laws against whites and Negroes are entering into the judicial procedures, and also such lacks in personal security of Negroes concomitant with those inequalities.

2. RELATIVE EQUALITY IN THE NORTH

There are deficiencies in the working of the machinery of the law in the North too. American justice is everywhere expensive and depends too much upon the skill of the attorney. The poor man has difficulty in securing his rights. Judges and police officers are not free from prejudices against people of lower economic and cultural levels. Experienced white and Negro lawyers have told the author that in criminal cases where only Negroes are involved there is sometimes a disposition on the part of the prosecutors, judges and juries to treat offenses with relative lightness. In matters involving offenses by Negroes against whites, Negroes will often find the presumptions of the courts against them, and there is a tendency to sentence them to a higher penalty than if they had committed the same offense against Negroes. Instances have been related to me in which Negro witnesses have been made the butt of jests and horseplay. I have, however, received

---

[a] One reason for this is that these persons are usually aware that their practice is inconsistent with their best ideals. Another reason is that such a disproportionately large part of the intellectuals of the region are liberals. (See Chapter 21, Section 5.)

the general impression that such differential treatment of witnesses is rather the exception than the rule, and that it will practically never happen to a Negro plaintiff or defendant who is assisted by good counsel.[5]

A more serious matter is the treatment of Negroes by the police. In most Northern communities Negroes are more likely than whites to be arrested under any suspicious circumstances. They are more likely to be accorded discourteous or brutal treatment at the hands of the police than are whites. The rate of killing of Negroes by the police is high in many Northern cities, particularly in Detroit.[a] Negroes have a seriously high criminality record,[b] and the average white policeman is inclined to increase it even more in his imagination. The Negroes are, however, not the only sufferers, even if they, as usual, reap more than their fair share. Complaints about indiscriminate arrests and police brutality are raised also by other economically disadvantaged and culturally submerged groups in the Northern cities. The attitudes of the police will sometimes be found among the most important items considered in local Negro politics in the North. Usually there is much less complaint about not getting a fair trial before the courts.

Another form of discrimination in the North against Negroes is in the market for houses and apartments; whites try to keep Negroes out of white neighborhoods by restrictive covenants. The legality of these covenants is open to dispute, but in so far as the local courts uphold them, the discrimination is in the legal principle, not in the individual cases brought to court.[c] In some Northern cities—as, for instance, Detroit—I have heard complaints that the police will sometimes try to restrict Negroes to the Negro districts, particularly at night. There have been bombings against Negroes who tried to invade white territory and even race riots, particularly in the wake of the sudden migration of great masses of rural Negroes from the South during and immediately after the First World War.[6] The police have not always been strictly impartial during such incidents.[7] But the courts have usually not shielded the white transgressors afterwards in the way which has become a pattern in the South.

Vigilantism occasionally occurs in the North. The Western frontier formerly saw much of it, but manifestations of it are rare now. During the 1920's the Ku Klux Klan operated in Indiana, Illinois, Michigan, and other Northern states almost as much as it did in the South. Immigrant sections of a few Northern cities occasionally witness such activities (e.g., the "Black Hand" society in Italian areas and the Tong wars in Chinese sections). Occasionally vigilantism of the Southern type will still occur in the North:

[a] See Chapter 27, Section 5.
[b] See Chapter 44, Section 2.
[c] See Chapter 29, Section 4.

On the night of August 11, 1939, seven Negro migratory workers including one woman were routed out of their sleep in an isolated one-room shack on a farm near Cranbury, New Jersey, by a mob of white men with handkerchief masks and guns. All seven were stripped naked, their hands tied and they were told to start across a field. The five single men escaped into the bushes, shots fired after them going over their heads. Jake and Frances Preston, the married couple, were threatened with mutilation and rape, were beaten with a rubber hose, had white enamel poured over them and were told to "head South."

Many believed prominent local citizens had instigated the attack. Local workers were aroused; migrants threatened to leave. Local farmers feared the loss of their laborers. The Workers Defense League offered a $100 reward for information leading to the arrest and conviction of the assailants. After two weeks the state police made ten arrests, one a minor. At first freed on $250 bail the nine self-confessed adult assailants were later given suspended sentences of three to five years. But intimidation of Negroes persisted. So civil suits were then instituted and on May 10, 1940, the Federal District Court of Newark awarded the Prestons damages of $2,000 each, and the other five $1,000 each.[8]

In many Northern cities Negroes relate that they find it difficult to get the courts to punish violations of the civil rights laws; for example, when Negroes are not permitted in certain restaurants and hotels. In such cases it is often difficult to obtain proofs which substantiate the charges, but this does not explain satisfactorily why those laws have as yet so largely remained paper decrees. In the over-all balance, however, infringements of Negro rights that are supposed to be prevented by the civil rights laws are of comparatively little importance.

There are, in many Northern places, Negro judges, Negro court officers and Negro policemen. Commonly there are Negroes on the jury lists. The large majority of all Negro lawyers find it to their advantage to practice in the North.[9] They generally plead cases before the courts and are not, like most of their Southern colleagues, restricted to trying to settle things outside of court. They occasionally have white people among their clientele. Negro lawyers in the North do not generally complain of being treated differently in court from their white colleagues or of meeting prejudice from the juries.[10]

Since, on the whole, Negroes do not meet much more discrimination from officers of the law than do white persons of the same economic and cultural level, *there is in the North no special problem of getting justice for Negroes, outside the general one of improving the working of the machinery of the law for the equal protection of the rights of poor and uneducated people.* The further reservation should be added that Negroes in Border cities—for instance, in Washington and St. Louis—meet relatively more prejudice both from the police and from the courts,[11] and the same thing holds for a city like Detroit which has a large population of white immigrants from the South.[a] In a comparable way, the Upper South is considerably more like the North in this respect than is the Lower South.

Part of the explanation of why the Negro gets more legal justice in the North is the fact that Negroes can vote in the North and, consequently, have a share in the ultimate control of the legal system. Nevertheless, the importance of political participation as a cause of equality before the law should not be exaggerated. The lack of discrimination in both respects has a common cause in a general inclination of white people in the North to regard Negroes as full citizens in their formal relations with public authority, even if not in economic competition or social intercourse. This is one point where the ordinary Northerner is unfailingly faithful to the American Creed. He wants justice to be impartial, regardless of race, creed or color.

The North is further removed from the memories of slavery, and its equalitarian philosophy became more rigorously formulated in the prolonged conflict with the South during and after the Civil War. Also, Northern Negroes are concentrated in big cities, where human relations are formalized and where Negroes are a small minority of the total population. The legal machinery in those cities might sometimes be tainted by the corruption of the city administration, but its size alone tends to objectify its operations and prevent its being influenced by the narrowest type of local prejudice. Other reasons would seem to be that Northern Negroes are better educated and have a higher economic status on the average, that Northern Negroes can be and are more inclined to stand up for their rights, and that most organizations fighting for the Negro have their headquarters in the North. Whatever the reasons, it seems to be a fact that *there is a sharp division between North and South in the granting of legal justice to Negroes.* In the North, for the most part, Negroes enjoy equitable justice.

3. THE SOUTHERN HERITAGE

Because the main problems of justice for the Negro are found in the South, this part of the book will deal almost exclusively with the South. *The difference in feeling of personal security between Negroes in the two regions is most striking to an observer. The Southern Negro seems to suspect a possible danger to himself or to other Negroes whenever a white stranger approaches him.* When you ask him where somebody lives, he will be slow and careful in giving information. When you knock at his door, particularly after dark, you will often see fear in his eyes until he comes to know your innocent intentions. It is not true, as is often maintained in the

[a] Detroit also seems to have a larger number of Southern-born policemen than most other Northern cities. In the recent clashes there between the police and the Negroes, many of the police were whites from Kentucky and Tennessee.

South, that this is his reaction only to strangers. I have often witnessed this undercurrent of fear and uncertainty in various undefined situations even when one or more of the white persons participating were personally known to the Negroes or were recognized by their dialect as having a Southern origin. The Northern Negro, in general, appears different in this respect. His self-assurance in behavior often seems preposterous or obstreperous to the Southern white man who has become accustomed to the submissive and guarded manners of the Southern Negro.

The reason for this, as we shall see, is that in the South the Negro's person and property are practically subject to the whim of any white person who wishes to take advantage of him or to punish him for any real or fancied wrongdoing or "insult." A white man can steal from or maltreat a Negro in almost any way without fear of reprisal, because the Negro cannot claim the protection of the police or courts, and personal vengeance on the part of the offended Negro usually results in organized retaliation in the form of bodily injury (including lynching), home burning or banishment. Practically the only check on white maltreatment of Negroes is a rather vague and unformulated feeling on the part of Southern public opinion that a white man should not be "mean" to a Negro except when he "deserves" it. But unless the white man acquires a reputation for being mean and unjust, his occasional violation of a Negro's legal rights is felt to be justified or—at most—"his own business."

The large element of chance and arbitrariness should be emphasized in a discussion of lawlessness in the South. Physical violence and threats against personal security do not, of course, occur to every Negro every day. Some Southern Negroes can probably go through life with only half a dozen "incidents." But violence *may* occur at any time, and it is the fear of it as much as violence itself which creates the injustice and the insecurity. The chance nature of the violence is illustrated by the fact that a nonconforming Northern Negro known to the author spent five years in the South without any trouble, while another Northern Negro, who went South with a determination to comply with all rules so as to avoid difficulty, met violence within a week.

When trying to understand the Southern situation as to law enforcement and the Negro's personal security, it is necessary to examine the historical heritage of the region. Under slavery the Negro was owned, bought, and sold as property; he was worked, housed, fed, and prevented from doing what he wished if it was contrary to the interests of his master. In general, the Negro slave had no "rights" which his owner was bound to respect.[a] Even if in legal theory the slave was given the status of a person under

---

[a] The North had a small amount of slavery in the early days of the nation, but it was restricted and was abolished by the first years of the nineteenth century. Its tradition was completely annihilated by the anti-slavery sentiment before and during the Civil War.

the law as well as the status of property, it was the latter viewpoint which, in practice, became the determining one. In the very relationship between master and slave it was inherent that—without recourse to courts—force and bodily punishment and, under certain circumstances, even the killing of the slave was allowed. ". . . all slaveholders are under the shield of a perpetual license to murder," exclaimed Hinton R. Helper in his unsparing onslaught on the plantation class and the slavery institution.[12] Thomas Jefferson saw clearly the moral danger of the slavery institution:

> The whole commerce between master and slave is a perpetual exercise of the most boisterous passions, the most unremitting despotism on the one part, and degrading submissions on the other. Our children see this, and learn to imitate it. . . . The man must be a prodigy who can retain his manners and morals undepraved by such circumstances. And with what execration should the statesman be loaded, who, permitting one half the citizens to trample on the rights of the other, transforming those into despots, and these into enemies, destroys the morals of one part, and the *amor patriae* of the other. . . . [Can] the liberties of a nation be thought secure when we have removed their only firm basis, a conviction in the minds of the people that these liberties are the gift of God? That they are not to be violated but with His wrath? Indeed, I tremble for my country when I reflect that God is just; that His justice cannot sleep forever."[13]

Most states, however, inaugurated statutes to protect the slave from unnecessary sufferings.[14] The master was obliged to provide food, clothing, and shelter, and to treat his slaves humanly. To the extent that these regulations were not sanctioned by the master's own economic interests and his feelings for his human property or by community sentiment, they seem not to have been enforced. The slave could generally not testify against a white man, and the white community was too much in collusion to permit the vindication of the slave's rights against his master. Considering the intensive criticisms of slavery laws and of the treatment of slaves which emanated from Abolitionist circles in the North—there are several learned treatises in the 'forties and 'fifties supporting the popular propaganda[15]— it is perhaps surprising that the Southern states did not build up a defense for their peculiar institution by legislating modernized slave codes, legalizing the humanized views which were expressed in the apologetic literature on slavery and, without doubt, even acted upon most of the time by the majority of slave owners.[16]

Most of the laws relating to the slavery institution were, instead, aimed at regulating in detail the behavior of the slaves, forbidding them to possess or carry weapons, to resist white persons, to assemble in the absence of whites, to leave the plantation without permission. Even those regulations seem not to have been enforced with too much rigidity as it was commonly left to the slave master, in whose interest they were enacted, to supervise his own slaves as he wished. Since all whites enjoyed a superior status, and since the assumption was upheld that they all shared the responsibility of keeping the Negroes in a lower status, they were given much the same unrestricted powers against the Negroes as the master, except in so far as these powers clashed with his property interests. A slave was not allowed to defend himself against any white man and if the slave were killed, it was considered as a property damage rather than murder and could be absolved by paying a fine.[17]

In this legal system, which was an outgrowth of slavery as an institution, the emergence of the free Negroes introduced an obvious anomaly which became more striking as slavery came more and more to be founded upon racial beliefs.[a] Under the constant fear of slave insurrection,[18] not only were restricting regulations of slave behavior continually elaborated, but the liberties and rights of free Negroes were severely limited.[19] This development is of particular importance for the legal status of the freedmen after Emancipation, as the nearest analogy was the *ante-bellum* status of free Negroes. Another tradition important for the future development was the function of the police. The police system in the South to a great extent served the explicit purpose of supervising Negro slaves and free Negroes and of hindering the former from escape. They were given the widest license to seize, whip and punish Negroes and generally to act as the agents of the masters. The police in the South were, by tradition, watchdogs of all Negroes, slave or free, criminal or innocent.

The psychic pressure upon white society of the slavery system and of the various devices necessary to uphold it against rebellious Negroes, envious poor whites, Northern Abolitionists, and world opinion, must have been intense. The South remained an unstable frontier civilization,[b] where the law was distant and wavering and human life was cheap. "Lynch law is essentially a fruit of frontier conditions with population sparse, officials few, amateurish, and easy-going, and legal machinery consequently inadequate," remarks Schrieke, and continues: "That it prevailed in the ante-bellum South to a degree comparable at all to that in the mining camps was doubtless due to the thinness of settlement and the occasional hysteria over rapes and rumors of revolts by Negroes."[20] But, in addition, the slavery system itself—and more particularly the right it gave and the custom it nurtured to punish bodily other adult human beings—must have conditioned people to violent and arbitrary behavior patterns. Probably more whites than Negroes were killed in the South during the three decades following Andrew Jackson's first administration, which generally is recognized as marking a beginning of increased tension and spreading violence in the South.[21] The Negro slaves had a protection, which the white men did not have, in their value as property.[22]

[a] See Chapter 4.
[b] See Chapter 20.

With these traditions and with all the tension and instability in its social fabric,[23] the South entered the long period of the Civil War and the convulsions which followed. The Negroes—having lost the protection for life and personal security which their property value had provided them, and also, in many cases, the personal relationship to their old masters, and being untrained for the new freedom—became the subjects of much greater violence. The whites—impoverished, bitter, fearful, thoroughly indoctrinated by their own defense ideology, and even more untrained to deal with their new fellow citizens in terms of legal equality—felt little check in practicing this violence. The Reconstruction Amendments, however, gave civil rights to Negroes for the first time. Even after the restoration of white supremacy was accomplished, all state legislation in the South had to be written upon the fictitious assumption that Negroes enjoyed full and equal protection under the law. The administration of justice had to proceed upon the same imaginary principle. In reality, legislation, courts, and police were, on the contrary, used to keep the Negroes "in their place." This intention had to be kept *sub rosa,* so as not to come into conflict with the Constitution. Serious and honest men had to pretend. On the other hand, the belief in legal inequality could never again be wholehearted. The upstanding Southern white men were compelled by their allegiance to their nation and its Constitution to observe a degree of both the form and the content of equality in justice.

So this unique phenomenon, unmatched in history, came into being: a strongly conservative democratic society where conservatism was harnessed to the practice of illegality and where the progressives, instead of the conservatives, had to become cautious defenders of the principle of legality. The South remained provincial and continued its fight against the Creed of the nation and the spirit of the age. The feeling grew, however, that—in this particular respect—it was fighting common sense and its own better conscience. When slavery once was abolished, and its reinstitution written off as undesirable or impractical, and when white men no longer had an economic interest in the persons of specific Negroes, the rational motives for keeping up a reserve of devices, outside the legal ones for keeping Negroes tractable, largely vanished.[24] These other devices served the positive purpose before the War of keeping the slave working for his master; now they mainly served the empty vanity of the weak white man and the desire for domination of the strong white man. The present writer has met few Southern white people—above the lowest level of education and culture—who have not declared themselves prepared *in principle* to abstain from illegality in the sphere of personal security and private property.

There is no question that the movement to normalize the legal order of the South is gaining momentum. The dynamic play of social forces behind this development has already been discussed.[a] In the legal sphere the influence of the federal courts and, in particular, the Supreme Court, is probably stronger than in the political sphere. The North has never compromised with the South on the principle of equality before the law to the same degree as it has on the principle of universal suffrage. And the group of people in the South who are prepared to take a stand for the former principle is—according to the present writer's definite impressions —considerably larger than the group standing for the latter principle. It may, therefore, be expected that there will be an even more rapid development in the field of justice in the near future than at the present time. *The lingering inequality in justice in the South is probably due more to low and lagging professional standards—certainly among the police, and in many regions even among the lawyers who are willing to enter into court service—than it is to opinion in favor of legal inequality.* Negroes in all classes perceive clearly and intensely that the best protection they can hope for is to receive the rights and privileges guaranteed them by law.

While lack of legal justice can be considered in itself as crucial to the peace and sanity of the South, this problem is interrelated with many others. When the Negro is discriminated against by the police, in court, and in private dealings with whites, this is made more possible by his poverty, his lack of political influence and his social abasement. An improvement in any of these fields will reflect itself in a greater security before the law. On the other hand, inequality in justice is undoubtedly responsible for no small part of the Negro's difficulties in rising economically and socially.[b]

[a] See Chapter 21, Section 4.

[b] The following survey of the facts relative to the administration of legal justice to the Negro in the South is based largely on a series of unpublished studies made for our inquiry by Arthur Raper, summarized in "Race and Class Pressures" (1940). These studies were made in localities all over the South, but emphasize conditions prevailing in the Lower South. For this reason, we shall sometimes fail to report in detail modifications of the general patterns that occur in many communities of the Upper and Border South. These modifications should not be underestimated as they are significant not only as frequent exceptions, but also as indications of change. In general, it might be said that the farther northward one goes in the South, the more similarities he finds to the stronger legal traditions of the North. This does not mean that the gradation is smooth as one travels northward from the Gulf of Mexico: the break at the Mason-Dixon line is so sharp that one cannot doubt that the Upper South is more like the Lower South than it is like the North. Too, many urban areas of the Lower South have as strong a legal structure as the average community in the Upper South.

CHAPTER 25

THE POLICE AND OTHER PUBLIC CONTACTS

1. LOCAL PETTY OFFICIALS

Practically all public officials in the South are whites. The principle is upheld that Negroes should not be given positions of public authority even on a low level. This situation is, of course, closely related to their disfranchisement. Even in the South, however, Negroes are sometimes appointed to minor offices in the localities where they are permitted to vote.[a]

The Negro's most important public contact is with the policeman. He is the personification of white authority in the Negro community.

> There he *is* "the law" with badge and revolver; his word is final; he is the state's witness in court, and as defined by the police system and the white community, his word must be accepted.[1]

In the policeman's relation to the Negro population in the South, there are several singularities to be observed, all of which have to be explained in the historical setting presented above. One is that he stands not only for civic order as defined in formal laws and regulations, but also for "white supremacy" and the whole set of social customs associated with this concept.[b] In the traditions of the region a break of the caste rules against one white person is conceived of as an aggression against white society and, indeed, as a potential threat to every other white individual. It is demanded that even minor transgressions of caste etiquette should be punished, and the policeman is delegated to carry out this function. Because of this sanction from the police, the caste order of the South, and even the local variations of social custom, become extensions of the law.

To enable the policeman to carry out this function, the courts are supposed to back him even when he proceeds far outside normal police activity. His word must be taken against Negroes without regard for formal legal rules of evidence, even when there are additional circumstantial facts supporting the contention of the Negro party. That this is so is freely admitted in conversation with both judges and police officers in the South.

[a] See Chapter 22, Section 5.
[b] See Part VII.

The reason is given in terms of social necessity. If the policeman were not given this extra-legal backing by the courts, his prestige and his ability to function as the upholder of the caste order would deteriorate. A constant pressure from the Negro people is recognized and is met in this way. Negroes are arrested and sentenced for all sorts of actual or alleged breaks of the caste rules, sometimes even for incidents where it is clear that their only offense was to resist a white person's unlawful aggression.[2] As this practice is against the formal rules of due process, and as, further, the social customs sanctioned in this way are themselves often directly contrary to the law, there is a strange atmosphere of consistent illegality around the activity of the officers of the peace and the whole judicial system in the South. A further result is that the police often assume the duty not only of arresting, but also of sentencing and punishing the culprit, and that the judges are grateful for being in this way spared from cases embarrassing to them as professional lawyers.

Other singularities in the activity of the Southern police system are, on the one hand, the availability of the police for sanctioning private white interests against Negroes and, on the other, the indulgence of private white persons in taking the law into their own hands. The boundary line between public functionaries and private citizens is thus blurred. The relation between master and slave was a relation of public and not only private law.[3] In the rural districts the plantation owners have tenaciously held to the old pattern of executing actual police power themselves over their Negro labor.[4] As in slavery a sort of delegated police power over Negroes is assumed to belong to other white persons than the employer. *All* white people in the neighborhood remain in a sort of taken-for-granted conspiracy to keep *all* Negroes "in their place," and they pretend a "right" to apply personal sanctions of intimidation and violence. The traveler in the rural districts of the Black Belt even today is startled to find how natural and regular it appears to many whites—and to Negroes—that personal threats and bodily punishments enter into employer-employee relations,[5] and, indeed, into most relations between whites and Negroes, even relatively casual ones.

As during slavery, the local police and the courts are expected to assist in upholding this caste pressure. On the one hand, the scope of police and court activity is limited in so far as the sentencing and punishing of Negroes for breaks against law and order in the plantation districts are taken care of by employers or white vigilantes. On the other hand, the peace officers tend to act as the agents of the planters and other white employers, prepared to appear on call and take charge of the case. To an extent these customs were transferred even to the cities. There the less personal and less stable relations between individuals in the two groups make the Negroes freer in their movement as long as they avoid white contacts, but, for the same reason, those contacts often become harsher.

The philosophies and traditions of the police have been borrowed, and a similar status and function have been assumed, by a large number of other functionaries, for instance, the operators and conductors on public carriers:

> When the Negro boards a street car, bus, or train he meets white operators, and legally they are quasi-officials; in dealing with Negroes and poorer whites they are real officials. For in addition to being legally empowered to carry out their duties, they readily exercise greater authority over the lower status folk.[6]

The Jim Crow regulations vary from city to city, or from state to state; they are complicated and technically impractical,[a] and a constant source of tension and friction. The operators and conductors—like the police officers —feel themselves obliged to sanction and enforce rules of racial etiquette and custom. They also are the watchdogs against "social equality."

Under these conditions it is no wonder that these functionaries often feel themselves—and white authority—challenged. As weak men (their economic and social status is low) with strong powers, they can seldom afford to take back a charge or an order. The nearest patrolman will be at hand to back up any white man having trouble with a Negro by arresting the Negro for "disturbing the peace." The courts will usually feel obliged to back up these functionaries even when it is apparent that they have transgressed their legitimate powers. Practically all Southern Negroes interviewed by the present writer on this question have complained about the arbitrary and high-handed manner in which the Jim Crow regulations in transportation are often handled. Incidents of illegal treatment are frequently reported in the Negro press. Such studies as have been made have largely confirmed these complaints.[7]

To the same category belong a great number of other functionaries.

> The meter readers for electric and gas subscribers, too, approximate quasi-officials when dealing with Negroes. They walk into Negro homes, and often make themselves obnoxious by refusing to remove their hats and show other civilities.[8]

The tax collectors and a number of petty officials at what the Negroes commonly refer to as "the white folks' courthouse" also belong to this group. The mass of Negroes in the South seem to be thoroughly convinced that, in the ordinary case, white solidarity would prevent them from getting justice even if they took their grievances to the higher-ups—if they cannot get some white person to intervene for them.

Practices vary a great deal, however, from community to community. Generally speaking, the Negroes seem to be treated more justly and

[a] See Chapter 28, Section 4.

courteously in the Upper South than in the Deep South. The observer feels that this whole problem of Negroes' public contacts with all the minor functionaries in private and municipal service would deserve intensive study. These contacts are of paramount practical importance: they represent the major part of all official relations of Negroes with the organized society in which they live, and they determine largely their attitudes to this society. A change to easier, friendlier, and more impartial public contacts would improve race relations immensely. As will be pointed out later in this chapter, there is a growing group of public contacts of a new type which meets these demands much better than the old type here reviewed.[a]

2. The Southern Policeman

The central relation in this system—and the prototype and sanction of all other public contacts—is that between Negroes and the local police. In purely rural districts the police consist of the sheriff and his deputies. Usually they are petty politicians with no police training at all except the experiences they get in their work. In the rural South the caste rules are so fixed, the contacts between whites and Negroes so continual, the caste control so pervasive, and so much of the daily suppression of the individuals of the lower caste is, as we pointed out, taken care of by employers and landowners themselves, that the peace officers' police duties are intermittent and restricted to occasional incidents. They then appear as the executors of the public will in the locality and are backed by the courts. In the Southern cities where the two racial groups are more separated, the duty of policing the population becomes a continuous and specialized task. The police then also become more directly important for interracial relations.

It is of great interest to study the qualifications and personality type of the Southern policeman who has been awarded this crucial position in the caste society. A special investigation was undertaken for this study by Dr. Arthur Raper, who made an inquiry as of 1940 into the personnel of the police force in 112 towns and cities, in 14 Southern states.[9] The level of general education among policemen is low.[b] In many small cities "almost anyone on the outside of the penitentiary who weighs enough and is not

---

[a] See Section 5 of this chapter.

[b] "Of the 112 Southern cities, towns and villages from which specific information about the police was secured for this study, 30 had no educational requirements for recruits to the force, while 20 specified grammar school. The remaining 62 required only high school or its equivalent. Even so, the 'equivalent' sufficed in a vast number of cases." (Arthur Raper, "Race and Class Pressures," unpublished manuscript prepared for this study [1940], p. 14.) Even in the largest cities a college graduate on the police force is a great rarity.

blind or crippled can be considered as a police candidate."[10] Even the formal police training is usually very deficient.[a]

Slightly over half the police systems studied are now using some form of civil service,[b] many of them for less than five years. But civil service requirements, as employed in Southern cities, reduce only slightly the influence of politics on the police system, for elected officials still run the civil service and select among the many who meet the formal requirements.[11] This means a low degree of personal and professional independence. "The fact that many police systems in the South are subject to politics puts a premium on the vote-getting qualities of the policeman."[12] Salaries of policemen rank somewhere between those of unskilled and skilled workers.[c] Less than half the police systems studied have worked out some sort of retirement fund.[d] Ambitious skilled workers like railroad workers, mechanics, carpenters, painters, plumbers, and electricians sometimes take police jobs when unemployed but try to get back to their old trades as soon as regular employment is assured.[13] The vast majority of policemen, however, do not belong to this category, and they hang on to the police force.[e] In the typical Southern police force the turnover is small and the average age high. Even when the police force is replaced for political reasons this does not generally mean a rejuvenation, "for older men can commonly deliver more votes."[14]

Although the policeman in the South is not considered a professional

[a] "Formal training for his duties is provided in only 33 of the 112 communities; in about half of the others, he works as a sort of apprentice under some older officer for a period of three to six months, and commonly at slightly reduced pay. In one-fourth of the communities no training is provided. One day he is a barber, textile worker, truck driver, mechanic, or private night-watchman; the next day, with uniform, badge and gun, he is a full-fledged police officer. In the meantime he may have promised to read a little booklet of four to sixteen pages, which contains rules of the police department." (*Ibid.*, pp. 17-18.)

[b] Sixty-five of 112. (*Ibid.*, p. 14.) In few cases do the Southern city police civil service systems approximate in rigor the systems employed by Northern cities.

[c] "The salary of patrolmen was $100 or below a month in 32 communities, $101 to $125 in 47, $126 to $150 in 24, and $150 or over in 10. Though these salaries are not large, they represent a real increase for most of the people who joined the police force." (*Ibid.*, pp. 14-15.)

[d] "In 13 instances, police are retired at more than half pay, while in 29 others it is one-half or less. Only 2 of the 21 villages studied (with fewer than 5 policemen each) had any retirement plan; 6 of the 32 systems with from 5 to 14 police each had some form of retirement pay, while retirement plans were found in 37 of the 59 communities with 15 or more policemen." (*Ibid.*, p. 16.)

[e] "In the last five years, among the 112 police systems studied, 41 had no police to resign for a better job, and 42 more had less than one-fifth resign for that reason. They stay because they are receiving more income than before—half again as much, often even twice as much. The policeman's salary runs for twelve months a year, too, and for more than a few of them, as will be seen later, there are opportunities for making money on the side." (*Ibid.*, pp. 15-16.)

man and is looked down on generally by the middle class whites, an appointment to the police force means an advance in income and economic security to poor white unskilled workers.

> Aside from the matters of monthly income and regularity of employment, it is quite clear that many policemen . . . are hungry for the opportunity to exercise authority. An ex-house-to-house salesman, clerk, truck driver, or textile worker not infrequently likes to have a gun handy, and enjoys the authority which his badge provides.[15]

The typical Southern policeman is thus a low-paid and dependent man, with usually little general education or special police schooling. His social prestige is low. But he is the local representative of the law; he has authority and may at any time resort to the use of his gun. It is not difficult to understand that this economically and socially insecure man, given this tremendous and dangerous authority, continually feels himself on the defensive. "He usually expects to be challenged when about routine duties. . . . This defensive attitude makes the policeman's job tedious and nerve-racking, and leaves the public with the feeling that policemen are crude and hard-boiled."[16] He is a frustrated man, and, with the opportunity given him, it is to be expected that he becomes aggressive. There are practically no curbs to the policeman's aggressiveness when he is dealing with Negroes whom he conceives of as dangerous or as "getting out of their place." He is accustomed also to deal roughly with "outside agitators," "Communists," "subversive influences," and in his mind there is a suspicion that there is a relation between these two groups of enemies of society.

3. THE POLICEMAN IN THE NEGRO NEIGHBORHOOD

This weak man with his strong weapons—backed by all the authority of white society—is now sent to be the white law in the Negro neighborhood. There he is away from home.

> He is an outsider, and there is such a thing as a "bad nigger." Fiction, of course, has dramatized the character, but there are facts which demand recognition. With the cop an outsider, the "bad nigger" an insider, a ready use of firearms is inevitable. The philosophies of the "outside" policeman and of the "bad nigger" contribute to the high homicide rate of Southern cities, for the records show that the police are most likely to get killed in the same cities where brutality, including killings, is most prevalent.[17]

As far as the cultural and social adjustment of the Negroes is concerned, *the Southern police system is undoing much of what Northern philanthropy and Southern state governments are trying to accomplish through education and by other means*. The average Southern policeman is a promoted poor white with a legal sanction to use a weapon. His social heritage has taught him to despise the Negroes, and he has had little education which could have changed him. His professional experiences with criminals, prostitutes, and loiterers in Negro joints and with such "good niggers" as can be used as informers, spotters, and stool pigeons—often petty criminals and racketeers who as an exchange for police immunity help locate Negroes desired by the police department[18]—are strongly selective and only magnify his prejudices. The result is that probably no group of whites in America have a lower opinion of the Negro people and are more fixed in their views than Southern policemen. To most of them no Negro woman knows what virtue is—"we just don't talk about prostitution among the Negroes," said one of the chiefs of police in a big Southern city to the present author—and practically every Negro man is a potential criminal. They usually hold, in extreme form, all other derogatory beliefs about Negroes; and they are convinced that the traits are "racial." This holds true of the higher ranks in the police departments as well as of the lower ranks. On the other hand, I have also found that some of the younger policemen, particularly if they have had any education, do tend to have slightly more modern views. But they have a hard time maintaining these views against the force of opinion among the older, more experienced men with whom they work.[19]

In many, but not all, Southern communities Negroes complain indignantly about police brutality. It is part of the policeman's philosophy that Negro criminals or suspects, or any Negro who shows signs of insubordination, should be punished bodily, and that this is a device for preventing crime and for keeping the "Negro in his place" generally.[20] It is apparent, however, that the beating of arrested Negroes[a]—frequently in the wagon on the way to jail or later when they are already safely locked up—often serves as vengeance for the fears and perils the policemen are subjected to while pursuing their duties in the Negro community. When once the beating habit has developed in a police department, it is, according to all experience, difficult to stop. It appeals to primitive sadistic impulses ordinarily held down by education and other social controls. In this setting the application of the "third degree" to get "confessions" from Negro suspects easily becomes a routine device.[b] Police brutality is greatest in the regions where murders are most numerous and death sentences are most frequent,[21] which speaks against its having crime-preventing effects. The observer who visits several communities and can make comparisons becomes convinced that, on the contrary, police brutality has thoroughly demoralizing effects on the Negroes.

[a] Policemen will also beat Negroes without arresting them. This occurs in cases of minor insubordination and when policemen are helping plantation owners keep their Negro tenants under control.

[b] Concerning the "third degree," see Raper, *op. cit.*, pp. 172-175.

The most publicized type of police brutality is the extreme case of Negroes being killed by policemen. This phenomenon is important in itself, but it constitutes only a minor portion of all police brutality, and the information available on Negro killings by the police does not even give a reliable index of the wider phenomenon.[22] More than half of all Negroes killed by whites, in both the North and the South, were killed by police.[a] But white policemen are also a great portion of all whites killed by Negroes.[b] Even if this information on reciprocal killings between Negroes and white policemen does not give adequate indication of the extent of police brutality, it tells something about the policeman's role in interracial relations.[23]

The majority of police killings of Negroes must be deemed unnecessary when measured by a decent standard of policemanship.[24] The victim is often totally innocent. But the white policeman in the Negro community is in danger, as the high casualty figures show, and he feels himself in danger. "In the mind of the quick-trigger policeman is the fear of the 'bad nigger.' . . . Sensing the danger of scared policemen, Negroes in turn frequently depend upon the first shot."[25] The situation is not this bad in every community of the South; many localities of the Upper South and some in the Lower South have advanced to higher standards.

The main reasons why Negroes want to have Negro officers appointed to police departments—besides the ordinary group interest of having more public jobs for themselves—are to have a more understanding, less brutal police supervision in the Negro community, and to have an effective supervision of Negro offenders against other Negroes. The second reason is not unimportant. Everywhere in Southern Negro communities I have met the complaint from law-abiding Negroes that they are left practically without police protection.

In 1930 there were 1,297 Negro policemen and 521 detectives, marshals,

[a] "Of the 479 Negroes killed in the South by whites [between 1920 and 1932], 260 or 54.3 per cent of the total were killed by peace officers; of 47 outside of the South, 32 or 68.1 per cent by officers." (Unpublished data compiled by H. C. Brearley in *ibid.*, p. 40.)

Of 202 Southern cities and towns studied by Raper for the period 1935-1940 "115 have had no one killed by the police . . . while 196 Negroes were killed in 61 cities and 67 whites in 40 cities." Northern cities with high figures for police killings are: ". . . Baltimore 13 Negroes and 4 whites, Kansas City 10 Negroes and 18 whites, Cleveland 12 Negroes and 16 whites, Boston 8 whites, and above all Detroit with 28 Negroes and 25 whites. In Washington, D. C., no less than 50 Negroes and 10 whites were killed by police from 1926 to 1938." (Raper, *op. cit.*, pp. 37-38.)

[b] "Of the 473 whites killed in the South by Negroes [between 1920 and 1932], 173 or 36.6 per cent were peace officers; of 63 outside the South, 18 or 28.6 per cent were officers." (Unpublished data compiled by H. C. Brearley in *ibid.*, pp. 40-41.)

". . . in 32 of the 202 Southern cities and towns from which information was secured 51 policemen had been killed since 1935; in the other 170 communities no policeman had been killed." (Raper, *op. cit.*, p. 38.)

sheriffs, constables, probation and truant officers in public service in the United States. Only 7 per cent were in the South outside the Border states. When the Border states and the District of Columbia are included in the South, the percentage rises to 18.[26] Apparently there was little increase, if any, between 1930 and 1940 in the South.[a] The reluctance to appoint Negro policemen in the South is reflected also in the restrictions put upon the authority of the few there are.[b] It is reported that the use of Negro police seems to be a factor making for a lowering of the crime rate in the Negro community. "They can arrest offenders with less show of force, partly because they know their way around in the community, and partly because they are personally respected."[27]

[a] "The geographic distribution of Negro policemen is in inverse relation to the percentage of Negroes in the total population. Mississippi, South Carolina, Louisiana, Georgia and Alabama—the only states with more than one-third Negro population—have not one Negro policeman in them, though they have nearly two-fifths of the total Negro population of the nation. Other states without regular Negro officers are Arkansas and Virginia, both with more than one-fourth of their population Negroes. Only two states with more than one-fourth Negro population have Negro policemen—North Carolina with one at Princeville, a Negro suburb of Tarboro, and Florida with three at Daytona Beach and one each at Fort Myers and Sarasota. In these states there is one Negro policeman to every 200,000 Negroes.

"In Maryland, Delaware, Tennessee and Texas, where Negroes make up from 10 per cent to 20 per cent of the population there are 39 Negro officers, or one to every 41,000 Negroes; while in the five states with from 5 per cent to 10 per cent of the population Negro, there are 165, or one to every 5,700 Negroes. In the remaining 32 states where the Negro accounts for less than 5 per cent of the total population, there are 756 policemen, or one to every 41,000 Negroes.

"The figures above do not include the District of Columbia, which seems to contradict the general pattern. It has 34 Negro policemen, one to every 3,800 Negroes. But the District, with 27 per cent Negroes in 1930, is very deep South in some respects, particularly in its record of police killings of Negroes.

"Excepting the District of Columbia, the South with slightly over three-fourths of the nation's Negro population has less than one-eighth of the nation's Negro policemen, while the North with one-fifth of the Negro population has four-fifths of the policemen, and the West with one per cent of the population has over 5 per cent of the Negro policemen." (*Ibid.*, pp. 24-25.)

The figures are as of 1940. One subsidiary reason why the South is hesitant about appointing Negroes as police officers is that, as a rule, they receive the same pay as the white officers. (*Ibid.*, p. 27.)

[b] "The province of authority of the Negro policeman varies with his location on the map. In most of the Northern and Western communities Negro policemen function as officers in any part of town, even though their special duties may often be more or less limited to the Negro section. Farther down the map, the Negro officers are restricted to Negro communities, while in most of the lower border cities with Negro policemen, their authority applies only to Negroes in the Negro section. When offending whites need to be arrested white officers are called in. It was with some feeling of victory that the Negroes in Louisville, a decade ago, won the right for Negro officers to go home in their uniforms as did the white police officers." (*Ibid.*, p. 26.)

4. Trends and Outlook

There are, however, some encouraging signs of change in the police systems of the South. The civil service system seems to be on the increase even in the South. This will tend to lower the age level and raise the educational level of persons appointed to the police force. It will also increase the independence of the police officers. Another factor is the growing influence of the federal police system.

> The F.B.I. is giving real stimulus to better-trained police personnel; many of the larger communities which have not yet set up training schools report that members of their staff are now taking the F.B.I. training course and upon their return will develop a local training school. This approach will in the course of a few years include all the cities of any size.[28]

The increase and improvement of the state police systems likewise tends to raise the standards of Southern policemanship and to set patterns for local police systems. The general influences of education, urbanization, and industrialization also are tending to modernize the administration of local governments in the South. Finally, the new functions of the policemen—answering questions for tourists, helping school children cross the streets, and so on—may serve as a humanizing force tending to counteract the stultifying effects of catching and beating criminals.[a]

The present writer has, from his contact with the Southern police system, become convinced that it represents a crucial and strategic factor in race relations. Could standards be raised—of education, specialized police training, independence of local politics, salary, and social prestige—some of the most morbid tensions in the South would be lessened. Legislators now take it for granted that teachers and social workers ought to have a college degree; *a college education should be even more urgently required for fulfilling the duties of a police officer.*[29] The policeman needs, besides a general education, a special training to make him a professional. This training should not be directed only on the technicalities of crime detection. Even more important is an understanding of the wider aims of crime

[a] *Ibid.*, p. 19.

". . . assistance in crossing streets is provided for Negro school children in scarcely 10 per cent of the communities in such representative Southern states as Arkansas, Mississippi, Alabama, Georgia, and the Carolinas, as reported by 88 Negro high school principals in these states. We noted above the friendly relations that develop between the school child and the policeman. When the typical chief of police was faced squarely with the question why it would not be a good thing to provide this avenue of understanding for Negro school children, who come from the highest crime sections in the city, the only answer was that he had not thought about it. Some rather haltingly suggested it could not be worked out because the Negro child would not be accepted in the same cordial fashion as the white child. One wonders, however, whether this is true. If it is, it further emphasizes the need for Negro policemen." (*Ibid.*, p. 22.)

prevention. *Ideally the policeman should be something of an educator and a social worker at the same time that he is the arm of the law.* Even in the police systems in the North, where standards of professional policemanship are highest, too little interest has been given to social and educational viewpoints. One result of this is that the policeman in America is not commonly liked and trusted as he rightly ought to be.[30]

Racial and social conditions make the policeman's task much more difficult in the South. *The South, particularly, needs a stress on the preventive aims and the peace-making functions of the police.* Few strategic moves to improve the Southern interracial situation would be more potent than the opening of a pioneering modern police college in the South on a high level, which would give a thorough social and pedagogical training as well as a technical police training. The South is changing, and it is the author's opinion that the graduates from such a school would not need to fear unemployment. The use of equally well-trained Negro policemen, particularly for patrolling the Negro communities, would be an especially wholesome reform. Public opinion in many Southern cities would tolerate such a reform: as in many other fields, local politicians and the public institutions lag behind the possibilities.

5. ANOTHER TYPE OF PUBLIC CONTACT

Besides the police and other functionaries who regard their chief function with respect to Negroes to be restraint and suppression, there are public officials in the South, as elsewhere, who regard their function to be service. Longest established among these are the postal officials, who are unique because they are under federal control and have to meet civil service standards. Southern Negroes know that they can rely upon having their letters duly delivered.[31] And they feel they can expect much more equal treatment and courteous service from Uncle Sam's agencies than from local authorities.

Other people who are building up a tradition of equal and just treatment of Negroes in public contacts are those concerned with social adjustment and social reform. They have become especially numerous and important under the New Deal. These officials have a relatively high level of general education and professional training and, what is even more important, have other goals than the perfunctory ones of preserving the social *status quo*. They are bent upon *preventing* individual and social inefficiencies and wrongs and upon *improving* conditions. Usually they are under some federal control. Even if, as we have seen,[a] they do discriminate against Negroes, they discriminate much less than has been the custom in the South.

[a] See Chapter 15.

To this practically new group of officials belong the relief administrator,[32] the county farm agent, the Farm Security supervisor, the home demonstration agent, and the doctors and nurses of local health programs. Some of these have Negro assistants to handle Negro cases, but many—including even the Farm Security Administration, which is one of the fairest of the New Deal agencies—restrict their personnel to whites. In the F.S.A. this is ". . . a concession which the agency felt obliged to make to ensure its being allowed to serve the pro rata number of Negro families."[33] The New Deal has not succeeded in stamping out discrimination against Negroes in its agencies in the South, but it has brought discrimination within some limits, and it has given the Negroes a new type of contact with public authority: educated and trained white men and women whose primary interest is not simply to keep them in their place, but to advise them and help them to a better life. This will, in time, stand out as a social and spiritual revolution.

CHAPTER 26

COURTS, SENTENCES AND PRISONS

1. The Southern Courts

William Archer, the sympathetic English traveler, who in 1908 criss-crossed the Southern states in order to inform himself on the Negro problem, summed up the part of his study which dealt with courts and justice in the following words:

> This is one of the few points on which there is little conflict of evidence—the negro, in the main, does not get justice in the courts of the South. The tone of the courts is exemplified in the pious peroration of the lawyer who exclaimed: "God forbid that a jury should ever convict a white man for killing a nigger who knocked his teeth down his throat!" Exceptions there are, no doubt; there are districts in which the negroes themselves report that they are equitably treated. But the rule is that in criminal cases a negro's guilt is lightly assumed, and he is much more heavily punished than a white man would be for the same offence; while in civil cases justice may be done between black and black, but seldom between white and black.[1]

and he quotes with endorsement an intelligent and conservative Negro informant:

> "A negro's case gets no fair hearing; and he is far more severely punished than a white man for the same offence. . . . There is only one court in which we think we get justice, and that is the Federal Court."[2]

Since Archer wrote, a generation has passed: things *have* changed somewhat but not fundamentally. Writing in 1932, Virginius Dabney could, without risking contradiction, refer to "the frequent failure of Southern blacks to obtain even elementary justice when they fall into the toils of the law."[3]

Apart from the basic institutional weakness already referred to,[a] that the courts are too directly controlled by a local public opinion where the Negroes are without a voice, there are some structural characteristics in the judicial procedure which operate against all poor and uneducated groups. The great number of courts, with higher or lower rank and with complicated jurisdictional boundaries between them, are likely to bewilder

[a] See Chapter 24, Section 1.

the unsophisticated citizen who attempts to get his rights protected.[4] Technicalities and legal fictions are allowed to play a great role, to the sacrifice of material justice. This is true of American justice in other parts of the country also,[a] but the very fact that the South after Reconstruction had to build up large parts of its legal system of discrimination against Negroes in evasion of the Constitution has particularly stamped Southern justice with this trait.

Under these circumstances a clever attorney can work wonders, particularly in those rural districts where the judge feels that the attorney knows more about law than he does himself.[5] The strength of the counsel a man can provide depends in general upon his wealth, and Negroes, as a poor group, suffer together with lower class whites. "The root of the evil is"—writes a prominent Southern white lawyer after having expressed his opinion that even the Negro can receive substantial justice in a Southern court if he is properly represented by competent counsel—"that so often his rights suffer because he cannot get into court in civil matters on account of financial want, and most frequently in criminal cases he is without funds to secure proper defense."[6] It is true that, in criminal cases, the court will appoint a lawyer for anybody who cannot afford to provide himself with proper legal aid. The court-appointed lawyer, however, in many cases, performs only perfunctory duties. Often the court will appoint some young lawyer without much experience. "Generally speaking, it is probably true that these charity lawyers are not as efficient as privately employed attorneys, but in many instances such is not the case."[7]

The American bond and bail system works automatically against the poor classes. The poor man, generally, cannot raise bail or bond himself to secure his release from jail pending trial. As the privilege of bail is discretionary, it is most often refused or made prohibitively high to accused Negroes, particularly when the alleged crime is against whites. Then there is what Raper calls "the dynamics of the fee system." Under this system—still in use in more than half the South—all the minor court officials, and in some instances the prosecuting attorneys, get their pay out of fines. This system ". . . puts a premium upon making those arrests and getting those convictions which will yield fees and costs without jeopardizing the political popularity of the fee-getting officials."[8] Equally bad conditions may prevail where there is no fee system: the judge may decide the punishment on the basis of a consideration as to the state's profit. Mississippi, for example, had a net profit of half a million dollars in 1939 from its penitentiaries,[9] and judges were inclined to send criminals to the penitentiary rather than fine them. Where the penitentiary system operates at a loss, the inclination is to fine Negroes and poor whites to reduce the burden of cost of the legal system.ª

Not only are all the court officials white, but the jury too is usually composed of whites only, except for cases in the federal courts and in some of the large cities. Yet to prohibit Negroes from jury lists is clearly unconstitutional. It has long been established that no statutes which barred Negroes from jury service were constitutional,[10] and higher court decisions have declared invalid convictions made by juries selected from lists which restricted Negroes. An impetus to using Negroes on juries came in 1935 when, in the widely publicized Scottsboro decision, the Supreme Court ruled that the trial was unconstitutional because Negroes had been systematically excluded from jury service. Courts want to have their decisions stand, and so a movement is under way to have Negroes on the jury list and call them in occasionally for service. Techniques are, however, being developed by which it is possible to fulfill legal requirements without using Negro jurors. In the Lower South the matter is usually disregarded. Dr. Raper reports, after a survey of the situation as of 1940, as follows:

> Inquiries about the use of Negro jurors have been made in the past year [1940] in numerous courts in Georgia, Alabama, Mississippi, Arkansas, Oklahoma, Texas, Florida, North and South Carolina. While Negroes are generally used on the federal grand juries and petit juries throughout most of these states, and in superior court grand and petit juries in the larger cities, the vast majority of the rural courts in the Deep South have made no pretense of putting Negroes on jury lists, much less

ª "Sometimes the incomes from fines take care of the cost of the police court and the police department. In DeKalb County, Georgia, for example, the local paper editorially boasted that in 1939 the county police department with 15 men on patrol duty, made 1,991 arrests during the year; only 10 of these were dismissed and only 20 were found not guilty. The total cost of operating the police department, including the police court, was approximately $40,000. The total fines collected amounted to $37,732.62, leaving a cost to the county of only $2,300. But this department collected stolen goods and property valued at $20,555.45.

". . . in this county, as is generally the case, the cost of the courts is borne by fines from the poorest people in the community. Negroes and poorer whites will be fined $10 to $40 for possessing a half pint of illegal liquor, while people with status have their liquor as they please, and everybody knows it. Disorderly conduct, loitering, vagrancy—all help pay for the court. Looked at purely from the point of view of maintaining race and class demarcations, the court is as effective as portrayed by the local paper.

"The recorder's courts in nearby Atlanta reported the collection of $236,285 in the first 8 months of 1939. At this rate the collections for the year would exceed $350,000. The cost of these courts for a year is slightly less than $21,000. The 1939 budget for the police department was $1,018,239.91. The fines for the year totalled about one-third of the cost of the police court and police department.

"A similar ratio obtained in Selma, Alabama, where the police budget was $35,000, fines $12,800. In Jackson, Mississippi, $61,000 and $40,000; Macon, Georgia, $141,715.34 and $47,852.85." (Arthur Raper, "Race and Class Pressures," unpublished manuscript prepared for this study [1940], pp. 160-162.)

calling or using them in trials. . . . North Carolina and Virginia have taken the
decisions more seriously. Even in these states, however, numerous courts have merely
ignored the matter.

It is the general assumption that the use of Negro jurors need not be considered
except in those court sessions in which Negro defendants are being tried on serious
charges. Even a capital offense against a Negro does not raise the all-white jury
issue unless local officials have reason to believe the case might be appealed on this
ground.[11]

To this should be added that Negro lawyers are scarce in the South.[a]
In some places, Negro lawyers are not allowed to appear in courts, and
even where they are allowed, they tend to stay away. Most of them seem
to be engaged in settling matters outside of court or working in real estate
or insurance offices or giving legal advice. Their white business is mainly
restricted to debt collection among Negroes. In law suits they may work
with white lawyers but do not appear much before the courts themselves.
Negro clients know that a Negro lawyer is not much use in a Southern
courtroom.[12] Lower class Negroes sometimes believe that Negro lawyers
are not permitted in courtrooms even where they are permitted. There
are other handicaps for Negro lawyers: their clients are usually poor; they
cannot afford extensive equipment;[13] they have not had the experience of
handling important cases; they cannot specialize.

2. DISCRIMINATION IN COURT

In a court system of this structure, operating within a deeply prejudiced
region, discrimination is to be expected. The danger is especially strong in
lower courts where the pressure of local public opinion is most strongly
felt, and where the judges often are men of limited education and provincial background.

In civil cases the average Negro will not only be up against the inability
of meeting the costs involved in a successful litigation—this he shares with
the poor white man in the South and elsewhere—but, when his adversary
is a white man, he also encounters white solidarity. Greater reliance is
ordinarily given a white man's testimony than a Negro's. This follows an
old tradition in the South, from slavery times, when a Negro's testimony
against a white man was disregarded; and the white judge may justify his
partisanship by what he feels to be his experience that Negroes are often
actually unreliable. It also fits into a pattern of thinking that it is dangerous
for the social order to allow Negroes to vindicate their rights against white
people. The writer has, however, frequently been told by Negroes and
whites in the South that it is becoming more and more common that
judges, with the consent of white society, stand up for giving the Negroes
what is due them as long as it concerns merely their property rights.

[a] See Chapter 14, Section 7.

In criminal cases the discrimination does not always run against a Negro defendant. It is part of the Southern tradition to assume that Negroes are disorderly and lack elementary morals, and to show great indulgence toward Negro violence and disorderliness "when they are among themselves." They should, however, not act it out in the presence of whites, "not right out on the street." As long as only Negroes are concerned and no whites are disturbed, great leniency will be shown in most cases. This is particularly true in minor cases which are often treated in a humorous or disdainful manner. The sentences for even major crimes are ordinarily reduced when the victim is another Negro.[14] Attorneys are heard to plead in the juries: "Their code of ethics is a different one from ours." To the patriarchal traditions belong also the undue importance given white "character witnesses" in favor of Negro offenders. The South is full of stories of how Negroes have been acquitted or given a ridiculously mild sentence upon recommendation of their white employers with whom they have a good standing.[15]

The leniency in punishment of Negro crime against Negroes has repeatedly been pointed out to the present writer by white Southerners as evidence of the friendliness of Southern courts toward Negroes. The same thing can be found in the writings of Southerners.[16] Yet the Southern Negro community is not at all happy about this double standard of justice in favor of Negro offenders. Law-abiding Negroes point out that there are criminal and treacherous Negroes who secure immunity from punishment because they are fawning and submissive toward whites. Such persons are a danger to the Negro community. Leniency toward Negro defendants in cases involving crimes against other Negroes is thus actually a form of discrimination.

For offenses which involve any actual or potential danger to whites, however, Negroes are punished more severely than whites.[17] Particularly the lower courts which work on a fee system are inclined to fine Negro defendants heavily without giving them much chance to explain their case. The inclination of the Southern court to make legal punishment a paying business[a] operates against Negroes who can be fined or sent to the penitentiary almost arbitrarily. Negroes alone are subject to a special form of legal injustice which is, however, now becoming rather rare: when white employers are short of workers, they inform the sheriff, who will suddenly begin to enforce vague laws such as that against vagrancy. Formerly the employers could rent prisoners from the state; now they make a deal with the Negro defendant to pay his fine if he will work a certain number of days—fewer than the number he would have to spend in jail.[18]

But quite apart from such pecuniary motives, the courts, particularly the

[a] See Section 1 of this chapter.

lower courts, too often seem to take for granted the guilt of the accused Negro.[a] The present author, during his visits to lower courts in the South, has been amazed to see how carelessly the Negro defendants—and sometimes also defendants belonging to the lower strata of whites—are sentenced upon scanty evidence even when they emphatically deny the charges. There is an astonishing atmosphere of informality and lack of dignity in the courtroom, and speed seems to be the main goal. Neither the judge nor the other court officers seem to see anything irregular in the drama performed; the observer is welcomed and usually asked to sit beside the judge to be better able to watch the interesting scene.

> Most of the Negroes seem to realize that their word in this machine-like courtroom is as nothing when weighed against the white officer's. The judge sometimes smiles understandingly as the arresting officer tells what the defendant did. And most Negroes simply take it. Now and then, however, one glances around until a sympathetic eye is caught and with a wordless stare says eloquently, "Oh, what's the use."[19]

It should be emphasized, however, that there are great differences between different courts, due partly to differences in the personality of the judge. A humane judge, whose mental horizon is not bound by the limits of his local community, will maintain a dignified court and administer impartial justice. As between rural and urban areas, it is difficult to say which is more prejudiced: urban courts have a greater familiarity with, and respect for, law; but rural courts retain some of the old aristocratic patriarchal traditions. According to Raper, in the rural courts, some Negro witnesses may also be used as character witnesses and there is, on the whole, less browbeating, derogatory joking, and open carelessness in the hearing of Negro witnesses, plaintiffs and defendants.[20] The higher state courts and the federal courts observe much more of judicial decorum and are, for this reason, less likely to discriminate against Negroes. The judges in these courts are usually also of a higher grade and are relatively independent of local opinion.

The jury, for the most part, is more guilty of obvious partiality than the judge and the public prosecutor. When the offender is a white man and the victim a Negro, a grand jury will often refuse to indict. Even the federal courts find difficulty in getting indictments in peonage suits,[21] and state courts receive indictments for physical violence against Negroes in an infinitesimally small proportion of the cases. It is notorious that prac-

---

[a] A white lawyer from a city in the Black Belt writes:

"On the criminal side of the court I think that a great many Negroes are convicted on testimony which would have resulted in the acquittal of a white defendant. A white defendant is presumed to be innocent until the contrary is proven; I am afraid that a Negro is presumed to be guilty until the contrary is proven. A jury which would find a white defendant guilty of a lesser grade of the offense involved will frequently find the Negro guilty of the highest grade." (Letter of July 2, 1940.)

tically never have white lynching mobs been brought to court in the South, even when the killers are known to all in the community and are mentioned by name in the local press. When the offender is a Negro, indictment is easily obtained and no such difficulty at the start will meet the prosecution of the case. The petit jury is even less impartial than the grand jury, since its range of powers is greater.

Public tension and community pressure increase with the seriousness of the alleged crime. A Southern student of law writes:

> One has only to visit a Southern community at a time when some Negro is on trial for the rape or murder of a white person to obtain a vivid picture of the hate and passion and desire for vengeance which is often aroused in the hearts of the Southern whites.
>
> Nowhere is the spirit of mob violence so strong as it is in the courtroom or just outside while a person who is accused of some particularly heinous crime is being tried. The air is charged with an undercurrent of tension and there is a feeling of suspense, as if some exciting incident may occur at any moment. Under circumstances of this kind it is rather difficult for the jury or even the judge to escape being influenced by the feeling which permeates the throng.[22]

There is thus even less possibility for a fair trial when the Negro's crime is serious. In the case of a threatened lynching, the court makes no pretense at justice; the Negro must be condemned, and usually condemned to death, before the crowd gets him. On the other hand, it is quite common for a white criminal to be set free if his crime was against a Negro. Southern whites have told the present author of singular occasions when a Negro got justice against a white man, even in a serious case, as something remarkable and noteworthy. This testifies that it still is an exception.[23] Kelly Miller reflected upon the situation as follows:

> Of the thousands of cases of murder of blacks by whites since emancipation there has been scarcely a legal execution, and comparatively few prison sentences. The offender usually escapes with the stereotyped verdict, "Justifiable homicide," or at best with a nominal fine. If the relations were reversed, whatever the provocative circumstances, the Negro would almost certainly be sentenced to death or to life imprisonment, if indeed the mob allowed the case to reach a judicial hearing. To say that these flagrant discrepancies have not their influence upon the black man's attitude toward the law, would be to deny that he is controlled by ordinary human motives. The best example that the South can set for the Negro would be punishment of white men for their crimes according to the requirement of the law. Mean white men will continue to mistreat Negroes just so long as they can do so with impunity by hiding themselves behind the cloak of racial arrogance.[24]

3. SENTENCES AND PRISONS

The South has the highest crime rates in the country.[a] Both Negroes and whites in the South have a higher crime rate than the average for the

[a] See Chapter 44, Section 2.

nation. *Within* the South, however, the number of convictions of Negroes is not much greater, on the average, than their proportion in the population: in 1939, Negroes constituted 44.0 per cent of the male prisoners convicted of felonies and received by state and federal prisons and reformatories in the three Southern census divisions.[25] In 1940, the proportion of Negroes in the total population of these areas was 23.8 per cent.[26] The main reasons why Negroes do not constitute an unusually large proportion of the criminals sent to prisons would seem to be that most of their crimes are trivial or are committed against other Negroes and so are considered to warrant only a fine or short local jail sentence. When Negroes commit crimes against whites, however, there is good reason to believe that the sentences are unusually heavy. The South makes the widest application of the death penalty,[a] and Negro criminals come in for much more than their share of the executions.[b] Although no conclusive evidence can be adduced, it would seem that Negro criminals serve longer terms for crimes against whites and are pardoned and paroled much less frequently than white criminals in comparable circumstances.[27]

America is world famous for the high aims and accomplishments of many of its progressive penal institutions in the North and West and, particularly, for the courageous scientific and practical discussion about treatment of crime and asociality. But America is famous also for the convict camps in the South. The generally very low level of Southern penal institutions is well known.[28] With the exception of the federal penitentiaries and one or two of the newer state penitentiaries, the Southern prison or prison camp is a place where prisoners are physically tortured for insubordination of any kind, where the guards are of the lowest stratum of society and receive extremely low pay, where the surroundings are dirty and the food abominable, where there is a tradition of callousness

---

[a] "North Carolina has a death penalty for burglary; Alabama and Virginia for robbery; of six states for arson, only two, Illinois and Delaware, are outside the South, the others being Alabama, North Carolina, South Carolina and Virginia. The death sentence for rape, too, is restricted almost wholly to the South and Southwest. The most common offense to be punished by death is murder. Eight states do not use capital punishment for any offense, and the homicide rates in these states are among the lowest in the nation; high homicide rates characterize the states that rely upon the death sentence. The states with no capital punishment are: Maine, Michigan, Minnesota, North Dakota, Rhode Island, South Dakota, Utah, and Wisconsin." (Raper, *op. cit.*, pp. 164-165.)

[b] "In 10 Southern states, for varying periods, 975 Negroes and 464 whites were sentenced to death. The Negro constitutes less than 30 per cent of the population in these states, but has more than twice as many death sentences imposed. Actual executions make the racial differential still greater, for 60.9 per cent of the Negro death sentences were carried out as compared with 48.7 of the white. The figures for life termers, by race, who actually die in prison are not available, but would most probably show the same race bias. For the Negro is given a more stern sentence and for the same reason is the less likely to have his sentence reduced." (*Ibid.*, p. 166.)

and brutality, where there is not the slightest attempt to reform but only to punish and get work out of the prisoners. Some of the Northern prisons are not good either, and there has been a long, hard struggle to improve very bad prisons in the North, but with the few exceptions noted, Southern prisons do not approximate Northern penal standards. There is no doubt that the average Southern prison is likely to make hardened criminals of all who fall into its clutches.[29] This inexpensive penal system in the South —from the point of view of budgetary income and outgo—is tremendously expensive from the point of view of real social costs.

Conditions are generally so bad in Southern prisons that it would be difficult to say whether Negro prisoners received poorer treatment than white prisoners. The penal institutions in the South are usually segregated for whites and Negroes. There is some opportunity, therefore, for state officials to purchase less food and equipment for Negroes than for whites and to discriminate in other ways. The wardens and guards are, in all cases, Southern poor whites. Probably the most harmful form of discrimination arises out of the fact that several states do not provide separate reformatories for Negro juvenile offenders as they do for white juvenile offenders, and the Negro youth must live with the hardened older criminal.

4. TRENDS AND OUTLOOK

This whole judicial system of courts, sentences and prisons in the South is overripe for fundamental reforms. It represents a tremendous cultural lag in progressive twentieth century America. Reform in this field—especially in the courts—would be strategic in the efforts to improve the Negro people and their living conditions and, consequently, to improve race relations.

There are signs of change. The Supreme Court is increasingly active in censoring the state courts when they transgress the principles of legal procedure: it is pressing the courts to include Negroes on the jury lists, to curb appeals to race prejudice on the part of public prosecutors and private attorneys, to reject evidence obtained by third degree methods, and so on. The attorneys of the federal government and the federal courts in the states have become more diligent in pursuing such offenses against civil liberties of Negroes as fall under their jurisdiction, thereby setting a pattern for the state courts also. Under these two sets of influences, the higher courts of the Southern states are tending increasingly to condemn the more blatant forms of deviation from fair trial in the lower courts.

A new generation of lawyers with a better general education and professional training is coming forward. I have been told that it is becoming easier for Negroes to get even the best local white lawyers to take on their defense in serious cases where there will be much publicity, and white lawyers have testified that their risk of meeting threats and ostracism from white society for so doing is decidedly diminishing. A first class counsel has great influence upon the morals of lower courts. The difficulty of the matter now is that most Negroes cannot afford good lawyers, even when they are available for a price. Probably the most effective means of bringing the Southern courts more rapidly to acquire a fixed pattern of carefulness and equity would be *the setting up of legal aid agencies everywhere in the South which, manned by high class professional lawyers, would be instructed not to work for any new legislation, but to assist poor whites and Negroes to enforce their rights under existing laws in civil and criminal cases.*[30] They should, to be effective, be kept entirely outside local politics and should be instructed to work not only upon application of clients but also to take the initiative, particularly in following the procedures at police courts and in prisons. Even one such agency, placed in a strategic city in the Black Belt—as, for instance, Atlanta, Georgia—would, without ever leaving purely professional routine work, and merely by the examples being set, change considerably the whole judicial atmosphere of the region.

The growth of the educated class of Negroes in the South[31] and the rising educational level of whites; the decreasing provincialism of the region, consequent to this and to industrialization, urbanization and migration; the increasing importance of Southern liberalism and generally the reflection of the humane spirit of the New Deal, the activity of such organizations as the National Association for the Advancement of Colored People and the Interracial Commission are all factors working in the same direction. The continuous influence of public opinion and the press of the North is also a major factor in reform. I have been told repeatedly, sometimes even by liberals in the South, that Northern criticism does more harm than good and is likely to drive Southern public opinion into sullen reaction. This might occasionally be the short-range effect, but I have also seen how, behind this defensive attitude in resenting Northern criticism, the average Southerner feels most embarrassed because of it, and how reform activity in the South is often spurred by considerations of national opinions. Another factor which is bound to have great influence in the future is the developing Negro vote. Already Negroes get more legal justice in those cities where they vote—even when that vote is bought.

It is the author's observation that, *in principle, the average white Southerner is no longer prepared to defend racial inequality of justice.* Much of the judicial discrimination against Negroes in the South seems to be backed or tolerated by public opinion because of carelessness and ignorance in regard to the Negro, rather than by an intentional and considered aim to discriminate. As far as public opinion is part of the problem, the task is, therefore, mainly one of adult education. White people must be taught to understand the damaging effects upon the whole society of a system of justice which is not equitable. Means must be found to bring the pressing problems of crime prevention, and of punishment and prison reform, into the awareness of the general public.

It is astonishing to observe how far to the background these problems are pushed in America, and how deep the common ignorance of them is even in the higher classes. Most people discuss crime as if it had nothing to do with social conditions and was simply an inevitable outcome of personal badness. Southern whites tend to exaggerate the extent of Negro crime and tend to under-estimate the extent of white crime: one of the results is that they consider crime and prison reform part of the Negro problem and therefore not to be discussed. Rape and sexual crimes play a great role in Southern thinking on the problem, but the idea that such crimes, when they occur, have to be suspected as symptoms of psychic abnormality seems to be entirely absent. I understand that even the great number of murder cases in the South are tried without a sanity hearing. Capital punishment is not a problem to the general American public; that it stimulates violence does not occur to the average American. In the South, even educated people, when they think of punishment for crime, have their minds fixed on vengeance and on the isolation or eradication of the criminal. Seldom do they discuss punishment as a means of general crime prevention. Other techniques of individual prevention—by rebuilding the criminal himself—are usually entirely ignored. Under these circumstances the problems of court and prison reform are considered only by a small minority of the highly cultured.

It is not difficult to understand the psychological mechanism behind this astonishing blind spot in the regional culture. These problems are unpopular because their discussion is bound to result in the rational demonstration that *it is in the interest of society to care for the Negro—and even for the criminal Negro.*

CHAPTER 27

VIOLENCE AND INTIMIDATION

1. THE PATTERN OF VIOLENCE

It is the custom in the South to permit whites to resort to violence and threats of violence against the life, personal security, property and freedom of movement of Negroes. There is a wide variety of behavior, ranging from a mild admonition to murder, which the white man may exercise to control Negroes. While the practice has its origin in the slavery tradition, it continues to flourish because of the laxity and inequity of the administration of law and justice. It would not be possible except for the deficient operation of the judicial sanctions in protecting Negroes' rights and liberties. Both the practice of intimidation and violence and the inadequate functioning of justice in the region are expressions of the same spirit of relative lawlessness; both are tolerated and upheld by the same public opinion. Both are rooted in this strange Southern combination of conservatism and illegality.[a] Both are expressions on the part of the Southern public of its dissatisfaction with formal laws, its disregard for orderly government.

The social pattern of subduing the Negroes by means of physical force was inherent in the slavery system. The master himself, with the backing, if needed, of the local police and, indeed, of all white neighbors, had to execute this force, and he was left practically unrestricted by any formal laws. After Emancipation the Black Codes,[b] of the period 1865-1867, were attempts to legalize a continued white control over the freedmen. Most of these laws were abolished during the Congressional Reconstruction, but their spirit prevailed in the complex of laws protecting the planters' interests—labor enticement laws, crop lien laws, vagrancy laws[c]—by which the states sanctioned the actions of the police and the courts in virtually upholding peonage, in spite of its being a federal offense. As the federal judiciary agencies have lately become active in stamping out peonage, and as the decline in the foreign market, the A.A.A. crop restriction policy, and other factors have made labor supply relatively abundant

[a] See Chapter 20, Section 7.
[b] See Chapter 10, Section 3.
[c] See Chapter 10, Section 4.

in the rural South and peonage unnecessary, these laws have become increasingly obsolete.

But quite apart from laws, and even against the law, there exists a pattern of violence against Negroes in the South upheld by the relative absence of fear of legal reprisal. Any white man can strike or beat a Negro, steal or destroy his property, cheat him in a transaction and even take his life, without much fear of legal reprisal. The minor forms of violence—cheating and striking—are a matter of everyday occurrence, but the major ones are infrequent enough to be talked about. Negroes, of course, try to avoid situations in which such violence is likely to occur, and if Negroes do incur the displeasure of a white man, a mere command or threat is usually enough to control them without the use of actual violence. The Negro's economic dependence upon whites makes these verbal controls especially potent. But accidental insult, and sometimes nothing at all except the general insecurity or sadism of certain whites, can serve as occasion for violence. Of course, there are certain checks on violence: most Southerners do not want to be mean or dishonest toward Negroes directly. Public opinion in the South tends to frown upon any white man who acquires a reputation for being consistently mean or dishonest, and on rare occasions may even ostracize him socially or encourage the application of legal sanctions against him. But the general attitude is one of *laissez faire*: if a plantation owner cheats or beats his Negro tenants, "that's his business"; if a Negro is the victim of a sudden outburst of violence, "he must have done something to deserve it." Above all, the Negro must be kept in his "place."

There is little that Negroes can do to protect themselves, even where they are a majority of the population.[a] They cannot easily secure the protection of police or court against white men. They cannot secure the protection of white employers against white men, unless the latter are poor or have had a bad reputation. They can, of course, strike back but they know that that means a more violent retaliation, often in an organized form and with danger to other Negroes. In an important sense, lynching and the wholesale destruction of Negro property are often merely the extreme forms of organized white retaliation against Negroes who have struck back when they were struck or cheated first by whites.[b] This retaliation more frequently takes a less violent form: the legal system may be called on to imprison the Negro for "attacking a white man"; white men may pretend that they are going to lynch the Negro but end up by only beating him or using the "tar and feather" technique; or the Negro may be "run out of town" and warned not to return.

[a] Negroes cannot protect themselves *especially* where they are a majority of the population, since this is for the most part in the Deep South.

[b] The causes of lynching are discussed in Sections 2 and 3 of this chapter.

The principles that the law and the law-enforcing agencies are supreme, impartial and above all groups in society has never taken strong root.[1] White people are accustomed—individually and in groups—to take the law into their own hands and to expect the police and the courts to countenance this and sometimes lend their active cooperation.[2] In the plantation areas where the social and political subordination of Negroes is solidified, there is not much need for special organizations of vigilantes to effectuate the extra-legal sanctions. The Ku Klux Klan and similar secret societies thrive, rather, in the border regions and in industrial communities.[3] But this is only a testimony that the extra-legal sanctions work more effectively where they are less challenged.

In this region the custom of going armed continually or having weapons within easy reach at home was retained from *ante-bellum* days. This custom was taken over also by the Negroes during Reconstruction days.[4] The writer has been astonished to see how firearms and slashing knives are part of the equipment of many lower class whites and Negroes in the South. The laws against carrying "concealed weapons" are not efficient, as they do not—and for constitutional reasons cannot[5]—forbid the owning, buying and selling of arms. White policemen have often complained to the author that it is not possible to disarm the civil population. They do not urge reforms, however, but take the prevailing situation as natural and inevitable. In the Negro community, where personal security is most lacking, this dangerous pattern of having knives and guns around is most widespread. It undoubtedly contributes to the high record of violent actions, most of the time directed against other Negroes.

2. LYNCHING

Lynching is spectacular and has attracted a good deal of popular and scientific[6] attention. It is one Southern pattern which has continued to arouse disgust and reaction in the North and has, therefore, been made much of by Negro publicists. It should not be forgotten, however, that lynching is just one type of extra-legal violence in a whole range of types that exist in the South. The other types, which were considered earlier in this chapter are much more common than lynching and their bad effects on white morals and Negro security are greater.[7]

Lynchings were becoming common in the South in the 'thirties, 'forties and 'fifties of the nineteenth century. Most of the victims in this early period were white men. The pattern of lynching Negroes became set during Reconstruction. No reliable statistics before 1889 are available. Between 1889 and 1940, according to Tuskegee Institute figures, 3,833 people were lynched, about four-fifths of whom were Negroes. The Southern states account for nine-tenths of the lynchings. More than two-thirds of the remaining one-tenth occurred in the six states which immediately border the South: Maryland, West Virginia, Ohio, Indiana, Illinois and Kansas. Since the early 1890's, the trend has been toward fewer and fewer lynchings. The annual average in the 'nineties was near 200; in the 'thirties it dropped to slightly over 10. In 1941 it was down to 4, but there are already more than this in 1942 (July). The decrease has been faster outside the South, and the lynching of whites has dropped much more than that of Negroes. Lynching has become, therefore, more and more a Southern phenomenon and a racial one. Against the decrease in number of victims there has been a marked trend toward greatly aggravated brutality, extending to torture, mutilation and other sadistic excesses.[8]

Lynching is a rural and small town custom and occurs most commonly in poor districts.[9] There are some indications that lynchings go in waves and tend to recur in the same districts.[10] The accusations against persons lynched during the period for which there are records were: in 38 per cent of the cases for homicide, 6 per cent for felonious assault, 16 per cent for rape, 7 per cent for attempted rape, 7 per cent for theft, 2 per cent for insult to white persons and 24 per cent for miscellaneous offenses or no offense at all.[11] In the last category are all sorts of irritations: testifying at court against a white man or bringing suit against him, refusal to pay a note, seeking employment out of place, offensive language or boastful remarks.[12] Regarding the accusations for crime, Raper testifies: "Case studies of nearly one hundred lynchings since 1929 convince the writer that around a third of the victims were falsely accused."[a] The meaning of these facts is that, in principle, a lynching is not merely a punishment against an individual but a disciplinary device against the Negro group.[b]

The danger of Negroes' desire to rape white women has acquired a special and strategic position in the defense of the lynching practice.[c] Actually, only 23 per cent of the victims were accused of raping or attempting to rape. There is much reason to believe that this figure has been

[a] Arthur Raper, "Race and Class Pressures," unpublished manuscript prepared for this study (1940), p. 274. Raper adds that it is his ". . . opinion that a great contribution could be made by some arrangement for immediate factual newspaper reports on each lynching and other race and class violence by trained newspaper men. At present the local representative of the news-gathering agencies sends in the story and usually says about what the community wants said. Expert reporters who could be sent wherever a mob threatened would be free to present the facts in the case." (*Ibid.*, pp. 274-275.)

Raper's idea is that such a service, to be really useful, should be sponsored and underwritten by an impartial agency.

[b] See Section 3 of this chapter.

[c] According to Sir Harry H. Johnston (*The Negro in the New World* [1910], p. 464), "Allusions to the rape or attempted rape of white women or girls, by negroes or mulattoes, are rare in the literature of the United States prior to 1870."

inflated by the fact that a mob which makes the accusation of rape is secure against any further investigation; by the broad Southern definition of rape to include all sex relations between Negro men and white women; and by the psychopathic fears of white women in their contacts with Negro men. The causes of lynching must, therefore, be sought outside the Southern rationalization of "protecting white womanhood."

This does not mean that sex, in a subtler sense, is not a background factor in lynching. The South has an obsession with sex which helps to make this region quite irrational in dealing with Negroes generally. In a special sense, too, as William Archer, Thomas P. Bailey, and Sir Harry Johnston early pointed out,[13] lynching is a way of punishing Negroes for the white Southerners' own guilt feelings in violating Negro women, or for presumed Negro sexual superiority. The dullness and insecurity of rural Southern life, as well as the eminence of emotional puritanical religion, also create an emphasis upon sex in the South which especially affects adolescent, unmarried, and climacteric women, who are inclined to give significance to innocent incidents.[14] The atmosphere around lynching is astonishingly like that of the tragic phenomenon of "witch hunting" which disgraced early Protestantism in so many countries. The sadistic elements in most lynchings also point to a close relation between lynching and thwarted sexual urges.[15]

Lynching is a local community affair. The state authorities usually do not side with the lynchers. They often try to prevent lynchings but seldom take active steps to punish the guilty. This is explainable in view of the tight hold on the courts by local public opinion. The lynchers are seldom indicted by a grand jury. Even more seldom are they sentenced, since the judge, the prosecutor, the jurors, and the witnesses are either in sympathy with the lynchers or, in any case, do not want to press the case. If sentenced, they are usually pardoned.[16] While the state police can be used to prevent lynching, the local police often support the lynching. From his study of 100 lynchings since 1929, Raper estimates that ". . . at least one-half of the lynchings are carried out with police officers participating, and that in nine-tenths of the others the officers either condone or wink at the mob action."[17]

The actual participants in the lynching mobs usually belong to the frustrated lower strata of Southern whites.[18] Occasionally, however, the people of the middle and upper classes take part, and generally they condone the deed, and nearly always they find it advisable to let the incident pass without assisting in bringing the guilty before the court.[19] Women and children are not absent from lynching mobs; indeed, women sometimes incite the mobs into action.[20]

3. THE PSYCHOPATHOLOGY OF LYNCHING

The psychopathology of the lynching mob has been discussed intensively in recent years.[21] Poverty and economic fear have been stressed as background factors.[22] It is generally held that the rise of lynchings and race riots during and immediately after the First World War had much to do with the increased mobility of, and competition from, Negroes during this period.[23] A substantial correlation from year to year between low cotton prices and high lynchings is demonstrated.[24]

Economic fear is mixed with social fear: a feeling that the Negro is "getting out of his place," and the white man's social status is being threatened and is in need of defense. ". . . lynching is much more an expression of Southern fear of Negro progress than of Negro crime," writes Walter White.[25] Tannenbaum observed that:

> The South gives indications of being afraid of the Negro. I do not mean physical fear. It is not a matter of cowardice or bravery; it is something deeper and more fundamental. It is a fear of losing grip upon the world. It is an unconscious fear of changing status.[26]

It is this feeling which is behind the common saying which a visitor to the South will hear even today from lower class whites that "a lynching now and then" is expedient or necessary in keeping the Negroes from becoming "uppity." It is commonly observed that after the First World War many lynchings of Negro soldiers—sometimes in uniform—were openly motivated by the fear that they had gotten "wrong ideas" about their social status while serving in France.[27]

The low level of education and general culture in the white South is another important background factor. Allied with it is the prevalence of a narrow-minded and intolerant, "fundamentalist" type of Protestant evangelical religion.[28] Occasional violently emotional revival services, and regular appeals in ordinary preaching to fear and passion rather than to calm reasoning, on the one hand, and denunciations of modern thought, scientific progress, and all kinds of nonconformism, on the other hand, help to create a state of mind which makes a lynching less extraordinary. Methodist and Baptist preachers were active in reviving the Ku Klux Klan after the First World War.[29] With but rare exceptions preachers and local religious leaders have not come out against lynchers.[30]

Another important background factor in the causation of lynching and other major forms of violence is the isolation, the dullness of everyday life and the general boredom of rural and small town life in the South.[31] There is a lack of wholesome recreation or even variation, which gives a real and sinister meaning to H. L. Mencken's statement that ". . . lynching often takes the place of the merry-go-round, the theatre, the symphony orchestra, and other diversions common to larger communities."[32]

Thus far we have considered the background factors and underlying causes of lynching. The causation is such that, when the time is ripe, almost any incident may touch it off. The incident is usually some crime, real or suspected, by a Negro against a white, or merely a "racial insult," such as when a Negro buys an automobile or steps beyond the etiquette of race relations in any way. Rumors will often start or accelerate a lynching. The lynching itself may take one or two main forms: in a *mob lynching* the whole community will participate with a high degree of frenzy;[33] in a *vigilante lynching* a restricted number of men, often disguised, will perform the deed with much ceremony.

The effects of lynchings are far-reaching. In the locality where it has happened and in a wide region surrounding it, the relations between the two groups deteriorate. The Negroes are terror-stricken and sullen.[34] The whites are anxious and are likely to show the assertiveness and suspicion of persons with bad, but hardened, consciences. Some whites are afraid of Negro retaliation or emigration. Every visitor to such a community must notice the antagonism and mutual lack of confidence between the two groups.

The long-run effects of lynching also are bad. As students of the Negro problem have long recognized, crime will not be hampered but rather stimulated by violence.[35] Far outside the locality where the lynching has occurred, in fact, all over the nation, it brutalizes feelings. Even in the North, some people have ceased to be concerned when another lynching occurs, and they jest about going South to see a lynching. It must have a particularly bad influence upon interracial attitudes of young people in the two groups.[36] Thus lynching has a psychological importance out of all proportion to its small frequency.

In every locality where there has been a lynching there are a great many people—sometimes a clear majority—who, when they think calmly, consider the incident most unfortunate. The nation-wide publicity created around a lynching community is, for one thing, commonly recognized to be damaging. The present writer has met few whites of the middle and upper classes in the South who have expressed themselves as in favor of lynch justice. But equally few have pretended that they would take any personal risks to hinder a lynching, and they make no effort to punish the lynchers. The ordinary Southerner apparently thinks that neither the upholding of the majesty of the law nor the life of even an innocent Negro is worth such a sacrifice. And, above all, Negroes must not have the satisfaction of seeing the whites divided or their assailants punished.

4. TRENDS AND OUTLOOK

It is possible to speculate about the causes for the decline in lynching. If our analysis of the background factors is correct, the rising standard of living and the improved education must have been of importance. The fundamentalism and emotionalism of Southern religion have been decreasing. Cultural isolation is being broken by radio, improved highways and cheap motor cars. There is more diversion from the drab and monotonous small town life, and the sex taboos have been somewhat relaxed. The national agitation around lynching, strengthened after the organization of the National Association for the Advancement of Colored People in 1909, has undoubtedly been of tremendous importance in awakening influential people in the South to the urgency of stopping lynching. The sharp decline in lynching since 1922 has undoubtedly something to do with the fact that early in that year the Dyer Anti-Lynching Bill was put through the House of Representatives. It was later killed in the Senate by the filibuster of the Southern senators, and the sell-out of Western and Northern senators,[37] but the continuous discussion of the measure from then on has probably been of great importance.[a] A prominent Negro leader confided to the present author that, as a force to stamp out lynching, the agitation around the bill is probably as effective, or more effective, than the law itself would be.

Southern organizations of whites have taken to condemning lynching. Some religious denominations of the South declare against lynching at their annual conventions and sponsor programs on racial matters for white youth. One of the most active fights of the Commission for Interracial Cooperation has been against lynching,[b] and, under its auspices, the Association of Southern Women for the Prevention of Lynching has collected nearly 50,000 signatures of Southern white women and of a few hundred peace officers to a pledge against lynching. Other women's organizations in the South also have been active in the propaganda against lynching. One of the most notable changes has been in the attitudes of the press. Today the great majority of Southern newspapers will come out openly against lynching. State authorities usually try to prevent lynchings, and they have an instrument in the state police systems which can be readily concentrated in any community where people are congregating for a lynching. Behind this movement is the growing strength of Southern liberalism, which we have considered earlier.[38]

[a] Bills against lynching have been introduced in Congress many times since 1922, but none of them has come so close to passage. Southern congressmen center their strategy against anti-lynching legislation by claiming that it would be unconstitutional and an infringement upon states' rights.

[b] See Chapter 39, Section 11.

It is often said that the decrease of lynching is only nominal, or partly so. There are several substitutes for lynching. One is the killing of Negro criminals by the police officers.[39] Similar to this is the precipitate and predetermined trial given to an accused Negro when there is danger that he will be lynched.[a] Another substitute is quiet murder without the formation of a mob.[40] A third substitute, "legal lynchings" proper, is that in which police and court officials promise to vigilante leaders that the accused Negro will receive a quick trial and the death penalty if he is not lynched.[41]

There is no way of finding out whether these substitute practices are really increasing. The present author is rather inclined to believe that they, too, have been declining. But there is no doubt that these substitutes have not declined as rapidly as lynching. All the other forms of violence against Negroes—striking, beating, robbing, destroying property, exiling, threatening—still occur in the South with great, though perhaps slightly decreasing, frequency. Such outrages do not get publicity in the white press and are not actively opposed by white organizations or state governments. Yet it would be easier to prevent and punish them with an adequate police and court system than it would be to curb lynching, for the white perpetrators of these outrages are more often individuals than groups. As in the case of lynching, an aroused Northern and Southern liberal public opinion would be effective in preventing them. In the last analysis, the true perspective of lynching as of these other forms of violence and intimidation is the inherited pattern of white society in the South not to respect the rights of Negroes on equal terms: the custom of tolerating the cheating of Negroes in economic deals and, generally, the insistence that he shall humbly pray for his due as a personal kindness, not proudly demand it as a right.

5. Riots

In one sense, the riot is the most extreme form of extra-legal mob violence used to prevent Negroes from getting justice. In another sense, however, the riot is quite different from all other forms of mob violence: it is not a one-way punishment but a two-way battle. The Negroes may be hopelessly outnumbered and beaten, but they fight back. There is danger to the white man participating in the riot as there usually is not when he engages in other forms of violence against Negroes. Sometimes the killing and beating of a large number of Negroes is called a riot: we prefer to call this a terrorization or massacre and consider it as a magnified, or mass, lynching. Its effects are those of a lynching. In this book we shall reserve the term "riot" to refer to mass violence in which Negroes fight as unreservedly as whites.

[a] Even the death sentence given by the courts to an accused Negro will not always deter a lynching mob.

The riot is as much, or more, characteristic of the North than it is of the South. It is generally only when Negroes think they might have something to gain that they will take the risk of fighting back, and in the North they know that some portion of the white population is on their side and that the police will ultimately restore order. The riot is primarily an urban phenomenon, as lynching is primarily a rural phenomenon, and the Northern Negro population is practically all urban. Housing segregation—or rather the concentration of Negroes in a few compact areas—is almost essential if Negroes are to fight back, and such segregation is more prevalent in Northern cities than in Southern cities.[a]

The pre-Civil War equivalents of the riot were the slave insurrection and its suppression.[b] Unusually bad conditions or the rare rise of bellicose Negro leaders would, not infrequently, provoke small spontaneous insurrections. The major insurrections of the early nineteenth century, led by Denmark Vesey and Nat Turner, were planned well in advance, and met with some success before their ultimate failure. In the North there were small-scale but vicious riots between 1829 and 1840, and again after 1880.[c]

It is impossible to say whether there is a trend in the number of riots. The great number of riots occurred during and just after the First World War, when the North was concerned with the tremendous migration of Negroes from the South and the South was concerned about the possible demands of returning Negro soldiers. According to W. E. B. Du Bois, there were riots in 26 American cities in 1919.[42] The most notorious was the Chicago riot in which 15 whites and 23 Negroes were killed, and 178 whites and 342 Negroes were injured.[43] The riot in Phillips County, Arkansas, in the same year, saw from 25 to 50 persons killed.[44] During the War, the most notorious riots were those in East St. Louis, Illinois, during which at least 39 Negroes and 8 whites were killed,[45] and in Houston, Texas, where 17 whites were killed and 13 Negroes were hanged, 41 were imprisoned for life, and 40 others held for trial.[46] Before the War, the most deadly riots were: the Atlanta, Georgia, riot of 1906 which killed 10 Negroes and 2 whites (more a one-way terrorization than a two-way riot);[47] and the Springfield, Illinois, riot of 1908, which cost the lives of 2 Negroes and 4 whites.[48]

Recent years have seen few race riots. They have become as unpopular as lynchings. The extreme tension of the First World War period has lessened, even if the northward migration and the existence of Negro soldiers continues. The beginning of the Second World War, however, shows some signs of recurrence of riots. There have been a number of

[a] See Chapter 29, Section 3.
[b] See Chapter 35, Section 1.
[c] See: W. E. B. Du Bois, *The Philadelphia Negro* (1899), pp. 26-27; James Weldon Johnson, *Black Manhattan* (1930), pp. 127-128.

incidents where Negro soldiers have clashed with Southern police and civilians with some fatalities on both sides.[a] In spring, 1942, there was a clash in the North: in trying to move into a government defense housing project built for them in Detroit, Negroes were set upon by white civilians and police. The project was built at the border between Negro and white neighborhoods but had been planned for Negroes. Encouraged by the vacillation of the federal government and the friendliness of the Detroit police (many of whom are Southern-born) and stimulated by the backing of a United States congressman and such organizations as the Ku Klux Klan, white residents of the neighborhood and other parts of the city staged protest demonstrations against the Negro housing project, which led to the riot. Whether these incidents presage another period of post-war riots, it is too early to say. On the whole, it does not seem likely that there will be further riots, of any significant degree of violence, in the North. Detroit is almost unique among Northern cities for its large Southern-born population and for its Ku Klux Klan. The main cause of riots in the North during the period after 1917 was the unusually large migration to the North and the consequent displacement of some whites by Negroes in jobs and residences. So far, the present war boom has seen no unusual northward migration of Negroes and relatively little displacement in jobs. A further reason why there probably will be no riots in the North after this War is that there is developing a new consciousness of the American Creed and of its significance for Negroes.

What may occur in the North, rather than the two-way conflicts which we are calling riots, are some sporadic and unorganized outbreaks on the part of the Negroes with little opposition from the whites. Such was the character of the so-called "Harlem Riot" of 1935 in New York City. If these occur, they will be due to continuing discrimination from the whites and to growing realization by Negroes that peaceful requests for their rights are not getting them anywhere. Whether or not these outbreaks will occur in the North will depend on whether or not the trend continues toward increased willingness to stand by the precepts of the American Creed.

While the future looks fairly peaceful in the North, there are many signs of growing race tension in the South. It seems almost probable that, unless drastic action is taken, severe race riots will break out in the South. We shall give some attention to this situation in the final chapter of this book.

The causation of riots would seem to be much like that of lynching. There is a background of mounting tension, caused by economic insecurity

---

[a] From the time of the inception of the draft in the fall of 1940 until April, 1942, there were three such clashes serious enough to get nation-wide publicity. These occurred in Fort Bragg, North Carolina, Gurdon, Arkansas, and Alexandria, Louisiana. In addition, there was a clash between Southern white soldiers and Negro soldiers at Fort Dix, New Jersey.

of whites, belief that the Negro is rising, sex jealousy, boredom on the part of the lower strata of the white population. The local police are often known to be on the side of the whites. The breaking point is caused by a crime or rumor of crime by a Negro against a white person, or by the attempt of a Negro to claim a legal right. The effects of riots may be even more harmful to amicable race relations than are those of lynching. Whites do not feel the twinge of bad conscience which they have when they have lynched helpless and unresisting Negroes. The feelings of fear and insecurity on the part of the whites are only increased when some of their own number have been killed or injured. The memory of a riot is much longer than that of a lynching, for both whites and Negroes. Their devastation and relative fewness make them landmarks in history.

PART VII

SOCIAL INEQUALITY

CHAPTER 28

THE BASIS OF SOCIAL INEQUALITY

1. THE VALUE PREMISE

The word "social" has two distinct meanings. There is the ordinary scientific usage of the term to refer to the whole range of relations between men. There is also the narrower but more popular usage which refers to personal relations, particularly those of an intimate sort. It is in the latter, more limited, sense that we shall use the term "social" in this part. Equality in "social relations" is commonly denied American Negroes. An elaborate system of measures is applied to separate the two groups and to prevent the building up of intimate relations on the plane of equality. Personal identifications of members of the two groups is thereby hindered. Some of these segregation measures have a spatial or institutional character, others are embodied in an etiquette of racial behavior.

Our main value premise in this part is again the precept of *equality of opportunity* in the American Creed. Race and color are not accepted as grounds for discrimination according to the Creed. Social discrimination is defined from this value premise as an arrangement which restricts opportunities for some individuals more than for others. Judged by the norm of equality in the American Creed, such practices are unfair and wrong. The Creed has, in this sphere, been given constitutional sanction in America as far as *public services* and *state regulations* are concerned.

But when segregation and discrimination are the outcome of individual action, the second main norm of the American Creed, namely, *liberty,* can be invoked in their defense. It must be left to the individual white man's own discretion whether or not he wants to receive Negroes in his home, shake hands with them, and eat with them. *If upheld solely by individual choice,* social segregation manifested by *all* white people in an American community can be—and is—defended by the norm of personal liberty. When, however, legal, economic, or social sanctions are applied to enforce conformity from *other* whites, and when Negroes are made to adjust their behavior in response to *organized* white demands, this violates the norm of personal liberty. In the national ideology, the point where approved liberty changes into disapproved restriction on liberty is left somewhat uncertain. The old liberal formula that the individual shall be left free to follow the dictates of his own will so long as he does not substantially hamper the liberty of other persons does not solve the problem, because it is not definite enough. As remarked in an earlier chapter, the American Creed is in a process of change from "rugged individualism." It is giving increasing weight to "the other fellow's" liberty, and thus narrowing the scope of the actions which become condoned by the individualistic liberty formula.

To apply the American value premises in this condition of internal conflict within the concept of liberty itself—which is only another aspect of its external conflict with the concept of equality—stress has to be laid on the actual amount of discrimination. When there is substantial discrimination present, liberty for the white person has to be overruled by equality. To discern discrimination we must take into account the indirect effects of segregation in terms of cultural isolation, political and legal disabilities, and economic disadvantages, which are often much more important than the direct social discrimination.

From these viewpoints there is hardly any doubt that the major portion of the system of social segregation and discrimination against Negroes is a challenge to the American Creed. As this system is administered in practice, most of it is unconstitutional and even contrary to the state laws which, in the South as in the North, are framed in terms of equality. There remains, however, a residual amount of idiosyncrasy in purely personal relations which may be upheld by the American liberty norm as it does not involve any substantial contradiction to the equality norm. In any case, these personal preferences and prejudices fall outside *res publica*; in Lord Bryce's words:

> As regards social relations, law can do but little save in the way of expressing the view the State takes of how its members should behave to one another. Good feeling and good manners cannot be imposed by statute.[1]

We must, however, also remember that the equalitarian, internally peaceful society, envisaged in the democratic Creed of this country, cannot exist when good feeling and good manners do not usually characterize the relations between members of the society.

We shall, in this chapter, attempt to study the mechanism of social segregation and discrimination, somewhat in detail, as it operates today in various regions of the country. But first we want to penetrate somewhat deeper into the rationalized ideologies behind its various manifestations and into the attitudes of different classes of white people who are upholding the color bar. We shall again have to devote the major part of our inquiry to conditions in the South where more than three-fourths of the Negro people live, and where segregation and discrimination are most prevalent.

2. THE ONE-SIDEDNESS OF THE SYSTEM OF SEGREGATION

I have heard few comments made so frequently and with so much emphasis and so many illustrations as the one that "Negroes are happiest among themselves" and that "Negroes really don't want white company but prefer to be among their own race." Even sociologists, educators, and interracial experts have informed me that, when the two groups keep apart, the wish for separation is as pronounced among Negroes as among whites.[2] In the South, many liberals are eager to stress this assertion as part of the justification for their unwillingness to give up the Southern doctrine that the Negroes must not be allowed to aspire to "social equality." Southern conservatives will usually give a somewhat different twist to the argument and actually insist that Negroes are perfectly satisfied with their social status in the South. But the conservatives are more likely to contradict themselves bluntly in the next sentence by asserting that in the back of the Negro's mind there is a keen desire to be "like white people" and to "marry white girls."

For the moment, we shall leave it an open question whether the whites understand the Negroes correctly on this point. We shall start from the evident fact that—quite independent of whether or not, to what extent, and how the Negroes have accommodated themselves—*social segregation and discrimination is a system of deprivations forced upon the Negro group by the white group*. This is equally true in the North and in the South, though in this respect, as in all others, there is more segregation and discrimination in the South, and thus the phenomenon is easier to observe.

That segregation and discrimination are forced upon the Negroes by the whites becomes apparent in the *one-sidedness* of their application. Negroes are ordinarily never admitted to white churches in the South, but if a strange white man enters a Negro church the visit is received as a great honor. The guest will be ushered to a front seat or to the platform. The service will often be interrupted, an announcement will be made that there is a "white friend" present, and he will be asked to address the Negro audience, which will loudly testify its high appreciation. Likewise, a white stranger will be received with utmost respect and cordiality in any Negro school, and everything will be done to satisfy his every wish, whereas a Negro under similar circumstances would be pushed off the grounds of a white school. Whenever I have entered a Negro theater in the South, the girl in the ticket office has regularly turned a bewildered face and told me that "it is a colored movie." But she has apparently done this because she thought I was making a mistake and wanted to spare me embarrassment. When I answered that I did not care, the ticket office girls usually sold the ticket and received my visit as a courtesy. I have never been refused service in a Negro restaurant in the South.

When the white conductor in a train has told me occasionally that I was in the wrong car, the underlying assumption has also been the same, that the separation was made in order to save white people from having to tolerate Negro company. Contrary to the laws—which are all written on the fiction of equality—he has, with a shrug of his shoulders, always left me where I was after I told him I had gone there purposely to have a look at the Negroes.[a] A Negro who would disclose a similar desire to observe whites would, of course, be dealt with in quite another way.[3] In the street-cars and buses the separation seems to be enforced fairly well in both directions. When, however, the conductor tells me, a white man, that I have taken the wrong seat, it is done in a spirit of respect and in order to help me preserve my caste status. The assumption is that I have made a mistake with no intention of overstepping the rules. In the case of a Negro the assumption is usually the contrary, that he is trying to intrude. In public buildings or private establishments of the South, I have never encountered any objection to my entering the spaces set aside for the Negroes, nor to my riding in the elevator set apart for Negroes if, for any reason, the white car was not there or was filled.

The rules are understood to be for the protection of whites and directed against Negroes. This applies also to social rituals and etiquette. The white man may waive most of the customs, as long as he does not demonstrate such a friendliness that he becomes known as a "nigger lover"; the reaction then comes, however, from the white society. He can recognize the Negro on the street and stop for a chat, or he can ignore him. He can offer his hand to shake, or he can keep it back.[4] Negroes often complain about the uncertainty they experience because of the fact that the initiative in defining the personal situation always belongs to the white man. It is the white man who chooses between the alternatives as to the character of the contact to be established. The Negro, who often does not know how the white man has chosen, receives surprises in one direction or the other, which constantly push him off his balance.[5]

The white man is not completely free either. He cannot go so far as to "lose caste" or to endanger the color line for the rest of the community. And when he takes certain freedoms, he must not allow the Negro to understand that he, the Negro, can claim them as a right. But each restriction on the white man's freedom is made to appear as a privilege, whereas each restriction on the Negro's freedom is culturally defined as an insult or a discrimination. Thus the one-sidedness of the segregation system is *felt* to hold, even when it does not so appear to the outsider.[6] The one-sidedness

[a] Cases could be cited where conductors have forced white men out of the Negro car into the white car. These would seem, however, to be extremely rare in the Lower South, although not uncommon in the Upper South.

of the system of segregation is apparent also in the fact that the better accommodations are always reserved for the white people.

The sanctions which enforce the rules of segregation and discrimination also will be found to be one-sided in their application. They are applied by the whites to the Negroes, never by the Negroes to the whites. Whites occasionally apply them to other whites who go too far, but the latter are felt to have already lost caste. The laws are written upon the pretext of equality but are applied only against the Negroes. The police and the courts, as we have pointed out in preceding chapters, are active in enforcing customs far outside those set down in legal statutes; the object of this enforcement is the Negro. Threats, intimidations, and open violence are additional sanctions, all directed against the Negroes and "nigger-loving" casteless whites. And there are economic sanctions: most Negroes are dependent for their livelihood on the good-will of white employers and white officials. The more perfectly the rules work, the less do the sanctions need to be applied.

In the North, where the whole system of social segregation and discrimination is kept *sub rosa*, the sanctions of the law are ordinarily turned the other way—to protect Negro equality. The Negroes in the North have, for these and other reasons, a greater margin for assertiveness. The author has observed that in the North, and particularly in New York's Harlem, he has occasionally been made to feel unwelcome in Negro restaurants. This attitude, however, is even there an exception. The Negroes who have attempted to "Jim Crow" me have explained their actions partly as revenge and partly as the result of suspicion against the intentions of white people who frequent Negro places. It has always disappeared and changed into the greatest friendliness when I have disclosed myself as not being an American.[7]

A major part of this chapter will be devoted to an analysis of the popular concepts, beliefs, and theories that are advanced by white people to motivate this one-sided system of segregation and discrimination. But before we proceed to this analysis, we shall have to return to the conditions in the *ante-bellum* South. In the field of personal and social relations—as in other fields of the Negro problem—what we are studying is in reality the survivals in modern American society of the slavery institution. The white Southerner is right when, in discussing every single phase of the Negro problem, he constantly falls back in his arguments on the history of the region.

3. THE BEGINNING IN SLAVERY

Inherent in slavery as a social arrangement was the principle that the slave was inferior as a human being. He was allowed certain indulgences but could claim nothing as a right or privilege. The paternalistic rule of the master who owned his body and all his abilities, including his propensity to procreate, stretched out over the most intimate phases of his life and was absolute, personal and arbitrary. The stamp of social inferiority on the Negro slave became strengthened by the race dogma, the functional importance of which we have studied in an earlier chapter.[a] This biological rationalization and the logic of the slavery institution itself also isolated the free Negroes and dragged them down into social inferiority.

In most relations a fairly complete social separation of the Negro group was enforced as a matter of policy and routine in a slavery society. The lives of the slaves were closely regimented in the interest of exploiting their labor and hindering their escape. Under the influence of the rising fear of slave revolts, the spread of abolitionism in the North, and the actual escape of many Negro slaves along the "underground railroad," the regimentation became increasingly strict during the decades preceding the Civil War. This regimentation of the slaves prevented, almost entirely, social contacts between the slaves and the whites who had no slaves. On the larger plantations the field slaves were usually constrained to the company of each other. Their main white contact was the overseer and, occasionally, the master and members of his family. On small holdings their contacts with the master and his family were more frequent and intensive.[8] Even the household slaves, however, never shared in the whites' life, except as servants whose humble station was made evident by all available means, including a ceremonial etiquette of obsequiousness which naturally developed between two groups of such different culture and such unequal status.

The slaves were provided with living quarters apart from the whites. Their religious activities also were usually separate. When allowed to attend religious services in the presence of white people, they had a segregated place in the church. They received no regular schooling. It was even forbidden by law to teach the slaves to read. They had their own amusements and recreations and never mixed in those of the whites. Their traveling was closely restricted. Marriage between the two groups was, of course, quite out of the question. There was a considerable amount of interracial sex relations, but they were usually of an exploitative type and restricted to those between white men and slave women. Most of these generalizations hold true also of the free Negroes in the South. They were forced into social isolation. White people did not, and could not in a slave society, accept them as equals.

4. THE JIM CROW LAWS

Emancipation loosened the bonds on Negro slaves and allowed them to leave their masters. The majority of freedmen seems to have done some

[a] See Chapter 4.

loitering as a symbolic act and in order to test out the new freedom.[a] Reconstruction temporarily gave civil rights, suffrage, and even some access to public office. It also marked the heroic beginning of the Negroes' efforts to acquire the rudiments of education.

There is no doubt that Congress intended to give the Negroes "social equality" in public life to a substantial degree. The Civil Rights Bill of 1875,[9] which, in many ways, represented the culmination of the federal Reconstruction legislation, was explicit in declaring that all persons within the jurisdiction of the United States should be entitled to the full and equal enjoyment of the accommodations, advantages, facilities, and privileges of inns, public conveyances on land and water, theaters, and other places of public amusement; subject only to the conditions and limitations established by law, and applicable alike to citizens of every race and color, regardless of previous condition of servitude.[10] The federal courts were given exclusive jurisdiction over offenses against this statute. Stephenson observes in *Race Distinctions in American Law* that "Congress apparently intended to secure not only equal but identical accommodations in all public places for Negroes and Caucasians."[11]

During Congressional Reconstruction some Southern states inserted clauses in their constitutions or in special laws intended to establish the rights of Negroes to share on equal terms in the accommodations of public establishments and conveyances.[12] Louisiana and South Carolina went so far as to require mixed schools.[13] From contemporary accounts of life in the South during Reconstruction, it is evident, however, that Negroes met considerable segregation and discrimination even during these few years of legal equality.[14] It is also apparent that nothing irritated the majority of white Southerners so much as the attempts of Congress and the Reconstruction governments to remove social discrimination from public life.

After Restoration of "white supremacy" the doctrine that the Negroes should be "kept in their place" became the regional creed. When the Supreme Court in 1883 declared the Civil Rights Bill of 1875 unconstitutional in so far as it referred to acts of social discrimination by individuals— endorsing even in this field the political compromise between the white North and South—the way was left open for the Jim Crow legislation of the Southern states and municipalities. For a quarter of a century this system of statutes and regulations—separating the two groups in schools, on railroad cars and on street cars, in hotels and restaurants, in parks and playgrounds, in theaters and public meeting places—continued to grow, with the explicit purpose of diminishing, as far as was practicable and possible, the social contacts between whites and Negroes in the region.[15]

We do not know much about the effects of the Jim Crow legislation. American sociologists, following the Sumner tradition of holding legisla-

[a] See Chapter 10, footnote 7.

tion to be inconsequential,[16] are likely to underrate these effects. Southern Negroes tell quite a different story. From their own experiences in different parts of the South they have told me how the Jim Crow statutes were effective means of tightening and freezing—in many cases of instigating—segregation and discrimination. They have given a picture of how the Negroes were pushed out from voting and officeholding by means of the disfranchisement legislation which swept like a tide over the Southern states during the period from 1875 to 1910.[a] In so far as it concerns the decline in political, civic, and social status of the Negro people in the Southern states, the Restoration of white supremacy in the late 'seventies—according to these informants—was not a final and consummated revolution but *the beginning of a protracted process which lasted until nearly the First World War. During this process the white pressure continuously increased, and the Negroes were continuously pushed backward.* Some older white informants have related much the same story.

Before the Jim Crow legislation there is also said to have been a tendency on the part of white people to treat Negroes somewhat differently depending upon their class and education. This tendency was broken by the laws which applied to *all* Negroes. The legislation thus solidified the caste line and minimized the importance of class differences in the Negro group. This particular effect was probably the more crucial in the formation of the present caste system, since class differentiation within the Negro group continued and, in fact, gained momentum.[b] As we shall find, a tendency is discernible again, in recent decades, to apply the segregation rules with some discretion to Negroes of different class status. If a similar trend was well under way before the Jim Crow laws, those laws must have postponed this particular social process for one or two generations.[c]

While the federal Civil Rights Bill of 1875 was declared unconstitutional, the Reconstruction Amendments to the Constitution—which provided that the Negroes are to enjoy full citizenship in the United States, that they are entitled to "equal benefit of all laws," and that "no state shall

[a] See Chapter 20.

[b] See Chapter 32.

[c] This problem of whether or not, and to what extent, the Jim Crow legislation strengthened and instigated Southern segregation and discrimination patterns is worthy of much more intensive study than has hitherto been given to it. The problem is important by itself as concerning a rather unknown phase of American history. In addition, it has a great theoretical interest. The common opinion among social scientists is that laws, particularly in the social field, are almost insignificant: "stateways cannot change folkways." This opinion is prevalent among Southern authors but is found, in one form or another, in most writings on the South and on the Negro problem even by Northern authors and by Negro writers. I believe this view to be exaggerated and to be an expression of the general American bias toward minimizing the effects of formal legislation, a bias in the *laissez-faire* tradition. (See Chapter 1, Section 11; and Appendix 2, Section 3.) The Jim Crow legislation represents an excellent test case for this *a priori* notion.

make or enforce any law which shall abridge the privileges and immunities of citizens of the United States"—could not be so easily disposed of. The Southern whites, therefore, in passing their various segregation laws to legalize social discrimination, had to manufacture a legal fiction of the same type as we have already met in the preceding discussion on politics and justice. The legal term for this trick in the social field, expressed or implied in most of the Jim Crow statutes, is "separate, but equal." That is, Negroes were to get equal accommodations, but separate from the whites. It is evident, however, and rarely denied, that there is practically no single instance of segregation in the South which has not been utilized for a significant discrimination. The great difference in quality of service for the two groups in the segregated set-ups for transportation and education is merely the most obvious example of how segregation is an excuse for discrimination.[17] Again the Southern white man is in the moral dilemma of having to frame his laws in terms of equality and to defend them before the Supreme Court—and before his own better conscience, which is tied to the American Creed—while knowing all the time that in reality his laws do not give equality to Negroes, and that he does not want them to do so.

The formal adherence to equality in the American Creed, expressed by the Constitution and in the laws, is, however, even in the field of social relations, far from being without practical importance. Spokesmen for the white South, not only recently but in the very period when the segregation policy was first being legitimatized, have strongly upheld the principle that segregation should not be used for discrimination. Henry W. Grady, for instance, scorned the "fanatics and doctrinaires who hold that separation is discrimination," emphasized that "separation is not offensive to either race" and exclaimed:

> . . . the whites and blacks must walk in separate paths in the South. As near as may be, these paths should be made equal—but separate they must be now and always. This means separate schools, separate churches, *separate accommodations everywhere —but equal accommodations where the same money is charged, or where the State provides for the citizen.*[18]

Further, the legal adherence to the principle of equality gives the Southern liberal a vantage point in his work to improve the status of the Negroes and race relations.[a] Last, but not least, it gives the Negro people a firm legal basis for their fight against social segregation and discrimination. Since the two are inseparable, the fight against inequality challenges the whole segregation system. The National Association for the Advancement of Colored People has had, from the very beginning, the constitutional provisions for equality as its sword and shield. Potentially the Negro is strong.

[a] See Chapter 21, Section 5.

He has, in his demands upon white Americans, the fundamental law of the land on his side. He has even the better conscience of his white compatriots themselves. He knows it; and the white American knows it, too.

5. Beliefs Supporting Social Inequality

In attempting to understand the motivation of segregation and discrimination, one basic fact to be taken into account is, of course, that many Negroes, particularly in the South, are poor, uneducated, and deficient in health, morals, and manners; and thus not very agreeable as social companions. In the South the importance of this factor is enhanced by the great proportion of Negroes in the total population. It is enhanced also by the democratic structure of public institutions in America.[19] William Archer, who, among the English observers of the Negro problem in America, probably better than anyone else was able to withstand the influence of race prejudice, declares himself for separation in railroad traveling for this reason:

> It is the crowding, the swamping, the submerging of the white race by the black, that the South cannot reasonably be expected to endure.[20]

This point is, however, much more complicated. For one thing, there is a great class of Southern whites who are also poor, uneducated, coarse and dirty. They are traditionally given various epithets, all with the connotation of social inferiority: "crackers," "hill-billies," "clay-eaters," "rednecks," "peckerwoods," "wool hats," "trash," "low-downers," "no 'counts." White farm laborers, sharecroppers, the permanently unemployed, and a great proportion of textile workers and other unskilled laborers are considered to be in this submerged group of lower class whites. Their presence in the South does not help the Negroes, however. It is, rather, the very thing which raises the need for a sky-high color bar. This class of whites knows that upper class whites are disposed to regard them as "just as bad as niggers," and they know, too, that they have always been despised by the Negroes, who have called them "poor white trash," "mean whites," or "po' buckra." It is in their interest, on the one hand, to stress the fundamental equality among all white people, which was the explicit assumption of the slavery doctrine, and, on the other hand, the gulf between whites and Negroes. The rising Negroes became an assault on the status of these poor whites.

The very existence of whites in economic and cultural conditions comparable to those of the masses of Negroes thus becomes a force holding Negroes down. Most middle and upper class whites also get, as we shall find, a satisfaction out of the subserviency and humbleness of the lower class Negroes. As Embree points out: "The attitudes of the aristocrat and of the poor white, starting from opposite motives, often result in the same discrimination."[21] The ordinary vicious circle—that the actual inferiority of the Negro masses gives reason for discrimination against them, while at the same time discrimination forms a great encumbrance when they attempt to improve themselves—is, in the social sphere, loaded with the desire on the part of lower class whites, and also perhaps the majority of middle and upper class whites, that Negroes remain inferior.

This fact that a large class of whites is not much better off than the masses of Negroes, economically and culturally, while whole groups of Negroes are decidedly on a higher level—in this situation when a general segregation policy protecting *all* whites against *all* Negroes has to be justified—makes the beliefs in the racial inferiority of Negroes a much needed rationalization. We have studied the racial stereotypes from this very viewpoint in an earlier chapter.[a] We pointed out that the racial inferiority doctrine is beginning to come into disrepute with people of higher education and is no longer supported by the press or by leading public figures. As a result, racial beliefs supporting segregation are undoubtedly losing some of their axiomatic solidity even among the masses of white people, although they still play a dominant role in popular thinking.

A tendency to exaggerate the lower class traits of Negroes also is apparent. This would seem to meet the need for justification of the caste order. We are being told constantly that all Negroes are dirty, immoral and unreliable. Exceptions are mentioned, but in an opportunistic fashion those exceptions are not allowed to upset the absolutistic theses. The fact that the average white man seldom or never sees an educated Negro[b] facilitates the adherence to the stereotypes. Even people who are modern enough not to regard these traits as biological and permanent find in them reasons to keep Negroes at a social distance. The feeling may be that Negroes have capacity but that it needs to be developed, and that takes a long time— "several centuries," it is usually said. Often it is argued that the low morals and the ignorance of Negroes are so prevalent that Negroes must be quarantined. It is said that at the present time any measure of social equality would endanger the standards of decency and culture in white society. It is also pointed out that Negroes are different in physical appearance even if they have the same basic mental capacity and moral propensities. These differences are claimed to be repugnant to the white man. Occasionally this repugnance is admitted to be an irrational reaction, as in the following comment by a young, middle class man of Savannah:

> You can't get a white man in the South to call them "Mr." I don't say "Mr." because it makes me feel uncomfortable. I know that's prejudice, but it's instinctive and not reasoning.[22]

[a] See Chapter 4.
[b] See Chapter 30, Section 2.

Besides these beliefs centering around Negro inferiority, there are a great number of other popular thoughts arranged to justify social segregation. One such belief was mentioned in the opening section of this chapter —namely, that Negroes like to be separated, that they are happy in their humble status and would not like to be treated as equals. Another idea with the same function is that separation is necessary in order to prevent friction between the two groups. This thought is usually supported by the reflection that the whites "would not stand for"—or "would not *yet* stand for"—another social order. Segregation thus becomes motivated directly by the whites' will to segregate and by certain untested assumptions regarding the state of public opinion. Segregation and subordination of Negroes are also commonly supported by the consideration that they have "always been" subordinate and that it is part of the mores and social structure that they remain subordinate for a long time. A remark by a machine shop manager in Newport News will illustrate this point of view:

> I explain it in this way. A mule is made to work; a horse is made for beauty. The Negro is the working man of the South. Plenty of Negroes here are much better than the whites. But as a class that is not as true for white people about being the workers.[23]

Earlier, and to some extent even today, this direct application of the conservative principle was bolstered with a religious sanction. Race prejudice is presented as "a deep-rooted, God-implanted instinct."[24] It is often said in the South that God did not create two distinct races without having some intention in so doing. This theological sanction may be illustrated by a remark by a state official in Arkansas:

> The Negro in his place is really an assistant in the South. He's what the Lord Almighty intended him to be, a servant of the people. We couldn't get along without them.[25]

This thought that Negro subordination is part of God's plan for the world has, however, never been uncontested. The Bible, especially the New Testament, is filled with passages supporting equality, and the heart of Christian teaching is to "love thy neighbor as thyself."

Two points need to be made about the beliefs mentioned thus far: First —with the exception of the racial and theological beliefs both of which are gradually losing out—they support segregation but not discrimination, not even that discrimination which arises out of segregation. Second, they do not support a wholesale segregation, for *some* Negroes are not educationally, morally, or occupationally inferior; *some* Negroes do not want to be segregated; and *some* whites feel no repugnance to the physical appearance of the Negro. If one held these beliefs alone, therefore, and were willing to act upon them, and if he were provided with relevant facts, he would not advocate complete segregation and would permit immediate social equality to some Negroes in their relations to some whites (at the same time he would want to restrict equality for some whites). Further, he would look forward to a time when segregation would be wiped out, and full equality permitted.[a] As this is not the attitude of most whites, we have an indication that those beliefs fundamentally are rationalizations of valuations.

It would, indeed, be possible to defend the caste order simply by arguing that it is in the white people's interests to keep the Negroes subordinate. Such a defense would be logically tight. It could not be challenged as an unscientific belief. Unlike the rationalizations mentioned in previous paragraphs, it need not look forward to an ultimate social equality as ideal. It differs from the other beliefs we have been considering also in that it demands discrimination primarily and segregation only incidentally.[26]

The remarkable thing, however, is that, *in America, social segregation and discrimination will practically never be motivated in this straightforward way as being in white people's interests.* Indeed, to judge from the discussion in all social classes of whites, and this is particularly true of the South, one is led to believe that such base and materialistic considerations never enter into their thoughts. The nearest approach one hears is oblique statements of the type: "This is a white man's country," or: "We've got to make these niggers work for us." Otherwise the matter is only touched by some liberal reformers who, interestingly enough, always try to prove to the whites that it is "in white people's own interest" to do away with this or that injustice against Negroes. I have become convinced that actually the interest motivation seldom explicitly and consciously enters the ordinary white man's mind. It is suppressed, as being in flagrant conflict with the American Creed and the Christian religion. But it is equally clear that most white people actually take good care of their interests and practice discrimination even when it is not required for segregation, and that segregation most often has the "function" of allowing a discrimination held advantageous to the whites.

Again a partial allegiance to the American Creed must be noted. Thomas P. Bailey talked about "the dissociation of a sectional personality."[27] The conflict between moral principles and actual conduct has its locus *within* persons; for this reason it will not be represented clearly in public discussion. The interests will have a part in setting the patterns of behavior and will give the emotional energy for the search for all the rationalizing beliefs we have mentioned. The Creed not only will prevent the interests from being explicitly mentioned and, indeed, from being consciously

---

[a] Even if one felt that the Negro was repugnant in his physical appearance to some white men, scientific knowledge could reveal to him that antipathies of this sort could be removed, and new ones avoided.

thought of, but will often qualify those rationalizing beliefs by hopes for improvement in Negro status toward greater equality and will actually also bend the behavior patterns considerably away from the crudest forms of outright exploitation.

But as yet we have not discussed the most powerful rationalization for segregation, which is the fear of amalgamation. It is this fear which gives a unique character to the American theory of "no social equality."

6. THE THEORY OF "NO SOCIAL EQUALITY"

In his first encounter with the American Negro problem, perhaps nothing perplexes the outside observer more than the popular term and the popular theory of "no social equality." He will be made to feel from the start that it has concrete implications and a central importance for the Negro problem in America. But, nevertheless, the term is kept vague and elusive, and the theory loose and ambiguous. One moment it will be stretched to cover and justify every form of social segregation and discrimination, and, in addition, all the inequalities in justice, politics and breadwinning. The next moment it will be narrowed to express only the denial of close personal intimacies and intermarriage. The very lack of precision allows the notion of "no social equality" to rationalize the rather illogical and wavering system of color caste in America.

The kernel of the popular theory of "no social equality"[a] will, when pursued, be presented as a firm determination on the part of the whites to block amalgamation and preserve "the purity of the white race."[28] The white man identifies himself with "the white race" and feels that he has a stake in resisting the dissipation of its racial identity. Important in this identification is the notion of "the absolute and unchangeable superiority of the white race."[29] From this racial dogma will often be drawn the *direct* inference that the white man shall dominate in all spheres.[30] But when the logic of this inference is inquired about, the inference will be made *indirect* and will be made to lead over to the danger of amalgamation, or, as it is popularly expressed, "intermarriage."

It is further found that the ban on intermarriage is focused on white women. For them it covers both formal marriage and illicit intercourse. In regard to white men it is taken more or less for granted that they would not stoop to marry Negro women, and that illicit intercourse does not fall under the same intense taboo.[31] Their offspring, under the popular doctrine that maternity is more certain than paternity, become Negroes anyway, and the white race easily avoids pollution with Negro blood. To prevent "intermarriage" in this specific sense of sex relations between white women and Negro men, it is not enough to apply legal and social sanctions against

[a] We have already touched the notion of "no social equality" in Chapter 3, Sections 3 and 4.

it—so the popular theory runs. In using the danger of intermarriage as a defense for the whole caste system, it is assumed both that Negro men have a strong desire for "intermarriage,"[32] and that white women would be open to proposals from Negro men, *if* they are not guarded from even meeting them on an equal plane. The latter assumption, of course, is never openly expressed, but is logically implicit in the popular theory. The conclusion follows that the whole system of segregation and discrimination is justified. Every single measure is defended as necessary to block "social equality" which in its turn is held necessary to prevent "intermarriage."[33]

The basic role of the fear of amalgamation in white attitudes to the race problem is indicated by the popular magical concept of "blood." Educated white Southerners, who know everything about modern genetic and biological research, confess readily that they actually feel an irrational or "instinctive" repugnance in thinking of "intermarriage."[a] These measures of segregation and discrimination are often of the type found in the true taboos and in the notion "not to be touched" of primitive religion. The specific taboos are characterized, further, by a different degree of excitement which attends their violation and a different degree of punishment to the violator: the closer the act to sexual association, the more furious is the public reaction. Sexual association itself is punished by death and is accompanied by tremendous public excitement; the other social relations meet decreasing degrees of public fury. Sex becomes in this popular theory the principle around which the whole structure of segregation of the Negroes—down to disfranchisement and denial of equal opportunities on the labor market—is organized. The reasoning is this: "For, say what we will, may not all the equalities be ultimately based on potential social equality, and that in turn on intermarriage? Here we reach the real *crux* of the question."[34] In cruder language, but with the same logic, the Southern man on the street responds to any plea for social equality: "Would you like to have your daughter marry a Negro?"

This theory of color caste centering around the aversion to amalgamation determines, as we have just observed, the white man's rather definite rank order of the various measures of segregation and discrimination against Negroes. The relative significance attached to each of those measures is dependent upon their degree of expediency or necessity—in the view of white people—as means of upholding the ban on "intermarriage."[b] In this rank order, (1) the ban on intermarriage and other sex relations involving white women and colored men takes precedence before everything else. It is the end for which the other restrictions are arranged as means. Thereafter follow: (2) all sorts of taboos and etiquettes in personal contacts; (3) segregation in schools and churches; (4) segregation

[a] See Chapter 4, Section 6.
[b] See Chapter 3, Section 4.

in hotels, restaurants, and theaters, and other public places where people meet socially; (5) segregation in public conveyances; (6) discrimination in public services; and, finally, inequality in (7) politics, (8) justice and (9) breadwinning and relief.[a]

The degree of liberalism on racial matters in the white South can be designated mainly by the point on this rank order where a man stops because he believes further segregation and discrimination are not necessary to prevent "intermarriage." We have seen that white liberals in the South of the present day, as a matter of principle, rather unanimously stand up against inequality in breadwinning, relief, justice and politics. These fields of discrimination form the chief battleground and considerable changes in them are, as we have seen, on the way. When we ascend to the higher ranks which concern social relations in the narrow sense, we find the Southern liberals less prepared to split off from the majority opinion of the region. Hardly anybody in the South is prepared to go the whole way and argue that even the ban on intermarriage should be lifted. Practically all agree, not only upon the high desirability of preventing "intermarriage," but also that a certain amount of separation between the two groups is expedient and necessary to prevent it. Even the one who has his philosophical doubts on the point must, if he is reasonable, abstain from ever voicing them. The social pressure is so strong that it would be foolish not to conform. Conformity is a political necessity for having any hope of influence; it is, in addition, a personal necessity for not meeting social ostracism.

T. J. Woofter, Jr., who again may be quoted as a representative of Southern liberalism, observes that ". . . unless those forms of separation which are meant to safeguard the purity of the races are present, the majority of the white people flatly refuse to coöperate with Negroes" and finds no alternative to "constant discontent and friction or amalgamation . . . , except the systematic minimization of social contacts."[35] But when Woofter has made this concession in principle to the segregation system of the South, he comes out with demands which, in practice, would change it entirely. He insists that all other forms of segregation than "those . . . which are meant to safeguard the purity of the races" be abolished, and that the administration of the system be just and considerate and, indeed, founded upon the consent of the ruled.[36]

. . . all that most Negroes see in separation is that it is a means to degrade, an opportunity to exploit them. So long as it presents this aspect to them, it will be galling and insulting, and they will oppose it. Stated positively, this means that, in the final

[a] As we pointed out in Chapter 3, Section 4, it so happens that Negroes have an interest in being released from segregation and discrimination in a rank order just the opposite of the whites' expressed rank order of having them retained. This is a principal fact in all attempts to change and reform race relations.

analysis, if segregation is to be successfully maintained, it must not be confused with discrimination and must finally be approved by the colored people themselves as beneficial to race relations.[87]

Virginius Dabney, to quote another prominent Southern liberal, actually goes so far as to assert that "there is . . . a growing conviction on the part of a substantial body of Southerners that the Jim Crow laws should be abolished,"[38] and argues that even if and in so far as the two population groups in the South should be kept apart, "the accommodations provided for Negroes should be identical with those provided for whites."[39]

It should be noted that neither Woofter nor Dabney takes up for discussion any segregation measure higher up on the white man's rank order than those imposed by the Jim Crow legislation. There they take their stand on the time-honored formula "separate, but equal," and insist only that separation should be rationally motivated, and that the constitutional precept of equality should be enforced.

7. CRITICAL EVALUATION OF THE "NO SOCIAL EQUALITY" THEORY

The sincerity of the average white person's psychological identification with the "white race" and his aversion to amalgamation should not be doubted; neither should his attitude that the upholding of the caste system, implied in the various segregation and discrimination measures, is necessary to prevent amalgamation. But the manner in which he constantly interchanges the concepts "amalgamation" and "intermarriage"—in the meaning of a white woman's marriage to, or sex relations with, a Negro man—is bewildering. Amalgamation both in the South and in the North is, and has always been, mainly a result, not of marriage, but of illicit sexual relations. And these illicit sex relations have in the main been confined to white men and colored women. It is further well known that Negro women who have status and security are less likely to succumb to sexual advances from white men.[40] Deprivations inflicted upon Negroes in the South must therefore be a factor tending to increase amalgamation rather than to reduce it. Together these facts make the whole anti-amalgamation theory seem inconsistent.

But here we have to recall the very particular definition of the Negro and white "races" in America.[a] Since all mixed bloods are classified as Negroes, sex relations between white men and colored women affect only the Negro race and not the white race. From the white point of view it is not "amalgamation" in the crucial sense. From the same point of view the race of the father does not matter for the racial classification of a Negro child. The child is a Negro anyhow. Sex relations between Negro men and white women, on the other hand, would be like an *attempt* to pour

[a] See Chapter 5, Section 1.

Negro blood into the white race. It cannot succeed, of course, as the child would be considered a Negro. But the white woman would be absolutely degraded—which the white man in the parallel situation is not. She must be protected and this type of amalgamation prevented by all available means. This is, of course, only an extreme case of the morality of "double standards" between the sexes. It is slowly withering away, and white men are gradually also coming to be censured for relations with women of the other group. Still, there is in popular sentiment an abysmal difference between the two types of sexual relations.

The statement frequently made by whites in the South that there is an instinctive and ineradicable sexual repulsion between the two groups is doubtful, in view of the present genetic composition of the Negro people. Besides, if it were true, the insistence upon the whole equipage of measures for racial separation for preventing "intermarriage" would be unnecessary, even to the white Southerner.[a] Even the more general allegation that there is an inherent repulsion to personal intimacies and physical contact between the two groups is unfounded. The friendly behavior of Negro and white children untrained in prejudice and also the acceptability of physical contact with favorite servants are cases in point. There are no reasons brought forward to make it likely that there are sex differentials in this respect, so that white men should react differently from white women. This brings us to a consideration of the extent to which the anti-amalgamation doctrine is merely a rationalization of purely social demands, particularly those concerning social status.

We have already observed that the relative license of white men to have illicit intercourse with Negro women does not extend to formal marriage. The relevant difference between these two types of relations is that the latter, but not the former, does give social status to the Negro woman and does take status away from the white man. For a white woman both legal marriage and illicit relations with Negroes cause her to lose caste. These status concerns are obvious and they are serious enough both in the North and in the South to prevent intermarriage. But as they are functions of the caste apparatus which, in this popular theory, is itself explained as a means of preventing intermarriage, the whole theory becomes largely a logical circle.

The circular character of this reasoning is enhanced when we realize that the great majority of non-liberal white Southerners utilize the dread of

---

[a] Race prejudice has, therefore, a "function" to perform in lieu of the absence of sex repulsion.

"It is just because primary race feeling is *not* deeply based in human instinct, whereas the mating instinct *is* so based, that a secondary racial feeling, race-pride, comes in from a more developed reflective consciousness to minimize the natural instinct for amalgamation . . ." (Thomas P. Bailey, *Race Orthodoxy in the South* [1914], p. 43.)

"intermarriage" and the theory of "no social equality" to justify discriminations which have quite other and wider goals than the purity of the white race. Things are defended in the South as means of preserving racial purity which cannot possibly be defended in this way. To this extent we cannot avoid observing that *what white people really want is to keep the Negroes in a lower status*. "Intermarriage" itself is resented because it would be a supreme indication of "social equality," while the rationalization is that "social equality" is opposed because it would bring "intermarriage."

Not denying the partial reality of the white person's psychological identification with the "white race" and his serious concern about "racial purity," our tentative conclusion is, therefore, that more fundamentally the theory of "no social equality" is a rationalization, and that the demand for "no social equality" is psychologically dominant to the aversion for "intermarriage." The persistent preoccupation with sex and marriage in the rationalization of social segregation and discrimination against Negroes is, to this extent, an irrational escape on the part of the whites from voicing an open demand for difference in social status between the two groups for its own sake. Like the irrational racial beliefs,[a] the fortification in the unapproachable regions of sex of the unequal treatment of the Negro, which this popular theory provides, has been particularly needed in this nation because of the strength of the American Creed. A people with a less emphatic democratic *ethos* would be more able to uphold a caste system without this tense belief in sex and race dangers.

The fixation on the purity of white womanhood, and also part of the intensity of emotion surrounding the whole sphere of segregation and discrimination, are to be understood as the backwashes of the sore conscience on the part of white men for their own or their compeers' relations with, or desires for, Negro women.[41] These psychological effects are greatly magnified because of the puritan *milieu* of America and especially of the South. The upper class men in a less puritanical people could probably have indulged in sex relations with, and sexual day-dreams of, lower caste women in a more matter-of-course way and without generating so much pathos about white womanhood.[42] The Negro people have to carry the burden not only of the white men's sins but also of their virtues. The virtues of the honest, democratic, puritan white Americans in the South are great, and the burden upon the Negroes becomes ponderous.[43]

Our practical conclusion is that it would have cleansing effects on race relations in America, and particularly in the South, to have an open and sober discussion in rational terms of this ever present popular theory of "intermarriage" and "social equality," giving matters their factual ground, true proportions and logical relations. Because it is, to a great extent, an

[a] See Chapter 4.

opportunistic rationalization, and because it refers directly and indirectly to the most touchy spots in American life and American morals, tremendous inhibitions have been built up against a detached and critical discussion of this theory. But such inhibitions are gradually overcome when, in the course of secularized education, people become rational about their life problems. It must never be forgotten that in our increasingly intellectualized civilization even the plain citizen feels an urge for truth and objectivity, and that this rationalistic urge is increasingly competing with the opportunistic demands for rationalization and escape.

There are reasons to believe that a slow but steady cleansing of the American mind is proceeding as the cultural level is raised. The basic racial inferiority doctrine is being undermined by research and education. For a white man to have illicit relations with Negro women is increasingly meeting disapproval. Negroes themselves are more and more frowning upon such relations. This all must tend to dampen the emotional fires around "social equality." Sex and race fears are, however, even today the main defense for segregation and, in fact, for the whole caste order. The question shot at the interviewer touching any point of this order is still: "Would you like to have your daughter (sister) marry a Negro?"

8. Attitudes among Different Classes of Whites in the South

Certain attitudes, common in the South, become more understandable when we have recognized that, behind all rationalizing stereotyped beliefs and popular theories, a main concern of the white man is to preserve social inequality for its own sake. One such attitude is the great sympathy so often displayed in the upper classes of Southern whites toward the "old time darky" who adheres to the patterns of slavery. The "unreconstructed aristocrat" after the Civil War believed with Carlyle that "[the Negro] is useful in God's creation only as a servant";[44] he remained paternalistic; he wanted to keep the Negroes dependent and resented their attempts to rise through education; he mistrusted the younger generation of Negroes; he had a gloomy outlook on the future of race relations. But he liked the individual Negro whom he knew personally and who conformed to the old relation of master-servant—who "stayed in his place."[45]

Even today this attitude helps to determine the relations between the two groups in rural districts.[46] It particularly forms the pattern of the relationship between employer and employee on the plantation and in household service. It is also the basis for the quasi-feudal use of white character witnesses for Negro offenders, and for the great leniency in punishing Negro offenders as long as they have not intruded upon white society.[a] One is amazed to see how often, even today, white people go out of their way to help individual Negroes and how many of them still take

[a] See Chapter 26, Section 2.

it for granted that Negro cooks shall be allowed to pilfer food for their own families from the white man's kitchen. The other side of this paternalistic relation is, of course, that servants are grossly underpaid. But it is not to be denied that on this point there is—in the individual case—a break in the bitterness of caste relations. Negro beggars who make their appeal to this old relationship will often be amply and generously rewarded by white people who are most stingy in paying ordinary wages and who deprive Negro children of their share of the state appropriations for schools in order to provide for white children.[47]

This is a survival of slavery society, where friendliness is restricted to the individual and not extended to the group, and is based on a clear and unchallenged recognition from both sides of an insurmountable social inequality. There are obvious short-term gains in such relations for the Negroes involved.[48] The whites in the South always stress that they, and not the Northerners, like and love the Negro and that they provide for him. The conservative Negro leaders in the Booker T. Washington line—and occasionally the others also—have endorsed this claim by pronouncing that the "best people of the South" always could be counted among "the friends of the race."[49] "No reputable Southerner is half as bad as Senator Tillman talks," exclaimed Kelly Miller,[50] and even the most violent Negro-baiting politicians occasionally show great kindness toward the individual Negroes who are under their personal control.[51]

The paternalistic pattern becomes particularly cherished by the white men as it so openly denotes an aristocratic origin. This gives it its strength to survive. It is a sign of social distinction to a white man to stand in this paternalistic relation to Negroes. This explains why so much of the conversation in the Southern white upper and middle classes turns around the follies of Negro servants. *Their Negro dependents and their own relations to them play a significant role for white people's status in society.*

To receive this traditional friendliness on the part of Southern white upper class persons, a Negro has to be a lower class Negro and to behave as an humble servant. James Weldon Johnson observed:

> . . . in fact, I concluded that if a coloured man wanted to separate himself from his white neighbours, he had but to acquire some money, education, and culture . . . the proudest and fairest lady in the South could with propriety—and it is what she would most likely do—go to the cabin of Aunt Mary, her cook, if Aunt Mary was sick, and minister to her comfort with her own hands; but if Mary's daughter, Eliza, a girl who used to run around my lady's kitchen, but who has received an education and married a prosperous young coloured man, were at death's door, my lady would no more think of crossing the threshold of Eliza's cottage than she would think of going into a bar-room for a drink.[52]

When the Negro rises socially and is no longer a servant, he becomes a stranger to the white upper class. His ambition is suspected. He is disliked.

The exceptions are when he, in spite of not being a servant, can establish a relationship of personal dependence and when he, in this relationship, can act out a role of deference and humility. He is then in the position to confer even more of a sense of status elevation to the white partner, and he is also rewarded by more protection and favors. Moton gives us the Negro angle of this situation:

> In a much more matter of fact way the Negro uses his intimate knowledge of the white man to further his own advancement. Much of what is regarded as racially characteristic of the Negro is nothing more than his artful and adroit accommodation of his manners and methods to what he knows to be the weaknesses and foibles of his white neighbour. Knowing what is expected of him, and knowing too what he himself wants, the Negro craftily uses his knowledge to anticipate opposition and to eliminate friction in securing his desires.[53]

The present author has time and again heard white men with a local public interest praise Negro college presidents and other white-appointed Negro leaders quite beyond any reasonable deserts, merely for their humble demeanor. One influential white editor in the Deep South indulged with zest in lengthy descriptions of the particular manner in which the principal and leading teachers of a nearby Negro educational institution—of which he spoke highly—walked, talked, and laughed, and he ended by exclaiming: "They bear themselves just like old field slaves." This was, in his opinion, a praiseworthy thing. The importance attached by white people to the forms of subservience on the part of Negroes can be measured by the degree to which they show themselves prepared to give in on material interests if those forms are duly observed. This attitude on the part of influential whites puts a premium on the individual Negroes most inclined and best gifted to flatter their superior whites, even if they lack other qualities. It is apparent that this attitude still represents a main difficulty in the effort to get Negro schools and other Negro institutions manned by Negro personnel with high professional standards.

Generally speaking, this attitude on the part of upper class whites has demoralizing effects on Negroes. In employment relations the paternalistic pattern tends to diminish the Negroes' formal responsibilities. The Negro worker has less definite obligations as well as more uncertain rights. He comes to be remunerated, not only for his work, but also for his humility, for his propensity to be satisfied with his "place" and for his cunning in cajoling and flattering his master. He has ready excuses for not becoming a really good worker. He is discouraged when he tries "to work his way up." It is considered better for him never to forget his "place," and he must scrupulously avoid even any suspicion that he seeks to rise above it. If successful, he might see good reasons to conceal it. Upper class Negroes in the South have often confided to me that they find it advantageous to simulate dependence in order to avert hostility from the whites and engage their paternalism. But even if the successful Negro puts on a show of dependence, he sometimes feels that he is less safe than if he had stayed at the bottom. A psychological *milieu* more effective in stifling spontaneous ambition is hardly thinkable.

This is one of the main roots of Negro "laziness and shiftlessness." And there are circular effects back on the whites[54]—on their own standards and on the standards they expect from the servants. Deference is bought for lowered demands of efficiency. Cable observed this long ago in his pamphlet, *The Negro Question,* and explained that:

> . . . the master-caste [in the South] tolerates, with unsurpassed supineness and unconsciousness, a more indolent, inefficient, slovenly, unclean, untrustworthy, ill mannered, noisy, disrespectful, disputatious, and yet servile domestic and public menial service than is tolerated by any other enlightened people.[55]

This might be slightly exaggerated even for his time, but it is true that patriarchalism breeds unambitious sycophants and keeps labor standards low.

This whole pattern was originally a rural pattern in the South. It fits best today into communities dominated by the semi-feudal plantation system. In the cities of the South, the tendency toward more casual and secondary relations is gradually breaking it up. But even in the cities, among the white upper classes in their relations to domestic servants, large parts of it are preserved today.

There is in the South, however, also another type of aristocratic attitude toward the Negroes, which is equally reluctant to modify the color bar but is prepared to allow the Negro people a maximum of possibilities for cultural growth and economic advancement behind the bar. This attitude, which involves a more unselfish friendliness and a truer social responsibility, not only to the individual Negro, but to the Negroes as a group, is perhaps best expressed by Edgar Gardner Murphy, who had the opinion that "there is no place in our American system for a helot class. . . . We want no fixed and permanent populations of 'the inferior.' "[56] As spokesman for the white South he declared:

> It is willing that the negro, within his own social world, shall become as great, as true, as really free, as nobly gifted as he has capacity to be.[57]

It was Murphy who coined the phrase "parallel civilizations."

This is a clear misinterpretation of the position of the majority of aristocratic white Southerners who most certainly do not look, and never have looked, upon the advancement of the Negro people with this equanimity and generosity. But it is a fair expression of what Murphy, himself, and many other white gentlemen of the region before and after him have felt.

This spirit has animated a growing number of white educators, churchmen, and politicians who, for a long time, in cooperation with Northern philanthropic organizations, have worked—"quietly and cautiously," as they always stress—to improve Negro schools and social conditions. This is also the ideological origin of modern Southern liberalism.[a] It has, from the beginning, stamped the work of the Interracial Commission. Fundamentally it is the attitude of the independent, secure, and cultured Southern upper class person who feels the social responsibility of his position and does not need to flatter his ego by the vulgar means of Negro subservience. He has good fences, and he keeps them up, but just because of this he can afford to be a good Christian neighbor to the poor Negro people around him.

He is well informed enough about social realities in his region to know also that such a policy, in the long run, is the best protection for the whites. He understands that the lower class Negroes, gradually losing their personal relations to the old master class among the whites, are a social menace and an economic liability to the South:

> But build him up. Make him sufficient in himself, give him within his own race, life that will satisfy, and the social question will be solved. The trained Negro is less and less inclined to lose himself in the sea of another race.[58]

The difference in attitude will show up significantly in relation to the upper and middle class Negroes. The ordinary white upper class people will "have no use" for such Negroes. They need cheap labor—faithful, obedient, unambitious labor. Many white Southerners will even today explain to the visitor that they prefer the Negro workers because they are tractable. When Negroes become prosperous, acquire education, or buy land, and when they are no longer dependent, this relationship is broken. But already, writing at the very beginning of this century, Page had pointed out "the urgent need . . . for the negroes to divide up into classes, with character and right conduct as the standard for elevation," and added the admonition: "When they make distinctions themselves, others will recognize their distinctions."[59] The younger school of Southern thinkers took up this idea, but had a greater trust in education and progress than Page, and a greater willingness to make it their own responsibility to do something to assist the rising Negroes in reaching, not only occasional landownership and education, but, in more recent times, to help get for them fair and equal justice, personal security and even political suffrage. Even for some of the modern liberals, however, it is apparent that they have great difficulties in freeing themselves entirely from the patronizing attitude which is the main tradition of the Southern white upper class. "I have frequently noted that with many white up-lifters the Negro is all

[a] See Chapter 21, Section 5.

right until he is up-lifted," James Weldom Johnson observed.[60] But great changes are under way. During this period of transition the ordinary upper class person, even if he is not touched by modern liberalism, will show a vacillating mind when judging the educated Negro trying to climb in social status: one moment hostility will hold sway—this Negro is "smart," "uppity," he "wants to be white"; the next moment respect becomes dominant—"this Negro is as good or better than many whites."

So far we have considered only white upper class people. It is the ambition of the white middle class people in the South to identify themselves with the aristocratic traditions of the region, and, for reasons already mentioned, their relation to the Negroes is crucial to the achievement of their ambition. They will hasten to inform even the casual acquaintance of their relationship to slave owners and of any old Negro servants—particularly if by any stretch of the definition a servant can be called "mammy." In their public contacts many middle class whites try to manifest benevolent condescension toward Negroes. On the other hand, some of them are in competition with Negroes, and many of them are able to rise economically only by exploiting Negroes. Too, their memories include fewer recollections of friendly contacts with Negroes than earlier fears and competitive attitudes. The attitudes of this white middle class toward the rising Negroes are decidedly less friendly than are those of the white upper class, and their attitudes even toward the subservient lower class Negroes are decidedly conflicting.

Lower class whites in the South have no Negro servants in whose humble demeanors they can reflect their own superiority. Instead, they feel actual economic competition or fear of potential competition from the Negroes. They need the caste demarcations for much more substantial reasons than do the middle and upper classes. They are the people likely to stress aggressively that *no* Negro can *ever* attain the status of even the *lowest* white. The educated Negro, the Negro professional or businessman, the Negro landowner, will particularly appear to them "uppity," "smart" and "out of place." They look on the formation behind the color line of a Negro upper and middle class as a challenge to their own status. They want all Negroes kept down "in their place"—this place is to them defined realistically as under themselves. They are naturally jealous of every dollar that goes to Negro education. They will insist that the caste etiquette be enforced upon the rising Negroes as well as upon lower class Negroes.[61]

The lower class whites have been the popular strength behind Negro disfranchisement, and are the audience to which the "nigger-baiting" political demagogue of the South appeals. They create the popular pressure upon the Southern courts to deny the Negroes equal justice. They form the active lynching mobs; they are responsible also for most of the petty outrages practiced on the Negro group. They are the interested party in economic discrimination against Negroes, keeping Negroes out of jobs which they want themselves. But even in their case, the general attitude of hatred toward Negroes collectively is modulated by occasional friendly relations with individual Negroes, and the most brutish of them have had some contact with the humanitarianism of the American Creed and of Christianity.[62]

The unfriendly attitudes on the part of the lower class whites become, as we have seen in earlier chapters, especially detrimental to the Negroes since upper and middle class whites are inclined to let them have their way. Plantation owners and employers, who use Negro labor as cheaper and more docile, have at times been observed to tolerate, or even cooperate in, the periodic aggressions of poor whites against Negroes. It is a plausible thesis that they do so in the interest of upholding the caste system which is so effective in keeping the Negro docile.[63] It is also difficult to avoid the further reflection that the hatred of lower class whites toward Negroes shows significant signs of being partly dislocated aggression arising from their own social and economic frustrations in white society:

> Although the poor white's antagonism toward the wealthy white is denied expression by considerations of economic and legal expediency, Negro dependents of hated landowners or other employers, offer vulnerable targets for suppressed antagonisms. The poor white utilizes every opportunity for asserting "white supremacy," partly because in his case it is a very meager and uncertain superiority, partly as an outlet for the hatreds generated by the social system of the South. Thus, the Negro is the target of the poor white not only because he is a competitor but also because of the Negro's identification with the upper-class white group of the South.[64]

Thus, in the three-cornered tension among upper class whites, lower class whites, and Negroes, the two white groups agree upon the Negroes as a scapegoat and the proper object for exploitation and hatred. White solidarity is upheld and the caste order protected. This hypothesis—if it could be confirmed by further research—would tend to raise some hope of a change for the better. Displaced aggression is less stable and less deep-rooted than other aggression. It cannot only be eradicated by such economic developments and reforms as mitigate the primary frustration, but it can also be redirected more easily by education.

The bitterness of racial feelings on the part of whites seems to be slowly declining, and the lower classes are probably following the trend. But still they are apparently the most prejudiced. There is one big factor of change, however, which works directly on the lower classes of whites. If labor unions should spread and increasingly come to include both white and Negro workers in a common solidarity, this development would revolutionize the situation. The author has seen how a quick and radical change in racial attitudes has been brought about in some places where the tie of a common organization has materialized. Aggression has been redirected and a certain amount of labor solidarity has taken the place of white solidarity. The labor movement is, however, still in its infancy in the South. The existing segregation in industrial work will, further, have the effect that, in many industries, trade unions will be white and will actually become an additional barrier against the intrusion of Negro labor, which will certainly not tend to diminish the urge for social discrimination but rather strengthen it. In the fields where there is actual competition for jobs, racial friction will remain one of the principal hindrances to successful unionization, and the odds are that it will often become successful only by eliminating the Negroes.[a] Negro labor will, however, hardly be driven out entirely from Southern industry. As we have shown, there will probably be an increasing pressure for jobs from the side of Negroes driven out of agriculture. If Negroes also become organized and if the collaboration between different unions increases, this might eventually prepare the ground for a growing labor class solidarity. There are great uncertainties involved in this problem and much will depend upon the educational forces in the South and the ideological trend in the whole nation.

9. SOCIAL SEGREGATION AND DISCRIMINATION IN THE NORTH

At the outbreak of the Civil War, most Northern states were nearly as far removed in time from actual slavery in their own realms as the Southern states are now. Their Negro populations were comparatively small in numbers. But slavery was a living institution within the nation. Though conditions were rather different in different Northern states, the general statement can be made that wherever Negroes lived in significant numbers they met considerable social segregation and discrimination. The Abolitionist propaganda and the gradual definition of emancipation as one of the main goals of the War undoubtedly tended to raise the status of Negroes somewhat. Still, one of the difficulties congressional leaders had in passing the Reconstruction legislation was the resistance in some Northern states where people found that they would have to change not only their behavior but also their laws in order to comply with the new statutes.[65]

In the social field—as in breadwinning, but not as in politics and justice —the North has kept much segregation and discrimination. In some respects, the social bars were raised considerably on account of the mass immigration of poor and ignorant Negroes during and immediately after the First World War. In the latter part of the 'twenties this movement was perhaps turned into a slight tendency in the opposite direction, namely, an appreciation of "The New Negro."[b] After a new wave of unpopularity during the first years of the depression, there seems again to have been a slow but

[a] See Chapter 18, Sections 3 and 4.
[b] See Chapter 35, Section 8.

steady development toward less social discrimination during the era of the New Deal. But quite apart from these uncertain fluctuations during the last couple of decades, it is obviously a gross exaggeration when it is asserted that the North is getting to be "like the South."

Even in the realm of social relations it is of importance that the average Northerner does not think of the Negroes as former slaves. He has not the possessive feeling for them and he does not regard their subservience as a mark of his own social status. He is, therefore, likely to let the Negroes alone unless in his opinion they get to be a nuisance. Upon the ideological plane the ordinary Northerner is, further, apparently conscious that social discrimination is wrong and against the American Creed, while the average Southerner tries to convince himself and the nation that it is right or, in any case, that it is necessary. The white newspapers in the North ordinarily ignore the Negroes and their problems entirely—most of the time more completely than the liberal Southern press. But when they have to come out in the open on the Negro problem, they usually stand for equality. Back of this official attitude, of course, is the fact that most Northerners are not in direct contact with Negroes. The patterns of social discrimination in the South have originally formed themselves as rural ways of life. In the North the rural sections are, and have always been, practically free of Negroes. Even in the big cities in the North, where there are substantial Negro populations, only a small part of the white population has more contacts with Negroes.

Lacking ideological sanction and developing directly contrary to the openly accepted equalitarian Creed, social segregation and discrimination in the North have to keep *sub rosa*. The observer finds that *in the North there is actually much unawareness on the part of white people of the extent of social discrimination against Negroes*. It has been a common experience of this writer to witness how white Northerners are surprised and shocked when they hear about such things, and how they are moved to feel that something ought to be done to stop it. They often do not understand correctly even the implications of their own behavior and often tell the interviewer that they "have never thought of it in that light." This innocence is, of course, opportunistic in a degree, but it is, nevertheless, real and honest too. It denotes the absence of an explicit theory and an intentional policy. In this situation *one of the main difficulties for the Negroes in the North is simply lack of publicity*. It is convenient for the Northerners' good conscience to forget about the Negro.

In so far as the Negroes can get their claims voiced in the press and in legislatures, and are able to put political strength behind them, they are free to press for state action against social discrimination. The chances are that they will meet no *open* opposition. The legislatures will practically never go the other way and attempt to Jim Crow the Negroes by statutes.

The federal Reconstruction legislation has taken better root in the North. When the Supreme Court in 1883 declared the Civil Rights Bill of 1875 unconstitutional, most states in the Northeast and Middle West, and some in the Far West, started to make similar laws of their own, while the Southern states, instead, began to build up the structure of Jim Crow legislation.[a]

With the ideological and legal sanctions directed *against* them, social segregation and discrimination have not acquired the *strength, persuasiveness or institutional fixity* found in the South. Actual discrimination varies a good deal in the North: it seems to be mainly a function of the relative number of Negroes in a community and its distance from the South. In several minor cities in New England with a small, stable Negro population, for instance, social discrimination is hardly noticeable. The Negroes there usually belong to the working class, but often they enter the trades, serve in shops, and even carry on independent businesses catering to whites as well as to Negroes. They belong to the ordinary churches of the community, and the children attend the public schools. Occasional intermarriages do not create great excitement. They fit into the community and usually form a little clique for themselves beside other cliques, but nobody seems to think much about their color. The interracial situation in such a city may remain even today very similar to that of Great Barrington, Massachusetts, some sixty years ago, which W. E. B. Du Bois portrays in his recent autobiography, *Dusk of Dawn*.[66]

In the bigger cities, even in New England, the conditions of life for the Negroes have probably never been so idyllic. Since the migration beginning in 1915, the status of Northern Negroes has fallen perceptibly.[67] In the Northern cities nearer the Mason-Dixon line there has always been, and is even today, more social segregation and discrimination than farther North.

One factor which in every Northern city of any size has contributed to form patterns of segregation and discrimination against Negroes has been residential segregation, which acts as a cause as well as an effect of social distance. This fundamental segregation was caused by the general pattern for ethnic groups to live together in Northern cities. But while Swedes, Italians, and Jews could become Americanized in a generation or two, and disperse themselves into the more anonymous parts of the city, Negroes were caught in their "quarters" because of their inescapable social visibility; and the real estate interest kept watch to enforce residential segregation. With residential segregation naturally comes a certain amount of segregation in schools, in hospitals, and in other public places even when it is

[a] See Section 4 of this chapter; see also Chapter 29. Maine, New Hampshire, and Vermont have no civil rights laws expressly relating to race and color. But there is little social discrimination against their small Negro populations.

not intended as part of policy. Personal contacts become, as a matter of course, more or less restricted to Negro neighborhoods. As the Negro sections grew during the northward migration, it became more and more possible for Negroes to have their entire social life in Negro neighborhoods, and white people became conditioned to look upon this as a natural and desirable situation.

In this process white Southerners who also moved northward have played a crucial role. To make a manager of a hotel, a restaurant, or a theater interested in trying to keep Negroes out of his establishment, it is not necessary that more than a tiny minority of customers object, particularly if they make a scene. Time and again I have, in my interviews with managers of various public places in the North, been told this same story: that they, themselves, had no prejudices but that some of their customers would resent seeing Negroes around. The fact that most Negroes are poor and residentially isolated and, hence, do not patronize white places often, and the further fact that upper class Negroes, who could afford to, abstain voluntarily from visiting places where they are afraid of being embarrassed, solidifies the situation. I have also noticed that Negroes often have an entirely exaggerated notion of the difficulties they would meet. They are conditioned to suspect discrimination even when there is no danger of it. So they abstain from going to places where they actually could go without any trouble. When once this pattern is set by themselves the result might later be discrimination when some Negro tries to break it.

The migrating Negroes have probably been even more influential in spreading Southern patterns in the North than the Southern whites. The low cultural level and poverty of the average Southern Negro stand out even more when he comes North where general standards are higher. If he comes without any other education, he is at least thoroughly trained in the entire ceremonial system of scraping his foot, tipping his hat, and using self-abasing vocabulary and dialect, and generally being subservient and unobtrusive in the company of whites. A Negro recently from the South is characterized as much by his manners and bearing as by his racial traits. He might get some ideas of a new freedom of behavior in the North and actually try his best to behave as a full man; and he might, indeed, easily succeed in becoming aggressive and offensive. But fundamentally it takes a radical reeducation to get him out of his Southern demeanor or the reaction to it. For a long time after migrating he will invoke discrimination by his own behavior. The submissive behavior of lower class Southern Negroes is usually not appealing at all to the white Northerner, who has not been brought up to have a patronizing attitude and who does not need it for his own self-elevation. The white Northerner also dislikes the slovenliness and ignorance of the Southern Negro. Thus the Negro often seems only strange, funny or repulsive to the white Northerner.

Even the poor classes of whites in the North come to mistrust and despise the Negroes. The European immigrant groups are the ones thrown into most direct contact and competition with Negroes: they live near each other, often send their children to the same schools, and have to struggle for the same jobs. Obviously attitudes among immigrants vary a good deal. Recent immigrants apparently sometimes feel an interest solidarity with Negroes or, at any rate, lack the intense superiority feeling of the native Americans educated in race prejudice. But the development of prejudice against Negroes is usually one of their first lessons in Americanization. Because they are of low status, they like to have a group like the Negroes to which they can be superior. For these reasons, it should not be surprising if now, since new immigration has been restricted for a considerable time, a study of racial attitudes should show that the immigrant groups are on the average even more prejudiced than native Americans in the same community.

I have an impression that the resentment against Negroes in the North is different from that in the South, not only in intensity, but also in its class direction. It does not seem to be directed particularly against the rising Negroes. In the more anonymous Northern cities, the Negro middle and upper classes do not get into the focus of public resentment as in the South. More important is the Yankee outlook on life in which climbing and social success are generally given a higher value than in the more static Southern society, and the ambitious Negro will more often be rewarded by approval and even by admiration, while in the South he is likely to be considered "smart," "uppity" or "out of his place."

Otherwise, the North is not original in its racial ideology. When there is segregation and discrimination to be justified, the rationalization is sometimes a vague and simplified version of the "no social equality" theory of the South which we have already discussed. It is continuously spread by Southerners moving North and Northerners who have been South, by fiction and by hearsay. But more often the rationalizations run in terms of the alleged racial inferiority of the Negro, his animal-like nature, his unreliability, his low morals, dirtiness and unpleasant manners. The references and associations to amalgamation and intermarriage are much less frequent and direct. This does not mean that the Northerner approves of intermarriage. But he is less emotional in his disapproval. What Paul Lewinson calls "the post-prandial non-sequitur"—if a Negro eats with a white man he is assumed to have the right to marry his daughter—practically does not exist in the North.

In this situation, however, not only is intermarriage frowned upon, but in high schools and colleges there will often be attempts to exclude Negroes from dances and social affairs. Social segregation is, in fact, likely to appear in all sorts of social relations. But there is much less social segregation and discrimination than in the South: there is no segregation on streetcars, trains, and so on, and above all, there is no rigid ceremonial governing the Negro-white relations and no laws holding the Negro down. The fact that there are no laws or defined rules of etiquette is sometimes said to cause friction and bitterness because some whites in the North will want Negroes to keep away from them, and Negroes cannot tell which whites these are. But the absence of segregating laws also keeps the system from being so relatively locked as in the South. It allows Negroes to be ambitious. And since Negroes in the North have the vote and a reasonable amount of justice in court, and since they can go to good schools and are, in fact, forced to get at least an elementary education, they can struggle for fuller social equality with some hope.

CHAPTER 29

PATTERNS OF SOCIAL SEGREGATION AND

DISCRIMINATION

1. Facts and Beliefs Regarding Segregation and Discrimination

In the preceding chapter we were primarily interested in the attitudes displayed in connection with segregation and discrimination and the popular concepts and theories advanced as motivation. Here we shall describe the actual patterns of social segregation. This we shall not be able to do in the detail we should like, partly because it is impossible to cover the whole of social life in a single chapter and partly because no studies have been made which quantify the extent of social segregation in any of its different forms or local variations.[1]

There is no little divergence of opinion as to the extent of segregation and discrimination in the interpersonal sphere. The literature tends to emphasize "interesting" individual experiences, which may be exceptions. In eliciting *opinions* as to the extent of segregation and discrimination, there exists enough divergence of interest to result in the collection of *beliefs* rather than *facts*. These beliefs are important data in themselves, but are no substitute for the facts. Both whites and Negroes in the South have a tendency to exaggerate the general scope and the local stability of segregation and discrimination patterns, to magnify unduly some occasional experience of their own and claim it as "characteristic." This varies considerably, however, depending upon political leanings and personality. The conservative white Southerner will often generalize what is merely occasional in his community and so also will the radical or dissatisfied Negro. The conservative Negro leader and his white friends in interracial work often show the contrary tendency to play down existing segregation and discrimination and to play up small favorable occurrences (that white and colored students meet for a discussion; that a prominent Negro, thanks to the influence of his white friends, can travel in a Pullman sleeper; that a supper is secretly shared). The lower class Negro in the South and in the North will usually be found to have vague and sometimes incorrect ideas of what he, as a Negro, can do and cannot do outside the narrow groove where he lives and where often his chief rule is merely that he

605

has to be subservient in every contact with whites and try to "keep out of trouble." As already mentioned, the white people in the North often do not realize the scope of actual segregation and discrimination against Negroes, while Negroes in the North, particularly in the upper and middle classes, have beliefs which are wrong in the other direction. These deviations of belief from reality are interesting and worth study. But, to repeat, statements purporting to describe general patterns of segregation and discrimination without systematic quantitative evidence—whether offered spontaneously or after questioning—may be expected to be deficient as descriptions of actual conditions.

We shall consider social segregation and discrimination under three categories: personal, residential, institutional. As we have seen, segregation in interpersonal relations is partly basic to most other forms of segregation and discrimination. Because of the strategic place it holds in the minds of white people, we shall consider it as the peak category of the rank order of social segregation and discrimination.[a] Much of what we shall have to say about the personal sphere is peculiar to the South and is unknown to Northerners. Residential and institutional segregation, on the other hand, are found in the North almost as much as in the South. Residential segregation is treated before institutional because it facilitates the latter by creating "natural" groupings of Negroes separate from whites.

2. Segregation and Discrimination in Interpersonal Relations

The ban on intermarriage has the highest place in the white man's rank order of social segregation and discrimination. Sexual segregation is the most pervasive form of segregation, and the concern about "race purity" is, in a sense, basic. No other way of crossing the color line is so attended by the emotion commonly associated with violating a social taboo as inter-marriage and extra-marital relations between a Negro man and a white woman.[2] No excuse for other forms of social segregation and discrimination is so potent as the one that sociable relations on an equal basis between members of the two races *may possibly* lead to intermarriage.

Intermarriage is prohibited by law in all the Southern states, in all but five of the non-Southern states west of the Mississippi River, but only in Indiana among the Northern states east of the Mississippi.[3] In practice there is little intermarriage even where it is not prohibited, since the social isolation from the white world that the white partner must undergo is generally intolerable even to those few white people who have enough social contact and who are unprejudiced enough to consider marriage with Negroes.[4] It is said that—as a reaction to the white attitude and as a matter of "race pride"—the Negro community also is increasingly likely to

---

[a] See Chapter 3, Section 4, and Chapter 28, Section 6.

ostracize mixed couples. This reaction is, however, much more pronounced toward illicit relations involving Negro women, and it has there the good reason that such relations are mostly of an exploitative type.

Extra-marital relations between Negro men and white women are all but nonexistent in the South.[5] If an incident occurs and is detected, it is either punished by the courts as rape, or the Negro is lynched, or he is run out of town. (The white woman is also run out of town if it becomes known that her action was voluntary.) In the North the sanctions are not so violent. There seems to be some small amount of interracial sexual experimentation in bohemian and radical circles involving Negro men and white women. There are also some white prostitutes catering to Negro men. The extent of extra-marital relations between white men and Negro women is a subject on which investigators give divergent estimates,[a] but there can be no doubt that it is a fairly common phenomenon throughout the South[6] and the North. Though tolerated, it is far from favored by public opinion and is usually clandestine.[b] It is also increasingly of a casual type. The old custom of white men keeping Negro concubines is disappearing in the South[7] and is rare in the North.

The prohibition of intermarriage in most states and the concomitant lack of effective legal protection—for claiming inheritance and alimony, for example—undoubtedly tend to decrease the deterrents on white men to take sexual advantage of Negro women. Miscegenation will thereby be kept on a higher level than under a system where the interests of Negro women and their mixed offspring were more equally protected.[c] The practically complete absence of intermarriage in all states has the social effect of preventing the most intimate type of acceptance into white society: if Negroes can never get into a white family, they can never be treated as "one of the family." Perhaps more important in the South as an effect of the lack of sanction for intermarriage is the regimentation of the whole gamut of contacts between adult members of the two races so that these contacts will be as impersonal as possible. This is commonly called "the etiquette of race relations."[8] This ceremonious attitude in race relations is especially striking when we consider that the American tends to be unceremonious in all his other relations. Although the racial etiquette

---

[a] See Chapter 5, Section 6.

[b] According to Jenks, one Southern (Louisiana) and two Northern (Nevada and South Dakota) states have laws against cohabitation and concubinage between members of the two races, as well as laws against intermarriage. (Albert E. Jenks, "The Legal Status of Negro-White Amalgamation in the United States," *The American Journal of Sociology* [March, 1916], p. 671.)

[c] This is the chief argument—besides general considerations of civil liberty and equality—of Negro spokesmen who want to have the ban on intermarriage abolished (See Walter White, *Rope and Faggot* [1929], pp. 77 ff.)

serves other functions,[a] its relation to the primary sex taboo is important enough to justify the ranking of the specific items of the etiquette according to their degree of intimacy or of closeness to the sex relation.[b] This would also seem to be the order in which any violation of the etiquette is likely to call forth excited condemnation and violent retaliation and, therefore, also the order of rigidity in the etiquette. The rank order and the correlation between degree of intimacy of the contact and degree of emotion caused by violation of the etiquette are hypotheses developed from impressionistic observations of white people's attitudes and behavior. The hypotheses are applied only to the South, but parallels in the North will be noted.

The relations which, outside of the purely sexual, are most intimate and are never tolerated between Negroes and whites in the South are those which imply erotic advances or associations, if the male partner is a Negro. Any attempt at flirtatious behavior in words or deeds will put him in danger of his life. Negro-white dancing as a heterosexual social activity with strong erotic associations is forbidden in the South whether the Negro partner be male or female. Even in the North interracial dancing seldom occurs. In high schools and colleges Negro students are usually expected not to attend social affairs where dancing is part of the entertainment. The same has been true of social functions given by mixed trade unions. If Negroes are allowed to come, they are often expected to bring partners of their own group. One can observe in the North that, when interracial dancing occurs, it intentionally has the significance for the white participants of demonstrating racial emancipation. The taboo against swimming together in the South is equally absolute, apparently for the reason that it involves the exposure of large parts of the body. In the North the taboo against using the same beaches or swimming pools is ordinarily also strong, though several public beaches, for instance, around New York, are open to both races.

The main symbol of social inequality between the two groups has traditionally been the taboo against eating together. It should at the outset be observed that, generally, the taking of meals in America has little social importance and is almost barren of all the rituals and ceremonial niceties commonly preserved in the older countries. In spite of frequent assertions

[a] One of the most important of the other functions of the etiquette in the South is to give whites—no matter how low in the social scale—a sense of power and importance. This "gain" has been excellently analyzed by John Dollard, *Caste and Class in a Southern Town* (1937), pp. 98 ff.

[b] This rank order is an expansion of the top layers of the rank order we proposed in Chapter 3, Section 4. It will be remembered that we placed the sexual sphere on top in the rank order of caste-defined relations, with the "social" sphere following it. This chapter gives consideration to these two orders, as previous chapters have considered the lower orders (justice, political and economic relations).

to the contrary, eating in the South when only white people are present is generally an even simpler affair than in the North. But in interracial relations eating together has been infused with a tremendous social signif-icance. "In the South, the table, simple though its fare may be," explains a Southerner, "possesses the sanctity of an intimate social institution. *To break bread together involves, or may involve, everything.*"[9] And, of course, even the less ritualized American eating is, in a degree, an equal-itarian activity; persons are forced to exhibit equal susceptibility to physiological needs, and if they are to sit facing each other for half an hour or so, they are inevitably thrown into social conversation.

For whites and Negroes to eat together would call forth serious con-demnation in the South. It is apparent—and well in accord with our hypoth-esis—that if a Negro man and a white woman should eat together, the matter would be even more serious. There are, however, occasions even in the South when upper class Negroes participate in interracial confer-ences—including the purely business or professional conferences—where eating takes place. In such cases the Negro participants are sometimes served in separate rooms or at separate tables in the same room. Even if there is only one Negro present and the conference is in a private home, the rule is that he must be served at a separate table. Liberal white educa-tors visiting Negro colleges sometimes take part in common meals, and they will not always be served at a separate table. Through this interracial activity, on a high level of social and cultural respectability, the eating taboo is slowly being broken down. People in the South generally know that such things are happening, and they are not as excited about it as they would have been a generation ago. In the case of eating incidental to the ordinary routines of life—such as in factory lunch rooms—Negroes regu-larly eat in separate rooms or have to wait until the whites have finished. Drinking is apparently less of an issue than eating. It is not considered quite so intimate since it requires less time, and it does not demand that participants sit down. At any rate, it would seem to be slightly less taboo for Negroes and whites to drink together than to eat together. For a white woman to take part in an interracial drinking party would, however, be worse even than eating with Negroes and it practically never occurs.

In the North, the taboo against interracial eating and drinking is weak: Negroes and whites will often be found eating together in restaurants, conferences and factory lunchrooms. Negro servants are practically never invited to eat at the same table with their white employers, but this is only slightly less true of white servants. In some Northern *milieus* it does seem to be considered objectionable for whites to invite Negroes to their houses for social gatherings, but the few occurrences seldom result in any reaction more violent than gossip.[10]

Next in order in degree of intimacy and in degree of reaction aroused by violation is a series of relations which involve at least one of the elements associated with eating: satisfying physiological needs, sitting down together, and engaging in sociable conversation. In public places, where there is a chance that whites and Negroes will want to use the facilities at the same time, there are separate rest rooms, toilets and drinking fountains all over the South. The use of the same toilet and drinking fountain does occur sometimes where it is not feasible to build separate facilities, as in some gas stations, factories and households. This indicates that the taboo is not quite so strong as in the case of eating and drinking. Separate rest rooms, toilets, and drinking fountains are not maintained in the North.

Perhaps allied with the prohibition against the use of the same facilities for the satisfaction of physiological needs is the prohibition against the participation of Negroes in activities where the human body is used. Dancing and swimming together are, as we have mentioned, especially taboo because of their erotic associations, but the prohibition extends—in a greater or less degree—to the various other sports and games.[a] The prohibition would seem to be less effective where social relations are least necessary—in group or professional sports. Also the prohibition does not extend to children, who often play together freely until puberty—a fact which shows the relation of this phase of the etiquette to sex. Playing together of children is reported to have been much more common in earlier times than now and extended then into the upper classes. Now it is increasingly becoming a lower class pattern both among whites and among Negroes. The Negro upper class families want to spare their children from early interracial experiences.[11] There is no general prohibition against Negroes taking part in sports and games in the North, although individual whites often refuse to play with Negroes. With the increase in sports and the greater preparation of Negroes for them, there has been an increase in interracial participation in them.

The conversation between whites and Negroes in the South is heavily regimented by etiquette. In *content* the serious conversation should be about

---

[a] Sometimes the prohibition against mixed sports is extended to mixed equipment. Charles S. Johnson (*Patterns of Negro Segregation*, prepared for this study [1943], p. 274) records the case of a principal of a white high school refusing to accept a basketball belonging to his school after the team of a Negro high school had borrowed it.

The principle of "not to be touched" extends in many directions. In a county in Georgia, where the Negro schoolhouses were dilapidated, I observed that in two cases there were good schoolhouses nearby which earlier had been used for white children but had been left vacant as a result of the recent centralization of the white school system. Upon my inquiry why they were not used for the Negro children, I was informed that this was impossible, for these reasons: in the one case, that there was a nearby old white graveyard and that white people in the community would not like to think of the barefoot Negro children passing by the graves and perhaps even treading upon them, and, in the other case, that the schoolhouse was used for occasional elections and that the white voters could not possibly be asked to enter a house used as a Negro school for casting their votes.

those business interests which are shared (as when a white employer instructs his Negro employee or when there is a matter to be discussed concerning the welfare of the Negro community) or it should be polite but formal inquiry into personal affairs (either a white or a Negro person may inquire as to the state of the other's health or business). There can generally be no serious discussion—although there can be the banter of polite conversation or joking—about local or national politics, international relations, or "news," on the one hand, or about items connected with the course of daily life, such as the struggle for existence or the search for pleasure, on the other hand. There are exceptions, of course. Some white women use their Negro servants as sources of gossip and local news.

The conversation is even more regimented in *form* than in content. The Negro is expected to address the white person by the title of "Mr.," "Mrs.," or "Miss."[12] The old slavery title of "Master" disappeared during Reconstruction entirely and was replaced by "Boss" or sometimes "Cap" or "Cap'n." From his side, the white man addresses the Negro by his first name, no matter if they hardly know each other, or by the epithets "boy," "uncle," "elder," "aunty," or the like, which are applied without regard to age. If he wishes to show a little respect without going beyond the etiquette, he uses the exaggerated titles of "doctor," "lawyer," "professor," or other occupational titles, even though the term is not properly applicable.[a] The epithets "nigger" and "darky" are commonly used even in the presence of Negroes, though it is usually well known that Negroes find them insulting. That there has been a slight tendency for this pattern to break down is shown by the use of the Negro's last name without title in many recent business relations. Too, a few salesmen will actually call Negroes by their titles of "Mr.," "Mrs.," and "Miss" in order to gain them as customers. Also significant is the fact that upper and middle class whites in the Upper South are beginning to call upper class Negroes by these titles.[b]

[a] In a small city I found the greatest difficulties in locating the principal of the Negro high school, whom I wanted to see (let us call him Mr. Jim Smith). The white people I asked had never heard about a Negro with that name and did not seem to know even where the Negro high school was. When I finally found him and told him about the difficulties I had met, he inquired. "Whom did you ask for?" I answered: "Mr. Jim Smith." He laughed and told me: "You should have asked for 'Professor Smith' or just for 'Jim'—sure, everybody knows me in this town."

[b] They are more inclined to use the titles of "Mr.," "Mrs.," and "Miss" for Negroes in private than in public. There is a deep and admittedly irrational aversion to using these titles on the part of some upper class whites. An educated Negro in a Southern Negro university was approached by an upper class white lady during the depression to ask for another Negro by his first name (let us call him Sam) who had charge of dispensing emergency relief for Negroes in the locality. Her interlocutor replied, "Sam who?" She did not know his last name and said, "You know who I mean, the nigger who sits at this desk and gives out the emergency relief. I want some relief for some of my niggers." Her interlocutor, wanting to tease her, went on: "Do you mean Mr. So-and-so or Mr. So-and-so," hoping to

Another aspect of the form of conversation between Negroes and whites is the rule that a Negro must never contradict the white man nor mention a delicate subject directly. That is, a good part of the Negro's conversation must be circumlocutory rather than direct. This is much less common now than formerly, but it has not disappeared. The *tone* of the conversation also was formerly fixed and still remains so to a certain extent: the Negro was to use deferential tones and words;[13] the white man was to use condescending tones and words. If the white man became angry or violent in his speech, the Negro could not reciprocate.

The apparent purpose of this etiquette of conversation is the same as that of all the etiquette of race relations. It is to provide a continual demonstration that the Negro is inferior to the white man and "recognizes" his inferiority. This serves not only to flatter the ego of the white man, but also to keep the Negro from real participation in the white man's social life. Conversation with other people is the principal way to participate in the lives of those people, to understand each other completely. In the North, the caste etiquette of conversation does not exist. That is, whites do not expect it. When Southern Negroes act it out they usually embarrass the average Northerner more than they please him. Where Negroes and whites meet socially on the same class level in the North (which they do relatively seldom because of residential and institutional segregation) they actually may come to understand one another. Southern whites have a myth that they "know" their Negroes. This is largely incorrect, and in their franker moments white Southerners will admit that they feel that Negroes are hiding something from them. They cannot know Negroes as they know other human beings because in all their contacts Negroes must, or feel they must, pose in a framework of etiquette. "What the white southern people see who 'know their Negroes' is the role that they have forced the Negro to accept, his caste role."[14] The racial etiquette is a most potent device for bringing persons together physically and having them cooperate for economic ends, while at the same time separating them completely on a social and personal level.

Closely allied to the forms of speech are the forms of bodily action when whites and Negroes appear before one another. For a Negro to sit down in the same room with a white person is not taboo, but it may be done usually

---

get her to say "mister" in designating a colored person. She finally broke down in tears and said, "Oh, please give me some relief for my niggers," but she refused to "mister" anybody.

Robert R. Moton, the late principal of Tuskegee, cites the case of "a distinguished Episcopal clergyman, a friend of mine and by everyone recognized as a friend of the race, [who] used to say that he always felt like laughing whenever he heard the principal of Hampton Institute, where he was a frequent visitor, refer to a coloured man as 'Mr.' To him, he said, it sounded just like saying 'Mr. Mule': it seemed no less ridiculous." (*What the Negro Thinks* [1929], p. 195.)

only at the request of the white person. Since the invitation is often not extended, it frequently happens that Negroes are standing in the presence of whites, even those who are of the same or lower socio-economic status as themselves. In conferences and public places, Negroes sit down without invitation, but there is usually segregation: Negroes will sit at one end of the conference table, or in the rear of or on one side of a courtroom, or in the balcony or gallery of a theater which they are permitted to enter. In the North, Negroes, when they are allowed to enter, take seats much in the same manner that whites do. Whatever segregation in seating there is in the North would seem to have a voluntary or class basis rather than a strict caste basis as in the South. Many theaters in the North, however, refuse to let a Negro enter, or, if they are in a state with a civil rights law, they try to find some excuse to make him stay away voluntarily. Where seats are reserved, the management will often try to sell seats to Negroes in a special section. Changing seats on the part of individual whites also will sometimes isolate Negroes in a Northern theater.

In general, the American is a great and indiscriminate hand-shaker. The ceremony is to him a symbol of friendliness and basic human equality. The partial taboo against shaking hands with Negroes is, therefore, significant. Formerly there was practically no hand-shaking between members of the two races except for that occurring when a Negro house servant would greet his returning master. The taboo is much less strong now, but the relation—in so far as it exists—is, as we have mentioned, entirely one-sided: the white man in the South may offer to shake hands with the Negro, but the Negro may not offer his hand to the white man. A white woman practically never shakes hands with a Negro man. The greeting of the Negro has traditionally been a bow and a removal of the hat. This, too, has become much less demanded. While talking, the traditional pattern was for the Negro to remain with hat off, with eyes directed on the ground, and with foot scraping the ground to "demonstrate" that he was incapable of standing and talking like a human being. This pattern, too, has rapidly been going into discard.

If he had to come into a white man's house, the rule was, and still is in most parts of the South, that the Negro must enter by the rear door. Since Negroes could plan this activity in advance they often avoided it by avoiding the need to talk to a white man in his house (by deliberately waiting until he came out to the street, or by going to his office, or by calling to him from the street or from the front yard). This etiquette form still exists for the most part, but many exceptions could be cited. Also, the increase in the number of houses without back doors is helping to break down the pattern. When a white man enters a Negro's house, he cannot be expected to show any signs of respect. He will enter without knocking; he will not remove his hat: he will not stand up when a Negro woman enters the room; he may even insist that the Negro occupants stand in his presence (the old-fashioned Negro will not presume to sit down anyway unless asked). There is little occasion for a white man to enter a Negro's house: if he wants to see a Negro he will send for him or call him on the telephone, or drive in his car to his house and blow the horn. White salesmen have found that they gained business if they showed Negroes some respect in their own homes, so they quite frequently violate the etiquette.[a] Practically nothing of any phase of the etiquette of bodily action, or of that associated with entering the houses of members of the other race, exists in the North.

In an essential and factual sense the cumbersome racial etiquette is "un-American." American civilization has received its deepest imprints from immigrants from the lower classes in Europe who were not much versed in the intricacies and shibboleths of upper class ceremonial behavior in the old countries and who often consciously resented them on ideological grounds. The equalitarian Revolutionary *ethos* also endorsed simple and unaffected manners. Aristocratic travelers from England and other countries during colonial times complained about the Americans not caring about social distinctions of birth and breeding. This is part of the historical background for the European (and American) myth of the Americans as being particularly "materialistic."[15] European observers with democratic leanings, from de Tocqueville on, have, on the contrary, found the lack of mannerisms of the typical American, his friendly, spontaneous, and equalitarian ways of meeting other human beings, a great charm of the new continent. The symbols a culture acquires are no accident and no forms are of more intrinsic importance than those of human contacts and relations. All these observers have, therefore, related this trait to the democratic and Christian *ethos* of the American Creed. When democratic European countries are said to become "Americanized," one of the positive elements in this change has commonly been recognized to be the throwing off of the inherited class etiquette, which is no longer functional in a modern democracy, and the breaking up of class isolation. Against this background,

[a] In violating the etiquette of caste, the white salesmen simply follow the normal etiquette of the society as a whole. Thus, the term "etiquette" as we have been using it is quite different from the term as understood by the man in the street, especially when applied to the behavior of the white man in the intercaste relation. But the term has a technical sociological meaning, and we are using it in this sense. The sociological term refers to all the formalisms which accompany interpersonal relations, regardless of whether or not they make for pleasant relations and increased mutual respect. But even when used by sociologists the term has the popular connotation of being a means of accommodation, and because of this the term is not the best one that could be used to describe the formalisms of Negro-white contacts: it is hard to see how the deliberate insults of the white man performing the actions required by the etiquette add to the "accommodation" of the intercaste relation.

the caste etiquette in America stands out as a glaring contradiction. It indicates the split in the American's moral personality.

The entire etiquette of interpersonal relations between Negroes and whites in the South is a systematic, integrated structure which serves to isolate the two groups from each other and to place the Negro group in an inferior social status. It formerly regimented practically every personal contact between members of the two races. It is breaking down to a certain extent—especially in those relations which are least intimate and most removed from the sexual.[16] It seems to be breaking down for two reasons: first, some Negroes are rising in class position so that many are above a good proportion of the whites, and class etiquette is chiseling in on caste etiquette; second, modern physical conditions (such as the absence of back doors, through which Negroes are supposed to enter whites' houses) prevent the full performance of an etiquette which developed under other conditions. Both of these conditions are more prevalent in the city than in the country. Coupled with the generally higher degree of secularization of attitudes in the city, they cause the etiquette to be somewhat less rigid in the city than in the country. As implied in the first cause of change, the etiquette is less rigidly applied to upper class than to lower class Negroes. This would not seem to be true, however, where a need was felt to reaffirm the caste line: when, for example, a white person of any class (usually the lower class) feels that a certain Negro or group of Negroes is getting too "uppity." Thus, while in everyday practice the upper class Negro need not abase himself in accordance with the full requirements of the etiquette, he must never be allowed to consider his privilege as a right. Even so, the very existence of the privilege is a sign of change.

Allied with change in the etiquette is uncertainty in its performance. Despite the basic uniformity of the pattern as we have described it, there has always been a great deal of local variation in detailed aspects of the etiquette.[a] This local variation *per se* should not, in most cases, be given too great importance in the study of the racial etiquette. The common denominator is not a stock of basic specific rules of behavior, but rather their common purpose, which is to isolate and subordinate the Negro group. One specific rule or another can equally well fill this function. But with increasing mobility of both Negroes and whites in the South it is becoming difficult for Negroes to follow the local requirements, and whites are in many cases unclear as to what they should expect or demand. Other influences which we have noted as modifying the etiquette also add to the uncertainty

[a] This variation has been a result not only of different local traditions, but also of the number and proportion of Negroes in the community, and the presence or absence of other minority groups. In many Texas communities where there are Negroes, their status is raised by reason of their small number and of the presence of a Mexican minority. In other Texas communities, prejudice against Negroes is very strong.

of its performance from both Negro and white points of view. While such a situation works hardships for individual Negroes—even to the extent of causing them to become innocent victims of police or court punishment or of mob violence—over a span of years it can be seen as a factor helping to break down the etiquette and to raise the status of Negroes in the attitudes of whites. Change from this source has occurred in the Border states to a greater extent than in the rest of the South.

Another area of life in which the patterns of segregation and discrimination are put under a strain is that in which they come in conflict with basically human inclinations. Negroes sometimes appear before whites in situations which evolve feelings of pity and sympathy. The inclinations of whites in these situations would be to help the Negroes were it not for the informal etiquette and formal rules of segregation. Of course, one of the effects of segregation and discrimination is to minimize the number of situations in which Negroes in desperate need of help appear before whites. Too, the etiquette is often so defined as to permit the white person to help the Negro. For example, the mistress could always administer any sort of bodily assistance to faithful servants who needed it without fear of violating the etiquette, whereas normally no white woman could touch a Negro man. There have always been situations, however, in which suffering Negroes have appeared before whites who were forbidden to help them because of the etiquette or formal rules. It is probable that, with the growing impersonality of the employer-servant relation and with the increase in the number of casual contacts, these situations are increasing in number. In such situations, the etiquette or rule is sometimes violated, sometimes not. We may cite illustrations of two types of these situations, where the etiquette was not violated, in order to bring out more fully the nature of the problem:

The other day I saw a good-looking, modest-appearing, well-dressed, but frail colored woman with a child in her arms attempt to board a street-car. She was about to fail. The conductor started to help her, then looked at the other passengers and desisted. His face was a study. Prejudice won; but it was a Pyrrhic victory.[17]

When I was working as a truant officer I was bitten by a dog. I went to a private physician. I had to go to the head of the welfare department (F.E.R.A.). The white woman in charge was very nice. She was as nice as white people can be. She sent me to the hospital. When I got there I had to wait a long time, and then I was sent to a white intern. He took me in a little room on one side. It looked like a storeroom. He told me to sit down and said that he wanted to look at my leg. My leg had a bandage on it, and the tape was stuck to the skin. He started tearing the bandage off. I asked him if he didn't have some ether to loosen the bandage with, and he said he didn't have any and that he could get it off without getting any. I was in this small room with the door shut. After he got the bandage off he refused to give me the Pasteur treatment. I got up and walked out. He followed me and called me everything but a child of God. He certainly did scare me. It is against the law to refuse the Pasteur treatment, but I never got it.[18]

Whether the rule or etiquette will be broken will obviously depend on the nature of the situation, on the presence or absence of white spectators and on the personality of the white man. A study of the effects on the white man's attitudes toward the etiquette and toward his own behavior would shed a great deal of light both on the nature of the etiquette and on human nature. Negroes seldom meet the problem since they are supposed to render assistance to whites under almost all circumstances. This fact only increases their bitterness when whites fail to reciprocate. There are certain situations, however, in which Negroes have the choice of refusing to aid a white person in need because they can avoid doing so without fear of detection. Such a revenge situation provides a subject for study parallel to that mentioned for whites. Even apart from the revenge motive, a Southern Negro, who is passing through territory where he is not known, has good reasons not to stop and offer his services, as he never knows what might come of it in the end. If the white person is a woman, he would be taking a considerable risk in offering to help her.

Conditions are sufficiently different in the *North* to lead us to regard the pattern of segregation and discrimination in interpersonal relations as having a different basis. It certainly does not cover the whole gamut of interpersonal relations but is spotty: it restricts marriage, but does not forbid it; it restricts dancing and swimming together but not eating and drinking together; it does not affect speech and body actions during speech. The Northern pattern could hardly be called an etiquette because it does not require that Negroes act in a special way toward whites or that whites act in a special way toward Negroes. Rather it takes the form of institutionalizing and rendering impersonal a limited number of types of segregation: Negroes are requested not to use bathing beaches reserved for whites; Negroes are requested not to patronize certain dance halls, hotels, and restaurants, and things are made unpleasant for them if they do. There is no organized force to stop intermarriage in most Northern states —whether legal or illegal. The pressure against intermarriage is simply, but effectively, the unorganized one of public opinion. Too, there seems to be little connection in motivation between the types of relations in which there is segregation and discrimination. It would seem much more reasonable in the North than in the South to accept the belief that Negroes are dirty as the main reason why they are not liked on the same bathing beaches. This belief is more natural for Northerners, since there is quite a bit of physical touch contact between Negroes and whites in the South and little in the North. Southerners tie up the bathing prohibition to the sexual prohibition—which Northerners less frequently do. Economic reasons seem to be important ones for demanding housing segregation in the North and are also more freely expressed, while in the South economic considerations are subordinated to, and all the specific segregations rationalized by, the closely interwoven theory of social equality.

For the most part, the etiquette of interpersonal relations between the races does not exist in law. In the South there are laws to segregate Negroes in institutions and to restrict interpersonal relations, but there are no laws to govern the behavior of Negroes and whites meeting on the street or in the house. The etiquette is enforced, however, to an extent by the police and the courts in the South as well as by public opinion and physical violence: policemen in the South consider the racial etiquette as an extension of the law, and the courts recognize "disturbance of the peace" as having almost unlimited scope.[a] The main sanctions are those of individual or group opinion and violence. Deprived of police and court protection, and usually dependent economically on white opinion, the Negro cannot take the risk of violating the etiquette.

3. Housing Segregation

If sexual segregation, or rather the concern about "race purity," is basic to most other forms of segregation psychologically—in so far as it gives them a main rationalization and an emotional halo which they otherwise should not have—residential segregation is basic in a mechanical sense. It exerts its influence in an indirect and impersonal way: because Negro people do not live near white people, they cannot—even if they otherwise would —associate with each other in the many activities founded on common neighborhood. Residential segregation also often becomes reflected in uniracial schools, hospitals and other institutions. It is relatively more important in the North than in the South, since laws and etiquette to isolate whites from Negroes are prevalent in the South but practically absent from the North, and therefore institutional segregation in the North often has only residential segregation to rest upon. For this reason, we shall emphasize the Northern situation in this section.

Housing segregation necessarily involves discrimination, if not supplemented by large-scale intelligent planning in the housing field of which America has as yet seen practically nothing. Housing segregation represents a deviation from free competition in the market for apartments and houses and curtails the supply available for Negroes. It creates an "artificial scarcity" whenever Negroes need more residences, due to raised economic standards or increased numbers of the Negro population. It further permits any prejudice on the part of public officials to be freely vented on Negroes without hurting whites. This last mentioned discriminating factor is more

[a] See Chapter 25, Section 1.

potent in the South than in the North, where race prejudice is less solidified and where Negroes have the vote. It is in Southern cities that Negroes receive few neighborhood facilities, such as paved streets, adequate sewage disposal, street lights, and so on. Rapid increases in the Negro population are much more prevalent in Northern cities, and residential segregation—by its curtailment of housing supply available for Negroes—prevents a proportional rise in housing facilities. In some neighborhoods of Northern cities housing conditions for Negroes are actually as bad as, or worse than, Southern ones.[a]

The available statistics refer directly to the actual concentration of Negroes in certain areas of a city and not to segregation in the sense of forced concentration. A sample study of 64 cities[19] in 1930 showed that 84.8 per cent of the blocks were occupied exclusively by whites. On the other hand, only 4.9 per cent of the blocks were completely occupied by nonwhite persons, some of whom were not Negroes. The percentage of blocks containing both whites and nonwhites was 10.3—over twice as large as the percentage of blocks having no whites. A large part of this lack of complete concentration is due to the fact that the data refer to entire blocks and not to individual houses. In many mixed blocks Negroes are concentrated in the backyards. Even so, we should not take it for granted that the concentration of Negroes is complete.[20] Most of the mixed areas, however, are cases of whites living in "Negro areas" and not of Negroes living in "white areas."

Residential concentration tends to be determined by three main factors: poverty preventing individuals from paying for anything more than the cheapest housing accommodation; ethnic attachment; segregation enforced by white people. Even in the absence of enforced segregation Negroes would not be evenly distributed in every city because as a group they are much poorer than urban whites. This applies with particular strength to the masses of Northern Negroes who are newly arrived from the South. Negroes would also be likely to cluster together for convenience and mutual protection. In the North this is again particularly true of Southern-born Negroes who have been brought up in a strict ethnic isolation enforced by the Jim Crow laws and the racial etiquette in the South. The three causal factors are closely interrelated. Even if initially the tendency on the part of whites to enforce segregation on Negroes was but slight, the actual concentration of a growing population consisting of poor uneducated Negroes

---

[a] See Chapter 16, Section 6. The discussion in this section will refer to cities. The residence of Negro tenants, sharecroppers, and farm laborers is controlled by the farm owners, who usually keep their Negroes separate from their whites when they have them both on the same land. Segregation operates on Negro farm owners in much the same way as it operates on city Negroes—they are seldom allowed to buy the more desirable land or land surrounded by white-owned property. (See Chapter 11, Section 6.)

in the slum sections would soon call forth more active intentions on the part of the whites to force segregation upon this group. These tendencies would become strongest in the middle and upper class areas. Generally it is true both in the South and in the North that segregation as a factor in concentrating the Negro population is a pattern that is most characteristic of higher class areas and is much weaker or totally absent in slum areas. Neither actual concentration nor segregation proper is restricted to Negroes. All the various national groups of immigrants have, for reasons of economy and ethnic cohesion, formed "colonies" in the poorer sections of Northern American cities. As long as they were poor and strange in language and other cultural traits, this concentration has been strengthened by segregation on the part of the older Americans. If this factor has not been noticed so much, the reason is not only that the first two factors were usually sufficient as causes, but also that the situation did not become permanent. For when the members of a national group become so "assimilated" that they no longer regard members of their ancestral group as closer than persons of the dominant group in the society—when they feel themselves to be more American than Italian, Polish, or Czech—they tend to disregard ethnic affiliation in seeking a residence and to pay more attention to their personal needs and their ability to pay rent. Within two or three generations, it has usually been the practice for families which stemmed from a certain section of Europe to forget about their ethnic background in seeking residences and to have the means of paying higher rents in almost the same proportion as Old Americans.

Negroes meet greater difficulties in rising economically, educationally and socially. But even apart from this, they are kept as aliens permanently. Otherwise Negroes who live in a Southern community and whose ancestors have been living there for several generations would no longer be living together, apart from the whites. Northern Negroes would similarly be expected to be distributed throughout Northern cities, rather than forced to remain in the Black Belts, if they were treated as members of ethnic groups from Europe are treated. Negroes who migrated from the South to the North in the last twenty-five years would be expected to live together because they are poor and because they feel less out of place among their own kind. But they would also be beginning to disperse themselves throughout the white population if it were not for segregation. Only Orientals and possibly Mexicans among all separate ethnic groups have as much segregation as Negroes.[21]

From this point of view residential segregation may be defined as residential concentration which, even though it were voluntary at the beginning or caused by "economic necessity," has been forced upon the group from outside: the Negro individual is not allowed to move out of a "Negro" neighborhood. The question whether the average Negro "wants" to live among his own kind then becomes largely an academic one, as we have no means of ascertaining what he would want if he were free to choose. In this sense practically all the statistically observed Negro housing concentration is, in essence, forced segregation, independent of the factors which have brought it about.

Southern whites do not want Negroes to be completely isolated from them: they derive many advantages from their proximity. Negroes, on their side, are usually dependent on whites for their economic livelihood, directly or indirectly. For these reasons, there are few all-Negro towns or villages in the South, and whites have never seriously endorsed the back-to-Africa and Kansas movements.[22] In some Southern cities, especially in the older ones, Negroes usually live in side streets or along alleys back of the residences of whites and sometimes in rear rooms of the whites' homes themselves—a practice surviving from slavery, when the slaves lived in shacks in the rear of the master's house. In such cases there is also segregation, but the segregation is based on what we may term "ceremonial" distance rather than spatial distance. Ceremonial distance occurs in Northern cities, too, when Negro servants live in or near the white employer's home.[a] In Northern cities, when Negroes were a small element in the population in numbers and in proportion and when they were practically all servants in the homes of wealthy whites (as they still are in many Northern cities outside of the largest ones), they also lived scattered throughout the city near the residences of their employers.

If, however, a Southern city received most of its Negro population after the Civil War, and if a Northern city has a large number of Negroes, such a city will tend to have large areas in which Negroes live separated in space from the whites. In other words, there are roughly two patterns of housing segregation in cities: one is found in Northern cities where there are few Negroes and in old Southern cities where the successors of local slaves make up the bulk of the Negro population; there Negroes live in practically all parts of the city but only along certain poorer streets or alleys. The other is found in Northern cities with a fairly large Negro population and in Southern cities where the proportionate bulk of the Negroes has come in since the Civil War; there Negroes live in a limited number of distinct Black Belts. This is a rather gross classification of types of residential segregation in cities: both patterns are to be found in the same city—and there are many variations.[23] In fact, as Woofter says:

[a] Ceremonial distance is regularly called into existence to preserve spatial segregation on the borderline between white and Negro neighborhoods. It becomes especially apparent when the accidents of city growth have brought wealthy white neighborhoods in close physical proximity to poor Negro neighborhoods. For example, New York's Harlem is adjacent to the Columbia University area and Chicago's small Near North Side Negro community is within a block or two of the Gold Coast.

> Each city has a pattern of its own determined by the percentage of Negroes in the total [population], the distribution of Negro employment, the distribution of the areas where property is within the means of colored families, the attitude of the people toward segregation, and the rate of expansion of business and manufacturing sections.[24]

The geography of a city also helps determine the pattern of segregation. In a flat city like Chicago, which expanded in practically all directions from a single center, Negroes are concentrated in the slums around the central business district and their better class neighborhood stretches out like a spoke from this slum base.[25] In a hilly city like Cincinnati, Negroes are concentrated in the lowlands. In a long, narrow city like New York, Negroes tend to live in a section of the strip, and the transportation lines go right through the Negro section. This latter variation should not lead us to believe that there is no segregation in such a narrow city as Manhattan, although some Negroes would like to believe that there is none. Claude McKay is in error when he says:

> Segregation is a very unfortunate word. It has done much harm to the colored group by paralyzing constructive thinking and action. Not by the greatest flight of the imagination could Negro Harlem be considered as a segregated area. Besides the large percentage of whites who do business there, quite a number of them also reside there in the midst of the colored people. Harlem is more like a depressed area. In my last book I compared it to the servant quarters of a great estate. The servants live on a lower level. But they are not segregated.[26]

To depict more clearly the character of residential segregation in American cities, Appendix 7 describes the pattern of Negro residences in selected cities.

4. SANCTIONS FOR RESIDENTIAL SEGREGATION

Probably the chief force maintaining residential segregation of Negroes has been *informal* social pressure from the whites. Few white property owners in white neighborhoods would ever consider selling or renting to Negroes; and even if a few Negro families did succeed in getting a foothold,[a] they would be made to feel the spontaneous hatred of the whites both socially and physically. The main reason why informal social pressure has not always been effective in preventing Negroes from moving into a white neighborhood has been the tremendous need of Negroes to move

---

[a] The first foothold of Negroes in a white neighborhood is often achieved by accident: a piece of property is deeded to an absentee landlord who has no interest in the neighborhood; a white real estate agent wishes to make the large profit involved in selling to harassed Negroes; one of the local white residents may not be morally integrated into the neighborhood (the strategic 3500 block on fashionable Grand Boulevard in Chicago was supposed to have been first opened to Negroes by a white prostitute who wished to retaliate on her neighbors for exposing her to the police).

out of their intensely overcrowded ghettos and their willingness to bear a great deal of physical and mental punishment to satisfy that need.

The clash of interests is particularly dramatic in the big cities of the North to which Negro immigrants from the South have been streaming since the First World War. When white residents of a neighborhood see that they cannot remove the few Negro intruders and also see more Negro families moving in, they conjure up certain stereotypes of how bad Negro neighbors are and move out of the neighborhood with almost panic speed. For this reason Negroes are dangerous for property values,[a] as well as for neighborhood business, and all whites are aware of this fact. In describing the succession of Negroes down the South Side in Chicago, an informant said, "This was not an incoming of the Negroes, so much as an outgoing of the whites. If one colored person moved into the neighborhood, the rest of the white people immediately moved out."[27]

Such a situation creates a vicious circle, in which race prejudice, economic interests, and residential segregation mutually reinforce one another. When a few Negro families do come into a white neighborhood, some more white families move away. Other Negroes hasten to take their places, because the existing Negro neighborhoods are overcrowded due to segregation. This constant movement of Negroes into white neighborhoods makes the bulk of the white residents feel that their neighborhood is doomed to be predominantly Negro, and they move out—with their attitudes against the Negro reinforced. Yet if there were no segregation, this wholesale invasion would not have occurred. But because it does occur, segregational attitudes are increased, and the vigilant pressure to stall the Negroes at the border-line is kept up.[b]

Various organized techniques have been used to reinforce the spontaneous segregational attitudes and practices of whites in keeping Negro residences restricted to certain areas in a city. These include local zoning ordinances, restrictive covenants and terrorism.

The earliest important legal step to enforce segregation was taken in 1910 when an ordinance was passed in Baltimore, Maryland, after a Negro family

[a] If white property owners in a neighborhood rush to sell their property all at once, property values naturally are hurt. After the transition to Negro occupancy is made, however, property values rise again at least to the level justified by the aging and lack of improvement of the buildings. No statistical study has been made which shows unequivocally that Negroes pay higher rents for equivalent apartments but this seems to be the opinion of all those—including white real estate agents—who have looked into the matter. Certain conditions, such as the lowering of rents to white tenants when there is a threat of Negro succession and the conversion into smaller apartments to meet the needs of Negro tenants, make it extremely difficult to measure the changes in rent that accompany a shift from white to Negro occupancy. (See Chapter 16, Section 6.)

[b] Negroes also get into neighborhoods which have deteriorated because industry, crime, or vice are moving in.

had moved into what had previously been an all-white block. Many Southern and Border cities followed suit,[28] after state courts upheld zoning ordinances. Even after the Louisville ordinance was declared unconstitutional by the Supreme Court of the United States in 1917,[29] certain cities put into effect other segregative laws designed to get around the decision. A more comprehensive and severe denunciation of segregation by law was made in the 1927 decision of the Supreme Court in the New Orleans case, but even as recently as 1940 the North Carolina State Supreme Court had to invalidate a residential segregation ordinance passed in Winston-Salem.

When the courts' opposition to segregation laws passed by public bodies became manifest, and there was more migration of Negroes to cities, organized activities on the part of the interested whites became more widespread. The restrictive covenant—an agreement by property owners in a neighborhood not to sell or rent their property to colored people for a definite period—has been popular, especially in the North. The exact extent of the use of the restrictive covenant has not been ascertained, but: "In Chicago, it has been estimated that 80 per cent of the city is covered by such agreements . . ."[30] This technique has come up several times for court review, but, because of technicalities, the Supreme Court has as yet avoided the principal issue of the general legal status of the covenants.[31] If the Court should follow up its action of declaring all local laws to segregate Negroes unconstitutional by declaring illegal also the private restrictive covenants, segregation in the North would be nearly doomed, and segregation in the South would be set back slightly.

In addition to restrictive covenants, neighborhood associations have served as organized extra-legal agencies to keep Negro and white residences separated. The devices employed by them range all the way from persuasion to bombing. The Washington Park Court Improvement Association in Chicago shifted its function from planting shrubbery and cleaning the streets to preventing Negroes from getting into the neighborhood, when the Black Belt began to expand in the direction of this community.[32]

But in spite of the white vigilance on the frontiers of the Negro districts, the line never gets absolutely fixed in all directions. Now and then a small break occurs, and the Negro community gains a little more space. Here and there some upper class Negroes succeed in moving out to a white neighborhood without causing a wholesale removal of the whites in the area or in building houses on vacant land at the outskirts of cities. If such cities expand, it is possible that these few Negroes will find themselves part of a large white neighborhood—at least in the North. Meanwhile more Southern Negroes move in and the pressure accumulates behind the main front line. The crowded lower class Negro ghetto remains alongside industry, vice and crime centers.[33] Because recent immigrants from Europe, especially

Italians and Jews, have been less prejudiced—and because they are poor and segregated themselves—foreign colonies also become their neighbors. But they are isolated from the main body of whites, and mutual ignorance helps reinforce segregative attitudes and other forms of race prejudice.

Opposed to this hypothesis has been the Southerner's theory that minimizing contacts means minimizing conflicts. In this particular respect, this theory is the less rational in view of the fact that the main distributive effect of segregation is to keep the few well-educated upper and middle class Negroes out of white neighborhoods. Segregation has little effect on the great bulk of poor Negroes except to overcrowd them and increase housing costs, since their poverty and common needs would separate them voluntarily from the whites, just as any European immigrant group is separated. The presence of a small scattering of upper and middle class Negroes in a white neighborhood would not cause conflict (unless certain whites were deliberately out to make it a cause of conflict), and might serve to better race relations. The fact is neglected by the whites that there exists a Negro upper and middle class who are searching for decent homes and who, if they were not shunned by the whites, would contribute to property values in a neighborhood rather than cause them to deteriorate. The socially more serious effect of having segregation, however, is not to force this tiny group of middle and upper class Negroes to live among their own group, but to lay the Negro masses open to exploitation and to drive down their housing standard even below what otherwise would be economically possible.

As pointed out in an earlier chapter,[a] recent government policies have, on the whole, served as devices to strengthen and widen rather than to mitigate residential segregation. The Federal Housing Administration, in effect, extends credit to Negroes only if they build or buy in Negro neighborhoods and to whites only if they build in white areas which are under covenant not to rent or sell to Negroes. This policy of the F.H.A. is the more important since it has been an ambition and accomplishment of this agency to make housing credit available to low income groups. The effect has probably been to bring about an extension of such "protection" to areas and groups of white people as were earlier without it. The United States Housing Authority and its local affiliates are not so intentionally restrictive. But they have been forced by public opinion to build separate housing projects for whites and Negroes, and even where they have mixed projects, they have been forced, in all but one or two instances, to keep the Negroes at one end and the whites at the other. Negroes have, however, had reasons to be grateful to the U.S.H.A. for the relatively large share of low cost housing this agency has given them

[a] See Chapter 15, Section 6.

even if it has not been effective in opening up new areas for the congested Negro populations in American cities.

The local government authorities have, for natural reasons—both in the South, where the Negroes are numerically strong but disfranchised, and in the North, where they have votes but are small minorities—rather sided with the white segregationalists. In the big Northern cities that have been the goal of the Negro migration northward, they have had the special and potent reason that they do not want to encourage more Negro migration. This reason—which, of course, in consideration of the Negro vote, has not often been announced openly, though, as the author has observed, it is freely admitted in conversation—has had a fateful influence on social policy generally. Even administrators, who on general principles have deplored the standards of public service in the Negro slums, have been inhibited from going in wholeheartedly for reform. They must tell themselves that even without reform the Negroes are much better off in Northern cities than in the South, and that any improvement is likely to attract more Negro migration. This attitude makes them also generally reluctant to enter into large-scale planning, and they use their influence to discourage even the Negro leaders from considering broad programs for social improvement. It is one of the factors which explains why both Negro and white leaders and experts in large Northern cities are found to be so barren of constructive ideas on policies in so far as Negro problems are concerned.[a]

This also explains why, in practice and often in discussion, the only two alternatives have been segregation and free competition. It must be emphasized that segregation *can* be "positive" or "negative." The average individual white's attitude is, of course, only negative: he wants to be "protected" from Negro neighbors.[b] But as long as the Negro population in a city is increasing—or even if it were stationary but the Negro group for some reason, such as higher income or an increased proportion of persons of marriageable age, were in need of more housing facilities—it is an irrational and, indeed, impossible policy in the long run only to "protect" white areas against Negro intrusion. The result will be "doubling up," scandalous housing conditions for Negroes, destroyed home life, mounting juvenile delinquency, and other indications of social pathology which are bound to have their contagious influence upon adjoining white areas. And inevitably the Negros will finally break through somehow and in some degree—this

[a] There is another problem after areas for Negro housing have been attained. This is the problem of finding capital to invest in such housing. (See Chapter 16 and Appendix 7.)

[b] In the opinion poll taken for this inquiry by *Fortune* magazine, from 77 to 87 per cent of the informants in various regions of America expressed themselves in favor of residential segregation of Negroes, based either on legislation or on social pressures. Only 10 to 19 per cent were against segregation. (See: Eugene L. Horowitz, "Race Attitudes," Table XX, in Otto Klineberg [editor], *Characteristics of the American Negro*, prepared for this study; to be published.)

eventual Negro invasion of white areas must actually be considered to be an insufficient "self-healing" which in Northern cities takes the place of intelligent political action. The impossible situation which prevails is being studied in excellent "ecological" research—a branch of social science and a direction of scientific interest which is itself a by-product of big cities' being allowed to grow without any plan. But in the practical field there is great lack of courage and interest. It must be stressed that if white people insist on segregation—and if society is assumed not to tolerate a socially costly sub-standard housing for Negroes—*the logical conclusion is that, in a planned and orderly way, either areas of old housing now inhabited by whites or vacant land must be made available for Negroes.* The F.H.A. has tended to tighten the present impossible situation. The U.S.H.A. has not been in a position to change it. The local city authorities avoid going into the problem. And the Negroes themselves are inarticulate and void of constructive ideas.

It seems of urgent importance that residential segregation and all the connected problems of Negro housing become the object of scientific research with more practical vision than hitherto. The general structure of this complex of problems is clear-cut and ready for social engineering. There is material available for the detailed statistical analysis needed for local planning. The field of conflicting and converging interests is easily mapped in every community. The strategic time for this planning work is now. After the War a great increase in private and public building is likely, since housing construction has been moribund for several years, and popular needs seemed about to cause a building boom when the War started and diverted the construction industries' efforts into the field of defense housing. Also, the War will leave in its wake a tremendous need for public works and private investment to prevent a new and more devasting world depression. To be maximally useful this housing boom should be planned in advance.[a] And it would be prudent not to overlook segregation and the abominable housing conditions for Negroes. Gross inequality in this field is not only a matter for democratic American conscience, but it is also expensive in the end.

5. The General Character of Institutional Segregation

While there is much segregation of Negroes in the North in public facilities and private commercial establishments—a segregation which we term "institutional," for convenience, to distinguish it from both personal and residential segregation—there is a tremendous difference between the North and the South in this form of segregation. The difference arises out of two facts.

[a] The National Resources Planning Board is now planning for post-war housing construction as a public works program.

One is that institutional segregation in the South is supported and, indeed, inspired by an elaborate racial etiquette and a clearly perceived popular theory of "no social equality." The etiquette is, as we have shown, for the most part entirely lacking in the North, while the theory of "no social equality" is perceived only vaguely and is not invested with the same deadly seriousness as in the South. For this reason institutional segregation fits in more "naturally" in the South, while in the North it is constantly challenging other elements of popular ideologies and customs. The North is more secularized in its way of thinking, and life is more anonymous. It is to a greater degree bent upon technical efficiency, which means that the economic irrationality of institutional segregation, when it does occur, is likely to appear more striking. This last mentioned point becomes the more important since the North, being more law-abiding and having to take the Negro vote into consideration, will usually have to carry on segregation without much financial compensation from discrimination. The second great cause of difference is that in the South institutional segregation is in the laws of the states and of the local communities and thus allows for few individual exceptions. In the North institutional segregation, arising out of personal distaste for Negroes and as a consequence of residential segregation, is entirely extra-legal and often illegal.

Every Southern state and most Border states have structures of state laws and municipal regulations which prohibit Negroes from using the same schools, libraries, parks, playgrounds, railroad cars, railroad stations, sections of streetcars and buses, hotels, restaurants and other facilities as do the whites.[a] In the South there are, in addition, a number of sanctions other than the law for enforcing institutional segregation as well as etiquette. Officials frequently take it upon themselves to force Negroes into a certain action when they have no authority to do so. The inability of Negroes to get justice in the courts extends the powers of the police in the use of physical force. Beating and other forms of physical violence may be perpetrated by almost any white man without much fear of legal reprisal.[b] Equally important sanctions are the organized threat and the risk of Negroes getting the reputation of being "bad" or "uppity," which makes precarious all future relations with whites. The Negro's reliance on the tolerance of the white community for his economic livelihood and physical security makes these threats especially potent.

As long as the Supreme Court upholds the principle established in its decision in 1883 to declare the federal civil rights legislation void, the Jim

[a] See Chapter 28, Section 9. For a survey of these laws and of the extent of the variations in law and judicial procedure in these matters, the reader is referred to Charles S. Mangum's recent book, *The Legal Status of the Negro* (1940).

[b] See Part VI.

Crow laws are to be considered constitutional. It is a notorious fact, however, that institutional segregation as it is actually practiced is the basis for gross discrimination, and this is unconstitutional. To prove discrimination before a court is always difficult, and such judicial procedures are expensive and can hardly be undertaken by private individuals. The Negro defense organizations, and primarily the National Association for the Advancement of Colored People, because of their limited funds—and also because they do not wish to call forth a new revolutionary movement in the South—have restricted themselves to attacks on selected strategic points. In the legal situation described, and particularly since the Supreme Court in recent years has become increasingly prepared to observe the intent of the Reconstruction Amendments, the defenders of the legal rights of Negroes go from victory to victory.[a]

It is often maintained—even by Negro intellectuals—that the fight for the Negroes' civil rights and against discrimination in institutional segregation is doomed to be fruitless, as the inequalities have much deeper roots and are upheld by other sanctions than law. This criticism, however, overlooks several points. The courts in the Southern states want to have their decisions upheld and the state authorities want to have their policies covered by law as far as possible. It is noticeable everywhere in the South that even the threat of legal action puts a certain restraint on institutional discrimination. And court decisions are increasingly exposing the Southern statutes backing the system of institutional segregation as unconstitutional. *This system is thus gradually losing its legal sanctions and increasingly depending upon extra-legal or illegal sanctions*. The parallel with disfranchisement should be observed.[b]

The dilemma of Southern whites in this field is accentuated by the fact that segregation, which is the proclaimed purpose of the Jim Crow legislation, is financially possible and, indeed, a device of economy only as long as it is combined with substantial discrimination. If institutional segregation should have to be made constitutional in practice—that is, by giving truly equal though separate facilities to both groups—it would in most cases turn out to be financially ruinous. Under the onslaught of legal action, which we shall have to expect to increase rather than to abate, and in the general trend toward legality which is visible in the South, this fundamental dilemma will become increasingly exposed and the stability of the entire system of institutional segregation will be gradually undermined. A factor which, on the contrary, works toward stabilizing the Southern Jim Crow system is the increasing amount of vested interest which the higher strata of the Negro community are acquiring in its preservation. The dilemma of the Negro business and professional class is that the segregation they are

[a] See Chapter 39.
[b] See Chapter 23, Section 4.

fighting against affords them the monopolistic basis of their economic existence.[a]

In the North the Jim Crow laws are absent. In addition, eighteen states have civil rights acts roughly similar to the kind which the federal government was prohibited from having by decision of the Supreme Court in 1883.[34] These laws are not rigorously enforced, and there are all sorts of ways of getting around them. But their very existence makes institutional segregation a qualitatively different problem in the North than in the South, and the scope of these laws is continually being increased.[35] Physical violence, organized threats, giving Negroes a bad reputation, extensions of police and court powers and laws are, further, seldom used in the North as sanctions in enforcing institutional segregation.[b] The main sanctions of institutional segregation in the North are individual protest and refusal to serve. The individual protester or refuser may be a white store or organization manager, a white customer, or even—at some risk of legal reprisal —a white public official. These sanctions are much weaker than any others used in the South.

Yet there is institutional segregation in the North, and its effects are far from negligible. Many institutions—such as schools, parks, playgrounds, stores, theaters, other places of amusement—have a community basis, and residential segregation is, therefore, an effective means of getting separate units for Negroes. Sometimes certain devices are employed artificially to increase the separating power of residential segregation. School boundaries, for example, are usually set at the boundary of the white and Negro neighborhoods: if a white child lives in a "Negro school district," he is readily given a permit to go to another school; if a Negro child lives in a "white school district," he is encouraged and sometimes coerced into going to a Negro school. Residential segregation is the main cause of institutional segregation also in other public facilities where it sometimes occurs, at hospitals, clinics, relief agencies, and so on, in the North.

In private facilities and organizations, however, there is the important added control of the manager's or group's desires. In states where there is no civil rights law, a manager of any private organization, commercial or noncommercial, can simply refuse to serve Negroes and may even put up a sign to that effect. In states where there are civil rights laws, no manager or employee may refuse to Negroes, theoretically, the service that he

[a] See Chapter 38, Section 10. A Southern white liberal pointed out to me that until comparatively recently Charleston, South Carolina, had employed white teachers in the Negro schools. He saw in this practice, in such places where the tradition from the *ante-bellum* South had been preserved, an example of white people helping the Negroes to rise. When I later visited Charleston, the Negroes related to me, as their main success in their fight to protect their interests, that they had succeeded in driving out the white teachers from the Negro schools and in giving these jobs to Negroes.

[b] See Chapter 24.

would offer to white persons. Actually, many stores, hotels, and other establishments refuse service to Negroes without excuse unless someone asks the police or courts to take action. Occasionally they even have signs up: "Whites Only." Even when the police and courts take action, the practice may be kept up, since the fine is usually small and the probability of being called before the law a second time also is small. Much more frequently employed than a direct violation of the law are the indirect devices of discouraging the Negro from seeking service in these establishments; by letting him wait indefinitely for service, by telling him that there is no food left in the restaurant or rooms left in the hotel, by giving him dirty or inedible food, by charging him unconscionable prices, by insulting him verbally, and by dozens of other ways of keeping facilities from him without violating the letter of the law.[36]

In addition to residential segregation and managerial refusal of services as techniques of effecting institutional segregation in the North, there are other means that should be mentioned. A voluntary organization, whether for civic, religious, political, economic, or associational purposes, will most often simply not invite Negroes to membership, even though they meet all other requirements. No state attempts to restrict the membership or service policies of voluntary associations. Even semi-public associations in Northern states with civil rights laws—such as the American Red Cross, the United Service Organizations, charities, universities[37]—grossly discriminate against Negroes. A fourth device is for individual whites to insult or stare at Negroes in restaurants or other public places where the management does not restrict service to them.

This all leads to a fifth, and equally important, cause of segregation: voluntary withdrawal of Negroes into their own group. This cause operates in the South, too. It is impossible to draw the line between voluntary withdrawal and forced segregation, and the latter is practically always contributory to the former, indirectly if not directly. The effects—in terms of cultural isolation and lack of equality of opportunity—are the same. In fact, the voluntary withdrawal often goes further than the demand for segregation on the part of the whites. Many Negroes in the upper and middle classes make it a policy to abstain as far as possible from utilizing the Southern Jim Crow set-ups in theaters, transportation, and the like, or from entering places in the North where they know that they are not welcome.

Institutional segregation and discrimination in the Border states is roughly between that of the North and that of the South. In some things, the Border is closer to the South and in others it is more like the North. In a few things, the Border is even harsher than the South: "In Baltimore and Washington, D. C., for example, there is more rigid segregation and rejection of Negro patronage in the large department stores than anywhere in the South."[38] In Washington the theaters for whites are completely closed to Negroes, but libraries, public buildings and parks are open.[39] The Border states have fewer restrictive laws than the Southern states but do not have the general civil rights laws found in the North. Still, there are a few laws both to restrict association and to prohibit discrimination, and even more laws making these things optional. According to Charles S. Johnson: "It is frequently necessary to be more explicit regarding segregatory intent [in the Border states] than in the South."[40] Still there is probably more confusion about the behavior required and more rapid breakdown of the various types of segregation and discrimination. But confusion and breakdown exist in other regions of the country also. The rules are complicated, and they vary locally even when they are kept stable in time. All Negroes point to this fact, some to argue the irrationality of the segregation system, others to explain how difficult it is for the Negro to find his way through the Jim Crow jungle.

6. Segregation in Specific Types of Institutions

It is in government-owned institutions that legal segregation is most complete in the South. One of the most inclusive definitions of the South—including all the Border states and some localities in such Northern states as Indiana and New Jersey—is that based on legal segregation in schools. Seventeen states and the District of Columbia have two complete sets of elementary and secondary schools as part of state law. With the exception of the District of Columbia, nearly every community in these states has a substantial amount of discrimination coupled with segregation in the provision of education for Negroes. The buildings and equipment are inferior; in rural areas most of the schools are not run during the planting or harvesting seasons; the teachers get a lower rate of pay;[a] Negroes have little control over their school;[41] many common academic subjects are not offered in the secondary schools in order to prevent Negroes from getting anything but a low grade vocational training.[b]

For higher education, Negroes are still worse off. Some of the Southern states support small Negro colleges—never comparable in facilities and personnel with even the average Southern state university. Other Southern states help to support privately run Negro colleges if these colleges agree to accept Negro students of that state at low tuition rates. Since many of these colleges do not have graduate departments, some of the state governments have paid tuition fees at any university in the United States for Negro students who wish to pursue certain studies provided for whites but not for Negroes by the state. Not only is it hard to obtain this out-of-

---

[a] See Chapter 14, Section 4. At the present time (winter, 1941-1942) Negro teachers in states of the Upper South are waging successful court battles to get equal pay.

[b] See Chapter 41.

state support, but Negro students are faced sometimes with the dilemma of whether to fight for their right to enter the state university or to seek the advantages of the superior Northern universities. In the recent (December, 1938) case of *Lloyd Gaines v. the University of Missouri*, the United States Supreme Court decided that a Negro could insist upon entrance into a regular state university if no separate but equal university were provided for Negroes by that state.[42]

There is little school segregation required by law in the Northern and Western states: Arizona requires it in elementary schools and makes it permissive in secondary schools;[43] Kansas, Wyoming, Indiana, and New Mexico make school segregation permissive in the elementary grades and sometimes also in the secondary grades.[44] Some communities in the southern parts of New Jersey, Indiana, Pennsylvania, Ohio, and Illinois use organized pressure contrary to law to segregate Negroes in at least the elementary grades.[45] In practically all other areas of the North there is partial segregation on a voluntary basis, caused by residential segregation aided by the gerrymandering of school districts and the system of "permits." This segregation is fairly complete for elementary schools, except where Negroes form only a small proportion of the population, but there is much less segregation in secondary schools. In few cases—if any—is this segregation accompanied by discrimination, however, except that form of discrimination which inevitably arises out of isolation. In fact there is probably more discrimination in the mixed schools than in the segregated ones in the North: frequently Negroes in mixed schools are kept out of swimming, dancing, and other athletics, and out of social clubs. There are, however, some Negro teachers in mixed schools in many Northern cities, and Negroes sit on the boards of education in a few big Northern cities.

No Northern state university prohibits the enrollment of Negroes, although a few practice minor forms of discrimination once they are enrolled. This is often a matter of individual prejudice rather than of official policy. Private universities in the North restrict Negroes in rough inverse relation to their excellence: the great universities—Harvard, Chicago, Columbia, and so on, restrict Negroes to no significant extent, if at all. A few exceptions exist: Princeton University, for example, has no Negro students, but this university has Southern traditions. Most of the minor private universities and colleges prohibit or restrict Negroes. Some of these permit the entrance of a few token Negroes, probably to demonstrate a racial liberalism they do not feel. Four or five Northern colleges or universities, outside the Negro ones, have a Negro on their instructional staff.[46] That there is no serious restriction on higher education for Negroes in the North is shown by the fact that there are only four Negro colleges in all the 30 non-Southern states, and two of these were started before the Civil War.

Most other public facilities—such as libraries, parks, playgrounds—are available to Negroes with about the same amount of discrimination and segregation, in the various regions of the country, as in schools. Negroes are not permitted to use these in the South unless they are acting in a servant capacity. Many Southern cities have separate parks, playgrounds, and libraries for Negroes, but in all cases they are poor substitutes for those available to whites. In a few cities in the Upper South Negroes are allowed to enter some of the general parks. In a few Southern cities, such as Nashville and Richmond, upper class Negroes are allowed to use the white library if they sit at a special table or in a special room. Interlibrary loans from the white to the Negro library also improve the situation in some cities.[47] In the North there is no segregation or discrimination in the use of these facilities, except that created by residential segregation and the unfriendliness of a relatively few white officials and members of the public.

Segregation of Negroes in jails, penitentiaries, reformatories, insane asylums, follows the same pattern found for schools and other public facilities, except that there is somewhat more segregation in the North in this respect than in others, and practically no exceptions to the segregational pattern in the South. When the institution has as its primary importance, not to protect white society, but to be of service to the Negro individual or community—as in the case of asylums for the insane and feeble-minded or specialized institutions for juvenile delinquents—many Southern states and localities do not have a Negro unit at all.[48] Charles S. Mangum comments on this last point: "This is one of the most flagrant violations of the spirit of the constitutional guarantee of equal treatment by the states discovered in this investigation."[49]

Negroes may enter public buildings in the South as well as in the North, but in the South the rules are that they must not loiter, must remove their hats, must not expect service until all whites have been accommodated (with the exception of many post offices and other buildings owned by the federal government), must sit in rear or side seats in most courtrooms, and in general must follow the etiquette most cautiously. Of all the institutions run by the government, public bathing beaches, pools and bath houses have the most complete segregation.

The pattern of segregation found in privately run public services is in the South often less rigid than in those operated by government. This differential—not great—occurs because businessmen are more solicitous about Negro customers than local governments are about Negro citizens. A good part of the segregation and discrimination that does occur in such facilities as railroad trains, railroad waiting rooms and ticket offices, street-cars, buses and taxicabs occurs because the law requires it. The law compels the transportation companies to bear the extra costs of maintaining two sets of facilities. This becomes the more expensive as many Negroes avoid Jim Crow facilities by using their own cars[50] or walking. On the other hand, it is notorious that the companies—with a few exceptions—save money by giving Negroes inferior service for equal charge. While white opinion would no doubt force these companies to maintain segregated facilities, there would be many exceptions and a slow trend toward a breakdown of segregation if there were no laws to keep the pattern rigid. This inference may be drawn from observation of segregation practices in privately run stores where there are no laws to prohibit or to segregate Negro customers.

Oklahoma and all the former slaveholding states, with the exception of Delaware, Missouri, and West Virginia, have laws requiring separation of whites and Negroes on railways operated in their jurisdiction.[51] Delaware has a law making it optional for railroad companies to Jim Crow, and a Missouri state court has upheld the validity of a railway's regulation directing a separation of the races on its coaches.[52] Although these laws could not be meant to apply to a Negro who was merely crossing the state without stopping in it, since such a law would be clearly unconstitutional even if the intra-state Jim Crow law would not, in practice it applies to such Negroes also. The conductors are given police power to enforce these statutes. Certain types of exceptions are commonly made: for nurses, police officers, railway employees. Sometimes the segregation is mainly ceremonial: Negroes may enter Alabama in Pullman cars but are given "Lower 13" (the drawing room in a Pullman with 12 sets of berths).[53] All the Southern states having railway Jim Crow laws, except Alabama, Kentucky, and Maryland, also require separate accommodations on street railways.[54] In those three states, the practice of Jim Crowing is left up to the streetcar companies: it is universal in Alabama, but does not occur in the Border states. It is a common observation that the Jim Crow car is resented more bitterly among Negroes than most other forms of segregation. In the North there is practically no segregation in public carriers.

Segregation is practically complete in the South for hotels and restaurants, places of amusement[a] and cemeteries.[b] The same is true of churches.[c] Many hospitals in the South receive Negro as well as white patients, but they are segregated; the Negro wards are mostly inadequate and inferior,

---

[a] Negroes are excluded from swimming pools, dance halls, skating rinks, pool parlors and bowling alleys patronized by whites. In theaters and assembly halls, where they are not excluded, they are segregated and usually given poorer seats.

[b] Before the Civil War it was not uncommon for Negro servants to be buried in the white family's plot. With the development of a new taboo in respect to mixed cemeteries, cases have occurred where Negro bones have been dug up and replaced in Negro cemeteries by white men. (Johnson, *Patterns of Negro Segregation*, p. 170.)

[c] In the *ante-bellum* South slaves often went to the churches of their masters. The exclusion on the part of the whites met a movement on the part of the Negroes to develop their own churches. Today the separation is complete. (See Chapter 40.)

and Negro doctors are not allowed to treat their patients there.[a] In the North the patterns vary a good deal. In all states where there are civil rights laws, hotels, restaurants, and amusement places are theoretically open to Negroes on equal terms with whites. In the states without such legislation, courts usually uphold the rights of proprietors to prohibit or segregate as they please.[55] In practice the higher priced establishments attempt to keep out Negroes all over the North, and the difference is not great in this respect between the South and the North, except for the presence of etiquette in the South. The low and moderate priced places probably most often accept Negro customers. Northern white churches do not prohibit Negroes, or even segregate them, but traditional adherence and residential segregation effectively keep Negroes practically separated in their own churches. Cemeteries are usually segregated even in the North.[56] The Y.M.C.A.'s ordinarily segregate Negroes even in the North, a main reason being that they are usually equipped with swimming pools; the Y.W.C.A.'s seem to show a tendency to be more liberal. There are separate hospitals for Negroes also in the North, and the hospitals which serve both races sometimes segregate Negroes but, on the average, the discrimination involved is slighter. In the North, Negro doctors are frequently given a chance to follow up their Negro cases in the hospitals.

As noted in Chapter 13 and Appendix 6, segregation in factories is usual throughout the South. It is not a matter of law in most cases, however, but is put into effect by the factory owners. If Negroes are allowed in an industry at all, they will usually be put either in a separate building or in a separate part of the regular factory building. The practice of giving Negroes only the hardest and least desirable jobs facilitates segregation. In most factories in the South, Negroes are required to use separate toilets and drinking fountains. Occasionally these things are put into law: a South Carolina law requires segregation in the cotton textile factories with respect to entrances, pay ticket windows, stairways, lavatories, toilets and drinking utensils.[57]

In the ordinary commercial establishments the variation is tremendous, since there are indefinite numbers of combinations of types and degrees of segregation in this field.[58] Only a few Southern communities have complete segregation for every commercial establishment,[b] just as only a few Northern communities have absolutely no segregation or discrimination. The situation is constantly changing in both North and South and is subject to a great variety of personal, customary and legal factors. It is reported from many localities, particularly in the South, that during the depression

[a] See Chapter 7, Section 5.

[b] Some Southern towns, especially in Texas, do not permit any Negro to spend over 24 hours within the town limits. Miami, Florida, and perhaps a few other Southern cities have laws forbidding Negroes to buy or to work outside the Negro district.

the competition for customers made store managers inclined to change their policy to greater compliance toward at least upper class Negroes.[59] There are possibly significant differences in the segregation patterns found for two distinct types of establishments—say, banks and department stores —but without detailed information we shall not risk saying that there definitely are.

We may generalize thus far, however: for each community there would seem to be less discrimination and segregation where the service is less personal and requires least manifestation of personality. Barbershops and beauty parlors will both in the North and in the South be most completely segregated. Stores for clothing will discriminate more than hardware stores. Gas stations will be least segregated; both in the South and in the North the rule is that the customer is to be served without regard to his color, but often with some regard to the quality or make of his car. Discrimination has many degrees: sometimes it will appear only in the way in which customers are served. Clothing stores, for example, may refuse to sell to Negroes, may have separate sections for them, may sell to them as to whites but refuse to let them try on clothing, may let them try on clothing if they keep the clothing from their bodies (for example, cloth over head before trying on hat) or may not discriminate at all. As a general conclusion, we can state that there is a good deal of difference between the North and the South in the discrimination practices of commercial establishments, but less here than in most other fields. The lack of laws, the impersonal nature of the relationship, and the profits to be made by commercial establishments if they cater to Negroes, all tend to weaken the patterns in the South. The present author has observed cities in the Deep South where the ordinary department store apparently discriminates less than in the North.

The prohibitions and restrictions on the Negro in the use of privately run establishments take two major directions: discrimination, and separate establishments for Negroes. There are usually not enough persons or wealth in the Negro community to provide Negroes with some of the more expensive services that are available to whites. This is especially true of theaters, concert halls, lecture halls and dance halls. When Negroes are permitted to go to these in the South—and seldom are they permitted to go to the best ones—they must occupy inferior sections, such as balconies. Segregated sections—whether of trains or of theaters—are commonly frequented by white men who often come there to engage in activities they would not dare to do in white sections (as, for instance, drinking or playing cards). The Negro sections usually have inferior equipment and are poorly cared for. In white stores where he may be served, the Negro customer is handicapped by not being allowed to try on clothing, by not being permitted to exchange any merchandise and by not being given the full services ordinarily volunteered by clerks. Too, in the South there is the abasing etiquette which is only slightly modified when the Negro is a customer. For all these reasons, Negroes are inclined to patronize establishments devoted exclusively to them.

These may be owned and operated by Negroes or by white men—Jews especially, in the North—but are seldom patronized by whites except those seeking unusual pleasures. Most Negro communities—except the smallest ones—now have the whole gamut of commercial establishments which cater to persons of low income. This is a relatively recent achievement in most cities, since Negroes had little capital to open businesses and Southern whites regarded with disgust any white man who served Negroes exclusively. Negroes of middle and high income are still under great handicaps except in the largest cities. For amusements they have often turned to social clubs rather than to commercial establishments, and they are inclined to stay at the home of a friend while traveling rather than to patronize the cheap restaurants and hotels which in larger cities are available to them. Thus, on the one hand, discrimination has helped to build up a separate Negro community; on the other hand, it has been an outcome of enforced segregation on the part of the whites. While there is less segregation and discrimination against upper class Negroes than against lower class Negroes, the former have isolated themselves more.

The services of white professional men have always been available to Negroes. There are relatively few Negro doctors, lawyers, dentists, pharmacists, nurses, and there are handicaps on the few there are: a Negro lawyer has little chance in a Southern courtroom, and a Negro doctor cannot get into most hospitals to operate.[a] Philanthropic organizations often refuse to hire Negro professionals to serve the members of their own group. Negro professionals are further handicapped by a low reputation in the Negro community. There is much more use of Negro professionals by Negroes in the North than in the South. But everywhere, white professionals are used more frequently by Negroes. Some white professionals refuse to serve Negroes for fear of lowering their prestige, but probably the majority will serve Negroes who can afford to pay their fee. There is one semi-professional service which is unique in that only Negroes serve Negroes: this is the undertaking service. The live Negro body may be handled by the white physician, but the dead one is handled only by the Negro undertaker. This is as much, or more, in accordance with desires of Negroes as of whites. Undertaking is consequently one of the most lucrative businesses open to Negroes.[b]

Voluntary associations—civic, social, business, and professional—almost

[a] See Chapter 14, Sections 6 and 7. A few Negro doctors—mainly in the North but also occasionally in the South—have a significant number of white clients.
[b] See Chapter 14, Section 2.

always prohibit Negro members in the South and sometimes even in the North, unless the association is concerned with some phase of the Negro problem. They simply refuse to invite Negroes to membership or to admit them when they apply for membership, whether by formal policy or by informal *ad hoc* action of the membership committee. Sometimes national organizations—dominated by Northerners—would be willing to admit Negroes but are prevented by their Southern minorities. The only types of groups that almost consistently take in Negroes without restriction are the scientific or other intellectual societies.[60] The professional associations, such as the state bar and medical societies, usually admit Negro members in the North but not in the South; the national organizations are built upon this compromise, where membership depends upon the policy of the local unit.

The position of trade unions has been dealt with earlier in this book;[a] it is still true that most of them exclude or segregate Negroes.

Because of their exclusion from the various associations, Negroes have formed their own associations. Every Negro community is abundantly supplied with social and fraternal organizations, and nearly every city has its Negro businessmen's group. Negro professionals have formed national associations which usually take the name *National* (Medical, Bar) Association in contradistinction to the white *American* (Medical, Bar) Association. Negro clergymen also are excluded from organizations of their white co-professionals, and in reacting have sometimes gone so far as to form new denominations. While the white groups lose a little of the strength which they might get by admitting all qualified persons, regardless of race, Negroes are materially hurt by not getting the advantages of membership in these bodies.

[a] See Chapter 18, Section 3.

CHAPTER 30

EFFECTS OF SOCIAL INEQUALITY

1. The Incidence of Social Inequality

The "function"—and in any case the effect—of the social mechanism discussed in the preceding chapter is to isolate the Negroes and to assign them to a lower social status. From this point of view, most of the minor variations in place and time are of little social significance. Significant only are those variations in the patterns which denote real differences in the degree of inferior status conferred. We have noticed such differences in relation to regions and social classes. But we have also noticed the "common denominator." Being a Negro involves—everywhere in America, and independent of social class—having an inferior status.

The Southern courts generally take judicial notice of the lower social status of Negroes by sentencing as defamation the act of insinuating a white person to be a Negro.[1] Stephenson quotes a South Carolina court as arguing:

> When we think of the radical distinction subsisting between the white man and the black man, it must be apparent that to impute the condition of the Negro to a white man would affect his [the white man's] social status, and, in case anyone publish a white man to be a Negro, it would not only be galling to his pride, but would tend to interfere seriously with the social relation of the white man with his fellow white men. . . .[2]

When Northern courts do not follow this practice, it does not mean that it is not at all injurious to a white person in the North to be called a Negro, but it indicates primarily that social inequality is not a matter of public policy in the North as it is in the South.

The lower social status of the Negro represents, apparently, a gain to the whites. Besides the direct deprivation it imposes on the Negro, it indirectly hampers his ambitions in spheres of life other than the purely "social." Whereas it was appropriate to center the discussion of the causation of segregation and discrimination around the attitudes of the whites, who enforce the system, it is expedient, when we now proceed to investigate the results of it, to view them as they affect the Negro people.

No responsible Negro leader ever accepted social discrimination or gave up the demand for *ultimate* full equality. Booker T. Washington—the great conciliatory leader of his people in its relation with white society during the period of grim reaction after Reconstruction—made it a point to observe scrupulously the customs of the South and always avoided offending the prejudices of the white Southerners in so far as was possible.[3] In his speeches and books he sometimes went far in his diplomacy. He not only formally accepted segregation and implicitly the entire racial etiquette, but presented excuses for much more than that. He pressed hard only for his most urgent demands.[a] But in principle he never gave up the Negro protest against social discrimination. His last article, published posthumously in 1915, "My View of Segregation Laws," brought out clearly that he saw that there were limits to the extent to which Negroes could accept segregation. It concluded with the following statement:

> Summarizing the matter in the large, segregation is ill-advised because:
> 1. It is unjust.
> 2. It invites other unjust measures.
> 3. It will not be productive of good, because practically every thoughtful negro resents its injustice and doubts its sincerity. Any race adjustment based on injustice finally defeats itself. The Civil War is the best illustration of what results where it is attempted to make wrong right or seem to be right.
> 4. It is unnecessary.
> 5. It is inconsistent. The negro is segregated from his white neighbor, but white business men are not prevented from doing business in negro neighborhoods.
> 6. There has been no case of segregation of negroes in the United States that has not widened the breach between the two races. Wherever a form of segregation exists it will be found that it has been administered in such a way as to embitter the negro and harm more or less the moral fibre of the white man. That the negro does not express this constant sense of wrong is no proof that he does not feel it.[4]

Robert R. Moton, Washington's successor as a conservative Negro leader trusted by the whites, went even further in his appeal for equality,[5] and the other outstanding Negro leaders have been outspoken in repudiating all social discrimination.

The Negro protest will be discussed in later chapters. For the moment we want to point out an intrinsic difficulty in the makeshift compromise with white society in the South, set forth by Washington in his Atlanta speech of 1895: "In all things purely social we can be separate as the five fingers, and yet one as the hand in all things essential to mutual progress." Segregation and the racial etiquette mean humiliation and this in itself is a severe discrimination. It has psychological effects. Only fifteen years after the Atlanta compromise, Archer declared the formula impossible:

> But to imagine it realized in perfection is to imagine an impossibility—almost a contradiction in terms. We are, on the one hand, to suppose the negro ambitious,

___
[a] See Chapter 35, Section 3, and Chapter 38, Section 4.

progressive, prosperous, and, on the other hand, to imagine him humbly acquiescent in his status as a social pariah. The thing is out of the question; such saintlike humility has long ceased to form any part of the moral equipment of the American negro. The bullet could never be thoroughly encysted; it would always irritate, rankle, fester.[6]

If the Negroes were to rise out of illiteracy, economic distress, and so on, they would no longer have the psychological basis for keeping themselves socially inferior and servile. It is possible that a limited social segregation, purified of all elements of discrimination—of the type the Southern white liberals have dreamed of—would perhaps solve the problem. But this is far beyond present-day practical discussion.

There is a fundamental flaw in that distinction between what is purely social and all the rest of discrimination against Negroes. *Social discrimination is powerful as a means of keeping the Negroes down in all other respects.* In reality it is not possible to isolate a sphere of life and call it "social." There is, in fact, a "social" angle to all relations. When the Negro is disfranchised or kept from public office, the motivation of the whites is partly that political activity is "out of place" for Negroes. When he is discriminated against in courts or by the police, the justification is that he is "inferior" and that he must be "kept in his place." If his citizenship rights were no longer infringed upon, the Negro's social status would immediately rise as well, and—quite apart from state action made possible by his political power—much of the psychological basis for social inequality would be undermined. The very existence of the heavy mechanism of social segregation and discrimination makes inequalities in politics and justice more possible and seemingly justifiable on grounds of inferiority.

The interrelations between social status and economic activity are particularly important. Occupations have numerous social connotations. In the first place, they help to give social status. As long as Negroes, solely because of their color, are forcibly held in a lower social status, they will be shut out from all middle class occupations except in their own segregated social world. White nurses, stenographers, bank clerks, and store attendants will decline to work with Negroes, especially when the white person is a woman and the Negro a man. If social segregation is to be carried out in the factories, it will be expensive to the employer since he will have to provide special coordinating facilities and separate toilets, washrooms and lunchrooms. The same tendencies will work in public employment, in the schools, and in the armed forces; the only difference being that in public employment the state authority might be made to interfere and enforce equality. If a Negro holds any high occupational position, he will seem pretentious.

At the lower end of the occupational scale the tendencies are more complicated. It is clear that white workers with a lower and more uncertain status in the occupational hierarchy may feel not less but more reason to object to Negro fellow workers. It is to be expected that the present trend of organizational stratification—giving more power over employment policy to the agents of the employees and attempting to raise standards of responsibility and respectability in all occupations—will tend to squeeze out the Negroes. This is not true, however, where they are already firmly entrenched, or their equality can be sanctioned by law, or an ideology of labor solidarity can be successfully invoked. This is the big question of what increasing unionization of labor will mean to the Negroes.[a] Everywhere in the labor market the very idea of their social inferiority is one of the Negroes' strongest handicaps in the competition for jobs. The vicious circle works here, too: the very fact that the masses of Negroes, because of economic discrimination—partly caused by social inequality—are prevented from entering even the bottom of the occupational hierarchy, are paid low wages and, consequently, are poor gives in its turn motivation for continued social discrimination.

The fact that social segregation involves a substantial element of discrimination will add its influence to this vicious circle. Negroes are given inadequate education, health protection, and hospitalization; they are segregated into districts where public services of water provision, sewage and garbage removal, street cleaning, street lighting, street paving, police protection and everything else is neglected or withheld while vice is often allowed. All this must keep the Negro masses inferior and provide reasons for further discrimination in politics, justice and breadwinning.

Under these circumstances there develops also what John M. Mecklin calls "the curious dualism in the social conscience or a double standard of conduct, one for the white and another for the black," which puts the Negro in a still more inferior social position.[7] This is partly the result of social segregation and discrimination but, at the same time, it gives justification to the whites for insisting upon their supremacy and for relegating the Negroes to a subordinate position. Here again we see the vicious circle in operation. It makes the task of the educator and reformer difficult. "As long as it is possible for a negro to violate half of the commands of the decalogue and still not lose social standing with his group, it is useless to hope for material improvement."[8] The ambition of the Negro youth is cramped not only by the severe restrictions placed in his way by segregation and discrimination, but also by the low expectation from both white and Negro society. He is not expected to make good in the same way as the white youth. And if he is not extraordinary, he will not expect it himself and will not really put his shoulder to the wheel.[9]

Segregation and discrimination have had material and moral effects on whites, too. Booker T. Washington's famous remark, that the white man could not hold the Negro in the gutter without getting in there himself, has been corroborated by many white Southern and Northern observers.[a] Throughout this book we have been forced to notice the low economic, political, legal, and moral standards of Southern whites—kept low because of discrimination against Negroes and because of obsession with the Negro problem. Even the ambition of Southern whites is stifled partly because, without rising far, it is so easy to remain "superior" to the held-down Negroes. The Southern whites are tempted to remain on low levels of sexual morals, thrift, industriousness, reliability, punctuality, law observance and everything else. This mechanism of descending self-adjustment in a system of moral double-dealing works also in the field of public affairs. There are few popular movements in the South to improve social conditions and standards of efficiency and morality partly because of the feeling that "we" are so much better than "they" and partly because any attempt at improvement is bound to help the Negroes as well as the whites.[b] Most of these things are true of the North as well as of the South, though to a much smaller extent and for reasons connected with other minority groups as well as the Negro.

One of the effects of social segregation is isolation of Negroes and whites. The major effects of isolation are, of course, on Negroes. Contrary to popular opinion, however, there are bad effects on whites also, and these are increasing as the level of Negro cultural attainment is rising. It is as much a misfortune for whites not to have contacts with Negroes of high education and achievement as not to have contacts with other whites of comparable attainment—perhaps more, since such Negroes have a unique range of experience. Whether they know it or not, white people are dwarfing their minds to a certain extent by avoiding contacts with colored people.

2. INCREASING ISOLATION

Against the obstacles of the powerful interlocking system of social, judicial, political, and economic inequalities and disabilities, and in spite of the desire on the part of the majority of Southern whites that the Negroes remain in an inferior social status, and the great indifference and ignorance about it all on the part of most Northern whites, *the Negroes*

[a] Next to Washington's, probably the most frequently quoted remark on this matter is that of Chancellor Kirkland of Vanderbilt University:

"In whatever form slavery may be perpetuated, just so far will it put shackles on the minds of Southern whites. If we treat the Negro unjustly, we shall practice fraud and injustice to each other. We shall necessarily live by the standards of conduct we apply to him. This is the eternal curse of wrong and injustice, a curse that abides on the ruler as well as the slaves. The South will be free only as it grants freedom." (Quoted from Mark Ethridge, "About Will Alexander," *The New Republic* [September 22, 1941], p. 366.)

[b] See Chapter 10, Section 2.

are rising. They are rising most rapidly in the North, but their rate of rise in the South is not inconsiderable. It is one of the paradoxes of the American situation, ultimately due to the split morality of the nation on the issue of racial democracy, that this rise of the Negroes to a great extent is the result of education and other public efforts, which—solicited by the Negro leaders, pushed by a small minority of Southern liberals, and assisted by Northern philanthropy—is largely provided by the Southern states themselves with the approval of the ordinary Southern whites in political power, acting in partial obedience to the American Creed.

The fundamental character of these efforts and their result have been to diffuse American middle class norms to the uneducated and crude Southern "folk Negroes," emerging out of the backwardness of slavery. Besides education, the persistent forces of industrialization and urbanization are having an impact on the Negro. Migration, occupational changes, the easy methods of communication, the Negro press, the growth of Negro organizations, the radio, the moving pictures, and all other vehicles of "modern life" are working upon the minds of Southern Negroes, gradually upsetting the older static tradition of compliance and introducing new thoughts and presumptions, dissatisfaction and unrest. In so far as the caste line remains comparatively fixed, one result of these changes is increasing isolation. The spiritual effects of segregation are accumulating with each new generation, continuously estranging the two groups.

One phase of the rise of the Negroes is the formation of a Negro middle and upper class.[a] A nucleus of such a class was already forming among free Negroes in slavery times. Since then it has been steadily, but slowly, growing, partly as a result of segregation itself, which holds down the Negro masses but opens petty monopolies for a few. These middle and upper class Negroes, who have stepped out of the servant status, live mostly by catering to their own people.[b] Not only have their economic contacts with whites been reduced but, because they know they are not liked by whites and are likely to feel humiliated in all contacts with them, they avoid whites in all other spheres of life. They even avoid, as we have had occasion to mention, the segregated set-ups where contact with whites is formalized and kept to a minimum.

It is the present writer's impression that, generally speaking, this tiny upper group of the Negro community often lives in a seclusion from white society which is simply extraordinary and seldom realized by white people. Measured in terms of the number of personal contacts with white people, there are Negro doctors, dentists, teachers, preachers, morticians, and druggists in the South who might as well be living in a foreign country: ". . . as the progressive colored people advance, they constantly widen the

[a] See Chapter 32.
[b] See Chapter 14.

gulf between themselves and their white neighbors."[10] Those contacts with whites which are unavoidable are becoming increasingly formal and impersonal. This means much for the development of Negro personality and cultural traits. In the present context it means that *white men in all classes usually have few occasions ever to meet a Negro above the servant classes*.[11] Certain minor exceptions will be discussed presently.

Parallel to this tendency is the habit of Southern whites to ostracize those white persons who work with Negroes in the field of education or who in other ways devote themselves to Negro welfare. This pattern was built up after the Civil War in animosity against the educational mission-aries from the North. The attitudes are now changing in some respects. One of the chief accomplishments of the Interracial Commission is to have given social respectability among whites to interracial work. But today there are no white teachers of Negroes below the college level in the South, and there is often a sphere of isolation around the white teachers in a Negro college, particularly in the Deep South. The maximum of tolerance given them is often to let them alone because "they are living with the niggers." More important is the related trend for Negro colleges to be manned by an all-Negro staff, which again means a growing separa-tion between the two groups on the middle and upper class level.

From the viewpoint of the popular theory of "no social equality" and the goal of preventing "intermarriage," this development must seem natural and, indeed, highly desirable. If any Negroes would be able to tempt white women to marry them, it would be the educated and econom-ically prosperous ones; it is against them that the bars are most necessary in the Southern whites' own theory of color caste.[a] Nevertheless, white Southerners who have been interested in promoting improved interracial relations have, for a long time, been complaining about the fact that the "races meet only on the lower plane."[12] On this point there is fundamental agreement between Negro and white spokesmen.[13]

The Interracial Commission, various universities, and religious bodies have attempted to counteract this tendency by arranging interracial meet-ings for representatives of the "best people" of both groups, by teaching white youth about Negro progress and by having college students of both races meet together. Of even greater importance is the growing number of liberal newspapers in the South which make a planned effort to give fuller and more sympathetic publicity to the Negro community.[b] But there is doubt in the present writer's mind whether these laudable efforts out-weigh the cumulative tendency in the segregation system itself, which continuously drives toward greater spiritual isolation between the two

[a] See Chapter 28, Section 6.
[b] See Chapter 42, Section 3.

groups. This is a heavy cost for Southern society, and it might create great dangers in the future.[14]

The behavior patterns and attitudes of the small Negro middle and upper class group are of greatest importance for the whole Negro people as they set the standards which are spread from the pulpit and the teacher's desk, by the influential Negro press and through social imitation. As has already been suggested, popular education in America is even more essentially directed on the dissemination of middle class views and ways of life than in most other countries. The cultural rise of the Negro masses means their gradual approach to middle class standards. Negro education is now segregated in the South nearly to the limit and is, consequently, in the hands of this spiritually isolated Negro middle and upper class group. White people do not know much about what goes on in Negro schools or what is printed in the Negro press. They would be shocked if they knew. But more fundamentally, white people are caught in the contradictions of their own thinking. The white control of the Negro schools cannot check, and cannot be intent upon checking, the spread among Negroes of the middle class attitudes leading to Negro social withdrawal. This is what the whites have asked for. Racial pride and voluntary isolation is increasingly becoming the pattern for the whole Negro people. Lower class Negro parents now teach their children to keep out of the way of white people.

Meanwhile the old bonds of intimacy between upper class white families and their Negro servants have been breaking down. This process started immediately after Emancipation but is not yet fully consummated. Contacts are becoming less personal and intensive, more formal, temporary and casual. In so far as Negro professionals increasingly are taking care of the souls and the bodies of Negroes generally, the result is not only the creation of a culturally isolated Negro middle and upper class but also, on the other side of the fence, a new barrier to communication between white people and lower class Negroes.[15] In their daily work also Negroes and whites have been becoming increasingly separated. The only exception in the South to the general trend of increasing separation is the recent coming together of Negro and white workers in the new labor unions.

Voluntary withdrawal is now becoming a habit in all social classes of Negroes.[16] It can be observed on the street. It can be seen in the stores. Raper describes a general store in the rural South, for example:

> Both races frequent the same store, at the same time, for the same purpose; whites and blacks stand together at the counter and buy. Negroes can buy anything, in any part of the store, at any time they have the money or credit to secure it. The members of the two races, however, mingle in the store only when they occupy the status of prospective purchasers, only when they are moving.
>
> As soon as the Negroes have finished their buying, they tend to move off to

themselves. When a Negro goes to sit down at the stove, he just naturally, it seems, sits by a member of his own race. Other Negroes drift in and the "Negro side" of the stove, which may be any side, reaches two-thirds around; half an hour later, the "white side," may take up two-thirds of the circle. All day long this circle around the stove gradually changes its racial complexion, with almost no intermixing of the races. The seating is not prearranged, and doubtless the sitters themselves are unaware of the typical arrangement, which anyone may observe for himself by "hanging around" a store in the rural portions of [a] county.[17]

Even the children keep apart. When occasionally they play together—only in very young ages and then only in the lower classes—the picture is usually one like that observed in Washington, D.C., by E. Franklin Frazier:

The colored children seemed to form a play group within a play group, the white children's talk almost all being addressed to other white children. Moreover, the colored children seemed to hang back and let the white children take the lead during the play. The colored children stood around and watched the white children as if admiring them. However, when the number of colored children increased and the two groups were about equal in numbers, the colored children showed much greater courage in swinging higher and longer on the limb, and much less fear than did the white children. . . . It is apparent from their overt behavior that the colored children hesitated to participate freely in the play group until they had the support of larger numbers of their own race. Even then it appears that they did not participate individually but rather as a group. Their self-consciousness was indicated not only by their initial hesitancy about participating freely in the play but also by their attempt to outstrip the white children.[18]

The present writer has made similar observations in all sorts of life situations:

I once visited a progressive prison in the North, one of the very finest institutions of its kind I have ever seen. The director pointed out to me that he was most eager to avoid every vestige of segregation between white and Negro prisoners. The individual cells where they slept during the night were allotted them in the alphabetic order of their names. But when I looked at the prisoners playing ball, the picture was one of separate cliques of whites and Negroes. Balls were passed from one clique to another but apparently always with minute observance of the color line. The director saw my reflection and explained to me that he has now given up fighting against the prisoners' self-segregation. He had even allowed the common rooms to be divided between the two groups. "The Negroes are nearly all born in the South," he commented. "If I were ignorant about the American race order in which they are all brought up, I should believe that this tenacious segregation is in their blood, or, at least, that the Negroes are just as eager to withdraw as the whites. In a sense they are. But in a deeper sense they are not. It is just social pressure congealed into habit."

This all seems to give a confirmation of the Southern white stereotype that "Negroes are happiest among themselves." and that by the mass of the Negro people "separation is not looked upon as a hardship but rather as a simple, natural fact, which is never questioned."[a] It is, however, my impression that this is a rationalization just as deceptive, and for a similar cause, as the belief that Southern Negroes are politically apathetic and do not care for suffrage. If they do not bother to try to vote, they have, as we found, in most cases good reasons in various sanctions they would meet and in the knowledge that elections do not have much importance anyhow under the system of the white primary. Likewise the Negroes have good reasons to keep to themselves socially, and the habit has grown into a stiff pattern. But this isolation is a consequence of segregation and discrimination and should not be construed as a cause (except in so far as it is part of a vicious circle), and still less as a moral support for the system. On this point Negroes are, in general, quite sophisticated.

The material presented in the American Youth Commission studies suggests a most important general observation: *there is almost a complete lack of reference in the interviews with young Negroes in the South to intimate and personal, friendly relations with white persons or families of the type so prevalent in earlier times. For the Negro youth growing up today in the Black Belt, both in cities and in the country, this old protective master-servant pattern seems to have almost entirely disappeared.* What still exists of it is felt by the older generation of Negroes and is bound to disappear with them. A social process is drawing to its close. A negative practical conclusion may be drawn from this observation: *in planning for future race relations in the South the factor of personal intimacy and friendliness between individual whites and Negroes upon the old patriarchal principle should be left out entirely as lacking in practical importance.* If it be deemed desirable to establish more positive human contacts in order to mitigate the dangerous accumulating estrangement between the two groups, this must be built on another foundation than the master-servant relation inherited from slavery.

In the North the Negroes have always been more isolated from whites.

[a] A much more representative statement of the Negro attitude toward segregation is that of A. Philip Randolph: "Jim Crow . . . is a moral, spiritual and intellectual insult to the very soul of the Negro." (Mimeographed address, at Madison Square Garden, New York City, June 16, 1942, p. 3.) Du Bois calls attention to what segregation means to the Negro in the South:

"In a world where it means so much to take a man by the hand and sit beside him, to look frankly into his eyes and feel his heart beating with red blood; in a world where a social cigar or a cup of tea together means more than legislative halls and magazine articles and speeches,—one can imagine the consequences of the almost utter absence of such social amenities between estranged races, whose separation extends even to parks and street-cars." (*The Souls of Black Folk* [1903], p. 185.)

A similar statement is made more recently by a prominent white man, Edwin R. Embree (*Brown America* [1933; first edition, 1931], p. 226.)

They have for generations had less of both patriarchal dependence and protection. Before the Great Migration accentuated segregation and discrimination, they had, however, established a place for themselves, in many cases not more isolated and subdued than the several immigrant groups. Their small numbers, their fairly high educational status, and their acceptable manners and personal habits in most places prevented a too severe exclusion. The children ordinarily went to the same schools as did whites; the grown-ups often belonged to the same churches and other organizations and not infrequently visited socially. With the formation of Black Belts in the metropolitan cities, isolation grew. In this particular respect the conditions of the Negro population in the two regions are approaching each other.

3. INTERRACIAL CONTACTS

The isolation we are speaking about—caused by all the barriers to contact involved in etiquette, segregation, and discrimination from the side of the whites and in voluntary withdrawal and resentment from the side of the Negroes—means a decrease of certain types of contacts between the two groups and a distortion of the ones that are left. It is useful here to put the reverse question: What contacts do remain? and what is their significance for interracial relations? To answer these questions there ought to be quantitative studies of the sort we have discussed previously.[a] Since no such studies have been made, our observations have to be general, tentative, and in the nature of somewhat schematic hypotheses for further research.

Negroes constitute about 10 per cent of the American population, and since there has been little[19] attempt to segregate them by region, there is naturally some contact. Of course, Negroes have been concentrated—for historical reasons—in the South, but there are enough Negroes throughout the North and in cities of the West for their appearance to be commonly recognized by the majority of the white inhabitants of these latter areas. The patterns of segregation and withdrawal are so effective, however, that even where Negroes are a common sight *there is actual contact with them in practically only three spheres of life: the casual, the economic and the criminal.*

By *casual contacts* we mean all those instances where Negro individuals and white individuals see each other but without the condition of recognizing each other as individuals, or at least for the whites to recognize the Negroes as individuals. Casual contacts would thus include passing on the street, passing or remaining briefly in the presence of each other in public buildings or public vehicles, having visual or auditory contact with each

[a] Chapter 29, footnote 1.

other by reason of independent relations with common third persons, or the like. Such contacts are the most numerous type, except possibly on the plantation and in other rural areas where either the Negro or the white population forms a small proportion of the total. Casual contacts are important in an urban civilization. But they are especially important in Negro-white contacts, since they are only slightly diminished by patterns of segregation and discrimination as compared to other types of Negro-white contacts. Since the casual contact is one in which the participants have no occasion to regard each other as individuals but only as members of a group, *the main effect of the casual contact would seem to be a strengthening of stereotypes*. Negroes, but not whites, have something of an antidote for the casual contact in their economic contact with whites. The main effect of casual contacts is, therefore, to create and preserve stereotypes of Negroes in the minds of the whites. This is not to say that casual contacts are the only, or even the most important, cause of stereotypes of Negroes. But the impersonality of the comparatively numerous casual contacts allows whites to see Negroes as a relatively uniform biological and social type and to ignore the great variations that would become apparent if observation were more attentive. All Negroes come to look alike to the average white person.

Casual contact between Negroes and whites is probably increasing as Negroes—and whites—are becoming more mobile and as the scope of Negro activity is becoming broader. Also it has been taking on a slightly different character as it enters the urban environment. In a city it is sometimes impossible to avoid close physical contact. Negroes and whites jostle each other unconcernedly on crowded streets, and Negroes have been observed to be standing in the white sections of crowded Jim Crow buses. The increase of casual contacts in Southern cities is undoubtedly wearing away somewhat the strictness of racial etiquette.

The increased range of casual contacts in recent years is not unrelated to the growth of a Negro upper class. This is especially important in the North, where there are no laws against Negroes using public facilities. A well-mannered Negro dressed in good taste who appears in a restaurant, a white church, or a railroad station is likely to weaken unfavorable Negro stereotypes rather than to strengthen them. In the South the effect of the appearance of the upper class Negro is somewhat more problematical. In the long run this will probably have a favorable effect, but in many known instances it has led to violence from lower and middle class whites who felt that the Negroes were getting too "uppity." The Negro's physical appurtenances—that is, his home, store, or automobile—will serve as a casual contact in the same manner as his person.

The effect of increased casual contacts due to increased Negro mobility has, thus far and when considered alone, probably hurt the Negro in the

North, even if other advantages for the Negro people as a whole from the northward migration have more than compensated for this disadvantage. The Northern white man, who formerly felt little prejudice against the few Northern Negroes and was inclined to idealize Negroes as part of his Civil War heritage, reacted unfavorably when the Great Migration brought up thousands of illiterate, dirty, and poor Negroes from the Deep South. In Chicago in 1910, for example, a few Negroes were scattered all over the city, and they were invited to many ordinary white homes as neighbors.ᵃ Now Negroes are forced to live in definite sections and practically the only white homes they are invited to are those of a few intellectuals and radicals.

Unlike casual contacts, *economic contacts*, though usually not intimate or protracted, are important enough for the whites and Negroes to see one another as individuals. In the great majority of economic contacts, whites see Negroes as economic inferiors, as when they are servants or other types of menial workers. More rarely they meet as economic equals, as when Negro and white workers work on the same level or when businessman meets businessman or salesman meets customer. Practically never do whites see Negroes as their economic superiors. This is due, of course, to the striking differential in economic and occupational status of whites and Negroes. In contacts arising out of economic relationships, the Negro partner is rarely employer, supervisor, skilled worker, merchant, or professional man. An additional reason for this is the fact that Negroes who occupy these higher economic positions tend to serve and to employ other Negroes. Of course, most whites are vaguely aware that there are Negroes in high economic positions. But it is probable that they everywhere underestimate the number of such Negroes, and it is certain that they rarely have enough contact with them to know them as individuals. From their side, Negroes have economic contacts with whites mainly as superiors and occasionally as equals. They thus tend to have their attitudes of inferiority and dependence—already in existence because of the slavery tradition—reinforced. The same can be said of their attitudes of resentment.

There is one sphere of economic relationship which is extremely important for several reasons. We refer to the Negro as a personal and domestic servant, a position in which he held practically a monopoly in the South until the depression of the 1930's, and in which he is numerically important in the North. The social importance of this relationship derives mainly from the fact that it is very intensive on one side. The Negro maid knows the life of her white employer as few white persons know it; and the Negro janitor and elevator operator knows a great deal of what goes on

---

ᵃ Gosnell informs us: "Before the Negro migration it was easier for a colored man to be elected to a county-wide position [in Chicago] than it has been since." (Harold F. Gosnell, *Negro Politicians* [1935], p. 369.)

in his building.[a] In slavery days the house servant learned the culture of his white master and—from a position on the top of the Negro class structure—transmitted it to the other slaves. Servants no longer have the highest socio-economic status among Negroes, but it can be safely said that Negroes know the white world very well, in its private, though not in its public, aspects.[20]

The white employer, on the other hand, does not know the Negro's world just because he has Negro servants. The white employer ordinarily is interested mainly in getting his servant to work, and his attitude toward the servant is, therefore, usually impersonal. We have already commented upon the fact that this relationship has in the main lost in intimacy and personal friendliness. Even if the white mistress takes an interest in her servant's well-being, she seldom gets first-hand acquaintance with the Negro's living conditions, and Negroes show an extreme suspicion of inquisitive whites, who, even though friendly, have a superior and sometimes insulting attitude.[21] In the South, there are also the barriers of etiquette: when the content of friendliness and mutual feeling of belonging is carved out from the system of etiquette, it becomes, to the Negroes, a cause for generalized resentment against the whites, and, to the whites, a formalization of their power over the Negroes. In both directions the etiquette works toward estranging the two groups. Even if, by some rare chance, a white employer should really come to know intimately his or her Negro servant, he would not thereby come to know the whole wide range of Negro life. What often happens in the employer-servant relationship is that—depending on the degree of friendliness or appreciation of the white employer and the degree of confidence felt by the Negro servant—the white man or woman makes an exception of his or her servant to the stereotyped conception of the "Negro in general." Similarly, the Negro servant might under happy conditions come to regard his or her employer as an exception to the general run of mean and exploitative white people. Too, the lower and dependent position of the Negro servant enhances the white person's belief that "the Negro is all right in his place."

The contacts between white and Negro workers were formerly of the same type. In the trades and handicrafts, the pattern in the South was, and is, that the white worker had a Negro helper. In factories the Negro workers are usually segregated or, in any case, held to certain jobs.[22] As we have pointed out, the mixed trade unions are a new adventure with an uncertain future. It is commonly reported that white workers, if they become accustomed to working with Negro workers, tend to become less prejudiced, and consequently that the Negro workers become less suspi-

---

[a] All service workers have, in one degree or another, this intimate type of contact with those they serve.

cious and resentful.[a] If, in later stages of the War, necessities in the nature of a national emergency should tend to open up new employment possibilities for Negroes in the war industries, this would probably have permanently beneficial effects on racial attitudes on both sides of the caste gulf. Our general hypothesis is that everything which brings Negro and white workers to experience intimate cooperation and fellowship will, on the balance, break down race prejudice somewhat and raise Negro status. The possibilities for Negroes to rise to the position of skilled workers have, therefore, not only economic significance but also a wider social import as this will tend to weaken the stereotype of the menial Negro.

There are other types of economic contacts between Negroes and whites in which the members of the two groups are of equal or near-equal status. Over a long time span Negro purchasing power has been increasing,[b] and the number of Negro businessmen who can deal as economic equals with whites in a similar position has been rising. The long-run effect of this is probably to make more whites realize that some Negroes have as much capacity as they, although some whites feel nothing but irritation and resentment that can turn into violence at the thought of Negroes rising in the economic scale. The effect, as usual, is cumulative: white merchants and salesmen in the South are chipping away at the etiquette in order to please their Negro customers, and the absence of the etiquette in a social relation helps to create a spirit of equality.

Another sort of economic relationship in which Negroes have a measure of near-equality with whites is that in which the Negro is an entertainer or artist. The Negro as a musician, actor, dancer, or other type of artist is allowed to perform almost freely for a white public in the North—and to some extent in the South[c]—in a way that he can in no other economic sphere outside of the service occupations. His excellence in these fields—cultivated by folk stimulation from earliest childhood and by the realization that other means of earning a living are closed—is recognized. In fact, it is even supported by the stereotypes: the Negro must make up for an intellectual lack by an emotional richness. Nevertheless, a Negro who achieves distinction or popularity in these fields is regarded as an individual, and there can be little doubt that he raises the general prestige level of the Negro population. What has been said of the entertainment and artistic

[a] See Chapter 17, Section 7.

[b] That is, the average Negro has more money to spend (holding constant the purchasing value of the dollar), although his increase has not paralleled that of the average white man.

[c] Negro entertainers may appear before white audiences in the South if there is no implication of social equality. Individual Negro artists appear before Southern white audiences without difficulty. All-Negro dance orchestras may play for white dancers. But Negro players are not allowed in large white bands. In September, 1941, the well-known white band leader, Artie Shaw, broke all his Southern engagements because he was not allowed to bring along his Negro trumpeter, "Hot Lips" Paige.

fields is true also of the athletic field, in which Negroes have achieved notable successes.[a]

Besides the respectable entertainment fields in which Negroes excel, there are the "low-brow" and shady ones. "Black-and-tan" cabarets are sought as amusement centers by many levels of urban whites, occasionally if not frequently. White cabarets, theaters, and burlesques in the North often have the popular attraction of Negro dancers and performers. Negro prostitutes are often considered to be especially desirable, in the South as well as in the North. More often they compete by underselling white prostitutes. The effect on white attitudes toward Negroes of contacts in these circumstances is problematical. Probably such contacts serve only to strengthen the stereotype that Negroes have wilder passions and that their excellence is limited to emotional activities. At most, they increase the favorableness of attitudes toward Negroes in individual cases only.

We mentioned *criminal contacts* as the third most important field of Negro-white relationship. Ordinarily in American societies, as in practically all other societies, criminal relationships are minor. The fact that it is so important in Negro-white relationships has unique causes and unique effects. The actual extent of Negro crime will be discussed in a subsequent chapter;[b] at this point we are interested only in the fact that whites *believe* the Negro to be innately addicted to crime.[c] The importance of Negro crime as a basis of social relations arises not only out of this fact, but also out of the fact that Negro crime gets great publicity. Even today a large proportion—perhaps a majority—of the news about Negroes that appears in the white newspapers of both South and North is about Negro crimes.[23] When a Catholic or Jew, Swede or Bulgarian, commits a crime that is serious enough to get into the newspapers, it is not usual for his religion or nationality to be mentioned. When a Negro commits a newsworthy crime, on the other hand, only rarely is an indication of his race not prominently displayed. To many white Northerners, this crime news is the most important source of information they get about Negroes. To white Southerners, the crime news reinforces the stereotypes and sometimes serves to unite the white community for collective violence against the individual Negro criminal or the local Negro community in general.

The crime news is unfair to Negroes, on the one hand, in that it emphasizes individual cases instead of statistical proportions (a characteristic of all news, but in this case unfair to Negroes because of the racial association with especially disliked crimes) and, on the other hand, in that all

[a] See Chapter 44, Section 5, for a discussion of Negro achievements.

[b] See Chapter 44, Section 2.

[c] This belief is connected with two more basic beliefs: that the Negro cannot control his passions and so is addicted to crimes against persons; that the Negro has no sense of morals and thus is addicted to crimes against property.

other aspects of Negro life are neglected in the white press which gives the unfavorable crime news an undue weight. Sometimes the white press "creates" a Negro crime wave where none actually exists. In the latter part of the summer of 1941, Washington, D.C. was disturbed by a Negro "rape-and-murder wave," according to white newspapers throughout the country. Actually only one Negro was found to be responsible for the several crimes.[24]

Crimes against Negroes outside of lynching receive no publicity in the white press. Lynching receives a wide but declining publicity, especially in the North, and such publicity probably serves to raise Negroes—by contrast with Southern whites—in the attitude of Northern whites.

We have emphasized the most important aspects of the three most important spheres of Negro-white contacts—the casual, the economic and the criminal. The casual contact is inevitable if Negroes live in the same communities as do whites; the economic contact is the main reason for not wanting to send Negroes back to Africa or to segregate them in an isolated region and is, therefore, "inevitable"; the criminal contact is the result of a prejudiced but news-interested society. Besides contacts in the casual, economic, and criminal spheres of life, there are a few contacts between Negroes and whites in almost every other sphere. Usually they are unimportant numerically, but they may be important in bringing about change. The personal relations arising out of Negro activity in science and literature are restricted to a small proportion of the white population, whose prejudice—if not already low—is diminished considerably by such contacts. Indirectly the effect may be greater. The scientific discoveries of a George Washington Carver or the literary product of a Richard Wright will achieve nation-wide publicity and acclaim and will affect people as far down as the lower middle classes. A second minor field of interracial contact of growing importance is that of professional interracial relations.[a] A third minor type of interracial contact is that between radicals. In the main our conclusion is that the lack of personal and intimate contacts between members of the two groups is extraordinary.

4. THE FACTOR OF IGNORANCE

In a sense, this isolation is the result of cultural assimilation itself. When the masses of the Negroes found out that they could acquire an education and make notable cultural achievements and—even more— when they absorbed the white American's ideals of democracy and equality,

[a] The work and significance of such organizations as the National Association for the Advancement of Colored People, the Urban League, the Commission on Interracial Cooperation, and the various local or temporary groups of similar purpose will be considered in Chapter 39.

they came to resent discrimination and felt it necessary to withdraw from white society to hold these advantages of America. Lord Bryce observed:

> Slaves or serfs who have been bred up to look upon subjection as their natural lot bear it as the dispensation of Nature. When they have attained a measure of independence, when they speak the tongue and read the books and begin to share the ideas of the dominant race, they resent the inferiority, be it legal or social, to which they find themselves condemned. Discontent appears and social friction is intensified, not only because occasions for it grow more frequent, but because the temper of each race is more angry and suspicious.[25]

The paradox is that *it is the very absorption of modern American culture which is the force driving the Negroes to self-segregation to preserve self-respect. It is, indeed, an impossible proposition to educate the American Negroes and at the same time to keep them satisfied with their lower caste position.* To try to make it possible, the white Americans should, at least, have given them a different kind of education. But this has not been possible in the face of the American Creed. The attempts to keep the Negroes shut out of the wider national and world culture by purposively stamping them with a low-grade vocational education for a servant and peasant life have never, after Reconstruction, been wholehearted enough[a] to prevent the kindling of unrest and resentment.

White Southerners are still proud of insisting that they "know the Negro," but the observer easily finds out that the actual ignorance about the other group is often astonishingly great. The average Southerner knows roughly—with many easily detected opportunistic gaps—the history of the Negro and the conditions under which Negroes live in the South. His lack of knowledge is of the Negro himself as an individual human being—of his ambitions and hopes, of his capacities and achievements. He zealously cultivates barren half-truths into rigid stereotypes about "the Negro race." Because of this pretentious ignorance, and because of the etiquette, the white Southerner cannot talk to a Negro as man to man and understand him. This, and the habit of living physically near this strange and unknown people—and resisting energetically the incorporation of it into the total life of the community—breeds among Southern whites a strained type of systematic human indifference and callousness. Although the Southerner will not admit it, he is beset by guilt-feelings, knowing as he does that his attitude toward the Negroes is un-American and un-Christian. Hence he needs to dress his systematic ignorance in stereotypes. The Southern whites need the sanctioning tradition: "the Negroes we have always with us." They need the ceremonial distance to prevent the Negroes' injuries and sufferings from coming to their attention. W. E. B. Du Bois comments bitterly:

[a] See Chapter 41.

It is easy for men to discount and misunderstand the suffering or harm done others. Once accustomed to poverty, to the sight of toil and degradation, it easily seems normal and natural; once it is hidden beneath a different color of skin, a different stature or a different habit of action and speech, and all consciousness of inflicting ill disappears.[26]

Under the old master-servant relationship, the white man's "understanding" of the Negro was not great, but with the disappearance of this relationship even this small amount of sympathetic knowledge declined. What remains is a technique of how to work Negroes and how to keep them "in their place," which is not a difficult task for a majority group which can dispose of all the social power instruments—economic, legal, political, and physical—and has made up its mind to use them for this purpose.[27] But insight into the thoughts and feelings of Negroes, their social organization and modes of living, their frustrations and ambitions is vanishing. Some white Southerners are aware of this fact. Baker reported that they were already so thirty years ago:

I don't know how many Southern people have told me in different ways of how extremely difficult it is to get at the real feeling of a Negro, to make him tell what goes on in his clubs and churches or in his innumerable societies.[28]

The present author has often met the same revealing curiosity on the part of white Southerners. In spite of human curiosity, however, Southerners do not really seek to know the Negro or to have intimate contacts with him, and consequently their feelings toward Negroes remain hard.

On their side, Negroes in the South instantaneously become reserved and secretive when they are in company with "their own whites." I have also witnessed how submissiveness, laughter, and fluent talking—which are sometimes displayed by Negroes in accordance with the rural tradition of interracial formality—most of the time, in reality, are nothing but a mask behind which they conceal their true selves.[29] Robert R. Moton, when writing a book on *What the Negro Thinks*, for white people, confirms the growing seclusiveness of his group. The Negro "seldom tells all the truth about such matters," he points out, and adds: "a great deal of it may not find its way into this volume."[30] Baker drew the conclusion, after observing the Negro's deliberate secretiveness, that this was a major source of deteriorating race relations.

The Negro has long been defensively secretive. Slavery made him that. In the past, the instinct was passive and defensive; but with growing education and intelligent leadership it is rapidly becoming conscious, self-directive and offensive. And right there, it seems to me, lies the great cause of the increased strain in the South.[31]

The Northerner also is ignorant about the Negro, but his ignorance is less systematic and, therefore, often less deep. As he is ordinarily less inhibited from looking upon the Negro as a normal human being, and as his observation of the Negro is not blinded by the etiquette, he is usually more cognizant of Negro attitudes and capacities and is more willing to lend a sympathetic ear to the Negro's plight. But he is much more ignorant of the conditions which the Negro faces. If the Southerner's whole race philosophy and even his kindliest thoughts are insulting to the new type of Negro emerging out of the cultural assimilation process, the Northerner is likely to insult him out of sheer ignorance. The average Northerner does not realize that to call a Negro woman a "Negress" is taken as an insult, and he does not understand in what high esteem the Negro holds the title "Mr." He does not see the discrimination under which the Negroes labor. Not knowing the patterns of violence and of laxness of law in the South, the Northerner does not comprehend the full reason for the Negroes' pathological bitterness and fear.

On his side, the Negro is inclined to be suspicious of the Northerner's good intentions and to retain in the North the cynical attitude and secretive manners that he has developed as a camouflage in the Southern race warfare. As a servant the Negro goes into middle and upper class homes even in the North and acquires a sort of knowledge about white people. But this knowledge is distorted, since it covers only the private life of the whites and not the public life. Seldom does a Negro know how white people on his own level live and think. In part, the Negro's ignorance is an effect of exclusion from white society. In part, it is the result of the Negro's having different interests and worries. He is preoccupied with Negro life and problems, and this makes him a little blind to the general American ones.

Mutual ignorance and the paucity of common interests is a barrier to, and a modifier of, social contact between even educated and liberal whites and Negroes in the North, even in the extraordinary circles where segregation and discrimination play no role. I have seen Negro and white social scientists together as friends and colleagues. But I know that when their minds meet it usually concerns some aspect of the Negro problem. The Negro is ordinarily not present—and if he is present, he is a stranger—when the whites meet to discuss more general problems. If this is true among liberal social scientists, it is still more true among prejudiced people in all classes. The Negro is an alien in America, and in a sense this becomes the more evident when he steps out of his old role of the servant who lives entirely for the comfort of his white superiors. Ignorance and disparity of interests, arising out of segregation and discrimination on the part of whites, increased by voluntary withdrawal and race pride on the part of Negroes, becomes itself an important element increasing and perpetuating isolation between the groups.

5. PRESENT DYNAMICS

Negroes adjust and have to adjust to this situation. They become conditioned to patterns of behavior which not only permit but call for discriminatory observance on the part of the whites. The people who live in the system of existing relations have to give it a meaning. The Negroes have the escape, however, that they can consider the system unjust and irrational and can explain it in terms of white people's prejudices, material interest, moral wrongness and social power. They can avoid contacts and in the unavoidable ones have a mental reservation to their servility. It becomes to them a sign of education and class to do so and thereby preserve their intellectual integrity. Many Negroes succeed in doing this, and their number is growing. *But the unfortunate whites have to believe in the system of segregation and discrimination and to justify it to themselves.* It cannot be made intelligible and defensible except by false assumptions, in which the whites force themselves to believe.

So the social order perpetuates itself and with it the sentiments and beliefs by which it must be expressed. The lower caste may with some exertion release themselves intellectually. The higher caste, on the contrary, is enslaved in its prejudices by its short-range interests. Without their prejudices, white people would have to choose between either giving up the caste system and taking the resultant social, political, and economic losses, or becoming thoroughly cynical and losing their self-respect. The whites feel the Negroes' resentment and suspect new attitudes. Formerly, the whites got some support for their false prejudices from the Negroes. This is becoming less and less true. Now they can hardly claim to "know their Negroes" and are forced to admit their ignorance. The social separation they asked for is becoming a reality. Thus the tragedy is not only on the Negro side.

But the system *is* changing, though slowly. Modern knowledge and modern industrial conditions make it cumbersome. The South is becoming "normalized" and integrated into the national culture. Like every other "normal" province, it is beginning to dislike being provincial. The world publicity around the Dayton trial, for instance, did much to censor fundamentalism in Southern religion. A great part of the region's peculiarities in its racial relations is becoming, even to the Southerner, associated with backwardness. The Southerner is beginning to take on an apologetic tone when he speaks of his attitude toward the Negro. To insist upon the full racial etiquette is beginning to be regarded as affectation.

The South has long eagerly seized upon every act of prejudice practiced against the Negro in the North and, indeed, all other social ills of the other region. The visitor finds even the average run of white Southerners intensely aware of the bad slum conditions in Northern metropolises and of the North's labor troubles. Even the Southern liberal has the habit of never mentioning a fault of the South without mentioning a corresponding condition in the North. Many a Northern visitor to the South gets the feeling that the South is "still fighting the Civil War." But, as Kelly Miller observed, the "you also" argument is never resorted to except in palliation of conduct that is felt to be intrinsically indefensible.[32]

Southerners travel and migrate and are visited by Northerners and Europeans. They listen to the radio[33] and read papers, magazines and books directed to the wider national audience. Southern writers—in social science, politics, and *belles-lettres*—aspire to national recognition and not only provincial applause. The thesis that the region is poor and culturally backward, and that this is largely due to the presence of the Negroes and to the Southern Negro policy, has been for a long time developed by Southern authors. The average Southerner is beginning to feel the need for fundamental reforms. Many Southern newspapers have become liberal. Interracial work is beginning to be recognized as socially respectable.

The diffusion of scientific knowledge regarding race cannot be regionalized any more effectively than it can be segregated along a color line. Racial beliefs are becoming undermined, at least for the younger generation in the middle and upper classes. Most of them never reach the printing press or the microphone any more, as they are no longer intellectually respectable. The educated classes of whites are gradually coming to regard those who believe in the Negro's biological inferiority as narrow-minded and backward. When a person arrives at the point where he says that he knows his views are irrational but that "they are just instinctive" with him, he is beginning to retreat from these views.

The capital N in "Negro" is finding its way into the Southern newspapers as it earlier did into books. It is becoming a mark of education in the white South to speak of Negroes as "niggras" and not as "niggers"—a compromise pronunciation which still offends the Yankee Negro but is a great step from the Southern white man's traditional point of view. In Southern newspapers Negro problems and Negro activity even outside crime are beginning to be commented upon, not only to draw Negro subscribers, but also because these matters are actually found to be of some general community interest. Letters from Negroes are not infrequently printed and sometimes the content discussed with respect. It would be no great revolution, at least not in the Upper South, if a newspaper one morning carried a portrait of a distinguished Negro on the front page. In liberal newspapers in the Upper South, Negro pictures have already occasionally been printed in the back pages.

The educated, respectable, self-possessed Negro is to the average white Southerner not so often as earlier just the "smart nigger" or the "uppity nigger." As the South becomes urbanized and some Negroes rise in status, it is becoming increasingly impracticable and, in some relations, actually impossible to bracket all Negroes together and treat them alike. Social classes among Negroes are becoming recognized. Titles of respect, the offer to shake hands, permission to use the front door and other symbols of politeness are more and more presented to certain Negroes who have attained social success.

We must not exaggerate these signs of wear and tear on the Southern color bar. *"Social equality" is still a terribly important matter in the region. But it is not as important as it was a generation ago.* One needs only to compare the tremendous upheaval in the South when President Theodore Roosevelt in the first decade of the twentieth century had Booker T. Washington to a luncheon at the White House[34] with the relatively calm irritation the white South manifested in the 'thirties when President Franklin Roosevelt and his gallant lady did much more radical things. It even continued to vote for him. The South is surely changing.

But the changes themselves elicit race prejudice. From one point of view, Robert E. Park is right, of course, in explaining race prejudice as "merely an elementary expression of conservatism," as "the resistance of the social order to change." When the Negro moves around and improves his status, he is bound to stimulate animosity.[35] The white South was—and is—annoyed whenever the Negro showed signs of moving out of his "place." And the white North definitely became more prejudiced when hundreds of thousands of crude Southern Negroes moved in. But conditions for Negroes are improving, Southerners are being jolted out of their racial beliefs, and the group of white people interested in doing something positive for the Negro has grown. The increase in prejudice due to the rise of the Negro is a local and temporary phenomenon in both the North and the South.

The Second World War is bound to influence the trends of prejudice and discrimination. At the time of revising this book (August, 1942) it is still too early to make a more definite prediction. It would seem though, that the War would tend to decrease social discrimination in the North. The equalitarian Creed has been made more conscious to the Northerners. Radio speeches and newspaper editorials keep on pointing to the inequalities inflicted upon the Negroes as a contradiction to the democratic cause for which America is fighting. There have been some incidents of racial friction in Detroit and other places but, generally speaking, race relations have rather improved. In New Jersey and other states the police and the courts have become more active in stamping out illegal discrimination in restaurants and other public places.

In the South, however, reports in the press as well as what we hear related by competent Negro and white observers point to a rising tension between the two groups. There seems to be an increased determination on the part of white Southerners to defend unchanged the patterns of segregation and discrimination. Even some Southern liberals fall in with the tendency toward a hardened white opinion. Mark Ethridge, former chairman of the President's Committee on Fair Employment Practice and editor of a liberal Southern newspaper, the Louisville *Courier-Journal*, declared at the Birmingham hearings of the F.E.P.C. in July, 1942, that:

> There is no power in the world—not even in all the mechanized armies of the earth, Allied and Axis—which could now force the Southern white people to the abandonment of the principle of social segregation. It is a cruel disillusionment, bearing the germs of strife and perhaps tragedy, for any of their [the Negroes'] leaders to tell them that they can expect it, or that they can exact it as the price of their participation in the war.[36]

There has been some friction between Negro soldiers and Southerners, and the South's old fear of the armed Negro is rising.

Much the same thing happened during the First World War. But this time the isolation between the two groups is more complete. White people in the South know less about Negroes and care less about them. This time the Negroes, on their side, are firmer in their protest, even in the South.[a] And this time the North is likely to be more interested in what happens to race relations in the South.

[a] See Chapter 35, Section 10.

Part VIII

SOCIAL STRATIFICATION

CHAPTER 31

CASTE AND CLASS

....

1. THE CONCEPTS "CASTE" AND "CLASS"

The Emancipation of 1863 stopped the practice of calling the Negroes "slaves." For a while "freedmen" and "ex-slaves" were popular terms, but it soon became evident that the nation wished to forget the issue which tore the country apart. Yet some term had to be found to describe the inferior status of the Negro, especially in scientific and literary circles. In the literature the term "caste," which was already in use before the Civil War, was increasingly employed.

As alternatives—often as synonyms—for denoting the Negro as a separate group in American society and its relationship with other groups, the term "race" and sometimes the term "class" have been used. The former term, "race," is, as we have shown in Chapter 5, inappropriate in a scientific inquiry, since it has biological and genetic connotations which are incorrect in this context and which are particularly dangerous as they run parallel to widely spread false racial beliefs. The latter term, "class," is impractical and confusing in this context since it is generally used to refer to a nonrigid status group from which an individual member can rise or fall. There is a class stratification *within* each of the two groups. When used also to indicate the difference *between* the Negro and white groups, the term "class" is liable to blur a significant distinction between the two types of social differences. The recently introduced terms "minority group" and "minority status,"[1] are also impractical as we have pointed out in Chapter 3, since they fail to make a distinction between the *temporary* social disabilities of recent white immigrants and the *permanent* disabilities of Negroes and other colored people.[a] We need a term to distinguish the large and systematic type of social differentiation from the small and spotty type and have throughout this book used the term "caste."

The sole criterion in defining scientific terms is practicality. Concepts are our created instruments and have no other form of reality than in our own usage. Their purpose is to help make our thinking clear and our observations accurate. The scientifically important difference between the terms "caste" and "class" as we are using them is, from this point of view, *a*

[a] See Chapter 3, Sections 1 and 2.

relatively large difference in freedom of movement between groups. This difference is foremost in marriage relations. Intermarriage between Negroes and whites is forbidden by law in 30 states of the Union and even where it is not legally forbidden it is so universally condemned by whites that it occurs extremely infrequently.[a] The ban on intermarriage is one expression of the still broader principle, which is valid for the entire United States without any exception, that *a man born a Negro or a white is not allowed to pass from the one status to the other as he can pass from one class to another.*[b] *In this important respect, the caste system of America is closed and rigid, while the class system is, in a measure, always open and mobile.* This has social significance because, as is evident from the preceding chapters, being a Negro means being subject to considerable disabilities in practically all spheres of life.

It should, however, be clear that the actual content of the Negro's lower caste status in America, that is, *the social relations across the caste line, vary considerably from region to region within the country and from class to class within the Negro group. It also shows considerable change in time.* But variation and change are universal characteristics of social phenomena and cannot be allowed to hinder us from searching for valid generalizations. It will only have to be remembered constantly that when the term "caste relations" is used in this inquiry to denote a social phenomenon in present-day America, this term must be understood in a *relative* and *quantitative sense.* It does not assume an invariability in space and time in the culture, nor absolute identity with similar phenomena in other cultures.[2] It should be pointed out, incidentally, that those societies to which the term "caste" is applied without controversy—notably the *ante-bellum* slavery society of the South and the Hindu society of India—do not have the "stable equilibrium" which American sociologists from their distance are often inclined to attribute to them.[c]

Much of the controversy around the concept caste seems, indeed, to be the unfortunate result of not distinguishing clearly between the caste *relation* and the caste *line.* The changes and variations which occur in the American caste system relate only to caste relations, not to the dividing line between the castes. The latter stays rigid and unblurred. It will remain fixed until it becomes possible for a person to pass legitimately from the lower caste to the higher without misrepresentation of his origin. The American definition of "Negro" as any person who has the slightest amount of Negro ancestry has its significance in making the caste line

[a] See Chapter 29, Section 2.

[b] A person can pass if he misrepresents his orgin, which it is impossible to do in most cases. For discussion of "passing" see Chapter 5, Section 7. Also see Section 4 of this chapter.

[c] A Hindu acquaintance once told me that the situation in the United States is as much, or more, describable by the term "caste" as is the situation in India.

absolutely rigid. Had the caste line been drawn differently—for example, on the criterion of predominance of white or Negro ancestry or of cultural assimilation—it would not have been possible to hold the caste line so rigid.

The general definition of caste which we have adopted permits us to infer a concrete definition for our particular problem. When we say that Negroes form a lower caste in America, we mean that they are subject to certain disabilities solely because they are "Negroes" in the rigid American definition and not because they are poor and ill-educated. It is true, of course, that their caste position keeps them poor and ill-educated on the average, and that there is a complex circle of causation, but in any concrete instance at any given time there is little difficulty in deciding whether a certain disability or discrimination is due to a Negro's poverty or lack of education, on the one hand, or his caste position, on the other hand. In this concrete sense, practically the entire factual content of the preceding parts of this book may be considered to define caste in the case of the American Negro.

We conceive of the social differentiation between Negroes and whites as based on tradition and, more specifically, on the traditions of slavery society. We have attempted to trace this cultural heritage in various spheres of life. The caste system is upheld by its own inertia and by the superior caste's interests in upholding it. The beliefs and sentiments among the whites centering around the idea of the Negroes' inferiority have been analyzed and their "functional" role as rationalizations of the superior caste's interests has been stressed. The racial beliefs and the popular theory of "no social equality" were found to have a kernel of magical logic, signified by the notion of "blood." We have been brought to view the caste order as fundamentally a system of disabilities forced by the whites upon the Negroes,[a] and our discussion of the Negro problem up to this point has, therefore, been mainly a study of the whites' attitudes and behavior. And even when we proceed to inquire about the internal social structure of the Negro caste, about Negro ideologies, Negro leadership and defense organizations, the Negro community and its institutions, Negro culture and accomplishments, and Negro social pathology, we shall continue to meet the same determinants. Little of this can be explained in terms of Negro characteristics. The Negro problem is primarily a white man's problem.[b] In this part we shall find that *the class order within the Negro caste is chiefly a function of the historical caste order of America.*

[a] The voluntary withdrawal and the self-imposed segregation were shown to be a secondary reaction to a primary white pressure.

[b] See Introduction, Section 3.

2. The "Meaning" of the Concepts "Caste" and "Class"

When attempting to define our value premise for the discussion of social stratification in this chapter, we have first to take notice of the fact that Americans in general in all castes and classes are outspoken in their disapproval of distinctions in social status. Leaving out of consideration for the moment the several subordinate castes (Asiatics and Indians, as well as Negroes), whose members have specific reasons for favoring an equalitarian social philosophy, the visitor from abroad meets everywhere in America an ideology denouncing class differences which is more pronounced and sanctioned by more patriotic pride than perhaps anywhere else in Western civilization. This ideology has clearly a definite intent to mark off American ideals from those of the Old World.

Even the educated Americans exaggerate the amount of class discrimination in Europe, especially with regard to England, the old mother country.[3] This is an old tradition from colonial times. But it has been adopted and strengthened by wave after wave of immigrants who partly rationalized their uprooting and transference to this country by a belief in the rigidity of the class system in Europe and the free competition and boundless opportunities in the New World. As we have pointed out, this equalitarianism was—for the whites—given a most prominent place even in the ideology of the *ante-bellum* South.[a]

This ideology permeates popular thinking to the degree that Americans in general do not recognize their own actual class status. Most Americans —in all social classes—believe they are "middle class."[4] Perhaps this national theory is responsible also for the fact that American sociology (which generally must be given the highest ranking in the world) is weak and undeveloped in regard to the problems of social stratification. When recently a group of social anthropologists and sociologists stressed caste and class,[5] their colleagues everywhere in America exhibited an interest in the adventure rather out of proportion to the specific scientific novelties involved. Also the tendency to exaggerate the rigor of the American class and caste system, which is sometimes apparent in the work of the group of investigators led by Professor W. Lloyd Warner, is more easily understood when it is recalled that they are out to challenge a popular national theory with deep historical anchoring in the American Creed.[6]

Before we proceed, it is necessary to consider some reasons why the popular theory that America has little class stratification is more plausible and, indeed, also more true than superficial observation of the tremendous socio-economic differentiation would lead one to believe. Because of the settling of the colonies largely by religious dissenters, the Revolution against England, the expulsion and voluntary exile of the Loyalist Tories,

* See Chapter 20, Section 4.

and the adoption of a democratic Constitution, the country started out without the heritage of royalty, a titled aristocracy or a church hierarchy. The frontier, the mobility, the relatively democratic structure of higher education, and the democratic form of government were factors hindering the emergence of rigid class distinctions.[a] Even today a higher percentage of Americans in the highest positions of wealth, authority, and culture have near relatives on the farms or in the factories than do people of similar status in most other capitalistic countries. A democratic simplicity and a great deal of formal equality in everyday contacts have been characteristic of America. The "American dream" and an optimistic outlook on the future for every individual have been cherished.

On the other hand, there have been factors which have accentuated social distinctions. These include: the immense and unprecedented differences in income and wealth, which until recently have been left comparatively undisturbed by taxation; the relatively unrestricted property rights inherited from English common law, which not only allowed monopolistic exploitation on a huge scale of the natural resources of the new continent, but also permitted types of consumption directly intended to demarcate social distance;[b] the relatively small scope of public ownership and controls over consumption and production generally and particularly over natural resources such as minerals, waterfalls, forests, and the means of transportation; the relative lack of producers' and consumers' cooperatives; the absence, until recently, of organized efforts to equalize economic and educational opportunities of rural and urban localities and of the major regions of the country; the continuous mass immigration until recently and the practice of ruthlessly exploiting immigrants; the consequent cultural and racial fragmentation of the lower strata of the population; and the lack of organized and persistent popular movements.

Even though there are tremendous differences in wealth and social position among Americans, this is not the predominant influence in the national *ethos*. The American Creed has insisted upon condemning class differences, and it continues to do so in the face of the facts. Part of the paradox is solved, however, when we observe that *the American Creed does not demand equality of economic and social rewards independent of an individual's luck, ability and push. It merely demands equality of opportunity*. Abraham Lincoln expressed this in concrete and pertinent terms:

[a] It is symbolic, but not directly important, that there is a provision in the Constitution forbidding the acceptance of titles of nobility.

[b] The unrestrictive property laws have, for instance, made it possible for rich people in America actually to keep out the common people not only from the spots where their homes are built but from whole sections of country including roads, lake shores, fields and forests.

What is the true condition of the laborer? I take it that it is best to leave each man free to acquire property as fast as he can. Some will get wealthy. I don't believe in a law to prevent a man from getting rich; it would do more harm than good. So while we don't propose any war upon capital, we do wish to allow the humblest man an equal chance to get rich with anybody else. When one starts poor, as most do in the race of life, free society is such that he knows he can better his condition; he knows that there is no fixed condition of labor for his whole life. . . . I want every man to have a chance—and I believe a black man is entitled to it—in which he can better his condition—when he may look forward and hope to be a hired laborer this year and the next, work for himself afterwards, and finally *to hire men* to work for him. That is the true system.[7]

The class differences denounced by the American Creed are the rigid and closed ones. The Creed demands *free competition,* which in this sphere of social stratification represents the combination of the two basic norms: "equality" and "liberty." And it is prepared to accept the outcome of competition—if it is really free—though there be some inequality. This demand is the essence of American economic and social liberalism. Behind it is the theory that lack of free competition results in social inefficiency. Rigid class distinctions, therefore, hamper social progress. And this gives us the clue to the more precise valuation of caste and class in the American Creed. A contemporary American sociologist, investigating the American minority problem, emphatically expresses and gives his allegiance to this national valuation:

Democracy is an empty word unless it means the free recognition of ability, native and acquired, whether it be found in rich or poor, alien or native, black man or white. Minorities in the United States consume as much of our national wealth as they are permitted by group prejudices and productive capacity. When their productivity is artificially held far below their potentialities, the final result is not that there is more left for a dog-in-the-manger majority, but that a selfish majority is defeating its own purpose by limiting the total national productivity to the detriment of the welfare of American residents as a whole. The days are gone when one class in the western world may long prosper, at the expense of the masses.[8]

Our value premise in this chapter will be the American ideal of free competition and full integration in this sense. Social distinctions which hamper free competition are, from the viewpoint of the American Creed, wrong and harmful. From this value premise we derive our more precise definition of caste and class. The "meaning" of social status and of distinctions in social status is not an *a priori* evident matter. It varies from one culture to another depending upon what is commonly considered important. It is not quite the same in England, France, Sweden and America. It has to be defined, or otherwise we do not know exactly what we are observing and measuring. And it is usually best defined in terms of the *ethos* in the particular national culture we are studying.

In a vague way we mean, of course, somewhat the same thing by social status in all the capitalistic democratic civilizations within the Western sphere, and we know that social status is ordinarily connected with income, wealth, occupation, education, family background, home ownership. Owing primarily to the great immigration to America, nationality, length of residence, language, and religion are additional factors indicating or determining class in this nation. These characteristics have different relative importance for the class structure in different national cultures. And none of them gives the full "meaning" of class in any one of the Western cultures.

One school of thought defines class in terms of class feeling: the consciousness of the individuals of a class that they belong together in a corporate unity, and that they have different interests from individuals in other classes. This criterion—which has been worked out partly under the influence of Marx's class sociology and which is closely related to the idea of "class struggle"—is obviously inadequate at least as far as America is concerned. In America, particularly in the lower strata, class feeling, in this sense of interest solidarity, is undeveloped. It does not give the true meaning or importance of class to any ordinary American.

The Warner group defines class as "the largest group of people whose members have intimate social access to one another."[9] This suggestive definition seizes upon the fact that, even when class consciousness and class solidarity are not developed,[10] people do feel social distance and act it out in their everyday life by forming more or less cohesive groups for leisure time activity.[11] This group formation centers around the family and has the most important effects in controlling the behavior of individuals even outside the leisure time spheres of their life, and particularly in determining the social orientation given children and youth.[12]

This viewpoint is certainly wholesome as a reaction against the tendencies to use the most easily available class indices—income and occupation—as more than approximate measures of social class.[13] But it obviously over-emphasizes the role of purely social contacts and under-emphasizes the importance of other criteria. It fails to consider such important things as the imperfect correlation of leisure groups, the continuity of the social status scale, the arbitrariness of class demarcations, the differential infrequency of social contacts, the difficulty of separating social from purely personal distances, the relation between social structures in all the various American communities, the desire of some individuals to gain a position of leadership in a lower class rather than rise to a higher one. The ordinary American—particularly the male American—will not recognize his own class concept in this definition.

Class is in America one of the "value-loaded" terms and has to be related to our value premise. *Classes and class differences in America are thus in this inquiry conceived of as the result of restriction of free competition* and, consequently, of the lack of full social integration. The upper classes enjoy their privileges because the lower classes are restricted in their "pursuit of happiness" by various types of relative or absolute social monopolies. Attaching importance to family background instead of, or in addition to, merit is one type of monopoly and the basic one for the degree of closedness and rigidity of a class system. The ownership of wealth and income and, in America, national origin or religion become other causes of monopolies, if education is not absolutely democratic and if positions in the occupational hierarchy are not filled with regard to merit only. In view of the inequality of opportunity in getting an occupation, and since occupational positions carry incomes roughly in proportion to their status associations, it is possible, in an approximate way, to determine social class by considering income or occupation as the chief index of social monopoly.

This view of the American class structure also gives a nucleus of a theory for the causal relations between income, wealth, occupation, education, family background, home ownership, national origin, language and religion, on the one hand, and the integration of them to form a class system, on the other hand. In America, as elsewhere in the Western world, the development of democracy and of economic and social technology, as well as the growth of occupational organizations and their increasing stress on professionalism, all tend to make education more and more important as a vehicle for social mobility. Education gives respectability by itself and opens the road to higher occupations and incomes. The "self-made man" without educational background and professional training is disappearing even in America. Higher education is held a monopoly practically closed not only to older generations who have passed their chance—which is not contrary to the American Creed with its stress on equality of opportunity—but often also to youth without a certain minimum amount of wealth, parental push, and all the other factors associated with high social status.

In a similar way each of the other factors can be linked to the rest and used as an index of social status in general. Participation in cliques, clubs, associations—which Warner considers to be most important for determining one's class position—is itself a factor determined in large part by these other factors and contributes to their significance by emphasizing them, by serving as a source of information that helps one to make money, by encouraging a certain type of social behavior. Class consciousness may or may not be present in this system of interrelated factors determining class position, depending, among other things, upon how shut up in their pigeon holes the individuals of a class actually feel themselves. If class consciousness is present, it will tend to have reciprocal influences with other factors.

Caste, as distinguished from class, consists of such drastic restrictions of free competition in the various spheres of life that the individual in a lower caste cannot, by any means, change his status, except by a secret and illegitimate "passing," which is possible only to the few who have the physical appearance of members of the upper caste. Caste may thus in a sense be viewed as the extreme case of absolutely rigid class. Such a harsh deviation from the ordinary American social structure and the American Creed could not occur without a certain internal conflict and without a system of false beliefs and blindnesses aided by certain mechanical controls in law and social structure. To the extent, however, that false beliefs in Negro inferiority are removed by education and to the extent that white people are made to see the degradations they heap on Negroes, to that extent will the American Creed be able to make its assault on caste.

Within each caste, people also feel social distance and restrict free competition, so that each caste has its own class system. The dividing line between two castes is by definition clear-cut, consciously felt by every member of each caste, and easily observable. No arbitrariness is involved in drawing it. The class lines, on the other hand, are blurred and flexible. The very fact that individuals move and marry between the classes, that they have legitimate relatives in other classes and that competition is not nearly so restricted in any sphere, blurs any division lines that are set. Lines dividing the classes are not defined in law or even in custom, as caste lines are. Therefore, it is probably most correct to conceive of the class order as a *social continuum*. In most communities, and certainly in the United States as a whole, class differences between the nearest individuals at *any* point of the scale cannot be easily detected. It is only differences between individuals further away from each other that are easily observable. This is true for practically every one of the factors that go to make up the class system—income, family background, social participation, and so on—and it is doubly true of the class system as a whole since the factors are not perfectly correlated. There are no "natural" class boundaries.

For scientific purposes, of course, we have to draw lines breaking up the social continuum of the class order. But they are arbitrary. It has been customary for a long time to divide the population into three classes: "upper class," "middle class," "lower class." It would be possible, however, to have four or five classes. The Warner group uses a system of six classes, dividing the conventional three classes each into two. For some purposes even more classes would be most convenient. But we should never imagine that there is any deeper reality in our measuring scale than there is in measuring a distance in kilometers instead of miles. If a conventional class division—for instance, the one in three classes—entered into the popular consciousness, people might come to think of themselves as organized in this way, which would undoubtedly have certain consequences for the actual class situation. In some European countries this might hold true. In America, where the social class structure is dimly intellectualized by the general public—in spite of much observance in actual life of small and big status differences— this is not quite so true.[a]

The actual class stratification differs much between different communities. This is particularly true between rural and urban communities, between communities in the different historical regions of the country, and between the white and Negro castes. Different class divisions for each of these would be appropriate. If for convenience's sake the same scale of division is being used, this should not lead us to exaggerate the similarity between the different class structures.[b] What is regarded as the upper class in one community or caste, for example, would not be regarded as upper class in another community or caste, even if community associations and caste marks were changed.

3. THE CASTE STRUGGLE

The Marxian concept of "class struggle"—with its basic idea of a class of proletarian workers who are kept together in a close bond of solidarity of interests against a superior class of capitalist employers owning and controlling the means of production, between which there is a middle class bound to disappear as the grain is ground between two millstones—is in all Western countries a superficial and erroneous notion. It minimizes the distinctions that exist within each of the two main groups; it exaggerates the cleft between them, and, especially, the consciousness of it; and it misrepresents the role and the development of the middle classes. It is "too simple and sweeping to fit the facts of the class-system."[14] In America it is made still more inapplicable by the traversing systems of color caste. The concept of "caste struggle," on the other hand, is much more realistic. Archer talked of a "state of war" between Negroes and whites in the United States;[15] James Weldon Johnson spoke about "the tremendous struggle which is going on between the races in the South."[16] The caste

[a] An exception to this occurs at the very top of the social status scale in America, where each big city, and some smaller ones, has its "400" and its social register and where, in recent years, part of the nation has become aware of "America's 60 families."

[b] Even where there is no caste division in a community, it sometimes requires doing violence to facts to consider all members of that community on a single social status continuum. Social status, as we have seen, is made up of many components, which do not correlate perfectly. One's position on the income continuum, for example, may be higher than his position on the family background continuum. To get a single social status continuum these components need to be weighted and combined. But sometimes even then the members of a community who are found to have equivalent social status will be found to follow different lines of social advancement. It may be found, for example, that a physician, an army captain and an artist have about the same social status. While none looks down on any of the others, and all may be invited to the same party, their interests, associations, and lines of advancement are so dissimilar that it is more convenient, for most purposes, to consider the community as having several parallel social status continua.

distinctions are actually gulfs which divide the population into antagonistic camps. And this is a conscious fact to practically every individual in the system.

The caste line—or, as it is more popularly known, the color line—is not only an expression of caste differences and caste conflicts, but it has come itself to be a catalyst to widen differences and engender conflicts. To maintain the color line has, to the ordinary white man, the "function" of upholding the caste system itself, of keeping the "Negro in his place." The color line has become the bulwark against the whites' own adherence to the American Creed, against trends of improvement in Negroes' education, against other social trends which stress the irrationality of the caste system, and against the demands of the Negroes. The color line has taken on a mystical significance: sophisticated Southern whites, for example, will often speak with compassionate regret of the sacrifices the Negroes "have to" make and the discriminations to which they "have to" submit—"have to" in order to preserve the color line as an end in itself. This necessitates a constant vigilance. Southern whites feel a caste solidarity that permits no exception: some of them may not enforce the etiquette against all Negroes in all its rigor, but none will interfere with another white man when he is enforcing his superiority against a Negro. A white man who becomes known as a "nigger lover" loses caste and is generally ostracized if not made the object of violence. Even a Southern white child feels the caste solidarity and learns that he can insult an adult Negro with impunity.[17]

An extreme illustration of white solidarity in the South is given every time the whites, in a community where a lynching has occurred, conspire not to let the lynchers be indicted and sentenced.[18] In less spectacular cases it operates everywhere. Davis and Gardner give a good description of its psychology and its relation to Negro pressure:

Although the whippings described above appear to be more or less routine punishments of Negroes for some specific violation of the caste rules, in many of them there is another factor involved. Periodically there seems to develop a situation in which a number of Negroes begin to rebel against the caste restrictions. This is not an open revolt but a gradual pressure, probably more or less unconscious, in which, little by little, they move out of the strict pattern of approved behavior. The whites feel this pressure and begin to express resentment. They say the Negroes are getting "uppity," that they are getting out of their place, and that something should be done about it. Frequently, the encroachment has been so gradual that the whites have no very definite occurrence to put their hands on; that is, most of the specific acts have been within the variations ordinarily permitted, yet close enough to the limits of variation to be irritating to the whites. Finally, the hostility of the whites reaches such a pitch that any small infraction will spur them to open action. A Negro does something which ordinarily might be passed over, or which usually provokes only a mild punishment, but the whites respond with violence. The Negro victim then becomes both a scapegoat and an object lesson for his group. He suffers for all the minor caste violations which have aroused the whites, and he becomes a warning against future violations. After such an outburst, the Negroes again abide strictly by the caste rules, the enmity of the whites is dispelled, and the tension relaxes. The whites always say after such an outburst: "We haven't had any trouble since then."[19]

In the North, a large proportion of the white population would never discriminate against Negroes, and there is a small number who stand up against violation of the Negro's rights even if the matter does not concern them personally. Since such friends of the Negroes are not ostracized, and are in fact looked up to as "fighters," the color line may be said to be broken at spots in the North. Further, as seen in the previous chapter, the color line in the North is not a part of the law or of the structure of buildings and so does not have the concre eness that it has in the South. But still there is a color line in the North: most white individuals and groups discriminate in one way if not in another; all feel a difference between themselves and Negroes even if the feeling is only that Negroes labor under a different history, different conditions, and a different problem, and no Negro can legitimately pass out of the Negro group. A crisis brings out the character of the color line in the North more distinctly: An example is provided by a struggle around a Negro housing project in Detroit that culminated in a minor riot in early 1942. The federal government (U.S.H.A.) built a housing project for Negro defense workers in Detroit and named it after the Negro poet, Sojourner Truth. The project was built in a mixed white and Negro neighborhood, and as the project neared completion the local whites—aided by the Ku Klux Klan—picketed the city hall in protest against Negro occupancy. The congressman for the district joined in the protest; the federal authorities temporarily abandoned the idea of giving the project to Negroes but later went back to their original intention. When Negroes tried to enter the homes for which they had paid rent, they were prevented from doing so by a white mob that used violence, and the Detroit police aided the mob and arrested Negroes. On the other hand, there was a nation-wide protest against this treatment of the Negroes, and even the common man of other Northern cities and towns could be heard to say that it was "pretty bad" when the police were beating Negroes and preventing them from moving into homes built for them. Public opinion helped to stiffen the backs of the federal authorities who, without this new and powerful backing, would probably have bowed to local sentiment. The caste line in the North exists, but has gaps.

The mechanism of the caste struggle in the South can be illuminated by observing more closely what happens when a person breaks caste solidarity. On the white side this exceptional person is called the "nigger lover." To be known by this characterization means social and economic death. Except for legal differences, such a person is virtually dealt with as a traitor in fundamentally the same sense as a citizen who, during the war, is in friendly contact with the enemy. The "scab" who goes over to the employer during a strike is another appropriate comparison. The disgrace and the persecution of the "nigger lover," the traitor and the labor "scab" is fundamentally independent of their motives. These will usually and unquestionably be presumed to be base. No explanation is accepted. The reason is in all three cases that they are considered dangerous to the interests of the group. In recent years the "nigger lover" has generally been associated with the "reds," and the "Communists," terms that in all America and particularly in the South are given a wide and vague meaning.

Interracial workers in the South have to tread carefully in order not to invoke this terrible condemnation of being "nigger lovers." They know— and their Negro friends "understand"—that they will have to avoid breaking such social etiquette as would "offend public opinion." I have repeatedly been informed by white participants in interracial work about the fine diplomacy involved, about the compliant understanding of the Negroes, and of the tremendous importance of this matter both to their own welfare and to the success of their interracial undertakings. The Negroes in the South, knowing the whites' treatment of "nigger lovers" and the probability that they themselves would come in for a share, often show considerable shyness with a friendly white man, until they feel sure that he is going to leave the community soon and that he will not advertise his friendliness. The fear of being stamped as "nigger lovers" on the part of the white interracialists accounts for their preference to "work quietly" and for their reluctance to appeal to the white masses. By working only with the "best people of both races" they hope, and have actually succeeded, in gaining social respectability for their strivings. But they always stress that they are treading upon a volcano, even if white solidarity is apparently losing some of its fury.[a]

The Negro, from his side, is even more aware of the caste line than is the white man. Because Negroes are a numerically smaller element in the population of most communities, the average Negro has more contacts with whites than the average white man has with Negroes. Too, the contact usually means more to the Negro; it is the Negro who must be prepared to meet the white man in the way demanded by etiquette, and an insult rankles longer than an expression of ego-superiority. Further: the Negro thinks and talks more about his caste position than the white man, especially in the North, and thus has many more caste experiences in his imagination. Since the caste line restricts the Negro without providing him with many compensating advantages, he feels it not only surrounding him but also

---

[a] Some white interracial workers have not been able to avoid the designation of "nigger lover." But they manage to exist by living in the anonymity of cities and by getting their economic support from Northern philanthropy.

holding him back. Du Bois has expressed the Negro's feeling of caste in poetic language:

> It is difficult to let others see the full psychological meaning of caste segregation. It is as though one, looking out from a dark cave in a side of an impending mountain, sees the world passing and speaks to it; speaks courteously and persuasively, showing them how these entombed souls are hindered in their natural movement, expression, and development; and how their loosening from prison would be a matter not simply of courtesy, sympathy, and help to them, but aid to all the world. One talks on evenly and logically in this way but notices that the passing throng does not even turn its head, or if it does, glances curiously and walks on. It gradually penetrates the minds of the prisoners that the people passing do not hear; that some thick sheet of invisible but horribly tangible plate glass is between them and the world. They get excited; they talk louder; they gesticulate. Some of the passing world stop in curiosity; these gesticulations seem so pointless; they laugh and pass on. They still either do not hear at all, or hear but dimly, and even what they hear, they do not understand. Then the people within may become hysterical. They may scream and hurl themselves against the barriers, hardly realizing in their bewilderment that they are screaming in a vacuum unheard and that their antics may actually seem funny to those outside looking in. They may even, here and there, break through in blood and disfigurement, and find themselves faced by a horrified, implacable, and quite overwhelming mob of people frightened for their own very existence.[20]

The counterpart to white solidarity on the Negro side of the caste gulf is the "protective community." It is revealing of the nature of the system of superior and subordinate castes that this Negro cohesion is defensive instead of offensive, and that, compared with white solidarity, it is imperfect. The individual Negro, as a member of the lower caste, feels his weakness and will be tempted, on occasion, to split Negro solidarity by seeking individual refuge, personal security and advantages with the whites. Commenting upon the Atlanta riot in 1906, when 10 Negroes were killed and 60 wounded, Ray Stannard Baker remarked:

> It is highly significant of Southern conditions—which the North does not understand—that the first instinct of thousands of Negroes in Atlanta, when the riot broke out, was not to run away from the white people but to run to them. The white man who takes the most radical position in opposition to the Negro race will often be found . . . defending "his Negroes" in court or elsewhere. . . . Even Hoke Smith, Governor-elect of Georgia, who is more distrusted by the Negroes as a race probably than any other white man in Georgia, protected many Negroes in his house during the disturbance.[21]

The historical background of this attitude lies in the patriarchal relations between master and slave.[a] Its tenacity is explained by the power situation.

On the other hand, there has been a growing tendency on the part of

---

[a] See Chapter 30, Section 2.

Negroes to fight back, to maintain solidarity in a crisis. Claude McKay wrote:

> If we must die, let it not be like hogs
> Hunted and penned in an inglorious spot,
> While round us bark the mad and hungry dogs,
> Making their mock at our accursed lot.
> If we must die, Oh let us nobly die,
> So that our precious blood may not be shed
> In vain; then even the monsters we defy
> Shall be constrained to honor us though dead!
>
> Oh, kinsmen! we must meet the common foe!
> Though far outnumbered let us show us brave,
> And for their thousand blows deal one death-blow!
> What though before us lies the open grave?
> Like men we'll face the murderous cowardly pack,
> Pressed to the wall, dying, but fighting back![22]

McKay tells how the poem was reprinted in every Negro publication of any consequence, that it was repeated in Negro clubs, cabarets, and at Negro mass meetings, and that ministers ended their sermons with it. The Negro statesman, James Weldon Johnson, in his *Negro Americans, What Now?* prompts his people:

> When we are confronted by the lawless, pitiless, brutish mob, and we know that life is forfeit, we should not give it up; we should, if we can, sell it, and at the dearest price we are able to put on it.[23]

Johnson is, of course, far from recommending force as a political means for Negroes. Just above the words quoted in the text he stated:

> We must condemn physical force and banish it from our minds. But I do not condemn it on any moral or pacific grounds. The resort to force remains and will doubtless always remain the rightful recourse of oppressed peoples. Our own country was established upon that right. I condemn physical force because I know that in our case it would be futile.[24]

But even today when the mob or the vigilantes are out for Negro blood in the South the ordinary effect will be that the Negroes in terror will individually stay where they are or run to seek escape. They will ordinarily not fight back.[a] Considering the power situation, they cannot be criticized. They are probably wise, not only individually but in the interest of their group.[25] In Northern cities, where the Negro population is more compact and

---

[a] Since the beginning of the Second World War, Southern Negroes have shown some inclination to organize and fight back when they are attacked. (See Chapter 27, Section 5; Chapter 35, Section 10; and Chapter 45, Section 7.)

where they have legal protection and the suffrage, the situation is becoming different. There they will fight.[a]

But Negro solidarity produced by caste pressure and appearing as a mutually protective cohesion has its function in more ordinary and everyday problems. Even then it has nothing of the strength and regularity of white solidarity. Perhaps we can best illustrate the difference by observing the Negro who breaks caste solidarity. The Negro counterpart to the "nigger lover" is the "white man's nigger." He is much less exceptional. In the Negro community there is no fuss about his motives: they are simply assumed to be the selfish ones of attempting to benefit from playing up to the whites. His crime is not that he "fraternizes" with individuals of the other caste, but, quite the contrary, that he submits to excessive subservience and that he takes orders and carries them out even against the interests of his own caste. He will usually not be universally condemned by the Negro community. There are regularly other Negroes who would be prepared to take the same role or are actually doing it. In a way he is only exaggerating the "natural" role of the lower caste individual. To the white man he is a "good" Negro, continuing the cherished tradition from slavery. He puts the white man into his "natural" aristocratic role and becomes rewarded with condescending benevolence.[b]

The disapproval of the "white man's nigger" in the Negro community will depend upon the relative material and cultural independence of the community and usually varies directly with the social and educational status of the reacting individual Negro. It never approaches the rage, on the other side of the caste line, against a "nigger lover." His white protection will make the "white man's nigger" powerful. I have observed in several instances, both in the South and in the North, that individuals who are notorious as "white man's niggers" or "Uncle Toms" have a status in the Negro community for this very reason. Negroes in general, even if they dislike them, and, in a sense, despise them, are nevertheless inclined to envy them and give them deference at the same time. Negroes ordinarily, it must be remembered, depend upon the good-will and help of whites in most matters. When Negroes want something done in their community, they will send their "Uncle Toms" as intermediaries. They will often do so even if they know in the individual case that those persons are thoroughly unreliable from the Negro point of view and, perhaps, that they actually act as spies and stool pigeons for the whites. The Negroes know that they will not succeed if they try to ignore the white man's trusted Negroes. The "white man's nigger" exists in the North as well as in the South, but he is rarer and has less influence in his own caste. In the South he is sometimes an humble uneducated servant or ex-servant,

[a] See Chapter 27, Section 5.
[b] See Chapter 34.

but may also be a businessman, a landowner, a school principal or a college president. He is then the white-appointed "leader" of his race.[a]

4. CROSSING THE CASTE LINE

Another interesting side glance on the American caste system is provided by observing the phenomenon called "passing." To cross the caste line from the white side would be a comparatively easy matter, since in America a Negro is not necessarily supposed to have any Negro features at all.[b] The passer would also be fairly unsuspected, as it is generally assumed that nobody would want to descend in caste status. And there is no reason—except race pride emerging as a reflection of and a reaction against white superiority—why Negroes would resent such passing. Passing from the white to the Negro caste occurs extremely rarely.[26]

For all practical purposes "passing" means that a Negro becomes a white man, that is, moves from the lower to the higher caste. In the American caste order, this can be accomplished only by the deception of the white people with whom the passer comes to associate and by a conspiracy of silence on the part of other Negroes who might know about it. A few persons with half of their ancestry Negro are known to have passed, and, of course, passing is much easier for those with smaller proportions of Negro ancestry.[c] Even if there are probably quite a substantial number of Ameri-

[a] For a discussion of Negro leadership, see Part IX.

[b] See Chapter 5, Sections 1 and 7.

[c] Louis Wirth and Herbert Goldhamer, "The Hybrid and the Problem of Miscegenation," in Otto Klineberg (editor), *Characteristics of the American Negro*, prepared for this study; to be published, manuscript pp. 82-83 and 100 ff.; and Caroline Bond Day, *A Study of Negro-White Families in the United States* (1932), pp. 10-11.

I have made numerous observations which discount the common notion that Southern whites are particularly trained to identify a Negro by his physical appearance. My opinion on this point, which is contrary to that of most Negro and white experts with whom I have discussed the matter, becomes more reasonable when it is recognized that, though Southern white people undoubtedly see more Negroes, they constantly see them in the relatively rigidly defined caste role of the Southern Negro. In the marginal case, when a strange person's physical appearance leaves room for doubt, they probably recognize the Negro mostly from his bearing and his way of doing things. If, however, a Negro throws off the Negro role and starts to walk, talk, and behave as an ordinary white man, he must, I believe, have quite distinct Negro features to be recognized as a Negro in the South, at least in the first encounter. On the other hand, the fact that Negroes in the South are trained to appear and behave in a very different way from white people must raise a great subjective and objective barrier for every Southern or Southern-reared Negro who would like to pass in the South or in the North.

Once I traveled by car for a considerable time all over the Lower South with a Negro colleague who was reared and trained in the West and the North to be a very "normal" person judged by white standards of behavior. As was, of course, necessary, we separated for the night, I staying in a hotel and he somewhere in the protective Negro community. We carried with us a portable dictaphone for recording our interviews, and we needed to work together for some hours now and then in my hotel room. My colleague, who has

can Negroes passing over permanently to the white caste every year,[a] a much greater number would be able to pass if they wanted to depart from the Negro community and were prepared to take the personal costs and the risks involved.

Passing requires anonymity and is, therefore, restricted to the larger cities where everyone does not know everyone else. A Negro from a small community can pass only if he leaves that community. Only a small portion of all passing is intentional and complete. There is a considerable amount of inadvertent and nonvoluntary passing. This must be particularly true in the

---

some unmistakable Negro features, found soon that it was not necessary to go through all the ordinary inconveniences with the hotel manager to get up to my hotel room. He just walked straight in, kept his hat on his head and behaved as a normal white person of the educated class. Nobody bothered him. My explanation is that the ordinary white Southerner, if he sees a man walking into a hotel and carrying himself with assurance and ease, actually *does not see his color.* He, literally, "does not believe his eyes." Behind the Southern whites' not seeing a Negro in my friend, might also—unconsciously—be the realization of all the trouble it would mean for them to effectuate the caste rules, if they recognized facts, and the great risk they incurred if they were mistaken.

My general conclusion is that the white Southerner, being accustomed to seeing all Negroes in a subservient caste role and living in a society where the inconvenience and risk involved in telling a person that he is a Negro are so considerable, will have greater difficulties in recognizing a Negro who steps out of his caste role. This hypothesis could be tested by properly controlled experiments.

I had once another experience which throws light on the same problem from the sex angle. The N.A.A.C.P. had, in 1939, their annual convention in Richmond, Virginia. I visited the meetings and took part in a boat excursion which ended the convention. On board I approached a group of officers and crew (whites) who held themselves strictly apart, looking on the Association members who had crowded their ship for the day with an unmistakable mixture of superiority, dislike, embarrassment, interest and friendly humor. My advance was first received coldly and deprecatingly—as I understood later, because they assumed I was a Negro. But when they had become aware of my foreign accent, and I had told them that I was a stranger who by chance had come on the boat, just for the excursion, they were most friendly and entertained me for more than an hour by telling me everything about the Negro and the Negro problem in America. During the course of our conversation I remarked that there were apparently a lot of white people, too, on the boat. At first they just laughed at my remark and insisted that all persons present were Negroes. Some Negroes are so fair, they told me, that only Southerners, who know them by lifelong intimate association can distinguish them from whites. I insisted and pointed to Mr. Walter White, the secretary of the N.A.A.C.P. and some other "white" Negroes, and actually succeeded in drawing an acknowledgment that he and some other men (who I knew were all Negroes) were, indeed, white upon closer observation. One of my interlocutors went to have a closer look at the persons I had pointed out, and came back and confirmed authoritatively that they were indeed white. "There are some 'nigger lovers' in the North and we have a few down here, too," he commented. When, however, I then pointed to a lady (whom I knew to be white) and intimated that she might be white, the whole company dismissed my idea as nothing less than absurd and, indeed, insulting. "No white woman would be together with niggers." Their theories of "white womanhood" obviously blinded them in a literal sense.

[a] See Chapter 5, Section 7.

North where segregation is not so complete and is actually illegal. Much passing is partial and sporadic, as when Negroes (in Washington, for example) pass for whites to attend theaters, lectures, concerts and receptions. To some extent such passing breaks the cultural and spiritual isolation of the Negro community and favors the dissemination of broader ideas and patterns into the Negro community.[27] In the Deep South passing for such purposes is so dangerous that it is much less common. Another type of temporary passing is that done by Negro youths to secure entrance to educational institutions where Negroes are not allowed, or where they are allowed but feel more comfortable appearing as whites. I have come across several such cases, all in the North. In the South the risk incurred would ordinarily be too great.

In the Northern and Border states it seems to be relatively common for light-skinned Negroes to "pass professionally" but preserve a Negro social life. Negro girls have practically no chance of getting employment as stenographers or secretaries, salesclerks in department stores, telephone operators, outside the establishments run by Negroes for Negroes.[a] In most communities their chances are slight even to become regular teachers, social workers, or the like, if they do not conceal their Negro ancestry. This practice is fairly widespread. Some establishments take the precautions through their personnel departments of making home visits and other inquiries in order not to get Negroes in their employment. Not only in these female middle class occupations but in all male and female trades where Negroes are excluded, there must be a similar incentive to attempt to "pass professionally." Since the middle and upper class occupations are almost all closed to Negroes, these occupations—especially medicine, dentistry, journalism, acting, in addition to those mentioned above—are most pervaded by "professional passers." The retention of a Negro social life while passing for white occupationally involves considerable difficulties in all sorts of personal relations with associates in the place of work, and there is a great risk of being found out. This explains why the practice seems to be so much more common in the North and the Border states than in the real South. In none of the regions, it should be emphasized, is it possible for the bulk of the Negroes to pass, because of their obviously Negroid physical appearance.

Professional passing often seems to be a transitional stage of life. Probably in most cases these passers voluntarily retreat from the higher caste's occupational life by getting married or employed in the segregated sphere, or they become detected after some time and have to flee the ground with shame. Sometimes professional passing is, however, only a step on the way to complete and permanent passing. By cutting off their Negro relations entirely they are able to decrease the risk of being exposed. But their fuller

[a] See Chapter 14.

participation in the life of the higher caste will mean that they will be hit the harder if they are found out.

In view of the advantages to be had by passing, it is not difficult to explain why Negroes pass, professionally or completely. It is more difficult, however, to explain why Negroes do not pass over to the white race more often than they actually do. On this point, as on all others concerning this necessarily secretive matter, our actual knowledge is most inadequate. It is probable that race pride and a missionary spirit of wanting to remain in the lower caste in order to fight its cause or otherwise work for its elevation might be a prominent motive for certain individuals. But for the great majority of passable Negroes such an explanation is not plausible and is seldom advanced. A young and gifted college graduate among my Negro friends, who had "passed" in college but later accepted a teaching position as a Negro in his home city, gave, upon my questioning, the following reasons why he preferred not to pass: (1) When passing as a white (with some Indian blood), he could never overcome a slight feeling of strain and nervousness when in company; he would have to make forced explanations concerning his family; and he always felt suspicion around him— probably more suspicion, he remarked, than there actually was. (2) Because of his teaching position and his "good looks" he is "tops" in the Negro community; while if he were white in a similar job, he would be one among many and far from the social ceiling. (3) Because his profession was one in which there are few qualified Negro workers, he got his position more easily as a Negro than he would have as a white man. He was aware that he could advance further in the white world, but observed that even a large advance as a white man would carry much less esteem than a correspondingly smaller advance as a Negro. (4) Social life was so much more pleasant in the higher ranks of the Negro community than in the corresponding ranks of the white community: a Negro had so many more intimate associates; there were so many more social affairs and family entertainments going on in the Negro community—due probably, he observed, to the Negro's reaction against segregation in public places.

I am inclined to believe that this young man's account of his reasons for preferring to be an upper class Negro, protected by the professional monopolies enjoyed by this class and surrounded by the social pleasantness of Negro society, rather than to be an isolated middle class white person with a minimum of initial contacts, was not only an honest statement on his own part, but is also fairly representative of many other passable young Negroes' motivation to stay Negro. Particularly important is his observation that light-skinned Negroes have great advantages in the Negro community and that a disproportionate number of them are in the upper strata or have hopes of getting there.[a]

[a] See Chapter 32.

Light-skinned and "good featured" Negro women are preferred as marriage partners by Negro men, while their chances on the white marriage market as lonely women without a known or presentable family must be slight. This explains why Negro women pass even less frequently than do Negro men.[28] Established personal relations, from family bonds to less intimate but still not meaningless relations, will to a degree always tie a Negro to his own caste, and will tend to do so more and more the older and better established he becomes. Quite often marriage will put a stop to all dreams of passing, since it is less likely that the mate is also capable of passing. The unfamiliarity with life conditions and expected patterns of behavior on the other side of the gulf also acts as a deterrent. As Wirth points out, this particular factor is likely to decline in importance as educational and cultural opportunities for Negroes widen.[29] Negroes believe that social life is generally more pleasant among Negroes than among whites: ". . . white people don't begin to have the good times that Negroes do. They're stiff and cold. They aren't sociable. They don't laugh."[30] Even if such pronouncements are often only compensating rationalizations, they have probably enough background in personal conviction to be of real importance in motivation. Finally, there is the important factor of inertia: complete passing is a major step that requires careful planning and decisive action, and it is not surprising that many Negroes who could take this step do not.

To the whites, passing is an insult and a social and racial danger. Most whites have heard about passing, but, for natural reasons, do not know any specific cases. Most Negroes, particularly in the upper strata, on the contrary, know of many other Negroes, sometimes half a hundred or more, who pass as whites. As they usually do not expose them, this shows a significant difference between the two castes in attitude toward passing. Many Negroes obviously take a sort of vicarious satisfaction out of the deception of the whites. It is a big joke to them. Some show envy. This is particularly apparent among darker Negroes who cannot think of passing. Negroes realize, of course, that as a mass they cannot find an escape from the lower caste by passing. Further, they are increasingly brought to the compensatory feeling of race pride:

> The Negro community is built around the idea of adjustment to being a Negro, and it rejects escape into the white world. Community opinion builds up a picture of whites as a different kind of being, with whom one associates but does not become intimate. Without much conscious instruction, the child is taught that his first loyalties are to the Negro group. He may criticize Negroes and even dislike them, but he is a Negro and must not even wish to be otherwise. This doctrine is reinforced by stories of the meanness and cruelty of white people. To wish to be white is a sacrifice of pride. It is equivalent to a statement that Negroes are inferior, and, consequently, that the youth himself is inferior.[31]

This, however, does not necessarily mean that a Negro becomes willing to disclose another Negro who is passing. The spirit of the protective community will usually work to help the ex-member to pass. If a passing Negro is disclosed by other Negroes, the cause is ordinarily not Negro solidarity but rather private envy, of which there is a great deal in a frustrated lower caste.

As a social phenomenon, passing is so deeply connected with the psychological complexes—built around caste and sex—of both groups that it has come to be a central theme of fiction and of popular imagination and story telling. The adventures of the lonesome passer, who extinguishes his entire earlier life, breaks all personal and social anchorings, and starts a new life where he has to fear his own shadow, are alluring to all and have an especially frightening import to whites. There is a general sentimentality for the unhappy mulatto—the "marginal man" with split allegiances and frustrations in both directions[a] which is especially applied to the mulatto who passes. From all we know about personality problems there is probably, as yet, substantial truth in the picture of the passer which our literary phantasy paints for us. But since there has been little observation of the personality problems of the passers, the picture of their difficulty is hard to define.

[a] See Chapter 32, Section 6.

CHAPTER 32

THE NEGRO CLASS STRUCTURE

1. The Negro Class Order in the American Caste System[a]

The caste principle, as insisted upon and enforced by white society would undoubtedly be best satisfied by a classless Negro community wherein all Negroes in all respects—educationally, occupationally, and economically—were in the lowest bracket and placed under the lowest class of whites. That "all Negroes are alike" and should be treated in the same way is still insisted upon by many whites, especially in the lower classes, who actually feel, or fear, competition from the Negroes and who are inclined to sense a challenge to their status in the fact that some Negroes rise from the bottom even if they professionally and socially keep entirely within the Negro community.[1] The popular theories rationalizing and justifying the caste order to the whites have been framed to fit this principle of a homogeneous lower caste. None of the Jim Crow legislation distinguishes between classes of Negroes.

This absolutistic principle has, however, never been fully realized even in the South. Already in slavery society there came to be a social stratification within the slave community, as house servants and skilled mechanics acquired a level of living and culture and enjoyed a social prestige different from that of the field slaves. The blood ties of the former group of slaves with the white upper class widened this difference. There may also have been some difference in status between the slaves owned by the aristocracy and the slaves owned by the small farmers.[2] Contemporary sources give us the impression that the hatred between Negro slaves and "poor white trash" was largely due to this social stratification in the Negro group.[3] It was mainly the superior slave who could be a challenge and danger to the poor whites, and it was he who, on his side, would have the social basis for a contemptuous attitude toward them. The early emergence of a

[a] In this chapter we shall confine ourselves to the relation between caste and *Negro* classes. This does not mean that caste has no effect on the white class structure. Attitudes and actions toward Negroes have always differentiated the various white classes in the South. (See Chapter 28, Section 8.) Also there have been concrete effects: for example, when practically all Negroes were below them during slavery, the lower class whites probably felt less social distance from upper class whites in the South than today when they realize that many Negroes have a class status above them.

class of free Negroes, which at the time of Emancipation had grown to one-half million individuals, strengthened this trend toward a social stratification of the Negro population in America. All sorts of restrictive laws were enacted and also partly enforced to keep the free Negroes down. But in spite of this, their condition of life and social status was different from that of the masses of slaves.[4]

After Emancipation this development continued. The measures to keep the Negroes disfranchised and deprived of full civil rights and the whole structure of social and economic discrimination are to be viewed as attempts to enforce the caste principle against the constitutional prescripts and against the tendency of some Negroes to rise out of complete dependence. The Constitution—and the partial hold of the American Creed even on the Southern whites' own minds—prevented effective caste legislation. All laws, even in the South, had to be written upon the pretense of equality. Education for Negroes was kept backward, but it was given in some measure and gradually improved. Some Negroes became landowners, often under the protection of individual white patronage. And, most important of all, social segregation itself—which has always been maintained as the last absolute barrier—afforded protection for a rising number of Negro professionals and businessmen. Negroes had to be ministered to, their educational institutions had to be manned, their corpses had to be washed and buried, and, as white people did not wish to take on these tasks and as Negroes gradually found out their own needs and chances, a Negro middle and upper class developed to perform these functions, and thus drew its vitality from the very fact of American caste. The dividing line between the two castes did not crack, however. Thus, this dual system of social class developed, *one class system on each side of the caste line.*

Robert E. Park has schematized this development as follows:

Originally race relations in the South could be rather accurately represented by a horizontal line, with all the white folk above, and all the Negro folk below. But at present these relations are assuming new forms, and in consequence changing in character and meaning. With the development of industrial and professional classes within the Negro race, the distinction between the races tends to assume the form of a vertical line. On one side of this line the Negro is represented in most of the occupational and professional classes; on the other side of the line the white man is similarly represented. The situation *was* this:

All white

All colored

It is *now* this:

White	*Colored*
Professional occupation	Professional occupation
Business occupation	Business occupation
Labor	Labor

The result is to develop in every occupational class professional and industrial bi-racial organizations. Bi-racial organizations preserve race distinction, but change their content. The distances which separate the races are maintained, but the attitudes involved are different. *The races no longer look up and down: they look across.*[5]

This description contains—as the author is probably well aware—several overstatements. The caste line is not vertical but rather "diagonal" (that is, a sloped line). The line has moved, and is moving, from horizontal, but it is still far away from the vertical position, as Warner has shown.[6] But Warner is not correct either, since he thinks of the caste line as a straight one, implying that the Negro group gets proportionately smaller

WARNER'S DIAGRAM[1]

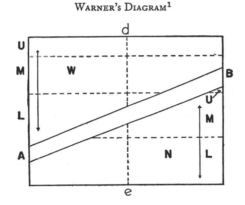

[1] W. Lloyd Warner, Introduction to *Deep South*, by Allison Davis, B. B. Gardner and M. R. Gardner (1941), p. 10.

Legend: W—White. N—Negro. U—Upper Class. M—Middle Class. L—Lower Class. AB—Caste Line. de—Ultimate Position of Caste Line.

as one goes up the social status scale. Actually, the Negro middle and upper class are *more than proportionately* smaller than their lower class. Du Bois brings this out clearly.

It goes without saying that while Negroes are thus manifestly of low average culture, in no place nor at any time do they form a homogeneous group. Even in the country districts of the lower South, Allison Davis likens the group to a steeple with wide base tapering to a high pinnacle. This means that while the poor, ignorant, sick and anti-social form a vast foundation, that upward from that base stretch classes whose highest members, although few in number, reach above the average not only of the Negroes but of the whites, and may justly be compared to the better-class white culture. The class structure of the whites, on the other hand, resembles a tower bulging near the center with the lowest classes small in number as compared with the middle and lower middle classes; and the highest classes far more numerous in proportion than those among blacks.[7]

We can diagram the caste-class situation in two ways: one, in terms of absolute numbers after the manner of the ordinary population pyramid—as in Du Bois' description; two, in terms of percentages at each social level —after the pattern of a box diagram. The latter diagram brings out the line, in temporal changes in which Warner and others have been interested. The pyramid and the line are drawn hypothetically—it would take an enormous amount of work to draw them with an approximation of empirical quantitative accuracy. But as to their general shape there can be

ABSOLUTE NUMBERS OF
WHITES AND NEGROES
AT EACH LEVEL OF
SOCIAL STATUS

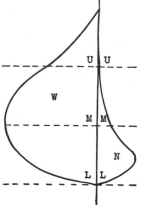

PERCENTAGE OF WHITES AND NEGROES
AT EACH LEVEL OF SOCIAL STATUS

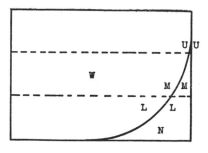

Legend: W—White. N—Negro. U—Upper Class. M—Middle Class. L—Lower Class.

little doubt: the pyramid is heavier at the bottom on the Negro side than on the white side, and the line is a *diagonal curve*, not a straight line diagonal.[8]

There is at least one weakness of all diagrams of this sort: they assume that the class structures of the two castes are exactly comparable, which they are not. On the same class level—that is, assuming white and Negro individuals with the same education, occupation, income, and so on—the white does *not* "look across" the caste line upon the Negro, but he definitely *looks down* upon him.[a] And this fundamental fact of caste is

[a] On the other hand, *within the Negro community*, the upper class Negro is placed higher than is the white man of comparable income, education, and so on, in the white community. Du Bois observed this:

materialized in a great number of political, judicial, and social disabilities imposed upon Negroes somewhat independent of their class, and in the rigid rule that the Negro is not allowed to pass legitimately from the one side to the other.

The diagonal and curved character of the caste line and this fact that whites can look down on Negroes of the same income, educational, or other level, form one of what Dollard calls the major "gains" of the caste order to the whites.[9] The difference between the South and the North and, in a degree, between rural and urban communities is, from this point of view, that the caste line tends to be somewhat more vertical in the latter than in the former regions and localities. The caste status of the Negro in the North and in cities generally has fewer rigid restrictions of free competition. In this direction the class system has been continually moving in the South and—except for the transitional extraordinary pressure of recent mass immigration—also in the North.

We have seen that Southern whites, especially in the lower brackets, often refuse to recognize class differences in the Negro community and insist upon distinguishing only between "bad niggers," "good niggers," and "uppity niggers," and that they, until recently, have succeeded in retaining a legal and political system which corresponds most closely to this view. But this uncompromising attitude is disappearing under the pressure of the facts of Negro social differentiation. Thus the actual import of caste is gradually changing as the Negro class structure develops— except in the fundamental restriction that no Negro is allowed to ascend into the white caste.

2. CASTE DETERMINES CLASS

While the Negro class structure has developed contrary to the caste principle and actually implies a considerable modification of caste relations, fundamentally this class structure is a function of the caste order. We have repeatedly had to refer to this important fact that, while the caste order has held the Negro worker down, it has at the same time created petty monopolies for a tiny Negro middle and upper class. Negroes understand this, although they seldom discuss it openly.[a]

". . . a white Philadelphian with $1,500 a year can call himself poor and live simply. A Negro with $1,500 a year ranks with the richest of his race and must usually spend more in proportion than his white neighbor in rent, dress and entertainment." (W. E. B. Du Bois, *The Philadelphia Negro* [1899], p. 178.)

[a] The author once attended a meeting in Detroit where one of the national Negro leaders gave a speech. The church where the meeting was held was filled with professionals and business people of the local Negro upper class with a sprinkling of humbler people. After the address, there was some discussion, and the eternal question of Negro strategy was brought up. The speaker in answering began to give the standard arguments for a cautious approach. In the middle of his answer he seemed to sense the futility of the ques-

The lower caste monopolies are strongest in some of the professions and in the service occupations near the professions (funeral work, beauty work, retail trade, and so on); some monopolistic leeway is also afforded small-scale Negro banking, insurance and real estate. For the rest of the occupations, the caste barriers block the way for Negroes.[a] It is thus understandable that, next to the small size of the middle and upper class, the Negro class system has its most characteristic feature in the fact that, on the whole, capitalist business and wealth mean so relatively little, and that general education and professional training mean so relatively much, as criteria for attaining upper class status.[b] This is evidently not due to a lower valuation of wealth among Negroes than among whites. Rather independent of the respectability of the source, wealth is as sure—and perhaps even a little more sure—to give upper class status among American Negroes as it does among whites. But there is so little of it in the Negro community. And education is such a high value to this group, which has to struggle for it, that it is understandable why education is more important, relatively, for Negro status than for white status. Among the consequences of the relative prestige of education among Negroes is that practically all Negro college teachers are upper class, and that most of the national Negro leaders are academic men. In both these respects, the American Negro world is strikingly different from the American white world.

One of the consequences of the small range of wealth and occupation in the Negro community, and of the importance of education, is that there is probably less social distance between bottom and top among Negroes than there is among whites. It is not uncommon for a Negro boy—especially in the North—to rise from the lowest to the highest social status in one generation. While a white boy could rise the same absolute social distance in the white caste during his lifetime—that is, he could attain the same increase in education, wealth, and manners—this distance would not appear so great because he would still be far from the top. This fact has tended to keep the various Negro classes in better contact with each other, except for the declining mulatto aristocracies, than is the case with the white classes. Other factors—such as caste pressure, the northward migration, and the

---

tion; he smiled and remarked that perhaps segregation should not be bullied so without qualifications: "How would you all feel if you awakened tomorrow morning and found yourself in the wild sea of white competition?" He cashed in a big laugh, somewhat nervous and bashful, but relieving.

[a] See Chapters 13 and 14.

[b] Two other characteristics that are rather unique make for upper class status in the Negro world: caste leadership and achievement in the white world. Marcus Garvey, Oscar DePriest, and Father Divine, on the one hand, and Joe Louis, Paul Robeson, and Rochester, on the other hand, have high status and would have had it even if they were neither rich nor educated.

existence of national organizations fighting for the whole caste—have had a similar effect.

Another characteristic of the Negro class structure—which would superficially seem contradictory to the previously mentioned trait, but is not on closer examination—is the smaller amount of pride in individual climbing among upper class Negroes. It is my impression that, in a sense, the typical Negro upper class person attaches more importance to family background than the typical Yankee. At least he is less likely to brag about his lowly origin. In this, as in many other respects, the American Negro seems more similar to the Southern white man, who also places a lower estimation on the self-made man. I should imagine that this is not only a cultural pattern borrowed from Southern white society but also, and more fundamentally, a trait connected with the fact that both Negroes and Southern whites are, though in different degrees, disadvantaged groups and do not feel the security of the Yankee, who can afford to brag about having started as newsboy or shoeshiner.[a]

Also important for the spirit of the Negro class structure is the fact that such a relatively large portion of the Negro middle class groups in all regions of America have positions in personal service of whites. In Southern cities some of the upper class Negroes still engage in some of the service occupations, as they did even in the Northern cities a generation ago. A great number of their sons and daughters have proceeded into the upper class professions. I have also been struck by the relatively high proportion of upper class professionals who during their college years, for lack of other employment opportunities open to Negroes, have done service work for whites. It appears plausible that both the refined and worldly-wise manners, especially in the older generation of upper class Negroes, and their often conservative social and economic views are not unconnected with such earlier experiences in personal service of well-to-do whites.[10]

An individual's relation to white society is of utmost importance for his social status in the Negro community. This aspect of the Negro class structure will be considered in the next part on Negro leadership and concerted action.

3. COLOR AND CLASS

The American order of color caste has even more directly stamped the Negro class system by including relative whiteness as one of the main

[a] A special reason why upper class Negroes often make so much of their family background is that if they had free Negro or upper class white ancestry it puts them above the hated slave background.

A few Negroes who have risen very high and who are secure may—like the white man—boast of their lowly origin. Frederick Douglass and Booker T. Washington did this.

factors determining status within the Negro community. This has a history as old as class stratification itself among Negroes. Mixed bloods have always been preferred by the whites in practically all respects. They made a better appearance to the whites and were assumed to be mentally more capable. They had a higher sales value on the slave market.[11] The select classes of trained mechanics and house servants who early came in closer contact with the dominant culture of the whites seem largely to have been drawn from the group of mixed bloods, and their superior training further raised their status.

A sexual selection added its influence to this occupational differentiation. The fair-skinned house girls were more frequently used as mistresses by men of the planter class than were the plantation hands. They became the mothers of successive generations of even whiter children. Many white fathers freed their illegitimate mulatto offspring and often also the children's mothers, or gave them the opportunity to work out their freedom on easy terms. Some were helped to education and sent to the free states in the North. Some were given a start in business or helped to acquire land.

For this reason the free Negro population everywhere contained a greater proportion of mixed bloods than did the slave population.[12] The mulattoes followed the white people's valuation and associated their privileges with their lighter color. They considered themselves superior to the black slave people and attributed their superiority to the fact of their mixed blood. The black slaves, too, came to hold this same valuation. The white people, however, excluded even the fairest of the mulatto group from their own caste—in so far as they did not succeed in passing—and the mulattoes, in their turn, held themselves more and more aloof from the black slaves and the humbler blacks among the free Negroes; thus the mulattoes tended early to form a separate intermediary caste of their own. Although they were constantly augmented by mulatto ex-slaves, they seldom married down into the slave group. In such cities as New Orleans, Charleston, Mobile, Natchez, and later Washington, highly exclusive mulatto societies were formed which still exist, to a certain extent, today. Color thus became a badge of status and social distinction among the Negro people.

Emancipation destroyed any possibility there might have been for the mulatto group to form an intermediary caste of their own in America as a substitute for their not being able to get into the white group.[a] Even their upper class position lost in relative exclusiveness as their monopoly of freedom was extinguished and white philanthropy began to aid the recently emancipated slave masses. The new definition of the Negro problem in the

[a] In South Africa, the mulatto group holds itself as a separate caste, even though the blacks are not slaves. A similar situation exists in many other countries. Our statement refers to conditions in the United States only.

South and the increased antagonism on the white side toward all Negroes who were "out of their place" made the whites less inclined to draw a distinction between light and dark Negroes.

But at the same time Emancipation broadened the basis for a Negro upper class and increased the possibilities for this class relatively even more than for the Negro masses themselves. What there was in the Negro people of "family background," tradition of freedom, education and property ownership was mostly in the hands of mulattoes. They became the political leaders of the freedmen during Reconstruction, as well as their teachers, professionals and business people. Compared with the newly freed slave population they had a tremendous head-start. In the social stratification of the Negro community their social distance toward the Negro masses perpetuated itself. Darker Negroes who rose from the masses to distinction in the Negro community by getting an education or by conducting successful business enterprises showed an almost universal desire to marry light-skinned women and so to become adopted members of the light-colored aristocracy and to give their children a heritage of lighter color. Blackness of skin remained undesirable and even took on an association of badness.[13]

Without any doubt a Negro with light skin and other European features has in the North an advantage with white people when competing for jobs available for Negroes.[14] It is less true in the South, particularly in the humbler occupations. The whites continue to associate the nearness to their own physical type with superior endowments and cultural advancement, and the preponderance of fair-skinned Negroes in the upper strata seems to give this prejudice a basis in fact. Perhaps of even greater importance is the fact that the Negro community itself has accepted this color preference.[15] In conversation Negroes often try to deny or to minimize this fact. But there are a number of indications which an observer cannot help recording. For one thing, many individual Negroes will be found, when speaking about themselves, to rate their own color lighter than it actually is, but practically none to rate it darker.[16] The desire on the part of Negro women of all shades and in all social classes to bleach their skin and straighten their hair—observed decades ago by Ray Stannard Baker and William Archer[17]—has been the basis for some of the most important Negro businesses and some of the largest fortunes. Cosmetics for such purposes are most prominently advertised in the Negro press. The pictures of the social lions displayed on the social pages of the Negro newspapers give evidence in the same direction, as does listening to the undertones of conversation in Negro society even when an outsider is present.

Cliques, clubs, and social life in general seem to be permeated by this color preference.[18] The color problem enters into the Negro home, where children show differences in shades, and into the schools.[19] In marriage selection, as we have had occasion to mention previously, it becomes a dominant factor. It is impossible not to observe that in the higher classes the wives regularly tend to be of a lighter shade of color than the husbands.[20] For a dark Negro woman, especially in the middle or upper classes, the chances of getting a husband are fewer than for a dark Negro man: men achieve more on the basis of merit and also take the initiative in marriage selection. A fair Negro woman, on the other hand, has such superior marriage chances that this fact is generally recognized as the major explanation of why passable women do not seem to pass out of the Negro caste as often as do passable men.

Fair-skinned Negroes have not been allowed by the white caste to establish an intermediary caste of their own. Their superior status has not been recognized. With great consistency they have been relegated to the Negro caste. In the Negro community their exclusiveness has been broken up by social mobility, aided by the growth of the Negro upper classes. Darker Negroes *can* rise to the top among Negroes in social status, and intermarriage with lighter Negroes *is* possible and actually not infrequent. But the marriage selection referred to and the greater opportunities generally for economic and cultural advance of fair-skinned Negroes have preserved an inherited situation where the darker individuals tend to form the lower classes while the fairer individuals tend to belong to the upper strata. The actual quantitative correlation between class and color is not known.[21] It would seem, however, as if it were higher in urban districts than in rural ones.[22] It is also probable that, in spite of the selective factors still working in favor of the fair-skinned individuals, the relative proportion of dark-skinned individuals in the upper classes is increasing as these classes are growing. The "blue-veined" societies are breaking up.

As the Negro community is becoming increasingly "race conscious" it is no longer proper to display color preferences publicly. The light-skinned Negroes have to pledge allegiance to the Negro race. There is and has always been much envy on the part of darker Negroes toward lighter ones. There is even some tendency to regard a light skin as a badge of undesirable illegitimacy, especially when the light-skinned individual has a dark-skinned mother or siblings.[23] There is also a slight tendency to attribute bad biological effects to miscegenation.[24] The Garvey Back-to-Africa movement appealed systematically to the darker Negroes and tried to impute superiority to an unmixed African heritage.[a] Other more recent movements have made similar appeals.[b] This reaction has, however, never outweighed the primary tendency, which has always been to regard physical and cultural similarity to white people with esteem and deference. And the reaction itself is in many cases a psychological defense against a dominant

[a] See Chapter 35, Section 7.
[b] See Chapter 39, Section 2.

belief in the desirability of light skin and "good" features. It has often been remarked that this tendency is not entirely unique among Negroes. It will appear in every disadvantaged group, for instance, among Jews in America. But Negro features are so distinct that only in the Negro problem does this factor become of great social importance.

Their color valuation is only one instance, among many, of the much more general tendency for the Negro people, to the degree that they are becoming acculturated, to take over the valuations of the superior white caste.[a] In other spheres this process can, on the whole, be regarded as a wholesome and advantageous adjustment of the Negroes to American life. In this particular respect, however, a conflict emerges which is unsolvable, as the average Negro cannot effectively change his color and other physical features. If the dark Negro accepts the white man's valuation of skin color, he must stamp himself as inferior. If the light Negro accepts this valuation, he places himself above the darker Negroes but below the whites, and he reduces his loyalty to his caste. The conflict produces a personality problem for practically every single Negro. And few Negroes accomplish an entirely successful adjustment.

There is a considerable literature on the personality problem of the light-skinned Negro.[25] He has been characterized as a "marginal man"—"one whom fate has condemned to live in two societies and in two, not merely different but antagonistic cultures"[26]—and he has been assumed to show restlessness, instability, and all sorts of deviations from a harmonious and well-balanced personality type.[27] This literature, which is largely of a speculative character,[28] probably reflects—like the great amount of fiction devoted to the mulatto—more the imaginative expectations of white people as they think of themselves with their white skin, if placed under the caste yoke, than the actual life situation of mulattoes in the Negro caste. It is forgotten that the Negro upper strata enjoy considerable protection behind the wall of segregation and that a light skin in all social strata of the Negro community has definite advantages, two factors which must tend to make mulattoes rather more satisfied to be Negroes than are the darker Negroes.[h] It should not be denied, of course, that there are fair-skinned Negroes in America who develop the personality traits traditionally ascribed to them.[e]

[a] See Chapter 44, Section 1.

[b] Another problem for dark-skinned Negroes who reach the upper class arises out of the fact that they are newly arrived and so have a tenseness which the light-skinned who, for the most part, are long established in the upper class, do not have.

The studies for the American Youth Commission (see footnote 9 of Chapter 30) corroborate the author's impression that the personality problems of the dark-skinned Negro are often greater than are those of the light-skinned Negro. This is especially true among the educated groups.

[e] I have met two violently anti-Negro mulattoes who identified themselves with the whites. One was a passer. The other was just a little bit too dark to pass safely. The latter proudly

But, as Wirth and Goldhamer point out, "It is important to recognize . . . that in a sense *every* Negro, whether light or dark, is a marginal man in American society."[29] And skin color is only one factor among many creating personality problems for Negroes.

4. THE CLASSES IN THE NEGRO COMMUNITY[a]

The static or cross-sectional configuration of the Negro class system, particularly as it is observable in the South, has recently been delineated in a number of community studies,[30] and we know much more on this topic today than we did ten years ago. In all these studies the conventional division of a population into three classes—"lower class," "middle class," "upper class"—has been applied to the Negro community.[31] Some of these studies, further, subdivide each of the three classes into two. It is quite convenient for the investigator to describe two extremes—the lower and upper classes—and then handle the great amount of variation by describing a middle class between them. We shall follow this pattern for the convenience of both ourselves and the reader. It should be understood that the description is in terms of the average, the general and the typical. Actually each class has a considerable amount of variation and there are often individuals who are complete exceptions. The actual situation, it must be remembered, is one of a continuum of social status, with an imperfect correlation between the factors making up social status and between social status and the other traits which are to be ascribed to the various classes. There are also differences between regions and communities, and the class structure is constantly changing.

The Negro *lower class,* as it is usually described, contains the large majority of Negroes everywhere.[32] Any reasonable criteria used to describe the white lower class would, when applied to Negroes, put the majority of the latter in the lower class.[33] They are the unskilled or semi-skilled laborers and domestic workers of the cities in the South and the North; and the agricultural wage laborers, tenants and household servants in Southern rural districts. During the 'thirties a large portion of this group has, permanently or temporarily, been on relief. Incomes are low and uncertain;

---

emphasized that he was "the descendant of slave owners," which, of course, is not uncommon in the Negro world, but in his announcement it had a definitely sadistic and hateful import. I have been with many passers; with the exception mentioned, they did not show any extraordinary hatred of Negroes or any abnormal fixation on "white blood." Fair-skinned nonpassing Negroes are generally conscious of their social advantage and are sometimes cautiously critical of the black masses. They do not ordinarily appear particularly off balance, but are rather inclined to belong to the complacent type of well-accommodated *petit bourgeois* Negro.

[a] For other dynamic interpretations of Negro classes, see: E. Franklin Frazier, *The Negro Family in the United States* (1939), pp. 393-475; and Allison Davis, Burleigh B. Gardner, and Mary R. Gardner, *Deep South* (1941), Chapters 9 and 10.

levels of living do not include most of what is considered cultural necessities according to the "American standard."[a] They generally have little education. The older generation is often illiterate or practically illiterate. Books, periodicals, and newspapers, social movements and ideas, play an almost insignificant role in their lives.

This class is Southern in origin and character. Even in the Northern cities the lower class of Negroes is largely made up of recent migrants from the South and of their children. Both economically and culturally the Southern origin projects into present time the attitude and behavior patterns from slavery to a great extent. Lower class Negroes have kept more of the mental servility and dependence of the slave population and developed less resourcefulness, self-reliance and sense of individual dignity. Their situation is not favorable for developing strong incentives to personal accomplishment and improvement. Standards of industry and honesty are generally low. Judged by American standards, their family life is disorganized and their sexual morals are lax.[b] Aggression and violence are neither rare nor censored much by community disapproval.[c] They are the group most subject to lack of legal protection in the South, and they probably have least respect for law and justice as it is applied in that region.[d]

Before the Civil War, ignorance and isolation probably kept most of the slaves accommodated to their inferior caste status. The bulk of this group remained in the lower class after the War. As the intimate servant-master relations have been progressively broken up, Negroes became increasingly resentful, in a sullen and concealed way, and behind their caste mask often manifested bitter resignation and suspicion against the whites. Some of them have been looked upon by the whites as the "good old darkies," but others are turning into "bad niggers," likely to fight back.[34] Their strangeness is increasingly felt. This process has gone much further in the North than in the South and, in the South, further in urban districts than in rural ones.

This Negro lower class is, to reiterate, not homogeneous. In respect to security of employment and level of income, but more fundamentally to variations in family circumstances and individual endowments and propensities, some are falling below the average class norm and some are managing to keep above. To a section of the lower class belong the chronic relief cases, the habitual criminals, prostitutes, gamblers and vagabonds. It is a matter of definition and, partly, a matter of unemployment cycles, where the dividing line is to be drawn. In some cases, a gambler will have the prestige

[a] Concerning occupational status, unemployment and relief, incomes and levels of living, see Chapters 15 and 16.

[b] See Chapter 43, Section 2.

[c] See Chapter 44, Section 2.

[d] See Part VI.

and wealth of a person in the middle or upper class, and during the depression of the 'thirties, the majority of the Negro population became either
actual or potential relief clients. For the rural districts, Charles S. Johnson
emphasizes rightly that a distinction should be made between the "folk
Negro" and the rest of the lower class. The "folk Negro" has a low degree
of assimilation to modern American standards but has, nevertheless, some
measure of family organization and internal group cohesion.[35] In the upper
levels of the lower class, there are many persons who have definite ambitions to better their own, or at least their children's, status. These people
will take care not to let their insurance lapse; they will have more permanent affiliation with churches and lodges; they will try to keep their children
in school. It is again a matter of definition as to how large a portion of the
Negro lower class should be included in this sub-group.

At the other end of the social status scale is the small Negro *upper class*.
In rural districts the ownership and successful management of a sizable
farm may be said to give a person upper class status. All over the country
the training for a profession or the carrying on of a substantial business,
particularly in the field of banking or insurance, but also in contracting, real
estate, and personal service, is the regular basis for an upper class position.
In smaller communities even today, and previously also in big cities, every
steady employment where some training or skill was required, and the
income was substantially above the average among Negroes, conferred
upper class status. Employment by public agencies, particularly federal
agencies like the United States postal service, has always carried high social
esteem in the Negro community, and if coupled with some home ownership
and some education, usually put the person in the upper class. Generally, in
the absence of wealth, higher education is becoming practically an essential
to an upper class position.[36]

Often family background is stressed in this class. The family is organized
upon the paternalistic principle, legal marriage is an accepted form, and
illegitimacy and desertion are not condoned. Children are shielded as far as
possible both from influences of the lower class Negroes and from humiliat-
ing experiences of the caste system. They are ordinarily given a higher
education and assisted to acquire professional training. As Negroes are
commonly believed to be loud, ignorant, dirty, boisterous, and lax in sexual
and all other morals, good manners and respectability become nearly an
obsession in the Negro upper class. If the community offers a choice, they
will tend to belong to Episcopal, Congregational, or Presbyterian churches,
or, in any case, to those churches where there is less "shouting" and where
the preacher also has some education and refinement. In Southern cities the
Negro upper class will often adhere more closely to strict puritanical
standards of conduct than the white upper or middle class.[37] In the larger
cities, however, the younger generation in the upper class shows allegiance

to the modern American fashion of being "smart" and "sporting." Conspicuous consumption in automobiles, dresses, and parties carried on with "good taste"—is becoming of increasing importance and may even supplant respectability as the major characteristic of upper class status.

The Negro upper class is most thoroughly assimilated into the national culture, but it is also most isolated from the whites.[a] They are the most race conscious. They provide the leadership and often almost the entire membership of the nationally established Negro defense organizations, such as the local branches of the N.A.A.C.P.[38] But they sometimes feel great difficulty in identifying themselves with the Negro masses whose spokesmen they are,[39] although, perhaps, no more than the white upper class with the white lower class. *The Negro upper class is characterized by many of the traits which are in complete contrast to those of the masses of Negroes in the lower class.* Their social ambition is to keep up this distinction. In private they are often the severest critics of the Negro masses. Their resentment against the "lazy, promiscuous, uneducated, good-for-nothing" lower class Negro is apparent to every observer. W. E. B. Du Bois talks about the "inner problems of contact with their own lower classes with which they have few or no social institutions capable of dealing."[40]

But their small numbers in rural districts and small cities of the South and the segregation everywhere enforce physical proximity to the lower class Negroes and make isolation difficult. The Negro masses, further, usually form the basis for their economic position and their income: usually they cannot afford too much exclusiveness. Moreover, they think of themselves, and are thought of by all other Negroes and by the whites, as the "Negro élite," membership in which confers the presumption of local leadership. This ties them spiritually to the protective Negro community. "Though the upper class is relatively small in numbers, ... it provides the standards and values, and symbolizes the aspirations of the Negro community; being the most articulate element in the community, its outlook and interests are often regarded as those of the community at large."[41] Not only as a basis for its economic livelihood but also as a sounding board for its role of leadership, the Negro upper class needs contact with the Negro masses. They have their social status and, indeed, their existence as an upper class only *by virtue of their relationship to the lower classes of Negroes.*

The conflict in their attitudes toward the lower class creates a tension and confusion in the political convictions of the upper class. Their wealth and security tend to make them conservative; their extreme dependence on the lower class forces them to sympathize with reforms which would aid the

[a] See Chapter 30, Section 2. This fact does not, however, prevent upper class Negroes from occasionally enjoying class solidarity over the caste line with upper class whites. See Davis, Gardner, and Gardner, *op. cit.*, p. 53; John Dollard, *Caste and Class in a Southern Town* (1937), p. 83; and Hortense Powdermaker, *After Freedom* (1939), p. 338.

lower class—and, therefore, themselves indirectly. Negro doctors, for example, have reasons to be against socialized medicine, as do many white doctors, since they might lose some of their clients. But they stand to profit enormously if the government should use Negro doctors to treat Negro patients under a socialized set-up.[a]

The Negro *middle class* is usually assumed to be larger than the upper class but smaller than the lower class.[b] There would be a good deal of difference of opinion among experts as to what occupations were associated with middle class status. They have usually achieved a small but, in comparison with the lower class, less insecure occupational position, but are characterized even more by a striving toward a better economic position. Usually they have had primary or secondary education, but few have been to college except the school teachers. Education has a high ranking in their scale of social values, and they want to give their children this means of fuller cultural emancipation. They also look down on the lower class Negroes and attempt to appear' respectable. Thrift, independence, honesty and industriousness are included in their standards. In the middle class, it becomes a proud boast never to have been in trouble with the law. Their family life is rather stabilized. Even if many of them are married under common law,[c] these marriages tend to be relatively stable. Extra-marital relations are not uncommon, at least for the men, but it is expected that affairs shall be carried on in decent secrecy. They are ordinarily energetic and loyal members of lodges and of churches—usually of the Baptist or Methodist variety.

In the bigger cities where prostitution, gambling, and other types of "protected" businesses reach considerable importance, there is, parallel to the ordinary "respectable" class structure, a less respectable, or "shady," class structure. Its upper class consists of the successful racketeers. The middle class may be said to consist of their lieutenants and the less successful independents. The lower class would then consist of hangers-on and petty criminals. Wealth and power is the main criterion of status in this society.

---

[a] See Chapter 15, Section 4.

[b] This arbitrary assumption would have an empirical justification if, as we assumed, the class pyramid has a tapering point and concave sides. See Section 1 of this chapter.

[c] There is a divergence of opinion among those who have studied the matter as to whether the middle class among Negroes tends to have formal marriage or only common-law marriage. Those who say that the Negro middle class tends to have legalized marriage probably consider that the middle class contains people occupied in skilled work and business. They are also probably thinking of Negroes in the North. We follow Powder-maker (*op. cit.*, pp. 152-153): "In the middle class, licensed marriages are few." We regard the middle class as consisting of mainly semi-skilled workers and workers in the "higher" service occupations, and we are giving main emphasis to conditions in the South. Practically all experts agree that the Negro middle class family is fairly stable, even where it has common-law marriage (see, for example Dollard, *op. cit.*, p. 87; E. Franklin Frazier, *Negro Youth at the Crossways* [1940], p. 278).

Education, family background, and respectability have no significance. The upper and middle classes of this shady society have a certain prestige with the lower classes of the general Negro society in the cities. For this reason, vice and crime can appear as a desirable career to almost any lower class urban youth. This shady Negro society has a parallel in the white world, but the shady white society probably has less general prestige.[a]

The foregoing picture of the Negro class structure is, like most other descriptions, static. Actually, however, the Negro class structure is dynamic: not only is there movement between the classes and changes within each of the classes, but also the entire class system is moving upward. We have set forth our specifications for a study of class structure and the Negro community, which takes into account this dynamic perspective, in Appendix 8.

[a] See Chapter 14, Section 10.

Part IX

LEADERSHIP AND CONCERTED ACTION

CHAPTER 33

THE AMERICAN PATTERN OF INDIVIDUAL
LEADERSHIP AND MASS PASSIVITY

1. "Intelligent Leadership"

Despite the democratic organization of American society with its emphasis upon liberty, equality of opportunity (with a strong leaning in favor of the underdog), and individualism,[a] the idea of leadership pervades American thought and collective action. The demand for "intelligent leadership" is raised in all political camps, social and professional groups, and, indeed, in every collective activity centered around any interest or purpose—church, school, business, recreation, philanthropy, the campus life of a college, the entertaining of a group of visitors, the selling of a patent medicine, the propagation of an idea or of an interest. As a standard demand it appears with great frequency in public speeches and newspaper editorials and will seldom be absent even when the social reformer or the social scientist speaks.

If an ordinary American faces a situation which he recognizes as a "problem" without having any specific views as to how to "solve" it, he tends to resort to two general recommendations: one, traditionally, is "education"; the other is "leadership." The belief in "education" is a part of, or a principal conclusion from, the American Creed.[b] The demand for "leadership" plays on a different plane of his personality. It is a result less of a conscious ideological principle than of a pragmatic approach to those activities which require the cooperation of many individuals. For this reason it is also much less a part of Americans' self-knowledge. While the democratic Creed and the belief in education are an ever present popular theory with highest national sanctions—held conscious not only by affirmative references in practically every solemn public utterance, but also maintained by an ever growing literature—it will be found that Americans in general are quite unaware that the leadership idea is a particular characteristic of their culture. Since the leadership concept—though, with a quite different import—has recently become associated with fascism and nazism, it is

[a] See Chapter 1.
[b] See Chapters 1 and 41.

understandable that Americans regularly show a marked reluctance to admit the fact even when it is pointed out by the observer.

What Americans display in their demand for leadership are primarily the general traits of their culture which may be referred to as individualism and romanticism. The ordinary American has a liking for the personal and the dynamic in collective activity, a longing for the uniquely human, the unexpected, the adventurous. He wants changes, and he likes to associate them with new faces. He hopes for individuals to step out of the mass, to find the formulas for directing the course of events, to take the lead. And he is prepared to create room for the exceptional individual's initiative. He is willing to gamble quite a bit on his choice. Not least important in his attitude toward the "outstanding" person is the inclination to be hopefully experimental. James Bryce observed:

> I doubt if there be any country [except the United States] where a really brilliant man, confident in his own strength, and adding the charm of a striking personality to the gift of popular eloquence, would find an easier path to fame and power, and would exert more influence over the minds and emotions of the multitude. Such a man, speaking to the people with the independence of conscious strength, would find himself appreciated and respected.[1]

In retrospect the American becomes rather pronouncedly a hero-worshiper. He usually conceives of the American Revolution as the deed of a group of outstanding, courageous and resourceful individuals. The Republic has its "Founding Fathers," such as few other democratic nations have. In fact, the American dramatizes and personifies the entire history of his country and of the world. Social changes are rarely looked upon as the outcome of broad trends and deep forces. The long toils and seemingly blind moves of anonymous masses are pushed into the background of his world view.[2]

Like no other people, Americans have continually succeeded in creating popular heroes—national, local and professional. Outstanding individuals may become heroes while they are still living. In no other part of Western culture is it less true that "no one is a prophet in his own country and his own time." A rising leader in America has quite commonly the backing of his home town and his own group: the American ideas of "favorite son" and "local boy who made good" are significant indications of this trait of American culture.

American individualism and romanticism have, in this particular respect, a personality basis to operate upon, which, for want of a better term, we shall call "personal generosity." On the average, Americans show a greater kindness and patience with others than Europeans do. This attitude is a natural product of the opportunities on the frontier and, more generally, in a rapidly expanding economy. Americans worship success. This peculiarity has been the object of their own and others' ironical and often scornful comments. What has less often been pointed out is that this success cult in America is not particularly self-centered; instead it is generous. *Usually it is not in his own but in other persons' success that the ordinary American rejoices and takes pride.* He identifies himself with those who succeed. He is inclined to "jump on the bandwagon," as the American expression runs, to "be on the winning side."

Americans have thus come to develop an unmatched capacity for vicarious satisfaction in watching others fight. The immense and agitated crowds of spectators, who can always be counted on to fill the stadiums when a hard struggle is staged, testify to this, as does also the manner in which international and national news is presented by press and radio to suit the American public. In America, as everywhere else, ninety-nine out of a hundred do not "succeed," of course—or "succeed" only if the standards are set low. But the extraordinary fact is that these ninety-nine less successful individuals in America, when they see their own hopes disappointed and their ambitions thwarted, are less likely than similar individuals in other countries to retreat into sour chagrin. The individual who is rising in America is not held back much by the mortification of his fellows and compeers. Occasionally he may even be pushed ahead.

Let us not be misunderstood. Of course there is personal envy in America, too. But there has been decidedly less of it than in the more static, less "boundless" civilizations of the Old World. Luck, ability and drive in others are more tolerated and less checked in America. Climbing is more generally acclaimed. Leadership is more readily accepted.

2. "COMMUNITY LEADERS"

So it becomes more natural, and more possible, in America, to associate the dynamic forces of society with individuals instead of with masses. In the Negro problem it is evident to the observer that the "community leaders" are given an astonishingly important role. When the white people want to influence Negro attitudes or behavior in one direction or another— to get the Negro farmers to plant a garden around their shacks, to screen their windows, to keep their children in school, to cure and prevent syphilis, to keep Negroes more respectful to the whites, to prevent them from joining trade unions, and to frighten them against "outside meddlers" or "red" seducers—the natural device (besides the long-range one of "education") is to appeal to the "community leaders." These leaders are expected to get it over to the Negro masses, who are supposed to be rather passive.

There are, as we shall point out, special reasons in the caste situation for this practice. But more fundamentally *this is a common American culture pattern.* Caste accentuates it, but in the sphere of the Negro problem both whites and Negroes display a general attitude toward leadership and followership which permeates the entire American nation. It is incorrect to discuss Negro leadership except in this general setting. If we should study Negro leadership as an isolated phenomenon, we should be inclined to ascribe to the Negro people certain cultural characteristics which are simply American. Actually the Negro, in this as in so many other respects, because of the peculiar circumstances in which he lives, is an "exaggerated American."

For in all America it is assumed that every group contains leaders who control the attitudes of the group. Everywhere—not least in idealistic pursuits—the method of reaching a goal is assumed to be the indirect one of first reaching the leaders and, through them, influencing the masses. The leaders are organized locally in civic clubs of all sorts, and they are conscious of their role. They create a "public opinion," the peculiarity of which becomes apparent when, for instance, it is said about a strike which has failed, in spite of the fact that practically all the workers—making up the majority of the population—participate, that "local opinion did not favor the strikers," or even more explicitly that "public opinion suppressed the strike."

3. MASS PASSIVITY

The other side of this picture is, of course, the relative inertia and inarticulateness of the masses in America. The remarkable lack of self-generating, self-disciplined, organized people's movements in America is a significant historical fact usually overlooked by American historians and social scientists.

The new continent has always offered fertile soil for "isms," including every possible "European-ism" and, in addition, a great variety of home-grown ones. Communist societies have been built by Shakers, Rappites, Zoarites, True Inspirationists, and other sects, and by secularized Owenites and Fourierists. The Mormons experimented with polygamy, as well as with communism, and the Oneida Community with idealistic unchastity. Fantastic slogans of easy money and cheap credit, "ham and eggs," "thirty dollars every Thursday," "share the wealth," "every man a king," have inflamed local sections of opinion and startled the world.

America has had its full share of utopians and idealists, and much more than its due of charlatans and demagogues. America is also the country of countless associations.[a] For every conceivable "cause" there is at least one association and often several. De Tocqueville and Bryce observed this, and it is true today. Americans in the upper and middle classes are great "joiners" and "supporters" of all sorts of schemes for the common good. If a proposal makes sense to people, their participation and purse can be counted on. But somehow the associations seldom reach down to the masses

[a] See Chapter 43, Section 5.

of people. In spite of all this lively organizational activity, America has had few protracted zealous movements among the people. There has frequently been popular unrest among farmers and workers in America; they have been dissatisfied and have dimly felt the need of one reform or another. Occasionally there have been bloody clashes: resort to violence both by employers and by workers in settling labor disputes has, until recently, been rather characteristic of America. Undoubtedly a general influence on the course of national and local politics has been exerted by the masses through democratic elections. But for some reason these forces, working in the masses, have seldom crystallized into orderly mass organizations.

The trade union movement is one of the oldest in the world, but in America it has always been comparatively inconsequential. Even with the active support of the federal government during the 'thirties, instituting protective legislation unmatched in other democratic countries, it has not even reached the size of the peak unemployment.[a] The observer is struck by the importance played by salaried "organizers" and the relative unimportance of, or often the lack of, a spontaneous drive from the workers themselves. There has never been much of a cooperative movement in America. Often cooperatives are still petty neighborhood organizations based on the activity of the individual idealists—the "leaders"—more than on the concerted effect of cold economic reasoning and of the desire for independence and economic power on the part of the mass of consumers. The diverse activities collectively known as "adult education" in America are often laudable strivings to disseminate education among the common people by universities, philanthropic organizations, state and federal agencies, radio companies, or groups of enlightened community leaders. There is still little concerted drive for self-education in civic affairs. There is no spontaneous mass desire for knowledge as a means of achieving power and independence.

The passivity of the masses in America is, of course, a product of the nation's history. The huge immigration through the decades has constantly held the lower classes in a state of cultural fragmentation. They have been split in national, linguistic, and religious sub-groups, which has hampered class solidarity and prevented effective mass organization. Folk movements require close understanding among the individuals in the group, a deep feeling of common loyalty, and even a preparedness to share in collective sacrifices for a distant common goal. Only on a basis of psychological identification with the interest group is it possible to ask the individual to renounce his own short-range interests for the group's long-range ones. The immigrants have felt social distance to other lower class persons with different cultural origin. Also because they have difficulty in communicating

[a] The top estimate of union membership in 1940 was 9 million. Estimates of peak unemployment in 1933-1935 ranged between 10 and 14 million.

with other Americans, immigrants have had to have leaders for this purpose. Bent on accommodation to social and economic pressure and on individual climbing, they have been conditioned to be even more individualistic
than the native Americans.

The open frontier[a] and the relatively good prospects for every able and
energetic individual to rise out of the lower classes kept down social discontent. Perhaps even more important, this social mobility drained the masses
in every generation of most of their organizational catalysts. Few potential
"leaders" remained in the lower classes to stimulate their loyalty and to
organize their resistance against pressure. Since American industry was
organized as it was, it required no sinister intention of the industrial executive to promote the rising labor leader to personnel expert or labor manager
to the great advantage of the enterprise, but at the expense of weakening
the energy of the workers. The way into independent business was even
more open. If the workers wanted to keep a man under these circumstances,
they had to give him a salary which raised him much above their economic
and social level.[b] A similar process worked on the potential organizers of
cooperatives, farmers' movements and, indeed, every germ of concerted
action on behalf of the lower classes in America.

Cultural fragmentation, the division of interest of the lower classes, and
their loss of leaders, thus stamped the masses with inertia. They are accustomed to being static and receptive. They are not daring, but long for
security. They do not know how to cooperate and how to pool risks and
sacrifices for a common goal. They do not meet much. They do not organize. They do not speak for themselves: they are the listeners in America.
They seldom elect representatives from their own midst to Congress, to
state legislatures or to city councils. They rather support friendly leaders
from the upper strata, particularly lawyers. Labor politics in America has
constantly held to the common minority pattern of supporting parties and
individual candidates who favored them and of assailing candidates who
opposed them. Labor has never—except in a few localities—successfully
sought political power for itself. It has never seriously tried to plan to
utilize its large potential share of the electorate to capture the government
of the country. Farmers' politics has, in the main, followed the same
minority scheme. Farmers' organizations in America have constantly been
in danger of being run by the small top group of big farmers, who, most
of the time, have different interests from the mass of small farmers. Gener-

---

[a] Pioneer communities also had to depend heavily on leaders to maintain law and
order, and these leaders have often remained after the legal order was more firmly
established.

[b] In no other democratic country is the salary scale of trade union officials so differentiated and the higher brackets so high, compared with workers' income, as in America.

ally speaking, the lower classes in America have been inarticulate and powerless.

This is the more striking when the lower classes are compared with the "Pullman class," which had greater cultural homogeneity, more self-confidence, and more of a tendency to pool its power than a similar class in most other countries. There are closer ties and a more easy understanding between upper class persons in the various professions and businesses in this country than anywhere else. They travel more than in other countries; being together on a Pullman train brings people together intimately. They meet constantly for conferences. They are accustomed to being dynamic and courageous and to taking big risks. They know how to cooperate and even how to sacrifice for a common cause. They feel responsibility for the whole nation, as they view its interests, partly because they usually have a long line of American ancestry. The "Pullman class" has been fairly open to talent from below and has contained a disproportionate amount of the nation's brains and courage. Its members have been willing and prepared to take the leadership made so easy for them by the inertia of the masses.

For judging future possibilities, it is important to note that the era of mass immigration has ended. The proportion of foreign-born white persons in the population is decreasing from decade to decade: it was 12.5 per cent in 1920, 10.9 per cent in 1930 but only 8.7 per cent in 1940.[3] The other main factors behind the political inertia of the American masses—the open frontier and the easy escape out of the lower classes—are also disappearing. There is no longer any free land, and agriculture is depressed and likely to remain depressed. The modern organization of American industry is not favorable to small independent enterprise, and no lower class person can accumulate the huge capital necessary to start a large enterprise. The control of production from Washington during the present War is inevitably stepping up this movement to eradicate small independent business. The growth and improvement of education and the trend toward professionalization in all desirable occupations also has helped to eliminate the "self-made man" even in America. Ambitions for children are real, but they cannot compensate entirely for the lessened possibilities for climbing of the parents themselves.

The class barriers are thus becoming higher and more unyielding, at the same time as the cultural heterogeneity within those barriers is continuously decreasing. The masses receive a steadily improved general education and keep a greater number of their own potential leaders. These trends might make them active and articulate. For the time being, however, there are only minor indications of such a change. If and when it comes, it is destined to remake the entire public and social life of America.

The present observer is inclined to view the American pattern of individual leadership as a great strength of this nation, but the passivity of the masses as a weakness. These two cultural traits of America have, in their historical development, been complementary. But individual activity and mass activity are not necessarily antagonistic principles. It is possible to envisage a future development where the masses in America participate more intensively in political activities of various sorts, but where, nevertheless, outstanding individuals are permitted to have wide space for their initiative according to the great American tradition. Such a social system, if it ever developed, would realize in the highest degree the age-old ideal of a vitalized democracy. It would result, not only in a decrease in the immense class differences in America, but more fundamentally, it would effect a higher degree of integration in society of the many millions of anonymous and atomized individuals: a strengthening of the ties of loyalty running through the entire social fabric; a more efficient and uncorrupted performance of all public functions; and a more intense and secure feeling on the part of the common citizen of his belongingness to, responsibility for, and participation in the commonwealth as a great cooperative human endeavor—a realization of a fuller life.

4. The Patterns Exemplified in Politics and Throughout the American Social Structure

This is a dream—and a dream well in line with the ideals contained in the American Creed—but the American patterns of individual leadership and mass passivity are a reality that can be studied in all social spheres. They are, of course, particularly apparent in the political life of the nation. In both local and national politics the individual officeholder is—for the period he is in office—awarded much more power than he would be in democratic European nations. What is even more important, he is allowed and, indeed, expected to follow the inclinations of his personal drives and ideas much more unhampered by laws and regulations or particularly by continuous and democratic participation from the people.[a]

In local politics, America has, on the whole, not spread political responsibility upon countless citizens' boards, as have, for example, the Northern

---

[a] This is another and most important aspect of the relative lack of an independent and law-abiding administration, commented upon in Chapter 20, Section 2. It is also closely related to the fact that the American political parties do not correspond closely to the broad divisions of ideals and interests among the people.

This American party system breaks up the natural groupings based on the ideals and interests of the American electorate. It can itself be explained only by taking the passivity of the masses into account. On the other hand, it results in elections being fought relatively much more over personalities than over programs, which, in its turn, enhances the importance of the personality of the individual candidates. Another effect is that citizens, in the masses, are not being trained to have systematic, consistent, and stable political ideas, which also is likely to make the electorate more easily moved by individual leaders. Again we see a social mechanism adhering to the principles of cumulative causation in a vicious circle. See Appendix 3.

European countries (including England), thereby widening political participation and making politics more anonymous and less dependent on outstanding leadership. Much more, not only of broad policy-making, but also of detailed decisions are, in America, centralized in the offices of salaried functionaries. *Political participation of the ordinary citizen in America is pretty much restricted to the intermittently recurring elections. Politics is not organized to be a daily concern and responsibility of the common citizen.* The relative paucity of trade unions, cooperatives, and other civic interest organizations tends to accentuate this abstention on the part of the common citizens from sharing in the government of their communities as a normal routine of life.[a] In this essential sense American politics is centralized. The same is even more true of national politics.

The basic democracy, however, is maintained in spite of the extraordinary power awarded to the individual officeholders and the equally extraordinary lack of participation by the common citizens in the running of public affairs. *While American democracy is weak from the aspect of the citizens' sharing in political action and responsibility, it is strong in the ultimate electoral controls.* And there is logic in this. Several elements of what, from the other side of the Atlantic, looks like "exaggerated democracy" in American measures of popular contral may be explained as having their "function" in preserving for the common man the ultimate political power in this system of government where he participates so little in its daily duties.[b] It is this trait which prevents the delegation of such tremendous power to leaders and the hero worship from degenerating into fascism.

[a] It should be observed that this American pattern of nonparticipation in government, the historical explanation of which we have hinted at above, does not have its roots in the American Creed. The development came to run contrary to the hopes of Thomas Jefferson. In his desire for a decentralized government there was an expectation of the growth of a close and never ceasing democratic collaboration in community affairs. John Dewey has recently pointed out:

"His project for general political organization on the basis of small units, small enough so that all its members could have direct communication with one another and take care of all community affairs was never acted upon. It never received much attention in the press of immediate practical problems." (*Freedom and Culture* [1939], p. 159.)

[b] The great political power awarded the President of the United States is prescribed in the Constitution. But this is a formal explanation. The head of the state in other countries also often has, according to the constitutions, great powers, which in the course of development he has not been allowed to retain. In America it has fitted well into the general leadership pattern to let the President retain this great power. But he is elected by popular vote—the device for indirect election provided in the Constitution broke down nearly at the beginning. And—most important from our viewpoint—it became the tradition to restrict the period of office to two terms. Both the power concentration in the Presidency and the restriction of the power period to eight years are a direct outflow of the common American attitude of leadership. Contrariwise, the actual development of this central conspicuous power institution in American politics has undoubtedly had its influence in molding attitudes in all other political spheres and in the entire American culture.

Americans have thus such "exaggerated" democratic devices as frequent elections, long ballots (so that even minor officers can be elected), the initiative and referendum, short terms of office, prohibitions against running for a second or third term. The intensive and ruthless publicity focused upon all officeholders—which does not even spare their private life—serves the same "function" of making officeholding precarious. Finally, the American system of "checks and balances" has not only gone into the federal and state constitutions but has become deeply entrenched in the American attitude toward all power problems even outside politics proper. Americans are inclined to give not only much power but *overlapping power* to two or more officials or agencies and then leave it up to them to work out a *modus vivendi* through cooperation, mutual hamperings and occasional stalls.

The Roosevelt administration, with all its duplication of offices for the same or similar functions, exaggerates only somewhat an American tradition. In a lesser degree this is a trait which runs through the whole gamut of social institutions in America.

To the foreign observer this American pattern of power control, built upon systematic friction and actual competition of competent people, looks sometimes not only cumbersome but wasteful of energy and dangerous to reasonable efficiency of government. In a system where such extraordinary powers are constantly being delegated to the functionaries and where so little is held for the participation of the common men, this device, like the others mentioned, serves the "function" of keeping the executives within popular control. For when competing holders of power come in conflict and eventually stall, the ultimate arbiter is the electorate at the next election. It is to this arbiter—and, in advance, to "public opinion"—that they plead when they are in danger of getting stuck.

The patterns of strong and competitive personal leadership and weak followership, which we have exemplified for politics, permeate the entire social structure. In most of these other fields the popular check on the system—that is, the strong electionary system—is much weaker. This gives much greater power to leaders. In large sectors of the labor union movement it is thus a problem of how to avoid complete boss rule and how to preserve that minimum of democracy which consists in the leaders' being regularly elected and having to report to meetings of the common union members. When in recent years the question of industrial unions *versus* craft unions finally was brought before the public, it appeared as a fight between William Green and John L. Lewis. Cooperatives, when they infrequently managed to get securely established in America, often degenerated into ordinary business partnerships. Universities in America have never been controlled by the professors but by their presidents—not elected by the professors—and their appointed deans, subject to the control of boards of trustees who are outside and above the university. In modern business corporations in America, shareholders have lost their power to directors and other "insiders."[4] Even in small groups—civic committees, research projects, or Sunday schools—the same pattern prevails: the leaders run the show, the masses are passive except for an occasional election.

The general public interest in personalities and in short-run developments manifests itself in government and business as well as in other phases of life. In Washington and in Wall Street, as well as in the other American centers of power control, the perspective is predominantly that of actual happenings yesterday and tomorrow and of individual persons in the spotlight: What effect will this minor event have? What one person is behind what other person? What idea has caught whom?

One earlier observation should be reiterated. The idea and reality of leadership is not an object for much reflection in America; indeed, it is almost not part of conscious knowledge. There is no popular theory to explain it or justify it. It is not a fortified and preached ideology like the American Creed.[a] Not only the unsophisticated common citizens but also the social scientists have observed these facts without much questioning or evaluation. The patterns of leadership and followership simply exist as things which are a matter of course. They have not yet been detected to be important problems.

In the following chapter we want to present a typology—a schematic but, if possible, realistic guide to the leadership traits of America as displayed in the Negro community—in the hope that it will be useful both for immediate orientation and for framing new research into this important aspect of the Negro problem which concerns power and power relations.

[a] There is, of course, much emphasis on character building, and training for leadership in America. But it is not recognized openly that there can be only a few leaders and the desire for a few trained leaders is not organized into an ideology or popular theory.

CHAPTER 34

ACCOMMODATING LEADERSHIP

1. Leadership and Caste

The Negro world conforms closely to the general American pattern just described. In fact, the caste situation—by holding down participation and integration of Negroes—has the effect of exaggerating the pattern.

We base our typology of Negro leadership upon the two extreme policies of behavior on behalf of the Negro as a subordinated caste: *accommodation* and *protest*. The first attitude is mainly static; the second is mainly dynamic. In this chapter we shall ignore almost entirely the dynamic attitude of protest and discuss the intercaste relation in terms of social statics. The object of study here is thus the role of the accommodating Negro leader. Our analysis will approach fuller realism only when we, in later chapters, bring in also the protest motive. This reservation should be held in mind when reading this chapter.

Accommodation is undoubtedly stronger than protest, particularly in the South where the structure of caste is most pervasive and unyielding. In a sense, accommodation is historically the "natural" or the "normal" behavior of Negroes and, even at present, the most "realistic" one. But it is practically never wholehearted in any American Negro, however well adjusted to his situation he seems to be. Every Negro has some feeling of protest against caste, and every Negro has some sort of conflict with the white world. Some Negroes are primarily driven by the protest motive. Social changes which affect Negro attitudes—for example, the development of Negro education, caste isolation, class stratification, and the northward migration—are all giving the protest motive increasing weight, at the same time as the economic, political, judicial, and ideological changes in American society tend to give an ever wider scope for Negro protest. Both main motives—or any intermediate one composed of a blend of these two—have their main origin in, and take their specific character from, the caste situation.

2. The Interest of Southern Whites and Negroes with Respect to Negro Leadership

The white caste has an obvious interest in trying to have accommodating Negro leaders to help them control the Negro group. Under no circumstances, in any community where the Negro forms a substantial portion of the total population, are the attitudes and behavior of the Negroes a matter of no concern to the whites. Negroes may be robbed of suffrage and subdued by partiality in justice, by strict segregation rules, by economic dependence, and by other caste sanctions; but it makes a great deal of difference to the whites how the Negroes—within the narrow margin of their freedom—feel, think and act.

The whites have a material interest in keeping the Negroes in a mood of wanting to be faithful and fairly efficient workers. They have an interest in seeing to it that the Negroes preserve as decent standards of home-making, education, health, and law observance as possible, so that at least contagious diseases and crime will not react back upon the whites too much. In this particular respect, whites formerly under-estimated the community of interest which follows from being neighbors, but they are increasingly becoming aware of it.

Further, as we have seen, the whites in the South have a strong interest that Negroes be willing, and not only forced, to observe the complicated system of racial etiquette. Southern whites also see a danger in that Negroes are becoming influenced by certain social ideas prevalent in the wider society. They want to keep them away from "red agitators" and "outside meddlers." In most Southern communities the ruling classes of whites want to keep Negroes from joining labor unions. Some are quite frank in wanting to keep Negroes from reading the Constitution or studying social subjects. Besides these and other interests of a clearly selfish type, many whites feel an altruistic interest in influencing Negroes to gain improved standards of knowledge, morals and conduct.

As the contacts between the two groups are becoming increasingly restricted and formalized, whites are more and more compelled to attempt to influence the Negro masses indirectly. For this they need liaison agents in the persons of Negro "leaders." This need was considerably smaller in earlier times when numerous personal and, in a sense, friendly master-servant relations were in existence. These personal relations of old times are now almost gone.[a] This means that the whites have seen their possibilities of controlling the Negro masses directly—that is, by acting themselves as "Negro leaders"—much diminished. The whites have increasingly to resort to leaders in the Negro group. They have, therefore, an interest in helping those leaders obtain as much prestige and influence in the Negro community as possible—as long as they cooperate with the whites faithfully.

On the other side of the caste gulf, the Negroes need persons to establish contact with the influential people in the white group. They need Negro leaders who can talk to, and get things from, the whites. The Negroes in

[a] See Chapter 30, Section 2.

the South are dependent upon the whites not only for a share in the public services, but individually for small favors and personal protection in a social order determined nearly exclusively by the whites, usually in an arbitrary fashion. The importance of Negro leaders to the masses of Negroes—as to the whites—is also increasing as it is becoming more rare for Negroes to have individual white friends to appeal to when they are in danger or in need of assistance.[a]

Under these circumstances it is understandable that the individual Negro who becomes known to have contact with substantial white people gains prestige and influence among Negroes for this very reason. Correspondingly, an accommodating Negro who is known to be influential in the Negro community becomes, because of this, the more useful to the whites. The Negro leader in this setting serves a "function" to both castes and his influence in both groups is cumulative—prestige in the Negro community being an effect as well as a cause of prestige among the whites. Out of this peculiar power system, a situation develops where Negro leaders play an even more important role than is usual, according to the common American pattern.

3. IN THE NORTH AND ON THE NATIONAL SCENE

In the North fewer white people are in a position where they have to care much about how the Negroes fare, or what they think and do. The Negroes, on their side, have the protection of fairly impartial justice and of the anonymity of large cities. They also have the vote and can press their needs in the regular fashion of American minority politics. They are, therefore, decidedly less dependent on accommodating leaders to court the whites. For neither of the two castes does the Negro leader fill such important functions as in the South.

But the pattern of pleading to the whites through their own leaders, who are trusted by the whites, is firmly rooted in the traditions of Southern-born Negroes who make up the great majority of adult Negroes in the North. Northern Negroes, also, are a poor group and are frequently in need of public assistance and private charity. They are discriminated against in various ways, particularly with respect to employment opportunities. They live in segregated districts and have few contacts with white people in most spheres of life. Though they have the vote, they are everywhere in a small minority. For all these reasons many of the Southern attitudes and policies in regard to Negro leadership can be observed to continue in the North.

[a] Factors which are decreasing the importance of accommodating Negro leaders to the Negro masses in the South are, on the other hand: the raised standards of legal culture in the region, the increasing professionalism and independence in state and local government administration, and particularly the growth of federal assistance and control. (See Parts V and VI of this book.)

Isolation breeds suspicion among Negroes against the majority group. And suspicion is, in fact, justified. For isolation bars the growth of feelings of mutual identification and of solidarity of interests and ideals in both groups. A white man's purposes when stepping down to lead Negroes must be scrutinized carefully before he can be trusted. This is a pragmatic truth obvious even to the most unsophisticated Negroes, and it has a basis in the Negro people's history through centuries. Northern Negroes will thus be reluctant to listen to white people with a thorough trustfulness and an entirely open mind. Indeed, they are able to give freer play to their suspicion than Southern Negroes as they are less controlled and dependent. Too, the growing race pride exerts its influence in this direction. Northern Negroes, therefore, also seek the intermediation of leaders from their own group.

On the white side, those politicians, public officials, philanthropists, educators, union leaders, and all other white persons in the North who have to maintain contact with and exert influence upon the Negro group must sense this suspicion. They usually also find the Negroes strange in many ways. Negroes seldom constitute the main interest in their various pursuits. They welcome the Negro leader as a great convenience, therefore, as a means of dealing with the Negroes indirectly.[1]

The Northern situation, however, is different from the Southern situation in two closely coordinated respects: (1) that the white majority is not motivated by an interest solidarity against Negroes, reaching practically every white individual,[a] and (2) that the Negro minority is not cramped by anything like the formidable, all pervasive, Southern system of political, judicial and social caste controls. One effect of this difference is that the Northern situation gives greater opportunity for the protest motive to come out in the open and not only, as in the South, to contribute its queer, subdued undertones to the pretended harmony of accommodation.[b]

A number of circumstances make the Negro look to the North in his national political interest. National power is centered in the North. In national politics the South is quite like a minority group itself—a "problem" to the nation and to itself—politically, economically and culturally. Negroes have the vote in the North. For these reasons the relations between whites and Negroes in national affairs tend to conform more to Northern than to Southern local patterns. But Negro leaders are needed. The Negro people are set apart; they have distinctive problems; and they are hardly represented at all in the policy-forming and policy-deciding private or public organs. The federal government and its various agencies, the political parties, and the philanthropic organizations have difficulty in reaching Negroes through their normal means of public contact. They must

[a] See Chapter 2, Section 8.
[b] See Chapters 35 and 37.

seek to open up special channels to the Negro people by engaging trusted Negroes as observers, advisers and directors of Negro opinion. The Negroes feel the same need for "contact" persons of their own.

The individual Negroes who are appealed to in the national power field immediately win great prestige in the Negro world. To deal with Negro leaders who have great influence among the masses of Negroes is, on the other hand, a great asset to the white-dominated national organizations, including the federal government. Fundamentally the same causal mechanism, therefore, operates in the national realm of intercaste relations as in the Southern or Northern local community.

4. THE "GLASS PLATE"

In the sphere of power and influence—in politics proper and outside of it, locally and nationally, in the South and in the North—the population thus becomes split into a white majority and a Negro minority, and the power relations running between these two blocs are concentrated and canalized in special liaison agents in the minority bloc. Whites who want to deal with the Negro masses do not have to go among them directly as they have to go among, say, Episcopalians. But it is, of course, just as difficult, and, in fact, more difficult, for Negroes to have direct contacts with the white population. Corresponding to the Negro leaders, there are white leaders.

The isolation implied in caste means thus, in the realm of power and influence, that *intercaste relations become indirect from both sides. Direct contacts are established only between the two groups of leaders, acting on behalf of the two blocs.* Except for those individuals, the invisible glass plate, of which Du Bois spoke,[a] is in operation. Common whites and blacks see each other, though usually only as strange stereotypes. But they cannot hear each other, except dimly. And they do not understand what they dimly hear from the other side of the glass plate. They do not trust and believe what they perhaps understand. Like two foreign nations, *Negroes and whites in America deal with each other through the medium of plenipotentiaries.*[b]

In a sense the white leaders have, from the Negroes' point of view, a similar "function" of acting as liaison agents to the Negro bloc. But there is this difference between the two groups of leaders: the white leaders are not "accommodating." They are not acting as "protest" leaders, either. The entire axis between the two extreme poles of accommodation and protest, which sets the orbit of Negro attitudes and behavior, exists only on the

[a] *Dusk of Dawn* (1940), pp. 130-131. Quoted in our Chapter 31, Section 2, p. 680.

[b] There are, of course, the exceptions of master-servant relations, but they are decreasing, and they have always been treated as exceptions. There are also the exceptions in the academic and artistic worlds, but they are few. (See Chapter 30, Section 3.)

Negro side. The white leaders' "function" to serve as liaison agents with Negroes is only incidental to their power in white society. Unlike the Negro leaders they have, in addition, to run the whole society. This is a consequence of all the power being held on the white side. The Negroes do not, therefore, pick their white agents in the same manner as the whites choose their Negro ones. The Negroes cannot confer much power upon whites of their choice. In the South they do not partake in the selection of even political leaders. The Negroes—through their leaders—have to accept the white leadership as it exists, determined exclusively by the whites. They have to try to "get in" with the ones who are already on top in white society.[a]

To this a few qualifications must be made. First, in some Southern communities white persons, distinguished by birth, education, or wealth, who have prestige but do not care to exert active leadership generally, may occasionally be induced to step in and use their potential power in favor of the Negroes or one individual Negro. When Negroes turn to such a person they might be said to pick him as a white leader for their purposes. The assumption is, however, that he already has latent power. The Negroes do not award him influence by selecting him, as whites do when they pick a Negro leader. He has, rather, to be careful not to assist the Negroes too often and too much, as this might wear out his prestige. He might even become known as a "nigger lover," which would be the end of his usefulness to the Negroes.

Second, some white persons actually specialize in becoming the fixers and pleaders for Negroes while they are not active as white leaders generally. They are the white interracialists of the South. In order to have protracted influence they require moral and financial backing from Northern philanthropists or, lately, from the federal government.[b] They should, in addition, preferably have upper class status because of birth, education or occupation. Even when they have both Northern backing and Southern status their influence in matters affecting Negroes is likely to be uncertain and narrow in scope. Acclaim from the Negroes is usually more a result of their activity than a basis for the assumption of it.

In the North, the fact of Negro suffrage means that in the sphere of politics proper Negroes participate in selecting the white officeholders (and occasionally add some Negro representatives). Support from Negroes,

---

[a] It is true that, according to Southern aristocratic traditions, to have Negro dependents—who, in servant fashion, display gratitude and attachment—gives status in white society. Negroes are, therefore, in the position to deliver something to the white leader which has social significance. But in the Southern caste situation, the Negroes will have to be prepared to pay this price to practically any possessor of white power and influence who asks for it.

[b] See Chapter 21, Section 5.

therefore, means something in the North. Their opposition might occasionally turn an election against a candidate. The actual and the still greater potential significance of the Negroes' sharing in the political power in the North has been discussed in Chapters 22 and 23. Negroes are, however, only a tiny minority everywhere in the North. Even if the difference from the South is enormous, Negroes are, most of the time and in most respects, dependent on white leaders who do not feel dependent on Negro opinion.

This is, generally speaking, still more true in other power spheres than in politics proper; for example, in philanthropy, in educational institutions, in professional associations. Poverty and cultural backwardness generally prevent Negroes from having practically any primary power over the selection of white leaders in these fields. An exception is the labor movement. In so far as unions are kept open to Negroes, and where unions are democratic, Negroes have their due portion of power much according to the rules in politics. National power relations are much like those in Northern communities.

The following discussion will deal only with Negro leaders. It must never be forgotten, however, that Negro leaders ordinarily do not deal with the white people but only with white leaders. Negro leaders are, in fact, even more isolated from the whites in general than are the white leaders from the Negroes. We shall find, however, that some of the protest leaders actually do try to reach white public opinion. Walter White, and the whole set-up of the N.A.A.C.P., is steadily hammering at the glass plate, as did James Weldon Johnson and W. E. B. Du Bois before him and Frederick Douglass still earlier. Such an effort is effective practically only on the national scene. The carefully worded "letters to the editor" by Negroes to liberal Southern newspapers, which are sometimes printed—reminding the whites of their Constitution, their democratic faith and their Christian religion, and respectfully drawing their attention to some form of discrimination—represent local attempts in the same direction.

The direct approach by Negroes to the white world stems almost entirely from the protest motive. The accommodating Negro leaders generally do not even attempt to reach white public opinion directly. On the national scene, Booker T. Washington and, after him, Robert R. Moton were exceptions. But Moton's errand, when disclosing to the general public "what the Negro thinks," was to give vent to a protest, modified by acceptable and soothing words, and, in a degree, the same can be said of Washington. Washington's main motive, however, was accommodation *for a price*. This was his message in the Atlanta speech of 1895 and in countless other addresses to white audiences in the North and in the South, where he promised Negro patience, boosted Negro efforts, begged for money for his school and indulgence generally for his poor people. He had become a personality with prestige whose voice could pierce the caste wall. And he was freely allowed audience since he toned down the Negro protest. On the local scene the accommodation motive by itself does not usually encourage Negro leaders to such adventures of trying to reach behind the white leaders to the white people. and there is generally no white public which wants to listen to them.

5. ACCOMMODATING LEADERSHIP AND CLASS

Negro leadership—as determined by caste in the way we have sketched—stands in an even closer relation to class than does white leadership. In a previous part of this book,[a] we saw that Negro classes generally were mainly a function of caste. One ramification of this thesis was touched upon only lightly and spared for the present discussion of Negro leadership: namely, that an individual Negro's relation to white society is of utmost importance for his class status in the Negro community.

It always gives a Negro scientist, physician, or lawyer prestige if he is esteemed by his white colleagues. Prestige will bring him not only deference but also clients and increased earnings. The Negro press eagerly records and plays up the slightest recognition shown a Negro by whites. A professional position outside the segregated Negro world, even if unpretentious, also carries high prestige. Being consulted by whites concerning Negro welfare, taking part in mixed conferences or having any personal relation to individual whites confers status.[2] This common view in the Negro community is, of course, realistic. White standards are, on the average, higher, and an indication that whites recognize a Negro as having approached or reached those standards means most of the time that he is exceptionally good in his line. More important still, the whites have the power, and friendly consideration from whites confers power upon the individual Negro participating in such a relation. The belief that whites have power has been exaggerated in the Negro community, so that friendly relations with certain individual whites confer status upon a Negro even when these whites actually have no power.

The import of this is that *leadership conferred upon a Negro by whites raises his class status in the Negro community*.[3] Correspondingly, it can be stated that an upper class position in the Negro community nearly automatically, with certain exceptions that we shall note later, gives a Negro the role of Negro leader.[4] He is expected to act according to this role by both whites and Negroes. Because most upper class Negroes are leaders, there is an extraordinarily close correlation between leadership and class position in the Negro community. On the other hand, there are more lower class leaders among Negroes than among whites—partly because a much greater proportion of Negroes are lower class and partly because of the

[a] See Chapter 32.

tradition of a strong lower class preacher and lodge leader among Negroes. Still, we believe that practically all upper class Negroes are leaders, something that is not true among whites. In order to understand this, several other things must be considered.

For one thing, the Negro upper class is—because of caste—such a small proportion of the total Negro population[a] that the scarcity value of upper class status becomes relatively high. In smaller communities only a handful of persons have upper class status; in all communities they are few enough to be in close contact with each other.

The upper class Negro is, furthermore, culturally most like the group of whites who have social power. Under a long-range view, the social classes represent various degrees of acculturation to dominant American culture patterns or gradations of lag in the assimilation process.[b] During this process standards of living have been raised, illiteracy and mortality rates have declined, the patriarchal type of family organization has made its influence felt, and, generally, white American middle class norms and standards have been filtering downward in the Negro people. The upper class represents the most assimilated group of Negroes. In part, they have status in the Negro community for the very reason that they are culturally most like upper class whites. It is natural also that upper and middle class whites feel most closely akin to this group of Negroes.

The attitude of whites in the Old South was, on the contrary, that the lowly "darky" was the favored and trusted Negro, while the educated, socially rising "Negro gentleman" was to be suspected and disliked. When a social stratification in the Negro people first appeared during slavery, the whole complex of legislation to suppress the free Negroes, to hinder the education of slaves, and to check the meetings of Negroes was expressly intended to prevent Negro individuals of a higher status from leading the Negro masses, and, indeed, to prevent the formation of a Negro upper class. The inclinations of white people remained much the same after the Civil War.[c] The Jim Crow legislation followed a similar tendency.[d] The white masses even today are usually most bitter and distrustful toward upper class Negroes.[e] This is still often the expressed opinion also of the upper class whites who are in control of the political and social power in Southern communities.[f]

But even in the South it has become more and more unfeasible to trust

[a] See Chapter 32, Section 4.
[b] We are referring to assimilation away from patterns in slavery, not patterns in Africa. See Hortense Powdermaker, *After Freedom* (1939), pp. 354, *passim*. See also Chapter 43, Section 1, of this book.
[c] See Chapters 10, 20 and 24.
[d] See Chapter 28, Section 4.
[e] See Chapter 28, Section 8.
[f] See Chapter 30, Section 2.

the Negro leadership to the lower class "Uncle Toms" of the old type. One reason has already been mentioned: the paternalistic personal relations in which they developed have decreased in frequency. There are fewer "good old darkies" available. Also, as wealth and education have become somewhat more attainable to Negroes, those who were favored with these things—the slowly growing upper class, who thus came to symbolize Negro advancement and race pride—supplanted the "darkies" in prestige in the Negro community. Even white backing could not entirely shield the "darkies" from ridicule and contempt on the part of the Negroes of superior wealth and education.

In this situation, the upholding of the old-time "darkies" as white-appointed Negro leaders would have implied an unyielding refusal to recognize the entire rising Negro class structure and the Negro's respect for education. It soon became apparent that such a policy would be ineffective and unrealistic. The development of a Negro upper class could not be checked: as we have pointed out, this class grew partly because of segregation itself. A protracted resistance to recognizing the growth of class stratification in the Negro community would also have run contrary to the dominant class pattern within American white society. By analogy a Negro class structure seemed the more natural as personal ties to white society became broken, and as the Negro group was more definitely set apart.

Finally, a large portion of the Negro upper class is actually appointed by the whites or is dependent for status upon the influential local whites. The whites soon learned that they could find as many "Uncle Toms" among Negroes of upper class status as among the old-time "darkies," and that educated persons often were much more capable of carrying out their tasks as white-appointed Negro leaders.

6. SEVERAL QUALIFICATIONS

Thus the whites accepted and strengthened the ever closer correlation between leadership and upper class status. But the correlation is still not perfect. Part of the explanation is the carry-over of old slavery attitudes among whites. I have observed communities, particularly in the Old South, where the leading whites have insisted on giving their ear even in public affairs to some old, practically illiterate ex-servant, while cold-shouldering the upper class Negroes. In the dependent situation of Southern Negroes, the Negro community is then willy-nilly compelled to use those old "darkies" as pleaders whenever the influential whites have to be appealed to.

Under such circumstances, a tremendous internal friction in the Negro community is likely to develop. The contempt of the upper class Negroes for the uneducated white-appointed "leaders" becomes increased by resentment born of a feeling of extreme humiliation. The "leaders," on their part, feeling the contempt and resentment of the "uppity" Negroes, often turn into thorough sycophants toward the whites and into "stuck-up" petty tyrants toward the Negro community.[5]

For reasons already touched upon, this arrangement is not the kind of leadership control of the Negroes which is most effective from the point of view of white interests. In the cases of this type I have observed, it has been apparent that the influential whites are motivated not only by their pride in adhering to traditional paternalistic patterns of the Old South, by their fear of ambitious capable Negroes, and by their personal liking for their favored "darkies," but also that they actually enjoy putting the Negro community in this situation. The humiliation of the "uppity" Negroes is, in other words, intentional.[a]

Such situations are becoming rare. I have observed, however, that another custom is still widespread everywhere in the South: to use servants, ex-servants, and other lower class Negroes as reporters and stool pigeons in the Negro community. Even if those spotters are usually not used in attempts to influence the Negroes positively, their spy activity and their being known "to be in with" white people give them a sort of power among their own people. Often they are utilized by the whites to "let it be known" in an informal way what the whites want and expect. This is a remnant of the old direct caste control. It is declining as employment relations are becoming more impersonal and as race solidarity in the Negro group is increasing.

More important reasons for an imperfect correlation in the South between leadership and upper class position are, however, certain facts within the Negro community itself. Many upper class Negroes do not care for the leadership role. It is true that they have superior status only in relation to the masses of other Negroes, and that they often depend economically on lower class Negroes as clients and customers. But they also may have a desire to isolate themselves from the Negro lower classes.[b] Many also do not have the easy manners, the engaging and spirited personality, and the ability to speak the language of "the people" necessary to approach and influence the Negro masses. Some have made themselves so personally unpopular with Negroes or whites that they cannot act as leaders.[6] Many are so filled by the protest motive that they feel a personal humiliation when this has to be put under cover in taking the role of accommodating Negro leaders. They retreat rather into the role of sullen, but personally watchful, individualists, nourishing hatred against the whites above them,

---

[a] This is an example of the element of sadism generally so visible in the white Southerners' paternalism. It is also reflected in the standard stories told and retold about Negro stupidity and immorality, always with an intense display of pleasure which the outsider does not feel.

[b] See Chapter 32, Section 4.

contempt for the Negro masses below them, and disgust—sometimes mixed with envy—for the accommodating Negro leaders beside them. Their "adjustment" is to "mind their own business."

In practically every Southern Negro community, there is this partial voluntary retreat of the Negro upper class from active leadership. Thus the common assumption among whites that upper class Negroes in general are leaders of their people is not quite true. Upper class Negroes pretend that it is true in order to gain prestige. It is also an expectation on the part of white community leaders who happen to know about them, observe their superiority in education, manners, standards, and wealth, and take their influence among the common Negroes for granted. It must always be remembered that the whites' actual knowledge about the Negroes in their own community nowadays is usually rudimentary. It is not unusual to find that a certain Negro has succeeded in impressing the local whites with an exaggerated belief in his actual influence among his own people.

More important than unwillingness or inability on the part of Negro upper class persons to play the leadership role is a more or less conscious repugnance on the part of the Negro lower classes against following them. "Too much" education often meets suspicion among lower class Negroes. Many Negro preachers, who usually do not suffer from over-education, have nourished this prejudice as they saw education draw people from religious faith and, particularly, from respect for themselves. The usual class envy between upper and lower class individuals in the Negro community is an ever present element in the situation, and is strengthened when, as in the case of the accommodating Negro leaders, the Negro protest against the whites cannot be invoked as a bond of race loyalty.[a]

The extreme result of this class conflict is that the Negro masses in the South—as well as large parts of the white masses in the same region —often become, not only as inactive as is necessary for accepting readily the leadership imposed upon them from the outside, but, indeed, so utterly passive that they simply do not care very much for anything except their animal demands and their personal security. Their economic, social, and cultural situation, as we have described it in previous chapters, makes this understandable. It is difficult indeed to reach the amorphous Negro masses at all, especially in rural districts.

It is often said that the Negro church and the fraternal and burial lodges are the only media by which those masses can be reached. The present observer is inclined to consider this statement as exaggerated in two directions: first, even the church and the lodges do not have a steady and strong influence on the lowest Negro classes; second, the Negro school, the Negro press, and the Negro professions are becoming vehicles which have considerable influence with the lower strata.

[a] See Chapters 35 and 37.

But there is enough truth in the statement to raise it above doubt that the Negro preacher—and, to a lesser extent, the lodge official—has more influence with the Negro masses than a white lower class preacher or lodge leader has with the white masses. The majority of Negro preachers and many local lodge leaders are not highly educated and do not belong to the upper classes. Particularly is this true of the ministers in the lower class churches and of the "jack-leg preachers," who are the ones who really reach down to the masses. Their uncouth manners, language,. and standards in general are assets in retaining a grip over lower class congregations. Negro ministers who are educated and who have upper class status actually often have to affect bad grammer and an accent and to use figures of speech taken from the cotton field and the corn patch in order to catch the attention of the masses and to exert some real leadership.[7] The great influence of the Negro preacher is exceptionally well known by the whites, and he is usually considered as a force for "good race relations," that is, for shepherding his flock into respect and obedience.[a] Such are the barriers to and inhibitions of the Negroes of upper class status in becoming effective mass leaders in the Negro community. But with these reservations—and keeping in mind that a large portion of the Negro masses is amorphous, utterly apathetic, and not "led" much at all, but more like Thomas Nelson Page's vision of a "vast sluggish mass of uncooled lava"[8]—it remains true that leadership and upper class status are strongly correlated in the South and that the tendency is toward an even closer correlation.

The author also has the impression that Negro leaders, more often than whites (among their own people), take on a rather dictatorial and paternalistic attitude toward their Negro followers. They seem to mimic, in a smaller degree, the role of the upper class white Southerner in his relation to his Negro dependents. There is often a considerable amount of bossing and ordering around in a Negro group assembled for any purpose. The Negro upper class person in a leadership position will often entertain the observer with much the same generalized derogatory statements about the common run of Negroes as white people use. When the Negro preacher in church starts out to elaborate the shortcomings of "the race," the implication of his being a Negro leader is most of the time apparent. The teacher's cadence when addressing children in the Negro school sounds more condescending than in white schools. The organization of life in Negro colleges seems to be definitely less democratic than in white colleges in America, even, and not least, when the staff of teachers is mainly Negro. The president in his relations to the

---

[a] The role of the preacher and the church as the pillars of caste observance among Negroes, but sometimes also as catalysts for the Negro protest, will be further discussed in Chapter 40.

professors and they in their relations to the students act more dictatorially and more arbitrarily.

7. Accommodating Leaders in the North

In the North, there has never been much love for the lowly "darkies" on the part of the whites. They have never felt much of an interest or inclination to lift poor, uneducated servants as leaders over the Negro community. There has been more acclaim of social climbing generally than in the South.[a] Almost from the beginning the Negro upper class was accepted by the whites, without resistance, as the source of Negro leaders.

On the other hand, probably a somewhat greater proportion of upper class Negroes in the North do not care for the responsibilities and rewards of being active Negro leaders. On the whole, the Negro masses are less passive. The preachers have, perhaps, rather less prominence as leaders and are, on the average, somewhat better educated and have a higher social status.

Negro suffrage in the North, however, creates space for a political leadership which, in order to be able to deliver the Negro vote to the party machines, must be chosen from people who really meet the common lower class Negroes. A good many of the petty politicians in Northern cities are lower class Negroes. Negroes who enjoy a sort of "upper class" status outside the respectable society—big-time gamblers, criminals, and so on—are often the machine lieutenants, precinct captains and bosses, or the "insiders" in the political game.

The odor of corruption and the connection with crime and vice which often surrounds American city politics, particularly in the slums, deter, of course, many upper class Negroes, as well as many upper class whites, from taking any active part in political leadership. This does not mean, however, that there is not a good deal of honest and devoted political leadership among Northern Negroes. It comes often from upper class Negroes. But proportionately the upper classes monopolize less of the actual leadership in local politics than in other fields. And the labor unions, which are stronger in the North, are training a new type of lower or middle class Negro leader of particular importance in politics. They can there often compete successfully with the upper class leaders. They are just as often as honest and as devoted to the Negro cause as are the upper class leaders.[9]

On the national scene, upper class status and, particularly, considerable education and personal ability are necessary for Negro leaders.

[a] See Chapter 28, Section 9.

8. THE GLAMOUR PERSONALITIES

One peculiar angle of the relation between Negro leadership and social class is high-lighted in the popular glamour and potential power of a Negro who has accomplished or achieved something extraordinary, particularly in competition with whites.

Attainments are apparently given a relatively higher rating in the Negro than in the white community. The Negro press eagerly publicizes "the first" Negro to win this or that degree, to be appointed to one position or another, or to succeed in a business or profession formerly monopolized by whites. This tendency among a subordinated group living in a society dominated by strong competitive motives is entirely natural; it has a close parallel in the women's world. In fact, the entire Negro upper class gets peculiar symbolic significance and power in the Negro community for the very reason that it consists of persons who have acquired white people's education and wealth and who are engaged in doing things which are above the traditional "Negro jobs." They have broken through the barriers, and their achievements offer every Negro a gloating consolation in his lowly status and a ray of hope.

Under this principle every Negro who rises to national prominence and acclaim is a race hero: he has symbolically fought the Negro struggle and won. Great singers like Roland Hayes, Marian Anderson, and Paul Robeson have their prestige augmented by the eager vibrations of pride and hope from the whole Negro people acting as a huge sounding board. So have successful Negro authors like Richard Wright and Langston Hughes; scientists like George Washington Carver and Ernest E. Just; athletes like Joe Louis and Henry Armstrong; entertainers like Bill "Bojangles" Robinson, the king of tap-dancing, and Duke Ellington, the famous jazz band leader.

Any one of them could, if he chose, exert a considerable power as an active Negro leader in a technical sense. Jesse Owens, who at the 1936 Olympics established himself as the world's fastest runner and one of the greatest track athletes in history, was young and inexperienced, in fact not yet out of college. But on the basis of his specialized mastery of running and the acclaim accorded him in the white and Negro press, Owens was considered a valuable political asset and employed by the Republican party to attract the Negro vote.

The situation of the Negro glamour personality is, however—and this must be noted if we want to observe true proportions—not different from what is ordinary in white America. The popularity of the "first" or the "oldest," the "biggest" or the "smallest," the "best" or the "worst," the "only" or the "most ordinary" specimen of a type has always given its particular color to American conceptions of things and persons. It is characteristic of a young culture. Negroes are only following a common American pattern, which, as usual, their caste status leads them to exaggerate somewhat. The early history of Charles Lindbergh is a case in point. The white public also influences Negroes to expect too much from a Negro who achieves something in a particular field. All Negroes look alike to many whites, and whoever, by whatever means, comes before the public eye becomes regarded as an outstanding Negro and is expected to hold a position of unwarranted importance in Negro affairs.

It must also be noted that Negro celebrities—actually perhaps even more carefully than white ones in America—generally show great restraint in avoiding the temptation of stepping outside their narrow field of competence. Marian Anderson is a good example of scrupulous adherence to this rule. When Paul Robeson and Richard Wright sometimes discuss general aspects of the Negro problem, they do so only after study and consideration. These two have deliberately taken up politics as a major interest. They act then in the same spirit and the same capacity as, for instance, Pearl Buck when she steps out of her role as a writer of novels and writes a social and philosophical essay on the women's problem. Although the possibilities and the temptations have been so great, glamour personalities have usually not exploited Negroes or the Negro problem.

It may be suggested that in the Negro world, and specifically in Northern Negro communities, women have a somewhat greater opportunity to reach active leadership than in white society. Negro women are not so often put aside into "women's auxiliaries" as are white women. If this hypothesis is correct, it corresponds well with the fact of Negro women's relatively greater economic and social independence.

CHAPTER 35

THE NEGRO PROTEST

1. THE SLAVE REVOLTS

There has always been another type of Negro leader than the "pussy-footing" Uncle Tom. And there has always been another main motive than accommodation for practically all Negro leadership: both as part of the leaders' own intuitions and as a conditioning demand from their Negro followers and from their white supporters.

The leaders of the numerous local slave insurrections[1]—Gabriel Prosser, Denmark Vesey, Nat Turner, and many others, known and unknown—represented early types of pure protest leaders, "race men" in the modern popular Negro terminology. They rose against overwhelming odds and succumbed with their followers. Many plots to revolt were prematurely revealed to the white masters by Negro stool pigeons who sought to curry favor by their betrayal. The chief short-range result of the persistent series of slave rebellions or attempts at rebellion was an ever closer regimentation of free and slave Negroes.[a]

These race martyrs can be said to have laid the foundations, not only for the tradition of Negro protest, but also—because of their regular and conspicuous failure—for the "realistic" theory of race relations. This theory is favored by Southern white liberals and is accepted by the great majority of accommodating Southern Negro leaders; it holds that everything which stirs up the resistance of the whites will deteriorate the Negroes' status, and that reforms must be pushed quietly and in such ways that the whites hardly notice them before they are accomplished facts comfortably sunk into a new *status quo*.[b]

American Negroes, in attempting to integrate themselves into American society, have had to pay the price of forgetting their historical heroes and martyrs. Charles S. Johnson makes the following interesting observation:

. . . Denmark Vesey, a Negro who resisted slavery and led an insurrection in the effort to throw off the oppression, is a type which contradicts the assumption that

[a] See Chapter 24, Section 3, and Chapter 28, Section 3. The rise of militant Abolitionism in the North was a complementary cause.
[b] See Chapter 21, Section 5, and Chapter 38, Section 4.

Negroes are innately docile as a race and were content with slavery. In a sense, Vesey represents the spirit of independence for which the founding fathers of America are praised—an insurrection is merely an unsuccessful revolution. But Denmark Vesey is a symbol of a spirit too violent to be acceptable to the white community. There are no Negro schools named for him, and it would be extremely poor taste and bad judgment for the Negroes to take any pride in his courage and philosophy. There is, indeed, little chance for Negro youth to know about him at all.[2]

2. THE NEGRO ABOLITIONISTS AND RECONSTRUCTION POLITICIANS

The Negro fighters in the Abolitionist movement in the North—William G. Allen, Dr. James McCune Smith, Martin Delany, William Wells-Brown, Sojourner Truth, Robert Purvis, Samuel E. Cornish, Charles Lenox Remond, Henry Highland Garnet, David Ruggles, William Still, Harriet Tubman, Charles Bennet Ray, John M. Langston, Frederick Douglass, and many others—represented a second early crop of Negro protest leaders. Unlike the slave insurgents, these leaders set the future pattern on which Negroes based their protest. The new pattern consisted of nonviolent legal activities in accord with the democratic principles of the American Creed and the Christian religion. Frederick Douglass, the outstanding Negro leader of this period, in 1852, in his 4th of July oration at Rochester, voiced the Negro protest thus:

What to the American slave is your 4th of July? I answer: a day that reveals to him, more than all other days in the year, the gross injustice and cruelty to which he is the constant victim. To him your celebration is a sham; your boasted liberty, an unholy licence; your national greatness, swelling vanity; your sounds of rejoicing are empty and heartless; your denunciation of tyrants, brass-fronted impudence; your shouts of liberty and equality, hollow mockery; your prayers and hymns, your sermons and thanksgivings, with all your religious parade and solemnity, are, to him, more bombast, fraud, deception, impiety and hypocrisy—a thin veil to cover up crimes which would disgrace a nation of savages. . . .

You boast of your love of liberty, your superior civilization, and your pure Christianity, while the whole political power of the nation (as embodied in the two great political parties) is solemnly pledged to support and perpetuate the enslavement of three millions of your countrymen. You hurl your anathemas at the crown-headed tyrants of Russia and Austria and pride yourselves on your democratic institutions, while you yourselves consent to be the mere *tools* and *bodyguards* of the tyrants of Virginia and Carolina. You invite to your shores fugitives of oppression from abroad, honor them with banquets, greet them with ovations, cheer them, toast them, salute them, protect them, and pour out your money to them like water; but the fugitives from your own land you advertise, hunt, arrest, shoot, and kill. You glory in your refinement and your universal education; yet you maintain a system as barbarous and dreadful as ever stained the character of a nation—a system begun in avarice, supported in pride, and perpetuated in cruelty. You shed tears over fallen Hungary, and make the sad story of her wrongs the theme of your poets, statesmen and orators, till your gallant sons are ready to fly to arms to vindicate her cause against the oppressor; but, in regard to the ten thousand wrongs of the American slave, you would enforce the strictest silence, and would hail him as an enemy of the nation who dares to make those wrongs the subject of public discourse![3]

During the Civil War the Abolitionist leaders had to argue and protest for two years before Negroes were given the right and chance to do their share of the fighting. When they were finally allowed into the Union Army, it was for reasons of military necessity.[a] The Emancipation Proclamation was issued mainly for the same reason and in order to win over world opinion for the Northern cause. The War was finally won, and freedom materialized for the four million slaves.

> The mass of slaves, even the more intelligent ones, and certainly the great group of field hands, were in religious and hysterical fervor. This was the coming of the Lord. This was the fulfillment of prophecy and legend. It was the Golden Dawn, after chains of a thousand years. It was everything miraculous and perfect and promising. For the first time in their life, they could travel; they could see; they could change the dead level of their labor; they could talk to friends and sit at sundown and in moonlight, listening and imparting wonder-tales. They could hunt in the swamps, and fish in the rivers, and above all, they could stand up and assert themselves. They need not fear the patrol; they need not even cringe before a white face, and touch their hats.[4]

During Reconstruction, Frederick Douglass, P. B. Pinchback, John Langston, and others of the Negro Abolitionist tradition constituted the center of a much larger group of Republican Negro politicians. As they were on the winning side, and as not only emancipation from slavery, but suffrage and other civil liberties, had been accorded to the Negroes by Congress, not protest but power consolidation and power exploitation became their main concern. In many minor issues they actually often followed a most accommodating pattern.

When, however, Restoration of white supremacy violently robbed the Negroes of suffrage and civil liberties in the South, the reasons for Negro protest again mounted. In the North, however, there was no immediate parallel to Southern Restoration and consequently no special incentive to protest. Too, the Northern Negroes lost their white co-fighters. A great deflation of ideals occurred, as is usual after a successful war. In a spirit of opportunistic optimism and ideological defeatism the Northerners wanted to get back to normalcy. The Negro was a thorn in their flesh. He stood in the way of a return to national solidarity and a development of trade relations between the two regions. With some guilt, but probably more relief the Northerners found out, when the compromise between the regions was a *fait accompli*, that apparently they did not care much about the Negroes, anyhow. A whole series of scientific, historical, and political writings—

[a] Lincoln is reported to have said: "Without the Negroes' help, neither the present nor any coming administration can save the Union."

reaching into the present time—got under way to rationalize the national compromise of the 1870's.[a]

Northerners sought to protect their conscience partly by means of the humanitarian work carried on by the reformers and philanthropists among Negroes in the South. And with some valid self-righteousness the Yankees could point out that in the North the scattered Negro population kept its suffrage and civil liberties. But the Negro problem as a national issue was dead in the North. In the South the protracted process of legalizing political and social discrimination continued its course. There was nothing left for the Negro protest but to fight a losing struggle and to go underground.

3. THE TUSKEGEE COMPROMISE

In this great calamity for the Negro cause, Booker T. Washington stepped forward and established himself as the national leader of a pragmatic and conciliatory school of thought, to which a great number of national and local Negro leaders, particularly in the South, adhered.

It is wrong to characterize Washington as an all-out accommodating leader. He never relinquished the right to full equality in all respects as the ultimate goal. But for the time being he was prepared to give up social and political equality, even to soft-pedal the protest against inequalities in justice. He was also willing to flatter the Southern whites and be harsh toward the Negroes—*if* the Negroes were only allowed to work undisturbed with their white friends for education and business. But neither in education nor in business did he assault the basic inequalities. In both fields he accepted the white doctrine of the Negroes' "place." In education he pleaded for vocational training, which—independent of whether or not it be judged the most advantageous direction of schooling for the Negroes—certainly comforted the whites in their beliefs about what the Negroes were good for and where they would be held in the occupational hierarchy.[b] Washington did not insist upon the Negroes rights, but he wanted a measure of tolerance and some material assistance. Through thrift, skill, and industry the Negroes were gradually to improve so much that, at a later stage, the discussion again could be taken up concerning his rights. This was Washington's philosophy. To quote a typical statement of his:

> I believe the past and present teach but one lesson—to the Negro's friends and to the Negro himself,—that there is but one way out, that there is but one hope of solution; and that is for the Negro in every part of America to resolve from henceforth that he will throw aside every non-essential and cling only to essential,—that

[a] See Chapter 20, Sections 6 and 7.
[b] See Chapter 41, Sections 4 and 5.

his pillar of fire by night and pillar of cloud by day shall be property, economy, education, and Christian character. To us just now these are the wheat, all else the chaff.[5]

Kelly Miller gives a characterization of Booker T. Washington in contradistinction to Frederick Douglass, which sets these two Negro leaders in a frame of the two spiritual tendencies of American culture at large: the uncompromising spirit of the American Creed and the spirit of business realism:

The radical and conservative tendencies of the Negro race cannot be better described than by comparing, or rather contrasting, the two superlative colored men in whom we find their highest embodiment—Frederick Douglass and Booker Washington, who were both picked out and exploited by white men as the mouthpiece and intermediaries of the black race. The two men are in part products of their times, but are also natural antipodes. Douglass lived in the day of moral giants; Washington lives in the era of merchant princes. The contemporaries of Douglass emphasized the rights of men; those of Washington, his productive capacity. The age of Douglass acknowledged the sanction of the Golden Rule; that of Washington worships the Rule of *Gold*. The equality of men was constantly dinned into Douglass's ears; Washington hears nothing but the inferiority of the Negro and the dominance of the Saxon. Douglass could hardly receive a hearing today; Washington would have been hooted off the stage a generation ago. Thus all truly useful men must be, in a measure, time servers; for unless they serve their time, they can scarcely serve at all. But great as was the diversity of formative influences that shaped these two great lives, there is no less opposability in their innate bias of character. Douglass was like a lion, bold and fearless; Washington is lamblike, meek and submissive. Douglass escaped from personal bondage, which his soul abhorred; but for Lincoln's proclamation, Washington would probably have arisen to esteem and favor in the eyes of his master as a good and faithful servant. Douglass insisted upon rights; Washington insists upon duty. Douglass held up for public scorn the sins of the white man; Washington portrays the faults of his own race. Douglass spoke what he thought the world should hear; Washington speaks only what he feels it is disposed to listen to. Douglass's conduct was actuated by principle; Washington's by prudence. Douglass had no limited, copyrighted programme for his race, but appealed to the Decalogue, the Golden Rule, the Declaration of Independence, the Constitution of the United States; Washington, holding these great principles in the shadowy background, presents a practical expedient applicable to present needs. Douglass was a moralist insisting upon the application of righteousness to public affairs; Washington is a practical opportunist, accepting the best terms which he thinks it possible to secure.[6]

It is a political axiom that Negroes can never, in any period, hope to attain more *in the short-term power bargain* than the most benevolent white groups are prepared to give them.[a] This much Washington attained. With shrewd insight, Washington took exactly as much off the Negro protest—and it had to be a big reduction—as was needed in order to get

[a] See Chapter 23, Section 1, and Chapter 39, Section 13.

the maximum cooperation from the only two white groups in America who in this era of ideological reaction cared anything at all about the Negroes: the Northern humanitarians[a] and philanthropists and the Southern upper class school of "parallel civilizations."[b] Both of these liberal groups demanded appeasement above all. And *so the Southern conservatives were actually allowed to set the conditions upon which Washington and the Southern and Northern liberals could come to terms.*

But this was hardly Washington's fault. It is not proven that he could have pressed the bargain he made for the Negro people more in their favor. Remembering the grim reaction of the period, it is difficult to study his various moves without increasingly feeling that he was truly a great politician, probably the greatest one the Negro people have ever had. For his time, and for the region where he worked and where then nine-tenths of all Negroes lived, his policy of abstaining from talk of rights and of "casting down your buckets where you are" was entirely realistic. Even today it is still—in local affairs where the short-range view must dominate—the only workable Negro policy in the South. Charles S. Johnson points out: "Practically all Southern Negroes *accept* racial segregation."[7] As we have seen in previous chapters, practically all Southern Negroes have actually to accept much more, including disfranchisement and gross arbitrariness and laxity in justice.

It is a different question, however, if *under the long-range perspective* it was true statesmanship or, more specifically, if it was all the statesmanship that was called for by the interests of the Negro people. The only reason why this problem needs to be raised is the fact that *Washington was not only a national Negro leader, but actually held a virtual monopoly of national Negro leadership for several decades.* Had this not been so, it is natural that a division of responsibility would have worked itself out, so that different individuals and groups would have taken care of the long-range and the short-range interests. The actual course of policy would have become the result of discussion and interaction between them. This view will be given considerable weight when, in Chapter 39, we come

---

[a] As an example of how far Northern humanitarians had left the Abolitionist tradition by 1900, see the speech of W. H. Baldwin to the American Association of Social Science ("Present Problems of Negro Education," *Journal of Social Science* [December, 1899], pp. 64-68). See also Chapter 21, Section 5, of this book.

[b] See Chapter 28, Section 4 and Section 8.

"A people, like a class, to advance must either be strong enough to make its way against all hostility, or must secure the friendship of others, particularly of those nearest it. If the Negro race in the South proposes, and is powerful enough to overcome the white race, let it try this method—it will soon find out its error; if not, it must secure the friendship of that race." (Thomas Nelson Page, *The Negro: The Southerner's Problem* [1904], pp. 306-307.)

to evaluate the different organized forces which are today shaping Negro policy.

4. THE SPIRIT OF NIAGARA AND HARPER'S FERRY

Among the Negro intellectuals, particularly in the North, Washington and the gradually fortified "Tuskegee Machine" met severe criticism.[8] It became vocal in 1901 when two Negro intellectuals, Monroe Trotter and George Forbes, began the publication of the Boston *Guardian*.[9] W. E. B. Du Bois soon was drawn more and more from his brilliant scientific pursuits,[10] and became the leader of this protest group. In *The Souls of Black Folk* (1903) he gave literary form to a philosophy antagonistic to Washington's. Du Bois demanded full social and political equality for Negroes, according to the Constitution, and complete cultural assimilation. And he offered his demands not as ultimate goals but as a matter of practical policy of the day.

In the summer of 1905, twenty-nine Negro intellectuals met at Niagara Falls (on Canadian soil, since they met discrimination in the Buffalo hotel at which reservations had been made for the conference). They had high hopes of forming a national protest organization with branches in the several states to wage a battle against all forms of segregation and discrimination, and, incidentally, against Washington's gradualist and conciliatory policy, which, they considered, sold out Negroes' rights for a pittance and even broke their courage to protest. A generation later, Du Bois, when writing his autobiography, gives the following concentrated expression to this criticism:

> At a time when Negro civil rights called for organized and aggressive defense, he [Mr. Washington] broke down that defense by advising acquiescence or at least no open agitation. During the period when laws disfranchising the Negro were being passed in all the Southern states, between 1890 and 1909, and when these were being supplemented by "Jim Crow" travel laws and other enactments making color caste legal, his public speeches, while they did not entirely ignore this development tended continually to excuse it, to emphasize the short-comings of the Negro, and were interpreted widely as putting the chief onus for his condition upon the Negro himself.[11]

The Niagara movement held two more meetings—one at Harper's Ferry —and issued proclamations. But it never grew to be anything more than a feeble junto. It had against it Booker T. Washington and all his Negro and white friends, and it was not discreet for ambitious young Negroes to belong to this movement.

The Niagara movement represented the first organized attempt to raise the Negro protest against the great reaction after Reconstruction. Its main importance was that it brought to open conflict and wide public debate two types of Negro strategy, one stressing accommodation and the other raising the Negro protest. Booker T. Washington and W. E. B. Du Bois became national symbols for these two main streams of Negro thought. Two groups of followers assembled behind them.

> Between these two groups there were incessant attacks and counter-attacks; the former declaring that the latter were visionaries, doctrinaires, and incendiaries; the latter charging the former with minimizing political and civil rights, with encouraging opposition to higher training and higher opportunities for Negro youth, with giving sanction to certain prejudiced practices and attitudes toward the Negro, thus yielding up in fundamental principles more than could be balanced by any immediate gains. One not familiar with this phase of Negro life in the twelve—or fourteen—year period following 1903 (the year of publication of *The Souls of Black Folk*) cannot imagine the bitterness of the antagonism between these two wings.[12]

Ray Stannard Baker, writing in 1908, observed: "It has come, indeed, to the point where most Negroes of any intelligence at all have taken their place on one side or the other."[13]

During this period, a pattern of Negro thinking and Negro controversy became established. I have found—particularly in the South, where conditions have changed less than in the North—that this discussion still goes on among intellectual and professional Negroes in much the same terms as at the beginning of the century.[a]

The agitation did not, for a long time, seriously encroach upon Booker T. Washington's power position. But he had increasingly to concede a place before the Negro public to astute critics of his conciliatory policy and to proponents of a more militant course of action. And he had to watch his own words and deeds carefully. He had, thereafter, to reckon not only with reactions from the whites, but also with reactions from the Negroes. As he grew older he increasingly took on symbolic dignity in his personal appearance. He also became more interested in stressing the principal demands of Negroes for ultimate equality. The irritation between the two groups remained, but when he died in 1915 he had moved considerably toward his opponents. And he knew that he no longer spoke alone for the whole Negro people. Robert R. Moton, his successor as head of the Tuskegee Institute—and symbolic conservative Negro leader in the eyes of the whites—could still less claim to be the sole Negro leader. Also, under the influence both of the criticism from the Du Bois group and of much changed conditions, he came increasingly to move toward an ideology which incorporated and expressed the Negro protest in cautious but no uncertain terms. Du Bois, on his side, had become prepared to accept

---

[a] Commenting upon this observation recently, a prominent Negro social scientist, well acquainted with Negro education in the South, remarked that the Washington-Du Bois controversy gives the Negro teacher in Southern high schools and colleges, where he has to watch carefully all his words, a protective historical front and an irreproachable excuse for discussing Negro policy with his students.

segregation in practice if it meant greater material advantage for Negroes. For example, he accepted segregation in the Army in order to get any Negro officers among the fighting forces at all. But the First World War and the post-war development fundamentally changed the psychology of the Negro people and the basic conditions for both accommodation and protest.

By the year 1909-1910, the Niagara movement had ceased to be an effective organization.[14] At this time, however, the stage was already set for the National Association for the Advancement of Colored People, which we shall consider in Chapter 39, and the Niagara movement merged with it. The N.A.A.C.P. has, since its foundation, been the central organization of Negro protest, carried on in the spirit of the Abolitionists and in collaboration with Northern white liberals. But the protest motive has also gone—to a varying degree—into the policy of all the other Negro betterment organizations. It has, in fact, become part of the ideology of the entire Negro people to an ever increasing extent.

5. The Protest Is Still Rising

It cannot be doubted that the spirit of American Negroes in all classes is different today from what it was a generation ago. The protest motive is still rising. It is bound to change considerably the conditions under which Negro leadership functions.

The main factors in this development toward greater "race consciousness" and increasing dissatisfaction with the caste position will be dealt with in later chapters in so far as they have not already been touched upon. The Negro betterment organizations have themselves helped this development even when the Negro protest has not been their central theme. When Negroes are brought together to discuss and plan for any purpose, this by itself makes them feel a new courage to voice, or at least to formulate to themselves, their protest. They cannot avoid reminding each other of the actually existing reasons for serious complaints.

The Negro press, which is reaching ever deeper down into the Negro masses, has, as one of its chief aims, to give a national account of the injustices against Negroes and of the accomplishments and aspirations of Negroes. Its existence, its popular spread, and its content are a testimony of Negro unrest. Its cumulative effect in spurring race consciousness must be tremendous.

Negro churches and lodges often may have served an escape purpose by deflecting attention from worldly ills and by diverting social dissatisfaction. On a more fundamental plane, however, they are vehicles for a teaching which is equalitarian. Christianity is a radical creed, even if its radical potentialities are kept suppressed. These institutions also move along with their membership. Generally they tend to give respectability to a form of life which is bound to strengthen the protest motive. Occasionally they are even more active. The school, merely by raising the general educational level, tends to influence the Negroes even more strongly in the same direction.

Generally speaking, every agency working for assimilation of the Negro people in the broader American civilization, which is democratic in its fundamental values, is bound to strengthen the Negro protest against caste. And so even is every agency that brings Negroes together for any kind of political, economic or social discussion. The growing isolation, which we commented upon in an earlier chapter,[a] is itself partly an expression of the Negro protest. As caste isolation becomes perfected and as the general education of the Negro people makes caste less bearable, sullen race consciousness and acute dissatisfaction increase.

6. THE SHOCK OF THE FIRST WORLD WAR AND THE POST-WAR CRISIS

The upheaval in Southern agriculture prior to the First World War, the mass migration to cities and to the North, and the War itself, all acted as stimulants to the rising unrest of the American Negro people. Urbanization and mobility are inimical to the traditionally peaceful and innocent accommodation of rural Southern Negroes. The War, too, made the whites place a higher value on democracy as "the American way of life." As part of this revival of democratic ideology among the whites, there was a certain amount of talk about lack of democracy at home which must be eliminated. These developments raised vague hopes among Negroes, or at least tended to fix their own attention on their anomalous position in American democracy.

The Negroes wanted to fight in that War, too. And they were needed: 400,000 Negro men were drafted. But they often found themselves segregated in labor camps or as servants. They met discrimination everywhere and derogatory rumors about their behavior as soldiers were spread.[15] Some 200,000 Negroes went to France to fight, and so got a vision of the larger world. Everything that happened was eagerly reported by the Negro press and was widely discussed.

After the War the homecoming Negro soldier met the suspicions and fears of the Southern whites. In the North their new footholds in industry were contested by anxious white job-seekers in the post-war depression. A wave of lynchings swept the South, and even more bloody race riots swept the North. Without doubt the accumulated experiences during and immediately after the First World War were a most severe shock to the American Negroes and had lasting effects.[16]

[a] See Chapter 30, Section 2.

7. The Garvey Movement

After the end of the First World War, America witnessed the first and, as yet, the only real mass movement of Negroes—[a] *The Universal Negro Improvement Association*—organized by a remarkable West Indian full-blooded Negro, Marcus Garvey. Garvey was a prophet and a visionary. From his early youth he had consecrated his life to the Negro protest. He had made a first unsuccessful attempt to start a Negro protest movement in America as early as 1916. In 1918 he returned to America after a visit to Europe.

Garvey understood how to capitalize upon the growing dissatisfaction among American Negroes.[17] He renounced all hopes of any assistance or understanding from the American whites. The white Americans might fight to save the world for democracy and to protect the rights of oppressed minorities in Europe, he told his listeners, but they would continue to oppress their own minorities and particularly the Negroes in the South. They might condemn Germany for treating an international agreement as a scrap of paper, while they bluntly ignored their own Constitution in so far as Negroes' rights were concerned. Racial prejudice was so ingrained in their whole civilization that it was absolutely futile to appeal to their sense of justice and their high-sounding democratic principles. Negroes, therefore, had to assert themselves against the whites:

> Being subservient to the will and caprice of progressive races will not prove anything superior in us. Being satisfied to drink of the dregs from the cup of human progress will not demonstrate our fitness as a people to exist alongside of others, but when of our own initiative we strike out to build industries, governments, and ultimately empires, then and only then will we as a race prove to our Creator and to man in general that we are fit to survive and capable of shaping our own destiny.[18]

He also denounced practically the whole Negro leadership. They were all bent upon cultural assimilation; they were all looking for white support in some form or another; and they were all making a compromise between accommodation and protest. Within a short time he succeeded in making bitter enemies of practically all Negro intellectuals.[b] Against him were mobilized most leaders in the Negro schools, in the Negro churches, the Negro organizations and the Negro press. He heartily responded by naming them opportunists, liars, thieves, traitors and bastards.

Over their heads he appealed to the common Negroes, and especially to the darker Negroes. He exalted everything black. Black stood for strength and beauty, not for inferiority. He even declared God and Christ

---

[a] There have been other local mass movements of Negroes, but the Garvey movement is the only one that has been on a national scale.

[b] A few intellectuals did come over to Garvey—notably Emmett Scott and the Rev. Dr. George A. McGuire. (See Claude McKay, *Harlem* [1940], pp. 152 and 162.)

black to spare the Negroes the humiliation of worshiping the images of white men. He preached the purity of the race and condemned amalgamation. He gave Africa a grand history and instilled a new pride of ancestry among even the downtrodden lower class Negroes in America:

> But when we come to consider the history of man, was not the Negro a power, was he not great once? Yes, honest students of history can recall the day when Egypt, Ethiopia and Timbuctoo towered in their civilizations, towered above Europe, towered above Asia. When Europe was inhabited by a race of cannibals, a race of savages, naked men, heathens and pagans, Africa was peopled with a race of cultured black men, who were masters in art, science and literature; men who were cultured and refined; men, who, it was said, were like the gods. Even the great poets of old sang in beautiful sonnets of the delight it afforded the gods to be in companionship with the Ethiopians. Why, then, should we lose hope? Black men, you were once great; you shall be great again. Lose not courage, lose not faith, go forward. The thing to do is to get organized; keep separated and you will be exploited, you will be robbed, you will be killed. Get organized, and you will compel the world to respect you. If the world fails to give you consideration, because you are black men, because you are Negroes, four hundred millions of you shall, through organization, shake the pillars of the universe and bring down creation, even as Samson brought down the temple upon his head and upon the heads of the Philistines.[19]

The only hope for American Negroes was to flee this country of oppression and return to Africa. In solidarity with all the Negro peoples in the world, they should then build up a country of their own. Negroes should become a nation and have the opportunity to live under their own leadership and to develop their own culture.

> Wake up Ethiopia! Wake up Africa! Let us work toward the one glorious end of a free, redeemed and mighty nation. Let Africa be a bright star among the constellation of nations.[20]

He appealed to the League of Nations and took up negotiations with the Republic of Liberia. An army would eventually be needed to drive out the white usurpers: and so Garvey founded the Universal African Legion, The Universal Black Cross Nurses, the Universal African Motor Corps, the Juvenile, The Black Eagle Flying Corps—all with uniforms and officers. A steamship line also was needed: and so he sponsored the organization of the Black Star Line and purchased ships.

The Empire of Africa was formally announced in 1921, and Garvey was inaugurated President-General of the Universal Negro Improvement Association and provisional President of Africa. He ruled with the assistance of one Potentate and one Supreme Deputy Potentate and created a nobility of Knights of the Nile, Knights of the Distinguished Service Order of Ethiopia, and Dukes of the Niger and of Uganda. He staged parades and consecrated a flag for his organization: black, red, and green—"black for the race," "red for their blood" and "green for their hopes." In the devices of ceremony, ritual, and pomp, Garvey only followed the romantic patterns of American secret orders, but he certainly made more effective use of them. All members of his organizations, even if they were not officers or noblemen, were "fellowmen of the Negro race" and collaborators in a worldwide struggle to free Negroes and erect again the great African culture.

Garvey set up his organization with local branches and a number of subsidiary organizations. He traveled and agitated. He published the *Negro World* as the official newspaper of the movement. He organized cooperative enterprises—grocery stores, laundries, restaurants, hotels, printing plants. He built a big meeting hall, all under the auspices of the Universal Negro Improvement Association. During 1920-1921 the movement reached its peak. It was strong in many parts of the country. In spite of having practically all the intellectual and organizational Negro forces working desperately against him, he assembled the Negro masses under his banner.[a]

Eventually his movement collapsed. His various business ventures failed or involved him in legal tangles. The counterpropaganda became increasingly effective. The Universal Negro Improvement Association began to decline toward the end of 1921. He was finally imprisoned by federal authorities on the charge of using the mails to defraud in connection with the sale of stock for his Black Star Line. After a long legal contest during which he foolishly insisted on pleading his own case and turning the trial into a farce, he was finally sentenced in 1925 and brought to the federal prison at Atlanta, Georgia, as a convict. After two years, he was released and deported as an undesirable alien. He continued to agitate from the West Indies but without any success. In 1940 he died in London, poor and forgotten.

The law suit marked the end of his organization as an important mass movement among American Negroes, even though there are some living off-shoots in religious sects[b] and also in some less important protest organizations.[c] There must also remain memories in the Negro community. The precise nature of these are not known. "When the curtain dropped on the Garvey theatricals, the black man of America was exactly where Garvey had found him, though a little bit sadder, perhaps a bit poorer—if not wiser," is Ralph Bunche's conclusion.[21] But the thinking and the feeling of the Negro masses on this point remains a mystery.

[a] "It is impossible to give an accurate estimate of the total membership of Garvey's organization at its peak. Garvey gave the probably exaggerated estimate of 6,000,000 members. William Pickens, on the other hand—one of Garvey's bitter enemies among the Negro intellectuals—charged that the organization never enrolled as many as 1,000,000. Kelly Miller cited the figure of 4,000,000." (Ralph Bunche, "Programs, Ideologies, Tactics, and Achievements of Negro Betterment and Inter-racial Organizations," unpublished manuscript prepared for this study [1940], Vol. 2, p. 398.)
[b] See Chapter 40, Section 2.
[c] See Chapter 39, Section 2.

Du Bois, Garvey's arch-enemy whom he had solemnly "excluded" from the race, has this to say in retrospect:

> It was a grandiose and bombastic scheme, utterly impracticable as a whole, but it was sincere and had some practical features; and Garvey proved not only an astonishing popular leader, but a master of propaganda. Within a few years, news of his movement, of his promises and plans, reached Europe and Asia, and penetrated every corner of Africa.[22]

James Weldon Johnson comments:

> Garvey failed; yet he might have succeeded with more than moderate success. He had energy and daring and the Napoleonic personality, the personality that draws masses of followers. He stirred the imagination of the Negro masses as no Negro ever had. He raised more money in a few years than any other Negro organization had ever dreamed of. He had great power and great possibilities within his grasp. But his deficiencies as a leader outweighed his abilities.[23]

Fascinating as Marcus Garvey was as a political prophet and as a mass leader, *the response from the Negro masses is even more interesting*. Negro intellectuals, for understandable reasons, show certain inhibitions in dealing with the topic as do the white students of the Negro problem. But it is worthy of intensive historical investigation and careful reflection. For one thing, it proves that it *is* possible to reach the Negro masses if they are appealed to in an effective way. It testifies to the basic unrest in the Negro community. It tells of a dissatisfaction so deep that it mounts to hopelessness of ever gaining a full life in America. It suggests that the effective method of lining up the American Negroes into a mass movement is a strongly emotional race-chauvinistic protest appeal. Considering the caste conditions under which Negroes live, this is not surprising.

On the other hand, the Garvey movement illustrates—as the slave insurrections did a century earlier—that a Negro movement in America is doomed to ultimate dissolution and collapse if it cannot gain white support. This is a real dilemma. For white support will be denied to emotional Negro chauvinism when it takes organizational and political form. This problem will be taken up for further discussion at the end of Chapter 39.

8. Post-War Radicalism among Negro Intellectuals

While the Garvey movement had its spectacular rise and fall, many other things happened on the intellectual Negro front which did not have much immediate effect upon the Negro masses but did set the patterns for Negro intellectuals until the present time.

After 1917 an attempt was made to organize and release the Negro protest into a political movement allied to radical white labor. Such young Negro socialists as Chandler Owen and A. Philip Randolph started left-wing organs, the principal of which were the *Messenger*, the *Emancipator*.

the *Challenge* and the *Crusader*. They preached labor solidarity across the race line.[a] The Communists, to the left of this group, later appealed to the Negroes as an oppressed people under imperialist exploitation and promised "self determination for the Negro in the Black Belt," to be realized by the setting up of an independent black republic. The new republic should comprise those more or less contiguous areas in the South in which the Negro population is a majority.[24] This fanciful construction failed utterly to strike the imagination of the Negro masses and is probably part of the reason why the Communist party did not catch more Negro intellectuals.[b]

More to the right of the *Messenger* group was "the New Negro movement," a somewhat undefined term to describe an outburst of intellectual and artistic activity and a tendency to glorify things Negro in a creative way. Although it was somewhat chauvinistically Negro and although it was nurtured by Negro intellectual leaders—especially by Du Bois, as editor of *The Crisis*, Charles Johnson, as editor of *Opportunity*, and Alain Locke, editor of the representative volume, *The New Negro* (1925)—it was primarily a white-sponsored movement. For a number of reasons—partly connected with the northward migration and partly with post-war escapism —Northern city whites suddenly became fascinated by the "exotic" African in their midst. The hiring of the Negro to furnish amusement—in literature and art as well as in jazz bands and burlesque shows—was characteristic of the "whoopee" period of the 1920's. The movement had its serious side also, since outstanding artists used the African motif in their work. It was serious from the side of the producers, but not from the side of the consumers.

This white patronage—which brought money and fame (and notoriety) to a relatively small number of Negroes—gave the Negro masses the beginnings of respect for their potentialities and their heritage.[c] Although Northern white opinion of the Negro was probably permanently raised by the movement, it was primarily a fad to most whites. It crashed with the stock market in 1929, although it has left permanent effects on the artistic tastes and entertainment interests of whites in the North and throughout the world. With the decline of white support, the movement largely broke up among Negroes, but its nucleus—an implicit understanding between Negro artists and intellectuals—has remained in a modified form until the present day.

9. NEGRO HISTORY AND CULTURE

The 'twenties and 'thirties also saw the rapid growth of a movement to discover a cultural tradition for American Negroes. When Garvey exalted

[a] This important theory will be discussed in Chapter 38, Sections 5, 6 and 7.

[b] See Chapter 23, Section 2.

[c] More specific effects of the New Negro movement are discussed in Chapter 44, Section 5.

the historical background of the Negro people, he stole weapons from his enemies, the Negro intellectuals.

For a long time, even before the Civil War, diligent work had been going on to provide the Negro people with a respectable past. In a sense the numerous slave biographies—the most important of which was *Narrative of the Life and Times of Frederick Douglass*[25]—served such a purpose. Any Negro who emerges to prominence has usually had a remarkable life, and autobiographies have always played an important role among Negro writings.[a] Still more directly the searching of historical sources to unveil the deeds of Negroes in the American Revolution and in other American wars is part of this movement. So is also the eager attempt to reveal partial Negro ancestry of prominent individuals all over the world (Pushkin, Dumas, Alexander Hamilton and others).

Much of all this is zealous dilettantism, sometimes of a quite fantastic nature.[26] But increasingly it is coming under the control of historical methods of research. White historians have usually been biased by their preconceptions about the Negroes' inherent inferiority and by the specific rationalization needs these preconceptions have been serving.[b] Even apart from this, they have not had much interest in the Negroes except as objects of white exploitation and contests. The Negro people have, in their hands, become more a part of the natural resources or the scenery of the country. Negro historians see tasks both in rectifying wrong notions of the white historians and in concentrating upon the neglected aspects of the Negroes' history.[c] This movement was given impetus in 1915 by the organization of *The Association for the Study of Negro Life and History* and its chief publication, *The Journal of Negro History*. The moving spirit behind the organization, and the editor of the *Journal*, is Dr. Carter G. Woodson.[d]

---

[a] These Negro autobiographies have sometimes ranked among the classic American autobiographies. Besides Douglass' *Autobiography*, there is Booker T. Washington's *Up From Slavery*; James Weldon Johnson's *Along This Way* (his famous *Autobiography of an Ex-Coloured Man* is fictional); James D. Corrother's *In Spite of the Handicap*; Claude McKay's *A Long Way from Home*; Langston Hughes' *The Big Sea*; Du Bois' *Dusk of Dawn* (and, in a sense, several earlier books, including the tremendously influential *The Souls of Black Folk*).

[b] See footnote 32 to Chapter 20.

[c] An excellent illustration of the "protest" nature of Negro history is given by the fact that one of the popular books of this type has the title *The Negro, Too, in American History* (by Merl R. Eppse [1939]).

[d] Dr. Mary McLeod Bethune is the present president, and there are other officers and directors.

Dr. Woodson is also the leader of the whole modern Negro History movement. Lawrence Reddick puts it: ". . . the history of Negro historiography falls into two divisions, *before* Woodson and *after* Woodson." ("A New Interpretation for Negro History," *The Journal of Negro History* [January, 1937], p. 21.)

The articles in the *Journal* meet all standards of historical scholarship, at least as much as in other historical journals.

In spite of all scholarly pretenses and accomplishments, this movement is basically an expression of the Negro protest.[27] Its avowed purpose is to enhance self-respect and race-respect among Negroes by substituting a belief in race achievements for the traditional belief in race inferiority. As Reddick puts it, ". . . Negro History is quite different from the study of the Negro. Frankly, the former differs from the latter in that Negro History has a *purpose* which is built upon a *faith*."[28] Propagandistic activities go on side by side with the scholarly ones. Various devices are used to bring the findings of historical research before the Negro public. Since 1937, the Association has been publishing the *Negro History Bulletin* which is for a wider audience than the scholarly *Journal of Negro History*. Summaries of articles from both journals in popular style are furnished Negro newspapers. Popular pamphlets and books are sold by house-to-house agents in the Negro community.[29] Displays are prepared for various types of Negro gatherings. Contact is made with certain types of Negro clubs. Perhaps the most successful single device is "Negro History Week,"[30] during which the written and spoken word is applied with concentrated effort, especially to Negro school children. If the teacher is Negro and at all aware of the historical research, the Negro school child gets this new angle on the history of the Negro throughout the year, but during Negro History Week, the Association makes a special effort to reach all Negro children.

> Just as the white American school child is taught American history from the point of view of the American chauvinist, the Negro school child is to see it from the point of view of the black racialist.[31]

When we call the activities of the Negro History movement "propaganda," we do not mean to imply that there is any distortion in the facts presented. Excellent historical research has accompanied the efforts to publicize it. But there has been a definite distortion in the emphasis and the perspective given the facts: mediocrities have been expanded into "great men"; cultural achievements which are no better—and no worse—than any others are placed on a pinnacle; minor historical events are magnified into crises. This seems entirely excusable, however, in view of the greater distortion and falsification of the facts in the writings of white historians. As propaganda, "Negro history" serves the same purpose for historical periods as the Negro newspapers serve for contemporary life: they both serve as a counterpoison to the false and belittling treatment of the Negro in newspapers and books written by whites.

In one phase of their activities, Negro historians have the support of some white scientists. This is in the field of African culture, for which anthropologists have recently manifested a new interest and a new appreciation. It was a basic means of satisfying white men's needs to justify slavery and white superiority that the "dark continent" be regarded as a place of cultureless savagery. This tradition of African inferiority has continued in the white world long after the American Indian, the Polynesian, and the Stone Age man were given applause for high cultural achievement. Only recently have even the anthropologists realized that African Negroes have surpassed most other pre-literate groups in at least the fields of government, law and technology. The general white public still does not realize this, but during the New Negro movement of the 1920's there developed something of an appreciation for modified African music and art. One white anthropologist, Melville J. Herskovits, has recently rendered yeoman service to the Negro History propagandists. He has not only made excellent field studies of certain African and West Indian Negro groups, but has written a general book to glorify African culture generally and to show how it has survived in the American Negro community. He has avowedly done this to give the Negro confidence in himself and to give the white man less "reason" to have race prejudice.

> To give the Negro an appreciation of his past is to endow him with the confidence in his own position in this country and in the world which he must have, and which he can best attain when he has available a foundation of scientific fact concerning the ancestral cultures of Africa and the survivals of Africanisms in the New World. And it must again be emphasized that when such a body of fact, solidly grounded, is established, a ferment must follow which, when this information is diffused over the population as a whole, will influence opinion in general concerning Negro abilities and potentialities, and thus contribute to a lessening of interracial tensions.[32]

Aside from the question of admiring their past achievements, Negroes are faced with the question of whether they should attempt to build morale by glorifying their present achievements or attempt to raise standards by criticizing the present low ones. Almost all Negroes, at least among the youth, are agreed that some of the traits for which they are praised by Southern whites (loyalty, tractability, happy-go-luckiness) are not the traits of which they should be primarily proud.[33] But there are other alleged Negro traits that white men praise which present more of a dilemma to Negroes. These are the so-called special Negro aptitudes for music, art, poetry and the dance. Not only have jazz, the blues, and tap-dancing captured the popular entertainment world, but spirituals have been adjudged "America's only folk music," and a few Negro actors, singers and poets have been counted among the best. In certain branches of sports, too, Negroes have come out on top. Because of white applause, Negroes can take heart in these achievements and can use them to protest against discrimination.

But some Negroes have doubts about some of these things. They feel that it is unwise for Negroes to specialize in so few fields, but rather that they should put more effort into breaking into new fields. They feel that there is something of a "double standard" when the white man applauds—that some lesser Negro poets and actors are getting applause because they are Negroes rather than because they have outranked the whites in free competition. They know that achievements in some of these fields merely strengthen the harmful stereotypes, that Negroes are innately more emo-tional and unrestrained and animal-like. They believe that the spirituals are a "badge of slavery" and retain the memories of slavery in both whites and Negroes, and that emphasis on things African is emphasis on the prim-itive background of Negroes. Finally, they are afraid of the "parallel civilizations" theory held by some whites: that Negroes should retain "their own" cultural heritage and not lose it for the general American culture.[a] All these things—feels this small group of Negroes, mainly intellectuals— will not redound to the ultimate advantage of Negroes but will tie them more strongly into a subordinate position. But even they, like the rest of the Negroes, take vicarious satisfaction in the present-day achievements of individual Negroes, and in so doing express their protest against their subordinate caste position.[b]

10. THE GREAT DEPRESSION AND THE SECOND WORLD WAR

The Great Depression struck the Negroes even harder than it did the whites. Not only did they lose jobs in the cities in greater numbers than did whites, but many of those who retained employment—especially in agri-culture—were driven down to starvation wages. Movements like the Black Shirts were organized to deprive Negroes of what jobs they had. Unem-ployed Negroes, unlike many unemployed whites, had no savings upon which they could fall back in the crisis. Also stinging in its effects was the collapse of the "New Negro" movement in the arts and entertainment field; this had been giving many Negroes long-range hope for a raised status. Between 1930 and 1933 there was utter distress and pessimism among Negroes; practically the only ones with hope were the few who turned to communism.

Negroes were frankly skeptical of the new President, Franklin D. Roosevelt, because he was a Democrat, and because rumors were spread that he was ill and his death would see the elevation of John N. Garner, the Vice-President from the South, to the Presidency. In Chicago, typical of Northern cities where Negroes voted, only about 23 per cent of the

[a] For a discussion of the "parallel civilizations" theory from the viewpoint of the white proponents, see Chapter 28, Sections 4 and 8.

[b] These achievements also encourage some Negroes and help build up a "tradition of success," the lack of which has helped to keep Negroes down in the past.

Negro vote went to Roosevelt in the 1932 election. Yet they swung rapidly around and became the strongest supporters of his politics.[a] With their new admiration for the New Deal, Negroes experienced a lift in their hopes for themselves. Unemployment relief removed much of the economic suffering, at least in the North. The United States Housing projects, Farm Security work, and other federal activities helped some Negroes to reorganize themselves. Politically, the Negroes were stimulated by their release from the Republican party and by the presence of Negroes in advisory positions in many government agencies. Above all, they were thrilled by Roosevelt's appeal to the underdog and by the obvious friendliness toward Negroes on the part of the President and Mrs. Roosevelt. There had been no race riots for several years; lynchings reached a new low; Southern liberalism—with federal government support—seemed to be growing. All these things made the late 1930's a period of somewhat less despair and pessimism for Negroes than the early 1930's. But there was little long-range hope: Negroes had relief, but no jobs; and there was no significant improvement in their position on any other front.

When the United States entered the Second World War in December, 1941, Negroes were not optimistic as to what its significance for them would be. They knew that the democratic war aims were not meant for them. The memories of the riots that followed the First World War rankled in their minds. Their difficulties in getting into the armed forces and into war industry in the period of preparation for war convinced them that an increase of activities would only mean that there were more fields in which Negroes would be discriminated against. But there was more reason and more opportunity to protest. The democratic ideology stimulated by the War and the heroic example of the colored peoples of China, the Philippine Islands, and elsewhere, outweighed the emphasis upon "wartime unity and harmony," and gave the Negro protest an ear among the whites, at least in the North. These same things made the Negro want to protest more.

We shall have more to say on the influence of the present War upon Negro attitudes in the last chapter. We shall find that the Negro protest has risen higher than ever. It is possible that at a later stage of the War, when the white unemployment reserve is worked off, the Negroes will see their employment opportunity rise. It is also possible that the white liberals will be able to open the doors somewhat more in the armed forces. It is possible that some more specific promises of measures against discrimination, not only in the economic field, but also in justice, politics, education, and other public services will be given to meet the low morale of the Negroes and to allay the uneasy feeling of many whites when faced before the world with the inconsistency between their democratic faith and their

[a] See Chapter 23, footnote 8.

treatment of Negroes. It is even possible that some real start will be made toward fulfilling the promises. Whether any promises to the Negro are fulfilled or not, it can be predicted with a fairly high degree of certainty that *this War, when and if it is won, and its sour aftermath will act like the First World War did—as a great shock to the Negro people and as a stimulant to their protest.*

CHAPTER 36

THE PROTEST MOTIVE AND NEGRO PERSONALITY

1. A MENTAL RESERVATION

The Negro protest is shut in by caste. Most of it is doomed to be introverted and self-consuming. An uproar like the Garvey movement is likely only to make the Negro protest appear intrinsically the more hopeless afterward.

Negroes are only a tenth of the American nation. As an effect of the perfected caste controls, described in earlier parts of the book, their political and social power is much less than a tenth. Therefore, Negroes can never cherish the healthy hope of coming into power. A Negro movement can never expect to grow into a democratic majority in politics or in any other sphere of American life. And to escape from America is a fantastic dream from which Negroes always awake and find that they do not even want it to happen. There is a sense of hopelessness in the Negro cause. Meanwhile the individual Negro has to find his path through life as it is.

But there is no wholehearted acceptance of the present situation. Deep down in the most dependent and destitute classes of Negroes in the rural South, the individual Negro of the masses ordinarily keeps a recess in his mind where he harbors the Negro protest. In the lower classes, and wherever the caste controls are severe, it is usually framed in the Christian ideals of human brotherhood and all men's fundamental equality before God. Church and religion is a much needed front to give respectability and acceptability to the suppressed Negro protest. The world can safely be claimed to be wrong in the light of Christian ideals. The rich and mighty white people are the possessors of this unrighteous world. Sometime, somehow, the wrongs are going to be corrected and "the last shall be first and the first shall be last." There is not only consolation and escape in this religious teaching, but it also serves as a means of guarding the democratic faith in the minds of downtrodden black people. It gives a supreme sanction to ideas from the American Creed, ideas which are unrealistic and fantastic in the light of the actual situation. This is the Negro protest in its most concealed form. In the upper strata, and generally in the North, the Negro protest is much more clearly thought out and overtly expressed in social, economic and political terms.

On a high intellectual level one way of preserving human dignity in the face of outward humiliation is to follow the well-known formula of James Weldon Johnson:

> The pledge to myself which I have endeavored to keep through the greater part of my life is:
>
> I will not allow one prejudiced person or one million or one hundred million to blight my life. I will not let prejudice or any of its attendant humiliations and injustices bear me down to spiritual defeat. My inner life is mine, and I shall defend and maintain its integrity against all the powers of hell.[1]

2. THE STRUGGLE AGAINST DEFEATISM

This attitude is not so uncommon as one would think, even among Negroes of humble status. But with the individual Negro there is always a tendency for the protest to become bent into defeatism. Negroes on all class levels give vent to this spirit of defeatism in expressions such as "niggers ain't for nothing," "niggers ain't got a thing," "we're the under-dogs," "Negroes can't win," "there is just no hope for Negroes," "why bother?"

This cannot be said publicly, though. The protest motive does not allow it. No Negro leader could ever preach it. No Negro newspaper could print it. It must be denied eagerly and persistently. But privately it can be said, and it *is* said.

Sometimes—and this also in all classes—the blame will be put on Negro inferiority: "niggers are no good," "niggers have no guts," "Negroes lack courage," "Negroes are lazy," "Negroes have no foresight and persistency," "Negroes can't work for themselves," "black is evil." This agrees with what most white people believe and want to believe. To Negroes it repre-sents the old caste accommodation pattern. It kills ambition and makes low standards of morals and accomplishments seem natural for Negroes.[a] It is a convenient philosophy and may, in a sense, be necessary for a balanced personality.

But Negro inferiority cannot be admitted publicly. It has been the result of the rising Negro protest that there is, in nearly the entire Negro popula-tion, a *theoretical* belief that Negroes are just as highly endowed with inherent capabilities and propensities as are white people. An emphatic assertion of equality of the Negro people's potentialities is a central theme in the propagation of Negro race consciousness and race pride. "The Negro is behind the white man because he has not had the same chance, and not from any inherent difference in his nature and desires,"[2] has been a thesis which for decades every Negro leader has found it necessary to assert. Not only Negro leaders and educators but all whites who address Negroes in a

---

[a] See Chapter 9, Section 2, and Chapter 30, Section 1.

spirit other than the oppressive one find it always of greatest importance to combat what has come to be known as the Negro "inferiority complex." As we have shown, science has supported the Negro position of equal average endowment, and even prejudiced whites, with any sense of responsibility, no longer *publicly* state that Negroes are inherently inferior.[a]

To admit Negro inferiority is thus treason to the race. But the lives of Negroes are filled with disappointments. Equality in endowment is not visibly demonstrated in accomplishment, except rarely. Even Negroes who are articulately race conscious have their moments of tiredness when they slip back into the inferiority doctrine, in the same way as religious persons have their moments of doubt about the existence of a divine providence. The inferiority doctrine remains, therefore, as an ever present undercurrent in Negro consciousness which must constantly be suppressed. It creeps up in conversation, and it flavors the jokes, particularly when Negroes are among themselves. It provides the terms of abuse and insult in intra-Negro quarrels. It plays an important role in the relations between the classes in the Negro community. It is no longer—and this is a result of the Negro protest—an attitude of carefree complacency, but a complacency tainted with much bitterness.

3. THE STRUGGLE FOR BALANCE

The standard explanation of Negro failures, and the only one publicly accepted, is to place the responsibility upon the caste system and the whites who uphold it: "the whites are mean to Negroes," "white people won't give the Negro a chance," "the whites are keeping Negroes down," "the American caste system degrades Negroes to half-men," "all odds are against us," "Negroes meet unfairness everywhere." As the Negro protest is rising and is becoming popularized, the view becomes more and more widespread that white oppression and the caste deprivations are to be blamed and not Negro inferiority.

In a way, this theory is an attempt at a rational explanation of the low status of Negroes. It preserves self-respect and does not necessarily damage ambition. Many Negroes who strive hard to keep up and improve their status actually succeed in holding to this theory without mental conflict. They place themselves and their group in a true perspective. They measure their failures and accomplishments in realistic terms: of their own abilities, of the caste deprivations, and of the factor of pure chance (which is always of major importance in the individual case but is balanced out for the group). Such persons thus keep a balanced personality, but in a way that is more pretentious and less demoralizing, because less complacent, than the old caste accommodation. It may be said to be the goal of all Negro educa-

[a] See Chapter 6.

tion to adjust Negro youth to this balanced state of realistic conception of one's self and the world and of *accommodation under protest.*

The temptations are great, however, to lose this precious balance, either by falling into the bitter complacency of the inferiority doctrine referred to above or by overdoing the equality doctrine and trying to build up a strained case that black is superior to white.[a] A third temptation is to exaggerate the accusation against the whites and so use the caste disabilities to cover all personal failures. The growing isolation makes such a self-deception the more easy to accomplish and, indeed, difficult to avoid. The whites' race prejudice and the general fact of belonging to a group that is discriminated against provide a ready excuse for sub-standard performance and for beliefs which are just as effective as the old inferiority doctrine and personally less unflattering.

The effects, however, are even more thoroughly demoralizing. There is not only complacency but more comforting self-pity. There is also at times a cynical disregard for "the rules of the game" when dealing with white people in such extraordinary circumstances where they cannot, or are not inclined to, hit back and put the screws on.[b] This is an angle of the general problem of the double standard to which we shall return.[c] It has a Negro side—in so far as Negroes accept the easy escape, with or without acceptance of the inferiority doctrine also—and is thus not caused only by white forbearance and paternalism.

The caste pressures thus make it exceedingly difficult for an American Negro to preserve a true perspective of himself and his own group in relation to the larger white society. The increasing abstract knowledge of the world outside—of its opportunities, its rewards, its different norms of competition and cooperation—which results from the proceeding acculturation at the same time as there is increasing group isolation, only increases the tensions. When once off balance in one direction or the other, it is easy to lose stability and to slide to and fro among various contradictory attitudes. There is irritation and resentment involved in each of them, except in the old naïve and easy-going inferiority belief, which hardly exists any more because of the Negro protest. Normal individuals do not like to find irritation and resentment in themselves. It thus becomes opportune and, indeed, highly practical to try not to think too much about it. For "what is the use?"

[a] See Chapter 35, Sections 7 and 9; Chapter 38, Section 12; and Chapter 39, Section 2.
[b] I once heard a white official of a philanthropic agency, who had discovered some financial double-dealing of a Negro research worker, comment upon his decision just to forget about it in somewhat the following words: "We must remember that these people are held down in a subordinate class. When we lift up one of them and deal with him as one of us, how can we assume that he should deal with us as a gentleman?"
[c] See Section 5 of this chapter.

4. Negro Sensitiveness

The upper classes are in many ways better protected, but they feel humiliations more intensively. It requires hard and continuous struggle to overcome the effects of the deprivations and humiliations. The intensity of this struggle is suggested by the fact that often a small personal incident has the power suddenly to infuriate even those Negroes who pretend that they are not "race men." They feel overwhelmed by the discriminations and the prejudice. This is what is called Negro "sensitiveness."[3]

Referring to the South, Charles S. Johnson gives the following interesting analysis of why upper class Negroes are more sensitive:

> The greater sensitivity of the upper-class Negro to racial discrimination is attributable to two factors: (1) his greater familiarity with political and social thought, and (2) the contradiction between his personal achievements and his social position. The upper-class Negro is more aware of the regional variations in racial prejudice. He sees the race system of the South as a local phenomenon, while the less educated Negro is apt to regard white domination as part of the order of the universe. The upper-class Negro also feels himself entitled by training and ability to achieve a high social position in the community—a position denied by reason of race alone.[4]

Much of the Negro sensitiveness is centered around the word "Negro" and its several synonyms. Even the lower class Negro in the rural South feels insulted when he is called a "nigger" by a white man. The word is hated because it symbolizes what prejudiced white people think of Negroes. It is often used, however, between Negroes of all classes not only as an insult but often in friendly joking. But it is insulting if it is used by a white person. In Chapter 29 we have discussed other names and modes of address to which Negroes are sensitive. All these words suggest to Negroes that the white man who uses them regards Negroes as inferior, and in the South white men who use them usually do have this attitude and express it intentionally in the words. The large number of these words and special ways of addressing Negroes indicate why Negroes have much to be "sensitive" about.

Indeed, the entire racial "etiquette" and system of segregation in the South are taken as insults by the Negro. At every hand the Southern white man has given the Negro much to be sensitive about. The mere assumption by the Southerner that his deprecation of the Negro is not taken as an insult helps to make the Negro sensitive. Ray Stannard Baker tells of the following occurrence:

> I was lunching with several fine Southern men, and they talked, as usual, with the greatest freedom in the full hearing of the Negro waiters. Somehow, I could not help watching to see if the Negroes took any notice of what was said. I wondered if they were sensitive. Finally, I put the question to one of my friends: "Oh," he said.

"we never mind them; they don't care." One of the waiters instantly spoke up: "No, don't mind me; I'm only a block of wood."[5]

The constant insulting in the South has developed the trait of sensitiveness in some Negroes to an unusually high degree. There is much cause for sensitiveness in the North also, but sometimes certain actions of Northern whites are taken as insults by Negroes when no insult is intended. This is understandable, of course, in view of the mutual ignorance of the two races in the North, but it nevertheless makes for mental unhealthiness on the part of some Negroes.

In the lower classes the protest motive is weaker and the equality doctrine not practical. The desire to maintain personal dignity and the social pressure to keep up respectability are not so strong. It is possible to take a more cynical, and even exploitative, attitude toward white people's pretenses of superiority. Frazier tells us how lower class parents in Washington "caution their children to avoid conflicts, to ignore insults, and to adopt techniques for 'getting by.' These techniques include 'acting like a monkey,' 'jibbering,' flattery, and plain lying."[6] One Negro youth expressed himself thus:

> I'm always being told I can't do something because I'm a "nigger." I don't feel badly about it all. I know being a "nigger" there are things I can't do, places I can't go, but I feel that where some tell me something I can't do, somebody will tell me I can do something I want to do. So I don't mind trying and if you know how to flatter and "jive" white people, you can get farther than they expect "niggers" to go. I usually make a big joke of it and act the part of a clown. I generally get just what I'm after. After all, I think that's all white people want anyway. They just want "niggers," to recognize them as superior, and I'm the man to play their game. I don't care what he says or does as long as he kicks in. One thing sure, he wouldn't call me "nigger" down on Delaware Avenue. Then, too, I usually remember even if he lets you do things, he really doesn't want you to, and you're still a "nigger" to him. I don't feel badly about being told I can't do something because if he lets me hang around long enough, I'll get something out of him.[7]

Another Negro boy who gave about the same account confessed however: "I hate myself, every time I say 'boss' or 'coat-tail' a peckerwood."[8]

Frazier brings this attitude into relation with the fact that so many of the lower class families were born in the South, and Davis and Dollard, studying Southern Negro youth, inform us that "the role of entertainer and clown is a familiar one to lower-class people."[9] Without doubt it is less common in the Northern cities, and it is becoming less common everywhere. The pattern that is becoming generally approved is an attempt at voluntary withdrawal. This pattern has become perfected in the upper classes; it is spreading into the lower classes.ᵃ In the unavoidable contacts

ᵃ See Chapter 30, Section 2.

with whites, however, their prejudices, and in the South the racial etiquette, must be accepted with good grace in order to avoid trouble and to get along.

5. NEGRO AGGRESSION

But some Negroes will openly tell the interviewer that: "I just get mad when I think about it all." Some really "get mad" occasionally and hit at the whites in the fury of frustration.

In the growing generation of Negroes, there are a good many individuals like Bigger Thomas, the hero of Richard Wright's popular novel, *Native Son*. They can be seen walking the streets unemployed; standing around on the corners; or laughing, playing, and fighting in the joints and pool-rooms everywhere in the Negro slums of American cities. They have a bearing of their whole body, a way of carrying their hats, a way of looking cheeky and talking coolly, and a general recklessness about their own and others' personal security and property, which gives one a feeling that carelessness, asociality, and fear have reached their zenith. In some cities they are known in the Negro community by the appropriate epithet "cats."

Some few Negroes even outside the world of the "cats" consciously think out their aggression against the white caste, at least as a temporary flight of the imagination to relieve inner tension. Ralph Bunche testifies:

> There are Negroes too, who, fed up with frustration of their life here, see no hope and express an angry desire to "shoot their way out of it." I have on many occasions heard Negroes exclaim: "Just give us machine guns and we'll blow the lid off the whole damn business." Sterling Brown's "Ballad for Joe Meek" is no mere fantasy and the humble Negro turned "bad" is not confined to the pages of fiction, granted that he is the exception. The worm does turn and a cornered rat will fight.[10]

But physical attack upon the whites is suicidal. Aggression has to be kept suppressed and normally is suppressed. It creeps up, however, in thousands of ways. The whites do not get as wholehearted a response from their Negroes as they would if the latter were well satisfied with the necessity of accommodation. Not only occasional acts of violence but much laziness, carelessness, unreliability, petty stealing and lying are undoubtedly to be explained as concealed aggression.[11] The shielding of Negro criminals and suspects, the dislike of testifying against another Negro, and generally the defensive solidarity in the protective Negro community has a definite taint of hostility.

The truth is that *Negroes generally do not feel they have unqualified moral obligations to white people.* This is an observation which a stranger visiting around in the Negro communities cannot help making time and again. The voluntary withdrawal which has intensified the isolation between the two castes is also an expression of the Negro protest under cover.

A less dangerous outlet for aggression is to deflect it from the white caste and direct it upon other Negroes.[12] This means that the caste protest turns inward upon the Negro community. The lack of police protection in the Negro community and the leniency toward Negro offenders if they restrict their activity to other Negroes makes this outlet for aggression even more inviting.[a] There are no reasons to assume that Negroes are endowed with a greater innate propensity to violence than other people.[b] The excess of physical assaults—and of altercations—within the Negro community is rather to be explained as a misplaced aggression of a severely frustrated subordinate caste.[18]

This outlet is, however, prohibited in the Negro middle and upper classes where respectability is a supreme norm and fighting and squabbling are severely censored. Hindered by caste, prudence, and respectability from taking it out on either the whites or on other Negroes in blows and scoldings, they have to store up their aggression. This is probably another cause of their greater sensitivity. Some few find an outlet in organizational activity for the Negro cause.

6. Upper Class Reactions

Caste solidarity is founded upon the entirely negative principle that all Negroes find themselves enclosed together behind the same caste bar and bruise their heads against it. Caste does not allow any Negro, when he has raised himself above the rest—and even if he then hates them—to leave the group. This is a background against which the relation between the different classes in the Negro community should be viewed. It is convenient to distinguish these relations, as seen by the minute upper class, from the conception held by the Negro masses.

As has already been indicated, there are many upper class Negroes who try to escape from race and caste.[14] They have arranged a little isolated world for themselves and want to hear as little as possible about their being Negroes or the existence of a Negro problem. They make it a point not to read Negro papers or Negro books; they keep themselves and their children apart from "common Negroes." They try to share the conservative political opinions of the whites of similar class status; they often over-do this considerably. They despise lower class Negroes, and they balance the account by despising lower class whites too.

In a sense this is a type of accommodation. It relinquishes the Negro protest but it does not accept the inferiority doctrine, at least not in so far as it applies to themselves. When people who hold this attitude play up class, it is instrumental in allowing them to play down caste. To preserve their attitude they keep as far as possible from interracial situations where the reality of caste would become acute. But, since whites of their class do

[a] See Part VI.
[b] See Chapter 6.

not accept them, they are doomed to loneliness together with some few like-minded and like-classed Negroes.

The students at Negro colleges enjoy a particularly protected life for some years, and it will be found that often the entire campus, or at least the majority cliques, arrange their life according to this pattern of isolation from the whites and from the Negro masses. They ordinarily meet difficulties in keeping it up in later life when they have left college. But many will try. The observer finds in Negro communities everywhere individual families or clusterings of families of this sort; in the bigger cities they form small exclusive societies. By their escape into class they have, however, only succeeded in isolating themselves from the Negroes, but have not succeeded in integrating themselves into the wider world, either socially and economically or ideologically. Their personality situation is usually more cramped than that of ordinary members of the Negro caste. While making it a policy to overlook caste humiliations, some small incident may, as we pointed out, cause them to flare up in accumulated resentment.

Most upper class Negroes cannot sustain and cannot afford for economic reasons even to attempt the isolation from the Negro caste which this type of escape presupposes. They must *identify themselves with "the race."* But their class is also important to them. They often then try to take the whole "race" along in an imaginary escape into class. Many Negroes who by individual ability, hard work, or luck have succeeded in climbing the social ladder in the Negro community—often thanks to social monopolies created by the segregation and discrimination they protest against—feel satisfied with their own exceptional success only to the degree that they generalize it and think of it as applicable to the whole race. They are then inclined to minimize the handicaps the Negro caste labors under. There is a considerable amount of accommodation in this attitude. I have often met Negro upper class persons who have idealized their own life history and, on this ground, come to entertain totally exaggerated notions about Negro progress in recent time and Negro opportunities for the future.[a]

This attitude seems to be quite common among individualistic businessmen and professionals. They borrow the spirit of the ordinary local American chamber of commerce, boast of their accomplishments and opportunities, and assume that they apply to the whole Negro people. Successful Negro preachers and educators, and some white friends of the Negro, join in the choir as it serves the good purpose of encouraging the Negro people to clamp down on the Negro protest somewhat, and to make a less resentful, more positive attitude toward life possible for the young and the rising. But there is little basis in reality for this attitude. It also is an escape. The boaster often reveals that he, himself, is not unaware of the self-deception

---

[a] There are perfect parallels in the white world among "self-made men" who have risen from poverty.

he has made into a "race philosophy" by showing in one way or another that he actually considers himself as a great exception while common Negroes are classed as inferior.

This last view is more consistently displayed by many upper class Negroes in the South who studiously build up their careers by pleasing white people and acquiring their patronage. In private they are often as overbearing to common Negroes as they are weak and unassertive to the whites. But they, too, usually cannot stand absolute loneliness, and they, too, usually need the Negro masses as a basis for their economy. As trusted "white men's niggers" they also need Negro followers to earn the patronage of their white "angels." For these reasons they, too, will have to keep their superiority feelings somewhat camouflaged.

Between this last type, the "white man's nigger," and the next to the last, the Negro boaster, fall most of the balanced and well-adjusted upper class Negroes. The types are not rigidly demarcated: most individuals move, to a certain extent, from one type to another according to the situation and to their own mood at the moment.

7. THE "FUNCTION OF RACIAL SOLIDARITY"

All upper class Negroes, except the first type, who tries to escape "the race," have their status defined in relation to the Negro masses, and practically all depend upon the lower classes of Negroes for their economy and their social position. The Negro masses are the only people they can influence, and to many upper class Negroes this is important not only in itself but also as a basis for influence with white people.

Upper class Negroes, further, share some of the disabilities of Negroes in general since many of the caste controls do not spare them. They undoubtedly feel the humiliation of caste more strongly, even if they suffer less from specific deprivations. Their formula for being accepted as "belonging" to the Negro caste is the appeal to "race." In order to gain their purpose, this appeal has to be invested with a certain amount of protest. It becomes an appeal to race solidarity.

The feeling of racial solidarity and the work for Negro betterment fill many of them with an altruistic urge. They experience the joy and consolation of identification with a wider goal than that of self-elevation. Many thus succeed in building up a balanced personality in striving unselfishly for the Negro group. But there should be no reason for surprise that in this narrow shut-in world, to which they are doomed, much envy and personal strife enters into all collaboration with their fellow Negroes. There is much mutual suspicion of one another's motives and reliability.

The Negro lower classes are, of course, likely to view the superior status and opportunities of upper class Negroes and their pretensions with envy. It is quite natural that the Negro upper class gets the brunt of the antagonism from the lower classes which arises out of the latters' poverty and dependence and which rightly should partly be directed against the caste system and the whites.[15] As the Negro protest becomes more articulate also among lower class Negroes, there is likely to be, however, a partial redirection of their antagonism in this latter direction and a mitigation of the class protest against the Negro upper class. *Upper class Negroes find it necessary to instigate a protest against caste on the part of the Negro masses as a means of averting lower class opposition against themselves and to steer it instead against the white caste.* For them the preaching of race solidarity is an instrument to assert Negro leadership.[16] It is also desirable in order to strengthen their economic monopolies behind the segregation wall.

The protest motive allows, on the other side of the bargain, the lower class Negroes to take vicarious satisfaction in the attainments of the upper class Negroes. It gives basis to the symbolic significance of upper class status which we mentioned earlier.[a] As we have repeatedly pointed out, the common Negroes need the Negro upper class as liaison agents to the whites.

In this way, *both upper class and lower class Negroes are likely to swing between, on the one side, desire for intense isolation and resentment against other Negro social classes and, on the other side, race solidarity based on the caste protest against white society.* For few individuals in any one of the various classes is the state of his feelings toward the rest of the Negro community a stable one. For all Negroes, the Negro protest fills a "function" of allowing a higher degree of caste solidarity.

[a] See Chapter 34, Sections 5 and 8.

CHAPTER 37

COMPROMISE LEADERSHIP

1. THE DAILY COMPROMISE

In discussing the accommodating Negro leader in Chapter 34, we assumed for the purposes of abstract analysis that the protest motive was absent. This assumption, however, has some real truth in it, as we shall show in the present chapter. The accommodation motive has predominant importance in the daily life of American Negroes. But it is true that the protest motive is ever present. In some degree it has reached practically all American Negroes. To many individuals it is a major interest. And the Negro protest is bound to rise even higher. But the influence of the protest motive is limited mainly to the propagation of certain ideas about how things *should* be. In any case but few Negro individuals are in a position to do anything practical about it. Everyone, however, has to get on with his own life from day to day, *now and here*. Even when the individual plans for future employment, for business, or for schooling, he has to reckon with the world as it is. He has to accommodate.

The Negro protest is thus mainly suppressed and turned inward. But it has effects upon Negro personality, upon the relations between the classes in the Negro community, and also upon caste relations. The whites, on their side, are accustomed to a certain amount of Negro unreliability, dishonesty, laziness, secretiveness, and even insolence and impudence. They shut their eyes to its explanation in Negro dissatisfaction and the other results of the caste system. The average white man, in the South, actually gets enjoyment out of observing and joking about Negro inefficiency and slyness. He knows that he gets the services of Negroes for a cheap price, and so he can afford to joke about this. But, apparently, he also wants to convince himself that the Negroes are well satisfied.[1] Now and then, however, he reveals to the observer, more or less incidentally, that he knows about and understands the Negro protest.

The Southerner keeps watching all the time for germs of unrest and dissatisfaction in the Negro community. He preserves the machinery of caste controls in a state of perpetual preparedness and applies it occasionally as an exercise or a demonstration. In this system, the Negroes *have to* accommodate individually and as a group. This is the situation in the South. As we shall observe later, the Northern situation is considerably different

2. THE VULNERABILITY OF THE NEGRO LEADER

In the protective Negro community much goes on which the white man does not know about. The reality of this reserve is well known to Negroes, and it is coming to effective use in the Negro church, the Negro school and the Negro press. But the Negro leader has stepped out of the anonymity, and the eyes of influential white people are focused on him. He has to watch his moves carefully in order not to fall out with them. This would end his usefulness to the Negro community as a go-between. And it would spell his own ruin, as the whites have a close control on his income and his status.

In the South practically all Negro teachers—from the lonely teacher in a dilapidated one-room school house isolated off somewhere in a rural county, to the president of a Negro college—are appointed by white leaders and they hold their position under the threat of being dismissed if they become troublesome.[a] The Negro church is often claimed to be the one independent Negro institution founded entirely upon the organizational efforts and the economic contributions of the Negro people themselves. But the observer finds that to an amazing extent there are ties of small mortgage loans and petty contributions from whites which restrict the freedom of the preachers. Negro professionals and Negro businessmen, operating in the tight areas behind the caste wall, are also dependent on the good-will, the indulgence, and sometimes the assistance of whites. The same is even more true of the successful Negro landowner, who in most Southern areas meets the envy of poor whites, and so needs the protection of the substantial white people in the community. And for all local Negro leaders, it is perhaps not the economic sanction that is most important, but the sanction of physical punishment, destruction of property and banishment.

In a sense, every ambitious and successful Negro is more dependent upon the whites than is his caste fellow in the lower class. He is more conspicuous. He has more to lose and he has more to gain. If he becomes aggressive, he is adding to all the odds he labors under, the risk of losing the good-will and protection of the influential whites. The Southern whites have many ways of keeping this prospect constantly before his mind. He knows he has to "go slow."

3. IMPERSONAL MOTIVES

This should not be construed to imply that there is a crude self-seeking opportunism on the part of Negro leaders or a cynical despotism on the part of the whites. The power situation is conducive to the creation of both, and the standards of power morals are low. But even the most right-minded ambitious Negro would be foolish not to realize that he has to keep in line

[a] See Chapter 41, Section 1.

if he wants to do something for his own people. Accommodation on his part can be, and often is, altruistically motivated. He can view it as a sacrifice of personal dignity and conviction which he undergoes to further, not only his own aspirations, but also those of his whole group. He can point out, rightly, that reckless opposition on his part might endanger Negro welfare.

There is much bitterness among Southern Negro leaders because they are criticized for being "Uncle Toms," especially by Northern Negro intellectuals. They will tell the observer that it takes little courage to stay in the safety of the North and to keep on protesting against Negro sufferings in the South. "They should come down here and feel the fears, uncertainties, and utter dependence of one of us in their own bones," said one prominent Negro banker in the Upper South. And he added: "If they then continued their outbursts, we would know that they are crazy, and we would have to try to get rid of them as a public danger. But, sure, they would come along. They would be cautious and pussy-footing as we are."[2]

On the white side, the motives are usually neither base nor crude. Often a Southern school board will try to appoint the best Negro they can get for teacher, school principal or college president. When they look for a "cautious," "sane," "sober," "safe," "restrained," and "temperate" Negro, they have in view a person who they honestly think will be good for "racial harmony." The same is true when they help a Negro preacher whom they consider a well-intentioned person. Mortgage loans and contributions to Negro churches are most of the time not given with the conscious intent to fabricate caste controls but to help religious work among Negroes by ministers who have their respect. But they operate within the framework of the Southern white philosophy of race relations.

According to this philosophy, the whites should "look after their Negroes." Negroes should not protest but accommodate. They should not demand their rights but beg for help and assistance. Everything then works out for the good of both groups. When they dismiss a "radical" professor from a Southern Negro college or put the screws on an incautious preacher, doctor, or businessman or do not listen to his requests any longer, they act "in the best interest of the Negro group." Even whites who personally would prefer to be more broad-minded, even Northern philanthropists who would help the South, have to take into account "the public opinion among whites," what "people will stand for down here."

The selection and the behavior of Negro leaders in the South is an outcome of this fact, that practically all the economic and political powers are concentrated in the white caste while the small amount of influence, status, and wealth that there is in the Negro community is derivative and dependent. The Negro masses are well aware of this situation. They need Negro leaders who can get things from the whites. They know that a Negro leader who starts to act aggressively is not only losing his own power and often his livelihood but might endanger the welfare of the whole Negro community.

In Southern Negro communities there is apparently much suspicion against "radical," "hot-headed" and "outspoken" Negroes. Negroes do not want to be observed associating with such persons, because they might "get in trouble." A barricade will often be thrown up around them by a common consent that they are "queer." The Negro community itself will thus often, before there is any white interference, advise individual Negroes who show signs of aggression that they had better trim their sails.

4. THE PROTEST MOTIVE

Nevertheless, the protest motive is not without influence on Negro leadership in the South. For one thing, some protest is almost a necessary ingredient in the leadership appeal to Negroes. The furthering of race pride and racial solidarity is the means of diminishing internal strivings in the Negro community and of lining up the community into a working unity. Whites sometimes understand this, and there is, therefore, also a certain amount of "tolerated impudence" which a trusted and influential Negro leader can get away with even in the presence of whites. If the Negro community feels sure that he, nevertheless, retains the ear of whites, such a guarded outspokenness will increase his prestige. Negro leaders are often keenly aware of just how far they can go with white people—just what they can afford to say, how they should say it, and when they should say it. Often a protest will be produced under the cover of a joke, or in a similar form, so that the whites do not quite get the full meaning or, anyhow, can pretend that they have not got it. There is a whole technique for how to "tell it right in the face of the whites" without being caught. The stories about such successful protests under cover form a mythology around a Negro leader who has the admiration and allegiance of his community.

But much more generally the Negro community enjoys the demonstration of the Negro protest—as long as it does not become too dangerous for racial harmony. The vicarious satisfaction taken in the victories of Negro athletes who have beaten white competitors has long been observed.[3] The esteem in the Negro community for the "bad nigger" is another point. The "bad nigger" is one who will deliberately run the risks involved in ignoring the caste etiquette, behaving impudently and threateningly toward whites and actually committing crimes of violence against them. Because he often creates fear in the white community, and because he sometimes acts the role of "Robin Hood" for lesser Negroes in trouble with whites, he is accorded a fearful respect by other Negroes.[4] He certainly does not become a Negro "leader." But, particularly in the lower classes, he is a race hero and will be protected by them by means of pretended ignorance as to his doings and whereabouts.

Whenever a Negro leader can afford—without endangering his own status or the peace of the Negro community—to speak up against, or behave slightingly toward, members of the superior caste, this will increase his prestige.[a]

5. THE DOUBLE ROLE

More generally, the presence of the protest motive in the Negro community tends to induce the Negro leader to take on two different appearances: one toward the whites and another toward the Negro followership. Toward the Negroes he will pretend that he has dared to say things and to take positions much in exaggeration of what actually has happened. The present author, when comparing notes from interviews in the Negro community with what the white community leaders have told him about their "good Negroes," has frequently observed this discrepancy.[5]

A dual standard of behavior is not unnatural for a Southern Negro. It is rather to be expected of anybody in the lower layer of the Southern caste system. But the Negro leaders especially are pressed into such a pattern as they are more regularly, and in a sense professionally, in contact with whites and have a more considerable stake in the game.

> They play two roles and must wear two fronts. . . . The adjustments and adaptations of the Negro leader are apt to be more pronounced and in bolder relief than those of the common Negro for the reason that the Negro leader clearly has much more to lose. He has two worlds to please and to seek his status in.[6]

There is a limit, though, to what an accommodating Negro leader can pretend in the Negro community of what he has been bold enough to say or do. What he says to the Negroes, if it is really startling, will most of the time be reported by servants and other stool pigeons to the whites, and might make them suspicious of him.

The Negro community gets a revenge against the whites not only out of the Negro leaders' cautious aggressions but also out of the whites' being

[a] A Negro school principal in one of the larger cities in the Deep South once took me around and showed me various aspects of Negro life in the community. All the time and even when we were alone he displayed towards me the usual cumbersome caste etiquette of the region. In the evening he had called together a meeting of some twenty leading Negro citizens for a conference with me, for which he acted as chairman. He now developed an entirely new personal relation to me and became bossy, careless, and even impudent, but under a general cover of exaggerated friendliness and great familiarity. The next day when we continued our explorations of the condition in the city he had again returned to his ordinary caste role of unobtrusive and overpolite Southern Negro. I even sensed a sort of excuse for the previous evening. My tentative explanation was that he had put on the show of superiority at the meeting to impress his Negro friends, after he had carefully surveyed me and, rightly, found that there was no risk involved.

deceived. The satisfaction when some member of the community has succeeded in "pulling the wool" over the eyes of trusting white men is apparent. If deception is achieved, the Negroes seem to enjoy their leaders' spreading the flattery thick when approaching the whites. This is the most concealed, the almost perverted, form of the Negro protest.

6. NEGRO LEADERSHIP TECHNIQUES

This situation is likely to make the Negro leader sophisticated and "wise." He becomes intensely conscious of all his moves. One Southern Negro leader outlined the most effective technique to use, when approaching influential white people to get them to do something for the Negro community, in the following words:

> Don't emphasize the Negro's "right" . . . don't *press* for anything . . . make him feel he's a big man, get to other white men to make him want to avoid seeming small, and you can make him jump through the barrel. You can make him a friend or a rattlesnake, depending on your approach.[7]

Another Negro leader told us:

> I'm a respectable citizen, but when I try to get my rights I do so in a way that will not be obnoxious, and not in a radical way. I don't believe in radicalism. We *ask* for things, but never *demand*. When I'm in Rome, I burn Roman candles . . . but I don't "Uncle Tom."[8]

A Negro editor in another Southern city explained:

> If a Negro goes so far as to make an enemy of the white man who has the power he is foolish. You can't hit a man in the mouth and expect him to loan you money. By all means keep in with the man who hires and pays you. A man wouldn't be head of a big concern if he weren't a smart man, and a smart man will always react to facts. My approach is to the fellow on top because he is going to have to take care of me and I must work with him——he has the stick.[9]

The successful Negro leader becomes a consummate manipulator. Getting the white man to do what he wants becomes a fine art. This is what is called "playing 'possum." The Negro leader gets satisfaction out of his performance and feels pride in his skill in flattering, beguiling, and outwitting the white man. The South is full of folklore and legend on this aspect of Negro leadership.[10] And the stories are told among whites too, just as are stories about clever children or animals.

Every person in this game has a double standard of understanding and behavior. The white leaders know that they are supposed to be outwitted by the subservient but sly Negro leaders. In the Southern aristocratic tradition they are supposed not only to permit and to enjoy the flattery of the Negro leaders but also to let them get away with something for themselves and for their group. It is the price due the Negro leaders for their adaptive skills and for their tactful abstention from raising the Negro protest. The Negro leaders also know their double role.

The Negro community is thus, on the one hand, filled by the Negro protest and it demands to be appealed to in terms of Negro solidarity. It also wants to feel that the protest is getting over to the whites. On the other hand, the Negro community knows the caste situation, is afraid of radical leaders and trouble-makers, and wants its go-betweens to be able to make some real deliveries.

7. Moral Consequences

This situation is pregnant with all sorts of double-dealing, cynicism and low morals in the Negro community. The leaders are under constant suspicion from the Negro community that they are dishonest, venal and self-seeking. One observing Negro citizen expressed a common view when he told us: "You give a few Negroes a break, hand them a job, and all problems are solved."[11] The complaints about "bad leadership"—"incompetent," "selfish," "treacherous," "corrupt"—were raised in every single Negro community the present author has visited. These complaints may, indeed, be said to constitute one of the unifying popular theories in the Negro world, a point upon which everybody can agree. "There are few Negro leaders," Ralph Bunche confirms, "who are not suspect immediately they attain any eminence. The racial situation has created a vicious circle in Negro reasoning on leadership, and the Negro leader is caught in it."[12]

The Negro community in the South cannot expect—and does not want—its leaders to act out the protest the common Negroes actually feel. There is, indeed, little reason to believe that the leaders are less militant than the community seriously wants them to be. But the common Negroes do feel humiliated and frustrated. And they can afford to take it out on their leaders by defaming them for their "kowtowing," "pussy-footing," and "Uncle Tomming"; by calling them "handkerchief heads" and "hats in hand"; and particularly by suspecting them for being prepared to barter away their own honor and the interests of the group for a job or a hand-out. *The Negro hates the Negro role in American society, and the Negro leader, who acts out this role in public life, becomes the symbol of what the Negro hates.*

The Southern Negro leader—not being allowed to state and follow a clear ideological line but doomed to opportunism, having constantly to compromise with his pride and dignity, and never being allowed to speak upon the authority of the strength of an organized group behind him but appearing as an individual person trusted by the adversary group before him—does not have the sanctions ordinarily operating to preserve the honor and loyalty of a representative leader. The temptation to sell out the group and to look out for his own petty interest is great. He thus easily comes to justify the common suspicions around him by becoming a self-seeker and opportunist. The anger in the Negro community against unscrupulous leaders is often directed against the fact that they do not get more for themselves out of their unscrupulousness in sacrificing the common interest:

> That [leadership] which can be bought . . . is usually purchaseable for "peanut money." The scorn for the practice among Negroes, frequently expressed is often less due to the fact that Negro leaders "sell out" than because they do so so cheaply.[13]

8. LEADERSHIP RIVALRY

Since power and prestige are scarce commodities in the Negro community, the struggle for leadership often becomes ruthless. Such is the situation even in those fields where there is little white interference.[14] White influence is likely to increase bitter personal rivalry, as the leader comes to operate as a single individual, trusted by the whites but generally without any organized backing or control in the Negro community and without a cause or an issue.

For the same reasons this rivalry does not provide a check on dishonesty. It rather loosens still more the loyalty of the Negro community. It also provides the influential whites with increased possibilities to "divide and rule." And it defiles still more the atmosphere around Negro leadership. The rivalry, the envy, and the disunity in the Negro community, and the destructive effects, are felt by even the poorest Negro, who will everywhere tell the inquirer that "Negroes just can't stick together." "Lambasting our leaders is quite a popular pastime," observes James Weldon Johnson.[15] Under those circumstances the attainment of Negro leadership also tends to "do something" to the individual Negro:

> For when a value is scarce its possession tends to inflate the possessor. The Negro leader often quickly puffs up when given power. He "struts" and puts up a big front, or puts on "airs," often indulges in exhibitionism. It is often truly said that the Negro leader "can't stand power." Actually, there is a sort of ambivalence which characterizes the attitudes of Negro leaders. The leader will pay lip-service to the concepts of democracy for he understands their significance and appeal to the Negro as a group. But in his personal views and relationship the Negro leader is ordinarily very allergic to democracy—he prefers to play the role of the aristocrat, or the dictator or tyrant. *For leadership itself is a form of escape.*[16]

9. QUALIFICATIONS

It should be observed that *these detrimental effects upon public confidence and morals in the Negro community are derivative from the basic lack of democracy inherent in the Southern caste situation,* and, further, that *they become increased by the rising Negro protest as long as it is denied free outlet.* They have close parallels in all other subordinate groups.

In this situation it is understandable why so many well-equipped upper class Negroes in the South withdraw voluntarily from attempting to play a leadership role. Bad odor around the whole activity is an additional reason for such withdrawal besides the ones mentioned in an earlier section.[a] But many cannot afford to withdraw entirely. So many of the vocations and positions which mean an economic and social career in the Negro community are under white control, directly or indirectly. And the influential whites reckon on their Negro college presidents, their Negro high school principals, their favored Negro ministers, farmers and businessmen to shepherd the Negro community.

This may, indeed, be a blessing to the Negro community as so many of the most devoted and capable Negro leaders in the South actually are persons who would prefer to stay away and mind their own business, if their position, and, especially, white expectations, did not draw them out as Negro leaders. It must never be forgotten—in spite of what many Negro interlocutors in their dismay and pessimism tell the interviewer to the contrary—that there are *in the South many honest and diligent Negro leaders* who unselfishly forward Negro interests by a slow, patient, but determined, plodding along against odds and difficulties. And an important aspect of the changing South is that—as the general educational level is raised, racial liberalism progresses, and federal agencies become important —*they are the Negro leaders to become increasingly trusted by the whites in power.*

10. In Southern Cities

In the rural South only accommodating Negro leadership is yet possible. In Southern cities—except in the smaller ones—the observer finds single individuals and small groups of followers around them who use the protection of the greater anonymity of the segregated urban Negro community to raise cautiously the banner of Negro protest.

They usually try to get the Negroes to attempt to register as voters. Upper class Negroes seldom become active protest leaders, as they would have too much to lose. Teachers or preachers are practically never active protest leaders. Such leaders seldom have conspicuous success, as the ordinary community leaders usually keep aloof, and as the Negro masses are apathetic.

The N.A.A.C.P., a national protest organization, has branches in most of the larger Southern cities. With exceptions, those branches are not active for a protracted period and they *cannot* be active, since the margin of freedom for the Negro protest is narrow. They have a social function and, in addition, the symbolic function of keeping the flame of protest burning in the community, and of collecting the contributions to be sent to the National

[a] See Chapter 36, Section 6.

Office in New York in order to make it possible for its staff to attack problems on the national front.[a]

The present writer once interviewed the president of the N.A.A.C.P. branch in one of the smaller capitals of the Deep South. He was a distinguished, elderly gentleman, a postal clerk who for many decades, upon the basis of his economic independence as a federal employee, had led a cautious fight for Negro interests in his community. During our conversation I asked him whether they had any other similar organizations in the city, and the following conversation ensued:

"Yes, there is the League for Civic Improvement."

"Why do you bother to have two organizations with the same purpose of trying to improve the position of Negroes?"

"Sir, that is easily explainable. The N.A.A.C.P. stands firm on its principles and demands our rights as American citizens. But it accomplishes little or nothing in this town, and it arouses a good deal of anger in the whites. On the other hand, the League for Civic Improvement is humble and 'pussy-footing.' It begs for many favors from the whites, and succeeds quite often. The N.A.A.C.P. cannot be compromised in all the tricks that Negroes have to perform down here. But we pay our dues to it to keep it up as an organization. The League for Civic Improvement does all the dirty work."

"Would you please tell me who is president of this League for Civic Improvement? I should like to meet him."

"I am. We are all the same people in both organizations."

This story revealed much of the political shrewdness by which the difficulties are sometimes met.

In a few places in the South there are appearing a few Negro labor leaders in new mixed unions, primarily in Birmingham and Baltimore and in other areas where Negroes are in mining and building construction. These Negro leaders usually keep faithfully and cautiously to their specialty. Toward the white union leaders they ordinarily act out the traditional accommodating Negro leader's role, though with considerably more backbone since they have an organized body of Negro workers behind them. The future of the Negro labor leader in the South, as well as the answer to the question whether he will have influence in broader spheres of politics and culture, remains uncertain.

11. IN THE NORTH

In the North the protest motive has a much freer scope and can come out into the open. Negro power in politics and in trade unions is more substantial. White people are not united, as in the South, in a systematic effort to keep the Negroes suppressed. The Negro community, therefore, demands a display of actual opposition from its leaders.

[a] See Chapter 39.

The Negro leaders are also much freer in their actions. They do not fear violence, intimidation and banishment. Even the controls over their economic prospects are much less tight. But white protection and assistance mean much in the North also. Negro preachers in the North get hand-outs, too. Negro teachers and other public employees are mostly appointed by whites in the North, too. But since the jobs are actually considered as concessions to Negro power and protest, the jobholders are not appointed entirely without consideration of the desires of the Negro community. And the civil service regulations are usually more effective in the North in protecting the independence of jobholders.

It is, thus, surprising that one meets in Northern Negro communities the same complaints about the great incompetence and venality of Negro leaders. One observes also much of the same keen and destructive personal rivalry of leaders. Part of this may be explained as a cultural heritage from the Southern situation. The greater freedom requires a radical reeducation which is far from finished among Southern-born Negroes in the North and among their children. Another part may be due to the fact that the Negro protest is not only much freer in the North but is also more widespread and more intensely felt. As the constructive outlets for this more intensive Negro protest are not too wide in the North either, it turns back on the Negro community and results in internal suspicion and vicious competition.

But more important in explaining dissatisfaction with leaders is the fact that the share in power which the Negroes hold in the North creates a much greater stimulus for various white interests to buy the Negro leaders. As the Negro people are poor and inexperienced in holding power, the temptations seem strong. Political parties have a reason in the North, which they do not have in the South, to bribe Negro newspaper editors, preachers, and other community leaders before elections. Employers occasionally feel inclined to do the same in order to keep Negro workers hostile to the trade unions. And even other white interests in the North, where it is less possible than in the South to frighten the Negro community in the direction wanted, will instead buy off its leaders.

It is possible—and, judging from the many sorry stories told to the present author, even probable—that there is just as much or more outright corruption in the Northern Negro leadership as in the Southern. And even in the absence of corruption, the Northern leaders, like the Southern ones, are apparently often interested in their own advancement more than in the cause they pretend to serve. Nevertheless, the Negro community also gets something—and indeed comparatively much—out of the greater freedom and out of its share in power. And the Northern situation is conducive to a gradual education of the Negro people to the opportunities and the duties of free citizenship. The masses can demand that their leaders be struggling protest leaders, clarifying and defining the Negro demands, and making the necessary compromises in the full light of publicity. In the North the recognition of full democracy in principle and unhampered rights to fight for its gradual realization in practice give Negroes a basis for hope.

12. ON THE NATIONAL SCENE

The conspicuousness of Negro leadership on the national plane and the severe demands on competence and devotion have a cleansing effect.

It is the writer's impression that national Negro leadership is no more corrupt nor more ridden with personal envy and rivalry than other national leadership. Indeed, it compares favorably in these respects with, for instance, national white labor leadership. The actual power situation will often induce national Negro leaders to be compromising and even accommodating. Considerations of personal advancement will sometimes make Negro advisors in government agencies and Negro aspirants for such jobs more interested in calming down the Negro protest than in giving it force and expression. But they are persistently watched by the Negro press and by the national Negro protest and betterment organizations. In politics and all other power fields the national Negro leaders, in conspiracy with their white allies, rather succeed in squeezing out more consideration for the Negro cause than corresponds to the actual strength of their organized backing—though, of course, far less than its potential future strength.

On the national scene—and also in the larger Northern cities—one often observes a phenomenon which has an exact parallel in the women's world, namely, that it is felt appropriate to have "one Negro" on boards, on committees, on petitions, and so on. Ralph Bunche comments:

> Not infrequently, Negroes are shoved into positions of leadership by white leaders for purely strategic reasons. It is common practice in numerous organizations and movements today, especially those of the liberal variety, to say "we must have a Negro on this." This attitude has even found reflection in the purely academic and scholarly organizations where it has been deemed necessary to project a Negro now and then into some position of prominence in order to demonstrate the liberality and tolerance of the group.[17]

The Negro appointed in this manner—for no other reason than that he is a Negro—often does not have the personal qualifications for holding a prominent position. This is an angle of the much broader problem of the "double standard" which we discussed in a previous chapter.[a] The caste situation generally works to the detriment of Negroes, but there are individual Negroes who are given recognition and advantages which they would not get if the measures were objective under a casteless system.

This sketch of Negro leadership is frankly impressionistic and partly speculative, as no intensive research on this topic has been made. It has been

[a] See Chapter 35, Section 9.

needed as a background for the account to follow on Negro ideologies and on Negro organizations and concerted action. In Appendix 9 we present a number of problems for research and a few methodological points, intended as a guide for future investigations.

CHAPTER 38

NEGRO POPULAR THEORIES[a]

1. INSTABILITY

Negro thinking is thinking under the pressure and conflicts to which the Negro is subjected. Du Bois pointed out:

> It is doubtful if there is another group of twelve million people in the midst of a modern cultured land who are so widely inhibited and mentally confined as the American Negro. Within the colored race the philosophy of salvation has by the pressure of caste been curiously twisted and distorted. Shall they use the torch and dynamite? Shall they go North, or fight it out in the South? Shall they segregate themselves even more than they are now, in states, towns, cities or sections? Shall they leave the country? Are they Americans or foreigners? Shall they stand and sing "My Country 'Tis of Thee"? Shall they marry and rear children and save and buy homes, or deliberately commit race suicide? [1]

Frustration and defeatism, forced accommodation under concealed protest, vicious competition modified by caste solidarity, form the main texture into which the patterns of Negro political and social thinking are woven. Upon the personality basis we have sketched in Chapter 36, these patterns cannot possibly become consistent and stable. And Negro political and social thinking does not have much connection with broader American and world problems. To an American Negro, there is little point in having definite opinions about the world.

To an extent this is true of the little fellow everywhere in a big world.

[a] Throughout this book, and especially in this chapter, we use the term "popular theories" to refer to a consciously thought-out, though not necessarily logical or accurate, system of ideas held by a large group of people concerning something that is important or interesting to them. Popular theories may be attempts at abstract explanation or attempts at practical solution of problems which bother these people. They include not only beliefs concerning facts but also valuations, and they are usually complex in that they contain many beliefs and valuations and in that they have far-reaching implications. Some writers have used the term "ideologies" in the same way that we use the term "popular beliefs," but there is no unanimity among those who use the term as to its definition, and the term is almost completely foreign to the man in the street. Other writers have used the terms "popular beliefs" and "mass beliefs" in somewhat the same way as we use the term "popular theories," but in this book we have restricted the term "belief" to a simple comprehension of facts, as distinguished from valuations.

Everyone who is not on top has to work out his compromise between accommodation and protest. But the average white American has a better chance to do this constructively. He can feel himself in power by identifying himself with the American nation of which he is a full-fledged citizen, and by aligning himself with a group that can struggle with hope of coming into power sometime in the future. Corresponding to these affiliations with the nation, with a political party, and with various opinion and interest groups, popular theories are being developed about how society *is* and how it *should be* conserved or changed. The feeling of belongingness and integration gives white men some stability and self-assurance. It is true that even the white masses in America show a relatively low degree of participation in, and responsibility for, the larger society.[a] Moreover, public opinion is relatively unstable in America, and propaganda an important factor. Even the ordinary white man in America has a less well-organized system of opinions on general matters than he would have in a social order with more democratic participation. But the difference between whites and Negroes is tremendous.

Negroes are denied identification with the nation or with national groups to a much larger degree. To them social speculation, therefore, moves in a sphere of unreality and futility. Instead of organized popular theories or ideas, the observer finds in the Negro world, for the most part, only *a fluid and amorphous mass of all sorts of embryos of thoughts. Negroes seem to be held in a state of eternal preparedness for a great number of contradictory opinions*—ready to accept one type or another depending upon how they are driven by pressures or where they see an opportunity. Under certain circumstances, the masses of American Negroes might, for example, rally around a violently anti-American, anti-Western, anti-white, black chauvinism of the Garvey type, centered around the idea of Africa as the mother country. But they might just as likely, if only a slight change of stimulus is provided, join in an all-out effort to fight for their native country, the United States of America, for the Western civilization to which they belong, and for the tenets of democracy in the entire world, which form their cherished political faith. Or they might develop a passive cynicism toward it all. Negro intellectuals usually do not have such a tremendous instability of opinion as the masses. But compared with white intellectuals they show the same difference as Negro masses compared with the white masses.

This is what white Americans perceive when they tell the observer that Negroes are "emotional" or "unstable." In a sense this judgment is correct. And this trait can be observed not only in Negroes' popular theories, or lack of theories, about the larger society, but also in the type of religious

[a] See Chapter 33

experience they seek, the news they read, the art they create, and in the disorganization and rivalry manifested in their families and social gatherings.[a] Most American whites believe that emotionalism and lack of rationality are inborn in the Negro race. But scientific studies have made such inherent temperamental differences between Negroes and whites seem improbable.[b] The present author is inclined, for these reasons, to view this characteristic of Negro thinking as a result of caste exclusion from participation in the larger American society.

2. NEGRO PROVINCIALISM

Another observable characteristic of the Negroes' thinking about social and political matters is its provincialism.

Here also we note an effect of caste exclusion, and not a racial trait. Provincialism in social and political thinking is not restricted to Negroes. Everybody is inclined to consider national and international issues from the point of view of personal, group, class or regional interests. The range of vision stands apparently in a close correspondence to the degree of participation in the larger society. And again, when comparing American whites and Negroes, we note a quantitative difference in both cause and effect that is so great as to become qualitative.

Negroes have so many odds directed against them and suffer so many injustices—and the dominant American Creed which provides the common floor for all social and political thinking in the country is so uncompromisingly democratic—that it is only natural that when Negroes come to think at all about social and political problems they think nearly exclusively about their own problems. The Negro protest defines the ills of the Negro group ever more sharply in their minds and emotionalizes narrowness. Race consciousness and race pride give it a glorification and a systematization. *As the Negro protest and race consciousness are steadily rising, Negro provincialism may even increase in the short run, in spite of the better educational facilities and a greater acculturation.*

The Negroes are so destitute of power in American society that it would, indeed, be unrealistic for them to try a flight into a wider range of problems. It seems functional and rational that they restrict their efforts to what is nearest home. They are not expected to have a worth-while judgment on national and international affairs, except in so far as Negro interests are concerned. To most groups of white Americans it would be preposterous and impudent, or at least peculiar, if Negroes started to discuss general problems as ordinary Americans and human beings. They are allowed—in various degrees—to protest; or it is, at any rate, taken for granted that they should protest. But they are neither expected nor allowed

[a] See Chapters 42, 43 and 44.
[b] See Chapter 6.

to participate. So the Negro protest and the white expectation harmonize and accumulate in their effects to narrow the range of Negro thinking.

This vicious circle of caste operates upon the finest brains in the Negro people and gives even to the writings of a Du Bois a queer touch of unreality as soon as he leaves *his* problem, which is the American Negro problem, and makes a frustrated effort to view it in a wider setting as an ordinary American and as a human being. A corresponding and complementary feeling of queerness is felt by the foreign observer when he turns over the leaves of the hundreds of recent books and articles by white Americans on American democracy and its implications. In this literature the subject of the Negro is a void or is taken care of by some awkward, mostly un-informed and helpless, excuses. This is, of course, seen clearly by the Negro intellectual. Ralph Bunche remarks:

. . . consciously or unconsciously, America has contrived an artful technique of avoidance and evasion. For example, American newspaper editorials carry glowing praise for the tenets of liberty and equality upon which the society is founded, but ignore completely the inconsistent Negro status. One author has recently written a book entitled *American Problems of Today*, and yet barely mentions the Negro in one or two incidental passages.[2]

The tragedy of caste is that it does not spare the integrity of the soul either of the Negro or of the white man. But the difference in degree of distortion of world view is just as great as the difference in size between the American Negro community and the rest of the world.

Negro thinking is almost completely determined by white opinions—negatively and positively. It develops as an answer to the popular theories prevalent among whites by which they rationalize their upholding of caste. In this sense it is a derivative, or secondary, thinking. The Negroes do not formulate the issues to be debated; these are set for them by the dominant group. Negro thinking develops upon the presuppositions of white thinking. In its purest protest form it is a blunt denial and a refutation of white opinions. Accommodation may bend the denial toward qualified denial or even qualified agreement. But Negro thinking seldom moves outside the orbit fixed by the whites' conceptions about the Negroes and about caste.

Restricted and focused in this way, the problem of housing becomes to Negroes a problem of residential segregation and their share in public housing projects. Education becomes Negro education. Politics concerns Negro disfranchisement and what the Negroes will get out of the kaleidoscopic and unintelligible chance play of strange national and world events. The fight between the C.I.O. and the A.F. of L. is a question of whether Negroes will be allowed into the labor unions. World trends in agricultural economics and American agricultural policy are seen only in terms of cotton and the Negro sharecropper.

The national budget and its short-range and long-range balancing, the principles of taxation, monetary policy, and banking, have no sensible meaning in the Negro world, except perhaps in terms of unemployment relief. The World War becomes translated into the administrative details concerning the extent to which Negroes will be kept from working in defense industries and from service in the armed forces. Being denied full fellowship by white America, the identification with the nation is somewhat uncertain and blurred by a constant reminder of color. Africa gets the American Negroes' loyalty to nation, besides the United States. Thus the Negroes ". . . must perpetually discuss the 'Negro Problem,' —must live, move, and have their being in it, and interpret all else in its light or darkness," Du Bois complains.[3] And Ralph Bunche observes:

> . . . when the Negro views any matter of broad governmental policy, he ordinarily weighs it not as an American citizen, but as a Negro American. His first queries will always be: "How will it effect 'Negroes'?" "Will it be so administered as to embrace Negroes fairly?" "What safeguards are taken to insure equal Negro participation in its benefits?" In other words, the Negro has learned from bitter experience that he must constantly be on the alert to hold his own in the society. . . . Thus there is a constant conflict between the Negro's . . . desire to be a full-fledged American citizen . . . and the necessity forced upon him by tradition and sentiment in the country, to "think Negro" first.[4]

The American caste situation being what it is, there should be nothing astonishing in the provincialism of the Negroes in their thinking or in their fixation on white opinions. The Negroes can even be said to act in a practical and rational way when they concentrate their efforts on their own worries and press their own local and national interests. It is also—from their point of view—only a matter of prudence if they feel inclined to view the white Americans' international ambitions and allegiances with skepticism and reserve. The Negro caste is, in a sense, "a nation within a nation," and an oppressed and exploited nation at that. It prays to become assimilated, but this is not permitted. It is thus understandable and, in some respects and some degree, even necessary that the Negroes fortify their souls with a dose of black chauvinism.

But all this does not make a half-truth into a truth. It does not wipe out the distorting effects of huge gaps in knowledge and interests. Negro provincialism damages the efficiency of the Negroes' own struggle for a larger share. But it cannot be helped, since it is rooted in caste. A balanced and integrated world view is denied American Negroes, together with many other good things in our social life. They will not be able to emerge completely from instability, provincialism, and distortion of opinions until that time in the future when American society itself is eventually delivered from caste.

3. The Thinking on the Negro Problem

Negro thinking in social and political terms is thus exclusively a thinking about the Negro problem. The formation of popular theories among
Negroes concerning the Negro problem also does not result in articulate,
systematized and stable opinions. Particularly in the lower classes, and
in the Southern rural districts, the ideological structure of Negro thinking—even in its own narrow, caste-restricted realm—is loose, chaotic
and rambling. This is understandable since the major determinants in the
Negro problem are outside the Negroes' control and usually outside their
vision.

Some main elements, and particularly the doctrine of Negro equality,
have, however, been fixed by the Negro protest, as far as public expressions go, even if it is a hard struggle for the individual Negro to keep
up this badge of Negro solidarity.[a] But for the other elements, the popular
Negro theories on their own problem have not only been developed and
formulated by the small fraction of articulate upper class professionals and
intellectuals but they have been reaching down to the Negro masses
only slowly. In this process they have become blurred and simplified:

> . . . there is little evidence that these articulated conceptions have filtered down into
> the inert Negro mass, whose intellectual muscles are lax. It is this "elite" group
> which alone indulges in vivacious theorizing on the "problem."[5]

The popular theories on Negro strategy all try to solve the fundamental
problem of how to make a compromise between accommodation and protest. Any workable policy has also to engender support from white groups.
One axis, convenient for our purpose of reaching a useful typology of
Negro ideologies, concerns *what social class or group among the whites
is chosen as a prospective ally.*

4. Courting the "Best People among the Whites"

The traditional alignment in the South, following a pattern inherited
from slavery and white paternalism, is for the Negroes to seek support
from the white upper class.

Both the lower class Negroes and the upper class Negro leaders feel that
the "quality folks," the "best people among the whites" are the friends of
the Negroes. They are held to be "too big" for prejudice. They are
secure and out of competition. The lower class whites, on the other hand,
have been considered as the Negroes' natural enemies. There is, as we
have seen, a portion of truth in this view.[b]

The Negroes have therefore looked to those whites who have secure

[a] See Chapter 36, Section 2.
[b] See Chapter 17, Section 6, and Chapter 18, Section 3.

social and economic positions to give them assistance and backing. On the labor market Negroes have usually trusted the employers and have expected them to give them jobs and to protect them from the antagonism of white workers. Negroes have seen the necessity of being tractable toward the employing class and of working for lower pay and keeping down demands in order to hold their jobs. Formerly Negroes gained entrance to jobs as labor scabs and strike-breakers. In education and business, too, and in interracial relations generally, their hopes have been focused on the better class of white people.

Booker T. Washington developed and utilized successfully this philosophy as a short-range strategy. He gave it an optimistic slant—and made a reservation for the Negro protest—by developing the idea that progress was possible if a strong Negro middle class could be founded upon white help and upon individual thrift and energy. If the Negro could become a good producer, his products would call forth a good price in return.

> Nothing else so soon brings about right relations between the two races in the south as the commercial progress of the Negro. Friction between the races will pass away as the black man, by reason of his skill, intelligence, and character, can produce something that the white man wants or respects in the commercial world.[6]

The results would be not only gradually higher standards of efficiency, earnings, and consumption, but also a growing respect from the whites who would finally give Negroes suffrage, equal justice and, if not "social equality," at least equal public services.[7]

This philosophy has been taken over without substantial change by the Negro leaders and organizations pursuing a policy of conciliation, expediency, gradualism and realism. It still forms part of upper and middle class, and even lower class, Negro thinking which is not too absorbed with protest. It was, naturally, never conducive to broadening the horizon for Negro opinions on general issues. It rather tied Negro thought to what was narrowly opportune for "getting along with white folks." By allying the Negro cause so exclusively with upper class white interests, it even kept Negroes, for a long time, from considering labor solidarity across the caste line. Booker T. Washington did much to raise the feeling for the dignity of labor so utterly destroyed by the institution of slavery. But he had no good words to say for labor unionism or labor solidarity between white and Negro workers. It should be remembered, though, that labor unions were nearly absent from the South in Booker T. Washington's time and very weak in the North and, further, that they did not usually show much friendliness toward Negroes.[a] Until after the First World War labor unions were looked upon as the natural enemies of Negroes.

[a] See Appendix 6.

The trends of change in American society have made this optimistic, gradualist philosophy increasingly unrealistic even as a short-range strategy. For one thing, the outlook for Negro progress along economic lines can no longer be presented as so bright. The Negro's economic position is deteriorating, while his legal, political, and social position is improving. In any case, much success cannot be hoped for along the directions Washington pursued. The whole middle class ideology of Washington turns out to be a blind alley. The best prospect for an average graduate of Tuskegee, or of any of the other schools like it, is to become a teacher, not a "doer," in business, crafts or agriculture.

The common Negroes, who cannot aspire to exploit the petty monopolies behind the segregation wall, as teachers, preachers, professionals or businessmen, have to compete for unskilled jobs and for the opportunity to advance to semi-skilled and skilled jobs in industry. Unemployment, meanwhile, has taken on proportions in America greater than ever before in history, which is serious for an unpopular labor group like the Negroes. The power over employment is increasingly held not by employers, but by labor unions. Many cities where Negroes live in tens of thousands or hundreds of thousands are now "union towns."

The functions of the philanthropic organizations—to which Booker T. Washington and his many successors pleaded and from which they so often got a helping hand—are in the process of being taken over by the states and the federal government. The federal government, particularly, is becoming a decisive factor as far as Negro interests as workers or unemployed workers are concerned. Even Negro education is becoming dependent upon the federal government. And the government is becoming less dependent upon the white upper classes. It depends upon the general electorate and, in labor issues, increasingly upon organized labor.

This new configuration was hardly visible before the First World War and is to a great extent the result of the Great Depression during the 'thirties and of the New Deal.

5. The Doctrine of Labor Solidarity

The wave of socialistic thought after the First World War, to which we have referred in Chapter 35, brought to the fore the demand for labor solidarity across the caste line.[8] But the American labor movement passed through a period of infirmity during the 'twenties and it was not until the New Deal that labor solidarity became a realistic basis for Negro policy.

The younger generation of Negro intellectuals, with few exceptions, supported by a gradually growing number of Negro trade unionists, have since 1930 preached labor solidarity as the cure-all of Negro ills. White labor is explained to be the Negroes' "natural" ally; the old alignment with the white upper class was a "bourgeois illusion."[9] Whether or not white labor is the Negroes' natural ally will be discussed presently. Before embarking upon this task it should, however, be remarked that, even if a reliance upon the white upper class today would be an "illusion," this does not prove that it was so in Booker T. Washington's time, fifty years ago, when, as we have pointed out, the power situation in America was a very different one.

Ralph Bunche, who, with reservations, is in fundamental agreement with the view that the Negroes' main hope lies in an alignment with white labor, explains this new view:

> This conception [that of class consciousness and class unity] . . . postulates the identity of interests of the working masses of the two races, and that these interests can be protected only by unity of action by both groups, against the employers and the capitalistic structure which dictate their exploitation.
> . . . This conception of the problem finds its immediate roots in the economic competition institutionalized by the capitalistic system. Under this system all workers are equally exploited, and division in the ranks of the working class is a fatal weakness. The employing class exploits the traditional hostility between black and white workers, deriving from the days of slavery, by playing black against white, keeping the two groups divided through fanning the flames of race hatred, and thus providing a mutual threat. Thus the Negro is often used as a scab and strike-breaker. This division decimates the strength of labor unions and reduces the collective bargaining power of all workers. The strength of the working class is in its unity and its ability to present a unified front to the bosses. Therefore, white and Negro workers must cast aside their traditional prejudices, in their own welfare; they must lock arms and march shoulder to shoulder in the struggle for the liberation of the oppressed working masses. The overwhelming majority of Negroes are working class, and most of these are unskilled. Thus, practically the entire Negro race would be included in the scope of this ideology. The black and white masses, once united, could employ the terrifying power of their numbers to wring concessions from the employers and from the government itself. Some visualize the formation of a powerful labor party in which all workers, of whatever race, color or creed, would work together for the exertion of that political influence, to which their numbers entitle them, on behalf of the masses of the people. Economic interest was thus to override conventional group prejudice, and the Negro worker would be accepted as a brother and equal. The basis of race conflict is economic competition, it is said, and as soon as the economic structure undergoes such alterations as are necessary in order to guarantee economic security to the working masses, the dynamic causes of race conflict will have been liquidated.[10]

The Negroes are advised to think less about race and more about class—not upper class, but working class. In this attitude there is evidently a tendency to explain away caste as far as possible. The caste disabilities are said to be due to the poverty and economic dependence of Negroes and not to their color. "The Negro sharecroppers suffer not because of their black face but because of exploitation, just like the white sharecroppers," is a thesis I have often heard developed by Negro intellectuals. They criticize

Negro "racialism," and particularly the fight carried on by the N.A.A.C.P. for suffrage and civil rights. It is said that the vote and the abolition of social segregation might have both a practical and still more a prestige value to the tiny Negro "élite," but these things have little significance for Negroes. Ralph Bunche explains the view:

> . . . it is not at all established that the Negro sharecroppers and the day laborer in the rural South, or the unskilled worker in Birmingham, is more exercised about being deprived of his right to vote, or being Jim Crowed on a street car, than he is about his inability to earn enough to make ends meet. These Negroes might well say that the poor white man of the South hasn't been able to do very much for himself with the ballot in all the years that he has had it.
>
> There is a tendency toward creating excessive illusions in this sort of thinking [along the line of civil liberties]. The inherent fallacy in the political militancy thus outlined is found in the failure to recognize that the instrumentalities of the State, —Constitution, government and laws,—can do no more than reflect the political, social and economic ideology of the dominant population, and that the political arm of the State cannot be divorced from the prevailing economic structure. Civil liberties are circumscribed by the dominant mores of the society.[11]

Speaking particularly about the redemption of the Negro masses in the South, Bunche stresses:

> This will never be accomplished at the Southern polls, not at least until labor, farm and industrial, black and white, has become so strongly organized and so bold as to present a forceful challenge to the authority of the entrenched interests. In other words the South must be subjected to a new agrarian and industrial revolution before any significant changes in the fundamental relationships—political, economic or racial—will occur.[12]

To this critical view of the fight for civil liberties we shall return in Chapter 39 when we come to analyze the activity of the N.A.A.C.P.[13]

6. SOME CRITICAL OBSERVATIONS

The assumption that race prejudice and caste conflict have their roots in economic competition and that the whole caste problem is "basically" economic has come to be widespread and is now accepted by practically all Negro and most white writers on the Negro problem.[a] It is always possible to point out numerous instances where economic competition or fear of competition have instigated or aggravated caste conflicts. Some employers have intentionally played off the two groups against each other in order to rule by division. And the white upper classes—even if their interests are not made conscious in this blunt way—have probably to a large extent been dominated by a fear that lower class whites and blacks might come to

---

[a] This statement, as far as the Negroes are concerned, is true for the 1930's. It has become slightly less true as the war spirit has rekindled a belief in values other than economic and has stimulated a new growth of variegated ideals.

terms and unite against them.[a] This motive is sometimes visible, for example, in the fight about the poll tax or the labor unions in the South.

Nevertheless, this hypothesis and, indeed, the very idea that one factor or another is "basic" or "primary" to the caste system, is erroneous. In the cumulative causation of interrelated social factors none of them is so unimportant that it should be neglected. Each factor can be made the object of induced change, and this will move the whole system—including the economic factors, whether they are the ones originally changed or not—in one direction or the other.[b] From a practical point of view, this reveals the fallacy of criticizing activities to improve Negro status because they do not attack the "basic" cause.

The further hypothesis that there exists a "natural" identity of interests between Negro and white workers is about as meaningful or meaningless a statement as the one that all mankind wants peace. It depends. The term "interest" when applied to a group of people is crude and ambiguous unless it is ascertained how the bonds of psychological identification are fixed. When it is said that all Negro and white workers have a "common interest," the assumption must be that they actually care about each other's welfare, that *they all feel as a group.*

> In economic discussion of group interests it seems often to be forgotten that such a conception has its ground in a purely psychological assumption of an actual experience of collectivistic feelings, which in reality may be absent or present in various degrees of intensity. When, for instance, it is argued that a special group of workers in the labor market, distinguished and visible on account of sex, age, color, culture, or what not, has common interests with other workers against the employers and not with the employers against the other workers, and that the other idea is an illusion, the truth of the statement is entirely dependent on the subjective factor: whether there is, in fact, a sentiment of solidarity in the entire labor group or not. The term "interest" is thus subjectively determined in two dimensions: first, of course, as to individual utility, as economic analysis has always assumed, and, second, as to the degree of factual emotional solidarity ties. Particularly in the weighing of remote *contra* immediate interests is this second factor of importance.[14]

If white and black workers do not feel united as a group, there is, of course, no "common interest." "Labor solidarity" is not a thing by itself; it exists, or does not exist, only in the feelings of the workers for each other. If white workers feel a group unity among themselves, from which they exclude Negroes, they are likely to try to push Negroes out of employment. If in such a situation white employers—for whatever reasons—are inclined to accept Negro workers, the interest solidarity actually ties the Negro workers to the white employers instead of to the white workers.

[a] See Chapter 17, Section 4, and Appendix 6 Compare Arthur Raper, "Race and Class Pressures," unpublished manuscript prepared for this study (1940), *passim.*
[b] See Chapter 3, Section 7, and Appendix 3.

It is argued, however, that, from an interest viewpoint, white workers "should" feel an identity with Negro workers, and that they are working against their own interests by wanting to discriminate against Negroes. Such a split prevents the formation of strong labor unions; if white workers want effective union power, they will have to try to align Negro workers with them. This is true in those fields of employment where Negroes are already entrenched, and where they cannot be pushed out by the whites. It is true, for instance, in longshore work and coal mining.[a] But it is not so true in the greater number of industries where Negroes are at present effectively excluded or safely segregated in "Negro jobs." In those latter fields this reason for labor solidarity with Negro workers will become even less significant for white workers to the degree that they come to control employment by their unions.

A feeling of "common interest" can be promoted, however, by the actual spread of the ideology of class solidarity. Of this there is as yet comparatively little in America. It is true that both the A.F. of L. and the C.I.O. are, in principle, committed to nondiscrimination. So is the whole American nation. Actually the record has been worse on the union front than in many other fields of American culture. We have reviewed these facts and discussed the relations between the American trade union movement and Negro workers.[b] Our tentative conclusion was that the future development of those relations is important for the welfare of the Negro people but also uncertain. The outcome will probably depend upon political decisions by governments and legislatures, which, in their turn, depend upon electorates in which labor is an important element but not the only one. For the outcome, the strength of the American Creed as a social force will be important. The civil rights and the votes which American Negroes will be able to hold are going to be important in this struggle to open further the labor unions to them.

7. The Pragmatic "Truth" of the Labor Solidarity Doctrine

The eager intent to explain away race prejudice and caste in the simple terms of economic competition, and the exaggerated notions about the relative unimportance of caste, is an attempt to escape from caste into class. As such, it is closely similar to the tendency of certain Negro upper class persons, already described, who also want to forget about caste and want to align themselves with the white upper class.[c] The differences are, however,

---

[a] See Appendix 6. It is true also in Southern agriculture, since *all* Negro sharecroppers can never be pushed out, even though many of them have been. There will always be enough Negro sharecroppers who can be used by the plantation owners to destroy an all-white union which excludes the Negroes.

[b] See Chapter 18, Section 3.

[c] See Chapter 36, Section 6.

significant. In the theory of labor solidarity the identification would include the whole Negro people. The aim of this theory is to unify the whole Negro people, not with the white upper class, but with the white working class. And the underlying ideology stems from Marxist proletarian radicalism instead of from American middle class conservatism.

The theory of labor solidarity has been taken up as a last "solution" of the Negro problem, and as such is escapist in nature; its escape character becomes painfully obvious to every member of the school as soon as he leaves abstract reasoning and goes down to the labor market, because there he meets caste and has to talk race and even racial solidarity. The theory is, however, increasingly becoming "realistic" and even pragmatically "true" as a Negro strategy, in the same sense that Booker T. Washington's theory was realistic and true in his time. With the power over employment opportunities increasingly held by the labor unions, the Negroes simply have to try to get into them in order not to be left out of employment. The Negro leaders have to try to educate the Negro masses to be less suspicious of unions. And they have to plead labor solidarity to white workers as the most important element of the American Creed.

It is also visible how not only the N.A.A.C.P., but also such conservative agencies for Negro collective action as the Negro church and the Urban League, in recent years have been becoming friendly to unions—provided they let the Negroes in. In practically the whole Negro world the observer finds that the C.I.O. is looked upon as a great Negro hope because it has followed a more equalitarian policy than the A.F. of L. Practically all articulate voices among Negroes are coming out in favor of unionism—with this one condition that they do not discriminate against Negroes.

This new policy preserves much more of the Negro protest but attempts to merge it with a class protest as far as possible. This attempt requires much accommodation and even humiliation. Many unions are as closed to Negro workers as the "quality folks" were to the Negro upper classes. Ralph Bunche faces this situation with a square realism which can well match what the old master politician, Booker T. Washington, must often have thought about the upper class Southerners he had to deal with, although he carefully avoided saying it in so many words:

> Negotiations with the poor whites on a national level is admittedly not easy, but the Negro has long exploited his humility, his ability to "take low," to bow and scrape, in his relations with the white employer and the white philanthropist. If he must, he can employ these artifices to much better advantage for himself in nudging into the good graces of organized labor. This is no time for picayunishness and displays of petty pride.[15]

If the dream should ever come true and if—under the influence of a growing labor solidarity and considerable government pressure—the Negro workers should become widely and wholeheartedly accepted in the American labor movement, be given fair chances for employment and advancement, and have a voice in affairs of the unions, one of the consequences of this tremendous break of the caste order would be the widening of the horizon of Negro social and political thinking. The Negro intellectuals and labor leaders, having the goal of aligning the Negroes to the labor movement, usually have concentrated their thinking on the practical question of how to get the Negroes into the unions. If this were once accomplished and an identification reached with the white laboring masses, it would mean the beginning of a liberation of the Negro soul. James Weldon Johnson wrote:

> Organized labor holds the main gate of our industrial and economic corral; and on the day that it throws open that gate . . . there will be a crack in the wall of racial discrimination that will be heard round the world.[16]

Granted that attempts toward an understanding with the white working class are of paramount importance, other sectors should not be forgotten. *The Negroes' status in America is so precarious that they simply have to get the support of all possible allies in the white camp.* In addition to the labor unionists, Negroes must seek the support of the civil liberties group in the North, the Southern liberals and interracialists in the South, and even the Southern aristocratic conservatives where they are prepared to give a helping hand. Furthermore, *the vicious circle keeping Negroes down is so perfected by such interlocking caste controls that the Negroes must attempt to move the whole system by attacking as many points as possible.*

Negro strategy would build on an illusion if it set all its hope on a blitz-krieg directed toward a "basic" factor. In the nature of things it must work on the broadest possible front. There is a place for both the radical and the conservative Negro leaders, for social workers and labor organizers, for organizations that can speak to the employers and those that can approach the workers, and for organizations that can lead the Negroes in politics. The practical conclusions from this eclectic principle will be drawn in the following chapter.

8. "The Advantages of the Disadvantages"

Repeatedly we have pointed out the fundamental dilemma of the Negro upper classes. On the one hand, upper class Negroes are the ones who feel most intensely the humiliations of segregation and discrimination. They are also in a position where they, more than the masses, can see the limits set by the caste system to their personal ambitions. They need to appeal to racial solidarity against caste if only to avert the aggression against themselves from the lower classes and to direct it upon the whites. On the other hand, segregation and discrimination create an economic shelter for them. In the main, they enjoy their economic and social status thanks to the petty monopolies behind the caste bar. This applies to ministers, teachers, and practically all other professionals, as well as to most Negro businessmen. Caste is their opportunity. They are exploiting "the advantages of the disadvantages."[a]

When we remember, further, that the upper class Negroes, even more than other upper class American groups, are responsible for the thinking on their group's problem, the question must be raised as to how this situation influences popular theories on the Negro problem. This is a viewpoint somewhat different from the viewpoint we have followed until now, when we have asked with what white group Negroes have sought allegiance. Here a crucial matter is the attitude toward segregation. It is the upper class Negroes who have felt and expressed most clearly and persistently the Negro protest against segregation. They have manned the chief organization to defend the civil rights of Negroes, the N.A.A.C.P.; they have developed the doctrine that all segregation is wrong and that full democratic participation and integration is right and is the ultimate goal to be fought for. The observer often finds them complaining that lower class Negroes do not resent strongly enough the Jim Crow restrictions.

The sincerity of the upper class Negroes' opposition to segregation cannot be doubted. The fact that they themselves thrive in its shelter is seldom discussed openly and publicly.[b] When occasionally it is brought up, the intellectual dilemma is projected into a distant future by the recognition that segregation will not be abolished soon, and by the reflection that such a change will lose opportunities for them in the Negro market but gain opportunities for them in the wider American market.

Nevertheless, the opposition against segregation in upper class circles is directed primarily against those sectors of the caste system where it functions least as a shelter to themselves. The protest is thus outspoken and unanimous in regard to exclusion from hotels, restaurants, theaters, concerts, and segregation in transportation facilities. It is ordinarily less unanimous with respect to segregation in education. Negro schools provide employment for Negro teachers who, with present prejudice, would most of the time have less chance in a nonsegregated school system. If there is a segregated school system, the main interest becomes to improve the Negro schools and to guarantee the Negro teachers equal salaries.

In regard to segregation in hospitals the observer finds the same ambivalence. As soon as separate Negro set-ups are provided at all, the Negro protest shows a tendency to become directed toward demanding better facilities in these set-ups and, particularly, toward the monopolizing of the jobs as

[a] This term was popularized by H. B. Frissell, the second principal of Hampton Institute.
[b] Except, of course, by the critics among the radical Negro intellectuals and by the social scientists.

doctors and nurses for Negroes. This, by the way, is a demand which is the more reasonable as Negro doctors and nurses are excluded practically everywhere from white hospitals, even where there are Negro wards. But the Negro protest has here accepted the segregation policy. "I was heart and soul . . . in [the] fight against segregation and yet I knew that for a hundred years in this America of ours it was going to be at least partially in vain," comments Du Bois with reference to a particular incident during his work with the N.A.A.C.P. and continues:

> . . . what Negroes need is hospital treatment now; and what Negro physicians need is hospital practice; and to meet their present need, poor hospitals are better than none; segregated hospitals are better than those where the Negro patients are neglected or relegated to the cellar. . . . I am certain that for many generations American Negroes in the United States have got to accept separate medical institutions. They may dislike it; they may and ought to protest against it; nevertheless it will remain for a long time their only path to health, to education, to economic survival.[17]

Ordinarily this policy is not expressed so bluntly, at least not publicly, but it is the guiding theory for most practical Negro policy on the local scene. It runs through the whole gamut of Negro professions and businesses. It was definitely part of Booker T. Washington's strategy:

> Let us in future spend less time talking about the part of the city that we cannot live in, and more time in making that part of the city that we live in beautiful and attractive.[18]

In judging this opportunistic policy it should be held in mind that, in the main, the economic and social interests of the articulate Negro upper class groups run parallel to obvious interests of the whole Negro people, as there is usually little prospect that segregation and discrimination will be stamped out in the near future. Excluded from, or separated and discriminated against, in all sorts of public and private institutions and facilities, Negroes need more and improved schools, parks, playgrounds, hospitals, Y.M.C.A.'s, funeral homes, taxi companies and all sorts of Negro professional and business activities.

The N.A.A.C.P. is by necessity caught in the same ideological compromise.[a] In principle the Association fights all segregation. As a long-range solution it demands that all color bars be torn down. Often its practical task, however, will be to defend the Negroes' interests that a reasonable equality is observed within the existing system of segregation:

> The NAACP from the beginning faced this bogey. It was not, never had been, and never could be an organization that took an absolute stand against race segregation of any sort under all circumstances. This would be a stupid stand in the face of clear and uncontrovertible facts. When the NAACP was formed, the great mass of Negro

[a] See Chapter 39, Section 8.

children were being trained in Negro schools; the great mass of Negro churchgoers were members of Negro churches; the great mass of Negro citizens lived in Negro neighborhoods; the great mass of Negro voters voted with the same political party; and the mass of Negroes joined with Negroes and co-operated with Negroes in order to fight the extension of this segregation and to move toward better conditions. What was true in 1910 was still true in 1940 and will be true in 1970. But with this vast difference: that the segregated Negro institutions are better organized, more intelligently planned and more efficiently conducted, and today form in themselves the best and most compelling argument for the ultimate abolition of the color line.

To have started out in this organization with a slogan "no segregation," would have been impossible. What we did say was no increase in segregation; but even that stand we were unable to maintain. Whenever we found that an increase of segregation was in the interest of the Negro race, naturally we had to advocate it. We had to advocate better teachers for Negro schools and larger appropriation of funds. We had to advocate a segregated camp for the training of Negro officers in the World War. We had to advocate group action of Negro voters in elections. We had to advocate all sorts of organized movement among Negroes to fight oppression and in the long run end segregation.[19]

Du Bois wrote this several years after he had left the N.A.A.C.P. as a result of a controversy with the Association mainly fought on this issue. He would not have said it in so many words fifteen years earlier, and the present leadership of the Association would probably not want to do it even today. But it is substantially a true characterization. Outside its important activity of defending full equality and democratic participation in politics, justice, and breadwinning, and besides its equally important long-range propaganda against all forms of segregation,[a] the Association finds itself, today as earlier, working for a more just administration of segregated set-ups.

As Negro institutions are improved and increasingly manned exclusively by Negro professionals, segregation itself is undoubtedly becoming fortified in America. And it should not be concealed either that powerful Negro vested interests in segregation are created. The trend is also in line with the rise of the Negro protest, which, on the one hand, means intensified "race pride" and, on the other hand, voluntary withdrawal and increasing isolation of Negroes from the larger American scene.[b] The Negro protest, primarily caused by and directed against segregation, thus comes to build up a new spiritual basis for segregation.

9. CONDONING SEGREGATION

"Whether self-segregation for his protection, for inner development and growth in intelligence and social efficiency, will increase his acceptability to white Americans or not, that growth must go on,"[20] writes Du

[a] See Chapter 39, Sections 5 to 9.
[b] See Chapter 30, Section 2.

Bois in his old age when he has become pessimistic about erasing the color bar in a reasonable future. Instead he urges the building up of a cooperative black economy for defense and mutual aid:

> To a degree, but not completely, this is a program of segregation. The consumer group is in important aspects a self-segregated group. We are now segregated largely without reason. Let us put reason and power beneath this segregation.[21]

A few important reservations must now be stressed. One is that few upper class Negroes are prepared to follow Du Bois into this open endorsement of segregation. A second is that Du Bois—like Booker T. Washington before him and practically all other Negro pleaders for a positive utilization of segregation—does not accept segregation as an ultimate solution but rather expects that the policy recommended will favor its earlier breakdown. Speaking particularly about segregated housing and rural settlement projects, he explains:

> Rail if you will against the race segregation here involved and condoned, but take advantage of it by planting secure centers of Negro co-operative effort and particularly of economic power to make us spiritually free for initiative and creation in other and wider fields, and for eventually breaking down all segregation based on color or curl of hair.[a]

A third reservation is even more important, though it can only by implication be inferred from what is said or written. Neither Du Bois nor any other Negro leader will be found prepared to urge the full utilization of segregation, which would be advantageous if segregation were accepted as an ultimate solution of the Negro problem.

A Negro leader, who really accepted segregation and stopped criticizing it, could face the dominant whites with a number of far-reaching demands. If, thus, Negroes accepted as final their disfranchisement in the South and condoned the exclusion of Negroes from politics, they could reasonably ask for a wide amount of self-government for Negroes. They could demand the right to elect their own school boards and governing bodies for their own hospitals and other public institutions. They could ask for Negro policemen to protect the Negro communities and perhaps even for separate lower Negro courts to settle civil and criminal cases between Negroes. Certain problems of fiscal clearing and white supervision would have to be settled, but with some legal ingenuity they could be solved. It would even be reasonable to ask for separate state and national representations of the disfranchised Southern Negroes. Even if such a representative body should have only the right to discuss and petition regarding legislation which

---

[a] W. E. B. Du Bois, *Dusk of Dawn* (1940), p. 215. The present writer does not share the optimism contained in the last part of this statement. Better utilization of segregation by Negroes will give the caste system a certain moral sanction and, probably even more important, will fortify it by Negro vested interests.

concerned Negro interests, it would not be without great importance to the Negro people.

If Negroes accepted residential segregation, they could reasonably demand that it be developed into a rationally planned policy, so that space is set aside for Negro sections. Residential segregation without such a positive policy is more cruel than it need be and than it is usually meant to be. Likewise, if Negroes accepted widespread economic discrimination, they could demand that at least certain "Negro jobs" be set aside and also be defended against white intruders. The present situation of one-sided competition and exploitation, where Negroes are excluded by the whites, but where the whites are free to squeeze Negroes out of even their traditional jobs, easily results in a concentration of unemployment among the Negro people and their gradual relegation to relief as a normal "occupation."

The outside observer of the irrational, inefficient, and cruel American caste system cannot help making such reflections. He finds, however, that an intelligent discussion along those lines is almost entirely absent from America. This absence reveals certain moral taboos of greatest importance. I have taken interest in discussing these matters with many American Negroes. Few of them have failed to see the sense of the proposals raised. But none has expressed approval of them. And they are never touched upon in Negro literature and in public discussion; they have never been thought through. The explanation is this: *Negroes feel that they cannot afford to sell out the rights they have under the Constitution and the American Creed, even when these rights have not materialized and even when there is no immediate prospect of making them a reality. At the same time Negroes show, by taking this position, that they have not lost their belief that ultimately the American Creed will come out on top.* Referring merely to the proposal of an isolated black economy, and not to the more general problem of complete segregation in all fields, which is never mentioned by Negroes, James Weldon Johnson once said:

> Clear thinking reveals that the outcome of voluntary isolation would be a permanent secondary status, so acknowledged by the race. Such a status would, it is true, solve some phases of the race question. It would smooth away a good part of the friction and bring about a certain protection and security. The status of slavery carried some advantages of that sort. But I do not believe we shall ever be willing to pay such a price for security and peace.[22]

More surprising, perhaps, is the fact that white writers—who usually implicitly condone segregation and who therefore might be expected to want to improve the present very wasteful caste system[23]—never say a word on this problem, which, from their point of view, should be so paramount.[a] Again the explanation of this lack of intellectual clarity and persistence cannot be given simply in terms of the relatively undeveloped state of scientific social engineering in America. For in most other fields at least attempts at rational practical thinking and social planning are present. The explanation will have to be sought in moral taboos. *The whites also are inhibited by the American Creed from thinking constructively along segregation lines.* They may observe and analyze scientifically the segregation system as it works; they may condone it implicitly or explicitly as advantageous or inevitable under the circumstances; they may do it with eyes open to the sufferings and inefficiencies in the system as it is. But they cannot permit themselves to think through carefully and in any detail how a segregation system could be rationally organized. For *this would imply an open break with the principles of equality and liberty.*

The extraordinary thing is how the national *ethos* works, in the short run, as a bar against clear and constructive thinking toward mitigating the inequalities which, contrary to the American Creed, are inflicted upon a weak group. In the long run, this same Creed might come to save, not only, as now, America's face, but perhaps also its soul.[b]

10. Boosting Negro Business

The idea that the development of a Negro middle class of landowners, businessmen, and professionals would have importance in the fight for equality and opportunity is old with the Negro people. It was pronounced before the Civil War. It played an important role in Booker T. Washington's philosophy:

> . . . wherever I have seen a black man who was succeeding in his business, who was a taxpayer and who possessed intelligence and high character, that individual was treated with the highest respect by the members of the white race. In proportion as we can multiply these examples, North and South, will our problem be solved.[24]

In 1900 he founded the National Negro Business League, which is still functioning. The resolution drawn up by the business section at the first meeting of the National Negro Congress, in 1936, made it equally clear that Negro business is much more than "business":

> The development of sound and thriving Negro business is most indispensable to the general elevation of the Negro's social and economic security . . . all Negroes consider it their inescapable duty to support Negro business by their patronage.[25]

The same advice has been given the Negro people by their white friends through generations. Upon this theory Negro education, particularly along

---

[a] Southern white writers are no real exception. It is true—as we have shown in earlier parts of this inquiry—that they often in *general terms* plead for certain alleviations of unnecessary suffering inflicted upon the Negroes at the same time as they hold to the necessity of the caste system. But there their thinking stops.

[b] See Chapter 1.

Tuskegee lines, has been aided and directed. Sir Harry Johnston, review-- ing the Negro problem in the beginning of this century, pointed to the Jews and drew this lesson:

> Money solves all human difficulties. It will buy you love and respect, power and social standing. With money you can create armies and build navies, you can control the votes of your fellow-citizens, found and shape their educational institutes, con- duct a Press, overcome disease, make actual the charity of early Christianity, achieve all purposes that are noble, and check the Devil at every turn; whether he crop up in the forms of alcoholism, disease, intestinal worms, religious intolerance, political oppression, waste of the earth's natural resources, or the misuse of corrugated iron. If you are rich you can roof your dwellings with tiles of the most beautiful, or stone slabs, or wooden shingles, marble terraces or leaden sheets; if you are poor you must content yourself with corrugated iron and know that your dwelling is a blot on the landscape.
>
> The one undoubted solution of the Negro's difficulties throughout the world is for him to turn his strong arms and strong legs, his fine sight, subtle hearing, deft fingers, and rapidly-developed brain to making of Money . . .[26]

And through the decades, Negroes have been told by white people and by their own leaders that in business they have fair chances. Moton stated it thus:

> It is in business, perhaps, that the Negro gets more honest consideration and a fairer deal than in any other of his contacts with the white men, not even excepting religion.[27]

Business will stimulate the Negro's initiative, give him valuable training and experience, increase his self-confidence, increase his wealth, create a relatively secure middle and upper class, give employment to Negroes in the lower classes, and provide a reservoir of resources which can be used in competition with the whites. "Business" in this popular theory includes all free professions. The scant success in building up a substantial Negro business and professional class and the explanations of this have been reviewed in Chapter 14. But the ideology is more alive than ever. Practi- cally all Negro businessmen and professionals met in the course of this study have this theory. It is preached in church and taught in school.

Its popularity is understandable. Negro professionals and business men —except those to whom caste gives an absolute monopoly, as it does to most teachers in Negro schools and colleges, preachers, morticians, beau- ticians—have to compete with whites and have to seek to build up a relative monopoly by appealing to racial solidarity. Their standards are often lower than those of their white competitors. And they meet suspicion from the Negro customers. The last phenomenon. observed by all students, is well stated by Bunche:

This placid acceptance of Negro inferiority is the refrain of the professional Negro's plaint. Negro doctors and lawyers, Negro businessmen, and even Negro teachers claim to suffer from the lack of confidence in the ability of Negroes typical of so many of the group. It is alleged that many Negroes go out of their way and even suffer humiliations from whites, in order to avoid going to the Negro doctor or hospital. A Negro lawyer will charge that the local Negro doctors, who themselves lose much of their potential Negro clientele to white doctors, will yet engage only white lawyers when they require legal service; and vice versa. Negro students at Negro private schools under white control, have, occasionally, when polled, indicated a preference for white teachers, though this is a sentiment that is fast changing. Negro businessmen allege that Negroes prefer to go downtown to white stores which do not want their trade, and often suffer insults, rather than trade in a Negro store. And even when, by circumstance, Negroes are compelled to turn to the Negro professional man, they not infrequently do so without confidence. I was seated in the outer office of a prominent Negro dentist in Richmond not long ago, when a Negro woman came in with an infected tooth. She informed the dentist that the "white lady" she works for had told her to come. After careful examination the dentist informed her that the tooth would have to be extracted. She became firm on hearing this and promptly informed him that he was quite wrong, as her "lady" had assured her that the tooth would not need to come out. The dentist could not convince her of the correctness of his trained judgment over that of her white "lady," so she stalked out angrily.[28]

Against this, Negro business and professional men have to appeal to their prospective clientele by developing race pride. They promise the advance of the whole race if Negroes only learn to stick together and to patronize race business.

In more recent times two new ideological arguments have been added. One is the program of a cooperative Negro economy set forth recently by Du Bois:[29]

We believe that the labor force and intelligence of twelve million people is more than sufficient to supply their own wants and make their advancement secure. Therefore, we believe that, if carefully and intelligently planned, a co-operative Negro industrial system in America can be established in the midst of and in conjunction with the surrounding national industrial organization and in intelligent accord with that reconstruction of the economic basis of the nation which must sooner or later be accomplished.[30]

Du Bois' blueprint of ". . . a racial attempt to use the power of the Negro as a consumer not only for his economic uplift but in addition to that, for his economic education,"[31] has remained in the realm of beautiful dreams and is likely to stay there. Americans in general have been weak in their cooperative endeavors, and there is little chance that the Negroes could take a lead in this field. The development of chain businesses in America has actually substituted for one of the chief accomplishments of consumers' cooperation in other countries to rationalize retail trade and lower consumers' costs, and at the same time, has made the prospect for consumers' cooperation in America, at this late stage, extremely unfavorable. But it should not be denied that even discussion among Negroes of Du Bois' proposal would mean an advance in economic education of the Negro people.

The second new idea is the use of the weapons of the boycott and picketing against white stores and other businesses in Negro districts which refuse to employ Negro workers. In numerous movements all over the country—sometimes with support from the local branches of the N.A.A.C.P. and the Urban League but usually directed by *ad hoc* organizations—the slogan "don't buy where you can't work" has been raised.[a] An unusual degree of militancy and tenacity has often been shown, and in some instances signal success has been won.

This last movement has, of course, limited possibilities. At most, it can increase the employment of a few more white collar workers in the segregated Negro districts. It turns on a petty middle class racial basis and might even have great dangers. The Negro masses must seek employment in the general labor market, and their hope is in nondiscrimination, not in apportioning jobs according to race. Speaking about this utilization of the boycott weapon, James Weldon Johnson remarks:

> In our case it might prove a boomerang; on the very argument for the employment of Negroes where we spend our money, Negro employees may be let out where we spend no money.[32]

11. CRITICISM OF NEGRO BUSINESS CHAUVINISM

The weaknesses of Negro business chauvinism are apparent from a consideration of the facts about existing Negro business.[b] In so far as Negro-owned business is inefficient compared to white-owned business, it cannot exist for a long time. James Weldon Johnson makes the following pointed observation:

> It is a common practice among us to go into business relying on "race pride." Now, "race pride" may be a pretty good business slogan, but it is a mighty shaky business foundation. A Negro American in business must give as excellent quality, as low a price, and as prompt and courteous service as any competitor, otherwise he runs a tremendous risk in counting on the patronage even of members of his own race. "Race pride" may induce them once or twice to buy . . . a pair of shoes that cost more and wear out quicker, but it won't keep them doing it. The Negro business men who have succeeded have been those who have maintained as high quality, as low prices, and as good service as their competitors.[33]

[a] See Chapter 14, Section 2. For a description of the movement in New York City, see Claude McKay, *Harlem* (1940), pp. 184-196. Another slogan of the movement is "double duty dollar"—referring to the fact that the dollar both buys good and helps the Negro.

[b] See Chapter 14, Section 2.

Aside from its capacity for maintaining itself, Negro business has been thought of as a means of improving the whole Negro people. As can be expected, the advocates of interracial labor solidarity are critical of this aspect of the ideology. Ralph Bunche develops the views of this school in criticizing Negro business ideology:

It would seem clear . . . that this hope for the salvation of the Negro within the existing ideological and physical framework, by the erection of a black business structure within the walls of white capitalism, is doomed to futility. In the first place, it would affect beneficially only a relative handful of Negroes, and these would mainly be those who have sufficient capital to become entrepreneurs. The advocates of Negro business have little to say about the welfare of Negro workers engaged in such business, except to suggest that they do not suffer from a discriminatory policy of employment. No one argues, however, that their wages and hours would be better, their working conditions improved, or their work less hard. What evidence there is points in quite the opposite direction. The apologists for the self-sufficiency ideology are in pursuit of a policy of pure expediency and opportunism through exploitation of the segregation incident to the racial dualism of America. They refuse to believe that it is impossible to wring much wealth out of the already poverty-stricken Negro ghettoes of the nation. Moreover, it should be clear that Negro enterprise exists only on the sufferance of that dominant white business world which completely controls credit, basic industry and the state. "Big" Negro business is an economic will-o'-the-wisp. Negro business strikes its appeal for support on a racial note, viz: the race can progress only through economic unity. But the small, individually-owned Negro businesses have little chance to meet successfully the price competition of the large-capital, more efficient and often nation-wide white business. The very poverty of the Negro consumer dictates that he must buy where buying is cheapest; and he can ill afford to invest in racial good-will while he has far too little for food. In this sense, Negro business looms as a parasitical growth on the Negro society, in that it exploits the "race problem." It demands for itself special privilege and parades under the chauvinistic protection of "race loyalty," thus further exploiting an already down-trodden group. It represents the welfare only of the pitifully small Negro middle-class group, though demanding support for its ideology from the race conscious Negro masses. Negro business may offer a measure of relief from racial and economic disadvantage to a handful of the more able or the more fortunate members of the race. But it is much more certain that the vast majority of Negroes in America will continue to till the soil and to toil in the industries of white America.[34]

This is sound reasoning. But when all this is said—when it is granted that there is no prospect that Negro business will ever develop to great importance and that, in any case, even if the business class is benefited, no great gains are assured to the mass of the Negro people—there are, nevertheless, some credit items which should not be ignored. *The chief advantage is the tiny Negro business and professional class itself, which lives by providing goods and services to Negroes.* It is this class which has the education and leisure necessary to articulate the Negro protest and to take up successful collective bargaining with white society.

In the long run, this class can be depended upon to voice the interests of the broad masses of Negroes, simply because its own interests are convergent with those of the masses of Negroes. The Negro preacher, doctor, lawyer, journalist, real estate dealer, insurance man, banker, mortician, and retail merchant has his business founded upon Negro purchasing power. If he serves only the upper strata, his interests are, nevertheless, indirectly tied to the interests of the masses, as the majority of his customers live off the common Negroes. He might sometimes exploit the masses mercilessly. But fundamentally he must want the Negroes to get employment and good pay or, if employment shrinks, he must want them to get public relief, because otherwise he will fail himself.

He must want the common Negroes to have the vote, because otherwise he will be less protected himself. He must want justice, because a prejudiced police and court system is a danger to him too. And when he fights against the humiliations of the Jim Crow system, which hurt him more than the Negro masses, even this is in the long run to the advantage of all Negroes. That there are exceptions and conflicts of interest is not denied. But neither should it be concealed that, in the main, the Negro masses can rely upon their upper class people to wage a fight that is in their interest.

12. "Back to Africa"

The idea of sending American Negroes back to Africa or to some other place outside the United States has, in the main, been confined to the whites. As Bunche observes: "The real significance of the colonization schemes is to be found in the conception of the Negro as an evil that had to be done away with."[35] This is true also in the case of such humanitarians and liberals as Thomas Jefferson and Abraham Lincoln when they showed interest in such projects.

The American Colonization Society was thus organized in 1817 to rid America of the free Negroes who were considered a danger to slavery in the Southern states. Its work proceeded parallel to the measures taken to regiment the slaves, to discourage manumission, to hinder slave and free Negroes from being taught to read, and generally to suppress the free Negro population.[a] There were individual sponsors who had a different view, but in general the Society took a pro-slavery attitude.

In spite of great efforts, the colonization scheme was a failure, owing to inadequate capital, the unwillingness of the free Negroes to emigrate, and the inability of those of them who did go to Liberia to develop any kind of prosperous community in that equatorial region—their failure, of course, being taken as conclusive evidence of the Negro's incapacity for self-government. The chief result of the Colonization Society's crusade was the passage of laws in the southern states prohibiting the education of Negroes, whether slave or free, under penalty of fine and imprisonment.[36]

[a] See Chapter 20, Section 4.

Most of the Abolitionists prior to the Civil War were critical of the movement, and Garrison pointed out that in the zenith of its activity a great many more slaves were brought illegally from Africa every year than the Society had ever sent there during all the years of its existence. After the Civil War and Emancipation the movement gradually vanished.

Most of the Negroes who went to Africa under the Society's auspices did so as part of a bargain with their masters in return for their freedom.[a] But there were some free Negroes who considered that colonization would be preferable to their anomalous and hopeless position in America. Since then there has always been some discussion among Negroes about the advisability of colonization.[37] The Garvey movement, referred to in Chapter 35, shows that the Negro masses are not immune to the idea. There have always been individual whites who have propagandized for it. Recently Senator Bilbo of Mississippi has made himself the white spokesman for it. He claims that more than two million Negroes signed a petition to the President endorsing his proposal, but this is probably a great exaggeration. In an interview with the present writer, he explained that he will wait for an increase of Negro support and for favorable circumstances, but when the question has so matured, he will take it up for more effective political pressure. Negro intellectuals are practically united against the back-to-Africa proposal. And this is understandable. They are entirely American in their culture; they want to stay in America and fight it out here.

The issue is dead at present but it might rise again. Should America enter into a period of protracted unemployment after the present War, and should this unemployment become more concentrated upon the Negro people—prospects which are not unlikely—then the Negro, who has traditionally been looked upon by the whites as cheap labor, might increasingly come to be looked upon as a relief burden. It is not beyond possibility that a large proportion of Southern whites might under certain circumstances come to demand the sending away of Negroes from America. And we know that if the pressure is hard, there will be considerable response in the Negro masses to Negro leaders who promise to take them back to Africa.[38]

However, under the perspective of present trends, there is also a more positive aspect of Negro colonization in Africa. Under the moral pressure of the present War, American and British statesmen are now making declarations that equality and liberty will be established in the whole world. The Atlantic Charter is only one example of a whole trend of public commitments to the freedom of suppressed peoples. Applied to Africa, these vague promises can have no other import than that the imperialistic exploitation of the Black Continent shall come to an end after the present War and that the century-old dreams of a true colonization of Africa will

[a] See Chapter 8, Section 2, especially footnote 4.

finally be realized. This cannot occur, however, until Africa is not a chess-board divided among European powers but is ruled in the interests of humanity and its own native population and with the goal that its various peoples will be independent as soon as possible, and until capital is invested in health and education and in the development of its natural resources. Lord Hailey, an Englishman, has already done some of the necessary spade work[39] of scientific inquiry for such practical work; a committee under his chairmanship is now preparing further plans. The problem is also being discussed in America. A committee of prominent white and Negro Americans under the chairmanship of Anson Phelps Stokes—The Committee on Africa, the War, and Peace Aims—has recently (1942) published a report, *The Atlantic Charter and Africa from an American Standpoint*, containing constructive proposals for a new African policy.

There are several factors which make it more probable, perhaps, that something positive will materialize out of the vague promises. One is that America has not taken any part in the African skin game. Another one is the fact that Russia and China are bound to play an important role in the peace. If anything in line with the promises would be carried out, it would be natural that American Negroes would take both a great interest in the adventure and an active part in its staging. Many Negroes in America feel an emotional attachment to Africa and its population. And because of their color they would, with greater ease, gain the confidence of the African Negroes. Until now there have been few such thoughts in the American Negro world. But Du Bois, who has become the most catholic of all Negro thinkers, with room for nearly every idea, remarks:

. . . my plan would not decline frankly to face the possibility of eventual emigration from America of some considerable part of the Negro population, in case they could find a chance for free and favorable development unmolested and unthreatened, and in case the race prejudice in America persisted to such an extent that it would not permit the full development of the capacities and aspirations of the Negro race.[40]

The post-war development might perhaps come to realize not only the second but also the first of these two conditions.

13. MISCELLANEOUS IDEOLOGIES

The white colonization schemes have practically never—even in the period when large regions of this country were unexploited—considered the possibility of settling the Negroes separately on the North American continent. Neither has there been much of a drive among Negroes to attempt to establish segregated Negro regions. The advocates of a Negro "Forty-Ninth State" have never found much of an audience. As we mentioned,[a] the Communist phantasmagoria of a liberated, Negro-governed Black Belt fell flat among the American Negroes.

[a] See Chapter 35, Section 8.

The account of Negro ideologies in this chapter is only selective. There are a great number of other loose ideas rambling around in the Negro world, on how to solve the Negro problem; some of them are referred to in other chapters of this part. Amalgamation and passing are sometimes referred to vaguely as an "ultimate solution." There are popular chauvinistic theories connected with religious ideas in the various churches and sects. Racialism of the Garvey type is harbored among the masses and, as Bunche observes, "there are, in the Negro universities, a good many 'academic Garveyites'."[41] Under this racial perspective the world may assume queer proportions:

> Thus many Negroes hold to a conception of the Negro problem that can be described only as an "optimistic fatalism." The burdens of the present are lightened in the conviction of the inevitability of the "black man's day" when all will be reversed. Whereas the Lothrop Stoddards bombard the white man with warning that the dark tide is rising, the black man considers this an augury of that future day when the world will see the "bottom rail on top," when black men will rule and their past will be vindicated. The heroic struggle of the British Indians for independence is acclaimed: Japan's rise to power in the East—even her invasion of China —is regarded as a source of great encouragement; every instance of rebellion in Africa, the Dutch East Indies, the West Indies, is hailed as a victory. Ethiopia was championed against Italy, and Liberia is a source of great pride. Every outbreak in Europe is considered of utmost importance to the dark races of the world. The internecine conflicts, the conflagrations in the white world are all regarded as certain signs of the ultimate decline and fall from dominance of the white races, upon which the dark peoples will invest the chancellories of the world. It is pointed out that the dark people greatly outnumber the whites in the population of the world. That all this will transpire is never doubted; it is not a product of reason or cold calculation, but is based upon blind faith. It is foretold in the stars, the scriptures, by the prophets; it is written and must come to pass.[42]

Even the most superb political brains of the Negro people, constantly holding themselves with intentional effort to positive thinking, must sometimes feel tired and pessimistic when facing the difficulties of getting a hearing from the dominant whites. Confesses James Weldon Johnson:

> There is in us all a stronger tendency toward isolation than we may be aware of. There come times when the most persistent integrationist becomes an isolationist, when he curses the white world and consigns it to hell. This tendency toward isolation is strong because it springs from a deep-seated, natural desire—a desire for respite from the unremitting, gruelling struggle; for a place in which refuge might be taken. We are again and again confronted by this question. It is ever present, though often dormant.[43]

What holds Negro thinking in a fairly consistent scheme and directs it most of the time upon positive goals is, in the final analysis, the determination to hold to the American Creed. Bowen summarizes a study of Negro opinion thus:

> But admitting the division of public opinion among Negroes, this survey found that on some matters Negro opinion is more united than white opinion is upon almost anything. It found for instance, that Negro opinion is, so to speak, completely united on the proposition that, given the necessary technical qualifications, Negroes should be equally eligible with whites for any job in the United States. It found Negro opinion united on the proposition that skin color should not be penalized in any way whatsoever. It found division of opinion as to how this can be brought about, but the division is as to ways and means, not as to objective. In other words, the color line itself is unjust and tyrannical.[44]

It is true that all Negroes down to the poorest Southern sharecropper are attached to Uncle Sam and expect more justice from Washington than from the state capitol, and more from the state capitol than from the county courthouse. The Negro people have a clear and unanimous view on the problem of "state rights *versus* federal rights." They are for centralization. "They feel themselves as Americans and want to be nothing else," observes Schrieke:

> But there is the real problem: they are American and Negro. As Negroes they see themselves constantly through American eyes. That unreconciled double-consciousness is their greatest trouble.[45]

This dual pull is the correspondence in the Negro world to what we for the white world have called the American Dilemma. Du Bois has expressed the tragedy of it:

> It is a peculiar sensation, this double-consciousness, this sense of always looking at one's self through the eyes of others, of measuring one's soul by the tape of a world that looks on in amused contempt and pity. One ever feels his two-ness—an American, a Negro; two souls, two thoughts, two unreconciled strivings; two warring ideals in one dark body, whose dogged strength alone keeps it from being torn asunder.[46]

CHAPTER 39

NEGRO IMPROVEMENT AND PROTEST ORGANIZATIONS

1. A GENERAL AMERICAN PATTERN

A rich vegetation of associations and organizations for worth-while causes is an American characteristic. Americans are great "joiners," and they enjoy "campaigns" and "drives" for membership or contributions. Social clubs are plentiful, and even they are taken with a seriousness difficult for a stranger to understand. Enthusiasm is invested in committee work of small importance in churches, lodges, clubs and civic organizations of all kinds.

Undoubtedly, this cultural trait is partly to be explained as an outflow of the idealism and moralism of the American people. Americans generally are eager to improve their society.[a] They also have a kindly spirit of neighborliness. They like to meet each other and to feel tied together for a common cause. For these things they are prepared to sacrifice freely of their time and their money. It is natural for the ordinary American, when he sees something that is wrong, to feel not only that "there should be a law against it,"[b] but also that an organization should be founded to combat it.

More fundamentally, this trait is an indication of political frustration. Americans are a politically minded people, and the traditions of democracy are strong. But they do not have much of an outlet for their public interests within their political system, as it has come to develop in practice. We have observed in a previous chapter that the degree of participation on the part of the common citizen in the daily duties and responsibilities of government is low in America—that is, *between* the recurrent elections and *except* for his part in forming the nebulous but powerful "public opinion."[c] This frustration is accentuated because the political parties are not built around broad ideals and common interests. The lack of political goals often goes to the extreme when parties become what the Americans call political "machines." Only to an unusually low degree can the ordinary American feel the political party to be a medium for his aspirations in the field of

---

[a] See Chapter 1, Section 12.
[b] See Chapter 1, Sections 8 and 9.
[c] See Chapter 33, Section 3.

social ideals. In so far as party politics is corrupt, it becomes the more understandable why the American wants to keep his efforts for worthy causes "outside party politics."[a] The huge amount of organizational activity is thus partly a sort of substitute satisfaction for the Americans' lively political interests which they find so thwarted in the American practice of government.

The lack of people's movements with broad well-integrated goals is part of this American setting.[b] The improvement and reform organizations usually have specialized aims, and an American who is using them to define himself with regard to his political leanings will have to—and often does—belong to a great number of them. In addition to such splits on issues, there is also a large overlapping of, and consequently competition between, organizations. Belonging to these organizations is, further, predominantly an upper and middle class pattern. The lower classes do not join organizations to the same extent. The organizations they do join are more likely to be merely social or religious.

No improvement or reform organization has ever developed a mass following for any length of time. If an organization should be able to build up a real mass following and keep it for any length of time, this would, of course, mean the formation of a new type of political party.[1] If this happened to a significant number of reform groups at the same time and if they came to join together in broader formations, it would effect a change in the political system. Natural outlets would be created for people's public interests, and most of the betterment organizations would have lost their excuse for existence. But the actual situation has never been thus.

In this setting the organizations actually have more of a "function" for the citizens' viewpoint than they would have in a system of democratic politics with more popular participation. Organizations are, in a sense, the salt of American politics. As there is so little idealism and, indeed, so few issues in ordinary party politics in America and, instead, often so much corruption, the ideals have to be pressed upon government from the outside. "Pressure groups" belong to this political system, where ideals and broad interests are so unsatisfactorily integrated into the democratic process.

This general American pattern will have to be kept in mind when we survey the Negro protest and improvement organizations. We shall find that, as usual, the Negro culture follows closely the American pattern with some differences in details, explainable in terms of the singular circumstances in which the Negro people live. As in other instances, those differences are of a type to make the Negro appear as an exaggerated American.

On the one hand, the Negroes must feel more frustrated in the American

[a] See Chapter 1, Section 10.
[b] See Chapter 33.

political system than the whites. The majority of Negroes live in the South and are disfranchised. In the North they live in big cities where machine rule is usual. Nationally as well as locally, the political parties give only scant attention to the Negroes' ideals and interests. Their extraordinary caste status gives Negroes tremendous grievances against society around which to rally. The Negro cause is conspicuously defined by the conflict between caste and the American Creed. On the other hand, there are certain factors which decrease interest in public affairs among Negroes. A greater proportion of the Negro people belong to the lower classes, and those classes among the Negroes are, on the average, poorer, less educated, more apathetic than in comparable white groups. There is more defeatism in all social classes of Negroes, and in the South there is even sheer fear of expressing an opinion. For these reasons, we might expect that the Negroes have plenty of organizations expressing the Negro protest, or some compromise between protest and accommodation; but we cannot expect much of a mass following.

We shall devote the major part of this chapter to a discussion of the three most important organizations for Negro protest and betterment: the National Association for the Advancement of Colored People (N.A.A.-C.P.), the Urban League, and the Commission on Interracial Relations. But we shall first mention the other organizations active in the field,[a] as they stood at the outbreak of the Second World War. Later we shall consider the development during the War. The value premises for our analysis are accounted for in a concluding section on Negro strategy.

2. NATIONALIST MOVEMENTS

There are still some remnants of the Garvey nationalist movement, officially entitled *The Universal Negro Improvement Association.*[b] A West

[a] In this chapter we shall not deal at all with certain white-dominated organizations. A number of left-wing organizations—the Communist party, the Socialist party, the American Civil Liberties Union, the International Labor Defense, the League for Industrial Democracy, the Workers Alliance of America, the American League for Peace and Democracy, the Independent Labor League of America, and others—have shown a more or less special interest in the Negro. (See Ralph Bunche, "The Programs, Ideologies, Tactics, and Achievements of Negro Betterment and Interracial Organizations," unpublished manuscript prepared for this study [1940], Vol. 4, pp. 675 ff.) Some movements—usually more to the right—have concentrated on the South, as the Southern Conference for Human Welfare (see Chapter 21, Section 5), the Southern Committee for Peoples' Rights of North Carolina, the Citizens' Fact Finding Movement in Georgia, the Committee on Economic and Racial Justice (with headquarters in New York) (see *idem*).

Finally, we shall not deal with the anti-Negro organizations—such as the Ku Klux Klan, the Women of the Ku Klux Klan, The Alabama Women's League for White Supremacy, The Alabama Women's Democratic Club, The National Association for the Preservation of the White Race, The White America Society. (For an analysis of these, see *ibid.*, Vol. 4, pp. 736 ff.)

[b] See Chapter 35, Section 7.

Indian Negro doctor, heading the New York division, which had established itself as an independent organization, explained its present-day (January, 1940) position to an interviewer for this study:

> We don't advocate going back to Africa. That will come in time. The main problem of the Negro is economic and that is what we must face. It's the Negro's problem and he must solve it by himself. . . . I say, if we can solve our economic problem, then to hell with the white man and that is exactly what we propose to do . . .
>
> Sir, the Negro must learn to keep his business to himself. He must be wise as a serpent and appear to be harmless as a dove. He must strike at the right moment. Let the European war start. Some Negroes are crying for peace. Peace, hell! Let them kill each other as long as they want to. The longer they do that, the better off the Negroes will be.[2]

This leader claimed for his own organization a membership of some 700 and referred to other small groups which carried on the original Garvey movement.[3]

The Peace Movement of Ethiopia is a back-to-Africa movement of a very different temper. It was founded at a meeting in Chicago at the end of 1932 and has been working in support of the "repatriation" bill of Senator Bilbo.[a] It is claimed that, within eight months, 400,000 names were obtained on a petition directed to the President of the United States requesting that he use relief funds to settle Negroes in Africa instead of supporting them as unemployed here. It is also claimed that a supplementary petition contains around 2,000,000 names from all states in the Union. The leaders of the movement are obscure.[4] The belief is strong in many quarters that they are the agents of Senator Bilbo.

In the memorial presented to the President at the end of 1933, the petitioners explained, among other things:

> We are simple minded, sincere, lowly, law-abiding workers who have maintained traditions of simple honesty, industry and frugality as much from choice as from necessity. Few of us have education, but we have learned not to heed the blandishments of self-seeking politicians, imposters, and the unworthy and undesirable products of the hectic civilization that is foreign to our nature. . . . Given an opportunity in our ancestral Africa, the knowledge of farming and of simple farm machinery and implements, which we have acquired here, would enable us to carve a frugal but decent livelihood out of the virgin soil and favorable climate of Liberia. . . . We are a liability now, and any cost of this project, no matter how great, would still, we sincerely believe, be a sound investment for the American people. . . . We, the subjoined and accompanying signatories, merely ask respectfully that we be eliminated from an over-crowded labor market and given a helping hand in establishing such social and economic independence as we are fitted for—establishing it where it will give no offense and where it may serve as an object lesson to tempt those who remain.[5]

[a] See Chapter 38, Section 12.

This sounds much more like the wishful dreaming of a kindly conservative Southern white man than an expression of thoughts and desires of American Negroes. In fact, I have nowhere seen any traces of this organization in the Negro communities I have visited. When the President found it impracticable to act favorably upon the petition, the memorialists turned to the General Assembly of Virginia, since Virginia had taken the initiative in acquiring the territory which is now Liberia. This legislative body resolved to recommend the proposal.[6]

The National Union for People of African Descent is another paper organization of American Negroes. It is extremely chauvinistic in the Garvey tradition. The aim of the organization is to create a sort of extra-territorial independence for the Negro people:

> . . . to obtain a nation, a flag, an army and navy exclusively of the black people, and through these media to ultimately throw off the yoke of white domination, white culture, and white mores.[7]

It has been helped by Negro unrest but does not seem to have made much headway.

The National Movement for the Establishment of the Forty-Ninth State wants to establish a territorial state in some less populated part of America:

> . . . not an isolated uncivilized hostile colony around which to build a figurative wall of China shutting out the possibilities of travel and growth from within and without; not a separate nation, but an interdependent commonwealth like any other of the present 48 states.[8]

In the Garvey tradition, this movement holds a fatalistic and pessimistic view of the Negroes' future in white America. White people do not consider giving Negroes justice and, therefore, Negroes will not get any unless they get off by themselves. Like all other organizations of this type—except the Garvey movement itself—it has never amounted to much.

During the present war crisis there have been rumors about various "fifth column" groups among American Negroes. For several years there have been attempts to disseminate Japanese propaganda to Negroes, but with minor success. Individual Negroes of the type who have been active in the small groups which are the remnants of the Garvey movement have given response, but their influence on Negro opinion is small. To our knowledge, only a few dozen Negroes have been arrested for advocating the cause of Japan.[a] There is undoubtedly a small group of Negroes who are in some degree friendly to Japan. A larger number take a vicarious satisfaction in imagining a Japanese (or German) invasion of the Southern

---

[a] In addition, some members of the Islamic cults have been arrested for failing to register for the draft. (*PM* [September 15, 1942 and September 22, 1942].) Two of the persons attempting to win Negroes to the cause of Japan were white. One was a follower

states.[9] But on the whole, while Negroes are dissatisfied, their protest has not turned in a treasonable direction. In fact, it may be said that their pro-democratic, anti-fascist ideology is at least as strong as that of most white groups in the United States.[a]

3. BUSINESS AND PROFESSIONAL ORGANIZATIONS

The National Negro Business League, founded by Booker T. Washington in 1900, has its purpose defined in the preamble to its constitution:

> That through the promotion of commercial achievement the race could be led to a position of influence in American life and thus pave the way to economic independence.[10]

The League functions as the national center for local business leagues, Negro chambers of commerce, and similar organizations of Negro business and professional men and women. Annually it conducts a three-day convention. Bunche reports about these conventions:

> The proceedings of these meetings consist mainly of informal business "life histories" given by the members, in which they trace the origin, development and present status of the business with which they are identified. This is in furtherance of the League's policy of stimulating and promoting business.[11]

It publishes a journal, *Negro Business,* and other propaganda material.[12] In 1929 the Business League launched *The Colored Merchants' Association* (C.M.A.) stores. This was a cooperative endeavor. The idea was to reduce costs and prices by cooperative buying and group advertising. But few Negro businesses were attracted, and the Negro consumers were generally not willing to accept the untested brands sold by the C.M.A. stores instead of the nationally advertised, standard brands offered by the white chain stores. The project failed during the depression.

We have discussed and criticized the ideology behind this movement in the preceding chapter.[b] Nothing the present writer has observed in Negro communities in various parts of America contradicts Bunche's evaluation:

> In terms of its influence on economic betterment of the Negro, the National Negro Business League has been inconsequential. As a factor in shaping the psychology and thinking of Negroes, however, it has been vastly important. . . . It has pursued the narrowest type of racial chauvinism, for it has organized, not business, but *Negro*

---

of the professional Fascist, Joe McWilliams. (*PM* [September 15, 1942].) The other owned the "Negro News Syndicate" and was supported by the Japanese. (*Time* magazine, [September 14, 1942], p. 46.)

[a] This is mainly an impression, but it has some substantiation in the various confidential polls of public opinion now being carried on, and in such small studies as that of Delbert C. Miller, "Effect of the War Declaration on the National Morale of American College Students," *The American Sociological Review* (October, 1942), pp. 631-644.

[b] See Chapter 38, Section 10.

business and has employed the racial situation as its main stock in trade in bidding for the support of Negro patronage.[13]

In 1918 Du Bois made an effort to create a national organization for consumers' cooperation. Upon his call, there met in the *Crisis* office "twelve colored men from seven different states" and they established *The Negro Co-operative Guild*.[14] Some abortive attempts to open cooperative stores in various cities were made, but nothing came out of it. Du Bois comments in 1940:

> The whole movement needed more careful preliminary spade work, with popular education both of consumers and managers; and for lack of this, it temporarily failed. It must and will be revived.[15]

We have touched upon the spontaneous movement, "don't buy where you can't work." There is no national organization behind this movement, but there are, or have been, several organizations with this purpose in many cities, as, for instance, *The Colored Clerks' Circle* in St. Louis and *The New Negro Alliance* in Washington.[16] The movement is a logical corollary of the Negro business philosophy. It is doomed to be rather inconsequential and even has potentialities damaging to Negro interests.[a]

Similar to the *National Negro Business League* are: *The National Negro Bankers' Association*, *The National Negro Insurance Association*, *The National Medical Association*, *The National Teachers' Association*, and *The National Bar Association*.[17] These organizations exist largely as substitutes for the ordinary professional organizations which to a large extent—and in the South regularly—exclude Negroes.[b] Also the Negro fraternities and sororities belong to this group of professional organizations. All of them are "race organizations" in the sense that they have as one of their purposes the improvement not only of their particular group's status but also that of the Negro people as a whole. Many of them do a considerable amount of lobbying and petitioning. In fact, even the churches, the lodges, and the social clubs are to a degree organizations for race defense. This tendency became intensified during the war crisis.

Special mention must be given to the *National Council of Negro Women* even though we cannot describe or evaluate it. It is under the presidency of Mrs. Mary McLeod Bethune, the outstanding Negro woman "race leader," president of Bethune-Cookman College in Florida, Negro advisor to the National Youth Administration and long head of the "Black Cabinet" in Washington.[c]

It is possible to view all the Negro organizations mentioned in this section as rather futile and inconsequential. This is the attitude prevailing

---

[a] See Chapter 14, Section 2, and Chapter 38, Section 11.
[b] See Chapter 29, Section 6.
[c] The "Black Cabinet" was discussed in Chapter 22, Section 5.

among the younger Negro intellectuals. When they are studied one by one and measured by their rather limited accomplishments, this view seems to be justified. Taken together, however, they mean that Negroes have increasingly become organized in natural social groups for concerted action, have become trained in orderly cooperation, and have become accustomed to plan and work together. All of them give an institutional sanction to protests against various kinds of discrimination. When seen in perspective, they represent bases for attempts at broader organizations.

To this category of Negro organizations belong Negro trade unions, but we have considered them in Chapter 38 and in Appendix 6.

4. THE NATIONAL NEGRO CONGRESS MOVEMENT

The Joint Committee on National Recovery was formed in the early days of the New Deal to watch out for Negro rights in the policy-making at Washington. Under the chairmanship of George Haynes, and with John P. Davis as executive secretary, it protested against wage differentials in industry and discriminatory administration of the agricultural programs, and it upheld the interests of Negroes in the code hearings under the N.R.A. It was supported financially by some twenty-two independent Negro organizations, though its major support came from the N.A.A.C.P.[18]

The National Negro Congress grew out of a conference in the spring of 1935 held at Howard University under the joint auspices of its Division of Social Sciences and of the Joint Committee on National Recovery. The idea was born that a national Negro agency, embracing all the existing Negro trade unions, religious, fraternal, and civic bodies, could give more strength and unity to all those organizations and, particularly, help awaken a response from the Negro masses. Stress was laid upon economic and social betterment as well as upon justice and citizens' rights.[19] For a time the National Negro Congress, which emerged out of these deliberations, actually showed prospects of becoming a strong Negro movement, though it finally failed.

The first National Negro Congress met in Chicago in February, 1936, for a three-day session. It was attended by 817 delegates, representing 585 organizations from 28 states and the District of Columbia. In a great number of resolutions, the Congress expressed the Negroes' dissatisfaction and protest and made practical proposals for change. Heading the list of resolutions was the general one to the effect that the Congress was not, and would never be, affiliated or dominated by any political faction or party.[20] A. Philip Randolph—the head of the Brotherhood of Sleeping Car Porters, who is not only the most prominent Negro trade unionist but one of the wisest Negro statesmen in the present generation—undertook the presidency and John P. Davis, who had been the secretary of the Joint Committee on National Recovery, became the executive secretary of the new organization. Local councils were established in many cities and seemed, in the beginning, to have been quite active. As late as 1939 and 1940, when the present writer traveled around in this country, the local councils of the National Negro Congress were the most important Negro organizations in some Western cities.

In October, 1937, the second National Negro Congress was held in Philadelphia. The delegates formed a total of 1,149 persons. Nothing important happened. Account was given of the progress in building up the organization. It is apparent that a chief difficulty was to get it on a sound financial basis. The third—and so far, the last—Congress meeting was held in Washington, D.C., in April, 1940. There were around 900 Negro and 400 white delegates representing organizations from all parts of the country. At this meeting the Congress sealed its doom by becoming simply a front organization for the Communist party.[21] Randolph was ushered from the presidency, and the Congress sank to unimportance, from which it will probably never rise again.[22]

The failure of the National Negro Congress seems due mainly to the following factors: lack of political training and understanding on the part of the rank and file of the Negro representatives for the various local Negro organizations; inability to raise even modest funds for the work of the organization; the skill, determination, and resources of the Communists, and their success in getting some of their group into the leadership of the Congress. Since 1940 the Congress has been kept up by the Communist party as a paper organization with some scattered local following, but it has largely lost its support from the other Negro organizations which originally furnished its basis.

The March on Washington Committee, led by A. Philip Randolph and created to voice the Negro protest in the war emergency, is in a sense a continuation of the nonpartisan general Negro movement represented by the Congress in its first year. We shall consider this Committee later.

The Southern Negro Youth Congress[23] was organized in Richmond, Virginia, in 1937, as a federation of Southern youth organizations. A yearly congress is held, the last one in April, 1942, at Tuskegee Institute.[24] Local councils are organized to conduct youth forums, work for crime reduction programs, health projects, vocational guidance campaigns, and similar activities in the interest of Negro youth. Owing to the "special problems" which face Negroes in the South, the local organizations have usually not been militant on questions of Negroes' rights. In spite of this, the author found that upper class Negroes in the South often considered the movement "radical" and dangerous for interracial peace.[25] Bunche gives, in 1940, this summary evaluation:

> The Southern Negro Youth Congress is a flame that flickers only feebly in a few Southern cities today. It started with promise but, lacking competent leadership, it

failed to catch the imagination of the young Negro of the South. Its program has been diffuse and recently, at least, seems to take its cue in the major essentials from the "line" laid down by the American Communist Party. . . . Moreover, no serious effort has been made to reach the lower class Negro youth of the South who are in dire need of guidance and encouragement. In its present form the Negro Youth Congress is run by and for a select group of Negro school boys and girls who are themselves terribly confused and often frustrated. It can contribute but little toward the progressive development of the Negro.[26]

This might be true enough, yet it should be recalled that any organization, even if its immediate accomplishments are small, represents a coming together of Negroes for concerted action, which gives training and vision.

5. THE NATIONAL ASSOCIATION FOR THE ADVANCEMENT OF COLORED PEOPLE

The National Association for the Advancement of Colored People is without question the most important agency for the Negroes in their struggle against caste. At several points in our inquiry, we have seen how it functions. It is an interracial movement. As a matter of fact, it was started on white people's initiative. In the summer of 1908 there had occurred a severe race riot in Springfield, Illinois, the home of Abraham Lincoln. Scores of Negroes had been killed or wounded and many had been driven out of the city. Wide publicity was given the affair in the press and one writer, William English Walling, threw a challenge to the nation: there was a need for a revival of the spirit of the Abolitionists to win liberty and justice for the Negro in America. The appeal was answered by Mary White Ovington. In January, 1909, Miss Ovington met with Mr. Walling and Dr. Henry Moskowitz in New York, and the plans were laid for the organization that was to become the N.A.A.C.P. Of these three, Miss Ovington is still active on the board of the N.A.A.C.P.[a]

Oswald Garrison Villard was asked to draft a call for a conference on February 12, 1909, the one hundredth anniversary of Abraham Lincoln's birth. Signed by many prominent white and Negro liberals, the document pointed in ringing phrases to the injustices inflicted upon the Negro against the letter and the spirit of the Constitution, and called upon

. . . all believers in democracy to join in a national conference for the discussion of present evils, the voicing of protests, and the renewal of the struggle for civil and political liberty.[27]

[a] Mary White Ovington, *How the National Association for the Advancement of Colored People Began* (1914), cited by Bunche, *op. cit.*, Vol. 1, p. 24. The following account of the N.A.A.C.P. has drawn heavily from Bunche's memorandum, compared with critical comments and information given by Walter White, the Secretary of the N.A.A.C.P., and Roy Wilkins, the Assistant Secretary of the N.A.A.C.P. and Editor of *The Crisis*. See also Paul E. Baker, *Negro-White Adjustment* (1934), pp. 43 ff.

At this first conference a committee of forty was formed to carry on the work. Mass meetings were held, pamphlets distributed, and memberships solicited. The following year, at a second conference, a merger was consummated of the forces of the Negro liberals of the Niagara Movement [a] and of the white liberals of Abolitionist traditions. Out of these two groups the National Association for the Advancement of Colored People was formed. Moorfield Storey of Boston was elected the first president. He and all other officers of the new organization were white, except Du Bois, who was to become the salaried Director of Publicity and Research. The platform adopted was practically identical with that of the Niagara Movement. It was at the time considered extremely radical.[28] "Thus," comments Bunche, "the N.A.A.C.P., propelled by dominant white hands, embarked upon the civil liberties course that the Negro-inspired Niagara Movement had futilely tried to navigate."[29] From the beginning Du Bois gave the tone to the new organization's activity. By 1914 there were thirteen Negro members on the Board of Directors, most of whom were veterans of the Niagara Movement. In 1910 the publication of the organization's journal, *The Crisis*, began and it soon became popular.

The long-run objective of the organization has always been to win full equality for the Negro as an American citizen. The specific objectives can best be presented by the following citation from its program as announced in 1940:

1. Anti-lynching legislation.
2. Legislation to end peonage and debt slavery among the sharecroppers and tenant farmers of the South.
3. Enfranchisement of the Negro in the South.
4. Abolition of injustices in legal procedure, particularly criminal procedure, based solely upon color or race.
5. Equitable distribution of funds for public education.
6. Abolition of segregation, discrimination, insult, and humiliation based on race or color.
7. Equality of opportunity to work in all fields with equal pay for equal work.
8. Abolition of discrimination against Negroes in the right to collective bargaining through membership in organized labor unions.[30]

The N.A.A.C.P. works through the National Office in New York City and through branches or local associations in cities everywhere in the country.[31] The National Office determines the policy of the organization and supervises the work of the branches.[32] The National Office, including *The Crisis*, employs 13 salaried executive officers and 17 other paid employees. All are Negroes. The president of the Association has always been a white man; at present he is Arthur B. Spingarn, who succeeded his brother, the late Joel E. Spingarn. The Board of Directors has mem-

[a] See Chapter 35, Section 4.

bers of both races; at present it is composed of 30 Negroes and 17 whites. There are 13 vice-presidents, 4 of whom are Negroes.[33] The main executive officer and the responsible head of the Association is the secretary. This office is now held by Walter White. Few branch officers are white, although some whites serve on executive committees of branches. It is estimated that about 10 per cent of the total membership of the Association is white. The Association is interracial only at the top, but practically all Negro at the base.

The war crisis is giving increasing importance to the Association and during the last few years there has been a remarkable increase in the number of local branches and in membership rolls. Currently there are 481 branches of the Association and, in addition, 77 youth councils[34] and 22 college chapters. The total membership of the Association is approximately 85,000. *The Crisis* has a circulation of about 17,500 copies. Since 1940 the Association has published a monthly paper, the *N.A.A.C.P. Bulletin,* which goes to all members. The National Office operates on a budget of around $85,000. Much the larger part of the budget is derived from membership fees, but a smaller part is raised by contributions from individuals and from a few foundations, most often given for specific purposes.[35]

The branches—and consequently the National Association—have nowhere been able to build up a real mass following among Negroes. The membership is still largely confined to the upper classes. It should be remembered, though, that lack of mass participation is not peculiar to the N.A.A.C.P. or even to the Negro world but is a characteristic of American public life as a whole. Few similar organizations have reached the organizational stability and the membership size of the N.A.A.C.P. It should also be stressed that, while the lack of mass following is a weakness, the high intellectual quality of the membership of the N.A.A.C.P. is an asset. Few organizations in the entire country compare with the N.A.A.C.P. in respect to the education and mental alertness of the persons attracted to it. In a study of 5,512 Negro college graduates from all areas and of all ages, Charles S. Johnson found that 25 per cent of them were members of the N.A.A.C.P.[36] No other organization for Negroes approached this percentage. The quality of the membership is reflected in the National Office. The national leaders of Negroes have generally been intellectuals,[37] and the N.A.A.C.P. represents the highest manifestation of this general tendency. In most branches Negro professionals and businessmen constitute almost exclusively the officers, boards and executive committees.

More fundamentally, however, this structure of the Association is a weakness. The Association should have a much larger popular support in order to be able to fight with greatest success. The national leaders of the movement, and also most of the local branch officers I have come in contact with, are aware of the fact that the Association, if it wants to grow, must gain more members in the lower and middle classes of the Negro people. In the present war crisis the Association is making great strides forward, and it is reported that Negro workers are increasingly coming to join the Association.[38] There is also in recent years a visible tendency to try to get workers, and, particularly, trade union officials, on the boards of the branches. It is not improbable that as a result of the rigors and exigencies of the War, the N.A.A.C.P. will come out as an organization much stronger in membership and with much more of a following among the masses.

6. The N.A.A.C.P. Branches

The activity of the Association depends largely upon the effective organization of its branches. They provide it with membership, the larger part of its financial support, and information from and contacts with its field of work. The branches are the lifeline of the Association, and the National Office is constantly struggling to maintain them in vigor and to found new branches, especially in recent years.[39]

It is a heavy task the Association demands from the branches. We quote from a summary made by Bunche from the instructions given by the National Office:

The branches are to assume responsibility for the general welfare of the Negro population of the particular locality. In carrying out the broad program enunciated by the National Office, they are local vigilante groups covering all of the ramifications of Negro life in a prejudice ridden *milieu*. The branches are to check on "biased and discriminatory legislation, biased and discriminatory administration of the law, and injustice in the courts." They are to combat attempts at racial discrimination in civil rights, parks, museums, theaters, conveyances and other public places, and in charitable and public agencies. They are expected to bring test cases on the rights of Negro citizens before the courts, where great injustice is done because of race or color prejudice. Instances of police brutality against Negroes are to be fought, and Northern branches are admonished to be on the alert for cases of extradition involving Negroes who have sought refuge in the North against Southern injustice. Branches are to seek to secure new laws and ordinances to protect the welfare of Negro citizens and to prevent race discrimination. . . . The branches are expected to assume responsibility for stimulating school attendance of Negro children, and encouraging Negro youth to attend high school and college, and also to see to it "that careful technical training in some branch of modern industry is furnished all colored children." The branches must oppose all forms of educational discrimination, and demand equal educational accommodations and facilities for Negro youth; direct educational segregation, and the subtle zoning of educational districts so as to segregate Negro children indirectly, should be fought, and the branches should cooperate in the current fight to equalize teachers' salaries in Southern schools, and to eliminate the Negro-white differentials in educational appropriations. Similarly the branches are to look after the health needs of the Negro communities; tax supported hospitals excluding Negro patients should be attacked, and efforts put forth to place Negro nurses and internes in municipal hospitals. The branches are to strive for wider employment opportunities and better wages for Negroes; discrimination in Civil Service employments should be opposed. The branches should cooperate with all community efforts touching the welfare of Negro citizens, and should combat unfavorable treatment of the Negro in the local press. They should cultivate cordial relations between the races in the community. Negroes should be encouraged to qualify for voting and to vote; all possible influence should be brought to bear toward the adoption and enforcement of civil rights laws; discriminatory practices in the administration of relief and on government work projects should be exposed and protested; and better housing for Negroes should be striven for.[40]

As suggested in this statement, the National Office advises its branches on tactics as well as aims. The branches are advised "that injury to one Negro on racial grounds affects the status of the whole group, and hence, the health and happiness of our American civilization."[41] The present War, with the many problems it raises or aggravates for Negroes, has, of course, increased the demands upon the branches.

When these things are considered: the immensity of the tasks set for the branches; the high demands made upon the time, interest, intelligence, and tact of the branch officers; the fact that those officers are not salaried but work on a voluntary basis in their free time; the inherent difficulties of minority tactics and, particularly, the power situation in the South; the fact that few white people outside the national center of the organization are prepared to give assistance or even sympathy to the work; while poverty, ignorance, and defeatism are widespread among the Negro masses—when all these adverse factors are considered, it should not be a surprise that hardly any branch even approaches the realization of the ideals envisaged for its active working.[42] If we consider the handicaps under which the branches work, we should classify them, before the War, as a few energetic branches, some dormant branches, and the majority of branches somewhere between.[43] As is natural, branches in the South had small membership rolls and showed little activity. They often seemed to run through a sort of irregular vitality cycle.

(1) The normal condition is local inactivity but with maintenance of a basic membership roll and more or less regular meetings, where the stress is usually given to the general goals of the Association more than to the specific problems of the locality. There are always social and educational entertainments. Belonging to the Association and paying dues is, in the upper classes, considered a minimum duty of a "race man" and a sign of community spirit and social respectability. "In the main," states a president of a local association in the Upper South, "we are concerned with collecting the dollar to aid the national group financially— you see we have so many organizations here to take up people's time."[44] Another head of a branch in the Deep South, whose policy is one of caution because he fears greater repression by local whites, explains it this way: "Our

task is to supply the material and the money; the folks up North have got to stick their necks out for us."[45]

(2) Now and then, ordinarily not for a period of many years, the local association flares up to importance in the community on account of a particularly self-sacrificing and energetic leader or group of leaders. Some actions are taken: In the North, these may be anything within the scope of the organization's aims. In the South they are usually restricted to the following things: a drive to get Negroes to register and vote; the organization of Negro voters to defeat a bond issue when Negro interests are flagrantly neglected; a representation to the authorities for more adequate schools or hospital facilities, for improved housing conditions, parks, and playgrounds, for the hiring of Negro policemen or firemen to serve in Negro districts, for the equalization of salaries of Negro teachers, against occasional police brutality; the instigation of a law suit to save a victim from the injustice of the region. No Southern branch could ever have the resources—or the boldness—to raise more than one or two such issues at a time. By its activity it receives publicity, and a membership drive will temporarily raise the enrollment considerably.

(3) After some time the activity falls again, either because the leaders move away or get disillusioned, or because of developing factionalism and internal strife and jealousy. Sometimes the cause is that influential white people in the community scare the leaders, or at least some of them, by telling them that they have to slow down. In either case the branch returns to its normal condition of relative ineffectiveness with maintenance and watchfulness. In extreme cases the branch can be totally destroyed.

In many Southern communities conservative or dependent upper and middle class Negroes shared the common white opinion in the region that the N.A.A.C.P. is a "foreign" or "radical" organization, that its policy is "tactless" and "tends to stir up undue hostility between the races." They stayed away from it entirely or made a compromise by paying dues but never attending meetings and by generally advising the organization to abstain from taking any action. I often heard the complaint that teachers are timid about identifying themselves with the Association for fear of jeopardizing their jobs, and that preachers are reluctant to join since their churches are often mortgaged by white people. In other communities, teachers and preachers were important in the local associations, but they did not usually urge action. Most other upper class Negroes also are dependent on the whites and have to proceed carefully. One prominent Negro leader in a city in the Deep South, which has a bad history of intimidation of Negroes, commented to us upon a recent unsuccessful effort to get a branch started again:

They went about it wrong. The best way to get an organization like that started here is to go talk to the white man first.[46]

This attitude should not be criticized in levity but must be understood against the background of the Southern caste situation.

Another difficulty of the typical N.A.A.C.P. branch is the competition for interest, time, and money from churches, lodges and social clubs of all sorts. Particularly as the N.A.A.C.P. cannot promise much in immediate returns for the individual, this competition is serious. Other competition comes from independent local civic organizations, often with the same local program.[47] There are hundreds of such organizations, often several in one city. The explanation of this is partly the same as of the great number of splits in sects and churches.[a] The local organizations sometimes thrive upon the spread of suspicion and even hostility against the N.A.A.C.P. as "foreign," "outside" or "meddling by a clique of New Yorkers." But more often the motives for the split are even more superficial and petty. Undoubtedly, it would mean a great increase in strength for the N.A.A.C.P. —and an equally great asset for the Negroes' organizational activity as a whole—if these organizations could be integrated as branches of the Association.

Sometimes, however, there are more objective reasons for organizational duplication. In an earlier chapter we have given an illustration from a city in the Lower South where a League for Civic Improvement was maintained to do the pussy-footing with which the N.A.A.C.P. could not be compromised.[b] In a city in the Upper South there is a powerful Committee on Negro Affairs with a membership of around a thousand, carrying on most of the Negro politics in the community. The N.A.A.C.P. branch has only about a hundred members. According to the president, the main function of the branch now seems to be one of patient waiting—it will step into the breach if the Committee fails or if the backing of the National Office is needed.[48] The leaders of the Committee on Negro Affairs, on the other hand, point out that the N.A.A.C.P. "helps us because the white man will do things for us to keep the N.A.A.C.P. out." A prominent Negro leader in one of the largest cities of the Deep South, who, himself, regards the N.A.A.C.P. as "radical," explains:

> The South doesn't like the N.A.A.C.P. and regards it as an alien force; but though whites won't give to the radical group what it demands, the conservative group can come behind and capitalize on the situation created by the "radicals." Therefore, both radical and conservative Negro groups are necessary—the radicals do the blocking and tackling and the conservatives "carry the ball."[49]

If all the difficulties under which a Negro protest movement has to work in the South are remembered, it is rather remarkable, in the final analysis, that the N.A.A.C.P. has been able to keep up and slowly build out its network of branches in the region, and that several of the Southern branches have been so relatively active. A strength of the organization is

[a] See Chapter 40.
[b] See Chapter 37, Section 10.

that, even if the formal membership is small, the great majority of Negroes in all classes in the South, as well as in the North, back its program.

The N.A.A.C.P. branches in the Northern cities usually have larger membership rolls than those in Southern cities, not only because there are many more Negroes in the average Northern Negro community, but also because most of the specific difficulties under which the Southern branches labor are absent. They are free to carry out campaigns and to take cases into court. The Negro vote gives them a backing for their demands. Considering the much more favorable conditions under which the Northern branches work, it should be no surprise that they are generally stronger and more active than Southern branches. The surprising thing is that they are not stronger and more active than they actually are.

7. THE N.A.A.C.P. NATIONAL OFFICE

The major part of the work carried on by the Association is performed by its National Office, which strikes the observer as unusually effective in its work. Owing to the National Office, the Association exerts—locally and nationally—an influence out of proportion to its small membership. The 33-year life span of the Association and the constant publicity it has received over the years give it prestige, stability, and respect, which the national officers know how to capitalize upon.

Generally, the National Office acts as a "watchdog" over Negro rights. When anything important develops on the national or on some local scene which is adverse to Negro interest, the Association promptly intervenes. A usual measure is that its secretary directs a telegram or letter to the responsible officials, which is made public through the press service of the Association. Of special importance is its watch on national legislation. The National Office tries to get hearings before Congressional committees and other investigating bodies and places on record its information and its demands on behalf of the Negroes. In the same way the Association fights for remedial legislation and for the adoption of changes in administrative practice. It is prepared to associate itself with other white or Negro organizations in cases touching Negro rights and interests.

Systematic lobbying, primarily in Washington, but also in state capitals, is kept up. Much of this work falls upon the shoulders of the secretary, Walter White. The Association tries to get on public record the opinions in crucial problems of federal administrators, congressmen, governors, other state officials, and important personalities in organizations and in business.

It loses no opportunity to place each and every elected or appointed official on record regarding specific cases affecting Negroes, such as lynching, riots, civil service discrimination, segregation, the right to vote, public works, unemployment relief, slander of the Negro race, etc. Where an official is derelict in his duty or openly prejudiced against Negroes, the National Office rallies the Branches to political action against him. In this way it has defeated for re-election many politicians guilty of race bias.[50]

The Association has successfully fought the appointment or election to public office of persons known to be prejudiced against Negroes.[51]

The Association puts its trust in publicity. A large part of the activity of the National Office is in the nature of educational propaganda. It not only publishes *The Crisis* and the *N.A.A.C.P. Bulletin*, but also a great many pamphlets, brochures and books on various aspects of the Negro problem. The officers of the National Office strive to present their case to the white public also through articles in outstanding national periodicals. The National Office provides data for research work on the Negro problem and for political work even when it is carried on outside the Association. From its staff or from a circle of active sympathizers, it furnishes speakers for important meetings. The officers of the Association travel widely on lecture tours all over the country. Most of the officers have traveled and lectured abroad, displaying the American Negro case to a world audience. Du Bois represented the Association as a lobbyist at the Versailles Peace Conference "in order to interpret to the Peace delegates the interests of the Negro peoples of the world."[52] The National Office has its own press service, which is used by the Negro press[a] and, occasionally, also by liberal white magazines and newspapers. In its publicity the National Office has a militant and challenging tone but is ordinarily—as far as the present author has been able to check during the course of this study—scrupulously correct in statements of fact.

In a broader sense, all the work of the Association is centered around creating favorable publicity for the Negro people and winning a hearing for their grievances from the general American public. Publicity is, therefore, an important aspect of all its moves. It succeeds rather well in reaching the alert strata of the Negro people—mainly through Negro newspapers—but it attempts also to reach the white public. There it is less successful, but more successful than any other agency. Its unceasing efforts are based upon the typical American democratic trust in the righteousness of the common man:

> . . . we must win the American public to want this right for us. They are a just people and if we could by education get them to see how silly and needlessly cruel it is to deny a person food and shelter, they would help enforce the law.[53]

In its lobbying the National Office pretends with grace to represent the Negro people and is not afraid of making threats by referring to the Negro vote. When we consider the weakness of its local branches and the general rivalry and apathy in the Negro communities, this appears to be largely

[a] See Chapter 42.

bluffing, and it is often successful bluffing. This is said not in criticism but in sincere admiration.[a]

From the very beginning, the Association has laid stress on its legal redress work, and this has always been a most important and, certainly, the most spectacular part of its activity.[54] The Association takes its stand on the legal equality of all the citizens of the country stipulated in the Constitution,[b] and in most of the laws of the several states of the South and the North. It brings selected cases of discrimination and segregation to the test of law suits.

In hundreds of cases, the lawyers of the N.A.A.C.P. have been instrumental in saving Negroes from unequal treatment by the courts, sometimes getting them acquitted when they were sentenced or in danger of being sentenced on flimsy evidence; sometimes getting death penalties or other severe penalties reduced.[55] The frequently successful fights to prevent the extradition of Negroes from Northern to Southern communities, when the likelihood of obtaining a fair trial for the Negroes sought could be shown to be questionable, has proved time and again an especially effective means of focusing national attention upon the low standards of legal culture in the South.[56] In numerous cases the exclusion of Negroes from grand and petit juries has been challenged, and the Association shares in establishing precedents by which the principle is now firmly established that the exclusion of Negroes from jury service is a denial of the equal protection of the laws guaranteed by the Fourteenth Amendment to the Constitu-

---

[a] Roy Wilkins comments on this point: ". . . the issues on which the N.A.A.C.P. uses the threat of reprisal by voters are carefully selected out of our long experience with items we know colored voters will resent at the polls, regardless of party affiliations or other distracting factors. But it must be remembered that we labor under no illusions so far as marshalling a complete bloc of Negro voters as such against any particular candidate or proposal. We know that party affiliation comes first with many colored people, just as it does with other racial groups. They are loyal, Democratic workers, for instance, first of all. We know that job-holding, or the hope of winning jobs will influence the vote more than consideration for racial ideals. We know that some communities will vote for segregated Negro schools on the excuse that only through those schools can they get jobs for their daughters as teachers. In other words, there is no such thing as a purely Negro vote. Nevertheless, on some broad questions, grievously aggravated in some community or by some politician, it is possible to swing a goodly section of the Negro vote in the way it should go, despite other factors operating." (Memorandum [August 11, 1942].)

[b] There is an interesting story from the First World War told by James Weldon Johnson. Du Bois, who was then editor of *The Crisis*, had been to the front in France and had a good deal to say about the treatment of the Negro soldier:

"The utterances of Dr. Du Bois in *The Crisis*, the organ of the association, brought a visit to the office from agents of the Department of Justice; in reply to the query: 'Just what is this organization fighting for?' Dr. Du Bois said: 'We are fighting for the enforcement of the Constitution of the United States.' This was an ultimate condensation of the program of the association." (*Black Manhattan*, p. 247.)

tion.[57] Police brutality, third degree methods in forcing confessions, and peonage have been fought.

The Association has likewise been continuously active in defending the Negroes' right to vote.[a] In 1915 it succeeded in having the "grandfather clauses" of Southern state constitutions declared unconstitutional. It has fought several other cases connected with the white primary and other means of disfranchising Negroes. As we know, it has not succeeded in hindering the wholesale disfranchisement of the Southern Negro population. But it has put a stop to Southern legislatures enacting the most bluntly discriminatory provisions against the suffrage of Negroes and has thus achieved a strategic situation where the white South increasingly bases disfranchisement upon extra-legal measures.[b] In the very year of the foundation of the Association a movement started to legalize residential segregation by city ordinance.[c] Challenging the constitutionality of this type of legislation was one of the main efforts of the Association during its first decade. In the famous Louisville Segregation Case, a decisive victory was won. The Association has been constantly vigilant, though with considerable caution, against the Jim Crow laws and, particularly, against inferior facilities for Negroes in segregated set-ups of various sorts. In recent years it has concentrated its attack on the barriers against Negro students[58] and on the unequal salaries of Negro teachers.[d]

The fights in court must not be viewed in isolation from the attempts to influence legislatures and administrators. Both types of effort are part of a grand strategy to win legal equality for the Negro people. The Association has spared no pains in pushing any and all Congressional action in favor of the Negro people, or in opposing measures having an actual or potential detrimental effect. Foremost among these efforts to influence legislation is the long fight for a federal anti-lynching law.[59] In this it has not succeeded as yet, but the important effect has been to keep the national conscience awake to lynching as a public scandal. In 1922, when the anti-lynching bill was first seriously considered in Congress, the number of lynchings dropped spectacularly.[e] The Association—which has employed a "watcher" in each branch of Congress and now has a bureau in Washington—has been able to stop much discriminatory legislation, including bills against intermarriage, Jim Crow bills, and residential segregation bills for the District of Columbia.[60] It has fought for increased federal aid to education, for an equal distribution of federal funds for education; against discriminatory provisions in the Wages and Hours Act; against discrimination

---

[a] See Chapter 22, Section 2.

[b] The importance of this is discussed in Chapter 23, Section 4.

[c] See Chapter 29, Section 4.

[d] See Chapter 14, Section 4.

[e] See Chapter 27, Section 4.

'n C.W.A., P.W.A., W.P.A. projects; against administrational discrimination in the T.V.A., local relief, and public utilities; and for many other
things.[61]

8. The Strategy of the N.A.A.C.P.

Both for strategic and for financial reasons the Association cannot afford
to be a legal aid society for Negroes. The cases pursued are selected because
of their general importance. The N.A.A.C.P. does not, therefore, substitute for institutions to enforce the laws and to aid poor people which we
suggested were needed.[a] This need is becoming less and less met by the
Association, as it has shifted its emphasis from legal defense to legal
offense.[62]

The author has found that some conservative Negroes and most conservative and liberal whites in the South accuse the N.A.A.C.P. of being
"reckless" in striking in all directions against the caste order of the region
without any thought whatever as to what can possibly be attained. When,
with this criticism in mind, I have studied the actions of the N.A.A.C.P.
over the decades, I have, on the contrary, come to the conclusion that the
Association is working according to a quite clearly conceived tactical plan,
which is only more far-seeing than is customary in America, particularly
in the South.[b] The Association has wisely avoided launching a wholesale
legal campaign against the Southern segregation system, as this would
have provoked a general reaction. It has selected its points of attack with
care and has pushed the front with caution; sometimes it has preferred
only to preserve a favorable defense position. On the other hand, when
the N.A.A.C.P. is striking—for instance, for a federal anti-lynching law or
for improved educational facilities for Negroes as in the Gaines Case—the
effect is not, as it is often asserted, an intensified reaction in the South, but,
on the contrary, a definite movement towards adjustment with the national
norms.

In this sense, the tactics of the N.A.A.C.P. are "opportunistic"—though
within the framework of a long-range policy to reach full equality for
Negroes. The Association has often accepted segregation, and in fact, has
sometimes had to promote further segregation, while it has been pressing
for increased opportunity and equality within the segregated system.[c] The
principle of opportunism, but also the integration of opportunism into the
long-range aims, is a conscious tactic:

> In cases where race discrimination is too strongly entrenched to be attacked at
> present, it [the branch] should secure at least equal rights and accommodations for
> colored citizens.[63]

[a] See Chapter 26, Section 4.
[b] See Chapter 33, Section 1.
[c] See Chapter 38, Section 9.

and it is:

> . . . convinced of the futility of any program to produce separate but equal educational opportunities for education for one-tenth of America's population, so they work for the day when the same and not equal opportunities are open to all. But on the way to the goal, the campaign to get those opportunities for all in states having laws requiring separate systems of education must be waged. Equal buildings, equal equipment in the buildings, equal salaries, equal length of school term, equal transportation facilities, equal per capita expenditure—all these are steps toward our goal.[64]

The N.A.A.C.P. has also been accused of being "radical." This criticism has been excellently evaluated by Bunche:

> The leadership and membership of the N.A.A.C.P., both Negro and white, is not recruited from the ranks of radicals. The program and tactics of the organization remain well within the bounds of respectability. It has, of course, been branded as radical by those who resent its militant demands for Negro equality and rights. But never, in the history of the organization, has there been aught but acceptance of the fundaments of the "American way" of life; the only demands for change have been directed toward Negro status. Its membership and its hold upon the black masses have never been strong enough to permit it to utter serious threats, nor to invoke mass pressure. Thus its tactics have had to conform to the dictates of expediency and opportunism; good strategy and the need for cultivating the prestige of the organization and the decree that demands shall be made and cases fought only when circumstances are of such favorable nature as to afford good chance of victory.[65]

9. CRITIQUE OF THE N.A.A.C.P.

The N.A.A.C.P. has been criticized by the most diverse groups for its concentration on publicity, suffrage and civil liberties. To the Northern sociologist with *laissez-faire* (do nothing) leanings, the N.A.A.C.P. and all the other organizations represent a superficial and inconsequential quackdoctoring of symptoms instead of a scientific treatment of causes. The "fundamental causes" are conflicts of "interests" which are not supposed to be touched by propaganda or law suits.[66] To the Southern liberal of a more contemplative temper, the struggle of the N.A.A.C.P. is a Don Quixotian battle against the unshakable "folkways and mores" of his unhappy region.[67] To the younger school of more or less Marxian-influenced Negro intellectuals, the N.A.A.C.P.'s policy is in the main only an evasion of the central problem, which is the economic one.[68] Different as these critical judgments are in motivation, they all express the fundamental defeatism in regard to the upholding of law and order which has become so widespread among American intellectuals of all colors and political creeds.[a]

This pessimism is exaggerated and, consequently, the criticism against the N.A.A.C.P. is largely unjustified. In our inquiry we started out by stressing the faltering systems of law and order in America. The low legal

[a] See Chapter 1, Sections 11 and 12.

culture, particularly in the South, was thereafter given great importance in nearly every specific aspect of our study. But we have also observed the definite trend toward a more equitable administration of the law in the South, and we have found that this trend is not unrelated to efforts of the type here discussed. With specific reference to the N.A.A.C.P., the present writer is inclined to agree with James Weldon Johnson who was once secretary of the organization:

> There is a school that holds that these legal victories are empty. They are not. At the very least, they provide the ground upon which we may make a stand for our rights.[69]

Very rightly Johnson points to the legal status of the Negro when the N.A.A.C.P. began to fight its battle, and the danger in the trend then under way, as the only basis for evaluating the organization:

> When the N.A.A.C.P. was founded, the great danger facing us was that we should lose the vestiges of our rights by default. The organization checked that danger. It acted as a watchman on the wall, sounding the alarms that called us to defense. Its work would be of value if only for the reason that without it our status would be worse than it is.[70]

Another Negro writer, Bertram W. Doyle, though of the "accommodation" school, testifies to the same effect:

> The significance of the agitation for rights and equality, as exemplified in, say, Mr. Du Bois, formerly a guiding spirit in the National Association for the Advancement of Colored People, was that under his scheme the races were not to be allowed to come to terms, and race relations were not again to be fixed in custom and formulated in codes before the Negro had fully experienced his freedom. Resistance to compromise has, then, helped to keep the racial situation in a state of flux and has tended to serve notice on the white man that weaker peoples expect him to live up to the principle established in his laws—those laws to which he proclaims loyalty.[71]

Thus, an evaluation of the N.A.A.C.P. requires us to examine the cases won by it and to note the effects of these victories. In the field of residential segregation, while the N.A.A.C.P. has not succeeded in getting the courts to outlaw private restrictive covenants, it has succeeded in having all laws to enforce residential segregation declared unconstitutional. This has meant that the Negroes are not completely ghettoized, and that they can expand in a city, though with much difficulty.[a] More important, the legal fight still goes on, and it is not improbable that the Supreme Court will soon come to reverse its stand on the constitutionality of even the private restrictive covenants. Similarly, in regard to suffrage: it is true that the Southern states have so far succeeded in evading the Supreme Court decisions on the

[a] See Chapter 29, Sections 3 and 4.

unconstitutionality of the white primary by having the primaries arranged as private party affairs.[a] But the fight is continuing, and even this barricade may fall as the "grandfather clauses" fell earlier. Perhaps the poll tax stipulations also will be declared unconstitutional if Congress does not make them illegal first. Likewise, though the decision in the Gaines Case will probably not open the Southern universities to Negroes in the near future, it is already forcing the Southern states to take action to improve the education situation for Negroes. Generally speaking, the fight against injustice and discrimination in the South and the keeping of national attention on the matter are social forces working for change which it seems unrealistic not to take into account.

The young Negro intellectuals who are critical of the N.A.A.C.P. have, however, a more positive point in mind.[b] On second thought they will usually concede the importance of the legal fight and also agree that it has crystallized the Negro protest.[c] But they insist that the N.A.A.C.P. has not attacked the fundamental economic problems.[d] They want the N.A.A.C.P. to come out with a radical economic program. They understand that this would alienate from the organizations many of their white and Negro supporters,[12] but apparently they do not care about this or about the loss in effectiveness of the present activity which would be a consequence.

This criticism is not new. Early in the history of the Association, the Socialists clamored against the narrow racial program of the N.A.A.C.P. They wanted it to attack the economic system, to embrace the economic and political philosophy of socialism. In later years, the Communist party has likewise been insisting that any Negro organization which does not devote itself to the revolutionary cause is futile. As an aftermath of this discussion, the young Negro intellectuals today—who are not Communists

[a] See Chapter 22, Section 2.

[b] We shall exemplify this widespread criticism of the N.A.A.C.P., as well as the other Negro betterment organizations, by statements made by Bunche in the work which has been basic to the description and analysis presented in this chapter. Even if we differ from Bunche on fundamental points, we want to stress that we have chosen to use his presentation as an object for criticism, not because it is weak, but, on the contrary, because it is the most clearly argued and ablest presentation of a view which we cannot share.

[c] "The N.A.A.C.P. unquestionably deserves full credit for setting a new pattern of thought among Negroes with respect to their problems. The vigor with which the Association, from the date of its inception, fought for the rights of Negroes before the courts opened the eyes of the Negro to an entirely new vista." (Bunche, *op. cit.*, Vol. 1, p. 141.)

[d] ". . . it [the N.A.A.C.P.] has ignored the fundamental conditions giving rise to the race problem. It has understood well enough that the Negro suffers from race prejudice, but has failed to concern itself with the root causes of race prejudice." (*Ibid.*, Vol. 1, p. 142; compare *ibid.*, Vol. 1, pp. 145, *passim*.)

". . . the South must be subjected to a new agrarian and industrial revolution before any significant changes in the fundamental relationship—political, economic or racial—will occur. This is what the N.A.A.C.P. apparently lacks the understanding and courage to face." (*Ibid.*, Vol. 1, p. 147.)

and often not even Socialists—deprecate the N.A.A.C.P. as "bourgeois" and "middle class."

To this criticism the N.A.A.C.P. answers that it considers its work in the civil liberties sphere important enough not to be lightheartedly jeopardized by radical adventures in other directions. It has machinery set up for this work, and three decades' experience has gone into perfecting it. This is a form of capital working for the Negro people which should not be squandered. It has "good-will" and a public "respectability" which might appear only as an object of ridicule to the radical intellectual but which, in the daily fight of the organization, is an asset. For a Negro protest or betterment organization to adopt a revolutionary program would be suicidal for the organization and damaging to the Negro cause.[a]

To the outside observer the reasons are strongly on the side of the N.A.A.C.P. against its critics. The American Constitution and the entire legal system of the land give the Negro a strategic strength in his fight against caste which it would be senseless not to utilize to the utmost. As it is possible to get the support of the Northern liberals—and of an increasing number of the Southern liberals, too—in the Negroes' fight for justice, this should be taken advantage of. A more or less radical economic program would not only jeopardize this support, but from a technical viewpoint, it is also impracticable to over-burden an agency with such divergent tasks.

Leaving aside their assumption that the economic factors are "basic,"[b] the critics are, of course, right in urging that there be organized efforts to tackle the Negroes' difficulties in breadwinning and, particularly, in gaining entrance into the labor unions. The question is, however, whether or

---

[a] "I feel very strongly that critics of the Association are not being reasonable where they maintain, in the light of the known American public opinion, and the known shackled condition of the Negro in the country, that an organization for his improvement should embark upon a political and economic revolutionary program.

"These organizations, if you will, must be somewhat opportunistic in their operation. The identification of the Negro's cause prominently and predominantly with a political and economic revolutionary program would be suicidal. The dangers inherent in such a procedure are but demonstrated by the fact that no racial group in America has adopted such a program.

"Indeed, it may be questioned whether the white masses have accepted such a philosophy as the way out of their obvious difficulties. Only an infinitesimal minority of persons in this country subscribes openly to and works actively in such a program. To ask the Negro, the most vulnerable, the poorest, the one most at mercy of the majority, to embark upon this is asking more than is practicable or sensible." (Roy Wilkins, in memorandum of March 12, 1941.)

"The white masses of America are not radical, to say nothing of the black masses. They are radical only with respect to the status of the Negro; on all other matters they are as conservative as the average American." (Roy Wilkins in memorandum of August 11, 1942.)

[b] See Chapter 3, Section 5, and Chapter 38, Section 6.

not this is the proper task for the N.A.A.C.P. To an extent it is, undoubtedly, and the Association has, during the New Deal, become increasingly active in fighting discrimination in public welfare policy and in the labor market. Outside such questions of discriminatory legislation and administration as the Association is particularly competent to handle, it leaves most of these problems to the Urban League, and the two organizations even have a gentleman's agreement of long standing to observe such a division of responsibility. The Urban League has, however, even stronger reasons for not embarking upon broad and fundamental economic reform programs, as we shall see shortly.

There is thus, unquestionably, room for more concerted action on the side of the Negro people. Particularly there is need of an agency attempting to integrate Negro labor into the trade union movement.[a] But the realization of this need should not be turned into criticism of the existing agencies serving other functions. Instead, the critics should go ahead and form the organizations they see the need of—soliciting advice and aid in their work from the experienced and established organizations. These critics—like most people who discuss the Negro protest and betterment organizations—assume without question that there should be just one unified Negro movement. We shall take up this important problem of Negro strategy later. Our conclusion will be that a suppressed minority group like the Negro people is best served by *several organizations* dividing the field and maximizing the support that can be gained from different groups of whites.

In this light should also be judged the criticism against the N.A.A.C.P. that it has "not become an important factor in the national political scene."[73] In our discussion of the Negro in politics, we have observed the need for organizing, locally and nationally, a collective bargaining agency for the Negro people to deal with the political parties.[b] But again there is a question whether the N.A.A.C.P. can undertake to carry out this task to a greater degree than it already does—which involves taking a stand in local and national political conflicts and supporting one party or the other —without losing in effectiveness in its primary function of fighting for legal equality for the Negro. Again it is a question of whether this task should not be given to another agency.

An indisputable weakness of the N.A.A.C.P. is its lack of mass support.[c]

---

[a] See Chapter 18, Section 3.

[b] See Chapter 23, Sections 1 and 2.

[c] ". . . the N.A.A.C.P. does not have a mass basis. It has never assumed the proportions of a crusade, nor has it ever, in any single instance, attracted the masses of people to its banner. It is not impressed upon the mass consciousness, and it is a bald truth that the average Negro in the street has never heard of the Association nor of any of its leaders. It has shown a pitiful lack of knowledge of mass technique and of how to pitch an appeal

This is, as we pointed out, admitted by the leaders of the Association.[a] When passing judgment on this problem of tactics, it should, in fairness, be recalled that we are actually asking why a severely disadvantaged group has not accomplished something which only rarely and imperfectly has been done among the whites in America. It should be borne in mind that the easiest means of rallying the American Negroes into a mass movement are such that they would destroy the organization. The Garvey movement demonstrated that the Negro masses can best be stirred into unity by an irrational and intensively racial, emotional appeal, the very thing which both the Association and its critics rightly shun. It is also questionable whether—as some of the critics of the Association hold—a greater stress on economic reform by itself has any more appeal than the fight against lynching and injustice. Poor and uneducated people all over the world are not particularly interested in economic revolution or even economic reform but must be educated to have such an interest.

When all this is said, it nevertheless stands out as a most pressing need for the organization to broaden its membership basis and to strengthen the activity of its branches.[74] There are, however, no easy panaceas available. It is the author's judgment that important steps are: (1) to have more working class members on the local boards; (2) to intensify propaganda in the schools and among the youth; (3) to stress adult education by organizing "study circles" and forums; (4) to get out more pamphlets and books on living issues and more printed directions both for individual studies and for adult education. More important, however, is the actual fighting done for the Negro. At present the war crisis is helping the Association win increasing support from the Negro people. Also in the somewhat longer perspective, the future seems promising for the Association. As the Negro masses are becoming educated and more articulate, and as the Negro protest is rising, this courageous organization with its experienced and cautious tactics will be able to count on increasing support.

---

so as to reach the ears of the masses. Were it able to stir the people, it could establish itself on a sound and independent financial basis; it could develop a feeling of solidarity among Negroes; and it could then employ an expanded paid professional leadership which would make possible the execution of an effective national program." (Bunche, *op. cit.*, Vol. 1, p. 151; compare *ibid.*, Vol. 1, pp. 142 ff.)

[a] "There are weaknesses in our branch structure and we have not yet found the formula for selling to the public the nature, the extent, the details, and the significance of the Association's program. Some have suggested that we might follow the example of Marcus Garvey and others in the utilization of fancy titles and robes. The Association, however, has felt that reverting to some of these methods of attracting the masses would do more harm in the long run to the organization, than good." (Walter White, in letter, March 15, 1941.)

"I believe that we recognize our lack of skill at mass appeal, and I believe we are on the way to doing something about it." (Roy Wilkins, in memorandum, March 12, 1941.)

10. THE URBAN LEAGUE

Much of what has been said of the N.A.A.C.P. applies also to the *Urban League*. Like the N.A.A.C.P., the Urban League is an interracial movement. Both organizations were started on white initiative. In 1906 a group of whites and Negroes formed *The Committee for Improving the Industrial Conditions of Negroes in New York City*. About the same time, another interracial group in New York formed *The League for Protection of Colored Women*. In 1910 a third interracial group held a conference which constituted itself into *The Committee on Urban Conditions Among Negroes*. The following year these three organizations decided to merge into one: *The National League on Urban Conditions Among Negroes*. The philanthropists, social workers, and professionals who made up the nucleus of the new organization "held that the Negro needed not alms but opportunity—opportunity to work at the job for which the Negro was best fitted, with equal pay for equal work, and equal opportunity for advancement."[75] The late professor, Edwin R. A. Seligman, became the first president of the organization.

The National Urban League is the parent organization. It has its central office in New York. In order to expand the work of the League in Southern communities, it has a Southern Field Branch Office in Atlanta, Georgia. The National Urban League is governed by an Executive Board of fifteen persons of whom seven are Negroes and eight whites. The president of the organization was for many years L. Hollingsworth Wood, and the executive secretary was Eugene Kinckle Jones, both of whom had been with the League since its beginning. They are now both retiring and are being replaced by William H. Baldwin and Lester B. Granger, respectively.[a] Besides the executive secretary there is a staff of eight executive officers and ten office workers. One of the officers is white but all the other employees of the National League are Negroes. The League publishes *Opportunity* and *The Secretariat*, the one directed to the general public, the other serving as house organ for the organization. The National League operates at present upon a budget of approximately $60,000 (including *Opportunity*). It is raised by contributions from foundations and from individuals.[76]

Local branches of the League are established in 46 cities. Of these, 12 are in the South, including the Border states, 2 are on the Pacific Coast, 12 are in the Northeast, and the remainder are in the Middle West. These figures reflect the history of the organization. It came into being to assist the unadjusted groups of Negroes migrating to Northern urban and industrial areas, but it has spread out to the Southern and West Coast cities which have similar needs.

The local Urban Leagues are governed by interracial boards. Sometimes

[a] Mr. Jones retains the office of General Secretary but is on leave from his duties.

there are other committees, usually interracial in composition. Many local Leagues, for example, have a committee on industrial relations. Each local office is staffed by a trained secretary, who is the responsible head of the work, and by specialized social workers and office workers, of a number determined by the financial resources of the local League. Thirty-nine of the forty-six local Urban Leagues are members of city-wide Community Chests, and most of these receive the greater part and often all of their financial resources from this source. Most local Leagues have incomes from individual contributions; some receive membership dues. For much of their work the local Leagues are able to solicit voluntary services from ministers, teachers, doctors, and other public spirited citizens in the Negro community. The National Office estimates that the combined budget of the local branches at present approximates half a million dollars annually.[a]

The activity of the local Urban Leagues is as wide in scope as modern social work when applied to the variegated needs of the poverty-stricken Negro communities. The outside observer cannot help but be impressed, not only by the urge to keep abreast of the latest developments in the broader social work field, but also with the attempts to find new solutions for the specialized problems of the Negro ghetto. It is apparent, however, that, particularly in the South, the Leagues work under tremendous handicaps on account of indifference and even hostility from most white people and halfheartedness on the part of even white sponsors and friends. It is also apparent that, all over the country, the efficiency of the work is kept down by inadequate financial resources.

Any detailed description of the activities of the local Leagues in attempting to get even the smallest economic openings for Negro workers and, generally, to heal the wounds of caste and mass poverty is out of the question in this book. They touch problems of education, home and neighborhood, problems of youth, recreation, vocational guidance and training, welfare work, housing, health, morals and manners. The Leagues carry on day nurseries, sometimes with baby clinics, child placement agencies, and, occasionally, schools for Negro girls who have become pregnant; they organize clubs for boys, girls, mothers, neighborhood and other groups; training schools for janitors or domestics; parent-teacher associations; study groups in trade unionism; health weeks, and so on. To mitigate delinquency among Negroes they offer to cooperate with the law-enforcement agencies and to perform such tasks as furnishing supplementary parole supervisors, safeguarding the interest of girls appearing in court, and, in some cases, finding homes for them. Fights are waged against commercialized prostitu-

---

[a] The statements in this and the following paragraphs are founded upon Bunche, *op. cit.*, Vol. 2, pp. 220 ff., upon information supplied by L. Hollingsworth Wood, Eugene Kinckle Jones, and Lester B. Granger of the National Urban League, and upon the writer's own observations.

tion in the vicinity of Negro homes, schools and churches. Much of this welfare work involves considerable "case work." Though not desiring to duplicate the work of the regular welfare agencies, the Leagues, nevertheless, find themselves involved in individual problems such as illness, old age, delinquency, unemployment, mental disorders, legal entanglement, drug addiction, illegitimacy and dependency.

None of the local Leagues can afford to become active in all these fields, but a primary task of all Leagues is to find jobs, more jobs, and better jobs for Negroes. They all function as employment agencies. The attempt is to run these agencies in an active way, opening up new jobs and preventing loss of jobs already held by Negroes. They have to get into contact with employers and trade union officers and try to "sell" Negro labor—impressing upon the employers that Negro labor is efficient and satisfactory, and upon the unionists that the Negro is a good and faithful fellow worker. A careful check-up has to be made on references, and a reputation must be gained and defended for the type of labor offered. The possibilities of vocational training have to be kept open to Negro youth, and the youths themselves have to be encouraged to be ambitious. The civil service boards have to be watched so that they do not discriminate against Negroes, and Negroes must be encouraged to take civil service examinations.

Not only in job placement activity, but also in attempting to get playgrounds, housing projects, schools, and other public facilities, the local Leagues work as pressure groups—with a tactic moderated by local circumstances and by their financial dependence on the white community. They engage in educational propaganda among whites as well as among Negroes. Sometimes regular campaigns are staged. Some Leagues have—openly or under cover—sponsored boycotts on the formula, "Don't buy where you can't work."

The National Urban League is the general staff for all this work. It directs and inspires it, coordinates and evaluates the experiments made in one place or another. It conducts community surveys and other research work. It educates and sometimes agitates: among the Negroes to improve themselves and among the whites to reduce prejudices and to give the Negroes a fair chance. Sometimes it concentrates on a pressure campaign to reach a particular goal. It uses its own publication, *Opportunity*, pamphlets and books, the radio, the pulpit and the lecture platform. It initiates conferences and investigations and furnishes government agencies with expert advice.

What the Urban League means to the Negro community can best be understood by observing the dire need of its activity in cities where there is no local branch. The League fills such an unquestionable and eminently useful community need that—were it not for the peculiar American danger of corruption and undue influence when something becomes "political"

—it is obvious that the activity should be financed, and financed much more generously, from the public purse: by the city, the state and the federal government. The League's activity among maladjusted Negroes in the industrial cities of America has national importance. It is concerned with the effects of such nation-wide American phenomena as the migration from rural areas—partly caused by national agricultural policy—and the almost universal economic discrimination against Negroes by whites.[a]

There are few informed persons in America, among either whites or Negroes, who do not appreciate the social service work done by the League. In many communities, however, white people often look upon the League as "dangerous," "radical" and too "friendly to labor." Among the younger Negro intellectuals, on the contrary, the League is commonly accused of being too "timid." The League has "made no serious effort to define its program in any fundamental way," it is said.[77] Because of its dependence upon white philanthropy, it advocates "a policy of racial expediency and conciliation, which is characterized by extreme opportunism."[78]

Against these charges the League retorts that "it is a social service organization attempting to perform a helpful task in a limited field."[79] Indeed:

> . . . the League could not be considered as a Negro movement, but an organization of American citizens who are convinced that an important development in our democratic institutions is that of according to the large Negro minority in America their economic rights. . . .
>
> The League is truly an interracial movement and cooperatively interracial at that. It would be expected, therefore, that the League should advocate conciliation in its highest sense. Any movement of this character which advocates understanding through conference and discussion must necessarily refrain from advocating mass action of one race calculated to force the other group to make concessions.[80]

The dispute has come to center about the League's attitude toward trade unionism. The National Urban League stated long ago that its official policy is in favor of collective bargaining and against strike-breaking, provided the unions are kept open to Negro workers.[81] There have been some incidents in which the League is alleged to have condoned strike-breaking.[82] More important is the general accusation that the League has not wholeheartedly worked to integrate Negro workers into the labor movement.[83]

I have found: (1) that almost everywhere the functionaries of the local Leagues are definitely in favor of trade unionism; (2) that in many cities, particularly in the South, local opinion—as represented by the Community Chests and the boards of the Leagues—hinders them from taking the action they would like to take to integrate Negro workers into labor unions; (3) that in still more cities, including many Northern cities, the unions do not take a very responsive attitude but are even more difficult to court than

[a] See Part IV, especially Chapter 12.

are local employers; (4) that a League which might organize actual strike-breaking against a union open to Negroes—if it has ever occurred—is now out of the question everywhere; (5) that such an action, even against a union that openly discriminates against Negroes, is extremely unlikely in most cities and is not likely to occur except as a last resort. Generally speaking, *local Urban Leagues change with the community, and, in most cities, change as much in advance of the community as is possible while maintaining community good-will and financial support for their program.* Much the same is true about the National Urban League. As the trade union movement and collective bargaining are gradually becoming normal and appreciated factors in American society, the Urban League is increasingly holding the lead as a pro-union force working among the Negro people.

This does not mean that it is likely that the League will ever become the agency needed in order to fight the Negroes' way into the labor unions. This should not be turned into a criticism of the League but into positive thinking and action on the part of interested Negro experts and leaders to form such an agency, utilizing the experience, the advice, and the good-will from the League as well as from the N.A.A.C.P. The Negro leaders who see the need for a Negro movement with a broader and more radical economic program should not—from their own point of view—spend their fire in criticizing this useful social service agency, which has been able to solicit so much help from the whites and to soothe so much suffering among the Negro people. They should, instead, appreciate what is obvious to any impartial observer: namely, that this organization, even though its tasks have been lowly, has been able to maintain a fighting spirit. It has been, and is now more than ever, pressing and fighting, intervening and proposing, educating and propagating for ideas and measures which—even from the point of view of its critics—are headed in the right direction even though they are not drastic enough in their opinion.[a] Again we observe that the critics of the Negro organizations are making the tactical blunder of assum-

[a] After reading this section, E. Franklin Frazier writes (letter, September 2, 1942):

"Although you have shown why the Urban League has not reached Negro workers as some critics have charged, I still feel that this is a defect in their program which is not attributable solely to lack of resources but rather to the general outlook of the leaders. I agree with you that much educational work must be done to secure the cooperation of Negro workers. In fact education of the upper layer of the Negro working class should have been and is still an important function of the Urban League. But still I feel that their general outlook and the class position of its leaders have been responsible to a large extent for their failure to carry on such an educational program. For example, I recall that in one city where they attempted to organize a Workers' Council they invited only professional people and neglected the more intelligent and more articulate members of the working class. As I was invited to the meetings I pointed out this defect but still the leaders insisted upon getting the professional class or educated people. I do not think that the Workers' Councils which the Urban League has formed have had much influence upon the Negro working class."

ing as self-evident that there should be only one unified Negro movement.[84]

11. THE COMMISSION ON INTERRACIAL COOPERATION[a]

The Commission on Interracial Cooperation, or the Interracial Commission, as it is commonly known, like the N.A.A.C.P. and the Urban League,
is not a Negro movement proper but a joint effort by whites and Negroes.[b]
While the two former organizations have a national scope and their central
offices are in New York, the Interracial Commission works in the South only
and has its center in Atlanta, which is also the headquarters of the Ku Klux
Klan and the capital of Georgia, one of the most backward states in the
Union.

This is indicative of much. The N.A.A.C.P. as a militant protest organization needs to work in an atmosphere where it can speak and act freely. The
Urban League as a social service institution for unadjusted Negroes in
industrial cities needs to be near the main concentrations of urban Negroes
as well as near the chief centers of white philanthropy. But the Interracial
Commission has set itself the much more difficult task of *working from
within* to improve race relations in the region they are worst. The other
two organizations can be "national." The Interracial Commission needs to
be recognized as "Southern." It can receive grants from Northern philanthropy, which is an established Southern pattern, but, in order not to
have its work appear as "outside meddling," the Commission must have
its seat in the South, its leaders and officers must be Southerners, and they
must lay stress on regional pride and patriotism.

There are more differences which should be understood in the same light.
In the other two organizations, Negroes played an important role almost
from the start and soon took over almost the entire political work. They
gradually became predominantly Negro organizations. The Interracial
Commission, on the other hand, has been much more exclusively the out-

---

[a] In our analysis of the interracial movement we choose to concentrate on the Commission
for Interracial Cooperation and its local affiliates. It should not be inferred that we underestimate the other agencies for interracial work even if we do not give any specific account
of them. Much of what we have to say on the Atlanta Commission has bearing on some of
the other agencies as well. Other agencies like the Commission on Race Relations of the
Federal Council of Churches of Christ in America and the Interracial Departments of
the Y. M. C. A. and Y. W. C. A. have different purposes, methods and sponsorship. (For
analyses of these agencies, see Bunche, *op. cit.*, Vol. 3, pp. 498 ff., and Paul E. Baker,
op. cit., pp. 24 ff.)

[b] The following short analysis of the Commission on Interracial Cooperation is based
upon the writer's own observations and upon Bunche, *op. cit.*, Vol. 3, pp. 444 ff., Paul E.
Baker, *op. cit.*, pp. 17 ff., various publications of the Commission, information given by
Howard W. Odum, Will W. Alexander, R. B. Eleazer. Jessie Daniel Ames, Emily H.
Clay of the Commission, and Arthur F. Raper, formerly the Research Secretary of the
Commission.

come of white people's activity. The Commission can employ Negro field workers, but it cannot, without endangering its good-will, have a single Negro employee working in its office.[85] The N.A.A.C.P. tries, at least, to get mass support and the Urban League works, of course, mostly with poor Negroes. The Interracial Commission, on the contrary, has had to direct its main effort on "the best elements of the two races." The two other organizations are, in a measure, opportunistic, as must be all minority organizations for concerted action. The Interracial Commission has to go much further in compromise in its practical work. These differences are all explained by differences in the tasks approached and the political conditions under which the organizations are working. No one who has read earlier parts of this inquiry will lightheartedly turn them into criticism against the Southern interracial movement.

Like Southern liberalism itself,[a] of which the interacial movement is an operative part, the attempt to bring representatives of the two groups together in constructive efforts to improve race relations in the South has a long history. Thomas Nelson Page wrote in 1904:

> A possible step in reaching the solution of the question might be for a reasonably limited number of representative Southern men to meet in conference a reasonable number of those colored men of the South who are more familiar with actual conditions there, and thus are representative of the most enlightened and experienced portion of that race. These, in a spirit of kindness and of justice, might confer together and try to find some common ground on which both shall stand, and formulate some common measures as to which both sides shall agree and which both shall advocate.[86]

Booker T. Washington and his white supporters in the South had the same vision. It is related that after the Atlanta riot in 1906, Washington boarded the first train for the city and interested the leading white people in conferring with a limited number of prominent Negroes in the local community.[87] Ray Stannard Baker said that "this was the first important occasion in the South upon which an attempt was made to get the two races together for any serious consideration of their differences."[88] There had, however, previously been some conferences on Southern education sponsored by Northern philanthropists. Too, many churches and other religious institutions had earlier sponsored interracial work, and they are still active in it.

Nevertheless, the Commission on Interracial Cooperation represented a new and courageous start. It was organized in 1919 as an effort to meet the great uncertainty and strain in the relations between whites and Negroes after the First World War.[89] The leading spirit of the movement and, later, the director of the work was W. W. Alexander. The purpose of the new organization was:

[a] See Chapter 21, Section 5.

. . . to quench, if possible, the fires of racial antagonism which were flaming at that time with such deadly menace in all sections of the country.[90]

Local interracial committees were started, and a series of ten-day schools for whites and Negroes, respectively, were held for the purpose of training leaders of both races to promote the interracial work. The schools concentrated upon community readjustment and care for the returning troops.[91] Started for the purpose of meeting a temporary emergency, the Commission's work was so successful and was deemed so important that it was decided to transform it into a permanent institution.

In the beginning the Commission sought to build up a network of local interracial committees. At one time there were state committees in every Southern state and local committees in more than eight hundred counties. A staff of salaried officers organized and directed great numbers of volunteer workers. During this early period a main emphasis in the Commission's program was placed on the correction of specific wrongs in the local communities. During the 'thirties the Commission encountered financial difficulties in keeping up its field staff. There was also some disappointment over the work in the local branches. The emphasis was then shifted to the educational approach and to the work of the Atlanta office. In 1938 only three of the Southern state commissions were even formally functioning.[92] At that time the Commission changed policy and started again to reorganize and revitalize state and local committees.[93] This reorganization work is still going on.

The center of the activity is the Atlanta office, which employs three white officers and four white office workers. The Executive Director is Will W. Alexander, and the Associate Director is C. H. Tobias; Alexander is white, Tobias is a Negro. Neither of these is actively engaged in the actual work of the Commission at the present time. The President is a prominent Southern white liberal, Howard W. Odum. The work is directed by a main governing Commission of 104 whites and 53 Negroes, representing the whole South.[a] The Commission meets annually. Abstaining from laying down any fixed constitution,[94] the main Commission and the Atlanta office carry on their own activity and assist in steering the activity of the state and local committees.[95] The Commission works on a yearly budget of around $70,000.[96] It is estimated that approximately 85 per cent of the financial support of the Commission comes from foundation grants.[97]

The Commission on Interracial Cooperation is the organization of Southern liberalism in its activity on the Negro issue. In its publications it demands a fair opportunity for the Negro as a breadwinner; equal participation in government welfare programs; equal justice under the law; suf-

[a] "Although the membership is composed of more white people than Negroes, our meetings are usually attended by a larger number of Negroes." (Emily H. Clay in letter, August 24, 1942.)

frage and other civil liberties. It does not attack segregation but stands up against discrimination.[a] The South is far from having achieved the Commission's aims, and the liberal forces of the region are weak. The Commission is, therefore, compelled to adopt in practice a gradualistic approach. "Sometimes asking for *all* you want is the best way to get nothing." R. B. Eleazer, the Educational Director of the Commission, has explained these tactics in the following words:

> The philosophy of the movement is not that of "seeking to solve the race problem," but simply that of taking the next practical step in the direction of interracial justice and good will.[98]

The chief political means of approaching the goal set up by the Commission are conciliation, moral persuasion and education. Its practical task is formulated as the attempt to promote:

> . . . the creation of a better spirit, the correction of grievances, and the promotion of interracial understanding and sympathy.[b]

[a] "The Commission has taken positive and public stands in its monthly paper *The Southern Frontier*, in its county forums, and at annual state conventions, on questions involving political and economic equality and extension of equal participation in all social and public welfare benefits. These include elimination of the white primary, abolition of the poll tax as a qualification for voting, Negro policemen, equal pay for equal work, including equalization of teachers' salaries, equal training in skilled and semi-skilled work, opening of tax-supported hospitals to Negro doctors, and equal provision of recreational centers for Negroes. Legislatively, the Commission, in cooperation with state committees, has worked to secure appropriations for graduate and professional training for Negroes and for the creation of training schools for Negro girls; in fact, the Commission's program, through its state and local committees, has included every field of public service supported wholly or in part with tax funds." (Memorandum by Jessie Daniel Ames, August, 1940.)

[b] *A Practical Approach to the Race Problem*, pamphlet issued by the Commission on Interracial Cooperation (1939); cited by Bunche, *op. cit.*, Vol. 3, p. 456.

The difference in tactics between the Commission and other organizations such as the N.A.A.C.P., as viewed by the Commission itself, is expressed in a recent report from the Commission's Negro field secretary, Dr. C. H. Bynum, communicated to me by Emily H. Clay (in a letter of August 24, 1942). Bynum says:

"In my opinion there is no fundamental difference in the programs of the Commission and other more vocal groups. The differences are in the approaches to the problem of race relations. We break down the general objective and others use the general compounded objective. We consolidate gains; others attempt 'blitz splits in the lines.' We use educational agencies; others seek greater concentration of governmental control. We balance permanent gains against probable imposed ruptures; others fight for violent ruptures predicated upon revolutionary changes.

"My personal predictions are without value, but history indicates that we may suffer heartbreaking reversals in race relations when peace comes. Southern culture patterns may bend, but they will not break. Who knows what will be the outcome of continued 'invasion of states rights'? No pessimist am I, but I prefer the surety of acceptance to the resentment of imposition. Acceptance may become a part of the general culture; imposition will

In this spirit the Commission has sponsored and carried out important researches on various phases of the Negro problem, such as cotton tenancy and lynching.[a] It publishes monthly *The Southern Frontier*[b] and a great number of pamphlets and educational material. It tries to influence the white press to give more favorable publicity to Negroes and to suppress such material as is likely to inflame white opinion. For this purpose it maintains a press service which goes to both the white and the Negro press. The Commission arranges interracial meetings for students and churchgoers. The Commission carries its message to conventions, conferences, and synods, and through the church press. The Commission has encouraged the introduction of courses on race relations in hundreds of colleges and high schools throughout the South. It has succeeded in getting pledges from 750 college professors, representing 400 white colleges of the South, to give rational discussions of race relations and of Negro capacity and achievement.[99] It attempts to influence strategic persons in state and local governments to give the Negroes more consideration. Sometimes the Commission enters legal redress work in selected cases which have broader applications. The Commission has thus recently, by following a peonage case to the Supreme Court, succeeded in getting Georgia's labor contract law pronounced unconstitutional,[100] and is at present carrying another case to the Supreme Court involving a young Negro accused of rape, whose guilt is very doubtful.[101]

From the beginning a main interest of the Commission was that of stamping out lynching. It has carried its attack through all the publicity agencies which could be used and especially directed it to women, officers of the law and of the courts, and to the church. In 1931 the Commission organized the *Association of Southern Women for the Prevention of Lynching*, headed by Jessie Daniel Ames, the Director of Field Work in the Atlanta Office. This organization has succeeded in aligning more than 40,000 women, who have pledged themselves to take certain active steps to help eliminate this blight on the South. Besides the prevention of lynching, the educational activity of the Commission covers health protection, sanitation, housing, relief, tenancy, agricultural adjustment, resettlement, and so on. The Commission has been active in securing Negro representation on boards and committees on government programs.

The Commission has a large share in the achievement of the dramatic

---

engender smoldering feelings which may at any hour leap into a blazing flame of madness."

[a] "The Commission's research program was abandoned in 1939 and no research work has been carried on since that time, a large number of our members being of the opinion that the greater results could be obtained by directing our efforts to activities in the field." (Memorandum by Emily H. Clay, August, 1942.)

[b] The circulation of *The Southern Frontier*, which began in January, 1940, has now reached 2,300. (Emily H. Clay, letter, August 24, 1942.)

decrease in lynching, and generally, in the greater enforcement of law in the South during the last two decades. The Commission was able largely to nullify the influence of the fascistic Black Shirt movement that grew up during the 1930's to eliminate Negroes from all jobs while there was any unemployment of whites. Few other organizations could have made the effective appeal to Southern whites which the situation called for. The Commission's surveys—for instance, of the tenancy problem—have been of great importance in the national discussion and for national policy. The work of the Farm Security Administration,[a] which for a long period was headed by W. W. Alexander, the Director of the Commission, is much in line with the efforts of the Commission and has set in effect many plans propagated and partly prepared by the Commission. The Commission has had its important part in the development of a friendlier attitude toward the Negro on the part of the white press in the South. The local interracial committees have also gotten much for the Negroes:

> . . . scores of Negroes have been extended legal aid in cases in which they were subjected to persecution, intimidation or exploitation; sewers, street paving, water, lights, library facilities, rest rooms, and other civic advantages, such as parks, playgrounds, pools and other recreation facilities, have been obtained for Negro communities; community chests have been induced to include Negro welfare agencies in their budgets; day nurseries and social centers have been conducted, and the appointment of colored probation officers has been secured.[102]

The fact that in most of these and other respects the Negro is still discriminated against in the South should not be allowed to conceal the fact that many small changes here and there have occurred, due to the activity of the interracial movement.

The Commission has not escaped criticism from conservative Southerners. The President of the Commission, Howard W. Odum, tells us:

> It [the Commission] has been investigated by the Ku Klux and by the Talmadge regime, and many efforts have been made "to get it." In recent years I have had very critical letters from some of the "best" people protesting against the radical viewpoint which the Commission has taken within the last few years.[103]

But, as we have pointed out earlier in this inquiry, one of the most important accomplishments of the Commission—which has a far-reaching cumulative effect—is to *have rendered interracial work socially respectable in the conservative South.* Liberal white Southerners, on their part, have usually backed the Commission. Whites in the North, outside the philanthropists, seldom know or care much about this work.

Negroes, on the other hand, tend to be critical of the Commission—even the older and more conservative Negro leaders. Few Negroes in the South have wholeheartedly praised its work. Several of the Negroes who have

[a] See Chapter 12, Section 12.

taken part in the local interracial committees or in the Atlanta Commission have privately made acid comments on the interracial movement. They complain that the white participants are not sincere enough, and that there is too much of the old paternalism in the whole approach. The Commission is frequently called a "face saving" device, a "gesture organization." But these observations were made in the years 1938-1939, when the activity in the local committees was at a low ebb and when the activity also of the main Commission was not as vigorous as earlier. The revitalization which the Commission has since gone through may have changed the attitudes of conservative Negro leaders.

By the younger Negro intellectuals the Commission is condemned for the "naïve assumption that when the two races know and understand each other better, the principal incidents of the race problem will then disappear."[104] The Commission is accused of having a "defeatist attitude, since it accepts the existing racial patterns while asking favors and exceptions with them."[a] The Commission is criticized for using "'influence'" instead of "pressure." They point out that the Commission does not reach, and has not even attempted to reach, the lower classes of whites and Negroes between whom the friction is most acute.[105]

This criticism seems too strong. It overlooks the power situation in the South. A movement which sets out to change public opinion and social institutions in the South and which wants to reap some fruit in the near future must make opportunism its tactical principle. It must develop an indirect approach instead of a direct attack. And it is no "naive assumption" that ignorance fortifies race prejudice, injustice and discrimination in the South. Education and cooperation will, therefore, have their effects even if they are slow to develop liberal political power which can force great reforms. The Commission *is* a useful agency. This, of course, should not exclude other and more radical efforts at the same time. Also it does not exclude a criticism that the Commission could work more effectively. But its

---

[a] Bunche, *op. cit.*, Vol. 4, pp. 557 ff.

"In the very nature of race relations in this country, the white members of the interracial groups must take upon themselves the responsibility for fixing the measures of values in inter-group relationships. It is not merely a question of *how much* the Negro is to ask for or to expect, but also *how* he is to ask for it, or indeed, whether he should *ask* for it at all, since it may often be more 'strategic' to permit his sympathetic white friends to act on his behalf. It is the whites alone who are in a position to advise the Negro that it is better for him to ask for little and to anticipate something than to ask for too much and gain nothing. It is the white, also, who can lean on realism and inform the Negro that if he goes before responsible officials in the community and demands or asks for benefits, his appeals are apt to be ignored. Whereas, if his white friends appear in his behalf, he has a better chance to receive the favor. That this half-a-loaf approach of the inter-racialist has won local benefits of various kinds for Negroes in particular communities is not denied; but this is no storming of the bastions of racial prejudice nor does it even aim toward them." (*Ibid.*, Vol. 4, pp. 559-560.)

main tactics must be condoned. These tactics *are* radical in the South, and among white people they can secure the backing of only the small group of Southern liberals.

If this is agreed, the question remains, however, whether the Commission could not be made into a more efficient organ for Southern liberalism. While liberalism generally has been on the advance, the interracial movement seems to have been losing out during the 'thirties. The Commission has not fulfilled the promises it once gave. The South has been changing[a] and there have been many new possibilities which the movement has not utilized. When the writer traveled in the South in 1938-1939 and observed the great needs and weak efforts, he felt strongly that there was room for more courage and vision in the work of the Commission. *The respectability the Commission has built up for interracial work in the South is a form of capital, but as such it is of no use at all if it is not invested, and even risked, in new ventures.* What is called for is, indeed, something of the spirit of the young W. W. Alexander when he first led the movement and before he was drawn into other important activities—that spirit, expanded and adjusted to the new situation. The post-war crisis in the South will not be minor. Already there are signs of unusual restlessness among both whites and Negroes in the South. A revitalized Interracial Commission will be much needed.

From this viewpoint the reestablishment of state and local committees, which has been started, seems to be an important move in the right direction. So as to be more influential in the political development of the region, *a broader appeal must be attempted, in order to reach directly even the middle and lower classes of whites.* Until recently the Commission has been working mainly with the "intelligent leadership" of the South and it admits that "the mass mind is still largely untouched."[106] The reservation should be made, however, that through the press, the churches, and the schools the Commission has already been influencing even the "mass mind." The new labor unions offer an opportunity for far-reaching work with the industrial workers.

The efforts to tie larger groups of the Southern people to the Commission's work are important also in order to *lay a firmer financial basis for its work.* It is demoralizing for the South to rely nearly exclusively on Northern philanthropy. The movement is working for interests which are vital for the future of the South. The liberals in the region should be made to feel that they are accomplishing something by their own sacrifices. There are people in the South with substantial incomes, and, while it is true that most of them are conservative and inclined to look upon any sort of activity in the field of race with apprehension, some are liberal and might be made to see their responsibility. But even apart from such gifts, ordinary people

[a] See Chapter 21, Section 4.

with moderate means can afford to pay membership dues.[107] If the Commission could raise its budget, this would greatly increase the possibilities of building up local organizations and of intensifying its work in all directions.

The present War and the peace crisis to follow it will severely test the whole work of the Commission. It is attempting to meet this test by increased activity.

12. THE NEGRO ORGANIZATIONS DURING THE WAR

A War fought in the name of "the four freedoms" is a great opportunity for Negro organizations. The exclusion of Negroes from defense jobs, the limited opportunities and maltreatment of Negro soldiers, the restrictions in the Army and Navy, bring home to every Negro individual the cause for which the Negro organizations are fighting.

In the First World War, Du Bois, then the leader of the N.A.A.C.P., wrote his famous article in *The Crisis*, "Close the Ranks," in which he virtually postponed the settlement of Negro grievances until the end of the War:

> We of the colored race have no ordinary interest in the outcome. That which the German power represents spells death to the aspirations of Negroes and all dark races for equality, freedom, and democracy. Let us not hesitate. *Let us, while the war lasts, forget our special grievances and close ranks shoulder to shoulder with our white fellow-citizens and the allied nations that are fighting for democracy.* We make no ordinary sacrifice, but we make it gladly and willingly with our eyes lifted to the hills.[108]

With few exceptions, Negro leaders in the Second World War have taken a different stand. They stress, of course, the loyalty of the Negro, but they do it more to inflate racial pride and to lay a basis for the accusations against the dominant whites who do not allow the Negro to make his full contribution to the war effort. They keep on emphasizing that Negro morale is low because of injustices and humiliations. They demand full civic, political and economic equality more strongly than ever. Walter White, in a statement issued a few days after the Pearl Harbor catastrophe, is typical of this Negro policy:

> Memories of all Negroes except those of the very young are bitter-green regarding the last World War. . . . I urge [Negroes] to remember that the declarations of war do not lessen the obligation to preserve and extend civil liberties here while the fight is being made to restore freedom from dictatorship abroad. . . .
>
> We Negroes are faced with a Hobson's choice. But there *is* a choice. If Hitler wins, every single right we now possess and for which we have struggled here in America for three centuries will be instantaneously wiped out by Hitler triumphs. If the Allies win, we shall at least have the right to continue fighting for a share of democracy for ourselves.[109]

For the Negro organizations, the War has provided more issues of immediate importance to attack. The organizations have increased in importance to the Negro people. Membership rolls have increased, particularly for the N.A.A.C.P. A new impetus to organizational cooperation has set in. Churches and fraternal organizations have increasingly been drawn into this cooperation. National conferences of organizational leaders are held from time to time, sometimes on governmental initiative, but usually without it. The N.A.A.C.P. has, on the whole, been in the lead in this activity.[a]

One of the most interesting effects of the War is the emergence of a new Negro organization: *The March-on-Washington Committee*. A. Philip Randolph, head of the Brotherhood of Sleeping Car Porters, in January, 1941, invited to a conference representatives of most of the Negro organizations. He proposed that a committee be formed to organize a march on the nation's capital to express the Negro protest against discrimination and to impress on the Administration the necessity of doing something about it. The Committee was formed, and preparation for the March made, when, on the initiative of Mrs. Eleanor Roosevelt, conferences were held between the President and members of the Administration, on the one hand, and members of the Committee, on the other hand.[110] The President issued an Executive Order intended to abolish all discrimination (on account of race, color, creed, or national origin) in employment in defense industries and government agencies, and appointed the Committee on Fair Employment Practice to implement his order.[b] Randolph, on his side, called off the March for the time being.

The March-on-Washington Committee, which, of course, gained a tremendous prestige among Negroes on account of its conspicuous success, did not dissolve. It did not even relinquish its idea of a March. The March-on-Washington movement remains a popular organization in many parts of the country. It is headed by a committee of national Negro leaders and has the backing of the major Negro organizations. It also has local affiliates. Its chief way of reaching the people is through mass meetings. The movement restricts its membership to Negroes. Randolph gives the reason for this:

> Just as the Jews have the Zionist Movement fighting on their specific problems; the workers have trade unions dealing with their specific problems; women have their movements handling their special problems, so the Negro needs an all-Negro movement to fight to solve his specific problems. . . . Nor does this all-Negro movement idea imply that interracial movements are not necessary, valuable and sound.

[a] At a conference, in January, 1942, of National Organizations on Problems of Negroes in a World at War, the N.A.A.C.P. was accepted as the clearing house for a number of committees appointed to make recommendations on various problems.

[b] See Chapter 19, Section 3.

It means that interracial movements need to be supplemented by specific religious groups of Jews and Catholics and Protestants. For no Negro is secure from intolerance and race prejudice so long as one Jew is a victim of anti-semitism or a Catholic is victimized as Governor Alfred E. Smith was by religious bigotry during the Presidential campaign against Herbert Hoover, or a trade unionist is harassed by a tory open-shopper.[111]

The March-on-Washington movement is interesting for several reasons. It is, on the one hand, something of a mass movement with the main backing from Negro workers, but has at the same time the backing of the established Negro organizations. Though a mass movement, it is disciplined and has not used racial emotionalism as an appeal. It demonstrates the strategy and tactics of orderly trade unionism. For the Negro cause it is prepared to use pressure even against the President. But it knows just how far it can go with the support that it has. Randolph, the leader of the movement, has so far (August, 1942) steered its course with admirable force and restraint.

The outside observer may be allowed to express the opinion that the Negro strategy during the war crisis has been skillful. The Negro leaders know full well that they have immense possibilities of putting pressure upon the American nation during this War for democracy. The plight of the Negro people is so great that they cannot afford not to make use of these possibilities. But they are wise enough to adjust the tactics to the terrain in various issues and regions of the country, and are careful not to lose the sympathy of the liberal forces among the whites. I have the feeling that, during the struggle for Negro rights, the Negro organizations—principally the N.A.A.C.P., the Urban League, and the trade unions—have trained a small group of devoted and accomplished politicians much superior to the average run of white politicians. It is a great pity, and a loss to the public life of the American nation, that these Negro leaders are limited to the Negro struggle alone and cannot get an outlet for their ability in tasks of more general importance.

13. NEGRO STRATEGY

Certain general observations and conclusions on Negro strategy should now be brought together. Before we do this, the value premises, which have been applied in the foregoing sections, should be made explicit. They are only an adaptation of the valuations contained in the American Creed which have been defined in the introductions to Parts III to VIII of this book. We are assuming that:

1. It is neither practical nor desirable for American citizens of Negro descent to be deported from this country. The problem is how to adjust race relations in America.

2. All concerted action by, or on behalf of, American Negroes should

be judged by the criterion of its efficacy in contributing to the ultimate extermination of caste in America. *The interests of the Negro people in winning unabridged citizenship in American society are taken for granted in the American Creed.* We are further assuming, as an evident matter of fact, that the power situation is such in America that Negroes can never hope to break down the caste wall except with the assistance of white people. Indeed, the actual power situation makes it *an obvious Negro interest and, consequently, a general American interest to engage as many white groups as possible as allies in the struggle against caste.*

It is a peculiar trait of much of the discussion of Negro concerted action in America that it usually proceeds upon the assumption that one unified Negro movement is the desideratum.[112] This assumption is unrealistic and impractical for several reasons. For one thing, a unified Negro movement would not appeal to the Negro masses except by an emotional, race-chauvinistic protest appeal. Such a movement, even if it were staged differently from the Garvey movement, would probably estrange the greater part not only of the Negro intellectuals, but also of the rest of the Negro upper class. It would definitely estrange practically all white groups. By this we do not mean that the racial appeal should not be used at all. It has to be used, but with caution. Still less do we mean that the Negro masses should not be appealed to. They should, but by movements with specific and limited practical aims. If, because of these reservations, the Negro masses are not reached within the near future to the same extent as would be possible in a race-chauvinistic, unified Negro movement, that is a price which will have to be paid.

When we look over the field of Negro protest and betterment organizations, we find that *only when Negroes have collaborated with whites have organizations been built up which have had any strength and which have been able to do something practical.* Except for the March-on-Washington movement—which has a temporary and limited purpose and which, in addition, is backed by the regular organizations—all purely Negro organizations have been disappointments. There are several explanations for this. One is that Negroes on the whole are poor. The completely Negro organizations have usually not had the sort of financial backing which has been available to interracial organizations. Another explanation is the lack of political culture in the traditions of the Negro people, because they have been subdued for generations. Political culture is one of the last accomplishments of any civilization, and there is not too much of it in this great and heterogeneous country as a whole, particularly on the state and municipal levels where Negroes have most of their political contacts. A third explanation is the existence of the interracial organizations. They have naturally drawn to themselves much of the individual talent for political leadership in the Negro people. A fourth, and basic, explanation is the obvious fact in the power situation, that it is advantageous and, indeed, necessary to have white allies in order to accomplish anything.

Leaving aside the interpretation of the history of concerted action for Negro interests and facing the problem as a question of political strategy, it will be apparent that *both the interest in keeping as allies as many white groups as possible and the interest in maintaining a high effectiveness in the work being done, speak for having, not one Negro organization, but a whole set of organizations specializing on different tasks and applying a different degree of opportunism or radicalism.* This means that none of the existing organizations should be criticized by applying the norm of an imaginary unified Negro movement, which would be expected to do *all* that the critics want done for the Negroes.

There is thus need for a militant organization like the N.A.A.C.P. to uphold the great Abolitionist tradition, taking its stand on the American Constitution and fighting for equality in justice and for suffrage, keeping alive the unabridged ideals of the American Creed, but having enough opportunism to take advantage of the possibilities of even minor improvements within the segregated setup if that can be done without violating the grand strategy aimed at exterminating segregation in the future. Such an organization will always have its influential white adherents. There is also need for a social service organization like the Urban League, doing its work among the victims of caste, educating and protecting Negroes, and exerting its pressure against the dominant white society from the welfare point of view. In America there will always be white supporters for such work, and they will be drawn from wider circles than the liberals of Abolitionist traditions who will come out for the N.A.A.C.P. In addition, there is in the South a pressing need for an interracial movement—indeed a need for a much more efficient agency than the present Commission on Interracial Cooperation—to exploit regional pride and the will to interracial understanding among white Southerners. Everything churches and other groups can do to increase the number of white people in the South and the North who are willing to do something for Negroes is a clear gain for the Negro cause.

There is little "overlapping" or "duplication" among the various existing Negro organizations. In so far as there is duplication, it is useful. It means that different white groups are being engaged for the same ultimate end who could not agree as to the immediate ends. Another important observation is that *there is actually little friction and rivalry among the three main organizations.* The N.A.A.C.P. and the Urban League have been able, most of the time, to work out both a division of responsibility and—in certain respects—a collaboration. Even in relation to the Interracial Commission, there has been surprisingly little rivalry and destructive competition.

Instead of unification there seems to be *need for further specialization*. It is a pressing need that concerted action be taken to integrate Negro workers into the labor movement.[a] It is a task of educating white and Negro workers and of fighting those labor organizations that discriminate against Negroes. This work cannot very well be done by any of the existing organizations without their becoming less efficient in the tasks they now perform and without their becoming weakened by losing some of their present white—and Negro—support. The Negro labor movement, which we thus propose, should also be interracial in order to be optimally strong and efficient. The chief difficulty in the way of its realization at present is the split in the American labor movement. Negro workers as a national group cannot afford to cast their entire lot in with the C.I.O., the A.F. of L., or with the John L. Lewis insurgents. Meanwhile, the local and occupational centers of a Negro labor movement that already exist are outposts, the importance of which should not be underestimated, nor should the services rendered for these groups by the N.A.A.C.P. and the Urban League.

Negroes also need an agency to carry on—locally and nationally—a political collective bargaining with the political parties.[b] This organization is the most difficult one to effectuate, since—unlike the others—it should preferably be a pure Negro organization. In order to work effectively it should be narrowly specialized to play the political game. It should, further, be manned by the most intelligent, the freest and the most respected Negro leaders. It should not be affiliated with any of the political parties. The National Negro Congress, in its short history, has shown how this task should not be approached.

There is also need for a legal aid agency concentrating its work on improving the law enforcement of the South. The N.A.A.C.P. cannot function as such. To the degree that it does, this weakens it by drawing too heavily on its financial and personnel resources. Such an agency should preferably *not* be set up separately for Negroes, but should be an agency to defend the rights of all poor and disadvantaged people.[c] It should not assist in the prosecution of strategic cases only, but of all cases where there has been injustice and illegality.[d]

Some of the wisest Negro thinkers have understood that the Negro

[a] See Chapter 18, Section 3; Chapter 38, Sections 6 and 7. Similar proposals are made by Horace R. Cayton and George S. Mitchell, *The Black Workers and the New Unions* (1939), especially pp. 425-434; and W. E. B. Du Bois, *Dusk of Dawn* (1940), p. 207.

[b] See Chapter 23, Sections 1 and 2.

[c] See Chapter 26, Section 4.

[d] The Civil Liberties Union does this sort of work, but its activity is not concentrated in the South and it restricts its work to defense of civil liberties rather than to all legal aid. The Union has some political ideals, which restrict its ability to get money. The organization we propose should be completely nonpolitical.

movement should split on several fronts and that it should make the most of possible allies among the whites. Kelly Miller has this to say:

> The progress of all peoples is marked by alterations of combat and contention on the one hand, and compromise and concession on the other, and progress is the result of the play and counterplay of these forces. Colored men should have a larger tolerance for the widest latitude of opinion and method. Too frequently what passes as "an irrepressible conflict" is merely difference in point of view.[113]

James Weldon Johnson wrote:

> We should establish and cultivate friendly interracial relations whenever we can do so without loss of self-respect. I do not put this on the grounds of brotherly love or any of the other humanitarian shibboleths; I put it squarely on the grounds of necessity and common sense. Here we are, caught in a trap of circumstances, a minority in the midst of a majority numbering a hundred and ten millions; and we have got to escape from the trap, and escape depends largely on our ability to command and win the fair will, at least, and the good will, if possible, of that great majority. . . .
>
> It seems to me that the present stage of our situation requires diversified leadership. I am certain that there are two elements which are necessary. We need an element of radicalism and an element of conservatism; radicalism to keep us from becoming satisfied and conservatism to give us balance; to the end that the main body will be steady, but alive, alert, and progressive. We should guard against being stagnant, on the one hand, or wild-eyed on the other.[114]

Negroes should attempt to develop that type of political culture which is ideal in any democratic nation. There must be radicals, liberals and conservatives. Viewed as a going system of collective action all three factions and many others have their "functions" in the concert. The intelligent citizen should be able to see this. It is required of him, of course, to take his own stand and to fight by his individual opinion, but, nevertheless, to be able, not only to "see the viewpoint of the other fellow," but actually to understand and appreciate his "function" in the system. When this mutual understanding is reached in a nation—which is a high stage of political culture—the radical or the conservative will find that it does not decrease in the least his efficiency in fighting for his own opinions. On the contrary, he can strike harder and better—at the same time as he becomes a little more careful about where he hits.

An American Negro should, in the same way, select the front where he wants to take his stand. But he should keep his eyes wide open to the desirability that other Negroes have other stands. The Negro labor organizer should be grateful that there are others who fight for his civil liberties and still others who do the welfare work for his potential members. The militant Negro should be able to see the usefulness—in some situations—of some Negro leaders who understand how to do the "pussy-footing," and contrariwise. The present writer has found many individual Negro leaders, most of them active in the organizations discussed in this chapter, who see this fundamental principle of democratic politics more clearly than is common among white Americans discussing national politics.

The fact that Negroes will have to seek a maximum number of white allies should not, however, be a reason for neglecting the organization of the masses of Negroes. All efforts of their own are required for the Negroes' advancement. A. Philip Randolph, speaking vainly to the National Negro Congress when it went down, rightly observed:

> The only rational conclusion, then, seems to be that the Negro and the other darker races must look to themselves for freedom. Salvation for a race, nation, or class, must come from within. Freedom is never granted; it is won. Justice is never given, it is exacted. Freedom and justice must be struggled for by the oppressed of all lands and races, and the struggle must be continuous, for freedom is never a final fact, but a continuing evolving process to higher and higher levels of human, social, economic, political and religious relationships.[115]

By this Randolph did not mean isolation in a black movement:

> But Negroes must not fight for their liberation alone. They must join sound, broad, liberal, social movements that seek to preserve American democracy and advance the cause of social and religious freedom.[116]

A word must be added on the moral aspect of Negro leadership. To the outside observer, one of the most discouraging facts in present-day America is the great indifference shown by the average white citizen toward corruption in politics, particularly in the states and municipalities where Negro concerted action will have to do most of its work. In the shut-in Negro world, there are, as we have observed,[a] so many special reasons for cynicism and amorality that dishonest leadership—except on the national level—is not unusual.

To the Negro people dishonest leadership is a most important cause of weakness in concerted action. It should be preached against and fought against. It should be a main topic in the teaching at Negro universities, in the Negro journals, in Negro adult education. If a generation of young Negroes could be brought up to understand how scrupulous honesty could tremendously strengthen the Negro cause—and, incidentally, in the long run advance them individually much more than the petty handouts by which they are now tempted—this would mean a great deal for Negro progress.

[a] See Chapter 36.

CHAPTER 40

THE NEGRO CHURCH

1. NONPOLITICAL AGENCIES FOR NEGRO CONCERTED ACTION

The primary functions of the Negro church, school, and press, which will be dealt with in this and the following two chapters, are not, of course, to be agencies of power for the Negro caste. Nevertheless, they are of importance to the power relations within the Negro community and between Negroes and whites. They bring Negroes together for a common cause. They train them for concerted action. They provide an organized followership for Negro leaders. In these institutions, theories of accommodation and protest become formulated and spread. These institutions sometimes take action themselves in the power field, attempting to improve the Negro's lot or voicing the Negro protest. Even more often they provide the means by which Negro leaders and organizations, which are more directly concerned with power problems, can reach the Negro people.

The Negro churches and the press are manned exclusively by Negroes. They are not interracial institutions as are the successful Negro protest and improvement organizations we analyzed in the preceding chapter. The school—when it is a "Negro school," that is, when it is segregated—is also almost always Negro-staffed, except for a few colleges. None of these organizations is, however, outside the control of the whites. The Negro press is the freest among these Negro agencies; the Negro school is the most tightly controlled. But *in all these institutions Negroes are among themselves.* They are usually away from the presence of whites, and this creates a feeling of freedom, in smaller matters even if not in major policies.

The very existence of these Negro institutions is, of course, due to caste. Without caste there would be no need in America for a specialized Negro press, for segregated schools or for separate churches. Under the caste system they all take on a defensive function for the Negroes, and sometimes they take on an offensive function. Generally speaking, the Negro press is, in this sense, more radical than the other nonpolitical agencies. Besides its primary function of replacing the old "grapevine telegraph" in the protective Negro community and of providing Negro news, it is one of the chief organs for the Negro protest. The other agencies are generally more accommodating. We have already expressed our conviction that all these agencies, however, in the long run tend to build up the Negro protest.[a]

Our treatment of these nonpolitical Negro institutions will be restricted mainly by the viewpoint of power and power relations followed throughout this part of our inquiry, and even in this respect it will not be so intensive as their importance warrants. The religious, educational, and cultural aspects of their activity will be almost entirely neglected. Some further considerations as to their role in the Negro community and as to what they indicate of Negro culture will be given in the next part of the book.

2. SOME HISTORICAL NOTES[b]

With few exceptions the Negro slaves brought to America had not been converted to Christianity.[1] For nearly a century many slaveholders felt reluctant to let the Negro slaves receive religious instruction as there was a belief that a baptized Christian could not be held as a slave. But when theologians, legislatures, and courts declared, around the year 1700, that conversion to Christianity was not incompatible with the worldly status of a slave, slaveholders went out of their way to provide a religious teaching and a place of worship for their slaves, or at least did nothing to hinder missionary work among them. Their primary motive undoubtedly was that the Christian religion, as it was expounded, suited their interests in keeping the slaves humble, meek and obedient. But the Christian duty to spread the gospel was probably also taken seriously, perhaps particularly so in order to compensate for many other deprivations to which the Negroes were subjected.

On many plantations the slaves were allowed to attend the same churches as did the whites, being seated sometimes in a gallery especially provided, sometimes in a separate section of the main floor. The service was then nearly always conducted by a white minister. But there were also Negro ministers, usually attending to the religious needs of only their own people, and separate worship soon became common. After the rebellion in 1831 led by Nat Turner, a Negro preacher, the fear of slave revolts and uprisings made masters endeavor to check the separate religious meetings of their slaves. But there was no complete stoppage of religion among Negroes. The idea of free worship and the advantages of having a slave work off his frustration in religion were too strong. Slaves were allowed into most white churches and could even meet by themselves if a white minister led them or if any white man observed them. Practically the only religious

---

[a] See Chapter 35.

[b] Most of the factual data for this section have been taken from Guion G. Johnson and Guy B. Johnson, "The Church and the Race Problem in the United States," unpublished manuscript prepared for this study (1940). Vol. 1.

meetings completely free of whites, however, were secret ones. Free Negroes, of course, continued to have their own churches, but a strong effort was made to separate them completely from the slaves. Some whites felt that only white ministers should be allowed to preach to Negroes, but on the whole, as long as the Negro preacher kept to the subjects of God and the other-world, and as long as he implanted a spirit of obedience to the existing order and the white master, there was little attempt to replace him. Undoubtedly the great bulk of the Southern Negro preachers advocated complete acceptance of slave status.

Still, the church service was one of the few occasions when slaves were allowed to congregate, when they could feel a spiritual union with other Negroes, when they could feel that they were equal to the white man—in the eyes of God—and when they could see one of their own number, the preacher, rise above the dead level of slavehood and even occasionally be admired by white people. The slaves on a plantation could regard the Negro preacher as their leader—one who could go to the white master and beg for trivial favors.

In the North, the few Negro churches before the Civil War served much the same functions as they do today. Many of them—like some white churches—were "stations" in the "underground railroad," at which an escaping slave could get means either to become established in the North or to go to Canada. The Northern Negro church was also a center of Negro Abolitionist activities. The slavery issue in national politics of these times actually gave the Negro church in the North as great an interest and stake in worldly affairs as it has today.

At the time of Emancipation probably only a minority of the Negro slaves were nominal Christians.[a] At the end of the Civil War, there was, on the one hand, an almost complete and permanent expulsion of Negroes from the white churches of the South and, on the other hand, a general movement among the Negroes themselves to build up their own denominations. This period witnessed another wave of conversion to Christianity of the Negroes and the firm establishment of the independent Negro church. Southern Negro religious leaders were helped much by white and Negro missionaries from the North. Observing the church situation in the 'seventies, Sir George Campbell gives the following picture of this religious activity:

> Every man and woman likes to be himself or herself an active member of the Church. And though their preachers are in a great degree their leaders, these preachers are chosen by the people from the people, under a system for the most part congregational, and are rather preachers because they are leaders than leaders because they are preachers. In this matter of religion the negroes have utterly eman-

[a] ". . . only one adult in six was a nominal Christian." (W. E. B. Du Bois, *The Negro* [1915], p. 227.)

cipated themselves from all white guidance—they have their own churches and their own preachers, all coloured men—and the share they take in the self-government of their churches really is a very important education. The preachers to our eyes may seem peculiar. American orators somewhat exaggerate and emphasize our style, and the black preachers somewhat exaggerate the American style; but on the whole I felt considerably edified by them. They come to the point in a way that is refreshing after some sermons that one has heard.[2]

Many Negro political leaders during Reconstruction were recruited from the preachers. After Reconstruction many of them returned to the pulpit. Under the pressure of political reaction, the Negro church in the South came to have much the same role as it did before the Civil War. Negro frustration was sublimated into emotionalism, and Negro hopes were fixed on the after-world. Negro preachers even cautioned their flocks to obey all the caste rules. But there was a new factor, which increased the possibility of the Negro church to serve as a power agency for Negroes; the white preachers and the white observer in the Negro church disappeared. There remained, however, the Negro stool pigeon who reported to the whites on the activities of Negroes in church and elsewhere.

In practically all rural areas, and in many of the urban ones, the preacher stood out as the acknowledged local leader of the Negroes. His function became to transmit the whites' wishes to the Negroes and to beg the whites for favors for his people. He became—in our terminology—the typical accommodating Negro leader.[a] To this degree the Negro church perpetuated the traditions of slavery.

In the actual power situation after Restoration of white supremacy, this was a realistic and, in a sense, necessary policy. If it becomes known that a Negro preacher in the South criticizes the caste system—except in very general terms—he is usually threatened and may be punished physically or exiled. His church is also in danger. If, on the other hand, he keeps in the good graces of the influential whites, he can reckon with their backing and support. To get money for his church and other advantages for himself and his group, the Negro preacher has to emphasize the patriarchal relationship—pointing out how "good" the Negro church is; that is, how the church keeps Negroes from going against the caste system.[3] Negro sermons in the South no longer contain any appeal to accept a slave status. They even seldom contain, directly at least, admonitions to accept caste subordination. But this advice is implied when the Negroes' attention is turned away from worldly ills.

The Negro church came to serve a vital role linked intimately with the status of the race. The doctrine of otherworldliness provided an essential escape from the tedium and tribulations, first of slavery and later of economic serfdom. . . . The

[a] See Chapter 34.

indifference of the Negro church to current social issues and its emphasis on the values of a future life lent indirect but vital support to the race patterns of the early post-slavery period.[4]

Accepting this role, the Negro church in the South has earned considerable good-will among the whites. Church and religion have a tremendous moral prestige in America, and the Negro church shares—on a lower level —in this appreciation. The white Southerner of today will often praise the Negroes for their "old time religion." Negroes are assumed to be endowed with particularly strong religious feelings. Religion is assumed to be a force for good in all respects and, particularly, for race relations. It is also taken for granted that the Negroes should be left a considerable freedom to develop their religious life as they want to, without interference. The Negro churches are, therefore, not closely controlled. The Negro preacher is trusted.

Thus the Negro church in the South did not become an institution that led the opposition to the caste system. Yet as an institution that received the sanction of Southern whites, the Negro church was able in some cases to modify the harshness of the system, and it has helped to maintain the solidarity of Negroes in their cautious pressure to ameliorate their position. In many cases, the churches helped to support schools, and education was one of the main ways that Negroes, individually and collectively, could rise in the world.

In the North the Negro church has, of course, remained far more independent. The ministers have been free to preach what they please without fearing intervention from the whites.[a] They have taken stands in local politics and in labor strife—though perhaps, more often than not, serving white benefactors primarily instead of the Negro cause. In not a few cases the Negro church became a center for social work in the Negro community.

[a] In more recent times there have developed some very minor sects which are openly anti-white, but since they take no overt action other than to prohibit whites from attending their services, few whites even know of their existence. Notable among the anti-white sects are the various "Islamic" cults. They claim to adhere to Mohammedanism instead of Christianity and look to the brown peoples of Asia Minor and North Africa to save them from the whites. One of these cults in Chicago, known as the Moors, is not only a religious group but an economic unit and a harem as well. Some 200 Negroes, mostly women, live together in a few ramshackle buildings in the Near North Side slum area.

Another anti-white group, the African Orthodox Church, is of somewhat greater numerical importance and has branches in many cities, but it has mollified its anti-white position somewhat in recent years. This church stemmed from the Garvey movement of the early 1920's (see Chapter 35, Section 7) and has affiliated itself with the Greek Orthodox Church. Its anti-white position was that of the whole Garvey movement, but recently it has permitted whites to attend service, although it still prohibits whites from becoming church leaders and emphasizes "segregated but equal." (J. G. St. Clair Drake, "The Negro Church and Associations in Chicago." unpublished manuscript prepared for this study [1940], pp. 288-290.)

Some ministers have taken the lead in expressing to the world the Negroes' needs and protest.[a] But on the whole even the Northern Negro church has remained a conservative institution with its interests directed upon otherworldly matters and has largely ignored the practical problems of the Negroes' fate in this world.[b]

3. THE NEGRO CHURCH AND THE GENERAL AMERICAN PATTERN OF RELIGIOUS ACTIVITY

To the outsider the main observation about Negro churches and Negro religious life is that they adhere so closely to the common American pattern. There are differences, and they are important; but more important are the similarities. Again we shall see how the caste system forces the Negro to become an "exaggerated American."

Americans generally are a religious people; Southerners are more religious than the rest of the nation, and the Negroes, perhaps, still a little more religious than the white Southerners. Negroes, on the whole, attend church probably in greater numbers than do whites although not in greater numbers than certain white groups like the Catholics. Among Negroes, as among whites, females attend more than males, the middle-aged and old attend more than the youth, the uneducated attend more than the educated, the lower and middle classes more than the upper classes.[5]

Particularly significant among these differentials is that between youth and age, since the tendency for Negro youth to abandon the church is perhaps even greater than among most white youth, with the exception of the Jews. This is explainable not only because of the general trend caused by increasing education and sophistication, but also by the very "backwardness" of the Negro church manifested in its emotionalism and puritanism. Still, as in white America, church membership confers respectability, and when young people marry and want to settle down, they are likely to join a church—though often one somewhat less attached to emotionalism and puritanism than the one attended by their parents. There is a trend toward a more intellectual and formal church service in the Negro as in the white

[a] An outstanding case is that of the Abyssinian Baptist Church in the Harlem section of New York City. It had 8,000 members in 1939, which made it by far the largest Negro church in the city. It claims many more thousands today. The young, popular, and ambitious minister, Rev. A. Clayton Powell, has not only taken a lead in sponsoring community welfare work, but has helped the workers' side in several strikes, has succeeded in getting jobs for Negroes, and has become a publisher of a Negro newspaper and a member of the New York City Council.

In Chicago, to take another exceptional case, the Good Shepherd Church sponsors a community center, which is directed by a Negro sociologist, Horace Cayton, and which ranks among the best of its kind. In several other instances upper class and educated Negroes have focused their efforts to improve the Negro community upon the large urban churches.

[b] See Section 5 of this chapter, especially the study by Mays and Nicholson cited there.

community. The difference is mainly that Negroes—together with some poor, isolated groups of whites—are lagging about half a century behind.[a]

Today it is probable that a greater proportion of Negroes than of whites belong to churches as formal church members. According to the United States Census of Religious Bodies, which is very inaccurate but has the best data available for the country as a whole, Negro churches claimed 5,660,618 members in 1936 and white churches 50,146,748.[6] Even if we make all the assumptions that work in the direction of under-enumerating Negro church membership, the Negroes still have a larger membership: 44.0 per cent of the Negro population are members of Negro churches, as compared to 42.4 per cent of the white population in white churches.[7] Actually the discrepancy is much greater, since we have neglected the significant number of Negroes who are members of white churches. The census overlooks many of the small denominations to which Negroes adhere more than whites; we have not subtracted Orientals and Indians from church figures but have done so for our population base; we have ignored the fact that whites belong, in greater proportion, to those churches that count membership from birth rather than from confirmation (for example, the Roman Catholic Church); we have neglected the fact that the Jewish churches report as members all persons living in communities in which local congregations are situated.

America as a whole is still predominantly Protestant in spite of the "new" immigration; Southern whites and Negroes are even more Protestant. In American Protestantism various low church denominations with less formalized ritual have always been predominant. The great majority of Negroes belong to the Baptist and Methodist churches or to small sects which have branched out from them, and the ritual of these churches tends to have little elaborateness or formality.[b] As in the white American population,

---

[a] See Chapter 43, Section 3.

[b] The only comprehensive statistics of religious affiliation for the United States are those of the Census of *Religious Bodies*, *1936*. (U. S. Bureau of the Census [1941].) This census reports that the various Negro Baptist bodies claimed 68.80 per cent of all members of Negro churches and the Methodist bodies 24.65 per cent. Next in size, according to this report, was the Roman Catholic Church with 2.43 per cent. The Protestant Episcopal Church, the Congregational churches, the Presbyterian churches, the Lutheran Church, and the Christian Science Church together claimed only 1.30 per cent. All the rest of the churches reported only 2.83 per cent of the church membership. Obviously there is something seriously wrong with these figures: many of the smaller sects are missing altogether; the African Orthodox Church certainly has more than 1,952 members, and the Holiness Church has more than 7,379 members. (*Ibid.*, Vol. 1, pp. 850-853.)

We guess that the actual percentage distribution of membership in Negro churches would show the Baptist proportion smaller, the Catholic proportion larger and the miscellaneous group's proportion larger. It should be remembered that the census figures refer to Negro churches only and do not include Negro members of white churches. According to *The Negro Handbook* there were 298,998 Negro Catholics in the United

among the Negroes the small upper class tends, more than the lower classes, to belong to the Episcopalian, Congregational, and Presbyterian churches.[a] Protestant religion in America has always had relatively more emotionalism than in other countries: revival meetings and evangelists have played a greater role, and the regular church services have exhibited more emotional traits. The South is somewhat extreme in this respect, too, and the Negroes

TABLE 1

NEGRO MEMBERSHIP IN HARLEM CHURCHES BY DENOMINATION: 1930

Denomination	Number	Per Cent
Baptist	27,948	41
Methodist	13,740	20
Protestant Episcopal	7,151	11
Roman Catholic[a]	4,990	7
Presbyterian	1,805	3
Adventist	1,000	2
Congregationalist	950	1
Moravian and Lutheran	900	1
Other	9,139	14
Total	67,623	100

Source: The Greater New York Federation of Churches, *The Negro Churches in Manhattan* (1930), pp. 17–18.
[a] Includes 5 churches having both Negro and white parishioners.

still more so.[b] As in the white population there is a class differential as well as a geographical one in regard to degree of emotionalism in religious service. Upper and middle class Negroes are likely to frown upon the old practices which still prevail in the lower classes.

States as of January 1, 1940. It was estimated that about one-third of them were in mixed churches. The 1936 Census of Religious Bodies reported only 137,684 Catholics in Negro churches. (Florence Murray [editor], *The Negro Handbook* [1942], p. 102; these figures were taken from John Thomas Gillard, *Colored Catholics in the United States* [1941].)

[a] The geographical distribution of Negro denominations is fairly even, on the whole, but there are significant exceptions that must be noted. In the South, Negroes have roughly the same denominational distribution as lower and middle class whites: they are mainly Baptist or Methodist with a concentration of Roman Catholic in southern Louisiana. In the North there is a much greater diversity: not only have Negroes gone into the established churches dominant in the North—the Episcopalian, Catholic, Presbyterian—but have started scores of new sects. Table 1 shows the distribution of Negro church membership in the Harlem section of New York City in 1930. Since 1930 we may guess that the Episcopal, Catholic and "Other" churches—"Other" being predominantly the new Negro sects but also some of the white-dominated churches such as the Christian Science Church—have increased their membership, partly at the expense of the Baptist and Methodist churches. The Father Divine Peace Mission has developed since 1932—mainly in New York but also in other Northern and Western cities—and it symbolizes the rapid growth of new Negro sects.

[b] See Chapter 43, Section 3.

In other respects than its emotionalism, the Negro church is quite like any lower class white Protestant church. Negro churches have made no innovations in theology or in the general character of the church service.[8] Some of the Negro cults—notably the one led by Father Divine—are exceptions, but for a long time there have been similar phenomena in the white world. The visitor to an average Negro church will see much the same type of service—with choir singing, hymns by the congregation, organ music (in the larger churches), prayer, sermon, collection—and hear the same theological terms that he does in the average white Protestant church. Except for a slight slant in the direction of "race,"[9] there is nothing in the formal content of the sermon to indicate that the church is a Negro church.

God and the angels are ordinarily white to Negroes, as they are to white churchgoers.[10] There is spiritual singing in Negro churches—especially in the rural Southern and the smaller Northern churches—and the spirituals *are* different from anything that can be found in the white churches.[a] But the ordinary hymns of the various Protestant churches are also in common use. The appeals used by the preacher, his way of handling his voice and the movements of his body, and the responses given by the audience in Negro churches also are different, but less so if the comparison is made with lower class white churches in isolated regions. Negro churches have, in addition to regular services, Sunday schools and various voluntary associations, and they provide some entertainment[11] and engage in an amount of educational and missionary work, just as most white churches do.

Americans are divided into a great number of denominations. In addition, each denomination often has several churches even in fairly small-sized communities. For these reasons individual congregations are, on the average, small in America. The split into miniature congregations is driven nearly to its limit in the Negro world.[b] With a relatively small congrega-

---

[a] See Chapter 44, Section 5.

[b] According to statistics, the 1936 Census of Religious Bodies (*Religious Bodies: 1936*, pp. 86, 850-851), the number of members per church were:

	Total churches	Urban	Rural
Negro	148	219	109
Non-Negro	311	616	139

Since the census figures on churches are usually not very accurate, we may cite three sample studies on the number of members in the average Negro church.

In 185 rural churches studied by Mays and Nicholson (Benjamin E. Mays and J. W. Nicholson, *The Negro's Church* [1933], p. 15), the average membership was 145 persons, of whom 50 per cent were actually contributing to the support of the churches. Compared to these figures, 609 urban churches had an average membership of 586 persons, of whom 43 per cent were contributing financial support. But in considering the size of the urban church, a sharp division must be made between the churches with edifices or halls and the "storefront" or residence churches.

In Harlem, for example, out of 163 Negro churches, 122 were meeting in residences or stores in 1930. These 122 churches claimed a total membership of 14,913, or 122 apiece

tion, and with no support from public funds, the individual minister in America is dependent on his church membership. The soliciting of contributions thus becomes an important part of the life of an American church. In the Negro church the collection of money becomes of pathetic importance, and a good portion of the time during an average church service is taken up by it.

For the same reasons the American church becomes forcefully stimulated to make itself as indispensable as possible to the people, and it undertakes many functions of a social nature in order to "sell" itself to the public. The church in the segregated Negro ghetto tends to take on even more functions of a nonreligious type than does the white church.

> The church has been, and continues to be, the outstanding social institution in the Negro community. It has a far wider function than to bring spiritual inspiration to its communicants. Among rural Negroes the church is still the only institution which provides an effective organization of the group, an approved and tolerated place for social activities, a forum for expression on many issues, an outlet for emotional repressions, and a plan for social living. It is a complex institution meeting a wide variety of needs.[12]

The Negro church was, from the beginning, the logical center for community life. It is thus much more than a place of worship.

> It is a social center, it is a club, it is an arena for the exercise of one's capabilities and powers, a world in which one may achieve self-realization and preferment. Of course, a church means something of the same sort to all groups; but with the Negro all those attributes are magnified because of the fact that they are so curtailed for him in the world at large. . . . Aside from any spiritual benefits derived, going to church means being dressed in one's best clothes, forgetting for the time about work, having the chance to acquit oneself with credit before one's fellows, and having the opportunity of meeting, talking and laughing with friends and of casting an appraising and approving eye upon the opposite sex. Going to church is an outlet for the Negro's religious emotions; but not the least reason why he is willing to support so many churches is that they furnish so many agreeable activities and so much real enjoyment. He is willing to support them because he has not yet, and will not have until there is far greater economic and intellectual development and social organization, any other agencies that can fill their place.[13]

The stronger dependence of the church and the minister on the active church members involves, of course, a fundamental democratization of organized religious life in America. American churches have had to come

---

on the average, and this was probably an over-statement. The other 41 churches had regular edifices or halls and claimed 51,220 members, or 1,250 apiece on the average. (See The Greater New York Federation of Churches, *The Negro Churches in Manhattan* [1930], pp. 11 and 17.)

In Chicago, a more careful study of 266 storefront churches in 1938 showed that they averaged only about 30 members apiece. (Drake, *op. cit.*, pp. 308-309.)

down to the people. In a veritable struggle for life they have had to go into competition with all other demands on peoples' money and time—and into competition with each other. Occasionally this is dangerous for the minister's integrity. He has to be a diplomat and a businessman and may have to compromise his ideals. The Negro churches are forced in the same direction as are white churches, but much more so.

In one particular respect the great split into denominations and individual congregations in America is anti-democratic in its results. It makes for a greater manifestation of social class distinction than there would be if most people belonged to the same state-supported church.[14] Belonging to one church or another serves in America as a means of class identification, just like membership in clubs. Even in this respect Negroes conform to the American pattern, but they exaggerate it slightly as high social status is rarer and respectability more precious in the lower caste.

4. A Segregated Church

Both the strength and the weakness of the Negro church as a power agency for the Negro people is related to the facts that the Negro church is a segregated church and that there is astonishingly little interracial cooperation between white and Negro churches. In both respects the South is extreme, but the situation in the North is not very different.

This virtual isolation between institutionalized religious life in the two castes is somewhat more easily explainable when we remember that churches in America have come to have significance for the social class the individual church member belongs to or aspires to belong to. Nevertheless, church segregation is a great moral dilemma to many earnest Christians among the whites. Embree explains to us:

> Segregation in Christian churches is an embarrassment. In a religion whose central teaching is brotherly love and the golden rule, preachers have to do a great deal of rationalizing as they expound their own gospel.[15]

Among Negroes all over the country this point is constantly made to prove the insincerity of white people.

Southern whites usually succeed in keeping the Christian challenge of religious brotherhood off their minds. The observer feels that the very incompatibility between the uncompromising Christian creed, on the one hand, and the actual caste relations, on the other hand, is a reason why white ministers in the South keep so aloof from the race problem and why the white church in the South has generally played so inconsequential a part in changing race relations. It is also a reason why the white minister has been closely watched by his congregation so that he does not start to draw practical conclusions from Christian doctrine that would favor the improvement of race relations. Bailey complained a generation ago:

Even in religion does the black blight of unfreedom appear. . . . Let a preacher in a Southern pulpit begin to plead for the negroes, and he at once endangers his popularity if not his support. Preachers do thus plead, on occasion, and are generously called "courageous" by some of their friends. Why should a minister of the church be "courageous" when he reminds his parishioners of the fundamental principle of Christianity, the priceless value of every human soul? And yet I should personally advise nine out of ten clergymen to leave this negro question severely alone. . . . If a special student of the negro question must submit to being called "brave" because he gently insinuates that, according to Christianity, negroes have immortal souls and that Christ died for those souls, although he has prefaced his remarks with a stiff statement of his adhesion to "Southern" principles, is it surprising that the people should want their ministers to keep clear of a subject which they ordinarily have not studied? On the other hand, I have heard esteemed and godly ministers make heartless remarks about negroes, remarks so cruelly harsh and unsympathetic that they aroused my indignation that alleged ambassadors of the Most High should speak so slightingly of any of God's children. . . . When men *must* use certain thought molds in politics, and *must* fear the effects of disturbing a bristling racial orthodoxy, it is natural that they should not be free in religion.[16]

The visitor to the South today finds Bailey's analysis of the moral dilemma of Southern ministers and church people still to the point. Things have changed, it is true, but not much. There are today more white ministers who dare to take an interest in their Negro neighbors, but the great majority of them keep astonishingly aloof—so much so that Moton could observe: "As a class, white ministers appear to have fewer contacts with Negroes than any group of their race."[17] Meetings of religious denominations for larger districts have acquired, under the influence of the interracial movement, the custom of "going on record" against lynching and for improved race relations. But the effects of this in the *local* community, where the minister faces the congregation which pays his salary, is usually slight.

As far as casual observations give a basis of judgment, sermons in Southern white churches are more "theological," less concerned with the citizen's daily problems, than in the North.[18] The average Southern white man, for natural reasons, can only be grateful not to have his stand on race relations exposed to the teachings of Christianity. It is commonly observed that the fundamentalism of the region is not unrelated to the moral difficulty of holding to Southern traditions in dealing with Negroes at the same time as being a Christian. Southern white church people have spent millions for foreign missions as against very small amounts for home mission work among their poor Negro neighbors.[19]

The moral situation is not altogether different in the North. It is true that the Northern whites since the Civil War have been generously supporting missionary work among Negroes in the South and denominational Negro schools and colleges. This is actually one of the great educational deeds of modern times. It is also true that many white churches in the

North have a few Negro members, and that they rarely would turn away Negro visitors who came to a service. But usually they cannot afford to let the Negro membership grow too large. Baker observed that he "found strange things in Boston": some Episcopal churches had had increased Negro attendance, and this created a serious problem. A prominent white church leader explained the matter to him in the following words:

> What *shall* we do with these Negroes! I for one would like to have them stay. I believe it is in accordance with the doctrine of Christ, but the proportion is growing so large that white people are drifting away from us. Strangers avoid us. Our organization is expensive to keep up and the Negroes are able to contribute very little in proportion to their numbers. Think about it yourself: What shall we do? If we allow the Negroes to attend freely it means that eventually all the white people will leave and we shall have a Negro church whether we want it or not.[20]

Similar situations and attitudes can be observed today everywhere in Northern cities with a heavy Negro population.

If this moral problem of organized American Christianity has not become more conspicuous and troublesome for white people's conscience, the explanation is that probably most Negroes—the caste situation being what it is—prefer to worship in Negro churches, even if they are against church segregation in principle. In the South they have no other choice anyway, and the question is not very practical. Even in the North Negroes usually feel more comfortable by themselves. And Negro preachers have a vested interest in segregated churches. It can be observed that Negro preachers suspect many of the projects looking toward interracial cooperation in church activities as attempts to deprive them of influence. They feel, often with some justification, that interracial religious activity would mean having white men as church leaders for Negroes but not Negroes as church leaders for whites.[21] Negro preachers have resented it when white denominations have sent white missionaries to convert Negroes.[22]

We find also that the white-dominated churches, which have been trying to keep their doors more open to Negroes and have sometimes made special efforts to convert Negroes, have not been too successful. The Roman Catholic Church belongs to this group. Although the Catholic Church can claim a greater proportion of Northern Negroes today than fifteen years ago, the proportion of all Northern Negroes with religious affiliations who were members of Catholic churches is probably still below 5 per cent.[23] On the whole, the Roman Catholic Church prefers to have Negroes attend all-Negro churches, on the basis of residential segregation and of attempts to dissuade them from attending white churches.[a]

---

[a] Gillard estimates that in 1940 about one-third of the Negro Catholics in the United States were in mixed churches. (Cited in *The Negro Handbook*, p. 102.)

In the South, especially in southern Louisiana where the French and Creole traditions are dominant, the Roman Catholic Church is the only one where Negroes are allowed

Of the Protestant churches, the Congregationalists and Quaker churches have probably been most nearly equalitarian,[24] but they have made little headway among Negroes. The Episcopalian and Christian Science churches have in the North much the same policy toward Negroes as does the Roman Catholic Church. A small but increasing proportion of upper and middle class Negroes have joined these churches and have some contact with the upper class whites who dominate them.[a]

The great majority of white churches, in the North as well as in the South, thus do not want to have a substantial Negro membership. The great majority of Negroes do not seem to want to join white churches, even if they are allowed. As usual the caste separation has been fortified by its own effects.

There is also astonishingly little interracial cooperation between the white and Negro churches of the same denomination. In the South there is practically no contact at all between Negroes and whites for religious pur-

---

to attend white churches. But even here, the dominant tendency is to keep Negroes in their own churches, to prevent Negroes from joining in interchurch Catholic meetings or celebrations, and to provide a separate set of white priests—who seldom mingle with the other priests—for the Negroes. (See Allison Davis, "The Negro Church and Associations in the Lower South," unpublished manuscript prepared for this study [1940], p. 15, *passim.*) The Catholic Negro churches have—with rare exceptions—white priests. According to Gillard, there were only 23 Negro priests in the Roman Catholic Church in 1941, and 6 of these were on foreign missions. (Cited in *The Negro Handbook*, pp. 102-103.)

[a] The Holiness Church, while predominantly white, has occasionally bi-racial congregations. It has not been attracting many new members lately.

The small Bahai Church is in America dominated by upper class Northern whites who have an explicit policy in favor of interracialism and internationalism. A small number of upper class Negroes have joined. It is the only white-dominated church in which there may be said to be absolutely no segregation or discrimination.

Similar to the Bahai Church in its principle against any form of racial discrimination, but quite different in that it is Negro-dominated and in that it is patterned after the emotional lower class type of Negro church, is the Father Divine Peace Mission movement. Estimates of the total membership of this bizarre sect, which has attracted members in significant numbers only since 1932, range up to 2 million (John Hoshor, *God in a Rolls Royce* [1936], p. xi), but there is good reason to believe that it was less than 15,000 in 1940 (Edward Nelson Palmer, "Father Divine Peace Mission," unpublished manuscript prepared for this study [1940], Appendix C of Guion G. Johnson and Guy B. Johnson, *op. cit.*, p. 6.) Over half the members are concentrated in New York City, and practically all the rest are in other Northern and Western cities; there are practically no adherents in the South. Most estimates have it that about 10 per cent of the members are white (*idem*), and one of the strongest injunctions of the sect is against recognition of color differences. The relation between the members is particularly intimate since they are enjoined to trade at "peace" stores and many of the members live together in the several "Heavens" which Father Divine has established in New York, New Jersey and Pennsylvania. While racial differences are not to be noticed, it must, of course, be important to his followers that God in the person of Father Divine, is a Negro.

poses,[a] except for some outcast white who can occasionally be seen attending Negro churches, the formal and restricted interracial work between ministers which is sometimes arranged for[b] and the white man who attends a Negro church for amusement or study. In the North there are more interracial contacts[c] but not enough to modify the basic fact of church separation. What little there is probably tends to improve race relations, to bring the Negro church closer to white norms of religious behavior, and to get money from the whites for the Negro church.[25]

5. ITS WEAKNESS

The Negro church is the oldest and—in membership—by far the strongest of all Negro organizations. Like the lodges, burial societies, and the great number of social clubs, the Negro church by its very existence involves a certain power consolidation. Meetings of the church officials in a denomination and church papers—read at least by most of the ministers—provide for an ideological cohesion, not only in religious matters but, to an extent, also in the common race interests. It also has some significance when, for instance, it is pointed out about Mr. Mordecai Johnson, the

[a] The Catholic Church in the region around New Orleans is an exception (see footnote a few pages back). Also, in the South occasionally a white preacher will visit a Negro Spiritualist Church to conduct a service (Davis, op. cit., p. 20.)

[b] Once a year some Southern churches participate in "Interracial Sunday" sponsored by the Commission on Race Relations of the Federal Council of Churches of Christ in America. Negro singers appear in white churches, occasionally a leading Negro will make a speech, and the white minister will devote his sermon to race relations. (Paul E. Baker, *Negro-White Adjustment* [1934], pp. 226-228.)

[c] The following five points of interracial contact in the North are taken, with slight modifications, from Drake, op. cit., p. 221. Drake made his summary on the basis of interviews with Negro pastors and other church officials in Chicago. The description is fairly representative for all large Northern cities:

1. There is occasionally an exchange of pulpits or choirs between Negro and white ministers on "Interracial Sunday" and a few other ceremonial occasions. In 1940, there were 45 exchanges in Chicago on Interracial Sunday. Only Negroes from large, well-established churches participate, and the white ministers are usually from small churches.

2. Young people's groups have "interracial programs," "good will activities," and so on. These are infrequent and informal except among the Congregationalists and Catholics (the Catholic Youth Organizations are particularly significant).

3. Where Negro churches belong to predominantly white denominations, there are the usual conferences, and similar meetings (especially in Holiness, Congregational, Episcopalian and Presbyterian churches).

4. Infrequent visits are made by white persons to Negro churches for special programs, money-raising events, or for political purposes.

5. Visits occur by both Negro and white persons to "unorthodox" or exotic churches. It might be said that only the curious and the maladjusted go (especially Holiness, Spiritualist and the smaller sects).

President of Howard University, that he is a Baptist minister and has the backing of the Negro Baptist world.

Potentially, the Negro church is undoubtedly a power institution. It has the Negro masses organized and, if the church bodies decided to do so, they could line up the Negroes behind a program. Actually, the Negro church is, on the whole, passive in the field of intercaste power relations. It generally provides meeting halls and encourages church members to attend when other organizations want to influence the Negroes. But viewed as an instrument of collective action to improve the Negroes' position in American society, the church has been relatively inefficient and uninfluential. In the South it has not taken a lead in attacking the caste system or even in bringing about minor reforms; in the North it has only occasionally been a strong force for social action.

This might be deemed deplorable, but it should not be surprising. Christian churches generally have, for the most part, conformed to the power situation of the time and the locality. They have favored a passive acceptance of one's worldly condition and, indeed, have seen their main function in providing escape and consolation to the sufferers. If there is any relation at all between the interest of a Negro church in social issues and the social status of its membership, the relation is that a church tends to be the more other-worldly the poorer its members are and the more they are in need of concerted efforts to improve their lot in this life. The churches where the poor white people in the South worship are similar to the common Negro churches.[26]

Even in this respect the Negro church is an ordinary American church with certain traits exaggerated because of caste. Of 100 sermons delivered in urban Negro churches and analyzed by Mays and Nicholson, only 26 touched upon practical problems.[a] The rural Negro church makes an even poorer showing in this respect.[b] Too, the Negro church is out of touch with

[a] Fifty-four others were classified as dealing with "other-worldly" topics, and the remaining 20 were doctrinal or theological. (*Op. cit.*, pp. 59 and 70.) Mays and Nicholson also reported, as have other students of the Negro church, that the sermons were characterized by poor logic, poor grammar and pronunciation, and an excessive display of oratorical tricks.

[b] Not only the sermons, but practically all the prayers, spirituals, and Church school literature of the three major Negro denominations support traditional, compensatory patterns, according to Mays. (B. E. Mays, *The Negro's God* [1938], p. 245.) Mays describes these patterns thus: "Though recognizing notable exceptions, they are compensatory and traditional in character because they are neither developed nor interpreted in terms of social rehabilitation. They are conducive to developing in the Negro a complacent, laissez-faire attitude toward life. They support the view that God in His good time and in His own way will bring about the conditions that will lead to the fulfillment of social needs. They encourage Negroes to feel that God will see to it that things work out all right; if not in this world, certainly in the world to come. They make God influential chiefly in the beyond, in preparing a home for the faithful—a home where His suffering servants will be free of the trials and tribulations which beset them on the earth." (*Idem.*)

current social life in the field of morals; the preaching of traditional puritanical morals has little effect on the bulk of the Negro population, and the real moral problems of the people are seldom considered in the church. Practically all Negro leaders have criticized the Negro church on these points. Booker T. Washington, for example, said:

> From the nature of things, all through slavery it was life in the future world that was emphasized in religious teaching rather than life in this world. In his religious meetings in *ante-bellum* days the Negro was prevented from discussing many points of practical religion which related to this world; and the white minister, who was his spiritual guide, found it more convenient to talk about heaven than earth, so very naturally that today in his religious meeting it is the Negro's feelings which are worked upon mostly, and it is description of the glories of heaven that occupy most of the time of his sermon.[27]

Ignorance, poverty, cultural isolation, and the tradition of dependence are responsible for this situation, in the same way as they are factors keeping Negroes down in other areas of life.

The frequent schisms in Negro churches weaken their institutional strength. New Negro churches and sects seldom begin because of theological divergences, but rather because a preacher wants to get a congregation,[28] because some members of a church feel that the minister is too emotional or not emotional enough, because some members feel that they have little in common with other members of the church, as well as because of outside missionary influences and division.[29] The competition between the preachers is intense and, as we said, most churches are small. There is little collaboration between the churches. Overhead expenses tend to be relatively high in the small church establishments.[30] Since, in addition, the membership of the churches is composed usually of poor people, the economic basis of most churches is precariously weak.[a]

Poverty often makes the Negro church dependent upon white benefactors. It also prevents paying such salaries[b] that ambitious young men could be tempted to educate themselves properly for the ministry.[c] In fact the

---

[a] Negro churches usually have poor business practices. There is little secretarial help, thus there is poor accounting, and the money is sometimes just given to the minister or to a few church officers to do what they please with it. There is probably a significant amount of misappropriation of funds under this system. (See Mays and Nicholson, *op. cit.*, pp. 168-197 and 259-265, and Hortense Powdermaker, *After Freedom* [1939], p. 238.)

[b] Mays and Nicholson (*op. cit.*, p. 189) reported from their 1930 sample study that 69.4 per cent of Negro ministers had an annual income of less than $2,000. The average rural preacher got only $266 per church per year, but often he served several churches or had some other outside source of income. See Chapter 14, Section 5.

[c] According to a sample study by Woodson, ". . . only seven-tenths of one per cent of Negro high school graduates contemplate taking up the ministry, and many of those who have been known to qualify themselves thus do not stay in the ministry." (Carter G. Woodson, *The Negro Professional Man and the Community* [1934]. p. 80.)

idea that a preacher should have education for his task is still usually lacking, and the average preacher has not much more of it than do the members of his flock.[31] The chief prerequisite for becoming a minister in most of the denominations to which Negroes belong is traditionally not education, but a "call" which is more often the manifestation of temporary hysteria or opportunistic self-inspiration than of a deep soul-searching. There are many exceptions, of course, and they are becoming somewhat more frequent, but the preachers who come to their profession through a "call" are still numerically significant. Such preachers tend to retain the emotionalism that has traditionally been identified with the Negro's religion.

The ministry was once the chief outlet for Negro ambition. Under slavery, as we have noted, the preacher stood out as the leader and spokesman for his group. After slavery his monopoly of status in the Negro community diminished as business and professional men increased in number.[32] Increasingly status within the Negro caste is being based on education. Since there is little in the way of special attention paid to the Negro minister's education—except for a minority, practically all in the cities—he is rapidly falling in relative status. Upper and middle class Negroes deprecate the common uneducated Negro preacher. Initiative and leadership in matters concerning the Negro community tend to pass to this new upper class of Negro businessmen and professionals. Meanwhile, taking up preaching is still one of the few possibilities of rising for the individual without a professional training.

As a class Negro preachers are losing influence, because they are not changing as fast as the rest of the Negro community. This is now on the verge of becoming a most serious problem, endangering the future of the Negro church. As improvements in education have been rapid in the last decades, the bulk of the old Negro preachers are today below the bulk of younger generation Negroes in education. Young people have begun to look down on the old-fashioned Negro preacher.[33] Lately the problem seems to have become as serious in rural areas as in cities. It is true that city youths are better educated and more sophisticated, but so also are city ministers who occasionally make some attempt to adjust to the needs of youth.[34]

It is difficult to see how the continuing decline of the minister's prestige and leadership can be stopped. Few college students are going into the ministry.[35] The ministry is no longer a profession which attracts the

Mays reports that there were 253 fewer students enrolled in Negro seminaries in 1939 than in 1924. Including 92 Negro students in Northern white seminaries, there were only 850 Negroes enrolled in all seminaries in 1939, and only 254 of these were college graduates. (Benjamin E. Mays, "The Negro Church in American Life," *Christendom* [Summer, 1940], pp. 389-391.)

brightest and most ambitious young Negroes.[a] The development under way will take a long time to manifest its complete effects. But it goes on and will spell the further decline of the Negro church as an active influence in the Negro community, if it does not begin to reform itself radically.

6. TRENDS AND OUTLOOK

The Negro church has been lagging ideologically, too. While for a long time the protest has been rising in the Negro community, the church has, on the whole, remained conservative and accommodating. Its traditions from slavery help to explain this. Its other-worldly outlook is itself an expression of political fatalism. In a city in the Deep South with a Negro population of 43,000 (Savannah), there are ninety Negro churches, one hundred active preachers and another hundred "jack legs"; here where the Negro ministry with few exceptions had been discouraging a recent movement to get the Negroes registered for voting, a Negro preacher explained:

> All we preachers is supposed to do is to preach the Lord and Saviour Jesus Christ and Him Crucified, and that's all.[b]

In most Negro communities visited by the present writer the progressive Negro leaders, trying to organize the Negro community for defense, complained about the timidity and disinterest on the part of the preachers. "They talk too much about heaven and too little about down here." Regularly the explanation was given that the churches were mortgaged to influential white people and that the preacher got small handouts from employers and politicians. Without doubt the preacher's old position of the white man's trusted Negro "leader" secures small advantages not only to himself but also to his group—and according to the scheme we analyzed

[a] In the last decade or so, there have been summer institutes established for Negro ministers—such as the one sponsored by the white Southern Methodist Episcopal Church—but relatively few Negroes participate, and even the education thus offered is completely inadequate for lack of time and money.

[b] Ralph J. Bunche, "A Brief and Tentative Analysis of Negro Leadership," unpublished manuscript prepared for this study (1940), pp. 79-80.

Sterner and I once attended a Sunday evening service in a Negro Baptist church in one of the capitals of the Upper South. The preacher developed the theme that nothing in this world was of any great importance: real estate, automobiles, fine clothes, learnedness, prestige, money, all this is nothing. It is not worth striving for. But an humble, peaceful heart will be remunerated in heaven. After the service we went up to the preacher for a talk. We asked him if he should not instead try to instil more worldly ambition in his poor and disadvantaged group. The preacher began to explain to us, as foreigners, that this would not do at all in the South. The role of the Negro church, he told us, was to make the poor Negroes satisfied with their lowly status. He finished by exclaiming: "We are the policemen of the Negroes. If we did not keep down their ambitions and divert them into religion, there would be upheaval in the South." This preacher is not typical in his philosophy of extreme accommodation or in his intellectual clarity. But it is significant that he exists.

in Chapter 34—it does give him prestige in the Negro community. But as the Negro protest rises, the traditional Negro preacher alienates a growing section of the Negroes from the church.

Care must be taken, however, not to over-state the criticism against the Negro church on this point. In both the North and the South one quite often meets Negro preachers who are active in the work for protest and betterment. Progressive ministers are still exceptions, but their existence might signify a trend. There seems to be less animosity against labor unions among Negro preachers—reflecting the increase in power of the unions referred to in Chapter 38. As the Negro protest is rising, the preacher finds generally that he has to change his appeal to keep his congregation in line.

When discussing the Negro church as it is and as it might come to be, it must never be forgotten that *the Negro church fundamentally is an expression of the Negro community itself*. If the church has been other-worldly in outlook and indulged in emotional ecstasy, it is primarily because the downtrodden common Negroes have craved religious escape from poverty and other tribulations. If the preachers have been timid and pussy-footing, it is because Negroes in general have condoned such a policy and would have feared radical leaders. The rivalry and factionalism, the organizational weakness and economic dependence of the Negro church, the often faltering economic and sexual morals of the preachers and their suspicion of higher education—all this reflects life as it is lived in the subordinate caste of American Negroes.

When the Negro community changes, the church also will change. It is true that the church has not given much of a lead to reforms but has rather lagged when viewed from the advanced positions of Negro youth and Negro intellectuals. But few Christian churches have ever been, whether in America or elsewhere, the spearheads of reform. That this fundamental truth is understood—underneath all bitter criticism—is seen in the fact that Negro intellectuals are much more willing to cooperate with Negro churches than white intellectuals with white churches.[36] The Negro protest and improvement organizations cooperate with all "respectable" Negro churches. The solidarity behind the abstract church institution in the Negro community is simply amazing. The visitor finds everywhere a widespread criticism, but this is focused mainly on the preachers. Few question the church as such, its benevolent influence and its great potentialities.

The Negro church is part of the whole circular process which is moving the American Negroes onward in their struggle against caste. The increasing education of the Negro masses is either making them demand something more of their church than praise of the other-world and emotional catharsis, or causing them to stand aloof from the institutionalized forms of religion. Not only the upper classes of Negroes are now critical of the shouting and noisy religious hysteria in oldtime Negro churches and new cults, but so are young people in all classes. The issue of emotionalism is still a keen divider but the dividing line now cuts deeper into the Negro community. In many Negro communities perhaps the majority still cling to the old patterns and resent persons—including ministers—who will not participate with them in the display of intense religious feeling. But, according to Mays and Nicholson, even in the rural South the revival meetings are less successful than they used to be, the professional evangelist is beginning to disappear, and the regular sermons attempt to be more thought-provoking.[37]

This is all part of the general process of acculturation. With considerable lag, the Negro clergymen, too, are acquiring a better education, which is reflected in their work. Negro preachers are increasingly in competition with professionals, businessmen, politicians, and labor union officials for local leadership. Competition is compelling them to try to do something positive for the Negro community. The social work programs of the relatively few churches which have them are mainly a development of the last decade or two, and we expect to see the trend continuing, especially in the North. The movement to the North and to the Southern cities also tends to emancipate the Negro preacher from white pressure. The fact that he gets more of his prestige from Negroes than from whites in the North is beneficial to the Negro community. These trends are making the Negro church a more efficient instrument for amelioration of the Negro's position at the same time as they are reducing the relative importance of the church in the Negro community.

CHAPTER 41

THE NEGRO SCHOOL

1. Negro Education as Concerted Action

The trend toward a rising educational level of the Negro population is of tremendous importance for the power relations discussed in this Part of our inquiry. Education means an assimilation of white American culture. It decreases the dissimilarity of the Negroes from other Americans. Since the white culture is permeated by democratic valuations, and since the caste relation is anything but democratic, education is likely to increase dissatisfaction among Negroes. This dissatisfaction strengthens the urge to withdraw from contact with prejudiced whites and causes an intensified isolation between the two groups.[a] Increasing education provides theories and tools for the rising Negro protest against caste status in which Negroes are held. It trains and helps to give an economic livelihood to Negro leaders.

In the Negro community, education is the main factor for the stratification of the Negro people into social classes.[b] The professionals who base their status upon having acquired a higher education form a substantial part of the Negro upper classes. And even in the middle and lower classes, educational levels signify class differences in the Negro community. In addition, education has a symbolic significance in the Negro world: the educated Negro has, in one important respect, become equal to the better class of whites.

These tendencies are most unhampered in the North. There Negroes have practically the entire educational system flung open to them without much discrimination. They are often taught in mixed schools and by white teachers; some of the Negro teachers have white pupils. Little attempt is made to adjust the teaching specifically to the Negroes' existing status and future possibilities. The American Creed permeates instruction, and the Negro as well as the white youths are inculcated with the traditional American virtues of efficiency, thrift and ambition. The American dream of individual success is held out to the Negroes as to other students. But employment opportunities—and, to a lesser extent, some other good things

[a] See Chapter 30, Section 2.
[b] See Chapter 32, Sections 1 and 2.

of life—are so closed to them that severe conflicts in their minds are bound to appear.

Their situation is, however, not entirely unique. Even among the youths from other poor and disadvantaged groups in the North the ideals implanted by the schools do not fit life as they actually experience it.[1] The conflicts are, of course, accentuated in the case of Negroes. Often they become cynical in regard to the official democratic ideals taught by the school. But more fundamentally they will be found to have drunk of them deeply. The American Creed and the American virtues mean much more to Negroes than to whites. They are all turned into the rising Negro protest.

The situation is more complicated in the South. The Negro schools are segregated and the Negro school system is controlled by different groups with different interests and opinions concerning the desirability of preserving or changing the caste status of Negroes. Looked upon as a "movement," Negro education in the South is, like the successful Negro organizations, an interracial endeavor. White liberals in the region and Northern philanthropists have given powerful assistance in building up Negro education in the South. They have thereby taken and kept some of the controls. In the main, however, the control over Negro education has been preserved by other whites representing the political power of the region. The salaried officers of the movement—the college presidents, the school principals, the professors, and the teachers—are now practically all Negroes; in the elementary schools and in the high schools they are exclusively Negroes. With this set-up, it is natural and, indeed, necessary that the Negro school adhere rather closely to the accommodating pattern.[a]

Negro teachers on all levels are dependent on the white community leaders. This dependence is particularly strong in the case of elementary school teachers in rural districts. Their salaries are low, and their security as to tenure almost nothing. They can be used as disseminators of the whites' expectations and demands on the Negro community. But the extreme dependence and poverty of rural Negro school teachers, and the existence of Negroes who are somewhat better off and more independent than they, practically excluded them from having any status of leadership in the Negro community. In so far as their teaching is concerned, they are, however, more independent than it appears. This is solely because the white superintendent and the white school board ordinarily care little about what goes on in the Negro school. There are still counties where the superintendent has never visited the majority of his Negro schools. As long as Negro stool pigeons do not transfer reports that she puts wrong ideas into the children's heads, the rural Negro school teacher is usually ignored.

In cities the situation is different. Negro elementary and high schools

[a] See Chapter 34.

are better; teachers are better trained and better paid. In the Negro community teachers have a higher social status. As individuals they also achieve a measure of independence because they are usually anonymous to the white superintendent and school board. In the cities, the white community as a whole does not follow so closely what happens among the Negroes. The Negro principal in a city school, however, is directly responsible to white officials and watches his teachers more closely than do superintendents of rural schools.

In state colleges the situation is similar, except that the professors have a still higher social status in the Negro community and except that the college tends to become a little closed community of its own, with its own norms, which tends to increase somewhat the independence of the teachers.

In the private colleges there is much more independence from local white opinion within the limits of the campus. A friendly white churchman belonging to the interracial movement recently told the students of Atlanta University, in a commencement address, that the teachers there enjoyed greater academic freedom than their white colleagues at the Georgia state institutions, and this is probably true. The influence exerted by the Northern philanthropists and church bodies who have contributed to the colleges —often exercised through Southern white liberals and interracialists and through outstanding conservative Negro leaders—is, to a great extent, effective as a means of upholding the independence of Negro college presidents and professors.

As conditions are in the South, it is apparent that this influence is indispensable for this purpose. Neither the Negro teachers themselves nor any outside Negro institution could provide a power backing effective enough to keep off local white pressure. This outside white control gives the Negro teachers a considerably greater freedom even to inculcate a protest attitude—if it is cautiously done—than is allowed in publicly supported educational institutions. But it is inherent in the Southern caste situation, and in the traditions of the movement to build up Negro education in the region, that even this control is conservatively directed when compared with Northern standards.

In spite of these controls, strongest at the bottom of the educational system but strong also in the higher institutions, there is no doubt, however, that *the long-range effect of the rising level of education in the Negro people goes in the direction of nourishing and strengthening the Negro protest.* Negro-baiting Senator Vardaman knew this when he said:

> What the North is sending South is not money but dynamite; this education is ruining our Negroes. They're demanding equality.[2]

This would probably hold true of any education, independent of the controls held and the direction given. An increased ability on the part of the

Negroes to understand the printed and spoken word cannot avoid opening up contact for them with the wider world, where equalitarian ideas are prevalent. But in the South there is not much supervision of Negro schools. And as we shall see later, Southern whites have been prohibited by their allegiance to the American Creed from making a perfected helot training out of Negro education.

2. EDUCATION IN AMERICAN THOUGHT AND LIFE

Even where the Negro school exists as a separate institution it is, like all other Negro institutions, patterned on the white American school as a model. It is different only for reasons connected with the caste situation. Even in their thinking on education, Negroes are typical, or overtypical, Americans.

As background for our discussion we shall have to remember the role of education in American democratic thought and life.[a] Education has always been the great hope for both individual and society.[b] In the American Creed it has been the main ground upon which "equality of opportunity for the individual" and "free outlet for ability" could be based. Education has also been considered as the best way—and the way most compatible with American individualistic ideals—to improve society.

Research in, and discussion of, education is prolific. In America, pedagogy anticipated by several generations the recent trend to environmentalism in the social sciences[c] and the belief in the changeability of human beings. It gave a basis for the belief in democratic values and expressed the social optimism of American liberalism. The major American contribution to philosophy—the theory of pragmatism—bears visibly the marks of having been developed in a culture where education was awarded this prominent role. And it was in line with American cultural potentialities when John Dewey turned it into a theory of education. No philosopher from another country would be likely to express himself as he did in the following:

> The philosophy of education is one phase of philosophy in general. It may be seriously questioned whether it is not the most important single phase of general

[a] See Chapter 9, Section 3.

[b] To many Americans the great stress on education early in the life of the new nation has become so commonplace that they do not see anything exceptional in it. Wilkerson, for instance, observes that the federal Constitution was silent on the question of education and that so were also many of the earlier state constitutions. (Doxey A. Wilkerson, "The Negro in American Education," unpublished manuscript prepared for this study [1940], Vol. 1, pp. 10-11.) The remarkable thing is, of course, that. on the contrary, some state constitutions in America did touch the question of public education. There were European countries where public education was introduced earlier than in America, or equally early. But nowhere would it have been considered important enough to deserve constitutional sanction.

[c] See Chapters 4 and 6.

philosophy . . . the whole philosophic problem of the origin, nature, and function of knowledge is a live issue in education, not just a problem for exercise of intellectual dialectic gymnastics.[3]

At least since the time of Horace Mann, Americans have been leading in the development of pedagogical thinking. The marriage between philosophy and pedagogy in Dewey and his followers has given America the most perfected educational theory developed in modern times. Under the slogan "education for a changing world" and supported by a whole science of "educational sociology," it requires that education be set in relation to the society in which the individual lives. The introduction of this value relation into discussions of educational goals and means is a paramount contribution of America. And this has remained not only an achievement of academic speculation and research but has, to a large extent, come to influence policy-making agencies in the educational field. America has, therefore, seen more of enterprising and experimental progressive redirecting of schools than has any other country.

The duty of society to provide for public education was early established in America, and private endowments for educational purposes have been magnificent. America spends more money and provides its youth, on the average, with more schooling than any other country in the world. America has also succeeded in a relatively higher degree than any other country in making real the old democratic principle that the complete educational ladder should be held open to the most intelligent and industrious youths, independent of private means and support from their family. Education has been, and is increasingly becoming, a chief means of climbing the social status scale. It is entirely within this great American tradition when white people, who have wanted to help the Negroes, have concentrated their main efforts on improving Negro education.

American Negroes have taken over the American faith in education. Booker T. Washington's picture of the freedmen's drive for education is classical:

Few people who were not right in the midst of the scenes can form any exact idea of the intense desire which the people of my race showed for education. It was a whole race trying to go to school. Few were too young, and none too old, to make the attempt to learn. As fast as any kind of teachers could be secured, not only were day-schools filled, but night-schools as well. The great ambition of the older people was to try to learn to read the Bible before they died. With this end in view, men and women who were fifty or seventy-five years old, would be found in the night-schools. Sunday-schools were formed soon after freedom, but the principal book studied in the Sunday-school was the spelling-book. Day-school, night-school, and Sunday-school were always crowded, and often many had to be turned away for want of room.[4]

Campbell observed in the 'seventies that ". . . the blacks are very anxious to learn—more so than the lower whites."[5] Bryce remarked some decades later that "there is something pathetic in the eagerness of the Negroes, parents, young people, and children to obtain education."[6] And Baker wrote at the beginning of this century:

> The eagerness of the coloured people for a chance to send their children to school is something astonishing and pathetic. They will submit to all sorts of inconveniences in order that their children may get an education.[7]

As self-improvement through business or social improvement through government appeared so much less possible for them, Negroes have come to affix an even stronger trust in the magic of education. It is true that some Negroes may lately have lost their faith in education, either because the schools available to them—in the South—are so inadequate or—in the North—because they achieve education but not the things they hoped to do with it. This attitude of dissatisfaction is probably part of the explanation why Negro children tend to drop out of high school more than do whites.[a] If both sources of dissatisfaction could be removed, there is reason to believe that American Negroes would revert to their original belief in education. And, aside from such dissatisfaction and even cynicism, the masses of Negroes show even today a naïve, almost religious faith in education. To an extent, this faith was misplaced: many Negroes hoped to escape drudgery through education alone. But it is also true that this faith has been justified to a large extent: education is one of the things which has given the Negroes something of a permanent advance in their condition.

The American zeal for education has always been focused on the individual's *opportunity*. The stress on enforcing a basic *minimum* standard of education for *all* young people in the nation has been less. In education as in many other fields of culture, America shows great disparity; there are at once many model schools and a considerable amount of illiteracy and semi-illiteracy. Bryce observed:

> If one part of the people is as educated and capable as that of Switzerland, another is as ignorant and politically untrained as that of Russia.[8]

And a similar statement holds true today.

This disparity is partly explainable in terms of size of the country and in terms of the administrative decentralization of the school system. But when one observes the tremendous differences in amount and quality of education between some of the cities and some of the rural districts in one single state, as, for instance, Illinois, he cannot avoid believing that more basic still is a general toleration by Americans of dissimilar status between regions and

---

[a] See Chapter 43, Section 4.

groups of people. In any case, these dissimilarities in educational facilities for whites in different regions are important for the Negro problem. A differential treatment of Negroes as a group has been less spectacular and has seemed less indefensible with this as a setting.

There is no doubt that a change of American attitudes in this respect is under way and that an increasing stress is placed upon the desirability of raising the educational level in the sub-standard regions to greater equality. This change—which is part of a much more general tendency of the American Creed to include ideals of greater economic equalization [a]—has taken form in the proposals for greater federal aid to education. The Negroes' chance of getting more equality in education is bound up with this movement.[b]

Considering the importance attached to education in America, it is surprising that the teacher has not been awarded a higher status in American society. Learning has never given much prestige, and until recently the teacher has been held on a relatively low economic level without much security of tenure, in most places. And even today he is, relatively speaking, not well paid, and his tenure is not secure, particularly in the South. Teachers in America have not even been allowed to have as much power over the government of their own schools as they have in comparable countries. Their status as employees is stressed. This applies to all teachers, though in different degrees. The teachers in grade schools, mostly women, are socially and economically placed at a disadvantage compared with other professionals with the same amount of preparation. The professors at colleges and universities are generally accorded middle class status, definitely below that of a successful businessman.

The Negro community is, in this respect, more similar to northern European societies. The teacher generally has a symbolic prestige from the importance of his calling. Because of the scarcity of business opportunities and of successful businessmen in the Negro community, the teacher is also more free from competition for prestige. It should be recalled, however, that the great personal dependency of the teacher, particularly in the rural South, and her low income tend to deflate her position in the Negro community.

Another peculiarity of America, which is not unconnected with the relatively low prestige of the teachers and of learning, is a common tendency to look upon education as something produced by the school and finished by graduation. The ordinary American does not conceive of education as a process which continues through adult life and is dependent upon the individual's own exertion. To few Americans does it seem to be an important goal in life continuously to improve their education. Few schools on any level direct much of their attention to preserving and developing the "educability" of the students. The very perfection of text books and too much teaching is likely to make the student more passive in his attainment of knowledge. Too little is generally asked of the students; too much—in teaching—is required of the teachers.[a] This is, perhaps, one of the reasons why the final educational results do not measure up to the great amount of funds and time which go into schooling in America. In this respect the Negro schools do not differ from white schools. In fact, they can, even less well than white schools, afford to disregard the more formal requirements and go in for experimentation.

In this connection should be noted the relative absence in America of a civic adult education movement upheld by the concerted efforts of the people themselves. We have related this to the relative political passivity of the American citizens between elections.[b] The government of American municipalities does not decentralize power and responsibility to a great number of boards and councils, and does not offer, therefore, much opportunity for participation to the ordinary citizen. This decreases the functional importance of civic adult education, as does also the relative absence of organized mass movements. If this is true of the white Americans, it is, of course, much more true of the Negroes, particularly in the South where they are largely disfranchised. Lack of participation in the wider community must depress interest in continued self-education, except when it is vocational or professional and motivated by narrow considerations of individual economic advancement.

America is, however, prominent in the type of passive mass education through such agencies as the radio, press, popular magazines and movies. The rise of the Negro population, not only to literacy but to a real capability of consuming the spoken and printed word, and the increasing efficacy of those agencies, must have a strong influence in raising the culture level of Negroes. Through these media, they are made more American.

[a] This is definitely true also of the ordinary college and, to an extent, also of the graduate school. There are too many arranged courses, too much "spoon feeding." The heavy lecturing—which the observer relates to the legislators' and the entire society's lack of respect for the learned profession and *their* demand to get labor for their money, as well as to the tradition of preaching kept in institutions which were almost all denominational seminaries in the beginning—is perhaps even more dangerous for the teachers than for the students as nothing is so indoctrinating as to listen to one's own voice. It keeps the professors from scientific work; and it keeps the students from finding their own way to the sources of knowledge. The "self-made man" is generally an American ideal, but in the schools it is less well realized than in other spheres of culture. The "spoon feeding" in higher institutions is the more important since they set the patterns, to a considerable extent, for the lower schools.

[b] See Chapter 33.

3. THE DEVELOPMENT OF NEGRO EDUCATION IN THE SOUTH

The history of Negro education in the South is one of heroic deeds as well as of patient, high-minded and self-sacrificing toil. In this context we can only present the outlines of the subject.

One of the cultural disparities between the North and the South at the outbreak of the Civil War was that the Northern states had established tax-supported public schools, while the public school movement was only in its beginning in the South.[9] The few Negroes in the North shared, on the whole, in the better educational opportunities in the region.[10] In the South most white people had little or no formal schooling. In all Southern states (except a few of the Border states and the District of Columbia) it was forbidden to teach slaves how to read and write, and several states extended the prohibition to free Negroes.[11]

Still, a few of the slave owners, or their wives and daughters, considered it a Christian duty to teach the slaves to read, and by 1860 perhaps as much as 5 per cent of the slaves could read and write.[12] A larger proportion of the free Negroes had acquired some schooling. The education of Negroes under slavery cannot be discussed without noting also the excellent training as artisans and handicraftsmen a small proportion of the slaves received. Each plantation was a more or less self-sufficient economy outside of its major crop export and food import, and, therefore, required slaves with each of the skills necessary to keep up the community. In the cities many slaves worked in the commercial handicrafts. The artisan tradition was passed on from person to person and usually did not require schools or the teaching of the more general arts.[a]

After the Civil War there came a tremendous demand for education in the South. Du Bois rightly points out that:

> The uprising of the black man, and the pouring of himself into organized effort for education, in those years between 1861 and 1871, was one of the marvelous occurrences of the modern world; almost without parallel in the history of civilization.[13]

A significant number of Union soldiers stayed in the South to teach the freedmen the "three R's." They were immediately assisted by better trained idealists—largely Abolitionists from the North, especially from New England.[14] Northern Negroes also came down to swell the number of teachers. As soon as these front-rank teachers had given their pupils an elementary education, the latter had no difficulty in finding positions as teachers. Wages were low and living conditions poor for teachers, but idealism was burning, and a rudimentary education spread.

The Freedmen's Bureau did some of its most important work in establish-

---

[a] See Appendix 6.

ing and supporting schools for Negroes. Missionary and church organizations in the North contributed not only by sending down teachers but
also by giving money for buildings and support of the students. Indeed,
most of the Negroes who received education in the South between 1865
and 1880 were schooled in institutions supported by the charity of Northern
churches.[15] Fisk, Atlanta, Howard and Hampton were founded in these
years. The Negro communities themselves collected much money for their
schools, particularly on the elementary level.

As a part of this movement the Reconstruction governments laid the basis
for a public school system in the South for both whites and Negroes. In all
Southern states the great American principle of free public schools for all
children was written into the new constitutions or other statutes. The
Restoration governments only continued what their predecessors had
organized for the whites. The Negroes were severely discriminated against;
in many parts of the South Negro education deteriorated for decades. This
period of reaction was a most crucial time for Negro education. Du Bois
is probably right when he says that "had it not been for the Negro school
and college, the Negro would, to all intents and purposes, have been driven
back to slavery."[16]

The great wonder is that the principle of the Negroes' right to public
education was not renounced altogether. But it did not happen. One
explanation is the persistency and magnanimity of Northern philanthropy.
But this activity was pursued under the indulgence of the Southern state
and municipal authorities. And, though their own contributions to Negro
education in many regions were not much more than face saving, *the
important thing is that face saving was deemed necessary and that the
Negroes' statutory right to public education remained unassailable in the
South.* The American Creed, backed by the Constitution, showed itself
strong enough not to allow the sacred principle of public education to
succumb. Even in the South—as it came out of the Civil War and Reconstruction—the caste interest could never be pursued wholeheartedly. The
moral dilemma, and the apologetic attitude, growing out of the partial
allegiance to the American Creed, is illustrated in a pronouncement like
the following from Thomas Nelson Page:

> The South has faithfully applied itself during all these years to giving the
> Negroes all the opportunities possible for attaining an education, and it is one of the
> most creditable pages in her history that in face of the horror of Negro-domination
> during the Reconstruction period; of the disappointment at the small results; in face
> of the fact that the education of the Negroes has appeared to be used by them only
> as a weapon with which to oppose the white race, the latter should have persistently
> given so largely of its store to provide this misused education.[17]

Almost as soon as the movement for the education of Negro youth began,
the quarrel started as to whether Negro education should be "classical" or

"industrial."[18] If the white Southerners had to permit the Negroes to get any education at all, they wanted it to be of the sort which would make the Negro a better servant and laborer, not that which would teach him to rise out of his "place." The New England school teachers—who did most of the teaching at first—wanted to train the Negroes as they themselves had been trained in the North: the "three R's" at the elementary level, with such subjects as Latin, Greek, geometry, rhetoric coming in at the secondary and college levels. But General S. C. Armstrong, a Union officer during the Civil War,[19] had established Hampton Institute in the tidewater region of Virginia as an "agricultural institution." He wanted to see continued the skilled artisan tradition that had existed among Negroes before the War. His most famous pupil, Booker T. Washington, founded the Tuskegee Institute in Alabama and became the apostle of industrial education for Negroes. There is no doubt that—quite apart from the pedagogical merits of this type of education—his message was extremely timely in the actual power situation of the Restoration. It reconciled many Southern white men to the idea of Negro education, and Washington has probably no small share in the salvaging of Negro education from the great danger of its being entirely destroyed. Meanwhile, the New England advocates of a classical education and their Negro followers carried on at Atlanta, Fisk, and at a few other Southern centers of Negro college education. The elementary schools—there were practically no secondary schools for Negroes in the South at this time—followed the patterns set by the dominant colleges.

The struggle between the conservative and the radical group of Negro leaders became focused on the issue: "industrial" *versus* "classical" education for Negroes. Washington became the champion for the former position, and he was backed by the white South and the bulk of Northern philanthropy. Du Bois headed the group of Negro intellectuals who feared that most often the intention, and in any case the result, would be to keep Negroes out of the higher and more general culture of America.[a] This dispute was important in the development of Negro ideologies. It scarcely meant much for the actual development of Negro education in the South,

[a] In this particular issue there was more heat and rivalry between the two groups than actual differences of opinion. Du Bois never deprecated in a wholesale manner vocational education; in later days he became, in fact, more and more positively in favor of it. Washington, on his side, had never accepted the dominant white man's idea that education for the Negro ought only to be training him to be a field hand or domestic servant and to know his lowly "place." In his famous Atlanta speech of 1895 he said:

"To those of my race who depend on bettering their condition in a foreign land or who underestimate the importance of cultivating friendly relations with the Southern white man, . . . I would say: 'Cast down your bucket where you are,—cast it down in making friends in every *manly* way of the people of all races by whom we are surrounded.

" 'Cast it down in agriculture, *mechanics, in commerce*, in domestic service, and *in the professions*.'" (*Up From Slavery* [1901; first edition, 1900], p. 219. Italics ours.)

which was dominated by the whites. If Negro education in the South did not become turned entirely into industrial education on the elementary level, the main explanation was, as we shall see, the growing expense of such training after the Industrial Revolution and the competitive interest of white workers to keep the Negroes out of the crafts and industry. On the higher level, a nonvocational Negro education had, as Du Bois always emphasized, its chief strength in the fact that Tuskegee Institute and other similar schools raised a demand for teachers with a broader educational background.

During all this time, from the Civil War until today, there has been a steady stream of money going from Northern philanthropy to Southern education. A large part of it has gone to white education. But a considerable portion has gone to Negro education, and it has had strategic importance: first, to give it a start during Reconstruction, later to hinder its complete destruction during Restoration, and to advance it in recent decades.

From about 1865 to about 1875, the period of "classical" education, most of the money came from Northern reform groups and churches, aided by state funds allocated by the Reconstruction governments. From about 1880 to about 1905 these sources were pretty dry, and educators of Negroes appealed to wealthy Northern businessmen, who had little interest in Negroes but could be relied upon to donate to most nonradical charitable causes. This was also the period when Negro college students formed singing groups which appeared before Northern audiences and took up collections.

In the first two decades of the twentieth century, Negro education received a great boost when the Northern philanthropic foundations stepped into the picture on a much larger scale.[20] Before then the George Peabody Fund (established in 1867) gave money to both white and Negro common schools and teacher-training schools in the South.[21] The John F. Slater Fund (established in 1882) supported industrial and teacher-training schools. Both Funds were small, and at first dominated by conservative principles. In 1908 a Quaker lady of Philadelphia, Miss Anna T. Jeanes, established a Fund to give impetus to the small rural Southern Negro school. Mr. Jackson Davis, then school superintendent of Henrico County in Virginia and now an officer on the General Education Board, and Miss Virginia Randolph, a Negro teacher in that county, worked out the plan for this Fund. This plan calls for a rural industrial supervisor who goes from school to school in a county and helps the teachers organize their domestic science, their gardening and their simple carpentry work. At first the Fund paid the salaries of these "Jeanes' teachers," but gradually many of the county school boards took over the function. The remnants of the Peabody, Slater, and Jeanes Funds have been recently integrated into the Southern Education Foundation, which still helps to pay part of the salaries of the Jeanes teachers.[22]

Another step was taken by the General Education Board, with money provided by John D. Rockefeller, under the direction of Wallace Buttrick. This foundation paid for state supervisors of Negro education who were to be under the state superintendents. The supervisors, who were white Southerners, had no official authority whatever, but they have been most important in raising the standards of the Negro public schools of the South. They plead to the state and county officials for improved educational facilities, and they get their authority out of their political independence, their intimate knowledge of their fields, and the fact that they act as the local agents for the several foundations interested in aiding Negro education.[23] They are now gradually becoming integrated in the state administration and are paid out of state funds.

Jackson Davis, N. C. Newbold, and several other leading educational statesmen of the South have been engaged in this work. The General Education Board has also given much money for fellowships, colleges, libraries, and other educational facilities for Southern Negroes and has made it possible for the Slater and Jeanes Funds to continue with their work. In 1911, Mr. Julius Rosenwald began the successful activity of giving one-third of the funds required for the erection of a rural school building, provided the school authorities, with the aid of white friends and the Negro people themselves, would furnish the other two-thirds.[24] The Rosenwald Fund has established libraries for Negroes, has assisted Negro universities and colleges and has given generously to Negro scholars for fellowships and research projects. The John F. Slater Fund, given a new direction after 1910 under the leadership of Dr. James H. Dillard, established the first "high schools" for Negroes in the rural South to give prospective teachers in the rural Negro elementary schools some education beyond that of the elementary school itself. The small Phelps-Stokes Fund (established in 1911) has devoted itself to assisting Negro and white college students, making studies of Negro problems and improving educational facilities for Negroes in the United States and in Africa. Andrew Carnegie, and the large foundation which he established, the Carnegie Corporation of New York, have given significant sums to Negro colleges and libraries, to various Negro improvement organizations, and to research projects on the Negro—including the present study.[a]

[a] In addition to the foundations mentioned in the text, there are others working in the field of Negro education:
 (1) The Daniel Hand Fund (established in 1888), directed by the American Missionary Association, aids Negro schools and colleges along with others;
 (2) The du Pont family has donated gifts for the education of the small Negro population of Delaware;
 (3) The Duke family has donated gifts to Negro colleges in North Carolina;

The support of Negro education in the South given by Northern philanthropic organizations has been important in terms of both the funds spent and the initiative taken. It has also spurred the Southern state and municipal authorities. Federal aid has had its importance and might come to mean more in the future. The general facts about this and about the discriminations in the South against Negro education in terms of financial expenditure have been reviewed in Chapter 15. We shall later add some notes on what this means for the actual character of education.

The stress then will be on elementary and secondary education. At the college level, Hampton and Tuskegee continue with their vocational emphasis but have recently tended to give a good basic education of the academic type. Most of the Negro liberal arts and teachers' colleges of the South are inadequate; more so even than the average white Southern college or university, which is notoriously inferior to the bulk of Northern colleges and universities.[25] The best Negro universities in the South—Howard (in Washington, D.C., supported by the federal government), Fisk (in Nashville, Tennessee, privately supported), Atlanta (in Atlanta, Georgia, privately supported)—are as adequate in many ways as the better Southern white universities. There are also one or two Negro colleges—for example, Talladega (in Alabama, privately supported)—that rank with the better white colleges. Only a half-dozen of the Southern Negro universities offer any training on the graduate or professional level and, with the exception of Howard University, graduate training is restricted to a few fields. Many Southern Negro students go to the great Northern universities. Many Northern Negro students go to Southern Negro colleges.

The control of Negro schools in the South has been shifting somewhat in recent years. As elementary and secondary education for Negroes is coming to be taken for granted by white Southerners, the support for it is coming less from Northern philanthropy and more from state and local tax funds assisted by federal grants-in-aid. With the support has gone the control, and the South now has complete control of Negro education on the elementary and secondary levels. Negroes hold some of the control over their own schools, partly because they help to pay for them by voluntary contributions, but mainly because they are the only teachers now in

---

(4) The Guggenheim Memorial Foundation provides research fellowships (some 20 outstanding Negroes have received these);

(5) There have been gifts by many Negro philanthropists. (See Horace M. Bond, *The Education of the Negro in the American Social Order* [1934], pp. 145-147);

(6) Church missions support a significant proportion of the secondary schools and colleges for Negroes in the South;

(7) The Harmon Foundation gives awards to Negroes for outstanding achievement, and holds exhibits of fine arts by Negroes. Other small foundations have special prizes for Negroes.

Southern Negro schools, and white school supervisors do not care to bother with Negro schools unless they hear that something is being taught that they do not like. But ultimate control is held by the white superintendents and school boards, subject only to the few restrictions entailed in accepting federal grants-in-aid and to the advice of the General Education Board supervisors. The same is true of the public colleges. The private colleges and universities for Negroes in the South are still supported, in large measure, by Northern philanthropy; control over them is still held by the trustees (who often come from outside the community where the colleges are located), by the foundations and other philanthropists, and by the Negro faculty itself which is expressly permitted a significant degree of autonomy.

4. THE WHITES' ATTITUDES TOWARD NEGRO EDUCATION

There are apparent conflicts of valuations between whites and Negroes in regard to Negro education. These conflicts, the interests involved, and the theories expressing them determine the forms of Negro education. But the situation is not so simple as just a difference of opinion. In fact, many whites are as eager to improve Negro education as is any Negro, and there are some Negroes who are rather on the other side of the fence, at least for the purpose of an opportunistic accommodation. The situation is complicated by the fact that both whites and Negroes are divided in their own minds. They harbor conflicting valuations within themselves. Only by keeping this constantly in mind can we understand the development of Negro education and correctly evaluate future prospects.

The American Creed definitely prescribes that the Negro child or youth should have just as much educational opportunity as is offered anyone else in the same community. Negroes should be trained to become good and equal citizens in a democracy which places culture high in its hierarchy of values. This equalitarian valuation is strong enough to dominate public policy in the North, in spite of the fact that probably most white people in the North, too, believe the Negroes to be inferior and, anyhow, do not care so much for their potentialities and possibilities as for those of whites. In the South the existing great discrimination in education is an indication that another valuation is dominating white people's actions. But it is a great mistake to believe that the American Creed is not also present and active in the motivations of Southern whites. Behavior is as always a moral compromise. Negroes would not be getting so much education as they are actually getting in the South if the equalitarian Creed were not also active.[a]

<hr>

[a] The division of white opinion with respect to Negro education is brought out by a poll of public opinion in July, 1940. (Planned by the American Youth Commission, interviews by the American Institute of Public Opinion; tabulations and analyses by several individuals and groups; published by the National Education Association. See *National Education*

By itself, the interest of upholding the caste system would motivate Southern whites to give Negroes practically no education at all or would restrict it to the transmission of only such lowly skills as would make Negroes better servants and farm hands. There is no mistake about this interest; it is real and has economic importance. Charles S. Johnson gives an account of it as it appears in the rural South:

> Literacy is not an asset in the plantation economy, and it was not only discouraged but usually forbidden. The belief that education spoiled the slave carried over with but little modification for many years into the belief that education spoils a field hand. The oldest members of the community are illiterate, and in those working relations which reveal least change from the past this lack has proved no important handicap. Reading and figuring carry elements of danger to established relations. Since the detailed direction of planting and handling of accounts are the sphere of the planter, theoretically it is he who can profit most from the technique of literacy. Too much attention to reading about the outside, and particularly to figuring, on the part of Negro tenants, would surely make them less satisfied with their status and bring them into harsh conflict with the system. The need of enough education to read and figure arises largely among those families desirous of escaping from the dependent relationship under the old plantation system.[26]

The poorer classes of whites in this respect have interests similar to those of the planters. They are in competition with Negroes for jobs and for social status. One of the things which demarcates them as superior and increases the future potentialities of their children is the fact that white children in publicly supported school buses are taken to fine consolidated schools while often Negro children are given only what amounts to a sham education in dilapidated one-room schools or old Negro churches by underpaid, badly trained Negro teachers. The observer, visiting Southern rural counties, gets clear statements of these interests on the part of all classes of whites who want to preserve the traditional caste order. The segregated school system of the South, in addition, allows a substantial saving by keeping Negro education low.

The caste interest is not merely economic. The whites have told themselves that education will make the Negro conscious of "rights" which he

---

Association Research Bulletin [November, 1940], p. 204.) A cross section of the nation was asked, "Do you think that the same amount of tax money should be spent in this state for the education of a Negro child as for a white child?" Southern whites were split equally: 45 per cent answered "yes"; 46 per cent answered "no" (9 per cent are reported as having "no opinion"). Northern whites were in favor of equal educational expenditures by a heavy majority: 86 per cent answered "yes"; 10 per cent answered "no" (4 per cent are reported as having "no opinion").

The large minority in favor of equality in the South is remarkable. As a guide for practical policy, however, it has to be discounted because of the peculiarity, which we noticed in Chapter 28 and elsewhere, that Southern whites often become convinced by their legal pretense "separate but equal" that Negroes actually get equal schooling.

should not know about. It will make him dissatisfied where he has been happy and accommodated. It will raise some Negroes above many whites in culture. It will make many more Negroes "uppity" and obnoxious. The supremacy of individual whites is bound up with Negro ignorance. If the Negro stays in the only "place" where he should be, then he does not need any education. These opinions also make sense in the light of the white caste's undoubted interest in keeping education away from the Negroes.

The white people have among themselves all the power, and so their convergent interests have molded Negro education in rural districts. The low standard of Negro schools is the result. But even in the rural South the observer sees the impact of the American Creed. Often it is revealed only in a bad conscience. This is apparent everywhere. In most localities there also seems to be a gradual improvement of Negro schools. In practically all places no obstacles are placed in the way of outside help if it observes the proper Southern forms, and it will even be encouraged either verbally or by "matching" it with local financial support. The scattering around the entire region of the Rosenwald schoolhouses is a case in point. Exertions by the Negroes to collect money among themselves for educational purposes are never discouraged but applauded by almost everybody. This is not said by way of excusing the bald and illegal discrimination in the rural school systems in the South, but only to stress the fact that the white caste interests are practically never driven to their logical end.

In the urban South, whites of the employing class do not have the same material interests in keeping the Negroes ignorant. They have rather to gain if their Negro servants and laborers have at least some education. The poorer classes of whites have scarcely any such gains to reap, however. They are interested in keeping Negroes as much as possible out of competition on the labor market. The general interest of keeping the Negroes down to preserve the caste order intact is present in the cities too. It is shared by all classes, but, of course, felt most strongly by the poorer whites. City populations are, however, more closely integrated in the life of the nation: the regional traditions are somewhat weaker, the cultural level among whites is higher, the American Creed is stronger. So we find that Southern cities offer the Negroes a substantially better education. In the Border states the integration in the national life and the strength of the American Creed are still stronger, and we find also that the educational facilities available to Negroes are more nearly equal to those of the whites.

The primary rationalization of this gradual deviation in the South from the policy representing the crude caste interest is usually phrased in the popular theory of the American Creed—that education of the youths of the poorer classes is beneficial not only to themselves but to society. Thomas Nelson Page presented the liberal Southerners' attitude toward the education of the Negro masses many years ago:

There is much truth in the saying that unless the whites lift the Negroes up, the Negroes will drag them down, though it is not true in the full sense in which it was intended. It is not true to the extent that the white must lift the Negro up to his own level; it is true to the extent that he must not leave him debased—at least must not leave him here debased. If he does, then the Negro will inevitably hold him, if not drag him down. No country in the present stage of the world's progress can long maintain itself in the front rank, and no people can long maintain themselves at the top of the list of peoples if they have to carry perpetually the burden of a vast and densely ignorant population, and where that population belongs to another race, the argument must be all the stronger. Certainly, no section can, under such a burden keep pace with a section which has no such burden. Whatever the case may have been in the past, the time has gone by, possibly forever, when the ignorance of the working-class was an asset. Nations and peoples and, much more, sections of peoples, are now strong and prosperous almost in direct ratio to their knowledge and enlightenment. . . .

Viewing the matter economically, the Negro race, like every other race, must be of far more value to the country in which it is placed, if the Negro is properly educated, elevated, and trained, than if he is allowed to remain in ignorance and degradation. He is a greater peril to the community in which he lives if he remains in ignorance and degradation than if he is enlightened. If the South expects ever to compete with the North, she must educate and train her population, and, in my judgment, not merely her white population but her entire population.[27]

This has been the main argument through decades for improving the educational facilities for Negroes in the South. Usually it is restricted by assertion of their lower capability of responding to education. Usually also it is qualified by the insistence on a particular kind of education as more suitable for Negroes.

There is petty pressure on Negro education in the South, but the truth is that the *Southern whites have never had the nerve to make of Negro education an accomplished instrument to keep the Negroes in their caste status.* It would have been possible, but it has not been done. The Southern whites' caste policy has been halfhearted all through, but particularly so in education. The explanation is again that they are also good Americans with all the standardized American ideals about education. The interest of educating the Negroes to become faithful helots has been obvious, but the Southern whites have not even attempted to make it effective in practice. Instead, they have merely kept Negro education poor and bad. And even on that point they have been gradually giving up resistance to the command of the Creed. This is the deeper dynamics of Negro education.

5. "Industrial" *versus* "Classical" Education of Negroes

Quite independent of how the specific value of "vocational" or "industrial" education, as compared with a more liberal education, is viewed, there is no doubt that the popularity among whites, now as earlier, of the former type of Negro education is mainly motivated by the interests of preserving the caste order. "Industrial" education for Negroes is the formula upon which Southern whites have been able to strike a compromise between their belief in education, which stems from the American Creed, and their interests as white Southerners in preserving the caste order of the region.

The argument runs: The Negroes are, and must be, servants, farm laborers, and industrial workers; they should, however, be trained to do their work better; then, in their "place," they would be better citizens too. What is needed, consequently, is a Negro education which bothers less with bookish learning and more with life in a humble status, daily duties, and the building up of character; the Negroes have to begin at the bottom and they will probably stay low, but they should be given the chance of moving upward slowly. The advocate of improved industrial training of Negroes also stresses the very material interest of the better class of white people to have more efficient servants. The play of these arguments can be observed today, when, for instance, one accompanies the State Agent for Negro Education in a rural county trying to persuade the local white leaders to spend money to improve Negro education.

The formula, "industrial education for Negroes," thus has a different meaning for different white people. There are some who have a genuine belief in the superiority generally of a practical stress in all public education. There are many more who see strong particular reasons for this educational goal in the actual situation of Southern Negroes. Many have their primary interest in improving Negro education as such and know that it is politically much more feasible if it is proposed in this way. To many the formula is, however, only a rationalization for discrimination and for holding appropriations low for Negro schools.[a]

> Industrial education becomes a byword. In the mind of one man it meant that the negro should be taught only to know the relative distance between two rows of cotton or corn, and how to deport himself with becoming behavior behind the chair while his white lord and master sits at meat; while, in the mind of another it stood for the awakening of the best powers and possibilities. To the white man of the South it may have meant that the negro was to be made more serviceable to him and more easily amenable to his imperious will. To the white man of the North it may have meant that the black man was to be made a competent worker, equipped with intelligence and skill such as are demanded of Northern workmen. However variant may have been the interpretations of the meaning of industrial education, there was a general agreement to discredit the higher culture of the race.[28]

This has, among other things, the implication that *in the South the problem of "industrial" versus "classical" education for Negroes is not, and has*

[a] Although, as we shall presently observe, true vocational education actually is more expensive.

never been, discussed merely in terms of pedagogical advantages and disadvantages. The political caste problem is always and necessarily involved. And the type of education to be given Negroes is always and necessarily connected with the amount of education and the financial obligations to be undertaken.[29]

Two factors complicate the issue even more: the high relative costs of modern vocational education and the white laborers' fear of the Negroes as competitors. In the period immediately after the Civil War, vocational education was—a fact now often forgotten—motivated also as a less expensive way of giving Negroes some schooling. General Armstrong, when founding Hampton Institute, stressed the agricultural and vocational line, not only for the reason that such a training best fitted the occupational possibilities of the freed slaves, but also because it allowed the students to earn something toward their maintenance at school.[30] In his appeals for funds for Tuskegee Institute, Booker T. Washington likewise always emphasized this element of economy, and particularly how the students, by their own work, erected many of the buildings and provided much toward the support of themselves and the school.

The pedagogical aim of vocational education outside agriculture in those days was to continue and build up the artisan tradition from slavery and to turn out young Negroes skilled in the old handicrafts—train them to be carpenters, masons, blacksmiths, shoemakers. When, however, the Industrial Revolution finally hit the South in full force, the demand of efficient industry was no longer for the artisan but for the skilled machine operator. The old handicrafts became relatively less important. Even agriculture did not show much demand for skilled Negro labor. On the plantations the employers continued to be best satisfied with the ignorant field hands who were not disturbingly ambitious, and the trend toward increased Negro landownership turned downward shortly after 1900. If Negroes—outside domestic service—were to be given effective vocational education, this would require such an elaborate equipment for the schools that it would become more expensive than "classical" education.

At the same time and partly for the same basic reasons, the interest of the white workers against allowing Negroes to acquire skills became stronger. In agriculture and in the stagnating crafts, new skilled Negro labor was not welcome; in industry it became a principle that all skilled jobs should be reserved for the whites.

What if the industrial education of the Negro should be found to conflict with the interests of the white laborer or skilled worker? Does any one suppose that it is the purpose of the South so to educate the Negro (or even allow him to be so educated) as to enable him to take the bread from the white man's mouth? And does any one suppose that the laboring white man of the arrogant and aggressive Anglo-

Saxon race will stand tamely by with folded arms while there is danger of its being done? This is the central point of the whole situation.[31]

By and large, *in spite of all the talk about it, no effective industrial training was ever given the Negroes in the Southern public schools,* except training for cooking and menial service. The expensive vocational training, which conflicted so harshly with the interests of the white workers, has never become much more than a slogan. Negro education has mostly remained "academic" and differs only in its low level of expenditure and effectiveness.

Even at the well-endowed centers of Hampton and Tuskegee, the industrial training offered was in demand almost solely because of a need for teachers in the lesser schools, rather than because of the needs of modern industry. This explains why they have been able to realize, in some lines at least, the vocational idea as well as they have, without coming into greater conflict with the interests of white workers. The schools to which those teachers have gone, and are now going, are usually not nearly so well equipped that they could be called "vocational" in any serious meaning of the term. They usually are poor schools, not deserving much of a classification into either "vocational" or "classical." A few exceptional schools excluded, they offer at best some training in domestic service for girls— which, for understandable reasons, meets more encouragement and less fear of competition—or a poor training in the technique of rapidly disappearing handicrafts, sometimes adjusted slightly to modern times by courses in "automobile repair work" or the like.[32]

The discussion of whether Negroes should have a vocational or a liberal schooling is thus only in part a real issue. Partly it is a cover for the more general problem as to what extent Negroes should have much education at all. The lines are blurred because the argument for vocational education is used both by the people who want to have more education for Negroes and by those who want to restrict it. The main conflict is between the ever present equalitarian American Creed, on the one hand, and the caste interest, on the other. The actual situation is different between regions; opinions are divided and confused within almost every individual. Let us, as an example, have a Southern liberal survey the field of opinions, as he sees it, and attempt to formulate his own attitude:

It is surprising to note the prejudice with which a great many southern whites view the whole subject of Negro education. Their sincere opinion that the Negro should not be given educational opportunities comparable to those which are provided for the white children is at least partly due to the strong belief that better facilities in the colored schools would not yield a proper return in human values. This belief is a heritage from slavery. Of course there is also the attitude that the educated Negro will lose the humility which has characterized his relations with the southern white man ever since Reconstruction. The white laboring man is no doubt influenced in his opposition to better educational facilities for Negroes by the fear that Negroes will enter skilled trades and thereby create a new and very effective rivalry in a field in which the whites have not had as much competition as they have where the task requires less training and education. However, certain farsighted leaders and some others realize that the Negro must be given better schools. They believe that improved colored school facilities will benefit not only the Negroes but also the whites. They feel that the colored man is entitled to a good high school education in subjects which may be selected with a view to the peculiar social situation in the South. The Negro must be trained for the jobs which are available under present conditions. Cultural training in the arts and sciences must for the present be subordinated to an education which is more suitable to his needs. In this way the greatest number will be benefited. The curriculum for the colored schools needs a great deal of study with a view toward revision.[33]

6. NEGRO ATTITUDES

The attitudes of the whites are of greatest importance for the growth of Negro education, as they have all the power. The Negroes are, however, not without influence, partly because the whites are divided among themselves and divided in their own conscience. The remarkable thing is that the Negroes are split in much the same way and on the same issues.

It is natural, to begin with, that the American Creed interest is more stressed with the Negroes. Deep down in their souls practically all Negroes feel that they have the right to equal opportunities for education. And the sanctity of the American Creed gives them the opportunity to express this opinion and to press the whites for concessions. The stress on education in American culture makes the Negro protest most respectable. But the observer finds also that there are a few upper class Negroes who express about the same opinion as whites, that common Negroes do not need and should not have much education. This is rare, however, and the opinion has to be concealed.

Much more important is the split in the Negro world as to what kind of education is desirable. On the one hand, they sense the caste motivation behind most whites' interest in industrial education for Negroes. They know also that they can hope to win the respect of the whites and take their place as equal citizens in American democracy only if they are educated in the nonvocational cultural values of the broader society. On the other hand, they see the actual caste situation as a reality and know that many lines of work are closed to them. In order to utilize fully the openings left, and in order eventually to open up new roads into industrial employment, they often conclude that Negroes are in particular need of vocational training. They realize also that the great poverty and cultural backwardness of their people motivate a special adaptation of Negro education. On this point there is a possibility of striking a compromise with the liberal white man. In the North most Negroes will not make this concession, and by no means all Negroes, perhaps not even a majority, in the South are prepared to take the stand. Even the ones who do, stress at the same time the necessity of raising educational opportunities and of improving the schools.

Concerning the content of teaching in other respects, Negroes are also divided. On the one hand, they are inclined to feel that the Northern system, where a standardized teaching is given students independent of whether they are whites or Negroes, is the only right thing. On the other hand, they feel that the students get to know too little about Negro problems. They thus want an adjustment of teaching toward the status of Negroes, usually not in order to make the Negroes weak and otherwise fit into the white man's wishful picture about "good niggers" but, on the contrary, to make Negroes better prepared to fight for their rights. They feel that education should not only be accepted passively but should be used as a tool of concerted action to gain the equal status they are seeking. For this reason many, if not most, Negro leaders desire that Negro students should get special training in Negro problems.

Du Bois, who originally was the most uncompromising advocate of the idea that no difference at all should be made in teaching Negro and white students, later came out with the opinion that the Negro student should not only be taught general history and social subjects as they were taught to white students, but also Negro history and Negro problems and, indeed, a special race strategy for meeting their individual and collective problems in America. Negro youth should even be taught to have pride in Africa.[34]

This opinion, except perhaps for the last point, is now commonly shared by most Negro intellectuals. The institution of "Negro History Week" has emanated from such attitudes.[a] Negro colleges and high schools are devoting an increasing interest to Negro problems. White interracialists condone these things.[35] Other whites do not care but feel, as we have said, that it is the Negroes' right to discuss their own problems if they want to.

There is a further controversy as to whether Negro education ought to be segregated or not. In the North the official opinion among whites is that segregation is not compatible with equality, but, as we have seen, much segregation is actually in effect as a consequence of residential segregation and of gerrymandering districts and granting permits to transfer. In the South direct segregation in schools is a necessary means of keeping up the tremendous financial discrimination against Negro schools. In recent years not even Southern liberals—with some rare exceptions—have stated that they favored mixed education. Segregation is usually not motivated by financial reasons but as a precaution against social equality.[36]

Negroes are divided on the issues of segregated schools. In so far as segregation means discrimination and is a badge of Negro inferiority, they are against it,[37] although many Southern Negroes would not take an open stand that would anger Southern whites. Some Negroes, however, prefer

[a] See Chapter 35, Section 9.

the segregated school, even for the North, when the mixed school involves humiliation for Negro students and discrimination against Negro teachers. Du Bois has expressed this point of view succinctly:

. . . theoretically, the Negro needs neither segregated schools nor mixed schools. What he needs is Education. What he must remember is that there is no magic, either in mixed schools or in segregated schools. A mixed school with poor and unsympathetic teachers, with hostile opinion, and no teaching concerning black folk, is bad. A segregated school with ignorant placeholders, inadequate equipment, poor salaries, and wretched housing, is equally bad. Other things being equal, the mixed school is the broader, more natural basis for the education of all youth. It gives wider contacts; it inspires greater self-confidence; and suppresses the inferiority complex. But other things seldom are equal, and in that case, Sympathy, Knowledge, and the Truth, outweigh all that the mixed school can offer.[38]

Other Negroes prefer the mixed schools at any cost, since for them it is a matter of principle or since they believe that it is a means of improving race relations.[a]

7. Trends and Problems

Schrieke, surveying Southern education a few years ago, sums up the situation in the following words:

. . . although there is some sort and some amount of Negro education everywhere, Negro education still does not have a fixed, legitimate, acknowledged place. It is realized that something must be done in order to keep the Negro satisfied and in order to uphold the American slogan of free schools for every child, but it is rare that a community has any real interest in planning or building a wise system of education for the race. Politically, it is not generally admitted that the Negro has a right to schools or to other public services. . . . The Negro is still not recognized as a citizen despite the Civil War amendments.[39]

This somewhat pessimistic evaluation is warranted by the facts. The educational facilities for Negroes, particularly in many rural regions, are scandalously poor.[b] The white community often blinds itself to the entire matter.

---

[a] There are many minor elements in the controversy. Frazier, for example, reports that some dark-skinned children in Washington and Louisville preferred mixed schools since the white teacher made no distinction between them and light-skinned Negroes—a distinction claimed to be made by some light-skinned Negro teachers. (E. Franklin Frazier, *Negro Youth at the Crossways* [1940], pp. 96-97.) On the other hand, some Negro upper class parents would like to keep their children away from the Negro schools, where prevail "dirt, noise, bad manners, filthy tales, no discipline," overcrowding and poorly trained teachers. (W. E. B. Du Bois, *Dusk of Dawn* [1940], p. 178.)

[b] The present writer has gone into many one-room, one-teacher Negro schools and hardly believed his eyes and his ears when he ascertained the primitive school building, the lack of practically all equipment, the extreme lack of contact with modern American civilization on the part of the untrained, poorly paid, Negro woman serving as teacher, and the bottomless ignorance of the pupils. I once visited such a school in a rural county of Georgia, not far from Atlanta. The building was an old Rosenwald school, dilapidated but far better

But in appraising the situation, it is equally important to recognize that there are dissimilarities in the level of educational facilities offered Negroes, and that there is a definite tendency upward.

This trend is gaining momentum and is pushed not only by Northern philanthropy and the intervention of federal agencies, but also by the growing force of Southern liberalism.[a] The rising educational level of the whites in the region gives an increasing basis for understanding the necessity of doing something for Negro education. The skillful strategy of the N.A.A.C.P. is probably going to enforce a raise in the wages of Southern Negro teachers over the next decade and will, if it does not open the door of the graduate schools to Negroes, at least compel the Southern states to

---

than many other school buildings in the region. The students were in all age groups from 6 to 7 years upward to 16 to 17. There was also an imbecile man of about 20 staying on as a steady student veteran. (The lack of institutions for old Negro mental defectives makes the great majority of them stay in their homes, and the homes find it often convenient to send them to school. There they are, of course, a great danger from several viewpoints.) The teacher, a sickly girl about 20 years old, looked shy and full of fear; she said she had had high school training.

The students seemed to enjoy the visit and it was easy to establish a human contact with them. No one could tell who was President of the United States or even what the President was. Only one of the older students knew, or thought he knew, of Booker T. Washington. He said that Washington was "a big white man," and intimated that he might be the President of the United States. This student, obviously a naturally very bright boy, was the only one who knew anything about Europe and England; they were "beyond the Atlantic," he informed me, but he thought that Europe was in England. No one had ever heard about Walter White, John Hope, Du Bois, or Moton. No one had heard of the N.A.A.C.P. One boy identified Carver as a "colored man who makes medicine." Several could identify Joe Louis, Ella Fitzgerald, and Henry Armstrong. Asked if they knew what the Constitution of the United States was and what it meant to them, all remained in solemn silence, until the bright boy helped us out, informing us that it was a "newspaper in Atlanta."

When telling such a horror story it must, at once, be added that it is not typical, though a large portion of rural Negro schools are at, or near, this cultural level. But it is remarkable, and a significant characteristic of the whole system, that it can exist even as an isolated case. It should also be said that there are a few white schools in some regions of the South which do not reach much higher. I recollect that some white school children in Louisiana believed that Huey Long was still living (autumn, 1938) and was the President of the United States.

A further reflection is that the usual measures of school efficiency (see Chapter 43, Section 4) are inadequate when the problem is to sound the bottom of ignorance in many Negro schools.

[a] As an example of what can now be publicly stated in the South concerning the low existing level of Negro educational facilities and the need for improved ones, we may note the excellent Louisiana Educational Survey. Charles S. Johnson and Associates prepared the monograph on the Negro public schools, and his report is summarized in popular form in the "summary report" prepared by Carleton Washburne (*Louisiana Looks at Its Schools* [1942]). Seldom has such an excellent survey appeared regarding the schools of any state, and the fact that this survey emanates from one of the Deep Southern states is a most hopeful sign.

initiate some sort of graduate training in the state-supported Negro colleges. In the beginning this graduate training will perhaps be merely a sham gesture, but a basis for further advance will have been created. Segregation will probably be upheld on all levels while discrimination is being fought and decreased. Segregation will less and less be a means of economy; gradually it will, instead, become a financial burden. It is not unlikely that segregation will then start to break down on the highest level. In the total view, the prospects are thus not entirely discouraging. In fact, *there have never been, since Reconstruction, fewer reasons for a defeatist attitude in regard to Negro education in the South.*

In spite of much and heated discussion regarding the type of Negro education, its actual development has never followed any plan or theory. The main problem has always been not what sort but *how much education the Negro should have and how much he gets.* Even today the chief problem is how to get increased appropriations and improved standards. As we have hinted, the theory of "industrial" training for Negroes has had its main function in being a bait for the powers of the purse in Northern philanthropy and in Southern public budgets. And the truth is that *any type of improved education for Negroes is salutary.*

There is an immense need of *new school buildings* for Negroes, particularly in rural districts but also in most Southern cities. There is also need for new *equipment* of all sorts, for *consolidated schools* and for *school buses.* After the close of the present war there is going to be, in all likelihood, a great necessity for public works to mitigate unemployment, and much of this activity is bound to be directed upon erecting buildings for public schools.

The only sound and democratic principle for distributing the benefits of the post-war public works policy in various districts and groups would be to build for those districts and groups in the nation whose old buildings are worst. Such a policy would, in the South, mean concentrating almost the whole activity on building Negro schools and other buildings for Negroes. The old Negro schools are generally so bad and inadequate that this kind of public construction would suffice to occupy the unemployed for quite a while. Such a policy will probably not be followed for political reasons. It is, however, not only a Negro interest but a general democratic interest that this policy be pressed, so that Negro schools get the maximum out of any post-war unemployment emergency. As communities usually want to have buildings erected independent of their purposes if they do not have to pay for them—because they mean work and income for the community— and as Southerners are not likely to object too much if Negro school buildings are built with federal money, it should be taken up for deliberation whether it would not be a wise policy to distribute federal aid to education in the form of taking over the responsibility for erecting and furnishing the buildings.

A second most important condition for progress is to improve *the standards of Negro teachers*. This has been seen by the Northern foundations and also by many of the Southern state authorities, and much effort has gone into improving teacher training in the South. Southern state and private Negro colleges largely serve this purpose. Many of the small Negro colleges in the South are inadequate and the whole system needs to be systematized. Many of them will, perhaps, succumb in the financial strain of the present War, and this might turn out to be a blessing in disguise if the remaining colleges are increased and improved correspondingly. The establishment of a new model teacher-training college in the South would be a great service which a farsighted federal policy could undertake in order to equalize educational opportunities for Negroes. Meanwhile the raised salary scales, to which the South will be compelled, will probably raise the standards of training Negro teachers. Negro teachers need not only better training and higher salaries; they also need more security of tenure. If the rural teacher could be given a greater independence and a higher prestige, this, by itself, would make her a better teacher and, particularly, increase the influence of the school over the community.

If the federal government undertakes further financial responsibility for education,[a] it will be up against a problem which has been bothering the philanthropic foundations for a long time, although it is seldom discussed openly: How is it possible to aid without decreasing local responsibility? In the author's judgment, *Northern philanthropy in its grand-scale charity toward the South, incidental to its positive accomplishments, has also had a demoralizing influence on the South.* The South has become accustomed to taking it for granted that not only rich people in the North, but also poor church boards, should send money South, thus eternally repaying "the responsibility of the North for Reconstruction." Thus far, rich people in the South have been less inclined to give away their money for philanthropic purposes.

For these moral reasons it is important, when the federal government steps in, that local financial responsibility be preserved as much as possible. *The ideal solution would be that the federal government pay certain basic costs all over the country,* such as original building costs and a basic teacher's salary. It is, of course, of special importance that, as far as possible, *absence of discrimination be made a condition for aid.* Otherwise the idea will become established that Negro education is the business of the federal government and less a concern of the state and the municipalities. In this sense there is a danger that the Negro people might become "the ward of the nation."

Our assumption was that, to improve Negro education, larger appropriations, better buildings, more equipment, better paid and trained teachers are essential. By this we did not want to discount altogether the problem of the direction of Negro education but only to retain true proportions. The main fault with Negro education is that it is undernourished and inadequate. As it is improved, however, the problem of its direction becomes important. Even when Negro education is on a low level, as in most rural districts at present, it is, of course, important not to have it misdirected. But the choice seems, for the most part, still to be between an antediluvian "industrial" education and an equally antediluvian "classical" education.[40]

The Jeanes teacher movement and other constructive attempts in Southern Negro education have tried to work out a makeshift policy in which the emphasis is laid upon maintaining and enriching the relations of the student to his community.[41] This is all very well, and entirely in line with modern educational theory as it has been developed in America. But one main point seems forgotten. With the present trends in Southern agriculture and American agricultural policy, it is fairly certain that many of the children born in a cotton county today are going to live and work not in cotton districts but in Northern and Southern cities. Many of the children born in a Southern city are going to live in the different environment of the Northern metropolis. If the American economy and economic policy are not going to stagnate, Negroes are going to work in new occupations within the next generation. *What is needed is an education which makes the Negro child adaptable to and movable in the American culture at large.*

Even the Negro child who will stay in Southern agriculture will need to use various types of machinery, to follow popular journals in his field, to deal with credit institutions and government agencies, and successfully to take part in organizations. He needs to be able to read, write, and reckon, and to be lifted so high above illiteracy that he actually participates in modern American society. Before all, he needs not to be specialized, but to be changeable, "educable." And *he needs it more than the white child, because life will be more difficult for him.*

The right balance between "industrial" and "classical" education can be struck if due weight is given to the prospect of mobility and change. The masses of Negro children are going to be laborers on the farms and in industries; some are going to be skilled laborers. We do not know where and in what occupation they are going to work, but we know there is going to be much moving around. They need to be taught skills; but the value of any vocational training should be judged in terms of the extent to which the skills acquired are transferable into skills in other trades. They need to be familiarized with the printed word and culture that is found in books, and, indeed, to get as much of the general American culture as they possibly can.

Meanwhile, Southern Negro schools are going to remain inadequate. The North will continue for many decades to get untutored and crude

Negro immigrants from the South. These uneducated masses of Southern-born Negroes will be a heavy burden on the social and economic order in the North. It is, therefore, an interest for Northern cities, and not only for the migratory Negroes, that *a program of adult education be instituted to teach the migrating Negro masses the elements of American culture and also, perhaps, elements of vocational skills.*

More significant in the dynamics of Negro education than the low average standards in some regions are the high standards in others, and the general trend toward improvement. The American nation will not have peace with its conscience until inequality is stamped out, and the principle of public education is realized universally.

CHAPTER 42

THE NEGRO PRESS

1. An Organ for the Negro Protest

Most white people in America are entirely unaware of the bitter and relentless criticism of themselves; of their policies in domestic or international affairs; their legal and political practices; their business enterprises; their churches, schools, and other institutions; their social customs, their opinions and prejudices; and almost everything else in white American civilization. Week in and week out these are presented to the Negro people in their own press. It is a fighting press.

> Negro papers are first of all race papers. They are first and foremost interested in the advancement of the race. A large percentage of the editorials are concerned with justice to the race, with equal privileges, with facts of race progress, or with complaint against conditions as they are. Of course there occur from time to time well written editorials on topics of general interest, such as world peace, better political adjustment, or the progress of civilization; but it still remains true that most of the editorials are distinctly racial. The articles in these papers are usually propaganda—that is, they follow the line of the editorials. A great many are genuinely inflammatory.[1]

The Negro papers offer something not found in the white press:

> Through all the Negro press there flows an undercurrent of feeling that the race considers itself a part of America and yet has no voice in the American newspaper. Members of this group want to learn about each other, they want the stories of their success, conflicts, and issues told, and they want to express themselves in public.[2]

The purpose of the press is clearly conceived. P. B. Young, the editor of one of the best Negro papers, the Norfolk *Journal and Guide*, expresses it thus:

> Traditionally our press is a special pleader; it is an advocate of human rights.[3]

There are at present about 210 Negro weekly, semi-weekly, or bi-weekly newspapers.[a] Some of these are for the general Negro public; others are

[a] Florence Murray (editor), *The Negro Handbook* (1942), p. 201. (The figures are taken from a U. S. Bureau of the Census report for 1940.) There have been repeated attempts to launch Negro dailies but they have regularly failed. (See G. James Fleming, "The Negro Press," unpublished manuscript prepared for this study [1940], Chapter IX.) The Atlanta

organs of Negro religious denominations and labor organizations. Most of the general newspapers have a circulation limited to the locality where they are published. But ten to twenty Negro papers have large circulations extending to whole regions and sometimes to all Negro America. In addition there are some 129 monthly, bi-monthly and quarterly magazines.[4] Two of these have outstanding national importance: *The Crisis*, published by the N.A.A.C.P., and *Opportunity*, published by the National Urban League.[a] The others are almost all organs of Negro religious denominations, fraternal orders, professional groups, colleges and schools. Only four Negro magazines are pictorial or theatrical.[5] The weekly press alone has a total circulation of around one and a half million.[6]

Practically all Negroes who can read are exposed to the influence of the Negro press at least some of the time. Perhaps a third of the Negro families in cities regularly subscribe to Negro newspapers,[7] but the proportion is much smaller in rural areas. The readers of the Negro press are, however, the most alert and articulate individuals who form Negro opinion. Newspapers are commonly passed from family to family, and they are sometimes read out loud in informal gatherings. They are available in barbershops, and sometimes in churches, lodges and pool parlors. Their contents are passed by word of mouth among those who cannot read.[8] Indirectly, therefore, even aside from circulation figures, this press influences a large proportion of the Negro population.

No unifying central agency directs the opinions expressed in the Negro press. Like white newspapers, Negro newspapers are in keen competition with one another for circulation. Without discounting either the idealistic zeal and the strength of personal opinion of many editors, columnists, and other Negro newspapersmen, or the influence of petty corruption in the Negro papers, by and large the Negro press provides the news and the opinions which its reading public wants. This inference has the corollary

---

Daily World is the only daily newspaper at the present time. In 1940 its daily circulation was about 5,000, but it had a weekly edition with a larger circulation. (*Ibid.*, Chapter IX, pp. 8 ff.)

[a] Among the magazines, *The Interracial Review*, an organ for Catholic Action, comes next perhaps in importance. *Silhouette* is a picture monthly, surviving *Flash* and *Candid*, which followed the *Life* pattern. A high place is held by *The Journal of Negro History*, edited by Carter G. Woodson; *Journal of Negro Education*, edited by Charles Thompson of Howard University; and *Phylon*, *The Atlanta University Review of Race and Culture*, edited by W. E. B. Du Bois. For some further notes on the publications or organizations and on the earlier appearances and disappearances of Negro magazines, see Fleming, *op. cit.*, Chapter XII. Also see: Sidney V. Reedy, "The Negro Magazine: A Critical Study of Its Educational Significance," *Journal of Negro Education* (October, 1934), pp. 598-604. In this chapter we shall concentrate our attention on the regular Negro weeklies, which, at least directly, are of greatest importance for the formation of Negro opinion. Most of what we have to say is, *mutatis mutandis*, valid for the periodicals also.

conclusion that Negro opinion—at least among the more alert and articulate groups—can be ascertained and studied in the Negro press.

The opinions expressed in the Negro press—directly in the editorials and columns and indirectly in the type of news selected—are remarkably similar all over the country. This is undoubtedly caused by the common demands of the reading public and the similarity of *milieu* of the competing journalists. Negro papers in the South tend to be more cautious and less belligerent. But a large proportion of all Negro papers bought and read in the South are published in the North.[9] This Northern competition explains to some extent why even Southern Negro newspapers give such a relatively blunt expression to the Negro protest. The more basic explanation, however, is that this is what the Southern Negro public wants to read, too. In the South, where concerted action on the part of Negroes is usually so severely checked, and where Negro leadership in all practical matters has to be accommodating, most of the time,[a] the Negro press serves as a safety-valve for the boiling Negro protest.

This is possible—like the great amount of Negro protest within the walls of the Negro church and the Negro school—because the whites seldom know much about it. Whites, apparently, very rarely see Negro papers. Even when they do come across them, there is a certain abstract feeling among all Americans for the freedom of the press which, even in the South, covers the Negro newspapers. The Southern Negro press, further, usually takes the precaution of not attaching its protest too much to local issues and news, but to general principles, national issues, and news from distant points. The local pages in Southern Negro papers are usually restrained.

Northern Negro papers are less afraid of carrying the Negro protest into local news and issues. But even in the North most of the local coverage tends to be restricted to news and gossip about the town. Indirectly, however, even the pages devoted to the local community have a protest purpose as well as an informational purpose in both the North and the South. All Negroes, and particularly the ambitious upper and middle classes of Negroes who make up most of the reading public, are aware that white Americans deny them social status and social distinction. This makes class and accomplishment seem tremendously important. The display of Negro "society news" in the Negro press is partly an answer to the social derogation from the whites.

The more important and open expressions of the Negro protest are to be found in the news coverage of the whole American Negro world and, to an extent, the Negro world outside the United States, and also in the columns and editorials on the status of the Negro people. It is a characteristic of the Negro press that if, on the one hand, it is provincial in focusing interest on the race angle, it, on the other hand, embraces the whole race

---

[a] See Chapters 34 and 37.

world. *The press defines the Negro group to the Negroes themselves.* The individual Negro is invited to share in the sufferings, grievances, and pretensions of the millions of Negroes far outside the narrow local community. This creates a feeling of strength and solidarity. The press, more than any other institution, has created the Negro group as a social and psychological reality to the individual Negro.

For this reason the Negro press is far more than a mere expression of the Negro protest. By expressing the protest, the press also magnifies it, acting like a huge sounding board. The press is also the chief agency of group control. It tells the individual how he should think and feel as an American Negro and creates a tremendous power of suggestion by implying that all other Negroes think and feel in this manner. It keeps the Negro spokesman in line. Every public figure knows he will be reported, and he has to weigh his words carefully. Both the leaders and the masses are kept under racial discipline by the press. This promotes unanimity without the aid of central direction.

The Negro press is thus strongly opinionated. This points to a difference between the Negro press and the foreign-language press supported by the various immigrant groups in America.[a] Both types of "minority press" serve the interest of their groups to read more news about themselves than the "majority press" cares to give them. Many individuals in the immigrant groups are also not familiar with the English language, and a foreign-language paper is to them a practical news agency. Many more feel a certain pride in a non-American origin and culture. But this attachment is usually experienced as a sentimental quality of distinction, besides that of being, or becoming, an American. Immigrants are usually bent on assimilation and, as good prospects are held out to them,[b] they feel little desire to protest.[c]

Negroes, on the contrary, have no language of their own, and their culture is American. But, however much culturally assimilated they are, they are not accepted as full-fledged Americans. They protest, not because they feel themselves different, but because they want to be similar and are forcibly held to be different.[d] The news in the Negro papers is selected and

[a] For a sociological analysis of the immigrant press, see Robert E. Park, *The Immigrant Press and Its Control* (1922).

[b] See Chapter 3, Section 1.

[c] This is true in all ordinary immigrant groups which do not feel very disadvantaged, and who are consequently not in opposition to their treatment in America. Exceptions are the papers of very disadvantaged groups or of extremely radical sub-groups.

[d] To the white American their pretensions are preposterous. "The impatient, all but militant and anti-social attitude of an influential section of the Negro press is to be condemned in this connection. These editors show an unfortunate lack of appreciation of the traits of the people they aspire to lead. Their language implies that the Negro is only an Anglo-Saxon who is so unfortunate as to have a black skin. Such a race philosophy only

edited to prove the theory that they are similar and that they should be treated as ordinary Americans.

In a sense, the Negro newspapers have, thus, an opposite purpose from the ordinary immigrant papers, which take full assimilation of the group for granted and cater only to temporary language difficulties and to a senti-mental pride in keeping up a cherished ethnic and cultural distinction. The foreign-language press is doomed to disappear as the immigrants become fully assimilated and are not replenished by new immigration. The Negro press, on the contrary, is bound to become ever stronger as Negroes are increasingly educated and culturally assimilated but not given entrance to the white world.

In spite of this basic difference in purpose and "function," the two types of press are interesting to compare. In many important technical respects they show similarities. Both the immigrant papers and the Negro papers usually have their reading public spread all over the country, and both tend to become regional or national in circulation. Both ordinarily serve a reading public below the average in income. Both, therefore, have diffi-culty in soliciting advertising, which tends to keep them marginal as economic enterprises. At present, the foreign-language press is often better protected against competition from the majority press; it can support many dailies.[a] With the decrease in the number of persons who read only a foreign language well, even the foreign-language papers will tend to become what the Negro papers already are, namely, papers read in addition to ordinary American newspapers. They will then also tend to be weekly and to be published in English, until they finally disappear altogether.[b]

2. THE GROWTH OF THE NEGRO PRESS[10]

The development of the Negro press follows closely two interrelated trends: the rising Negro protest and the increase of Negro literacy. The Negro press was born in the struggle against slavery as a Negro branch of the Abolitionist propaganda organs in the North. The first Negro news-paper, *Freedom's Journal*, was launched in 1827 in New York by John B. Russwurm and Samuel E. Cornish. Detweiler counts 24 Negro journals appearing before the Civil War. Some of them were rather short-lived.[11]

---

works injustice to the Negro himself and it is high time to discard it." (John M. Mecklin, *Democracy and Race Friction* [1914], p. 46.)

[a] In Chicago alone there are some 20 to 25 foreign-language daily newspapers (Elizabeth D. Johns, "The Role of the Negro Newspaper in the Negro Community," unpublished manuscript made available through the courtesy of the author [1940], p. 24), while the Negroes have not succeeded in keeping up dailies. There is at present only one Negro daily (see footnote a few pages back). This is in spite of the fact that there are nearly 13 million Negroes in the country, as compared to only 11 million foreign-born whites and the latter are split up into many nationalities.

[b] This process has proceeded far, for instance, in the Scandinavian language groups.

The most famous of them was the *North Star*, edited by Frederick Douglass. It continued to be published—later as *Frederick Douglass's Paper*—until Emancipation, and had some white subscribers. Emancipation marked the end of this first period of Negro journalism. For the later development of the Negro press the tradition of militancy set during this first period was important. Many of those journals had been protesting, not only against slavery but also against discrimination in the North, and had advocated full civil liberties. They generally kept a high intellectual standard. James Weldon Johnson testifies:

> It is astounding on glancing backward to see how well written and edited were the majority of these periodicals. They stated and pleaded their cause with a logic and eloquence which seldom fell below the highest level of the journalism of the period. And yet it is not, after all, astounding—there was the great cause, the auspicious time; and, by some curiously propitious means there were, too, the men able to measure up to the cause and the time. There were among the editors of these papers, especially in New York, men of ability and men of learning.[12]

After Emancipation, Negro papers could be published and distributed in the South. The campaign of Negroes to learn to read and the high prestige of the printed word provided a steadily growing Negro public. Negro papers started after Emancipation were "organs" for the Republican party. The Restoration was a hard blow for the Negro press, but the slow migration to the North and the gradually rising proportion of literates in the Negro population sustained a rising number of Negro newspapers.

In 1870 there were only about 10 Negro journals in America; in 1880 there were 31; and in 1890 there were 154.[13] In 1880 there were Negro publications in nineteen states; in 1890 in twenty-eight states. Most of these journals had a small circulation; many were only fly-by-night enterprises. Some of them, as the Washington *Bee*, the Cleveland *Gazette*, the Philadelphia *Tribune*, and the New York *Age*, were, however, destined to have many years of national influence. Their success was largely the result of the "force of the personalities of their editors."[14]

From the Negroes' point of view, this period was a time of reaction and pessimism. The Negro press was not belligerent according to present standards, but followed Booker T. Washington's conciliatory course.[a] But in 1901 the Boston *Guardian* was launched by William Monroe Trotter as an uncompromisingly militant organ in the Abolitionist tradition. It got

---

[a] When the Niagara movement started, one of the main points of the reform program launched by the radical Negro intellectuals was to fight the corruption of the Negro press. More specifically, they accused the "Tuskegee Machine" (see Chapter 35, Section 3) of exerting undue pressure upon the Negro press. In 1904 Du Bois published a statement in the Boston *Guardian* concerning the venality of certain Negro papers which he charged had sold out to Mr. Washington. In his autobiography he reiterates the charges. (See *Dusk of Dawn* [1940], pp. 76 ff., 86 ff., *passim*).

a nation-wide reading public among the Negro intellectuals and was a force behind the Niagara movement.[a] In 1905, Robert S. Abbott started his Chicago *Defender*, which was destined to revolutionize Negro journalism. The foundation of the N.A.A.C.P. in 1909 and the publishing of *The Crisis* in 1910 gave further impulse to racial radicalism in the press.

But it was the First World War that provided the tide of protest upon which the press rose in importance and militancy. It was largely the Negro newspapers that made the Negroes fully conscious of the inconsistency between America's war aims to "make the world safe for democracy" and her treatment of this minority at home. It was also the Negro press that made the northward migration into a Negro protest movement.[b]

There was a more immediate personal interest in the contents of the press. Negroes wanted to read about employment possibilities and the stream of migration; about what happened to the 400,000 drafted Negro men and the 200,000 Negro soldiers in France. As riots increased in number and bloodiness, they wanted to read about them. The government believed that the Negro press was dangerous for morale during the War, and had to call a conference of Negro editors and other Negro leaders. It was staged as an important move and provided headlines in the Negro press. "With 'copy' like this to work on, every paper could exploit the war, and could benefit from it if its publisher was capable or willing to make the most of the circumstances."[15]

The Negro, due to the War and to the Great Migration, had moved out of the isolated Negro community. In some places in the South attempts were made to keep out Negro newspapers from the North.[16] This, again, provided stories and grievances and gave additional emotional value to the Northern Negro newspaper in the eyes of Southern Negroes. The circulation of the Negro press swelled.

After the War there were other things to keep up this interest in Negro newspapers: the continued wave of lynchings and riots, the Garvey movement, the friendliness on the part of the Communists and other radical groups emerging during the 'twenties, the continuing migration and the problems that accompanied it. During the 'thirties Negro welfare was deeply involved in most government policies, and there was a new type of discrimination. The shift of the Negro vote from the Republican party to the New Deal Democrats was a dramatic move of Northern Negroes.

The Second World War again increased unrest, suspicion, and dissatisfaction, which it is the opportunity of the press to stir up and organize. Again the inconsistency between expressed war aims and domestic policy becomes glaring. Again there is discrimination in the Army, Navy, and Air Force, and in the war industries. Again there are Negro heroes, unrec-

[a] See Chapter 35, Section 4.
[b] See Chapters 8 and 35.

ognized by the whites, to praise. And again the low war morale of the Negro people becomes a worry to the government. Again white leaders come out with declarations that justice must be given to Negroes. The Administration makes cautious concessions. Negro leaders are more determined. All this makes good "copy."

Now the color question is involved in the world conflagration. There is probably not a single issue of any one of the big weeklies which does not point out the failure of the British to give India independence, or contain editorial reflections to the effect that the defeat in Singapore and elsewhere was due to the Britishers' having maltreated and lost the confidence of the natives. China, moreover, cannot be expected to have too much trust in America which discriminates against all colored people. There is plenty of psychological compensation which the Negro press can now offer, and the opportunity is well exploited. There is little doubt that the Negro press is again making headway—carried along upon the rising tide of the protest.

3. CHARACTERISTICS OF THE NEGRO PRESS

Negro newspapers are similar to ordinary American newspapers, particularly those circulating among the lower classes. Many of the dissimilarities are only the exaggerations of common American traits, called forth by the caste situation. For a true perspective, it is important to keep this constantly in mind when discussing the characteristics of the Negro press in terms of dissimilarities.

As already mentioned, the Negro newspaper is typically an "additional paper." More white papers are probably bought and read by Negroes than Negro papers. The Negro papers, therefore, largely supplement the ordinary papers with Negro news and opinions.

Even in this field they are not without competition. A few liberal white newspapers in the South present noncontroversial news from the local Negro world and, occasionally, some from other places. Some Southern newspapers sell a special edition, often marked with a star or several stars, in the Negro community, which is never seen in the white section of the city. Not only are most whites unaware of these "black star" editions, but many Negroes believe they are buying the regular white newspaper. In these special editions Negroes get a whole page or more for themselves, often substituting for the financial news. There they may be called by the titles of Mr. and Mrs. and have plenty of information on local Negro social life, associations and churches. These white newspapers do not give as much Negro news from the rest of the nation as Negro newspapers, and they do not express the Negro protest.

It is difficult to determine how much competition the white press in the South—of both the liberal and "black star" types—offers to the Negro press. The fact that the Negro newspaper is only an "additional" paper that comes out once a week may cause Negroes to neglect it. The limited coverage of the Negro press and its reporting of news that is usually a few days old work against it. Also, some Negroes get "fed up" with the problem and protest news, and turn with relief to a general newspaper that contains the little social news about Negroes in which they are interested. On the other hand, because the Negro paper is only an "additional" one, like a magazine, Negroes may be willing to buy both papers if they buy any at all. The fact that the Negro press in the whole country has a circulation of about one and a half millions, which includes about one-third of all Negro families in the country,ª is a reason for believing that their weekly newspapers are not greatly hurt by competition from the Southern white daily press.

There are, however, two types of indirect competition. First, the provision of some Negro news in "black star" editions and in the regular liberal newspapers prevents the Negro press from carrying on a completely effective campaign against the white press on grounds of discrimination. Second, because of this and because Negro newspapers could not afford to provide general national and local news in addition to Negro news, the existence of the white press prevents the success of a daily Negro newspaper. Indeed, there is much soundness in the argument that the Negro newspaper remain a weekly one, since it could not hope to compete in providing general news as a daily paper. Many Negroes claim to get "fed up" on the Negro newspaper. This attitude would become accentuated if the Negro newspaper should appear daily.

In the North there are no special Negro editions of the white daily press, and, with rare exceptions, white papers give even less attention to Negro life than is becoming standard in the Southern liberal press. One exception that should be mentioned is the New York newspaper with a national circulation, *PM*.[17] Although they do not give space to Negro news, it is possible that the Hearst newspapers attract a good many lower class Negroes. It is not known how much the white daily press competes with the Negro weekly press in the North, but it is probable that the competition is even less than in the South. The stronger "race pride" in the North and the high quality of many of the large Northern Negro newspapers are also factors.

As the Negro newspaper is a weekly paper, as Negro news is not too plentiful because of the paucity of agencies and reporters to communicate it, and as much of the news is several days old when it appears in the weekly press, it is natural that editorials, columns, and other non-news

---

ª This equation is not quite justified, of course, because some families subscribe to more than one Negro newspaper. But it will do for rough calculations, since one and a half million persons, if they were no more than one person from each family, would include more than one-third of all Negro families.

items are given a proportionally larger space than in an ordinary daily newspaper, and that the news itself is more "edited." This is true, incidentally, of all weeklies, whether Negro or not. In the Negro weekly it is further motivated by the strong propaganda purpose: the news is presented mainly to prove the thesis of the Negro protest.

The Negro weekly is ordinarily a "sensational" paper. It is true that there are degrees: The highly respected and respectable Norfolk *Journal and Guide* is more conservative in its appearance, and many of the poor Negro organs in smaller cities do not reach the technical standard where sensationalism is possible. But by and large, the statement is true. Sensational journalism is, however, not an un-American trait. The Negro press has merely adopted a technique from the white press with which it is in competition. The most sensational white newspapers are found in the big cities, and there they appeal to the masses. Fleming observes:

> It is not by accident, it should be pointed out, that the Negro papers which traditionally and consistently feature big, black headlines across Page One and show other marks of sensationalism are in the cities where Hearst papers are also published with their striking headlines making appeal also to the Negro and other mass readers. For instance, there are Negro papers which have lost circulation because Hearst papers, and others, could do a better job of carrying features giving "number" tips to policy players and bringing the daily reports of the stock market for betting purposes.[18]

The Negro editors and publishers give the same type of defense for the sensationalistic technique in journalism as do their white colleagues:

> . . . they want to reach the largest possible number of readers, in order to use that following as an instrument for improving and advancing the race.[19]

Thus the main factor in the explanation of why the Negro press exaggerates the American pattern of sensational journalism is, of course, that the Negro community, compared with the white world, is so predominantly lower class. It is true that the lower half of the Negro community probably does not belong to the regular and direct audience of the Negro press.[20] Even if practically all persons belonging to the upper class were to buy Negro papers, this could not sustain them. The main reading public must belong to the middle class and the upper layers of the lower class. Hence, in the main, an expansion of the circulation, which every paper aims at, must be obtained in the lower strata of the Negro community. In this struggle to increase circulation, sensationalism is a rational policy.

Sensationalism also occurs in the Negro press because it is an "additional" Negro paper. Its excuse for existing is to select those items with a race angle and to "play them up," as they are "played down" in the ordinary white press. In hammering the Negro protest week after week, the press is constantly in danger of becoming abstract and tedious. It must, therefore, attempt to "personalize" the news as much as possible. It must accentuate the human-interest angle, and create a feeling that people are fighting and that big things are happening. Much space is thus devoted to crime. This might seem surprising since Negroes rightly accuse white newspapers of giving too much space to Negro crime and too little to all other Negro activities. But most Negroes, like other lower class persons, want to read about crimes.[a] Furthermore, the white papers write much about crimes committed by Negroes against whites, but little about crimes in the Negro community and about crimes committed by white persons against Negroes. The last item, particularly, is important to the Negro newspapers seeking to combat and, if possible, to reverse the white stereotypes of "the criminal Negro." Crimes against Negroes by whites are always "played up" greatly. Lynchings are, of course, and have always been, a specialty for the Negro press. In the other direction, the Negro press is likely to treat as sensational individual accomplishments of Negroes and public statements by whites for or against the caste system. It will also dramatize the society news.

Few features in the Negro press seem more ridiculous to the ordinary white American than the display of Negro society. At the same time, no other news items in the Negro press demonstrate better how the social patterns and interests of Negroes are typically, and even over-typically, those of ordinary Americans. Fleming observes rightly:

> Many a sermon has been preached about Negro "sassiety" and of the way Negroes fritter away their time in the frivolities recorded on the society page. The answer lies

[a] It is interesting to observe, on the other hand, that "sex" is played up less in the Negro press than in the white tabloids appealing to lower class people. The Negro newspapers have more pictures of women, but almost generally they are dressed and they are presented in a social setting. These pictures are displayed in order to show off Negro society. The great social role given women is a general American trait and is, in the Negro world, particularly understandable when we remember the close ideological association between "white supremacy" in the South and "Southern womanhood." There seem, however, to be fewer pictures of alluring women displayed to tempt the sexual appetite of the readers. This impressionistic observation is corroborated by Susan M. Kingsbury, Hornell Hart, and Associates, *Newspapers and the News* (1937); four Negro papers (the Chicago *Defender*, the New York *Amsterdam News*, the New York *Age* and the Baltimore *Afro-American*) were found to give "less attention" to sex interests than did the white tabloid. (*Ibid.*, p. 88.) To the outside observer the lively interest in everything with "sex-appeal" in America appears as a backwash of puritanism. The observation has also been made by Negroes. James Weldon Johnson comments:
"An examination of the vast number of salacious white periodicals published in the U.S. would incline one to think that sex has gone to the white man's head, transferred its seat to the imagination. When sex goes to the head, it loses its lusty, wholesome quality and begins to fester, to become maggoty. Sex with us is, in a large measure, still in the lusty, wholesome stage. Let's keep it there as long as we possibly can." (*Negro Americans. What Now?* [1934], pp. 29-30.)

in the background of the Negro: a people whose tastes, goals and ideals—both from formal training and informal ideals—are strictly American, with no special religious or nationalistic heritage being passed on to them in a way comparable to the experience of the Jew or the offspring of more recent immigrants. In addition, Negroes in America have been largely a servant class, coming into close contact with the "cream" of American social position. From the days of slavery, therefore, they have known what is considered good taste and fine manners, and have sought to make their own lives after the pattern of the masters. Negroes also read the magazines and newspapers and see the same moving pictures as does the rest of America! There is more truth than jest in the saying among Negroes that if you visit a Negro's home where the dinner service is complete in every detail and where the host and hostess know what to do with every piece of dinnerware, behold! there is a household where someone, at some time, has been a butler, valet, maid or cook to some of the best families of America (not wholly true, but suggestive).[21]

The "society" page of the Negro newspaper is a direct copy of that of the white paper. It is certainly no more exaggerated than the gossip pages of the small-town American newspaper. Whites are amused by it partly because of their belief in the inferiority of the Negro, but also partly because they are seldom aware of the existence of a Negro upper class, especially one so attentive to the social niceties.

Most upper and middle class Negroes "over-do" their social activity because they are struggling for status as individuals. Social mobility is great. Negroes stress "society" because whites deny them social prestige. They have to create prestige and distinctions of prestige among themselves, and there is an element of the caste protest in demonstrating that they have done it. But apart from this, Negroes, in their isolated and cramped world, enjoy reading about themselves in pleasant situations just like other small-town Americans. The society pages in a Negro paper are, indeed, most similar to the small-city white newspaper. While the Negro paper has the character of a small-town paper, at the same time, by covering the whole country and the world from the race angle in its general news, it keeps the character of a general race paper.

It seems probable that the society news in a Negro paper—as also in the small-city white paper—is of greatest importance for keeping up its sale. Many editors say that they feel that Negroes buy their papers partly because there they can read about themselves and their friends or social competitors. The Negro paper gives almost every upper or middle class Negro family a chance now and then to see one of the family displayed with name and picture, at least as a member of a club, a church, a committee, a high school class, or as attending a tea, a dance, a bridge party or a sports event. Fleming observes:

> In the large, anybody not in the criminal class, can get a "personal" or "social note" in the Negro paper.[22]

This personal publicity in many cases also gives the editor or, in bigger Negro papers, his usually underpaid employees, some additional income.[a]

Usually it is not so much the arrived upper class persons who strive for publicity in this Negro press as the people who are striving and aspire for recognition. But the former group gets its share because it is the pride of the Negro community and most often it dominates the civic organizations like the N.A.A.C.P., even if it leaves the churches and the lodges to the ambitious middle class. The news about all this organizational activity in the isolated Negro community—of churches, clubs, associations—serves primarily a purely practical purpose of giving certain information which is not offered in the ordinary press. It also defines the Negro community as an institutionalized society to the individual Negro, who is excluded so much from white society, and it gives him a feeling of security and belongingness. In all organizational activity there is also usually a "race cause" present, and even this news serves the protest motive in some degree. And, more or less incidentally, it supplements the society news in reporting on personal status and accomplishments of prominent individuals.

The sports columns, likewise, have for their purpose to record and exalt Negro performances. Even the comics usually have, in addition to their regular purpose to distract and amuse, also a race message to tell: that the Negro is witty, that he is clever, that he is strong, and occasionally, that the whites are mean and inferior. When the Negro press indulges in self-criticism of the "race," there is often a prefatory repudiation of the white stereotypes of the "lazy" or "criminal" Negro and an attempt to redefine the characteristics in Negro terms: that Negroes are too good-hearted, too easily deceived and cannot "keep together." The Negro press makes an emphatic appeal to the Negroes to show in life and deed that the whites are mistaken. The Negro newspapers do what the national press in every country can be observed to do: they flatter the group and appeal to group-pride even when admonishing; they help to make it feel self-confident and superior.

4. THE CONTROLS OF THE NEGRO PRESS

The Negro press is primarily controlled by the *active members* of the upper and middle classes of the Negro community. As we have mentioned, these classes make up a great part of its subscribers. The people who publish and write the Negro newspapers belong to the upper class. It is the doings and sayings of people in the upper and middle classes that are recorded in the Negro press. They, therefore, set its tone. Indeed, the

---

[a] I have met this practice of demanding a small amount of money for taking society news and even associational material in many Negro communities, but can, of course, neither know about its financial importance nor if it is also a practice in the comparable white press.

Negro newspapers are one of the chief agencies for the Negro upper class to spread its opinions among the lower classes of the Negro community.

In the Negro newspapers one can see displayed the dilemma of the upper class which we have often commented upon. They react with even more resentment than lower class Negroes against the humiliation of Jim Crow segregation. However, the caste barriers serve partly as a protection to give them special opportunities and status. They need to appeal to racial solidarity to avert lower class hostility against themselves and to perfect their economic and social monopolies. But they also must desire to stress accomplishments and distinctions within the Negro community behind the caste wall, and they want to have painted in the Negro press the pleasantness of the life they enjoy. Frazier observes:

> The Negro upper class, as we have remarked, has an essentially middle-class outlook (that is, in the historic sense), but in their philosophy and behavior one finds all forms of antiquated aristocratic attitudes toward work and expenditures as well as a "sporting complex." On the other hand, this class places great emphasis upon success and conspicuous consumption. Because of their isolation, members of this class overemphasize the importance of their position in the Negro world and speak contemptuously of poor whites (who incidentally include public school teachers). They exhibit an almost childish awe toward professional men, especially physicians. The confusion in ideals and values is also vividly represented in Negro newspapers. These news organs are intensely race conscious and exhibit considerable pride in the achievements of the Negro, most of which are meager performances as measured by broader standards. In addition to carrying a large number of advertisements of products designed to conceal Negro characteristics, these papers constantly play up the slightest recognition shown the Negro by whites. The confusion in ideologies is shown in other respects. For example, a casual reader of the *Afro-American* might get the impression that this newspaper is far to the "left" and espouses working class ideals, but a regular reader would find that upon occasions it is likely to play up the activities of Negro "society" or voice some reactionary religious or economic ideal.[23]

The upper class control of the Negro press gives it an essential conservatism, which only the casual white reader will not observe. The Negro lower classes, however, are caught in the same dilemma. They have accepted white values, even when they are brought to protest against white exclusion. They thus take a vicarious satisfaction out of reading about Negro accomplishments and even about the conspicuous consumption of the Negro upper classes. The lower classes also are radical only in the race question.

The upper class should not, therefore, be held entirely responsible for the ideology of the Negro press. The lower classes also play a part in its control, since they contain the bulk of potential readers. As the educational level is raised and the circulation of Negro newspapers broadened, their control can be expected to have increasing weight. In all political matters which have a bearing upon the welfare of the poorer classes, the majority of Negro papers take a "radical" stand. The same is becoming true on the issue of labor unionism. The fact that most persons in the upper class are dependent, directly or indirectly, upon the economic welfare of the masses for their livelihood tends to bend the political opinions of the Negro upper class toward economic "radicalism."

Park, in his study of the immigrant press, pointed out: "In many cases the advertisements reveal the organization of the immigrant community more fully than does the rest of the paper,"[24] and the same is true also of the Negro paper. The main observation about the advertising in the Negro press is that there is so little of it. And there does not seem to be much of a trend toward an increase.[a] In the almost complete absence of much ordinary commercial advertising, the ads for "hair-straighteners," "skin-bleachers," and other cosmetics, patent medicines, dream books and "occults" become the more conspicuous.[25] They often include half or more of all advertising in a Negro paper.

The paucity of advertising, of course, makes the economy of a Negro newspaper precarious.[b] It cannot keep the copy price too high, either, if it wants a substantial circulation. These factors explain why some Negro papers are so weak economically. It is often pointed out by Negro newspapermen that the paucity of advertising at least has one good effect, that the Negro press becomes freer from any outside controls. It depends more exclusively on its readers. There is undoubtedly some truth in this. On the other hand, the weak economy of the average Negro newspaper must make it easier to buy it for little money, if anybody cares to. There is gossip in the Negro communities about how one or another Negro paper has "sold out for an ad." It is significant that small Negro newspapers often start up in Northern cities just before an important election and disappear after the election is over.[26]

[a] Fleming reports from the 1940 meeting of the Negro Newspaper Publishers' Association in Chicago:

"At the recent meeting . . . publisher after publisher reported his paper's losing fight to get advertising for soap, dental cream and chain grocery stores—and even now such copy is for the most part scant and infrequent, while there are even beer and whiskey concerns which turn down every suggestion to advertise in Negro papers.

"Department store copy is absent because so many such stores are not anxious to have any, or any large numbers of, Negroes trying on hats, shoes and clothing; or they believe Negroes with capacity to buy will read their advertisement in the daily. New automobiles are missing because the industry does not believe that the Negroes are able to buy a new car. Other advertisers do not use any weekly paper whatever and see no difference between the white weekly and the Negro paper. In still other instances there are some dailies which so thoroughly cover the Negro community that advertisers can be convinced that advertising in the Negro paper is a needless duplication." (*Op. cit.*, p. VI:2).

[b] The economic weakness of Negro newspapers is partly reflected in their large death rate. Detweiler (Frederick G. Detweiler, *The Negro Press in the United States* [1922], p. 24) points out that of 288 periodicals existing in 1910, only 163 remained in 1921, and only 59 of these went back to 1900.

As no studies of the finances and controls of the Negro press have been made, it is impossible to present a factual statement on this point. One important thing seems clear, however: the financial controls do not concern its stand on the racial question. In this main issue of the Negro press, it is free. Few white business enterprises have any interest in toning down the Negro protest.ᵃ It may be expected that, on the contrary, a white firm which bribed a Negro paper to favor its interest in some particular respect would rather want the paper's expression of the Negro protest to be accentuated in order to preserve confidence on the part of its readers.²⁷ The same holds true, on the whole, of political parties in the North and a few places in the South which pay in cash for support from the Negro papers before elections.²⁸

As Negro newspapers specialize in Negro news, they become dependent upon the agencies which provide such news. A Negro newspaper covers its own locality. Some few can afford to send staff writers to places where important national events are occurring and to have regular correspondents in certain main centers. But for the rest, all Negro papers must depend for their news on syndicate and organizational releases. There are a number of Negro news agencies: some giving their services for nothing, some exchanging news for free advertising space, and some asking a small fee.²⁹ Before every election they tend to increase in number and efficiency. The main agency is the Associated Negro Press, in existence since 1919.³⁰ The N.A.A.C.P. sends out its own news releases every week, and they are important for the Negro press.

5. OUTLOOK

The importance of the Negro press for the formation of Negro opinion, for the functioning of all other Negro institutions, for Negro leadership and concerted action generally, is enormous. The Negro press is an educational agency and a power agency. Together with the church and the school—and in the field of interracial and civic opinions, more than those two institutions—it determines the special direction of the process through which the Negroes are becoming acculturated. The Negro press causes, on the one hand, an intense realization on the part of the Negroes of American ideals. On the other hand, it makes them realize to how small a degree white Americans live up to them.

As the educational level of the Negro masses rises, as those masses become less dissimilar in culture from other Americans, as the isolation between the two groups increases under voluntary withdrawal on the part of the Negroes, as race consciousness and race solidarity are intensified, as the Negro protest is strengthened, and disseminated even among the lower

---

ᵃ Negro businesses will rarely have such an interest, either, and few Negro businesses could afford to spend money on it, anyhow.

classes—as all these closely interrelated processes are proceeding, partly under the influence of the Negro press itself, the Negro press will continue to grow. With larger circulation, there will be increased possibilities of getting advertising. With a fortified economic basis the Negro press will be able not only to buy better equipment but also to engage better-trained journalists and to organize a better national news service. When the Negro press can produce a better product than now, it will sell even better. The Negro newspaper will probably remain a weekly, though perhaps in some regions it will become possible to launch Negro dailies. This is the prospect we see for the Negro press. It will flourish and become more conspicuous when the foreign-language papers die out. We are assuming that American society will not rapidly become so thoroughly reformed that it will be of no importance whether a man is black or white. We believe that there is a trend in America away from racial discrimination, and in Chapter 45 we shall summarize the reasons why we believe that this is so. But there is a long way to go before the Negro will be secure in enjoying his full constitutional rights. It will probably not happen in this generation and, perhaps, not in the next. Meanwhile, gradual improvements will only strengthen Negro concerted action as they will seem to prove that the Negro protest is effective. All improvements will give the Negro press more big news and important issues to discuss.

In the South the white press has been undergoing a great change in its treatment of the Negro problem. Most liberal white newspapers are today more generous in reporting favorable news from the Negro world than white newspapers in the North and often open their columns for Negro letters to the editor. Northern newspapers are frequently more liberal in their editorials, especially since the outbreak of the War, but give only scant space to Negro news. This process of change in the white press is continuing. The present war emergency seems only to have speeded it up. But— aside from the Southern "black star" editions—this change does not mean serious competition for the Negro press since the latter serves to give "additional" news on the Negro. No feasible widening of the reporting of Negro activities in the white press will substitute for the Negro press. What happens to Negroes will continue to have a relatively low "news value" to white people, and even the most well-meaning editor will have to stop far short of what Negroes demand if he wants to satisfy his white public. It is likely also that with increased race consciousness among Southern Negroes, the "black star" editions will lose in popularity.

Whether or not this forecast of an increasing circulation for Negro papers comes true, the Negro press is of tremendous importance. It has rightly been characterized as "the greatest single power in the Negro race." [31]

PART X

THE NEGRO COMMUNITY

CHAPTER 43

INSTITUTIONS

1. The Negro Community as a Pathological Form of an American Community

Until now the Negro community has not been the primary object of our study. But we have not been able to avoid dealing with the community and with various, alleged or real, cultural and personality traits of the American Negro. There are a number of problems, however, such as those of the Negro family, crime, insanity, and cultural accomplishments, which have been touched upon only incidentally. We shall now take up these nonpolitical aspects of the Negro community. The treatment will be incomplete and condensed, for three reasons. First, these problems are not focal in our inquiry. Second, many sides of them have already been dealt with in other parts of the book. Third, several of those problems have recently been treated extensively in the scientific literature. It would obviously be impossible to describe and analyze the hundreds of specific communities in which Negroes live. We must content ourselves instead with a general account of the basic community institutions and activities, noting the major contrasts between the white and the Negro pattern of community organization, depicting the salient historical trends, and indicating the most striking divergences between the Northern and Southern and the urban and rural ways of life.

The value premise for this Part is derived from the American Creed. America was settled largely by persons who, for one reason or another, were dissatisfied with conditions in their homelands and sought new opportunities. Until 1921 the nation welcomed immigrants almost unreservedly. They came from everywhere and brought with them a diversity of institutions and cultural patterns. It was natural that the "melting pot," "Americanization"—or, to use a more technical term, "assimilation"—became a central element in the American Creed. To make a homogeneous nation out of diverse ethnic groups, the immigrants were to abandon their cultural "peculiarities"—or to contribute them to American culture as a whole, as some would have it—and to take on the cultural forms of America. There could be diversity, to be sure, but this diversity was not to have a strictly ethnic basis; individuals should be free to be part of any community they wished. Ideally, Americanization was to take place immediately, or, rather, in the five years required to achieve citizenship. But it was realistically recognized that in some cases it might require two or three generations.

Negroes have been living here for over three hundred years, and practically all of the ancestors of present-day Negroes came to this country more than a hundred years ago. It is probable that, on the average, Negroes have been Americans longer than any immigrant group except the British. They should be well assimilated by now. Negroes, however, together with the Orientals and, to some extent, Indians and Mexicans, have not been allowed to assimilate as have European immigrants. There is intense resistance on the part of the white majority group to biological amalgamation; and the lower caste status of Negroes is rationalized to prevent miscegenation.[a] Negroes have been segregated, and they have developed, or there have been provided for them, separate institutions in many spheres of life, as, for instance, in religion and education. Segregation and discrimination have also in other ways hampered assimilation. Particularly they have steered acculturation so that the Negroes have acquired the norms of lower class people in America.

Negro institutions are, nevertheless, similar to those of the white man. They show little similarity to African institutions. In his cultural traits, the Negro is akin to other Americans. Some peculiarities are even to be characterized as "exaggerations" of American traits. Horace Mann Bond has characterized the American Negro as a "quintessential American."[1] Even the "exaggeration" or intensification of general American traits in American Negro culture is explainable by specific caste pressures. In his allegiances the Negro is characteristically an American. He believes in the American Creed and in other ideals held by most Americans, such as getting ahead in the world, individualism, the importance of education and wealth. He imitates the dominant culture as he sees it and in so far as he can adopt it under his conditions of life. For the most part he is not proud of those things in which he differs from the white American.

True, there has developed recently a glorification of things African, especially in music and art, and there was a back-to-Africa movement after the First World War.[b] But this is a reaction to discrimination from white people, on the one hand, and a result of encouragement from white people, on the other hand. Thus, even the positive movement away from American culture has its source in that culture. Negro race pride and race prejudice serve to fortify the Negro against white superiority. *In practically all its divergences, American Negro culture is not something independent of general American culture. It is a distorted development, or a pathological condition, of the general American culture.* The instability of the Negro family, the inadequacy of educational facilities for Negroes,

[a] See Chapters 3 and 28.

[b] See Chapter 35, Sections 7 and 9, and Chapter 38, Section 12.

the emotionalism in the Negro church, the insufficiency and unwholesomeness of Negro recreational activity, the plethora of Negro sociable organizations, the narrowness of interests of the average Negro, the provincialism of his political speculation, the high Negro crime rate, the cultivation of the arts to the neglect of other fields, superstition, personality difficulties, and other characteristic traits arc mainly forms of social pathology which, for the most part, are created by the caste pressures.

This can be said positively: *we assume that it is to the advantage of American Negroes as individuals and as a group to become assimilated into American culture, to acquire the traits held in esteem by the dominant white Americans.* This will be the value premise here. We do not imply that white American culture is "higher" than other cultures in an absolute sense. The notion popularized by anthropologists that *all* cultures may be good under the different conditions to which they are adaptations, and that no derogatory association should *a priori* be attached to primitive cultures, is a wholesome antidote to arrogant and erroneous ideas closely bound up with white people's false racial beliefs and their justification of caste. But it does not gainsay our assumption that *here, in America,* American culture is "highest" in the pragmatic sense that adherence to it is practical for any individual or group which is not strong enough to change it.

Also not to be taken in a doctrinal sense is the observation that peculiarities in the Negro community may be characterized as social pathology. As a reaction to adverse and degrading living conditions, the Negroes' culture is taking on some characteristics which are not given a high evaluation in the larger American culture. Occasionally the Negro culture traits are appreciated by the whites. The Negro spirituals—called by James Weldon Johnson, though with some exaggeration, "America's only folk music"— are a case in point.[a]

From the practical point of view, the problem of the historical origin of the divergences of American Negro culture becomes irrelevant. The con-

[a] Similar exceptions can be noticed in every lower class culture. There has been, for instance, in most industrial countries in recent decades, a "proletarian" branch of literature, which draws its themes and its inspiration from life in the lower classes. This literature is often, characteristically enough, appreciated more by members of the higher classes than by the proletarians themselves. Generally pastoral romanticism, which has been a part of urban civilization since the time of the ancient Greeks, has idealized lower class life. The tendency is tainted with sentimentality, and this is frequently displayed by people who show a particular interest in Negro culture. Among the radically inclined, this romanticism serves to express their sympathy for the underdog; among conservatives it serves as a rationalization for continuing the inequalities. To Negroes it serves as an expression of their protest and their "race pride." As usual it appeals much more to upper and middle class Negroes than to lower class Negroes. The sentimentality involved in idealizing lower class traits has, of course, nothing to do with scientific observation. The residuum of truth in the tendency is, however, that even if generally the result of adverse living conditions are bad, exceptionally they may be good—"good" and "bad" defined according to our value premise of placing the general American culture "higher."

troversy on social causation has come to turn on the question of the importance of the African heritage. To a long line of writers, the African heritage
has been regarded as a sign of the Negro's lack of capacity for higher civilization. Those writers usually attached their interest to the unfavorable
traits they attributed to the Negro: criminality, amorality, lack of ability for
organized social life, little talent for inventiveness, and so on. On the other
hand, a modern school of anthropologists and historians, trying to appreciate
the Negro, shows an equal, though opposite, selectiveness in their interest.
They attempt, for instance, to derive Negro music, dancing, and art from
Africa and to describe peculiarities in religion and the mother-centered
family as an African heritage, while they leave crime and amorality to be
explained by white pressure. Melville J. Herskovits and Carter G. Woodson represent this tendency.[a] Others, like E. Franklin Frazier, have
regarded the African heritage as insignificant and have sought the explanation in the special circumstances connected with slavery and caste.[2] The
latter theory may be said to be predominant in sociological literature.
There are certain variations of the latter theory: some would prefer to
think of Negro institutions as "accommodations" to slavery and caste
conditions; some would prefer to think of them as the results of isolation
due to slavery and caste; others would prefer to think of Negro institutions
as a case of "cultural lag" because of the existence of slavery and caste.[b]

Here the interest is in the fact that American Negro culture is somewhat
different from the general American culture, that this difference is *generally
created* by American conditions even if some of the *specific forms* are
African in origin, and that the difference is significant for Negroes and for
the relations between Negroes and whites.[c]

2. The Negro Family

The recent book by E. Franklin Frazier, *The Negro Family in the United
States* (1939), is such an excellent description and analysis of the American

[a] See Chapter 35, Section 9.

[b] It cannot be said that either of these theories, or the theory of a predominant African
heritage, is scientifically proved. The historical evidence is usually so incomplete that, with
some selectiveness on the part of the particular writer, it can easily be fitted into any theory
without proving it. Also, there is no reason why all the theories could not be correct to a
certain degree. For example, the practice of baptism is prevalent among American Negroes
and is also to be found among African Negroes and American whites: it may have been that
the African cult sensitized and predisposed Negroes to like baptism, but the specific pattern
was adopted from white Americans. The scientific problem, which is largely unsolved, is to
show comprehensively how, in specific respects, present-day Negro culture developed when
the Negro slaves—who were certainly not without culture when they reached America—had
to live on for generations under the specific circumstances created for them in America.

[c] We do not mean to say that the difference between the two theories is not important in
either a theoretical or a practical sense. We have considered the practical significance of
Herskovits' theory in Chapter 35, Section 9.

Negro family that it is practically necessary only to relate its conclusions to our context and to refer the reader to it for details.

The uniqueness of the Negro family is a product of slavery. Most slave owners either did not care about the marital state of their slaves or were interested in seeing to it that they did not form strong marital bonds. The slave owners who did not want some of their slaves to marry were: those who had Negro mistresses, those who bred mulattoes or strong slaves, and those who did not want to make it difficult when they sold slaves individually rather than in family units. The internal slave trade broke up many slave families—even those belonging to masters who encouraged stable marriages, when death or economic disaster occurred—and the threat of it hung over all slave families. Certain cultural practices grew up in slavery which retain their influences up to the present day in rural Southern areas: marriages sometimes occur by simple public declaration or with a ceremony conducted by a minister but without a marriage license. Coupled with this was the popular belief that divorce could occur by public declaration or simply by crossing state or county lines.

After slavery there emerged certain new obstacles in the way of marital stability. Mobility was increased, work was not readily available, and there began a migration to cities with an attendant increase in desertion, prostitution and temporary marriage. Yet coincident with these developments the stability of the Negro family grew. Even before the Civil War there had been certain masters who encouraged stable marriages among their slaves, and the freed Negroes, especially in the North, began to develop their own strong family units. The strong hold of religion on the Negro tended to stabilize his family life. At the close of the Civil War, the slave states legalized all existing common-law marriages [a] and, with the disappearance of the master's interests and of forced sale, there was a great increase in family stability. But the starting point was so low that Negroes never caught up. Isolation, poverty and ignorance were again the obstacles to acculturation.

There are two outstanding types of exceptions to the general observation that the average Negro family is more disorganized than the white family. In rural areas of the South, especially in isolated areas, there is a large class of Negro families which is so like the ideal type of the monogamous patriarchal Christian family that Frazier calls them "Black Puritans." The impetus for this family form probably came from the religious slave owner. Much more significant is the upper class Negro family in the towns and cities. Upper class Negroes probably have fewer extra-marital relations and

---

[a] Some states required that the couple be remarried; others required only that they declare their marriage before a public officer and get a certificate; but the majority of Southern states legalized all Negro common-law marriages without any action on the part of the couple. A few states left it to the courts to recognize legality as cases arose. (Gilbert T. Stephenson, *Race Distinctions in American Law* [1910], pp. 67-68.)

TABLE 1

NUMBER AND RATE OF ILLEGITIMATE BIRTHS, BY NATIVITY, SECTION AND RURAL-URBAN RESIDENCE: 1936

Section	Total Births[a]	Number				Total Births[a]	Rate Per 1,000			
		Totals	White Mother Native	Mother Foreign	Other Races		Totals	White Mother Native	Mother Foreign	Other Races
United States[b]	72,338	31,850	30,597	806	40,488	39.8	20.3	20.6	9.9	162.1
Cities of 10,000 or more	30,461	16,441	15,615	583	14,020	40.5	24.3	25.2	10.2	182.9
Cities of 2,500 to 10,000	5,741	2,969	2,894	44	2,772	28.8	16.1	16.4	6.1	182.1
Rural	36,136	12,440	12,088	179	23,696	41.8	17.6	17.6	10.3	150.5
Southern States[c]	49,353	13,137	12,564	244	36,216	58.6	20.9	20.4	18.4	170.0
Cities of 10,000 or more	15,320	4,752	4,421	176	10,568	67.9	27.0	26.3	23.5	213.8
Cities of 2,500 to 10,000	3,656	1,041	1,006	12	2,615	46.4	16.0	15.8	8.4	191.4
Rural	30,377	7,344	7,137	56	23,033	56.4	18.9	18.6	12.9	153.7
Northern and Western States[b]	22,985	18,713	18,033	562	4,272	23.6	20.0	20.8	8.2	117.6
Cities of 10,000 or more	15,141	11,689	11,194	407	3,452	28.7	23.4	24.9	8.2	126.8
Cities of 2,500 to 10,000	2,085	1,928	1,888	32	157	17.3	16.2	16.7	5.5	100.6
Rural	5,759	5,096	4,951	123	663	17.7	16.0	16.2	9.4	87.8

Source: U.S. Bureau of the Census, *Births, Stillbirths and Infant Mortality Statistics: 1936*, pp. 9–13.

[a] Includes "Country not stated."
[b] Exclusive of California, Massachusetts, and New York. These states do not require a statement concerning legitimacy of child.
[c] Includes: Alabama, Arkansas, Delaware, District of Columbia, Florida, Georgia, Kentucky, Louisiana, Maryland, Mississippi, Missouri, North Carolina, Oklahoma, South Carolina, Tennessee, Texas, Virginia, West Virginia.

less divorce than upper class whites.[3] They have reacted against the reputation of lower class Negroes and have not permitted themselves the marital laxness of some upper class whites. This has been more or less a spontaneous trend, developing not so much with a positive model from white society,[a] but more with the negative stimulus of white derisiveness. Whites do not realize that one of the most stable types of urban families is that of the Negro upper class, so in one sense the effort to build a reputation is wasted. But ammunition for white derision is lessened and a model for the Negro lower class is provided. Thus the efforts of the small Negro upper class may yet have an important effect.

There are no perfect indices of family disorganization, since there are no official statistics on extra-marital relations, on "temporary" marriages without benefit of clergy, or on unofficial desertion. Perhaps the best direct index of family stability that is available is that of illegitimacy. There is far from complete reporting of illegitimate births, there is even serious under-reporting of all types of births. But the figures are available for the whole country and are relatively more complete than for any other direct index of family disorganization. Table 1 brings out strikingly the difference between Negro and white illegitimacy.[b] For the United States as a whole, the figures indicate that Negroes have about eight times as much illegitimacy as native whites and about sixteen times as much illegitimacy as the foreign-born whites. Differentials between various groups of Negroes are not so certain, but there would seem to be fewer cases of illegitimacy in the North than in the South (despite lack of regional differences among whites) and fewer in the rural areas than in the urban areas.

There are no nation-wide statistics on divorce by race, and even the scattered statistics available are of limited significance because most Negro couples who separate do so without a divorce and because the states have different legal practices in divorce. The same is true of legal desertion statistics.[4] All census data on this problem are somewhat inaccurate, and the figures cited suggest conditions rather than measure them precisely. The census information on the marital status of Negroes is especially inaccurate, since unmarried couples are inclined to report themselves as married, and women who have never married but who have children are inclined to

[a] The model for the upper class Negro family was, in a sense, the white upper class family of an earlier generation. In this case, as in so many other cases, Negroes were assimilated with a cultural lag.

[b] "Other races" are predominantly Negro and so may be used as an index of Negro. Frazier has data on illegitimacy for selected cities which have better statistics than the rest of the nation and which separate Negroes from whites. These data show roughly the same things as the table presented here. (See E. Franklin Frazier, The Negro Family in the United States [1939], Appendix B, pp. 568-569.) For a summary of studies of Negro illegitimacy in special localities, see Eleanor C. Isbell, "Memorandum on the Negro Family in America," unpublished manuscript prepared for this study (1940), pp. 63-64 and 84-89.

report themselves as widowed. It is suggestive that the proportion of "widows" among Negro women in 1930 was 15.9 per cent, as compared to 9.7 per cent among native white women of native parentage. If a legal or common-law marriage had broken up, the partners became either unattached individuals (if they had no children or had abandoned them) or members of broken families (if they stayed with their children). Unattached individuals and "one-person families" constituted about 13 per cent of the Negro population in 1930, whereas the corresponding figure for the white population was 9 per cent. Broken families were 30 per cent of all Negro families, but only 20 per cent among native white families, despite the greater concentration of Negroes in rural-farm areas where broken families are least frequent (Table 2).

TABLE 2

Proportion Broken Families[a] of All Families: 1930

	Negro	Native White
All families	29.6	19.5
Rural farm families (South)	20.1	12.8
Rural nonfarm families (South)	34.1	16.8
Urban families (South)	38.4	19.8

Source: Richard Sterner and Associates, The Negro's Share, prepared for this study (1943), p. 50. Sterner computed these figures from unpublished data of the U. S. Bureau of the Census.
[a] Includes married if spouse is not present, widowed, divorced, and single heads of families.

In addition to the direct indices of family disorganization, there are several other signs that Negroes have a larger share of the factors contributing to family disorganization. Lodgers, for example, are often a disruptive factor in family life. In Northern urban areas 29 per cent of the Negro families reported lodgers in their homes in 1930, as compared to 10 per cent of the native white families. In Southern urban areas the proportions were 20 per cent for Negroes and 11 per cent for whites.[a] "Doubling up" of families in a single household is another factor contributory to family disorganization, and Negroes have more of it.[5] Similarly, as we have noted in Chapter 16, Negroes have more over-crowding and less home ownership.

While the Negro masses undoubtedly have much more of all those characteristics which define family disorganization in the traditional American sense, they have certain other cultural traits which tend to reduce the disorganizing effect of those characteristics. Although the census would not bring out the fact, since there is a confusion over common-law marriage and temporary marriage, there are probably significantly fewer unattached Negro adults than unattached white adults. In a small community in rural

[a] Richard Sterner and Associates, The Negro's Share, prepared for this study (1943), p. 55. For the United States as a whole, 15.2 per cent of the Negro families had lodgers, as compared to 9.0 per cent of the native white families.

Alabama, Charles S. Johnson found no spinsters and extremely few older bachelors among the Negroes (612 families).[6] He also found only two divorced persons who had not remarried. Further: common-law marriage and illegitimacy are not seriously condemned within the Negro community —except among the upper classes—and they have, therefore, fewer disorganizing effects on the individual. The Southern Negro community defines divorce in a broad sense—to include most cases of desertion or mutual agreement to separate and also the crossing of state or county lines —so that there is no moral guilt attached to remarriage even if there is legal guilt. The Negro community also has the healthy social custom of attaching no stigma to the illegitimate child and of freely adopting illegitimate children and orphans into established families. A high value is placed on children generally, and those who mate outside of marriage do not have a tendency to prevent the coming of children. There are few unwanted children. Another healthy social attitude found by Charles Johnson is that of regarding a forced marriage as less respectable than desertion after a forced marriage. The erring daughter is forgiven by her parents and is not ostracized by the community.

The existence of these practices does not mean that the Negro community has no moral standards, even in the traditional American sense. "Fast women," philandering men and "fly-by-night" affairs are condemned. In the rural South, the rule is that a person may cohabit with only one other person during a given period: there is little promiscuity.[7] But the important thing is that the Negro lower classes, especially in the rural South, have built up a type of family organization conducive to social health, even though the practices are outside the American tradition. When these practices are brought into closer contact with white norms, as occurs when Negroes go to the cities, they tend to break down partially and to cause the demoralization of some individuals.

3. THE NEGRO CHURCH IN THE NEGRO COMMUNITY[a]

At least 44 per cent of American Negroes were claimed as members of Negro churches in 1936. Actually, the proportion is considerably higher, for several reasons.[8] Although church membership means different things to different people, it is quite obvious—not only from total membership figures, but also from the character of the church service, the religious nature of many of the Negro's songs, the great use to which the church building is put, the diversity of voluntary activities organized around the church—that religion and church play an important role in the Negro

[a] The most useful general sources of information on the Negro church that we have found and the ones we have relied upon for most of our factual data are: B. E. Mays and J. W. Nicholson, *The Negro's Church* (1933); and J. G. St. Clair Drake, "The Negro Church and Associations in Chicago," unpublished manuscript prepared for this study (1940).

community, probably more important than in the average white community. In this section we shall seek to sketch this role.

Probably the chief "function" of the Negro church has been to buoy up the hopes of its members in the face of adversity and to give them a sense of community. This is, of course, true of any church, but it is especially true of Negroes, who have had a hard lot and to whom so many channels of activity outside the church have been closed. Negroes have had to place their hopes for a better life in religion. As a Negro poet puts it, "Our churches are where we dip our tired bodies in cool springs of hope, where we retain our wholeness and humanity despite the blows of death from the Bosses. . . ."[9] It is this need, perhaps more than anything else, which has attached the Negro so strongly to his church and accounts for his reputation as a religious person. In the colder and more critical words of Mays and Nicholson,[10] "It is not too much to say that if the Negro had experienced a wider range of freedom in social and economic spheres, there would have been fewer Negroes 'called' to preach and fewer Negro churches."

The denominations to which Negroes belong do not tend to have a heavy, formal ritual.[a] It is true that a significant proportion of church-going Negroes belong to the formalized Episcopalian and Catholic churches, but the great majority belong to the Baptist and Methodist churches or to the many little sects that have grown up in recent years. Lower class Negroes more than middle and upper class Negroes adhere to these latter churches. The small upper class of Negroes tends to belong to the Episcopalian, Congregational, and Presbyterian churches, since for them a main function of church membership is to give prestige.[11]

The religious service in Negro churches is often characterized by extreme emotionalism. The old-fashioned preacher employs gestures, intonation of the voice, sobbing, and words calculated to arouse emotion.[12] His audience aids with interjections at certain points and with stamping of the feet. There is a great deal of choir and congregational singing, and use of musical instruments of the percussion type.[b] These "rousements" bring most of the congregation into some degree of "possession."

[a] For the facts concerning the distribution of Negro churches by denominations, see Chapter 40, Section 3.

[b] Allison Davis lists the rituals of Negro churches which arouse emotions as follows:

"1. Narration of 'visions' or 'travels' as public evidence of individual's religious conversion.

"2. Highly dramatized baptism in public setting, in a river, creek, or (usually in Old City and its environment) in a hog-wallow.

"3. Communion service in which members shake hands with one another, and march around minister and church officers in a closely packed circle, while they sing and stamp feet.

"4. Communal participation by members in both sermon and *prayers*, with antiphonal structure in which members reply to preacher or deacon, or interrupt him. Communal singing, of same antiphonal form.

"5. Funeral service in which all congregation views corpse, and participates in both

Whites, in searching for rationalizations to justify the subordination of the Negro, have seized upon the fact of religious emotionalism and ascribed it to "animal nature" and even to "excessive sexuality." Even Northerners —or we could perhaps say, *especially* Northerners—have done this, since the Negro's religion is so different from their own, and they are at a loss to account for this behavior. Southerners, on the other hand, are accustomed to seeing extreme emotionalism in many lower class white churches and revival meetings.

Two things are important in attempting to explain this emotionalism. In the first place, it has been exaggerated. A large minority of Negroes do not attend church, and another large minority do not have emotionalism in their church service. There are wide differences among the various Negro denominations in degree of emotionalism manifested.[13] Emotionalism is uncommon in the upper and middle class Negro churches—which are quite like white churches of the same class level in this respect—and it is uncommon in the Catholic Church and other large, well-established urban churches where there are more lower class Negroes than middle and upper class Negroes. There is a definite trend for Negro youth to avoid the emotional type of church, and the same is true of the social "climbers" of all ages and occupations.[14] Emotionalism is most common in the rural Southern Negro churches and in the "storefront"[a] churches of the cities. These form the great bulk of the Negro churches, but since their congregations are small, they do not include such a large proportion of the Negro churchgoers. But even in the churches of the rural South, emotionalism is declining. According to Mays and Nicholson, revival meetings in the rural South are less successful than they used to be; the professional evangelist is disappearing; and the regular sermons attempt to be more thought-provoking.[15]

---

sermon and prayers; a highly communal service with violent demonstrations such as shouting and 'getting happy.'

"6. Marching of usher board of church, or of visiting usher boards, around seated congregation up to chancel, where donation is made by each member of usher board. Repeated several times, while both usher board and congregation sing.

"7. Intoning, or at times the singing, of sermon or prayer by minister. Use by minister of sobbing technique, or of triumphant laugh in preaching; walking into congregation or elaborate physical dramatization of sermon by preacher.

"8. Devotion of a large part of the service to the collection of money.

"To these may be added rituals of the Sanctified, Spiritualist, Holiness, and other esoteric sects found among both Negroes and whites of the lower class positions, such as the practices of 'sacred dancing,' rolling in a sawdust pit in state of ecstasy, tambourine playing, reading of the future, healing of the sick, use of images of saints, foot-washing, use of drum and of jazz music, etc." ("The Negro Church and Associations in the Lower South," unpublished manuscript prepared for this study [1940], pp. 83-84.)

[a] The term "storefront" churches is commonly used to include churches in residences as well as in stores.

The second point is that the great periods of Negro conversion to Christianity were periods when the emotional forms of religion were taking hold of the whites too. In the Great Revival of 1800, it was common to see large groups of whites, gathered in a field upon the advertisement of a traveling revival leader, shouting, crying, laughing, "speaking with tongues," barking, dancing, rolling around, and manifesting all the traits associated with extreme "possession." Negroes occasionally participated, but more often just watched from a distance or had their own imitations with the help of white missionaries.[16] Negroes—and lower class whites in isolated communities in the South—have retained these religious practices in a relatively subdued form. Negroes have been losing them, but not as rapidly as have whites. Certain practices of the Negro Baptist and Methodist churches—such as permitting persons to become clergymen without having an education—and the geographical and cultural isolation of Negroes in the rural South, have helped to keep the Negroes behind the whites in the trend toward less emotionalism.

It may be that emotionalism in religion is well suited to take the Negro's mind off his degradation and frustration. It is commonly said that it is religion that "keeps him going." The feeling of "possession" is used the world over to produce euphoria when circumstances are unduly unpleasant —although in most groups, drugs and drink rather than religious excitement produce the effect. Whether or not there is any relation between the decline of emotionalism in religion and the growing resentment and caustic bitterness among Negroes could not be proved, although it is plausible.

Just as emotionalism was borrowed from and sanctioned by religious behavior among whites, so were the smaller religious sects taken over by Negroes after they were started by whites. The generation following 1880 saw the origin of a large number of lower class religious movements, especially among whites in the Middle West.[17] These movements gained most headway, perhaps, among the poor whites and the Negroes of the South. To this group of sects belong the Holiness Church, the Disciples of Christ, the Church of God and twenty-odd others.[18]

The Negro church is a community center *par excellence.* In the South, there are few public buildings for the recreation of Negroes, except some of the schools, upon the use of which many limitations are laid. Negroes are usually too poor to build special community centers. Only in large cities does private enterprise provide halls for Negro meetings and recreation. Negro homes are almost always too small to have more than two or three guests at one time. Only the church is left, and in many ways it is well fitted to serve as a community center. It is usually located in the heart of the community it is meant to serve, often closer to most of the homes than is the school. It is owned by the Negroes themselves, and they can feel free to do what they please in it. The white man's respect for religion gives it a freedom from intrusion that is not enjoyed even in the Negro home. In the rural churches, often the preacher himself does not participate in the social activities that go on in his church, since he often has three or four other churches to attend to.[a] In fact, the Negro church is such a good community center that it might almost be said that anyone who does not belong to a church in the rural South does not belong to the community.[19]

The school is often located in a church in the rural South. Lodges and clubs frequently hold their meetings in the church, more often in rural areas than in the cities. Lectures and meetings for discussion of civic problems—including political meetings in the North—are probably most often held in churches. The large Negro churches in Northern, and sometimes Southern, cities often have the full gamut of social and recreational activities that is found in large white churches.[20] And, finally, the church, like the barbershop and the pool parlor, is a place to which one wanders when he has nothing else to do.

The denominations to which Negroes predominantly belong—Baptist and Methodist—attempt to exercise a strict control over morals, and have a rather broad definition of morals. For want of a better term, we may say that they have "puritanical" standards of behavior. Negroes have taken over these standards but have modified them somewhat to suit Negro customs and white demands. For example, Negro preachers condemn extra-marital sex relations, but they seldom take any specific steps to stop them because usually so many of their congregation engage in the condemned behavior. Too, they dare not say anything against relations between Negro women and white men in the South for fear of physical punishment. In addition to extra-marital sex relations, the practices of gambling, drinking, drug-taking, smoking, snuff-dipping, card-playing, dancing and other minor "vices" are condemned. Sometimes even ordinary sports and picnics come under a religious ban. These injunctions seem to have effect on middle class Negroes, especially those who are ready to settle down. The upper class among Negroes also tends to avoid some of these practices, but more because they individually want to or because they want to maintain status, rather than because of any specific injunction against them by the church. The bulk of the lower class, and the youth of all classes, seems to pay little attention to them. Females, as greater churchgoers, and as the traditional guardians of morals, obey them more than males.

The Negro church, in respects other than its emotionalism, is like any lower class white Protestant church. In its relation to the Negro community,

[a] The churches may often be scattered over the countryside, and the ministers have difficulty in getting to them. Mays and Nicholson report that, of 159 rural churches studied, only 5.7 per cent of the preachers lived within 10 miles of the church. (*Op. cit.*, p. 251.)

however, the Negro church tends to be different from the white church in relation to its community.

The Negro preacher's stand on problems of caste and on all "political" problems is equivocal. On the one hand, he must preach "race solidarity" because his congregation demands it and because he himself stands to gain if the economic and political situation of his community improves. On the other hand, he is not only a focus of caste pressure, but his position of leadership depends upon the monopoly given him by segregation. Although the Negro preacher is "other-worldly" in his sermons,[a] he has a closer relation to politics than has the white clergyman. In accordance with Baptist and Methodist tenets, he preaches puritanical morals, and yet is often far from exemplary in his own life and sometimes has connections with the underworld. These paradoxes exist because the Negro preacher is not only a clergyman, but also, as Du Bois puts it, "a leader, a politician, an orator, a 'boss,' an intriguer, an idealist."[21] These divergent interests make the Negro preacher shift his actions fairly frequently with respect to controversial questions, so that he appears inconsistent.

Negro preachers usually support Negro business. But at least one case is known where they have received threats from white business competitors for doing so.[22] And there is the fact that the Negro church often receives more money from white businessmen (since there are more of them even in Negro neighborhoods) than from Negro businessmen. In advertising Negro business, preachers use the pulpit as well as written endorsements and the church paper.[23] Some of the Negro businessmen are known racketeers: their legitimate businesses are sometimes a "front" for gambling rackets and even vice. The churches are, of course, officially against such things, but gambling (especially "policy") among the members of the congregation is too widespread to be stamped out, and often the contributions from Negro policy racketeers—especially in the North—are a major source of support for the church. Some Negro ministers in Chicago meet the situation by ignoring the policy playing that goes on; others openly endorse it on the grounds that it provides jobs for Negroes and that "gambling isn't the worst sin." Some Spiritualist churches actually give out lucky numbers to be played.[24]

Where Negroes vote, preachers frequently take a stand and use their influence and their pulpit to swing Negro votes.[25] Although the feeling is prevalent among Negroes, as among whites, that clergymen should have nothing to do with politics, the Negro preacher's position as a community leader, as well as his desire to get money for his church and even for himself, often leads him to have some sort of tie with a political machine or candidate. A minister who has a political tie gains in power, since he can "fix" minor difficulties with the law for members of his congregation and

[a] See Chapter 40, Section 5.

sometimes even has control over a few jobs, political or otherwise. Politicians, both white and Negro, realizing that Negroes are in great need and are easily influenced by any display of friendliness or of power, often make use of the large churches even without the minister's express assent. They make an appearance at a church service and conspicuously donate large sums of money at collection time. Many of the church members interviewed by Gosnell did not resent a white politician even in the pulpit, since they felt that the Negro needs all the white influence he can get, and since they do not have time to attend regular political meetings in which they are interested.[26] The church, as the community's most central public institution, seems to many Negroes to take on political functions, as other non-religious functions, quite naturally.

The Negro community is so poor, and the number of Negro churches so large in relation to the number of churchgoers,[a] that the upkeep of the church is a financial drain. A good portion of the time during an average church service is taken up with the collection, and there is a tendency to emotionalize the collection so as to elicit more money.[27] Both in the South and in the North, there is importuning of white churches, white businessmen, and other white individuals for money to support the churches. Still the average Negro does not get much back from his church in the way of community services.[28] Relatively few of the churches—even the urban churches—offer facilities for recreation, and the amounts spent on charity, education and social service are pitifully small. This is partly due to the fact that there are too many churches, which makes the overhead expense too high.[b] Too, the urban Negro church often gets itself into great debt when it buys or builds a church edifice. In Mays and Nicholson's sample of urban Negro churches in 1930, 71.3 per cent had debts on their buildings.[29] Finally, Negro churches have poor business practices.[c] For all these reasons, and relative to the poverty of the congregation, the Negro church is more expensive to the average Negro than the white man's church is to him. Most Negroes are aware of this fact and are not happy over it.

The Negro church is at once modeled after the white church and yet fitted into the needs and culture of the Negro community. Theology and church service are the same as in white Protestant churches. Emotionalism was borrowed from the whites but has been retained after most whites have abandoned it, and is now considered a Negro "characteristic." Although Negroes do not, on the whole, pay much attention to the moral injunctions of the church, the church has been the major center of community life, and the preacher has been the major leader of the community. But this is

[a] For statistics on the number of members per church, see Chapter 40, Section 3.
[b] For the facts on church expenditures, see footnote 30 of Chapter 40.
[c] See Chapter 40, Section 5.

changing rapidly as the Negro community becomes diversified, as other professionals are becoming more numerous, as upper and middle classes develop among Negroes, as the minister does not advance as rapidly in education and sophistication as do the youth of his community. The Negro church has declined in relative importance since 1880, and the prospects are for a continued decline. Nevertheless, the Negro church means more to the Negro community than the white church means to the white community—in its function as a giver of hope, as an emotional cathartic, as a center of community activity, as a source of leadership, and as a provider of respectability.

4. The Negro School and Negro Education[a]

As we have pointed out in Chapter 41, there were few educational facilities for Negroes before the Civil War. Since then the proportion of Negro children attending school has gone up so rapidly that now it is not far behind the also increasing proportion of white children attending school

TABLE 3

School Attendance in the United States, Ages 5-20, by Race: 1850-1940

	NEGROES		WHITES
Year	Number	Per cent of Population aged 5-20	Per cent of Population aged 5-20
1850	26,461	1.7	52.9
1860	32,629	1.8	56.0
1870	180,372	9.2	51.2
1880	856,014	32.5	58.2
1890	999,324	32.0	55.4
1900	1,083,516	31.0	53.6
1910	1,644,759	44.7	61.3
1920	2,030,269	53.5	65.7
1930	2,477,311	60.0	71.5
1940	2,698,901	64.4	71.6

Sources: The figures for 1850-1890, inclusive, are from E. George Payne, "Negroes in the Public Elementary School of the North," *The Annals of the American Academy of Political and Social Science* (November, 1928), p. 224.
The figures for 1900 to 1940, we have calculated from the following sources: (1) U. S. Bureau of the Census, *Negroes in the United States, 1790 to 1914*, p. 377; (2) U. S. Bureau of the Census, *Negroes in the United States, 1920-1932*, pp. 209-210; (3) *Sixteenth Census of the United States: 1940, Population*. Preliminary Release, Series P-10, No. 17, Table 2. From the decennial censuses of population of 1850 to 1890, we have corroborated Payne's figures on number of Negroes and whites attending school for every year but 1890 (where we have a discrepancy of some 7,500 in the figure for Negroes), but we have not attempted to get the base figures on the number aged 5 to 20 for these years. For Negroes alone, Bond corroborates Payne's percentages within 1.3 per cent. (Horace Mann Bond, *The Education of the Negro in the American Social Order* [1934,] p. 178.)

[a] The most useful general study of Negro education is that of Horace Mann Bond, *The Education of the Negro in the American Social Order* (1934). Also useful in more specialized problems are: (1) Charles S. Johnson and Associates, "The Negro Public Schools," Section 8 of the *Louisiana Educational Survey* (1942); (2) Buell G. Gallagher, *American Caste and the Negro College* (1938); (3) Doxey A. Wilkerson, *Special Problems of Negro Education* (1939); (4) David T. Blose and Ambrose Caliver, *Statistics of the Education of Negroes: 1933-1934 and 1935-1936*, U. S. Office of Education Bulletin No. 13 (1938).

(Table 3). These figures are deceptive, however, since the bulk of Negro children live in the South, and education for Negroes in the South is generally inferior to that for whites. Too, school attendance is something that can be misrepresented to a census-taker. The main reason for the discrepancy still existing is that Negroes do not attend high school and college to the same extent as do whites. As we shall see later in this section, elementary school attendance is about the same for Negroes and whites, except in the rural South.

TABLE 4

School Attendance, Ages 7–20, by Race and Region: 1930

| Region[a] | Per cent of Population aged 7–20 attending school April 1, 1930 | |
	Negroes	Whites
United States	64.4	75.4
Urban	67.0	75.8
Rural	63.0	74.9
North and West	71.1	76.4
Urban	71.2	—
Rural	70.6	—
South	63.2	72.8
Urban	64.5	—
Rural	62.7	—

Sources: Calculated from U.S. Bureau of the Census, Negroes in the United States, 1920–1932, p. 212; and Fifteenth Census of the United States: 1930, Population, Vol. 2, pp. 1099, 1106–1107.
[a] South defined as the three census divisions: South Atlantic, East South Central, West South Central; North and West defined as the rest of Continental United States (including Missouri).

Table 4 shows that Negroes are below whites in school attendance to the extent of about 9.6 per cent in the South and 5.3 per cent in the North. Within the South, rural areas have a greater discrepancy (between whites and Negroes) than do urban areas.[30]

While the quantitative, though not qualitative, discrepancy between Negro and white education is disappearing, the lack of schools for Negroes in the past is reflected today in the statistics on educational status of adults (Table 5). The average Negro past the age of 25 years is reported to have had 5.7 years of schooling, as compared to 8.8 years for the average native white person. The education of rural-farm Negroes (practically all Southern) has been least complete: 15 per cent have had no formal education at all, and almost 60 per cent never reached the fifth grade. Only 5.5 per cent of rural-farm Negroes (compared to 28.1 per cent of rural-farm native whites) have received any high school training whatsoever. In the country as a whole only 1.2 per cent of adult Negroes are college graduates (compared to 5.4 per cent of native whites) and only 7.1 per cent can claim to be high school graduates (compared to 28.6 per cent of the native whites). Clearly the formal education of the Negro population is greatly inferior to

TABLE 5

YEARS OF SCHOOL COMPLETED, BY PERSONS 25 YEARS OLD AND OVER, BY RACE,
FOR THE UNITED STATES, RURAL AND URBAN AREAS: 1940

| | PERCENTAGE DISTRIBUTION | | | | | | | |
| | United States | | Urban | | Rural Nonfarm | | Rural Farm | |
Years Completed	Native White	Negro	Native White	Negro	Native White	Negro	Native White	Negro
Persons 25 years and over	100.0	100.0	100.0	100.0	100.0	100.0	100.0	100.0
No school years completed	1.3	10.0	0.8	6.6	1.7	12.7	2.5	15.0
Grade School:								
1 to 4 years	6.1	31.3	3.7	23.7	7.3	35.5	11.1	44.1
5 and 6 years	9.7	21.5	7.5	21.3	10.8	21.4	14.6	21.9
7 and 8 years	36.0	19.8	33.6	24.8	36.1	16.5	42.7	11.7
High School:								
1 to 3 years	17.3	8.5	18.7	11.5	16.9	6.4	13.7	3.6
4 years	16.6	4.1	20.1	6.2	14.5	2.4	8.9	1.0
College:								
1 to 3 years	6.6	1.8	7.5	2.6	6.5	1.4	4.0	0.6
4 years and more	5.4	1.2	7.0	1.8	4.7	0.9	1.5	0.3
Not reported	1.1	1.8	1.0	1.5	1.4	2.7	1.1	1.8
Median school years completed	8.8	5.7	9.6	6.8	8.6	5.0	8.0	4.1

Source: *Sixteenth Census of the United States: 1940, Population,* Preliminary Release, Series P-10, No. 8

that of the native white population even in number of school years completed—disregarding the still more inferior *quality* of Negro education in the South.

The situation is dynamic: education for Negroes is improving. The percentage of Negro children who remain in school beyond the fourth grade rose from 18 in 1921 to 20 in 1936.[31] At a later point we shall note the striking recent increase in high schools for Negroes. But Negro children

TABLE 6

RATIO OF NEGRO TO WHITE PUPILS IN PUBLIC SCHOOLS BY GRADES
IN 18 SOUTHERN STATES: 1933–1934

Grade	Ratio of Negro to White Pupils Enrolled	Grade	Ratio of Negro to White Pupils Enrolled
1	.631	8	.141
2	.396	9	.135
3	.360	10	.112
4	.328	11	.099
5	.288	12	.091
6	.252	Post-Graduate	
7	.200	High School	.013
		Kindergarten	.087

Source: Calculated from data in Doxey A. Wilkerson. *Special Problems of Negro Education* (1939) pp. 166-168. Wilkerson takes his data from U.S. Office of Education, *Biennial Survey of Education in the United States: 1932-1934,* Bulletin No. 2 (1935), pp. 56-57 and 96.

still lag far behind white children in education. There is a much stronger tendency for Negroes than for whites to drop out of school at lower grades. While the ratio of Negroes to whites in the first grade in the 18 Southern states (1933-1934) is .631, the ratio drops to .141 in the eighth grade and to .091 in the twelfth grade (Table 6). The "holding power" of the Negro school is low at all levels. The reasons for this are in the whole character of the caste relation in the South. This tendency for Negroes to drop out of school more than do whites stops at the college level. Of all high school graduates over 25 years of age in the country (1940), a slightly greater proportion of Negroes than of whites have gone to college (42.6 per cent compared to 41.9 per cent).[32] Of course, a much smaller proportion of all Negroes than of whites goes to college, but once Negroes have attained high school graduation, they have a slightly better chance of going to college. This reversal is probably due to the tremendous difficulties the Negro child encounters in getting as far as high school graduation, to the relative lack of opportunities for Negro high school graduates, and to the relatively better opportunities for college-trained Negroes.[a]

It is unnecessary to take up the Negro school in the North since it hardly exists as a separate entity. Most of the Negro children in the North are separated from white children because of a small amount of legal segregation, a moderate amount of forced illegal segregation, and a large amount of coercive but not illegal separation (connected with housing segregation and the system of gerrymandered districts and permits).[b] But there is little difference between Negro and white schools in the North either in quality of instruction and facilities or in the content of the courses. What there is, is due to the rapid migration of the Negroes to the North, which has caused an undue over-crowding of schools and an over-burdening of teachers. But this lag in adjusting facilities to increased enrollment would seem to carry with it no discrimination, and would probably disappear shortly after the end of large-scale migration. The teachers of Negro children are as well trained as the teachers of white children, except possibly for the selection which occurs when a white teacher avoids teaching in a school attended almost entirely by Negro students.

There is practically no attention paid to Negro problems or Negro students' needs in the Northern school. Except for a few all-Negro colleges, Negroes in Northern colleges are a small proportion of the student population, and except for a certain amount of social ostracism, they are not

[a] See end of Chapter 13. The explanation is not that college enrollment is so much more common in the North generally. The proportion of those over 25 who have had at least one year of college is the same in the South as in the North (not including the Pacific or Mountain states): 9.2 to 9.5. (*Sixteenth Census of the United States: 1940, Population*, Preliminary Release, Series P-10, No. 8.)

[b] See Chapter 29, Section 6.

treated differently than are white students.[a] The main reason why the average Negro gets an education inferior to the average white in the North is that poverty and disease keep him out of school more and force him to leave school at an earlier age. The rising legal minimum age for leaving school—all Northern states having some sort of compulsory attendance law since the Civil War—and the lack of employment opportunities, especially during the depression of the 1930's, have tended to reduce this differential, except at the college level. The school, outside of the activity of educating the young, is not important in the life of the Northern Negro community —a general characteristic of all schools in Northern cities where Negroes live. Only one aspect of Northern education for Negroes requires special attention: like white students, Negro students in the North are inculcated with the American Creed and with the traditional American virtues of efficiency, thrift, ambition, and so on. But employment opportunities—and to a lesser extent, some of the other "good" things of life—are so closed to them that these school-bred attitudes create special conflicts in their minds and cause them to become especially cynical with regard to them.[b] But this cynicism is by way of defense, and their deprivations cause the Northern Negro youth to place the highest value on the American Creed and the American virtues.

The situation in the South, however, is different. While the federal and state constitutions require equal educational facilities for Negroes and whites, and the pretense is kept up that the constitutional requirements are met by "separate but equal" school systems: actually, however, the educational facilities for Negroes are far inferior to those for whites except at a few universities supported by Northern philanthropy or by the federal government. To a great degree this is inevitable where two parallel segregated school systems must be maintained.[c] The richer Northern communities, with a smaller proportion of Negroes, find it a drain on the budget to support a single decent school system, much less two. The insufficient support of Negro schools in the South is reflected in a complete lack of schools in some rural areas, an insufficient number of schools in other areas, a grave lack of equipment, a lack of enforcement of the truancy laws for Negroes, an inferior quality of teacher training, differential payment to teachers, and miserably poor standards all around. The situation has been so bad that Southern Negroes have lost much of the faith in education they once had.

In the rural South the one-room school house for Negroes is fairly typical, with the whole range of elementary grades taught by a single teacher in a

---

[a] Except at the graduate level, when instructors in the social sciences expect Negro students to study Negro problems.

[b] See Chapter 36.

[c] See Chapter 15, Section 3; and Chapter 41.

single room. Where Negroes are a small element in the population, Negro school houses may be far apart (cases have been reported where an elementary school child has had to travel up to eighteen miles every day). The authorities are very discriminatory in providing bus services for Negro pupils.[a] School buses are generally provided for rural whites, but are rarely provided for Negroes. Some Negro families have to pay for private bus service, and others board their children in town.[33] The alternative is not to go to school at all, an alternative followed by some discouraged Negro families. There is a special need for school bus service in rural areas, since adequate schools cannot be paid for unless they serve many children residing over a wide area. But the "consolidation of schools" movement has hardly begun for rural Negro schools in the South, although it is well-developed for the white schools.

Another handicap of a financial nature is that Negro children must sometimes provide all their own books and other school supplies; white children get these things free. The content of the elementary education in the rural South is almost unbelievably poor in the eyes of the outsider; a poorly trained[b] and poorly paid[c] Negro woman[d] must control and teach a group of children from a poor and uncultured home background, in an overcrowded,[e] dilapidated,[f] one-room[g] school house, where she must perform at least some of the janitorial and administrative duties. She is also subject to unusual outside pressure.[h]

The Negro school in the rural South is kept open only about seven

[a] While Negroes constituted 28 per cent of the pupils enrolled in the public schools of 10 Southern states (1935-1936) and were 34 per cent of the rural-farm population aged 5 to 17 (1930), they received only 3 per cent of the total expenditures for transportation (1935-1936). (Compiled from a variety of government reports by Wilkerson, *op. cit.*, p. 19.)

[b] See Chapter 14, Section 4.

[c] See Chapter 15, Section 3.

[d] Of all teachers in public elementary and secondary schools in the 18 Southern states in 1935-1936, 80.6 per cent were women. (Blose and Caliver, *op. cit.*, p. 12.)

[e] The average pupil load per teacher in 18 Southern states in 1933-1934 was 43 for Negroes and 34 for whites. (*Biennial Survey of Education: 1932-1934*, pp. 64-65, and 93-94 and 99; compiled by Wilkerson, *op. cit.*, p. 21.)

[f] The average value of school property in 10 Southern states in 1935-1936 was $36 per Negro pupil and $183 per white pupil. (Compiled from various government publications by Wilkerson, *op. cit.*, p. 31.)

The literature is replete with descriptions of how dilapidated the rural Negro school houses are: see, for example, *ibid.*, pp. 28-29; Ambrose Caliver, *Rural Elementary Education among Negroes under Jeanes Supervising Teachers*, U. S. Office of Education, Bulletin No. 5, (1933); John G. Van Deusen, *The Black Man in White America* (1938), pp. 164-166.

[g] Sixty-five per cent of all the Negro public schools in Louisiana are one-teacher schools, and another 27 per cent are two- or three-teacher schools (Charles S. Johnson, "The Negro Public Schools," p. 43).

[h] See Chapter 40, Section 1.

months a year; Negro children must work in the fields in planting and harvesting seasons, and the white planters give the signal for the Negro school to curtail its session, to close or to open. There is a low attendance generally because transportation is so poor for Negroes, because they must help around the house, because they are frequently ill or have insufficient clothing, because there is practically no enforcement of truancy regulations.[a] The white schools, in contrast, operate for eight or nine months a year, with fixed opening and closing dates, and with fairly rigorously applied truancy regulations. The secondary school situation for Negroes in the rural South is much worse, since there are so few secondary schools, and they are so far apart. As a consequence, Negro children come out of their school system—both elementary and secondary—very poorly educated. All studies show them to be far below the national average in scholastic achievement.[34]

Standards of teacher selection are low in the rural South. If a Negro girl knows a white member of the school board or any influential white person, she can be fairly sure of getting a teaching job even though she never completed high school. Sometimes there is the formality of passing an "examination" to get a teacher's certificate. The low standard of selection of the Negro school teacher, her usually inadequate ability to teach, and her extreme dependence on white men, give her a fairly low status in the rural Negro community. To the extent that she has been educated, however, she can attain a higher status. The teacher and the school house are usually integrated into the Negro community, since the teacher's social life is bound up with that of the parents of her pupils, and the school house is usually used for community purposes. Although all rural people probably have a sense of possessiveness for their local school house and use it for a variety of purposes, rural Southern Negroes have a special pride in theirs since they help to collect the money for it and sometimes they actually build and furnish it. Some teachers have succeeded in organizing Parent-

[a] The average number of days in a school year in 18 Southern states in 1935-1936 was 167 for whites and 146 for Negroes. The worst state was Mississippi, where the average school term was 145 for whites and 119 for Negroes. The discrepancy was even greater in Louisiana and South Carolina, although the absolute figures were not so low. In addition, Negro children failed to attend classes quite as frequently as white children so that their average number of days attended was only 113, as compared to 136 for whites. (See Blose and Caliver, *op. cit.*, p. 35.) These figures are so high because no separation is made between rural and urban schools. In Southern cities, Negro and white schools usually have the same length of term, but in rural areas of the Deep South, "terms of three and four months' duration are by no means uncommon . . ." (Bond, *op. cit.*, p. 291.) Further, as one superintendent in Louisiana said, "You can't afford to enforce compulsory school laws for the Negro children. As it is, their schools are too crowded, and we hardly know what to do with the ones we have. If all of them were in school that should be there, we'd have a school problem that the school board just wouldn't know how to handle." (Cited in Charles S. Johnson, "The Negro Public Schools," p. 125.)

Teacher Associations, and these have been of material advantage to both parents and teachers.[a]

There is a clear tendency to avoid civics and other social sciences in the Southern Negro public schools. They are not taught to any extent in the white schools, but a special effort is made to prevent Negroes from thinking about the duties and privileges of citizenship. In some places there are different school books for Negroes and whites, especially in those fields that border on the social. Where white students are taught the Constitution and the structure of governments, Negroes are given courses in "character building," by which is meant courtesy, humility, self-control, satisfaction with the poorer things of life, and all the traits which mark a "good nigger" in the eyes of the Southern whites. The content of the courses for Negroes throughout the South, except at the colleges with a tradition dating back to the "classical" influence of the New England "carpetbagger," is molded by the caste system at every turn. For example: a leaflet sent out by a privately controlled and privately supported North Carolina "Institute"— something meant to be a cross between a technical high school and a technical college—describes its course of study as follows:

> While the school gives a thorough English Education, it must be remembered that it is strictly moral, religious and industrial. Every boy and girl is taught practical Politeness, Farming, Housekeeping, Laundry, Dressmaking, Printing, Cooking, Brickmasonry, Plastering, and Automobile Mechanics. Students are taught self-reliance, race pride, independent man and womanhood. They are encouraged to remain at their homes in the South, to buy land, assist their fathers and mothers and to educate their fellows.

To repeat: this is the course of study at a privately supported school at almost the college level. It is probably an exceptionally poor school, but it illustrates what does exist. Publicly supported elementary schools for Negroes in the South put out no such statements regarding courses of study.

There is a strong element of the vocational in the education of Southern Negroes. Rural boys are given courses in agriculture; urban boys are given courses in the manual arts; and girls are given courses in home economics. Since little money is made available to teach such courses[b]—and adequate teaching of them requires a good deal of expensive equipment—and since the teachers are often inadequately trained, the courses are usually on a low level. The range of these courses, too, is restricted: for the most part, Negroes are taught only how to be farmers, semi-skilled workers and

[a] While rural Negro teachers are integrated into the community, they are usually not active in it and belong to few civic organizations other than the P.T.A. (Charles S. Johnson, "The Negro Public Schools," pp. 100-101.)

[b] Negroes receive little of the money made available for vocational education by the federal government, since the state legislatures misappropriate the funds. See Chapter 15, Section 3

servants. Negroes who have succeeded in becoming businessmen have usually gone through the regular academic curriculum rather than the vocational schools. Except for the private schools, which train for skilled work, vocational education for Negroes in the South has usually meant training to do more efficiently the traditional menial "Negro job." Little attention has been paid to the fact that a changing economy has created a serious over-population in agriculture and even in domestic service. The teaching of *new* occupations to Negroes is even further from whites' minds than the teaching of the older, but desirable, occupations. Vocational education in the public schools of the South has also served as a means to keep Negroes from getting the general education given to whites, since it is felt —with good reason—that an academic education would make Negroes ambitious and dissatisfied with a low occupation, would "ruin a good field hand." Vocational education for Negroes in the North has had none of these degrading traits, and a larger proportion of Negroes in high schools has been getting vocational training in the North than in the South.[35]

Educational conditions for Southern Negroes are better in the cities than in the rural areas. Negroes live closer together, and the local governments are thus more willing to build more and better schools. There are no problems of having the schools too far apart, of closing down the schools for planting and harvest season, of having all grades under one teacher in one room. The teachers are better trained, in some cases better trained than white teachers in the same cities, since Negro women who go to college have few opportunities outside of the city school systems.[36] They also achieve a measure of independence.[a] While the quality and quantity of education in the city schools is better than in the country schools, the subjects taught and their content are about the same. The Negro school teachers in the Southern cities usually have a high status in the Negro community and often are looked up to as leaders in social life and general activities.[37]

High schools for Negroes in the South have existed in significant numbers for only about twenty years[b] and are still inadequate. In 18 Southern states (1933-1934), only 19 Negro children out of 100 aged 14 to 17 (1930) were attending public high schools, as compared to 55 white children in the same Southern states and to 60 children in the nation as a whole.[c] These low figures are not entirely due to the lack of public high schools for Negroes, but are tied up with the whole educational and social

---

[a] See Chapter 41, Section 1.

[b] In 1915-1916 there were only 64 *public* high schools for Negroes in the 18 Southern states and more than half of these were in 4 states—Kentucky, West Virginia, Tennessee and Texas. There were also 216 *private* high schools in that year. In 1935-1936 there were 2,305 *public* high schools in these states, and in 1932-1933, 92 *private* high schools. (Blose and Caliver, *op. cit.*, p. 8.)

[c] The worst state for Negroes was again Mississippi, where 7 Negro children out of 100, as compared to 66 white children out of 100, attended public high school. (Wilkerson, *op. cit.*, pp. 36-37.)

structure of the South: Negro children tend to drop out of elementary school, partly because the family is poor and they are needed for work, partly because schools are so inaccessible, and partly because instruction is so inferior. But the lack of high schools is also important: Wilkerson points out that there was one white high school teacher for every 11 white seventh grade (elementary school) pupils but only one Negro high school teacher for every 20 Negro seventh grade (elementary) school pupils.[38] Although two-thirds of all Southern Negroes live in rural areas, only 508 of the 1,077 Negro high schools in 18 Southern states (1933-1934) were in rural areas, and they enrolled only 21 per cent of the total number of Negro pupils in public high schools in these states.[39]

The Negro public junior college is practically nonexistent in the South, since there were only 5 of them in 16 Southern states (1933-1934), enrolling only 706 students.[40] In addition, Negroes had 17 private junior colleges, enrolling another 1,344 students. The colleges proper present a comparable situation. Negroes constituted 25 per cent of the population 18 through 21 years of age in 17 Southern states (1930) but only 6 per cent of the public college enrollment (1933-1934).[41]

Of the 117 Negro institutions of higher learning in the United States (1932-1933), only 36 were public. More than half of these public colleges were land-grant institutions—largely stimulated and supported by the federal government; of the 81 private colleges, all but seven were church-affiliated. Most of these colleges did not have the teachers and school facilities to provide an adequate education.[a] Before 1937, only 5 Negro institutions offered instruction at the graduate level.[42] After that year, when the federal courts declared that a state must offer equal educational opportunities to Negroes, several Southern states forced ill-equipped public Negro colleges to assume graduate instruction. For all practical purposes, however, it may still be claimed that only 3 or 4 Negro institutions have real graduate instruction, and none of them offers the Ph.D. degree.

The whole Southern Negro educational structure is in a pathological state. Lack of support, low standards, and extreme dependence on the whites make Negro education inadequate to meet the aims of citizenship, character or vocational preparation. While illiteracy is being eliminated, this is only in a formal sense—since children who are taught to read and write and do arithmetic seldom make use of these abilities. Still there are many educational opportunities for Negroes, and the situation is far better than it was at the close of the Civil War. The concept of education for

---

[a] By 1939, the Southern Association of Colleges and Secondary Schools had awarded Class "A" rating to only 18 Negro colleges, and 4 Negro junior colleges. (Fred McCuistion, *Graduate Instruction for Negroes in the United States* [1939], pp. 29-30.) In addition to these, 3 public and 2 private institutions had been accredited in 1938 by the North Central Association and the Middle States Association. In the 11 states under the Southern Association, 46 per cent of the white colleges are accredited but only 22 per cent of the Negro colleges. (Wilkerson, *op. cit.*, p. 70.)

Negroes is hardly questioned any longer. The complete educational ladder is available to practically all Northern Negroes and to most of the Southern Negroes who live in large Southern cities. At least the rudiments of an education are available even to the rural Southern Negroes. There is considerable educational opportunity at the college level, even in the South. The general trend toward improved education is helping the Negro, even if he does not share in the new opportunities as much as do whites.

5. VOLUNTARY ASSOCIATIONS

As many foreign observers have pointed out,[43] America has an unusual proliferation of social clubs, recreational organizations, lodges, fraternities and sororities, civic improvement societies, self-improvement societies, occupational associations, and other organizations which may be grouped under the rubric of "voluntary associations." While this is true of Americans generally, Negroes seem to have an even larger relative number of associations. In Chicago in 1937, when the total Negro population of the city was less than 275,000, there were over 4,000 formal associations, the membership of which was wholly or largely Negro.[44] In Natchez, Mississippi, where the total Negro population was about 7,500, there were more than 200 Negro associations discovered in one week in 1935.[45] This characteristic of the Negro community becomes even more striking when it is realized that generally upper and middle class people belong to more associations than do lower class people.[46] Thus, despite the fact that they are predominantly lower class, Negroes are more inclined to join associations than are whites; in this respect again, Negroes are "exaggerated" Americans. Only a small number of the Negro associations had as their primary purpose to protest against caste or to improve the Negro community in some way;[47] these protest and improvement associations were considered in Chapter 39. Here we shall give brief consideration to the many associations which have a "sociable" or "expressive" function. With rare exceptions, these associations have only Negroes as members, and their large number is in some measure a product of the prohibitions against having Negro members in white associations.

Max Weber has sought to explain the numerous social clubs in America as a means of helping people to business, political and social success.[48] This is only partly true for American Negroes. It is undoubtedly the reason why upper and middle class Negroes belong to more voluntary associations than do lower class Negroes.[49] But it does not serve to explain why Negroes have relatively more associations than do whites, or why lower class Negroes are members of as many associations as they are. Membership in their own segregated associations does not help Negroes to success in the larger American society. The situation must be seen as a pathological one: Negroes are active in associations because they are not allowed to be active in much of the other organized life of American society. As Robert R. Moton pointed out,[50] the tremendous amount of club activity among Negroes is, in one sense, a poor substitute for the political activity they would like to participate in but cannot because of caste. Negroes are largely kept out, not only of politics proper, but of most purposive and creative work in trade unions, businessmen's groups, pressure groups, large-scale civic improvement and charity organizations, and the like.

A second reason why we regard the huge number of voluntary associations among Negroes as pathological is that some of them—especially the lodges—would seem to follow a pattern which is about a generation behind the general American pattern. Whereas in white America the lodges—with their secret rites and elaborate ritual—began to become unpopular at least thirty years ago, the decline of Negro lodges occurred, not because they became unpopular, but because they failed to pay insurance premiums. The most serious decline of Negro lodges has occurred in the last ten years.[51] And when lodge membership did decline among Negroes, the lower class people who left lodges simply joined religious sects, rather than disentangle themselves completely from such old-fashioned groups, as did whites.[52] The content of the meetings of the Negro sociable groups, even outside the old-fashioned lodges, also reveals the lag in their adaptation to modern American standards. The meetings are often heavily formalized, in the manner of white upper class clubs of a generation or two ago. Strict rules of parliamentary procedure are followed in the "business" meetings; the "entertainment" consists, with little variation, of card-playing, lectures, or recitals; a complete roster of officers is elected even if there are less than a dozen members in the entire club; in upper class clubs formal dress is required at certain of the meetings.[a]

Another reason why we regard the great number of Negro voluntary associations as a sign of social pathology is that they accomplish so little in comparison to what their members set out to achieve by means of them. A large number of the associations—including not a few of the "social"

---

[a] "Behavior at club meetings is rather rigidly stereotyped—(1) business, while visitors wait in another room, (2) card playing, (3) eating, (4) a period of rather general unorganized conversation and hilarity. There are wide variations, however, in the nature of the 'business' discussed and in the amount of formality involved. The bulk of the clubs are very formal in their conduct of business, having a parliamentarian to correct the group on points of order, even when only four or five members are present. Since there is a great deal of inter-club visiting, the clubs are careful about 'doing things in an orderly manner' so that they will not get a 'bad reputation.' Some clubs play whist, but the bulk of them play auction bridge; a few play contract. A few vary the procedure by the use of popular games such as 'Pick-up-sticks,' 'Lexicon,' or 'Pit.'

"Ranking within the club world depends partly upon the elaborateness of the entertaining and the orderliness of meetings. Clubs range from the very formal middle-aged women's groups of upper-middle class to the rather rough behavior of younger upper-lower class (or even middle-aged lower class groups.) On the whole, however, the standards of the club world operate to stereotype the behavior." (Drake, "The Negro Church and Associations in Chicago," pp. 466-467.)

clubs—claim to be "civic-minded" or interested in improving the "race."[a] They collect money and hold dances or card-parties for such purposes, and they drain off a large part of the Negroes' spare time.[b] Even when they do not claim to be engaged in protest or amelioration, the social clubs and lodges divert to themselves a larger part of the Negro people's time and money than do comparable associations among the whites.[53] This is accentuated by their intense rivalry and heavily formalized activity. Since, as we noted, Negro clubs and lodges do not help their members to business, political, or social success in the same way that white clubs do, much of their activity is wasted effort. Many Negroes are aware of this and talk against it. But the pattern of a "heavy" social life is so traditional in the Negro community that even those who do not like it cannot escape it without cutting off much of their relationship with their fellows and without losing some of their prestige. It is probable that the bulk of the Negroes, including those who make no overt protest against the great proliferation of clubs with ritualized social activity, feel frustrated by it at times. The average sociable club has only one or two dozen members; there is an intense rivalry between clubs for status and an equally intense rivalry between members within any given club for office; the club is often short-lived; it seldom aids the individual to achieve success or raises the level of the "race"; it is time-consuming and the activities undertaken are heavily formalized.

Aside from the above-mentioned differences between Negro and white voluntary associations, they are much alike. Negro associations are apparently modelled after white associations, even if those white models are remnants of a past generation[c] and so appear ludicrous to some white people today.

[a] The athletic associations, the occupational associations, and the Parent-Teacher Associations have definite and limited functions, so that much of what is said about the social clubs, church clubs, "welfare" clubs, and lodges in this paragraph does not apply to the former groups.

[b] Much of the money collected for "charity" by the social clubs goes to pay for the heavy expenses of the entertainment and of the club. (See Drake, "The Negro Church and Associations in Chicago," p. 477 and Davis, op cit., p. 163.)

[c] As we noted above, the Negro social clubs are modelled after upper class white social clubs of the period 1880-1910 or the small town social clubs of today. The Negro lodges were modelled after the white lodges as they have been since 1865. The Negro lodges began when the white lodges refused to take in Negro members, and when white insurance companies refused to accept Negroes as insurance policyholders. There was no attempt to hide the fact that they were imitations of the white lodges: the Eighth Annual Report of the Improved Benevolent and Protective Order of Elks of the World states:

"Like all other secret and benevolent organizations that have been organized, the white order of Elks will not permit colored persons to become members. But there are colored Elks now. . . . Some may try to deprecate the colored Elks but we have the same ritual that the white Elks have. . . . The difference between the white and colored Elks is this: The white order is known as the Benevolent and Protective Order of Elks. Ours is known as the Improved Benevolent and Protective Order of Elks of the World." (Cited by W. E. B. Du Bois (editor), *Economic Cooperation among Negroes* [1907], p. 126).

The distinctive thing about Negro associations has been the death benefit and sickness insurance features of some Negro lodges and benevolent societies. Even this was not a unique trait of Negro organizations, since white lodges frequently have them too. But it was much more developed among Negroes,[54] and it made the lodges of almost equal importance with the churches in the period around 1890.[55] The insurance features of many lodges elicited the only serious praise that has been bestowed upon Negro sociable organizations. A survey edited by Du Bois in 1898 said that the lodges represented the "saving, banking spirit among the Negroes and are the germ of commercial enterprise of a purer type," but at the same time he castigated their "extravagance and waste in expenditure, an outlay for regalia and tinsel."[56] Booker T. Washington saw the secret society as the Negro's means of creating capital, learning business techniques, and teaching the "masses of people habits of saving and of system which they would not otherwise have been able or disposed to learn."[57] But owing to the frequent failure of the lodges and benevolent societies to pay insurance premiums,[a] which has been noticeable since the beginning of the depression in 1929,[58] the lodges have been declining in popularity.[b] Especially the lower classes have left; the middle classes remain for the prestige, power and recreation that the lodges provide. But even the middle classes, and especially the upper classes, are being attracted away from the lodges and toward the business and professional associations, the college and high school fraternities and sororities. Typical of the highest sort of evaluation of the lodges heard today is the one expressed by the secretary of a local Urban League in a Northern city:

> Not much practical value to the community at large but vastly important to the individual who is thereby associated with a definite group. There are a few visionary optimists in each order who think their group can become "a great force for the political and social betterment of the Negro people," but the rest are there because they like to have a good time with the boys, or the girls, and who like the pomp and ceremony and mumbo-jumbo of the meetings—which is as good a reason for joining as any.[59]

Thus, aside from the fact that all Negro groups are inevitably forced to be "race conscious" and that most of them at least pretend to improve the position of the "race," "there is a pronounced tendency . . . for mutual aid associations and civic groups to become recreational associations."[60] It is, therefore, only as a means of recreation that Negro voluntary associations can be given a high evaluation. To determine whether or not such a high evaluation is justified, we shall have to consider, briefly, the general character of recreation and amusement in the Negro community. This we shall do in the following chapter.

[a] See Chapter 14, Section 3.
[b] See footnote 52 to this chapter.

CHAPTER 44

NON-INSTITUTIONAL ASPECTS OF THE
NEGRO COMMUNITY

1. "PECULIARITIES" OF NEGRO CULTURE AND PERSONALITY

The increasing isolation between Negroes and whites has, as we noted,[a] increased the mutual ignorance of the two groups. Lower class Negroes know much of the private side of the lives of the whites since so many of them are servants to whites; upper and middle class Negroes know very little about either the private or the public life of whites. Whites of all classes know even less about Negroes. Because of their lack of intimate contact with Negroes, whites create and maintain stereotypes about them. Most of the stereotypes have no basis in fact, but even those that are superficially true are not understood by whites in terms of their motivation and cultural origin. Even when they do not mean to be unfriendly to Negroes, whites observe that certain aspects of Negro life are "different" or "peculiar." Some of these cultural peculiarities bother whites; all of them are taken into account—consciously or unconsciously—when whites act in regard to Negroes. Since the whites are the dominant group, it is important for Negroes to determine what whites find peculiar about their culture. In this chapter, we shall not attempt to describe all the ways in which the Negro community differs from the white community, but only those non-institutional differences in Negro culture which whites find most unusual or disturbing. We shall start from our conclusion in Chapter 6 that these differences have no basis in biological heredity, that they are of a purely cultural nature.

In this section, we shall sometimes be writing about Negro culture traits as though they applied to all Negroes. This is, of course, incorrect, and it angers many Negroes. There is a diversity of behavior patterns among Negroes, perhaps as great as in white American society with all its diverse national backgrounds. Negro communities range from the folk societies of isolated rural Southern areas to the highly sophisticated wealthy night club groups of Harlem. Much of the diversity among Negroes arises out of a tendency of upper class Negroes to act in a manner just the opposite of lower

[a] See Chapter 30.

class Negroes, and some of it arises out of diverse historical background. We shall try to take account of the diversity, but we feel we are justified in writing of Negro culture traits because *average* Negro behavior differs from *average* white behavior. From a practical standpoint it is necessary to take account of these differences in averages because white people see them and use them to buttress their prejudices.

Because of the isolation between the two groups and because of the fear and suspicion on the part of Negroes toward the whites, it is practically impossible for any white investigator to get completely into the Negro community. We do not claim that we completely understand the Negro community, and no doubt many Negro readers will find some of our observations about them to be naïve or mistaken. Yet the white investigator has two advantages: First, he knows what white people do *not* know about Negroes. Negroes do not realize how ignorant most white people are about the Negro community, and they do not understand how even their white friends may be unaware of certain things about them. Second, Negroes are so thoroughly isolated from white society that they have little basis for comparing their society with white society. Without the objectivity acquired by stepping outside of their own culture, they often cannot see how the Negro community differs from the white. For these two reasons, it may be that the white investigator can more easily determine what whites find "peculiar" in the Negro community and can more easily interpret these peculiarities to the whites. This is not inevitably so, however, and there is need for Negro scholars, with their greater ability to get inside the Negro community, to understand the white man's point of view when they study and describe the Negro community.

The trait which the whites perhaps associate most with Negroes is a tendency to be aggressive.[a] This tendency is remarked about whenever Negroes commit crimes, whenever they are insulting and even whenever they try to rise out of their "place." The tendency is exaggerated in the minds of the whites, and whites are ambivalent in their beliefs since they also frequently speak of the Negroes as docile, subservient and dull. The tendency is exaggerated partly because white newspapers give relatively little news about Negroes other than crime news,[b] partly because of the

[a] Some of the culture traits frequently associated with Negroes have been discussed at length in other chapters and will not be taken up again at this point. For a consideration of Negro immorality, see Chapter 43, Section 2. For a discussion of Negro religious emotionalism, see Chapter 43, Section 3. For a discussion of Negro aping of white manners, see Chapter 32; Chapter 42, Section 3; and Chapter 43, especially Section 5. For a discussion of Negro laziness, inefficiency, and lack of ambition, see Chapter 9, Section 2, and Chapter 10, Section 2. For a consideration of the causes of Negro servility, see Chapter 29, Section 2. For a discussion of racial beliefs in general, see Chapter 4, especially Sections 7 and 8.

[b] See footnote 23 of Chapter 30.

traditional racial stereotypes and partly because many whites do not attribute to Negroes the natural human reactions to insult and deprivation.

Except for the sullen criminal youths found mainly in Northern cities,[a] Negroes seem to be no more aggressive than whites. In view of the fact that they are so frequently discriminated against and insulted, Negroes are remarkably passive and polite toward whites. Negroes have never, since the Civil War, organized to revolt against white domination. They are generally courteous to whites who do not insult them, and even to whites who do. It probably can be generalized that when noncriminal Negroes are called "bumptious," especially in the South, they are merely trying to get their rights as citizens and thus are attempting to rise out of their lower caste status. Another reason why whites, especially Northern whites, find Negroes aggressive or unpleasant is because they have unwittingly insulted them[b] or because they do not understand the Negro's suspicion and fear of whites arising out of the uncertainty of life and property in the South. In the North, too, Negroes may do unpleasant things out of ignorance or appear "bumptious" because they are glad to be free of Southern restrictions.[c]

[a] See Chapter 36, Section 5.

[b] We have noted several times in this book that Negroes are sensitive to insult and that whites, especially Northern whites, insult them unwittingly. When, in November, 1942, Irving Berlin wrote a patriotic song, he used the word "darky" in it and precipitated a storm of protest. He quickly changed the word to Negro and said he had not meant to insult anyone. The following excerpt from a letter to the editor of *Time* magazine is interesting both as an example of unwitting insult and for the list of names by which Negroes like to be described.

"First it was your constant use of the abortive term *Negress*; your farfetched designation of *pickaninnies* in a Chicago department store. . . . Now it is your use of "darky-driven" trucks! . . . Damn!! What is wrong with *Time's* policy toward the American Negro in the last year and a half? It's getting so I can't read an article about the race without being insulted! . . .

"Some terms (adjectives) that might be used in describing Negroes:

"bronzed (conventional but well liked)	coal black (trite)
mighty black	smooth yellow (don't use 'high yaller')
jade black	golden tinted
blue black	mellow (current '38-'40)
huskies	smooth (in place of 'shiny')
Zigaboo (coined by Negroes)	golden brown
Senegambian	chocolate brown (trite)
coffee-colored (used by *Time*)	(*you* add to the list)

Don'ts

"Nigger	darky
Negress	octoroon
pickaninny	quadroon, etc."

(A letter to the editor, *Time* [August 25, 1941], p. 8.)

[c] "If the Negroes in Harlem show at times less courtesy toward white visitors than is required by the canons of good taste, this is bad, but understandable. It was remarked shortly after the first migration that the newcomers on boarding street cars invariably

Next to aggressiveness, probably the most striking trait of Negroes noticed by whites is emotionality and spontaneous good humor. This is given both a high and a low evaluation. On the one hand, the ability to enjoy life is recognized as desirable, and the Negro's music, dancing, literature and art are appreciated by the whites. But on the other hand, lack of self-control and the tendency to act on impulse are deprecated. Negroes have acquired the art of enjoying life more than have whites.[1] Because they have no direct background in puritanism, they have taken sex more as it comes, without all the encumbrances and inhibitions. The relative economic independence of the Negro woman allows her to mate more in the spirit of equality and mutual enjoyment, and less out of a sense of duty or to get economic advantages. Because they have so little money to spend on entertainment and because the white masters in slavery times did not bother to regiment the small amount of free time of the Negroes, the Negroes have learned to enjoy small and inexpensive things and to get as much pleasure as they can out of their free time. The habit of spending a good deal of leisure time out-of-doors, due in part to the over-crowdedness of the Negro home, has contributed to the social pleasantness of Negro life, since being outside involves meeting friends and having no worries about destroying furniture.[a] Negroes also try much harder than do whites to get as much pleasure out of their work as they can.

There is something of the "devil-may-care" attitude in the pleasure-seeking of Negroes. They know that all the striving they may do cannot carry them very high anyway, and they feel the harshness of life—the caste pressures are piled on top of the ordinary woes of the average white man. "So you might as well make the most of it"; "what the hell difference does it make." In this spirit, life becomes cheap and crime not so reprehensible. Thus both the lack of a strong cultural tradition and the caste-fostered trait of cynical bitterness combine to make the Negro less inhibited in a way which may be dangerous to his fellows. They also make him more indolent, less punctual, less careful, and generally less efficient as a functioning member of society.

Because of the false racial belief that Negroes had innate emotional talents to compensate for their low intellectual capacities, whites have seldom hindered the development of the Negro in the artistic fields. In

---

strode to the front even if there were seats in the rear." (Charles S. Johnson, "New Frontage on American Life," in Alain Locke [editor], *The New Negro* [1925], p. 287.)

[a] Negroes do not hesitate to tell how they enjoy life in spite of caste. Claude McKay, for example, says:

"The prison is vast, there is plenty of space and a little time to sing and dance and laugh and love. There is a little time to dream of the jungle, revel in rare scents and riotous colors, croon a plantation melody, and be a real original Negro in spite of all the crackers. Many a white wretch, baffled and lost in his civilized jungles, is envious of the toiling, easy-living Negro." (*A Long Way from Home* [1937], pp. 145-146.)

fact, whites have enjoyed a paternalistic feeling in fostering this development. Negroes have been able to find an economic market for their artistic achievements, and this has fostered still more their development in this field, especially as opportunities are so closed to them in other fields. The pattern of uninhibited singing and dancing into which the Negro child is brought from his earliest years also gives a superb training for achievement in these fields. This trait of singing and dancing is so deep in the American Negro's culture that he sometimes falls into the white man's error of thinking of it as a racial trait: "white people have no rhythm"; "they can't dance with feeling"; "whites are naturally cold."

The good humor that is associated with the Negro's emotionalism is the outcome, not only of the attempt to enjoy life to its fullest, but of stark fear of the white man. Much of the humor that the Negro displays before the white man in the South is akin to that manufactured satisfaction with their miserable lot which the conquered people of Europe are now forced to display before their German conquerors. The loud high-pitched cackle that is commonly considered as the "Negro laugh" was evolved in slavery times as a means of appeasing the master by debasing oneself before him and making him think that one was contented. Negroes still "put it on" before whites in the South for a similar purpose. They also use it when they are entirely among themselves—in the same way as they use the hated term "nigger."

In a similar manner, the Negro slave developed a cleverness in language which is akin to the "bright sayings" of children. Like the "Negro laugh," he found that a clever remark amused the white man and often staved off punishment or brought rewards.

No master could be thoroughly comfortable around a sullen slave; and, conversely, a master, unless he was utterly humorless, could not overwork or brutally treat a jolly fellow, one who could make him laugh. The famous black-face minstrels by white performers get their suggestion from the plantation entertainers. The most important use of humor to the Negro, however, was in his personal relations with his white master. The master says to a young slave, "You scoundrel, you ate my turkey," and the slave replies, "Yes, suh, Massa, you got less turkey but you sho' got more nigger." The slave lives to eat another turkey and the master has another entertaining story.[a]

[a] W. D. Weatherford and C. S. Johnson, *Race Relations* (1934), p. 284. Preceding the statement quoted in the text, Johnson gives the following analysis of Negro humor:

"The humor of the Negro has been regarded as one of his native characteristics. It is, indeed, one of the useful contributions of the race to the grim struggle of America for progress and wealth. This humor has enlivened the public and private stage, the joke columns of the press, and countless after-dinner speeches. It has made entertainment without end for the smoking cars of the railroad trains. Since the native African is not a very humorous person, it seems most likely that this quality of humor was developed in slavery, and there is just as good reason for regarding it as a survival trait."

In one other way the Negro's humor has grown out of the caste situation, not out of fear of it but out of contempt for it: the Negro tries, in all sorts of ways, to express his hatred of the prejudiced white man. Such cynical humor travels in the Negro community as do the anti-dictator jokes in the totalitarian countries of Europe:

> "It says in the white folks' newspaper that our women are trying to ruin the white folks' homes by quitting their jobs as maids."
> "Yeah. A lot of white women are mad because they have to bring up their own children."

Like the Negro's cackling laugh and appeasing humor, his "dumbness" has been developed as an accommodation to caste. There is no gainsaying the fact that most Negroes are extremely ignorant: they have no tradition of learning; they have had unusually bad schools in a region generally noted for the poverty of its education; their interests are often so closely restricted to the Negro problem that they have not developed knowledge of other things; they are forcibly isolated from white society so that they often cannot know what is expected from them in the way of manners. Yet, in addition to all this actual ignorance, there is a good deal of pretended ignorance on the part of the Negro. To answer certain questions posed to them by white people in the South is a way of getting both themselves and their fellows in trouble. So they feign inability to understand certain questions. To volunteer information is often a sure way of being regarded as "uppity" by whites. So they restrict their conversation to what is necessary or customary. And they act humble, which also gives them an air of "dumbness." The aggressive Negro, the one who talks the most in an effort to impress others with his cleverness, is likely to be more ignorant and less intelligent than most of the humble or reserved Negroes. Actually, Negroes tend to be clever in their petty guilefulness. Some of the falsehoods told by Negroes—and lying is another of the traits in the stereotype of the Negro—have their cause in the fear or suspicion of the white man.[2] In other cases Negroes may lie to whites in resentment against the caste system. Among themselves, Negroes are probably not given to lying, humility, "dumbness" or reservedness any more than whites are. In fact, they are inclined to be talkative and witty. Some of their talk is malicious gossip and detraction of others: there is naturally much jealousy among the members of a suppressed group when one of them rises or gets any privileges. There is intense competition among all those Negroes who feel that they have a chance to rise. The individualism of Negroes, their inability to "hang together," their bitter competition and jealousy are commented upon by white observers and deplored by Negro leaders.[3]

Another trait attributed to the Negro and connected with emotionalism is a love of the gaudy, the bizarre, the ostentatious.[a] The lower and middle class Negroes have their lodges with all their pomp and ceremony. If they can afford it, they wear colorful clothing of unusual style. Their social gatherings are made expensive by good food, display and excellent entertainment. The Negro's reputation for conspicuous display is, of course, exaggerated, because most Negroes do not have the money to be ostentatious: so many of them wear the cast-off clothing of white people and live in tiny shacks and flats. White people often generalize about the Negro race from a single observation: a Negro racketeer driving a gaudy, expensive car will cause thousands of white people to remark about the ostentatiousness of Negroes. What there is of color and pomp in their lodges and social gatherings is a sort of lag in acculturation, a misguided attempt to gain status by conspicuous consumption. Negroes have no more of this than do immigrant white groups and even many poor *native* white groups. Some of what appears exotic to whites is simply a result of the development of unique culture traits: a group which is kept so forcibly isolated as are the Negroes is bound to initiate a few such traits even though the great bulk of their behavior patterns are those which are common to all Americans. An example of such a trait is that which has come to be known as a "zoot suit": a man's suit with broad-seated and narrow-cuffed trousers and a long suit-coat, usually worn with a wide-brimmed hat. This suit, inci-

---

[a] This trait, as well as the connected Negro trait of audaciousness, is characteristic of white Southerners too, and it may be that Negroes have taken on the trait from the whites.

"White southerners employ many of the same defense mechanisms characteristic of the Negro. They often carry a 'chip on the shoulder'; they indulge freely in self-commiseration; they rather typically and in real Negro fashion try to overcome a feeling of inferiority by exhibitionism, raucousness, flashiness in dress, and an exaggerated self-assertion. An air of belligerency, discreetly employed when it can be done without risk, is one means of release for the individual who feels himself the underdog. A casual observation of the conduct of southern law-makers in the chambers of Congress will be sufficient to demonstrate that southern legislators, taken as a group, are more abusive, indulge in personalities and more rough and tumble repartee than the legislators from any other section. What spice there is in the Congressional Record is furnished by the southerners, whether it be a Cole Blease, a Heflin or a 'Cotton Ed' Smith delivering one of the notorious diatribes against the Negro, (including a discourse on how permanent is the odor of the Negro), or a Huey Long giving one of his opponents a 'dressing down' with enough insulting innuendo to have caused gun-play in the old days (and enough even today to have gotten Huey's nose punched now and then, it was rumored). The southerner is proficient too, at conjuring up arguments to show how shabbily the South has been treated. Like the Negro, the white South holds out its hands for alms and special privilege. A Georgia planter, bitterly anti-New Deal, was not at all moved by the assertion that a lot of northern money was being sent South in relief and other New Deal activities. 'We *oughta* be gittin' some of it back; they stole enough from us in the war,' he drawled. It is well-known in the inside circles of some of the national academic societies that southern members put in special claims for representation among the office-holders on the grounds that 'the South is discriminated against,' and they often got recognition." (Ralph J. Bunche, "Memorandum on Conceptions and Ideologies of the Negro Problem," unpublished manuscript prepared for this study [1940], pp. 71-73.)

dentally, has been borrowed by white youths in America who consider themselves experts on jazz music (also of Negro origin) and by pseudo-sophisticated lower class youths of certain European countries.

There are some special reasons why Negro clothing may look bizarre to white people: first, pieces of cast-off clothing may not go well together even though each piece looked all right when it was worn with its original counterpart. Second, that clothing which looks well on most white people may look foolish or odd on Negroes, because of the different skin color and features. Third, those who try to fit their clothing to their skin color and features may select things that are strange and exotic to conservative whites. Sometimes the adjustment of clothing to physical traits is successful: white clothing on dark skin often achieves a beautiful effect. Another interesting adjustment is the Negro woman's use of red lipstick on the eyelids to make her eyes appear larger, whereas white women use blue, brown, or black eye shadow to achieve the same effect.

Upper class Negroes, in their attempt to avoid the unfavorable traits commonly associated with Negroes, are conservative in their dress and public behavior. They avoid everything that is loud, gaudy and cheap. But they also are driven by a desire for status and so engage in conspicuous consumption of another type. They imitate the staid, old-fashioned patterns of those upper class white people who have not become emancipated. Their clothes are most "respectable" and most expensive; their homes—though small—are furnished in "good taste"; their social gatherings are costly and ceremonial. They even go to extremes of conspicuous consumption in their desire to gain status, as many other channels of gaining status are closed to them.[4] They try to copy the "highest" standards of white people and yet get absolutely no recognition for doing so.

The struggle for status manifests itself frequently in speech and this, too, may become ostentatious. With education valued so highly, and with so little of it available to them, Negroes often try to exhibit an education which they do not have. In speech this takes the form of the misuse of big words. The trait is manifested not only in the pompous oratory of many Negroes but also in their everyday conversations. On other occasions the big words are used properly, but they are out of place in simple conversation. The correct but misplaced use of big words also originates in an attempt to gain status, and is probably a survival of nineteenth century florid oratory.

The eating of chicken, 'possum, watermelon, corn pone, pork chops is part of the stereotype of the Negro, at least in the North. These things are, of course, either common or delicate foods in the South for both whites and Negroes, and there is no special reason why their consumption should be regarded as a "Negro trait." As a matter of fact, the foods generally consumed by Negroes are far from bizarre: they can seldom afford any but the most prosaic types of foods. And Negroes are at least as cautious as are whites in their distribution of expenditures.[a] The belief that they have so much of the foods they desire seems to have the opportunistic purpose of hiding the fact that Negroes are too poor to buy all the foods they actually need.[b]

Another commonly observed trait of Negroes is their lack of poise, their inability to act in the conventional yet free and easy way expected of adult men and women in America. Much of this is a product of Southern caste etiquette, of course, where Negroes are presumed to be "uppity" if they stand up straight, look into the eyes of the person they are talking to and speak distinctly and to the point. Even in the North, many Southern-born Negroes keep their eyes on the ground, shuffle their feet, wiggle their bodies, and talk in a roundabout manner. Even when they want to get away from the Southern caste etiquette, many Negroes lack poise in their contacts with whites out of a sense of insecurity. Like adolescent youths, many Negroes will either exhibit a startling lack of poise or appear to gain it by putting on a cold front and acting mechanically. The uncertainty of the caste etiquette is another factor making for lack of poise: how a Negro is supposed to act before a white man varies with time, locality and the character of the white man. Among themselves, of course, Negroes are as much at ease as white people are.

At all times, even when they have poise, Negroes are secretive about their community when talking to whites.[5] They are suspicious of questions, and, except for stool pigeons who gain something by telling whites what goes on among Negroes, they are loyal to their group. They will usually protect any Negro from the whites, even when they happen not to like that individual Negro. They do not like to talk to whites about their community or about Negroes in general, for fear that anything they say will be twisted around to disparage Negroes. This is true even of Negro intellectuals when they talk to friendly white intellectuals. Negroes are suspicious of whites, even when there is not the slightest ground for being so, and whites seldom realize this.

The Negro's superstitiousness has been given much attention by whites. It is generally assumed that the Negro's superstitions and magical practices are of African origin. There is probably some truth in this assumption, but it has led whites to search out these superstitions and magical practices and to exaggerate them. As Powdermaker says, in referring to the large litera-

[a] Chapter 16, Sections 3 and 5.

[b] Somewhat like the belief that Negroes are addicted to certain foods is their association with dice-throwing. City Negroes do engage in much dice-throwing, but rural Negroes and upper class Negroes do not often engage in this pastime. Crap-shooting is now so much engaged in by whites that there is some doubt whether Negroes shoot craps any more than whites do.

ture on the subject: "It seems doubtful, however, that this emphasis on superstition is in proportion to its importance in the life of the Negro today."[6] As among white people, superstition among Negroes is a survival of an earlier period, and as such it is disappearing as Negroes assimilate modern American culture traits. Upper class Negroes are about as free from superstition and magical practices as upper class whites are, and Negro youth of the lower classes adhere to them only loosely. It is only in the rural areas of the South that these beliefs and practices have a powerful hold on Negroes. It is there that the "voodoo" doctors are still to be found,[7] who use incantations and charms, but often add advice in love or economic cases, and pills in sickness cases in imitation of real doctors. Quack doctors find Negroes easy prey, even in Northern cities.[a]

To the Northern white man, although seldom to the Southern white man, the speech of the Negro seems unusual. In fact, the "Negro dialect" is an important cause of the Northern whites' unconscious assumption that Negroes are of a different biological type from themselves. The present writer found many Northern whites who were amazed when they learned that Negroes could and did speak perfect English. It is not realized that the so-called "Negro dialect" is simply a variation of the ordinary Southern accent which so many Northerners like so well. It is this accent in lower class slang form, with a very small number of uniquely Negro cultural additions. There is absolutely no biological basis for it; Negroes are as capable of pronouncing English words perfectly as whites are.

Northern whites are also unaware of the reasons why they practically never hear a Negro speaking perfect English: First, at least three-fifths of Negroes living in the North are Southern-born,[8] and Negroes tend to retain the accent of their childhood, just as others do. Second, even most Northern-born Negroes were brought up in households and communities where they heard nothing but the "Negro dialect" spoken. School was the only place to learn good English, and many Negroes did not, or could not, take adequate advantage of it. Third, Negroes seem to be proud of their dialect, and frequently speak it even when they know how to speak perfect English. Some upper class Negroes do this to retain prestige and a following among lower class Negroes. In the South a few educated Negroes do

---

[a] A recent case of quackery in New York City is reported in the New York *Herald Tribune* of March 13, 1942 (p. 10). A West Indian Negro ". . . complained that he went to Byron [the quack] last October for treatment for recurrent headaches. The treatment consisted of copious draughts of herbs and bites on the neck, and was neither particularly effective nor worth the $59 charge, according to the complainant. . . . Byron also is known as Saibu Sudens. When using that name he wears a fez, on the grounds that he is part Egyptian, and at other times dons a skullcap in token of his claim that the other part is Jewish." Byron gave his age as 99 years.

For a discussion of superstition and occultism among Negroes in Harlem, see Claude McKay, *Harlem* (1940), pp. 82-85; 105-110.

it to avoid appearing "uppity" in the eyes of the whites. Few Negroes seem to realize that the use of the dialect augments white prejudice, at least in the North. Fourth, most of those who know how to speak perfect English are members of the upper classes, and these are so segregated that a large proportion of the whites can go through their entire lives without hearing one of them speak. The high-toned, pleading voice of the Negro is also associated with his speech. This trait was, of course, developed by the demands of the caste etiquette.

There are only a few dozen words and phrases that are uniquely Negro, except possibly in some isolated Southern rural areas.[9] Some of these words refer to things which are unique to the Negro community—such as "peola" and "high yaller" which refer to skin colors found among Negroes but not among whites. Others refer to things or conditions for which there is no adequate English word—such as "dicty" which means trying to put on airs and act upper class without having the basis for doing so. "Muck-ety-muck" and a few other Negro words have been taken over into general American slang. For the most part, the white American is not aware that there are uniquely Negro words, although he may be vaguely aware that there are some things said when Negroes talk among themselves that he cannot understand.

As more Negroes become educated and urbanized, it may be expected that they will lose their distinctive cultural traits and take over the dominant American patterns. The trend will work slowly, since caste serves to isolate Negroes from American culture and so hampers their assimilation. Still, there is reason to believe that it is more rapid today than it was before. As the trend proceeds, and as there emerges a class of Negroes which is recognized by whites to have the same cultural traits as themselves, the Negro will be thought to be less "peculiar" than he is now. Recognition of increased cultural similarity is not unimportant in the general attitude of whites toward Negroes. Thus cultural assimilation plays a role in the general circular process determining the Negro's status in America.

CRIME[a]

Negro crime has periodically been the subject of serious debate in the United States and, at least since 1890, has often been the object of statistical measurement. Just as the past year has seen an epidemic of reports in New York newspapers of assault and robbery by Negroes, so other periods have seen actual or alleged "crime waves" among Negroes in other areas.

---

[a] In preparing this section we have relied most heavily on an unpublished manuscript prepared for this study: Guy B. Johnson and Louise K. Kiser, "The Negro and Crime" (1940). A part of this study was incorporated in an article by Guy B. Johnson, "The Negro and Crime," *The Annals of the American Academy of Political and Social Science* (September, 1941), pp. 93-104.

At all times the stereotyped notion has prevailed that Negroes have a criminal tendency, which manifests itself in acts ranging all the way from petty thievery by household servants to razor-slashing homicide. The statistical studies of Negro crime have not been consistent in their findings, and each has evoked much criticism in scientific circles. The census of 1890 contained a criticism of its own crime statistics:

> The increase in the number of prisoners during the last 40 years has been more apparent than real, owing to the very imperfect enumeration of the prison population prior to 1880. Whatever it has been, it is not what it might be supposed to be, if we had no other means of judging of it than by the figures contained in the census volumes.[10]

Since that time, there have been many pertinent criticisms of Negro crime statistics.[11] Johnson and Kiser express the attitude of all honest students of Negro crime toward these statistics:

> The statistical data upon which we are forced to base our knowledge of Negro crime measure only the extent and the nature of the Negro's contact with the law and is of value for that purpose. However, our information relates to apparent crime only and not to the actual amount of crime committed by any one group or by the population in general. There is no consistent and measurable relation between apparent and real criminality and, as a result, it is not possible to estimate from available criminal data the amount and proportion of Negro crime or the extent to which it is increasing or decreasing.[12]

This attitude, as well as the conflict of conclusions, is not difficult to understand when one realizes the nature of the statistics on Negro crimes and the character of the legal process which defines a given act as a crime. Crime statistics are generally inadequate, despite a tremendous improvement within the last decade, and Negro crime statistics are further complicated by discrimination in the application of the law and by certain unique traditions. It may be stated categorically that there are no statistics on crimes *per se*: there are only statistics on "crimes known to the police," on arrests, on convictions, on prisoners. Honest studies based on different sets of statistics will give different findings. Crime is not uniformly defined from state to state and from time to time. Statistics on one area at one time will show different conclusions from statistics on another area at another time. Finally, the conclusions of a given study are largely determined by the "factors" one takes into account in analyzing the statistics.

It is necessary to consider all the weaknesses of the statistics on Negro crime because these statistics have been used to buttress stereotypes of Negro criminality and to justify discriminatory practices. Even capable and honest scientists like Walter Willcox have used the available statistics to "prove" Negro criminality.[13] But Willcox did this in 1899; competent scientists are no longer so uncritical of their data. Incompetent popularizers, however, continue to misuse the statistics. In this situation it becomes more important to criticize the statistics than it is to present them. To such a criticism we shall now proceed.

Statistics on Negro crime have not only all the weaknesses of crime statistics generally—such as incomplete and inaccurate reporting, variations between states as to definitions and classification of crimes, changes in policy—but also special weaknesses due to the caste situation and to certain characteristics of the Negro population. One of the basic weaknesses arises out of the fact that those who come in contact with the law are generally only a selected sample of those who commit crimes. Breaking the law is more widespread in America than the crime statistics indicate and probably everyone in the country has broken some law at some time. But only a small proportion of the population is arrested, convicted and sent to prison. Some major crimes (such as violation of the Sherman Anti-Trust Act and avoidance of certain tax payments) are even respectable and are committed in the ordinary course of conducting a business;[14] others (such as fraud and racketeering) are not respectable but are committed frequently and often go unpunished. It happens that Negroes are seldom in a position to commit these white collar crimes; they commit the crimes which much more frequently result in apprehension and punishment. This is a chief source of error when attempting to compare statistics on Negro and white crimes.

In the South, inequality of justice seems to be the most important factor in making the statistics on Negro crime and white crime not comparable. As we saw in Part VI,[a] in any crime which remotely affects a white man, Negroes are more likely to be arrested than are whites, more likely to be indicted after arrest, more likely to be convicted in court and punished. Negroes will be arrested on the slightest suspicion, or on no suspicion at all, merely to provide witnesses or to work during a labor shortage in violation of anti-peonage laws. The popular belief that all Negroes are inherently criminal operates to increase arrests, and the Negro's lack of political power prevents a white policeman from worrying about how many Negro arrests he makes. Some white criminals have made use of these prejudices to divert suspicion away from themselves onto Negroes: for example, there are many documented cases of white robbers blackening their faces when committing crimes.[15] In the Southern court, a Negro will seldom be treated seriously, and his testimony against a white man will be ignored, if he is permitted to express it at all. When sentenced he is usually given a heavier punishment and probation or suspended sentence is seldom allowed him.[16] In some Southern communities, there are no special institutions for Negro juvenile delinquents or for Negro criminals who are

---

[a] Quantitative evidence for this and the following paragraphs may be found not only in Part VI of this book, but also in Johnson and Kiser, op. cit., pp. 65-192.

insane or feeble-minded. Such persons are likely to be committed to the regular jails or prisons, whereas similar white cases are put in a separate institution and so do not swell the prison population.

Some of the "crimes" in the South may *possibly* be committed only by Negroes: only Negroes are arrested for violations of the segregation laws, and sometimes they are even arrested for violation of the extra-legal racial etiquette (the formal charge is "disturbing the peace," "insolence to an officer," "violation of municipal ordinances," and so on). The beating of Negroes by whites in the South is seldom regarded as a crime, but should a Negro lay hands on a white man, he is almost certain to be apprehended and punished severely. As Frazer points out: "In the South, the white man is certainly a greater menace to the Negro's home than the latter is to his."[17] Similarly, when white lawyers, installment collectors, insurance agents, plantation owners, and others, cheat Negroes, they are never regarded as criminals.[18] But stealing by Negroes from whites—beyond that petty stealing which is part of the patriarchal tradition from slavery—is almost always punished as a crime.

In one respect, Southern discrimination against Negroes operates to reduce the Negro's crime record. If a Negro commits a crime against another Negro, and no white man is involved, and if the crime is not a serious one, white policemen will let the criminal off with a warning or a beating, and the court will let him off with a warning or a relatively light sentence. In a way, this over-leniency stimulates greater crimes since it reduces risks and makes law enforcement so arbitrary. Life becomes cheap and property dear in the Negro neighborhood—a situation conducive to crime.

These things occur in the North, too, although in much smaller degree. In the North it is not so much discrimination which distorts the Negro's criminal record, as it is certain characteristics of the Negro population. In the first place, unorganized crime is much more prevalent in the South than in the North, both among whites and among Negroes, and when the Negro migrates North, he brings his high crime rate along with him. Specific cultural practices brought from the South also affect the Negro's crime record in the North: a member of New York's grand jury told the author that part of the high Negro juvenile delinquency and crime rate was due to the Negro practice of fighting with knives instead of with fists, as whites do. "The fights start in the same way among both groups, but the law defines the Negro's manner of fighting as a crime, and the white's manner of fighting as not a crime."[19]

A third impersonal cause of distortion of the Negro's crime record is his poverty: he cannot bribe the policeman to let him off for a petty offense; he cannot have a competent lawyer to defend him in court; and when faced with the alternatives of fine or prison by way of punishment, he is forced to choose prison. The Negro's ignorance acts in a similar fashion: he does not know his legal rights and he does not know how to present his case; thus even an unprejudiced policeman or judge may unwittingly discriminate against him. Also associated with the Negro lower class status in distorting his crime record is his lack of influential connections: he does not know the important people who can help him out of petty legal troubles. In the North, the fact that an unusually large proportion of Negroes are in the age group 15-40, which is the age group to which most criminals belong, operates to make the Negro crime rate based on total population figures deceptively high. Negro concentration in the cities in the North, where the crime rate is generally higher than in rural areas, acts in the same manner. The Negro crime rate is further inflated by greater recidivism: a given number of Negro criminals are sent to jail more often than are the same number of white criminals.[20] The longer prison sentence meted out to Negroes raises the number of Negroes in prison at any one time beyond what it would be if crime statistics reflected only the total number of criminals.

In general, our attitude toward crime statistics must be that they do not provide a fair index of Negro crime. Even if they did, a higher crime rate would not mean that the Negro was more addicted to crime, either in his heredity or in his culture, for the Negro population has certain external characteristics (such as concentration in the South and in the young adult ages) which give it a spuriously high crime rate. With this attitude in mind, we may examine some of the statistics. The most nearly complete, and the most reliable, set of statistics on crime for the nation are the recent annual reports of the United States Bureau of the Census, *Prisoners in State and Federal Prisons and Reformatories*. We shall use the set for 1939, the most recent set available at the time of writing. These statistics have two important weaknesses (in addition to those just reviewed): First, they do not include criminals in local jails, but only those in state and federal prisons and reformatories. For this reason, they do not include most of the petty crimes, and to get a relatively complete picture of types of offense we shall have to turn to other sources. Second, prisoners are a very selected group of criminals: they have been apprehended, arrested, indicted, convicted and committed. Criminologists generally hold that the further the index from the crime, the poorer it is as a measure of crime. This may be true for white prisoners, but it is not nearly so true for Negro prisoners. So many Negroes are arrested on the vaguest suspicion that those who are actually sent to prison may more likely be a representative group of criminals than those who are only arrested.

Table 1 shows that there are about three times as many Negro males in prisons and reformatories as there are native white males, in proportion to the sizes of their respective populations, and that the rate for Negro

TABLE 1

PRISONERS RECEIVED FROM COURTS BY STATE AND FEDERAL PRISONS
AND REFORMATORIES BY SEX, RACE AND NATIVITY: 1939

Race and Nativity	Number Received from Courts			Rates per 100,000 Population [a]		
	Total	Male	Female	Total	Male	Female
White	47,971	45,796	2,175	42.3	77.0	3.7
Native	45,280	43,257	2,023	42.4	80.9	3.8
Foreign-born	2,691	2,539	152	23.6	42.2	2.8
Negro	17,324	16,135	1,189	134.7	257.4	18.0
Other Races	729	698	31	123.8	202.9	12.7

Sources: U.S. Bureau of the Census, *Prisoners in State and Federal Prisons and Reformatories: 1939* (1941),
p. 11; and *Sixteenth Census of the United States: 1940, Population,* Preliminary Release, Series P–10, No. 6.
[a] The population bases are as of 1940.

women is more than four times as great as that for native white women.
Foreign-born whites have rates much lower than native whites and members of races other than white and Negro (that is, Indians, Chinese, Filipinos, and others) have rates almost as high as do Negroes. Table 2
reveals that the difference between Negroes and whites is much larger
in the North than in the South. In the South the number of Negro male
felony prisoners is only between two and two-and-a-half times as great
(in proportion to population) as the number of native white male felony
prisoners. In the North, however, the Negro rate is almost five times as
large as the white rate. This would seem to be due mainly to the fact
that Northern Negroes are concentrated in cities, where social disorganization is greater and law enforcement is more efficient. We shall return to
the problem of causes of crime after considering the types of offenses
which are most characteristic of Negroes.

TABLE 2

MALE FELONY PRISONERS RECEIVED FROM COURTS BY STATE AND FEDERAL PRISONS
AND REFORMATORIES, BY GEOGRAPHIC AREAS AND BY RACE AND NATIVITY: 1939

Race and Nativity	Number		Rate per 100,000 Population [a]	
	Southern States [b]	Northern and Western States	Southern States [b]	Northern and Western States
Total	19,430	28,894	46.6	32.1
Native White	10,659	22,759	34.3	30.0
Foreign-born White	132	1,435	21.1	13.3
Negro	8,548	4,402	86.3	148.7
All Other Races	91	298	88.6	61.3

Sources: U.S. Bureau of the Census, *Prisoners in State and Federal Prisons and Reformatories: 1939*
(1941), p. 28; and *Sixteenth Census of the United States: 1940, Population,* Preliminary Release, Series P–10,
No. 1.
[a] Population bases are as of 1940.
[b] Southern states include, according to this census publication: Delaware, Maryland, District of Columbia,
Virginia, West Virginia, North Carolina, South Carolina, Florida, Kentucky, Tennessee, Mississippi, Arkansas,
Louisiana, Oklahoma and Texas. Georgia and Alabama did not report. All Northern states reported.

Negroes tend to commit certain types of crimes and not others; on the average the distribution of their crimes according to type differs from that of the white population. We have already mentioned that Negroes do not tend to commit "white collar" crimes; they do not have the opportunity to commit these large-scale, almost respectable crimes. Another significant omission is organized crime by gangs; Negro criminals commit their crimes as individuals, often more spontaneously than do white criminals.[a] There are Negro racketeers, of course, but most of the big rackets operating in the Negro community (mainly connected with gambling) are run by whites.[b]

Statistics on offenses by type are faulty because of variations in definition and classification used by different states. But they can be used to give a rough picture of the differences between whites and Negroes according to type of offense. We shall use the *Uniform Crime Reports* of the Federal Bureau of Investigation, since these offer the only available nation-wide information classifying arrests both by race and by specific offenses, including minor offenses. From Table 3, we can see that the Negroes' proportion was particularly high in crimes of homicide, assault, carrying and possessing weapons, robbery, burglary, larceny, receiving and possessing stolen goods, prostitution, disorderly conduct, "suspicion," violation of liquor laws, gambling. On the other hand, the contribution of Negro offenders was noticeably low in cases of embezzlement and fraud, forgery and counterfeiting, auto theft, sex offenses other than prostitution, drunkenness and driving while intoxicated.

In view of the fact that whites generally believe that Negroes are especially responsible for rape and sex crimes, it is important to note that these offenses seem to be relatively unimportant among Negroes (although the rate is higher among Negroes than among whites). All existing studies bear out this point, so that the low rate of sex offenses is not just a quirk of these specific statistics.[21] Like other Negro crime rates, the Negro rape rate is fallaciously high: white women may try to extricate themselves from the consequences of sexual delinquency by blaming or

---

[a] The following statement refers to the Harlem Negro Community of New York City: "In regard to adult delinquency we find no organized criminal gangs, but a preponderance of such crimes as flourished among poverty stricken and disorganized people. Moreover, the fact should be stressed that the very economic impotence of the community and its subjection to exploitation by outside interests, such as the policy racket and the location of institutions in the community for the pleasure and vices of whites, who seek this means of escape from the censure of their own groups, encourages anti-social behavior and nullifies the efforts of responsible citizens to maintain social control." (The Mayor's Commission on Conditions in Harlem, "The Negro in Harlem: A Report on Social and Economic Conditions Responsible for the Outbreak of March 19, 1935," typescript [1936], p. 115.)

[b] See Chapter 14, Section 10, for a discussion of racketeering, gambling and other "shady" occupations.

TABLE 3

DISTRIBUTION OF ARRESTS ACCORDING TO RACE AND TYPE OF OFFENSE (EXCLUDING THOSE
UNDER FIFTEEN YEARS OF AGE): 1940

Offense Charged	Per Cent Negro of Total in Each Offense	Rate per 100,000 Population [a]	
		Negro	White [c]
Criminal homicide	40.1	19.8	3.2
Robbery	30.8	31.7	7.6
Assault	44.0	116.4	15.7
Burglary—breaking or entering	24.5	66.3	22.0
Larceny-theft	28.4	138.1	37.4
Auto-theft	14.8	15.4	9.6
Embezzlement and fraud	11.5	17.1	14.2
Stolen property; buying, receiving, etc.	27.3	7.6	2.2
Arson	17.4	1.5	0.8
Forgery and counterfeiting	9.1	5.0	5.4
Rape	22.1	10.4	3.9
Prostitution and commercialized vice	25.4	17.7	5.6
Other sex offenses	14.9	11.1	6.8
Narcotic drug laws	19.3	7.5	2.9
Weapons, carrying, possessing, etc.	45.8	20.3	2.5
Offenses against family and children	15.6	9.7	5.7
Liquor laws	47.2	36.5	4.4
Driving while intoxicated	6.8	15.3	22.4
Road and driving laws	21.6	10.0	3.9
Parking violations	14.3	b	b
Other traffic and motor vehicle laws	21.0	15.5	6.2
Disorderly conduct	28.1	64.2	17.6
Drunkenness	12.3	110.3	84.8
Vagrancy	19.5	81.5	36.0
Gambling	41.9	43.2	6.0
Suspicion	27.1	130.6	37.9
Not stated	19.5	6.5	2.9
All other offenses	23.5	69.2	24.1
Total	22.8	1,078.4	391.6

Sources: U.S. Department of Justice, Federal Bureau of Investigation, *Uniform Crime Reports* (Fourth Quarterly Bulletin, 1940), p. 223; and *Sixteenth Census of the United States: 1940, Population,* Preliminary Release Series P-10, No. 1.
a Population bases taken as of 1940.
b Less than one-tenth of one per cent.
c White includes both foreign-born and native-born, and it includes Mexicans (who are separated in the original statistics).

framing Negro men; a white woman who has a Negro lover can get rid of him or avoid social ostracism following detection by accusing him of rape; neurotic white women may hysterically interpret an innocent action as an "attack" by a Negro.[22] Real cases of Negro raping of white women probably involve only psychopathic Negroes, at least in the South, for punishment is certain and horrible.

As among whites, most of the crimes committed by Negroes are of a petty type; it is only by comparison with the white crime rates that the Negro crime rates for serious offenses stand out.

One of the most noticeable features of the Negro offenses is the small number of vicious or serious crimes in the period studied—that is, most of the cases studied were misdemeanors rather than felonies. There were, it is true, a rather considerable number of assault cases but a large proportion of these were in connection with drunkenness. . . . The comparatively large numbers in for possession and selling liquor and for fraud . . . are partly explained by the fact that quite a number of the former merely had in their possession a little liquor which they had not yet drunk, and that most of the fraud cases were instances of jumping small board bills.

There was very little difference noted between the percentages of various crimes of the two races. In general, the crimes which one committed, most frequently, the other also tended to commit frequently.

If any one feature . . . may be thought of as characterizing most of the Negro's crimes, it is not their viciousness or even their immense numbers, but merely their petty qualities. . . .

The relatively small proportion of violent crimes committed by Negroes, and the large proportion of cases of drunkenness, petty larceny, vagrancy, and other lesser offenses, further enhances the conclusion that there is no innate racial criminal tendency.[23]

The study for the Mayor's Commission on Conditions in Harlem, made by E. Franklin Frazier, showed that in the first six months of 1935, 6,540 Negro men and 1,338 Negro women were arrested in Harlem.[24] Of the male arrests, 31.9 per cent were for policy gambling and 30.9 per cent were for disorderly conduct. Only 7 per cent were for burglary, robbery, grand larceny, assault and robbery, and pickpocketry combined; 5.0 per cent were for felonious assault; and only 0.5 were for homicide. About 80 per cent of the Negro women arrested were charged with immoral sex behavior. Another study showed that 54 per cent of the arrests of all women for prostitution in New York City were of Negro women, and that the rate for Negro women was 10 times that for white women.[25]

Theft, burglary, and other property offenses are committed mainly against whites; assault, murder, and other crimes against persons are committed mainly against other Negroes. "Premeditated crimes or those requiring education and cunning do not seem to be so prominent among colored offenders as do those crimes likely to involve some emotional flare-up, or some immediate desire or economic necessity."[26]

Explanations of Negro crime have usually started out from the statistical finding that Negroes commit more crimes than do whites. If this is done, the first group of "causes" of Negro crime to be considered are the discriminations in justice which we summarized at the beginning of this section. Because the criminal statistics reflect police and court practices as much as they do crime, it is impossible to prove whether or not the Negro crime rate would be higher than the white crime rate if there were no discrimination. In the same way, the general characteristics of the Negro population—poverty, ignorance of the law, lack of influential connections,

Southern patterns of illegality and use of weapons in fights, concentration in the cities and in young adult ages in the North—operate to make the Negro crime rate higher than the white crime rate, and so may be thought of as another group of causes of Negro crime. Existing data are insufficient to hold these factors constant in order to determine whether Negroes would still have a higher crime rate if they did not have these general characteristics in any greater degree than does the white population.

A third group of causes of Negro crime is connected with the slavery tradition and the caste situation. It has always been expected of Negro servants in the South that they should pilfer small things—usually food but sometimes also clothing and money. In fact, their money wages are extremely low partly because the white employers expect them to take part of their earnings in kind. Something of the same custom prevails between all white employers and Negro employees in the South. This custom has had two effects which operate to raise the Negro's criminal record: First, it has developed in the Negro a disrespect for the property of others, which sometimes leads him to pilfer things from people to whom he does not stand in the relationship of indulged servant. If he may take a pair of socks from one employer, why may he not take a screw driver from another employer? This feeling is strengthened by the fact that Negroes know that their white employers are exploiting them. If they cannot get decent regular wages, they feel they should be allowed to get what they can by pilfering.[27] The second way in which this Southern custom gets the Negro in trouble is when he moves North. In the North any type of taking of property without express permission is regarded as stealing and it may sometimes lead to arrest: Negro servant women in the North have a bad reputation for petty pilfering, and this adds to bad interracial feeling.

Much more deeply based in the caste situation than this custom is the Negro's hatred of whites. A not insignificant number of crimes of Negroes against whites are motivated by revenge for discriminatory or insulting treatment. Such a crime may be emotional, as when a Negro suddenly feels that he has stood enough in the way of deprivation and insults and that he only desires to make white people suffer too, even at the cost of his own punishment by law or by a mob. Negro literature is filled with stories of Negroes suddenly breaking out in such a manner. The revenge motive may also lead to a cold and calculating crime: it is said by many Negro social scientists that "mugging"—the robbing and beating of a victim in a certain way by a group of three or four petty professional criminals—was originally practiced only in Negro neighborhoods on white men who were thought to be searching for Negro prostitutes. The revenge motive is seen in the unnecessary and cruel way in which the victim is beaten.

The Negro's reaction to caste is much more general than can be expressed by calling it a revenge motive. Caste, especially when it operates to cause legal injustice and insecurity of life and property, prevents the Negro from identifying himself with society and the law. Because the white man regards him as apart from society, it is natural for a Negro to regard himself as apart. He does not participate in making the laws in the South, and he has little chance to enforce them. To the average lower class Negro, at least in the South, the police, the courts, and even the law are arbitrary and hostile to Negroes, and thus are to be avoided or fought against. The ever-present hostility to the law and law-enforcement agencies on the part of all Southern Negroes and many Northern Negroes does not often manifest itself in an outbreak against them because the risks are too great. But occasionally this hostility does express itself, and then there is crime. The Negro community tends to be sympathetic toward an individual Negro who commits a crime against whites, since he is only expressing a hostility which is felt generally. Sometimes the hostility toward the white community is expressed in crimes against Negroes who turn traitor to their group and work with the whites.[a]

The slavery tradition and the caste situation are also reflected in the low regard for human life that characterizes lower class Southerners generally, and especially Negroes. A slave's life had only a money price, not a legal or ethical price. After Emancipation, the use of violence to support the caste system and the general Southern pattern of illegality maintained this low regard for human life. Negroes have taken over the white man's attitude and have even exaggerated it. Assault and murder are relatively more common among Negroes. Such crimes are rarely premeditated; they are the result of a moment's anger when it is not inhibited by a developed respect for life and law. The fact that the law is arbitrary, in the South, further depreciates the value of a Negro's life and property. For crimes committed against other Negroes, Negro criminals often go unpunished or are lightly punished, especially if they can get white men to act as "character" witnesses. Sometimes even a white man will not insist on having a Negro who steals from him arrested, usually because he needs this Negro as a worker.[28]

Certain traits, present everywhere, but more developed in the Negro as a consequence of his slavery background and his subordinate caste status, have also been conducive to a high Negro crime rate. Sexual looseness, weak family bonds, and poverty have made prostitution more common among Negro women than among white women. Carelessness and idleness have caused the Negro to be the source of a disproportionate amount of accidental crimes and of vagrancy. Negroes also have a high record in crimes connected with gambling and the use of liquor, although it is not certain whether their record is higher than that of other lower class groups.

Social organization is generally at a low level among Southern Negroes,

[a] This includes "stool pigeons," "Uncle Toms" and petty racketeers looking for immunity.

but disorganization only reaches its extreme when Negroes migrate to cities and to the North.[a] The controls of the rural community are removed; and the ignorant Negro does not know how to adjust to a radically new type of life. Like the European immigrant, he comes to the slums of the Northern cities and learns the criminal ways already widely practiced in such areas. The high crime rates in the Northern cities that successively characterized the slum dwellers of German, Scandinavian, Irish, Polish, and Italian descent, are now characteristic of Negroes and Mexicans as the most recent of a series.[29] Negroes are especially prone to take over the criminal patterns of the urban slums since they have such difficulty in getting regular and decent jobs. More Negro mothers than white mothers have to work for a living and so cannot have the time to take care of their children properly. Negro children, more than white children, are forced to engage in street trades, where they can easily pick up the arts of robbing and prostitution. The over-crowdedness of the homes and the consequent lack of privacy prevent the growth of ideals of chastity and are one element in encouraging girls to become prostitutes. The friction that is bound to develop in a poverty-stricken household, especially where there are no strong family traditions, weakens still further the family controls over the children, and the children then become more subject to the influences of the streets. Poverty is thus an important breeder of crime among Negroes.

Partly because Negro neighborhoods are slum areas and partly because Negroes are supposed to be masters of sensuous pleasure, Negro neighborhoods are frequented by whites who wish to do something illicit or immoral. White criminal gangs in Northern cities often have their headquarters in Negro neighborhoods. White men come to Negro neighborhoods to find both white and Negro prostitutes. Gambling dens and cabarets (during the Prohibition era, elaborate speakeasies) are often concentrated in Negro neighborhoods. All sorts of tastes, including those which are regarded as immoral and perverted, are catered to in Negro sections. Illegal selling of narcotics is much simpler in Negro neighborhoods. The owners of these enterprises are practically all whites, although the "entertainers" and subordinates are often Negroes. The police do not stand on the law so much in Negro neighborhoods; what goes on is too much for them to handle, and they come to expect graft for "protection." In such a neighborhood Negroes, especially children,[b] develop a distorted sense of values. Much of

---

[a] The prison system of the South—bad for whites and especially bad for Negroes—acts like migration in fostering criminality among Negroes. Negroes have a higher recidivism rate than do whites, which means that Negro criminals have become more addicted to crime and less corrigible. (See Johnson and Kiser, *op. cit.*, pp. 364-367 and 258-263.)

[b] Recently Northern cities have become especially concerned about juvenile delinquency among Negroes. In New York City in the autumn of 1941, for example, there were a large number of newspaper reports about a serious new delinquency wave in Harlem. In addition to the daily newspaper stories, there were statements and speeches by public officials, meetings

the crime and vice among Negroes in cities, and sometimes even in smaller towns, exists because the white man brings his own crime, vice and disrespect for law to the Negroes.[a]

The intense competition between Negroes and the relatively unfixed moral standards serve to encourage crimes inflicted by Negroes on other Negroes. With so few opportunities available to them Negroes are willing to take greater risks to obtain some of them. With uncertain sex mores and a great deal of family disorganization, Negroes are more likely to act with motives of sexual jealousy. The over-crowdedness of the home and the lack of recreational facilities augment the effect of all these disorganizing and crime-breeding influences.

We know that Negroes are not biologically more criminal than whites. We do not know definitely that Negroes are culturally more criminal, although we do know that they come up against law-enforcement agencies more often. We suspect that the "true" crime rate—when extraneous influences are held constant—is higher among Negroes. This is true at least for such crimes as involve personal violence, petty robbery, and sexual delinquency—because of the caste system and the slavery tradition. The great bulk of the crime among Negroes has the same causes as that among whites. It is only the differences between the two rates for which we have had to seek special explanation. There are the same variations in

---

of Negro and white civic groups, special investigating committees, and other means of arousing the public to the high Negro delinquency rate. The Negro rate had always been considerably higher than the white rate, and now it seemed that the Negro rate was increasing while the white rate was steady and even declining. According to a Report of the Sub-Committee on Crime and Delinquency of the City-Wide Citizens' Committee on Harlem, there were "five times as many Negro juvenile delinquents arraigned in Children's Court as white delinquents in proportion to their respective numbers in the population, and 1941 saw an increase of 23 per cent in Negro juvenile delinquency in the city." ([August, 1942] p. 2. The Negro rate had risen steadily before 1941, too, because of continuing immigration from the South [Ibid., p. 3].) This public agitation apparently had some effect, for the Negro delinquency rate fell while the white rate rose following the entrance of the United States into the War. (Ibid., p. 3.) Newspaper interest in Negro delinquency has continued and efforts to diminish it have not slackened. New job opportunities for Negroes, as a consequence of the war boom, may also be a factor in lowering the juvenile delinquency rate.

[a] In their positions as servants to whites, Negroes see further into the seamy side of the white man's life.

"Many of the moral Negroes have a very low opinion of white sexual and family standards. In their positions as butlers, maids, waiters, and bellhops, they have had exceptional opportunity to view the seamy intimacies of high life. Since servants are supposed not to see or hear, their presence is no deterrent, and they tell among themselves lurid tales of drunkenness and promiscuity, some of which are undoubtedly true. There is a saying among male Negroes of the better class that all white girls are loose and many diseased. But caste resentment enters into their judgment just as race prejudice is likely to color similar generalizations about Negro morality by white men." (Robert A. Warner, New Haven Negroes [1940], p. 218.)

the crime rate between social classes among Negroes as among whites: The upper and middle classes among Negroes are at least as law-abiding as the corresponding classes among whites; much of the differential in gross crime rate lies in the fact that the proportion of lower class Negroes is so much greater. Upper and middle class Negroes make a special effort to be law-abiding just as they try to avoid most of the typical and stereotyped patterns of behavior associated with the Negro lower classes. But, like the lower class, they meet prejudiced treatment from the police and the courts and so add to the crime rate.

3. MENTAL DISORDERS AND SUICIDE

As we observed in Chapter 6, there is no indication that Negroes are innately more susceptible than are whites to mental disorder generally or to certain specific types of mental disorder. The circumstances under which Negroes live, however, have a definite influence on their mental health. We shall be able to give only a limited demonstration of this influence, since the data we are forced to use are extremely poor.[a]

There is no proof that there was an increase in mental disease among Negroes after Emancipation, but if there was—as is likely—it may simply have been a manifestation of the general trend toward increased mental disease that was characteristic of whites also.[30] Even if the increase was unusually sharp, this may be regarded as an instance of how Negroes started to "catch up" to whites after Emancipation, rather than as a proof that Negroes "could not take" freedom.

Until 1933, there was a greater proportion of whites than of Negroes in *state* hospitals [b] for the insane, in the country as a whole, though in most of the Northern states the reverse was true for at least a decade previously.[31] The Census of 1933 showed that the proportion of Negroes in state hospitals was higher than the proportion of whites in state hospitals in the country as a whole). This also was true in all but four of the Southern states, despite discrimination against Negroes in admitting them to state hospitals. Because whites made some use of private hospitals and because state hospitals discriminated against Negroes, it cannot be inferred from these figures

[a] Statistics on mental disorder in the United States refer to cases in institutions, not to all cases or even to all cases known to doctors. Since institutional policy varies more with time and place than with mental disease itself, the statistics must be used with extreme caution. It is impossible, for example, to present meaningful figures comparing Negroes and whites in the whole country (or in the South alone), Southern Negroes with Northern Negroes, or rates at present with rates a few decades ago.

[b] Throughout this section we shall use statistics for state hospitals only. Private hospitals not only have a differential policy by race and region, but require a fee that prohibits most Negroes from using them. Fortunately for comparative purposes, most whites also use the state hospitals. But the mere fact that whites use private hospitals to a certain extent makes the comparison of Negroes and whites in state hospitals of limited usefulness.

that Negroes now have a higher true rate of mental disease than do whites in the South. But the discrimination, if any, is so minor in the North, and the discrepancy in the rates between Negroes and whites is so great, that it is practically certain that Negroes have more mental disease in the North than do whites.

The only detailed and comprehensive study of the mental disease of Negroes is that by Benjamin Malzberg for New York State in 1929-1931.[32] He found the Negro rate of first admissions to state hospitals to be 151 per 100,000 population, as compared to 74 for whites. Even for New York City alone, Negroes had a much higher rate than did whites.[33] These great discrepancies existed in spite of the fact that the Negroes were a younger population and the young generally have less insanity. The Negro rate in New York State, standardized to hold age constant, was 225 per 100,000 population, as compared to 97 for whites. The Negro rates exceeded the white rates at every age.

It is clear that the great discrepancy between Negroes and whites in New York State is due to migration. There was practically no difference in the rate of Negroes and whites born in New York State (40 as compared to 45).[a] Also there was only a relatively small difference between Negroes and whites born in states other than New York (186 as compared to 151), and this difference was probably due to the greater divergence in the places that Negroes came from. Conditions of life in the South, from which most Negroes in the North have come, are the most important reason for the higher mental disease rate of Negroes, as we shall see when we come to consider specific types of mental diseases. Also it is disorganizing to have to change one's home, job, friends, manner of living, especially if that change is as great as that from the rural South to the urban North. Too, the people who make these moves are generally the least satisfied and least secure; otherwise they would not be making the change.[b]

The conditions under which Negroes live are reflected in the types of mental diseases predominant among them. There are two types of mental disease which are 3 or 4 times as prevalent among Negroes as among whites (New York State, 1929-1931):[34] general paresis, which is a consequence of syphilis, and the psychoses that sometimes follow too great indulgence in alcohol. Clearly the high syphilis rate among Negroes—and the family disorganization and poor health facilities in the South, which are behind it—is a major cause of the high mental disease rate of Negroes in the North. The poverty of Negroes in both South and North, and the disorganization

[a] The slightly higher rate for whites is undoubtedly due to the fact that the white population was 8 years older, on the average, than the Negro population.

[b] It is not necessary to claim that migrants are least successful or most successful. For purposes of explaining the correlation between migration and mental disorder, it is enough to claim that migrants are least satisfied, irrespective of their degree of success.

associated with migration, would seem to be behind the greater indulgence in alcohol. In New York State the standardized rates were also significantly greater for Negroes than for whites in the following mental diseases: psychosis with cerebral arteriosclerosis (ratio: 2.9 to 1), dementia praecox (ratio: 2.0 to 1), senile psychoses (ratio: 1.9 to 1), manic-depressive psychoses (ratio: 1.5 to 1).[a] Dementia praecox and manic-depressive phychoses, at least, would seem to be due in part to migration and urbanization.[35]

According to a preliminary report of a study in progress, by Mandel Sherman and Irene C. Sherman, the specific symptoms of mental disease also are related to social background.[36] Delusions of psychotic Negroes tend to center around the topics of religion, possession of great wealth (often used to help other Negroes), attainment of superiority in the literary and educational fields, and outstanding assistance to the race. Delusions of whites, on the other hand, center around possession of great wealth (usually for personal benefit only) and somatic reactions (for example, false belief that one has a serious physical illness). In this connection it is interesting to note that Negroes have much less paranoia (the "disease of egotism") than do whites. Another significant trait of the delusions is that those of Negro men and women are much less divergent than are those of white men and women. Negroes are also reported to have more hallucinations (errors in perception) than do whites, probably because they are less well educated and more superstitious.

This presentation of a few selected facts regarding the distribution and differential character of mental disease is a sketchy reflection of a whole trend in psychiatric research. Experts are far from unanimous regarding the causation of mental disease or of the specific forms which it takes, but there is a growing feeling among them that the tensions and crises of life, as well as more objective social conditions, such as the presence of syphilis and the excessive use of hard liquor, are directly connected with mental disease. Negroes and whites lead different sorts of lives, to a certain extent and on the average, and this may be expected to reflect itself in differentials in the incidence of mental disease and of its specific manifestations. The average lower class Negro has, on the one hand, a more carefree life and fewer inhibitions, as so little is expected of him by the whites, by other Negroes, and by his own conscience. On the other hand, he meets the most severe frustrations along the caste line. The situation is different in different social classes: upper and middle class Negroes may feel the latter frustrations more intensively at the same time as they are not allowed the com-

---

[a] Institutionalization is an even poorer index of feeble-mindedness than it is of mental disease. The rate of first admissions is much higher for whites than for Negroes in the country as a whole, but this is clearly due to discrimination against Negroes in the South. In New York and New Jersey, where there is something like impartiality in institutional policy, Negroes have a higher rate than do whites.

pensation of carelessness in personal behavior. If these and other group experiences are reflected in the incidence of mental disease, it may be possible to learn about Negro culture and personality through a study of characteristic mental aberrations of Negro individuals.

In contrast to the high mental disease rate, Negroes apparently have a very low suicide rate. It is only 4.0 per 100,000 population (1940), as compared to 15.5 for whites, 8.4 for Indians, 45.2 for Chinese and 26.0 for Japanese.[37] One of the reasons for the low suicide rate for Negroes is a younger age composition, since suicide rises rapidly with age. But it also seems that Negroes are actually less prone to escape their problems by taking their lives.[a]

4. RECREATION

Negro recreation is conditioned by three factors: First, Negroes are barred from using public recreational and amusement facilities in many places even in the North, and are inadequately supplied with private facilities.[b] Second, their geographical concentration in the South means that many of their recreational patterns follow those of the rural South. These are carried over to the urban North by the migrants from the South and are further shaped by the fact that the great bulk of the Negro population is of low economic status and lives in slum areas. Third, because recreation and amusement must be carried on almost entirely within the isolated Negro community, Negro recreation has developed peculiar traits of its own, different from those that characterize recreation in the white community. One of the most striking characteristics of Negro amusements and recreation is their tendency to be informal, intimate and sociable.

Life in rural areas is generally dull and uneventful.[38] There is little to do during a large part of the year; at other times farm work takes up all the time.[39] Recreation may become the means of filling up empty, dull days or serve as relief from long, hard, monotonous labor. Because of the lack of facilities, recreation tends to be informal and unorganized. Besides swimming, hunting, and fishing,[40] a considerable amount of time is spent in loafing, talking, boasting, telling tall stories, singing. Everybody participates, and the behavior is free, easy, and spontaneous. Loud good-natured "banter" is part of it; it often deteriorates, however, into aggression and obscenity.[41] The laughing, boisterous groups, frequently seen by the whites, give them the idea that Negroes have a wonderfully happy time. While it is true that the Negroes' recreational behavior is relatively unrestrained

---

[a] This is especially striking in view of the fact that few Negroes are Catholics, and Catholics have a low rate because of religious injunctions.

[b] See Chapter 15, Section 5. For a full discussion of the inadequate recreational facilities provided for Negroes, see E. Franklin Frazier, "Recreation and Amusement among American Negroes," unpublished manuscript prepared for this study (1940).

and uninhibited, it is not a constructive form of amusement; it is monotonous and offers no chance to develop skills, physical or mental. Whenever commercial amusements invade the rural areas, no matter how cheap and sordid, the young people flock to them, thankful for any brightly lighted, stimulating place to meet people and to dance.

One of the chief amusements in rural areas is "going to town" which may be to the nearest town, to the general store, to the "ice-cream parlor" (for the young people), or to the railroad station, either in the evenings or on Saturdays.[42] The time is spent in shopping, meeting acquaintances, sitting around the stove in the general store, or standing on the street corners laughing and joking.[a] The men and young people participate in these activities, but the older women rarely do.

For the older women, church activity is usually the only form of recreation.[43] They go to church to meet friends, display their new clothes when they have them, and enjoy the rivalries and strivings for prestige and position in the church. If the church is at all primitive in its service and music, it offers the additional experience of emotional catharsis. For the most part, rural women lead an even more monotonous and isolated life than do men.

One would expect that in the absence of other recreational facilities there would be many radios, but this does not seem to be so.[44] More use is made of the phonograph.[45] Even the limited use of radios and phonographs, however, is healthy in that it helps to break down the isolation of these communities; and, since many of the successful, popular musicians are Negroes, it stimulates the ambition of Negro youth. Rural Negroes see few movies. Where there are movie houses in rural areas, they do not provide accommodations for Negroes. Although movies offer a limited type of experience (and not always a wholesome one) to urban youth, they do give them some idea of other ways of living, other sections of the country and other historical periods. Even this minor broadening experience is absent from rural experience.

The informal gatherings to talk and joke and meet one's friends are carried over from the rural areas to the city. There the barbershop, the street corner, and most frequently, the poolroom become the gathering places for the lower class men and boys. In the cities, the men and boys who have the time for such activity are usually unemployed, and the atmosphere is much less wholesome and innocent than that which surrounds the same sort of loafing and talking in the country. The proprietor of the poolroom is often a petty criminal engaged in gambling and commercial vice, and the

---

[a] Again we may point out that the gaiety of these informal groups may be deceiving, since much of the conversation is bitter and angry about incidents that have happened in town or on the plantations. The whites never hear this, as it ceases when they approach. The boisterousness and unrestrainedness of conversation is customary in uneducated people; and the laughter may be at the expense of the whites and bitter rather than humorous.

young people become involved in criminal activities through his influence. The banter, loafing, wrestling, and working off of animal spirits, natural and harmless in wide country spaces, become stealing and gang activity in the city. Too, the free and easy sex contacts of the rural areas are classified as juvenile delinquency in the city.[46] On the other hand, Y.M.C.A.'s, settlement houses, city playgrounds, and athletic clubs in the North do provide organized and wholesome recreation, although not enough of it. Since Joe Louis' rise to fame and fortune, any place that provides gymnasium facilities attracts boys.

Negro people in the city, even of the respectable middle class, spend much of their time on the streets, partly because of their rural background, partly because of the crowdedness and unattractiveness of their homes. One of the favorite Negro pastimes is "strolling." James Weldon Johnson describes it in Harlem:

> The masses of Harlem get a good deal of pleasure out of things far too simple for most other folks. In the evenings of summer and on Sundays they get lots of enjoyment out of strolling. . . . Strolling in Harlem does not mean merely walking along Lenox or upper Seventh Avenue; . . . it means that those streets are places for socializing. One puts on one's best clothes and fares forth to pass the time pleasantly with the friends and acquaintances and, most important of all, the strangers he is sure of meeting. One saunters along, he hails this one, exchanges a word or two with that one, stops for a short chat with the other one. He comes up to a laughing, chattering group, in which he may have only one friend or acquaintance, but that gives him the privilege of joining in. He does join in and takes part in the joking, the small talk and gossip, and makes new acquaintances. He passes on and arrives in front of one of the theatres, studies the bill for a while, undecided about going in. He finally moves on a few steps farther and joins another group and is introduced to two or three pretty girls who have just come to Harlem, perhaps only for a visit; and finds a reason to be glad that he postponed going into the theatre. The hours of a summer evening run by rapidly. This is not simply going out for a walk; it is more like going out for adventure.[47]

There is also much casual visiting back and forth in the respectable lower and middle class community, especially among the women.

Urban Negroes find most of their amusement and recreation in the social clubs, athletic clubs, churches and lodges.[a] Sports, dancing, card-playing and other games, petty civic improvement activities, and, in the churches, singing and dramatics [48] are the chief forms of amusement. In the large Northern (but not the Southern) cities, movies, theaters, concert halls, night clubs, and restaurants are generally available to Negroes (if they can afford them); but there is always the possibility of insult or unpleasantness, and no Negro section, even in New York or Chicago, can support a complete set of recreational facilities. The voluntary organizations, therefore, continue

---

[a] For a discussion of these voluntary associations, see Chapter 43, Section 5.

to be a chief source of Negro recreational life. Clubs support each other by buying tickets to the other's dances, style shows, plays, and so on; consequently, a full (sometimes too full) social and recreational life is provided the club members.[a] Since the same small group of people with the same interests constantly intermingles socially; since these people participate little in other activities; and since clubs frequently meet in private homes, a highly personalized and socialized recreational life is the result. This feeling of intimacy and "at homeness" pervades all the sociable and recreational life that is peculiarly Negro and is what the whites see and remark about when they say that Negroes have a good time. Negroes among themselves act as if they were in a small family group, often even in commercial places. They know everybody and have a personal interest in everybody; they feel that they are part of a small community. This looks cozy and cheerful and intimate to whites accustomed to impersonal, formalized, overorganized social relations.

A few other characteristics of Negro recreation may be noted. One of the main forms of recreation among lower class Negroes is gambling. Besides playing the numbers,[b] Negroes are traditionally expert poker players and crap-shooters.[c] The excitement of gambling coupled with the chance of gain is easily understandable in the light of the monotony of rural life and of the unemployment in cities. These games, also, can be played anywhere with little equipment and with anybody who happens to be around. It should be noted, further, that crap-shooting is the invariable accompaniment of traditional "Negro jobs," those of waiter, bell-boy, porter, jobs where the over-all hours are long and where the men must be on call at all times, but where there is much unoccupied time.

Among the urban youth and lately among rural youth, dancing is a favorite pastime. Dancing is one of the favorite forms of recreation among the upper class and in the clubs and equally so in the commercialized dance halls frequented by lower class young people. Negroes have developed most of the modern jazz dances which are now popular in the white world.

Most Negroes do not follow the usual American pattern of taking a vacation. The great majority of them are too poor.[49] The upper classes who can afford to are usually barred from those vacation resorts which meet their standards.

Before the World War Negroes were developing summer resorts for their exclusive use on a relatively large scale. There is an excellent Negro summer resort in

[a] See Chapter 43, Section 5; also see J. G. St. Clair Drake, "The Negro Church and Associations in Chicago," unpublished manuscript prepared for this study (1940), pp. 473-475.
[b] See Chapter 14, Section 10.
[c] Whites now play these gambling games extensively, also; see the footnote on crap shooting in Section 1 of this chapter.

Michigan, and another in Mississippi. Several colored seaside resorts flourish along the Atlantic coast. On the whole, however, these can be patronized only by the few who have the time and money to spend a good portion of the year away from home on vacation. While there are some Negro resorts which can be enjoyed by poor Negroes, the number of this class actually able to patronize them is small. A pseudo-vacation is obtained by many of the working colored people by securing jobs at seashore or other resorts where they can earn their living and still have vacation in off hours and through a change of scene. In Philadelphia, for illustration, it is common for colored cooks and maids to go to Atlantic City and other nearby resorts for summer work, thus breaking the monotony of their routine and obtaining some semblance of a real vacation away from the home city and without starving. This is no doubt better than no vacation at all but the problem has not been faced. The majority of this group must continue to think of vacation as a short period free from work but otherwise no different from the rest of the year.[50]

One of the most wholesome aspects of Negro recreation and amusement is that it is not a separate part of their lives, but is well integrated into the daily routine. Part of this seems to be that Negroes, having little time free from hard work, devised relaxing accompaniments to their work. Singing, for example, accompanies all work, even on the chain gang; gambling while working is another example. Part of it is that so many of the usual recreational forms were denied them that they learned to enjoy the everyday things they did.[51] Whatever the cause, this integration of fun and work has undoubtedly made life possible for many Negroes under the difficult situations they face.

5. Negro Achievements[a]

Opportunity is a most important prerequisite for achievement; and since the Negro's opportunities in America have been kept low, his achievements are also small. In 1929-1930, there were only 98 Negroes listed in *Who's Who in America*.[52] No Negro is outstanding in national, state or local politics. Few Negroes have been outstanding in business, and these have become successful usually by catering to special needs of the Negro group. At present, when the federal government is asking capable and wealthy businessmen to work for it as "dollar-a-year" men, only one Negro has been included in the group. There have been but one or two outstanding Negro military leaders. No Negro has been an outstanding jurist, although a few Negro lawyers deserve fame for the way they have handled cases involving Negro rights. Since scientific achievement requires not only a superior education but also a secure position and facilities in a university or large

---

[a] We shall not attempt to give a systematic survey of Negro achievements in this section. Rather we shall single out the main fields in which Negroes have made notable achievements and give examples of the achievements and the achievers. In order to be concrete, we shall mention names. The persons named are merely outstanding examples; they do *not* include all Negroes who have made notable achievements.

industrial concern, there have been only half a dozen outstanding Negro natural scientists, and perhaps a dozen or so outstanding Negro social scientists.[a] And so it goes, down the list of fields in which superior performance is regarded as noteworthy. Most of the fields in which Negroes commonly attain superior performance are regarded as lowly—such as agriculture and personal service—and so no attention is paid to the high performance, and it is not recognized as an achievement. The esteemed fields in which Negroes have made many achievements are those of the arts, of the sports and of entertainment.

Before we go on to these, we call attention to the high performance of Negroes in a field that is often overlooked by whites. We refer to the fighting for the Negro cause—the field of race leadership. If we include this field with politics, we can honestly say that some of the most capable statesmen in the United States are Negroes, whatever we may think of their policies. If these men, with their training in practical politics, were white, they would no doubt be national leaders just as they are now race leaders. This was almost recognized of Frederick Douglass and Booker T. Washington, but the two other Negro statesmen of equal stature—W. E. B. Du Bois and James Weldon Johnson—have been virtually ignored by whites. On a second level, still high when compared with most white national leaders, are such men as Elmer Carter, Lester Granger, Charles Johnson, A. Philip Randolph, and Walter White. A woman, Mary McLeod Bethune, belongs on this level. Younger men, with no small achievement and still greater promise, are Earl Dickerson, Adam Clayton Powell and Roy Wilkins. In addition to these, there are wise Negro politicians all over the country, in the national offices of the betterment and protest organizations, and in the federal government in Washington. Working on the Negro problem gives one a set of practical ideals, a training in strategy, and a respect for courage, patience, and loyalty, that are necessary to a first-rate politician.

It is in the field of entertainment that the Negro's achievements are most widely recognized, and the opportunities made available to him there have made it possible for him to develop excellence in the economically subsidiary fields of arts and sports. The Negro has not only provided entertainment and art but also material for entertainment and art by whites: the Negro folk tales of Uncle Remus were set in writing by Joel Chandler Harris; many of the rhythmic songs of the Negro have provided the basic themes for white composers (Stephen Foster, for example); the greatest popularizers of ragtime music were Al Jolson and Irving Berlin; some of the best dramas of Negro life are by Du Bose Heyward; the Negro's

---

[a] It may be remarked, in passing, that in sociology, which is the branch of science under which most of the studies of Negro life and problems have gone on, Negroes have occasionally made first-rank achievements in the field

abstract painting and sculpture have been one of the sources of modern cubism and surrealism.[53] But Negroes themselves do not take second rank in these fields. Joe Louis is now the world's champion heavyweight prizefighter, and Jack Johnson held this title a generation ago. Negroes have held several of the lesser boxing championships (notably Henry Armstrong and John Henry Lewis) and have achieved first rank in running (notably Jesse Owens), football (notably Paul Robeson), and some of the other sports. Among the ten highest paid concert artists of the year 1941, three were Negroes: Marian Anderson, Dorothy Maynor and Paul Robeson.[54] Roland Hayes ranked not far below the first ten. The stage has long witnessed front-rank Negro actors, and it is now graced with such figures as Todd Duncan, Canada Lee, Paul Robeson and Ethel Waters. On the dance stage there are such masters of their respective talents as Katherine Dunham and Bill (Bojangles) Robinson. Negroes have invented a whole series of dance steps, including the fox trot, cake walk, Charleston, black bottom, turkey trot, the shag, jitterbugging; and Latin American Negroes have contributed the tango, rhumba, samba, conga. The screen and radio are practically closed to serious Negro actors—there being only three or four pictures in the entire history of film-making that have portrayed Negroes, even as minor characters, in roles other than those of buffoons or criminals.[a] But some Negroes have achieved huge success in the role of buffoon—notably Hattie McDaniels and Rochester. Negro musicians of various types are also popular on the radio. Negro jazz band leaders are among the most popular—Louis Armstrong, Count Basie, Cab Calloway, Duke Ellington, Fletcher Henderson, Jimmie Lunceford, King Oliver and Fats Waller.

[a] There is a definite improvement, in the last year or so, in the treatment of Negroes in movies. Before 1940, there had been, in addition to the movies in which Negroes were portrayed as clowns, criminals, or incidental servants, only such special movies and shorts as were meant for purely Negro consumption. (For a history of these all-Negro pictures, see James Asendio, "History of Negro Motion Pictures," *International Photographer* [January, 1940], p. 16.) There had been only one or two full-length movies in which Negroes were portrayed in more favorable or more human roles and which were meant for general white consumption. Ignorance on the part of film producers and fear of offending white Southerners were the main reasons for this treatment. After 1940, patriotic motives, stimulated by the growing war spirit, as well as definite pressure from the federal government, moved Hollywood to treat Negroes a little more favorably in the movies. In 1940 and 1942 there were produced: *Syncopation*, showing the role of the Negro in the creation of jazz music; *In This Our Life*, an Ellen Glasgow story in which a Negro youth incidentally tells his ambition to be a lawyer and in which he is almost executed for a crime committed by one of the white heroines; *Tales of Manhattan*, which shows Negroes as superstitious peasants but withal some cleverness and human emotion. In the week of July 31, 1942, some Negro leaders held a conference with "70 top executives of the screen world" to try to get them to assign to Negroes "roles in motion pictures more in keeping with their status and contribution to American life and culture." (*N.A.A.C.P. Press Service* [July 31, 1942], p. 4.) It is likely that such efforts, if continued, will have some effect, especially when further pressure comes from war agencies of the federal government.

Negroes have contributed such popular musical forms as ragtime, jazz, the blues, swing and boogie-woogie.

Negroes have been greatly hampered in more serious music, but in the past year Dean Dixon has emerged as a symphony orchestra conductor under the sponsorship of the white music critic, Samuel Chotzinoff. Negroes have achieved moderate success in composing serious music (for example, William Grant Still) and much greater success in composing lighter music (for example, Will Marion Cook, Duke Ellington, James Reese Europe, W. C. Handy and Rosamund Johnson). In art, Negroes have had most influence as subjects for and influences on white artists, but there have been a few front-rank American Negro painters and sculptors (Richmond Barthé, Aaron Douglas, Augusta Savage, Henry O. Tanner). In literature, Negroes have a forte, and in all branches of literature Negroes have made really outstanding achievements. The names of Countee Cullen, Langston Hughes, Claude McKay, Sterling Brown, and Richard Wright (and in the past Paul Lawrence Dunbar and James Weldon Johnson) are well known to the white reading public, and there are at least a score of other Negro writers of equal merit but little known to the white reading public.

To understand why Negroes have made outstanding achievements in these fields, it is necessary to go into their history. We find that there are two distinct lines of development, which have begun to converge only in the last twenty years. One is the buffoonery practiced for the entertainment of whites; the other is the great variety of expressive activity practiced for the artists' own enjoyment.

Under slavery, the chief form of entertainment in the large, isolated plantation was the slave show. The Negro was the court jester, who pleased his master by singing, dancing, telling jokes and generally "acting up." James Weldon Johnson describes the earliest Negro entertainment:

> Every plantation had its talented band that could crack Negro jokes, and sing and dance to the accompaniment of the banjo and the bones, the bones being the actual ribs of a sheep or some other small animal, cut the proper length, scraped clean and bleached in the sun. When the wealthy plantation owner wished to entertain his guests, he needed only to call his troupe of black minstrels.[55]

Even during slavery, but especially after it, there developed the "nigger minstrel show" which had the same features as the entertainment furnished by slaves. Practically all these shows which were successful had white actors who put burnt cork on their faces and spoke with a Negro accent; only Bert Williams among the Negroes achieved success as a minstrel comedian.[56] These shows, which still exist in a modified form,[57] appealed to the crudest tastes and accentuated all the Negro stereotypes. Their heyday lasted from 1875 to 1900, and during this period Negro musicians, song and play writers, and dancers stooped low to appeal to the popular taste.[58] Only the songs developed into something better. These songs—known as "coon songs" because they were funny at the expense of Negroes, stressing their supposed chicken-eating, wife-beating, razor-slashing traits—had a rhythm which made them popular. Later they developed into ragtime. After receiving a further influence from Negro secular folk-music—especially that kind fostered by vagrant Negro troubadours along the Mississippi River—ragtime was to have a meteoric career culminating in Irving Berlin's "Alexander's Ragtime Band" (1911), and it ultimately developed into jazz.[59] After the turn of the century, Negro entertainment began to improve in quality: the minstrel show gradually gave way to the musical comedy. Musical comedies written and acted by whites were popular in the period just before the First World War; and under the stimulus of the general popularity, shows written and acted by Negroes were successful. A high level of achievement was reached at this time by the writing and acting team of Cole and Johnson. These shows were still funny, but they also contained some serious art and appealed to a more cultivated audience.

After the War, Negro entertainment began to climb to new heights of popularity and quality. The jazz fad was on, and Negro singers, dancers and orchestras were much in demand. There was a great opportunity for Negro composers and musicians to supply jazz and blues music, and sometimes more classical variations. The African theme in art was suddenly the object of great admiration. *Opportunity* and *Crisis* magazines offered prizes for the best poetry and prose writing by Negroes, and the successful candidates found themselves swept up in adulation by thrill-seeking whites. To the Negroes, it was the period of the "New Negro," when their capacities and achievements were beginning to be recognized by the whites. To most of the whites who were giving this recognition to the Negroes, it was the period of the "gay 'twenties": the patronage they gave to Negro artists and performers was only part of the general seeking, on the one hand, after thrills and novelties and, on the other hand, after really good art, music and literature. They sponsored artists with little ability along with artists of great ability. They encouraged Negroes to develop African and pseudo-African themes because they were so exotic and bizarre. They also encouraged the noisy, the sexy and the perverted. When the Great Depression ended the "gay 'twenties," the patronage of the Negroes was greatly diminished, and the Negro arts were left with certain traits that they could not easily change.

Negro entertainment and the arts were, however, far from stopped completely during the 1930's. There were still many serious white devotees, and the Negroes themselves formed an increasingly appreciative audience. The "swing" and "boogie-woogie" period came into popular music, and the blues enjoyed a new burst of popularity. Negro stage comedians were still popular, although there was less money available to pay for them. It was the serious arts of poetry, the drama, painting and sculpture which were most affected by the depression. During the 1920's they had been supported by the intellectuals and the pseudo-intellectuals; during the 1930's these people either had little money left or no longer cared for the Negro arts. The fad of adulating things Negro was definitely over, and Negro performers and artists had to compete with others without any special advantage. The best held on and strengthened their popularity; the mediocre dropped out and were soon forgotten. The Negro artists themselves developed higher standards and sought to base their art on something more secure than the white man's demand for the exotic and the bizarre. General anti-Negro prejudice makes it somewhat harder for a Negro artist or performer to get a position than for a white person of equal talent, but on the whole there is less prejudice in this field than in practically any other field.[a] Some whites are inclined to have a double standard in judging Negro achievements; they applaud mediocrity and thereby foster it.

The federal government provided special opportunity between 1935 and 1939, when the Federal Theater aided unemployed Negroes by putting on all-Negro shows: there was a chance not only for Negro actors, but also for Negro writers, musicians and producers. The shows were successful and they strengthened both white and Negro recognition of Negro talent. The Negro painter was also given his chance when the W.P.A. and the N.Y.A. required the designing and decoration of such public works as schools, libraries, hospitals and parks. These federal agencies also offered art classes of various sorts, mostly in practical arts, and many Negroes participated.[60] The Federal Writers' Project provided further opportunities for Negro writers.

Today Negroes have a high record of performance and popularity in both serious and comic entertainment. Negro dancers, singers, orchestras, comedians, strip-teasers, and acrobats are used in theater stage shows and night club floor shows in all the large Northern cities. There are all-Negro shows and shows with both white and Negro performers (in the last 6 or 7 years Negroes have even been permitted to play in predominantly white orchestras).[61] Negro sections of cities often contain a few entertainment places which are popular with white audiences. In the South Negro performers are much more restricted, but are sometimes used if strictly segre-

---

[a] Negroes cannot get on the opera stage, and they are occasionally restricted on the concert stage (witness the famous incident in 1939 when the Daughters of the American Revolution prevented Marian Anderson from singing in Constitution Hall in Washington, D. C.). More serious restrictions against the Negro occur in the field of sports. Negroes cannot get into big league baseball and rarely have they been allowed into competitive tennis or golf games. They are generally kept out of competitive sports which require teams. Even in boxing, the sport in which they have achieved such notable success, they have been seriously restricted (for example, Jack Dempsey, when champion, consistently refused to let Harry Wills battle for his crown).

gated. Negro minstrel shows are still found, and the Negro buffoon is often part of vaudeville shows. Negro tap-dancers are in fairly wide demand, as are Negro burlesque dancers. Serious Negro artists and writers have a reasonably wide audience: one of the most popular novels of the past five years has been Richard Wright's *Native Son*.

Although most of the contemporary Negro literature received its stimulation from white sponsorship beginning in the first decade of the twentieth century and greatly increased during the 1920's, it has in addition a purely Negro history. Since 1760, when Jupiter Hammon, a slave in Long Island, New York, published "An Evening Thought: Salvation by Christ, with Penitential Cries," there has hardly been a decade when some Negro has not published something. The early writing by Negroes was perhaps not so good, but few white Americans then were accomplishing anything of note. Frederick Douglass, however, attained a high level of prose writing in some of his Abolitionist oratory. By the last decade of the nineteenth century, a Negro poet, Paul Lawrence Dunbar, was recognized as on a level with the best white American poets of the century.

Another serious strain in Negro art was that of folk-music. In this, Negroes have probably surpassed white Americans. The folk-songs are generally classified into two types: the spirituals and the secular songs. After some early experimentation, the spirituals emerged as the distinctively Negro religious music after 1830.[62] Negroes sang them practically only for their own benefit until the Fisk Jubilee Singers sang them around the country to get money for their school. By the 1890's they were recognized by whites as an outstanding form of music. This recognition was no doubt helped by Dvořák, the great Bohemian composer, in his use of some of them as main themes in his New World Symphony (1895). Since then, they have been favorite songs with all levels of white society, and many an outstanding Negro singer has got his start by fulfilling the demand of whites for spirituals.

The secular folk-songs began mainly as work-songs or leisure-time songs. There were no musical instruments, of course, and the people kept time by clapping or stamping, or if they were working, they kept time by the movements needed in their work. Thus there developed an emphasis on rhythm, and Negroes became masters of the possibilities in rhythm. The songs were begun by whole groups of people: usually some song leader would start off with a likely line; if it caught, the rest of the group would take it up and it became a theme for the chorus; other individuals would chime in with a rhyming line to keep the song going.[63] Some of the songs are more individualized in character—especially the love songs, the blues and the clever satires. Each song had many variations and was continually in the process of change until someone wrote it down. Sometimes the words did not make sense, or the consecutive lines would not follow each other logically. But they were cheerful, rhythmical songs which expressed much of the Negro's interests, problems and attitudes. These songs are still being created. They have achieved a great popularity in the white world: sometimes they are "jazzed up" or "swung" and become popular songs; sometimes they became popular in their original form (for example, most of the blues); sometimes they are sung as semi-popular folk-songs; sometimes they are mistakenly grouped with the spirituals because they have a few religious words. It was a white man, Stephen Foster, who was the chief popularizer of the secular Negro folk-songs.

Until recently, the puritanical spirit has been a powerful influence on entertainment and the arts in America. To a large degree white Americans have considered it somewhat immoral to be an entertainer, and white American men have considered it beneath their dignity and their capacity to cultivate the arts. Nevertheless, practically all Americans have enjoyed stage entertainment, and many Americans show "appreciation of the arts." Since whites stereotype the Negroes as immoral and somewhat bestial, they have been willing to let Negroes entertain them. They could enjoy the bawdy and frivolous songs, dances and jokes without "sinning" themselves.[64] White men have also been willing to let their women and their Negroes cultivate the arts.[a]

Negroes, on their side, have developed entertainment and the arts because they were relatively free of puritanical traditions and because there they were offered relatively attractive economic opportunities. Also without the means of paying for entertainment, they have learned how to entertain themselves. They have been so successful at this that they have taken over the whites' false racial belief that Negroes are innately superior in emotional expression. This has, however, helped to provide a tradition of success which has spurred them on. Further, novels, poetry, songs, and even painting and sculpture have proven excellent media for expressing the Negro protest or rationalizing the Negro's accommodation to caste.[65] Even the spirituals often have these themes, sometimes under the guise of religious words to avoid censure from the whites ("Didn't my Lord deliver Daniel, and why not every man?" "Let My People Go"). The race issue is often a source of inspiration, and it provides a limitless set of high ideals. Whether all these influences make Negroes superior to whites in the arts we are not in a position to judge. We are merely interested in explaining why Negro achievements in this field are so much greater than in other fields, and why they have been so popular among whites. There are

---

[a] At first, whites may have thought it a little presumptuous of Negroes to go into the arts, but even under slavery, "Negro craftsmen were well-known as cabinet-makers, marquetry setters, wood carvers and iron-smiths as the workmanship of many colonial mansions in Charleston, New Orleans and other colonial centers of wealth and luxury will attest." (Alain Locke, *Negro Art: Past and Present* [1936], pp. 1 and 3.)

many negative factors to be considered in judging relative excellence: Negroes can seldom get the training usually considered necessary to highest achievement in the arts; their segregated schools are usually inadequate; they are restricted in their contacts and, much more than whites, lack the atmosphere congenial to creative work; they are seldom allowed to get far from the race problem; many white critics have a double standard—more indulgent to Negroes—when comparing the products of Negro and white artists; there are still some restrictions against Negro artists, especially in the South.

Whatever the reason for the success of Negroes in the fields of entertainment and the arts, the success has had predominantly beneficial effects for the Negroes. It has enabled them to get a measure of self-confidence, even though it may have had the secondary effect of stimulating a false pride in race. It has made the whites more friendly, and sometimes it has made them have a measure of respect for Negroes.[a] It has opened a significant number of excellent economic opportunities for Negroes, and is thus the economic basis for a sizable portion of the Negro upper and middle class. Interest in the arts may have improved the taste and poise of Negroes; but interest in entertainment may have degraded their tastes. In a number of ways, never analyzed by students of Negro social life, entertainment and the arts have had a pervasive influence on practically all Negroes.

When white support of Negro literature and art was partially withdrawn after 1929, Negroes tended to react away from doing the things whites wanted them to do. Paul Robeson, for example, declared:

> I believe where the Afro-American made his mistake was when he began trying to mimic the West instead of developing the really great tendencies he inherited from the East. I believe the Negro can achieve his former greatness only if he learns to follow his natural tendencies, and ceases trying to master the greatness of the West. My own instincts are Asiatic.[66]

This is only petulance, of course, but many Negro writers and artists have come to believe that they can develop an art quite distinct from the white American's art and from what the white American is willing to pay for. But, as George S. Schuyler wrote in 1926, "Negro art there has been, is, and will be among the numerous black natives of Africa; but to suggest the possibility of any such development among the ten million colored people in this republic is self-evident foolishness."[67] Negro art will continue to be American because its creators are American and American influences continually mold it. Whether Negro artists will turn out products which differ from those of white artists will depend on those individual artists, and on the audiences willing to pay for the art.

[a] See Chapter 30, Section 3.

Part XI

AN AMERICAN DILEMMA

CHAPTER 45

AMERICA AGAIN AT THE CROSSROADS

1. The Negro Problem and the War

The three great wars of this country have been fought for the ideals of liberty and equality to which the nation was pledged. As a consequence of all of them, the American Negro made great strides toward freedom and opportunity.[1] The Revolutionary War started a development which ultimately ended slavery in all Northern states, made new import of slaves illegal and nearly accomplished abolition even in the South—though there the tide soon turned in a reaction toward fortification of the plantation system and of Negro slavery. The Civil War gave the Negro Emancipation and Reconstruction in the South—though it was soon followed by Restoration of white supremacy. The First World War provided the Negro his first real opportunity as a worker in Northern industry, started the Great Migration out of the South, and began the "New Negro" movement —though the end of the War saw numerous race riots and the beginning of a serious decline in employment opportunities. After the advances on all three occasions there were reactions, but not as much ground was lost as had been won. Even taking the subsequent reactions into account, each of the three great wars in the history of America helped the Negro take a permanent step forward.

Now America is again in a life-and-death struggle for liberty and equality, and the American Negro is again watching for signs of what war and victory will mean in terms of opportunity and rights for him in his native land. To the white American, too, the Negro problem has taken on a significance greater than it has ever had since the Civil War. This War is crucial for the future of the Negro, and the Negro problem is crucial in the War. There is bound to be a redefinition of the Negro's status in America as a result of this War.

The exact nature of this structural change in American society cannot yet be foreseen. History is not the result of a predetermined Fate. Nothing is irredeemable until it is past.[a] The outcome will depend upon decisions and actions yet to be taken by whites and Negroes. What we can know definitely, however, are the trends as they developed up to the War and

[a] See Appendix 1, Section 3.

the changes so far during the War. On the basis of this knowledge, we can discern the gamut of possibilities for the future. If, in addition, we have some insight into the temper and inclination of the people who are both the actors and the spectators of the drama being staged, we can estimate which are the most probable developments.

2. SOCIAL TRENDS

Looking back over the ground we have mapped in our inquiry, we can make two general observations. One is the following: *What we usually call "social trends" have their main significance for the Negro's status because of what is in white people's minds.* It is true, for instance, that the decreasing relative demand for unskilled work, compared with skilled and semi-skilled work, and the change of much dirty and heavy labor to clean and easy labor, have dangerous implications for the Negro's employment opportunities. But if these technological and economic trends have disastrous effects on the Negro, the cause of this is the persistency with which white people want to keep him out of skilled and pleasant work. It is also true that the trend toward mass unemployment in America tends to turn Negro labor into a relief burden. But, again, the concentration of unemployment upon the Negro people is explainable only as the direct and indirect effects of discrimination. The restricted immigration of white Europeans to America and other population changes are reversing the century-old trend, in which the Negro was becoming a smaller portion of the total population of the United States, into a trend in which the Negro is becoming a slightly increasing proportion of the population. But if this change of trend will disappoint some white Americans and perhaps tend to increase racial friction, the cause is again race discrimination.

The second observation is this: *The important changes in the Negro problem do not consist of, or have close relations with, "social trends" in the narrower meaning of the term but are made up of changes in people's beliefs and valuations.* We started by stating the hypothesis that the Negro problem has its existence in the American's mind. There the decisive struggle goes on. It is there that the changes occur. Our investigation has amply confirmed our basic assumption, as an abbreviated summary of some of our main findings regarding recent trends will demonstrate.

In the field of *"social"* relations we traced a slow but visible decrease of discrimination in the South during recent decades up until the outbreak of the present War. The racial etiquette was gradually loosening. White people were beginning to take cognizance of distinctions in education and class within the Negro community and becoming prepared to treat Negroes somewhat differently according to their individual worth. The "no social equality" theory was not quite so rigid as in earlier generations. The entire Jim Crow apparatus was maintained, but its motivation was no longer so unquestioned. Southern liberals were demanding with increasing courage and determination that the doctrine "separate, but equal" should be followed out in its "equality" aspect as well as in its "separateness" aspect— that segregation should not be utilized as a means of discrimination.

The separation of the two groups in the South was, meanwhile, becoming more and more perfected as the frequency of personal master-servant relations was decreasing and as the segregated Negro institutions and Negro professions were being built up. There even seemed to be a growing mental isolation between whites and Negroes. Behind this potentially most dangerous development was not only the exclusionist policy of the whites, but also the sullen dissatisfaction and bitter race pride of the Negroes themselves. They were "withdrawing" themselves as a reaction to the segregation and discrimination enforced by the whites.

In the North the sudden influx of Southern Negroes during the Great Migration caused a temporary rise in social discrimination. Since, in spite of this, there was much less of it in the North than in the South, the migration meant a decrease of social segregation and discrimination for the Negro people as a whole. It also seemed that, despite the sharp temporary rise on account of the migration, the trend in the North, too, was toward decreasing race prejudice.

In the administration of *justice* there was a definite improvement in the South, even if Negroes in that region are still far from enjoying equality before the law. There was a slow rise in the quality of the police and the courts. Lynching, peonage, and other conspicuous aberrations of justice were becoming stamped out. This development was spurred by the increasing interest and interference in the judicial order of the region, shown by the federal courts and other federal agencies, and also by the state governments. The activity of such private organizations as the N.A.A.C.P. and the Interracial Commission were also of paramount importance for this development. More fundamentally the prestige of law was rising in the South and people were becoming more law-abiding. These changes were related to a general rise in education of the Southerners and to their fuller participation in the larger American culture.

In the North the Negro continued to enjoy full equality before the law. There was some strain in the North during the Great Migration, sometimes mounting to race riots during which the arm of the law was not always just and impartial. But on the whole the judicial order of the region was upheld, and equality in justice was not a major problem.

In the *political* sphere, the South continued to disfranchise the Negro, contrary to the clear precept of the American Creed and the Constitution. The masses of whites were also kept from political participation. Real issues were kept out of politics and there was a great amount of corruption. But these things proved increasingly difficult to keep up. Economic and ideological changes, related to the region's rapid industrialization, urbanization, and labor unionization, stepped up by the Great Depression and the New Deal, caused political splits in the Southern Democratic party machines. The splits usually remained latent, but here and there, now and then, they forced themselves into the open. The "Solid South" seemed definitely endangered. The poll tax was under fierce attack in all Southern states, and some had already abolished it.

Meanwhile such things as the rise of the price level since the 'nineties and the improved educational level of Southern Negroes made the statutory devices to keep Negroes from the polls—by property and literacy requirements as well as by the poll tax—less and less effective. Negro disfranchisement came increasingly to depend upon extra-legal and illegal sanctions. We viewed this situation as extremely unstable for several reasons: the legal culture of the South was rising; there were no more loopholes left for legalizing Negro disfranchisement; the Solid South was showing signs of breaking up; the liberal forces in the North were getting increasingly exasperated with the South; and the Supreme Court was starting to enforce the Constitution as it applied to voting in the South. Southern liberals were standing up, not only against the poll tax, but often also against the one-party system and the exclusion of Negro voters from the primaries. Even conservative Southerners were occasionally found to hold the opinion that sometime in the future the Negro was going to vote in the South. While the Negro was almost as effectively disfranchised in the South in the years before the outbreak of the present War as he has ever been, our judgment, when taking all these changes into account, thus was that his political position was potentially much stronger and that his gradual enfranchisement was bound to come.

In the North the Negro enjoyed uninfringed his right to vote, and the steadily continuing migration to the North meant that the Negro vote was growing.

In the enjoyment of *public services* the Negro was discriminated against severely in the South in blunt repudiation of the Constitution and the state laws. But even in this sphere we saw a slow improvement of his status as a result of the rising legal culture of the region; the pressures from the Negroes, from public opinion in the North, from the federal courts and administration as well as from the white Southerners' own better conscience. It was becoming somewhat less unusual that a playground or even a little park was arranged for Negroes in some cities. The Negro schools were greatly improved even if they usually still remained inferior. Without question the New Deal was of tremendous importance for the Negro in respect to the share he received of public services. It is true that the Washington administration did not dare and, in any case, did not succeed in stamping out discrimination in relief, agricultural policies, or anything else in the South, but it definitely decreased it. It also brought a new kind of public servant to the South, educated and zealous officials who were not primarily interested in "keeping the Negro in his place" but in encouraging and advancing him. This introduced a new and wholesome type of public contact for the Negro people in the South, and Negroes got a feeling that public authority could be other than arbitrary and suppressive.

In the North public services were, on the whole, granted to Negroes as to other citizens in similar circumstances.

While in all these spheres the trends at the outbreak of the present War were definitely in the direction of a rise in the status of the Negro in America,[a] the same cannot be said about those relating to his occupational status. In Southern agriculture the Negro's plight had been becoming continually worse and showed no prospects for a brighter future. His low place on the occupational ladder usually as a plantation tenant—the increase of Negro landownership had stopped 40 years earlier—his dependence on cotton, his lack of education, and the intense race prejudice in the blighted rural regions of the South made him the main sufferer of the boll weevil, of Southern over-population and "white infiltration," of mechanization and, during the 'thirties, of the collapsing world market and the contractionist national agricultural policy. Yet there were no wholehearted attempts on a mass scale, either by the federal government or by any other agency, to reeducate rural Southern Negroes to take up new occupations in other areas. America was under the spell of economic defeatism so far as a belief in continued rapid industrialization was concerned, and there was no hope of placing the dislocated Negro sharecropper in the industrial cities.

Some rural Negroes moved to Northern and Southern cities, increasing unemployment there. Monopoly of jobs by the whites increased during the Great Depression, and Negroes did not find any new employment openings. Various national policies, such as the Wages and Hours Law, instituted to stamp out sweatshop conditions, could not avoid hurting the employment opportunities of Negroes since they were marginal workers. Under these conditions it is a wonder that Negroes were able to retain as many of their jobs as they did. But Negro unemployment mounted in all cities, particularly in the North, and the Negro workers increasingly became a relief burden. The whole country, and particularly the North, was much more generous toward the Negro in doling out relief to him than in allowing him to work and earn his bread by his own labor.

Meanwhile, the new unions in the mass production industries gave Negro workers hope by organizing them together with whites in fields in which

[a] Coming back to South Carolina after an absence of twenty years, John Andrew Rice noted as one of the outstanding changes: "The Southerner's attitude toward the Negro is incredibly more humane than it was in the South I knew as a child." (*I Came Out of the Eighteenth Century* [1942], p. 195.)

Negroes were already working. But, with few exceptions, they did not open up new industries for Negro employment during the 'thirties, neither did they pave the way for Negroes to rise by promotion from the level of unskilled workers to that of the semi-skilled and skilled. Negro business did not flourish either, and the small gains made in a few professions were quantitatively insignificant. There is no question but that the development in the economic sphere was grave. But as discrimination was slowly decreasing in all other spheres, as there were good prospects that national politics would remain liberal and progressive, as Negro defense organizations and the Negro advisors in the federal administration were hammering on the inequalities, and as the new unions were pledged to nondiscrimination, there seemed to be good prospects that even the threatening trends respecting the Negro's economic status could have been turned, if the country had got out of the long stagnation in a normal way and had entered a new era of continued industrialization. Some of the economic policies of the New Deal were poorly thought out and badly integrated; in some respects they were damaging to the Negro. But administrators and experts were eager to learn from their mistakes and could be expected to accomplish better economic planning and direction when they were relieved of the pressure of emergency and improvisation.

3. The Decay of the Caste Theory

The problem of what would have occurred if there had been no war is now purely academic. The Second World War is bound to change all trends. But before we analyze the implications of the War for the Negro problem, we need to take a still broader perspective and ask: what has happened to white opinions on the Negro problem in the span of three generations since Emancipation?

In the South three generations ago white people had for their defense a consistent and respectable theory, endorsed by the church and by all sciences, printed in learned books and periodicals, and expounded by the South's great statesmen in the Capitol at Washington. The Negro's subordinate status was a principle integrated into a whole philosophy of society and of human life. The Negro was a completely different species of mankind: undeveloped, "child like," amoral, and much less endowed with intellectual capacities than the white man; he was meant by the Creator to be a servant forever; if kept in his "place" he was useful or at least tolerable, and there he was also happy; "social equality" was unthinkable as it implied intermarriage which would destroy the white race and Anglo-Saxon civilization. Much of this theory—which acquired an elaborate structure to satisfy the specific needs to justify discrimination in various spheres of life—remained through Reconstruction, and it was again hailed in the Restoration of white supremacy. Indeed, much of it remained until a couple of decades ago. But now it is almost destroyed for upper class and educated people. Its maintenance among lower class and uneducated people meets increasing difficulties. *The gradual destruction of the popular theory behind race prejudice is the most important of all social trends in the field of interracial relations.*

It is significant that today even the white man who defends discrimination frequently describes his motive as "prejudice" and says that it is "irrational." The popular beliefs rationalizing caste in America are no longer intellectually respectable. They can no longer, therefore, be found in current books, newspapers or public speeches. They live a surreptitious life in thoughts and private remarks. There we have had to hunt them when studying the matter in this inquiry. When they were thus drawn out into the open they looked shabby and ashamed of themselves. Everybody who has acquired a higher education knows that they are wrong. Most white people with a little education also have a hunch that they are wrong. There is today a queer feeling of *credo quia absurdum* hovering over the whole complex of popular beliefs sustaining racial discrimination. This makes the prejudiced white man nearly as pathetic as his Negro victim.

The white man is thus in the process of losing confidence in the theory which gave reason and meaning to his way of life. And since he has not changed his life much, he is in a dilemma. This change is probably irreversible and cumulative. It is backed by the American Creed. The trend of psychology, education, anthropology, and social science is toward environmentalism in the explanation of group differences, which means that the racial beliefs which defended caste are being torn away. It also means, by implication, that the white majority group in power is accused of being the cause of the Negro's deficiencies and unhappiness. Authority and respectability are no longer supporting the popular beliefs. The beliefs are no longer nourished from above. Instead they are increasingly fought. There is a considerable time-lag between what is thought in the higher and in the lower social classes. But as time passes the lower social strata also will change their beliefs. These ideas are spread by the advance of education.

All of this is important. People want to be rational, and they want to feel that they are good and righteous. They want to have the society they live in, and their behavior in this society, explained and justified to their conscience. And now their theory is being torn to pieces; its expression is becoming recognized as a mark of ignorance.

On the other side of the caste gulf the development leads to increased bitterness. To the Negro the white man's trouble with his conscience cannot but seem to be insincerity or something worse. The Negro protest is rising, spurred by the improvement in education. The Negro group is being permeated by the democratic and equalitarian values of the American culture. Since at the same time there has been increasing separation between the two groups, Negroes are beginning to form a self-conscious "nation within the nation," defining ever more clearly their fundamental grievances against white America.

America can never more regard its Negroes as a patient, submissive minority. Negroes will continually become less well "accommodated." They will organize for defense and offense. They will be more and more vociferous. They will watch their opportunities ever more keenly. They will have a powerful tool in the caste struggle against white America: the glorious American ideals of democracy, liberty, and equality to which America is pledged not only by its political Constitution but also by the sincere devotion of its citizens. The Negroes are a minority, and they are poor and suppressed, but they have the advantage that they can fight wholeheartedly. The whites have all the power, but they are split in their moral personality. Their better selves are with the insurgents. The Negroes do not need any other allies.

This moral process had proceeded far when the Second World War broke out.

4. Negroes in the War Crisis

This War is an ideological war fought in defense of democracy. The totalitarian dictatorships in the enemy countries had even made the ideological issue much sharper in this War than it was in the First World War. Moreover, in this War the principle of democracy had to be applied more explicitly to race. Fascism and nazism are based on a racial superiority dogma—not unlike the old hackneyed American caste theory—and they came to power by means of racial persecution and oppression. In fighting fascism and nazism, America had to stand before the whole world in favor of racial tolerance and cooperation and of racial equality. It had to denounce German racialism as a reversion to barbarism. It had to proclaim universal brotherhood and the inalienable human freedoms. The fact that the Japanese utilize anti-white feelings in Asia and elsewhere made it even more necessary to stress the racial equality principle.

In the internal political struggle before America became involved in the War, the isolationists had worked up the idea that there was much to improve at home without trying to improve the rest of the world. They did not disdain even to point to the injustices inflicted upon the Negro; many isolationists to the left put the Negro cause to the forefront. A Georgia senator who had made a lengthy talk about the danger to democracy abroad was challenged by an isolationist co-senator with the question whether the fight for democracy should not begin in Georgia. The plight of the Negro sharecropper and the presence of peonage and lynching were brought up to stress the unsolved tasks at home and to win Negro sympathies for the isolationist cause.[2] One permanent result of this pre-war discussion was that, in this War, the promises to establish the full democratic liberties, not only abroad but also in America, played an even more prominent role than in the First World War.

For the Negroes this new War carried unpleasant reminiscences of the earlier one. The situation looked bitterly ironical. This time, too, the Negro had to fight desperately to get the right to fight for his country. In the armed forces Negroes were discriminated against in the usual ways and to almost the same extent. Mobs had attacked Negro soldiers and war workers, and a Southern senator had requested the Army to keep Negro soldiers out of the South. Negroes also had to fight to get into the war industries and had only partial success. In the First World War they actually made considerable advances in industrial employment, and the Great Migration was a welcome consequence. But this time the nation was well stocked with unemployed whites at the beginning of the defense boom. A technological development had also intervened, decreasing the industrial demand for unskilled labor—the type of jobs for which Negroes are least unwelcome. Up to the time when this is being written (August, 1942), the Negro has been almost excluded from the great bulk of the war industries. Discrimination is the rule practically everywhere.

Under the threat of a Negro march on Washington, skillfully staged by A. Philip Randolph, the President made a solemn proclamation against discrimination in the defense industries and government agencies and appointed a committee, having both Negro and white members, to see that it was observed. Other branches of the Administration made declarations and issued orders against discrimination: some of these statements were apparently sincere in their intention, some were face-saving moves, and most had their locus somewhere in the wide range between. The Republican National Committee resolved that racial discriminations are "wrongs under the Constitution" and pledged the opposition party to work to correct them. The national labor unions also lined up for nondiscrimination. The Negroes heard and read the kindly promises. They again noted the public acceptance of their own reading of the Constitution and the American Creed. But they knew the grim reality.

In the twenty years between the two World Wars the general level of education of the American Negroes had become considerably higher, and so had their capacity for democracy. The Negro press had become better equipped, and it reached farther. The Negro organizations had grown in strength. The national Negro leaders had become firmer, and they were more resentful. This time they were not willing cheerfully to postpone their complaints until the War was over. The elderly Du Bois renounced with bitterness the credulous advice he once gave his people in the First World War to "close ranks." In this new War the Negro leaders advertised freely—and sometimes provocatively—the danger of a low morale among Negroes.

In this War there was a "colored" nation on the other side—Japan. And that nation started out by beating the white Anglo-Saxons on their own ground. The smoldering revolt in India against British rule had significance for the American Negroes, and so had other "color" incidents in the world conflict: the wavering sympathies of several native populations in the Dutch and British possessions in the Pacific, the mistrust against Great Britain among the Arab peoples, the first abandonment of Ethiopia, and the ambiguity of the plans for the colonial chessboard of Africa. Even unsophisticated Negroes began to see vaguely a color scheme in world events, although their thoughts are usually not yet organized in a definite pattern.[3] In a "letter to the editor" by a Negro, which crept into a liberal white paper in the Upper South, the concluding sentences read:

> The Negro races on earth are very suspicious of the white man's good intentions. This is very likely to be the last war that the white man will be able to lead humanity to wage for plausible platitudes.[4]

And this low-toned threat from a single Southern Negro became occasionally more shrill in the North: all colored people should be united in their interests against the whites, and the aim should not be "national unity" but a real color war which would definitely end white imperialism and exploitation.

But this was exceptional. World politics and the color issue are, in the final analysis, of secondary importance to American Negroes, except as avenues for the expression of dissatisfaction. The American Negro is thoroughly Americanized; his complaint is merely that he is not accepted. What really matters to him is his treatment at home, in his own country. A Negro journalist, explaining the feeling of the Negro to the white public, has this to say:

> Because he must fight discrimination to fight for his country and to earn a living, the Negro to-day is angry, resentful, and utterly apathetic about the war. "Fight for what?" he is asking. "This war doesn't mean a thing to me. If we win I lose, so what?"[5]

Reading the Negro press and hearing all the reports from observers who have been out among common Negroes in the South and the North convince me that there is much sullen skepticism, and even cynicism, and vague, tired, angry dissatisfaction among American Negroes today. The general bitterness is reflected in the stories that are circulating in the Negro communities: A young Negro, about to be inducted into the Army, said, "Just carve on my tombstone, 'Here lies a black man killed fighting a yellow man for the protection of a white man.'" Another Negro boy expressed the same feeling when he said he was going to get his eyes slanted so that the next time a white man shoved him around he could fight back.[6] Their caste status being what it is in America, Negroes would, indeed, not be ordinary human beings if such dissatisfaction and bitterness were not their reaction to all the morale talk about democracy, the four freedoms, the American way of life, all the violent denunciations of Nazi race hatred and the lack of freedom under totalitarian rule. We should also remember, however, that, even if Negroes are still mainly excluded from work in the manufacturing industries and from employment offering much future prospect, the war boom has created a lot of secondary employ ment for Negroes, too. There is more money in circulation and some trickles down to the Negroes. With a little money in his pocket even the poor Negro day laborer or domestic worker feels that he can afford to stiffen himself. Many white housewives notice strange thoughts and behavior on the part of their Negro servants these days.

The loyalty of the American Negro in war and peace is, however, prover-bial. The only thing Negroes ask for is to be accepted as Americans. The American Constitution is even dearer to them than to their white compa-triots. They are more unreservedly anti-fascist. Few American Negroes want the Axis powers to win the War. But this is not much of an issue to Negroes, as they, about as much as white Americans, are convinced of the invincibility of their country. Negroes have never doubted the strength and resourcefulness of the whites. Even more, they know that America offers more possibility of democracy, even for themselves, than do the Axis nations. In one of the most thoughtful statements on the question of Negro loyalties since the beginning of the war crisis, Ralph Bunche says:

> There should be no illusions about the nature of this struggle. . . . The fight now is not to save democracy, for that which does not exist cannot be saved. But the fight is to maintain those conditions under which people may continue to strive for realiza-tion of the democratic ideals. This is the inexorable logic of the nation's position as dictated by the world anti-democratic revolution and Hitler's projected new world order.[7]

But it is quite common that Negroes feel a satisfaction in the temporary adversities and want the War to become as serious a matter as possible to the white people in power. There have been reports that poor Negro share-croppers in the South sometimes indulge in dreams of a Japanese army marching through the South and killing off a number of "crackers." They do not want them to land in the North, though, and they certainly do not want them to stay. But much more common is a glowing ill-concealed satisfaction over the war adversities on various fronts. Practically every issue of any Negro newspaper gives proof of this attitude. It must be conceded that Negroes have also some good rational reasons for this feeling. They know, of course, that, as a Northern Negro social scientist explains:

... the graver the outside danger to the safety of this country, the more abundant the gains will be likely to be [for the Negroes]. But until such time as this country is actually in grave danger most of the attention given to the problem of [Negro] morale will be that of conjuring up the right type of propaganda to allay their discontent.[8]

A white commentator complained some months ago that the Negro press is something of a fifth column. He received the unanimous and angry answer in all Negro papers that this is exactly contrary to the truth. Negroes are standing only for the democratic principles, to defend which America is waging war. They are dissatisfied because these principles are ignored in America itself. They are just the opposite of war dodgers and traitors: they pray to have the right to fight and die for their country and to work in the war industries, but they are excluded. They can, with new reason, point to the inconsistency between American ideals and practices, as does one of their wisest editors, Elmer A. Carter: ". . . this strange and curious picture, this spectacle of America at war to preserve the ideal of government by free men, yet clinging to the social vestiges of the slave system."[9] This ideological attack is so clear-cut and simple and so obviously to the point that it appeals even to the least educated Negro. The cause of the American Negro has supreme logical strength. And the Negro is better prepared than ever before in his history to fight for it.

5. The War and the Whites

This simple logic is, of course, apparent to white Americans, too. And the whites were on the way, even before the War, to lose their caste theory and their complacency in the face of obvious abuses of the American Creed. They are also stirred up by the War and the great cause of human liberties at stake. In the North the question can be publicly approached in only one spirit, that of the American Creed. A newspaper editorial reads like this:

If the United Nations win this war the principle of the world-wide legal equality of races will have to be recognized. Since this is largely a war of ideas, and since racial equality before the law has become one of the central ideas on the democratic side, we can almost say that this principle, in itself, may be the deciding factor. The Chinese, the East Indians, the numerous African peoples and many other groups are on our side, or would be so if they were completely convinced that we mean what we say by equality just as unreservedly as the Nazis mean what they say by inequality. But we Americans cannot very well talk convincingly in these terms unless we prove our sincerity in our own country. Our largest recognizable racial minority is the Negro.[10]

The titular leader of the Republican party, Wendell Willkie, speaking in July, 1942, at the annual conference of the N.A.A.C.P. in Los Angeles, California, had this to say:

Today it is becoming increasingly apparent to thoughtful Americans that we cannot fight the forces and ideas of imperialism abroad and maintain a form of imperialism at home. The war has done this to our thinking. . . . So we are finding under the pressures of this present conflict that long-standing barriers and prejudices are breaking down. The defense of our democracy against the forces that threaten it from without has made some of its failures to function at home glaringly apparent. Our very proclamations of what we are fighting for have rendered our own inequities self-evident. When we talk of freedom and opportunity for all nations the mocking paradoxes in our own society become so clear they can no longer be ignored.[11]

The world conflict and America's exposed position as the defender of the democratic faith is thus accelerating an ideological process which was well under way. In this dramatic stage of the American caste struggle a strategic fact of utmost importance is this, that the entire caste order is extra-legal if not actually illegal and unconstitutional. The legal order of the land does not sanction caste but, on the contrary, is framed to guarantee equality and to suppress caste. The only important exceptions are the Jim Crow laws in the Southern states. But even they are written upon the fiction of equality, although, if equality were enforced, they would not only lose in efficacy as means of expressing caste subordination, but also become tremendously burdensome economically for society and, consequently, the whites would be robbed of one of their main interests in upholding them.

The whites are aware of the tremendous social costs of keeping up the present irrational and illegal caste system. Among other things, this anomaly is one of the main factors keeping the respect for law and order and the administration of laws at such a low level in America. The whites investigate these irrationalities and the consequent social wastage; they build scientific systems to explain their social causation, in fact, they know all about it and deplore it. They have the political power to make caste legal and orderly, whether with Negro consent or without it. But practically never will whites be heard making such proposals, and still less will they seriously discuss and plan for such a change. They cannot afford to compromise the American Creed.

Caste may exist, but it cannot be recognized. Instead, the stamp of public disapproval is set upon it, and this undermines still more the caste theory by which the whites have to try to explain and justify their behavior. And *the Negroes are awarded the law as a weapon in the caste struggle.* Here we see in high relief how the Negroes in their fight for equality have their allies in the white man's own conscience. The white man can humiliate the Negro; he can thwart his ambitions; he can starve him; he can press him down into vice and crime; he can occasionally beat him and even kill him; but he does not have the moral stamina to make the Negro's subjugation legal and approved by society. Against that stands not only the Constitution and the laws which could be changed, but also the American Creed which is firmly rooted in the Americans' hearts.

6. The North Moves Toward Equality

In the North the Creed was strong enough long before the War to secure for the Negro practically unabridged civic equality in all his relations with public authority, whether it was in voting, before the courts, in the school system or as a relief recipient. But he is discriminated against ruthlessly in private relations, as when looking for a job or seeking a home to live in. The white Northerner, in his private dealings with people to whom he does not feel akin, has dangerous traditions derived from the exploitation of new immigrants. But even in those nonpublic spheres, and particularly in the problem of breadwinning, the white Northerner is becoming prepared, as a citizen, to give the Negro his just opportunity. But apparently, as a private individual, he is less prepared to feel that he himself is the man to give the Negro a better chance: in his own occupation, trade union, office or workshop, in his own residential neighborhood or in his church. The social paradox in the North is exactly this, that almost everybody is against discrimination in general but, at the same time, almost everybody practices discrimination in his own personal affairs.

It is the cumulation of all these personal discriminations which creates the color bar in the North and for the Negro causes unusually severe unemployment, crowded housing conditions, crime and vice. About this social process the ordinary white Northerner keeps sublimely ignorant and unconcerned. This aloofness is, of course, partly opportunistic but it can be fought by education. When now, in the war emergency, the Negro is increasingly given sympathetic publicity by newspapers, periodicals, and the radio, and by administrators and public personalities of all kinds, one result is that the white Northerner is gradually waking up and seeing what he is doing to the Negro and is seeing also the consequences of his democratic Creed for his relations with Negroes. We have become convinced in the course of this inquiry that the North is getting prepared for a fundamental redefinition of the Negro's status in America. The North will accept it if the change is pushed by courageous leadership. And the North has much more power than the South. The white South is itself a minority and a national problem.

Also working in favor of the Negro is another trend, namely, the concentration of responsibility. Particularly in the crucial economic sphere this trend is rapid. Labor relations are coming increasingly to be planned and regulated by broad union policies and by national legislation and administration. The War will force this change forward step by step. After the War, in the great crisis of demobilization and liquidation, mass unemployment will be a main problem. Large-scale public intervention will be a necessity. In this endeavor no national administration will dare to allow unemployment to be too much concentrated upon the Negro.

The average white Northerner will probably agree with a policy which holds open employment opportunities for Negroes, because, as we said, he is against economic discrimination as a general proposition. There is also—together with all opportunistic ignorance and unconcernedness—a bit of rational defense for the distance he preserves between his political and his private opinion. In the individual shop where he works or the residential section where he lives, he sees the danger in admitting a few Negroes, since this will bring an avalanche of Negroes on his shop or his neighborhood. This danger is, of course, due to the fact of the Negro's general exclusion. It is part of the vicious circle holding the Negro down.

If government policy prevents general discrimination, however, there will be no avalanche of Negroes on any one white employer or group of employers. The Negroes, who comprise less than 10 per cent of the population, must be given their chance in private enterprise or be supported by public funds. "Buck-passing" is no longer possible when the problem comes to be viewed nationally. And the planning and directing agencies will be compelled to make the white public see the problem nationally in order to get public support for the policy they must pursue. As private relations are increasingly becoming public relations, the white Northerner will be willing to give the Negro equality.

These are the reasons why we foresee that the trend of unionization, social legislation, and national planning will tend to break down economic discrimination, the only type of discrimination which is both important and strong in the North. Other types of discrimination will then tend to decrease according to the law of cumulative causation which has been frequently referred to in this book.

7. Tension in the South

The situation in the South is different. Unlike the white Northerner, who is most inclined to give the Negro equality in public relations and least inclined to do so in private relations, the white Southerner does not differentiate between public and private relations—the former as well as the latter have significance for prestige and social equality. Moreover, he is traditionally and consistently opposed to Negro equality for its own sake, which the Northerner is not. He may be privately indulgent much more than the white Northerner, but he is not as willing to give the Negro equal treatment by public authority. This is one of the romantic principles behind the legal inequity in the South. But the Southerner is a good American, too, and the region has been becoming rapidly "Americanized" during the last generation.

The ordinary conservative white Southerner has, therefore, a deeper split in his moral personality than does the white Northerner. The War is stirring up the conflict in his soul. The air is filled with reminders of the great cause of democracy and the equality of peoples, which is the main issue in the War America is waging against nazism, fascism, and Japanese imperialism. His "own Negroes" are making some money, reading the Negro press and getting restless. The N.A.A.C.P. and other protest organizations are fighting ever more daringly in his own cities. In his newspapers he reads how the national leaders, from the President down, come out with blunt denunciations of racial discrimination. He is finding that Northern leaders are increasingly getting interested in the poll tax, the white primary, Negro disfranchisement, injustices against Negroes, and other peculiar institutions of the South which he guards behind the doctrine of "states' rights."

What is he supposed to do? Give up Jim Crow and so perhaps allow a Negro to marry his daughters; build good schools for Negroes, though the schools are not too good for his own children; punish white invaders of Negro rights, though they otherwise may be perfectly good and upright citizens; relinquish white supremacy? Is he supposed to retreat from all "Southern traditions"? He sees "outside aggression" wherever he turns.

This is an old story and a phase of a mental cycle through which the unfortunate South has often passed before. The fact that this time the white Southerner's caste theory is weaker than ever and does not inspire much of his own intellectual confidence makes his dilemma worse. His emotions on the color issue are less stable also because his personal ties to the Negro group have been decreasing, and racial isolation has been intensified during the last generation. He "knows the Negro" less well than did his father and grandfather, though he continues to pretend that he knows him well, because to "know the Negro" is also a Southern tradition. Having fewer personal contacts with Negroes he is likely to exaggerate the signs of opposition from the Negroes, for he feels that the Negroes have good reason to develop opposition. The presence in Southern communities of Negro soldiers, many from the North, increases his uneasiness. Du Bois, writing about the First World War, talks about:

> . . . the deep resentment mixed with the pale ghost of fear which Negro soldiers call up in the breast of the white South. It is not so much that they fear that the Negro will strike if he gets a chance, but rather that they assume with curious unanimity that he has *reason* to strike, that any other persons in his circumstances, or treated as he is would rebel. Instead of seeking to relieve the cause of such a possible feeling, most of them strain every effort to bottle up the black man's resentment.[12]

In the present crisis, Guion G. Johnson, a liberal Southern white historian, could already in July, 1941, report from the South that

> . . . there has been some uneasiness that "our Negroes" are being tampered with, and white advocates of racial goodwill have occasionally found it more difficult

within the last year to speak out boldly. White persons who have for decades been working toward interracial cooperation may now find themselves charged with fifth column activity and Negro leaders may be denounced as communists or nazis.[13]

Another prominent white Southern liberal describes in a letter to the author the mental state of the white South as of summer, 1942:

. . . we are in the midst of a situation in the South where we seem to have been thrown back with great losses where we had expected great gains: and . . . the situation in the South may be of the proportions of a crisis greater than we have had in many years. For the first time in my experience the situation is so complex that we do not know how to proceed to next steps. Just a few years ago we almost had unanimity in plans for cooperative arrangements, in which Negroes and whites were enthusiastic and in which representatives of nearly all phases of the South were participants. We had worked into entirely new patterns of fellowship and participation, and there were many evidences that the South was beginning to be proud of this progress. Today, as far as I know, there is practically none of this left. The South is becoming almost unanimous in a pattern of unity that refers to white unity. The thousands of incidents and accidents in the South are being integrated into the old pattern of Southern determination against an outside aggression.[14]

In the approaching conflict between the Negro and the South, this writer sees that

. . . a South which was just coming into its own, getting ready for an enriched agriculture, a more balanced economy, a more liberal viewpoint will sacrifice all this in a pathetic blood and sweat episode reminiscent of the Civil War and Reconstruction.

Similar to this deeply concerned statement of a liberal white Southerner, we may cite the equally troubled view of a Negro clergyman, Dr. J. S. Nathaniel Tross:

I am afraid for my people. They have grown restless. They are not happy. They no longer laugh. There is a new policy among them—something strange, perhaps terrible.[15]

The situation is so critical in the South today that fifty Southern Negro leaders have seen fit to gather together, deliberately excluding Northern Negroes, and to plead for racial amity. They accept social segregation, but request the elimination of all other inequalities. This development was made necessary by the fearful backing away of some Southern liberals—notably Mark Ethridge, John Temple Graves, and Virginius Dabney—from the social segregation issue. The meeting of the Southern Negroes serves both as an attempt to prevent the racial lines from being drawn more sharply and as a disclaimer of responsibility for future violence.

An important element in the situation is that the Southern Negroes, if they are attacked, are more prepared to fight this time than they have ever been before. A competent Negro social scientist, who has recently been studying conditions in the Upper South, confirms this view and, in May, 1943, confides that he expects the outbreak of serious race riots in the South within the next year.

The situation is grave, and the years to come will provide a serious test of the political resourcefulness of white public authorities and of other white and Negro leaders. But regardless of what happens, we do not believe that this is a turn for the worse in race relations in the South. Even if there are going to be serious clashes and even if their short-run effects will be devastating to the Negroes involved and, perhaps, to Negroes in the whole region, we believe that the long-run effect of the present opinion crisis in the South, because it is a catharsis for the whites, will be a change toward increased equality for the Negro. When we make this judgment, we recall a remark once made in a conversation by a prominent and conservative Negro social scientist in the South. He stated as his considered opinion that tensions are not necessarily bad and that under certain conditions even race riots may have wholesome effects in the long run. He continued in about the following way: "They stir up people's conscience. People will have to think matters over. They prevent things from becoming settled. If the race situation should ever become fixed, if the Negro were really accommodated, then, and only then, would I despair about a continued great improvement for Negroes. As long as there is friction and fighting, there is hope."

At this juncture the white North is moving in a direction contrary to the South. The white South is becoming increasingly isolated. There has not been such a great distance in the views of the Negro problem between the white majority groups in the two regions since Reconstruction. Though it is seldom expressed clearly, the outside observer feels convinced that an increasing number of white Northerners mean business this time. It is true, as James Weldon Johnson once observed, that "essentially the status of the Negro in all other sections will depend upon what it is in the South,"[16] but the North will find it increasingly necessary to have its say about the Negroes' status in the South. The North cannot well afford any longer to let the white Southerners have their own way with the Negroes as completely as they have had.

The national compromise has lasted for two generations; it may now be approaching its end, at least relatively. Ten years from now this period in the history of interracial relations in America may come to look as a temporary *interregnum*. The compromise was not a stable power equilibrium. Signs of its end have been frequent during the 'thirties: a whole set of Supreme Court decisions, the New Deal in the South, the increasing activity of federal agencies to stamp out peonage, the agitation for a federal lynching law and for an abolition of the poll tax by Congress, the repeal of the two-thirds majority rule for the nomination of the Democratic candidate for the Presidency, and so on.

The Negro problem is becoming national in scope in a different sense than was meant when white Southerners expressed a belief that the Negro migration to the North would give the North more of a share in the trouble of having Negroes as neighbors and that then the North would understand the racial philosophy of the South better. The Negro vote and the labor vote in the North also have considerable weight in checking Southern conservatism and have increasing power to do so. But aside from all that, national planning cannot leave out the South or humor too much its irrationality. As a matter of fact the South, particularly its agriculture and its population pressure, will continue to remain one of the main national worries.

Because of this development, spurred by the war crisis and the coming peace crisis, it seems justifiable to predict a growing tension between the two regions, one which will not be restricted to the Negro issue. There is not going to be a civil war, of course. The South is this time relatively much weaker in all respects. The North will probably not become more considerate if the interracial tension in the South gets out of hand and results in bloody clashes. As recourse to civil war is out of the question and as things thus have to be settled by political means, the fact becomes of importance that the white South is not united against a redefinition of the Negro's status. The South has been, and is, changing rapidly, and Southern liberalism has been coming to be a force though it was practically nowhere in political power and today is fearfully timid on the Negro issue. Even the ordinary conservative white Southerner has a deeply split personality. In the short run this can be suppressed, and the tension can lead to violent reactions. But in the long run it means that the conservative white Southerner himself can be won over to equalitarian reforms in line with the American Creed.

8. INTERNATIONAL ASPECTS

What has actually happened within the last few years is not only that the Negro problem has become national in scope after having been mainly a Southern worry. It has also acquired tremendous international implications, and this is another and decisive reason why the white North is prevented from compromising with the white South regarding the Negro. The situation is actually such that any and all concessions to Negro rights in this phase of the history of the world will repay the nation many times, while any and all injustices inflicted upon him will be extremely costly. This is not yet seen clearly by most Americans, but it will become increasingly apparent as the War goes on.

We mentioned in passing that the American Negro cannot help observing the color angle to this War. He is obviously getting vicarious satisfaction out of this perspective, and he is also testing some vague feelings of solidarity and allegiance to the cause of other colored peoples involved in the world conflagration. But this is a minor part of the international implications. The American Negro is thoroughly American in his culture and whole outlook on the world. He is also loyal to America, and there is no danger that he will betray it. This is at least certain in the short-range view, which covers this War and the coming peace. How the Negro would react if he were left dissatisfied and if later a new war were to be fought more definitely along color lines is more difficult to predict.

The main international implication is, instead, that America, for its international prestige, power, and future security, needs to demonstrate to the world that American Negroes can be satisfactorily integrated into its democracy. In a sense, this War marks the end of American isolation. America has had security behind the two protecting oceans. When now this isolation has been definitely broken, the historians will begin to see how it has always greatly determined the development of America. Statesmen will have to take cognizance of the changed geopolitical situation of the nation and carry out important adaptations of the American way of life to new necessities. A main adaptation is bound to be a redefinition of the Negro's status in American democracy.

It is commonly observed that the mistrust of, or open hostility against, the white man by colored people everywhere in the world has greatly increased the difficulties for the United Nations to win this War.[a] Many old sins and stupidities are today staring back upon the white man, and he continues to commit them, though he now knows better. The treatment of the Negro in America has not made good propaganda for America abroad and particularly not among colored nations. That good American who has acquired such a rare understanding for the Asiatic people's mind, Pearl S. Buck, comments:

Japan . . . is declaring in the Philippines, in China, in India, Malaya, and even Russia that there is no basis for hope that colored peoples can expect any justice from the people who rule in the United States, namely, the white people. For specific proof the Japanese point to our treatment of our own colored people, citizens of generations in the United States. Every lynching, every race riot, gives joy to Japan. The discriminations of the American army and navy and the air forces against colored soldiers and sailors, the exclusion of colored labor in our defense industries and trade unions, all our social discriminations, are of the greatest aid today to our enemy in Asia, Japan. "Look at America," Japan is saying to millions of listening ears. "Will white Americans give you equality?"[17]

[a] Not only colored peoples have been disturbed by America's treatment of her Negroes. The German radio often mentions America's harsh treatment of Negroes in its propaganda broadcasts to European peoples. (New York *Times* [September 2, 1942], p. 3.)

And she assures her compatriots:

> We cannot . . . win this war without convincing our colored allies—who are most of our allies—that we are not fighting for ourselves as continuing superior over colored peoples. The deep patience of colored peoples is at an end. Everywhere among them there is the same resolve for freedom and equality that white Americans and British have, but it is a grimmer resolve, for it includes the determination to be rid of white rule and exploitation and white race prejudice, and nothing will weaken this will.[18]

This is perhaps an exaggeration. Perhaps the War can this time be won even without the colored people's confidence. But the absence of their full cooperation, and still more their obstructive activities, will be tremendously costly in time, men and materials. Caste is becoming an expensive luxury of white men.

It seems more definitely certain that it will be impossible to make and preserve a good peace without having built up the fullest trust and goodwill among the colored peoples. They will be strong after the War, and they are bound to become even stronger as time passes. For one thing, this is certain in so far as numbers are concerned. During the short span of the last three centuries, which include almost the entire epoch of white power expansion, the peoples of European stock increased sevenfold, while the others increased only threefold. The whites grew from a bare 100 millions, or a fifth of the globe's total, to over 700 millions, or a third of all mankind. The increase for the whites was fastest during the last century when they gradually became able to control deaths but had not as yet brought births under control. The whites are, however, now in the second phase of this dynamic sequence: the white birth rate is falling so fast that it is catching up with the relatively stable death rate. The population expansion of the whites is now slowing down, absolutely and relatively. Many of the Western nations, including America and all those other peoples on the highest level of industrial civilization, will probably start to shrink in population numbers within a few decades. The colored nations, on the other hand, are just entering the first stage where expansion is likely to be pushed by an increasingly improved control over death, and it is unlikely that the increase in birth control will keep pace with the improvement of the control over death. The whites will, therefore, from now on become a progressively smaller portion of the total world population. If we except the Russian peoples, who are still rapidly increasing, the rapid change in proportion stands out still more dramatically.

Another broad trend is almost as certain, namely, that the "backward" countries, where most colored people live, are going to become somewhat industrialized. The examples of Japan and, more recently, of Russia and China give support to the view that in the future we shall see many backward countries industrialized at a tremendously more rapid rate than were the pioneer Western countries, who had to find out everything for them-selves. The same examples illustrate also how such backward nations can advantageously use the newly created industrial apparatus for producing war materials, and they illustrate, too, how they can fight with them.

Particularly as Russia cannot be reckoned on to adhere to white suprem-acy, it is evident from these facts—though nobody in our countries seems to take it seriously—that within a short period the shrinking minority of white people in our Western lands will either have to succumb or to find ways of living on peaceful terms with colored people. If white people, for their own preservation, attempt to reach a state in which they will be tolerated by their colored neighbors, equality will be the most they will be strong enough to demand.

History is never irredeemable, and there is still time to come to good terms with colored peoples. Their race pride and race prejudice is still mostly a defensive mental device, a secondary reaction built up to meet the humiliations of white supremacy. This is apparent in the case of the American Negro. It probably holds true even for other colored people who have not yet had a taste of power. A Chinese propaganda leaflet assures the Americans:

> Chinese nationalism or race-consciousness is essentially defensive in character. It has developed out of continuous fight for freedom, and has never been offensive.[19]

It should be apparent that the time to come to an understanding on the basis of equality is rapidly running out. When colored nations have once acquired power but still sense the scorn of white superiority and racial discrimination, they are likely to become indoctrinated by a race prejudice much more akin to that of the whites—a race prejudice which can be satisfied only by the whites' humiliation and subjugation.

9. MAKING THE PEACE

Americans in general are concerned with the task of making a constructive peace after the War. It is commonly understood that this task is fraught with immense and unprecedented difficulties and, particularly, that the flagrant mismanagement of international affairs by the great democracies in the period between the two World Wars, the devastation caused by the Second World War, the breaking up of the state structures of Europe, and the approaching liquidation of colonial imperialism in the Far East have created a psychological state in mankind which, aside from all physical and economic deficiencies, raises almost insurmountable obstacles for the peace-makers. Americans generally recognize also that the protection of the two oceans is gone forever, that American isolationism will never more be possible, that America is in world politics for better or for worse, and that this time it has to stick to the making and upholding of the peace which is yet to be written.

Americans also recognize that America has to take world leadership. The coming difficult decades will be America's turn in the endless sequence of main actors on the world stage. America then will have the major responsibility for the manner in which humanity approaches the long era during which the white peoples will have to adjust to shrinkage while the colored are bound to expand in numbers, in level of industrial civilization and in political power. For perhaps several decades, the whites will still hold the lead, and America will be the most powerful white nation.

America goes to this task with the best of intentions. Declarations of inalienable human rights for people all over the world are now emanating from America. Wilson's fourteen points were a rehearsal; Roosevelt's four freedoms are more general and more focused on the rights of the individual. The national leaders proclaim that the coming peace will open an age of human liberty and equality everywhere. This was so in the First World War, too. This time something must be done to give reality to the glittering generalities, because otherwise the world will become entirely demoralized. It will probably be impossible to excite people with empty promises a third time. It is commonly agreed, and taken as proved by the coming of this War, that peace cannot be preserved if the development of a democratic life in every nation is not internationally guaranteed and the possibility of oppression is not checked. It is anticipated that international agencies will be created to sanction such a development.

In view of the clarity and unanimity in America on these fundamental points, few white Americans fully realize all the obvious implications. I have, for instance, met few white Americans who have ever thought of the fact that, if America had joined the League of Nations, American Negroes could, and certainly would, have taken their cases before international tribunal back in the 'twenties. Some versatile Negro protest leaders are, however, familiar with the thought. After this War there is bound to be an international apparatus for appeal by oppressed minority groups. In America, Negro organizations like the N.A.A.C.P. are excellently equipped for such conspicuous litigation. It is, indeed, possible that such implications of the coming democratic peace, when they become better seen and publicly discussed, will act as deterrents and as a motive for isolationism in some American circles. But there is no way back. America is irredeemably in world politics.

Behind her two protecting oceans America has until now lived an exuberant and carefree life without having to bother much about its international reputation. Probably no other modern people has cared less about what impression it makes on other nations. The ordinary American might have been interested to know, but has not bothered much about, the fact that lynchings and race riots are headlines in Bombay; that Huey Long and Father Coughlin, the wave of organized crime during and after Prohibition, the fiscal bankruptcy of Chicago some years ago, the corrupt political machines in Philadelphia, the Dayton trial of Darwinism, provided stories for the Sunday papers in Oslo; that many men and women in democratic countries around the entire world have had their first and decisive impression of American public life from the defense of Sacco and Vanzetti and the Scottsboro boys. Friends of America abroad have tried to make the picture of American life more balanced and more accurate by fixing public attention on the numerous good sides, on American accomplishments, on all the good intentions and on the favorable trends. But they have been only partly successful, and America itself has—until this War—never cared to advertise America abroad.

This—like America's openness to criticism, which is the positive side of this unconcernedness—is a sign of great strength, but it was the strength of a departed isolation. There was also ignorance behind the attitude. Aware of all the good things in his country and rightly convinced that, on the whole, they greatly outweigh all the imperfections, the ordinary American takes it for granted that America is liked and trusted abroad.

The loss of American isolation makes all this most serious. America has now joined the world and is tremendously dependent upon the support and good-will of other countries. Its rise to leadership brings this to a climax. None is watched so suspiciously as the one who is rising. None has so little license, none needs all his virtue so much as the leader. And America, for its own security, cannot retreat from leadership.

There is, of course, another possible solution besides good-will, and that is power. In some quarters in America the observer finds exaggerated notions about the power which America's financial strength after the War will allow her. Americans have not commonly taken to heart what was conclusively proved by experience in the period between the two World Wars, namely, that, after the loans are given, the power belongs to the debtor and not to the creditor.

Military power, however, can be substituted for good-will. But America does not have the will or stamina for real imperialism. The farmer, the laborer, the merchant, the intellectual, in one word, the common man who ultimately makes political decisions is against suppression abroad. In the international field the Southerner is not unlike his Northern compatriot. All American adventures in imperialism give abundant proofs of half-heartedness and show again the power over the Americans of the American Creed. If America does not go fascist, American militarism will not be an adequate substitute for good-will.

The treatment of the Negro is America's greatest and most conspicuous scandal. It is tremendously publicized, and democratic America will continue to publicize it itself. For the colored peoples all over the world, whose rising influence is axiomatic, this scandal is salt in their wounds. In all white nations which, because of the accident of ethnic homogeneity or for other causes, have not been inculcated with race prejudice, the color of the victim does not provide any excuse for white solidarity. That this is so in Russia is well known and advertised. It holds true also in many other white nations.

10. AMERICA'S OPPORTUNITY

But these consequences of the present course of America's and the world's history should not be recorded only in terms of compelling forces. The bright side is that the conquering of color caste in America is America's own innermost desire. This nation early laid down as the moral basis for its existence the principles of equality and liberty. However much Americans have dodged this conviction, they have refused to adjust their laws to their own license. Today, more than ever, they refuse to discuss systematizing their caste order to mutual advantage, apparently because they most seriously mean that caste is wrong and should not be given recognition. They stand warmheartedly against oppression in all the world. When they are reluctantly forced into war, they are compelled to justify their participation to their own conscience by insisting that they are fighting against aggression and for liberty and equality.

America feels itself to be humanity in miniature. When in this crucial time the international leadership passes to America, the great reason for hope is that this country has a national experience of uniting racial and cultural diversities and a national theory, if not a consistent practice, of freedom and equality for all. What America is constantly reaching for is democracy at home and abroad. The main trend in its history is the gradual realization of the American Creed.

In this sense the Negro problem is not only America's greatest failure but also America's incomparably great opportunity for the future. If America should follow its own deepest convictions, its well-being at home would be increased directly. At the same time America's prestige and power abroad would rise immensely. The century-old dream of American patriots, that America should give to the entire world its own freedoms and its own faith, would come true. America can demonstrate that justice, equality and cooperation are possible between white and colored people.

In the present phase of history this is what the world needs to believe. Mankind is sick of fear and disbelief, of pessimism and cynicism. It needs the youthful moralistic optimism of America. But empty declarations only deepen cynicism. Deeds are called for. If America in actual practice could show the world a progressive trend by which the Negro became finally integrated into modern democracy, all mankind would be given faith again—it would have reason to believe that peace, progress and order are feasible. And America would have a spiritual power many times stronger than all her financial and military resources—the power of the trust and support of all good people on earth. *America is free to choose whether the Negro shall remain her liability or become her opportunity.*

The development of the American Negro problem during the years to come is, therefore, fateful not only for America itself but for all mankind. If America wants to make the second choice, she cannot wait and see. She has to do something big and do it soon. For two generations after the national compromise of the 1870's between the North and the South on the Negro problem, the caste status of the Negro was allowed to remain almost unchanged. It was believed by most well-meaning people that self-healing would work, that the Negro problem would come to solve itself by the lapse of time. George Washington Cable wrote in the 'eighties:

> There is a vague hope, much commoner in the North than in the South, that somehow, if everybody will sit still, *"time"* will bring these changes.[20]

Two decades later, Ray Stannard Baker reported from the South:

> All such relationships will work themselves out gradually, naturally, quietly, in the long course of the years: and the less they are talked about the better.[21]

Most of the literature on the Negro problem continues to this day to be written upon this same static assumption.

We have given the reasons why we believe that the *interregnum*, during which the forces balanced each other fairly well, is now at an end. The equilibrium, contrary to common belief, was unstable and temporary. As American Negroes became educated and culturally assimilated, but still found themselves excluded, they grew bitter. Meanwhile the whites were in the process of losing their caste theory. The international upheavals connected with the two World Wars and the world depression brought these developments to a crisis. American isolation was lost. Technical developments brought all nations to be close neighbors even though they were not trained to live together.

We are now in a deeply unbalanced world situation. Many human relations will be readjusted in the present world revolution, and among them race relations are bound to change considerably. As always in a revolutionary situation when society's moorings are temporarily loosened, there is, on the one hand, an opportunity to direct the changes into organized reforms and, on the other hand, a corresponding risk involved in letting the changes remain uncontrolled and lead into disorganization. To do nothing is to accept defeat.

From the point of view of social science, this means, among other things, that social engineering will increasingly be demanded. Many things that for a long period have been predominantly a matter of individual adjustment will become more and more determined by political decision and public regulation. We are entering an era where fact-finding and scientific theories of causal relations will be seen as instrumental in planning controlled social change. The peace will bring nothing but problems, one mounting upon another, and consequently, new urgent tasks for social engineering. The American social scientist, because of the New Deal and the War, is already acquiring familiarity with planning and practical action. He will never again be given the opportunity to build up so "disinterested" a social science.

The social sciences in America are equipped to meet the demands of the post-war world. In social engineering they will retain the old American faith in human beings which is all the time becoming fortified by research as the trend continues toward environmentalism in the search for social causation. In a sense, the social engineering of the coming epoch will be nothing but the drawing of practical conclusions from the teaching of social science that "human nature" is changeable and that human deficiencies and unhappiness are, in large degree, preventable.

In this spirit, so intrinsically in harmony with the great tradition of the Enlightenment and the American Revolution, the author may be allowed to close with a personal note. Studying human beings and their behavior is not discouraging. When the author recalls the long gallery of persons whom, in the course of this inquiry, he has come to know with the impetuous but temporary intimacy of the stranger—sharecroppers and plantation owners, workers and employers, merchants and bankers, intellectuals, preachers, organization leaders, political bosses, gangsters, black and white, men and women, young and old, Southerners and Northerners—the general observation retained is the following: Behind all outward dissimilarities, behind their contradictory valuations, rationalizations, vested interests, group allegiances and animosities, behind fears and defense constructions, behind the role they play in life and the mask they wear, people are all much alike on a fundamental level. And they are all good people. They want to be rational and just. They all plead to their conscience that they meant well even when things went wrong.

Social study is concerned with explaining why all these potentially and intentionally good people so often make life a hell for themselves and each other when they live together, whether in a family, a community, a nation or a world. The fault is certainly not with becoming organized *per se*. In their formal organizations, as we have seen, people invest their highest ideals. These institutions regularly direct the individual toward more cooperation and justice than he would be inclined to observe as an isolated private person. The fault is, rather, that our structures of organizations are too imperfect, each by itself, and badly integrated into a social whole.

The rationalism and moralism which is the driving force behind social study, whether we admit it or not, is the faith that institutions can be improved and strengthened and that people are good enough to live a happier life. With all we know today, there should be the possibility to build a nation and a world where people's great propensities for sympathy and cooperation would not be so thwarted.

To find the practical formulas for this never-ending reconstruction of society is the supreme task of social science. The world catastrophe places tremendous difficulties in our way and may shake our confidence to the depths. Yet we have today in social science a greater trust in the improvability of man and society than we have ever had since the Enlightenment.

APPENDICES

A METHODOLOGICAL NOTE ON
VALUATIONS AND BELIEFS

1. The Mechanism of Rationalization

People have ideas about how reality actually is, or was, and they have ideas about how it ought to be, or ought to have been. The former we call "*beliefs.*" The latter we call "*valuations.*" A person's beliefs, that is, his knowledge, can be objectively judged to be true or false and more or less complete. His valuations—that a social situation or relation is, or was, "just," "right," "fair," "desirable," or the opposite, in some degree of intensity or other—cannot be judged by such objective standards as science provides. In their "*opinions*" people express both their beliefs and their valuations. Usually people do not distinguish between what they think they know and what they like or dislike.

There is a close psychological interrelation between the two types of ideas. In our civilization people want to be rational and objective in their beliefs. We have faith in science and are, in principle, prepared to change our beliefs according to its results. People also want to have "reasons" for the valuations they hold, and they usually express only those valuations for which they think they have "reasons." To serve as opinions, specific valuations are selected, are formulated in words and are motivated by acceptable "reasons." With the help of certain beliefs about reality, valuations are posited as parts of a general value order from which they are taken to be logical inferences. This value hierarchy has a simple or elaborate architecture, depending mainly upon the cultural level of a person. But independently of this, most persons want to present to their fellows—and to themselves—a trimmed and polished sphere of valuations, where honesty, logic, and consistency rule. For reasons which we shall discuss, most people's advertised opinions are, however, actually illogical and contain conflicting valuations bridged by skewed beliefs about social reality. In addition, they indicate very inadequately the behavior which can be expected, and they usually misrepresent its actual motivation.

The basic difficulty in the attempt to present a logical order of valuations is, of course, that those valuations actually are conflicting. When studying the way in which the valuations clash, and the personal and social results brought about by the conflicts, we shall, moreover, have to observe that the valuations simply cannot be treated as if they existed on the same plane. They refer to different levels of the moral personality.[a] The moral precepts contained in the respective valuations correspond to

[a] This hypothesis is presented more fully in the Introduction to this volume (Sections 1 and 2).

different degrees of generality of moral judgment. Some valuations concern human beings in general; others concern Negroes or women or foreigners; still others concern a particular group of Negroes or an individual Negro. Some valuations have general and eternal validity; others have validity only for certain situations. In the Western culture people assume, as an abstract proposition, that the more general and timeless valuations are morally higher. We can, therefore, see that the motivation of valuations, already referred to, generally follows the pattern of trying to present the more specific valuations as inferences from the more general.

In the course of actual day-to-day living a person will be found to focus attention on the valuations of one particular plane of his moral personality and leave in the shadow, for the time being, the other planes with their often contradicting valuations. Most of the time the selection of this focus of evaluation is plainly opportunistic. The expressed valuations and beliefs brought forward as motives for specific action or inaction are selected in relation to the expediencies of the occasion. They are the "good" reasons rather than the "true" reasons; in short, they are "rationalizations."

The whole "sphere of valuations"—by which we mean the entire aggregate of a person's numerous and conflicting valuations, as well as their expressions in thought, speech, and behavior—is thus never present in conscious apperception. Some parts of it may even be constantly suppressed from awareness. But it would be a gross mistake to believe that the valuations temporarily kept in the shadow of subjective inattention—and the deeper-seated psychic inclinations and loyalties represented by them—are permanently silenced. Most of them rise to consciousness now and then as the focus of apperception changes in reaction to the flow of experiences and impulses. Even when submerged, they are not without influence on actual behavior. They ordinarily bend behavior somewhat in their direction; the reason for suppressing them from conscious attention is that, if obeyed, they would affect behavior even more. In this treatise, therefore, behavior is conceived of as being typically the outcome of a moral compromise of heterogeneous valuations, operating on various planes of generality and rising in varying degrees and at different occasions to the level of consciousness. To assume the existence of homogeneous "attitudes" behind behavior would violate the facts, as we must well know from everyday introspection and from observation and reflection. It tends to conceal the moral conflicts which are the ultimate object of our study in this book.

The individual or the group whose behavior we are studying, moreover, does not act in moral isolation. He is not left alone to manage his rationalizations as he pleases, without interference from outside. His valuations will, instead, be questioned and disputed. Democracy is a "government by discussion," and so, in fact, are other forms of government, though to a lesser degree. Moral discussion goes on in all groups from the intimate family circle to the international conference table. Modern means of intellectual communication have increased the volume and the intensity of such moral interrelations.

When discussion takes the form of moral criticism by one person or group or another, it is not that the one claims to have certain valuations that the other does not have. It is rather an appeal to valuations which the other keeps in the shadow of inattention, but which are assumed, nevertheless, to be actually held in common. This assumption, that those with opposing opinions have valuations in common, is ordinarily correct. As we observed in the Introduction,[a] cultural unity in America consists in the fact that most Americans have most valuations in common, though they are differently arranged and bear different intensity coefficients for different individuals and groups. This makes discussion possible and secures an understanding of, and a response to, criticism.

In this process of moral criticism which men make upon each other, the valuations on the higher and more general planes—referring to *all* human beings and *not* to specific small groups—are regularly invoked by one party or the other, simply because they are held in common among all groups in society, and also because of the supreme prestige they are traditionally awarded. By this democratic process of open discussion there is started a tendency which constantly forces a larger and larger part of the valuation sphere into conscious attention. More is made conscious than any single person or group would on his own initiative find it advantageous to bring forward at the particular moment. In passing, we might be allowed to remark that this effect—and in addition our common trust that the more general valuations actually represent a "higher" morality—is the principal reason why we, who are convinced democrats, hold that public discussion is purifying and that democracy itself provides a moral education of the people.

When thus even the momentarily inopportune valuations are brought to attention, an element of indecision and complication is inserted. A need will be felt by the person or group, whose inconsistencies in valuations are publicly exposed, to find a means of reconciling the inconsistencies. This can be accomplished by adjusting one of the conflicting pairs of valuations. If the valuation to be modified is on the less general plane, a greater moral harmony in the larger group is brought about. Specific attitudes and forms of behavior are then reconciled to the more general moral principles. If, on the other hand, an attempt is made to change or reinterpret valuations which are more general in scope and most of the time consciously shared with all other groups in society, the deviant group will see its moral conflict with other groups becoming increasingly explicit (that is, if the other groups are not themselves prepared to change their general valuations toward a moral compromise). This process might go on until discussion no longer becomes feasible. In the extreme case such a moral isolation, if the dissenting group is powerful enough, may break the peace and order of society and plunge a nation into civil war.

In the short-run day-to-day conflicts, usually no abrupt changes of valuations will occur. The need for reconciling conflicting valuations brought into the open through public discussion will, for the time being, only result in quasi-logical constructions. In the very nature of things, these constructions must be fantastic, as they represent an attempt to reconcile the illogicalities by logical reasoning.

The temptation will be strong to deny the very existence of a valuation conflict. This will sometimes bring in its wake grossly distorted notions about social reality. There is a sort of social ignorance which is most adequately explained as an attempt to avoid the twinges of conscience. It is, for instance, an experience of every social scientist, who has been working on problems of social policy and has taken some interest in people's reactions, that the strongest psychic resistance is aroused when an attempt is made to teach the better situated classes in a society about actual lower

[a] Section 2.

class standards of living and what causes them. This particular type of moral escapism works, sometimes with extraordinary effectiveness, in the American Negro problem.

The feeling of need for logical consistency within the hierarchy of moral valuations—and the embarrassed and sometimes distressed feeling that the moral order is shaky—is, in its modern intensity, a rather new phenomenon. With less mobility, less intellectual communication, and less public discussion, there was in previous generations less exposure of one another's valuation conflicts. The leeway for false beliefs, which makes rationalizations of valuations more perfect for their purpose, was also greater in an age when science was less developed and education less extensive. These historical differentials can be observed today within our own society among the different social layers with varying degrees of education and communication with the larger society, stretching all the way from the tradition-bound, inarticulate, quasi-folk-societies in isolated backward regions to the intellectuals of the cultural centers. When one moves from the former groups to the latter, the sphere of moral valuations becomes less rigid, more ambiguous and also more translucent. At the same time, the more general valuations increasingly gain power over the ones bound to traditional peculiarities of regions, classes, or other smaller groups. One of the surest generalizations is that society, in its entirety, is rapidly moving in the direction of the more general valuations. The speed stands in some relation to, and can be gauged by, geographical mobility, the development of intellectual communication, the decrease of illiteracy and the funds spent on education.

During this process of growing intellectualization, people's awareness of inconsistencies in their own spheres of valuations tends to be enhanced. At the same time—if moral cynicism does not spread, a possibility which we shall consider presently—they are increasingly reconditioned to demand consistency in their own valuations and, particularly, in those of other people. They learn to recognize and to avoid the use of illogicalities and misconceptions of social reality for overcoming the incongruities in their valuations. The impatient humanitarian might find this process exasperatingly slow, and the results meager. The perspective of decades and generations, however—providing moral catastrophes do not interrupt the growth process—yields a more optimistic impression.

We have already hinted at the fact that valuations are seldom overtly expressed except when they emerge in the course of a person's attempts to formulate his beliefs concerning the facts and their implication in relation to some section of social reality. Beliefs concerning the facts are the very building stones for the logical hierarchies of valuations into which a person tries to shape his opinions. When the valuations are conflicting, as they normally are, beliefs serve the rationalization function of bridging illogicalities. The beliefs are thus not only determined by available scientific knowledge in society and the efficacy of the means of its communication to various population groups but are regularly "biased," by which we mean that they are systematically twisted in the one direction which fits them best for purposes of rationalization.

There are in the Negro problem whole systems of popular beliefs concerning the Negro and his relations to the larger society which are crudely false and can only be understood in this light. These "popular theories," or ideologies, are themselves important data in our study, as they represent strategic social facts in the practical and political problems of race relations. A legitimate task of education is to attempt to correct popular beliefs by subjecting them to rigorous examination in the light of the factual evidence. This educational objective must be achieved in the face of the psychic resistance mobilized by the people who feel an urgent need to retain their biased beliefs in order to justify their way of life.

If this educational effort meets with success, the illogicalities involving valuations become exposed to the people who hold them. They are then pressed to change their valuations to some degree or other. For if popular beliefs depend upon valuations, as we have shown, the valuations also depend upon the beliefs in our civilization bent upon rationalism. When supporting beliefs are drawn away, people will have to readjust their value hierarchies and, eventually, their behavior. As the more general norms in our culture are given supreme moral sanction, this means—if we assume that this "valuation of the valuations" is upheld, and moral cynicism counteracted—that the valuations on a more specific level (often called "prejudices") will yield to them. This is the reason, and the only reason, why we generally assume that improved knowledge will make for "better" citizens. Facts by themselves do not improve anything.

There is a question of terminology which should be touched upon, as it is not without importance for our scheme of thinking. The term "value" has, in its prevalent usage, a loose meaning. When tightened it is generally taken to refer to the object of valuations, rather than to the valuations themselves. Unfortunately it has a connotation of something solid and homogeneous while our hypothesis is that the valuations are conflicting. We shall avoid using the term "value." The term "attitude" has the same connotation of solidity. Too, it is often used to denote beliefs as well as valuations. When used in this book "attitude" should be understood as simply a convenient synonym for valuation.[a]

2. THEORETICAL CRITIQUE OF THE CONCEPT "MORES"

We must voice our grave skepticism toward the simple explanatory scheme concerning the role of valuations in social life typified by William Graham Sumner's concepts, "folkways" and "mores."[b] Since his time these concepts—or one of their several synonyms—have been widely used by social scientists and have, in particular, determined the approach to the Negro problem. The formula will be found to be invoked with some regularity whenever an author expresses his attitude that changes will be slow, or, more particularly, that nothing practical can be done about a matter. It is closely related to a bias in social science against induced changes, and especially against all attempts to intervene in the social process by legislation. The concept of mores actually implies a whole social theory and an entire *laissez-faire* ("do-nothing") metaphysics,[c] and is so utilized.

Leaving aside for the present the political connotations of Sumner's construction, and focusing our interest only on its usefulness as a scientific tool, our main criticism

[a] This paragraph will, perhaps, explain why the author has not been able to avoid the term "valuation" though knowing well that it is not widely used in America. The term has been used, however, by John Dewey in several of his works, by Charles H. Cooley in his *Social Process* (1918), by Robert M. MacIver in his *Social Causation* (1942), and probably by others.

[b] William Graham Sumner, *Folkways* (1911, first edition 1906).

[c] See Appendix 2, Section 3, and Chapter 1, Section 11.

is the following: By stowing the commonly held valuations into the system of mores, conceived of as a homogeneous, unproblematic, fairly static,[a] social entity, the investigator is likely to underestimate the actual difference between individuals and groups and the actual fluctuations and changes in time. He is also likely to lose sight entirely of the important facts, that even within a single individual valuations are operative on different planes of generality, that they are typically conflicting, and that behavior is regularly the outcome of a moral compromise.

It might be that Sumner's construction contains a valid generalization and offers a useful methodological tool for studying primitive cultures and isolated, stationary folk-communities under the spell of magic and sacred tradition. It might even be that the most convenient definition of such a folk-culture is the applicability of the theory of folkways and mores. The theory is, however, crude and misleading when applied to a modern Western society in process of rapid industrialization, moving in swift trends rippled by indeterminate cyclical waves: a society characterized by national and international mobility, by unceasing changes and differentiations of all valuations and institutions, by spreading intellectualization, by widening intellectual communication and secularization, by ever more daring discussion even of fundamentals and intimacies, and by a consequent virtually universal expectation of change and a firm belief in progress. If Sumner's construction is applied to such a society, except as a contrast conception to mark off some remaining backward cultural isolates which are merely dragged along and do not themselves contain the active factors of social dynamics, it is likely to conceal more than to expose. It conceals what is most important in our society: the changes, the conflicts, the absence of static equilibria, the lability in all relations even when they are temporarily, though perhaps for decades, held at a standstill. The valuation spheres, in such a society as the American, more nearly resemble powder-magazines than they do Sumner's concept of mores.

3. VALUATION DYNAMICS

In our view, changes in valuations—of the type known as "revolutions," "mutations," or "explosions"—are likely to occur continuously in modern society. "Stability," or rather lack of change, when it reigns, is the thing which requires explanation. Individual persons in modern society are in the same sort of labile equilibrium as the molecules of explosives. Their valuations are inconsistent, and they are constantly reminded of the inconsistency. Occasionally the moral personalities of individuals burst, and a modification and rearrangement of the valuations in the direction of a more stable equilibrium is accomplished.

Since similar influences work upon all individuals in the society, the cumulative results include continuous changes of "public opinion." Such changes are "intentional," in a sense, and part of a democratic development. The trend of opinions and changes in institutions in a democracy—the "reforms"—usually have their core in the cumulation of such valuation explosions in the minds of people. When the inconsistency between people's valuations is large and has effectively been exposed, the change might occasionally be sudden and quite big, and we speak then of a social

[a] Sumner recognized a "strain toward consistency" within the mores because of conflicting principles, but his main emphasis—and the same is true when the concept is used by contemporary writers—is always upon stability, inertia, and resistance against induced change. Compare Appendix 2, Section 3.

revolution. But the more evolutionary social changes, if they are dissected into their elements, are not very different except in magnitude.

The history of every nation and of every community, in fact, of every group, is, in one sense, the record of the successive waves of such opinion explosions. Even societies have their catharses and, like individuals, they have them almost all the time. It is the weakness, not only of the static and fatalistic traditions in social science attached to the great names of Marx and Sumner, but of our common tendency to look for explanations in terms only of natural forces and material trends,[a] that we blind ourselves to the dynamics of opinion as it develops from day to day; or, in any case, we become inclined to deal with human opinions more as the result of social change than as part of the cause of it.

By stressing that opinions are not passive elements in the social process, we have, of course, not meant to make them altogether independent of material forces. The very fact that opinions to an extent are opportunistic implies that they will change as a result of every other change in social environment. Changes in the technique of production, of communication and of consumption force individual and group revaluations. But so, also, does spread of knowledge, as well as moral discussion and political propaganda. Ideas have a momentum of their own; they are partly primary causes in the social process; or rather, they are integral factors in an interdependent system of causation.

In an opinion catharsis—of an individual or a group—a new, temporary, and labile equilibrium of conflicting valuations is established. The direction in a normal and peaceful process of popular education is toward decreasing inconsistency. We said that ordinarily the new balance gives greater weight to the more general valuations. But our reason for the conclusion was that those valuations were generally agreed to be morally "higher" and have supreme social sanction, and we added the reservation that our conclusion assumes that moral cynicism does not spread. If moral cynicism should spread, however—that is, if people become willing to throw aside even their most cherished general valuations, such as their faith in democratic liberty, equality, and Christian brotherhood—the situation permits almost any type of reconstruction. Instead of a rebirth of democracy and Christianity such that those terms acquire new personal meanings for every individual, there may be a revulsion to fascism and pagan gods.

When a sudden and great opinion catharsis occurs in society, customs and social trends seem to the participants to be suspended or radically changed, as they actually are to a certain extent. In this sense history is undecided; it can take several courses. Ideological forces take on a greater importance. Leaders—whom we call either "statesmen," "thinkers" and "prophets" or "demagogues" and "charlatans," depending upon our valuation of their aims and means—capture the attention of the masses and manage to steer the upheaval in one direction or the other. On a smaller scale the same occurs in every group at all times, and the "leaders" are legion; in a sense we are all "leaders." In the explanation of this type of process, where ideological factors, together with all other factors, are active forces within an interdependent system of causation, the materialistic conception of history breaks down. Indeed, any mechanical philosophy of human dynamics is inadequate—except when looking

[a] See Appendix 2, Section 3.

backward, because in looking backwards, *any* development can be organized into *any* scheme, if it is general enough.

Before leaving the subject of social dynamics, we must qualify our remarks to recognize the existence of social statics. By stressing the instability of valuations we do not deny that there is an enormous amount of resistance to change. There *is* a great deal of practically mechanistic causation in human life, almost completely divorced from valuations. People do strive to keep their valuation conflicts under control. They want to keep them off their minds, and they are trained to overlook them. Conventions, stereotypes, and convenient blind spots in knowledge about social reality do succeed in preserving a relative peace in people's conscience. Even more important, perhaps, is the fact that there are only a few hours a day free from the business of living, and that there are so many "pleasant" things to do during these few hours. Most people, most of the time, live a routine life from day to day and do not worry too much. If it could be measured, the amount of both simple and opportune ignorance and unconcernedness about social affairs would undoubtedly be greater than the amount of knowledge and concern.

But to stress these things is not to invalidate the dynamic theory we have presented. Modern people *do* have conflicting valuations, and the spread of knowledge and the increase of interrelations *are* more and more exposing them. Changes in the material environment also keep minds from becoming settled. If we call the relative absence of change in modern society "stability," we must recognize that it is not such as is envisaged in the theory of the folkways and mores. There is *instability* at bottom, a *balancing of forces in conflict with each other*, and there is continuously the possibility of rapid, and even induced, change, the direction of which is not altogether predetermined by trends and natural forces.

A METHODOLOGICAL NOTE ON FACTS AND VALUATIONS IN SOCIAL SCIENCE

1. BIASES IN THE RESEARCH ON THE AMERICAN NEGRO PROBLEM

The biases in popular beliefs about social reality and the deeper conflicts of valuations rationalized by these popular theories can be made apparent through comparison with "objective" truth as this is revealed by scientific research.[a] But the scientist himself is not necessarily immune to biases. In the light of the history of scientific writings on the American Negro problem, the biased notions held in previous times and the opportunistic tendencies steering them stand out in high relief against the better controlled scientific views of today. Our steadily increasing stock of observations and inferences is not merely subjected to continuous cross-checking and critical discussion but is deliberately scrutinized to discover and correct hidden preconceptions and biases. Full objectivity, however, is an ideal toward which we are constantly striving, but which we can never reach. The social scientist, too, is part of the culture in which he lives, and he never succeeds in freeing himself entirely from dependence on the dominant preconceptions and biases of his environment.

Race problems, generally, and the Negro problem in America, particularly, are to an extraordinary degree affected by conflicting valuations of high emotional tension. Keeping in mind the actual power situation in the American nation and observing the prevalent opinions in the dominant white group, we are led, even by a superficial examination, to expect that even the scientific biases will run against the Negroes most of the time. This expectation has been confirmed in the course of our study.[b]

The underlying psychology of bias in science is simple. Every individual student is himself more or less entangled, both as a private person and as a responsible citizen, in the web of conflicting valuations, which we discussed in Appendix 1. Like the layman, though probably to a lesser extent, the scientist becomes influenced by the need for rationalizations. The same is true of every executive responsible for other people's research and of the popular and scientific public before which the scholar performs, and whose reactions he must respect. Against the most honest determination

[a] See Appendix 1, Section 1.
[b] The fact that most of the literature on the Negro problem is biased one way or the other is commonly understood in America and often stated; see, for example, E. B. Reuter, *The American Race Problem* (1938; first edition, 1927), pp. 17 and 27; John Dollard, *Caste and Class in a Southern Town* (1937), pp. 33-41.

to be open-minded on the part of all concerned and, primarily, on the part of the scientists themselves, the need for rationalization will tend to influence the objects chosen for research, the selection of relevant data, the recording of observations, the theoretical and practical inferences drawn and the manner of presentation of results.

The method of detecting bias also is simple. As the unstated premises are kept hidden, the inferences drawn from them and from the factual data contain logical flaws. The general method of detecting biases is, therefore, to confront conclusions with premises and find the *non sequitur* which must be present if inferences are biased. If all premises are not stated explicitly, the inferences must be inconclusive. This method works as long as the biases are restricted to the plane of inferences. If the biases have influenced the very observations, so that the observed data are wrongly perceived and recorded, the method is to repeat the observations. If they have influenced the selection of data collected, the viewpoints and hypotheses applied, or the demarcation of the field of study, the check consists in the application of alternative hypotheses and the widening of the scope of research to embrace the neglected fields. The awareness of the problem of bias is a most important general protection.

Certain tendencies toward scientific bias are apparent on the surface.[a] These biases may be classified into groups, each of which may be regarded as a continuum along which the specific biases fall.[b]

(a) *The Scale of "Friendliness" to the Negro.* Various authors show a different degree of "friendliness" to the Negro people and to the Negro cause. It will often be visible in the very style of presentation, but its more important locus is, of course, in approaches and conclusions. This applies not only to general books on the Negro problem but to special researches and to researches primarily centered on other topics but involving some aspect of the Negro problem.

White scholars until the last two or three decades worked more or less consistently in the interests of the dominant white group's need for rationalization or justification of the system of color caste. Even the friends of the Negro people were moved by the dominant public opinion to assume, without much questioning, views which were unduly unfavorable to the Negroes. They were, in other words, "friendly" to the Negroes only when compared with the very unfriendly general public opinion, but not when compared with what disinterested scholarship should have demanded. This general bias is most easily detected in the question of the Negro's racial traits, but it also operated in other fields, for instance in the writing of history.

In the course of a general movement in the American social sciences toward increasing emphasis upon the "environment" as a cause of differences between social groups the scientific treatment of the Negro problem has, during the last few decades, become vastly more friendly to the Negroes. Without any doubt many white

[a] Under a more penetrating analysis all tendencies to bias will be found to have involved relations among themselves and with deeper ideological tendencies which have even shaped our main conceptual tools in social science; see Section 3 of this Appendix. These ideological tendencies are biased in a static and do-nothing (*laissez-faire*) conservative direction, which, in the main, works against a disfavored group like the American Negroes.

[b] The statements made in the following paragraphs grew out of the author's reflections upon the literature on the Negro problem. For further explanation and substantiation the reader is referred to the specific chapters of our inquiry.

scientists in the field, perhaps the majority, have attached their research interests to the Negro problem or to various aspects of it because of a primary reform interest. In the national *ethos* there is traditionally, as we often have occasion to point out, a strong demand for "fair play" and for consideration toward "the underdog." Since Negroes are severely suppressed, even today, and since by virtue of that fact they often fall below the mark in conduct and accomplishments, and since public opinion is still prejudiced against the Negroes, even a friendliness which stands out as exceptional may allow views which are rather on the unfriendly side of true objectivity. The range of scientific opinions, therefore, does not even today necessarily include the unbiased opinion.

Negro social scientists can be assumed, naturally, to have been biased in the friendly direction. Generally speaking, they have most of the time reached results more favorable to their group. Public and academic opinion in the dominant majority group, the Negro scientists' desire to lean backwards and be strictly scientific, and other reasons, may often cause even the Negro scientist to interpret the facts in a way which is actually biased against his own people.

(b) *The Scale of "Friendliness" to the South.* Most Negroes still live in the South, and, what is more important, all economic, social, and political problems of this region are connected with the Negro problem to a degree without comparison in other regions. The historical tradition through slavery, Civil War, Reconstruction, and Restoration also ties together the judgments on the South and on the Negro. The same is true of the caste restrictions to which the Negro in the South is subjected. In general, a friendly attitude toward the South carries with it unfavorable views toward Negroes or at least a tendency to minimize the fact that they are a substantial proportion of the South's people. Conversely, a sympathetic attitude toward Negroes, their shortcomings, their grievances, and their problems, and especially the attempt to explain them on any basis other than racial inferiority, will be taken as a criticism of the social and moral order of the South.

The first tendency is conspicuous in practically all writings on the Negro problem by Southern writers—at least until recently. The natural interest to defend the white South will be reflected in adverse biases in the discussion about the Negro. Because of the present trend in social sciences toward fewer adverse biases against the Negro, Southern social scientists have increasingly taken a critical attitude toward Southern institutions and morals. This second tendency runs parallel to, and supports, Southern liberalism.[a]

A pro-Southern bias, is, however, not restricted to Southern writers. Ever since the great national compromise of the 1870's, when Reconstruction was liquidated, the need for rationalization of the anomalous position and treatment of the Negro has been national in scope. Contrary to the belief commonly held in the South, the present writer has reached the conviction that not only the general public in the North but also Northern social scientists are rather pro-Southern in their biases.[b]

[a] Southern liberalism is discussed in Chapter 21, Section 5.

[b] This impression is based upon the writer's comparative studies of the literature on the Negro problem. The more precise significance of the statement is the belief that if a statistically reliable sample from Northern scientific literature were made of statements which twisted truth somewhat in one direction or the other, there would be a considerable preponderance of twists in favor of the South. Usually those twists are in the nature of avoid-

Because the existence of the Negro problem is so widely held to be a blot upon Southern civilization, this common tendency in favor of excusing or explaining the South gives rise to biases adverse to the Negro. The recent trend toward increased friendliness to the Negro has been connected with rising criticism against the South. Negro writers have naturally never shared much in the pro-Southern bias.

(c) *The Scale of Radicalism-Conservatism.* The place of the individual scientist in the scale of radicalism-conservatism has always had, and still has, strong influences upon both the selection of research problems and the conclusions drawn from research. *In a sense it is the master scale of biases in the social sciences.* It can be broken up into several scales, mutually closely integrated: equalitarianism-aristocratism, environmentalism-biological determinism, reformism—*laissez-faire*, and so forth. There is a high degree of correlation between a person's degree of liberalism in different social problems. Usually the more radical a scientist is in his political views, the more friendly to the Negro cause he will feel and, consequently, the more inclined he will be to undertake and carry out studies which favor the Negro cause. The radical will be likely to take an interest in refuting the doctrine of Negro racial inferiority and to demonstrate the disadvantages and injustices inflicted upon the Negro people.

The tendency toward increased friendliness to the Negro people, already referred to, is undoubtedly related to a general tendency during the last few decades, in American society and its social science, toward greater liberalism. In a particular problem where public opinion in the dominant white group is traditionally as heavily prejudiced in the conservative direction as in the Negro problem, even a radical tendency might fail to reach an unprejudiced judgment; whereas under other circumstances or in other problems the objective truth might lie beyond the most extreme conservative position actually held. The prevalent opinion that a "middle-of-the-road" attitude always gives the best assurance of objectivity is, thus, entirely unfounded.

(d) *The Scale of Optimism-Pessimism.* Without doubt most social scientists are under the influence of the general tendency of any man or any public not to want to be disturbed by deeply discouraging statements about the social situation and impending trends or by demands for fundamental changes of policy.[a] In the Negro problem, which has extremely disturbing prospects, indeed, this tendency to defend the "happy end-

---

ance of facts and conclusions which would be embarrassing to the South; sometimes the avoidance takes the form of understatements, euphemistic expressions or concealment of such data and conclusion in unduly abstract and complicated formulations. Pro-Southern biases in the studies of Southerners, when they occur, take the same expression; in addition, their presentations of facts will often be softened by tributes to the regional romanticism. This bias is more prevalent in the fields of history and sociology than in the other social sciences.

[a] This tendency can be illustrated from many other fields. When an economic depression turns into a prolonged stagnation of industry as in America during the 'thirties, economists are likely to begin to talk about "maturity" of the economy, and to direct their interests to minor waves of ups and downs within the stagnation. When the industrialization process is checked for a time, some agricultural economists will always be found to give themselves and the general public consolation in a new enthusiasm for self-sustaining farming or even an American peasantry. When sound forecasts of the reproduction trend point to a cumulatively declining future population, the statisticians in all countries turn out for a time to talk about the approach of a "constant population."

ing," for white America and the Negro people will generally make for a soft-pedaling of such adverse facts in the interracial situations as offer little prospect of becoming changed within a reasonable time. This minimization or suppression of discouraging facts may occur when they refer to either the white or the Negro group. At the same time encouraging signs will be unduly played up. Practically the whole literature on the Negro, as on all other social problems, is influenced by this tendency.[a]

This optimistic bias may work against the Negro or for him. It may be connected with a radical or a conservative inclination. In some respects this tendency will gain strength as people's interest in reforms increases; they do want to believe in them. A skeptical conservative is, sometimes, more likely to face facts as they are, than is a fervent liberal. On the other hand, a conservative is interested in presenting actual conditions in a favorable light, while the reformer takes his very start in revealing unfavorable facts. The tendencies here cross each other in a most complicated pattern.

The majority of people do resist having matters which they regard as unfortunate depicted as hopelessly closed. They usually do not want, either, to be confronted with demands for fundamental reforms in deeply ingrained social usages. The reluctance on the part of many Negro and white social scientists to accept the term "caste" to describe the white-Negro relationship—and the remarkable charge of emotion invested in this minor terminological question—apparently has part of its explanation in the common dislike of a term which carries associations of permanency to an institution incompatible with the American Creed and in the unwillingness to face a demand for fundamental reforms.

The optimistic bias becomes strengthened, paradoxically enough, by the scientist's own critical sense and his demand for foolproof evidence. The burden of proof is upon those who assert that things are bad in our society; it is not the other way around. Unfortunate facts are usually more difficult to observe and ascertain, as so many of the persons in control have strong interests in hiding them. The scientist in his struggle to detect truth will be on his guard against making statements which are unwarranted. His very urge to objectivity will thus induce him to picture reality as more pleasant than it is.

(e) *The Scale of Isolation-Integration.* In the Introduction we pointed out the opportune interests and factual circumstances which must make both white and Negro scientists inclined to treat the Negro problem in isolation from the total complex of problems in American civilization.[b] The maximum integration represents absence from bias along this line. Objectivity is reached the more completely an investigator is able to interrelate the Negro problem with the total economic, social, political, judicial and broadly cultural life of the nation.

[a] An illustration on a high level of an adjustment to the general demand for a "happy end" is Lord Bryce's famous study of American local and national politics, *The American Commonwealth,* published in 1893 and republished in 1910 and 1919. Bryce had to engage in a close investigation of many deeply disturbing phases of American public life, and the greatness of his work is due largely to his successful effort never to shun the facts and never to present his conclusions in uncertain terms. But in short paragraphs sprinkled throughout his text he played up the reform tendencies somewhat. This became visible when, in later editions, he could retain most of his text unchanged—including the optimistic forecasts about "impending" reforms.

[b] Introduction, Section 4.

(f) *The Scale of Scientific Integrity.* The degree to which a scientist is prepared to study unpopular subjects and to state plainly and clearly unpopular conclusions derived from his findings depends, naturally, on his own political inclinations, his personal courage and the relative freedom awarded him by society. These factors, however, are not independent of each other. In communities where academic freedom is low, the scientist normally will, in adjustment to the environment where he works, develop, on the one hand, a dislike for controversial matters and for clear and bluntly scientific statements concerning them, and, on the other hand, an unduly high valuation of agreement and conformity as such. Quite independent of the favorable or unfavorable judgment society passes upon such an attitude, it is, of course, detrimental to scientific clarity and objectivity and to scientific progress.

It is apparent that the social and political situation in the South, and particularly in the Deep South, is still not very favorable to a disinterested and objective study of the Negro problem. Until recently this problem, in spite of its supreme importance to the region, was avoided as an object for research. Even at present, and even at the academic fortresses where a considerable amount of academic freedom has been realized, it requires personal courage on the part of a scientist to investigate objectively such aspects of the Negro problem as are heavily loaded with emotions; for example, those connected with sex or religion. Similar influences work upon the Negro scientist in the South. He will often have to become an artist in interracial diplomacy, which, on the whole, will tend to make him rather diplomatic even in his scientific research. The interracial situation in the South will thus tend to lay political inhibitions on both white and Negro scientists.

In the North, and particularly at the great and famous institutions, such inhibitions are not found. Where there are remnants of inhibitions in social research they will rather be applied to other fields—economic and political—more important to the social forces in control of universities and other research institutions, than to the Negro problem.

Quite generally it must be remembered, however, that the Negro problem is something of a skeleton in the American closet. Objective studies are liable to show up situations which are scandalous, not only to the community but also to the nation. A certain apprehension is natural. On the whole, *however, the American public is remarkably scandal-proof.*[a] But it seems as if the closet has first to be opened, and the scandal, so to speak, be publicly "established." Certain scandals are public, as a matter of tradition and convention, and investigations of them do not meet with violent protest. Lynching, for example, is such a public scandal in connection with the Negro problem. The phenomenon can be investigated and written about rather freely everywhere, even in the South. The same is true, to a great extent, of the seamy sides of politics. These scandals have become notorious and recognized. The national conscience has dissociated itself from them, even if it has not been possible to stamp them out of existence. There are, however, other scandals which are not, at least not as yet, "established." It seems to be rather accidental and, to some extent, a result of private initiative on the part of an investigator who originally opens the issue, which scandals

---

[a] The extraordinary high degree of openness to criticism which characterizes American culture above every other national culture in the Western world is discussed in Chapter 1.

are, and which are not, established enough to move the national conscience and leave the scientists free for their work.[a]

2. METHODS OF MITIGATING BIASES IN SOCIAL SCIENCE

Since Benjamin Franklin's day, American science has quite distinctly leaned toward a healthy trust in "hard facts." The inclination to stress empirical "fact-finding" has characterized the magnificent rise of American social sciences. As a trend it has become accentuated during the last generation by the huge funds made available for research, the unprecedentedly rapid growth of universities and research institutions, the equally rapid increase of the number of persons engaged in scientific pursuits, and the specialization thereby made possible.

By subjecting popular beliefs and scientific assumptions to the test of facts, specific biases in the research on the Negro have time and again been unmasked. The recent history of research on racial differences offers excellent examples. Incidentally, it also gives a clue as to the direction in which the biases in the Negro problem would tend to go if unchecked. Generally speaking, our attempts to eradicate biases by stress on factual research have been the more fruitful, the simpler the problems involved are from a methodological point of view and the more successfully we have been able to utilize controlled research methods such as have been developed in the natural sciences.

It must be maintained, however, that *biases in social science cannot be erased simply by "keeping to the facts" and by refined methods of statistical treatment of the data.* Facts, and the handling of data, sometimes show themselves even more pervious to tendencies toward bias than does "pure thought." The chaos of possible data for research does not organize itself into systematic knowledge by mere observation. Hypotheses are necessary. We must raise questions before we can expect answers from the facts, and the questions must be "significant." The questions, furthermore, usually have to be complicated before they reach down to the facts. Even apparently simple concepts presume elaborate theories. These theories—or systems of hypotheses—contain, of necessity, no matter how scrupulously the statements of them are presented, elements of *a priori* speculation. When, in an attempt to be factual, the statements of theory are reduced to a minimum, biases are left a freer leeway than if they were more explicitly set forth and discussed.

Neither can biases be avoided by the scientists' stopping short of drawing practical conclusions. *Science becomes no better protected against biases by the entirely negative device of refusing to arrange its result for practical and political utilization.* As we shall point out, there are, rather, reasons why the opposite is true.

When perhaps a majority of the foremost social scientists in America have an ambition toward, and take pride in, keeping entirely free from attempting to reach practical and political conclusions from their research, part of the explanation is their high professional standards. The quest for scientific objectivity is, I believe, more lively, and kept more explicit, in America than elsewhere. The position is also more understandable when considered from an historical perspective. Social science in America in its modern form developed as a conscious reaction to an earlier highly normative and teleological doctrine. Monumental theories were built without resort to the observa-

[a] There are other scales along which biased views fall, such as the scales of dogmatism—eclecticism, long-run—short-run perspective, practicality—impracticality. They have been incidentally taken up in the various chapters.

tion of social facts, and radical changes in social life were demanded without due consideration of the actual forces and processes through which social life exists and changes. The reaction against reformism and philosophical system-building has been particularly violent in American sociology where a concerted drive to build a social science on the model of the natural sciences is clearly apparent. This tremendous reaction is so recent that many of the older generation of present-day sociologists took part in it.[a] Among the less influential social scientists, the old-fashioned "practical" doctrine is actually still alive.

In seeking to explain why American social science avoids conclusions that are practical, we must also recall its high degree of specialization. Practical conclusions must always draw on a much more comprehensive range of insights into many fields than is necessary for good work in most specialties. Many excellent social scientists honestly feel incompetent before the broader practical tasks.[b] Finally, there has been in America, until the New Deal at least, a great personal and institutional isolation between the scholars and the political agencies of the nation. In America the general public has not developed a strong tradition of looking to its academicians for leadership of national thought in the broader issues. It has not given them the ear and prestige—and especially in the earlier period, not even the freedom—which was due them.[c]

This attempt at explanation of the fact that most outstanding social scientists want to keep strictly to the principle of avoiding practical conclusions does not weaken

[a] In a significant sense this advance in social science knowledge was part of the general modern trend toward secularization of thought. Many of the earlier sociologists—against whose teachings contemporary sociologists are still reacting—were clergymen, as were the fathers of some of our outstanding contemporary sociologists. The recent trend toward facts and naturalistic explanations is, therefore, a movement toward emancipation. In both the radical wing of previous social speculation—represented by such reform movements as Perfectionism, Positivism, and Telesis—and the conservative do-nothing (*laissez-faire*) wing—Utilitarianism, Malthusianism, and Social Darwinism—there was an assumption of the freedom and rationality of the individual. The reaction of modern sociologists has been against this assumption as well as against the similar "freedom of the will" doctrine of their clerical predecessors. Such a reaction alone would tend to make social science less interested in the practical sphere of its subject matter.

[b] Specialization and the handling of the large research funds and of the correspondingly large personnel resources also make cooperative work more possible and more necessary. Serving on committees of all sorts usually belongs to the responsibilities of the best men in every field. American social scientists have broken new paths and carried out huge tasks, which earlier could not have been dreamt of, by successfully applying cooperation to research. But in committee work it is always the easier to reach agreement on factual aspects of research, whereas the more practical aspects—particularly when the matter is controversial—are kept out of vision or left open.

[c] In this light one also better understands the high emotions contained in such denunciations of "pulpit orators," "well-meaning theorists," "arm-chair philosophers," "ardent evangelists," "artists," "social reformers," "religionists," "journalists," "promoters," "advertisers," "advocates," "flag-wavers," "day-dreamers" and "idealists," as are frequently used by social scientists when they assert that they are going to be strictly factual and avoid practical conclusions.

The strong anti-practical inclination to which such denunciations testify is also to be understood as a reaction against the particularly "practical" and moralistic culture in which the social scientists are living—the reaction itself thereby becoming moralistic.

the present author's conviction that the principle is arbitrary as a methodological rule and is detrimental to true scientific objectivity in its application. The main reasons for this conviction are the following:

Although the social scientist attempts to make his initial observation of a phenomenon as factual as possible, he finds it difficult to adhere strictly to this principle. Our whole literature is permeated by value judgments despite prefatory statements to the contrary. To the knowledge of the present writer, there is no piece of research on the Negro problem which does not contain valuations, explicit or implicit. Even when an author writing on, let us say, Negro education, politics, business, or labor attempts to give us only the data he has collected and the analysis he has made, he can rarely refrain from value judgments on them.

These practical judgments are usually relatively simple. They are not presented as inferences from explicit value premises plus the data, but rather, in the age-old fashion, as being evident from the nature of things: *actually as part of the objective data.* They are not marked off properly from theoretical knowledge of truth, but are most often introduced by loading part of the terminology with valuations, valuations which are kept vague and undefined. Sometimes the reader is told what is right or what is wrong, desirable or undesirable, only by implication. It should be stressed that this criticism often applies even to the most ostentatiously "pure" fact-finding research. Man is, as Aristotle told us, a political animal, and social science is a political science, in this sense. Valuations are present in our problems even if we pretend to expel them. The attempt to eradicate biases by trying to keep out the valuations themselves is a hopeless and misdirected venture.

Attaching importance to the presence or absence of practical conclusions also fosters a dangerously superficial view of what biases really are. I have often observed that social scientists who are responsible for the publications of other author's works or who utilize them in their own writings, when they apprehend biases, believe that these can be "edited away," by modifying certain expressions used or cutting out or revising certain practical conclusions drawn. Similarly, a general tendency toward understatement is observable in most social science literature. When an author has set down something which he feels to be unfavorable about a social class or a region, he looks for something favorable to say in order to "balance the picture." A "balanced view," a colorless drawing, is considered to be more "scientific." Particularly in governmental investigations great care is usually taken to spare the readers. The deliberate attempt that is made in such reports not to offend anyone will often make them difficult to use for scientific purposes. This tendency is, of course, not only ineffective in mitigating biases, but, even worse, it is itself one of the main types of bias in research.

Biases in research are much deeper seated than in the formulation of avowedly practical conclusions. They are not valuations *attached* to research but rather they *permeate* research. They are the unfortunate results of *concealed* valuations that insinuate themselves into research in all stages, from its planning to its final presentation. The valuations will, when driven underground, hinder observation and inference from becoming truly objective. This can be avoided only by making the valuations explicit. *There is no other device for excluding biases in social sciences than to face the valuations and to introduce them as explicitly stated, specific, and sufficiently concretized value premises.* If this is done, it will be possible to determine in a rational way, and openly to account for, the direction of theoretical research. It will further be possible to cleanse the scientific work shop from concealed, but ever resurgent, distorting valuations. Practical conclusions may thus be reached by rational inferences from the data and the value premises. Only in this way does social engineering, as an advanced branch of social research, become a rational discipline under full scientific control.

The method of working with explicit value premises has a very evident advantage in this last respect of laying a rational foundation for practical research. There are only two means by which social scientists today avoid practical and political conclusions: (1) neglecting to state the value premises which, nevertheless, are implied in the conclusions reached; (2) avoiding any rational and penetrating analysis of the practical problems in terms of social engineering (which would too visibly distract from the announced principles of being only factual). By the first restraint the doors are left wide open for hidden biases. The second inhibition prevents the social scientist from rendering to practical and political life the services of which he is capable.

Regarding the last point, social scientists have become accustomed to answer that "very much more detailed factual research is necessary before wise action can be planned upon the basis of scientific knowledge." This statement, which, with few verbal variations, will be found so often in our literature, is an expression of scientific modesty. But it also expresses escape. From the point of view of the practical man and of society, the rejoinder must be made: first, that practical action or inaction must be decided from day to day and cannot wait until eventually a lagging social science has collected enough detailed data for shouldering its part of the responsibility for social action; second, that, even with much more money and exertion spent on research, social science will, in this complicated and rapidly changing world, probably always be able to present this same alibi; and, third, that the scientist—even if his knowledge is only conjectural in certain respects—is in a position to assist in achieving a much wiser judgment than the one which is actually allowed to guide public policy.

The third point is the decisive one. Without doubt we know quite enough in most social problems to avoid a great number of wasteful mistakes in practical life and, consequently, to have a better world. Even in science, although we may strive toward the absolute, we must always be prepared to deliver the incomplete knowledge we have on hand. We cannot plead that we must wait "until all the facts are in," because we know full well that *all* the facts will never be in. Nor can we argue that "the facts speak for themselves" and leave it "to the politician and the citizen to draw the practical conclusions." We know even better than the politician and the ordinary citizen that the facts are much too complicated to speak an intelligible language by themselves. They must be organized for practical purposes, that is, under relevant value premises. And no one can do this more adequately than we ourselves.

There is a common belief that the type of practical research which involves rational planning—what we have ventured to call "social engineering"—is likely to be emotional. This is a mistake. If the value premises are sufficiently, fully, and rationally introduced, the planning of induced social change is no more emotional by itself than the planning of a bridge or the taking of a census. Even prior to the stage of social engineering proper, the research technique of accounting openly for one's value premises actually de-emotionalizes research. Emotion and irrationality in science, on the contrary, acquire their high potency precisely when valuations are kept suppressed or remain concealed in the so-called "facts."

The primary task in the present inquiry on the Negro problem has been to ascertain relevant facts and to establish the causal relations between facts. The viewpoints and, consequently, the principle of selection in regard to both direction and intensity of analysis, however, have been determined by certain value premises. In the practical sphere it has been our main task to ascertain how situations and trends, institutions and policies, have to be judged when a given set of value premises is applied.

The question of the selection of value premises remains to be settled. Values do not emerge automatically from the attempt to establish and collect the facts. Neither can we allow the individual investigator to choose his value premises arbitrarily. *The value premises should be selected by the criterion of relevance and significance to the culture under study.* Alternative sets of value premises would be most appropriate. If for reasons of practicability only one set of value premises is utilized, it is the more important that the reservation is always kept conscious: *that the practical conclusions—and, to an extent, the direction of research—have only hypothetical validity* and that the selection of another set of value premises might change both.

The formulation of specific valuations to be utilized as instrumental norms in a scientific investigation is likely to emphasize the tremendous moral responsibility placed upon social scientists. A number of points already made should, however, be borne in mind. First, the same responsibility is actually carried by every student, whether he chooses to make his value premises explicit or not. Second, if he makes his value premises explicit, his responsibility is, in fact, smaller, as he then fixes his readers' attention on the matter and thus aids them to criticize his value premises and conclusions. Third, the research part of the work is mainly dependent on the value premises as to viewpoints and direction. Fourth, his method means that he has taken precautions to avoid hidden valuations, that is, biases.

3. The History and Logic of the Hidden Valuations in Social Science

In the preceding section we have given our main reasons why social science is essentially a "political" science; why practical conclusions should not be avoided, but rather be considered as a main task in social research; why explicit value premises should be found and stated; and how, by this technique, we can expect both to mitigate biases and to lay a rational basis for the statement of the theoretical problems and the practical conclusions. The remainder of this note brings together under one head what is virtually a series of footnotes to the previous section. It contains arguments which are in the nature of digressions from the main argument in the text as technical qualifications.

Probably everyone with mastery of the writings in any large field of social science will agree with the description we have given of the present situation. We emphatically denounce valuations in social science, but they are constantly creeping into our work. Most of us declare just as emphatically that we want to abstain from any practical conclusions and to direct our effort wholly to the discovery of the truth of the matter, but in spite of this intention we make value judgments in a general, vague, hidden and unwitting manner. We have briefly hinted at certain facts in the social situation of science and scientists in America which make this situation more understandable.[a]

[a] Professor Robert S. Lynd has discussed the other-worldliness of social science in a suggestive manner from a somewhat different viewpoint in his challenging book, *Knowledge for What?* (1939).

In various degrees this tendency has characterized social research in all Western countries since its beginning in the eighteenth century. Leaving the question open for a moment as to how to cure this methodological confusion, we might point to some of its major historical determinants. In this short note we shall have to be inconclusive.[a] The problems of doctrinal history and the sociology and psychology of science involved are, in addition, so complex that we prefer to have our remarks considered as suggestions.

Basic to the eagerness in trying to drive valuations underground is the rationalism of our Western culture. Even the man in the street, when he wants to appear enlightened, will attempt to avoid expressing primary and personal valuations. He wants to be "objective" and to avoid arbitrariness. He will, therefore, give "reasons" for his desires, and he tries to make the reasons appear purely "factual" so that they will be acceptable to any "rational" man.[b] He wants, in other words, to suppress his valuations *as valuations* and to present them as systems of rational beliefs concerning reality. The same tendency has for centuries driven the philosophers in their scholarly exertions to base systems of morals and politics upon "the nature of things" and, later, upon the "sensations," that is, in this context, upon empirical observations and rational inferences. The difference between the various moral philosophies which fought and superseded each other is—on this central point—not great. The philosophies of the seventeenth, eighteenth, and early nineteenth centuries—and, in particular, the then perfected systems of Natural Rights and Utilitarianism—became the foundations, not only of our later moral and political thinking as it has developed in America among other countries, but also of the modern social sciences. The latter have, indeed, been a chief expression for the rationalistic desire in our culture to eradicate valuations and lay the basis for a factual and objective view of social problems.

The social sciences thus developed as branches of the philosophies of Enlightenment. New philosophical ideas have later been inserted; for instance, the ideas of social development attached to the names of Darwin, Hegel, Marx and Spencer. But certain central normative and teleological ideas of the philosophies of Natural Rights and Utilitarianism have been preserved. One such idea is the thought that there is a *communum bonum*, a "general" or "common welfare," and that it can be ascertained by scientific investigation. Another one is the thought that basically human interests are in harmony.

The idea that there is such a thing as a "common welfare," an "interest of society," which can be known, has followed us up to present times. It is seldom discussed but rather taken for granted. When during the 'twenties the criticism of classical economics in America asserted itself, and the so-called institutionalists apparently followed a tendency to find as many faults as possible with the old school of economists, the most central concept of classical economics, the "general welfare," was practically never challenged. Most work done in economics even today assumes tacitly the existence of such an entity. The availability of this concept makes it easy and natural for the economist, and also for other social scientists, to apply a concealed valuation, cov-

[a] For a fuller treatment of some of the problems dealt with in this section, we refer to the present author's *Das Politische Element in der Nationalökonomischen Doktrinbildung* (1932), and "Das Zweck-Mitteldenken in der Nationalökonomie" in *Zeitschrift für Nationalökonomie* (1932), pp. 305 ff.

[b] See Appendix 1.

ered only by this vague phrase, directly to his material or factual data. Statements that something is, or is not, desirable from the viewpoint of "society" will surprisingly often appear even in statistical work without any conclusive argument about how such a value judgment has been reached and precisely what it means.

From the beginning of social science the idea of a "harmony of interests" was closely associated with the idea of "common welfare." "Social value" was originally conceived of as a value common to all participants in a society. The harmony doctrine, obviously, made the calculation of the social value out of individual interests so much easier, and this fact, undoubtedly, has been an advantage in its use which has given it much of its survival strength.[a] We want to believe that what we hold to be desirable for society is desirable for all its members.

The harmony doctrine is essential to "liberalism" as it has historically developed out of the philosophies of Enlightenment (the term "liberalism" is here used in its most inclusive sense). From the very beginning liberalism was split into two wings, a radical one and a conservative one. The radical wing upheld the opinion that a harmony of interests would exist only in a society where the institutions—and primarily the distribution of property—were changed so as to accord with the precepts of these philosophies. The "natural order" studied by the radical liberals was, therefore, a hypothetical society where the "natural laws" functioned undisturbed by "corrupted institutions": where, thus, for example, all "natural" titles to property—with Locke the "fruits of labor"—were retained, but society was purified of all monopolies and privileges and, consequently, from "exploitation." The conservative wing, on the other hand, proceeded to apply the harmony doctrine directly to the unreformed society (which, incidentally, was a corruption of thought, as they all usually adhered to a philosophy which reserved the concepts "natural order" and "social harmony" for a society purged as severely as the radicals wanted it). The radical wing became the reformers, the visionaries, and the utopians: it gave birth to various schools of communism, socialism, syndicalism and anarchism. The conservative wing profited from its "realism." In its practical work it abstained from speculating about a "natural order" other than the one that existed; it studied society *as it was* and actually came to lay the foundations for modern social science. For this we have to be grateful to conservative liberals. But they perpetuated in modern social science, also, their static and fatalistic political bias, a do-nothing liberalism. The harmony doctrine in this setting was, of course, even less well founded than the radical liberals' idea that only in a very different "natural order" would human interests be mutually compatible.

Economics—or "political economy," to use the old-fashioned but much more adequate term (the attribute "political" has been dropped for convenience and as a tribute to the purity of science)—is the oldest branch of social science in the sense that it was the earliest to develop into a system of observations and inferences organized under the principle of social laws.[b] In economics we can most conveniently study the influence of the static and fatalistic general bias upon the development of a social science discipline. From natural science it early borrowed the concept of "equilibrium." This concept, as well as the derived concepts of "balance," "stability," "normal," are all often heavily loaded with the static and fatalistic valuations. To an extent these

[a] Myrdal, *Das Politische Element in der Nationalökonomischen Doktrinbildung.*

[b] History and political science are, of course, older, but they never reached agreement upon a system of causation.

concepts have taken over the role of the conservative variant of the old harmony doctrine. It is, of course, possible to utilize them in a purely instrumental manner and the success of generations of economists in gradually perfecting our knowledge of economic relations is due to such a utilization of the various notions of social equilibrium and disequilibrium. The "assumptions" of economic theory have been useful. But their load of inherited static and fatalistic valuations is heavy, and they will often turn into convenient covers for biases in this direction.

The direction is loose and general, however. Like "welfare" and "harmony of interest," those concepts can be bent considerably. Their role for the underhand presentation of practical conclusions is rather the formal one of providing objective-sounding, technical terms for the subjective valuations which are actually pressing for expression. They thus permit entrance of the biases of a time, a social setting or a personality. These biases may be conservative or "radical" (radical in the sense of being Marxian). The relation between, on the one hand, the specific biases in research and, on the other hand, these value-metaphysical thought-structures forming the frame for economic theory and research, is primarily this: that the arbitrariness inherent in the structures allows the specific biases room for play which, under the rules of scientific strictness, they should not have had. But it is equally important to remember that they do not give absolutely free leeway. They are headed in one definite direction. As long as economics keeps its valuations implicit and hidden, the utilization of those concepts will tend to insert in scientific work a do-nothing bias.

The younger social sciences have followed much the same track. A few remarks, mainly by way of illustration, will be made concerning American sociology, particularly as it has influenced the study of the Negro problem.

Few have had more influence on contemporary American social science thinking than William Graham Sumner. He was a political economist of strong *laissez-faire* leanings before he became a sociologist, and he continued to indoctrinate generations of Yale undergraduates with the economic doctrines of Manchester-liberalism.[a] Sumner is usually believed to have had two sides: on the political side he advocated Social Darwinism[b] and was a conservative; on the scientific side he was the great observer of "folkways and mores." These two sides were closer than is commonly thought. His observations that there were folkways and mores which gave societies a static stability buttressed his belief that social change was difficult to achieve. His desires to maintain the *status quo* led him to conclude that there should be no attempt to change the folkways and mores. The unification of the two streams in Sumner's thinking gives us an example of the fallacious attempt to draw practical conclusions from purely factual premises:

> The great stream of time and earthly things will sweep on just the same in spite of us . . . Everyone of us is a child of his age and cannot get out of it. He is in the stream and is swept along with it. All his science and philosophy come to him out of it. Therefore the tide will not be changed by us. It will swallow up both us and our experiments

[a] Charles A. and Mary R. Beard, *The Rise of American Civilization*, Vol. II, (1927), pp. 236-237, 429 and 430.

[b] Social Darwinism refers to that continuation of the *laissez-faire* movement after it took on the Darwinian terminology of "struggle for existence" and "survival of the fittest." The ideological father of Sumner was the founder of Social Darwinism—namely, Herbert Spencer.

. . . That is why it is the greatest folly of which a man can be capable, to sit down with a slate and pencil to plan out a new social world.[a]

Sumner could not fail to have a particularly strong influence on social science thinking about the problems of the South and, specifically, about the Negro problem. The theory of folkways and mores has diffused from the scientists and has in the educated classes of the South become a sort of regional political *credo*. The characterization of something as "folkways" or "mores" or the stereotype that "stateways cannot change folkways"—which under no circumstances can be more than a relative truth—is used in the literature on the South and on the Negro as a general formula of mystical significance. It is expressed whenever one wants to state one's opinion that "what is, must be" without caring to give full factual reasons. To a large extent the formula has also been taken over by the Negro writers. We may note a recent example of the same sort of reasoning on the part of a writer, who, if he had not been influenced by Sumner, is in perfect agreement with him. The example is the more striking because it is taken from the pages of the radical Negro periodical, *The Crisis*, and is part of a review of a book whose author is trying to improve the lot of the Negro—though perhaps in a naïve manner.

It is the belief, on the other hand, of our author and a considerable group of educators, largely members of the "social frontier group" at Teachers' College, that education can lead in social reform instead of following in the wake of social trends. This belief is a form of wish-fulfillment thinking based upon the assumption that social life can be rationalized and that the *processus social* can be rid of its irrational elements and brought under the control of a previously established plan. *Res est ridicula et nimis iocosa.* Such a belief is not a product of scientific observation, but of the educator's *faith*, and one as naïve as any ever inherited by man. If the researches of science have established anything, it is that man is at bottom a most irrational animal; a rationalizing rather than a reasoning creature.[b]

Much less conservative than Sumner but still bound by a similar fatalism have been Robert E. Park and some of his followers. Park's influence on the research on the Negro problem has been great and direct, as so many of the contemporary students of this problem are his pupils or recognize his guidance as their most important inspiration. Park is not, as was Sumner, moved by any deeply felt desire to maintain the *status quo*. But his keen observation of social conditions—and, perhaps, also some disillusions from his reform activities—have made him realize the tremendous force exerted by "natural" influences.[c] Not observing much in the way of conscious and organized planning in his

[a] William Graham Sumner, "The Absurd Attempt to Make the World Over," *Essays of William Graham Sumner*. Edited by A. G. Keller and Maurice R. Davie (1934), Vol. I, pp. 105-106.
[b] James W. Ivy, review of *An Analysis of the Specific References to Negroes in Selected Curricula for the Education of Teachers* by Edna Meade Colson, in *The Crisis* (October, 1941), p. 331.
[c] Park, of course, recognizes the possibility of rapid and radical social change. His theory concerning such change is centered around the concept of "crisis." This theory was first developed by W. I. Thomas, *Source Book for Social Origins* (1909), pp. 17-22. The theory, simply stated, is that under certain circumstances habits, mores, and folkways are recognized by people to be no longer useful as ways of meeting situations and needs, and, after a brief period of amoral disorganization, people come together to build up a new type of "socially acceptable" behavior, or such a new folkway develops naturally "without

contemporary America except that which was bungling and ineffective because it did not take due account of the natural forces, he built up a sociological system in terms of "natural" causation and sequence. Probably because he has no intentional conservative bias, it is difficult to find simple statements in Park's writing which exemplify the fallacy of drawing practical conclusions from factual premises alone. What we do find is a systematic tendency to ignore practically all possibilities of modifying—by conscious effort—the social effects of the natural forces.[a] Occasionally the do-nothing (*laissez-faire*) implications of Park's assumptions are revealed:

The races of high visibility, to speak in naval parlance, are the natural and inevitable objects of race prejudice.[b]

Accommodation, on the other hand, is the process by which the individuals and groups make the *necessary* internal *adjustments* to social situations which have been created by competition and conflict. . . . Eventually the new order gets itself fixed in habit and custom and is then transmitted as part of the established social order to succeeding generations. Neither the physical nor the social world is made to satisfy at once all the wishes of the natural man. The rights of property, vested interests of every sort, the family organization, slavery, caste and class, the whole social organization, in fact, represent accommodations, that is to say, limitations of the natural wishes of the individual. These socially inherited accommodations have presumably grown up in the pains and struggles of previous generations, but they have been transmitted to and accepted by succeeding generations as part of the natural, inevitable social order. All of these are forms of control in which competition is limited by status.[c]

. . . the political process can only proceed in a relatively orderly way in so far as it generates a political power and authority capable of enforcing a certain degree of order and discipline until a new equilibrium has been achieved and the changes which the new programs initiated have been assimilated, digested and incorporated with the folkways of the original and historic society.[d]

Race relations . . . might comprise . . . all those situations in which some relatively stable equilibrium between competing races has been achieved and in which the resulting social order has become fixed in custom and tradition.

Under such circumstances the intensity of the race consciousness which a struggle for status inevitably arouses, where it did not altogether disappear, would be greatly diminished. The biracial organizations of certain social institutions that have come into existence in Southern states since emancipation exhibit the form which such racial accommodations sometimes take.[e]

---

discussion and organization." The whole period is called a "crisis." This theory is not very clearly presented in Park's published writings, but the nearest thing to a complete statement of it may be found in the article on "Collective Behavior" in the *Encyclopedia of the Social Sciences* (1935), Vol. 3, pp. 631-633.

[a] With the same qualifications for the "crisis" theory of social change, it can be said that William I. Thomas, who has had a great influence on practically all contemporary American sociologists, shows the same lack of interest for problems of induced change.

[b] "Behind Our Masks," *The Survey* (May 1, 1926), p. 136.

[c] Robert E. Park and Ernest W. Burgess, *Introduction to the Science of Sociology* (1921), pp. 510-511. (Italics ours.)

[d] Robert E. Park, "Social Planning and Human Nature," *Publications of the American Sociological Society* (August, 1935), p. 28.

[e] Robert E. Park, "The Nature of Race Relations," in Edgar T. Thompson (editor), *Race Relations and the Race Problem* (1939), pp. 4-5.

Park's naturalistic and, therefore, fatalistic philosophy has been transmitted to some of his students who have been working on the Negro problem. Throughout the writings of Edward B. Reuter, for example, we find statements similar to the following taken from a recent consideration of race relations:

> It is in the nature of a competitive order, and every natural and social order is competitive, to place groups and individuals in the position where they can survive, and it is in the nature of individuals and groups to develop the characters essential or conducive to survival in the natural and cultural area in which they are placed and in which they struggle to exist. Whether we consider plants, animals, or human beings we find that, in the large, they are in those areas where each is best fitted to thrive and prosper, and that each is somewhat nicely adapted in its structures and in its habit system to the special conditions of existence in the habitat . . . Adaptation is the price of survival.[a]

What has been said of Park could be said also of William F. Ogburn. The tremendous social influence of inventions and changes in economic organization and the march of social trends have convinced him that man's intentional efforts to do something about the world are futile.[b]

> . . . much of our difficulty is due to the fact that the different parts of our highly interrelated civilization are changing at unequal rates of speed, bringing maladjustments and social problems that would not occur in a stationary society or in one where the different parts moved along simultaneously. When one part of our culture, as for instance, the technological-economic organization, changes rapidly while another part, as for instance, government, changes more slowly, there comes a time when the maladjustment is sufficiently serious to occasion a whole series of rapid changes in the lagging institutions. In such times and for such changes the word "Revolution" is often used.
>
> For the future, there is no particular reason to think that the technological inventions and scientific discoveries will slow up. Indeed, they are likely to come faster. However, we may, perhaps, be able to speed up the changes in other institutions slightly more quickly, by greater use of the communication inventions. But on the other hand, the process of keeping up with the pace set by technology may be slowed up because of the increasing heterogeneity of society and the possible greater number of institutional lags to be caught up. Therefore, no prospective integration of state and industry is expected to deliver us in the future from grave social disturbances.[c]

[a] E. B. Reuter, "Competition and the Racial Division of Labor," in Thompson, *Race Relations and the Race Problem*, pp. 46-47.

[b] It should be noted in passing that the Marxian teleology implied in the materialistic conception of history is, from our point of view (however catastrophic the trends are pictured) of the do-nothing (*laissez-faire*) variety; that is, it is biased in the static and fatalistic direction as we have used these terms in this note. In his principal writings Marx shows—contrary to what is often popularly assumed—no interest whatsoever in social planning. He expected "the reign of freedom" in the classless communistic society to arise full-fledged by natural force out of a political revolution caused by trends in technology and production. The interest in social reforms which he showed particularly in later days were a result of an ideological compromise. Modern social engineering has actually had practically no inspiration from Marx's "scientific" socialism, actually less than from the early French and English socialists whom Marx repudiated as dilettantes and utopians.

The liberalistic character of Marxism is easily understood when its ideological roots are scrutinized. (It explains why elements of Marxian teleology have had such an easy access into modern American sociology and history.)

[c] William F. Ogburn, "Man and His Institutions," *Publications of the American Sociological Society* (August, 1935), pp. 39-40.

The materials of social planning may, in general, be summed up in the phrase "social forces." They are what social planners have to deal with. What social forces may consist of does not concern us at the moment, but the effect of social forces is to produce motion. In the case of the above illustration the motion is in population growth. In fact, motion is the principal characteristic of our age, for we call it the "age of change." Social planning deals with changes, either with changes already started, or in planning new changes. It is difficult to name a single phase of our contemporary civilization that is not undergoing change. Some parts are changing more rapidly than others. It is this fact that we are living in a changing world which is the justification for asking the question: What is likely to happen? . . .

Technology enters the analysis at this point because these changes which are taking place are in large part instigated by invention. Thus many of the changes in international relations are affected by the airplane, just as in an earlier generation changes taking place in the relations of warring peoples were affected by gunpowder. Hence the knowledge of inventions supplies us partly with the answer to the question of what is going to happen. The wishes of human beings are relatively stable from age to age insofar as heredity or the physiological foundations are concerned. They take different expressions, however, because of the different social conditions in which men live. New inventions start changes in the behavior of mankind. They are new stimuli to which human beings respond.[a]

The social scientists we have cited could not have reached their negative views on planned and induced social change unless guided by a set of general assumptions in their selection and interpretation of the empirical data. This implies that they have introduced valuations along with facts in deriving conclusions relative to what can be and should be the nature of man's practical efforts. We all claim that our factual or theoretical studies alone cannot logically lead to a practical recommendation. A practical or valuational conclusion can be derived only when there is at least one valuation among the premises. When our premises consist exclusively of facts, only a factual conclusion can result. If we proceed otherwise, and if we, further, denounce valuations, we are thus constantly attempting the logically impossible: From certain observations concerning the causation of a social phenomenon we jump to the valuational conclusion that we can do nothing to change this phenomenon because it has such and such a causation. To illustrate this common fallacy we have chosen examples from the writings of only a few leading sociologists. The specific error that is common to these three men—Sumner, Park, and Ogburn—has been with social science from the beginning and is still quite general in contemporary social science. This specific error is not that of observing a deep-rooted and all-pervasive social causation. The observations of such causation made by the particular authors chosen for exemplification are rather monumental contributions to knowledge of a most significant nature. The specific logical error is that of inferring from the facts that men can and should make no effort to change the "natural" outcome of the specific forces observed. This is the old do-nothing (*laissez-faire*) bias of "realistic" social science.

To bring out the nature of this bias and demonstrate the arbitrariness thereby inserted into research, we may consider the same facts that have been observed by Sumner, Park, and Ogburn and add to them an explicit and dynamic value premise

[a] William F. Ogburn, "Technology and Planning," in George B. Galloway and Associates, *Planning for America* (1941), pp. 179-180.

(instead of the implicit fatalistic and static one) and from these deduce a quite different practical conclusion. Recognizing the folkways and mores,[a] for example, and having a desire to *change some of them* in one direction or another, we should be interested in studying the range and degree of inertia; all the exceptions to the folkways; the specialization of groups; the conflicts (between persons and within persons); the changes, the flexibilities, and the manageability of some factors in the social system; instead of, as Sumner usually [b] does, stressing and exemplifying the great over-all inertia. On the practical plane we should make not only the negative inference that a plan for social change should expect to be time-consuming and to meet strong resistance, but also the positive inference that it has to direct its attack on certain points where the mores are weakest and where people are already beginning to question them (or have a divided conscience with respect to them). We should also infer that it should not attack them directly but should create situations where the people themselves will strain the mores. Similarly, if we recognize the tremendous force of certain processes and sequences we might, with a dynamic value premise, deduce that strategy demands a redirection or stoppage of processes which contain within themselves a motive power in a certain direction, and an effort *against* individuals coming to "adjust" themselves to the processes. Finally, a recognition of the sweep of social trends and of the basic role of invention and economic organization in social causation, coupled with a dynamic instead of static valuation, would lead one to facilitate the perfection and adoption of those inventions which have the greatest promise of moving the society in a desired direction and to seek *social* inventions which would modify economic organization and the effects of mechanical inventions. Social scientists are so habituated to using static and fatalistic value premises with such facts as the mores, social processes, and social trends, and they are so prone to associate radical valuation premises with a complete disregard of the facts, that they often do not realize that it is quite possible to couple dynamic value premises with factual knowledge of mores, social processes or social trends. The static and fatalistic value premises have actually imbedded themselves into the data.[c] And it should not surprise us that the great development of social sciences in recent decades in America has not been accompanied by any correspondingly important development of social engineering.

In the theory of folkways and mores the heavy load of do-nothing (*laissez-faire*) valuation becomes particularly apparent when Sumner and his many followers[d] set

[a] We stand in critical opposition to these concepts on theoretical grounds, as they tend to give an impression of a homogeneous and unproblematic valuational background for behavior, which we think is mistaken (see Appendix 1, Section 3), but this does not deeply concern our present argument.

[b] See Appendix 1, Section 2.

[c] The fact of static and fatalistic valuations in social science research may be accepted even though the analysis of its historical causation, presented on previous pages, may be questioned by some.

[d] Many other sociologists outside the Sumner tradition considered man-made legislation as ineffectual and dangerous. Franklin H. Giddings, the leader of the Columbia School, for example, had this to say about "stateways":

"Because the folkway is adaptive it is variable, and folkways, therefore, become various, not only because new ways from time to time arise out of new circumstances and demands, but also through differentiation. One has only to call to mind the fluctuations of fashion, the changing forms of address and ceremony, the rise and fall of recreations, the fleeting

out with the purpose of proving the inefficacy of legislation. With reference to race relations in the South after the Civil War, Sumner said:

> The two races have not yet made new mores. Vain attempts have been made to control the new order by legislation. The only result is the proof that legislation cannot make mores. . . . It is only just now that the new society seems to be taking shape. There is a trend in the mores now as they begin to form under the new state of things. It is not at all what the humanitarians hoped and expected. . . . Some are anxious to interfere and try to control. They take their stand on ethical views of what is going on. It is evidently impossible for any one to interfere. We are like spectators at a great natural convulsion. The results will be such as the facts and forces call for. We cannot foresee them. They do not depend on ethical views any more than the volcanic eruption on Martinique contained an ethical element.[a]

It should be noted that—in spite of its psychologism, its ethical relativism, its modernized terminology, and the abundant anthropological illustrations—this theory is nothing else than a reformulation and slight modification of the old *laissez-faire* doctrine of the "natural order" as it was more naïvely set forth in the Enlightenment period: human relations are governed by "natural laws"; "natural laws" are not only the right laws but are also, in the main, and in spite of all the interferences of foolish governments, actually permeating real life; they do not need to be legalized—if legislation adheres to the "natural laws," it is not exactly damaging but useless; if legislation conflicts with the "natural laws" it will be inefficacious though slightly damaging

---

fads in games and sports, to realize the enormous flexibility of folkways. Stateways tend toward uniformity. Governments attempt to standardize not only rights at law but also legal procedure, administrative rules, and the conduct of citizens. Legislators are intolerant of exceptions, bureaucrats abominate them, and courts, while finding precedents for them when moral justice or the rule of reason requires, do not otherwise make them. Trial by jury, however, which mediates between folkways and stateways, is a venerable if not always a venerated defense against the governmentalists, who would dictate and ration our food and drink, write our medical prescriptions, cut our clothes, tell us what we may read and look at, and send us to bed at curfew.

"Stateways are instituted by command, backed up by physical force. They are formal, as machine-like as they can be made, and relentless. Folkways exert pressure which may be resistless, but it is indefinite, elastic, and automatically variable." (*Studies in the Theory of Human Society* [1922], p. 193.)

[a] William Graham Sumner, *Folkways* (1906), pp. 77-78. Other statements by Sumner, in his least opinionated book, revealing his attitude toward legislation, are the following:

"Acts of legislation come out of the mores. . . . Legislation, however, has to seek standing ground on the existing mores, and it soon becomes apparent that legislation, to be strong, must be consistent with the mores. Things which have been in the mores are put under police regulation and later under positive law. It is sometimes said that 'public opinion' must ratify and approve police regulations, but this statement rests on an imperfect analysis. The regulations must conform to the mores, so that the public will not think them too lax or too strict." (*Ibid.*, p. 55.)

"[The mores] never contain any provision for their own amendment." (*Ibid.*, p. 79.)

"The combination in the mores of persistency and variability determines the extent to which it is possible to modify them by arbitrary action. It is not possible to change them, by any artifice or device, to a great extent, or suddenly, or in any essential element; it is possible to modify them by slow and long-continued effort if the ritual is changed by minute variations." (*Ibid.*, p. 87.)

as it will disturb somewhat the smooth operation of the "natural laws." This is, for instance, the doctrine back of Adam Smith's well-known dictum that trade barriers, though, of course, irrational and cumbersome, will, in the broad overview, not amount to much, as the smugglers will pierce them, acting here as the agents of the "natural laws" with the same immutability as water seeking its level. The "invisible hand" will inevitably guide human activity. On this central point, which apparently is much of the political purpose of the whole theory of folkways and mores, Sumner simply expresses a common American prejudice against legislation which we have discussed in Chapter 1, Section 5, and in other places.

The presence of this same static and fatalistic valuation in the hidden *ethos* of contemporary social science is suggested by some of the terminology found throughout the writings of many sociologists, such as "balance," "harmony," "equilibrium," "adjustment," "maladjustment," "organization," "disorganization," "accommodation," "function," "social process" and "cultural lag." While they all—as the corresponding concepts in economics, mentioned above—have been used advantageously to *describe* empirically observable situations, they carry within them the tendency to give a do-nothing (*laissez-faire*) valuation of those situations. How the slip occurs is easily understandable: When we speak of a social situation being in harmony, or having equilibrium, or its forces organized, accommodated, or adjusted to each other, there is the almost inevitable implication that some sort of ideal has been attained, whether in terms of "individual happiness" or the "common welfare." Such a situation is, therefore, evaluated as "good" and a movement in the direction is "desirable." [a] The negative terms—disharmony, disequilibrium, maladjustment, disorganization—correspondingly describe an undesirable

---

[a] There is practically no discussion in the literature on the value connotation in the terms exemplified in the text. When raising the question with representative social scientists, I have often met the following reaction: first, an acknowledgment that many authors in speaking of adjustment, accommodation, disorganization, and so forth, imply valuations of "good" or "bad" and that this is unscientific, but, second, that sometimes—even when a valuation is implied—this is so general that it is self-evident. "Accommodation, for example," it is said, "is a process whereby people are able to cooperate and thereby maintain some social order; accommodation grows out of a conflict of interest and is only established after each party to the conflict has accepted a place in the social order and developed appropriate or reciprocal attitudes; but there always remains a latent conflict. The only 'goodness' implied in accommodation is that thereby cooperation under social order is maintained." Against this argument there are several criticisms to be raised: (1) the value given to cooperation and social order should be given explicitly rather than implicitly in the connotation of a term; (2) this valuation is certainly not under *all* conditions self-evident from the viewpoint of every party involved (to one party a continued conflict can under circumstances be preferable, if only for reaching another and more favorable status of accommodation); (3) this valuation is not, just because it is so general, precise enough to serve a scientific purpose even if it were made explicit (the status to which conflicting parties are actually brought to "accommodate" is not given *a priori* but is the outcome of a social process, the actual result of which becomes condoned because "accommodation" in general is condoned; this result could have been different not only because of a prolonged conflict but also because of a different type of accommodation behavior by one person or the other). In the Negro problem practically every situation, except where a race riot is on, can be, and is often actually in the literature, described as an "accommodation," and *status quo* in every aspect can thus be, and is, implicitly justified because it preserves cooperation and the social order.

situation, as indicated by the etymological connection of their prefixes to the word "bad." A great arbitrariness—allowing for the more specific biases of a personality and a cultural setting—is present in deciding upon just *what* shall be considered as equilibrium and *what* disequilibrium in a process of social change. The following quotation has been chosen to illustrate the working of a political bias through the vehicle of such terms, not only because the bias—directed against the Negro as his interests are commonly conceived—is expressed in a particularly blunt form, but also because it happens to be from the pen of a Negro sociologist:

> In the face of these opposing views, then, conclusions concerning the effect of education upon Negroes during this period may be reserved. If education brought disorganization among the former slaves, it may be counted as a liability. If, on the other hand, it served as an outlet for feelings that might otherwise have been directed into politics, where discord might have resulted, it may be counted on as an asset. The situation doubtless varied in different places at different times—assisting or retarding adjustment in areas where the one effect or the other, already mentioned, preponderated.[a]

Similarly, if a thing has a "function" it is good or at least essential.[b] The term "function" can have a meaning only in terms of a presumed purpose; if that purpose is left undefined or implied to be the "interest of society" which is no further defined, a considerable leeway for arbitrariness in practical implication is allowed but the main direction is given: a description of social institutions in terms of their functions must lead to a conservative teleology. If there is a "cultural lag," there is likewise a presumption that the elimination of the lag is desirable. While social processes and mores may not be good, in terms of certain arbitrary standards, they are believed to exist or develop with an inevitability that defies all efforts directed toward their modification.

These and similar static terms constitute much of the basic descriptive and theoretical terminology in all the social sciences. It is certainly an important task of self-scrutiny for social science to determine why such terms and not more dynamic ones have been given such a strategic position in social science thinking. The present author has suggested above that the origin of social science out of the philosophies of Enlightenment and the greater "realism" of the *laissez-faire* wing of early liberalism is of central importance. The very fact that the evaluative nature of these terms has gone almost unnoticed suggests that the explanation of their choice must go deep into the roots of Western culture. Whatever the reason for their predominance, the fact that such terms —without much care to preserve for them a strictly theoretical meaning—are widely used to describe much of social life and serve as keystones in theoretical explanations of social structure and change, inserts into social science an implicit static and fatalistic value premise. The use of such terms makes it appear that a given situation is desirable or inevitable without the explicit specification by the social scientist of what he considers desirable or of the possibilities of the modification of "inevitability."

There is nothing to be criticized when a scientist explicitly states that he hopes a certain situation will develop, that such a situation is a good one according to certain standards which he sets up, or that a certain situation or development is inevitable beyond

[a] Bertram W. Doyle, *The Etiquette of Race Relations in the South* (1937), p. 127.

[b] How easily even a radical social scientist may slip over to the expression of approval of something that he says has a function is illustrated by Durkheim's discussion of crime and punishment: Emile Durkheim, *The Rules of Sociological Method* (1938; first edition, 1895), translated by Sarah A. Solovay and John H. Mueller, pp. 66-70.

all possibility of modification by any contingency or directed effort whatsoever. What is to be criticized is the use of terms to hide the fact that there is a value premise in a value judgment. The observation of the facts of a given existing situation alone will never permit the conclusion that such a situation is good or desirable or even that this situation is inevitable in the future. In other words, we are making a plea for explicit value premises. We are also making a plea for unbiased research. The relation between these two *desiderata* is this, that it is the hidden valuations which give entrance to biases in social science.

The author is well aware that some of his criticisms and suggestions in the preceding pages on the history and logic of the hidden valuations in social science are controversial and would ask the reader to note that the following remarks on a positive methodology for social science as well as Sections 1 and 2 of this Appendix do not depend on the correctness of Section 3.

It should also be reiterated as a concluding remark that when we have illustrated our thesis by citing prominent American sociologists, this is only because American sociology has provided the main scientific frame for the scientific study of the Negro problem which is our particular concern in this book. The tendencies criticized are, however, common in all social sciences in the entire Western world. Too, not all American sociologists have a do-nothing (*laissez-faire*) bias. In earlier generations Lester F. Ward, Simon Patten, and many others were reformers, and Ward thought of social science as social engineering. Their methodological principles were not clear, however. In the present generation Louis Wirth, to mention only one prominent representative of a growing group holding a dissenting view, has expressed opinions in fundamental agreement with this appendix.[a]

4. THE POINTS OF VIEW ADOPTED IN THIS BOOK

Scientific facts do not exist *per se*, waiting for scientists to discover them. A scientific fact is a construction abstracted out of a complex and interwoven reality by means of arbitrary definitions and classifications. The processes of selecting a problem and a basic hypothesis, of limiting the scope of study, and of defining and classifying data relevant to such a setting of the problem, involve a choice on the part of the investigator. The choice is made from an indefinite number of possibilities. The same is true when drawing inferences from organized data. Everything in the world is connected with everything else: when shall one stop, and in what direction shall one proceed when establishing causal relations? Scientific conventions usually give guidance. But, first, convention itself is a valuation, usually a biased one, and it is the more dangerous as it is usually hidden in tacit preconceptions which are not discussed or even known; second, progress in science is made by those who are most capable of freeing themselves from the conventions in their science and of seeking guidance from other sciences and nonscientific endeavors.

[a] Louis Wirth, "Preface" in Karl Mannheim, *Ideology and Utopia* (1936), pp. xiii-xxxi and his article "Ideological Aspects of Social Disorganization," *American Sociological Review* (August, 1940), pp. 472-482. John Dollard's *Criteria for the Life History* (1935) and *Caste and Class in a Southern Town* (1937) also exemplify a conscious interest in making biases explicit even if they do not reach a methodology centered on explicit value premises. Robert MacIver's *Social Causation* (1942) and Robert Lynd's *Knowledge For What?* (1939) are other sociological books which are free of implicit value premises.

Prior to research, therefore, are complicated theories. The architecture of these theories is arbitrary except when they are intentionally founded upon a definition of relevant interests. This is true no matter how much effort is invested in selecting terms of low valuational content and no matter how remote from public interest the causal analysis is. When one is out to determine such a simple thing as the level of "real wages" in a community, for example, he has to rack his soul to decide whether to base his calculations on hourly rates or on annual wages: whether to consider articles outside of the staple commodities as necessities of consumption, whether to consider certain items, the consumption of which is not "customary," as necessities because all dieticians think so, and generally speaking, how to decide the weights in the consumption budgets used for constructing a cost of living index. In a world of change and variation there can be no such thing as an "ideal index"; in the final analysis, the weights have always to be *chosen* upon the basis of what one's interest in a study is. In comparing Negroes and whites, decisions must be taken in such problems as: is it more proper to make the comparison directly or to take into account the fact that Negroes are concentrated in the lower occupational brackets, in poorer and more backward regions of the country, and that they have been discriminated against in education and in other respects? [a]

These considerations sound trite to any scientist who is at all aware of his methodology. What we wish to point out, however, is that every choice involves valuations. One does not escape valuations by restricting his research to the discovery of "facts." The very attempt, so prevalent in recent years, to avoid valuations by doing research that is simply factual and without use for practical or political efforts involves in itself a valuation. We hasten to explain that we are not criticizing pure fact-finding. Fact-finding is indispensable for the solution of most of the problems—both practical and theoretical—that we encounter. The criticism is directed against fact-seeking that is done without a problem. The full statement of a problem, including the decision of scope, direction, hypothesis, classification principles, and the definition of all terms used, renders explicit the valuations necessary in fact-finding research. The author can, of course, explicitly disavow any practical interest and declare that he personally finds that the topic and the hypothesis appeal to him esthetically—or that he has made all his choices at random. If, however, practical usefulness is an aim in science, even the direction of research becomes dependent upon much wider valuations concerning society.

It should be stressed that this complication of a science which is not mere "art for art's sake" does *not* in the least decrease the demands upon objectivity in research. On the contrary, specification of valuations aids in reaching objectivity since it makes explicit what otherwise would be only implicit. Facts may be scientifically recorded and analyzed with explicit value premises as well as without them, and this can actually be accomplished the better in the former case since the explicit value premises focus the investigator's attention upon the valuations which, if hidden, are the roots of biases, since they generally set a standard of relevance and significance. This is true also when the analysis proceeds to draw practical conclusions. The conclusions must simply be remembered to be only as valid as the premises, which is true in all science. In fact, only when the premises are stated explicitly is it possible to determine how valid the conclusions are.

[a] See Richard Sterner and Associates, *The Negro's Share* (1943), prepared for this study; pp. 3-9.

1. *Theoretical and Practical Research.* Our entire discussion is based upon a distinction between two aspects, or stages, of social science research: the "theoretical" and the "practical." By "theoretical" research we mean here all the research which is directed purely and exclusively toward ascertaining facts and causal relations between facts. By "practical" research we mean the logical procedure of relating value judgments to factual situations and to actual trends of change and, from their combination, deriving scientific plans for policies aimed at inducing alterations of the anticipated social trends ("social engineering").

The relations established in theoretical research are simply *causal.* In practical research the causal relations are transposed into *purposeful* relations. The sequence in theoretical research—from cause to effect—is in social engineering turned into the reverse order from ends to means. In practical research the causal relations established by theoretical research are taken as facts.

Theoretical research is primarily concerned with the *present* situation and the *past* development. It attempts to establish, out of systematized experience of the present and the past, a rational knowledge, in as general terms as possible, of the causal relations between elementary factors in the social process. Its final goal is to be able on this basis to forecast the *future* by rational prognoses.

Practical research is exclusively concerned with the *future.* Its principal viewpoint is that the future represents a set of alternatively possible trends of development. What future development will actually occur is, from the practical point of view, a matter of choice, in so far as decisions and actions on the part of the citizen and society can determine this development. Its final goal, therefore, is the scientific planning of "induced changes."

Between the two aspects, or stages, of social research there exist the following main relations:

(a) The direction of theoretical research is determined by the practical purposes held in view. In a study of the American Negro problem which is as predominantly practical in its intentions as ours, the frame for all our theoretical research thus consists of certain practical questions concerning the future status of the Negro and the future of race relations in America.

(b) Practical problems can, on the other hand, be approached only on the basis of the theoretical analysis of actual facts and their causal interrelations.

(c) On theoretical grounds some practical goals can be shown to be futile—that is, impossible of execution. Theoretical research thus sets the scope of practical research by determining what is feasible.

(d) Knowledge of facts is never enough for posing the practical problems concerning what is right, just, desirable and advisable. Practical conclusions are, by logical necessity, inferences from value premises as well as from factual premises.

In our study it is our ambition, first, to keep this distinction between theoretical and practical research clear throughout the various specific problems we are dealing with; and, third, to treat the practical problems as problems of scientific research. We shall, second, not to shun the practical problems but rather make them central in our work; therefore, have to devote the closest attention to value premises.

2. *Value Premises.* Value premises in research have to satisfy the following criteria:

(a) They must be *explicitly stated* and not hidden as tacit assumptions.

(b) They must be as *specific and concretized* as the valuation of reality in terms of factual knowledge requires.

(c) They cannot be derived directly from factual research but they will have to be *purposively selected.*

(d) They cannot be *a priori*, self-evident, or generally valid; they can have only an *hypothetical* character.

(e) Since incompatible valuations are held in society, the value premises should ideally be given as a number of sets of *alternative* hypotheses. The value judgments reached as conclusions from factual data and from these value hypotheses consist of a corresponding number of alternative plans for practical policy.

(f) In a scientific treatment of the practical aspects of social problems, the alternative sets of hypothetical value premises should not be chosen arbitrarily. The principle of selection should be their *relevance*. Relevance is determined by the interests and ideals of actual persons and groups of persons. There is thus no need of introducing value premises which are not actually held by anybody.[a]

(g) Within the circle of relevance so determined a still more narrow circle of *significance* may be taken to denote such valuations which are held by substantial groups of people or by small groups with substantial social power. Realistic research on practical problems will have to concentrate its attention upon value premises corresponding to valuations which have high social significance or are likely to gain in social significance. On the other hand, it is certainly not necessary to adopt only those valuation premises which are held by a majority of the population or by a politically dominant group.

(h) The goals set by the value premises must also be *feasible*. Some courses of future development might be proved—by theoretical investigation of relevant data—to be impossible or highly improbable. Valuations bent upon the impossible should, of course, not be chosen as valuation premises but be theoretically criticized as unfeasible. This theoretical criticism in terms of feasibility of people's actual valuations is, indeed, one of the most important tasks of social science.

(i) The set of value premises selected must not include mutually incompatible ones but must be *consistent*. In this context we must observe that sometimes a balance or a compromise in the set of value premises must be worked out and defined (to take an over-simplified example, progress may mean a sacrifice of stability and order). Some value premises are more inclusive than others and subsume others under them. Some value premises stand in a proximate relationship to others (as means to ends).

If these rules could be observed, the analysis of social problems in theoretical terms would become released from arbitrariness in the setting of problems and protected from the unconscious effect of biases. The analysis in practical terms would be elevated to the rational plane and made specific and realistic. *The aim of practical research*—starting out from the data revealed by theoretical research and from sets of explicitly stated, concretely specified, alternatively assumed, hypothetical value premises which are relevant, significant, and attainable—is, in general terms, *to show precisely what should be the practical and political opinions and plans for action from the point of view of*

[a] This is a rule of economy. There are, of course, no logical reasons why we might not anticipate combinations, syntheses, mutual modifications of existing value premises or even conjure up new ones and thus enlarge still more our perspective. Certainly we could go outside the culture and epoch under study and use the value premises operating there and see what would happen if they were in the culture and epoch.

*the various valuations if their holders also had the more correct and comprehensive
factual knowledge which science provides.*

3. *Prognoses and Programs.* A study of valuations as they, in the form of interests
and ideals, are actually held in various racial, regional, economic, and social groups of
American society is, naturally, an important task in itself in the theoretical exploration
of social reality. As the future social development will, in part, depend upon the reactions of the various groups and upon their relative power, the *prognoses* of future trends
—which represent the ultimate goal for theoretical research—must include an investigation of the valuations and of the power behind valuations.

Prognoses and programs are in this scheme of thinking naturally interdependent: (a)
the prognoses will partly depend on the actually conceived programs of various individuals and groups with diverse valuations and with various amounts of power; (b) rational
programs must, on the other hand, be built upon the prognoses of trends which these
various groups and individuals intend to bend in one way or the other; (c) even the
existing programs of individuals and groups are, of course, founded upon ideas about
future trends; (d) practical research tries to rationalize the existing programs by connect-
ing the valuations basic to those programs with available scientific knowledge; (e) to the
degree that practical research is successful in this, and to the extent that the educational
agencies in society are effective in disseminating knowledge, it will influence trends and,
consequently, be a cause of change of programs to be considered in theoretical prognoses.

Existing programs are multiple and conflicting, at least in a democratic society where
no one group has all the power.[a] Practical research cannot, therefore, proceed on the
old liberalistic doctrine that there is a "harmony of interest" and that there is only one
program which is directed toward all the good in the world. Theoretical analysis reveals
that there is actual struggle and competition between individuals and between groups,
and that social trends take their form as an outcome of this struggle and competition.
For practical analysis, therefore, there must be alternative programs.

4. *The Selection of Value Premises.* The scheme of principles for selecting value
premises and introducing them into scientific research, presented in the last two sections,
represents an ideal for social science. The possibilities of approaching it, however, are
severely restricted by a number of circumstances:

(a) The scientific basis for constructing our "field of valuations" is poor. Public
opinion with respect to the Negro problem has not been studied much, and the studies
made do not meet our requirements.[b] For the most part we have been forced to base
our generalizations on impressionistic observations of the values held by different groups
and individuals.

(b) Many of the valuations held with respect to the Negro problem have much

---

[a] The more "normal" conditions are, the greater is the number of conflicting programs.
In a crisis situation—economic, social, or political—there really is an approximation to
"interest harmony" in society because interests have, for the time being, been taken away
from long-range objectives and concentrated upon one, mutually shared, short-range objective. In a depression both employers and employees can be shown to have a common interest
in economic expansion, raising volume of credit, demand, prices, production, employment
and wage-earnings. In war the common interest rising above all other goals is to win
victory. In a crisis the methodological problem for practical research is, therefore, relatively simple.
[b] See Appendix 10, Section 2.

broader application than this problem, and consequently cannot be completely restricted to a uni-linear pro- and anti-Negro scale of valuations. They branch out into the whole complex of economic, social, and political problems where the Negro has a stake in contemporary American civilization. Valuations which can be observed in behavior and opinions are not formed with respect to the Negro in abstraction, but to the Negro in specific social relations. This difficulty is, however, somewhat relieved, as there apparently is a high degree of correlation between the valuations along various scales.

(c) Valuations concern not only goals or "ends" in the treatment of the Negro, but also the "means" of achieving these goals and the "by-effects" of the achievement.

(d) We cannot assume that the conflicts of valuation are raging only *between* individuals and *between* groups. It is too significant to overlook that these conflicts are actually housed *within* single individuals.[a] This makes both the observation of valuations and the imputation of power to various valuations a most delicate problem.

(e) Partly because a single individual may hold several logically incompatible valuations, a set of valuations is seldom systematized and made self-consistent.

(f) Another difficulty in extracting value premises arises out of the fact that they are bound up with beliefs.[b] People's beliefs represent not only their volitional attitudes to social problems but also their incomplete and incorrect views as to the facts of social reality. Beliefs may influence valuations, just as valuations influence beliefs. Because we can get at only expressed opinions, which are themselves a much modified form of complexes of beliefs and valuations, it is a complicated task to detect valuations. From behavior and expressed opinions we must infer back to those complexes. From them we must infer back to basic valuations. This latter step includes the speculation as to what people's valuations would be if they were juxtaposed with correct knowledge instead of incorrect knowledge. The tracing out of a set of existing valuations, and a determination of their relevance and significance, is—for this reason alone—a difficult undertaking.

(g) Aside from all this, the very multiplicity of relevant and significant sets of valuations will, of course, raise great operational difficulties in research. The number of sets of value premises applied will have to be reduced much by way of abstraction. As there is a high correlation between valuations along different scales, some main composite axes can be defined. On each axis not every point need be represented but only a few, so that one can see what difference it makes in scientific approach and practical conclusions when one moves to the one extreme or the other. But even after a reduction of the sets of value premises to a few, the analysis will tend to be complicated.

5. _The "Instrumental Norm."_ With these complications and difficulties in view, it becomes evident that to try to consider all the existing, relevant, and significant sets of valuations with respect to the Negro problem, to relate them to relevant facts, and to draw up various sets of practical programs is a task which cannot be accomplished within the confines of present research resources. The ideal should, however, be held clearly and uncompromisingly before our eyes as the goal for research.

In this situation we have seen fit to adopt the following solution: *that one single set of relevant and significant value premises be selected for utilization in a preliminary analysis* and *that other significant sets of value premises be introduced at a later stage*

[a] See the Introduction and Appendix 1.
[b] See Appendix 1, Section 1.

of the investigation to make possible judgments in terms of alternative valuations and policies.

The purely *technical and instrumental character* of the preliminary set of value premises must be borne in mind constantly. The valuations of situations and trends, institutions and policies reached in terms of the instrumental value premises also are only preliminary.

But we must not deceive ourselves on this point: the selection of the instrumental norm *has* material significance. The whole direction of our theoretical research actually becomes determined by this norm. We have given one particular set of valuations a *strategically favorable position* in the study. This is not a characteristic of our study in particular but of all research working under the same limits of research resources. It is not a bias, as the direction of research has been determined under conscious control and by help of explicit valuations. But measured by the standards of our ideal for research and keeping in mind all other possible sets of value premises, it is a one-sidedness in approach, and we should be fully aware of it. In the present volume time and space have, further, prevented the subsequent complementation of our results by applying alternative sets of value premises, except at a few points.[a]

Under these circumstances the utmost importance must be attached to the choice of the instrumental norm. In Chapter 1, Section 13, we have given the reasons why we have organized this book around a set of valuations which we have called the "American Creed."

6. *The Value-Loaded Terms.* This very set of dynamic valuations contained in the American Creed has actually, to a great extent and despite compromises with the inherited static valuations of social science, determined the object and direction of previous research on the Negro problem. We are thus keeping to the tradition, only attempting to clarify what we are doing. The scientific work on the Negro in politics has been centered upon disfranchisement. This means that the interest has been defined out of the notion that the extraordinary thing to be studied is the fact that often in America the Negro is not given the right to suffrage as other citizens. In the same vein the work on the Negro's legal status has been focused upon the specific disabilities of the Negro under the law. Negro education has likewise been studied under the main viewpoint of discrimination. The same is true of the research on the Negro as a breadwinner. Negro standards of living have been compared with those of the whites. His share in social welfare policy has been measured by the standards of equality. *Discrimination* has been the key word for most studies on the Negro problem. This very term—and all its synonyms and specifications—and the theoretical approach which it signifies are derived out of the precepts of the American Creed.

It has often been observed that these terms, and a great many other terms of more general import for social research, as, for instance, class and caste, are all value-loaded. Many scientists attempt to avoid what they rightly (as they are not specifying the value premises involved) conceive of as biases by choosing new terms for the same things which do not carry such apparent connotations of valuation. This attempt is in our view misdirected. Biases are not so easily eradicated. And in this case they signify— though in a concealed and therefore uncontrollable way—valuations necessary for the setting of scientific problems. "Without valuations," Professor Louis Wirth writes,

[a] See, for example, Chapter 23, Section 6.

"we have no interest, no sense of relevance or of significance, and, consequently, no object." [a]

The value-loaded terms have a meaning and represent a theoretical approach, because the theoretical approach itself is determined by the valuations inherent in the governing *ethos* of a society. When this is seen clearly, and when those valuations are made explicit and, consequently, *the terms are defined in relation to the valuations,* then, and only then, are we in the position to use the terms freely without constantly endangering the theoretical analysis by permitting biases to slip in. There is thus no sense in inventing new scientific terms for the purpose. New terms for old things can only give a false security to ourselves and bewilder the general public. In the degree that the new terms would actually cover the facts we discussed in the old familiar terms—the facts which we *want* to discuss, because we *are interested* in them—they would soon become equally value-loaded in a society permeated by the same ideals and interests. Scientific terms become value-loaded because society is made up of human beings following purposes. A "disinterested social science" is, from this viewpoint, pure nonsense. It never existed, and it never will exist. We can make our thinking strictly rational in spite of this, but only by facing the valuations, not by evading them.

[a] In a letter to the author, September 29, 1939.

A METHODOLOGICAL NOTE ON THE PRINCIPLE
OF CUMULATION

In social science we have been drawing heavily on the notions and theories of the much farther developed natural sciences, particularly physics. The notion of equilibrium, for instance, has been in all our reasoning for centuries. Actually it is present in most research of the present day, even when it is not formally introduced. In most social research we have restricted our utilization of the equilibrium notion to that simple and static variant of it, the *stable equilibrium*. It is this equilibrium notion which is implicit in the sociological constructions of "maladjustment" and "adjustment" and all their several synonyms or near-synonyms, where equilibrium is thought of as having a virtual reality in determining the direction of change.[a] We propose the utilization of *other equilibrium notions* besides this simplest one. For dynamic analysis of the process of change in social relations, it is highly desirable that we disengage our minds from the stable equilibrium scheme of thinking. The other types of equilibrium notions are often better descriptions of social reality than the stable one.

If we succeed in placing a pencil upright on its end, it is also in equilibrium, but an unstable one, a "labile status" of balancing forces, as we easily find if we touch it. No "adjustment," "adaptation," or "accommodation" toward the original position will follow the application of a push, but only an accelerated movement away from the original state of balance. A third type of equilibrium is present when a pencil is rolling on a plane surface: it may come to rest anywhere. A fourth type is what we might call "created equilibrium," that is, arranging a disordered pile of pencils into a box by intelligent social engineering.

The most important need is to give place in our hypothetical explanatory scheme to a rational recognition of the cumulation of forces. In one branch of social science, economics, these various types of equilibrium notions have lately been used with great advantage. The principle of cumulation has given us, for the first time, something which approaches a real theory of economic dynamics.[b] In Chapter 3, Section 7, we referred to the theory of the "vicious circle" as a main explanatory scheme for this inquiry into the Negro problem; the scheme reappears in every part of our book. The following

---

[a] These equilibrium concepts have been used also as vehicles for introducing hidden valuations—i.e., bias—into research; see Appendix 2. Our interest in this appendix is directed only upon their usefulness as theoretical tools. To explain these other notions it is convenient to think in terms of analogies. The stable equilibrium is like a hanging pendulum, unmoving, and with no tendency to move unless jolted.

[b] For a simplified model of cumulative economic causation, see Gunnar Myrdal, *Monetary Equilibrium* (1939), pp. 24 ff.

brief notes are intended to give an abstract clarification of the theory and a perspective on some of its future potentialities as a method of social research.

In considering the Negro problem in its most abstract aspect, let us construct a much simplified mental model of dynamic social causation. We assume in this model society of our imagination a white majority and a Negro minority. We assume, further, that the interrelation between the two groups is in part determined by a specific degree of "race prejudice" on the side of the whites, directed against the Negroes. We assume the "plane of living" of the Negroes to be considerably lower than that of the whites. We take, as given, a mutual relationship between our two variables, and we assume this relationship to be of such a type that, on the one hand, the Negroes' plane of living is kept down by discrimination from the side of the whites while, on the other hand, the whites' reason for discrimination is partly dependent upon the Negroes' plane of living. The Negroes' poverty, ignorance, superstition, slum dwellings, health deficiencies, dirty appearance, disorderly conduct, bad odor and criminality stimulate and feed the antipathy of the whites for them. We assume, for the sake of simplicity, that society, in our abstract model, is in "balance" initially. By this we mean that conditions are static, that our two variables are exactly checking each other: there is—under these static conditions—just enough prejudice on the part of the whites to keep down the Negro plane of living to that level which maintains the specific degree of prejudice, or the other way around.

If now, in this hypothetically balanced state, for some reason or other, the Negro plane of living should be lowered, this will—other things being equal—in its turn increase white prejudice. Such an increase in white prejudice has the effect of pressing down still further the Negro plane of living, which again will increase prejudice, and so on, by way of mutual interaction between the two variables, *ad infinitum*. A cumulative process is thus set in motion which can have final effects quite out of proportion to the magnitude of the original push. The push might even be withdrawn after a time, and still a permanent change will remain or even the process of change will continue without a new balance in sight. If, instead, the initial change had been such a thing as a gift from a philanthropist to raise the Negro plane of living, a cumulative movement would have started in the other direction, having exactly the same causal mechanism. The vicious circle works both ways.

The Negroes' "plane of living" is, however, a composite entity. Let us, while retaining our major assumptions, approach a more realistic conception by splitting up this quantity into components, assuming that the cumulative principle works also in their causative interrelations. Besides "relative absense of race prejudice on the side of whites," we introduce a number of variables: levels of "Negro employment," "wages," "housing," "nutrition," "clothing," "health," "education," "stability in family relations," "manners," "cleanliness," "orderliness," "trustworthiness," "law observance," "loyalty to society at large," "absence of criminality" and so on. All these variables—according to our hypotheses—cumulate. In other words, we assume that a movement in any of the Negro variables in the direction toward the corresponding white levels will tend to decrease white prejudice. At the same time white prejudice is assumed to be, directly or indirectly, one of the causative factors effective in keeping the levels low for the several Negro variables. It is also our hypothesis that, on the whole, a rise in any single one of the Negro variables will tend to raise all the other Negro variables and thus, indirectly as well as directly, result in a cumulatively enforced effect upon white prejudice. A rise in employment will tend to increase earnings; raise standards of living; and improve health, education, manners and law observance and *vice versa*; a better education is assumed to raise the chances of a higher salaried job, and *vice versa*; and so all the way through our whole system of variables. Each of the secondary changes has its effect on white prejudice.

If, in actual social life, the dynamics of the causal relations between the various factors in the Negro problem should correspond to our hypotheses, then—assuming again, for the sake of simplicity, an initially static state of balanced forces—*any change in any one of these factors, independent of the way in which it is brought about, will, by the aggregate weight of the cumulative effects running back and forth between them all, start the whole system moving* in one direction or the other as the case may be, with a speed depending upon the original push and the functions of causal interrelation within the system.

Our point is not simply that many forces are "working in the same direction." Originally we assumed that there was a balance between these forces, and that the system was static, until we introduced one push coming in at one point or the other. When the system starts rolling, it is true that *the changes in the forces*—though not all the forces themselves—work in one direction; but this is because the variables are assumed to be interlocked in such a causal mechanism that a change of any one causes the others to change *in the same direction*, with a secondary effect upon the first variable, and so on.

We may further notice that the "balance" assumed as initial status was not a stable equilibrium at all—of the type which is tacitly assumed in the notions of "maladjustment," "adjustment," "accommodation," "social lag"—and, further, that in our scheme of hypotheses there is not necessarily assumed to exist any new "balance," or "equilibrium," or "harmony," toward which the factors of the system "adjust" or "accommodate." In the utilization of this theoretical model on problems of actual social reality, the initial state of labile balance, which we assumed for simplicity in our demonstration, will, of course, never be found. What we shall have to study are *processes of systems actually rolling* in the one direction or the other, systems which are constantly subjected to all sorts of pushes from outside through all the variables, and which are moving because of the cumulative effect of all these pushes and the interaction between the variables.

The individual factors into which we split the Negroes' plane of living can, of course, be split again, and it is the purpose of scientific analysis to do so. The causal relations between the sub-factors, and between them and all other factors, will be assumed to be ruled by the same cumulative principle. White race prejudice, here assumed as the "cause" of discrimination, is not a solid and static factor. To begin with, it depends upon discrimination itself. If, for some reason—for example, the demand of the employer during a war emergency, or the ruling of a trade union—white workers actually come to work with Negroes as fellow workers, it has been experienced that prejudice will often adjust to the changed amount of discrimination. White prejudice itself can be split into a great number of beliefs and valuations; to a degree, both of these two types of factors are dependent upon each other, as we hinted at in Appendix 1, and, consequently, are under the rule of the cumulative principle.

Throughout this treatise on the Negro problem the model of dynamic causation— and the implied skepticism toward the idea of stable equilibrium—is kept steadily in the back of our mind. A main viewpoint in our study of every single factor in the Negro problem is thus its interrelation with all other factors and their cumulative effect upon the status of the Negro. The principle of cumulation allows us to see that there is sense in the general notion of the "status of the Negro." We should, indeed, have liked to present in our study a general *index*, year by year or at least decade by decade, as a quantitative expression of the movement of the entire system we are studying: the status of the Negro in America. Such an index would have about the same significance as the general indices of production or prices or any other complex systems of interdependent variables. The index is an average. It should, for the same principal reasons, have to be broken down for regions, classes, and items, and this breaking down would have the same scientific function in an analysis. It would give quantitative precision to the concept of the general status of the Negro—a concept which, because of the cumulative principle, we cannot escape. And it always clarifies our reasoning to be compelled to calculate a quantitative value for a notion we use. Materials for such an index of (relative and absolute) Negro status are, to a great extent, available, and the general theory of the index offers a methodological basis for its construction. But the work of constructing and analyzing a general index of Negro status in America amounts to a major investigation in itself, and we must leave the matter as a proposal for further research.

Our chief task is to analyze the causal interrelation within the system itself as it works under the influence of outside pushes and the momentum of on-going processes within. The system is much more complicated than appears from our abstract representation. To begin with, all factors must be broken down by region, social class, age, sex and so on. As what we are studying is a race relation, the number of combinations increases by multiples for each classification applied. White prejudice, for instance, varies not only with the status of the white man, but also with the Negro's social class and the field of Negro behavior in relation to which race prejudice is active. There are also Negro prejudices in the system.

Each factor has its peculiarities and irregularities. White prejudice, for instance, changes not only as a reaction to actual changes in Negro plane of living, but also to expectations of such changes. The latter reaction may be totally different from the former: a higher plane of living among Negroes, when it is actually achieved, may be expected to effect a *decrease* of white prejudice, but the *expectation* of it for the future might *increase* prejudice, particularly in the South (even if its long-run effects—when it actually comes—will be, as we have assumed, a decrease of prejudice). It is possible, finally, that certain social classes of whites—say poor whites in the South—even in the fairly long-range perspective will react with increased prejudice against the Negro's approaching the white man's status.

The system thus becomes complicated, but the fundamental principle of cumulative causation remains. The scientific ideal is not only to define and analyze the factors, but to give for each one of them a measure of their actual quantitative strength in influencing the other factors, as well as a measure of their ability to be influenced themselves by outside forces. The time element becomes of paramount importance in these formulas. As we have exemplified for the factor of white prejudice, the effects might have different signs in the short and in the long run. Even when this is not the case, the effects will be spread differently along the time axis. A rise of employment, for instance, will almost immediately raise some standards of living, but a change in levels of education or health are slow to be achieved, and their effects back on the other factors are in turn delayed, which slows up the whole process of cumulation. The system regularly develops under a great multitude of different outside pushes, primarily directed against almost every single factor. The actual pushes go in both directions, thus often *turning the system around on its axis as it is rolling.* Ideally, the scientific solution of the Negro problem should thus be given in the form of an interconnected series of quantitative equations, describing the movement of the actual system under various influences. That this complete, quantitative and truly scientific solution is far beyond the horizon does not need to be pointed out. But in principle it is possible to execute, and it remains as the scientific ideal steering our endeavors.

This conception of a great number of interdependent factors, mutually cumulative in their effects, disposes of the idea that there is *one* predominant factor, a "basic factor." This idea—mainly in the form of a vague conception of economic determinism—has been widely accepted in the writings on the Negro problem during the last decade. As we see the methodological problem, this one-factor hypothesis is not only theoretically unclear but is contradicted by easily ascertainable facts and factual relations. As a scientific approach it is narrow.[a]

The theoretical system of dynamic social causation we have selected corresponds more closely to the practical man's common-sense ideas about things than it does to the apprehension of reality met in many scientific writings on the Negro problem. The social scientist tends to rely too much on static notions and *a priori* to give too dominant a role to a "basic factor." The professional philanthropist, the Negro educator, the Negro trade unionist, the leaders of Negro defense organizations like the N.A.A.C.P., the Urban League, or the Interracial Commission, and, indeed, the average well-meaning citizen of both colors, pragmatically applies this same hypothesis.[b] To use once more

[a] The usual economic one-factor theory is available in two extreme versions, depending upon the type of political teleology involved: (1) a radical Marxist version, where the expectation is an economic revolution which will change everything and even eradicate race prejudice; (2) a liberalistic version which does not expect an economic revolution and which—as the assumption is that no significant change can be brought about except by tackling the "basic factor," the economic system—is pessimistic about any type of induced change. There are all sorts of intermediary positions and also compromises toward recognizing that factors other than the economic one have some influence. But the one-factor theory always implies a fatalistic tendency and prevents a rational conception of interdependence and cumulative dynamic causation. See Appendix 2, Section 3.

[b] The best formulation of our hypothesis available in the literature is, thus, to be found in a book by a practical man writing without scientific pretensions but out of lifelong experiences: "There is a vicious circle in caste. At the outset, the despised group is usually inferior in certain of the accepted standards of the controlling class. Being inferior, members of the degraded caste are denied the privileges and opportunities of their fellows and so are pushed still further down and then are regarded with that much less respect, and therefore are more rigorously denied advantages, and so around and around the vicious circle. Even when the movement starts to reverse itself—as it most certainly has in the case of the Negro—there is a desperately long unwinding as a slight increase in good will gives a little greater chance and this leads to a little higher accomplishment and that to increased respect and so slowly upward toward equality of opportunity, of regard, and of status." (Edwin R. Embree, *Brown America* [1931], p. 200.) To this it should only be added that even if the unwinding process is working with time lags so is the opposite movement. In spite of the time lags, the theory of the vicious circle is a cause rather for optimism than for pessimism. The cumulative principle works both ways.

our parallel from modern economic theory: when the economists during the last two decades abandoned the classical static equilibrium approach and went ahead to construct a dynamic theory of causal interrelations in a process of change, what they actually did was to apply the pragmatic notions of bankers, businessmen, and labor leaders and try to systematize them. This revolutionized economic theory and had great importance for the scientific planning of economic policy. A rational strategy in the Negro problem also assumes a theory of dynamic causation.[a]

[a] Some remarks on this problem are made in Chapter 3, Section 7.

APPENDIX 4

NOTE ON THE MEANING OF REGIONAL TERMS AS
USED IN THIS BOOK

The word *America* is used as a synonym for continental United States.

The word *South* is not used consistently throughout the whole book, since various investigators upon whose work we have drawn have had variant definitions. In each case we have tried to make the definition clear by context or footnotes. In a sense the geographical boundaries of the South are "ideal-typical," and it is in this sense that we shall speak of the South when we are not using statistics. Some have stressed that there are many Souths, but in the Negro problem there are also reasons for speaking about one South.

> . . . if it can be said there are many Souths, the fact remains that there is also one South. That is to say, it is easy to trace throughout the region (roughly delimited by the boundaries of the former Confederate States of America, but shading over into some of the border states, notably Kentucky, also) a fairly definite mental pattern, associated with a fairly definite social pattern—a complex of established relationships and habits of thought, sentiments, prejudices, standards and values, and associations of ideas, which, if it is not common strictly to every group of white people in the South, is still common in one appreciable measure or another, and in some part or another, to all but relatively negligible ones.[a]

The roughness of these ideal-typical boundaries for the South is suggested when we examine various criteria for defining the South, as in Table 1. When we use statistics, we refer either to the census definition of the South (16 states and the District of Columbia) or to the school-segregation-law definition (17 states and the District of Columbia). These definitions differ solely by the inclusion of Missouri in the latter. Sometimes statistics for all these states are not available, and we are forced to use an artificially abbreviated definition but without pretense that this includes all of the South.

The *North* is a residual term, comprising all states not in the South: it thus includes all Western states in the historical period being discussed. Sometimes, in order to call special attention to the Western states, we speak of the "North and West." When we wish to restrict our discussion to the northeastern quadrant of the country, we speak of "the Northern states east of the Mississippi River."

Many authors have defined different regions *within* the South. When we cite them we use their definitions. When we use regional terms on our own authority, we follow these definitions unless necessity forces us to specify other definitions: *Lower South*, or

[a] W. F. Cash, *The Mind of the South* (1941), p. viii.

1071

Deep South, includes Florida, Texas, Georgia, Alabama, Mississippi, Louisiana, Arkansas, Oklahoma, and South Carolina; *Upper South* includes North Carolina, Tennessee, and Virginia; *Border states* include Kentucky, West Virginia, Maryland, Delaware, District of Columbia and sometimes Missouri.

TABLE 1

VARIOUS DEFINITIONS OF THE SOUTH

State	Seceded in Civil War	Slave States, 1860	Laws prohibiting inter-marriage (excluding Western States)	School segregation laws	Legal and illegal forced school segregation (excluding Western States)	Jim Crow railways	Jim Crow street cars	South of Mason-Dixon Line 39°43′26″	Census	White Primary
Oklahoma	Choctaw Nation	Not a State	x	x	x	x	x		x	
Texas	x	x	x	x	x	x	x	Equivalent to Slave States east of Ohio. Boundary between Pennsylvania and Maryland.	x	part
Louisiana	x	x	x	x	x	x	x		x	x
Arkansas	x	x	x	x	x	x	x		x	x
Mississippi	x	x	x	x	x	x	x		x	x
Alabama	x	x	x	x	x	x	x		x	x
Tennessee	x	x	x	x	x	x	x		x	part
Florida	x	x	x	x	x	x	x		x	x
Georgia	x	x	x	x	x	x	x		x	x
South Carolina	x	x	x	x	x	x	x		x	x
North Carolina	x	x	x	x	x	x	x		x	part
Virginia	x	x	x	x	x	x	x		x	x
West Virginia		Not a State	x	x	x				x	
Maryland		x	x	x	x		x		x	
Kentucky		x	x	x	x		x		x	
Delaware		x	x	x	x		optional		x	
Missouri		x	x	x	x					
District of Columbia		x		x	x				x	
New Jersey					part					
Indiana			x		part					
Kansas					part					
Illinois					part					
Ohio					part					
Pennsylvania					part					

A PARALLEL TO THE NEGRO PROBLEM

In every society there are at least two groups of people, besides the Negroes, who are characterized by high social visibility expressed in physical appearance, dress, and patterns of behavior, and who have been "suppressed." We refer to women and children. Their present status, as well as their history and their problems in society, reveal striking similarities to those of the Negroes. In studying a special problem like the Negro problem, there is always a danger that one will develop a quite incorrect idea of its uniqueness. It will, therefore, give perspective to the Negro problem and prevent faulty interpretations to sketch some of the important similarities between the Negro problem and the women's problem.

In the historical development of these problem groups in America there have been much closer relations than is now ordinarily recorded. In the earlier common law, women and children were placed under the jurisdiction of the paternal power. When a legal status had to be found for the imported Negro servants in the seventeenth century, the nearest and most natural analogy was the status of women and children. The ninth commandment—linking together women, servants, mules, and other property —could be invoked, as well as a great number of other passages of Holy Scripture. We do not intend to follow here the interesting developments of the institution of slavery in America through the centuries, but merely wish to point out the paternalistic idea which held the slave to be a sort of family member and in some way—in spite of all differences—placed him beside women and children under the power of the *paterfamilias*.

There was, of course, even in the beginning, a tremendous difference both in actual status of these different groups and in the tone of sentiment in the respective relations. In the decades before the Civil War, in the conservative and increasingly antiquarian ideology of the American South, woman was elevated as an ornament and looked upon with pride, while the Negro slave became increasingly a chattel and a ward. The paternalistic construction came, however, to good service when the South had to build up a moral defense for slavery, and it is found everywhere in the apologetic literature up to the beginning of the Civil War. For illustration, some passages from Georg⸱ Fitzhugh's *Sociology for the South*, published in 1854, may be quoted as typical:

> The kind of slavery is adapted to the men enslaved. Wives and apprentices are slaves; not in theory only, but often in fact. Children are slaves to their parents, guardians and teachers. Imprisoned culprits are slaves. Lunatics and idiots are slaves also.*

A beautiful example and illustration of this kind of communism, is found in the

* P. 86.

instance of the Patriarch Abraham. His wives and his children, his men servants and his maid servants, his camels and his cattle, were all equally his property. He could sacrifice Isaac or a ram, just as he pleased. He loved and protected all, and all shared, if not equally, at least fairly, in the products of their light labour. Who would not desire to have been a slave of that old Patriarch, stern and despotic as he was? . . . Pride, affection, self-interest, moved Abraham to protect, love and take care of his slaves. The same motives operate on all masters, and secure comfort, competency and protection to the slave. A man's wife and children are his slaves, and do they not enjoy, in common with himself, his property?[a]

Other protagonists of slavery resort to the some argument:

In this country we believe that the general good requires us to deprive the whole female sex of the right of self-government. They have no voice in the formation of the laws which dispose of their persons and property. . . . We treat all minors much in the same way. . . . Our plea for all this is, that the good of the whole is thereby most effectually promoted. . . .[b]

Significant manifestations of the result of this disposition [on the part of the Abolitionists] to consider their own light a surer guide than the word of God, are visible in the anarchical opinions about human governments, civil and ecclesiastical, and on the rights of women, which have found appropriate advocates in the abolition publications. . . . If our women are to be emancipated from subjection to the law which God has imposed upon them, if they are to quit the retirement of domestic life, where they preside in stillness over the character and destiny of society; . . . if, in studied insult to the authority of God, we are to renounce in the marriage contract all claim to obedience, we shall soon have a country over which the genius of Mary Wolstonecraft would delight to preside, but from which all order and all virtue would speedily be banished. There is no form of human excellence before which we bow with profounder deference than that which appears in a delicate woman, . . . and there is no deformity of human character from which we turn with deeper loathing than from a woman forgetful of her nature, and clamourous for the vocation and rights of men.[c]

. . . Hence her [Miss Martineau's] wild chapter about the "Rights of Women," her groans and invectives because of their exclusion from the offices of the state, the right of suffrage, the exercise of political authority. In all this, the error of the declaimer consists in the very first movement of the mind. "The Rights of *Women*" may all be conceded to the sex, yet the rights of *men* withheld from them.[d]

The parallel goes, however, considerably deeper than being only a structural part in the defense ideology built up around slavery. Women at that time lacked a number of rights otherwise belonging to all free white citizens of full age.

So chivalrous, indeed, was the ante-bellum South that its women were granted scarcely any rights at all. Everywhere they were subjected to political, legal, educational, and social and economic restrictions. They took no part in governmental affairs, were without

[a] *Ibid.*, p. 297.

[b] Charles Hodge, "The Bible Argument on Slavery," in E. N. Elliott (editor), *Cotton Is King*, and *Pro-Slavery Arguments* (1860), pp. 859-860.

[c] Albert T. Bledsoe, *An Essay on Liberty and Slavery* (1857), pp. 223-225.

[d] W. Gilmore Simms, "The Morals of Slavery," in *The Pro-Slavery Argument* (1853), p. 248. See also Simms' "Address on the Occasion of the Inauguration of the Spartanburg Female College," August 12, 1855.

legal rights over their property or the guardianship of their children, were denied adequate educational facilities, and were excluded from business and the professions.[a]

The same was very much true of the rest of the country and of the rest of the world. But there was an especially close relation in the South between the subordination of women and that of Negroes. This is perhaps best expressed in a comment attributed to Dolly Madison, that the Southern wife was "the chief slave of the harem."[b]

From the very beginning, the fight in America for the liberation of the Negro slaves was, therefore, closely coordinated with the fight for women's emancipation. It is interesting to note that the Southern states, in the early beginning of the political emancipation of women during the first decades of the nineteenth century, had led in the granting of legal rights to women. This was the time when the South was still the stronghold of liberal thinking in the period leading up to and following the Revolution. During the same period the South was also the region where Abolitionist societies flourished, while the North was uninterested in the Negro problem. Thereafter the two movements developed in close interrelation and were both gradually driven out of the South.

The women suffragists received their political education from the Abolitionist movement. Women like Angelina Grimke, Sarah Grimke, and Abby Kelly began their public careers by speaking for Negro emancipation and only gradually came to fight for women's rights. The three great suffragists of the nineteenth century—Lucretia Mott, Elizabeth Cady Stanton, and Susan B. Anthony—first attracted attention as ardent campaigners for the emancipation of the Negro and the prohibition of liquor. The women's movement got much of its public support by reason of its affiliation with the Abolitionist movement: the leading male advocates of woman suffrage before the Civil War were such Abolitionists as William Lloyd Garrison, Henry Ward Beecher, Wendell Phillips, Horace Greeley and Frederick Douglass. The women had nearly achieved their aims, when the Civil War induced them to suppress all tendencies distracting the federal government from the prosecution of the War. They were apparently fully convinced that victory would bring the suffrage to them as well as to the Negroes.[c]

The Union's victory, however, brought disappointment to the women suffragists. The arguments "the Negro's hour" and "a political necessity" met and swept aside all their arguments for leaving the word "male" out of the 14th Amendment and putting "sex" alongside "race" and "color" in the 15th Amendment.[d] Even their Abolitionist friends

[a] Virginius Dabney, *Liberalism in the South* (1932), p. 361.
[b] Cited in Harriet Martineau, *Society in America* (1842, first edition 1837), Vol. II, p. 81.
[c] Carrie Chapman Catt and Nettie Rogers Shuler, *Woman Suffrage and Politics* (1923), pp. 32 ff.
[d] The relevant sections of the 14th and 15th Amendments to the Constitution are (underlining ours):

14th Amendment

Section 2. Representatives shall be apportioned among the several States according to their respective numbers, counting the whole number of persons in each State, excluding Indians not taxed. But when the right to vote at any election for the choice of Electors for President and Vice President of the United States, Representatives in Congress, the executive and judicial officers of a State, or the members of the Legislature thereof, is denied to any of the *male* inhabitants of such State, being twenty-one years of age, and citizens of the United States, or in any way abridged, except for participation in rebellion, or other crime, the basis of representation therein shall be reduced in the proportion

turned on them, and the Republican party shied away from them. A few Democrats, really not in favor of the extension of the suffrage to anyone, sought to make political capital out of the women's demands, and said with Senator Cowan of Pennsylvania, "If I have no reason to offer why a Negro man shall not vote, I have no reason why a white woman shall not vote." Charges of being Democrats and traitors were heaped on the women leaders. Even a few Negroes, invited to the women's convention of January, 1869, denounced the women for jeopardizing the black man's chances for the vote. The War and Reconstruction Amendments had thus sharply divided the women's problem from the Negro problem in actual politics.[a] The deeper relation between the two will, however, be recognized up till this day. Du Bois' famous ideological manifesto *The Souls of Black Folk*[b] is, to mention only one example, an ardent appeal on behalf of women's interests as well as those of the Negro.

This close relation is no accident. The ideological and economic forces behind the two movements—the emancipation of women and children and the emancipation of

---

which the number of such *male* citizens shall bear to the whole number of *male* citizens twenty-one years of age in such State.

15th Amendment

Section 1. The right of citizens of the United States to vote shall not be denied or abridged by the United States or by any State on account of *race, color or previous condition of servitude.*

[a] While there was a definite affinity between the Abolitionist movement and the woman suffrage movement, there was also competition and, perhaps, antipathy, between them that widened with the years. As early as 1833, when Oberlin College opened its doors to women —the first college to do so—the Negro men students joined other men students in protesting (Catt and Shuler, *op. cit.*, p. 13). The Anti-Slavery Convention held in London in 1840 refused to seat the women delegates from America, and it was on this instigation that the first women's rights convention was called (*ibid.*, p. 17). After the passage of the 13th, 14th, and 15th Amendments, which gave legal rights to Negroes but not to women, the women's movement split off completely from the Negroes' movement, except for such a thing as the support of both movements by the rare old liberal, Frederick Douglass. An expression of how far the two movements had separated by 1903 was given by one of the leaders of the women's movement at that time, Anna Howard Shaw, in answer to a question posed to her at a convention in New Orleans:

" 'What is your purpose in bringing your convention to the South? Is it the desire of suffragists to force upon us the social equality of black and white women? Political equality lays the foundation for social equality. If you give the ballot to women, won't you make the black and white woman equal politically and therefore lay the foundation for a future claim of social equality?' . . .

"I read the question aloud. Then the audience called for the answer, and I gave it in these words, quoted as accurately as I can remember them·

" 'If political equality is the basis of social equality, and if by granting political equality you lay the foundation for a claim of social equality, I can only answer that you have already laid that claim. You did not wait for woman suffrage, but disfranchised both your black and white women, thus making them politically equal. But you have done more than that. You have put the ballot into the hands of your black men, thus making them the political superiors of your white women. Never before in the history of the world have men made former slaves the political masters of their former mistresses!' " (*The Story of a Pioneer* [1915], pp. 311-312.)

[b] 1903.

Negroes—have much in common and are closely interrelated. Paternalism was a preindustrial scheme of life, and was gradually becoming broken in the nineteenth century. Negroes and women, both of whom had been under the yoke of the paternalistic system, were both strongly and fatefully influenced by the Industrial Revolution. For neither group is the readjustment process yet consummated. Both are still problem groups. The women's problem is the center of the whole complex of problems of how to reorganize the institution of the family to fit the new economic and ideological basis, a problem which is not solved in any part of the Western world unless it be in the Soviet Union or Palestine. The family problem in the Negro group, as we find when analyzing the Negro family, has its special complications, centering in the tension and conflict between the external patriarchal system in which the Negro was confined as a slave and his own family structure.

As in the Negro problem, most men have accepted as self-evident, until recently, the doctrine that women had inferior endowments in most of those respects which carry prestige, power, and advantages in society, but that they were, at the same time, superior in some other respects. The arguments, when arguments were used, have been about the same: smaller brains, scarcity of geniuses and so on. The study of women's intelligence and personality has had broadly the same history as the one we record for Negroes. As in the case of the Negro, women themselves have often been brought to believe in their inferiority of endowment. As the Negro was awarded his "place" in society, so there was a "woman's place." In both cases the rationalization was strongly believed that men, in confining them to this place, did not act against the true interest of the subordinate groups. The myth of the "contented women," who did not want to have suffrage or other civil rights and equal opportunities, had the same social function as the myth of the "contented Negro." In both cases there was probably—in a static sense—often some truth behind the myth.

As to the character of the deprivations, upheld by law or by social conventions and the pressure of public opinion, no elaboration will here be made. As important and illustrative in the comparison, we shall, however, stress the conventions governing woman's education. There was a time when the most common idea was that she was better off with little education. Later the doctrine developed that she should not be denied education, but that her education should be of a special type, fitting her for her "place" in society and usually directed more on training her hands than her brains.

Political franchise was not granted to women until recently. Even now there are, in all countries, great difficulties for a woman to attain public office. The most important disabilities still affecting her status are those barring her attempt to earn a living and to attain promotion in her work. As in the Negro's case, there are certain "women's jobs," traditionally monopolized by women. They are regularly in the low salary bracket and do not offer much of a career. All over the world men have used the trade unions to keep women out of competition. Woman's competition has, like the Negro's, been particularly obnoxious and dreaded by men because of the low wages women, with their few earning outlets, are prepared to work for. Men often dislike the very idea of having women on an equal plane as co-workers and competitors, and usually they find it even more "unnatural" to work under women. White people generally hold similar attitudes toward Negroes. On the other hand, it is said about women that they prefer men as bosses and do not want to work under another woman. Negroes often feel the same way about working under other Negroes.

In personal relations with both women and Negroes, white men generally prefer a less professional and more human relation, actually a more paternalistic and protective position—somewhat in the nature of patron to client in Roman times, and like the corresponding strongly paternalistic relation of later feudalism. As in Germany it is said that every gentile has his pet Jew, so it is said in the South that every white has his "pet nigger," or—in the upper strata—several of them. We sometimes marry the pet woman, carrying out the paternalistic scheme. But even if we do not, we tend to deal kindly with her as a client and a ward, not as a competitor and an equal.

In drawing a parallel between the position of, and feeling toward, women and Negroes we are uncovering a fundamental basis of our culture. Although it is changing, atavistic elements sometimes unexpectedly break through even in the most emancipated individuals. The similarities in the women's and the Negroes' problems are not accidental. They were, as we have pointed out, originally determined in a paternalistic order of society. The problems remain, even though paternalism is gradually declining as an ideal and is losing its economic basis. In the final analysis, women are still hindered in their competition by the function of procreation; Negroes are laboring under the yoke of the doctrine of unassimilability which has remained although slavery is abolished. The second barrier is actually much stronger than the first in America today. But the first is more eternally inexorable.[a]

[a] Alva Myrdal, *Nation and Family* (1941), Chapter 22, "One Sex a Social Problem," pp. 398-426.

APPENDIX 6

PRE-WAR CONDITIONS OF THE NEGRO WAGE EARNER IN SELECTED INDUSTRIES AND OCCUPATIONS[a]

═══

1. GENERAL CHARACTERISTICS OF NEGRO JOBS

Many of the generalizations made in Chapter 13 will be corroborated in this Appendix by data on conditions in particular lines of work. The selection of industries and occupations that we shall use may be somewhat arbitrary. The reason is that we do not intend to give anything like an exhaustive description; our purpose is rather to emphasize the fact that general industrial trends, race prejudice, and other factors have worked out somewhat differently for different industries and occupations. For that reason, we need include only examples on how the Negro has fared in different types of cases.[b] On the one hand, there are the so-called "Negro jobs," i.e., those industries in which, as far as the South is concerned, most of the workers are Negro. On the other hand, there are those industries which, even in the South, have only a minority of Negro workers. Finally, there are industries which are exclusively or almost exclusively for whites.[c]

[a] The subsequent "case studies" are based, mainly, on a previously cited series of unpublished research memoranda on "Negro Labor and Its Problems," prepared by and under the direction of Paul H. Norgren. He was assisted by Lloyd H. Bailer (automobiles), James Healy (lumber), Herbert R. Northrup (tobacco and longshore work) and Arnold M. Rose (service industries exclusive of domestic service and slaughtering and meat packing). Most of the data on the Negro in domestic service have been drawn from a memorandum by Gladys L. Palmer ("A Memorandum Report on Negroes in Domestic Service") which was worked out in conjunction with this series. For more recent information, we have depended in part on an unpublished doctor's thesis by Herbert R. Northrup, "Negro Labor and Union Policies in the South" (Harvard University), in which certain parts of Dr. Norgren's materials have been supplemented and brought forward to the beginning of 1942.

(Editor's Note: Since Dr. Myrdal's book went to press, Dr. Northrup has rewritten his thesis for publication by Harper & Brothers under the title, *Organized Labor and the Negro*.)

[b] The length of each section, for the same reason, is not determined by the actual importance to the Negro of the various lines of work.

[c] Obviously there are no distinct borderlines between these various groups. There are no Negro jobs in the sense that the Negro, at least in the South, has a complete job monopoly in certain occupations. On the other hand, when Negroes do compete with white workers in "non-Negro jobs," there is usually some concentration of Negroes in certain specific occupations. Even industries excluding Negroes may use Negroes exclusively for work carrying a social stigma (charwomen, toilet attendants). The question of what occupations should be considered as Negro jobs is to be answered somewhat differently depending upon what kind of occupational or industrial classification is used for the analysis. An enumeration of "Negro jobs," for these reasons, must be arbitrary to some extent.

Even those should be considered, for it is just as important to find out why the Negro has failed to gain a foothold in a particular industry as it is to describe his condition in occupations where he has been allowed to work.

Table 1 shows the industries in which significant numbers of Negroes are employed. A reference to it, as each of the specific industries is taken up, will serve to give basic facts relevant to the discussion and to place the industry under consideration in perspective.

We intend to begin with the "Negro jobs," in which the bulk of the Negro workers are concentrated. Those segregated or semi-segregated occupations in which, as far as the South is concerned, one-half or more of the workers are Negro, include the following principal groups: domestic service; home laundering; certain other service occupations; home sewing; lumber milling; turpentine farming and distilling; fertilizer manufacturing; unskilled work in building construction; maintenance-of-way work on railroads; longshore work; delivery and messenger work; work as helpers and laborers in stores; unskilled work in blast furnaces and steel rolling mills; tobacco rehandling and other unskilled work in tobacco factories.[a] To this list could be added two traditionally Negro jobs which have been expanding rapidly since 1910, but in such a way that the Negroes have gained less than the whites, so that their share in the employment has been cut to less than one-half. These are unskilled work in building, repairing, and maintenance of roads, streets, and sewers; and work as teamsters, truck drivers and so forth. In the South, the proportion of Negro workers in these occupations, by 1930, was 42 and 32 per cent, respectively.[b] It is apparent that motorization was the cause both of the increase in total numbers thus occupied and of its growing attractiveness to white labor. As we shall find, there is a similar development under way in some of the other "Negro job" industries as well. In other such industries, Negroes have been able to maintain their traditional position, at least up until 1930.

Virtually all these "Negro job" industries have the common feature that they are regarded as undesirable from one or several viewpoints. Many of them carry a social stigma, particularly in the South, where they tend to be despised not only because they are located at the bottom of the occupational ladder, but also because of the very fact that they are traditionally "Negro jobs." The average wage level is low; in the South it tends to be even lower in relation to what is paid for skilled work than it is in the North. Most of the male Negro jobs call for outdoor work. They are usually

. . . characterized by a much greater degree of intermittency in employment than most white jobs in the South. . . . Thus, all of the outdoor occupations are subject to frequent "layoffs" in rainy weather. Winter cold curtails employment in turpentine extraction and, to some extent, also in building work; and seasonal variations in demand seriously affect work opportunities in lumber and fertilizer production. Business depressions infringe far more heavily on the lumber and construction industries than on textiles, garment-making, and most of the other southern industry-sectors where whites hold the bulk of the jobs.

Moreover, several of the Negro jobs are characterized

. . . by a high degree of physical and psychological disutility. Practically all of the occupations are "day labor" jobs, involving long and strenuous muscular exertion,

[a] *Fifteenth Census of the United States: 1930. Population*, Vol. 4; Table 11 of state tables. See also *Thirteenth Census of the United States: 1910, Population*, Vol. 4; pp. 434-534.
[b] *Idem.*

TABLE 1

Nonagricultural Industries and Service Groups Having 15,000 Negro Workers or More: 1930

Industry and Service Group[a]	Number of Negro Workers, 1930 (in thousands)			Negro Workers as per cent of All Workers, 1930	Per cent Females Among Negro Workers, 1930	Number of Workers in 1930 to Number of Workers in 1910 ×100	
	United States	The South	The North and West			All Workers	Negro Workers
Forestry	26	25	1	13.3	1.2	109	100
Coal mines	58	46	12	8.4	.1	103	143
Building industry	181	97	84	7.0	.1	101	77
Chemical and allied industries	48	34	14	7.7	1.9	270	241
Fertilizer factories	17	b	b	60.4	.7	201	220
Cigar and tobacco factories	34	31	3	22.9	54.0	77	135
Clay, glass and stone industries	29	15	14	7.8	2.6	101	101
Clothing industries	35	11	24	4.4	48.0	116	303
Suit, coat, and overall factories	15	b	b	4.8	16.7	82	158
Food and allied industries	57	31	26	6.2	20.8	169	278
Slaughter and packing houses	18	5	13	11.2	7.6	187	349
Iron, steel, vehicle and machinery industries	177	69	108	5.4	1.0	183	368
Automobile factories	26	3	23	4.0	1.1	606	4,551
Blast furnaces and steel rolling mills	53	15	38	8.5	.6	155	291
Car and railroad shops	16	b	b	7.2	.8	174	368
Lumber and furniture industries	139	132	7	16.1	2.4	108	110
Saw and planing mills	114	112	2	25.1	1.4	97	102
Paper, printing and allied industries	17	8	9	2.2	12.3	161	302
Textile industries	26	21	5	2.1	24.4	132	231
Cotton mills	16	15	1	3.9	18.0	118	226
Miscellaneous manufacturing industries	141	100	41	6.7	22.4	120	114
Independent hand trades	28	19	9	7.8	76.2	42	53
Turpentine farms and distilleries	33	b	b	75.2	.9	111	103
Construction and maintenance of roads, streets, sewers and bridges	64	48	16	14.1	.5	191	174
Garages, greasing stations and automobile laundries	44	19	25	10.4	.4	b	b
Postal service	18	6	12	6.3	3.3	167	301
Steam railroads	163	105	58	10.3	1.1	102	175
Truck transfer and cab companies	41	b	b	8.5	.6	131	98
Water transportation[d]	45	b	b	15.0	.7	135	139
Wholesale and retail trades, except automobiles[e]	192	121	71	3.6	8.4	150	158
Public service (not elsewhere classified)[f]	62	38	24	5.9	5.6	197	238
Recreation and amusement	35	16	19	7.9	16.0	b	b
Other professional and semiprofessional services[g]	138	103	35	4.7	48.1	b	c
Hotels, restaurants, boarding houses	228	124	104	16.8	46.4	b	b
Laundries and cleaning, dyeing and pressing shops	78	43	35	18.6	65.3	h	h
Other domestic and personal service[i]	1,174	806	368	38.6	83.6	b	b

Sources: Fifteenth Census of the United States: 1930, Population, Vol. 3, Part 1, p. 23, and Vol. 5, pp. 408–587. Thirteenth Census of the United States: 1910, Population, Vol. 4, pp. 302–433.
    a Heterogeneous sub-groups, such as "other iron and steel and machinery factories," are not listed, even when they had more than 15,000 Negro workers in 1930.
    b Data not available.
    c Includes 20,000 Negro seamstresses.
    d Largest group of Negro workers were longshoremen and stevedores (25,000).
    e Includes truck drivers, delivery men, laborers, porters, and helpers in stores (100,000 Negro workers)
    f Largest group of Negro workers was 32,000 "other laborers."
    g Includes 25,000 Negro clergymen and 54,000 Negro school teachers.
    h Figures available only for laundries: all workers—199; Negro workers—395.
    i Largest groups of Negro workers were: cooks (206,000); other servants (404,000); home launderers and laundresses (270,000).

usually in the form of "identical motions," continuously repeated. The high subjective undesirability of such work, as compared with even the most monotonous factory production-machine job, is universally acknowledged. In addition, there are other "disagreeableness factors" attached to the conditions of work in particular Negro jobs which push them even farther down in the utility scale. In logging it is chiefly risk of accident and disease; in sawmills, accident risk and noise; in fertilizer plants, dust and disagreeable odors; in road construction, excessive exposure to the elements, and so on.[a]

Before we go further in our description of the male "Negro jobs" we should consider the one occupation which is most important of all to the nonfarm female Negro: domestic service.

2. DOMESTIC SERVICE

The range of job opportunities, as previously stated, is more limited for Negro women than for Negro men. There is a similar sex differential in the white population, but the hardship worked on Negro women is much more pronounced. We have already emphasized the fact that, in 1930, as many as 1,150,000 Negro women earned their living as workers in domestic service and other service industries. This means that only one in seven of all Negro female workers gainfully occupied in nonagricultural pursuits worked in manufacturing, commerce, trade or any other nonservice occupation. The largest group among the female Negro service workers consisted of those employed by private households. They numbered 690,000 and thus constituted somewhat more than half of all Negro female workers in nonagricultural pursuits. Including males, there were about 750,000 Negroes working as servants of private families, which means that almost 40 per cent of all workers in this field were Negro.[b] It was much lower, however, for certain groups of higher and "intermediate" servants like "housekeepers and stewards" (8 per cent) and "nurses, not trained" (11 per cent) than for cooks and other household servants, of which almost half were Negro.

About two-thirds of the Negro servants reside in the South and one-third in the North and West.[c] The South had shown an increase of over 40 per cent from 1910 to 1930, but outside the South there were between two and three times more Negro servants in 1930 than in 1910. Indeed, more than half the total increase occurred in the North and the West.[d] There were seven Northern states, where one-fourth or more of the

[a] Paul H. Norgren and Associates, "Negro Labor and its Problems," unpublished manuscript prepared for this study (1940), Part 1, pp. 6-7.

[b] U.S. Bureau of the Census, *Negroes in the United States: 1920-1932*, pp. 303 and 325-326. See also *Fifteenth Census of the United States: 1930, Population*, Vol. 5; pp. 412-587. It is somewhat difficult to ascertain which service workers can be considered as employees of private households. The following groups were included in the figure cited in the text: cooks, other servants, housekeepers, and stewards which were not employed by hotels, restaurants, etc., and nurses (not trained).

[c] The census definitions of North, South and West are used throughout this Appendix.

[d] *Fifteenth Census of the United States: 1930, Population*, Vol. 4, State Table 11; *Negroes in the United States: 1920-1932*, pp. 303-309; and *Thirteenth Census of the United States: 1910, Population*, Vol. 4, pp. 434-534. The comparison is not quite exact. In the first place the Census designation "servants" includes not only employees in private families but also cooks, maids, etc. (but not waiters and waitresses), in hotels, restaurants, eating places and lodging houses; housekeepers and nurses, on the other hand, are not included. Second, data for 1910 and 1930 are not quite comparable.

servants were Negro. The percentage of Negroes was still higher in the South; in ten states it was 85 per cent or more, and there were four Southern states where only one servant out of twenty was a white person.

The gain in employment of Negro servants in private families, which may have amounted to more than 300,000 new jobs, was due to several factors. One was the enlargement of the market for the Negro domestic servant brought about by the northward migration of Negroes, and the simultaneous decline in the number of young immigrant girls in the North. A second was a general expansion in the field. It has been estimated that the total number of domestic workers in private families has increased by about one-third from 1910 to 1930.[a] It seems that but a small part of this increase was for white workers; most of the expansion was a Negro gain.[b]

It should be noted, however, that this general expansion was only half as great, proportionally, as the increase in number of nonfarm families.[c] This circumstance should be considered, for it may serve as a warning against any exaggerated hopes that the Negroes, even if they fail to get a real place in other parts of the nonagricultural economy, can always be assured of having an increasing number of job opportunities as servants to private families. True, we have reason to assume that the increase in the number of nonfarm families will continue for a long time and that there will be a smaller number of white girls willing to work as domestics. If the Negro population becomes more dispersed over the entire North and West—which probably will happen gradually, but only in so far as some jobs can be found also for Negro men—this, too, will increase the opportunities for Negro domestics. Yet, it should never be overlooked that the proportion of families having full-time servants is probably shrinking, owing to a number of factors: smaller number of children; higher wages for domestics; mechanization of home work and increased use of processed foods; transfer of service work from homes to specialized service establishments. These trends will limit the job opportunities for Negro women particularly where they now have a near-monopoly on this kind of work. As for the North and the West, we should not take it for granted that the chances of Negro domestics will increase in exact proportion to the difficulties of finding white workers. Many housewives outside the South have a prejudice against using Negro women in their homes, partly because they believe them to be less dependable, partly because they shun the contact with an alien race. It is quite probable that the opening up of a public discussion on venereal diseases during recent years has increased the reluctance of many white women to have colored help. Those who do use Negro domestics are increasingly insisting on "health cards." The prevalence of such attitudes has never been adequately studied, but we have reason to assume that such attitudes con-

[a] David Weintraub and Harry Magdoff, "The Service Industries in Relation to Employment Trends," *Econometrica* (October, 1940), p. 304. These authors made these computations from data in Daniel Carson, assisted by Henriette Liebman, *Labor Supply and Employment, Preliminary Statement of Estimates Prepared and Methods Used*, W.P.A. National Research Project (November, 1939).

[b] At this writing there are no data on household servants available from the 1940 Census which could be compared with those in the 1930 Census. It seems, however, that the proportion of Negroes among the domestic workers in the South has been declining (see Chapter 13, Table 3).

[c] There were about 14,000,000 nonfarm families in 1910 and over 23,000,000 in 1930. (*Fifteenth Census of the United States: 1930, Population*, Vol. 6; p. 11.)

stitute a factor of some significance. The depression of the 'thirties seems to have brought about a great decline in household employment. A survey of subscribers to *Fortune* magazine revealed that half the families who had had a servant in 1933 had none in 1938.[a]

It must be considered that the market for domestic service is much more restricted in the North and West than it is in the South. According to the Study of Consumer Purchases for 1935-1936, no less than 61 per cent of the nonrelief white families in a sample of Southeastern villages had some expenditure for household help. For a sample of small cities in the North Central region, on the other hand, the corresponding proportion was only 22 per cent, and it was but 17 per cent for a group of villages in the Middle Atlantic and North Central areas.[b] Large cities also show a similar differential between the South and the rest of the country. It is particularly interesting to find that, in the South, among families with an income of less than $1,000, or even less than $500, there is a significant number who have domestics (Table 2). Among well-to-do

TABLE 2

Percentage of Nonrelief White Families, in Selected Income Groups, Who Had Expenditure for Household Help: 1935-1936

Income group	Atlanta	New York	Chicago	South-eastern villages	North Central small cities	Middle Atlantic and North Central villages
$ 500— 749	8	..	..	23	4	8
750— 999	20	..	..	39	7	9
1,000—1,249	17	3	5	57	10	11
....						
2,000—2,499	51[a]	22	15[a]	80	34	29
....						
5,000—7,499[b]	99	89	78	100	89	70

Sources: Bureau of Labor Statistics, *Study of Consumer Purchases,* "Family Expenditure in Chicago, 1935-36" (1939), Bulletin No. 642, Vol. 2, p. 35; "Family Expenditure in New York City, 1935-36" (1939), Bulletin No. 643, Vol. 2, p. 36; "Family Expenditure in Three Southeastern Cities, 1935-36" (1940), Bulletin No. 647, Vol. 2, p. 39, and United States Department of Agriculture, *Family Expenditure for Housing and Household Operation,* Miscellaneous Publication No. 432, Urban and Village Series (1941), pp. 50-51.
[a] Approximate figure.
[b] For the three last columns: $5,000-9,999.

families in the South, the practice of having hired help is almost universal. In the North and West, on the other hand, there are quite a few households in the higher income brackets which get along without any servants, and it is extremely rare that low income families have any expenditures for outside assistance in their homes. Moreover, it seems that in the South, oftener than elsewhere, servants are hired on a full-time basis. According to the samples for small cities and villages, half the Northern families having

[a] "The Servant Problem," *Fortune,* March, 1938, p. 114 This figure and other references in this section to the *Fortune* article are quoted by permission of *Fortune* magazine.

[b] U.S. Department of Agriculture, *Family Expenditure for Housing and Household Operation,* Miscellaneous Publication No. 432, Urban and Village Series (1941), pp. 50-51.

servants hired them for only a few hours a day, or a few days a week, but in the South more than two-thirds of these families had full-time domestics.[a]

These findings are highly significant. They confirm the impression that there is a limit to further increases in the employment of Negro domestics. In the South, where such a large part of the demand comes from families in the middle, or even lower, income groups, the situation must be characterized as unstable. Any decline in family income or any improvement in working conditions that add to the expense of having a servant may actually bring about a curtailment of the job opportunities for servants. And it is particularly in the South that the working conditions for domestics need to be improved. According to the previously quoted village and small city samples from the Consumer Purchases Study, cash wages for domestics showed a marked tendency to be low when the income of the family they worked for was low.[b]

By and large, domestic work is a low wage industry. The estimates of the state employment offices, for instance (Table 3), indicate that wages as low as $3-5 per week occur even in the North. Some of the largest Northern cities, however, have "typical" wage rates of $15-20, but these figures do not indicate a uniform level. Even in New York

TABLE 3

RANGE BETWEEN LOCAL WAGE RATES FOR DOMESTIC WORK, IN SELECTED STATES, ACCORDING TO ESTIMATES BY STATE EMPLOYMENT OFFICES: JANUARY, 1939

| State | Cooks | | General Maids | |
	Resident	Board Only	Resident	Board Only
New York	$5.00–21.00	$5.00–20.00	$4.00–12.00	$4.00–15.00
Illinois	4.00–15.00	4.00–15.00	4.00–12.00	4.00–13.00
Minnesota	5.00–10.00	a	3.00– 6.00	3.00– 5.50
North Carolina	3.00– 7.00	3.00– 6.50	3.00– 5.00	3.00– 8.00
Georgia	1.75– 5.00	2.50– 5.00	2.75– 5.00	2.75– 6.00
Alabama	2.00– 7.00	3.00– 5.00	2.50– 6.00	2.50– 5.00

Source: Gladys L. Palmer, "A Memorandum Report on Negroes in Domestic Service," unpublished manuscript prepared for this study, (1940), pp. 249–251. Based on reports to U.S. Employment Service. The State Employment Offices had indicated the wage rate most typical in about 6 to 12 different places in each state which were considered as representative of the various labor market situations existing within the State
a Complete data not available.

wages are often low. It is a well-known fact that the wages at the "slave-markets" for Negro domestics in the Bronx and other places[c] are frequently far below what is considered to be typical for the better organized part of the domestic service market in New York. In the South, however, wages are low much more generally, and there are even localities where the usual wage is scarcely $2 per week.

There are few data on wages for Negro and white domestics separately. Nevertheless, since Negroes are largely concentrated in the South, there is no question but that on the average they receive lower wages than whites. They do have some representation, how-

[a] *Idem.*
[b] *Idem.*
[c] Carl Offord, "Slave Markets in the Bronx," *The Nation* (June 29, 1940), pp. 780-781.

ever, among the better paid servants, but as Dr. Palmer finds, partly on the basis of the same survey, they do not get their proportionate share of the more worth-while jobs.[a]

The fact that wages are seldom higher, and are sometimes lower, for servants who live in their own homes than for domestics who get living quarters in addition to the cash wage and meals makes the real wage of the Negro household employees lower than that of their average white colleagues. Negroes seldom have "live-in" jobs. This may be due, in some measure, to race prejudice on the part of their employers. One major reason for it is the fact that only a minority of the Negro servants are single. In 1930 no less than 70 per cent of the Negro servants were married, widowed, or divorced, whereas the corresponding figure for native white servants was 46 per cent.[b] The fact that Negro domestics seldom leave their occupation after having married explains why their average age is so much higher than that of white domestics. About one-fourth of the Negro domestics were under 25 years of age, as compared to almost half the native white domestics. This means that the average Negro servant should have more experience than most white domestics. It means, further, that they are in greater need of adequate wages, since they more often have to contribute to the family income. Yet their average wages are lower rather than higher than those of the young white girls.

It is a well-known fact that hours of work often tend to be long in domestic service —something which is of particular importance when the servant has a family of her own. Dr. Palmer quotes a study covering many sections of the country, according to which the general average would be around "72 hours a week, with many instances of 80 or more weekly hours."[c] *Fortune's* study of upper class servants gave somewhat lower averages, but several other studies cited by Dr. Palmer tend to confirm the higher estimates.[d] It is evident, particularly from the *Fortune* study, that hours of work tend to be particularly long in the South, which means that Negroes, by and large, have a longer working week than white servants. According to the *Fortune* sample, twice as many Negroes as whites work long hours. "On the other hand, it is held by some persons that the two o'clock dinner hour, usual in small towns throughout the South, shortens the day for servants. Cooks may come at the 'crack of dawn' but they are free to leave after that early dinner."[e] The fact that Negro servants seldom live with their employers means that they do not have to be "on call" after ordinary working hours.

Domestic service is an unorganized industry. The elimination of exploitative conditions of work has lagged in this occupation compared with the development in manufacturing industries. Adequately performed, domestic work requires a rare combination of various skills and social talents. Yet it has a social stigma which places it far below most unskilled occupations in people's appreciation. For this reason, it cannot offer any appeal to the ambition of those who want to make a career, and this affects the quality

[a] "A Memorandum Report on Negroes in Domestic Service," unpublished manuscript prepared for this study (1940), pp. 194-204.

[b] U.S. Bureau of the Census, *Negroes in the United States: 1920-1932*, p. 334. *Fifteenth Census of the United States: 1930, Population*, Vol. 5, p. 299.

[c] Dorothy P. Wells, article in *Occupations*, February, 1938, quoted in Palmer, *op. cit.*, p. 206.

[d] Palmer, *op. cit.*, pp. 207-212.

[e] *Ibid.*, p. 207.

of the workers and their performance in a way which perpetuates the low status of the occupation. Domestic service is not covered by any federal laws about social security, minimum wages and maximum hours. The Employment Service sometimes sets unofficial wage minima by refusing to refer registrants to employers who pay salaries below a certain scale. Relief agencies often consider the value of a job offer before deciding whether or not a client should be offered the alternative of either accepting it or being taken off the relief rolls. Several of the Northern states have made some efforts to improve the situation by introducing protective legislation, but this legislation is not extensive and it has not been adequately enforced.[a] In the South there is still less legal or administrative protection. Because so many middle income and low income families in the South have domestic servants, the problem of improving the conditions of work in this occupation without endangering the work opportunities is much more difficult in the South than anywhere else.

Among the most constructive efforts are the attempts to give adequate vocational training to an increased number of white and colored girls. The Work Projects Administration has been training thousands of girls every year. Local organizations, such as the Y.W.C.A., have sponsored a number of training centers. Negro vocational institutions have done their bit. So far these attempts are minimal compared with the size of the market. Also, there is no guarantee that the best trained students will work as domestics; they may prefer such jobs as cooking in restaurants. Even at best, the chances to improve the conditions of workers and the status of the occupation appear rather slim; it goes without saying that only in those families which are able and willing to pay adequate wages can domestic work become "professionalized" in this way. The number of such families may increase, particularly because of the rising proportion of gainfully occupied married women in the white population. This trend cannot fail to increase both the need for reliable and competent domestic workers and the ability to pay high salaries to such workers. Some of the underlying forces—such as the higher employment rates of the housewives—will precipitate the trend toward greater dependence on specialized service industries such as commercial laundries, cleaning and dyeing shops, processed food production, child nurseries, hotels and restaurants. And this change, as we shall see, may tend to put the Negro in a still more disadvantageous position.

3. OTHER SERVICE OCCUPATIONS

The most significant example of how the Negro has lost out through the "industrialization" of service work is the displacement of the Negro home laundress by commercial laundries. This group of Negro service workers, the second largest among all groups, has declined from 368,000 in 1910 to 271,000 in 1930.[b] Since in 1930 not much more than one-tenth of these workers resided in the North and West, where there had been about as many in 1910, it is evident that the northward migration failed to give the Negro laundress any new job opportunities which could compensate for the displacement in the South. The main reason for this is probably that commercial laundries are particularly well developed in the large Northern centers; the competition of the

[a] *Ibid*, pp. 225-232.
[b] U.S. Bureau of the Census, *Negroes in the United States: 1920-1932*, p. 326. *Thirteenth Census of the United States: 1910, Population*, Vol. 4, pp. 430-431. Some of the Negro home laundresses may work as employees of private households. It is probable, however, that the majority of them did the laundering in their own homes.

Chinese laundryman and the home washing machine may have been an additional factor; the pattern of Negro residential segregation in cities like New York and Chicago, finally, may have made it more difficult for the Negro home laundress to solicit patrons. The commercial laundries, on the other hand, have increased their Negro labor forces from 15,000 in 1910 to 60,000 in 1930. Compared to this four-fold increase for Negroes, the number of white workers only doubled. Yet even this gain was small compared with the loss.

Dressmakers and seamstresses (not in factories)[a] constitute a similar case. The number of Negro workers in this group declined from 38,000 in 1910 to 20,000 in 1930.

It is extremely difficult to get an idea of the development in most of the other service industries, since the census statistics are seldom quite comparable from one decade to another, and few adequate studies have been made. In 1930, 228,000 Negro workers, constituting 17 per cent of all workers in the industry, were employed in hotels, restaurants, and boarding houses, the majority of them as porters, waiters, cooks and other servants.[b] All these occupations have experienced a rather rapid growth during the last few decades, but the Negroes have had but a small share in these gains.[c] The consequence, in the case of waiters and waitresses, is that the proportion of Negroes has declined from 22 per cent in 1910 to 15 per cent in 1930. What little part the Negro had in the general increase was mainly in the North, where, by 1930, there were more Negro waiters than in the South. Negro waitresses made somewhat more progress than the waiters but were nevertheless much fewer than their male counterparts by 1930. In the white group, too, it was the women who made the largest gains. Thus, the loss of the Negro male waiters was largely the gain of the white waitresses. During the 'thirties Negroes continued to lose in relative position. In the South, in 1930, 40 per cent of the workers in hotels, restaurants, and similar places were Negroes, but in 1940 only 32 per cent were Negroes.[d] Negro bell-boys, too, have lost out, at least relatively. Travelers in the South often have occasion to observe that, nowadays, the most modern and busiest hotels and restaurants tend to have white bell-boys and white waitresses, whereas the old-fashioned places tend to have Negro servants. In hotels and restaurants, generally, it seems that workers behind the scenes—cooks, porters, and so forth—are often Negro, even when those who come into direct contact with the customers are white.

The barbershop and hairdressing occupations have undergone a tremendous development since 1910, particularly in the female branch, the beauty shop business. The total number of workers in the whole group of occupations almost doubled between 1910 and 1930, but the Negro gain was only about 50 per cent. The Negro barber has lost most of his white business in the South. His gains have been restricted to the segregated Negro neighborhoods, where the beauty shops have experienced a faint counterpart to

[a] U.S. Bureau of the Census, *Negroes in the United States: 1920-1932*, p. 310; *Thirteenth Census of the United States: 1910, Population*, Vol. 4, pp. 312 and 313. Most of these Negro seamstresses usually work in their own homes. Some may work in homes of white families where they are temporarily employed.

[b] U.S. Bureau of the Census, *Negroes in the United States: 1920-1932*, p. 358.

[c] *Thirteenth Census of the United States: 1910, Population*, Vol. 4, pp. 430-433; *Fifteenth Census of the United States: 1930, Population*, Vol. 5, pp. 412-587.

[d] See Chapter 13, Table 3.

the boom in white areas. Under such circumstances, there is nothing surprising in the fact that almost half the Negro workers are in the North.

The most important group among other service occupations from the viewpoint of Negro employment were the janitors and sextons. No less than 78,000 Negro workers were enumerated under this heading in 1930. It appears that there had been a big increase in this work since 1910, and slightly more so for Negroes than for whites. Among elevator tenders, on the other hand, there was a decreasing proportion of Negroes. Among charwomen and cleaners the Negro maintained his relative position pretty well; and among bootblacks he improved it.

Such is the story we can read in the census reports. It is not encouraging. By and large, the displacement of work from homes to service and manufacturing industries brings a definite loss to the Negro. The main reason for this seems to be that it makes the work more pleasant, and thus more attractive to the white worker. When there is an expansion, the Negro usually fails to get his full share of it, except in particularly lowly occupations. Sometimes there is an actual decline in the number of Negro workers. Had more complete data from the 1940 Census been available at this writing, we should probably have been able to document these conclusions even more convincingly. For, because of the unemployment among white workers during the 'thirties, these trends, if anything, must have become more pronounced.

4. TURPENTINE FARMS

Turpentine farms and distilleries are not a large industry, but they have the highest proportion of Negroes in the whole nonservice group. Of the total labor force of 43,000 in 1930, no less than 75 per cent was Negro. It is almost entirely a Southern industry, mainly located in Georgia and Florida. At present it is experiencing a pronounced war boom. Otherwise it has been almost stationary for several decades. Turpentine, which is used mainly for making paint, has been increasingly substituted for by petroleum products. There is, however, a growing demand for rosin, formerly considered only as a by-product of turpentine manufacture, so that it has become more valuable than the turpentine itself.[a] Certain technical innovations have made the existence of the ordinary turpentine farms rather difficult. Norgren points out that:

> There has been developed in recent years a new method of producing turpentine, known as the wood distillation process. This process consists in removing and pulping the stumps of pine trees in "logged-over" areas, and distilling the pulp in large centrally-located stills. Since modern labor-saving devices are used throughout, the number of man-hours required to produce a given quantity of product by this method is only a small fraction of what it is in the average gum-turpentine establishment; and it is consequently not surprising to learn that wood turpentine has become a serious competitor of the gum-distilled product.[b]

There are obvious reasons why the turpentine industry employs predominantly Negro workers. It is located in rather isolated rural areas. The work is strenuous. The main part of it is "chipping," which means cutting of V-shaped gashes through the bark with a heavy knife. A normal day's work may mean cutting some 1,000 to 1,500 trees in this way during 8 to 12 hours. Other chores are performed by children. Wages are

[a] Norgren and Associates, *op. cit.*, Part 1, p. 106.
[b] *Ibid.*, Part 1, p. 108.

low. On the basis of field work and various spot studies,[a] Norgren estimated the normal wage at between 90 cents and $1.25 per day; the annual wage income, because of slack work during the winter and during rainy days, is probably little more than $200. Housing facilities in the camps are often extremely unsatisfactory. The commissary system is widely used, just as on Southern plantations. Prices are kept high, and workers easily become indebted to the employers. Not even Negroes are easy to get under such conditions. There is a general complaint among employers that labor is scarce. Such a situation must tempt employers to indulge in practices of peonage, and there are definite reports to the effect that these temptations have not always been resisted. It has even happened that workers have been induced to come to the camps under false pretenses and then forced into contracts and debts and thereby retained as workers.

> Labor is recruited for these camps by a man, usually a Negro, who makes glowing speeches of high wages and easy hours. But soon the unsuspecting Negro youth, who thought he was getting on a truck headed for a distant city, finds he is headed toward a turpentine or lumber camp. Once there he gets into debt and can leave only upon threat of a six months' chain gang sentence. For, according to the law, jumping a debt is defined as "intent to injure and defraud."[b]

The claim that the Florida peonage law was sponsored by turpentine farm interests sounds plausible.[c]

The turpentine farm workers have no protection from any federal labor legislation, as the turpentine industry, except for the distilleries, is considered part of agriculture. Employers receive, for the same reason, certain benefits under the new agricultural programs. Indirectly, the workers may have received some part of these benefits. Yet, by and large, the gum industry is characterized by extraordinarily exploitative conditions of work, and it has an uncertain future. The implications of the situation are especially serious for Negroes because this industry employs mostly Negroes.

5. LUMBER

Next to building construction and the iron and steel industries, lumber is the most important of all manufacturing industries from the point of view of the number of Negroes employed. The lumber industry proper had in 1930 almost 140,000 Negro workers. In addition, there were about 26,000 Negro forest workers, most of whom were registered as "lumbermen, raftsmen and woodchoppers."[d] A large part of these were employed by the rapidly growing Southern paper and pulp industry. In this work, however, it is only the wood-cutting activity which is a Negro occupation. In the paper and pulp mills themselves there were less than 8,000 Negro workers in 1930.[e] These

[a] See, for example, Work Projects Administration, *Part-Time Farming in the Southeast*, Research Monograph 9 (1937), pp. 212-213.

[b] Arthur Raper, "Race and Class Pressures," unpublished manuscript prepared for this study (1940), p. 186.

[c] Arthur Raper (*idem*) quotes an article by Orland K. Armstrong (New York *World*, November 26, 1929), according to which the man, who was president of the Florida Senate when the peonage bill was passed, acknowledged that "the influence behind the passage of this law was the naval stores and lumber operators of this state."

[d] U.S. Bureau of the Census, *Negroes in the United States: 1920-1932*, pp. 337-359. According to the 1940 figures, which are not quite comparable, there were in the South 156,000 Negro workers employed in logging, sawmills and planing mills, manufacturing of furniture, store fixtures and miscellaneous wooden goods. (Chapter 13, Table 3.)

[e] U.S. Bureau of the Census, *Negroes in the United States*: 1920-1932, p. 348.

were mainly in laboring jobs, at wages which were lower, compared with the pay of skilled and semi-skilled workers, than was true in other parts of the country.[a] The wage level is still lower for wood cutters; prior to 1938, the average was less than $1 for a day of 10 to 14 hours. It is not clear whether the Wages and Hours Law has brought any significant improvement. The employers have succeeded fairly well in postponing its enforcement. An industry committee, set up in 1940 for the purpose of regulating labor conditions under the law, even excluded production of pulpwood from the paper and pulp industry, which means that the wood cutters cannot get any benefit from the minimum wage of 40 cents an hour decided upon by the committee.[b]

Only a small minority of the 140,000 Negroes in the lumber and woodworking industry proper were in processing work. Furniture and piano factories had few Negro workers (8,000), but box factories and miscellaneous plants had a somewhat greater number (17,000). The bulk of the Negro workers, or 114,000, were employed by saw and planing mills, where they constituted one-fourth of the national, and one-half of the Southern, labor force.

This situation, of course, is rather unfortunate for the Negroes. The saw and planing mills have been a stationary, sometimes even a regressive, industry since about 1910. The expansion in the Pacific, and particularly in the Northwestern areas, has made it still more difficult for the Southern mills. Moreover, Southern pine timber stands have been exploited in a rather shortsighted manner, causing serious denudation. The increased use of iron, steel, cement, and bricks in building construction, the substitution of barbed wire for wood in farm fencing, of fiber for wood in boxes and crates, the use of mesh-bags instead of boxes for packing of fruits, as well as other similar changes, have brought about serious limitations in the demand. Nevertheless, there may be some hope for the future. Timber stands in other parts of the country may become so exhausted that the rapid growth in the Southern climate will give the Southern industry a competitive advantage. New uses for the product (e.g., plywood-built airplanes) may bring about an increased demand.

During the early 'thirties lumber production in the South was reduced by almost two-thirds, and the recovery was very slow.[c] Owing to the present war emergency, the production is large for the time being, but this boom, of course, is not going to last. The insecurity in the situation is further enhanced by the fact that mechanization, which has proceeded rather far in other areas, has been less pronounced in the South, mainly because low wages prevailed until recently. For this reason, and also because of the denudation of many Southern timber stands, the productivity of the worker in the Northwestern region has been estimated to be about 60 per cent higher than that of the Southern worker.[d] Mechanization has not always caused displacement of labor; in some cases, it is claimed, mechanization has increased job opportunities by making it possible

[a] Norgren and Associates, *op. cit.*, Part 1, pp. 100-101. The section on the lumber industry in Norgren's manuscript was written by James Healy.

[b] *Ibid.*, Part 1, pp. 102-104. Information on prevailing wages based on an interview, May 30, 1940, with Mr. Richter, Field Investigator in the Wage and Hour Division, U.S. Department of Labor.

[c] *Ibid.*, Part 1, p. 26; based on data from the *Biennial Census of Manufactures*. Also pp. 31-32 and letter from Paul H. Norgren, August 16, 1942.

[d] *Ibid.*, pp. 60-63. Information based on brief submitted to Office of National Recovery Administration, Division of Review, Yost *et al*, "Economic Problems of the Lumber and Timber Products Industry" (March, 1936), Work Materials #79, p. 151.

to utilize stands of timber which otherwise would have been economically inaccessible. Still, the regional differential in this regard constitutes a constant threat to the job opportunities for Negroes. It is hard to see how an equalization of labor conditions could fail to encourage such technological changes as would curtail employment in the South.[a]

The insecurity of the individual worker is made still greater because of the loose structure of the Southern lumber industry. A large part of the production comes from small, marginal mills with a high bankruptcy rate. They employ a somewhat greater proportion of Negroes than do the large mills, partly because they have to depend on cheap labor, but also because they cannot always afford to segregate white and Negro workers in the mill towns.[b] These conditions contribute to the extremely high labor turnover; the separation rate in 1934 was as high as 88 per cent.[c] The rapid labor turnover must also be seen in conjunction with the fact that the number of working days per year ranges around 200 days, according to a survey for 1939.[d] The lumber industry is really nothing but an outgrowth of agriculture. Labor flows continually back and forth between these two industries.

The wage structure has long been characterized by a great differential between skilled workers, such as sawyers, who are predominantly white, and unskilled laborers, most of whom, in the South, are Negroes. Various studies quoted by Norgren and Associates indicate that, in the South, sawyers (head, band) during the 'twenties and early 'thirties, earned more than three times and sometimes almost four times as much per hour, on the average, as did laborers. In the Far West, on the other hand, sawyers earned somewhat more than twice the average wage of laborers.[e] The wage level, further, has been particularly low and unstable in the South. The average hourly earnings for all workers in Southern logging camps and sawmills, according to certain sample studies, seem to have decreased from roughly 30 cents in 1928 to 18 cents in 1932. It was about twice as high in the Northwest in 1928, and the regional differential was even greater in 1932 in that the relative decrease was more pronounced in the South than in the Northwest.[f]

The Wages and Hours Law, in conjunction with the business recovery, had brought about a great improvement by 1939-1940. The whole wage structure in the Southern lumber mills seems to have become somewhat more concentrated; sawyers (head, band) earned "only" about two-and-a-half times more than the low wage labor groups.[g] Even

[a] See Work Progress Administration, National Research Project, "Mechanization in Lumber" (March, 1940), Report No. M-5, pp. 79-93.

[b] Norgren and Associates, op. cit., Part 1, pp. 21-26 and 69.

[c] Ibid., p. 47, and Monthly Labor Review (May, 1935), pp. 1285-1287.

[d] Norgren and Associates, op. cit., Part 1, p. 46.

[e] A. Berglund, et al., Labor in the Industrial South (1930), p. 41. Bureau of Labor Statistics, "Wages and Hours of Labor in the Lumber Industry in the United States: 1932" (1932), Bulletin #586, pp. 24-33. Quoted in Norgren and Associates, op. cit., Part 1, p. 59.

[f] See Bureau of Labor Statistics, "Wages and Hours of Labor in the Lumber Industry in the United States: 1928" (1928), Bulletin #497, and "Wages and Hours of Labor in the Lumber Industry in the United States: 1932" (1932), Bulletin #586. Several other studies quoted by Norgren (op. cit., Part I, p. 64) confirm the impression of the low wage level in the South; some averages are even lower than those quoted in the text.

[g] Bureau of Labor Statistics, unpublished tabulations, September 16, 1941. The writer is indebted to Acting Commissioner of Labor Statistics, A. F. Hinrichs, for permission to use these data, and to Dr. Norgren for certain suggestions concerning their interpretation.

TABLE 4

AVERAGE EARNINGS AND HOURS OF WORK FOR LUMBER WORKERS IN THE SOUTH BY TYPE AND BRANCH OF INDUSTRY AND BY COLOR: 1939-1940

Type and Branch of Industry	Number of Workers		Average Hourly Earnings		Average Weekly Hours		Average Weekly Earnings	
	Negro	White	Negro	White	Negro	White	Negro	White
Establishments with 20 or more employees:								
Logging branch	3,835	2,766	$0.32	$0.37	35.8	39.3	$11.33	$14.58
Sawmill branch	10,356	4,325	0.30	0.39	38.4	41.1	11.66	16.05
Maintenance and service occupations	2,366	3,872	0.30	0.41	42.2	45.0	12.80	18.46
Establishments (small logging camps) with fewer than 20 employees	555	415	0.24	0.28	37.6	38.8	9.02	10.99

Source: U.S. Bureau of Labor Statistics, unpublished tabulations, September, 1941. (Permission to publish tables obtained from Acting Commissioner A. F. Hinrichs.)

more important is the fact that the average wage level had been brought up above the pre-depression level (Table 4). The high proportion of workers earning exactly 30 cents an hour (Table 5) indicates that this improvement is due to a great extent to the Wages and Hours Law. At the same time it is evident that the law was still evaded frequently, particularly by small mills and in the case of Negroes.[a] This evasion is not always illegal, however; many small mills have simply withdrawn from interstate commerce. But other small mill owners fail to comply, pointing to their inability to pay higher wages. The Wages and Hours officials have found it practical to abstain from

TABLE 5

PERCENTAGE DISTRIBUTION OF LOGGING AND SAWMILL WORKERS BY AVERAGE HOURLY EARNINGS, BY TYPE AND BRANCH OF INDUSTRY AND BY COLOR, IN THE SOUTH: 1939-1940

Hourly Earnings	Establishments with 20 or More Employees				Establishments with fewer than 20 Employees			
	Logging		Sawmilling		Logging		Sawmilling	
	Negro	White	Negro	White	Negro	White	Negro	White
Total	100.0	100.0	100.0	100.0	100.0	100.0	100.0	100.0
Under 20.0 cents	3.2	1.2	4.3	1.8	27.6	11.4	34.2	18.7
20.0-29.9 cents	2.8	3.4	4.0	4.4	24.1	26.3	17.8	24.8
Exactly 30.0 cents	52.8	25.9	64.0	32.5	40.2	40.4	44.1	36.2
30.0-39.9 cents	32.5	41.4	23.8	31.6	7.2	14.7	3.4	10.5
40 cents and over	8.7	28.1	3.9	29.7	0.9	7.2	0.5	9.8

Source: U.S. Bureau of Labor Statistics, unpublished tabulations, September, 1941. (Permission to publish table obtained from Acting Commissioner A. F. Hinrichs.)

[a] The problem has been stated succinctly in a memorandum of a Wages and Hours inspector in the Southern area: "The lumber industry in this area is perhaps our biggest headache *as an industry.* . . . Wages in the southern branch of the industry have been traditionally substandard and 25 and 30 cents an hour minus the privilege of gettting 15 cents of it back through the commissary devices, necessitated greater adjustments than in many other industries. . . . Also, . . . the scene of operation is more or less isolated, which condition doesn't contribute towards cooperation in working out of problems that confront the industry." (Memorandum prepared by Robert K. Miller, Inspector, Atlanta, Georgia [May 10, 1940], p. 1. Quoted by Norgren, *op. cit.*, Part 1, p. 81.)

using forceful means against such financially weak operators[a] and have, for the most part, concentrated their efforts on the larger mills—with great success, as we see from the statistics.

There is no evidence concerning the extent to which there has been any displacement of labor because of the wage increase. Owing to the present war boom, employment has so far increased rather than decreased. What is going to happen after the war, however, is a different matter entirely. Unless this wage increase is wiped out by inflation—which may well happen—it is hard to visualize how it could fail to bring about, eventually, considerable mechanization as well as elimination of financially weak establishments.

The hourly earnings tended to be somewhat lower for Negro than for white lumber workers. Such a difference usually appears even when Negroes and whites in the same occupational sub-group are compared (Table 6). This does not prove, however, that

TABLE 6

OCCUPATIONS IN LUMBER MILLS (Sawmills, Logging, Maintenance and Service Branches) BY AVERAGE HOURLY EARNINGS OF WHITE WORKERS, AND DIFFERENCE BETWEEN AVERAGE EARNINGS OF WHITE AND NEGRO WORKERS, IN THE SOUTH: 1939-1940

(The original data are based on establishments with 20 or more employees.)

Average hourly earnings of white workers by occupation	All occupations[a]	Higher than for whites	Equal to earnings of whites	Lower than earnings of whites by specified amounts				
				0.5–1.9 cents	2.0–3.9 cents	4.0–5.9 cents	6.0–7.9 cents	8.0 cents & over
Total	60	5	3	21	11	6	4	10
Under 35.0 cents	38	5	3	19	10	1	..	..
35.0-39.9 cents	12	..	..	2	1	5	3	1
40.0-44.9 cents	5	..	..	..	..	..	1	4
45 cents or more	5	..	..	..	..	..	..	5

Source: Adapted from U.S. Bureau of Labor Statistics, unpublished tabulations, September, 1941. (Permission to publish table obtained from Acting Commissioner A. F. Hinrichs.)
[a] Only occupations which had 25 or more Negro and 25 or more white representatives in the sample were included

Negroes are paid less on an hourly basis when performing the same duties as white workers in the same establishments. It is possible that these wage differentials in specified occupational groups are caused by the tendency of low wage establishments to hire a greater proportion of Negroes than do high wage establishments. Besides, in most of the cases, these differences are rather small, except—and this is rather significant—in occupations where wages are far above the general average. The only chance for a Negro to get into a high wage occupation usually is to accept a wage considerably lower than that paid to white employees for the same kind of work. Yet, the main reason why Negroes, by and large, have lower pay than whites is that they are relatively more concentrated in low wage work.[b] The proportion of Negroes is particularly low in

[a] *Ibid.*, Part 1, pp. 84-85.
[b] In part, there is a reversed causation. The wage differential between "high" and "low" occupations, as we have seen, is more pronounced in the South than elsewhere. In other words, the wages for unskilled work are particularly low in the South *because* most of the unskilled workers are Negroes.

maintenance and service occupations, which include such groups as electricians, machinists, mechanics, millwrights and sawfilers. If we classify all the occupations by the average hourly wages for all workers, we find that the proportion of Negroes diminishes regularly as the average earnings increase, from 69 per cent in occupations paying less than 35 cents an hour to 6 per cent in work paying 50 cents or more.[a]

Earnings per week differ more than wages per hour, due to the fact that the working week is somewhat shorter for Negro than for white workers. Even so, it must be said that the $9-13 earned per week by Negro lumber workers—as against the $11-18 earned by whites—is not so bad compared to what they have been used to before. The main problem is how much work they will have when the war boom is over.

Lumber mills located in isolated areas have to provide housing for their workers. In these "mill villages" Negroes are usually segregated, and the accommodation for them tends to be inferior to that offered to whites. Most of the workers have to pay rent for their housing facilities. There is a commissary system, but nowadays it does not seem to be used for the purpose of exploiting the workers, except in unusual cases. Peonage, by the same token, is reported to be rare.[b] Increases in rents and commissary prices, however, have been used, in some instances, as one of the devices for evasion of the Wages and Hours Law, but Wages and Hours officials are gradually wiping out practices of this kind.[c]

There have been several attempts to unionize the Southern lumber mill workers, but, so far, unions have little power in this field. There are four principal reasons for this: The pronounced anti-union attitudes of most Southern employers, together with the political impotency of the workers; the great number of small establishments, many of which have an isolated location; the high labor turnover and the constant interchange of labor between agriculture and lumber camps; and the presence of the Negro. The Brotherhood of Timber Workers, organized in 1910 and soon affiliated with the International Workers of the World, worked among both Negroes and whites in Louisiana, Arkansas and Texas. The employers defeated it, capitalizing on the race issue.[d] The International Timber Workers' Union, an A.F. of L. affiliate, entered the

---

[a] The complete series was:

Occupations classified by average hourly earnings	Percentage of Negro workers
Under 35.0 cents	69.3
35.0-39.9 "	36.1
40.0-44.9 "	18.3
45.0-49.9 "	12.6
50.0-cents & over	5.8
All occupations	59.9

Adapted from: U. S. Bureau of Labor Statistics, unpublished tabulations for sawmill and logging workers in establishments having 20 or more employees. Figures made available through the courtesy of Acting Commissioner A. F. Hinrichs.

[b] Norgren and Associates, *op. cit.*, Part 1, pp. 69-72.

[c] *Ibid.*, Part 1, p. 86, and *Wage and Hour Reporter* (May 27, 1940), p. 223.

[d] That Southern employers have long been aware of the value of the race issue in the fight against unions is suggested by the following statement:

" '. . . if the labor organizations pursue their policy of injustice and disturbance, the time will come when the industries of the South . . . will be filled with Negroes.' In Negro

field in 1919, organizing both Negroes and whites, but this union, too, had no success in spite of an offer of the white leaders to "sell the Negroes out." During the N.R.A. period, the A.F. of L. made some new attempts to organize Southern lumber workers. A C.I.O. union, the International Wood Workers of America, which has come into existence during recent years, seems to have been more successful. It has several locals in many Southern states and has even obtained some contracts. Yet it is safe to say that the overwhelming majority of the Southern lumber workers are still unorganized.[a]

6. THE FERTILIZER INDUSTRY

The fertilizer industry differs from the turpentine and lumber industries in that it is a comparatively new industry which has been expanding during recent decades. The number of Negro workers more than doubled between 1910 and 1930, whereas the white labor force increased to a somewhat smaller extent. The reason for this difference is that the expansion was particularly pronounced in the South, which has the bulk of all fertilizer factories in the country.[b] In 1930 about 60 per cent of all workers and 81 per cent of the unskilled workers were Negro; in the South, of course, only a small minority of the workers were white.[c] Even the North has a large proportion of Negro workers.[d]

The Negro's predominant position in the Southern branch of the industry is probably due to the unpleasantness of the work. The odors are bad, the atmosphere dusty and, in all likelihood, unhealthy. Employment for most workers is seasonal, the period of highest activity occurring prior to the planting in the spring. Then, too, it is a low wage industry, at least in the South, and especially for Negroes. According to a sample study for 1938,[e] the average hourly earnings for Negro workers in the South were 25 cents, as against 37 cents for white workers. In the North, on the other hand, there was but a small wage differential and a much higher general level (49 and 52 cents, respectively). Even in specific occupations the earnings of Negro workers in the South were markedly lower than those of white workers. Skilled workers earned twice as much as unskilled workers in the South, whereas the corresponding difference in the North was not much over 50 per cent. Whereas in the North virtually all workers received wages in excess of the legal minimum, 2 per cent of those in the Upper South and no less than 43 per cent of those in the Lower South received wages lower than 25 cents an hour, which was the minimum wage at that time according to the Wages and

---

labor lies the panacea for the wrongs frequently committed by organized labor, and a reserve force from which can be supplied any needed number of workers when the time shall come that they will be needed '. . . [The Negro] is absolutely loyal to his employer; he is not given to strikes; he does his work faithfully, and can be depended on.' He [Mr. Coffin] believes that labor agitation can be largely kept out of the South because the Southern manufacturers will 'Negroize' their industries rather than submit to unjust domination by the unions." *U. S. Industrial Commission Reports* (1900), Vol. 7, statement of Mr. Coffin, p. 62.

[a] Norgren and Associates, *op. cit.*, Part 1, pp. 50-54.

[b] According to the 1937 *Census of Manufacturers*, 73 per cent of all workers in the fertilizer industry were in the South.

[c] *Fifteenth Census of the United States: 1930, Population*, Vol. 4, pp. 27-28.

[d] Bureau of Labor Statistics, "Wages and Hours in the Fertilizer Industry 1938," *Monthly Labor Review* (March, 1939), pp. 666-681.

[e] *Idem.*

Hours Law. This figure, however, does not necessarily indicate widespread noncompliance; since the fertilizer factories work for local markets to a great extent, it is probable that many of them seldom enter interstate trade. In spite of this condition, it seems most likely that the subsequent rise in the legal minimum, as well as the enforcement work of the Wages and Hours Division in the Department of Labor, has brought about a certain increase in the average Southern wage since 1938.[a]

7. Longshore Work

The Negro longshoreman has a somewhat different position from that of the workers in most other Negro jobs.[b] His wages are comparatively high, although much less so on an annual than on an hourly basis. There is an old union tradition in this trade which includes racial collaboration. While such collaboration is by no means perfect, it is far superior to anything that can be found in most other typical Negro jobs. The Negro has even managed to get an increased proportion of these jobs. In those South Atlantic ports of Virginia, South Carolina, and Florida where he has traditionally had at least nine out of every ten jobs, he has maintained that proportion. He has even improved his position as indicated by the following figures:

TABLE 7

PERCENTAGE OF NEGROES AMONG LONGSHOREMEN AND STEVEDORES IN SELECTED STATES: 1910 AND 1930

State	1910	1930	State	1910	1930
New York	6.0	15.2	Alabama	80.5	95.8
New Jersey	2.7	22.2	Louisiana	59.8	74.3
Pennsylvania	40.5	51.8	Texas	35.3	69.8
Maryland	65.0	68.6			

Sources: Thirteenth Census of the United States: 1910, Population, Vol. 4, State Table 7.
Fifteenth Census of the United States: 1930, Population, Vol. 4, State Table 11.

The total number of Negro longshoremen and stevedores increased from 16,000 in 1910 to over 25,000 in 1930, or from one-fourth to one-third of the total national labor force in the occupation. All of this increase occurred between 1910 and 1920 when there was a general boom in port activities. During the 'twenties, on the other hand, there was a decline in employment which hurt the white workers more than the Negroes. There was a decline during the 'thirties, of course, and both racial groups must have suffered heavily from it, but Northrup, during his fieldwork, gained the definite impression that the relative position of the Negro workers had not been impaired, at least not in the South. The only possible exception would be New Orleans.[c]

There are definite reasons why the Negro does not have his usual inferior position in water-front work. No great differences exist between various skilled groups. All that

[a] All data in this paragraph have been drawn from Norgren and Associates, *op. cit.*, Part 1.

[b] This section is based on Herbert R. Northrup, "Negro Labor and Union Policies in the South," unpublished Ph.D. thesis, Harvard University (1942). Some preliminary work for this thesis was done for our study.

[c] Northrup, *op. cit.*, p. 117.

counts is physical strength and endurance as well as certain training in the art of apply-ing it. The popular beliefs in Negro inferiority never refer to his physical condition, so it is quite natural that they have hampered him less in this field than in most others. In only a few cases have white workers been able, for a time, to monopolize higher jobs; this happened with respect to cotton screwmen in New Orleans, but the white monopoly was broken at the beginning of this century, and the whole craft was eventu-ally eliminated through technological development.[a] Racial competition, in the main, has been a question of sharing jobs of the same type or, at least, of about the same general status. In the South the Negro had from the outset such a numerical superiority that it soon proved difficult not to treat him as an equal or near-equal. Then, too, the big expansion during the First World War was accompanied by a scarcity of white labor. There was no way of stopping the Negro from making gains.

There are disagreeable aspects of this occupation which have made it unattractive to white workers. The work is extremely strenuous. There is little chance for the older worker. Accident risks are high. Job opportunities are irregular and subject to severe business cycle fluctuations. Periods of idleness are broken by hours and days of rush work. Those who have a job try to keep it in order to make full use of it. This, at times, makes them work as much as 36 hours at a stretch, which increases the accident risk.

Moreover, most ports have the so-called "shape-up" system of hiring [b] which means that there is no even distribution of work opportunities. The workers become entirely dependent on the hiring agents and foremen. This leads to favoritism. It opens the way to discrimination against the Negroes, who, for the most part, work in separate gangs and often have been segregated in separate positions when working on the same ship with whites.[c] It also leads to "kick-backs" to hiring agents and foremen and to other forms of corruption, graft and sometimes plain racketeering on the water front. Some of the labor unions have become undemocratic because of the power of the foremen.

The trade union history of the longshoremen is long and turbulent, full of racial strife, with whites attempting to exclude Negroes or Negroes breaking the strikes of whites. But almost from the very beginning there were some successful attempts to organize racial cooperation on a basis of mutual solidarity and equality. There was a strong Negro union in Charleston, South Carolina, in the 1860's, and during the 1870's at least two noteworthy Negro unions were formed, one in New Orleans and one in Baltimore. In 1865 Negro and white longshoremen collaborated in a strike in New Orleans,[d] and there was a much bigger strike in the 1880's in which workers of both races participated. About that time a noted foreign observer commented on how "despite occasional outbreak of racial antipathy," the unions in New Orleans had been able to "harmonize the opposing factors, and have undertaken, through the recognition of black labor, a problem in civilization whose solution they will probably not live to see."[e]

The International Longshoremen's Association (I.L.A.), organized during the 1890's,

[a] Sterling Spero and Abram L. Harris, *The Black Worker* (1931), pp. 185-187.

[b] In this system of hiring, the worker must find out for himself where work is available each day and there is no assurance that the foreman will select him.

[c] *Ibid.*, p. 197.

[d] *Ibid.*, pp. 182-183.

[e] A. S. von Waltershausen, *Die Nordamerikanischen Gewerkschaften unter dem Einfluss der fortschreitenden Produktionstechnik* (1886), p. 94; quoted in Spero and Harris, *op. cit.*, p. 184.

has dominated the field during the last decades and is still the most important organization, except on the West Coast where the longshoremen's locals have joined the C.I.O. Negroes and whites are usually organized in separate locals. It is asserted that even Negroes like it better this way, in that it gives them the opportunity to work under foremen of their own race and also to bring organized pressure against the white part of the unions.[a] Negroes are heavily represented in the national leadership of the union. This does not mean, however, that discrimination and racial antagonism have been eliminated. It is frequently charged that the white workers get more and better work opportunities than Negro workers. Writing about present-day conditions in New Orleans, Northrup states that the 800 members of the white local get more steady work than the 2,100 members of the Negro local.[b] In Houston the work is divided evenly between the white and the Negro locals, in spite of the fact that they are of different size (300 and 400 members, respectively). Similar arrangements with similar results exist also in other ports. Negroes have been hampered by the fact that unions in most Southern ports were more or less crushed during the early 'twenties and remained comparatively powerless until the New Deal. Some Southern Negro locals are still suffering from internal strife, graft, and corruption, even sometimes from the embezzling of union funds by unfaithful leaders. The national union directed by a powerful machine has taken a clear position on the race issue but has done little to tackle the basic problem of work distribution. The main reason is probably that a rotation system would necessitate a limitation in the number of workers and, hence, in the dues-paying membership; also, it would hurt the vested interests of those now favored. Only in a few of the Negro-dominated ports, like those in Texas (where the unions managed to remain strong throughout the 'twenties), on the West Coast, and, to a certain extent, in Baltimore, have rotation systems been introduced. The C.I.O. unions on the Pacific Coast seem to be the only ones which have gone the whole way on the race issue. Negroes are completely unsegregated, and the unions support them in every way, even going so far as to make water-front restaurants accept Negro union members as patrons. Only a handful of Negro longshoremen, however, work on the Pacific Coast.[c]

The ordinary hourly wage rate in work for deep-sea traffic, as of April, 1942, was $1.20 in the Northern ports and in Norfolk, $.70 in Charleston and Savannah, $.95 in Mobile, and $1.10 in New Orleans and Galveston. The North-South differential is due to the weakness of most Southern unions during the 'twenties and early 'thirties.[d] The employment opportunities certainly must be good at the present time; we have no data on the extent to which the Negro longshoreman has been able to improve even his relative position because of the war boom. The future prospects, however, must be extremely doubtful in this work with its pronounced booms and depressions.

8. BUILDING WORKERS

Except for agriculture and domestic service, there is no industry which gives employment to as many Negroes as does building construction and related work, such as con-

[a] *Ibid.*, pp. 72-73.

[b] *Op. cit.*, pp. 175 and 178.

[c] Interviews with union leaders in San Francisco made by Gunnar Myrdal, March, 1940.

[d] Northrup, *op. cit.*, p. 129. The data for 1942 are based on information from the International Longshoremen's Association (letter from John R. Owens, Secretary-Treasurer, January 30, 1942).

struction and maintenance of highways, streets, railroads. In 1930 there were 181,000 Negro workers in building construction alone, almost half of them in the North and the West. In construction and maintenance of roads, streets, sewers, and bridges, there were 64,000 Negro workers, four-fifths of whom lived in the South. Finally, there were 98,000 Negro laborers employed by steam railroads, most of them in the maintenance-of-way departments.[a] This last group will be discussed in the next section.

It has been pointed out already that the Negro, in spite of migration to the North, has lost in relative position both in ordinary building construction (which had about the same total number of workers in 1930 as in 1910) and in construction and maintenance of streets, highways, and so forth, which is an expanding industry. The almost complete cessation of residential and factory construction during the 'thirties has hastened the elimination of the Negro building worker in that white competitors became still more eager to monopolize whatever job opportunities were left. In the South less than one-fifth of all persons employed in construction work in 1940 were Negroes.[b]

The situation is somewhat different in skilled and unskilled building trades. In the laboring jobs the Negro workers are still in the majority in the South, even if their numbers have been decreasing for a long time. In 1910 almost three-fourths of the building laborers and helpers in ten Southern states were Negro, but this proportion had declined to less than two-thirds by 1930. Among Southern street and highway workers the proportion of Negroes decreased from over three-fourths in 1910 to somewhat more than one-half in 1930,[c] although in this case there was a considerable increase in actual numbers even for Negroes. It seems that Negroes have smaller chances than whites to secure employment with municipalities. Unpublished data from the United States Bureau of Employment Security, quoted by Norgren, indicate that while 73 per cent of "private" placements of building and construction laborers in six Southern states during the period from mid-1937 to mid-1938 were of Negroes, the corresponding proportion for "public" placements was considerably lower—60 per cent.[d] Yet, there is no doubt but that this is still a "Negro job" in the South.

There are many Negroes in skilled building occupations as well. Indeed, in 1930 there were some 80,000 of them, which means that about half of all Negro skilled workers are in the building trades. But not even in the South did they dominate these skilled occupations. On the contrary, most of them had by 1930 become predominantly "white jobs" even in the South; in only one of them did the Negro have more than half the work opportunities.[e] We can take it for granted that the situation has further deteriorated since that time.

This condition is the result of a long development. Although occupational census data were not tabulated by race until 1890, it is generally believed that "in the *ante-*

---

[a] *Fifteenth Census of the United States: 1930, Population*, Vol. 4, State Table 11.

[b] Chapter 13, Table 3.

[c] Norgren and Associates, *op. cit.*, Part 1, p. 5. Based on the decennial censuses.

[d] *Ibid.*, p. 152.

[e] *Ibid.*, Part 3, p. 289, based on census data. It should be emphasized that the Negro's share in employment in the skilled building trades was certainly smaller than this information indicates, in that the proportion of skilled workers who were either unemployed or had to accept unskilled work was greater among Negroes than among whites.

bellum South the bulk of the building work was . . . performed by Negroes." [a] The South was even more rural then than now. Plantations were self-sufficient economic entities, and the only way to get construction work done was to train a few slaves for it. Even in the cities the white building workers suffered from competition with free Negroes and Negro slaves who were hired out by their owners or allowed to work independently on the condition that they give the owners part of their earnings. It goes without saying that the white workers protested against this state of affairs, but as long as the politically most powerful class had a considerable interest in letting Negroes have a large share of the work, there was no way for the white worker to drive the Negro out. A survey for 1865, made under the auspices of the federal government, indicated that 80 per cent of all skilled mechanics (including building tradesmen) in the South were Negroes.[b]

The end of slavery meant the end of this protection of the Negro worker. It also meant that plantation owners and other employers lost much of their interest in giving training to Negroes,[c] for they were no longer assured of retaining the services of Negro workers whom they had trained. The change, of course, was not completed in one stroke. The Black Codes, and particularly the laws about apprenticeship, still gave employers a vested interest in Negro labor for a long time.[d] This only cushioned the effects of Emancipation. Negroes moved about as they had never done before, and the old master-servant relationship meant much less than it had during slavery.

Already by 1890 the white workers were in the majority in the skilled building occupations in the South.[e] Only one-fourth of the carpenters, for example, were Negro at that time, and among the painters the proportion of Negroes was even lower. The corresponding proportion for 1930 for these two groups had declined to 17 per cent. The Negro has never had a chance to enter the ranks of the electricians, a comparatively new occupation; by 1930, less than 2 per cent of the electricians in the South were Negroes. Plumbing, which has been a rapidly expanding trade, has likewise given but few opportunities to Negroes; in 1930 only 12 per cent of all plumbers in the South were Negroes. Negroes also managed to maintain their relative position in plastering and bricklaying jobs, at least until 1930; no less than 44 per cent of the bricklayers and 61 per cent of the plasterers in the South in 1930 were Negro. Yet if we add the number of workers for all these six trades together, we find that the Negro's relative position in the South had become much worse during the period 1910-1930, in that the whites had got almost all the benefit of the big general expansion which occurred during this period. That the Negroes received a smaller share than did whites of the dwindling job opportunities during the 'thirties is indicated by several studies. Analyzing data from the United States Employment Service for five Southern states in

[a] *Ibid.*, p. 285. See also Lorenzo J. Greene and Carter G. Woodson, *The Negro Wage Earner* (1930), pp. 14-17; Spero and Harris, *op. cit.*, pp. 5-10; Raymond B. Pinchbeck, *The Virginia Negro Artisan and Tradesman* (1926), pp. 17-54.

[b] Norgren and Associates, *op. cit.*, Part 3, p. 286. Norgren's main sources are: Charles H. Wesley, *Negro Labor in the United States, 1850-1925* (1927), p. 142; *The Freedmen's Record* (July, 1868), pp. 108-109; and *The New Era* (January 13, 1870).

[c] Northrup, *op. cit.*, p. 28.

[d] See Chapter 10.

[e] Norgren and Associates, *op. cit.*, p. 289 and Northrup, *op. cit.* See also Walter F. Willcox, "Negro Criminality," *Journal of Social Science* (December, 1899), pp. 85-86.

1937-1938, Norgren found that the proportion of Negroes among the "placements" was invariably much lower than the corresponding proportion among those registering for work. For carpenters, they were 5 and 10 per cent, respectively; for bricklayers, 35 and 44 per cent; for painters, 9 and 12 per cent; for plumbers, 8 and 20 per cent; and for plasterers, 53 and 75 per cent.[a] The same data show that the skilled Negro building worker has great difficulty in getting employment in the increasingly important public building projects.[b] It is believed that plasterers, who have allowed Negroes a better position than has any other building craft, are threatened, more than the rest, by competition from pre-fabricated materials, such as plasterboard.[c]

There is no doubt that the decline in the relative position of the skilled Negro building worker is due largely to the attitude of white workers.

> The intense anti-Negro sentiment which arose in the South during and immediately after the Reconstruction Period was . . . undoubtedly the most significant factor in displacing Negroes from the building crafts.[d]

Many employers have come up from the ranks of the white workers and share their views. Trade unions, however, had little to do with the big displacement of Negro skilled workers which occurred between the end of the Civil War and the 'nineties, for until that time they remained rather powerless in the South. They are largely responsible, on the other hand, for the fact that the Negro has been kept from sharing in the expansion of the building trades which occurred in the South during this century. The discriminatory attitude of the organized building crafts is the more significant at the present time, since they dominate the American Federation of Labor—a circumstance which is behind the reluctance of this organization to take any definite action against exclusionist and segregational practices.

All building crafts are not equally bad. The leaders of the Bricklayers, Masons and Plasterers' International Union as well as the Operative Plasterers' and Cement Finishers' International Association have fought discriminatory practices in a rather consistent way.[e] This, no doubt, is the principal reason why Negroes have fared much better in these crafts than in other skilled building trades. We can also, in all probability, assume that the basic reason for the favorable behavior in the organized trowel trades toward the Negro was the fact that the Negro had managed to maintain a substantial position in these occupations before the time when the unions started to become powerful in the South. Consequently, it was difficult to disregard him.[f] However that might be, it remains a fact that it was in the 1890's that the national leadership of the bricklayers' union started to take strong action against locals which excluded Negroes. Sometimes it uses the separate Negro local, but, according to Northrup, mainly "as a club with which to force local unions to admit colored bricklayers." Out of 28 Southern and

---

[a] Norgren and Associates, *op. cit.*, Part 3, p. 293. The five states were Alabama, Georgia, Louisiana, North Carolina and South Carolina

[b] *Ibid.*, Part 3, p. 325.

[c] Northrup, *op. cit.*, pp. 91-92.

[d] Norgren and Associates, *op. cit.*, Part 3, pp. 287-288.

[e] *Ibid.*, Part 3, p. 321, and Northrup, *op. cit.*, pp. 80-96.

[f] "The extent of the opposition of the labor unions toward the black mechanics . . . varied in inverse proportion to the numerous strength of the Negroes in the trades." (Greene and Woodson, *op. cit.*, pp. 188-189; see also Northrup, *op. cit.*, pp. 96-98.)

Border cities studied by Norgren, Northrup, and others, in 1940-1941, 22 had mixed locals, 3 (Atlanta, Richmond, and Charleston, South Carolina) had separate Negro and white locals, and 3 (St. Louis, Baltimore, and Tampa) had white locals indulging in various degrees of exclusionist policies. It is said that the race relations are usually good in the mixed Southern locals.[a] The plasterers' union shows similar conditions. Of 26 Southern and Border cities surveyed by Northrup in 1940-1941, only 2 (Birmingham and St. Louis) had separate locals for Negroes and whites; 2 had exclusively white locals; whereas the remaining 22 cities had unsegregated local unions (in 12 of these unions Negroes were in the majority). Discriminatory tendencies appear here and there, but the national leadership takes strong action against them.[b]

These examples show that there is nothing inherently "natural" in the exclusionist and segregational attitudes dominating other organized building crafts, except that the Negro worker was so powerless to begin with in these other trades that it was comparatively easy to keep him out. The United Brotherhood of Carpenters and Joiners, for over forty years representing the most important of all the building crafts, usually organizes Negroes and whites into separate locals—that is, in so far as Negroes are allowed to belong to the union. In the South there seems to be no exception to this rule, and it is often practiced in Northern cities as well. This segregation works considerable hardship on the Negro worker, for there seems to be little attempt to divide the work evenly between the Negro and the white locals. In the South, white locals are often allied with the municipal political machines, and this is one of the reasons why it is so much easier for white workers to secure employment on public construction projects; the political bosses know, of course, that white workers can vote, and that Negroes cannot. Also, it is easier for white than for the colored locals to be in constant contact with private contractors. It even happens that white locals import white workers from other cities rather than allow Negroes to get a share of especially attractive work opportunities. Sometimes they have excluded Negroes altogether from work in white neighborhoods, which means that Negro carpenters are restricted to maintenance and repair work and the building of small unpretentious homes; they seldom get any share of the work on larger projects. It is extremely hard for the colored workers, under such circumstances, to maintain their skills. There are Southern cities where few, if any, Negro craftsmen are competent to use newer techniques and newer materials. During the 'thirties a great number of Negro locals disappeared, whereas the white locals usually managed to survive. As a consequence, in many Southern cities colored workers are completely excluded. During the latter part of the 'thirties and the present war boom, a reversal in this trend has been brought about, thanks to the efforts of the federal government.[c] In spite of these efforts, Northrup did not find more than 18 colored locals in 33 Southern and Border cities in 1940-1941, and most of those seemed to depend entirely on the protection of the federal government.[d]

The Brotherhood of Painters, Decorators, and Paper-hangers seems to be even worse than the Carpenters. Negro workers are not often organized even in separate locals.

[a] Northrup, *op. cit.*, pp. 83-85.

[b] *Ibid.*, pp. 94-96.

[c] All data in this paragraph are based on Northrup, *op. cit.*, pp. 50-57. Concerning the efforts of the federal government, see Chapter 19, Section 3. Norgren and Associates, *op. cit.*, pp. 314-316, and ff.

[d] Northrup, *op. cit.*, p. 65.

When Negroes tend to undercut the going union rate, the white locals sometimes allow Negroes to organize a local of their own; but they then make contracts with the former employers of Negro labor, thereby depriving Negroes of many of the work opportunities they formerly had. Recently, certain changes have been adopted in the constitution of the union which give the greater power to the national leadership; this may facilitate the setting up of more auxiliary Negro locals, but it may not mean that Negroes will get a larger share of the work.[a]

Yet even the Painters are relatively liberal when compared with the Electricians and the Plumbers, which exclude Negroes almost completely. Norgren, writing in 1940, had not found any single Negro local in the South, whereas a few of the Northern cities had a handful of colored members in white locals. Moreover, these unions, particularly the Plumbers, have backed state and municipal legislation establishing public licensing boards. Since the unions are usually represented on these boards, they have been able to restrict the granting of licenses almost exclusively to white plumbers and electricians in all localities where this set-up is functioning.[b] We have seen the results of these exclusionist practices: Negroes have never been able to get any significant representation among the electricians; even in the South Negro plumbers are a very small and decreasing minority.

According to the general rule that Negroes are less discriminated against where they had a substantial portion of the work at the time when union activities began, the union for building laborers treats Negroes rather well. The International Hod Carriers', Building and Common Laborers' Union had a total membership in 1941 of 250,000, of which some 70,000 were Negroes.[c] With few exceptions, Negroes and whites are organized in the same locals. There are certain complaints that many locals are administrated by the national union rather than by the members themselves, but there seems to be no evidence that this state of affairs would work any particular hardship on Negro members. Negroes are represented in the national leadership.[d]

The federal government, as mentioned earlier, has, during recent years, attempted to secure for Negroes a share of the work on public housing projects for Negroes. During 1933-1937 these projects were built by the Public Works Administration; and from 1937 to 1942 they were built under the auspices of the United States Housing Authority. The proportion of Negroes employed is the same as the proportion of Negroes in the population of the locality where the project is built, and it applies to workers of all kinds. The contractors have not had any difficulty in filling their "Negro quota" of unskilled workers and of such skilled workers as bricklayers, plasterers, and so forth, but when it comes to the other skilled workers, either they usually declare themselves unable to find enough competent Negro skilled workers; or the opposition of the white unions was so strong that the U.S.H.A. had to permit the application of a "blanket" quota for the whole project rather than of a specific quota for each occupation. Even if the claims about the nonexistence of competent Negro craftsmen were exaggerated, they were probably well founded in many instances; we have to remember that Negro craftsmen

---

[a] *Ibid.*, pp. 67-79.

[b] Spero and Harris, *op. cit.*, pp. 59-60; Norgren and Associates, *op. cit.*, Part 3, pp. 312-313; Northrup, *op. cit.*, pp. 49-50.

[c] *Ibid.*, p. 111. Information based on American Federation of Labor, *Report of Proceedings, 1941*, p. 492.

[d] Northrup, *op. cit.*, pp. 113-114.

had been rather systematically kept out of the larger construction projects where they could have learned newer techniques. Until the end of 1940 Negroes received 13 per cent of the total payroll on the U.S.H.A. projects, but only 5 per cent of the payroll for skilled work.[a] Even so, it helped Negro workers in the South to maintain unions which otherwise would have disappeared and even to revive some unions which had disappeared during the previous depressions.

9. RAILROAD WORKERS

In 1930 there were 163,000 Negro workers employed by steam railroads, constituting slightly more than 10 per cent of the total labor force in the industry. About 98,000 of these Negroes were designated as laborers; 37,000 were porters, waiters, and cooks; less than 11,000 were firemen, brakemen, switchmen, and flagmen; and most of the rest belonged to minor categories of unskilled workers. Less than 200 were conductors or locomotive engineers.[b]

Railway service expanded during the First World War but declined afterward, owing to competition with motor traffic. The end result, by 1930, was that the total number of employees was about the same as in 1910. The number of Negro workers had increased by 25 per cent, but this was due to their inroads in the North. The number of laborers, for instance, increased from about 8,000 to 24,000 in the North and West, but declined from 78,000 to 73,000 in the South.[c] Most other categories, such as locomotive firemen and brakemen, had fewer Negro workers in 1930 than in 1910. In the South, particularly, the decline in the proportion of Negroes employed in such occupations was very noticeable. The development during the 'thirties meant that the Negro's opportunities for advancement became still more insignificant than before; also, the groups in which Negroes were concentrated were severely hit by the depression and by competition with motor traffic. The total number of maintenance-of-way employees in the South declined by more than 50 per cent from 1928 to 1938,[d] and since Negroes constituted about three-fourths of this labor force in the South, it must have meant a tremendous loss in Negro employment. The census data show that in the South Negroes constituted only 21 per cent of the railroad workers in 1940, as compared with 25 per cent in 1930.[e] This decrease is, of course, in addition to the decrease in actual numbers of Negro railroad workers.

Most of the railroad brotherhoods are among the leaders in Negro exclusionism. The Brotherhood of Locomotive Engineers and the Order of Railway Conductors have been almost completely successful in keeping the Negro out. The Brotherhood of Locomotive Firemen and Enginemen is equally exclusionistic. Until the beginning of this century, however, the fireman's job was generally considered too dirty for a white man in the

[a] Robert C. Weaver, "Racial Employment Trends in National Defense," *Phylon* (Fourth Quarter, 1941), p. 347. See also Norgren and Associates, *op. cit.*, Part 3, pp. 331-335.

[b] U. S. Bureau of the Census, *Negroes in the United States: 1920-1932*, pp. 353-354; *Fifteenth Census of the United States: 1930, Population*, Vol. 4, State Table 11.

[c] U. S. Bureau of the Census, *Negroes in the United States: 1920-1932*, pp. 303-309; *Thirteenth Census of the United States: 1910, Statistics*, Vol. 4, pp. 434-534. These figures do not include female workers, who numbered only about 1,000 in 1930.

[d] Interstate Commerce Commission, *Annual Statistical Report* for 1928 and 1938. Quoted by Norgren and Associates, *op. cit.*, Part 1, p. 129.

[e] See Chapter 13, Table 3.

South, but technical developments soon made it more attractive.[a] The removal of racial wage differentials in 1918 made the employers lose their interest in having Negro firemen, which, of course, hastened the elimination of Negroes.[b] Few, if any, Negroes are getting into such occupations at the present time. It is possible, however, that the present war boom has brought about a temporary change in this situation. Some Negroes are even being driven out, and the probability is that the Negro, before long, will have but a handful of representatives in these groups. This process of elimination has been accompanied by physical intimidation and even murder. Charles S. Johnson has found trustworthy accounts and records of no less than 21 shootings and murders of firemen and brakemen during the short period 1931-1934.[c]

The Brotherhood of Railway and Steamship Clerks, Freight Handlers, Express and Station Employees (A.F. of L.), which formerly excluded Negroes, changed its policy in 1940 by accepting segregated Negro "auxiliaries," directed by white officers.[d] Even more unfavorable to Negroes is the fact that a similar policy is followed by the Brotherhood of Maintenance of Way Employees (A.F. of L.), which represents the occupation including the bulk of the Negro railroad workers. This union was orginally started by the foremen who are still dominating it. Since the foremen are always white, the Negro workers feel that the organization serves the purpose of keeping them subjugated under their white bosses.[e] This condition is the more deplorable since maintenance-of-way workers are the largest low wage group in the railway industry.[f] In 1935 over two-thirds of them earned 35 cents per hour or less in the South and almost one-fifth received 20 cents or less.[g] Thanks to the Wages and Hours Act, there have been improvements since then, at least for those lowest down on the wage scale. The average in 1939 for 15 Southern states was 33 cents, as against 47 cents in the "Eastern district."[h] The application of the Wages and Hours Law has been delayed, in some cases, because of evasion. At least one great Southern road used the device of charging their workers undue amounts for rent and other expenses, but was forced, through court action, to refrain from such practices.[i] The wage increases, on the other hand, are encouraging mechanization, particularly in the South where, so far, there has been comparatively little mechanization and where the rise in wage cost counts most.[j] After the present war boom the Negro railroad worker, more likely than not, will have even less employment than he had before this emergency.

[a] Charles S. Johnson, "Negroes in the Railway Industry, Part 2," *Phylon* (Second Quarter, 1942), p. 204.

[b] Northrup, *op. cit.*, pp. 348-349.

[c] "Negroes in the Railway Industry, Part 2."

[d] Northrup, *op. cit.*, p. 353.

[e] *Ibid.*, pp. 357-358.

[f] Charles S. Johnson, "Negroes in the Railway Industry, Part 1," p. 6.

[g] Federal Coordinator of Transportation, *The Extent of Low Wages and Long Hours in the Railroad Industry* (November, 1936), quoted in Norgren and Associates, *op. cit.*, Part 1, pp. 140-142.

[h] *Ibid.*, p. 141. Information secured from Wages and Hours Division, Department of Labor. The "Eastern District" encompasses New England, the Great Lakes region and the Central East.

[i] *Ibid.*, pp. 141-143.

[j] *Ibid.*, pp. 144-145, and Charles S. Johnson, "Negroes in the Railway Industry, Part 2," pp. 196-198.

One group of Negro railroad workers stands somewhat apart: the Pullman porters, dining car waiters, redcaps, and other railroad service workers. In spite of the fact that total railroad employment was no larger in 1930 than in 1910, the number of Negro railroad service workers doubled during this period, and the absolute number of Negro workers in the group (37,000) was larger than is to be found in most manufacturing industries. The reason is that Negroes have a near-monopoly on these jobs, even though there has been some competition from Mexicans and Filipinos during recent years, and even from whites in certain cities.[a]

This has been the field of the most successful independent Negro unionism. After trying in vain for more than a decade to institute an efficient organization, the Pullman porters, under the leadership of A. Philip Randolph, finally succeeded in 1925 in organizing the Brotherhood of Sleeping Car Porters, which now has about 10,000 members. In 1936 it got an international A.F. of L. charter, and after great difficulties, because of the unwillingness of the Pullman Company to recognize it as bargaining agent for the porters, it succeeded in 1937 in making the company sign a contract in which certain improvements in the conditions of work were granted. The wage rates for Pullman porters now vary between $89.50 and $114 per month, depending on years of service and type of work. Extra pay is received when the working time exceeds 240 hours a month. In addition, porters receive tips.[b] Another powerful Negro union is the United Transport Workers of America which includes redcaps, dining car waiters and others.[c]

10. TOBACCO WORKERS

There have been two opposing trends affecting the Negro's position in the tobacco industry. From a national viewpoint, he has often gained, but only for the reason that Southern manufacturing, both absolutely and relatively, has become more important. On the other hand, in those Southern states where the majority of the Negro tobacco workers are occupied, white workers have, at times, made substantial gains at the expense of the Negro.

Let us consider, first, the national trend during the last decades. The tobacco industry underwent a rapid expansion during the First World War, but during the 'twenties there was a tremendous decline in employment due, largely, to mechanization. The net effect was that the total number of workers dropped 23 per cent between 1910 and 1930.[d] The depression in the 'thirties, of course, brought about further declines. According to the *Census of Manufacturers*, the tobacco industry had 25 per cent fewer workers in 1939 than in 1929.

In 1930 there were 34,000 Negroes in the industry, only one-tenth of whom resided outside the South. The Negro had had a larger share in the employment gains during the First World War and a smaller share in the subsequent losses than the white worker. By 1930 there were 35 per cent more Negro workers in the industry than in 1910, and

[a] Charles S. Johnson, "Negroes in the Railway Industry, Part 2," p. 202. Interview by Gunnar Myrdal with white "redcap" Kansas City, Kansas, March 20, 1940.

[b] "A Brief History of the Organizing of the Brotherhood of Sleeping Car Porters, an International Union," undated typescript issued by the Brotherhood of Sleeping Car Porters. See also, Charles S. Johnson, "Negroes in the Railway Industry, Part 2," pp. 203-204.

[c] Florence Murray (editor), *The Negro Handbook* (1942), p. 136.

[d] *Thirteenth Census of the United States: 1910, Population,* Vol. 4, p. 396.

the proportion of Negroes in the industry had increased from 13 per cent to 23 per cent.[a] This difference, however, was entirely due to the condition that those states where the Negro is predominant in the tobacco industry (principally North Carolina, Virginia, and Kentucky) have fared much better than most of the others. The Negro has but few representatives among the cigar makers in Florida, Pennsylvania, New Jersey, and elsewhere, a group which constituted more than half of all tobacco workers in 1939, and has suffered more than most other groups, partly because of the mechanization, but also because of the declining relative importance of cigar consumption. Moreover, part of the Northern tobacco industry has migrated to the South—a trend which, of course, would tend to improve the Negro's relative position.[b]

Let us now turn our attention to the Southern scene. It is believed that originally almost all the tobacco workers in the South were Negro slaves, but from 1850 on there is evidence of Negroes being displaced by whites. This trend was precipitated, after the Civil War, by the development of a new type of production which did not have the tradition of being a "Negro job" industry: cigarette manufacturing. The introduction of machinery was another factor encouraging the hiring of white workers, in that it made the work less strenuous, less dirty and, generally, more attractive. Negroes were retained as tobacco stemmers, however, and in all sorts of common labor jobs, whereas most other processing work was handled by white operatives.[c] Yet, by 1890, the first year for which census data on occupations by race are available, about two-thirds of all tobacco workers in Virginia, Kentucky and North Carolina were Negro. It seems, also, that a certain stabilization in the apportionment of jobs between the two races had been attained at that time, for the same two-thirds ratio was maintained until 1930.[d] The number of Negro workers almost doubled between 1910 and 1920. There was a decrease by one-fourth between 1920 and 1930.

Concerning the development during the 'thirties, it may be noted that the total number of tobacco workers in Virginia and North Carolina was more than one-tenth higher in 1939 than in 1929.[e] The fact that the development was so much more favorable in these states than for the nation as a whole should, of course, make for a further improvement of the Negro's relative position in the tobacco industry. It is possible, however, that the proportion of Negro workers has declined in Virginia, North Carolina, and Kentucky; for, during the 'thirties, there has been a definite tendency to mechanize tobacco stemming, which previously has been much less affected by

[a] *Fifteenth Census of the United States: 1930, Population*, Vol. 5, p. 440.

[b] Northrup, *op. cit.*, pp. 194-195. Information based on J. P. Troxell, "Labor in the Tobacco Industry," unpublished Ph. D. thesis, University of Wisconsin (1931); and U.S. Women's Bureau, *The Effect on Women of Changing Conditions in the Cigar and Cigarette Industries*, Bulletin No. 100, p. 20.

[c] Northrup, *op. cit.*, pp. 181-186. See also, Pinchbeck, *op. cit.*, pp. 54-59; and Joseph C. Robert, *The Tobacco Kingdom* (1938).

[d] Northrup, *op. cit.*, p. 190. Information based on the decennial censuses. It is possible that the data for 1900 and 1910 are not quite comparable with those for 1920 and 1930, but the possible error in the comparison seems not to be significant.

[e] *Sixteenth Census of the United States, Census of Manufactures, 1939, Tobacco Manufacturers Group*, p. 3; and *Fifteenth Census of the United States, Census of Manufactures, 1929*, Vol. 2, pp. 388 and 537. The figures for 1939 include cigarette workers only; those for 1929 include both cigar and cigarette workers. Parallel data for Kentucky are not yet available.

mechanization than have other operations. The main reason for this is the wage increase which has been brought about under the N.R.A., the Fair Labor Standards Act, and through the efforts of trade unions.[a]

A trend in this direction has been under way, but there seems to be little statistical evidence available at this writing on how far it had proceeded before it became submerged in the present war boom. So far, the main effect seems to have been that the Negro has received a somewhat smaller share than the white workers in the employment gains brought about through an increased demand. The number of colored workers in Virginia tobacco manufacturing increased by 27 per cent between 1931 and 1938; the corresponding figure for whites was somewhat higher, or 33 per cent.[b] There is reason to believe that the trend became more pronounced after 1938.[c] Prior to that year, the independent stemmeries which during the peak season of 1939 gave employment to an estimated 40,000 workers, predominantly Negroes (whereas the average for the whole year was less than 19,000) had been exempt from all minimum wage regulations.[d] The failure of these independent stemmeries to be excluded from the wages and hours regulations brought about a considerable increase in the earnings of their workers; the average for 11 stemmeries was 16 cents in 1935 and 33 cents in 1940-1941.[e] A similar wage increase had already occurred in the stemmery departments of the cigarette factories between 1933 and 1935, because of N.R.A. regulations, and there are several cases known when this has caused such plants to mechanize their stemmery departments.[f]

In spite of these wage increases, Negroes still receive much lower wages than whites. Worse than that, the work season is much shorter in rehandling work, where almost all the workers are Negro, than in other operations. In Virginia rehandling plants it averaged only 153 days (1939) whereas it was 234 days in cigar and cigarette manufacturing where two-thirds of the labor force was white. Although both labor groups were of about the same size during the time of operation, the rehandling workers received a total annual payroll less than half as large as that received by cigar and cigarette workers.[g] It is a well-known fact that female Negro tobacco workers have to supplement their factory earnings by doing domestic work during off seasons.

The Tobacco Workers' International Union was organized in the 1890's. It was a weak union most of the time until the late 1930's. Except for short periods, such as the First World War, it has seldom, until lately, taken a strong stand against employers, nor made any rigorous efforts to organize more than limited sections of the industry.

[a] Northrup, op. cit., pp. 197-207.

[b] Manuscript table based on the annual reports by the Virginia State Department of Labor and Industry. Courtesy, Dr. Lorin A. Thompson, Virginia Population Study.

[c] From 1938 to 1939 the number of white tobacco workers in Virginia increased by 8 per cent and the number of Negro tobacco workers by 3 per cent. (Ibid., and Department of Labor and Industry, Commonwealth of Virginia, Labor and Industry in Virginia, 43rd Annual Report, year ending September 30, 1940 [1941], p. 31.)

[d] U.S. Department of Labor, Wages and Hours Division, "The Tobacco Industry" (mimeographed, 1941) p. 11. Quoted in Northrup, op. cit., p. 203.

[e] "Hours and Earnings of Employees of Independent Leaf-Tobacco Dealers," Monthly Labor Review (July, 1941), p. 7. Quoted in Northrup, op. cit., p. 206.

[f] Ibid., pp. 200-201. Wage data based on U.S. Bureau of Labor Statistics, "Earnings in Cigarettes, Snuff, and Chewing- and Smoking-Tobacco Plants, 1933-1935," Monthly Labor Review (May, 1936), pp. 1322 and 1331.

[g] Department of Labor and Industry, Commonwealth of Virginia, op. cit., p. 27.

Its main strategy seems to have been to sell the right of using the union label to a few employers, who did not have to pay a high price for getting their conditions of work accepted by the union. Then, too, it has been one of the most consistently undemocratic of all American organized labor groups. Between the years 1900 and 1939 there was not a single national convention, and the leadership was fundamentally the same during this whole time. The leaders would not retire even because of old age; the rank-and-file membership had to institute prolonged legal proceedings to reintroduce democracy and establish a new, more liberal and more efficient leadership. Before this certain significant successes had been won in the form of increased membership and contracts with large employers, particularly after the Supreme Court had upheld the National Labor Relations Act in 1937. The change in leadership strengthened this trend still further.[a]

It is evident that the Negro could not expect any great advantages from the union as it functioned before this reorganization. Where Negroes were organized, they were, and still are, for the most part kept in segregated locals. This system, of course, may appear as much more "natural" in the tobacco industry than in many other lines of work, since there is a strict occupational race segregation in tobacco, but it has made racial cooperation more difficult. The new regime has been much more friendly to Negroes than the old one. For the first time since 1900 a Negro has been elected vice-president. Negroes and whites are to be organized in the same locals "whenever possible" and, in actual practice, this policy has been followed in at least one case (Memphis). In the Virginia-North Carolina area there is a "joint shop committee" representing white and colored locals. These beginning interracial efforts may promise something for the future, but so far there has not been any complete understanding, nor grounds for the hope that the union will help the Negro in breaking up the occupational pattern of segregation in the tobacco industry. In some places, particularly in Richmond, it has been difficult to make the white local leaders interest themselves in the Negro. Few attempts were made to get Negroes organized, and this made Negro workers at some of the local stemmeries start a series of successful strikes on their own in 1937-1938. They were encouraged by the C.I.O., which helped them organize themselves independently. A group of white workers, members of the Amalgamated Clothing Workers (C.I.O.), at one time joined their picket line. The C.I.O. has competed with the T.W.I.U. in other places, and this threat has helped to make the local leadership of the A.F. of L. union more aware of the necessity of admitting the Negro to membership.[b]

11. TEXTILE WORKERS

We shall consider the textile industry, not because it is a major "Negro industry," but—quite the opposite—because it is the main Southern industry excluding Negroes. It is the largest of all manufacturing branches in the South, yet it fails to use any Negro labor, except for limited menial purposes, such as sweeping, cleaning and yard labor. The Southern textile industry underwent a continued expansion during the 'thirties but Negroes derived little, if any, gain from it. The proportion of Negro workers in

[a] Northrup, *op. cit.*, pp. 207-235. Northrup has brought together his material on the tobacco workers union in an article, "The Tobacco Workers International Union," *The Quarterly Journal of Economics* (August, 1942), pp. 606-626. The references here, however, are to the thesis.

[b] *Idem.*, and Federal Writers' Project, *The Negro in Virginia* (1940), pp. 308-311.

Southern textile mills and clothing factories declined from 7 per cent in 1920 to 4 per cent in 1940. The absolute number of employed Negro workers in the South was 26,000 in 1940.[a]

Before the Civil War the textile industry in the South was unimportant. It was largely manned by Negroes, and often owned by planters who used their own slaves. It was not until about a decade after the Civil War that the real growth began. This growth, however, was not a matter of an expansion of the old plants. Instead, there were new plants built, mainly in the upper Piedmont area, where there is a big supply of white labor. Yet around many of the new textile mills there was a large potential Negro labor force as well. Norgren, on the basis of the 1880 Census, finds that Negroes constituted about one-third of the population in the upland counties of Georgia, Alabama and the two Carolinas. Yet no appreciable share of the jobs was given to the Negro.[b]

The explanation of this phenomenon seems to be that the origin of the cotton industry in the South was not a matter of individualistic enterprise alone. Regular "cotton mill campaigns" were organized by "citizens' committees" which often raised funds for the purpose. The entrepreneurs depended on the moral and financial backing of their white fellow citizens and had to consider their viewpoints, which were colored by the anti-Negro sentiments bred during the Reconstruction period.[c] The very fact that the industry was a new one and not a descendant of the pre-war textile plants was enough to leave the Negro out. Only in rare instances has the Negro had a chance in any Southern industry where he had not become entrenched before or just after the Civil War, when the moneyed whites had a direct financial interest in him.

As soon as this exclusionist pattern was established, the white working population acquired a vested interest in it which was difficult to remove. That the majority of the white workers are women, while the majority of the Negro workers are men, may have contributed to the resistance. There is an even greater reluctance against allowing Negroes of either sex to work with white women than there is against letting Negro men work with white men. Some employers have tried to employ more Negroes, but have met with such vigorous protests that they have had to abandon the idea.[d] The Negro, thus, has been unable to share in the benefits of the spectacular rise of the Southern textile industry. Although it has hurt the working population in the New England and Middle Atlantic states, it has not helped the Southern Negro to any appreciable extent.

An energetic unionization campaign in the South was inaugurated in 1937 by the Textile Workers' Union. Like other C.I.O. unions, it admits Negroes on a basis of equality, and membership in this union often protects the Negro from losing the few jobs that he now has in the Southern textile mills. It is not likely, however, that the union will ever do anything positive in order to help the Negro get a share in the ordinary production jobs. Even if unionism in Southern textile mills is based on a working class

[a] Chapter 13, Table 3.

[b] Norgren and Associates, *op. cit.*, Part 3, pp. 254-261. Norgren's description of the historical development of the Southern textile industry is largely based on Broadus Mitchell, *The Rise of Cotton Mills in the South* (1921); and Broadus Mitchell and George S. Mitchell, *The Industrial Revolution in the South* (1930).

[c] *Ibid.*, Part 3, pp. 262-265.

[d] *Ibid.*, Part 3, p. 269, and Greene and Woodson, *op. cit.*, pp. 146-148.

ideology, one can scarcely expect the membership to accept major sacrifices in order to help the Negro.[a]

12. COAL MINERS

Bituminous coal mining,[b] except for a temporary recovery during the present war boom, has been a declining industry for the past few decades. This is due to over-expansion during the First World War, mechanization, and increased use of fuel substitutes, particularly oil and electricity. Nevertheless, the Negro is better off in this occupation than in most others. Writing before the present war boom, Norgren says:

> Considered as a source of employment, bituminous coal mining is decidedly a declining industry. During the past two decades, the number of persons earning their livelihood in this branch of economic activity has decreased by more than 200,000 or approximately one third[*]; and there is little prospect of any reversal of the trend in the near future.
>
> Despite this fact, there are good grounds for the contention that Negro coal miners constitute one of the more favorably situated groups in the colored working-class world. In the first place, while total employment has shrunk drastically, employment of Negroes has decreased only to a minor extent. Secondly, the occupational status of the Negro coal mine worker has always been, and still is, practically on par with that of the white worker—a state of affairs almost unknown outside of this industry. And, finally, as we have already intimated, he is afforded the protection of a union organization which proclaims, and adheres to, a policy of full racial equality.[c]

In 1930 there were 58,000 Negro coal miners,[d] or 43 per cent more than in 1910, whereas the number of white workers was about the same as in 1910. The bulk of the Negro workers was in West Virginia, Alabama, Kentucky and Pennsylvania. Most of the Negro miners in Pennsylvania had come there after 1910, often as strike-breakers, and since total employment in the Pennsylvania mines decreased between 1910 and 1930, they had actually displaced some white workers. In spite of this northward migration, the number of Negro miners remained insignificant in the North. In no Northern state did they constitute as much as 3 per cent of the labor force in the coal mines, and about four-fifths of them were still in the South in 1930. Negroes had been able to better their relative position because the Southern fields had gained much at the expense of Northern mines (even to the extent of having more mine workers in 1930 than in 1920, whereas the country as a whole showed a loss in employment during this period). The Southern mines had been unimportant around 1900, but by 1927 the coal production in West Virginia, Kentucky, and Virginia alone temporarily surpassed that of Pennsylvania, Ohio, Indiana and Illinois. These gains were partly due to improvements in the transportation facilities in the South and to technical factors.

A third and very significant reason was the regional wage differential. The South, most of the time, had nonunion labor, whereas Northern operators had to pay higher union rates. As a result, the number of days worked per year was usually higher in the South than in the North, where it dwindled to 130-140 days during the depressions of the

[a] Norgren and Associates, *op. cit.*, Part 3, pp. 270-271.

[b] There are but few Negroes employed in anthracite coal mining.

[c] Norgren and Associates, *op. cit.*, Part 4, p. 396. Norgren's reference (*) is to: National Labor Relations Board, *The Effect of Labor Relations in the Bituminous Coal Industry upon Interstate Commerce* (1938), Bulletin No. 2, p. 59.

[d] Anthracite coal mining included.

early 'twenties and 'thirties. In 1927, the Northern employers managed to get rid of the union contract and were able to cut their wage costs so that they regained a large part of their previous losses to the Southern fields. They have been able to maintain this position. When the New Deal brought about new wage minima and gave new power to the unions, the regional wage differential was kept small [a] and, in 1941, it was virtually eliminated.

By and large, the Negroes failed to get their proportionate share of the employment gains in the South. Therefore, the proportion of Negroes among the Southern coal mine workers declined from 35 per cent in 1910 to 19 per cent in 1930, whereas the Northern coal fields accepted a somewhat increased proportion of Negro workers. During the 'thirties there was a continual loss in relative position for Negro miners in the South. About 46,000 Negro workers (including unemployed persons) were registered as coal miners in the 1930 Census, and they constituted 19 per cent of the total. In 1930 there were 35,000 employed Negro coal miners in the South, making up 16 per cent of the total. There was only a small difference between the corresponding absolute numbers for white workers.[b]

The outlook for the Negro is doubtful. It is possible that the general long employment trends will not go as steeply downward as they did during most of the period 1920-1940. On the other hand, the South has lost the competitive advantage of a nonunion wage scale. Since the increase in wages has been greater in the South than elsewhere, it is likely that mechanization will be particularly pronounced in the South. Norgren and Northrup have noticed a tendency to mechanize the loading operations in Southern coal fields. It will probably hurt Negroes more than whites for several reasons: first, because Negroes are concentrated both in the South and in the hand-loading jobs; second, because whites are usually selected as operators of mechanical loaders. (One factor in this selectivity is that mechanical loading is crew work while hand loading is a highly individualized occupation.) The United Mine Workers Union, which otherwise protects Negroes, has been reluctant to resist such favoritism.[c] The present war boom may

[a] Norgren and Associates, *op. cit.*, Part 4, pp. 406-417.

The wage level in West Virginia, Kentucky and Virginia declined from an average of 82 cents an hour in 1921-22 to 70 cents in 1924, whereas the Northern fields (Pennsylvania, Ohio, Indiana, and Illinois) almost maintained their level of 1921-1922 (89 cents) up until about 1927, when union conditions were abolished in most of them. The average wage, by 1933, hit a low of 37 cents in the Upper South, as against 46 cents in Illinois, Indiana, Ohio and Pennsylvania. Then followed an increase under the New Deal. By 1936 the averages were 77 cents in the North and 74 cents in the Upper South. In 1941 a basic daily wage rate of $7 was adopted for both Northern and Southern Appalachian area. The rate in Alabama, however, is lower ($5), partly because this state does not compete with the others, but probably also because it has the highest proportion of Negro workers in the coal mines. (See: F. E. Berquist and Associates, *Economic Survey of the Bituminous Coal Industry under Free Competition and Code Regulation* [mimeographed], National Recovery Administration, Work Materials No. 69 [1936], 2 vols. Also, Table 4 in Norgren, *op. cit.*, Part 4, p. 436, and Northrup, *op. cit.*, p. 290.)

[b] *Fifteenth Census of the United States: 1930, Population*, Vol. 3, Part 1, p. 23; *Sixteenth Census of the United States: 1940 Population*, Second Series, State Tables 18a and 18b.

[c] Norgren and Associates, *op. cit.*, Part 4, pp. 417-419, and letter from Paul H. Norgren, August 16, 1942. See also Northrup, *op. cit.*, pp. 296-301.

counteract this trend temporarily; it is possible that the scarcity of white labor will give the Negroes an increased share of the jobs. On the other hand, there is the danger of overexpansion which will increase the general post-war unemployment. It is impossible to say anything definite on these important matters.

As previously mentioned, unionism, until the New Deal era, was much weaker in the South than in the North. Yet there have been determined attempts since the 1880's to unionize the Southern coal industry. These attempts were sometimes successful, but only for short periods. Time and again the union was defeated by employers, who utilized all sorts of brutal tactics. In this they were usually supported by groups of white citizens who were incited by the race issue.[a] These defeats, as well as the subsequent abolishment of union contracts in the northern Appalachian area, could not fail to weaken the United Mine Workers, but the organization was by no means crushed. It had been fighting hard and from the very beginning had developed a technique of equalitarian collaboration between white and black labor which turned out to be highly useful. The continued wage cuts during the Great Depression of the 'thirties, the unemployment which eventually brought great numbers of mine workers to starvation, as well as memories of the previous fight, all prepared the ground for a determined comeback. The opportunity came with the New Deal. With the institution of the N.R.A. a big organizing campaign was launched, North as well as South. The response was impressive. Within a few months the overwhelming majority of mine workers was unionized. The employers tried to play up the race issue, and they spread rumors to the effect that either Negroes or whites would lose everything by putting the union into power. This time it failed. Then, too, the mine operators were weak. Many of them were impoverished, and some had come to realize the futility of using the wage-cut method as a competitive instrument. Pressure from the government aided the union. Almost the whole field is now covered by contracts. Negroes and whites are organized in the same locals, often with a white president and a Negro vice-president—an arrangement which has been adopted in order to have a white representative to contact employers and yet give the Negroes a voice in the decisions whenever they constitute an appreciable proportion of the workers. There may still be a small amount of bad racial feeling, but the leadership takes energetic action against any local which does not recognize the principle of racial equality and collaboration. The policy of "gradualism" adopted by the union has given results. At the beginning, when employers had to get used to the idea of discussing work problems with representatives of labor, the unions were sometimes reluctant to include Negroes among their representatives at these discussions. Today, even in Alabama, Negroes take part in all such discussions and argue quite as freely as whites. They probably have gained more than whites through the collective settlement of all sorts of petty grievances, since they were formerly more easily subjected to arbitrary treatment by foremen. Then, too, more than whites, they are concentrated in piece-rate work, where there is need for constant adjustments because of the variation in yield of different work places. These policies seem to have brought about an increased mutual understanding between the two racial groups. Speaking of the conditions in Birmingham, Norgren says:

> Informants among both leaders and rank-and-file members testify that social intercourse between workers of the two races is much more common to-day than it was prior to the

[a] Spero and Harris, *op. cit.*, pp. 357-375.

advent of organization. Colored unionists contribute freely to discussions at union business meetings; white delegates shake hands with Negro delegates at district council assemblages without displaying repugnance or embarrassment; Negroes and whites ride together in the mine cages. Only in social gatherings is the "jim crow" custom retained unchanged.[a]

Perhaps still more important is the fact that seniority rules—regardless of race—have been adopted in both the dismissal and the rehiring of workers.[b]

13. IRON AND STEEL WORKERS

The iron, steel, vehicle, machinery, and other metal industries had, in 1930, 177,000 Negro workers, over 60 per cent of whom resided outside the South. Except for the building industry, no other manufacturing branch had as many Negro workers. The increase since 1910 was tremendous; the number of Negro workers was between three and four times greater in 1930 than two decades earlier; whereas the number of white workers had not even doubled. Still, Negroes constituted but 5 per cent of the total labor force in the iron, steel and vehicle industries.[c]

The largest industries in the group, from the point of view of Negro employment, were blast furnaces and steel rolling mills, which had 53,000 Negro workers in 1930; automobile factories (26,000); and car and railroad shops (16,000).[d] In this section, we focus our attention on the first group, and we shall consider the second one in a following section.

The condition of the Negro in the basic steel industry is rather similar to that in the coal mining industry. Both are "heavy" industries, in need of great numbers of unskilled workers and subject to pronounced business cycle variations. Of great practical importance for the Negro is the somewhat accidental fact that the present union leaders have been recruited from United Mine Workers officials and, therefore, are more likely to adhere to a philosophy of racial cooperation. There are also striking dissimilarities: whereas most Negro mine workers are in the South, no less than 72 per cent of the Negro steel mill workers were employed in the North and West in 1930. More important is the fact that the occupational pattern in the steel mills is much more heterogeneous than in the mine fields. There are marked wage differentials between various skilled groups. This made it more difficult to organize white and black labor on the basis of equalitarianism. This fact, in conjunction with the great power of the large concerns dominating the production of steel, has made it difficult to organize any union at all.[e]

Steel production, except for cyclical fluctuations, is an expanding industry. Therefore, to achieve equality in the steel industry would be worth more to the Negro than the progress he has made as a mine worker. By 1910 there were almost as many Negro workers in basic steel plants in the North as in the South, where the steel industry was unimportant. The number of Negro workers in Northern steel plants was between four

[a] Norgren and Associates, *op. cit.*, Part 4, p. 445.
[b] The last three paragraphs are based on *ibid.*, Part 4, pp. 441-448, and Northrup, *op. cit.*, pp. 280-301.
[c] *Fifteenth Census of the United States: 1930, Population*, Vol. 5, pp. 408-411.
[d] *Fifteenth Census of the United States: 1930, Population*, Vol. 3, Part 1, p. 23; U.S. Bureau of the Census, *Negroes in the United States: 1920-1932*, pp. 343-346.
[e] Norgren and Associates, *op. cit.*, Part 4. pp. 451-452.

and five times greater in 1920 than in 1910, largely because of the expansion of the steel industry during the First World War. In the South, Negroes gained much less, or about 80 per cent, although the general expansion in blast furnaces and steel rolling mills was much more pronounced than in the North. Negroes, however, got somewhat more than their proportionate share of the new jobs in Southern mills. The 'twenties brought a general decline in the basic steel industry. Again, Negroes fared better in the North, where they had almost the same number of steel workers in 1930 as in 1920. In the South, the decrease was somewhat more pronounced for Negro than for white workers. During the 'thirties, also, the Negro lost in relative position in the South. If we add together the figures for both basic steel production and manufacturing of machinery and transportation equipment (except automobiles), we find that, in 1940, the number of *employed* white workers in the South was almost as high as the number of *both employed and unemployed* white workers in 1930; for Negroes there was a substantial difference between the two figures. The 40,000 Negro employed workers in 1940 constituted only 15 per cent of the total in the South; whereas the proportion of Negroes among those registered as gainful workers in steel and machinery production in 1930 had amounted to 19 per cent.[a]

More than three out of every four Negro workers in blast furnaces and steel rolling mills were classified as unskilled in 1930. One in seven was a semi-skilled worker, and one in fourteen a skilled worker. On the other hand, about one-half of the native whites and one-fourth of the foreign-born whites were skilled, clerical or managerial workers. The Negroes had a higher representation in the skilled crafts than they had in most other industries, but this was largely a result of the composition of the labor force in this industry. In relation to other groups, their position was about as unfavorable as in most other industries. The skilled Negro workers are largely concentrated in hot and disagreeable work, such as furnace jobs. There is reluctance to use Negroes in such skilled work as machinists do; little more than 1 per cent of those workers were Negroes. The situation, if anything, seems to have deteriorated rather than improved. There had been a slightly greater proportion of skilled craftsmen among Negro steel workers in 1910 and a lower proportion of semi-skilled workers. The proportion that Negro workers constituted of all workers had more than doubled in the unskilled and semi-skilled categories from 1910 to 1930, but increased only to a small extent for skilled and higher groups. Indeed, the major part of the increased need for common laborers had been met by hiring more Negro workers. But the general expansion in unskilled occupations was much smaller than that in higher categories, so that the habit of using Negroes predominantly in the lower jobs put a limit to their chance of increasing their share in the total employment.[b]

The wage level in the steel industry, as previously noted, is characterized by great differences in earnings between skilled and unskilled workers. This is particularly true in the South, where the general level is comparatively low, especially for common

[a] *Fifteenth Census of the United States: 1930, Population,* Vol. 3, Part 1, p. 23. *Sixteenth Census of the United States: 1940, Population,* Second Series, State Tables 18a and 18b. Norgren and Associates, *op. cit.,* Part 4, p. 456.

[b] U.S. Bureau of the Census, Alba M. Edwards, *Social-Economic Grouping of the Gainful Workers of the United States, 1930* (1938), pp. 100 and 130. *Thirteenth Census of the United States: 1910, Population,* Vol. 4, Table 6. Norgren and Associates, *op. cit.,* Part 4, pp. 471 and 473.

laborers. There has been some equalization of both the regional and the occupational wage differentials; at the same time the general level has been raised considerably.[a] Most of the traditional characteristics of the wage structure still persist, however, and they are behind the racial wage differentials mirrored in the following figures for April, 1938:

	Negro	White	Differential
North	$.74	$.86	$.12
South	.54	.75	.21

Source: U.S. Bureau of Labor Statistics, "Earnings of Negro Workers in the Iron and Steel Industry April, 1938", *Monthly Labor Review*, (November, 1940), p. 1140.

Comparing these figures with an earlier sample study for 1935, one finds that there has been a general increase in wages for both Negro and white workers. The Negro-white differential seems to have become somewhat smaller in the South even in terms of cents per hour but has remained almost unchanged in the North.[b] The main impression conveyed by these data, however, is that, in spite of all racial injustice in the apportionment of jobs, the Negro steel worker, particularly in the North, enjoys relatively high wages compared with other Negro wage earners. It should be kept in mind that the increase in cost for unskilled labor may influence mechanization trends in a way which may be unfavorable to the Negro. He cannot be assured of any real future in the steel industry unless allowed the benefit of a wider range of occupational opportunities.

Behind the wage increases during the 'thirties were the new federal minimum wage regulations and the Steel Workers Organizing Committee (S.W.O.C.)—later called The United Steel Workers of America. This union has been the first which has consistently given real protection to the Negro. There was a long and hard struggle to organize this union, and during the early stages Negroes were excluded. The only time before the 'thirties when the Negro was shown any real consideration was in 1918, when the first noteworthy attempt was made to organize unskilled steel workers in Alabama; employers, playing up the race issue and using violence and intimidation, managed to defeat the unions completely.[c] In 1919 an attempt was made to organize the whole steel industry on a broad basis under the leadership of a joint committee representing several unions in the field. The unions were disastrously defeated in this year, and thereafter the Amalgamated was completely inactive. Negroes were frequently

[a] U.S. Bureau of Labor Statistics, "Earnings and Hours in Bar, Puddling, Sheet-Bar, Rod, Wire, and Sheet Mills, 1933 and 1935," *Monthly Labor Review* (July, 1936), p. 117; "Earnings and Hours in the Iron and Steel Industry, April, 1938," *Monthly Labor Review* (August, 1940), pp. 421-442; "Earnings and Hours in the Iron and Steel Industry," Part 2, *Monthly Labor Review* (September, 1940), pp. 709-726; "Annual Earnings in the Iron and Steel Industry, 1937," *Monthly Labor Review* (October, 1940), pp. 823-833; "Earnings of Negro Workers in the Iron and Steel Industry, April, 1938," *Monthly Labor Review* (November, 1940), pp. 1139-1149.

[b] U.S. Bureau of Labor Statistics, "Earnings of Negroes in the Iron and Steel Industry," *Monthly Labor Review* (March, 1937), p. 566. Quoted in Norgren and Associates, *op. cit.*, Part 4, p. 476.

[c] Spero and Harris, *op. cit.*, pp. 247-252.

used in strike-breaking in the steel industry. It is said that the employers used some 30,000 Negro strike-breakers in the 1919 strike, and although the union gave some attention to obtaining Negro support, no considerable number of Negroes was ever organized.

The N.R.A. brought about an extremely rapid increase in unionism, but the leadership of the Amalgamated Association of Iron, Steel and Tin Workers (A.F. of L.) failed to give this movement much encouragement and even showed some hostility to it. A decision of the A.F. of L. convention of 1934 to organize the iron and steel industry was sabotaged by the A.F. of L. leadership, which permitted craft unions to "raid" newly organized units dividing the workers among the various crafts. In 1936 the C.I.O. organized the Steel Workers' Organizing Committee (S.W.O.C.), which started an energetic and successful membership drive. In 1937 it won its most spectacular victory when the United States Steel Corporation signed a contract.[a] Now nearly all major steel plants are covered by union contracts.

This new unionism in steel meant a change in the position of the Negro. He had been taken in as an equal by many of the company unions during the N.R.A. period, and also by communist and independent local leaders. The fact that the leadership of the S.W.O.C. was largely recruited from the Mine Workers meant that his position became even more secure. Negroes in most cases responded enthusiastically to unionization efforts. Wherever Negroes constitute a large part of the workers they get some representation in the local leadership, often, as in the Alabama district, a vice-presidency. The employers in the South have tried to play up the race issue and they encouraged some municipalities to pass city ordinances forbidding joint meetings of white and Negro workers; this time it availed little.[b]

The standard S.W.O.C. contract stipulates that seniority shall be followed for dismissals and in rehiring.[c] It is doubtful whether a similar principle will be adhered to in the case of promotions even though the contract contains a clause to that effect. Norgren points to the heterogeneous occupational pattern in the steel industry which makes it difficult to induce the white workers to go the whole way in racial equalitarianism. He adds:

If this problem [abolishment of racial discrimination in promotion] does not iron itself out in the local unions—and it is hardly probable that it will—it would seem to fall to the national union leaders to lead the way in solving it. As far as the writer has been able to learn, the heads of the S.W.O.C. have not, up to now, given the question serious consideration. This neglect is probably justified to a considerable extent, since the steel union has as yet scarcely developed beyond the organization stage. There is little doubt, however, that sooner or later the problem will come to the fore. And the manner in which it is handled should provide an acid test of the workability of the racial equality idea in the union movement.[d]

In 1940 an A.F. of L. union succeeded in winning an election at a Birmingham plant by promising the Negro workers help in getting promoted.[e] This seems to indicate

[a] Norgren and Associates, op. cit., Part 4, pp. 490-502.
[b] Northrup, op. cit., p. 326.
[c] Norgren and Associates, op. cit., Part 4, p. 505, and Horace R. Cayton and George S. Mitchell, *Black Workers and the New Unions* (1939), pp. 202-212.
[d] Norgren and Associates, op. cit., Part 4, p. 506.
[e] Northrup, op. cit., p. 342.

that the problem has made itself felt rather severely in some places. Even if the union's present policy of "gradualism" in this matter [a] can easily be understood, there is no doubt that the issue will soon have to be faced. It is obvious that Negro workers need a larger share of the semi-skilled and skilled jobs to minimize their risk of technological displacement.

14. AUTOMOBILE WORKERS [b]

In 1930 there were 26,000 Negro workers in the automobile industry, constituting 4 per cent of the total number of workers. The automobile industry does not, therefore, constitute a major source of Negro employment. It is, however, one of the few industries in which the Negro has managed to get a foothold since the Civil War. Even if the Negro's gains in the automobile industry are not spectacular, it is remarkable that he has done as well in this Northern industry as he has in the Southern textile mills.

The explanation of this phenomenon is not difficult to find. It was during the First World War, with its accompanying scarcity of labor, that the automobile industry started to become of major importance in American manufacturing. Recruiting of labor was a major problem, particularly in Detroit where there was no large local labor supply to begin with. That almost 60 per cent of all Negro automobile workers were employed in Michigan in 1930 and that some concerns which have plants in several places give no employment to Negroes except in or around Detroit confirms the contention that it was because of an initial shortage of labor in Detroit that the Negro was able to make so much headway in the automobile industry. It should not be overlooked that Southern whites have come in even greater numbers to Detroit.

> It is common today for automobile factory employment officials to estimate that anywhere from 20 to 60 per cent of their employees are Southern whites while Negroes seldom exceed more than 10 per cent except in individual foundry establishments.[c]

Not only are the Negro automobile workers distributed geographically in an uneven way but also the distribution among various concerns and plants is anything but proportionate. This, of course, suggests that the Negro gains may be accidental. Negroes constitute a rather high proportion among the employees of the parts manufacturers which are subject to severe price competition and cannot afford to pay high wages. The leading employer of Negroes among the main manufacturers is the Ford Motor Company which, at the beginning of 1940, had almost 10,000 Negro workers in Michigan. Almost all of them were employed in the River Rouge plant, where they constituted almost 12 per cent of the labor force. Next came the Briggs Manufacturing Corporation which had 3,000 Negro workers in the Detroit area, where they constituted more than one-fifth of the total labor force. General Motors Corporation, on the other hand, had a much smaller proportion of Negro workers, about 2,500, or 2.5 per cent of

[a] Herbert R. Northrup has certain scattered and impressionistic evidence to the effect that the union actually has helped Negroes get promoted in several Northern plants (*ibid.*, p. 344).

[b] The extensive material on the Negro in the automobile industry contained in Norgren and Associates, *op. cit.*, Part 4, pp. 513-642, was collected by Lloyd H. Bailer, who, under the supervision and guidance of Dr. Norgren, conducted an extensive series of interviews in Detroit, and wrote the main part of the chapter.

[c] Norgren and Associates, *op, cit.*, Part 4, p. 534. See, also, pp. 533, 541-544.

all its workers in Michigan and Indiana. Chrysler had 2,000 Negroes, making up 4 per cent of its Detroit labor force.[a]

Nearly three-fourths of all Negro workers in the automobile industry in 1930 were in unskilled occupations; the corresponding proportion for white workers was less than one-fifth. One-eighth of the Negro workers, but almost one-half of the white workers, were in skilled and clerical occupations. The range of job opportunities for Negro automobile workers is usually narrower than these figures suggest. Negroes are invariably concentrated in service jobs, foundries and paint departments.[b] Some of the Negro foundry workers and painters are in skilled jobs, but Norgren and Bailer say:

> Negro operatives and skilled workers in these departments . . . are almost invariably employed in such hazardous occupations as shear operators, heaters, spraymen, chippers, rough snag grinders and sand blasters and in other operations undesirable because they are dirty, dusty, extremely hot, or are accompanied by fumes.[c]

An inquiry among company officials and workers suggested that the main reason for this condition was the opposition of the white workers—many of whom are Southerners—to collaboration with Negroes. Concerning the attitudes of employers' representatives, there are certain data assembled by Norgren and Bailer. Most employers' representatives who had any appreciable experience with Negro workers seemed inclined to think that Negroes were about as efficient as whites, although some added qualifications to the effect that Negroes compared "favorably with whites on the work they perform."[d] Several officials believed, of course, in the general stereotype that Negroes are particularly able to stand hot work.[e] One employers' representative pointed to the difficulty of Negroes' getting training as skilled workers. He believed, in addition, that it was possible to secure a higher percentage of skilled workers from a group of white workers than from a group of Negro workers; for this reason, he explained, employers preferred to get their craftsmen from the whites, although there are individual Negroes who are potentially just as good. Another informant gave this very interesting viewpoint:

> It seems to me the average colored worker is more loyal to his boss than to his job. If he likes his boss, he will work himself to death, but if he doesn't like him he won't do a thing. The white worker is different. I've known white workers who simply hated their foremen but they did good work out of loyalty to the job itself.[f]

The River Rouge plant of the Ford Motor Company, which has the largest proportion of Negroes of all major Detroit automobile factories, differs in other respects from the general pattern. The Negro has a share of the jobs in almost all departments. He

---

[a] *Ibid.*, Part 4, pp. 526 and 539-545.

[b] U. S. Bureau of the Census, Alba M. Edwards, *Social-Economic Grouping of the Gainful Workers of the United States, 1930* (1938), pp. 98-99.

[c] Norgren and Associates, *op. cit.*, Part 4, p. 549. The statement is backed up by a detailed analysis of job specifications in several of the major Detroit plants (*ibid.*, pp. 552-559 and 649-652).

[d] *Ibid.*, Part 4, pp. 572-589.

[e] Such a capacity has been attributed to all marginal groups of workers such as South Europeans, Negroes, and Mexicans who have had to content themselves with such jobs as appeared unattractive to the dominant group. (Glen E. Carlson, "The Negro in the Industries of Detroit," unpublished doctoral dissertation, University of Michigan (1929). Quoted in Norgren and Associates, *op. cit.*, Part 4, p. 573.)

[f] *Ibid.*, Part 4, p. 574.

does not, however, have full equality of opportunities; the occupational status of the Negro worker at the Ford plant differs only in degree from that of Negro workers in other plants. In 1937 about half the Negro workers were in the foundry of the River Rouge plant, where they constituted 47 per cent of all the workers. In the tool rooms scarcely 1 per cent of the workers were Negro. Still, the Negroes have a better chance to advance in this factory than they have almost anywhere else.[a]

This difference between the River Rouge plant and other major automobile factories is not accidental. In 1921, when layoffs occurred because of the post-war depression, some Negro leaders approached Henry Ford asking him not to dismiss Negroes in any discriminatory manner. Ford then set down the policy that Negroes should make up the same proportion of the workers as corresponded to their proportion in the population of Detroit, and that they should be represented in all departments of his company. He has appointed some Negro officials in his personnel department who do the hiring of Negroes and have the right to interfere should any discriminatory practices occur. It is claimed that these Negro personnel officials have put pressure on the workers in political matters and, until Ford gave in to the union in 1941, in matters of labor organization. Although conditions even in other respects are not ideal, they are far better than in other automobile plants, and Negro leaders generally characterize them in this way.[b] Negro and white Ford workers are not segregated in the work rooms, which sometimes happens in other factories. White workers may object to this condition, but the opposition is not nearly as widespread nowadays as it used to be in the early 'twenties when Negroes started to become a prominent part of the Ford labor force. The fact that the company's policy on this issue is well known makes the white workers realize that opposition would be of little avail. The Ford training school was, until about 1940, the only major automobile trade school in Detroit which admitted Negro workers.[c]

Daily wage rates are comparatively high in the automobile industry, but work has been insecure. There are seasonal variations in the need for labor. Since the beginning of the 'thirties, the cyclical variations have been worse. The drive for efficiency has put a premium on youth. It is frequently claimed that new workers are being hired while good, well-trained workers are walking the streets.[d]

The automobile industry was not well organized until the C.I.O. organized the United Automobile Workers' Union in 1936-1937. The United Automobile Workers' Union (now the United Automobile, Aircraft and Agricultural Implements Workers' Union) includes the Negro on a basis of equality. Negroes have been represented in the leadership from the beginning. Yet for a long time the Negro was a poor union member. Bailer, when making a survey of all U.A.W. locals in Detroit in 1940, found that more than three-fourths of the white workers, but not much more than one-half of the Negroes, in plants under the jurisdiction of these locals were organized by that time. Moreover, there were general complaints about Negroes showing less interest than whites in union work. Some Negroes served as strike-breakers at a Dodge walk-out in 1939, and the same thing happened in the Ford factories in 1941. The reasons for this condition are obvious. Negroes have been unaccustomed to union work. As long as Ford

[a] *Ibid.*, Part 4, pp. 559-570 and 649-652.
[b] *Ibid.*, Part 4, pp. 589 and 599-652.
[c] *Ibid.*, Part 4, pp. 589 and 599-624.
[d] *Ibid.*, Part 4, pp. 527-531.

held out against unionism, it is quite understandable that many Negroes were reluctant to join in the fight. The high proportion of white Southerners in the Detroit labor force made the union members disinclined to accept the equalitarian philosophy of the leaders. Segregation in social affairs of workers had been customary. It could not be abolished immediately, partly because real estate and restaurant owners who catered to union social affairs often supported segregational practices. Bailer found, however, in 1940 and again in 1942, that conditions were constantly improving. Ford's surrender to the unions has probably precipitated this development.[a]

The problem of promotion remains a major difficulty. White workers would probably not object to the granting of departmental seniority rights to the Negro. In order to get full equality of opportunity the Negro must have a chance for promotion not only within departments, but also from one department to another. In 1940, according to Bailer, the white workers objected so much to the granting of such rights to Negroes that it seemed impossible that they would get them in the near future.[b] Definite progress has been made during the present war boom. It is reported that Negroes have been moved from foundry shop in one establishment to skilled work in other departments of other establishments.[c]

This description of the conditions in the automobile industry is largely historical. The conversion to war use has brought about an entirely new situation, which, at the present time, is rather difficult to survey. Elsewhere we have assembled some scattered information on this development.[d]

15. THE SLAUGHTERING AND MEAT-PACKING INDUSTRY

The slaughtering and meat-packing industry had 18,000 Negro employees in 1930, constituting 11 per cent of its total labor force. It is not of great importance as a source of employment to Negroes, and yet it is the only food industry which has any appreciable number of Negro workers. The story of labor in the slaughter and packing houses is full of racial strife. It is a good illustration of how race prejudice, while usually limiting opportunities for the Negro, sometimes helps him.[e]

About three-fourths of the Negro workers in 1930 were employed outside the South, and one-third of the Northern workers were in Illinois, where they constituted roughly 30 per cent of the total unskilled and semi-skilled labor force. The proportion of Negroes among such workers was as high or almost as high in some of the secondary Northern slaughtering centers located in Missouri, Kansas and Nebraska. Among the skilled workers, Negroes generally had few representatives, and at each occupational level they tended to be more concentrated in heavy or distasteful work than were white employees.[f]

This, however, is less surprising than is the fact that the Negro makes up such a large

[a] *Ibid.*, Part 4, pp. 626-639. Interview with Lloyd H. Bailer, August 3, 1942.
[b] *Idem.*
[c] Interview with Lloyd H. Bailer, August 3, 1942.
[d] See Chapter 19.
[e] The chapter on the slaughtering and meat-packing industry in Norgren and Associates, *op. cit.*, Part 4, pp. 653-698, was written by Arnold M. Rose. The basic sources were census reports, Alma Herbst, *The Negro in the Slaughtering and Meat-Packing Industry in Chicago* (1932), and Cayton and Mitchell, *op. cit.*, pp. 228-279.
[f] Norgren and Associates, *op. cit.*, Part 4, pp. 659-671.

part of the labor force in some of the Northern centers. This was not so originally. Kansas and Missouri had an appreciable proportion of Negro workers in 1910, but the increase during the First World War was such that by 1920 this proportion had become two or three times higher. Even more spectacular was the development in Chicago. Negroes had been used as strike-breakers in 1894 and, particularly, in 1904. Few of these Negro strike-breakers were allowed to stay, and by 1910 there were only about 500 Negro workers in the Chicago stockyards. The subsequent increase was due to three factors: (1) the scarcity of labor during the First World War; (2) the interest the packers had in keeping the labor force heterogeneous when a unionization drive was started in 1916 and 1917 by the Amalgamated Meat Cutters and Butcher Workmen, and the Stockyards Labor Council; and (3) the fact that, while some unions did accept Negroes, there were several others which "drew the color line sharply" or discriminated against them in other ways, and this alienated many Negro workers.[a] In other words, the packers made a definite policy of increasing the proportion of Negro workers, and the equivocal stand of the unions on the race issue ensured them of success. The unions could not fail to see this danger, and an energetic attempt was made to win the Negro workers over. It met with some response from the Negroes, but the race riot of 1919, due in part to the increase in the proportion of Negro workers in the stockyards and to "the conflict between union workers and packing house employers for the allegiance of Negro workers," made these attempts fail.[b] During a strike in December, 1921, and January, 1922, Negroes were used as strike-breakers. The workers were completely defeated, and unionism in the Chicago stockyards was practically eliminated for a decade.[c]

During the 'twenties Negroes lost in relative position in some of the secondary Northern meat-packing centers. In Chicago, on the other hand, they continued to gain, in that the actual number of Negro workers was slightly increased between 1920 and 1930, although the total labor force in the stockyards showed some decrease.[d] When unionism returned to the Chicago packing houses during the New Deal, Negroes continued to be rather "poor union material." There was a three-cornered battle among company unions, the Amalgamated Meat Cutters and Butcher Workmen (A.F. of L.) and the Packing House Workers' Industrial Union (C.I.O.) The Amalgamated was still unable to go the whole way on the Negro issue; often there was racial segregation in social affairs, and the representation of Negroes among the leaders was not high enough to appeal to the Negroes. The Packing House Workers are said to have been dominated (at least formerly) by communist leaders. Employers continued to intimidate union members to such an extent that Negroes, who had always gained more by siding with the employers, were reluctant to join the independent unions in large numbers.[e] Recently, there have been reports that the C.I.O. union has become a dominant influence in the major Chicago plants,[f] and this may have increased the prospects for a final victory for the kind of unionism which will appeal to Negro workers.

[a] Cayton and Mitchell, op. cit., pp. 242-246.

[b] Ibid., p. 247.

[c] Norgren and Associates, op. cit., Part 4, p. 676.

[d] Ibid., Part 4, pp. 661-665.

[e] Ibid., Part 4, pp. 689-694. Cayton and Mitchell, op. cit., pp. 262-279.

[f] Information from Howard D. Gould of the Chicago Urban League (letter of May 21, 1942).

Concerning the wage level, we may refer to the following average figures contained in a study in 1937 by the Department of Labor.

| Section and Race | Males | | | | Females |
	Total	Skilled	Semi-skilled	Unskilled	
The North					
Negroes	$.71	$.84	$.71	$.63	$.53
Whites	.69	.82	.67	.60	.51
The South					
Negroes	.46	.54	.49	.40	a
Whites	.53	.67	.50	.45	.38

Source: U.S. Bureau of Labor Statistics, "Earnings and Hours in the Meat-Packing Industry, December 1937," Monthly Labor Review (October, 1939), p. 953.
a Number of workers in sample too small for computing of average.

We find that the wage structure is characterized by a rather large differential between North and South. In Northern states there is the rather exceptional phenomenon that Negroes at each occupational level and also in general, earned slightly more per hour than did whites. This is probably due to the fact that Negro workers, more than whites, are concentrated in some of the largest plants. In the South, on the other hand, Negroes usually earned less than whites, not only generally but also at each occupational level.

DISTRIBUTION OF NEGRO RESIDENCES IN
SELECTED CITIES

This description of the distribution of Negro residences in selected cities should be read in connection with the description of residential segregation in Chapter 29, Section 3.

There have been Negroes in New York for hundreds of years.[a] At first they tended to live in close proximity to the homes of the wealthy whites in whose residences they were employed as servants. This caused them to live in little concentrations in several sections of the city. Some of these nests still persist, but the new migrants to New York tended to live together in a section which moved northward on Manhattan Island in the wake of the upper class whites. About 1900 the main Negro center was in the vicinity of West Fifty-third Street and was no longer a satellite community to that of the rich whites. It contained "three rather well-appointed hotels"[b] and was as much an independent community as can be found among any ethnic group in New York except the Chinese. At the same time, the large Brooklyn Negro community also was developing. The last and biggest shift was from the middle of Manhattan to Harlem. Commerce and industry were moving uptown, and new residential opportunities opened to Negroes in Harlem after 1900:

> Harlem had been overbuilt with large, new-law apartment houses, but rapid transportation to that section was very inadequate—the Lenox Avenue Subway had not yet been built—and landlords were finding difficulty in keeping houses on the east side of the section filled. Residents along and near Seventh Avenue were fairly well served by the Eighth Avenue Elevated. A colored man, in the real estate business at this time, Philip A. Payton, approached several of these landlords with the proposition that he would fill their empty or partially empty houses with steady colored tenants. The suggestion was accepted, and one or two houses on One Hundred and Thirty-fourth Street east of Lenox Avenue were taken over. Gradually other houses were filled. The whites paid little attention to the movement until it began to spread west of Lenox Avenue; they then took steps to check it. They proposed through a financial organization, the Hudson Realty Company, to buy in all properties occupied by colored people and evict the tenants. The Negroes countered by similar methods. . . .

[a] This description of the distribution of Negroes in New York is taken largely from the following two sources:

James Weldon Johnson, "Harlem: the Culture Capital," in Alain Locke (editor), *The New Negro* (1925), pp. 301-311.

E. Franklin Frazier, "Negro Harlem: An Ecological Study," *American Journal of Sociology* (July, 1937), pp. 72-88.

[b] James Weldon Johnson, *op. cit.*, p. 302.

The situation now resolved itself into an actual contest. Negroes not only continued to occupy available apartment houses, but began to purchase private dwellings between Lenox and Seventh Avenues. Then the whole movement, in the eyes of the whites, took on the aspect of an "invasion"; they became panic-stricken and began fleeing as from a plague. The presence of one colored family in a block, no matter how well bred and orderly, was sufficient to precipitate a flight. House after house and block after block was actually deserted. It was a great demonstration of human beings running amuck. None of them stopped to reason why they were doing it or what would happen if they didn't. The banks and lending companies holding mortgages on these deserted houses were compelled to take them over. For some time they held these houses vacant, preferring to do that and carry the charges than to rent or sell them to colored people. But values dropped and continued to drop until at the outbreak of the war in Europe property in the northern part of Harlem had reached the nadir.

In the meantime the Negro colony was becoming more stable; the churches were being moved from the lower part of the city; social and civic centers were being formed; and gradually a community was being evolved. Following the outbreak of the war in Europe Negro Harlem received a new and tremendous impetus.[a]

The Great Migration from the South greatly expanded [b] and stabilized the Harlem area. To a limited extent, Negroes bought houses—often fine old mansions—as well as rented them, and opened their own stores as well as traded with local white store-keepers. With the continuing migration of Negroes into New York, Harlem is still expanding, but not in proportion to the increase in its population. Outside pressures and the growth of a well-to-do Negro class has forced and permitted the building of large structures containing many small apartments.

It is difficult and hazardous to make predictions. If, as is generally assumed, New York's commerce and industry do not expand to any considerable extent in the future, Negroes are not likely to be pushed out of Harlem. Harlem can grow spatially also. Harlem has a glamour of its own which will continue to attract Negroes from all over the country even if employment opportunities are not too bright, and they might become better off than they were during the 'thirties, particularly if the New York Negroes can more effectively use their political power to break down economic discrimination. The newcomers will, as usual, be forced to seek residence in established Negro communities. The Brooklyn settlement is growing, but so is Harlem, and it is likely that Harlem will remain the center of New York's Negro population and, in a sense, the cultural capital of all American Negroes. Aside from the couple of other large Negro communities in the metropolis, and the half dozen small communities which have developed in vacant land at the outskirts of the city,[c] the few Negroes who live in scattered sections of New York represent the older pattern which prevailed when Negroes were few in number and engaged in serving wealthy whites.

Negroes have been living in Chicago [d] since the city was incorporated in the 1830's.

[a] James Weldon Johnson, op. cit., pp. 303-305.

[b] The center of Harlem was 135th Street and 7th Avenue. The expansion was outward from this center. See Frazier, op. cit., pp. 74-75.

[c] There is, for example, the Jamaica area of Queens, and three or four small Negro areas in the Bronx.

[d] This description of the Negro community in Chicago is based on personal observation by Arnold Rose and on a large number of historical sources, including a collection of unpublished interviews with old residents (in possession of the Social Science Research Committee of the University of Chicago).

They were few in number until the meat-packing industries brought them up from the South during the stockyards strikes of 1894 and 1904, and even then they formed an insignificant proportion of the population until the war industries' boom, beginning in 1915. Before 1915 Chicago Negroes lived in practically every section of the city, usually in small concentrations at the edge of areas inhabited by wealthy whites. It is interesting to observe that, except for a few settlements at the very outskirts of the city, the Negroes have not been able to get into any new areas in the rapidly growing city since 1910, despite a more than six-fold increase in the Negro population since that time. The South Side area—largest in 1910—has expanded enormously in a thin strip, which has come to be known as Chicago's "Black Belt," and the other areas also have expanded slightly, but no new areas within the city proper have been opened to Negroes. As in the case of New York, segregation has been increasing: even the upper class Negroes whose ancestors lived in Chicago on terms of almost complete social equality with their white neighbors are now forced into the Negro ghettos and are hardly differentiated from the impoverished Negro just arrived from the South.

The history of the expansion of the Chicago South Side Black Belt has exhibited the full gamut of Negro housing problems. The constant immigration of Southern Negroes into this segregated area caused doubling-up of families, the taking in of lodgers, the conversion of once spacious homes and apartments into tiny flats, the crowding of an entire family into a single room, the rapid raising of rents, the use of buildings which should be condemned. The careless attitude of the health and sanitary inspection authorities toward Negroes and toward poor people generally is especially serious where an ignorant population took over the homes abandoned by another population group. Light industry, wholesale commercial establishments, gambling and vice resorts have been pressing the poorer Negroes southward from the direction of the downtown area. The holding of land for speculation, the high cost of building, the lack of capital have left huge gaps of vacant land in the midst of the most over-crowded Negro areas in the northern half of the Black Belt. The west boundary of the section is sharply deline-ated by a series of railroad tracks which cut off the Negroes from their poorer white neighbors. The southward expansion has been marked by bitter conflict between the dispossessed whites and the harassed Negroes. Organizations have been set up to prevent any white owners from selling or renting to Negroes; Negroes who succeeded in getting a foothold, or whites who seemed inclined to give them one for large sums of money, were terrorized and physically maltreated; bitter fear and hatred has marked many of the other contacts between whites and Negroes because of the whites' beliefs that the Negroes were dangerous to their persons and property. There has been practically no expansion to the east despite all Negro pressures and needs. The housing difficulties of the Negroes in Chicago are apparent at every point, and yet neither the City Council nor any other white group has been willing to do anything about it.

Southern cities usually have such a large Negro population that when the Negro community grows, it is near enough to the outskirts of the city that it can expand into vacant land and not simply inherit white areas. Many Southern cities have traditionally had their Negro communities at the edge of town. This is not true of Washington, D.C., however, for this rapidly expanding city has many of the segregation patterns and problems of the typical Northern cities with large Negro populations, though in Washington the locations of the Negro districts are more scattered. Nor is it true of the old Southern cities, like Charleston, South Carolina, or Baton Rouge, Louisiana, where

Negro residences are so interspersed among white residences that it is difficult to find a large Negro community as a spatial unit.[a]

While Birmingham, Alabama, has received the major part of its Negro population since the Civil War, the Negro population of the city is not concentrated in a few areas.[b] Negroes, however, are not distributed at random throughout the city either, but rather are to be found in a large number of small segregated areas. This may be simply explained by the fact that the city developed out of twelve originally separate towns, each of which had its one or two Negro areas, with some scattering of Negro families throughout.

In Nashville, Tennessee,[c] Negroes are concentrated in a half dozen or so communities adjacent to white lower class or lower middle class areas. In upper class areas, a few Negro servants occupy quarters provided by their employers. There are practically no Negroes in the white upper middle class areas of West End, Hillsboro and Belle Meade. In the white lower middle class area east of the Cumberland River there are two adjacent but distinctly defined Negro communities. In the white lower class area of South Nashville, there are large Negro communities with poorly defined boundaries. North Nashville, too, has a large Negro community surrounded by white lower class areas. According to Johnson, Negroes in Nashville (unlike Negroes in Northern cities) do not separate themselves into economic groups.

[a] While 45 per cent of Charleston's population is Negro, only 5 per cent of the Negroes there live in blocks with 100 per cent Negro occupancy, and nearly 40 per cent live in blocks with less than 50 per cent colored occupancy. See Federal Housing Administration, *The Structure and Growth of Residential Neighborhoods in American Cities* (1939), pp. 66-67.

[b] For the facts of the distribution of Negroes in Birmingham, see Mabel L. Walker, *Urban Blight and Slums* (1938), pp. 43-44.

[c] For the facts of the distribution of Negroes in Nashville, see Charles S. Johnson, *Patterns of Negro Segregation*, prepared for this study (1943), Chapters 1 and 2. Also see materials on Nashville gathered for this book (available in Schomburg Collection).

RESEARCH ON CASTE AND CLASS IN A
NEGRO COMMUNITY

We have presented only the barest outlines of the Negro class structure. Like all outlines, and like all descriptions in terms of "the average" and "the typical," the description is somewhat distorted. There are exceptions to every statement. For fuller descriptions, the reader is referred to the community studies made in recent years.[a] While these studies are excellent, further research is necessary to get an adequate picture of the Negro class system. We shall append a few suggestions for further research.

"What constitutes the race problem," observes Charles S. Johnson, "is not the fixed character of the relations, but their dynamic character. There would be no race problem if the Negro group uniformly accepted the status assumed for it. The present patterns of these relations are, in the large, different from what they were fifty years ago or even twenty years ago. They vary with localities and backgrounds and with social classes within the Negro and white groups."[b] Moreover, in this process of social change *the class and caste structures are themselves changing.* The studies of the Negro class structure so far have been, on the whole, of a static type and have contributed little to our knowledge of the social dynamics actually involved. Even when viewed as cross-sectional investigations, a general weakness of those studies has been that the correlation between the factors giving status—occupation, income and wealth, education, family background, complexion and so on—have been observed and recorded only in a vague and general way and, in any case, no attempt has been made to weight them quantitatively. From the point of view of social dynamics, this is serious since we do not have a basis for forecasting trends in social mobility, and we cannot properly make certain practical proposals we should like to make.[c]

[a] See footnote 9 in Chapter 30, and footnote 5 in Chapter 31.

[b] *Growing up in the Black Belt* (1941), p. 276.

[c] Charles S. Johnson gives the broad outline of the dynamic problem as it appears to the *individual:*

"In the present situation of the Negro in the South, the two values within control of an individual which can do most to facilitate class mobility are wealth and education. Ancestry and color, which are sometimes associated with social status, are factors beyond the control of living individuals struggling for status. Wealth is theoretically possible of control, but actually a remote possibility. Education is within reach and, consequently, it is invested with almost magical properties by both the ambitious parents and the youth." (*Ibid.*, p. 77.)

What we want to know in some detail is how this causal mechanism actually functions, and how it determines change in the social class system. In a sense the things mentioned by Johnson represent the "causes and conditions" of social stratification.

The ideal community study should start out from a careful *statistical analysis* of vital, social, and economic data concerning the individuals and families making up the community being studied. The less measurable data on attitudes, cultural traits, behavior patterns in which social stratification is expressed, and the "feeling" of social status or toward social status on the part of members of the various groups, should then be observed and the results *integrated into the framework of statistical knowledge*. Only when so treated do they reveal their full meaning. The entire analysis should be dominated by the recognition that the Negro class structure is rapidly changing. The dynamics of the problem do not consist merely in the tensions, frictions and movements *within* the class structure. Even more important is the resultant *movement of the whole class structure* and, incidentally, the actual import of a position in this structure for Negroes in various social classes.

In such an approach it is of importance to keep clear at the outset that our class concepts have no other reality than as a conceptual framework. They should, therefore, be given *instrumental* definitions (*in relation* to the questions asked and the instruments used for observations). Fundamentally we are studying a series of continua—on the one side, incomes, occupations, educational levels, complexions, and so on; on the other side, family organization, ambition, moral standards, regard for respectability, social prestige, class and caste attitudes, and so on. We know that there are monopolistic elements in the social situation. Because of a causal mechanism—which constitutes the very problem of class dynamics to be investigated—there is a specific, but changing, correlation between all these various series, and we attempt to observe the result of this correlation in terms of social classes. But neither the particular series themselves nor the integration of the series into a composite "social status" reveal any gaps from which we can infer "natural" classes.[a] If there are gaps in some of the series, they can be assumed, in a rapidly changing society, to vary from community to community and from one time to another. We must choose our class lines arbitrarily to answer certain specific questions.

Further, as usual, we must observe *the differences in social stratification* between South and North, rural and urban districts, and city communities of varying size and age. It is true that every Negro community—no matter how small, and no matter how insignificant are the apparent differences in wealth, education, and color—has its social cleavages. But the differences between different Negro communities are so great that

---

[a] The authors of the Warner group—to whom American social science is indebted, not only for much of the recently acquired detailed knowledge about the Negro class structure, but also for the impetus to overcome the popular American theory of the absence of class in this country—often give the reader the impression that they believe that there are *in reality* clearly demarcated social classes: ". . . well-defined upper, middle, and lower social classes exist within each caste. Each of these classes has its distinctive pattern of familial, recreational, and general social behavior." (Allison Davis, Burleigh B. Gardner, and Mary R. Gardner, *Deep South* [1941], p. 49, footnote.)

Because of this misconception—which is sometimes called reification—these authors became tempted to give us a somewhat oversimplified idea about social stratification in the Negro community. The fault is not the simplification, which is an almost necessary method when dealing with complicated social relations, but the reluctance to admit it and to make adequate reservations. What they are actually presenting is an ideal-typical—and, therefore, over-typical—description, based on much detailed observation which is all organized under the conceptual scheme applied. By unduly insisting upon the realism of this analysis, however, they come to imply a rigidity in the class structure which is not really there.

the application of a too hard and fast conceptual frame of class structure will do violence to the facts. When only a single community can be studied, it should not be assumed to be typical nor should the question of its uniqueness or typicality be ignored. Rather, the investigator must attempt to place it in the Southern scene, or in the American scene, or even in the whole Western civilization scene, by comparing it with the average and range in many significant respects. This he will be enabled to do by his general knowledge and—more important—by the great volume of census and other existing bodies of statistical data. In the same way he should make use of the often great volume of historical, descriptive, and statistical material, so that he can place the community in time and see its dynamics. A community is in constant flux, and a cross-sectional picture involves a distortion.

Caste and class are never the only bases for cleavage in a community. A community is a complex thing. Social life occurs in the form of human experience and is not neatly boxed according to the criterion in which the social scientist studies it. No two persons are alike, and the range of variation in many respects is great. Except for a few things like sexual differentiation, human beings do not divide themselves into "natural" classes. Not only must the social scientist abstract from social reality, note variation in his abstractions, and classify within the variations before he can begin to draw conclusions, but he must also make a decision as to what abstractions, variations and classifications are significant. All these actions of the scientist are ultimately arbitrary. When we choose "caste" and "class" as tools to organize our observations and conclusions about American communities, we must be on our guard lest we put blinders on our observations.

While we do believe the concepts of caste and class are important tools for the study of American communities, there are *other* ordering concepts which are significant and which must be related to caste or class to make even *their* role clear. Such traits as age, sex, "personality," "race philosophy," rural or urban background, and perhaps others, are important to the study of any Negro community. For the purposes of illustration, we may indicate briefly how "age" is an important concept for the study of such a community. The continuous advancement of education and related factors of change make the younger Negroes different from the older ones. Age differentials are a basis of solidarity and create tension within the class structure. As time passes, the young become the old and move the entire class structure. Taking a cross-sectional view, the constellation of caste, class and age may give a configuration like the one which Hortense Powdermaker compresses in the following statement:

> The White aristocrats are the least, and the Poor Whites are the most, hostile toward the other race. Among the Negroes the upper class is the most, and the lower class the least, antagonistic toward the Whites. Again, the older generation of Whites are the ones in whom most affect is aroused by the inter-racial situation, while the younger generation is inclined to view the problem more casually. The reverse is true for the Negroes: the older generation shows the tolerance and calmness traditionally associated with age, while the young people are the ones who feel most intensely on racial issues.[a]

Such a situation is, of course, fraught with impending changes for the fundamental class and caste relations. Taking a long-range view, the Negro class structure of today is only the passing arrangement of a society in transition.

[a] *After Freedom* (1939), p. 334.

We cannot close this description of what a study of a Negro community should be without calling attention to the study which best meets our requirements, a study which is now all but forgotten. We refer to W. E. B. Du Bois, *The Philadelphia Negro*, published in 1899.

RESEARCH ON NEGRO LEADERSHIP

The study of leadership and followership should not start out from an attempt to define on *a priori* grounds the two principal concepts involved. In this tangled and uncultivated field of study such an attempt would almost inevitably land the investigator in hollow and doctrinal squabbles on the meaning of words. We have only to settle that *we are discussing the role and importance of individual persons in the sphere of social and political power and—as a power basis for these individuals as well as a concept for contrast—the role of the masses.* This statement of the problem has to be made more definite by a realistic conception of the general pattern of leadership and followership in American culture as a whole.

The general American pattern has to be assumed to be modified considerably in the Negro people because of caste. In this problem, caste particularly implies two things: First, that the identification on the part of Negroes with the American nation as a whole and with national groups of various types, as, for instance, the workers, becomes abnormally weak or totally lacking.[a] Second, that Negroes, because of their subordinate caste position, find all their power relations confined to the narrow orbit of accommodation or protest, or to a compromise between accommodation and protest. Besides this realistic axis of behavior in power relations, there are unrealistic outlets in extrovert or introvert aggression and in psychological and ideological escapism. As we saw in Chapter 38, Negro popular theories generally, because of caste, become fixated, negatively or positively, on white theories on the Negro; outside the Negro problem these popular theories become amorphous and unstable.

The primary effect of the caste situation on Negro leadership—compared with a "normal" American situation—is to enhance tremendously the importance of Negro leaders as liaison agents between the two groups. Negro leaders have a "function" to fulfill for both castes. As the Negro class structure is also closely determined by caste, there is a relation to be investigated between class and leadership. The Negro leaders should be viewed from the standpoints of the two castes and their interests. The white caste has an interest in supporting those Negro leaders who can transfer their influence upon the lower caste. The Negro caste has two interests: one, to express the Negro protest as far as it does not damage its immediate welfare; two, to get as much as possible from the whites. The partly contradictory interests of the Negro community can be taken care of by the same individual leaders or by several different leaders in a division of responsibility.

A most important problem, which, to be solved, would require much more factual research, concerns the operation of the selective social mechanism by which Negro

---

[a] The chapter on Negro ideologies enlarges upon this topic (Chapter 38).

leaders are chosen and permitted to exercise influence. It is apparent to the observer that the white caste controls the appointment and eventual dismissal of a number of Negro leaders and greatly promotes or hinders the rise of most of the others. This is partly a matter of tradition, but to a greater extent it corresponds to real interests of the whites. There are also, of course, other forces in action: partly "objective" ones, such as individual merit, Negro class monopolies, and the factor of change, and partly subjective attitudes held by the Negro masses.

The way to study this important aspect of our problem is to analyze—against the background of a survey of the entire social *milieu* in which Negro leaders develop and operate—the factors actually responsible for the elevation of a selected sample of Negroes to prominence in church, education, business, politics, and also in vice and racketeering. This would, incidentally, because of the close relation between class and leadership in the Negro community, also reveal much of the internal dynamics of the Negro class structure.

We might be allowed to illustrate the type of study suggested by formulating a number of questions, some of which have been given a conjectural answer in Chapters 34 to 37. How does the selective mechanism operate differently in the various fields of social activities? in rural and urban districts? in the South and the North? on the local and the national plane? What are the trends of change?

To what extent, specifically, and by what means, do white caste interests interfere? What are the specific interests in Negro leadership of white politicians, planters, merchants, bankers, manufacturers, philanthropists, in a given community? What rewards do they hold out for Negro leaders and what effective demands do they make upon them? How tractable must those leaders be in order to become successful? What demands upon the Negro leaders, and with what effectiveness, are raised by the Negro community? How is a compromise struck between submission and aggression, accommodation and protest? What are the chances under various circumstances for a really independent Negro leadership? In other words, we should want a full analysis of the social controls operating on the individual Negro who is attempting to rise to prominence.

What effect do the various influences on the selective social mechanism determining the rise of Negro leaders have on the racial, social and political attitudes of the Negro masses? What is the effect of the masses—through their partial influence on the selective mechanism and as the object for leadership influence—on the behavior and the popular theories of the leaders? How far down in the Negro class structure do various Negro leaders reach by their influence and from how far down in the masses do influences emanate upon the leaders? What influence do Negro leaders have on white leaders with whom they are in immediate contact?

These questions open up the problems of the interrelations between functioning Negro leaders and the white community leaders, on the one hand, and between Negro leaders and Negro followers, on the other hand. More specifically we want to know, how much influence and what sort of influence do those prominent Negroes have? In what circles of the white and the Negro population is the influence exerted? What deliveries to the whites and to the Negroes do they promise, and which do they actually make?

How does the Negro leader operate? To what extent and how does he utilize the white and the Negro press, the Negro organizations and the various "fronts"? To what extent does the Negro leader become pressed into a dual standard of behavior in order to serve his two constituencies: the white leaders and the Negro community? How does he make a choice among necessary compromises, advantageous compromises and plain selling out of the Negro interests? How does he strike a balance between personal and group opportunism? What techniques of adaptive manipulation does he develop?

To what extent does the peculiar situation of the Negro leader in the American caste system further corruption and destructive personal rivalry? What does the Negro community think of its leaders? How does that influence the Negro leaders?

These problems are hardly touched upon in our tentative analysis in the text. They lend themselves well to a treatment in terms of "leadership types."

QUANTITATIVE STUDIES OF RACE ATTITUDES

1. EXISTING STUDIES OF RACE ATTITUDES

Quantitative studies of race attitudes are summarized in a monograph prepared for this study by Eugene L. Horowitz.[a] In this Appendix we shall briefly indicate the direction of work that has been done and offer a few suggestions as to the type of attitude studies which would be in accord with the methodological principles presented in Appendix 1.

One of the early classic efforts to measure race attitudes was that of Emory S. Bogardus.[b] His questionnaire offered a list of races and nationalities and a list of seven degrees of social intimacy (e.g., proximity of residence, marriage). The interviewee was to check off the degree of social intimacy to which he would be willing to admit a member of each race or nationality. By this means Bogardus could present a rank order of races and nationalities according to the degree of preference for them by a given group of Americans. The problem of degree of friendliness toward the Negro and of comparative friendliness toward various races and nationalities became a major concern for those interested in the quantitative approach to the study of attitudes, especially after L. L. Thurstone[c] introduced a series of major technical improvements into the measuring process. In 1929, E. D. Hinckley devised a scale of attitudes toward the Negro which presumably could be administered to any group of whites.[d]

With techniques developed for measuring the degree of friendliness or social distance toward the Negro, students began to investigate differences in attitudes as measured by the scales. There have been studies correlating the scores on these scales with region, rural-urban residence, age, sex, church affiliation, social class, intelligence, general education, general social and political outlook. The scales have also been used to measure the effect of experiments: students were given courses in race relations or were brought into social contact with Negroes, and the change in their performance on the attitude test was noted.[e]

[a] " 'Race' Attitudes" in Otto Klineberg (editor), *Characteristics of the American Negro*, prepared for this study, to be published.

[b] "Race Friendliness and Social Distance," *Journal of Applied Sociology* (January-February, 1927), pp. 272-287.

[c] The first article in the series on race attitudes by Thurstone was "An Experimental Study of Nationality Preferences," *The Journal of General Psychology* (July-October, 1928), pp. 405-425.

[d] E. D. Hinckley, "The Influence of Individual Opinion on the Construction of an Attitude Scale," *The Journal of Social Psychology* (August, 1932), pp. 283-295.

[e] On this point, see, in addition to Horowitz (*op. cit.*, manuscript pages 214-218), Mapheus Smith, "A Study of Change of Attitudes toward the Negro," *Journal of Negro Education* (January, 1939), pp. 64-70.

The studies correlating friendliness toward the Negro with educational status and with experience regarding Negroes do in a general way what certain other studies do in a more specific way. These latter studies attempt to find out whether the possession of certain information or misinformation about Negroes in a given situation affects a white person's attitudes toward Negroes in that situation. There are relatively few studies of this type. Related to these studies are those which attempt to find out whether race prejudice is a general attitude which applies to most situations or whether it is a group of attitudes each of which applies only to a specific situation. An interesting study of this sort was that by Bolton in which the conclusion was drawn that a "group of Southern students are much more liberal toward the economic, the political and the educational rights of the Negro than towards social intermixture with the race," and, therefore, that the latter should be measured as a distinct attitude.[a]

2. THE EMPIRICAL STUDY OF VALUATIONS AND BELIEFS

The paramount importance attached to observing and measuring valuations and beliefs in the Negro problem by means of scientifically controlled research must be clear from the Introduction and Appendix 1 of this book. Unfortunately the results of quantitative studies of opinions and attitudes regarding this aspect of the Negro problem are meager. The most general conclusion from a survey of the existing studies regarding the relation between valuations and beliefs is that they have not added anything significant to our knowledge.[b] They have not yet succeeded in quantifying our general common-sense notions on the subject. The main explanation is undoubtedly that, until now, not much work has been done in this particular field.[c]

Another general defect is that the studies which have been made usually have been planned in isolation from both the general social study of the Negro and the political battle about his status. They have, therefore, not had a perspective which gives relevance to the questions asked, and they have not been prepared by the working out of consistent schemes of scientific hypotheses. This is the more natural and, indeed, the more defensible, since the studies carried out have usually had an experimental character and have been more concerned with perfecting the tools of measurement than with the conclusions to be obtained. In the main this holds true also of the mass public opinion polls. Particularly when asking Negroes for their opinions—but also when asking whites for theirs on the Negro problem—there are a number of purely technical difficulties which as yet have not been overcome.

Instead of indulging in further negative criticism, we shall develop briefly certain positive suggestions for opinion research as they have arisen in our study of the Negro problem. At the outset it should be remembered that an average opinion in regard to the Negro problem, as does every other opinion, contains two elements which are of different character: (1) beliefs concerning reality which can be true or untrue, com-

[a] Euri Relle Bolton, "Measuring Specific Attitudes towards the Social Rights of the Negro," *The Journal of Abnormal and Social Psychology* (January-March, 1937), p. 396.

[b] A summary and evaluation of these studies has been made for our study by Horowitz. *op. cit.*, manuscript pages 115, 123-148.

[c] It should be clear that our statement does *not* apply to the whole range of attitude and public opinion measurement, but solely to this activity regarding the Negro problem. The measurement of attitudes and public opinion has contributed much both to scientific and to practical knowledge outside the Negro problem, and is now showing amazingly rapid advancement in present achievement and tremendous possibilities for future achievement.

plete or incomplete; (2) valuations of an actual or hypothetical reality which can vary in intensity, clarity, and homogeneity but in themselves are neither complete nor incomplete, neither true nor untrue. There are, of course, opinions, which are only beliefs or only valuations. But more usually, opinions are combinations of both: on the one hand, beliefs are, as we have seen, nearly always influenced by the valuations for which they serve as rationalizations (which in logical terms means that they are "biased"), and, on the other hand, beliefs influence valuations.

Reacting to the earlier schools of rationalistic psychology, we became several decades ago so impressed by the fact that people did not act and think rationally that something of a tradition became established not to split opinions into two components relating to the cognitive and to the volitional sides of mental processes. This is part of the background for the present loose usage of the word "attitude" as a scientific term.[a] In many questionnaires one finds questions concerning knowledge, concerning almost pure valuations, and concerning both combined—all these three types mixed together without much distinction. And the subsequent analysis does not take into account the difference between them. Such a differentiation is of great importance, however, since a study of people's beliefs throws light not only on what they know or do not know but, in addition, on the structure of their entire valuation sphere.

The fact that people's beliefs, unlike their valuations, can be directly judged by the objective criteria of correctness and completeness offers us a clue for analyzing scientifically the complexes of struggling valuations that exist in the minds of people. It is a sound hypothesis that, since the beliefs of men serve an opportunistic function, both the direction and the degree of their deviation from "objective" knowledge will tell us how people are trying to reconcile their valuations on a lower plane, implicit in their daily behavior, with the more general valuations which are recognized as morally higher in our society. From this point of view, it becomes of great importance to chart quantitatively people's knowledge and ignorance on controversial subjects. For this purpose the questions to be utilized in certain types of opinion studies should be purged as far as possible of all valuations; they should only test the respondent's conception of this particular part of reality. It is fairly easy to prepare a standard norm of what represents objective knowledge; in the many problems where we are still ignorant or hesitant, consciousness of our ignorance constitutes true knowledge. For testing knowledge as to its degree of completeness, some sort of graduated scale can be worked out with the help of available techniques.

If properly carried out, such a study of factual knowledge regarding the Negro problem—differentiated in relation to certain main axes: white-Negro, North-South, urban-rural, social class, education, sex, age—would be revealing. Its practical importance for education is obvious. It will also have great theoretical importance in explaining white people's behavior with respect to Negroes. The hypothesis is that we are not facing a question merely of more or less meager and incorrect knowledge. There is an emotional load of valuation conflicts pressing for rationalization, creating certain blind spots—and also creating a desire for knowledge in other spots—and in general causing conceptions of reality to deviate from truth in determined directions. If such an analysis of the degree of knowledge and ignorance and also of their localization and

---

[a] As used by Thomas and Znaniecki in *The Polish Peasant*, the term "attitude" was a part of the reaction to the complete irrationalism emphasized by the instinctivist and behaviorist schools.

concrete character is carried out, the valuations and their conflicts can be recorded, indirectly but quantitatively—just as the heat of distant stars is measured by observing their spectra. From our inquiry of the Negro problem we are convinced that ignorance is *not* always simple; it is often opportune.[a]

But the valuations should, of course, also be studied directly. For this purpose questions should be selected which relate to opinions that do not contain any reference to reality. A main consideration in the analysis of answers to such questions should be that valuations are complex and ordinarily conflicting, and that an individual's focusing of attention in the valuation sphere may be opportune. In most cases the indirect analysis of the valuation sphere, through the study of the deviations of beliefs from true knowledge, is likely to reach deeper than does the direct analysis. An individual continually tends to arrange his valuations so that they may be presented in an acceptable form. But in his beliefs concerning social reality—which are shaped to give the appearance of rational organization to his morals—he reveals himself.

3. "Personal" and "Political" Opinions

When studying valuations there is another distinction the observance of which is of utmost significance in the Negro problem as in other problems where human valuations are sharply conflicting, namely, the distinction between a person's "private," or "personal," opinion and his "public," or "political," opinion on the same question.[b] They do not need to agree; in fact they seldom agree. This, in itself, is a reason for a clear distinction to be upheld, since otherwise a major source of systematic error is contained in the observations. A further reason is that the very registration and measuring of this difference is an important part of an opinion analysis.

A man's opinion as to the desirable size of a normal family might be totally different,

[a] As examples of how opportune ignorance and knowledge may be, it might be pointed out that Negroes are amazingly sophisticated with respect to the incidence of indirect taxation and the environmental influences on intelligence test scores. Even ordinary Negroes with little formal schooling can explain to the satisfaction of the economist just how taxes on real estate are passed on to the tenant, and can often do better than the trained psychologist in revealing just how lack of incentive and intellectual stimulation can keep intelligence tests from revealing "innate ability." It is apparent that the reason Negroes know these things is that they have been victimized by indirect taxation and the intelligence tests—that is, it is claimed that Negroes pay practically no taxes, because they pay practically no *direct* taxes, and that they are biologically inferior because their I.Q. scores are lower. It is apparent, too, that whites—especially the dominant ones, the ones who pay direct taxes and who have, or think they have, high I.Q. scores—have an opportune ignorance with respect to these things. Even when simple facts are presented to ruffle their ignorance, they reject them.

[b] There has been much discussion about the distinction between "opinion" and "attitude," with the assumptions that the former is measurable while the latter is not and that the former is a mere verbalization while the latter directs action. Our distinction between personal and political opinions is different, and should not be confused with the distinction between opinion and attitude. It is no easier to measure political opinions than personal opinions; both direct action—although different kinds of action; and one is not more a mere verbalization than is the other.

Schanck has attempted to investigate statistically the distinction between public and private attitudes, although without relation to the Negro. (R. L. Schanck, "A Study of a Community and Its Groups and Institutions Conceived of as Behaviors of Individuals," *Psychological Monographs* [1932].)

on the one hand, when he faces the problem as a citizen taking a stand on the population issue if this is brought to the political forefront and, on the other hand, when he faces his own family limitation problem.[a] Exactly this same thing is true in the Negro problem. Many white people would be prepared to stand for and practice changed relations to Negroes *if* they were made the common rule in society, while they are not prepared to practice them as exceptions to the rule. Some of the apparent confusion and contradiction in nearly every individual's attitude to the Negro problem becomes explainable by applying this distinction.[b]

Part of the actual differences between personal and political attitudes is *rational*. The very aim of a person's political opinion is to ask for and, eventually, to cause such institutional changes in society that the circumstances under which he lives and forms his personal opinions are modified, and, consequently, to change his personal behavior and attitudes also. A positive stand on the political population question—say a demand that the average nonsterile marriage produce four children—may be the center of a complex of political opinions demanding legal and economic changes in the family institution. There is no contradiction between a four-child norm in one's political opinion and, say, a two-child norm in one's personal opinion and actual family limitation behavior.

Similarly in the Negro problem. In numerous conversations with white Americans in the North and in the South, the observer is informed by the man he talks to that he himself would be prepared to act in such and such a way different from his ordinary behavior *if* society, the local community, or "public opinion" would not react in such and such a way; and, second, that he would favor this and this social change implying such and such alterations of the caste relations in society, although he is not prepared to live up to those alterations as an individual *unless* the social changes are first carried out. It should be noticed that political opinions are thus regularly of a conditional character and that they usually refer to a more distant future. There are few white

[a] See Gunnar Myrdal, *Population: A Problem for Democracy* (1940), Chapter 5, "People's Opinions," particularly pp. 106 ff. and 115 ff.

[b] The distinction between public and private attitudes also comes out with regard to what one will or will not admit with respect to the Negro. Baker tells a story which illustrates this aspect of the distinction. It is from ". . . the discussions of the Alabama legislature then in session. A compulsory education bill had been introduced; the problem was to pass a law that would apply to white people, not to Negroes. In this connection I heard a significant discussion in the state senate. I use the report of it, for accuracy, as given the next morning in the *Advertiser:*

" 'Senator Thomas said . . . he would oppose any bills that would compel Negroes to educate their children, for it had come to his knowledge that Negroes would give the clothing off their backs to send their children to school, while too often the white man, secure in his supremacy, would be indifferent to his duty.

" 'At this point Senator Lusk arose excitedly to his feet and said:

" ' "Does the Senator from Barbour mean to say that the Negro race is more ambitious and has more aspirations than the white race?"

" ' "The question of the gentleman . . . is an insult to the senate of Alabama," replied Senator Thomas deliberately. "It is an insult to the great Caucasian race, the father of all the arts and sciences, to compare it to that black and kinky race which lived in a state of black and ignorant savagery until the white race seized it and lifted it to its present position." ' " (Ray Stannard Baker, *Following the Color Line* [1908], p. 248.)

Americans even in the South who do not declare themselves in favor of much more equality for the Negro in politics, education, and everything else—but they want them far in the future when certain conditions are changed. (The inconsistency in their attitudes often consists only in their being unwilling to do anything—not even in the political sphere and often least of all there—to change those conditions.) Generally, it can be assumed that being able to keep more of a rational and conscious distinction and relation between one's personal and political opinions is a function (1) of education and intelligence on the part of the individual, (2) of his identification with society (being a "good citizen"), and (3) of his training to think of himself as a would-be legislator, that is, as a participant in inducing the social change.

But part of this difference between personal and political opinions is *irrational*, and there is then inadequate intellectual connection between the two. In many countries, again to use an illustration from the population problem, it is possible to prove statistically that a large number of people, who publicly condemn birth control as immoral and who back legislative measures to prohibit it, must practice it privately. In the Negro problem there are equally flagrant contradictions between people's opinions about how society ought to be and the opinions whereby they defend their own daily behavior.

4. THE PRACTICAL STUDY OF RACE PREJUDICE

In a footnote on page 52, in Chapter 3, we indicated that we preferred to use the word "discrimination" rather than "race prejudice." [a] Discrimination is generally considered to be the objective aspect of prejudice, and in many areas of life we could objectively observe discrimination. Race prejudice is a much more controversial subject; many persons who practice discrimination, consciously or unconsciously, claim they have no race prejudice. We have not neglected, however, the subjective aspect of discrimination, even though we have not associated our analysis with the term "race prejudice." In Chapter 28, for example, we presented the theory of "no social equality" which, in a sense, is a theory of a certain type of race prejudice.

In this section we shall use the term "race prejudice" as a conceptual tool for analysis of the motivation of white people's negative attitudes toward Negroes. We believe it necessary to continue the practice followed in most attitude measurement studies, of measuring variations in race prejudice and relating this variation to variations in other significant variables. We should like to suggest an innovation in these studies: that the assumption be made that there are several types of race prejudice, types which are differentiated from each other for practical reasons. It may be discovered that two white persons, having an equal degree of race prejudice according to an attitude scale, have different motivations for this prejudice, in such a manner that a given program of action will reduce the prejudice of one but not of the other. If such be discovered, we may claim to have a pragmatic classification of race prejudice. Presumably a judicious choice of questions on an attitude measurement scale would classify white people according to the type of prejudice they hold toward Negroes.

Many psychological theories of race prejudices have been advanced. [b] Implicit throughout our book has been the theory that it is useful to consider race prejudice as

[a] We have occasionally used the term "race prejudice" in a common-sense way, not in an analytic way.

[b] For an excellent brief summary of these theories, see Henry A. Davidson, "The Anatomy of Prejudice," *Common Ground* (Winter, 1941), pp. 3-12.

of three types, which we have described as that of the white Southerner, that of the white Northerner, that of the Negro. In holding this theory, we do not claim that other theories are incorrect or that no other classification of race prejudice is useful. It is merely that we happen to find this theory and this classification most useful, and we have organized our book around them. Our description and classification are, of course, based on impression and need to be verified and modified by further research. Further, we do not claim that all white Southerners have the kind of prejudice which we characterize as being typical of prejudiced white Southerners, or that no Northerners have this kind of prejudice. It is merely that we find the race prejudice characteristic of most prejudiced Southern whites different, on the average, from that characteristic of most prejudiced Northern whites. Similarly, we believe that the prejudice of most Negroes is to be analyzed in different terms.

The prejudice of the white Southerner has a complex basis. The Southerner holds that all Negroes are inferior to all whites, and he has a great variety of racial and social beliefs to support this valuation. The character of his prejudice is revealed in his "rank order of discriminations": [a] It is surely significant that the white Southerner is much less willing to permit intermarriage or to grant "social equality" than he is to allow equality in the political, judicial and economic spheres.[b] The violence of the Southerner's reaction to equality in each of the spheres rises with the degree of its relation to the sexual and the personal, which suggests that his prejudice is based upon fundamental attitudes toward sex and personality. An attempt to reduce race prejudice of this sort requires a profound strategy. Attitude measurement devices could not only get at the specific character of the race attitudes but could also help to test various experimental devices used in attempting to modify these attitudes.

The race prejudice of the typical Northerner seems to be of a much simpler character. It is based mainly on ignorance, both simple and opportune, and is much less bound up with fundamental conceptions of society and self. The Northerner seldom gets a chance to see the Negro's good points, and he does not understand the social background of the Negro's bad points. The Southerner's prejudice also has much of ignorance in it, but the Southerner's ignorance is more opportune because it is tied to fundamental motives. The Northerner has little of the Southerner's rank order of discriminations: he favors equality in justice and politics, and he finds the etiquette of race relations obnoxious. The Northerner is against intermarriage and equality in the economic sphere. But even here his motives seem to be largely different from those of the Southerner: he avoids intermarriage mainly for reasons of social status and personal antipathy, not because he believes that intermarriage will disrupt society;[c] he is against

[a] See Chapter 3, Section 4.

[b] See Chapters 28 and 29.

[c] "Potential equality is of the essence of democracy. Extirpate 'race prejudice' in a democracy and social communion and intermarriage are bound to follow. One of the reasons why Northerners fail to understand this is their aesthetic antipathy to the negro. Most Southerners like individual negroes that 'keep their place'—and I daresay that the negroes, like all more or less primitive folk, are likable. The Northerner is protected from social communion and intermarriage by his feelings; the Southerner is protected by what he calls his principles—the superiority of the whites, and the like." (Thomas P. Bailey, *Race Orthodoxy in the South* [1914], p. 63.)

economic equality largely out of ignorance of the Negro's capacities.[a] These hypotheses need to be tested by attitude questionnaires. If we are correct in judging the Northerner's prejudice to be based so largely on ignorance, and if a distinction is made between questions of belief and questions of valuation,[b] the attitude measuring process can itself serve as an experiment. If two similar groups of Northerners are presented with the same set of valuation questions, and one group is also given relevant factual information, there should be a noticeable difference in their performance.[c]

The Negro's prejudice toward whites or toward other Negroes seems to be a secondary reaction. Because he has taken over American culture, the average Negro has also taken over something of the white American's attitude toward the Negro.[d] There is nothing of the "rank order" in the Negro's prejudice but something of ignorance. There is also much in it of considerations of personal social status. It may also be that some of the hostility felt toward the whites is deflected from them to the Negro group.

The Negro's negative attitude toward the white man may better be described as hatred or fear rather than prejudice. It is the hatred or fear toward those who humiliate him and deprive him of many of the good things of life. If the deprivation or humiliation were to cease, the hatred and fear also would cease. This is even true of the anti-Semitism found among Negroes: It happens that Jews are the leading retail merchants in many Negro neighborhoods and are the leading employers of Negro servants in Northern cities. The natural dislike of the dominant person by the subordinate person in an unequal economic bargain thus seems to be the cause of any striking anti-Semitism that appears in certain Negro groups. Negroes practically never feel that whites are inferior, and they do not connect racial equality with sexual and personality fears. Negro prejudice toward whites is based partly on ignorance, but it is much more a matter of fear and hatred of the oppressor. This secondary character of the Negro's[e] race prejudice could be tested by wisely administered questionnaires.

[a] Probably both the Northern employer and the Southern employer are ignorant of the Negro's economic potentialities. But where the Northern employer would like to know of them, the Southerner employer would not.

[b] See Section 2 of this Appendix.

[c] Our distinction between the Southerner's and the Northerner's prejudices implies that two similar groups of Southerners would not manifest such a difference in performance due merely to the administration of simple, direct, factual information.

[d] Du Bois describes the prejudice of Negroes toward other Negroes:

"Negroes, particularly the better class Negroes, are brought up like other Americans despite the various separations and segregations. They share, therefore, average American culture and current American prejudices. It is almost impossible for a Negro boy trained in a white Northern high school and a white college to come out with any high idea of his own people or any abiding faith in what they can do: or for a Negro trained in the segregated schools of the South wholly to escape the deadening environment of insult and caste, even if he happens to have the good teachers and teaching facilities, which poverty almost invariably denies him. He may rationalize his own individual status as exceptional. He . . . cannot ordinarily believe that the mass of Negro people have possibilities equal to the whites." (W. E. B. Du Bois, *Dusk of Dawn* [1940], p. 191.)

LIST OF BOOKS, PAMPHLETS, PERIODICALS AND OTHER
MATERIAL REFERRED TO IN THIS BOOK

Books and manuscripts prepared for this study are listed in the "Author's Preface."

ABBOTT, GRACE, *From Relief to Social Security: the development of the new public welfare services and their administration.* Chicago: The University of Chicago Press, 1941.

ADAMS, JAMES TRUSLOW, *America's Tragedy.* New York: Charles Scribner's Sons, 1934.

ADAMS, JAMES TRUSLOW, *The Epic of America.* Boston: Little, Brown and Company, 1931.

ADAMS, JAMES TRUSLOW, "Our Lawless Heritage," *Atlantic Monthly,* vol. 142, no. 6; December, 1928; pp. 732-740.

"Africa." *The Encyclopaedia Britannica,* eleventh edition; vol. 1; pp. 325-330.

ALILUNAS, LEO, "Legal Restrictions on the Negro in Politics." *The Journal of Negro History,* vol. 25, no. 2; April, 1940; pp. 152-202.

ALLEN, JAMES S., *The Negro Question in the United States.* New York: International Publishers, 1936.

The American Academy of Political and Social Science, *The Annals.* Vol. 124, "Legal Aid Work." March, 1926.

American Federation of Labor, *Report of Proceedings of the Sixty-First Annual Convention.* October, 1941.

AMES, JESSIE DANIEL, *The Changing Character of Lynching.* Atlanta: The Commission on Interracial Cooperation, Inc., July, 1942.

AMES, JESSIE DANIEL, *Democratic Processes at Work in the South, Report of Commission on Interracial Cooperation, 1939-1941.* Atlanta: The Commission on Interracial Cooperation, Inc., October, 1941.

ANDREWS, H. L., "Racial Distinctions in the Courts of North Carolina." Unpublished M.A. thesis, Duke University, 1933.

Anonymous, *Lynching Goes Underground.* January, 1940.

ANTHONY, DAVID W., "The Cranbury Terror Case." *The Crisis,* vol. 46, no. 10; October, 1939; pp. 295-296, 314-315.

ARCHER, WILLIAM, *Through Afro-America; an English reading of the race problem.* London: Chapman and Hall, Ltd., 1910.

ARNESON, BEN A., "Non-Voting in a Typical Ohio Community." *The American Political Science Review,* vol. 19, no. 4; November, 1925; pp. 816-825.

ASENDIO, JAMES, "History of Negro Motion Pictures." *International Photographer,* vol. 2, no. 12; January, 1940; p. 16.

ASHBY, WILLIAM M., "No Jim Crow in Springfield Federal Housing." *Opportunity,* vol. 20, no. 6; June, 1942; pp. 170-171, 188.

Ayer, N. W., and Son's Directory of Newspapers and Periodicals. Philadelphia: N. W. Ayer and Son, Inc., 1942.

BABCOCK, J. W., "The Colored Insane." *Alienist and Neurologist,* vol. 16; 1895; pp. 423-447.

BAILEY, THOMAS PEARCE, *Race Orthodoxy in the South and Other Aspects of the Race Question.* New York: The Neale Publishing Company, 1914.

BAKER, J. N., "Alabama's Program for Planned Parenthood." Address delivered at the Third Southern Conference on Tomorrow's Children, Nashville, Tennessee: October 31, 1941.

BAKER, PAUL E., *Negro-White Adjustment; an investigation and analysis of methods in the interracial movement in the United States; the history, philosophy, program, and techniques of ten national interracial agencies. Methods discovered through a study of cases, situations, and projects in race relations.* New York: Association Press, 1934.

BAKER, RAY STANNARD, *Following the Color Line; an account of Negro citizenship in the American democracy.* Garden City, New York: Doubleday, Page and Company, 1908.

BAKWIN, HARRY, "The Negro Infant," *Human Biology,* vol. 4, no. 1; February, 1932; pp. 1-33.

BALDWIN, W. H., "Present Problems of Negro Education." *Journal of Social Science,* vol. 37; December, 1899; pp. 48-64.

BALLAGH, JAMES C., *A History of Slavery in Virginia.* Baltimore: Johns Hopkins University Press, 1902. (Johns Hopkins University Studies in History and Political Science.)

BANCROFT, GEORGE, "Memorial Address on the Life and Character of Abraham Lincoln. Delivered at the Request of Both Houses of the Congress of America, Before Them, in the House of Representatives at Washington on the 12th of February, 1866." Washington, D. C., 1866.

BANCROFT, H. M., *Retrospection, Political and Personal.* New York: Bancroft Company, 1912.

BARKER, TOMMIE DORA, *Libraries of the South; a report on developments, 1930-1935.* Chicago: American Library Association, 1936.

BATES, ERNEST S., *American Faith; its religious, political, and economic foundations.* New York: W. W. Norton and Company, Inc., 1940.

BEAN, ROBERT B., "Some Racial Peculiarities of the Negro Brain." *American Journal of Anatomy,* vol. 5, no. 4; September, 1906; pp. 353-432.

BEARD, CHARLES, *An Economic Interpretation of the Constitution of the United States.* New York: The Macmillan Company, 1913.

BEARD, CHARLES A. and MARY R., *The Rise of American Civilization.* 2 vols. New York: The Macmillan Company, 1933. (First vol., 1927.)

BENEDICT, RUTH, *Race: Science and Politics.* New York: Modern Age Books, 1940.

BENTLEY, ISAAC MADISON and E. V. COWDRY (editors), *The Problem of Mental Disorder.* New York: McGraw-Hill Book Company, Inc., 1934.

BERGLUND, ABRAHAM, and Associates, *Labor in the Industrial South; a survey of wages and living conditions in three major industries of the new industrial South.* University, Virginia: The Institute for Research in the Social Sciences, 1930. (Institute Monograph no. 9.)

BERLE, ADOLPH A. and GARDINER C. MEANS, *The Modern Corporation and Private Property*. New York: Commerce Clearing House, Inc., 1932.

BLAINE, JAMES G., *Twenty Years of Congress: from Lincoln to Garfield. With a review of the events which led to the political revolution of 1860*. 2 vols. Norwich, Connecticut: H. Bill Publishing Company, 1884-1886.

BLAINE, JAMES G. and Others (Symposium) "Ought the Negro to be Disfranchised? Ought He to Have Been Enfranchised?" *The North American Review*, vol. 128; March, 1879; pp. 225-283.

BLAYTON, JESSE B., "Are Negro Banks Safe?" *Opportunity*, vol. 15, no. 5; May, 1937; pp. 139-141.

BLAYTON, JESSE B., "The Negro in Banking." *The Bankers Magazine*, vol. 133, no. 6; December, 1936; pp. 511-514.

BLEDSOE, ALBERT TAYLOR, *An Essay on Liberty and Slavery*. Philadelphia: J. B. Lippincott and Company, 1856.

BOAS, FRANZ, U. S. Immigration Commission, *Changes in Bodily Form of Descendants of Immigrants*. Washington, D. C.: 1910. (Senate Document 208.)

BOAS, FRANZ, "The Half-Blood Indian, an anthropometric study." *The Popular Science Monthly*, vol. 45; October, 1894; pp. 761-770.

BOAS, FRANZ, *The Mind of Primitive Man*. New York: The Macmillan Company, 1911. (Also 1938 edition.)

BOAS, FRANZ, "The Mind of Primitive Man." *The Journal of American Folk-Lore*, vol. 14, no. 52; January-March, 1911; pp. 1-11.

BOGARDUS, EMORY S., "Race Friendliness and Social Distance." *Journal of Applied Sociology*, vol. 11, no. 3; January-February, 1927; pp. 272-287.

BOIE, MAURINE, "An Analysis of Negro Crime Statistics for Minneapolis for 1923, 1924 and 1925." *Opportunity*, vol. 6, no. 6; June, 1928; pp. 171-173.

BOLTON, EURI RELLE, "Measuring Specific Attitudes towards the Social Rights of the Negro." *The Journal of Abnormal and Social Psychology*, vol. 3, no. 4; January-March, 1937; pp. 375-397.

BOND, HORACE MANN, *The Education of the Negro in the American Social Order*. New York: Prentice-Hall, Inc., 1934.

BOND, HORACE MANN, "Should the Negro Care Who Wins the War?" *The Annals of the American Academy of Political and Social Science*, vol. 223; September, 1942; pp. 81-84.

BOWEN, TREVOR, *Divine White Right; a study of race segregation and interracial coöperation in religious organizations and institutions in the United States*. With a Section on "The Church and Education for Negroes" by Ira DeA. Reid. New York: Harper and Brothers, 1934. (Published for the Institute of Social and Religious Research.)

BRANDT, KARL, "Fallacious Census Terminology and Its Consequences in Agriculture." *Social Research: An International Quarterly of Political and Social Science*, vol. 5, no. 1; February, 1938; pp. 19-36.

BRIGHAM, CARL C., "Intelligence Tests of Immigrant Groups." *Psychological Review*, vol. 37, no. 2; March, 1930; pp. 138-165.

BRIGHAM, CARL C., *A Study of American Intelligence*. Princeton: Princeton University Press, 1923.

BRINTON, HUGH P., "Negroes Who Run Afoul the Law." *Social Forces,* vol. 11, no. 1; October, 1932; pp. 96-101.

Brotherhood of Sleeping Car Porters, "A Brief History of the Organizing of the Brotherhood of Sleeping Car Porters, an International Union." Undated typescript.

BROWN, EARL, "American Negroes and the War," *Harper's Magazine,* vol. 184, no. 1103; April, 1942; pp. 545-552.

BROWN, EARL and GEORGE R. LEIGHTON, *The Negro and the War. Public Affairs Pamphlets* no. 71; 1942.

BROWN, STERLING A., *The Negro in American Fiction.* Washington, D. C.: The Associates in Negro Folk Education, 1937. (Bronze Booklet no. 6.)

BROWN, STERLING A., "Negro Character as Seen by White Authors." *Journal of Negro Education,* vol. 2, no. 2; April, 1933; pp. 179-203.

BROWN, W. O., "Rationalization of Race Prejudice." *The International Journal of Ethics,* vol. 43, no. 3; April, 1933; pp. 294-306.

BROWN, WILLIAM MONTGOMERY, *The Crucial Race Question.* Little Rock: The Arkansas Churchman's Publishing Company, 1907.

BRYANT, CAROLYN, "The Cincinnati Clinic." *The Birth Control Review,* vol. 16, no. 6; June, 1932; p. 177.

BRYANT, IRA B., JR., "News Items about Negroes in White Urban and Rural Newspapers." *Journal of Negro Education,* vol. 4, no. 2; April, 1935; pp. 169-178.

BRYCE, JAMES, *The American Commonwealth.* New York: The Macmillan Company, 1893.

BRYCE, JAMES, *The Relations of the Advanced and the Backward Races of Mankind.* Oxford: The Clarendon Press, 1902. (Romanes Lecture.)

BUCK, PAUL H., *The Road to Reunion, 1865-1900.* Boston: Little, Brown and Company, 1937.

BUCK, PEARL, *American Unity and Asia.* New York: The John Day Company, 1942.

BUCKMASTER, HENRIETTA (Henrietta Henkle), *Let My People Go; the story of the underground railroad and the growth of the abolition movement.* New York: Harper and Brothers, 1941.

BUNCHE, RALPH J., "The Negro in the Political Life of the United States." *Journal of Negro Education,* vol. 10, no. 3; July, 1941; pp. 567-584.

BURGESS, ERNEST W., "Residential Segregation in American Cities." *The Annals of the American Academy of Political and Social Science,* vol. 140, no. 229; November, 1928; pp. 105-115.

BURGESS, ERNEST W., "The Romantic Impulse and Family Disorganization." *The Survey,* vol. 57, no. 5; December 1, 1926; pp. 290-294.

BURNS, ROBERT E., *I Am a Fugitive from a Georgia Chain Gang.* New York: The Vanguard Press, 1932.

CABLE, GEORGE W., *The Negro Question.* New York: American Missionary Association, 1888.

CABLE, GEORGE W., *The Silent South, together with the freedman's case in equity and the convict lease system.* New York: Charles Scribner's Sons, 1885.

CAMPBELL, SIR GEORGE, *White and Black in the United States.* London: Chatto and Windus, 1879.

CANADY, HERMAN G., "The Effect of 'Rapport' on the I. Q.: A New Approach to the

Problem of Racial Psychology." *Journal of Negro Education*, vol. 5, no. 2; April, 1936; pp. 209-219.

CANTOR, NATHANIEL, "Crime and the Negro." *The Journal of Negro History*, vol. 16, no. 1; January, 1931; pp. 61-66.

CAREY, HENRY C., *The Slave Trade, domestic and foreign; why it exists, and how it may be extinguished*. Philadelphia: A. Hart, 1853.

CARLYLE, THOMAS, *Occasional Discourse on the Nigger Question*. London: T. Bosworth, 1853.

Carnegie Institution of Washington, *Documents Illustrative of the Slave Trade to America*. Washington, D.C., 1930-1935. (Carnegie Institution Publication no. 409, 4 vols.)

CARPENTER, MARIE E., *The Treatment of the Negro in American History School Textbooks; a comparison of changing textbook content, 1826 to 1939, with developing scholarship in the history of the Negro in the United States*. Menasha, Wisconsin: George Banta Publishing Company, 1941.

CARPENTER, NILES, "The New American Immigration Law and the Labor Market." *The Quarterly Journal of Economics*, vol. 45, no. 4; August, 1931; pp. 720-723.

CARTER, ELMER A., "Eugenics for the Negro." *The Birth Control Review*, vol. 16, no. 6; June, 1932; pp. 169-170.

CARTER, ELMER A., "Shadows of the Slave Tradition." *Survey Graphic*, vol. 31, no. 11; November, 1942; pp. 465-467, 553-555.

CASEY, ALBERT E., "Research Activity and the Quality of Teaching in Medical Schools." *Science*, vol. 96, no. 2483; July 31, 1942; pp. 110-111.

CASH, WILBUR J., *The Mind of the South*. New York: Alfred A. Knopf, 1941.

CATT, CARRIE CHAPMAN and NETTIE ROGERS SHULER, *Woman Suffrage and Politics; the inner story of the suffrage movement*. New York: Charles Scribner's Sons, 1923.

CAYTON, HORACE R., "Fighting for White Folks?" *Nation*, vol. 155, no. 3; September 26, 1942; pp. 267-270.

CAYTON, HORACE R., "The Morale of the Negro in the Defense Crisis." Paper read to the Twentieth Annual Institute of the Society for Social Research, The University of Chicago, August 15, 1941.

CAYTON, HORACE R. and GEORGE S. MITCHELL, *Black Workers and the New Unions*. Chapel Hill: The University of North Carolina Press, 1939.

CHAMBERLAIN, BERNARD P., *The Negro and Crime in Virginia*. Charlottesville: University of Virginia, 1936.

CHAMBLISS, ROLLIN, *What Negro Newspapers of Georgia Say about Some Social Problems, 1933*. Published M.A. thesis, University of Georgia, 1934. (Phelps-Stokes Fellowship Studies no. 13.)

The Chicago Commission on Race Relations, *The Negro in Chicago*. Chicago: The University of Chicago Press, 1922.

COBB, W. MONTAGUE, "The Negro as a Biological Element in the American Population." *Journal of Negro Education*, vol. 8, no. 3; July, 1939; pp. 336-348.

COBB, W. MONTAGUE, "Physical Anthropology of the American Negro: Status and Desiderata." Unpublished manuscript, Department of Anatomy, Howard University. Washington, D. C.: 1942.

COBB, W. MONTAGUE, "The Physical Constitution of the American Negro." *Journal of Negro Education*, vol. 3, no. 3; July, 1934; pp. 340-388.

COLLINS, HENRY HILL, JR., *America's Own Refugees; our 4,000,000 homeless migrants.* Princeton: Princeton University Press, 1941.

COLLINS, WINFIELD H., *The Truth about Lynching and the Negro in the South, in which the author pleads that the South be made safe for the white race.* New York: The Neale Publishing Company, 1918.

The Commission on Interracial Cooperation, *The Interracial Commission Comes of Age.* Atlanta: The Commission on Interracial Cooperation, Inc., February, 1942.

The Commission on Interracial Cooperation, *The Mob Still Rides, a review of the lynching record, 1931-1935.* Atlanta, Georgia: 1936.

The Commission on Interracial Cooperation, *A Practical Approach to the Race Problem.* Atlanta: The Commission on Interracial Cooperation, Inc., October, 1939.

The Commission on Interracial Cooperation, *The Southern Frontier,* vol. 3, no. 6; June, 1942.

Committee on Africa, the War and Peace Aims, *The Atlantic Charter and Africa from an American Standpoint.* 1942.

Contemporary China. Reference Digest, published by Chinese News Service, Inc.; vol. 2, no. 6; August 10, 1942.

COOLEY, CHARLES HORTON, "Genius, Fame, and the Comparison of Races." *The Annals of the American Academy of Political and Social Science,* vol. 9; May, 1897; pp. 317-358.

COOLEY, CHARLES HORTON, *Social Process.* New York: Charles Scribner's Sons, 1918.

COOPER, GEORGE M., "Birth Control in the North Carolina Health Department." *North Carolina Medical Journal,* vol. 1, no. 3; September, 1940; pp. 463-466.

COOPER, GEORGE M., F. R. PRATT, and M. J. HAGOOD, "Four Years of Contraception as a Public Health Service in North Carolina." *American Journal of Public Health,* vol. 31, no. 12; December, 1941; pp. 1248-1252.

Council for Democracy, *The Negro and Defense. Democracy in Action Pamphlets,* no. 3; 1941.

Council on Medical Education and Hospitals, "Hospitals and Medical Care in Mississippi." *Journal of the American Medical Association,* vol. 12, no. 22; June 3, 1939; pp. 2317-2332.

CRANE, A. L., "Race Differences in Inhibition." *Archives of Psychology,* no. 63; March, 1923.

The Crisis, Editorial, vol. 46, no. 7; July, 1939; p. 209.

The Crisis, Editorial, vol. 46, no. 9; September, 1939; pp. 271-272.

The Crisis, "Iron Ring in Housing." Vol. 47, no. 7; July, 1940; pp. 205-210.

CROSSWAITH, FRANK R., and ALFRED BAKER LEWIS, "Discrimination Incorporated." *Social Action,* vol. 8, no. 1; January 15, 1942; pp. 4-37.

DABNEY, VIRGINIUS, *Below the Potomac, a book about the new South.* New York: D. Appleton-Century Company, Inc., 1942.

DABNEY, VIRGINIUS, *Liberalism in the South.* Chapel Hill: The University of North Carolina Press, 1932.

DANIELS, JONATHAN, *A Southerner Discovers the South.* New York: The Macmillan Company, 1938.

DANIELS, JOSEPHUS, *Tar-Heel Editor.* Chapel Hill: The University of North Carolina Press, 1939.

DAVENPORT, CHARLES B., and A. G. LOVE, *Army Anthropology, based on observations made on draft recruits, 1917-1918, and on veterans at demobilization, 1919.* The Medical Department of the U. S. Army in the World War. Vol. 15, *Statistics.* Part I. Washington, D. C.: 1921.

DAVENPORT, CHARLES B. and M. STEGGERDA, *Race Crossing in Jamaica.* Washington, D. C.: Carnegie Institution of Washington, 1929.

DAVIDSON, HENRY A., "The Anatomy of Prejudice." *Common Ground,* vol. 1, no. 2; Winter, 1941; pp. 3-12.

DAVIS, ALLISON, and JOHN DOLLARD, *Children of Bondage; the personality development of Negro youth in the urban South.* Washington, D. C.: American Council on Education, 1940. (Prepared for the American Youth Commission.)

DAVIS, ALLISON, BURLEIGH B. GARDNER and MARY R. GARDNER, *Deep South; a social anthropological study of caste and class.* Chicago: The University of Chicago Press, 1941.

DAY, CAROLINE BOND, *A Study of Some Negro-White Families in the United States.* Cambridge: Peabody Museum of Harvard University, 1932.

DEDRICK, CALVERT L., and MORRIS H. HANSEN, *The Enumerative Check Census.* Vol. 4 of *The Final Report on Total and Partial Unemployment, 1937. Census of Partial Employment, Unemployment, and Occupations.* Washington, D. C.: 1938.

DE LEEUW HENDRIK, *Sinful Cities of the Western World.* New York: J. Messner, Inc., 1934.

Detroit Bureau of Governmental Research, *The Negro in Detroit.* Detroit: Detroit Bureau of Governmental Research, Inc., 1926.

DETWEILER, FREDERICK G., *The Negro Press in the United States.* Chicago: The University of Chicago Press, 1922.

DEWEY, JOHN, "The Determination of Ultimate Values or Aims through Antecedent or A Priori Speculation or through Pragmatic or Empirical Inquiry." *The Thirty-Seventh Yearbook of the National Society for the Study of Education.* Part II, "The Scientific Movement in Education." 1938; pp. 471-486.

DEWEY, JOHN, *Freedom and Culture.* New York: G. P. Putnam's Sons, 1939.

DEWEY, JOHN, "Interpretation of Savage Mind." *The Psychological Review,* vol. 9, no. 3; May, 1902; pp. 217-230.

DICKINSON, ROBERT L., and WOODBRIDGE E. MORRIS, *Techniques of Conception Control.* New York: Birth Control Federation of America, Inc., 1941.

DODD, WILLIAM E., *The Cotton Kingdom, a chronicle of the Old South.* New Haven: Yale University Press, 1919.

DODD, WILLIAM E., "Freedom of Speech in the South." Communication to the Editor of *Nation,* vol. 84, no. 2182; April 25, 1907; pp. 383-384.

DODD, WILLIAM E., *Statesmen of the Old South; or, from radicalism to conservative revolt.* New York: The Macmillan Company, 1911.

DOLLARD, JOHN, *Caste and Class in a Southern Town.* New Haven: Yale University Press, 1937. (Published for the Yale Institute of Human Relations.)

DOLLARD, JOHN, *Criteria for the Life History, with analyses of six notable documents.* New Haven: Yale University Press, 1935. (Published for the Institute of Human Relations.)

DOLLARD, JOHN and Associates, *Frustration and Aggression.* New Haven: Yale University Press, 1939. (Published for the Institute of Human Relations.)

Donaldson, W. T., "Compulsory Voting." *National Municipal Review*, vol. 4, no. 3; July, 1915; pp. 460-465.

Donnan, Elizabeth, "The Slave Trade into South Carolina before the Revolution." *The American Historical Review*, vol. 33, no. 4; July, 1928; pp. 804-828.

Douglass, Frederick, "The Claims of the Negro, Ethnologically Considered." An address before the Literary Societies of Western Reserve College, at Commencement, July 12, 1854. Rochester: Lee, Mann, and Company, 1854.

Douglass, Frederick, *Life and Times of Frederick Douglass, written by himself.* Boston: De Wolfe, Fiske and Company, 1895. (Expanded from *Narrative of the Life of Frederick Douglass*, published in 1845.)

Doyle, Bertram Wilbur, *The Etiquette of Race Relations in the South.* Chicago: The University of Chicago Press, 1937.

Doyle, Bertram Wilbur, "Racial Traits of the Negro as Negroes Assign Them to Themselves." Unpublished M.A. thesis, The University of Chicago, 1924.

Drake, J. G. St. Clair, "Churches and Voluntary Associations in the Chicago Negro Community." W.P.A. District 3, Chicago: project under the supervision of Horace R. Cayton, December, 1940. (Mimeographed.)

Dubin, Robert, "Factors in the Variation of Urban Occupational Groups." Unpublished M.A. thesis, The University of Chicago, 1940.

Dublin, Louis I., *Health and Wealth, a survey of the economics of world health.* New York: Harper and Brothers, 1928.

Dublin, Louis I., and Alfred J. Lotka, *Twenty-Five Years of Health Progress, a study of the mortality experience among the industrial policyholders of the Metropolitan Life Insurance Company, 1911 to 1935.* New York: Metropolitan Life Insurance Company, 1937.

Du Bois, W. E. Burghardt, "Black Folk and Birth Control." *The Birth Control Review*, vol. 16, no. 6; June, 1932; pp. 166-167.

Du Bois, W. E. Burghardt, *Black Folk, Then and Now; an essay in the history and sociology of the Negro race.* New York: Henry Holt and Company, 1939.

Du Bois, W. E. Burghardt, *Black Reconstruction, an essay toward a history of the part which black folk played in the attempt to reconstruct democracy in America, 1860-1880.* New York: Harcourt, Brace and Company, 1935.

Du Bois, W. E. Burghardt, *Darkwater; voices from within the veil.* New York: Harcourt, Brace, and Howe, 1920.

Du Bois, W. E. Burghardt, "Does the Negro Need Separate Schools?" *Journal of Negro Education*, vol. 4, no. 3; July, 1935; pp. 328-335.

Du Bois, W. E. Burghardt, *Dusk of Dawn; an essay toward an autobiography of a race concept.* New York: Harcourt, Brace and Company, 1940.

Du Bois, W. E. Burghardt (editor), *Economic Cooperation among Negro Americans. Report of a social study made by Atlanta University.* Atlanta, Georgia: The Atlanta University Press, 1907.

Du Bois, W. E. Burghardt, Editorial, *The Crisis*, vol. 19, no. 3; January, 1920; p. 106.

Du Bois, W. E. Burghardt, "The Hosts of Black Labor." *Nation*, vol. 116, no. 3018; May 9, 1923; pp. 539-541.

Du Bois, W. E. Burghardt, *The Negro.* New York: Henry Holt and Company, 1915. (Home University Library of Modern Knowledge, no. 91.)

Du Bois, W. E. Burghardt, "A Negro Nation within the Nation." *Current History*, vol. 45, no. 4; June, 1935; p. 265.

Du Bois, W. E. Burghardt, *The Philadelphia Negro: a social study. Together with a special report on domestic service, by I. Eaton.* Philadelphia: The University of Pennsylvania Press, 1899. Publications of The University of Pennsylvania series in Political Economy and Public Law, no. 14.

Du Bois, W. E. Burghardt (editor), *Some Efforts of American Negroes for their Own Social Betterment.* Atlanta, Georgia: Atlanta University Press, 1898. (Atlanta University Publication, no. 3.)

Du Bois, W. E. Burghardt, *The Souls of Black Folk.* Chicago: A. C. McClurg and Company, 1903.

Duggan, I. W., "Cotton, Land and People: A Statement of the Problem." *Journal of Farm Economics*, vol. 22, no. 1; February, 1940; pp. 188-197.

The Duke Endowment, *Fourteenth Annual Report of the Hospital Section, 1938.* Charlotte, North Carolina: The Duke Endowment, 1939.

Durkheim, Émile, *The Rules of Sociological Method.* (Translated by Sarah A. Solovay and John H. Mueller.) Chicago: The University of Chicago Press, 1938. (First French edition published in 1895.)

East, Edward M., *Heredity and Human Affairs.* New York: Charles Scribner's Sons, 1927.

Eckenrode, Hamilton J., *Jefferson Davis, President of the South.* New York: The Macmillan Company, 1923.

Eddy, Walter A. and Gessner G. Hawley, *We Need Vitamins.* New York: Reinhold Publishing Company, 1941.

Educational Policies Commission, *Education and Economic Well-Being in American Democracy.* Washington, D.C.: Educational Policies Commission, National Education Association of the United States and the American Association of School Administrators, 1940.

Elliott, E. N. (editor), *Cotton Is King, and Pro-Slavery Arguments.* Augusta, Georgia: Pritchard, Abbott and Loomis, 1860.

Embree, Edwin R., *Brown America: the story of a new race.* New York: The Viking Press, 1931.

Embree, Edwin R., *Julius Rosenwald Fund: Review of Two Decades, 1917-1936.* Chicago: 1936.

Embree, Edwin R., *Julius Rosenwald Fund: Review for the Two-Year Period 1940-1942.* Chicago: 1942.

Eppse, Merl R., *The Negro, Too, in American History.* Chicago: National Educational Publication Company, Inc., 1939.

Ethridge, Mark, "About Will Alexander." *The New Republic*, vol. 105, no. 12; September 22, 1941; pp. 366-367.

Ferebee, Dorothy Boulding, "Planned Parenthood as a Public Health Measure for the Negro Race," Address at Annual Meeting of the Birth Control Federation of America. New York: January 29, 1942.

Ferguson, G. O., "The Psychology of the Negro, an experimental study." *Archives of Psychology*, no. 36; April, 1916.

Fisher, Constance, "The Negro Social Worker Evaluates Birth Control." *The Birth Control Review*, vol. 16, no. 6; June, 1932; pp. 174-175.

FITZHUGH, GEORGE, *Sociology for the South: Failure of Free Society*. Richmond: A. Morris, Publisher, 1854.

FLORANT, LYONEL C., "Memorandum re: Negro Housing in Norfolk, Virginia." Unpublished manuscript, Population Study, Virginia State Planning Board; June 3, 1942.

FORD, NICK AARON, *The Contemporary Negro Novel, a study in race relations*. Boston: Meador Publishing Company, 1936.

FORTUNE, T. THOMAS, Answer to speech of W. H. Baldwin, "The Present Problems of Negro Education." *Journal of Social Science*, vol. 37; December, 1899; pp. 64-68.

Fortune, "Fortune Quarterly Survey: XIII." Vol. 18, no. 1; July, 1938; pp. 36-37, 74-80.

Fortune, "Fortune Quarterly Survey: XXVII." Vol. 21, no. 2; February, 1940; pp. 14, 20, 28, 133-136.

Fortune, "Harlem." Vol. 20, no. 1; July, 1939; pp. 78, 168-170.

Fortune, "The Negro's War." Vol. 25, no. 6; June, 1942; pp. 77-80, 157-164.

Fortune, "The Servant Problem, Women's Labor Problem." Vol. 17, no. 3; March, 1938; pp. 81-85.

FOWLES, GEORGE MILTON, *Down in Porto Rico*. New York: Eaton and Mains, 1910.

FRAENKEL, OSMOND K., "Restrictions on Voting in the United States." *The National Lawyers' Guild Quarterly*, vol. 1, no. 2; March, 1938; pp. 135-143.

FRAZIER, E. FRANKLIN, "Children in Black and Mulatto Families." *The American Journal of Sociology*, vol. 39, no. 1; July, 1933; pp. 12-29.

FRAZIER, E. FRANKLIN, *The Free Negro Family*. Nashville, Tennessee: Fisk University Press, 1932.

FRAZIER, E. FRANKLIN, *The Negro Family in Chicago*. Chicago: The University of Chicago Press, 1932.

FRAZIER, E. FRANKLIN, *The Negro Family in the United States*. Chicago: The University of Chicago Press, 1939.

FRAZIER, E. FRANKLIN, "Negro Harlem: An Ecological Study." *The American Journal of Sociology*, vol. 43, no. 1; July, 1937; pp. 72-88.

FRAZIER, E. FRANKLIN, *Negro Youth at the Crossways, their personality development in the middle states*. Washington, D.C.: American Council on Education, 1940. (Prepared for the American Youth Commission.)

FRAZIER, E. FRANKLIN, "The Pathology of Race Prejudice." *The Forum*, vol. 77, no. 6; June, 1927; pp. 856-862.

FRAZIER, E. FRANKLIN, "Review of *The Myth of the Negro Past*." *Nation*, vol. 154, no. 7; February 14, 1942; pp. 195-196.

FRY, C. LUTHER, *The U.S. Looks at Its Churches*. New York: Institute of Social and Religious Research, 1930.

GABRIEL, RALPH H., *The Course of American Democratic Thought*. New York: The Ronald Press Company, 1940.

GALLAGHER, BUELL G., *American Caste and the Negro College*. New York: Columbia University Press, 1938.

GALLOWAY, GEORGE B., *Postwar Planning in the United States*. New York: The Twentieth Century Fund, 1942.

GALLOWAY, GEORGE B., and Associates, *Planning for America*. New York: Henry Holt and Company, 1941

GALLUP, GEORGE, and SAUL FORBES RAE, *The Pulse of Democracy*. New York: Simon Schuster, 1940.

GARDNER, WILLIAM J., *A History of Jamaica*. London: T. Fisher Unwin, 1909.

GARTH, THOMAS R., *Race Psychology; a study of racial mental differences*. New York: McGraw-Hill Book Company, Inc., 1931.

GARVEY, AMY JACQUES (editor), *Philosophy and Opinions of Marcus Garvey*. Vol. 1. New York: The Universal Publishing House, 1923.

GIDDINGS, FRANKLIN H., *Studies in the Theory of Human Society*. New York: The Macmillan Company, 1922.

GIST, NOEL P., "The Negro in the Daily Press." *Social Forces*, vol. 10, no. 3; March, 1932; pp. 405-411.

GIST, NOEL P., "*Racial Attitudes in the Press.*" *Sociology and Social Research*, vol. 17, no. 1; September-October, 1932; pp. 25-36.

GLEASON, ELIZA ATKINS, *The Southern Negro and the Public Library*. Chicago: The University of Chicago Press, 1941.

GOODELL, WILLIAM, *The American Slave Code in Theory and Practice*. New York: American and Foreign Anti-Slavery Society, 1853.

GOODRICH, CARTER, and Associates, *Migration and Economic Opportunity; the report of the study of population redistribution*. Philadelphia: The University of Pennsylvania Press, 1936.

GOSNELL, HAROLD F., *Getting Out the Vote; an experiment in the stimulation of voting*. Chicago: The University of Chicago Press, 1927.

GOSNELL, HAROLD F., *Negro Politicians, the rise of Negro politics in Chicago*. Chicago: The University of Chicago Press, 1935.

GOSNELL, HAROLD F., "The Negro Vote in Northern Cities." *National Municipal Review*, vol. 30, no. 5; May, 1941; pp. 264-267.

GOSNELL, HAROLD F., and NORMAN N. GILL, "An Analysis of the 1932 Presidential Vote in Chicago." *American Political Science Review*, vol. 29, no. 6; December, 1935; pp. 967-984.

GOULD, CHARLES W., *America: A Family Matter*. New York: Charles Scribner's Sons, 1920.

GRADY, HENRY W., *The New South*. New York: Robert Bonner's Sons, 1890.

GRANGER, LESTER B., "The Negro Congress—Its Future." *Opportunity*, vol. 18, no. 6; June, 1940; pp. 164-166.

GRANGER, LESTER B., "Negroes and War Production." *Survey Graphic*, vol. 31, no. 11; November, 1942; pp. 469-471, 543-544.

GRANT, MADISON, *The Passing of the Great Race*. New York: Charles Scribner's Sons, 1916.

GRAVES, JOHN TEMPLE, "The Southern Negro and the War Crisis." *Virginia Quarterly Review*, vol. 18, no. 4; Autumn, 1942; pp. 500-517.

The Greater New York Federation of Churches, *The Negro Churches of Manhattan*. New York: The Greater New York Federation of Churches, 1930.

GREEN, H. M., "Hospitals and Public Health Facilities for Negroes." *Proceedings of the National Conference of Social Work*. Chicago: The University of Chicago Press, 1928, pp. 178-180.

GREENE, HARRY W., *Negro Leaders*. Institute, West Virginia: West Virginia State College, November, 1936. West Virginia State College Bulletin, series 23, no. 6.

GREENE, LORENZO J. and CARTER G. WOODSON, *The Negro Wage Earner*. Washington, D.C.: The Association for the Study of Negro Life and History, Inc., 1930.

GROVES, ERNEST R., and WILLIAM F. OGBURN, *American Marriage and Family Relations*. New York: Henry Holt and Company, 1928.

HAILEY, MALCOLM. *An African Survey; a study of problems arising in Africa south of the Sahara*. London: The Oxford University Press, 1938.

HAMILTON, HORACE C., "The Social Effects of Recent Trends in the Mechanization of Agriculture." *Rural Sociology*, vol. 4, no. 1; March, 1939; pp. 3-25.

HAMILTON, JAMES A., *Negro Suffrage and Congressional Representation*. New York: The Winthrop Press, 1910.

HAMPTON, WADE and others (Symposium): "Ought the Negro to Be Disfranchised? Ought He to Have Been Enfranchised?" *The North American Review*, vol. 128; March, 1879; pp. 225-283.

Hampton Normal and Agricultural Institute, *Report of the Hampton Normal and Agricultural Institute for the Fiscal Year Ending June 30, 1875*. Hampton, Virginia: Normal School Steam Press, 1875.

HANKINS, FRANK H., *The Racial Basis of Civilization; a critique of the Nordic doctrine*. New York: Alfred A. Knopf, 1926.

HARPER, CHANCELLOR WILLIAM, *Memoirs on Slavery*. Paper read before the Society for the Advancement of Learning of South Carolina, annual meeting at Columbia, South Carolina, 1837. Charleston: James S. Burges, 1838.

HARRIS, ABRAM L., *The Negro as Capitalist: a study of banking and business among American Negroes*. Philadelphia: The American Academy of Political and Social Science, 1936.

HART, ALBERT BUSHNELL, *The Southern South*. New York: D. Appleton and Company, 1910.

HART, HORNELL NORRIS, *Selective Migration as Factor in Child Welfare in the United States with Special Reference to Iowa*. Iowa City: The University of Iowa, 1921.

HASTIE, WILLIAM, "The Negro in the Army Today." Typewritten public statement. War Department; August, 1942.

HAUSER, PHILIP M., "Differential Fertility, Mortality, and Net Reproduction in Chicago, 1930." Unpublished Ph.D. thesis, The University of Chicago, 1938.

HAYES, LAURENCE J. W., *The Negro Federal Government Worker*. Washington, D.C.: The Graduate School, Howard University, 1941. (Howard University Studies in the Social Sciences, vol. 3, no. 1.)

HECKSCHER, ELI F., *Mercantilism*. (Translated by Mendel Shapiro.) London: G. Allen and Unwin, Ltd., 1935. (First published, 1931.)

HELPER, HINTON, *The Impending Crisis of the South: how to meet it*. New York: Burdick Brothers, 1857.

HENDERSON, ELMER W., "A Study of the Basic Factors Involved in the Change in the Party Alignment of Negroes in Chicago, 1932-1938." Unpublished M.A. thesis, The University of Chicago, 1939.

HERBERT, HILARY A. (editor), *Why the Solid South? or, Reconstruction and its results*. Baltimore: R. H. Woodward and Company, 1890.

HERSKOVITS, MELVILLE J., *The American Negro, a study in racial crossing*. New York: Alfred A. Knopf, 1928.

HERSKOVITS, MELVILLE, J., *The Anthropometry of the American Negro*. New York: Columbia University Press, 1930.

HERSKOVITS, MELVILLE J., "On the Provenience of the New World Negroes." *Social Forces*, vol. 12, no. 2; December, 1933; pp. 247-262.

HERSKOVITS, MELVILLE J., "Review of *The Negro Family in the United States*." *Nation*, vol. 150, no. 4; January 27, 1940; pp. 104-105.

HERSKOVITS, MELVILLE J., V. K. CAMERON, and H. SMITH, "The Physical Form of Mississippi Negroes." *The American Journal of Physical Anthropology*, vol. 16, no. 2; October-December, 1931; pp. 193-201.

HICKS, JOHN D., *The Populist Revolt; a history of the Farmers' Alliance and the People's Party*. Minneapolis: The University of Minnesota Press, 1931.

HIGH, STANLEY, "How the Negro Fights for Freedom." *Reader's Digest*, vol. 41, no. 243; July, 1942; pp. 113-118.

HILL, ROBERT T., *Cuba and Porto Rico, with the other islands of the West Indies; their topography, climate, flora, products, industries, cities, people, political conditions, etc.* New York: The Century Company, 1898.

HIMES, NORMAN, "Clinical Service for the Negro." *The Birth Control Review*, vol. 16, no. 6; June, 1932; pp. 176-177.

HINCKLEY, E. D., "The Influence of Individual Opinion on the Construction of an Attitude Scale." *The Journal of Social Psychology*, vol. 3, no. 3; August, 1932; pp. 283-295.

HOFFMAN, FREDERICK L., *Race Traits and Tendencies of the American Negro*. New York: The Macmillan Company, 1896.

HOLMES, SAMUEL JACKSON, "The Negro Birth Rate." *The Birth Control Review*, vol. 16, no. 6; June, 1932; pp. 172-173.

HOLMES, SAMUEL JACKSON, *The Negro's Struggle for Survival, a study in human ecology*. Berkeley, California: University of California Press, 1937.

HOOT, JOHN WELDON, "Lynch Law, the Practice of Illegal Popular Coercion." Unpublished Ph.D. thesis, The University of Pennsylvania, 1935.

HORST, PAUL, and Associates, *The Prediction of Personal Adjustment*. New York: Social Science Research Council, 1941. (Social Science Research Council Bulletin no. 48.)

HOSHOR, JOHN, *God in a Rolls Royce; the rise of Father Divine, madman, menace, or messiah*. New York: Hillman-Curl, Inc., 1936.

HRDLIČKA, ALEŠ, *The Old Americans*. Baltimore: The Williams and Wilkins Company, 1925.

HRDLIČKA, ÁLEŠ, "The Full-Blood American Negro." *American Journal of Physical Anthropology*, vol. 12, no. 1; July-September, 1928; pp. 15-53.

HUGHES, HENRY, *Treatise on Sociology, Theoretical and Practical*. Philadelphia: the author, 1854.

HUGHES, LANGSTON, *The Big Sea, an autobiography*. New York: Alfred A. Knopf, 1940.

HURD, JOHN CODMAN, *The Law of Freedom and Bondage in the United States*. Boston: Little, Brown and Company; vol. 1, 1858; vol. 2, 1862.

HURSTON, ZORA NEALE, *Mules and Men*. Philadelphia: J. B. Lippincott Company, 1935.

Hurston, Zora Neale, *Tell My Horse*. Philadelphia: J. B. Lippincott Company, 1938.

Hurston, Zora Neale, *Their Eyes Were Watching God: a novel*. Philadelphia: J. B. Lippincott Company, 1937.

Huxley, Julian S., and A. C. Haddon, *We Europeans*. New York: Harper and Brothers, 1936.

Irish, Marian D., "The Southern One-Party System and National Politics." *Journal of Politics*, vol. 4, no. 1; February, 1942; pp. 80-94.

Ivy, James W., "Review of *An Analysis of the Specific References to Negroes in Selected Curricula for the Education of Teachers* by Edna Meade Colson." *The Crisis*, vol. 48, no. 10; October, 1941; p. 331.

Jackson, L. P., "Elizabethan Seamen and the African Slave Trade." *The Journal of Negro History*, vol. 9, no. 1; January, 1924; pp. 1-17.

Jaffe, A. J., "Population Growth and Fertility Trends in the United States." *Journal of Heredity*, vol. 32, no. 12; December, 1941; pp. 441-445.

Jaffe, A. J., "Urbanization and Fertility." *American Journal of Sociology*, vol. 48, no. 1; July, 1942, pp. 48-60.

James, William, *On Some of Life's Ideals; on a certain blindness in human beings; what makes a life significant*. New York: Henry Holt and Company, 1912.

James, William, "The Will to Believe," *The New World: A Quarterly Review of Religion, Ethics, and Theology*, vol. 5, no. 18; June, 1896; pp. 327-347.

Jarvis, J. Antonio, *Brief History of the Virgin Islands*. St. Thomas, Virgin Islands: The Art Shop, 1938.

Jefferson, Thomas, *The Writings of Thomas Jefferson: being his autobiography, correspondence, reports, messages, addresses, and other writings official and private*. Vols. 1 and 8. (H. A. Washington, editor.) Washington, D.C.: Taylor and Maury, 1853-1854.

Jenkins, William Sumner, *Pro-Slavery Thought in the Old South*. Chapel Hill: The University of North Carolina Press, 1935.

Jenks, Albert Ernest, "The Legal Status of Negro-White Amalgamation in the United States." *The American Journal of Sociology*, vol. 21, no. 5; March, 1916; pp. 666-678.

Jernegan, Marcus Wilson, *Laboring and Dependent Classes in Colonial America: 1607-1783; studies of the economic, educational, and social significance of slaves, servants, apprentices, and poor folk*. Chicago: The University of Chicago Press, 1931.

Johns, Elizabeth D., "The Role of the Negro Newspaper in the Negro Community." Unpublished manuscript, 1940.

Johnson, Charles S., *Growing up in the Black Belt; Negro youth in the rural South*. Washington, D.C.: American Council on Education, 1941. (Prepared for the American Youth Commission.)

Johnson, Charles S., "The Negro." *The American Journal of Sociology*, vol. 47, no. 6; May, 1942; pp. 854-864.

Johnson, Charles S., *The Negro in American Civilization; a study of Negro life and race relations in the light of social research*. New York: Henry Holt and Company, 1930.

JOHNSON, CHARLES S., *The Negro College Graduate*. Chapel Hill: The University of North Carolina Press, 1938.

JOHNSON, CHARLES S., "The Negro Public Schools." Section 8 of Louisiana Educational Survey: Survey of Elementary and Secondary Education, vol. 4. Baton Rouge: Louisiana Educational Survey Commission, 1942. (Mimeographed.)

JOHNSON, CHARLES S., "Negroes in the Railway Industry." Part I. *Phylon*, vol. 3, no. 1; First Quarter, 1942; pp. 5-14. Part II. *Phylon*, vol. 3, no. 2; Second Quarter, 1942; pp. 196-204.

JOHNSON, CHARLES S., *Shadow of the Plantation*. Chicago: The University of Chicago Press, 1934.

JOHNSON, CHARLES S., and HORACE M. BOND, "The Investigation of Racial Differences Prior to 1910." *Journal of Negro Education*, vol. 3, no. 3; July, 1934; pp. 328-339.

JOHNSON, CHARLES S., EDWIN R. EMBREE and W. W. ALEXANDER, *The Collapse of Cotton Tenancy*. Chapel Hill: The University of North Carolina Press, 1935.

JOHNSON, GUION GRIFFIS, "The Impact of War upon the Negro." *Journal of Negro Education*, vol. 10, no. 3; July, 1941; pp. 596-611.

JOHNSON, GUY B., "Commencement Address." *Virginia State College Gazette*, vol. 45, no. 3; December, 1939; pp. 10-16.

JOHNSON, GUY B., "The Negro and Crime." *The Annals of the American Academy of Political and Social Science*, vol. 217; September, 1941; pp. 93-104.

JOHNSON, GUY B., "Negro Racial Movements and Leadership in the United States." *The American Journal of Sociology*, vol. 43, no. 1; July, 1937; pp. 57-71.

JOHNSON, GUY B., "Some Factors in the Development of Negro Social Institutions in the United States." *The American Journal of Sociology*, vol. 30, no. 3; November, 1934; pp. 329-337.

JOHNSON, JAMES WELDON, *Along This Way; the autobiography of James Weldon Johnson*. New York: The Viking Press, 1933.

JOHNSON, JAMES WELDON, *The Autobiography of an Ex-Coloured Man*. Boston: Sherman, French and Company, 1912.

JOHNSON, JAMES WELDON, *Black Manhattan*. New York: Alfred A. Knopf, 1930.

JOHNSON, JAMES WELDON, *Negro Americans, What Now?* New York: The Viking Press, 1934.

JOHNSON, JAMES WELDON, "A Negro Looks at Politics." *The American Mercury*, vol. 18, no. 69; September, 1929; pp. 88-94.

JOHNSTON, SIR HARRY H., *The Negro in the New World*. London: Methuen and Company, Ltd., 1910.

The Journal of Negro History, vol. 27, no. 1, January, 1942.

KATZ, DANIEL, and KENNETH BRALY, "Racial Stereotypes of One Hundred College Students." *The Journal of Abnormal and Social Psychology*, vol. 28, no. 3; October-December, 1933; pp. 280-290.

KELLER, ALBERT G., and MAURICE R. DAVIE (editors), *Essays of William Graham Sumner*. New Haven: Yale University Press, 1934.

KENNEDY, JOHN B., "So This Is Harlem." *Collier's*, vol. 92, no. 18; October 28, 1933; pp. 22 and 50-52.

KENNEDY, LOUISE V., *The Negro Peasant Turns Cityward; Effects of Recent Migration to Northern Centers*. New York: Columbia University Press, 1930.

Kenney, John A., "The Inter-Racial Committee of Montclair, New Jersey." *Journal of the National Medical Association*, vol. 23, no. 3; July-September, 1931; pp. 97-109.

Kester, Howard, *Revolt among the Sharecroppers*. New York: Covici, Friede, 1936.

Key, V. O., Jr., *Politics, Parties and Pressure Groups*. New York: Thomas Y. Crowell Company, 1942.

Kingsbury, Susan M., Hornell Hart and Associates, *Newspapers and the News, an objective measurement of ethical and unethical behavior by representative newspapers*. New York: G. P. Putnam's Sons, 1937.

Kiplinger, Willard M., *Washington Is Like That*. New York: Harper and Brothers. 1942.

Kiser, Clyde V., "Birth Rates and Socio-Economic Attributes in 1935." *The Milbank Memorial Fund Quarterly*, vol. 17, no. 2; April, 1939; pp. 128-151.

Kiser, Clyde V., "Fertility of Harlem Negroes." *The Milbank Memorial Fund Quarterly*, vol. 13, no 3; July, 1935; pp. 273-285.

Kiser, Clyde V., *Sea Island to City, a study of St. Helena Islanders in Harlem and other urban centers*. New York: Columbia University Press, 1932.

Klineberg, Otto, *Negro Intelligence and Selective Migration*. New York: Columbia University Press, 1935.

Klineberg, Otto, *Race Differences*. New York: Harper and Brothers, 1935.

Krout, Maurice H., "Race and Culture: A Study in Mobility, Segregation, and Selection." *The American Journal of Sociology*, vol. 37, no. 2; September, 1931; pp. 175-189.

Kurtz, Russell H. (editor), *Social Work Yearbook: 1941*. New York: Russell Sage Foundation, 1941.

Lamar, L. Q. C. and others (Symposium): "Ought the Negro Be Disfranchised? Ought He to Have Been Enfranchised?" *The North American Review*, vol. 128; March, 1879; pp. 225-283.

La Piere, Richard T., *Collective Behavior*. New York: McGraw-Hill Book Company, Inc., 1938.

Lester, Richard A., *Economics of Labor*. Seattle, Washington: The Washington Book Store, 1940. (Mimeographed; now printed.)

Lester, Robert M., *Corporation Grants for Education of the Negro*. Carnegie Corporation of New York pamphlet, privately printed, 1941.

Lewinson, Paul, *Race, Class, and Party; a history of Negro suffrage and white politics in the South*. London: The Oxford University Press, 1932.

Lewis, Julian H., *The Biology of the Negro*. Chicago: The University of Chicago Press, 1942.

Lewis, Matthew G., *Journal of a West India Proprietor, 1815-17*. Boston: Houghton Mifflin Company, 1929.

Leyburn, James G., *The Haitian People*. New Haven: Yale University Press, 1941.

Life Magazine, vol. 12, no. 11; March 16, 1942; pp. 40-41.

Lightfoot, Robert M., *Negro Crime in a Small Urban Community*. Charlottesville: University of Virginia, 1934. (Phelps-Stokes Fellowship Paper of the University of Virginia No. 12.)

Lincoln, Abraham, "Speech at New Haven, March 6, 1860." *The Complete Works of Abraham Lincoln*, vol. 5 (John G. Nicolay and John Hay, editors). New York: Francis D. Tandy Company, 1894.

LITCHFIELD, EDWARD H., "A Case Study of Negro Political Behavior in Detroit." *The Public Opinion Quarterly*, vol. 5, no. 2; June, 1941; pp. 267-274.

LOCKE, ALAIN, *Negro Art: Past and Present*. Washington, D.C.: The Associates in Negro Folk Education, 1936.

LOCKE, ALAIN, *The Negro and His Music*. Washington, D.C.: The Associates in Negro Folk Education, 1936.

LOCKE, ALAIN, *The New Negro: an interpretation*. New York: Albert and Charles Boni, 1925.

LOCKE, ALAIN, "Who and What Is a Negro." *Opportunity*, vol. 20, no. 2; February, 1942; pp. 36-41.

LOGAN, RAYFORD W. (editor), *The Attitude of the Southern White Press toward Negro Suffrage: 1932-1940*. Washington, D.C.: The Foundation Publishers, 1940.

LORIMER, FRANK, ELLEN WINSTON and LOUISE K. KISER, *Foundations of American Population Policy*. New York: Harper and Brothers, 1940.

LOVE, A. G., and C. B. DAVENPORT, "A Comparison of White and Colored Troops in Respect to Incidence of Disease." *Proceedings of the National Academy of Sciences*, vol. 5, no. 3; March, 1919; pp. 58-67.

LYND, ROBERT S., *Knowledge for What? The place of social science in American culture*. Princeton: Princeton University Press, 1939.

McALPIN, ALICE S., "Changes in the Intelligence Quotients of Negro Children." *Journal of Negro Education*, vol. 1, no. 1; April 1, 1932; pp. 44-48.

McCARROLL, E. MAE, "A Report on the Two-Year Negro Demonstration Health Program of the Planned Parenthood Federation of America, Inc." A talk delivered at the annual convention of the National Medical Association, Cleveland, August 17, 1942.

McCUISTION, FRED, *Graduate Instruction for Negroes in the United States*. Nashville: George Peabody College for Teachers, 1939.

McDOUGALL, WILLIAM, *The Group Mind, a sketch of the principles of collective psychology*. New York: G. P. Putnam's Sons, 1920.

McDOUGALL, WILLIAM, *Is America Safe for Democracy?* New York: Charles Scribner's, 1921.

MacIVER, ROBERT M., *Social Causation*. Boston: Ginn and Company, 1942.

MacIVER, ROBERT M., *Society; Its Structure and Changes*. New York: Ray Long and Richard R. Smith, Inc., 1931.

McKAY, CLAUDE, *Harlem: Negro Metropolis*. New York: E. P. Dutton and Company, Inc., 1940.

McKAY, CLAUDE, *A Long Way from Home*. New York: L. Furman, Inc., 1937.

McKAY, CLAUDE, " 'Segregation' in Harlem?" *Column Review*, vol. 13, no. 4; December, 1941; pp. 5-7.

MAGUIRE, JOHN MACARTHUR, "Legal Aid." *Encyclopedia of the Social Sciences*; vol. IX; pp. 319-324.

MALL, FRANKLIN P., "On Several Anatomical Characters of the Human Brain, Said to Vary according to Race and Sex, with Especial Reference to the Weight of the Frontal Lobe." *The American Journal of Anatomy*, vol. 9, no. 1; February, 1909; pp. 1-32.

MANGUM, CHARLES S., JR., *The Legal Status of the Negro*. Chapel Hill: The University of North Carolina Press, 1940.

MANINGTON, GEORGE, *The West Indies with British Guiana and British Honduras*. London: L. Parsons, 1925.

MANNHEIM, KARL, *Ideology and Utopia, an introduction to the sociology of knowledge*. London: K. Paul, Trench, Trubner and Company, Ltd., 1936.

MARTINEAU, HARRIET, *Society in America*, 2 vols. New York: Saunders and Otley, 1837.

The Mayor's Commission on Conditions in Harlem, "The Negro in Harlem: A Report on Social and Economic Conditions Responsible for the Outbreak of March 19, 1935." New York: 1936. (Typescript.)

MAYS, BENJAMIN E., "The Negro Church in American Life." *Christendom, an ecumenical review*, vol. 5, no. 3; Summer, 1940; pp. 387-398.

MAYS, BENJAMIN E., *The Negro's God as reflected in his literature*. Boston: Chapman and Grimes, Inc., 1938.

MAYS, BENJAMIN E., and JOSEPH W. NICHOLSON, *The Negro's Church*. New York: Institute of Social and Religious Research, 1933.

MEAD, MARGARET, *Coming of Age in Samoa, a psychological study of primitive youth for Western civilization*. New York: W. Morrow and Company, 1928.

MECKLIN, JOHN M., *Democracy and Race Friction: a study in social ethics*. New York: The Macmillan Company, 1914.

MERRIAM, CHARLES E., "The Meaning of Democracy." *Journal of Negro Education*, vol. 10, no. 3; July, 1941; pp. 309-317.

MERRIAM, CHARLES E., and HAROLD F. GOSNELL, *Non-Voting; causes and methods of control*. Chicago: The University of Chicago Press, 1924.

Metropolitan Life Insurance Company, *Statistical Bulletin*, vol. 20, no. 6; June, 1939.

MILLER, DELBERT C., "Effect of the War Declaration on the National Morale of American College Students." *American Sociological Review*, vol. 7, no. 5; October, 1942; pp. 631-644.

MILLER, KELLY, "Government and the Negro." *The Annals of the American Academy of Political and Social Science*, vol. 140, no. 229; November, 1928; pp. 98-104.

MILLER, KELLY, *Out of the House of Bondage*. New York: The Neale Publishing Company, 1914.

MILLER, KELLY, *Race Adjustment—Essays on the Negro in America*. New York: The Neale Publishing Company, 1908.

MIMS, EDWIN, *The Advancing South, stories of progress and reaction*. Garden City, New York: Doubleday, Page and Company, 1926.

MITCHELL, BROADUS, *The Rise of Cotton Mills in the South*. Baltimore: The Johns Hopkins Press, 1921.

MITCHELL, BROADUS, and GEORGE S. MITCHELL, *The Industrial Revolution in the South*. Baltimore: The Johns Hopkins Press, 1930.

MITCHELL, H. L., "The Southern Tenant Farmers Union in 1941." Report of the Secretary, 1942. (Mimeographed.)

Modern Industry, "Found: A Million Manpower." Vol. 3, no. 5; May 15, 1942; pp. 28-31.

MOFFAT, R. BURNHAM, "The Disfranchisement of the Negro, from a lawyer's standpoint." *Journal of Social Science*. vol. 42; September, 1904; pp. 31-62.

MONTAGUE, LUDWELL LEE, *Haiti and the United States, 1714-1938*. Durham: Duke University Press, 1940.

MOORE, WILBERT E., and ROBIN M. WILLIAMS, "Stratification in the Ante-Bellum South." *American Sociological Review*, vol. 7, no. 3; June, 1942; pp. 343-351.

MOTON, ROBERT RUSSA, *Finding a Way Out; an autobiography*. Garden City, New York: Doubleday, Page and Company, 1921.

MOTON, ROBERT RUSSA, *What the Negro Thinks*. Garden City, New York: Doubleday, Doran and Company, Inc., 1929.

MOWRER, ERNEST R., *Family Disorganization; an introduction to a sociological analysis*. Chicago: The University of Chicago Press, 1927.

MURCHISON, CARL A. (editor), *A Handbook of Social Psychology*. Worcester, Massachusetts: Clark University Press, 1935.

MURPHY, EDGAR GARDNER, *The Basis of Ascendancy, a discussion of certain principles of public policy involved in the development of the Southern states*. London: Longmans, Green, and Company, 1909.

MURPHY, EDGAR GARDNER, *Problems of the Present South, a discussion of certain of the educational, industrial, and political issues in the Southern states*. New York: The Macmillan Company, 1904.

MURRAY, FLORENCE (editor), *The Negro Handbook, 1942*. New York: Wendell Malliet and Company, 1942.

MYERS, GUSTAVUS, *America Strikes Back: a record of contrasts*. New York: Ives Washburn, Inc., 1935.

MYRDAL, ALVA, *Nation and Family, the Swedish experiment in democratic family and population policy*. New York: Harper and Brothers, 1941.

MYRDAL, ALVA and GUNNAR, *Kontakt Med Amerika*. Stockholm: Albert Bonnier, 1941.

MYRDAL, GUNNAR, *Monetary Equilibrium*. London: W. Hodge and Company, Ltd., 1939.

MYRDAL, GUNNAR, *Das Politische Element in der Nationalökonomischen Doktrinbildung*. Aus dem Schwedischen Übersetzt von Gerhard Mackenroth. Berlin: Junker und Dünnhaupt, 1932.

MYRDAL, GUNNAR, *Population, a problem for democracy*. Cambridge: Harvard University Press, 1940.

MYRDAL, GUNNAR, "Das Zweck-Mitteldenken in der Nationalökonomie." *Zeitchrift für Nationalökonomie*, bund IV. Vienna, Austria: 1932.

Nation, "Prostitution in New York City." Vol 142, no. 3690; March 25, 1936; p. 369.

National Association for the Advancement of Colored People, "Bulletin." New York: June, 1942. (Mimeographed.)

National Association for the Advancement of Colored People, *N.A.A.C.P. Annual Report for 1941*. New York: National Association for the Advancement of Colored People, 1942.

National Association for the Advancement of Colored People, "Press Service." New York: December 12, 1941. (Mimeographed.)

National Association for the Advancement of Colored People, "Press Service." New York: February 13, 1942. (Mimeographed.)

National Association for the Advancement of Colored People, "Press Service." New York: February 27, 1942. (Mimeographed.)

National Association for the Advancement of Colored People, "Press Service." New York: July 17, 1942. (Mimeographed.)

National Association for the Advancement of Colored People, "Press Service." New York: July 31, 1942. (Mimeographed.)

National Association for the Advancement of Colored People, *Teachers' Salaries in Black and White. A Pamphlet for Teachers and Their Friends.* New York: National Association for the Advancement of Colored People, September, 1941.

National Association for the Advancement of Colored People, *Thirty Years of Lynching in the United States, 1899-1918.* New York: National Association for the Advancement of Colored People, 1919.

National Education Association of the United States, Research Division, *Research Bulletin.* Vol. 18, no. 5; November, 1940.

National Industrial Conference Board, *The Economic Almanac for 1942-1943.* New York: National Industrial Conference Board, 1942.

The National Urban League, "Report of Progress in the War Employment of Negro Labor." July, 1942. (Mimeographed.)

Neff, Lawrence W., *Race Relations at Close Range; watching the Negro problem settle itself.* Emory University, Georgia: Banner Press, 1931.

Nettels, Curtis P., *The Roots of American Civilization: a history of American colonial Life.* New York: F. S. Crofts and Company, 1938.

The New Republic, "The Revolt of the Evil Fairies." Vol. 106, no. 14; April 16, 1942; pp. 458-459.

New York *Herald Tribune,* October 16, 1941, p. 5.

New York *Herald Tribune,* March 13, 1942, p. 10.

New York *Herald Tribune,* April 5, 1942, p. 3.

New York *Herald Tribune,* May 10, 1942.

New York *Herald Tribune,* June 10, 1942.

New York *Post,* January 20, 1939.

New York *Post,* November 9, 1939.

New York *Times,* January 11, 1939.

New York *Times,* May 26, 1941.

New York *Times,* April 3, 1942.

New York *Times,* Editorial, April 3, 1942.

New York *Times,* May 26, 1942, p. 20.

New York *Times,* July 20, 1942.

New York *Times,* September 2, 1942, p. 3.

New York City's Welfare Council, "Report of the Sub-Committee on Crime and Delinquency of the City-Wide Citizens' Committee on Harlem." New York: 1942. (Mimeographed).

Newsweek, vol. 12, no. 5; August 1, 1938; pp. 7-8.

Nixon, Herman Clarence, *Forty Acres and Steel Mules.* Chapel Hill: The University of North Carolina Press, 1938.

Norfolk *Journal and Guide,* February 28, 1942.

Northrup, Herbert R., "Negro Labor and Union Policies in the South." Unpublished Ph. D. thesis, Harvard University, 1942.

Northrup, Herbert R., "The Tobacco Workers International Union." *The Quarterly Journal of Economics,* vol. 56, no. 4; August, 1942; pp. 606-626.

Notestein, Frank W., "Differential Fertility in the East North Central States." *The Milbank Memorial Fund Quarterly*, vol. 16, no. 2; April, 1938; pp. 171-191.

Nourse, Edwin G., Joseph S. Davis and John D. Black, *Three Years of the Agricultural Adjustment Administration*. Washington, D. C.: The Brookings Institution, 1937.

O'Connor, William Barnes, "The Use of Colored Persons in Skilled Occupations." *The Conference Board Management Record*, vol. 3. no. 12; December, 1941; pp. 156-158.

Odum, Howard W., *Social and Mental Traits of the Negro; research into the conditions of the Negro race in Southern towns, a study in race traits, tendencies and prospects*. New York: Columbia University, 1910.

Odum, Howard W., and Harry E. Moore, *American Regionalism; a cultural-historical approach to national integration*. New York: Henry Holt and Company, 1938.

Offord, Carl, "Slave Markets in the Bronx." *Nation*, vol. 150, no. 26; June 29, 1940; pp. 780-781.

Ogburn, William F., "Man and His Institutions." *Publication of the American Sociological Society*, vol. 29, no. 3; August, 1935; pp. 29-40.

Olmsted, Frederick L., *The Cotton Kingdom; a traveller's observations on cotton and slavery in the American slave states*, 2 vols. New York: Mason Brothers, 1861-1862.

Opportunity, "The Vanishing Mulatto." Vol. 3, no. 34; October, 1925; p. 291.

Osborn, Frederick, *Preface to Eugenics*. New York: Harper and Brothers, 1940.

PM, February 10, 1942, p. 20.

PM, February 13, 1942, p. 14.

PM, May 7, 1942.

PM, June 23, 1942, p. 22.

PM, August 16, 1942, p. 17.

PM, September 15, 1942.

PM, September 22, 1942.

Page, Thomas Nelson, *The Negro: The Southerner's Problem*. New York: Charles Scribner's Sons, 1904.

Panunzio, Constantine, "Intermarriage in Los Angeles, 1924-1933." *The American Journal of Sociology*, vol. 47, no. 5; March, 1942; pp. 690-701.

Park, Robert E., "The Bases of Race Prejudice." *The Annals of the American Academy of Political and Social Science*, vol. 140, no. 229; November, 1928; pp. 11-20.

Park, Robert E., "Behind Our Masks." *The Survey: Graphic Number*, vol. 56, no. 3; May 1, 1926; pp. 135-139.

Park, Robert E., "Collective Behavior." *Encyclopedia of the Social Sciences*; vol. III; pp. 631-633.

Park, Robert E., *The Immigrant Press and Its Control*. New York: Harper and Brothers, 1922.

Park, Robert E., "Social Planning and Human Nature." *Publication of the American Sociological Society*, vol. 29, no. 3; August, 1935; pp. 19-28.

Park, Robert E., and Ernest W. Burgess, *Introduction to the Science of Sociology* Chicago: The University of Chicago Press, 1921.

Parrington, Vernon L., *Main Currents in American Thought*. New York: Harcourt

Brace and Company; vol. 1, *The Colonial Mind, 1620-1800*; vol. 2, *Romantic Revolution in America, 1800-1860*; vol. 3, *The Beginnings of Critical Realism in America, 1860-1920* (completed to 1900 only), 1927-1930.

PAYNE, GEORGE E., "Negroes in the Public Elementary Schools of the North." *The Annals of the American Academy of Political and Social Science*, vol. 140, no. 229; November, 1928; pp. 224-233.

PEARL, RAYMOND, "Fertility and Contraception in Urban Whites and Negroes." *Science*, vol. 83, no. 2160; May, 1936; pp. 503-506.

PEARL, RAYMOND, *The Natural History of Population*. London: The Oxford University Press, 1939.

PEIRCE, PAUL S., *The Freedmen's Bureau. A Chapter in the History of Reconstruction*. Iowa City: The University of Iowa, 1904.

PENN, IRVINE GARLAND, *The Afro-American Press and Its Editors*. Springfield, Massachusetts: Willey and Company, 1891.

PHILLIPS, ULRICH B., *American Negro Slavery; a survey of the supply, employment and control of Negro labor as determined by the plantation regime*. New York: D. Appleton and Company, 1918.

PIERCE, BESSIE L., *Public Opinion and the Teaching of History in the United States*. New York: Alfred A. Knopf, 1926.

PIERCE, CLAUDE C., "State Programs for Planned Parenthood." Address read at the Conference of State and Provincial Health Authorities of North America. Washington, D.C.: March 23-24, 1942.

PINCHBECK, RAYMOND B., *The Virginia Negro Artisan and Tradesman*. Richmond: The William Byrd Press, Inc., 1926.

PINCKARD, GEORGE, *Notes on the West Indies, including observations relative to the Creoles and slaves of the western colonies, and the Indians of South America; interspersed with remarks upon the seasoning or yellow fever of hot climates*, 2 vols. London: Baldwin, Cradock, and Joy, second edition, 1816.

PINTNER, RUDOLPH, *Intelligence Testing—Methods and Results*. New York: Henry Holt and Company, 1923.

Planned Parenthood Federation of America, Inc., "Distribution of Birth Control Centers and Services." New York: July, 1942. (Mimeographed.)

Planned Parenthood Federation of America, Inc., "The Legal Status of Contraception." New York; July, 1942. (Mimeographed.)

POINDEXTER, H. A., "Special Health Problems of Negroes in Rural Areas." *Journal of Negro Education*, vol. 6, no. 3; July, 1937; pp. 399-412.

POLLOCK, H. M., "Frequency of Dementia Praecox in Relation to Sex, Age, Environment, Nativity, and Race." *Mental Hygiene*, vol. 10, no. 3; July, 1926; pp. 596-611.

PORTER, KENNETH W., "Notes Supplementary to 'Relations Between Negroes and Indians.'" *The Journal of Negro History*, vol. 18, no. 3; July, 1933, pp. 282-321.

PORTER, KENNETH W., "Relations Between Negroes and Indians Within the Present Limits of the United States." *The Journal of Negro History*, vol. 17, no. 3; July, 1932, pp. 287-367.

POUND, ROSCOE, *Criminal Justice in the American City—A Summary*. Cleveland: The Cleveland Foundation, 1922. (Part 7 of the Cleveland Foundation Survey of Criminal Justice in Cleveland.)

Powdermaker, Hortense, *After Freedom; a cultural study in the deep South*. New York: The Viking Press, 1939.

Pro-Slavery, the argument as maintained by the most distinguished writers of the southern states. Philadelphia: Lippincott, Grambo, and Company, 1853.

The Public Opinion Quarterly, vol. 3, no. 4; October, 1939; pp. 586-587, 592.

The Public Opinion Quarterly, vol. 4, no. 1; March, 1940; pp. 91; no. 3; September, 1940; p. 547.

The Public Opinion Quarterly, vol. 5, no. 3; Fall, 1941; p. 477.

PUCKETT, NEWBELL N., *Folk Beliefs of the Southern Negro*. Chapel Hill: The University of North Carolina Press, 1926.

PYLE, W. H., "The Learning Capacity of Negro Children." *The Psychological Bulletin*, vol. 13; 1916; pp. 82-83.

Quillin, Frank U., *The Color Line in Ohio; a history of race prejudice in a typical northern state*. Ann Arbor: George Wahr, 1913. (University of Michigan Historical Series.)

Raleigh *News and Observer*, May 3, 1942.

RANDOLPH, A. PHILIP, Address, March on Washington Movement, in Madison Square Garden. June 16, 1942. (Mimeographed.)

RANDOLPH, A. PHILIP, *The World Crisis and the Negro People Today*. Speech to the Third National Negro Congress. Washington, D.C.: April, 1940.

RAPER, ARTHUR F., *Preface to Peasantry; a tale of two black belt counties*. Chapel Hill: The University of North Carolina Press, 1936.

RAPER, ARTHUR F., *The Tragedy of Lynching*. Chapel Hill: The University of North Carolina Press, 1933.

REDDICK, LAWRENCE D., "A New Interpretation for Negro History." *The Journal of Negro History*, vol. 22, no. 1; January, 1937; pp. 17-28.

REDDICK, LAWRENCE D., "Racial Attitudes in American History Textbooks of the South." *The Journal of Negro History*, vol. 19, no. 3; July, 1934; pp. 225-265.

REDDING, J. SAUNDERS, "Playing the Numbers." *The North American Review*, vol. 238, no. 6; December, 1934; pp. 533-542.

REEDY, SIDNEY V., "The Negro Magazine: A Critical Study of Its Educational Significance." *Journal of Negro Education*, vol. 3, no. 4; October, 1934; pp. 598-604.

REID, IRA DEA., *In A Minor Key; Negro Youth in Story and Fact*. Washington, D.C.: American Council on Education, 1940. (Prepared for the American Youth Commission.)

REID, IRA DEA., *Social Conditions of the Negro in the Hill District of Pittsburgh*. Pittsburgh: General Committee on the Hill Survey, 1930.

REUTER, E. B., *The American Race Problem; a study of the Negro*. New York: Thomas Y. Crowell Company, 1927.

REUTER, E. B., *The Mulatto in the United States: including a study of the rôle of the mixed-blood races throughout the world*. Boston: R. G. Badger, 1918.

REUTER, E. B. (editor), *Race and Culture Contacts*, New York: McGraw-Hill Book Company, Inc., 1934.

REUTER, E. B., *Race Mixture, studies in intermarriage and miscegenation*. New York: Whittlesey House, McGraw-Hill Book Company, Inc., 1931.

RICE, JOHN ANDREW, *I Came Out of the Eighteenth Century*. New York: Harper and Brothers, 1942.

RICHARDS, HENRY I., *Cotton and the AAA*. Washington, D.C.: The Brookings Institution, 1936.

Richmond *News Leader*, "The News Leader Forum." December 6, 1941.

RINCHON, DIEUDONNÉ, père, *Le Trafic Négrier, d'après les livres de commerce du capitaine Gantois Pierre-Ignace Liévin van Alstein. L'organisation commerciale de la traite des noirs.* Uccle Bruxelles: Les Éditions Atlas, 1938.

RIVERS, W. H. R., "Observations on the Senses of the Todas." *The British Journal of Psychology*, vol. 1, part 4; December, 1905; pp. 321-396.

ROBERT, JOSEPH C., *The Tobacco Kingdom; plantation, market, and factory in Virginia and North Carolina, 1800-1860*. Durham: Duke University Press, 1938.

ROBERTSON, WILLIAM J., *The Changing South*. New York: Boni and Liveright, 1927.

ROGERS, JOEL A., *This Mongrel World, a study of Negro-Caucasian mixture throughout the ages, and in all countries*. New York: J. A. Rogers, publisher, 1927.

ROMAN, CHARLES V., *American Civilization and the Negro; the Afro-American in relation to national progress*. Philadelphia: F. A. Davis Company, 1916.

ROSENSTEIN, JOSEPH, "Government and Social Structure in a Deep South Community." Unpublished M.A. thesis, The University of Chicago, 1941.

ROSENTHAL, SOLOMON P., "Racial Differences in the Incidence of Mental Disease." *Journal of Negro Education*, vol. 3, no. 3; July, 1934; pp. 484-493.

Ross, F. H., and L. V. KENNEDY, *A Bibliography of Negro Migration*. New York: Columbia University Press, 1934.

ROUSSÈVE, CHARLES BARTHELEMY, *The Negro in Louisiana, aspects of his history and his literature*. New Orleans: The Xavier University Press, 1937.

ROYCE, JOSIAH, *Race Questions, Provincialism and Other American Problems*. New York: The Macmillan Company, 1908.

RUSSELL, JOHN H., *The Free Negro In Virginia, 1619-1865*. Baltimore: Johns Hopkins Press, 1913. (Studies in History and Political Science, series 31, no. 3).

SAIT, EDWARD McCHESNEY, *American Parties and Elections*. New York: The Century Company, 1927.

"A Salary Study for the Lexington Public Schools." Bulletin of the Bureau of School Service, vol. 7, no. 3; University of Kentucky, March, 1935.

SANGER, MARGARET, *Margaret Sanger: An Autobiography*. New York: W. W. Norton and Company, 1938.

SANGER, MARGARET, *My Fight for Birth Control*. New York: Farrar & Rinehart, Inc., 1931.

SCHANCK, R. L., "A Study of a Community and Its Groups and Institutions Conceived of as Behaviors of Individuals." *Psychological Monographs*, vol. 43, no. 195; 1932.

SCHMIDT, CARL T., *American Farmers in the World Crisis*. New York: The Oxford University Press, 1941.

SCHRIEKE, B., *Alien Americans*, New York: Viking Press, 1936.

SCHURZ, CARL, "For the Great Empire of Liberty, Forward!" Speech delivered at Concert Hall, Philadelphia, September 16, 1864. Washington, D.C.: Union Congressional Committee, 1864.

SCHUYLER, GEORGE S., "Views and Reviews." The Pittsburgh *Courier*, May 9, 1942.

SCHUYLER, GEORGE S., "Views and Reviews." The Pittsburgh *Courier*, June 13, 1942.

SCHUYLER, GEORGE S., "The Negro-Art Hokum." *Nation*, vol. 122, no. 3180; June 16, 1926; pp. 662-666.

Schuyler, George S., "Quantity or Quality." *The Birth Control Review*, vol. 16, no. 6; June, 1932; pp. 165-166.

Schuyler, George S., "Who is 'Negro'? Who is 'White'?" *Common Ground*, vol. 1, no. 1; Autumn, 1940; pp. 53-56.

Scott, Emmett J., *Scott's Official History of the American Negro in the World War*. Chicago: Homewood Press, 1919.

Scott, Emmett J., and Lyman Beecher Stowe. *Booker T. Washington, Builder of a Civilization*. Garden City, New York: Doubleday, Page and Company, 1916.

Seibels, Robert, "The Integration of Pregnancy Spacing into a State Maternal Welfare Program." *Southern Medicine and Surgery*, vol. 102, no. 4; May, 1940; pp. 230-241.

Seibels, Robert, "A Rural Project in Negro Maternal Health." *Human Fertility*, vol. 6, no. 2; April, 1941; pp. 42-44.

Shaler, Nathaniel S., *The Neighbor; the natural history of human contacts*. Boston: Houghton Mifflin and Company, 1904.

Shapiro, Harry L., *Migration and Environment; a study of the physical characteristics of the Japanese immigrants to Hawaii and the effects of environment on their descendants*. New York: The Oxford University Press, 1939.

Shaw, Anna Howard, *The Story of a Pioneer*. New York: Harper and Brothers, 1915.

Shaw, Clifford R., and Henry D. McKay, *Juvenile Delinquency and Urban Areas*. Chicago: The University of Chicago Press, 1942.

Shaw, George Bernard, *Man and Superman, A Comedy and Philosophy*. New York: Brentano's, 1904. (First edition, 1903).

Shay, Frank, *Judge Lynch, his first hundred years*. New York: Ives Washburn, Inc., 1938.

Shufeldt, Robert W., *America's Greatest Problem: The Negro*. Philadelphia: F. A. Davis Company, 1915.

Siegfried, André, *America Comes of Age, A French Analysis*. (Translated by H. H. and Doris Hemming.) New York: Harcourt, Brace and Company, 1927.

Simkins, Butler, "Ben Tillman's View of the Negro." *The Journal of Southern History*, vol. 2, no. 2; May, 1937; pp. 161-174.

Simms, W. Gilmore, *Address on the Occasion of the Inauguration of the Spartanburg Female College, August 12, 1855*. Spartanburg: Published by the Trustees, 1855.

Simpson, George Eaton, *The Negro in the Philadelphia Press*, Philadelphia: University of Pennsylvania Press, 1936.

Sinckler, Edward G., *The Barbados Handbook*. London: Duckworth and Company, 1914.

Smith, Mapheus, "A Study of Change of Attitudes toward the Negro." *Journal of Negro Education*, vol. 8, no. 1; January, 1939; pp. 64-70.

Smith, Reginald Heber, *Justice and the Poor, a study of the present denial of Justice to the poor and of the agencies making more equal their position before the law, with particular reference to legal aid work in the United States*. New York: Carnegie Foundation for the Advancement of Teaching, 1919. (Bulletin, no. 13.)

Smith, Samuel Denny, *The Negro in Congress 1870-1901*. Chapel Hill: The University of North Carolina Press, 1940.

Smith, Thomas Lynn, *The Sociology of Rural Life*. New York: Harper and Brothers, 1940.

Social Science Research Committee of the University of Chicago, "History of Douglas." Unpublished document, no. 15.

Social Science Research Committee of the University of Chicago, "History of Grand Boulevard." Unpublished document, no. 7.

Southern Tenant Farmers' Union, "History of S.T.F.U." Memphis, no date. (Mimeographed).

Southern Tenant Farmers' Union, *The Tenant Farmer*.

Spero, Sterling D., and Abram L. Harris, *The Black Worker; The Negro and the Labor Movement*. New York: Columbia University Press, 1931.

Spier, Leslie, *Growth of Japanese Children Born in America and in Japan*. Seattle, Washington: University of Washington Press, 1929.

Steiner, Jesse F., and Roy M. Brown, *The North Carolina Chain Gang; a study of county convict road work*. Chapel Hill: The University of North Carolina Press, 1927.

Stephens, Oren, "Revolt on the Delta." *Harper's Magazine*, vol. 183, no. 1098; November, 1941; pp. 656-664.

Stephenson, Gilbert T., *Race Distinctions in American Law*. New York: D. Appleton and Company, 1910.

Stewart, J., *A View of the Past and Present State of the Island of Jamaica; with remarks on the moral and physical condition of the slaves and on the abolition of slavery in the colonies*. Edinburgh: Oliver and Boyd, 1823.

Stoddard, Lothrop, *The Rising Tide of Color Against White World Supremacy*. New York: Charles Scribner's Sons, 1920.

Stone, Alfred Holt. *Studies in the American Race Problem*. Garden City, New York: Doubleday, Page and Company, 1908.

Stonequist, Everett V., *The Marginal Man; a study in personality and culture conflict*. New York: Charles Scribner's Sons, 1937.

Stoney, George E., "Suffrage in the South, Part II: The One Party System." *Survey Graphic*, vol. 29, no. 3; March, 1940; pp. 163-167, 204-205.

Storey, Moorfield, *Problems of To-day*. Boston: Houghton Mifflin Company, 1920.

Strong, Edward K., *The Second-Generation Japanese Problem*. Stanford University, California: Stanford University Press, 1934.

Strong, Samuel M., "The Social Type Method: Social Types in the Negro Community of Chicago." Unpublished Ph.D. thesis, The University of Chicago, 1940.

Stroud, George M., *A Sketch of the Laws Relating to Slavery in the Several States of the United States of America*. Philadelphia: Kimber and Sharpless, 1827.

Sumner, William, *Folkways*. Boston: Ginn and Company, 1906.

Sumner, William, *What Social Classes Owe to Each Other*. New York: Harper and Brothers, 1883.

Sutherland, Edwin H., "White-Collar Criminality." *American Sociological Review*, vol. 5, no. 1; February, 1940; pp. 1-12.

Sutherland, Robert L., *Color, Class, and Personality*. Washington, D.C.: American Council on Education, 1942. (Prepared for the American Youth Commission.)

Taeuber, Conrad and Irene B., "Negro Rural Fertility Ratios in the Mississippi Delta." *The Southwestern Social Science Quarterly*, vol. 21, no. 3; December, 1940; pp. 210-220.

TANNENBAUM, FRANK, *Darker Phases of the South*. New York: G. P. Putnam's Sons, 1924.

TARKINGTON, BOOTH, *Penrod*, Garden City, New York: Doubleday, Page and Company, 1914.

TAYLOR, A. A., "Historians of the Reconstruction." *The Journal of Negro History*, vol. 23, no. 1; January, 1938; pp. 16-34.

THOMAS, NORMAN, "How Democratic are Labor Unions?" *Harper's Magazine*, vol. 184, no. 1104; May, 1942; pp. 655-662.

THOMAS, WILLIAM H., *The American Negro, A Critical and Practical Discussion*. New York: The Macmillan Company, 1901.

THOMAS, WILLIAM I., *Sex and Society. Studies in the Social Psychology of Sex*. Chicago: The University of Chicago Press, 1907.

THOMAS, WILLIAM I., *Sourcebook for Social Origins. Ethnological materials, psychological standpoint, classified and annotated bibliographies for the interpretation of savage society*. Chicago: The University of Chicago Press, 1909.

THOMAS, WILLIAM I., and FLORIAN ZNANIECKI, *The Polish Peasant in Europe and America; Monograph of an Immigrant Group*, 5 vols. Chicago: The University of Chicago Press; vol. 3, Boston: R. G. Badger, 1918-1920.

THOMPSON, CHARLES H., "The Conclusions of Scientists Relative to Racial Differences." *Journal of Negro Education*, vol. 3, no. 3; July, 1934; pp. 494-512.

THOMPSON, CHARLES, H., "The Status of Education *Of* and *For* the Negro in the American Social Order." *Journal of Negro Education*, vol. 8, no. 3; July, 1939; pp. 489-510.

THOMPSON, EDGAR T., "Population Expansion and the Plantation System." *The American Journal of Sociology*, vol. 41, no. 3; November, 1935; pp. 314-326.

THOMPSON, EDGAR T., (editor), *Race Relations and the Race Problem, A Definition and An Analysis*. Durham: Duke University Press, 1939.

THOREAU, HENRY DAVID, *A Yankee in Canada, with Anti-Slavery and Reform Papers*. (Sophia Thoreau and W. E. Channing, editors.) Boston: J. R. Osgood and Company, 1878.

THURSTONE, L. L., "An Experimental Study of Nationality Preferences." *The Journal of General Psychology*, vol. 1, nos. 3 and 4; July-October, 1928; pp. 405-425.

Time, vol. 22, no. 9; August 28, 1933, p. 32.

Time, vol. 38, no. 8; August 25, 1941; p. 8.

Time, vol. 38, no. 10; September 8, 1941; p. 13.

Time, vol. 40, no. 4; July 27, 1942, p. 17.

Time, vol. 40, no. 11; September, 14, 1942; p. 46.

TINGSTEN, HERBERT, *Political Behavior; studies in election statistics*. London: P. S. King and Son, Ltd., 1937.

TOCQUEVILLE, ALEXIS DE, *Democracy in America*. (Translated by Henry Reeve), 2 vols. New York: The Colonial Press, 1899. (First edition, 1835.)

TODD, T. W., "Entrenched Negro Physical Features." *Human Biology*, vol. 1, no. 1; January, 1929; pp. 57-69.

TODD, T. W., and ANNA LINDALA, "Dimensions of the Body: Whites and American Negroes of Both Sexes." *American Journal of Physical Anthropology*, vol. 12, no. 1; July-September, 1928; pp. 35-119.

Tolnai, B. B., "Abortions and the Law." *Nation*, vol. 148, no. 16; April 15, 1939; pp. 424-427.

Turner, Frederick Jackson, *The Frontier in American History*. New York: Henry Holt and Company, 1920.

Turner, Frederick Jackson, "The Significance of the Frontier in American History." Address delivered at the forty-first annual meeting of the State Historical Society of Wisconsin, December 14, 1893. Madison, Wisconsin: The State Historical Society of Wisconsin, 1894, pp. 79-112.

Twelve Southerners, *I'll Take My Stand: the South and the agrarian tradition*. New York: Harper and Brothers, 1930.

The Twentieth Century Fund, *Facing the Tax Problem*. New York: The Twentieth Century Fund, 1937.

Underhill, Edward B., *The West Indies: their social and religious condition*. London: Jackson, Walford and Hodder, 1862.

U.S. Bureau of the Census, *Births, Stillbirths and Infant Mortality Statistics: 1936*. Washington, D. C.: 1938.

U.S. Bureau of the Census, *Census of Agriculture: 1935*, vol. 3.

U.S. Bureau of the Census, *Census of Manufactures: 1937*.

U.S. Bureau of the Census, *A Century of Population Growth in the United States: 1790-1900*. Washington, D.C.: 1909.

U.S. Bureau of the Census, Alba M. Edwards, *Social-Economic Grouping of the Gainful Workers of the United States: 1930*. Washington, D.C.: 1938.

U.S. Bureau of the Census, *Eleventh Census of the United States: 1890. Population*, vol. 2.

U.S. Bureau of the Census, *Eleventh Census of the United States: 1890. Report on Crime, Pauperism and Benevolence in the United States*, Part. 2.

U.S. Bureau of the Census, *Fifteenth Census of the United States: 1930. Agriculture*, vols. 2, 3, and 4.

U.S. Bureau of the Census, *Fifteenth Census of the United States: 1930. Manufactures: 1929*, vol. 2.

U.S. Bureau of the Census, *Fifteenth Census of the United States: 1930. Population*, vols. 2, 3, 4, 5, and 6.

U.S. Bureau of the Census, *Fifteenth Census of the United States: 1930. Unemployment*, vol. 2.

U.S. Bureau of the Census, *Fourteenth Census of the United States: 1920. Population*, vol. 3.

U.S. Bureau of the Census, *Negro Population in the United States: 1790-1915*. Washington, D.C.: 1918.

U.S. Bureau of the Census, *Negroes in the United States: 1920-1932*. Washington, D.C.: 1935.

U.S. Bureau of the Census, *Prisoners in State and Federal Prisons and Reformatories: 1939*. Washington, D.C.: 1941.

U.S. Bureau of the Census, *Religious Bodies: 1936*. 2 vols. Washington, D.C.: 1941.

U.S. Bureau of the Census, *Sixteenth Census of the United States: 1940. Agriculture*. United States Summary, First Series and United States Summary, Second Series.

U.S. Bureau of the Census, *Sixteenth Census of the United States: 1940. Manufactures: 1939, Tobacco Manufacturers Group*.

U.S. Bureau of the Census, *Sixteenth Census of the United States: 1940. Population.* First Series; Second Series; and Preliminary Releases, Series P-4, nos. 4, 5, 8; Series P-4a, nos. 14, 16; Series P-5, nos. 3, 4, 10, 13, 14, 16; Series P-10, nos. 1, 6, 8, 17.

U.S. Bureau of the Census, *Sixteenth Census of the United States: 1940. Retail Trade. Retail Negro Proprietorship—The United States—1939.* Preliminary Release, August 29, 1941.

U.S. Bureau of the Census, *Statistical Abstract of the United States: 1938.* Washington, D.C.: 1939.

U.S. Bureau of the Census, *Statistical Abstract of the United States: 1941.* Washington, D.C.: 1942.

U.S. Bureau of the Census, *Thirteenth Census of the United States: 1910. Agriculture,* vol. 5.

U.S. Bureau of the Census, *Thirteenth Census of the United States: 1910. Population,* vol. 4.

U.S. Bureau of the Census, *Twelfth Census of the United States: 1900. Agriculture,* vol. 5.

U.S. Bureau of the Census, *Vital Statistics: Special Reports: 1940.* Vol. 14, no. 2; Washington, D.C.: 1941.

U.S. Bureau of the Census, *Vital Statistics-Special Reports, Mortality Summary for U.S. Registration States: Suicide.* Washington, D.C.: September 19, 1942.

U.S. Census Office, *Agriculture of the United States in 1860: Compiled from the Original Returns of the Eighth Census.* Washington, D.C.: 1864.

U.S. Census Office, *Eighth Census of the United States: 1860.* Vol. 1.

U.S. Census Office, *Statistics of the United States in 1860.* Washington, D.C.: 1866.

U.S. Committee on the Costs of Medical Care, C. Gebhard, *Funeral Costs.* Washington, D.C.: 1930. (Miscellaneous Contributions on the Costs of Medical Care, no. 3.)

U.S. Committee on Discrimination in Employment, "History of the Committee on Discrimination in Employment." Washington, D.C.: August 14, 1942. (Mimeographed.)

U.S. Committee on Negro Housing, Charles S. Johnson (editor), *Negro Housing.* Washington, D.C.: 1932. (Report of the Committee on Negro Housing to the President's Conference on Home Building and Home Ownership.)

U.S. President's Committee on Fair Employment Practice, Negro Employment and Training Branch, Labor Division, O.P.M., Minority Groups Branch, Labor Division, O.P.M., *Minorities in Defense.* Washington, D.C.: October, 15, 1942.

U.S. Department of Agriculture, *Agricultural Statistics: 1940.* Washington, D.C.: 1941.

U.S. Department of Agriculture, *Agricultural Statistics: 1941.* Washington, D.C.: 1942.

U.S. Department of Agriculture, Bureau of Agricultural Economics, *The Agricultural Situation.* Vol. 26, no. 3, March, 1942; no. 4, April, 1942; no. 8, August, 1942.

U.S. Department of Agriculture, Bureau of Home Economics, *Consumer Purchases Study, Farm Series, Urban and Village Series,* and *Urban, Village and Farm Series.* Washington, D.C.: 1941.

U.S. Department of Agriculture, M. R. Cooper and Associates, "The Causes: Defects in Farming Systems and Farm Tenancy." *Yearbook of Agriculture: 1938.* Washington, D.C.: 1938, pp. 137-157.

U.S. Department of Agriculture, *Crops and Markets.* Washington, D.C.: July, 1942.

U.S. Department of Agriculture, "Extension Work With Negroes." Washington, D.C.: no date. (Mimeographed.)

U.S. Department of Agriculture, J. C. Folsom and O. E. Baker, *A Graphic Summary of Farm Labor and Population.* Washington, D. C.: November, 1937. (Miscellaneous publication, no. 265.)

U.S. Department of Agriculture, F. L. Langsford and B. H. Thibodeaux, *Plantation Organization and Operation in the Yazoo-Mississippi Delta Area.* Washington, D. C.: 1939. (Technical Bulletin, no. 682.)

U.S. Department of Agriculture, *Yearbook of Agriculture: 1938.* Washington, D. C.: 1938.

U.S. Department of Agriculture, *Yearbook of Agriculture: 1940.* Washington, D. C.: 1940.

U.S. Department of Commerce, Bureau of Foreign and Domestic Commerce, *Causes of Negro Insurance Company Failures.* Washington, D. C.: 1937. (Bulletin, no. 15.)

U.S. Department of Commerce, *Consumer Use of Selected Goods and Services, By Income Classes.* Washington, D. C.: 1935-1937. (Market Research Series, no. 5.)

U.S. Department of Justice, Federal Bureau of Investigation, *Uniform Crime Reports for the United States and Its Possessions.* Fourth Quarterly Bulletin, 1940, vol. 11, no. 4; January, 1941.

U.S. Department of Labor, Bureau of Labor Statistics, "Earnings and Hours in Bar, Puddling, Sheet-Bar, Rod, Wire, and Sheet Mills, 1933 and 1935." *Monthly Labor Review*, vol. 43, no. 1; July, 1936; pp. 113-149.

U.S. Department of Labor, Bureau of Labor Statistics, "Earnings in Cigarette, Snuff, and Chewing-and-Smoking-Tobacco Plants, 1933-35." *Monthly Labor Review*, vol. 42, no. 5; May, 1936; pp. 1322-1335.

U.S. Department of Labor, Bureau of Labor Statistics, "Earnings in the Iron and Steel Industry, 1937." *Monthly Labor Review*, vol. 51, no. 4; October, 1940; pp. 823-833.

U.S. Department of Labor, Bureau of Labor Statistics, "Earnings and Hours in the Iron and Steel Industry, April, 1938." *Monthly Labor Review*, vol. 51, no. 2; August, 1940; pp. 421-442.

U.S. Department of Labor, Bureau of Labor Statistics, "Earnings and Hours in the Iron and Steel Industry, April, 1938." Part 2. *Monthly Labor Review*, vol. 51, no. 3; September, 1940; pp. 709-726.

U.S. Department of Labor, Bureau of Labor Statistics, "Earnings and Hours in the Meat-Packing Industry, December, 1937." *Monthly Labor Review*, vol. 49, no. 4; October, 1939; pp. 936-959.

U.S. Department of Labor, Bureau of Labor Statistics, "Earnings of Negro Workers in the Iron and Steel Industry, April, 1938." *Monthly Labor Review*, vol. 51, no. 5; November, 1940; pp. 1139-1149.

U.S. Department of Labor, Bureau of Labor Statistics, "Labor Turnover in the Sawmill Industry, 1933 and 1934." *Monthly Labor Review*, vol. 40, no. 4; May, 1935; pp. 1285-1287.

U.S. Department of Labor, Bureau of Labor Statistics, "Wages and Hours in the Fertilizer Industry, 1938." *Monthly Labor Review*, vol. 48, no. 3; March, 1939; pp. 666-681.

U.S. Department of Labor, Bureau of Labor Statistics, *Study of Consumer Purchases, Urban Series and Urban Technical Series.* Washington, D. C.: 1939-1941.

U.S. Department of Labor, Wages and Hours Division, *Wage and Hour Reporter*, May 27, 1940.

U.S. Farm Security Administration, *Report of the Administrator: 1941.* Washington, D. C.: 1942.

U.S. Federal Emergency Relief Administration, Harold Hoffsommer, "Landlord-Tenant Relations and Relief in Alabama." Washington, D. C.: 1935. (Division of Research, Bulletin, series 2, no. 9, mimeographed.)

U.S. Federal Emergency Relief Administration, *Monthly Report, May 1, through May 31, 1934.* Washington, D. C.: 1934.

U.S. Federal Housing Administration, *Eighth Annual Report.* Washington, D. C.: 1942.

U.S. Federal Housing Administration, Homer Hoyt, *The Structure and Growth of Residential Neighborhoods in American Cities.* Washington, D. C.: 1939.

U.S. Federal Housing Administration, *Seventh Annual Report.* Washington, D. C.: 1941.

U.S. Federal Housing Administration, *Successful Subdivisions.* Washington, D. C.: 1941 (Land Planning Bulletin, no. 1).

U.S. Federal Housing Administration, *Underwriting Manual: With Revisions to February, 1938.* Washington, D. C.: 1938.

U.S. Federal Security Agency, Social Security Board, Bureau of Employment Security, *The Labor Market.* May, 1942.

U.S. Federal Security Agency, Social Security Board, Bureau of Employment Security, *The Labor Market*, June, 1942.

U.S. Federal Security Agency, Social Security Board, Bureau of Employment Security, *The Labor Market*, September, 1942.

U.S. Federal Security Agency, Social Security Board, Bureau of Employment Security, "Negro Workers and the National Defense Program." Washington, D. C.: September 16, 1941. (Mimeographed.)

U.S. Federal Security Agency, Social Security Board, Bureau of Employment Security, "Survey of Employment Prospects for Negroes." Washington, D. C.: no date. (Mimeographed.)

U.S. Federal Security Agency, Social Security Board, Bureau of Employment Security, "USES Operations Bulletin." No. C-45. Washington, D. C.: July 1, 1942. (Mimeographed.)

U.S. Federal Security Agency, Social Security Board, Bureau of Employment Security, "Vocational Training Activities of Public Employment Offices." Washington, D. C.: January, 1942. (Mimeographed.)

U.S. Federal Security Agency, Social Security Board, Wayne F. Caskey, "Workers with Annual Taxable Wages of Less than $200 in 1937-39." *Social Security Bulletin*, vol. 4, no. 10; October, 1941; pp. 17-24.

U.S. Federal Security Agency, Social Security Board, *Old Age and Survivors Insurance Statistics, Employment and Wages of Covered Workers, 1938.* Washington, D. C.: 1940.

U.S. Federal Security Agency, Social Security Board, "Operation of the Employment Security Program." *Social Security Bulletin*, vol. 4, no. 10; October, 1941.

U.S. Federal Works Agency, *Second Annual Report.* Washington, D. C.: 1941.

U.S. Housing Authority, *What Does the Housing Program Cost?* Washington. D. C.: 1940.

U.S. Industrial Commission, *Reports.* Vol. 8. Washington, D. C.: 1900-1902.

U.S. National Emergency Council, *Report on Economic Conditions of the South.* Washington, D. C.: 1938.

U.S. National Recovery Administration, F. E. Berquist and Associates, "Economic Survey of the Bituminous Coal Industry Under Free Competition and Code Regulation." 2 vols. Washington, D. C.: 1936. (Work Material, no. 69, mimeographed.)

U.S. National Resources Committee, *Consumer Incomes in the United States: Their Distribution in 1935-36.* Washington, D. C.: 1938.

U.S. National Resources Committee, *Farm Tenancy, Report of the President's Committee.* Washington, D. C.: 1937.

U.S. National Resources Committee, *Our Cities; Their Role in the National Economy,* Washington, D. C.: 1937.

U.S. National Resources Committee, *The Problems of a Changing Population; Report of the Committee on Population Problems to the National Resources Committee.* Washington, D. C.: 1938.

U.S. National Resources Committee, *Supplementary Report to Our Cities.* Vol. 1, *Urban Government.* Washington, D.C.: 1939.

U.S. National Resources Committee, Warren S. Thompson and P. K. Whelpton, "Estimates of the Future Population of the United States—1940-1980." *Population Statistics. 1. National Data.* Washington, D. C.: 1937.

U.S. National Resources Planning Board, *National Resources Development, Report for 1942.* Washington, D. C.: 1942.

U.S. Office of Education, Advisory Committee on Education, *The Federal Government and Education.* Washington, D. C.: 1938.

U.S. Office of Education, Advisory Committee on Education, *Federal Relations to Education,* 2 vols. Washington, D. C.: 1931.

U.S. Office of Education, Advisory Committee on Education, Clarence Heer, *Federal Aid and the Tax Problem.* Washington, D. C.: 1939. (Staff Study, no. 4.)

U.S. Office of Education, Advisory Committee on Education, *Report of the Committee, February, 1938.* Washington, D. C.: 1938.

U.S. Office of Education, Advisory Committee on Education. Doxey A. Wilkerson, *Special Problems of Negro Education.* Washington, D. C.: 1939. (Staff Study, no. 12.)

U. S. Office of Education, *Biennial Survey of Education in the United States: 1934-36.* Washington, D. C.: 1938. (Bulletin, 1938, no. 2.)

U.S. Office of Education, David T. Blose and Ambrose Caliver, *Statistics of the Education of Negroes, 1933-34 and 1935-36.* Washington, D. C.: 1939. (Bulletin, 1938, no. 13.)

U.S. Office of Education, Ambrose Caliver, *Rural Elementary Education Among Negroes Under Jeanes Supervising Teachers.* Washington, D. C.: 1933. (Bulletin, 1933, no. 5.)

U.S. Office of Education, Ambrose Caliver, *Vocational Education and Guidance of Negroes.* Washington, D. C.: 1938. (Bulletin, 1938, no. 38.)

U.S. Public Health Service, The National Health Survey 1935-36, Bernard D. Karpinos,

The Socio-Economic and Employment Status of the Urban Youth of the United States 1935-1936. Washington, D. C.: 1941.

U.S. Public Health Service, The National Health Survey, 1935-36. Preliminary Reports. *Adequacy of Urban Housing in the United States As Measured by Degree of Crowding and Type of Sanitary Facilities.* Washington, D. C.: National Institute of Health, 1939. (Sickness and Medical Care Series, Bulletin, no. 5.)

U.S. Puerto Rico Reconstruction Administration in Cooperation with the Writers' Program of the Work Projects Administration, *Puerto Rico, A Guide to the Island of Boriquén.* New York: The University Society, Inc., 1940.

U.S. Senate, Second Session on S. Res. 266. *Violations of Free Speech and Assembly and Interference With Rights of Labor.* Report of LaFollette Committee. Hearings before a Sub-committee of the Committee on Education and Labor. Washington, D. C.: 1936.

U.S. Senate, Seventy-sixth Congress, first session on S. 1970. *Oppressive Labor Practices Act.* Report of the LaFollette Committee. Hearings before a Sub-committee of the Committee on Education and Labor. Washington, D. C.: 1939.

U.S. War Production Board, Statistics Division, "State Distribution of War Supply and Facility Contracts, June, 1940 through May, 1942." Washington, D. C.: 1942. (Mimeographed.)

U.S. Works Progress Administration. R. H. Allen and Associates, *Part-Time Farming in the Southeast.* Washington, D. C.: 1937. (Research monograph, no. 9.)

U.S. Works Progress Administration, Anne E. Geddes, *Trends in Relief Expenditures, 1910-1935.* Washington, D. C.: 1937. (Division of Social Research, monograph, no. 10.)

U.S. Works Progress Administration, Margaret Loomis Stecker, *Intercity Differences in Costs of Living in March, 1935, 59 Cities.* Washington, D. C.: 1937. (Research monograph no. 12.)

U.S. Works Progress Administration, Margaret Loomis Stecker, *Quantity Budgets of Goods and Services for a Basic Maintenance Standard of Living and for Operation under Emergency Conditions.* Washington, D. C.: 1936 (Research bulletin, series 1, no. 21.)

U.S. Works Progress Administration, Thomas J. Woofter, Jr. and Associates, *Landlord and Tenant on the Cotton Plantation.* Washington, D. C.: 1936. (Research monograph, no. 5.)

U.S. Work Projects Administration, William C. Holley, Ellen Winston, and Thomas J. Woofter, Jr., *The Plantation South, 1934-1937.* Washington, D. C.: 1940. (Division of Research, monograph, no. 22.)

U.S. Work Projects Administration, Roman L. Horne and Eugene G. McKibben, *Changes in Farm Power and Equipment, Mechanical Cotton Picker.* Philadelphia: 1937. (National Research Project on Re-employment Opportunities and Recent Changes in Industrial Techniques. Studies of Changing Techniques and Employment in Agriculture, Report A, no. 2.)

U.S. Work Projects Administration, *Mechanization in Lumber.* Washington, D. C.: 1940. (National Research Project, Report no. M-5.)

U.S. Work Projects Administration, Federal Writers' Projects, *The Negro in Virginia.* New York: Hastings House, 1940.

U.S. Work Projects Administration, Federal Writers' Projects, *These Are Our Lives*. Chapel Hill: The University of North Carolina Press, 1939.

Vance, Rupert B., "Cotton and Tenancy." *Problems of the Cotton Economy*. Dallas, Texas: Southern Regional Committee of the Social Science Research Council, 1936. (Proceedings of the Southern Social Science Research Conference. New Orleans, Louisiana, March, 1935.)

Vance, Rupert B., *Human Factors in Cotton Culture; a study in the social geography of the American South*. Chapel Hill: The University of North Carolina Press, 1929.

Vance, Rupert B., *Human Geography of the South: a study in regional resources and human adequacy*. Chapel Hill: The University of North Carolina Press, 1932.

Vance, Rupert B., "The Regional Approach to the Study of High Fertility." *The Milbank Memorial Fund Quarterly*, vol. 19, no. 4; October, 1941; pp. 356-374.

Van Deusen, John G., *The Black Man in White America*. Washington, D. C.: Associated Publishers, Inc., 1938.

Veblen, Thorstein, *The Theory of the Leisure Class; an economic study in the evolution of institutions*. New York: The Macmillan Company, 1899.

Virginia Department of Labor and Industry, *Forty-Third Annual Report; Industrial Statistics, Calendar Year, 1939*. Richmond, 1941.

Virginia Department of Labor and Industry, *Thirty-Fourth Annual Report; Industrial Statistics, Calendar Year, 1930*. Richmond: 1932.

Vollmer, August, *The Police and Modern Society*. Berkeley, California: University of California Press, 1936.

Walker, Harry J., "Negro Benevolent Societies in New Orleans." Unpublished manuscript, Fisk University, 1936.

Walker, Ira De., and Associates, *Thus Be Their Destiny*. Washington, D. C.: American Council on Education, 1941. (Prepared for the American Youth Commission.)

Walker, Mabel L., *Urban Blight and Slums; economic and legal factors in their origin, reclamation and prevention*. Cambridge: Harvard University Press, 1938.

Wallace, Henry, "The Price of Free World Victory." Speech before Free World Association, 1942. (Mimeographed press release from the Office of the Vice-President.)

Walsh, John Raymond, *C.I.O.: industrial unionism in action*. New York: W. W. Norton and Company, 1937.

Ware, Caroline F., *Greenwich Village, 1920-1930; a comment on American civilization in the post-war years*. Boston: Houghton Mifflin Company, 1935.

Warner, Robert Austin, *New Haven Negroes, a social history*. New Haven, Yale University Press, 1940.

Warner, W. Lloyd, Buford H., Junker, and Walter A. Adams, *Color and Human Nature, Negro personality development in a Northern city*. Washington, D.C.: American Council on Education, 1941. (Prepared for the American Youth Commission.)

Warner, W. Lloyd, and Paul S. Lunt, *The Social Life of a Modern Community*. New Haven: Yale University Press, 1941.

Washburne, Carleton, *Louisiana Looks at Its Schools*. Baton Rouge: Louisiana Educational Survey Commission, 1942.

WASHINGTON, BOOKER T., *The Future of the American Negro*. Boston: Small, Maynard and Company, 1899.

WASHINGTON, BOOKER T., "My View of Segregation Laws." *The New Republic*, vol. 5, no. 57; December 4, 1915; pp. 113-114.

WASHINGTON, BOOKER T., *The Story of the Negro: the rise of the race from slavery*, 2 vols. Garden City, New York: Doubleday, Page and Company, 1909.

WASHINGTON, BOOKER T., *Up from Slavery; an autobiography*. Garden City, New York: Doubleday, Page and Company, 1900.

WASHINGTON, GEORGE, *Letters and Addresses of George Washington*. (Jonas Viles, editor.) New York: The Unit Book Publishing Company, 1908.

WASHINGTON, FORRESTER B., "Recreational Facilities for the Negro." *The Annals of the American Academy of Political and Social Science*, vol. 140, no. 229; November, 1928; pp. 272-282.

WEATHERFORD, WILLIS D., *Negro Life in the South; present conditions and needs*. New York: Young Men's Christian Association Press, 1910.

WEATHERFORD, WILLIS D., *Present Forces in Negro Progress*. London: Association Press, 1912.

WEATHERFORD, WILLIS D., and CHARLES S. JOHNSON, *Race Relations; adjustment of whites and Negroes in the United States*. Boston: D. C. Heath and Company, 1934.

WEAVER, ROBERT C., "Racial Employment Trends in National Defense," Part I. *Phylon*, vol. 2, no. 4; Fourth Quarter, 1941; pp. 337-358. Part II. *Phylon*, vol. 3, no. 1; First Quarter, 1942; pp. 22-30.

WEAVER, ROBERT C., "With the Negro's Help." *Atlantic Monthly*, vol. 169, no. 6; June, 1942; pp. 696-707.

WEBB, JAMES MORRIS, *The Black Man the Father of Civilization; proven by Biblical history*. Seattle, Washington: Acme Press, 1910.

WEBER, MAX, "Geschäftsbericht." *Verhandlungen des Ersten Deutschen Soziologentages vom 19-22 Oktober, 1910 in Frankfort a. M.* 1911. (Translated for private use by E. C. Hughes, 1940.)

WECTER, DIXON, *The Hero in America, a chronicle of hero-worship*. New York: Charles Scribner's Sons, 1941.

WEINTRAUB, DAVID, and HARRY MAGDOFF, "The Service Industries in Relation to Employment Trends." *Econometrica*, vol. 8, no. 4; October, 1940; pp. 289-311.

WERTENBAKER, THOMAS J., *The Old South; the founding of American civilization*. New York: Charles Scribner's Sons, 1942.

WESLEY, CHARLES H., "The Concept of Negro Inferiority in American Thought." *The Journal of Negro History*, vol. 25, no. 4; October, 1940; pp. 540-560.

WESLEY, CHARLES H., *Negro Labor in the United States, 1850-1925; a study in American economic history*. New York: Vanguard Press, 1927.

WHELPTON, P. K., "An Empirical Method of Calculating Future Population." *Journal of the American Statistical Association*, vol. 31, no. 195; September, 1936; pp. 457-473.

WHITE, WALTER, *The Fire in the Flint*. New York: Alfred A. Knopf, 1924.

WHITE, WALTER, "It's Our Country, Too." *The Saturday Evening Post*, vol. 213, no. 24; December 14, 1940; pp. 27, 61-68.

WHITE, WALTER, *Rope and Faggot, a biography of Judge Lynch*. New York: Alfred A. Knopf, 1929.

Willcox, Walter F., "Negro Criminality," *Journal of Social Science*, vol. 37; December, 1899; pp. 78-98.

Williams, William H., "The Negro in the District of Columbia During Reconstruction." *The Howard Review*, vol. 1, nos. 2-3; June, 1924; pp. 97-148.

Winslow, Vernon, "Negro Art and the Depression." *Opportunity*, vol. 19, no. 2; February, 1941; pp. 40-42, 62-63.

Wirth, Louis, "Ideological Aspects of Social Disorganization." *American Sociological Review*, vol. 5, no. 4; August, 1940; pp. 472-482.

Wish, Harvey, "American Slave Insurrections before 1861." *The Journal of Negro History*, vol. 22, no. 3; July, 1937; pp. 299-320.

Witmer, A. H., "Insanity in the Colored Race in the United States." *Alienist and Neurologist*, vol. 12, no. 1; January, 1891; pp. 19-30.

Witty, P. A., and M. A. Jenkins, "The Case of 'B'—A Gifted Negro Girl." *Journal of Social Psychology*, vol. 6, no. 1; February, 1935; pp. 117-124.

Witty, P. A., and M. A. Jenkins, "The Educational Achievement of a group of Gifted Negro Children." *The Journal of Educational Psychology*, vol. 25, no. 8; November, 1934; pp. 585-597.

Witty, P. A., and M. A. Jenkins, "Intra-Race Testing and Negro Intelligence." *Neurologist*, vol. 12, no. 1; January, 1891; pp. 19-30.

Witty, P. A., and H. C. Lehman, "Racial Differences: the Dogma of Superiority." *Journal of Social Psychology*, vol. 1, no. 3; August, 1930; pp. 394-418.

Woodbury, Coleman (editor), *Housing Officials' Yearbook: 1940.* Chicago: National Association of Housing Officials, 1940.

Woodson, Carter G., "The Beginnings of the Miscegenation of the Whites and Blacks." *The Journal of Negro History*, vol. 3, no. 1; October, 1918; pp. 335-353.

Woodson, Carter G., *A Century of Negro Migration.* Washington, D. C.: The Association for the Study of Negro Life and History, Inc., 1918.

Woodson, Carter G., *The History of the Negro Church.* Washington, D. C.: The Associated Publishers, Inc., 1921.

Woodson, Carter G., "Insurance Business among Negroes." *The Journal of Negro History*, vol. 14, no. 2; April, 1929; pp. 202-226.

Woodson, Carter G., *The Mis-Education of the Negro.* Washington, D. C.: The Associated Publishers, Inc., 1933.

Woodson, Carter G., *The Negro Professional Man and the Community with special emphasis on the physician and the lawyer.* Washington, D. C.: The Association for the Study of Negro Life and History, Inc., 1934.

Woodworth, Robert S., *Heredity and Environment; a critical survey of recently published material on twins and foster children.* New York: Social Science Research Council, 1941. (Bulletin no. 47, prepared for the Committee on Social Adjustment.)

Woofter, Thomas J., Jr., *The Basis of Racial Adjustment.* Boston: Ginn and Company, 1925.

Woofter, Thomas J., Jr., *Black Yeomanry; life on St. Helena Island.* New York: Henry Holt and Company, 1930.

Woofter, Thomas J., Jr., *Races and Ethnic Groups in American Life.* New York: McGraw-Hill Book Company, Inc., 1933.

WOOFTER, THOMAS J., JR., and Associates, *Negro Problems in Cities*. Garden City, New York: Doubleday, Doran and Company, Inc., 1928.

WORK, MONROE N. (editor), *Negro Year Book, an annual encyclopedia of the Negro, 1931-1932*. Tuskegee Institute, Alabama: Negro Year Book Publishing Company, 1931.

WORK, MONROE N. (editor), *Negro Year Book, an annual encyclopedia of the Negro, 1937-1938*. Tuskegee Institute, Alabama: Negro Year Book Publishing Company, 1937.

World Almanac: 1942, The. Published by the New York *World-Telegram*.

WRIGHT, MARION M. THOMPSON, *The Education of Negroes in New Jersey*. New York: Columbia University, 1941.

WRIGHT, RICHARD, *Native Son*. New York: Harper and Brothers, 1940.

WRIGHT, RICHARD, *12 Million Black Voices; a folk-history of the Negro in the United States*. New York: The Viking Press, 1941.

WRIGHT, RICHARD, *Uncle Tom's Children, four novellas*. New York: Harper and Brothers, 1938.

YOUNG, DONALD R., *American Minority Peoples; a study in racial and cultural conflicts in the United States*. New York: Harper and Brothers, 1932.

YOUNG, DONALD R., *Research Memorandum on Minority Peoples in the Depression*. New York: Social Science Research Council, 1937. (Bulletin no. 31, prepared under the direction of the Committee on Studies in Social Aspects of the Depression.)

YOUNG, EARLE F., "The Relation of Lynching to the Size of Political Areas." *Sociology and Social Research*, vol. 7, no. 4; March-April, 1928; pp. 348-353.

YOUNG, P. B., "The Negro Press—Today and Tomorrow." *Opportunity*, vol. 17, no. 7; July, 1939; pp. 204-205.

Chapter 24. *Inequality of Justice*

[1] "In many a small town and city [of the South], the mayor and councilmen offer for election with a complete list of police and other public officers."[d]

[2] Willis D. Weatherford and Charles S. Johnson, *Race Relations* (1934), p. 61.

[3] W. E. B. Du Bois, *The Souls of Black Folk* (1903), p. 176. Italics ours.

[4] As early as 1904, Murphy recognized the "morbid and exaggerated solidarity" among Negroes against the white agencies of justice as the "blind moving of the instinct of self-protection."[e] Weatherford observes how the reaction breaks down " . . . one of the most powerful deterrents of crime; namely, the loss of status among those who are of the same class as the possible criminal."[f]

The Negro spokesmen generally do not deny the charges against their people of being inclined to shield criminals of their own race. But they unanimously point to the defects in the working of justice as the explanation:

"The Negro feels that he cannot expect justice from Southern courts where white and black are involved. In his mind accusation is equivalent to condemnation. . . . The very spirit in which, he feels, the law is administered makes it difficult for the colored

[a] *Negro Americans, What Now?* pp. 56-57.

[b] T. J. Woofter, Jr., *The Basis of Racial Adjustment* (1925), p. 167.

[c] Statement by Association of Southern Women for the Prevention of Lynching, in Jessie Daniel Ames, *The Changing Character of Lynching*, published by Commission on Interracial Cooperation (July, 1942), p. 70. See also Dabney, *op. cit.*, pp. 253-254.

[d] Arthur Raper, "Race and Class Pressures," unpublished manuscript prepared for this study (1940), p. 14.

[e] Edgar Gardner Murphy, *Problems of the Present South* (1909; first edition, 1904), p. 174.

[f] Weatherford and Johnson, *op. cit.*, p. 430.

citizen to exercise cheerful co-operation and acquiescence."[a] Robert R. Moton, a most conservative Negro educator and leader, writes in the same vein:

"In the light of these facts [the attitudes and activities against the Negro in the First World War] it ought not be difficult to understand why the reproach is so often hurled at the Negro that he does not cooperate with officers of the law in apprehending criminals and those accused of crime. To the Negro the law where these practices obtain appears not as an instrument of justice, but as an instrument of persecution; government is simply white society organized to keep the Negro down; and the officers of the law are its agents authorized to wreak upon the helpless offender the contempt, the indignation, and the vengeance that outraged law and order feels when stimulated by prejudice. There is no such hue and cry over crime when the victim is a Negro and the perpetrator either white or black as when the victim is white and the suspect is black or supposed to be black."[b]

and:

"The Negro knows, perhaps better than he knows anything else, that his chances of securing justice in the courts in those sections of the country where discrimination is in other things legal and common are so slim that in most instances he has nothing to gain by resorting to the courts even for litigation with members of his own race; while it is accepted by most as a foregone conclusion that no court anywhere will render a judgment against a white man in favour of a Negro plaintiff. A Negro defendant may occasionally get a favourable judgment as against a white plaintiff, but the reverse is a far more frequent possibility, so much so that a Negro very rarely brings suit against a white man for any cause in those states where relations between the two races are more or less strained. It is figured that to do so will involve a man in fruitless litigation, with the original loss augmented by the cost of the action. In spite of all the injustices and abuses from which Negroes suffer, one seldom hears of a court action brought by Negroes against any white person in our Southern states."[c]

A recent investigator of a Southern community, Hortense Powdermaker, testifies concerning the attitudes among the Negroes:

". . . many of the Negroes have long since concluded that their best course is to keep clear of legal complications wherever possible. To go to court for any cause would be to solicit more trouble than the matter at issue might be worth. Since no Negro can expect to find justice by due process of law, it is better in the long run to suffer one's loss—or to adjust it oneself. From this angle, the 'lawlessness' sometimes ascribed to the Negro may be viewed as being rather his private and individual 'law enforcement' *faute de mieux*. The feeling against going to court has in it an element of race-solidarity. Some Negroes will criticize one of the race who takes legal action against another Negro. Such criticism is part of a definite counter-current against the still prevalent tendency to take one's troubles to a white man."[d]

On this point the Southern white liberals—who, in this region, have to defend the principle of legality, since conservatism there is married to the tradition of illegality—agree without reservation with the Negro leaders. Baker reported this more than thirty years ago. One of the Southern liberals told him frankly:

"We complain that the Negroes will not help to bring the criminals of their race

[a] Kelly Miller, *Race Adjustment* (1908), p. 79.
[b] *What the Negro Thinks* (1929), pp. 154-155.
[c] Moton, *op. cit.*, pp. 141-142.
[d] *After Freedom* (1939), p. 126.

to justice. One reason for this is that the Negro has too little confidence in our courts. We must give him that, above all things."[a]

Woofter eloquently expresses the view of Southern liberalism today when he says:

"In the successful adjustment of the legal relationships of the two races democracy is vitally involved. The right to a fair trial by an impartial jury of peers is one of the bed-rocks upon which freedom rests, and if it cannot be preserved when the courts serve two races, then democracy itself rests on quicksand. The problem of legal justice is, therefore, fully as important to the white race as to the Negro race. Any tendency to weaken the feeling that the court system is entirely impartial, unaffected by passion or prejudice, and meticulously just, or any tendency to strengthen the feeling that the court can be biased or made the instrument of a particular class, is a tendency which may wreck society."[b]

[5] For example, Robert A. Warner describes the situation in New Haven, Connecticut, in these terms:

"Only occasionally are justice betrayed and the colored people robbed of the protection of the law, when the judges of the city court suspect acts of violence in which Negroes are involved are simple assaults. One such case was appealed to Criminal Superior Court successfully. A white man, drunk, was surprised in the act of stealing the car of a reputable Negro couple. When they chased and overtook him, he slashed the woman so severely that a blood transfusion was necessary to save her life. The city court disposed of the case with a cursory $25 fine and costs for breach of the peace, and suspended judgments or penalties for the motor vehicle violations involved. The higher court gave the miscreant a deserved year in jail." (*New Haven Negroes* [1940], p. 224.)

[6] The classic case study on this subject is the survey undertaken by The Chicago Commission on Race Relations. (*The Negro in Chicago* [1922].)

[7] In Detroit a federal housing project, the Sojourner Truth Homes, was the scene of a riot between whites and Negroes. The project was designed for Negro defense workers. On the day set for occupancy, February 28, whites who lived nearby picketed the project. Moving vans containing the furniture of prospective Negro tenants were stopped. When one van tried to pass the line, the white men climbed all over the truck; a stone was thrown, hitting a Negro driver. Then mounted police charged in. *Life* magazine reports: "Cops charged down on Negro sympathizers of excluded tenants. Police devoted most attention to Negroes, made no effort to open picket lines for vans. Said one inspector: 'It would be suicide if we used our sticks on any of them [the whites].'" (*Life* [March 16, 1942], pp. 40-41.)

[8] Henry Hill Collins, Jr., *America's Own Refugees* (1941), p. 156. See also, David W. Anthony, "The Cranbury Terror Case," *The Crisis* (October, 1939), pp. 295-296.

[9] Of 1,247 Negro lawyers, judges, and justices reported in the United States in 1930, only 436 were from the whole South, where over three-fourths of the Negro population were concentrated. (U. S. Bureau of the Census, *Negroes in the United States: 1920-1932*, pp. 9 and 293.)

[a] Ray Stannard Baker, *Following the Color Line* (1908), p. 49. The statement was made by a Mr. Hopkins, leader of the Civic League of Atlanta, composed of the foremost white citizens of that city.

[b] T. J. Woofter, Jr., *The Basis of Racial Adjustment* (1925), p. 125.

[10] Statements in this paragraph are the conclusions the present author has reached after having interviewed a great number of white and Negro lawyers in Northern cities.

[11] E. Franklin Frazier, *Negro Youth at the Crossways* (1940), pp. 34-35 and 169.

[12] Hinton Rowan Helper, *The Impending Crisis of the South* (1860; first edition, 1857), p. 140.

[13] "Notes on Virginia: 1781-1782," in *The Writings of Thomas Jefferson*, H. A. Washington (editor) (1859), Vol. 8, pp. 403-404. In two paragraphs Cash, in his *Mind of the South*, gives the common sense of the long-drawn-out discussion about whether slavery was cruel or not:

"Wholly apart from the strict question of right and wrong, it is plain that slavery was inescapably brutal and ugly. Granted the existence, in the higher levels, of genuine humanity of feeling toward the bondsman; granted that, in the case of the house-servants at least, there was sometimes real affection between master and man; granted even that, at its best, the relationship here got to be gentler than it has ever been elsewhere, the stark fact remains: It rested on force. The black man occupied the position of a mere domestic animal, without will or right of his own. The lash lurked always in the background. Its open crackle could often be heard where field hands were quartered. Into the gentlest houses drifted now and then the sound of dragging chains and shackles, the bay of hounds, the report of pistols on the trail of the runaway. And, as the advertisements of the time incontestably prove, mutilation and the mark of the branding iron were pretty common.

"Just as plain was the fact that the institution was brutalizing—to white men. Virtually unlimited power acted inevitably to call up, in the coarser sort of master, that sadism which lies concealed in the depths of universal human nature—bred angry impatience and a taste for cruelty for its own sake, with a strength that neither the kindliness I have so often referred to (it continued frequently to exist unimpaired side by side, and in the same man, with this other) nor notions of honor could effectually restrain. And in the common whites it bred a savage and ignoble hate for the Negro, which required only opportunity to break forth in relentless ferocity; for all their rage against the 'white-trash' epithet concentrated itself on him rather than on the planters." (Wilbur J. Cash, *The Mind of the South* [1941], pp. 82-83.)

[14] John Codman Hurd, *The Law of Freedom and Bondage in the United States* (1858-1862), Vol. 1, pp. 222-309; Vol. 2, pp. 2-218.

[15] See: William Goodell, *The American Slave Code in Theory and Practice* (1853); John Codman Hurd, *The Law of Freedom and Bondage in the United States* (1858-1862); and George M. Stroud, *A Sketch of the Laws Relating to Slavery in the Several States of the United States of America* (1856).

[16] Compare William Sumner Jenkins, *Pro-Slavery Thought in the Old South* (1935), pp. 153-154.

[17] Goodell, *op. cit.*, pp. 122-127, 201-224; Stroud, *op. cit.*, pp. 20-28, 67-75; Hurd, *op. cit.*, Vol. 2, pp. 79-80 and 96.

[18] For a summary of these insurrections and their effects on the whites, see Harvey Wish, "American Slave Insurrections before 1861," *The Journal of Negro History* (July, 1937), pp. 299-320. See also Chapter 35, Section 1, of this book.

[19] Gilbert T. Stephenson, *Race Distinctions in American Law* (1910), pp. 36 ff.

[20] B. Schrieke, *Alien Americans* (1936), pp. 135-136.

[21] See Frank Shay, *Judge Lynch* (1938).

[22] Guy B. Johnson, "Patterns of Race Conflict," in *Race Relations and the Race Problem*, Edgar T. Thompson (editor) (1939), pp. 131 ff.

[23] It has become customary in sociological literature to refer to the slavery system and the ante-bellum South as a social order in balance and equilibrium. "There was no serious race problem under slavery. The problem arose with the sudden and complete destruction of the old social arrangement, and the necessity for making a new racial adjustment under the irreversible conditions of a tremendous Negro population growth, economic interdependence, and the partial acculturation of the Negro group." (Charles S. Johnson in Weatherford and Johnson, *op. cit.*, p. 543. Compare William Graham Sumner, *Folkways* [1906], pp. 77 and 90; Robert E. Park, "The Bases of Race Prejudice," *The Annals of the American Academy of Political and Social Science* [November, 1928], pp. 13-15; Bertram W. Doyle, *The Etiquette of Race Relations in the South* [1937], pp. 7 ff.) This view is considerably exaggerated, to say the least.

[24] There are, however, advantages to be gained by holding the Negro in a subordinate position. "Three gains are seen as accruing to the middle-class white group; they are the economic, sexual, and prestige gains. The white middle class is so placed that it makes all of these gains from the Negroes and some of them from the lower-class whites." (John Dollard, *Caste and Class in a Southern Town* [1937], p. 99.)

Chapter 25. *The Police and Other Public Contacts*

[1] Arthur Raper, "Race and Class Pressures," unpublished manuscript prepared for this study (1940), p. 20.

[2] A great many of these arrests occur on streetcars and buses. A Negro may be arrested for demanding the right change from the conductor or for refusing to give up his seat in the colored section of the car to a white person.[a] He may be arrested for being in the white section of town after dark.[b] Raper cites the following case.

". . . Mrs. Edna Lewis, prominent Negro Baptist from Akron, Ohio, . . . was attending the Baptist World Alliance in Atlanta in August, 1939. When driving downtown she had asked a policeman how to reach Fort Street. Instead of directing her, he said, 'All you darkies want to go to darkeytown.' 'Well,' replied Mrs. Lewis, 'I happen not to be any more darkey than you are.' The policeman, indignant and amazed stammered out, 'Why—why—I'll have you put in jail for that.' Whereupon, he arrested her, called a nearby patrol wagon and sent her off to the police station on a charge of 'disturbing the peace.' At the sergeant's desk she was told she could post a bond of $12 or remain in jail until Monday."[c]

In July, 1942, in Rome, Georgia, Mrs. Roland Hayes, wife of the famous tenor, went with her daughter into a shoe store where she had dealt for three years. It was a hot day, and they sat under the fan. A clerk asked them to move back into the section reserved for Negroes. Mrs. Hayes refused, saying it was hot, and that she preferred to remain under the fan. Words were exchanged, and Mrs. Hayes told the clerk he was behaving like Hitler.

[a] Raper, *op. cit.*, pp. 6-7.
[b] *Ibid.*, pp. 56-57.
[c] *Ibid.*, pp. 57-58.

When Mr. Hayes later went into the store to rectify the matter, a policeman caught him by the belt as he started to leave. When he stated that his wife did not curse (as the clerk contended that she had), an un-uniformed man hit him in the mouth. The policeman handcuffed Mr. Hayes and took him and his wife and daughter to the police station. In the car, Mr. Hayes was struck again. Mr. Hayes and his wife were put in a cell, later released on $50 bond.[a]

In both Mrs. Lewis' and Mr. Hayes' cases, further action did not follow because of the ensuing publicity, but the ordinary Negro in similar circumstances would have been fined or imprisoned.

[3] Guy B. Johnson observes:

". . . for the most part each plantation or household was a little realm in which the slaveowner was lord and master and had jurisdiction over the punishment of his slaves for all except those serious offenses which were recognized as crimes against the state. This fact is of great significance for the understanding of racial conflict, for it means that white people during the long period of slavery became accustomed to the idea of 'regulating' Negro insolence and insubordination by force with the consent and approval of the law."[b]

[4] "In the rural areas the punishment of Negroes is largely in the hands of white planters. They whip Negroes both for infractions of the caste rules and for minor crimes, such as fighting or theft. Furthermore, the planter for whom the Negro works either participates in the punishment himself or gives his permission. Some planters assert that they are solely responsible for their own Negroes and that no one else has any right to punish them."[c]

[5] Compare John Dollard, *Caste and Class in a Southern Town* (1937), pp. 122 ff. and Chapter 8, and Davis, Gardner, and Gardner, *op. cit.*, pp. 55-56, 336 ff., *passim.* See also Chapter 27, Section 1.

[6] Raper, *op. cit.*, p. 6. "The conductors in charge of trains operated in these [Jim Crow] states are in practically every instance given police powers to enforce the regulation."[d] Some street car conductors in Southern cities carry guns and use them to threaten Negroes.

[7] Raper, *op. cit.*, especially pp. 6-10 and 35-63.

[8] *Ibid.*, p. 7.

[9] *Ibid.*, pp. 13-18 and appendices 1, 6, and 9.

[10] *Ibid.*, p. 14.

[11] "When a department goes on civil service, the more flagrant abuses of 'log rolling' are eliminated, but the department even then is not immune to political bias. Civil service commissions sometimes reflect factionalism. Even if the commissioners achieve absolute impartiality, there is still plenty of opportunity to leave off the person with a high civil service ranking and appoint others with lower ratings, for the common practice is to make a selection from the three highest ranking applicants, which means the third highest may secure the appointment. The other two would then remain on the list, to be called back along with a new third, and again the first and second ranking applicants can be

[a] See *Time* (July 27, 1942), p. 17.
[b] "Patterns of Race Conflict" in *Race Relations and the Race Problem*, Edgar T. Thompson (editor) (1939), p. 130.
[c] Allison Davis, B. B. Gardner, and M. R. Gardner, *Deep South* (1941), pp. 55-56.
[d] Charles S. Mangum, Jr., *Legal Status of the Negro* (1940), p. 183.

ignored. And so on until the desired number of appointments have been made. The only circumstances under which the highest ranking applicant would necessarily be appointed is for all eligible persons on the list to be appointed."[a] It is understood that Negroes cannot apply for police positions.

[12] *Ibid.*, p. 14. "Where the police department is directly under the city administration, that is, 'in politics,' each political faction has its own list of prospective officers, who work in the campaign on promise of a job if successful at the polls. But this does not mean that the particular person who becomes a policeman took an interest in the election; he may have been sponsored by a politically potent father, uncle, lodge buddy, or perhaps a former employer. Under such a system, victory for the contesting political party may mean the dismissal of half or more of the force."[b]

[13] *Ibid.*, p. 15.

[14] *Ibid.*, p. 14.

[15] *Ibid.*, p. 16.

[16] *Ibid.*, pp. 19 and 20.

[17] *Ibid.*, p. 20.

[18] *Ibid.*, p. 21.

"The fact that Negroes are used unofficially by the police force seems to contribute to the high homicide rate among Negroes, simply because the lives of the Negro informers, spotters, and stool pigeons are cheap to the Negroes who are wanted by the police and who are being reported, often as not, by fellow criminals trying to protect their own skins. The law is white. So too are the officials who administer it. The Negro who works with the police becomes a party to the 'crime' of subjecting a member of his group to an unfriendly court. He is by definition of the hunted man, a traitor to his own race—and his life may be the price."[c]

[19] The hardships of the white policeman should not be forgotten when accounting for his intense race prejudice. When he patrols the Negro sections of Southern cities, he is in considerable danger of personal violence and knows it. Dr. Raper describes the daily routine as follows:

"Police service to Negro communities is limited largely to radio cruising cars. A map of their routes through Atlanta's Negro sections, however, shows that they do not go through the areas where most Negro homicides occur, but rather stay on the main thoroughfares which are given over largely to business purposes. Too often the police go into the Negro community only when called, as it were, to umpire Negro brawls, or even more often to pick up members of the 'enemy' faction. When poolroom operators or restaurant keepers are unsympathetic with boisterousness, the whole group may be taken off together in 'Black Maria.' Managements do not, as a rule, follow such a practice, however, for to do so would be to go out of business shortly.

"The real function served by the police in many Southern Negro communities seems to be limited to rounding up vagrants, loiterers, crap shooters, non-cooperating prostitutes, and drunks. These occasional arresting excursions serve several purposes: they keep the Negroes intimidated, they maintain arrest quotas, they earn money for the police court, and sometimes they help preserve order. For, as pointed out by more than one police official, most of the Negro killings grow out of these social gatherings.

[a] Raper, *op. cit.*, p. 17.
[b] *Ibid.*, p. 16.
[c] *Ibid.*, pp. 21-22.

Though nearly all responsible Negro people want better police services in their communities, they do not commonly agree that the picking up of people for trivial offenses is desirable. They expect the police officers to be quite discriminating and perhaps to use more insight than they have, for from the white policeman's point of view, Negro gangs must be broken up upon sight or there is likelihood that banter will be challenged by heavy threats, and somebody fatally wounded with a razor, ice pick, or pistol."[a]

[20] "It is a common belief of many whites that Negroes will respond only to violent methods. In accordance with their theory of the 'animal-like' nature of the Negro, they believe that the formal punishments of fines and imprisonment fail to act as deterrents to crime."[b]

"Much of the beating of Negroes by the police is based on the general belief that formal punishments by fine or jail sentence fail to act as deterrents to Negro criminals. This belief is combined with the feeling that legal technicalities frequently prevent Negro lawbreakers from being punished through the courts. Thus, the police tend to revert to direct action and to administer punishment themselves. They claim that their action is justified because it reduces crime."[c]

[21] Raper, *op. cit.*, p. 35.

[22] In the North, there is much killing of Negroes by the police, but it seems to be more a part of the regular warfare against criminals than it is an expression of race prejudice. It is the present writer's impression that brutality other than killing is much less common in the North than in the South. It is to be regretted that no quantitative information is available on police brutality other than killing.

[23] Raper, *op. cit.*, pp. 52-53. Compare *ibid.*, p. 35.

[24] For substantiation, see *ibid.*, pp. 41-52.

[25] *Ibid.*, p. 53.

W. E. B. Du Bois sums up the situation thus:

"These districts are not usually protected by the police—rather victimized and tyrannized over by them. No one who does not know can realize what tyranny a low-grade white policeman can exercise in a colored neighborhood. In court his unsupported word cannot be disputed and the only defense against him is often mayhem and assassination by black criminals, with resultant hue and cry."[d]

[26] U.S. Bureau of the Census, *Negroes in the United States: 1920-1932*, pp. 322-324; and *Fifteenth Census of the United States: 1930, Population*, Vol. IV, Table 13. The census figures for the South do not include Negro women officers who are, however, few in number.

[27] Raper, *op. cit.*, p. 27.

[28] *Ibid.*, p. 18.

"The Universities of North Carolina, Virginia, Alabama and perhaps other states sponsor institutes for police officers." (*Ibid.*, p. 18.)

[29] I have been made aware that this recommendation seems utopian. Even most Northern police systems are far from reaching this standard. But considering both the very large proportion of all young men who go through college and the high crime rate which makes the police so particularly important in America, it seems to the foreign

[a] *Ibid.*, pp. 22-23.
[b] Davis, Gardner, and Gardner, *op. cit.*, p. 46.
[c] *Ibid.*, p. 502.
[d] *Dusk of Dawn* (1940), pp. 182-183.

observer that it is an irrational practice to keep the policemen's professional standard so unusually low.

[30] For discussions on the problem of improving the police standards, see August Vollmer, *The Police and Modern Society* (1936), especially pp. 216-234; and the National Resources Committee, *Urban Government* (1939), pp. 276-291.

[31] "After several years' experience in rural Black Belt communities, the writer is thoroughly convinced that the local whites would be thrown into a panic if they knew the contents of the letters regularly going in and out of the Negro community. No matter how poor and illiterate the small town Negro family may be, and how cowed by the potential mob, regular inquiry will be made at the general delivery window.

"Most sharecropper families have at least one member who can read and write, and all have mail boxes by the roadside. The R.F.D., however, may not be considered dependable in times of strife, and especially important, or should we say delicate, letters are carried personally to the post office.

"Sometimes the local post office may not be considered safe, and letters may be posted in the nearest city. This is particularly true when people are under surveillance, for whatever reason, and wish to conceal the destination of their letters. The files of Washington officials, as well as the Commission on Interracial Affairs and the N. A. A. C. P., bear eloquent testimony to the sense of security that Negroes and poorer whites feel even in the local postal service in the rural South."[a]

[32] Raper testifies that they sometimes start out by approximating federal standards but sooner or later become appreciative of local practices, and continues:

"On the basis of wide personal observation, the writer knows of only one instance in the South where absolute equality between the races was practiced by a local administrator. This was in Atlanta, for a few months shortly after the emergence of the New Deal, when Miss Louisa deB. Fitzsimmons was in active charge of relief administration."[b]

[33] Raper, *op. cit.*, p. 12.

Chapter 26. *Courts, Sentences and Prisons*

[1] *Through Afro-America* (1910), pp. 97-98.

[2] *Ibid.*, pp. 96 and 97.

[3] Virginius Dabney, *Liberalism in the South* (1932), p. 256.

[4] Arthur Raper, "Race and Class Pressures," unpublished manuscript prepared for this study (1940), pp. 64 ff.

[5] *Ibid.*, p. 89.

[6] Letter, April 15, 1940.

[7] Charles S. Mangum, Jr., *The Legal Status of the Negro* (1940), p. 343.

[8] Raper, *op. cit.*, p. 67. Compare *ibid.*, pp. 156 ff.

[9] *Ibid.*, p. 155.

[10] Mangum, *op. cit.*, Chapter 12.

[11] Raper, *op. cit.*, pp. 79 and 80.

[12] "In most courts where Negro jurors will not be used or will be used only under

---

[a] Raper, *op. cit.*, pp. 10-11.
[b] *Ibid.*, p. 8, footnote 1.

the sternest instructions from the judge, a Negro lawyer would be a real handicap to a client. The general white populace, including the jurors, would feel that such a Negro client was uppity—if not actually trying to insult the community." (*Ibid.*, p. 91.)

[13] A Northern Negro lawyer complains:

". . . many of them [Negroes] who have the means prefer white lawyers in the same manner that a person prefers to buy at a big, well-equipped store. My office is not so well equipped and manned as to indicate that I could handle very important and intricate cases . . ." (Letter, March 20, 1940.)

[14] A white lawyer from the Upper South writes in a letter:

"When the cases involve no such issues [on the race question] but are merely cases, I have noted that cases between Negro and Negro are handled somewhat differently than cases between white and white. I mean a spirit of levity, an expectation of something 'comical' appears to exist. The seriousness in the white vs. Negro case is decidedly lacking. As you know it is a rare case indeed in which a Negro who has murdered a Negro receives the extreme penalty, either death or life imprisonment here, regardless of the facts. Only the other day in a local case a Negro who murdered another with robbery as motive, a charge that would have been as between white and white, or Negro and white victim, good for the electric chair, was disposed of by a jury with a 15 year sentence. The punishment as between Negro and Negro, as distinguished from white vs. white, or Negro vs. white victim, is decidedly different and clearly shows the racial approach to the question. In short the court-room feeling is that the Negro is entirely inferior, with punishment for crimes by him against his own kind punished with less punishment than when the white man is involved." (Letter of June 19, 1940.)

[15] The author can personally testify to a few cases of a white upper class person securing leniency for a Negro accused of a crime against another Negro.

[16] Edgar G. Murphy, for example, wrote:

"Petty crimes are often forgiven him, and in countless instances the small offences for which white men are quickly apprehended are, in the negro, habitually ignored. The world hears broadly and repeatedly of the cases of injustice, it hears little of those more frequent instances in which the weaknesses of a child-race are accorded only an amused indifference or a patient tolerance by their stronger neighbors." (*Problems of the Present South* [1909; first edition, 1904], p. 176.)

[17] A generation ago Baker observed:

"One thing impressed me especially, not only in this court but in all others I have visited: a Negro brought in for drunkenness, for example, was punished much more severely than a white man arrested for the same offence. The injustice which the weak everywhere suffer—North and South—is in the South visited upon the Negro. The white man sometimes escaped with a reprimand, he was sometimes fined three dollars and costs, but the Negro, especially if he had no white man to intercede for him, was usually punished with a ten or fifteen dollar fine, which often meant that he must go to the chain-gang." (Ray Stannard Baker, *Following the Color Line* [1908], p. 49.) See also Allison Davis, B. B. Gardner, and M. R. Gardner, *Deep South* (1941), p. 504.

[18] See Chapter 10, Section 4. The Southern legal codes contain a number of laws making it possible for the employers in rural districts to utilize the legal machinery for their own economic purposes. Among them the vagrancy laws:

". . . they afford a legal means for recruiting temporary peons. The device is simple:

Employers let it be known that they need additional laborers. If such an announcement brings out a sufficient number of workers, there is no excuse for invoking the vagrancy laws; but if a sufficient number is not forthcoming, any person without visible and obvious means of support is subjected to choosing between accepting the local labor opportunity or being drawn into court, where he may readily be fined or imprisoned. If fined, however, he may still be forced to accept local employment, for an employer may arrange with court officials to pay his fine and let him work it out. Such prisoners are ready victims of peonage, they are court wards and their employers exercise close surveillance over their movements, having virtual license to keep them in debt at the commissary. The worker has little choice, for the prison sentence hangs over his head should he not work out the fine satisfactorily.

"The inclusiveness of the vagrancy charge may be seen from the Florida statute which defines persons subject to arrest for vagrancy as 'rogues, vagabonds, idle or dissolute persons, common pipers and fiddlers . . . persons who neglect their calling, or are without reasonably continuous employment or regular income, and who have not sufficient property to sustain them.' Under such a law a dozen potential workers can be picked up at a crap game or just around the corner, for being unoccupied. And should they not readily submit, they can be picked up for disorderly conduct or resisting arrest." (Raper, *op. cit.*, pp. 187-188.) In April, 1942, the United States Department of Justice began investigating such a case in Georgia.

[19] Raper, *op. cit.*, p. 107.

[20] *Ibid.*, pp. 137-141.

[21] *Ibid.*, pp. 189-195.

[22] Mangum, *op. cit.*, p. 274.

[23] On February 18, 1936, at Raleigh, North Carolina, a white man was executed for killing a Negro. This datum was so important because it was recorded in the press to be the first time that such a thing had ever occurred in the South. (See Raper, *op. cit.*, p. 166.)

[24] Kelly Miller, *Race Adjustment* (1908), p. 80.

[25] U.S. Bureau of the Census, *Prisoners in State and Federal Prisons and Reformatories: 1939*, p. 29. In 1938, the proportion was 45.0; in 1937 it was 44.5.

[26] *Sixteenth Census of the United States: 1940, Population*, Preliminary Release, Series P-10, No. 1.

[27] Raper, *op. cit.*, pp. 163-168.

[28] Frank Tannenbaum, *Darker Phases of the South* (1924), Chapter 3; Raper, *op. cit.*, pp. 171-172; George Washington Cable, *The Silent South* (1885); Robert E. Burns, *I Am a Fugitive From a Georgia Chain Gang* (1932); Jesse F. Steiner and Roy M. Brown, *The North Carolina Chain Gang* (1927); John L. Spivak, *Georgia Nigger* (1932).

[29] See Raper, *op. cit.*, Appendix 10, "Women Criminals in Atlanta, August 1939."

[30] See: *The Encyclopedia of the Social Sciences*, "Legal Aid," Vol. 9, pp. 319-324; Reginald Heber Smith, *Justice and the Poor* (1919). *The Annals of the American Academy of Political and Social Science* (March 1926) are entirely devoted to a discussion of legal aid societies in the United States. For a discussion of the relative lack of these societies in the South, see *ibid.*, pp. 20-26.

[31] Reports from several Negro lawyers, even in the Deep South, suggest that the mere presence of a large, interested, and well-behaved Negro audience in court has

a beneficial influence upon the impartiality of the legal procedures. It also stimulates the Negro lawyer. One of them, from a small city in the Lower South, writes:

"I have found that a courtroom of Negro spectators gives the Negro lawyer a feeling of support. He has potential clients, and certainly he will override any fears which may reside in his heart and soul to win more clients. So, he becomes more effective at the bar. Then too, the Negro spectators convey an interest which is compelling to the judge, in deciding cases which are affected with a public interest." (Letter, April 14, 1940.)

Chapter 27. *Violence and Intimidation*

¹ The patterns of extra-legal violence and intimidation have been felt by poor whites, to a certain extent, as well as by Negroes—in spite of the fact that, in recent years, poor whites have come to employ violence against Negroes more than do upper class whites. Even during slavery white aggression turned against other white people who did not conform or who were obnoxious for one reason or another. The class angle became more important when, in the later decades of the nineteenth century, small white farmers were pressed down into tenancy, or, as industry developed, became a white proletarian class of industrial workers. Southern white sharecroppers and textile workers could certainly not be dealt with as Negro labor, but part of the sanctions against the lower caste were transferred and applied to the lower class. Nearly one-half of the fatalities in labor struggles for each year between 1934 and 1940 occurred in the South which had scarcely one-fourth of the nation's population and less than one-fourth of its industrial workers. Nearly one-half of the Southern labor fatalities have been Negroes, though they constitute only one-fifth of the Southern industrial population. (Arthur Raper, "Race and Class Pressures," unpublished manuscript prepared for this study [1940]; and *Fifteenth Census of the United States: 1930, Population,* Vol. IV, Table 18 and State Table 11.)

² The custom of dueling when one's "honor" was challenged was quite common among the upper classes of the South in the nineteenth century. This was part of the Southern pattern of taking the law into individual hands, but it is one type of extra-legal violence which has been completely done away with. Dueling never had any significance for Negroes or poor whites.

³ Raper, "Race and Class Pressures," pp. 278-295.

⁴ To the average Northerner, who has little contact with poor white Southerners but some contact with Southern Negroes, the carrying of knives and other weapons is a "Negro custom." Actually, of course, it is a Southern custom.

"Most men, Negro and White, carry guns, and many of them also have knives. The most common type, familiarly called a 'crab-apple switch,' is a rather long pocket knife with a sharp four-inch blade." (Hortense Powdermaker, *After Freedom* [1939], pp. 169-170.)

⁵ Amendment II of the United States Constitution reads in part "the right of the people to keep and bear arms shall not be infringed."

⁶ Excellent studies of lynching include: The National Association for the Advancement of Colored People, *Thirty Years of Lynching in the United States: 1889-1918* (1919); Frank Shay, *Judge Lynch* (1938); Walter White, *Rope and Faggot* (1929);

Arthur Raper, *The Tragedy of Lynching* (1933); John Weldon Hoot, "Lynch Law, the Practice of Illegal Popular Coercion," unpublished Ph.D. thesis, University of Pennsylvania (1935).

[7] Compare Donald R. Young, *American Minority Peoples* (1932), pp. 254 ff., and, by the same author, *Research Memorandum on Minority Peoples in the Depression* (1937), pp. 172 ff.

[8] White, *op. cit.*, pp. 19 ff.

[9] Earle F. Young, "The Relation of Lynching to the Size of Political Areas," *Sociology and Social Research* (March-April, 1928), pp. 348-353; and National Resources Committee, *Our Cities* (1937), p. 16.

[10] Commission on Interracial Cooperation, *The Mob Still Rides* (1935), pp. 15-16, and Raper, *The Tragedy of Lynching*, pp. 29-30.

[11] Raper, *The Tragedy of Lynching*, p. 36.

[12] *Ibid.*, pp. 36-37.

[13] William Archer, *Through Afro-America* (1910), pp. 216-217; Thomas P. Bailey, *Race Orthodoxy in the South* (1914), p. 44; Sir Harry H. Johnston, *The Negro in the New World* (1910), p. 462. Similar statements have been made by E. G. Murphy, *The Basis of Ascendancy* (1909), p. 52, and more recently by Frank Tannenbaum, *Darker Phases of the South* (1924), pp. 32-33; Walter White, *Rope and Faggot* (1929), pp. 62 ff.; John Dollard, *Caste and Class in a Southern Town* (1937), pp. 163-164; Hortense Powdermaker, *After Freedom* (1939), p. 52; E. Franklin Frazier, "The Pathology of Race Prejudice," *The Forum* (May, 1927), pp. 856-862; W. F. Cash, *The Mind of the South* (1941), pp. 114-117.

[14] White, *op. cit.*, pp. 57 ff.; Tannenbaum, *op. cit.*, pp. 34 ff.

[15] Dollard, *Caste and Class in a Southern Town*, pp. 321-326 and 338; White, *op. cit.*, Chapter 4.

[16] Raper, *The Tragedy of Lynching*, pp. 16-19 and 32-33, *passim*.

[17] Raper, "Race and Class Pressures," p. 275. Also see Raper, *The Tragedy of Lynching*, pp. 13-14.

[18] Raper, *The Tragedy of Lynching*, pp. 10 ff. *passim*.

[19] *Ibid.*, pp. 11-12.

[20] *Ibid.*, pp. 12-13; White, *op. cit.*, pp. 3, 26 and 38.

[21] Raper, *The Tragedy of Lynching*, pp. 8 ff. and 44 ff.; White, *op. cit.*, pp. 3-18 and 54-81; Tannenbaum, *op. cit.*, 25-26.

[22] Willis D. Weatherford and Charles S. Johnson, *Race Relations* (1934), p. 57; White, *op. cit.*, pp. 103-105 *passim*.

[23] Weatherford and Johnson, *op. cit.*, p. 57; White, *op. cit.*, p. 111; Tannenbaum, *op. cit.*, pp. 19-20.

[24] T. J. Woofter, Jr., in Raper, *The Tragedy of Lynching*, pp. 30-31; C. I. Hovland and R. R. Sears, "Minor Studies of Aggression: VI. Correlation of Lynchings with Economic Indices," reported in John Dollard *et al.*, *Frustration and Aggression* (1939), p. 31; and Buell G. Gallagher, *American Caste and the Negro College* (1938), pp. 381 ff.

[25] *Op. cit.*, p. 11. Compare p. 12. Ray Stannard Baker (*Following the Color Line* [1908]) earlier made a similar statement: ". . . a community will rise to mob Negroes or to drive them out of the country . . because the Negro is becoming educated,

acquiring property and 'getting out of his place'" (*ibid.*, p. 81), and he talks about their "fear" of the Negro. (*Ibid.*, pp. 7-8.)

[26] Tannenbaum, *op. cit.*, pp. 8-9.

[27] White, *op. cit.*, pp. 111 ff.

[28] *Ibid.*, pp. 40 ff.

[29] William J. Robertson, *The Changing South* (1927), p. 99. The phenomenon was observed also by André Siegfried, who pointed out that the Klan movement was inspired by the Protestant clergy; see *America Comes of Age* (1927) pp. 132-135.

[30] Raper, *The Tragedy of Lynching*, pp. 2, 21 *passim.*

[31] "Village life is dull everywhere, but in the South the situation is in many respects worse than in any other part of the country. The single crop so characteristic of the South has its influence in denying the rural population varied interests. The single crop, with its reduction of the farmer to the status of a city worker, who has to depend upon a money economy for nearly all of his needs, with its greater emphasis upon a money crop for sale rather than a varied crop for use, with its tendency to neglect the other subsidiary activities that are the very foundation of diversified farming, with its large tenancy, its frequent change of place, its intermittent periods of idleness, its monotonous food, its indebtedness, lack of interest in the farm, in its appearance, and the too frequent absence of numerous cattle and their almost human appeal to tenderness and care—the single crop has made the rural community in the South much more a burden spiritually and has meant much greater need for external excitement, partly expressed in intense religious emotions and protracted meetings." (Tannenbaum, *op. cit.*, pp. 21-22.)

[32] White, *op. cit.*, pp. 9 ff.

[33] For a general consideration of the nature of the lynching mob, see Richard T. LaPiere, *Collective Behavior* (1939), pp. 538-542.

[34] Charles S. Johnson describes the effects on the Negro community:

"During and shortly after a lynching the Negro community lives in terror. Negroes remain at home and out of sight. When the white community quiets down, the Negroes go back to their usual occupations. The incident is not forgotten, but the routine of the plantation goes on. The lynching, in fact, is part of the routine. . . . The effect on children is profound and permanent. After a time the Negro community returns to 'normal.' Life goes on, but Negro youth 'let white folks tend to their business.' Contacts with whites are avoided as far as possible. The youth may work for white people but intimacy is avoided. The Negro servant or laborer continues friendly to his employers. The employers may even be liked and regarded as 'good white folks,' but ultimate trust is held in abeyance." (*Growing Up in the Black Belt* [1941], pp. 317-318.)

[35] Murphy wrote:

"It has become increasingly obvious, however, that whatever the practise of lynching may or may not be, it is not a remedy. It does not prevent crime. Through the morbid interests which it arouses, and through the publicity which it creates, it inflames to the utmost the power of criminal suggestion and aggravates all the conditions of racial suspicion and antagonism. The so-called 'remedy' has always been followed by new outbreaks of the disease, the most atrocious crimes coming at short intervals after the previous exercise of the mob's philosophy of 'prevention.'" (Edgar G. Murphy, *Problems of the Present South* [1909; first edition, 1904], p. 178.)

Miller observed:

"In the first place it causes the whites to hate the Negro, as it is a part of human nature to hate those whom we have injured. In the second place it causes the Negro to hate the whites. It is universally conceded that lynching has no deterrent effect upon the class of crimes alleged to excite its vengeance. On the contrary, it probably has the opposite effect. The criminals and outlaws of the Negro race, who care nothing for life or death, may be thus hardened into resolves of revenge, and lie waiting to strike the hated race where the blow will be most keenly felt." (Kelly Miller, *Race Adjustment* [1908], p. 69.)

Similarly Stone:

"But the point I would urge is that the illegal execution of Negroes by lynching, even when torture is added, has an inciting rather than a deterring influence upon the large number of potential criminals." (Alfred H. Stone, *Studies in the American Race Problem* [1908], p. 465.)

[36] Moorfield Storey, *Problems of Today* (1920), pp. 128 ff.; Weatherford and Johnson, *op. cit.*, pp. 437 ff.

[37] James Weldon Johnson, *Along This Way* (1934), pp. 361-374.

[38] Donald Young points to the conflict of "interests" as a basic cause of lynching and suggests that the decrease in Negro lynchings in the South "may be ascribed not so much to a recognition of the evils of lynching, *per se*, as to decreasing clashes of interests between black and white in the South." (*American Minority Peoples*, p. 256.) He follows out the thought by stating:

"This suggests the futility of anti-lynching laws, of interracial commissions, and of educational programs in warring against mob action. Laws taking the prosecution of mob members out of the local courts into the federal would be only a well meant gesture, for even federal judges are human, reflect local sentiment, and must depend on the cooperation of local witnesses who are convinced that lynching is justified to preserve group welfare. It is for this reason that local legal authorities are usually without either the power or the will to prevent or prosecute such offenses. To impose a heavy fine on the county in which lynchings take place, a suggestion based on the theory that the substantial property owners of the community would be spurred to prevent them in order to save their pocketbooks, could have but little effect, for the stronger belief would still persist that such coercion was necessary to protection.

"Interracial commissions and other educational programs are valuable to the extent that the clash of group interests is fictitious, and can be shown to be so. Usually such programs reach only the more substantial elements in a community, people who as a rule are neither leaders of nor participants in mob action. Why should they be? They have achieved personal security, and are not directly in conflict with the minorities who are the object of lynchings. Their interest is a secondary one, derived from the masses directly in conflict with Negroes, Chinese, strikers, or other competing groups. This is the fundamental explanation of the fact that mobs, with few exceptions, are composed of the handicapped social classes who cannot be reached by appeals to justice and humanity." (*Ibid.*, pp. 256-257.)

This reasoning—which, incidentally, is also adhered to by many among the young Negro intellectuals under Marxist influence—is not convincing to us. Collective "interests" do not exist as solid and unchangeable social entities. The "interests," as they are felt, depend upon the actual bonds of identification; a "redefinition of the situation" will change the "interest." Such a redefinition can be accomplished by education and propaganda, and also by laws and the administration of laws. (See Chapter 38, Section 6.)

[39] See Chapter 25, Section 3. Allison Davis and John Dollard mention five incidents in New Orleans between 1936 and 1938:

"Three of these men [five colored men killed by white policemen] were killed in city jails while awaiting trial. The other two were shot while in custody. All were accused of having attacked white men or women. By means of detailed accounts in the newspapers, these symbolic 'legal lynchings' were made known to the colored population and served as a means of further intimidation." (*Children of Bondage* [1940], p. 248.)

[40] ". . . lynchings often happen. They are different to what they used to be though. They used to be big mobs hunting for a nigger, but now you just hear about some nigger found hanging off a bridge." (Interview in Charles S. Johnson, *Growing Up in the Black Belt*, p. 5.) Also see Jessie Daniel Ames, *The Changing Character of Lynching* (1942), pp. 8-9.

The following quotation suggests that secret vigilante lynching has become quite significant. It is from a pamphlet entitled *Lynching Goes Underground* ([January, 1940], pp. 7-8), sponsored by Senators Wagner and Capper and by Representatives Gavagan and Fish. The title page reads: "The author of this report, who must remain anonymous, is a native white Southerner who has lived all his life in the South and still lives there. He has made a number of investigations of lynchings."

"With regard to the whole problem of lynching your investigator desires to make the following statement. It is his considered judgment that, for various reasons, lynching is entering a new and altogether dangerous phase. Lynchings in the past have been characterized by the mob, the faggot, the rope. Hundreds of people, often thousands, poured out to participate or witness the lynching of a man or woman accused of some crime, often of the most trivial nature and often without any real charge at all. Pictures of the mobbed and mobbers have been taken and widely circulated. Souvenirs of the lynched man or woman, in the form of fingers, toes and other parts of the body, have been brazenly displayed by members of the mob.

"Public opinion is beginning to turn against this sort of mob activity. Sentiment is growing against lynching. Agitation for Federal and state anti-lynching laws gives pause to the lynching crowd. Lynching, they say, must go on, but it must be done quietly so as not to attract attention, draw publicity. Thus those who must rule by terror and intimidation turn to new methods. The old mob is disappearing but the work of the mob goes on. A Negro is accused of some crime, real or alleged. A few white men gather, formulate their plans, seize their victim. In some lonely swamp a small body of men do the job formerly done by a vast, howling, bloodthirsty mob composed of men, women and children. The word is then passed that the matter has been handled to the satisfaction of those in charge of such matters.

"Your investigator has probed numerous lynchings. His acquaintance with lynchers and the lynched extends over a lifetime. It is his judgment that countless Negroes are lynched yearly, but their disappearance is shrouded in mystery, for they are dispatched quietly and without general knowledge. . . .

"Your investigator was informed by competent observers that since the notorious double blow torch lynching which occurred at Duck Hill, Mississippi, in 1937, word has been passed that in the future all difficulties between Negroes and whites will be handled by a small group of white men already appointed for that purpose. He was similarly advised that in the vicinity of Cleveland, Mississippi, at least four Negroes had been lynched within the past four or five months."

41 " 'Let the law take its course,' under mob surveillance, is doubtful gain, for in such a situation the courts are virtually prostituted to mob demands." (Raper, "Race and Class Pressures," p. 277.) See also Chapter 26, Section 2, of this book.

42 W. E. B. Du Bois, *Dusk of Dawn* (1940), p. 264.

43 The Chicago Commission on Race Relations, *The Negro in Chicago* (1922), p. 1. There were 17 other persons injured whose race was not recorded, bringing the total of injured up to 537.

44 Du Bois, *Dusk of Dawn*, p. 264.

45 The Chicago Commission on Race Relations, *op. cit.*, p. 72.

46 Du Bois, *Dusk of Dawn*, p. 252.

47 Baker, *op. cit.*, p. 15.

48 The Chicago Commission on Race Relations, *op. cit.*, p. 67.

Chapter 28. *The Basis of Social Inequality*

1 James Bryce, *The Relations of the Advanced and the Backward Races of Mankind* (1902), p. 43.

2 This assertion has also been expressed in the literature; see, for instance, E. B. Reuter, *The American Race Problem* (1927), p. 388.

3 James Weldon Johnson, in his autobiography, discusses the Jim Crow arrangement in railway traveling and gives the following exemplification of the point in the text:

"It was the usual 'Jim Crow' arrangement: one-half of a baggage coach, unkempt, unclean, and ill smelling, with one toilet for both sexes. Two of the seats were taken up by the pile of books and magazines and the baskets of fruit and chewing gum of the 'news-butcher.' There were a half-dozen or more Negroes in the car and two white men. White men in a 'Jim Crow' car were not an unusual sight. It was—and in many parts still is—the custom for white men to go into that car whenever they felt like doing things that would not be allowed in the 'white' car. They went there to smoke, to drink, and often to gamble. At times the object was to pick an acquaintance with some likely-looking Negro girl." (*Along This Way* [1934], pp. 86-87.)

4 "The practice depends upon the individual white man. Negroes and whites occasionally shake hands under a variety of conditions: when a salesman is trying to sell goods, when a former employer meets a respected Negro who has worked for him, when whites are attending public programs or meetings of Negroes, and occasionally on the streets. The white man makes the first approach." (Charles S. Johnson, *Growing Up in the Black Belt* [1941], p. 277.)

5 See W. E. B. Du Bois, *Dusk of Dawn* (1940), p. 259; James Weldon Johnson, *Along This Way*, pp. 298, 299; R. E. Park and E. W. Burgess, *Introduction to the Science of Sociology* (1921), pp. 250-251; Charles S. Johnson, *Patterns of Negro Segregation*, prepared for this study (1934), p. 6.

6 The one-sidedness of the segregation system is so entrenched that it also dominates the interracial work. Particularly in the South and when more than one individual

from each group is involved, this activity can ordinarily be observed to take the form of white people coming to the Negroes—attending their church meetings, concerts, lecture programs, or arranging an interracial conference of leaders or students in a Negro college. Negroes are not supposed to take the initiative. James Weldon Johnson observes:

"There, interracial intercourse, when it does take place, is more often than not a one-sided arrangement. In such instances, the whites come into our midst, but, no matter how sincerely they desire the closer relationship, they fear to offend public sentiment by having us go into their midst. Few there are who dare defy that sentiment. The situation of those who genuinely wish to defy it and dare not is near to pathetic. The cultivation of social and intellectual intercourse between members of the two races in the South cannot progress very far until the whites are as free to act as we are." (*Negro Americans, What Now?* [1934], p. 83.)

The greater freedom of the Negro of which Johnson speaks is the freedom to receive white people without being ostracized by his own group.

[7] This sudden change of attitude has, as is well known, its exact counterpart on the white side. It has been repeatedly pointed out by Negro authors that a dark-looking man who speaks Spanish, French, or some other foreign language and appears as a South American (or Italian, or Indian) will be excepted from the ordinary Jim Crow practices against American Negroes. This story from Booker T. Washington's *Up from Slavery* may illustrate the point:

"I happened to find myself in a town in which so much excitement and indignation were being expressed that it seemed likely for a time that there would be a lynching. The occasion of the trouble was that a dark-skinned man had stopped at the local hotel. Investigation, however, developed the fact that this individual was a citizen of Morocco, and that while travelling in this country he spoke the English language. As soon as it was learned that he was not an American Negro, all the signs of indignation disappeared. The man, who was the innocent cause of the excitement, though, found it prudent after that not to speak English." ([1929; first edition, 1900] p. 103.)

[8] Booker T. Washington tells us about his early childhood:

". . . the plantation upon which I was born, in Franklin County, Va., had, as I remember, only six slaves. My master and his sons all worked together side by side with his slaves. In this way we all grew up together, very much like members of one big family. There was no overseer, and we got to know our master and he to know us." (*The Story of the Negro* [1909], Vol. 1, p. 149.)

[9] 18 Stat. L. 335, Chap. 114.

[10] Gilbert T. Stephenson, *Race Distinctions in American Law* (1910), p. 10; Charles S. Mangum, Jr., *The Legal Status of the Negro* (1940), p. 28.

[11] Stephenson, *op. cit.*, p. 11.

[12] *Ibid.*, pp. 115 ff.; Mangum, *op. cit.*, p. 29.

[13] Stephenson, *op. cit.*, pp. 171 ff.

[14] See W. E. B. Du Bois, *Black Reconstruction* (1935), especially pp. 674 ff.

[15] For an up-to-date account of the Jim Crow legislation, see Mangum, *op. cit.*, especially pp. 181-222.

[16] "The two races have not yet made new mores. Vain attempts have been made to control the new order by legislation. The only result is the proof that legislation cannot make mores." (William Graham Sumner, *Folkways* [1906], p. 77.)

[17] "No small part of the motive back of the South's legal separation of the races in transportation and education is the fact that services for the two races can be made unequal only when administered to them separately. The phrase 'separate and equal' symbolizes the whole system, fair words to gain unfair ends." (Arthur Raper, "Race and Class Pressures," unpublished manuscript prepared for this study [1940], p. 3.)

[18] Henry W. Grady, *The New South* (1890), pp. 244-246; italics ours. In this context Grady furnishes his audience the following illustrative information:

"The Negroes of Georgia pay but one-fortieth of the taxes, and yet they take forty-nine per cent of the school fund. Railroads in Georgia provide separate but equal cars for whites and blacks, and a white man is not permitted to occupy a colored car." (*Ibid.*, p. 246.)

This information is, of course, inaccurate even today and was still more so in Grady's time.

[19] Referring to the Jim Crow arrangement in the railway system, William Archer remarks:

"Remember that the question is complicated by the American's resolute adherence to the constitutional fiction of equality. As there are no 'classes' in the great American people, so there must be no first, second, or third class on the American railways. Of course, the theory remains a fiction on the railroad no less than in life. Everyone travels first class; but those who can pay for it may travel in classes higher than first, called parlour-cars, drawing-room cars, and so forth. The only real validity of the fiction, it seems to me, lies in the unfortunate situation it creates with regard to the negro. If our three classes (or even two) were provided on every train, the mass of the negro population would, from sheer economic necessity, travel third. It might or might not be necessary to provide separate cars on that level; but if it were, the discrimination would not be greatly felt by the grade of black folks it would affect. In the higher-class cars there would be no reasonable need for discrimination, for the number of negroes using them would be few in comparison, and personally unobjectionable. The essential elbow-room would seldom be lacking; conditions in the first and second class would be very much the same as they are at present in the North." (*Through Afro-America* [1910], pp. 72-73.)

[20] *Idem.* "But elbow-room is just what the conditions of railway traveling preclude; wherefore I hold the system of separate cars a legitimate measure of defense against constant discomfort. Had it not been adopted, the South would have been a nation of saints, not of men. It is in the methods of its enforcement that they sometimes show themselves not only human but inhuman." (*Ibid.*, p. 72.)

[21] Edwin R. Embree, *Brown America* (1933; first edition, 1931), p. 205.

[22] Cited in Charles S. Johnson, *Patterns of Negro Segregation*, p. 207.

[23] Quoted from *ibid.*, pp. 195-196. Similar remarks are: "We have always had caste in the world"; "I imagine the average [Negro] is probably happiest when he is waiting on white folks and wearing their old clothes." (See *idem.*)

[24] William M. Brown, *The Crucial Race Question* (1907), p. 118.

[25] Charles S. Johnson, *Patterns of Negro Segregation*, p. 195.

[26] The full gamut of interest motives is suggested by John Dollard (*Caste and Class in a Southern Town* [1937], pp. 98-187) in his theory of gains. It should be noted that Dollard considers these gains—which he classifies as economic, sexual, and prestige—as a means of interpreting and ordering the facts of Negro-white relations in the South.

He does not mean that the gains theory is held consciously and unqualifiedly by the majority of Southern whites who receive these gains from Negro subordination.

[27] *Race Orthodoxy in the South* (1914), p. 48.

[28] The popular theory usually does not reach the level of articles and books any more; even the recent scientific literature on the Negro problem is likely to avoid this central notion. Thomas P. Bailey, a Mississippi professor writing just before the First World War, gives perhaps the clearest pronouncement in print of the prevalent view:

"Some representatives of the humanitarian group feel it difficult to understand why an illiterate and even vicious white man should object to dining with a highly cultured negro gentleman. To them the attitude of the 'low' white man seems essentially illogical and absurd; but it is not so to the men who know the 'low-grade' white man from the *inside.* The whole picture changes when one knows 'what it is about.' *Social attitudes at bottom are concerned with marriage,* and all it stands for. Now, race conscience may prevent the enlightened humanitarian from encouraging in any way the interbreeding of the two races. Race-pride will deter the average man who is willing to acknowledge the excellence of certain individual negroes. *But may it not require race enmity to prevent the amalgamation* of the 'lower' grades of the higher race with the higher grades of the lower race?" (*Op. cit.,* pp. 11-12; second and third italics ours.)

[29] Thomas N. Page, *The Negro: The Southerner's Problem* (1904), p. 292. See also Chapter 3, Section 3, and Chapter 4. Under the influence of modern research this doctrine is in process of disappearing from the literature but it lives on in the conviction of white people. It has even today the gist exemplified by the quotation in the text.

[30] Again the prevalent sentiment is best exemplified by a citation of old literature. The rhetorical intensity of the following paragraphs from Henry W. Grady gives something of the emotional tone of even present-day popular views:

"But the supremacy of the white race of the South must be maintained forever, and the domination of the negro race resisted at all points and at all hazards, because the white race is the superior race. This is the declaration of no new truth; it has abided forever in the marrow of our bones and shall run forever with the blood that feeds Anglo-Saxon hearts." (*Op. cit.,* p. 104.)

"Standing in the presence of this multitude, sobered with the responsibility of the message I deliver to the young men of the South, I declare that the truth above all others to be worn unsullied and sacred in your hearts, to be surrendered to no force, sold for no price, compromised in no necessity, but cherished and defended as the convenant of your prosperity, and the pledge of peace to your children, is, that the white race must dominate forever in the South, because it is the white race, and superior to that race with which its supremacy is threatened." (*Ibid.,* pp. 107-108.)

[31] See Chapter 3, Section 2. James Weldon Johnson observes that in the South ". . . a white gentleman may not eat with a colored person without the danger of serious loss of social prestige; yet he may sleep with a colored person without incurring the risk of any appreciable damage to his reputation," and concludes, "Social equality signifies a series of far-flung barriers against amalgamation of the two races; except so far as it may come about by white men with colored women." (*Along This Way,* pp. 312-313.)

[32] "The intelligent Negro may understand what social equality truly means, but to the ignorant and brutal young Negro, it signifies but one thing: the opportunity to enjoy, equally with white men, the privilege of cohabiting with white women. This the whites of the South understand; and if it were understood abroad, it would serve

to explain some things which have not been understood hitherto. It will explain, in part, the universal and furious hostility of the South to even the least suggestion of social equality." (Page, *op. cit.*, pp. 112-113.)

[33] "Even the most liberal Whites in the community claim that the equality for which the Negroes ask is not possible without the 'social equality'—the intermingling and inter-marriage—they so deeply fear. They also hint that the Negroes 'unconsciously' do desire this sort of social equality." (Hortense Powdermaker, *After Freedom* [1939], p. 350.)

[34] Bailey, *op. cit.*, p. 42.

[35] *The Basis of Racial Adjustment* (1925), pp. 240-241. Woofter distinguishes between contacts which are "helpful" and those which are "harmful." In the latter category he places "social intermingling" along with "vice" and "crime," "violence, economic exploitation, unfair competition, and demagogic or exploitative political contacts." (*Ibid.*, p. 215.)

[36] *Ibid.*, pp. 235 ff.

[37] *Ibid.*, p. 239.

[38] *Liberalism in the South* (1932), p. 254. Dabney continues:

"The argument runs that such laws were desirable twenty or thirty years ago when the great majority of blacks were unclean in person and slovenly in attire, and when the ubiquitous saloon and its readily purchased fire water were conducive to clashes between the lower orders of both races. It is contended that these reasons for separating the races in public gatherings and on public conveyances do not now obtain to anything like the same extent, and that the Negroes should no longer be humiliated in this manner."

[39] *Ibid.*, p. 255.

[40] "Here, as elsewhere, however, it has been rather the social inequality of the races, than any approach to equality, which has been responsible for the mixture, in so far as such has occurred. It was the social inequality of the plantation days that began the process of mixture. . . . If race-amalgamation is indeed to be viewed as always an evil, the best way to counteract the growth of that evil must everywhere be the cultivation of racial self-respect and not of racial degradation." (Josiah Royce, *Race Questions, Provincialism and Other American Problems* [1908], pp. 21-22.)

[41] See Chapter 27, Section 3. W. F. Cash, in his *The Mind of the South* (1941), gives, with much insight and understanding, the story of how in the Old South the sex relations of white men with Negro women tended to inflate white womanhood (pp. 84 ff). The Negro woman, torn from her tribal restraints and taught an easy complaisance, was to be had for the taking:

"Boys on and about the plantation inevitably learned to use her, and having acquired the habit, often continued it into manhood and even after marriage. For she was natural, and could give herself up to passion in a way impossible to wives inhibited by Puritanical training. And efforts to build up a taboo against miscegenation made little real progress." (*Ibid.*, p. 84.)

The white women were naturally disturbed by what they could not help knowing about. The Yankees were not slow to discover the opening in the Southern armor:

"And the only really satisfactory escape here, as in so many other instances, would be fiction. On the one hand, the convention must be set up that the thing simply did not exist, and enforced under penalty of being shot; and on the other, the woman must be compensated, the revolting suspicion in the male that he might be slipping into bestiality got rid of, by glorifying her; the Yankee must be answered by proclaiming from the housetops that Southern Virtue, so far from being inferior, was superior, not alone to the North's but to any on earth, and adducing Southern Womanhood in proof." (*Ibid.*, p. 86.)

After the War this led to "the Southern rape complex." (*Ibid.*. pp. 116 ff.) Every attempt to rise socially on the part of the Negro became an insult to the white woman:

"What Southerners felt, therefore, was that any assertion of any kind on the part of the Negro constituted in a perfectly real manner an attack on the Southern woman. What they saw, more or less consciously, in the conditions of Reconstruction was a passage toward a condition for her as degrading, in their view, as rape itself. And a condition, moreover, which, logic or no logic, they infallibly thought of as being as absolutely forced upon her as rape, and hence a condition for which the term 'rape' stood as truly as for the *de facto* deed." (*Ibid.*, p. 116.)

". . . the increased centrality of woman, added up with the fact that miscegenation, though more terrifying than it had been even in the Old South, showed little tendency to fall off despite efforts to build up standards against it, served to intensify the old interest in gyneolatry, and to produce yet more florid notions about Southern Womanhood and Southern Virtue, and so to foster yet more precious notions of modesty and decorous behavior for the Southern female to live up to." (*Ibid.*, p. 128.)

[42] The "woman on the pedestal" pattern is found outside the American South, of course. It is a general trait in Western civilization and had extreme expression among the feudal nobility of the Middle Ages and the court nobility of France after Louis XIV. It was given added impetus by the loss of the economic function of middle class women at the end of the 18th century. But nowhere did it appear in such extreme, sentimental, and humorless form and so far down in the social status scale as in the American South. (For a general description of the Romantic "pure woman" ideology, see Ernest W. Burgess, "The Romantic Impulse and Family Disorganization," *The Survey* [December 1, 1926], pp. 290-294.)

[43] All the moral conflicts involved in preserving the institution of color caste in a democracy, but quite particularly the association of the caste theory with sex and social status, explain the fear complex upon which most investigators of the race problem in the South have commented. Thomas P. Bailey was early outspoken on this point:

"But the worst has not been told. The veriest slavery of the spirit is to be found in the deep-seated anxiety of the South. Southerners are afraid for the safety of their wives and daughters and sisters; Southern parents are afraid for the purity of their boys; Southern publicists are afraid that a time will come when large numbers of negroes will try to vote, and thus precipitate race war. Southern religionists are afraid that our youth will grow up to despise large numbers of their fellow-men. Southern business men are afraid that agitation of the negro question will interfere with business or demoralize the labor market. Southern officials are afraid of race riots, lynchings, savage atrocities, paying not only for negro fiendishness but also for the anxiety caused by fear of what might be." (*Op. cit.*, pp. 346-347.)

[44] Thomas Carlyle, *Occasional Discourse on the Nigger Question* (1853; first printed in *Fraser's Magazine* [December, 1849]), p. 28.

[45] Quite ordinarily this attitude is directly associated with cherished memories from slavery. The pattern was set early after the Civil War. Again Henry W. Grady can be

used to illustrate the consolidation of white thinking on race relations after Reconstruction. He talked touchingly of the relations that "did exist in the days of slavery":

". . . how the negro stood in slavery days, open-hearted and sympathetic, full of gossip and comradeship, the companion of the hunt, frolic, furrow and home, contented in the kindly dependence that has been a habit of his blood, and never lifting his eyes beyond the narrow horizon that shut him in with his neighbors and friends. But this relation did exist in the days of slavery. It was the rule of that *regime*. It has survived war, and strife, and political campaigns in which the drum-beat inspired and Federal bayonets fortified. It will never die until the last slaveholder and slave have been gathered to rest. It is the glory of our past in the South. It is the answer to abuse and slander. It is the hope of our future." (*Op. cit.*, pp. 152-153; compare Page, *op. cit.*, pp. 80, 164 *passim*.)

[46] "For those still living in the county there is, it would appear, one unfailing rule of life. If they would get along with least difficulty, they should get for themselves a protecting white family. 'We have mighty good white folks friends, and ef you have white folks for your friends, dey can't do you no harm.' " (Charles S. Johnson, *Shadow of the Plantation* [1934], p. 27.)

[47] Woofter remarks:

"The liberality with which these colored beggars are treated is often more of a liability than an asset to racial adjustment, because such emotional but unscientific giving often leaves the givers with a paternalistic feeling toward the whole race and a belief that by giving small alms they have discharged their full civic duty toward their colored neighbors." (*Op. cit.*, p. 199.)

[48] Dollard, *op. cit.*, pp. 389-432.

[49] It was part of Washington's tactics to exaggerate this point. An interesting comparison can be made between his first book, published in 1899, and his later writings. In the former, *The Future of the American Negro*, he painted the cruelties of slavery in glaring terms; in the latter he rather elaborated on the lighter sides of the institution. This was part of his attempt to gain the assistance or at least the tolerance of the Southern whites, and he had found out that this appealed to the Northern philanthropist also. In his last book, *The Story of the Negro* (1909), he wrote, for instance, in explaining why "a mob in the South . . . does not seek to visit its punishment upon the innocent as well as upon the guilty":

"In the South every Negro, no matter how worthless he may be as an individual, knows one white man in the town whose friendship and protection he can always count upon; perhaps he has gained the friendship of this white man by reason of the fact that some member of the white man's family owned him or some of his relatives, or it may be that he has lived upon this white man's plantation, or that some member of his family works for him, or that he has performed some act of kindness for this white man which has brought them into sympathetic relations with each other. It is generally true, as I have said before, that in the South every white man, no matter how bitter he may seem to be toward the Negro as a race, knows some one Negro in whom he has complete confidence, whom he will trust with all that he has. It is the individual touch which holds the two races together in the South, and it is this individual touch which the races which is lacking, in a large degree, in the North." (Vol. 1, p. 189.)

This was a gross overstatement even when Washington wrote, and is still less accurate today. (See Chapter 27, Section 2.)

[50] Kelly Miller, *Race Adjustment—Essays on the Negro in America* (1908), p. 92.

[51] "Vardaman, declaiming violently against Negro colleges, has actually, in specific instances, given them help and encouragement. I was told how he had cut off an $8,000 appropriation from Alcorn College because he did not believe in Negro education: but he turned around and gave Alcorn College $14,000 for a new lighting system, because *he had come in personal contact with the Negro president of Alcorn College, and liked him.*" (Ray Stannard Baker, *Following the Color Line* [1908], p. 250.)

[52] *Autobiography of an Ex-Coloured Man* (1927; first edition, 1912), p. 79.

[53] Robert R. Moton, *What the Negro Thinks* (1929), p. 27.

[54] "The very existence of a lazy, shiftless, incompetent, irresponsible mass of laborers that require the closest supervision all the time necessarily lowers the economic energy and standards of the white people. Many a white man excuses his easy, sauntering way of transacting business by speaking of the ridiculous rush and hurry-scurry of the North. But much of our Southern lassitude is caught from the ways of the negro rather than the wiles of the hookworm. . . . In a thousand ways negro economic inefficiency retards the development of the South. And this constant doing of less than our best, this easy-going lack of regard for time, this willingness to put up with inefficient service and to overlook small pilfering because one 'expects that from a negro'—what is all this but an insidious form of psychological economic unfreedom?" (Bailey, *op. cit.*, p. 342.)

[55] George W. Cable, *The Negro Question* (1903; first edition, 1890), p. 23.

[56] *The Basis of Ascendancy* (1909), p. 233.

[57] *Problems of the Present South* (1909; first edition, 1904), pp. 274-275. Murphy continued:

"It has fixed its barriers—in no enmity of temper but in the interest of itself and its civilization, and not without regard to the ultimate welfare of the negro. It cannot base its social distinctions on an assertion of universal 'inferiority'—for in that case every gifted or truly educated negro might shake the structure of social usage. It bases its distinctions partly upon the far-reaching consideration that the racial stock of the two families of men is so unlike that nothing is to be gained and much is to be lost from the interblending of such divergent types; partly upon the broad consideration of practical expediency, in that the attempt to unite them actually brings unhappiness; partly upon the inevitable persistence of the odium of slavery; partly upon a complex indefinable, but assertive social instinct." (*Ibid.*, pp. 275-276.)

[58] Willis D. Weatherford, *Negro Life in the South* (1915), p. 173.

[59] Page, *op. cit.*, p. 307.

[60] *Negro Americans, What Now?* p. 84.

[61] John Dollard reports from his study of a community in the Deep South that it is rather the white middle class that shows the most bitter resentment against the Negroes (*op. cit.*, p. 77). But Dollard reports that there were very few lower class whites in this community, and he did not study them intensively (*ibid.*, p. 99). Davis, Gardner, and Gardner also report from their community study that "it is the lower-middle-class whites who take it upon themselves to control the urban Negroes and to keep them in hand." (Allison Davis, B. B. Gardner, and M. R. Gardner, *Deep South* [1941], pp. 56-57.)

[62] "In many instances it was noticed that lower-class whites living in Negro neighborhoods treated their Negro neighbors in much the same way as they did their white neighbors. There were the usual gossiping, exchange of services, and even visiting." (Davis, Gardner, and Gardner, *op. cit.*, p. 50.)

[63] Charles S. Johnson, *Growing Up in the Black Belt*, p. 284.

[64] *Ibid.*, pp. 283-284.

[65] Frank U. Quillin, *The Color Line in Ohio* (1913), pp. 97-104.

[66] *Dusk of Dawn*, pp. 8 ff. Du Bois tells about when he entered high school ". . . there came some rather puzzling distinctions which I can see now were social and racial; but the racial angle was more clearly defined against the Irish than against me. It was a matter of income and ancestry more than color." (*Ibid.*, p. 14.) Another description of the status of Negroes in a small New England city may be found in Robert A. Warner's *New Haven Negroes* (1940).

[67] According to some observers, there was a noticeable decrease of friendliness toward Negroes in the North even before the Great Migration. Ray Stannard Baker, for example, expresses this opinion in *Following the Color Line* (pp. 188 ff.). It may have been due to the passing of the Abolitionist fervor or to the beginning of the Negro migration from the South (partly for the purpose of breaking strikes) or to the "new immigrants" from Southern and Eastern Europe. Counterbalancing factors were the improved educational and economic status of Northern Negroes and the practical absence of forced residential segregation. If there was such a trend, it was not important, and the increase of anti-Negro sentiment in the North may—for all practical purposes—be said to have begun with the Great Migration.

Chapter 29. *Patterns of Social Segregation and Discrimination*

[1] The actual patterns of segregation and discrimination—even if not their motivation —are facts subject to simple observation and, consequently, to quantitative measurement and analysis. When the attitudes and popular theories of white persons with respect to Negro persons are manifested in such concrete acts as passing laws, signing restrictive covenants, and demanding certain signs of deference, these actions can be counted and classified, and differences noted in them relative to type, region, time periods, social class, sex, age and so on. Residential segregation is visible in the layout of the community, and some of its concomitants—such as a differential in the proportion of Negroes seen on various streets or in various stores—can be made graphic by simple enumeration. Studies have been made—using census data—of the proportions of Negroes residing in the different sections of cities. (See, for example, T. J. Woofter, Jr., and Associates, *Negro Problems in Cities* [1928]; and United States Federal Housing Administration, Homer Hoyt, *The Structure and Growth of Residential Neighborhoods in American Cities* [1939].) There has not been, however, a systematic effort to relate the facts of residential distribution to differentials in patterns of ways of limiting contacts with Negroes and treating them as inferiors. The provision of such things as separate public toilets, drinking fountains, and railroad station entrances for Negroes is visible in signs and posters or in the structure of buildings. Prohibitions against intermarriage and against the use of the same schools or the same railway cars are easily detectible in laws and court decisions, as well as in collected statistics and by direct observation. The extent of separation of Negroes and whites in business and in professional and friendly associations can be discerned by scanning membership lists or by brief interviews with secretaries. For the measurement of segregation and discrimination in interpersonal relations, the investigator could obtain short-period diaries of Negroes, and perhaps whites, living in

different areas and of different statuses and with different personal characteristics. This source would provide exact information on such things as the use of the term "nigger" and the refusal to let Negroes enter by the front door and sit in the presence of whites. It is especially important to get precise information about interpersonal relations between Negroes and whites since these probably form the most sensitive index of the condition of and trends in the Negro problem as a whole. Only quantitative data could really indicate how segregation and discrimination curtail the number and scope of personal contacts over the color line, and how they change the character of those contacts which remain. Only quantitative data—along with other information—could permit an empirical analysis of the causation of those patterns.

Since no systematic quantitative study has been made, we shall be forced to give the same sort of impressionistic survey which we have just criticized. We have the advantage, however, of Charles S. Johnson's summary of general patterns of segregation and discrimination in thirteen communities (*Patterns of Negro Segregation* [1943]; this study was carried out as part of our inquiry), as well as a diverse variety of local studies and of published and unpublished statements. For the etiquette of race relations, there is the study by Bertram Wilbur Doyle, *The Etiquette of Race Relations in the South* (1937).

[2] Mississippi has ". . . a criminal statute punishing anyone for publishing, printing, or circulating any literature in favor of or urging interracial marriage or social equality." (Charles S. Mangum, Jr., *The Legal Status of the Negro* [1940], p. 237.)

[3] Louis Wirth and Herbert Goldhamer, "The Hybrid and the Problem of Miscegenation," in Otto Klineberg (editor), *Characteristics of the American Negro*, prepared for this study; to be published, manuscript page 160.

The Supreme Court has never directly passed upon the constitutionality of the laws against intermarriage. It is, however, commonly upheld on the ground that the proscription is not discrimination but applies to both the Negro and the white partner. (Compare Mangum, *op. cit.*, pp. 288 ff.)

[4] The existing statistical knowledge about recent intermarriage is limited to three areas. Wirth and Goldhamer have complied in detail statistics for Boston and for New York State outside of New York City. (*Op. cit.*, manuscript pages 37-71.) Panunzio has calculated summary figures for Los Angeles County. (Constantine Panunzio, "Intermarriage in Los Angeles, 1924-1933," *The American Journal of Sociology* [March, 1942], p. 699.) Of all marriages involving Negroes in Boston in 1934-1938, 3.7 per cent were with whites. For New York State exclusive of New York City, the corresponding figure in 1934-1936 was 1.7 per cent. For Los Angeles County in the period 1924-1933, there were only four cases, although there were 51 cases of intermarriage with Asiatics and Indians. California has had a law prohibiting Negro-white intermarriage since 1850, but there were three cases of Negro males born outside the United States and one case of a white female born outside the United States, who were allowed to marry into the other group. If the number of intermarriages be considered, not as relative to the total number of marriages involving Negroes but as relative to the total number of marriages involving whites, the percentage drops to an insignificant fraction. Thus even the relative numerical significance of intermarriage is much greater for Negroes than for whites. The data show intermarriage higher in urban than in rural areas, but this is only among marriages between Negro males and white females, and not between white males and Negro females. The former type of intermarriage is much more common, and the light female finds she can get a better man among her own

people—especially from the ranks of dark superior Negroes, while the light male can also marry "upward" by seeking a white wife, from whom he does not expect economic advantage anyway. It may also be that the white woman has more sexual attraction for the Negro male than the white man has for the Negro female, since sex contact between the former pair is more forbidden, even in prostitution. In socio-economic status, the Negro male who intermarries is high, while the white male, the white female, and the Negro female are low. The white females, by marrying into the lower caste, go upward in class, but the white male usually cannot get such an advantage because the better class Negro female finds it to her advantage to marry the darker Negro of high socio-economic status. Whites who intermarry are not predominantly foreign-born as is some-times thought. Among white males who marry Negroes, there are about as many native-born of native parentage as there are foreign-born, relative to their respective population. Among white females who marry Negroes in Boston and New York State (outside of New York City) the relative proportion of native-born of native parentage is actually higher than that of foreign-born. Among both males and females, the native-born of foreign parentage have the least amount of intermarriage, which fact perhaps reflects the general ambitiousness of this element of the population. Finally, it should be mentioned that those who intermarry tend, to an unusual extent, to be marrying for a second or third time. Over 30 per cent of Wirth's sample of Negro and white brides were pre-viously married. The proportion was almost as high for Negro grooms though much smaller for white grooms.

It is possible to get trends in intermarriage for Boston only. In that city, between 1900 and 1904, 13.6 per cent of all marriages involving Negroes were interracial. (Alfred Holt Stone, *Studies in the American Race Problem* [1908], p. 62.) Between 1914 and 1918, this percentage had dropped to 5.2, and between 1919 and 1923 to 3.1. In 1934-1938, it had risen slightly to 3.7. (Wirth and Goldhamer, *op. cit.*, Table IV, manuscript page 41.) Needless to say, Boston is not typical of the entire United States, and it experienced accretions to its Negro population since 1900.

Holmes cites a study by Hoffman which indicates that intermarriage was declining already in the last few decades of the nineteenth century in four Northern states. (S. J. Holmes, *The Negro's Struggle for Survival* [1937], p. 174.)

⁵ According to W. J. Cash (*The Mind of the South* [1941], p. 313), when the red light districts of Southern cities were suppressed, prostitution took to hotels, where Negro bellboys took on the economic and sexual functions of pimps. There are also isolated cases recorded of more permanent relations between Negro men and white women. (See, for example, Walter White, *Rope and Faggot* [1929], pp. 71 ff., and Allison Davis, Burleigh B. Gardner, and Mary R. Gardner, *Deep South* [1941], pp. 33-37.)

⁶ The toleration in the South is abetted by prohibiting Negro men from protecting their women against the white man's advances. In the city studied by Allison Davis and John Dollard (*Children of Bondage* [1940], pp. 245-246), a Negro minister who protested in his pulpit against interracial liaisons was warned by a group of white busi-nessmen.

⁷ John Dollard, *Class and Caste in a Southern Town* (1937), pp. 141-142; Hortense Powdermaker, *After Freedom* (1939), pp. 181 ff.

⁸ For an excellent description of the scope and rigorousness of this etiquette, see Doyle, *op. cit.* This book interprets the etiquette as a means of accommodating what

was previously, and might again become, a conflict relation between Negroes and whites. This interpretation, in our opinion, is quite in error since only a small proportion of Negroes feel accommodated when performing self-abasing actions demanded by the etiquette. Actually, the majority of Negroes are at bottom embittered by the performance of these actions and keep it up only to avoid violence and greater humiliation. Not only are Negroes resentful, but they are also in constant fear—despite the etiquette and perhaps because of the etiquette. It is easy to slip and to violate a complex etiquette or to have one's actions misinterpreted as a violation of the etiquette. Such a situation creates a fear in the Southern Negro which is not known to the Northern Negro. In one sense, therefore, the Northern Negro without the etiquette and with police and court protection is better "accommodated" than the Southern Negro with his etiquette. Even whites cannot be said to be "accommodated" to Negroes by the existence of the etiquette, since they are—for the most part—acutely aware of the deference accorded them and are constantly on their guard lest it be neglected—indicating that the Negroes are attempting to leave their lowly place. On neither side is there accommodation in the sense that the course of race contacts runs so smoothly—oiled by the performance of the etiquette—as to pass unnoticed. Rather, the course of race contacts is the result of an oblique and repressed but continuous struggle—for most Southern Negroes and whites— with the performance of the etiquette being one of the tributes demanded by the whites for being on top in the struggle.

[9] Edgar Gardner Murphy, *Problems of the Present South* (1909; first edition, 1904), p. 278. Italics ours.

[10] Violence did occur, however, in the upper middle class area of Kenwood in Chicago, in December, 1940, when a white family had a party where Negroes were present. Lower class persons in a neighboring block learned of the event while it was in progress and formed a mob outside the home. After windows were broken, police protection had to be sought to evacuate the members of the party. When the white owner returned to his home the next day, he was shot at. He moved to a new residence under police protection. This incident is, of course, far from typical and it was complicated by the fact that the Kenwood area was being threatened by Negro residential invasion and by the fact that the white person in question was known to be a Jewish radical.

In Princeton, New Jersey, a white woman who proposed to have a dinner to which Negroes would be invited was visited by a delegation of leading white women of the town and was told that such things were just not done.

[11] Charles S. Johnson, *Patterns of Negro Segregation*, pp. 145-146.

[12] In America the modern usage of one common set of titles (outside the caste sphere) has developed out of an earlier system of differentiated titles, where the ones now used referred to upper class status:

"Class lines in New England were also indicated by the forms of address in vogue. Some of the titles denoting good repute were: 'esquire' or 'gentleman' for wealthy landowners and merchants who had belonged to the English upper middle class; 'master' for clergymen who possessed the degree of master of arts; 'mister' for professional people and substantial landowners and merchants (about one man in fourteen was addressed as Mr.); and 'goodman' for ordinary yeoman farmers. Such military titles as captain and ensign also signified an honorable station. Indentured servants, tenants, and wage-earners were unceremoniously called by their family or given names. Church pews were assigned on the basis of social status, while the names on the student register at Harvard College were listed, not alphabetically, but according to family rank." (Curtis P. Nettels, *The Roots of American Civilization* [1938], p. 327.)

[13] John Dollard describes typical Negro behavior in relation to whites in Southerntown as "white-folks manner":

"There is a continual flow of agreement by the Negro while a white man is talking, such as 'Yes, boss,' 'Sho nuff,' 'Well, I declare,' and the like. The Negro must maintain a position of continuous affirmation of the white man's wishes and ideas, showing thereby his lack of contrary intent, independence, aggressiveness, and individuality. A 'good nigger' from the white man's point of view is one who has mastered this technique." (*Op. cit.*, p. 180.)

When whites tell jokes about Negroes a main point is to "give an image of a hightoned, pleading voice, full of uncertainty, begging for favor. Evidently this whining, cajoling tone is one of the badges of inferiority which Negroes accept and cultivate. The whites imitate it with an evident hostile relish. It establishes at once by its difference from ordinary white speech the inferior position of the Negro as a suppliant." (*Ibid.*, p. 257.)

[14] *Idem.*

[15] Gustavus Myers, *America Strikes Back* (1935). It is interesting to note that the South has similarly been accustomed to accusing the Northern Yankees of "materialism."

[16] To illustrate the extent to which the etiquette has broken down—or never existed —we may cite Charles S. Johnson's summary of the etiquette in eight counties of the rural South. (*Growing Up in the Black Belt* [1941], pp. 277-280.)

"Where taboos are rigid:

1. Negroes may never marry whites in any of the counties studied.
2. Negroes may never dance with whites in any of the counties studied.
3. Negroes may never eat with whites in any of the counties except Bolivar and Coahoma (Mississippi) and Davidson (Tennessee).
4. Negroes may never play games with whites in any counties except Bolivar, Davidson, and Madison (Alabama).
5. Negroes must always use 'Mr.' and 'Mrs.' when addressing whites in all counties.
6. Whites never use 'Mr.' and 'Mrs.' when addressing Negroes in Bolivar, Coahoma, Johnston (North Carolina), Macon (Alabama) and Shelby (Tennessee).
7. Negroes never drink with whites in Madison and Shelby counties except occasionally among the lower classes.
8. Negroes never enter white people's houses by the front door in Coahoma and Johnston.
9. Negroes must give whites the right-of-way on the sidewalks in Bolivar and Madison.
10. Negro men must take off their hats in banks, stores, and so forth, where whites need not, in Madison.
11. Negroes cannot touch a white man without his resenting it in Bolivar and Madison.
12. Negroes must always say 'Yes, sir,' and 'Yes, ma'am,' when addressing whites in all counties except Davidson and Johnston."

"Where the etiquette is relaxed:

1. Negroes drink with whites sometimes in Bolivar, Coahoma, Davidson, Greene, Johnston, and Macon.

2. Negroes and whites shake hands sometimes in all counties.

3. Negroes enter white people's houses by the front door sometimes in Bolivar, Davidson, Greene, Madison, and Shelby.

4. Whites use 'Mr.' and 'Mrs.' sometimes in Davidson, Greene, and Madison when addressing Negroes.

5. Whites and Negroes play games together sometimes in Bolivar, Davidson, and Madison.

6. Negroes must use 'Yes, sir,' and 'Yes, ma'am,' sometimes in Davidson and Johnston.

7. Negroes may touch a white man without causing resentment in Davidson, Johnston, Macon, and Shelby."

"Where the etiquette is confused:

1. Negroes attend theaters patronized by whites in all counties but Madison.

2. Negroes can try on hats in all stores in all counties but Shelby.

3. Negroes can try on gloves in all stores in Bolivar, Davidson, Johnston, and Macon, and in no stores in Greene.

4. Negroes must occupy a separate section while being waited on in all stores in Coahoma, Macon, and Madison; in some stores in Davidson, Greene, Johnston, and Shelby; and in no stores in Bolivar.

5. Negroes may sit in all public parks in Bolivar, Coahoma, Greene, and Macon; in some parks in Davidson and Shelby; and in none in Johnston and Madison.

6. Negroes use hotels with whites in none of the counties.

7. Negroes use some restaurants with whites in Coahoma, Davidson, Madison, and Shelby only, and these are separated by partition.

8. Negroes serve on juries sometimes in Coahoma, Greene, and Shelby, never in Bolivar, Johnston, and Madison.

9. Negro lawyers may try cases in all counties except Madison.

10. Negroes are segregated in all courts except in Coahoma.

11. Whites work *for* Negroes sometimes in Bolivar, Davidson, Greene, Johnston, and Madison; never in Coahoma, Macon, and Shelby.

12. Whites work *with* Negroes usually in Coahoma and Greene; sometimes in Davidson, Johnston, and Madison; seldom if ever in Shelby.

13. Whites are served by Negro doctors in Davidson, Greene, Johnston, Madison, and Shelby; not in Bolivar, Coahoma, and Macon.

14. Negroes usually vote in Coahoma, Davidson, Johnston, Macon, and Shelby; sometimes in Greene and Madison.

15. Negroes and whites worship together sometimes in Coahoma, Davidson, Greene, Macon, and Madison; never in Bolivar, Johnston, and Shelby.

16. Negroes drink with whites in drug and liquor stores in Coahoma; at beer 'joints' in Bolivar; when each party is about half drunk from whisky in Greene; and among the lower classes occasionally in all counties."

[17] C. V. Roman, *American Civilization and the Negro* (1921; first edition, 1916), p. 58.

[18] Interview by Charles S. Johnson, *Patterns of Negro Segregation*, pp. 52-53. Other cases of this sort are cited by Johnson (*ibid.*); by R. R. Moton (*What the Negro Thinks* [1929], p. 181); and by John A. Kenney ("The Inter-Racial Committee of Montclair, New Jersey," *Journal of the National Medical Association* [July-September, 1931], pp. 102-103).

[19] U.S. Federal Housing Administration, *op. cit.*, p. 63. These cities do not constitute a representative sample of American cities, as Hoyt is well aware. They do not include the seven most important cities in the country from the standpoint of total numbers of Negroes. They are especially biased for the North: although 40 of the 64 cities were in the North, they included only 3 of 28 Northern cities containing the largest numbers of Negroes. New York, Chicago, or Philadelphia alone—none of which was included in the sample—had more Negroes than all the included 40 Northern cities put together. Of the 32 cities in the study containing the smallest proportions of non-whites, all were in the North except two in the Border states; of the 16 cities containing the largest proportions of nonwhites all but one were in the South. For these reasons we shall not draw the conclusion that Hoyt does, that ". . . the degree of nonwhite concentration in any city increases directly with the number and proportion of non-white persons in the population." (*Ibid.*, p. 68.) On the basis of our own impressionistic observations of cities not in Hoyt's sample, we are inclined to believe that the correlation between concentration and proportion of Negroes is not large, and whatever correlation there is would be due to the relation between number and proportion. In other words, we should guess that the concentration of Negroes in a city is far more related to their number than to their proportion in a city. We should also guess that any generalization of this sort would have to be qualified for differences between South and North.

[20] Using an even less refined technique, one based on wards rather than blocks, Burgess reported that Negroes showed the greatest concentration of any ethnic group in a group of major cities—except for Philadelphia where the Italians were more concentrated than the Negroes. (Ernest W. Burgess, "Residential Segregation in American Cities," *The Annals of the American Academy of Political and Social Science* [November, 1928], pp. 108-109.) For Chicago alone, there is a study of residential concentration of Negroes by Mary Elaine Ogden, "The Chicago Negro Community—A Statistical Description" (mimeographed), Chicago: W.P.A. District 3 (1939). This study was done under the direction of Horace Cayton and W. Lloyd Warner.

[21] See Burgess, *op. cit.*, p. 110.

[22] For a discussion of these movements and the forces behind them, see Lyonel C. Florant in Chapter 2 of Samuel A. Stouffer and Associates, "Negro Population and Negro Population Movements, 1860-1940," unpublished manuscript prepared for this study (1940).

[23] Woofter has adopted a four-fold classification of cities based on the patterns of residential segregation found in them. This is better than our two-fold classification in many respects and deserves to be quoted here:

"The first group is typified by New York and Chicago, where the concentration of Negroes is great and yet where it affects only a small part of the whole city area. In Chicago this pattern seems to be changing as the Negroes spread more southward. . .

"The second group is typified by Richmond, and includes most of the large southern cities where Negroes are highly concentrated in several rather large parts of the city and lightly scattered in others, thus leaving a large proportion of the white people in areas from 10 to 90 per cent. Negro . . .

"The third group is typified by Charleston, and is limited to the older southern cities and towns which have a heavy percentage of Negroes in their total population, and consequently a heavy scattering of Negroes throughout the city. . .

"Group four is composed of cities with light colored infusion, where the diffusion of Negroes affects only a very small area of the city and is somewhat scattered within this area . . ." (T. J. Woofter, Jr., and Associates, *Negro Problems in Cities* [1928], p. 38.)

[24] *Ibid.*, p. 37.

[25] Woofter's maps show this concentration of Negroes outside the central business districts of cities to be typical. (*Ibid.*, pp. 40-67.) See also Burgess, *op. cit.*, p. 108.

[26] " 'Segregation' in Harlem?" *Column Review* (December, 1941), p. 5. While McKay is incorrect in saying that there is no segregation of Negroes in New York, he is correct in pointing out that Harlem is not a self-sufficing community in the sense that New York's Chinatown is. Chinatown has not only segregation, but also an alien culture and its own internal government. Negro communities are, on the other hand, more of an integral part of American life than even Greek and Italian communities. (Burgess, *op. cit.*, p. 110.)

Harlem is, in one sense, less integrated into New York than the Black Belt is into Chicago: Harlem's cultural and commercial center is near its geographical center at 135th Street and 7th Avenue and zones of decreasing concentration of Negroes and Negro activities encircle it. The Chicago community, on the other hand, is a long thin strip, with poor Negroes at one end near poor white areas and wealthy Negroes at the other end near wealthy white areas. (See E. Franklin Frazier, *The Negro Family in Chicago* [1932], and "Negro Harlem: An Ecological Study," *American Journal of Sociology* [July, 1937], pp. 72-88.)

[27] Document in possession of the Social Science Research Committee of the University of Chicago. ("History of Grand Boulevard," document number 7.)

[28] See Charles S. Johnson, *Negro Housing* (1932), pp. 35-37.

[29] This was the famous case of *Buchanan* v. *Warley*. 245, U.S. 60, 38 S.Ct. 16, Nov. 5, 1917. For a discussion of the laws and court cases, see Richard Sterner and Associates, *The Negro's Share*, prepared for this study (1943), pp. 205-209.

[30] "Iron Ring in Housing," *The Crisis* (July, 1940), p. 205. This and other descriptions of the extent and legal status of restrictive covenants may be found in Sterner and Associates, *op. cit.*, pp. 207-208.

[31] Some have mistakenly thought that the Supreme Court's decision in the recent (1940) case of *Hansberry* v. *Lee* made restrictive covenants illegal. Actually nothing was decided except that Negroes could move into the West Woodlawn area of Chicago. The case was so decided because 95 per cent of the white property owners of that area had not signed the restrictive covenant, which—by its own terms—called for 95 per cent of the signatures.

[32] From document in possession of the Social Science Research Committee of the University of Chicago.

[33] Woofter brings out the nature of the surroundings to a Negro neighborhood in his maps in *Negro Problems of Cities*. Burgess adds corroborating facts (*op. cit.*, p. 108).

[34] See Chapter 28, Section 4. Mangum describes these laws thus:

"These states are California, Colorado, Connecticut, Illinois, Indiana, Iowa, Kansas, Massachusetts, Michigan, Minnesota, Nebraska, New Jersey, New York, Ohio, Pennsylvania, Rhode Island, Washington, and Wisconsin. The statutes are more or less specific concerning places which are meant to be regulated. Some of them contain long lists of places of public resort, while others mention only a few or none at all. The statutes differ in the type or types of remedy to be employed in seeking redress. Thus seven states provide for a criminal prosecution only, one makes a provision for a civil action alone, seven allow both a criminal action and either a suit for a penalty or a civil action for damages, while the remaining three permit both types of redress but state that success in an action of either kind shall bar all other proceedings." (*Op. cit.*, pp. 34-35.)

[35] For example, in May, 1942, New York State added prohibitions against discrimination by public golf courses and by sports promoters in state-wide contests.

[36] The partial futility of the civil rights law in New Jersey is indicated by the following comment made by a city official in Atlantic City:

" 'I think the southerners handle them better because they don't assert their rights. They are not permitted in the bars, etc. This equalization law is not a benefit for the man who runs the place. In New Jersey they have a state law that they are to be admitted to restaurants and theaters, but the courts wouldn't recognize it here. It is seldom a sensible colored man will thrust himself in where he is not wanted. In New York they have hired lawyers and prosecute such cases to the bitter end; they do not succeed in getting very far, not for the present time. I was in a restaurant in Philadelphia one time and a colored couple came in. The manager told them all the tables were reserved. They walked out. That's what overcomes the law. I kept a hotel for thirty years. They knew I didn't care for their trade, and they never came. I told them, "You know it is not fair to make me lose my trade." You can't throw them out, but the majority are satisfied to keep to themselves. They understand in the moving pictures that they are to sit on the left side. Our colored people are a nice class.' " (Quoted in Johnson, *Patterns of Negro Segregation*, pp. 200-201.)

[37] For example, Princeton University, in New Jersey—a state with a civil rights law —permits no Negro to enroll as a student.

The American Red Cross refuses to permit Negro women to assist in its civilian first-aid training program unless they can form their own segregated units on their own initiative. It has also refused to accept Negro blood donors. After protests it now accepts Negro blood but segregates it to be used exclusively for Negro soldiers. This is true at a time when the United States is at war, and the Red Cross has a semi-official status.

The United Service Organizations—a body created to give civilian aid in the present war effort—refuses to let Negroes participate in many of its activities in several Northern states. For that matter, so does the Office of Civilian Defense—a government agency which has refused to permit Negroes to serve as volunteer airplane spotters in at least one Northern state.

[38] Johnson, *Patterns of Negro Segregation*, p. 7.

[39] *Idem.*

[40] *Idem.*

[41] While the teachers and principals of Negro schools in the South are uniformly Negro, the controlling and supervising officials are white. In 1940, Wilkerson found Negroes on the school boards only in Washington, D. C., West Virginia, Oklahoma and Missouri among all Southern states. He was able to find only 18 Negroes holding state administrative or supervisory positions. (Doxey A. Wilkerson, "The Negro in American

Education," unpublished manuscript prepared for this study [1940], Vol. 1, pp. 163-174.)

[42] In another important case (*Donald Murray v. the University of Maryland*, 1936), the Maryland Circuit Court of Appeals decided that Negroes must be admitted to the law school of the University of Maryland, and several Negroes have taken advantage of the ruling.

[43] Mangum, *op. cit.*, p. 79.

[44] *Ibid.*, pp. 80-82.

[45] Wilkerson, *op. cit.*, Vol. 1, pp. 209-212. Concerning the illegal situation in the southern half of New Jersey, see Marion M. T. Wright, *The Education of Negroes in New Jersey* (1941), pp. 183-193.

[46] In May, 1942, a Negro minister of New York City was named to the board of Union Theological Seminary. This was apparently the first time since Reconstruction that a Negro attained such a position in a predominantly white educational institution.

[47] Only two Southern states make legal provision for the extension of public library service to Negroes.

"In West Virginia, a state law requires all libraries receiving public funds to give service to Negroes, and in Texas the law requires commissioners' courts to make proper provision for library service to Negroes through branches of the county free library." (Tommie Dora Barker, *Libraries of the South* [1936], pp. 51-52.) As a result, over one-third of the public libraries serving Negroes in 13 Southern states in 1935 were in West Virginia and Texas.

[48] Referring to what happened to the proposed training school for delinquent Negro girls in Georgia, Dabney reports:

"Talmadge even vetoed an appropriation voted almost unanimously by the Georgia Legislature in 1941 for the operation of a training school for delinquent Negro girls. The building had been paid for with the nickels and dimes of Georgia's Negro women, and had been presented by them to the state four years before. It had never been opened, for lack of funds—and doubtless won't be, as long as Georgia sends Talmadges to the gubernatorial mansion, although Georgia has a training school for delinquent Negro boys. So has every other Southern state except Mississippi, which has practically as many Negroes as whites, but no training school for either delinquent colored boys or delinquent colored girls." (Virginius Dabney, *Below the Potomac* [1942], p. 214.)

[49] *Op. cit.*, p. 234.

[50] Many authors have observed that the coming of the cheap automobile has meant for Southern Negroes, who can afford one, a partial emancipation from Jim Crowism.

"Race is most completely ignored on the public highway; there a Negro in a moving automobile has not only a legal right to half the road, but in practice is accorded it. The mechanics of the situation ensures that only the person careless of his own life will dare claim more than his share. Some [white] people, observing this equality, fear it is a bad precedent. Effective equality seems to come at about twenty-five miles an hour or above. As soon as the car is stopped by the side of the road, to pick wild flowers or fix a puncture, the color of the occupants places them in their traditional racial roles." (Arthur Raper, "Race and Class Pressures," unpublished manuscript prepared for this study [1940], p. 9.)

[51] Mangum, *op. cit.*, pp. 181-182.

[52] *Ibid.*, pp. 182 and 203-204.

[53] Johnson, *Patterns of Negro Segregation*, p. 47.

[54] In Atlanta formerly, Negroes not only had to sit in separate sections of the car, but also had to enter by a different door. With the adoption of the one-man car this practice was abandoned. According to Johnson (*ibid.*, p. 50), the one-man car has reduced friction since there is no confusion as to where to enter and conductors do not fuss with the seating.

[55] Mangum, *op. cit.*, pp. 32-65.

[56] Only in New York and New Jersey do the Civil Rights Acts prohibit racial segregation in cemeteries. (*Ibid.*, p. 156.)

[57] *Ibid.*, p. 175.

[58] See Mangum, *op. cit.*, pp. 26-68, *passim*.

[59] See, for example, Davis, Gardner, and Gardner, *op. cit.*, p. 463.

[60] There are exceptions: In the first half of 1942, there was a fight to get Negroes and Orientals into the American educators' national honor fraternity, Phi Delta Kappa. After numerous debates, threats of secession, and temporary compromises the fight was won. Previously, however, even the local chapters could not admit Negroes.

Chapter 30. *Effects of Social Inequality*

[1] Gilbert T. Stephenson, *Race Distinctions in American Law* (1910), pp. 20 ff.; Charles S. Mangum, Jr., *The Legal Status of the Negro* (1940), pp. 18 ff.

[2] Stephenson, *op. cit.*, p. 28.

[3] Emmett J. Scott and Lyman Beecher Stowe, *Booker T. Washington* (1916), pp. 108 ff.; see particularly Washington's correspondence with Edgar Gardner Murphy, *idem*.

[4] *The New Republic* (December 4, 1915), pp. 113-114.

[5] "He [the Negro] feels that it is a libel against his race to say that segregation and discrimination are necessary to protect the white man's civilization, the sanctity of his home, or the integrity of his race. He feels that it is an unwarranted insult both to his person and to his character to establish that there is any place to which the public is admitted that will be defiled by the mere presence of a black man in the enjoyment of equal privileges with others. He maintains that prejudices of individuals that make for discrimination against his race should be properly regarded as purely private and personal without any title whatsoever to recognition and support by public authority." (Robert R. Moton, *What the Negro Thinks* [1929], pp. 238-239.)

[6] William Archer, *Through Afro-America* (1910), p. 212.

[7] *Democracy and Race Friction* (1914), pp. 184-185.

"Any one acquainted with southern conditions in the 'black belt' today will realise that this is no mere possibility, but is to a very large extent a reality. There exist in the minds of both blacks and whites two conceptions of conduct, recognised as valid in two different spheres and with little in common. This explains the paradoxical fact that a moral lapse of a negro often does not make him lose social standing with the negroes nor with the whites, while the condemnation of a white by his fellows for committing the same offence will often be shared by the negroes also. Each is judged by the social standards of his group and the other group accepts those judgments as valid for the individual and the case concerned; there is little free immediate functioning of social sanctions independent of race distinctions." (*Ibid.*, pp. 14-15.)

[8] *Ibid.*, p. 110.

[9] See the series on present Negro youth problems prepared for the American Youth Commission: Ira DeA. Reid, *In a Minor Key* (1940); Allison Davis and John Dollard, *Children of Bondage* (1940); W. Lloyd Warner, Buford H. Junker, and Walter A. Adams, *Color and Human Nature* (1941); E. Franklin Frazier, *Negro Youth at the Crossways* (1940); Charles S. Johnson, *Growing Up in the Black Belt* (1941); Ira D. Walker, Vincent J. Davis, Donald W. Wyatt, and J. Howell Atwood, *Thus Be Their Destiny* (1941); and Robert L. Sutherland, *Color, Class, and Personality* (1942). These studies have confirmed and given definiteness to the observation of Booker T. Washington:

"The Negro boy has obstacles, discouragements, and temptations to battle with that are little known to those not situated as he is. When a white boy undertakes a task, it is taken for granted that he will succeed. On the other hand, people are usually surprised if the Negro boy does not fail. In a word, the Negro youth starts out with the presumption against him." (*Up from Slavery* [1929; first edition, 1900], p. 36.)

[10] James Weldon Johnson, *The Autobiography of an Ex-Coloured Man* (1927; first edition, 1912), pp. 79-80.

"Beyond that there is a type of Negro already referred to, whom the majority of whites never see and consequently do not know. They own their own homes, so the white landlord does not see them; they carry insurance with a Negro insurance company, so no white collector comes to the door; their groceryman is a coloured man; they travel by auto rather than by street car or train; as a rule they live in the segregated residence districts; their physician, lawyer, dentist, and often their banker is a Negro. As a result of all this, there is a constantly diminishing contact between the corresponding classes of the two races, which for the whites as a whole is fast approaching the zero point." (Moton, *op. cit.*, pp. 17-18.)

[11] Ray Stannard Baker observed long ago:

" Here is a strange thing. I don't know how many Southern men have prefaced their talks with me with words something like this:

" 'You can't expect to know the Negro after a short visit. You must live down here like we do. Now, I know the Negroes like a book. I was brought up with them. I know what they'll do and what they won't do. I have had Negroes in my house all my life.'

"But curiously enough I found that these men rarely knew anything about the better class of Negroes—those who were in business, or in independent occupations, those who owned their own homes. They did come into contact with the servant Negro, the field hand, the common laborer, who make up, of course, the great mass of the race. On the other hand, the best class of Negroes did not know the higher class of white people, and based their suspicion and hatred upon the acts of the poorer sort of whites with whom they naturally came into contact. The best elements of the two races are as far apart as though they lived in different continents; and that is one of the chief causes of the growing danger of the Southern situation." (*Following the Color Line* [1908], p. 44.)

[12] Edgar G. Murphy may again be used to express the views of the enlightened and responsible Southerner.

"Of the destructive factors in negro life the white community hears to the uttermost, hears through the press and police courts; of the constructive factors of negro progress—the negro school, the saner negro church, the negro home—the white community is in ignorance. Until it does know this aspect of our negro problem it may know more or less accurately many things about the negro; but it cannot know the negro. . . . Seeing the negro loafer on the street, the negro man or woman in domestic service, the negro laborer in the fields, is not seeing the negro. . . . And at the point where this lower contact ceases, at the point where the negro's real efficiency begins, and he passes out of domestic service or unskilled employment into a larger world, the white community loses its personal and definite information; the negro passes into the unknown. As the negro attains progress, he, by the very fact of progress, removes the tangible evidence of progress from the immediate observation of the white community. Thus the composite idea, the social conception of the negro which is beginning to obtain among us, is determined more largely by the evidences of negro retrogression or negro stagnation than by the evidence, the real and increasing evidence, of negro advancement." (*Problems of the Present South* [1909; first edition, 1904], pp. 167-168.)

[13] Du Bois may be quoted to illustrate the Negro point of view:

"And here is a land where, in the higher walks of life, in all the higher striving for the good and noble and true, the color-line comes to separate natural friends and co-workers; while at the bottom of the social group in the saloon, the gambling-hall, and the brothel, that same line wavers and disappears." (W. E. B. Du Bois, *The Souls of Black Folk* [1903], p. 186.)

[14] W. E. B. Du Bois gives the Negro angle to the situation when he writes of the "best elements" of the two groups:

". . . it is usually true that the very representatives of the two races, who for mutual benefit and the welfare of the land ought to be in complete understanding and sympathy, are so far strangers that one side thinks all whites are narrow and prejudiced, and the other thinks educated Negroes dangerous and insolent. Moreover, in a land where the tyranny of public opinion and the intolerance of criticism is for obvious historical reasons so strong as in the South, such a situation is extremely difficult to correct. The white man, as well as the Negro, is bound and barred by the color-line, and many a scheme of friendliness and philanthropy, of broad-minded sympathy and generous fellowship between the two has dropped still-born because some busybody has forced the color-question to the front and brought the tremendous force of unwritten law against the innovators." (*The Souls of Black Folk*, p. 184.)

[15] Moton, *op. cit.*, pp. 4-5.

[16] The series of investigations on Negro youth recently prepared for the American Youth Commission (see footnote 9 in this chapter) present a large amount of interview material in which this view is confirmed.

Charles S. Johnson, whose study concerned the rural Deep South and who has most explicitly analyzed his findings as to the attitudes of Negro youth toward the dominant caste controls, concludes:

"Among the youth of all areas, social classes, and individual temperaments, two characteristics were observed which were fairly common: (a) they were race conscious to the extent of recognizing themselves as different and apart from the rest of the community; and (b) they entertained a conviction that Negroes, as a race, were treated unfairly and were suppressed economically." (*Growing Up in the Black Belt* [1941], p. 285.)

The Southern caste order makes the expression of antagonism inadvisable and even dangerous. "Outward submissiveness and respect may thus be, as often as not, a mask behind which these youth conceal their true attitudes." (*Ibid.*, p. 296.) In this situation voluntary withdrawal becomes the natural solution. Johnson observes that: "In most cases the youth expressed themselves as preferring not to associate with whites, and viewed their segregation with indifference." (*Ibid.*, p. 288.)

Davis and Dollard, who studied two small cities in the Deep South, give much the same picture, except that the urban youth seem to invest more explicit dislike and even hatred in their attitude of withdrawal:

"This finding runs counter to the widespread social dogma which states that the southern Negro does not experience his caste restrictions as punishments. The dogma, popular as it may be, is not borne out by the thousands of pages of interviews which have been recorded for Negroes of all social classes in Old City and its rural background, in Natchez, and in New Orleans. Within their conversation groups these Negroes in the Deep South were often found detailing the instances in which they had been threatened or humiliated by white people and expressing great hostility and resentment toward the local white group. In fact, the antagonism voiced by the local white people toward Negroes, although it was certainly violent, and fully supported by group approval, was scarcely more violent than that which Negroes, including the youngest adolescents, expressed to the white group as a whole.

". . . indeed it becomes clear that only a vested societal interest in caste can account for the established dogma that most Negroes are completely 'accommodated' to their caste status and that they are simple-natured, childlike beings with childish needs. It is necessary for the society to inculcate strong defensive teachings of this kind to prevent general human recognition of the basic deprivations and frustrations which life in a lower caste involves. But it is certain that the sting of caste is deep and sharp for most Negroes." (*Op. cit.*, pp. 244-245.)

[17] Arthur F. Raper, *Preface to Peasantry* (1936), p. 276.

[18] *Negro Youth at the Crossways* (1940), pp. 70-71.

[19] Some communities—notably in Texas, the Far West and New England—exclude Negroes entirely.

[20] "Across the Tracks is a life but little known to the Whites, who rarely go there. Everything that happens on the white side, however, is known to the Negroes, who have constant access to white homes and business places. This disparity of information is both a natural and a significant factor in the relations of the two groups." (Hortense Powdermaker, *After Freedom* [1939], pp. 11-12.)

[21] "Almost every white woman feels that she knows all about her cook's personality and life, but she seldom does. The servant is quite a different person Across the Tracks and is not as a rule communicative about the life she leads there. She, on the other hand, has ample opportunity to know intimate details concerning her mistress's life and family. Under her mild 'Yes, Ma'am,' and 'No, Ma'am,' there is often a comprehension which is unsuspected and far from mutual." (*Ibid.*, p. 119.)

[22] This is somewhat less true in the coal and steel industry in the South and, generally, in the North. See Appendix 6.

[23] There are some quantitative studies which bear out this point. The Chicago Commission on Race Relations made a study of all articles dealing with Negroes in three leading Chicago newspapers during 1916-1917. Of the 1,338 articles, 606 dealt with crime and vice, riots and clashes. In 1918, the same three newspapers published

275 articles "favorable" to Negroes and 165 "unfavorable." (The Chicago Commission on Race Relations, *The Negro in Chicago* [1922], pp. 524, 532.)

In a study of 28 Texas newspapers, Ira B. Bryant, Jr., classified news about Negroes as social, anti-social and neutral. The "anti-social" news was practically all about crime. In the 16 urban newspapers, 84.4 per cent of all Negro items were anti-social, 12.8 per cent were social and 6.6 per cent were neutral. In the 12 rural newspapers, 59.8 per cent of all Negro items were anti-social, 24.5 per cent were social, and 15.7 per cent were neutral. ("News Items about Negroes in White Urban and Rural Newspapers," *Journal of Negro Education* [April, 1935], pp. 169-178.)

On the other hand, Robert A. Warner reports that the newspapers of New Haven, Connecticut, are uniformly friendly to Negroes and do not report any undue selection of crime news to the exclusion of other types of news. (*New Haven Negroes* [1940], p. 275.)

In a study of 60 issues of 17 white newspapers from various sections of the United States, from July 15, 1928, to March 21, 1929, Gist found that 46.9 per cent of all news space devoted to Negroes was "anti-social." Gist felt that this was unusually low since at that time newspapers were giving an unusual amount of space to Negro voting in the election of 1928. (Noel P. Gist, "The Negro in the Daily Press," *Social Forces* [March, 1932], pp. 405-411.)

In a study of 4 Philadelphia newspapers for the years 1908, 1913, 1918, 1923, 1928, and 1932, Simpson found that the percentages of Negro crime news in all Negro news space ranged from 51.1 per cent to 73.6 per cent. He further found that the total amount of news space devoted to Negroes was progressively declining over this 25-year period: the number of Negro news inches per 10,000 Philadelphia Negroes fell from 159 in 1908 to 32 in 1932. (George E. Simpson, *The Negro in the Philadelphia Press* [1936], pp. 115-116.)

[24] *Time* (September 8, 1941), p. 13.

[25] James Bryce, *The Relations of the Advanced and the Backward Races of Mankind* (1902), pp. 31-32.

[26] W. E. B. Du Bois, *Black Reconstruction* (1935), p. 52.

[27] Concerning the Southerner who says he knows the Negro, Moton observes:

"When one of these says he 'knows the Negro' it means that he has had them under his control for very practical purposes and has come to a pretty wide and thorough knowledge of the habits, mannerisms, foibles, weaknesses, defects, deficiencies, virtues, and excellencies of this particular type of the race. It means, too, that he is thoroughly familiar with the ethical, social, and moral code that obtains among white men of his class in dealing with Negroes of this class and under the conditions obtaining in these fields. In such a declaration he means to say that he knows how to get the required amount of work from any given group of such Negroes, that he knows the conditions under which they will work best, the amount of pressure they will stand, what abuse they will submit to, what they will resent, under what conditions they will remain cheerful, when they will become sullen, what and when to pay them, what food to provide, what housing to furnish, what holidays to recognize, and what indulgences to grant. Such a man knows, too, to what extent public opinion in his own race will support him in his relations with his men. He is familiar with all the local prejudices and practices involved in race adjustments; he is adept according to these in 'keeping the Negro in his place'; and above all else he can be counted on to be firm and resolute in all his dealings with black folk of every type and class. . . .

"Thus a great part of 'knowing the Negro' is a thorough understanding of the operations of this type of interracial sentiment and of how to employ it in managing the Negro and 'keeping him in his place.' Where firmness is required rather than sympathy, where ruthlessness is the order of the day rather than consideration, a white man who 'knows the Negro' is the most effective agent procurable. What he *doesn't* know about the Negro is the factor that produces the race problem." (*Op. cit.*, pp. 6-7 and 8.)

"Perhaps no single phrase has been more frequently used in discussing the race problem in America than the familiar declaration, 'I know the Negro . . .'

"Negroes have always met this remark with a certain faint, knowing smile. Their common experience has taught them that as a matter of fact there are vast reaches of Negro life and thought of which white people know nothing whatever, even after long contact with them, sometimes on the most intimate terms." (*Ibid.*, p. 1.)

[28] Baker, *op. cit.*, pp. 38-39. As early as 1899, ex-Governor Northen of Georgia, in a speech at Boston, noted that the two races were drifting apart in the South. ("The Negro at the South," p. 7, quoted by Walter F. Willcox, "Negro Criminality," *Journal of Social Science* [*December*, 1899], pp. 87-88.)

[29] For an example of how laughter is a part of the interracial etiquette, see Jonathan Daniels, *A Southerner Discovers the South* (1938), pp. 255-259.

[30] P. 67.

[31] Baker, *op. cit.*, p. 39.

[32] Kelly Miller, *Race Adjustment, Essays on the Negro in America* (1908), p. 92.

[33] I have the impression that Southern radio stations make less use of national networks than do Northern radio stations. If this were found to be a fact, an analysis of the reasons for it would be suggestive.

[34] Scott and Stowe, *op. cit.*, pp. 115 ff., and Alfred Holt Stone, *Studies in the American Race Problem* (1908), pp. 242 ff.

[35] "The Bases of Race Prejudice," *The Annals of the American Academy of Political and Social Science* (November, 1928), p. 13.

[36] Quoted from John Temple Graves, "The Southern Negro and the War Crisis," *The Virginia Quarterly Review* (Autumn, 1942), pp. 504-505. This article, too, is an example of the recent tendency toward increased unfriendliness toward the Negro on the part of Southern liberals.

Chapter 31. *Caste and Class*

[1] ". . . the Negro group has gradually ceased to exhibit the characteristics of a caste and has assumed rather the character of a racial or national minority." (Robert E. Park, "Introduction" to Bertram Wilbur Doyle, *The Etiquette of Race Relations in the South* [1937], p. xxii.) See Donald R. Young, *American Minority Peoples* (1932) and, by the same author, *Research Memorandum on Minority Peoples in the Depression* (1937).

[2] Many Negro social scientists, and some white ones, are reluctant to use the term "caste" because of its connotations of invariability and accommodation. They point out, with good reason, that the use of the term "caste" has sometimes blinded social

scientists to many important facts about the relations between Negroes and whites and has sometimes been used as an excuse for conditions which are undesirable from the Negroes' point of view. Charles S. Johnson, for example, ably presents the case against the concept of "caste" (*Growing Up in the Black Belt* [1941], pp. 325-327). He points out that there is much tension and friction between Negroes and whites, and some social scientists seem to presume that a caste system is so "accommodated" that there is little or no tension or friction. The Negro in the South occupies a subordinate position, but "he is struggling against this status rather than accepting it." There is constant change, contrary to the beliefs of many who use the term "caste": ". . . the attitudes of the white group are constantly changing, and at many points in the relationship between the two races there is a blurring of caste distinctions." Thus, he says, the term "caste" is inapplicable since: "A caste system is not only a separated system, it is a stable system in which changes are socially impossible; the fact that change cannot occur is accepted by all, or practically all, participants."

We are in agreement with Charles Johnson's description of the facts, and we respect his right to choose any definition of caste he desires, but we do not agree with his definition; we do not believe that such a caste system as he has defined ever existed, and we point out that he is forced to use some other word to mean what we mean by caste. Johnson uses the older terms "race" and "race system" in exactly the same way as we use "caste" and "caste system." While the former terms now enjoy a peculiar popularity in Negro circles (for example, certain militant Negroes use the term "race man" to refer to any Negro), partly in reaction to white prejudice, we believe the term "caste"—with its socially static connotation—is less dangerous and inaccurate than the term "race"—with its biologically static connotation.

[3] To this censoring attitude corresponds, as a reaction, an exaggerated interest in European nobility. A Scandinavian, conditioned for a long time to look upon nobility with complete unconcernedness—sensing only a slight, pleasant and favorable association to the old history—will invariably be much astonished the first time he sees his democratic American friend make so much fuss over a prince or a count who happens to be around. The author has observed that European governments, public agencies, and business concerns have not been slow to adapt themselves to this American peculiarity by attempting, whenever practical, to include nobility as political or business representatives to this country. All wavering from the principle of merit and efficiency must, however, in the long run, be expensive to those countries, particularly as it tends to preserve the American misconception of the role played by nobility in Europe.

The point has, however, a much closer bearing to the problem under study in this book. To the author it has become apparent that the Northern romanticism for the "Old South" has the same basic psychology. It is, likewise, only the other side of Yankee equalitarianism. The North has so few vestiges of feudalism and aristocracy of its own that, even though it dislikes them fundamentally and is happy not to have them, Yankees are thrilled by them. Northerners apparently cherish the idea of having had an aristocracy and of still having a real class society—in the South. So it manufactures the myth of the "Old South" or has it manufactured by Southern writers working for the Northern market. Henry W. Grady, Southern spokesman to the North, describes the *ante-bellum* South in dithyrambs:

"That was a peculiar society. Almost feudal in its splendor, it was almost patriarchal in its simplicity. Leisure and wealth gave it exquisite culture. Its wives and mothers, exempt from drudgery, and almost from care, gave to their sons, through patient and constant training, something of their own grace and gentleness, and to their homes beauty and light. Its people, homogeneous by necessity, held straight and simple faith, and were religious to a marked degree along the old lines of Christian belief. This same homogeneity bred a hospitality that was as kinsmen to kinsmen, and that wasted at the threshold of every home what the more frugal people of the North conserved and invested in public charities. The code duello furnished the highest appeal in dispute. An affront to a lad was answered at the pistol's mouth. The sense of quick responsibility tempered the tongues of even the most violent, and the newspapers of South Carolina for eight years, it is said, did not contain one abusive word. The ownership of slaves, even more than of realty held families steadfast on their estates, and everywhere prevailed the sociability of established neighborhoods. Money counted least in making the social status, and constantly ambitious and brilliant youngsters from no estate married into the families of planter princes. Meanwhile the one character utterly condemned and ostracized was the man who was mean to his slaves. Even the coward was pitied and might have been liked. For the cruel master there was no toleration. . . .

"In its engaging grace—in the chivalry that tempered even Quixotism with dignity —in the piety that saved master and slave alike—in the charity that boasted not—in the honor, held above estate—in the hospitality that neither condescended nor cringed— in frankness and heartiness and wholesome comradeship—in the reverence paid to womanhood and the inviolable respect in which woman's name was held—the civiliza- tion of the old slave *regime* in the South has not been surpassed, and perhaps will not be equaled, among men." (*The New South* [1890], pp. 153-159 *passim.*)

It would be interesting to investigate in further detail the role of this projected Yankee class romanticism in the original creation and the tenacious upholding of the myth of the "Old South" and the whole "*pauvres honteux*" mentality of the region. As in the case of the Europeans, it is only natural that the Southerners, when they found out that they could sell their region with all their troubles, sorrows, and unsolved problems as "glorious," to the Yankees, availed themselves of this easy escape. And, both in the defensive position before the Civil War and the poverty and drudgery afterward, they had, of course, also reason of their own to indulge in mythological romanticism. But it is likewise natural that it has been Southerners who themselves have found that this easy way of appealing to the North is too expensive in the long run and hinders both progress at home and a real understanding on a deeper level with the powerful Yankees.

[4] When the *Fortune* survey asked the question, "If you had to describe the class to which you belong with one of these three words [upper, middle, lower], which would you pick?" they obtained the following results:

| "Answered that they are: | Pros- perous | "People who are actually— | | | |
		Upper Middle	Lower Middle	Poor	Negro
Upper Class	23.6%	7.9%	4.6%	4.5%	16.1%
Middle Class	74.7	89.0	89.4	70.3	35.7
Lower Class	0.3	0.6	3.1	19.1	26.2
Don't Know	1.4	2.5	2.9	6.1	22.0"

Fortune commented: ". . . every class and occupation, including even the unemployed and the lowly farm hand, decisively considered itself middle class . . ." (These figures are reprinted through the courtesy of *Fortune* magazine and are from "Fortune Survey: XXVII," *Fortune* [February, 1940], p. 20.) For a further discussion, see George Gallup and Saul Forbes Rae, *The Pulse of Democracy* (1940), pp. 169-170.

[5] The leading users of the concepts of caste and class have been a group of investigators centered around Professor W. Lloyd Warner of the University of Chicago: John Dollard, *Caste and Class in a Southern Town* (1937) (This book was only slightly influenced by Warner and used the concepts of caste and class in a less doctrinal way than the following books); Allison Davis and John Dollard, *Children of Bondage* (1940); W. Lloyd Warner, Buford H. Junker, and Walter A. Adams, *Color and Human Nature* (1941); Allison Davis, Burleigh B. Gardner, and Mary R. Gardner, *Deep South* (1941); W. Lloyd Warner and Paul S. Lunt, *The Social Life of a Modern Community* (1941).

In addition there are a few sociologists outside the Warner group who stress problems of class stratification—notably Louis Wirth and Robert S. Lynd. Many writers have employed the concept of caste as central to a study of some aspect of the Negro problem. Few have done this with such insight as Buell G. Gallagher (*American Caste and the Negro College* [1938].)

[6] There has been some attempt to consider "social classes" in America before Warner, however. Those interested in philanthropy did so early. William G. Sumner had a class stratification scheme borrowed from Galton, based on biological ability (*Folkways* [1913; first edition, 1906], pp. 39-53) and he wrote an essay on "What Social Classes Owe to Each Other" (1883). Far more realistic was Thorstein Veblen in his *Theory of the Leisure Class* (1899). In recent years, much influence in the direction of thinking in terms of class stratification emanated from the work of Alba M. Edwards of the United States Census Bureau (*Social-Economic Grouping of the Gainful Workers in the United States: 1930* [1938].)

[7] Speech at New Haven, March 6, 1860, in the *Complete Works of Abraham Lincoln*, John G. Nicolay and John Hay (editors) (1905; first edition, 1894), Vol. V, pp. 360-361.

[8] Young, *American Minority Peoples*, p. 417.

[9] Davis and Dollard, *op. cit.*, p. 13. Compare the other works cited in footnote 5 of this chapter. Davis and Dollard continue:

"A class is composed of families and of social cliques. The interrelationships between these families and cliques, in such informal activities as visiting, dances, receptions, teas, and larger informal affairs, constitute the structure of a social class.

"The forms of participation of the social clique and class are of an intimate type which implies that the individuals included have *equal status in the sense that they may visit one another, have interfamily rituals such as meals or tea together, and may intermarry*. Other types of cliques and larger groups which are organized upon a different basis, such as by common occupation, or recreation (card-playing, golfing, etc.) or church membership, or lodge membership, are not necessarily class-typed. Social participation of this kind, therefore, may not be used by the observer as a reliable index of class position." (*Idem.*)

From a scientific point of view this definition of class has the advantage that: "Social classes may be determined objectively by using records of intimate social participation between the inhabitants [of a community]." (*Idem.*)

Social classes, but not castes, are supposed to overlap somewhat in their membership. "Participation lines are not rigidly drawn. In this respect, social classes are to be contrasted with the color castes, of Negroes and whites, which are mutually exclusive in their social life." (*Idem.*)

Warner himself is not so explicit about how one class can be distinguished from another, although he is quite clear as to the criteria of status.

"Great wealth did not guarantee the highest social position. Something more was necessary.

"In our efforts to find out what this 'something more' was, we finally developed a class hypothesis which withstood the later test of a vast collection of data and of subsequent rigorous analysis. By class is meant two or more orders of people who are believed to be, and are accordingly ranked by the members of the community, in socially superior and inferior positions. Members of a class tend to marry within their own order, but the values of the society permit marriage up and down. A class system also provides that children are born into the same status as their parents. A class society distributes rights and privileges, duties and obligations, unequally among its inferior and superior grades." (Warner and Lunt, *op. cit.*, p. 82.)

"We eventually became convinced that the cliques were next in importance to the family in placing people socially. . . . As we define it, the clique is an intimate nonkin group, membership in which may vary in numbers from two to thirty or more people. As such it is a phenomenon characteristic of our own society. When it approaches the latter figure in size, it ordinarily breaks up into several smaller cliques. The clique is an informal association because it has no explicit rules of entrance, of membership, or of exit. It ordinarily possesses no regular place or time of meeting. It has no elected officers nor any formally recognized hierarchy of leaders. It lacks specifically stated purposes, and its functions are less explicit than those of the family, the association, or the institution. The clique may or may not include biologically related persons; but all its members know each other intimately and participate in frequent face-to-face relations." (*Ibid.*, pp. 110-111.)

[10] In Davis, Gardner, and Gardner we find a statement which suggests that class consciousness is a basic criterion of class: "Members of any one class thus think of themselves as a group and have a certain unity of outlook." (*Op. cit.*, p. 71.) In general, however, members of the Warner group do not emphasize class consciousness.

[11] "In both Yankee City and Old City, individuals recognize their class members by characteristic traits, ranging from dress and speech to education and family connections. Class distinctions are always made on the basis of possible social intimacy, as in the following typical expressions: 'They go around with our friends.' 'We don't go around with those people. They don't fit in with our group.' 'I know I can't class with the big shots.' 'They are ignorant people, and we don't have anything to do with them.' Social classes are thus operating in our society as groups between which there is not intimate participation." (Davis and Dollard, *op. cit.*, p. 259.)

[12] "In the study of human motivation in our society, the analysis of the social class pressures and rewards is of major importance. A child is trained principally by his family, his family's social clique, and his own social clique; the goals and sanctions of

both the family and the intimate social clique are determined principally by the class-ways, that is, by the criteria of status in *their part of the society*." (*Ibid.*, p. 16.)

"For it is the members of the child's and his family's cliques who actually constitute that 'social environment' of which we have talked so loosely, and which, we have said, reinforces the child's habits. Through the demands and pressures of the family and of the clique, class learning is instilled and maintained." (*Ibid.*, p. 262.)

[13] Actually, of course, there is a strong correlation between "social class" in Warner's sense, on the one hand, and income and occupation, on the other hand. One student has taken the population of Yankee City, grouped by Warner into classes on the basis of his information, and reclassified it according to Alba Edwards' socio-economic census group-ings. He found a high correlation between the two classifications. (Robert Dubin, "Factors in the Variation of Urban Occupational Structure," unpublished M.A. thesis, The University of Chicago [1940].)

[14] R. M. MacIver, *Society: Its Structure and Changes* (1931), p. 89.

[15] William Archer, *Through Afro-America* (1910), pp. 234 ff.

[16] *Autobiography of an Ex-Coloured Man* (1927; first edition, 1912), pp. 75-76. Johnson continues:

"It is a struggle; for though the black man fights passively, he nevertheless fights; and his passive resistance is more effective at present than active resistance could possibly be. He bears the fury of the storm as does the willow-tree.

"It is a struggle; for though the white man of the South may be too proud to admit it, he is, nevertheless, using in the contest his best energies; he is devoting to it the greater part of his thought and much of his endeavour. The South today stands panting and almost breathless from its exertions."

[17] Robert R. Moton, *What the Negro Thinks* (1929), p. 8.

[18] As this is being written the Negro press is still vibrating over the first lynching for the year 1942, which occurred in Sikeston, Missouri, January 25.

The N.A.A.C.P. reports that: "White citizens in Sikeston will not testify against each other in any prosecution for guilt in the lynching . . . and they use the threat of a race riot to prevent further investigation and publicity. . . .

"The make-up of the mob was described as being 'just folks' . . . The investigators said: 'We were given the definite impression that the lynchers would not be ostracized by the community; on the other hand those who might *testify against* the lynchers would be ostracized. . . .

" 'Young Prosecuting Attorney Blanton will hardly sacrifice both his career and personal friends, by prosecuting those friends who elected him to office. Even the most liberal of the planters said he would "not be inclined to testify." ' " (N.A.A.C.P. Press Release [February 13, 1942], pp. 1-2.)

Although Governor Forrest C. Donnell of Missouri ordered an immediate investiga-tion, and the Federal Bureau of Investigation sent their investigators into Sikeston, no indictments were ever brought.

The way in which this solidarity on the white side elicits a corresponding solidarity on the Negro side is beautifully illustrated in this case. Negro columnists are com-plementing the American war slogan: "Remember Pearl Harbor" with the Negro slogan: "Remember Sikeston."

[19] Davis, Gardner, and Gardner, *op. cit.*, pp. 48-49.

[20] W. E. B. Du Bois, *Dusk of Dawn* (1940), pp. 130-131.

[21] *Following the Color Line* (1908), p. 11.

[22] Claude McKay, *A Long Way from Home* (1937), p. 227.

[23] (1934), p. 7.

[24] *Negro Americans, What Now?*, p. 6.

[25] Archer observes:

"Once let a dozen white men be killed by armed negroes in any city of the South, and a flame would burst out all over the land which would work untold devastation before either authority or humanity could check it. The incident would be taken as a declaration of racial war; everywhere the white mob would insist on searching for arms in the negro quarters; the negroes would inevitably attempt some panic-stricken defensive organization; and the more effective it proved, the more terrible would be the calamity to their race. Not even in the wildest frenzy, of course, could the race, or a tenth part of the race, be violently wiped out; but they might be so dismayed and terrorized as to lose that natural buoyancy of spirit which has hitherto sustained them, and enabled them to increase and multiply. The prophets of extinction already read hopelessness and a prescience of doom in the negro tone of mind; but, so far, I think the wish is father to the thought. The race, as a whole, is confident, in its happy-go-lucky way. But would their spirit survive a great massacre, followed by an open and chronic *Negerhetze?* I doubt it . . ." (*Op cit.*, pp. 206-207.)

[26] The only white passers the author has personally observed were two cases of white women married to Negro men, who found it convenient to call themselves Negroes. Donald Young informs us: ". . . occasionally persons of unmixed white ancestry have deliberately passed themselves off as Negroes, presumably in the main because of a preference for Negro associations and for employment opportunities, as in a colored orchestra." (*Research Memorandum on Minority Peoples in the Depression*, p. 28.) Sometimes white orphans have been brought up in Negro households and voluntarily retain the caste status of their foster parents. See a special investigation by Louis Wirth and Herbert Goldhamer, "The Hybrid and the Problem of Miscegenation," in Otto Klineberg (editor), *Characteristics of the American Negro*, prepared for this study; to be published, manuscript page 75.

[27] See *ibid.*, manuscript pages 97-98 and quoted sources.

[28] *Ibid.*, manuscript pages 83-84.

[29] *Ibid.*, manuscript page 89.

[30] A Negro's comment cited by Baker, *op. cit.*, p. 161.

[31] Charles S. Johnson, *op. cit.*, p. 301.

Chapter 32. *The Negro Class Structure*

[1] The resentment against the rising Negro takes concrete forms: ". . . 'even the reasonable Southerner,' " William Archer quotes a Southerner as saying, " 'feels a certain bitterness on the subject of education when he sees the black child marching off to a school provided by Northern philanthropy, while the child of the "poor white" goes into the cotton-factory.' " (*Through Afro-America* [1910], p. 17.) The fact that this is an exception, that white children on the average are much better provided for, and that employment in the cotton industry is one of the best protected caste monopolies in

breadwinning, does not meet the white wish that *all* Negroes should be below *all* whites, and no exception allowed.

² Hortense Powdermaker, *After Freedom* (1939), pp. 5-6.

³ See Wilbert E. Moore and Robin M. Williams, "Stratification in the Ante-Bellum South," *American Sociological Review* (June, 1942), pp. 350-351.

⁴ E. Franklin Frazier, *The Free Negro Family* (1932).

⁵ "The Bases of Race Prejudice," *Annals of the American Academy of Political and Social Science* (November, 1928), p. 20. (Italics ours.) Park is, of course, not the first one to have pointed out the presence of caste and class structures in Southern society, nor to indicate the trend toward parallelism in class structures.

⁶ W. Lloyd Warner, "Introduction," to *Deep South* by Allison Davis, Burleigh B. Gardner, and Mary R. Gardner (1941), pp. 10 ff.

⁷ W. E. B. Du Bois, *Dusk of Dawn* (1940), p. 183.

⁸ Buell G. Gallagher has also suggested diagrams to describe caste and class in the South in recent years. He presents two diagrams: (1) "Economic," which is much like our second, or percentage, diagram. (2) "Social," which shows all Negroes below all whites.

"Two caste patterns prevail, each governing etiquette and fixing status in its sphere. In economic status (1), the Negro caste is integrated (as an encysted group, not assimilated); but in all other respects (2) every Negro is judged inferior to all whites in status." (*American Caste and the Negro College* [1938], p. 87.)

CASTE AND CLASS IN THE AMERICAN SOUTH OF THE 1930's
(1) ECONOMIC   (2) SOCIAL

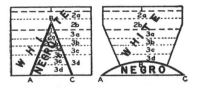

Legend: A, B, C = Caste Line.
1, 2, 3, a, b, c, d = Classes.

Since Gallagher separates these two things, instead of integrating them into "status" —as do Park and Warner—he is considering something a little different than we are at this point: he is considering Southern white theory as well as practice, and neglecting factors other than "economic" and "social" that might go to make up status (such as status in court). Gallagher's presentation may be the most useful for many purposes, and it brings out the fact that a person may have one status in one situation and another status in another situation.

Another caste-class diagram is suggested by Wilbert E. Moore and Robin M. Williams, but since it refers only to the pre-Civil War period and not to present conditions, we may neglect it here. (*Op. cit.*, p. 349.)

⁹ John Dollard, *Caste and Class in a Southern Town* (1937), pp. 98 ff. and 173 ff.

¹⁰ There were, of course, also other relations than that of servant-master to the better class of whites which molded this personality type.

Ralph Bunche pays his tribute to a passing generation in the following words:

"The fine old gentlemen of the earlier days, with all of their old-fogeyism, tolerance and patience, worshipped a different god. They were under the spell of the aristocratic whites of their day; they took as their model the best educated and most cultured men of their period, and they attempted to acquire and did acquire many of the graces and talents of this group without, through lack of riches, being able to cultivate their more costly vices.

"It does seem that the current generations of Negroes have lost something valuable in the transition, and this not merely in poise, dignity and the graces, but also to a damaging degree in the qualities of honor, principle, integrity and intellectual honesty." ("Conceptions and Ideologies of the Negro Problem," unpublished manuscript, prepared for this study [1940], p. 111.)

[11] Marcus Wilson Jernegan, *Laboring and Dependent Classes in Colonial America, 1607-1783* (1931), p. 9. See also Chapter 5, Sections 4 and 5; and Louis Wirth and Herbert Goldhamer, "The Hybrid and the Problem of Miscegenation" in Otto Klineberg (editor), *Characteristics of the American Negro*, prepared for this study; to be published, manuscript pages 208 and 138-139.

[12] Wirth and Goldhamer, *op. cit.*, manuscript page 134 and sources cited by them.

[13] "Along with the advantageous social position of the mulatto there has been a pronounced disadvantage for blacks in the ideological heritage of society generally. The concept of blackness has held, in the popular mind, an unfavorable connotation. 'Black is evil,' 'black as sin,' 'black as the devil,' are phrases which suggest the emotional and aesthetic implications of this association. The evil and ugliness of blackness have long been contrasted in popular thinking with the goodness and purity of whiteness. Whether with respect to men or things this color association has been deeply meaningful; it is an inescapable element of the cultural heritage." (Charles S. Johnson, *Growing Up in the Black Belt* [1941], p. 257.)

"The interviews revealed results similar to those of the tests. Some of the reactions to blackness were as follows: 'Black is too black,' 'Black is ugly,' 'Black people are mean,' 'Black isn't like flesh,' 'Black is bad because people make fun, and I don't think it looks good either,' 'Black people can't use make-up,' 'Black people are evil,' 'White looks better than black,' 'No black people hold good jobs,' 'Black people can't look nice in their clothes,' 'You can't get along with black people,' 'Black looks dirty,' 'Black people have to go to the kitchen and scrub,' 'Even in college they don't want to take in black students.' Black youth are called by such derisive names as 'Snow,' 'Gold Dust Boys,' 'Blue Gums,' 'Midnight,' 'Shadow,' 'Haint,' 'Dusty,' 'Polish,' and 'Shine.' . . .

"In the second place, the belief that 'black people are mean' can easily make such people 'mean' if the behavior toward them is habitually based on such an assumption. In the end the reaction of such dark persons reinforces the stereotype." (*Ibid.*, pp. 259-262.)

[14] Donald R. Young observes rightly: "The common preference for the 'mammy' type of servant or the 'darkey' type of gardener, butler, odd-job man, and flunkey is not in opposition to this statement, for the very preference of these types helps keep them in the dead-end employments just mentioned, certainly not employments which lead to advancement." (*American Minority Peoples* [1932], p. 397.)

[15] Davis, Gardner, and Gardner tell us about the supreme importance of the complexion for class status in a Southern city. "Other qualifications being nearly equal.

colored persons having light skin and 'white' types of hair will be accorded the highest station within the lower caste. This fact does not prevent the expression of strong antagonisms to light-skinned persons by the rest of the group. Such antagonism is an expression of the envy and humiliation of the darker individuals.

"Since the system of classes operates within a caste system, the physical traits of the white caste must be accorded highest value; the darker individuals cannot but be conditioned to the all-important symbols of the upper caste, and so give them highest rank. The upper class, on the other hand, thinks of the lower class as black and woolly-haired, thus mentally associating the lowest social rank with the 'lowest' physical traits." (*Op. cit.*, p. 235.)

"The high social value placed upon light skin color and white hair-form is even more clearly related to the operation of caste sanctions. While it is not true that these physical traits alone assure a colored person an upper-class status, it is certain that, in most of even the older colored communities, social mobility proceeds at a faster pace for persons with these physical traits. It is commonly said by colored men of the upper and upper-middle classes today that they marry women for their 'looks,' while white men of parallel status marry for family status, money, and education." (*Ibid.*, p. 244.)

[16] "It was observed in the testing program and in the direct interviews with the youth that they consistently rated their own complexions a shade or more lighter than they appeared to be. This prompted the study to attempt a more careful measurement of a tendency which seemed to have some significance. It suggested a type of unconscious response to the color evaluations which they gave in other situations. They could escape, in their own minds at least, some of the unfavorable association, by appraising themselves as lighter than they were." (Charles S. Johnson, *Growing Up in the Black Belt*, p. 265.)

[17] *Following the Color Line* (1908), pp. 157 ff.; *Through Afro-America* (1910), pp. 225 ff.

[18] This "peculiar inconsistency" on the color question has been observed and discussed by every author on the Negro problem during recent decades. Recently much new material has been made available by the studies on Negro youth, prepared for the American Youth Commission (see footnote 9 to Chapter 30), all of which have attached great importance to the color factor in the personality development of Negro youth. One of the studies—*Color and Human Nature* (1941) by W. Lloyd Warner, Buford Junker, and W. A. Adams—was mainly directed on this problem. This new material rather tends to confer the impression that color and color preference in the Negro community is even more important than was earlier assumed in the general literature on the Negro problem.

[19] "It often happens that darker children in families feel that their parents give preference to the children of lighter complexion. Even such inadvertent and casual comparisons as 'better hair,' 'nicer complexion,' 'prettier skin,' 'nicer shade' affect the more sensitive young people and contribute to their feelings of inferiority. Children may apply color values unfavorably to one or the other of the parents and find themselves apologizing for the dark complexion of a parent. They may even harbor resentment against the parent who was biologically responsible for their own undesirable appearance. By far the most frequent instances of color sensitivity, however, occur outside the home as the child attempts to make adjustment to new groups." (Charles S.

Johnson, *Growing Up in the Black Belt*, p. 267. Compare Allison Davis and John Dollard, *Children of Bondage* [1940], p. 254 *passim*.)

For a discussion of how the color problem enters in the school see, Davis and Dollard, *op. cit.*, p. 253; E. Franklin Frazier, *Negro Youth at the Crossways* (1940), pp. 96 ff.; and Anonymous, "The Revolt of the Evil Fairies," *The New Republic* (April 6, 1942), pp. 458-459.

[20] The few attempts made to tabulate and correlate color of Negro husbands and wives confirm this observation. See: M. J. Herskovits, *The American Negro* (1928), p. 64; E. B. Reuter, *Race Mixture* (1931), pp. 158-159; E. Franklin Frazier, *The Negro Family in the United States* (1939), pp. 572 ff.

[21] Wirth and Goldhamer have surveyed the various studies bearing on the problem; *op. cit.*, pp. 142-147.

[22] ". . . dark color is widely looked down upon in the Chicago Negro community. Instead of being regarded as a proud racial distinction, it is taken as a reminder of traditional servitude and as a badge of lowly status. The distribution of our cases in each social class according to color also suggests . . . that dark-skin persons in the higher ranks of Negro society find themselves a minority in competition with individuals of lighter color. These higher positions call for personalities strong enough to cope with potential conflicts over appearance in relation to social acceptability." (Warner, Junker, and Adams, *op. cit.*, p. 31.)

"Our results indicate that there is little correlation between class and color in the southern rural area. Differences in complexion and hair create problems of adjustment, but do not mark class lines within the rural Negro group." (Charles S. Johnson, *Growing Up in the Black Belt*, p. 272.)

[23] Before Emancipation and, in the mulatto societies, for a considerable time afterward, it was a point of pride to have a white (illegitimate) father, particularly if he belonged to the aristocratic classes. This is not true any more. The studies of Dollard, Powdermaker, and others show that even in the South it is rather a disgrace. Davis, Gardner, and Gardner, for example, say: "Whereas in Old County of a generation ago an individual's status was increased by his kinship to white persons of the middle or upper classes, today both miscegenation and illegitimacy are rather heavily tabooed in the colored upper and upper-middle classes." (*Op. cit.*, p. 247.)

[24] "Although mulattoes on the whole appear to be proud of their lighter complexions, they are at a disadvantage when the question of paternity is raised by their darker associates. Such derisive terms as 'Yellow Pumpkin,' 'Yellow Bastard,' are used in this connection. The youth commenting on this shade of complexion made such statements as these: 'Yellow people are not honest' (meaning that they are probably illegitimate), 'Yellow is the worst color because it shows mixture with whites,' 'Yellow is too conspicuous' (like black), 'Yellow people don't look right,' 'Real yellow people ain't got no father,' 'Yellow don't have no race, they can't be white and they ain't black either,' 'Anything that is too light looks dirty,' 'Yellow is mixed bad blood,' 'Light people get old too quickly,' 'Yellow don't hold looks so long,' 'White colored people is all bastards.' " (Charles S. Johnson, *Growing Up in the Black Belt*, pp. 262-263.)

[25] See E. B. Reuter, *The Mulatto in the United States* (1918), especially pp. 19, 102-104, and Everett V. Stonequist, *The Marginal Man* (1937), especially Chapter 6.

[26] Robert E. Park in the "Introduction" to Stonequist, *op. cit.*, p. xv.

[27] Stonequist writes about the mulatto that he is ". . . not the dejected, spiritless

outcast; neither is he the inhibited conformist. He is more likely to be restless and race-conscious, aggressive and radical, ambitious and creative. The lower status to which he is assigned naturally creates discontented and rebellious feelings. From an earlier, spontaneous identification with the white man, he has, under the rebuffs of a categorical race prejudice, turned about and identified himself with the Negro race. In the process of so doing, he suffers a profound inner conflict.

"After all, does not the blood of the white man flow in his veins? Does he not share the higher culture in common with the white American? Is he not legally and morally an American citizen? And yet he finds himself condemned to a lower caste in the American system! So the mulatto is likely to think to himself. Living in two such social worlds, between which there is antagonism and prejudice, he experiences in himself the same conflict. In his own consciousness the play and the strife of the two group attitudes take place, and the manner in which he responds forms one of the most interesting chapters in the history of the Negro." (*Op. cit.*, pp. 24-25.) Stonequist makes similar statements about the unhappiness of mulattoes as over against dark Negroes, on pages 24-27, 110-113, 144-145 and 184-189 of *The Marginal Man.*

[28] The theory of the "marginal man" was originally developed for Jews and other white immigrants in America, and for them it probably has validity and a strong empirical basis. It was transferred uncritically to the Negro situation where its validity it questionable. Stonequist uses two types of evidence to support his theory that the mulatto has greater personality difficulties than the full-blooded Negro.

(1) He quotes autobiographical statements by mulattoes who complain bitterly about being colored. Du Bois' famous statement is quoted, for example:

"It is a peculiar sensation, this double-consciousness, this sense of always looking at one's self through the eyes of others, of measuring one's soul by the tape of a world that looks on in amused contempt and pity. One feels his two-ness—an American, a Negro; two souls, two thoughts, two unreconciled strivings; two warring ideals in one dark body, whose dogged strength alone keeps it from being torn asunder." (*The Souls of Black Folk* [1903], p. 3. Quoted in *ibid.*, p. 145.)

In practically all these quotations (many of them are from Du Bois), however, the mulatto is not complaining because he wants to be associated with the white world over against the black world. He is complaining because of the treatment accorded him as a Negro. When Du Bois speaks about his "double consciousness"—having loyalties and feelings of both Negroes and Americans—he means Negroes and Americans, not—as Stonequist makes out—Negroes and whites. It is the antithesis between the American Creed and the Negro's actual status to which Du Bois calls attention, not the mulatto's character as a marginal man. It may justly be said that the American Negro is a marginal man, but it cannot be claimed, from these quotations, that the mulatto is any more "marginal" than is the black man.

(2) Stonequist reports the results of a questionnaire study. He finds, for example, that the 45 Negroes who could possibly pass for white or Indian or Mexican in a sample of 192 Negro college students had greater "psychological difficulties with which to contend" than the darker Negro students. This sample, however, cannot be regarded as representative of the entire Negro population. (*Op. cit.*, pp. 189-190.)

It should be noted that there is some pragmatic truth in the theory that the mulatto has more *Weltschmerz.* In so far as there is still a correlation between color and class status, this is true, because upper class Negroes are more articulate and more sensitive to the discriminations directed against all Negroes. But as far as his color is concerned, the mulatto has less of a personality problem than does the dark Negro, and he certainly has no loyalty to his white ancestors.

[29] *Op. cit.*, p. 135.

[30] Dollard, *op. cit.*; Powdermaker, *op. cit.*; and Davis, Gardner, and Gardner, *op. cit.* Also the studies of Negro youth prepared for the American Youth Commission, cited in footnote 9 of Chapter 30, have been framed with a main view on the Negro class system.

[31] Many earlier studies of the Negro, which could not be described as "community studies," also divided the Negro population into three classes.

[32] If we add together all the following occupational groups of male Negroes, we arrive at a figure of 80 per cent of all male Negro gainful workers in 1930: owners of less than 20 acres of land used for agriculture, agricultural cash tenants having less than 50 acres, agricultural share tenants having less than 50 acres, all agricultural share-croppers and wage laborers, and all nonagricultural gainful workers in the unskilled and semi-skilled groups in Edwards' social-economic classification. For purposes of general description, this would seem to be a most useful description of the Negro lower classes defined in purely occupational terms. One of the major weaknesses of the definition is that it includes all servant employees, and in the Negro world some of these have middle or even upper class status. On the other hand, some skilled workers with restricted employment opportunities—especially in building construction—will have lower class status in the Negro community. (Sources: (1) United States Bureau of the Census, *Negroes in the United States: 1920-1932*, pp. 602-605. (2) United States Bureau of the Census, Alba M. Edwards, *Social-Economic Grouping of the Gainful Workers of the United States, 1930* [1938], pp. 58-59.)

For the Southern rural population Charles S. Johnson estimates—". . . on the basis of occupation, income, education, family organization, relationship to property, and general community recognition of standing"—that the lower class amounts to 82 per cent, while the middle class takes 12 per cent and the upper class only 6 per cent (*Growing Up in the Black Belt*, p. 77). Johnson's criteria could, of course, be varied according to the needs of the investigator and different percentages would result, but no one has ever said that the bulk of Southern rural Negroes are not lower class. Frazier informs us that in urban communities in the Border cities like St. Louis and Washington, the lower class comprises "about two-thirds of the Negro population." (Frazier, *Negro Youth at the Crossways*, p. 263.) Warner, Junker, and Adams tell us that the "great masses of Chicago Negroes belong to the lower class." (*Op. cit.*, p. 22.) Davis, Gardner, and Gardner state that "the overwhelming majority of colored persons are considered lower class, *according to the colored group's own standards.*" And that "in most American colored societies the middle and upper classes together . . . do not include more than one-fourth of the population." (*Op. cit.*, p. 222.) These estimates are not very exact and they are apparently not made on similar criteria. In this context our only point is that all authors include the majority of the Negro population in the lower class.

[33] "The critical fact is that a much larger proportion of all Negroes are lower class than is the case with whites. This is where caste comes to bear. It puts the overwhelming majority of Negroes in the lowest class group and keeps them there." (Davis and Dollard, *op. cit.*, p. 65.)

[34] Thomas Nelson Page's vision was ". . . a vast sluggish mass of uncooled lava

over a large section of the country, burying some portions and affecting the whole. It is apparently harmless, but beneath its surface smoulder fires which may at any time burst forth unexpectedly and spread desolation all around." (*The Negro: The Southerner's Problem* [1904], p. 64.)

[35] Charles S. Johnson, *Growing Up in the Black Belt*, pp. 75 ff., 98, 280 *passim*. Compare Charles S. Johnson, *Shadow of the Plantation* (1934), p. 6.

"Within the lower classes a distinction should be made between the 'folk Negro' and the rest of the population. This distinction is important and more cultural than economic; it refers to the family habits and values evolved by the Negro culture under the institution of slavery. Many of the naive traits and customs of the 'folk Negro' are out of line with the practices of the larger society, but were at times in the past essential to group survival in cultural isolation. Stripped of their basic African culture by the exigencies of life in America, they evolved a social life and a culture of their own which was adequate for survival in their peculiar status in America. The customs, beliefs, and values developed have been a response to their limited roles within the American social order, even when many of the traits of the group have been borrowed from early American settlers and crude pioneers in the cotton country. In a sense, they have been repositories of certain folkways now outgrown by those groups which were more rapidly absorbed into the larger currents of American life. The patterns of life, social codes and social attitudes, set in an early period, have because of the cultural as well as geographical isolation continued to be effective social controls. In the social consciousness of the group and in its social life, there has been a considerable degree of organization and internal cohesion.

"The 'folk Negro' organization of life and of values has been essential to survival and to the most satisfying functioning of the members of the group in their setting. Many things for which the larger dominant society has one set of values, meanings, and acceptable behavior patterns—marriage, divorce, extra-marital relations, illegitimacy, religion, love, death, and so forth—may in this group have quite another set. This helps to explain types of personalities developed under the peculiar circumstances of life of the 'folk Negro' and makes their behavior more intelligible. The increase of means of communication and the introduction of some education is breaking down the cultural isolation of this group." (Charles S. Johnson, *Growing Up in the Black Belt*, pp. 75-76.)

[36] "The upper class of the Negro population is that group possessing in general a family social heritage known and respected by the community, a substantial amount of education, an occupational level which is achieved by special formal preparation, a comfortable income, ownership of property, stability of residence, superior cultural standards, a measure of personal security through influential connections, or the ability to exert economic or other pressure in the maintenance of this security, or *any combination of most of these characteristics*. Further, this group is conceived by itself as a class and is so recognized by others; it is recognized by similar groups in other areas; and is regarded, whether with approval or disapproval, by other classes as a different and an exclusive society. In this classification are usually the Negro doctor's families, some teachers and school principals, successful landowners, and even families without large possessions but with superior education and a significant family history. The distinction may be clarified by the observation that the typical rural preacher, although a 'professional,' does not normally belong in the class. The physician almost always does. Most of the preachers, especially in the Southern rural areas, are about as unlettered as their

congregations. Further, the economic and social limitations of their calling restrict their entree to this class." (*Ibid.*, pp. 73-74.)

[37] Hortense Powdermaker speaks of a "lag" in a process of acculturation. "The upper class enforces strict Puritanical standards formed after the white model. The morals they enforce, however, correspond to those of a generation ago more closely than those of today. While they observe and inculcate in their children the Puritanical code of which their ancestors were deemed incapable, the descendants of the whites from whom they learned these ideals of behavior are tending to greater laxity." (*Op. cit.*, p. 355.)

[38] See Chapter 39, Section 6. Hortense Powdermaker sees an interesting parallel which emphasizes the paradoxical situation of the Negro upper class in the caste conflict:

"There is a further analogy between the position of the Negro upper class and that of the Poor Whites, one at the top, the other at the botton of the social ladder within its group. Each serves as agent for its race toward the other, taking actions and expressing sentiments to which the group as a whole is not ready to commit itself. The Poor White, in his occasional violent expressions of race antagonism, acts for those Whites who tacitly condone and overtly deplore such behavior. He is rewarded by his fellows chiefly in resentment, since he embodies, in addition to traits of his own which they dislike, their own least worthy impulses. The Negro upper class acts out for its race the denial that Negroes are inferior; it demonstrates that they too can be educated, moral, industrious, thrifty. This class also reaps a share of resentment from other members of its race, but here resentment is far less keen and less conscious, and is offset by substantial advantages, among which is to be numbered a very gratifying prestige. Each of these two classes is set apart from the rest of its race, experiencing different conflicts and holding different attitudes; and each awakens in the other race a special hostility strongly tinged with fear." (*Op. cit.*, pp. 334-335.)

[39] Writing of the upper class in 1899—when he could still speak of it as "the germ of a great middle class"—Du Bois observed:

". . . in general its members are curiously hampered by the fact that, being shut off from the world about them, they are the aristocracy of their own people, with all the responsibilities of an aristocracy, and yet they, on the one hand, are not prepared for this role, and their own masses are not used to looking to them for leadership. As a class they feel strongly the centrifugal forces of class repulsion among their own people, and, indeed, are compelled to feel it in sheer self-defense. They do not relish being mistaken for servants; they shrink from the free and easy worship of most of the Negro churches, and they shrink from all such display and publicity as will expose them to the veiled insult and depreciation which the masses suffer. Consequently this class, which ought to lead, refuses to head any race movement on the plea that thus they draw the very color line against which they protest." (*The Philadelphia Negro*, p. 177.)

[40] *Dusk of Dawn*, p. 185.

[41] Frazier, *Negro Youth at the Crossways*, p. 28.

Chapter 33. *The American Pattern of Individual Leadership and Mass Passivity*

[1] *The American Commonwealth* (1910, first edition, 1893), Vol. 2, p. 373.

[2] The contrary tendency in American history and social science in recent decades is evidently a reaction to this popular attitude. It goes, as reactions usually do, to the

opposite extreme; and so American social speculation, on the scientific level, is dominated by a rather doctrinal stress on trends and mechanical forces and by an underestimation of, not only the personal accidents in history, but also the importance of ideas and ideals. Charles and Mary Beard's *The Rise of American Civilization* (1927) is visibly marked by a materialistic conception of history as dominated by economic interests. They do this even though they are good Americans, and as authors have enough feeling for their audience to populate their pages with outstanding personalities, to paint them a little in the fashion of angels and devils, and often to forget their philosophical intention to show up individuals as marionettes in the power of deeper forces. A sociologist such as William Ogburn is even more typical of this scientific reaction toward a mechanical view of social change. The reaction has influenced a small group of intellectuals around the great universities and the periodicals devoted to social criticism and reform, but has as yet not disturbed the ordinary American's ways of thinking. And even the little crowd of intellectuals themselves are influenced only on a rather abstract plane of their thinking. In their daily affairs they usually think and act according to the popular attitude, and, indeed, they have to do so if they do not want to doom themselves to isolation.

[3] *Fifteenth Census of the United States: 1930, Population*, Vol. II, p. 37; and *Sixteenth Census of the United States: 1940, Population*, Preliminary Release, Series P-10, No. 1.

[4] See the classic study by A. A. Berle and Gardiner C. Means, *The Modern Corporation and Private Property* (1932), especially pp. 277-287.

It is not surprising that big business in America, organized as it is, has been unusually reluctant to share its control over labor conditions with trade unions or to allow government interference in the public interest.

Chapter 34. *Accommodating Leadership*

[1] An interesting parallel, which cannot be followed up here, would be with similar problems and tendencies in the relations between the wider society and other distinct minority groups such as the other color castes—Japanese, Chinese, Filipinos, Mexicans—and immigrant groups—Jewish, Czech, Polish, Italian.

[2] This pattern has sunk deep into the entire class structure of the Negro community. It is commonly known that Negro domestics often consider it a degradation of their social status to work in a Negro family. An upper class Negro friend of mine testifies:

"I know of a good many instances, especially in Washington, and one or two of them are personal, where Negro domestics flatly refuse to work for Negroes, for fear that they will lose caste by doing so. My wife, who happens to fall in the category of the 'voluntary' or 'sociological' Negro, once hired a domestic at a wage admittedly higher than this girl had ever gotten before, when I chanced into the room. The young lady, a dark brown skin, promptly arose, exclaimed: 'Oh, I didn't know you were *colored*—I don't work for colored,' and left without further ado. On another occasion we had employed a nice, inefficient but highly religious old lady in the same capacity. She had to attend church each Sunday morning, and would cook the dinner early and depart. After a few Sundays, she explained to us the reason for the generous portions of our larder with which she sallied out these Sunday mornings. She had a long tram ride to her home, she said, and on her car she would always encounter a number of her friends who were employed as domestics in white families. These friends were always well laden with tidbits, it seems, and she solemnly declared that this was the first time she had ever worked for colored; none of her friends ever had, though they knew she was so engaged, and that she wanted to show her friends that 'colored folks are just as good to work for as white folk.' Thus we sacrificed half of each Sunday dinner to maintain the prestige of the race."

[3] It should be noted that Negro leadership does not *per se* raise an individual's status in the eyes of white people in general. Only a few white people know about the leadership function he performs; to others he is just another Negro. His class status, on the other hand—which might be a function of his leadership—is easier to observe from his dress, manners, occupation, and so on, and may more generally command white respect. (See Chapter 30, Section 2, and Chapter 32, Section 4.) Whites will, however, regularly show respect if they come to know about an individual Negro's accomplishments or even if they come to know quite *in abstracto* that he is a "distinguished Negro."

[4] In this analysis of the relation between social class and leadership, color will be left out of account. It is true that most Negro leaders, particularly on the national plane, have been mulattoes and sometimes near-white or passable. (Compare E. B. Reuter, *The Mulatto in the United States* [1918].) This fact is, however, the less astonishing when we remember (1) how greatly mixed the entire Negro population is (Chapter 5), and (2) how color is an important factor in determining social class in the Negro community (Chapter 32). It is plausible that a light color is often an asset to a Negro leader in his dealings with both whites and Negroes, but it is also certain that a dark color is sometimes advantageous for a Negro leader. The two tendencies do not cancel each other since they occur in different types of leadership.

But color, independent of its relevance for class, is probably a minor factor for Negro leadership. Reuter's assertion that the mulatto is "the most vital point" in the race problem (*ibid.*, p. 87, *passim*) seems, for the reasons given, much exaggerated. An analysis directed to this particular relationship could only be warranted in a study which proceeded to distinguish between *all* the different factors determining leadership in the Negro community, that is, besides color: education, occupation, wealth, family background, and so forth. This we cannot undertake in the present abstract overview.

A story related to us by E. Franklin Frazier (conversation, July 11, 1942) might be repeated, however, to illustrate that dark color is sometimes an asset for a Negro leader. At a convention called to elect a bishop of one of the major Negro denominations, two candidates presented their qualifications. The first was very dark in color, and his keynote speech was that a dark man should lead the Negro people. The electors were predominantly dark and their applause indicated that his election was practically clinched. The other candidate, a light man, met a hostile audience. He agreed that dark Negroes needed dark leaders, but said that sometimes admiration for dark skin was more important than dark skin itself. He then pointed to his opponent's wife and to his own wife in the audience. The opponent's wife had light skin, but his own wife had dark skin. He won the election.

Marcus Garvey's dark skin was an asset, but so may be Walter White's extremely light skin, since there may be a feeling that this man who could pass is making a personal sacrifice by being a "voluntary" Negro.

[5] A field interview by Ralph Bunche and myself with a local Negro leader of the

type characterized in the text, and with some other people in the Southeastern coast city where he lives, is presented in excerpts in: Ralph Bunche, "A Brief and Tentative Analysis of Negro Leadership," unpublished manuscript prepared for this study (1940), pp. 94-111.

[6] A word might also be said about the "shady" upper class—the big-time gamblers and lords of vice and crime. In spite of the fact that they have, in a sense, upper class status and may be personally popular, they cannot be used as regular leaders because they do not fit the American idea of what a leader should be. They do act as "behind the scenes" political leaders, especially in the North.

[7] J. G. St. Claire Drake, "The Negro Church and Associations in Chicago," unpublished manuscript prepared for this study (1940), p. 402; and Allison Davis, Burleigh B. Gardner, and Mary R. Gardner, *Deep South* (1941), pp. 236-239. This theme appears in literature, too. See Walter White, *The Fire in the Flint* (1924).

[8] *The Negro: The Southerner's Problem* (1904), p. 64.

[9] The best published study of Northern Negro political leaders is Harold F. Gosnell's *Negro Politicians* (1935).

Chapter 35. *The Negro Protest*

[1] See Melville J. Herskovits (*The Myth of the Negro Past*, prepared for this study [1941], pp. 91 ff.) for a short survey of the slave revolts and for references to the literature.

[2] *Growing Up in the Black Belt* (1941), p. 243.

[3] Quoted from W. E. B. Du Bois, *Black Reconstruction* (1935), pp. 14-15.

[4] *Ibid.*, p. 122.

[5] Booker T. Washington, *The Future of the American Negro* (1902; first edition, 1899), p. 132.

[6] *Race Adjustment, Essays on the Negro in America* (1908), pp. 17-18.

[7] *Patterns of Negro Segregation*, prepared for this study (1943), p. 263.

[8] From a perspective of almost 40 years after he first opened attack on the "Tuskegee Machine," Du Bois comments upon it as follows:

"It arose first quite naturally. Not only did presidents of the United States consult Booker Washington, but governors and congressmen: philanthropists conferred with him, scholars wrote to him. Tuskegee became a vast information bureau and center of advice. It was not merely passive in these matters but, guided by a young unobtrusive minor official who was also intelligent, suave and far-seeing, active efforts were made to concentrate influence at Tuskegee. After a time almost no Negro institution could collect funds without the recommendation or acquiescence of Mr. Washington. Few political appointments were made anywhere in the United States without his consent. Even the careers of rising young colored men were very often determined by his advice and certainly his opposition was fatal. How much Mr. Washington knew of this work of the Tuskegee Machine and was directly responsible, one cannot say, but of its general activity and scope he must have been aware. . . . The control was to be drastic. The Negro intelligentsia was to be suppressed and hammered into conformity. The process involved some cruelty and disappointment, but that was inevitable. This was the real force back of the Tuskegee Machine. It had money and it had opportunity, and it found in Tuskegee tools to do its bidding. . . . Things came to such a pass that when any Negro complained or advocated a course of action, he was silenced with the remark that Mr. Washington did not agree with this. Naturally the bumptious irritated, young black intelligentsia of the day declared, 'I don't care a damn what Booker Washington thinks. This is what I think, and *I have a right to think.*' " (W. E. B. Du Bois, *Dusk of Dawn* [1940], pp. 73-75).

⁹ Du Bois testifies: "The *Guardian* was bitter, satirical, and personal; but it was well-edited, it was earnest, and it published facts. It attracted wide attention among colored people: it circulated among them all over the country: it was quoted and discussed. I did not wholly agree with the *Guardian*, and indeed only a few Negroes did, but nearly all read it and were influenced by it." (*Ibid.*, p. 73.)

¹⁰ Du Bois was then professor at Atlanta University. He had there started what has been called "the first real sociological research in the South" (Guy B. Johnson, "Negro Racial Movements and Leadership in the United States," *American Journal of Sociology* [July, 1937], p. 65.) When he did not get the support he hoped for to fulfill his plan to study the Negro problem—because Booker T. Washington and his group did not endorse it, or so he believed— and later, when the N.A.A.C.P. was founded, he left the University entirely. Another reason why he left was that he thought that his connection with the University increased its difficulties in getting foundation support. (See Du Bois, *Dusk of Dawn*, pp. 68-95 *passim*.)

¹¹ *Ibid.*, p. 72.

¹² James Weldon Johnson, *Along This Way* (1934), p. 313.

¹³ *Following the Color Line*, p. 219.

¹⁴ For the history of the Niagara Movement, see Ralph J. Bunche, "The Programs, Ideologies, Tactics, and Achievements of Negro Betterment and Interracial Organizations," unpublished manuscript prepared for this study (1940), Vol. I, pp. 15 ff., and W. E. B. Du Bois' autobiography, *Dusk of Dawn*, pp. 88-95.

¹⁵ Emmett J. Scott, *The American Negro in the World War* (1919), pp. 92-104 and 426-457; Du Bois, *Dusk of Dawn*, pp. 245-256; James Weldon Johnson, *Along This Way*, pp. 318-319.

¹⁶ James Weldon Johnson describes "the spirit of defiance born of desperation" after the First World War and attributes to it the new racial radicalism of the period:

"With the close of the war went most of the illusions and high hopes American Negroes had felt would be realized when it was seen that they were doing to the utmost their bit at home and in the field. Eight months after the armistice, with black men back fresh from the front, there broke the Red Summer of 1919, and the mingled emotions of the race were bitterness, despair, and anger. There developed an attitude of cynicism that was a characteristic foreign to the Negro. There developed also a spirit of defiance born of desperation. These sentiments and reactions found varying degrees of expression in the Negro publications throughout the country; but Harlem became the centre where they were formulated and voiced to the Negroes of America and the world. Radicalism in Harlem, which had declined as the war approached, burst out anew. But it was something different from the formal radicalism of pre-war days; it was a radicalism motivated by a fierce race consciousness." (*Black Manhattan* [1930], p. 246.)

¹⁷ For the history of the Garvey movement and a bibliography, see Bunche, *op. cit.*,

Vol. 2, pp. 393 ff. The descriptive facts about the movement in this section are taken from Bunche.

[18] Quoted from Amy Jacques Garvey (editor), *Philosophy and Opinions of Marcus Garvey* (1923), pp. 8-9.

[19] Quoted from *ibid.*, p. 77.

[20] Quoted from *ibid.*, p. 5.

[21] *Op. cit.*, Vol. 2, p. 412.

[22] *Dusk of Dawn*, p. 277.

[23] *Black Manhattan*, p. 256.

[24] James S. Allen, *The Negro Question in the United States* (1936), especially pp. 177-194.

[25] First edition 1845. In its final form, after many additions through the decades until Douglass' death in 1895, it is called *The Life and Times of Frederick Douglass*.

[26] An example of pseudo-history, fantastically glorifying the achievements of Negroes is: James Morris Webb, *The Black Man the Father of Civilization; Proven by Biblical History* (1910).

[27] The combination of scholarly and protest motives in the work of the Association is seen in its statement of purposes and achievements (taken from the inside cover of *The Journal of Negro History* for January, 1942):

"Its purposes:

1. To collect sociological and historical data.
2. To publish books on Negro life and history.
3. To promote the study of the Negro through clubs and schools.
4. To bring about harmony between the races by interpreting the one to the other. . . .

"Its achievements:

1. It has directed the attention of investigators to this neglected field.
2. It has extended the circulation of *The Journal of Negro History* and *The Negro History Bulletin* into South America, Europe, Asia and Africa.
3. It has published twenty-seven volumes of articles and documents giving facts which are generally unknown.
4. It has produced twenty-nine monographs on Negro Life and History.
5. It has organized and stimulated the studies of local clubs and classes, which have done much to change the attitude of communities toward the Negro.
6. It has collected thousands of valuable manuscripts on the Negro which have been made accessible to the public in the Library of Congress.
7. It has had thirteen young men and women trained for research in social science and for instruction in colleges and universities."

The protest purpose of the Association is more revealed in its annual meetings and in its other activities than in the *Journal*.

[28] Lawrence Reddick, "A New Interpretation for Negro History," *The Journal of Negro History* (January, 1937), p. 17.

[29] The Association is connected with *The Associated Publishers*, a publishing firm also headed by Dr. Woodson. This firm publishes many scholarly and popular books on the Negro—some at the direction of the Association—and has agents to increase their sale in Negro communities all over the country.

[30] This occurs in the week which includes Lincoln's birthday, February 12. It has been going on since 1926 and seems to be growing rapidly in popularity.

[31] E. B. Reuter, *The American Race Problem* (1927), p. 300.

[32] Herskovits, *op. cit.*, p. 32. In reviewing this book, Alain Locke has pointed out that Herskovits' type of propaganda might come to increase race prejudice rather than to decrease it, in that if white people come to believe that Negroes have a strong African heritage they would think that Negroes were unassimilable. (Alain Locke, "Who and What Is a Negro?" *Opportunity* [March, 1942], p. 84.) Frazier further criticizes the practicality of Herskovits' propaganda by asserting that if whites came to believe that the Negro's social behavior was rooted in African culture, they would lose whatever sense of guilt they had for keeping the Negro down. Negro crime, for example, could be explained away as an "Africanism" rather than as due to inadequate police and court protection and to inadequate education. (E. Franklin Frazier, speech to the West Harlem Council of Social Agencies, New York City [December 5, 1941].) There is, perhaps, a measure of truth both in the claims of Herskovits and in those of his critics, but both make certain assumptions about the causes of race prejudice which are not only unproved but are not stated explicitly.

[33] "In the South the prestige of the Negro group suffers from persistently unfavorable judgments on the part of the white community; of equal significance is the fact that Negro youth do not as a rule take pride in the qualities for which Negroes are most appreciated by the whites. Only a few of them, for example, recognize loyalty, uncomplaining industry, and patience as having racial prestige value comparable to the importance given these traits by the white group when they wish to speak favorably of Negroes. It is a convenience in the biracial situation to be regarded as loyal, tractable, happy and hard working; few of the interviews with these youth revealed, however, that they were proud of these racial virtues. Indeed, few of the comments assumed these virtues to be racial, or the qualities to be virtues." (Charles S. Johnson, *Growing Up in the Black Belt*, p. 242.)

Chapter 36. *The Protest Motive and Negro Personality*

[1] James Weldon Johnson, *Negro Americans, What Now?* (1934), p. 103. This formula has many variations. Booker T. Washington retells from a conversation he once had with Frederick Douglass:

"At one time Mr. Douglass was traveling in the State of Pennsylvania, and was forced, on account of his colour, to ride in the baggage-car, in spite of the fact that he had paid the same price for his passage that the other passengers had paid. When some of the white passengers went into the baggage-car to console Mr. Douglass, and one of them said to him: 'I am sorry, Mr. Douglass, that you have been degraded in this manner,' Mr. Douglass straightened himself up on the box upon which he was sitting, and replied: 'They cannot degrade Frederick Douglass. The soul that is within me no man can degrade. I am not the one that is being degraded on account of this treatment, but those who are inflicting it upon me.'" (Booker T. Washington, *Up from Slavery* [1901; first edition, 1900], pp. 99-100.)

[2] Booker T. Washington, *The Future of the American Negro* (1902; first edition, 1899), p. 26.

³ Our discussion of Negro sensitiveness does not assume that light-colored Negroes, because of their color, are any more sensitive or emotionally unbalanced on the average than dark Negroes. (See Chapter 32, Section 3, for a criticism of this theory.) It may be, however, that upper class Negroes are more sensitive because of their status and education, and since upper class Negroes tend to be of lighter color, there is an apparent—but no directly causal—connection between color and sensitiveness.

⁴ Charles S. Johnson, *Growing Up in the Black Belt* (1941), p. 312.

⁵ *Following the Color Line* (1908), p. 27.

⁶ E. Franklin Frazier, *Negro Youth at the Crossways* (1940), pp. 44-51.

⁷ *Ibid.*, pp. 50-51.

⁸ *Ibid.*, p. 56. "Coat-tail" is the Negro word for flatter, and a "peckerwood" is a lower class white man.

⁹ Allison Davis and John Dollard, *Children of Bondage* (1940), pp. 87-88.

¹⁰ "Conceptions and Ideologies of the Negro Problem," unpublished manuscript prepared for this study (1940), p. 161.

¹¹ See John Dollard, *Caste and Class in a Southern Town* (1937), pp. 250 and 286 ff.

¹² Dollard, *op. cit.*, pp. 267 ff.

¹³ ". . . since the hostility of Negroes against whites is violently and effectively suppressed, we have a boiling of aggressive effect within the Negro group." (Dollard, *op. cit.*, p. 269.) Dollard goes even further and suggests a purpose on the side of the whites: "One cannot help wondering if it does not serve the ends of the white caste to have a high level of violence in the Negro group, since disunity in the Negro caste tends to make it less resistant to the white domination. If this should be a correct observation, it need not follow that the tolerance of violence is a matter of conscious policy on the part of the white group; instead it would seem to be pragmatic, unformalized, and intuitive, but nonetheless effective." (*Ibid.*, p. 280; compare p. 285.)

¹⁴ This phenomenon is often commented upon in the Negro world:

"It is common for educated and upper class Negroes to develop an aloofness, a social exclusiveness and snobbishness, which is at times even more sharp than in the white society, because the Negro finds in it both a means of defense against inferiority feeling and a form of escape. Negroes who hold good jobs, as for instance, teachers, are notoriously passive and comformist. Their jobs give them economic and social status which they are determined to hold even at the expense of surrendering their intellectual independence. The Negro radicals, few as they are, have rarely been recruited from among Negroes holding good jobs." (Bunche, *op. cit.*, p. 174.)

¹⁵ Just as lower class Negroes manifest their frustrated antagonism against whites by showing antagonism against upper class Negroes, so upper class Negroes do the same against lower class Negroes. They sometimes even go so far as to blame the whole caste system on the low standards of behavior of lower class Negroes. Charles S. Johnson quotes an illustrative statement by a senior postal clerk in Indianapolis:

"We have a very low class of Negroes in Indianapolis. That is one reason why it is difficult for us to insist on all of our rights. We can't go to the white people and ask that certain Negroes be admitted to places and others refused. I can't blame white people, though, for drawing a line." (*Patterns of Negro Segregation*, prepared for this study [1943], p. 283.)

¹⁶ "It is interesting to notice here that the chief device employed by upper-class

colored speakers for dissolving the antagonism of a lower-class audience was to emphasize the *solidarity of the caste*, to invoke the ideals, that is, of 'race pride' and 'race loyalty.' " (Allison Davis, Burleigh B. Gardner, and Mary R. Gardner, *Deep South* [1941], p. 236.)

Chapter 37. *Compromise Leadership*

[1] "In many respects the Negro is a model prisoner—the best in this country. He accepts the situation—generally speaking—bears no malice, cherishes no ill will or resentment, and is cheerful under conditions to which the white man refuses to reconcile himself.

"This adaptability of the Negro has an immediate bearing on the question before us. It explains why the Negro masses in the Southern states are content with their situation, or at least not disturbing themselves sufficiently over it to attempt to upset the existing order. In the main, the millions in the South live at peace with their white neighbours." (Alfred Holt Stone, *Studies in the American Race Problem* [1908], p. 235.)

[2] For another statement in the same direction, see Booker T. Washington, *The Story of the Negro* (1909), Vol. 1, pp. 190-191.

[3] Thus Joe Louis enables many lower class youths (in fact, many Negro youths and adults in all classes) to inflict vicariously the aggressions which they would like to carry out against whites for the discriminations and insults which they have suffered. A 19-year-old Washington youth, a high school graduate, said:

" 'I've tried to follow in Louis' footsteps, but I'm not big enough. I've heard all of his fights and seen him several times here in Washington. I've thrilled at every damned "peck" he knocked over and helped raise hell in the U street celebrations after each one. When he lost, I felt pretty bad, though I'll ever feel something was wrong— crooked. He sure proved something was wrong the way he beat up Schmeling the second time!' " (E. Franklin Frazier, *Negro Youth at the Crossways* [1940], p. 179.)

"Likewise, a ten year old son of a laborer would rather be Joe Louis than any other Negro in the country because he 'would get a lot of fun going in the ring and beating up somebody.' He added, 'Joe Louis has done a lot to make the colored race recognized.' " (*Ibid.*, p. 180.)

An upper class lad—a 17-year-old and college freshman—spoke of Joe Louis' fight with Schmeling as follows:

" 'I was hitting every blow with him and taking with him those he got. And when he lost, I really felt sick. Somehow I didn't even want to go on the street the next day. One thing he's done, he's certainly made the so-called white fighters have a wholesome respect for his fists. I suppose symbolically that's the only way white people can be made to respect Negroes in other walks of life.' " (*Ibid.*, p. 190.)

Charles S. Johnson observes:

"In a few areas of the South, the disposition of Negro youth to celebrate too jubilantly the fistic triumphs of Joe Louis has been brusquely and sometimes violently discouraged, indicating that the symbolism was as significant for the white as for Negro youth." (*Growing Up in the Black Belt* [1941], p. 246.)

⁴ Arthur Raper, "Race and Class Pressures," unpublished manuscript prepared for this study (1940), pp. 54-55.

⁵ Ralph Bunche also observes that "It is common for Negroes to have one set of ideas which they express before Negroes and a totally different set for use when in the presence of whites," and tells the following story:

"I once heard a Negro black-face comedian on the stage of the Howard Theatre in Washington enact this phenomenon most humorously. He was mimicking a 'big Negro leader' in an address to a Negro audience. After citing the grievances of the Negro people, the speaker, first looking about very cautiously to make sure there were no white eaves-droppers present, proclaimed (loudly at first, stentorian in the middle, and then dwindling to a bare stage whisper at his climax): 'What we cullud folks has to do is to RISE UP AND STRIKE DOWN these, hyah, *damned* white folks!' (last two words written in very small type.)" ("Memorandum on the Conceptions and Ideologies of the Negro Problem," unpublished manuscript prepared for this study [1940], p. 97.)

⁶ Ralph J. Bunche, "A Brief and Tentative Analysis of Negro Leadership," unpublished manuscript prepared for this study (1940), pp. 34-35.

⁷ Quoted in *ibid.*, p. 81.

⁸ *Idem.*

⁹ Quoted in *ibid.*, p. 82.

¹⁰ "The stories of the demeanor of Negro college presidents and the administrators of other Negro institutions, when they appear before white legislators, governors, educational officials of the state and philanthropic foundations, are legion, and these would be extremely revealing sources of information on how the Negro leader can 'go into an act' when he wants something from responsible white men. . . . Just recently a prominent Negro Republican politician demonstrated to the Committee how Negroes can 'strut' as a means of winning their favor—and he got it. The strategic personal adjustment to the attitudes of the dominant group made by the individual Negro leaders afford a wide vista and a very challenging subject for research." (*Ibid.*, p. 35.)

¹¹ Quoted in *ibid.*, p. 125.

¹² *Ibid.*, p. 126.

¹³ *Ibid.*, p. 11. See also Chapter 22, Section 5, of this book.

¹⁴ "As an example, note the frantic scramble for the Negro bishoprics and the leadership contests within the lodges." (Bunche, "A Brief and Tentative Analysis of Negro Leadership," p. 10.)

¹⁵ *Negro Americans, What Now?* (1934), pp. 85-86.

¹⁶ Bunche, "A Brief and Tentative Analysis of Negro Leadership," p. 10 (italics ours). See also, Chapter 36, Section 5, of this book.

¹⁷ *Ibid.*, p. 32.

Chapter 38. *Negro Popular Theories*

¹ W. E. B. Du Bois, *Black Reconstruction* (1935), p. 703.

² Ralph J. Bunche, "Memorandum on Conceptions and Ideologies of the Negro Problem," unpublished manuscript prepared for this study (1940), p. 23.

³ W. E. B. Du Bois, *The Souls of Black Folk* (1903), p. 202.

⁴ "Programs, Ideologies, Tactics, and Achievements of Negro Betterment and Inter-

racial Organizations," unpublished manuscript prepared for this study (1940), Vol. 1, p. 13.

[5] Bunche, "Conceptions and Ideologies of the Negro Problem," p. 98.

[6] Booker T. Washington, *The Future of the American Negro* (1899), pp. 86-87.

[7] *Ibid.*, pp. 85, 93, 176, 177 *passim*.

[8] There were some Negro leaders (Isaac Myers, Josiah Weirs, Peter H. Clark, John M. Langston, Sella Martin) even during the Reconstruction period who advocated labor solidarity and trade unionism as a vital concern for the Negro people. Du Bois says: "The Negroes, especially the Northern artisans, tried to keep in touch with the white labor movement." (Du Bois, *Black Reconstruction*, p. 360.) The Negro unions sent delegates to the National Labor Union Convention in New York in 1869, and Isaac Myers, their leader, appealed for solidarity between the white and Negro laborers. The white labor movement responded rather coolly and in December of 1869 the Negroes held their own convention (The National Negro Labor Convention) in Washington at which 159 delegates were present. (*Ibid.*, p. 362.)

There was even some interest in the international labor movement. In 1870 Sella Martin was sent as a delegate of the colored workers to the World Labor Congress in Paris, but international labor was as uninterested in Negro labor as was the American movement, and interest in international labor soon died among American Negro labor unionists. (*Ibid.*, pp. 360-361.) For a complete account of the Negro labor movement during Reconstruction, see *ibid.*, pp. 354-367; see also, Guion G. Johnson, "History of Racial Ideologies in the United States with Reference to the Negro," unpublished manuscript prepared for this study (1940), Vol. 2, pp. 239-244, especially p. 239.

[9] Harris, in discussing the young intellectuals, says: "To have confined their propaganda to the Negro bourgeoisie would have caused the Negro radicals to compromise with the theories to which they were committed. Their acceptance of the theory of the class struggle and their application of it to the race question caused them to champion labor solidarity between white and black workers." (Sterling D. Spero and Abram L. Harris, *The Black Worker* [1931], p. 391.)

[10] "Conceptions and Ideologies of the Negro Problem," pp. 131-133.

[11] *Ibid.*, p. 130.

[12] "Programs, Ideologies, Tactics and Achievements of Negro Betterment and Interracial Organizations," Vol. 1, pp. 147-148.

[13] In passing it should be observed that the academic radicalism of Negro intellectuals, exemplified by the citation from Bunche, can easily come to good terms with the type of liberal but skeptical *laissez-faire* (do nothing) opinion so prevalent among white social scientists writing on the Negro problem. Both groups are critical of the fight for suffrage and civil rights. (See Chapter 39, Section 9.) Both assume that the economic factor is basic. And—since neither party is very active in trying either to induce or to prevent an economic revolution—it does not make much difference if the Negro radicals look forward to an economic revolution and the white sociologists do not. (See Appendix 2.)

[14] Gunnar Myrdal, *Population: A Problem for Democracy* (1940), pp. 87-88.

[15] "Programs, Ideologies, Tactics and Achievements of Negro Betterment and Interracial Organizations," Vol. 4, p. 778.

[16] *Negro Americans, What Now?* (1934), pp. 66-67.

[17] W. E. B. Du Bois, *Dusk of Dawn* (1940), p. 309.

[18] Emmett J. Scott and Lyman Beecher Stowe, *Booker T. Washington* (1916), p. 40.

[19] Du Bois, *Dusk of Dawn*, pp. 309-310.

[20] *Ibid.*, p. 306.

[21] *Ibid.*, p. 215.

[22] James Weldon Johnson, *op. cit.*, p. 15.

[23] Examples are: E. B. Reuter, in the last chapter of *The Mulatto in the United States* (1918), and Donald R. Young, *American Minority Peoples* (1932), pp. 578-593 *passim*.

[24] Quoted in Scott and Stowe, *op. cit.*, p. 189.

[25] Cited in Bunche, "Conceptions and Ideologies of the Negro Problem," p. 121.

[26] *The Negro in the New World* (1910), pp. xi-xii.

[27] Robert R. Moton, *What the Negro Thinks* (1929), p. 38.

[28] "Conceptions and Ideologies of the Negro Problem," pp. 113-114.

[29] *Dusk of Dawn*, pp. 173-220 *passim*.

[30] *Ibid.*, p. 321.

[31] *Ibid.*, p. 208.

[32] James Weldon Johnson, *op. cit.*, p. 71.

[33] *Ibid.*, pp. 77-78.

[34] "Conceptions and Ideologies of the Negro Problem," pp. 122-124.

[35] *Ibid.*, p. 55.

[36] Ernest Sutherland Bates, *American Faith* (1940), p. 438.

[37] Samuel A. Stouffer and Lyonel C. Florant, "Negro Population and Negro Population Movements, 1860 to 1940, in Relation to Social and Economic Factors," unpublished manuscript prepared for this study (1940), pp. 44-50 (revised by Lyonel C. Florant under the title, "Negro Migration—1860-1940" [1942]). See also, Bunche, "Conceptions and Ideologies of the Negro Problem," pp. 51-55.

[38] Du Bois observes that "there is no likelihood just now of [the Negroes] being forcibly expelled" but continues:

"So far as that is concerned, there was no likelihood ten years ago of the Jews being expelled from Germany. The cases are far from parallel. There is a good deal more profit in cheap Negro labor than in Jewish fellow citizens, which brings together strange bed-fellows for the protection of the Negro. On the other hand one must remember that this is a day of astonishing change, injustice and cruelty; and that many Americans of stature have favored the transportation of Negroes and they were not all of the mental caliber of the present junior senator from Mississippi. As the Negro develops from an easily exploitable, profit-furnishing laborer to an intelligent independent self-supporting citizen, the possibility of his being pushed out of his American fatherland may easily be increased rather than diminished. We may be expelled from the United States as the Jew is being expelled from Germany." (*Dusk of Dawn*, p. 306.)

Unlike Du Bois, I am inclined to believe that it is less the economic rise of American Negroes to economic independence and more their submergence into unemployment and public relief which will spell the danger. If I am right, the security for the American Negro will be, first, an economic policy which will avert more unemployment, and second, a continued fortification of the American Creed.

[39] Malcolm Hailey, *An African Survey* (1938).

[40] *Dusk of Dawn*, p. 199.

[41] Ralph J. Bunche, "A Brief and Tentative Analysis of Negro Leadership," unpublished manuscript prepared for this study (1940), p. 29.

[42] Bunche, "Conceptions and Ideologies of the Negro Problem," pp. 140-141.

[43] James Weldon Johnson, *op. cit.*, p. 13.

[44] Trevor Bowen, *Divine White Right* (1934), pp. vi-vii.

[45] Bertram Schrieke, *Alien Americans* (1936), p. 151.

[46] Du Bois, *The Souls of Black Folk*, p. 2.

Chapter 39. *Negro Improvement and Protest Organizations*

[1] Reform groups have occasionally become political parties in the United States. In a sense the Republican party began as a rather radical reform group. All but one or two of the small "third parties" in the history of the United States have been radical, and many of them had a nucleus in a reform group. The reforms sought have been specific —as in the case of the Prohibition party—or general—as in the case of the Socialist party. The third parties have been both short- and long-lived. Their death has not always meant failure to attain the reforms sought: in some cases one or the other of the major parties has incorporated some of the third party's aims into its own program and has succeeded in bringing it into law.

[2] Ralph Bunche, "The Programs, Ideologies, Tactics and Achievements of Negro Betterment and Interracial Organizations," unpublished manuscript prepared for this study (1940), Vol. 2, pp. 419-423.

[3] *Ibid.*, Vol. 2, p. 423.

[4] *Ibid.*, Vol. 3, pp. 425 ff.

[5] *Ibid.*, Vol. 3, pp. 427-428.

[6] *Ibid.*, Vol. 3, pp. 428 ff.

[7] *Ibid.*, Vol. 3, p. 434.

[8] "49th State," *Compass* (March, 1936), p. 17. Cited in Bunche, *op. cit.*, Vol. 3, p. 439.

[9] The highest proportion of Negroes, of all Negroes interviewed, who have admitted pro-Japanese inclinations, in a confidential poll conducted by Negro interviewers, is 18 per cent. But in a similar poll of Southern white industrialists, asked to choose between complete Negro equality and German victory, they chose the latter by a heavy majority.

[10] Bunche, *op. cit.*, Vol. 2, p. 301.

[11] *Ibid.*, Vol. 2, p. 307.

[12] Affiliated is *The Housewife's League*, working for the promotion of race business. According to a pamphlet published by The Housewife's League: "A belief in the future of Negro Business and a desire to assist in every way by patronizing and encouraging the same, is all that is necessary to become a member." (*Ibid.*, Vol. 2, p. 305.)

[13] Bunche, *op. cit.*, Vol. 2, p. 314.

[14] Du Bois, *Dusk of Dawn* (1940), p. 280.

[15] *Ibid.*, p. 281.

[16] See Bunche, *op. cit.*, Vol. 2, pp. 380 ff., for a critical account of the latter organization.

[17] *Ibid.*, Vol. 2, p. 306; Vol. 4, pp. 672 ff.

[18] *Ibid.*, Vol. 4, pp. 668 ff.

[19] *Ibid.*, Vol. 2, pp. 319 ff.

[20] *Ibid.*, Vol. 2, pp. 323 ff.

[21] *Ibid.*, Vol. 2, pp. 355 ff.

[22] The Congress had gotten into debt to the Communist party. Davis, who as secretary had carried the chief responsibility for its work, had apparently become skeptical about the possibility of carrying on the Congress according to the original plans. (See Bunche, *op. cit.*, Vol. 2, pp. 369-371. See also Lester B. Granger, "The Negro Congress—Its Future," *Opportunity* [June, 1940], pp. 164-166.)

The third Congress was much affected by the international situation. This was the time of the Hitler-Stalin pact, which opened the Second World War, and the American Communists agitated violently against American participation in the "imperialist" war, against Roosevelt's aggressive policy toward Germany, his rearmament program for America, and the aid to Great Britain. The Communists staged the Congress excellently for their purposes. According to Bunche:

"The Negro rank and file did not know what it was all about except when perfervid speeches were made demanding anti-lynching legislation, the franchise, and full democracy for the Negro. The more subtle aspects of the line that was being followed were over the heads of most of the rank and file, but the Congress was well organized and the speeches were all of a pattern." (*Op. cit.*, Vol. 2, p. 360.)

John L. Lewis, though not a Communist himself, gave the tone of the meeting in his keynote speech. He came out violently against the President's foreign policy and wanted the Congress to join forces with Labor's Non-Partisan League. President A. Philip Randolph spoke after Lewis and gave a carefully prepared address, later printed under the title *The World Crisis and the Negro People Today*. He pointed out that the Soviet Union was a totalitarian country pursuing power politics, and that the Communist party depended on Russian orders. He warned the Congress to stick to its principle and remain nonpartisan. Only if the Congress abstained from any political alignment and retained a minimum program of action was there hope that it could establish an effective national Negro pressure group on the basis of all Negro organizations.

"The procedure, conduct and policies of the Negro Congress, as set up in this third national meeting, will make its influence in the affairs of the American Negroes, short lived. The American Negroes will not long follow any organization which accepts dictation and control from the Communist Party. The American Negro will not long follow any organization which accepts dictation and control from any white organization." (*The World Crisis and the Negro People Today* [1940], p. 25.)

During Randolph's speech the Communists arranged a demonstration and walked out, leaving only a third of the audience when he finished talking. Thereafter nearly all speeches followed the "party line," and the Negro protest was skillfully draped in Communist slogans.

[23] Bunche, *op. cit.*, Vol. 2, pp. 372 ff.

[24] *The Southern Frontier* (June, 1942).

[25] Like the National Negro Congress, with which it has strong relations, it has partly been under Communist influences.

[26] Bunche, *op. cit.*, Vol. 2, pp. 378-379.

[27] Cited in *ibid.*, Vol. 1, p. 27.

[28] James Weldon Johnson, *Black Manhattan* (1930), pp. 140 ff.

[29] *Op. cit.*, Vol. 1, p. 29.

[30] *The Acid Test of Democracy*, Leaflet (1940); cited in *ibid.*, p. 44.

[31] In the following states and regions the branches have formed conferences which hold periodic state or regional conventions: Virginia, Oklahoma, Pennsylvania, New Jersey, South Carolina, Ohio, Illinois, Iowa, Maryland, Michigan, New York, Texas; and Southern, Northwest and New England regions. (Information from Roy Wilkins, memorandum [August 11, 1942].)

[32] A branch is ". . . a constituent and subordinate unit of the Association, subject to the general authority and jurisdiction of the Board of Directors of the Association. Its objects shall be to promote the economic, political, civic and social betterment of colored people and their harmonious cooperation with other peoples." (Quoted in Bunche, *op. cit.*, Vol. 1, p. 36.)

[33] Information from Roy Wilkins, memorandum (August 11, 1942).

[34] The local Youth Councils are an intrinsic part of the structure of the Association. "This is an attempt by the Association to canalize . . . the current tendencies of restless youth to organize and to attract young Negroes to the organization. . . . The Youth Councils devote themselves to the broad program of the Association, with special attention to the problems of youth and employ similar tactics." (Bunche, *op. cit.*, Vol. 1, p. 42.)

[35] Information from Roy Wilkins, memorandum (August 11, 1942).

Concerning the last point, Wilkins comments: "Offhand, I do not believe we receive contributions from more than five foundations, and the largest gift from any of them is less than 1/80 of our total budget."

[36] *The Negro College Graduate* (1938), p. 349.

[37] Greene found that only 10 out of 367 Negro "leaders" were not college or professional school graduates. His complete figures are as follows:

Academic Preparation of Negro Leaders as Determined by the Number of Degrees they Received "In Course"

Degree	Number
Bachelor's	127
Master's	104
Doctoral	33
Professional	87
No degree indicated	10
No report	6

(Harry W. Greene, *Negro Leaders* [1936], p. 12.)

Some of the persons in Greene's sample were selected because they were outstanding in academic fields. Still, the high educational level of nearly everyone on Greene's list is nothing less than phenomenal and is probably not paralleled among white leaders.

[38] The Detroit branch has secured 12,000 new members in a recent membership campaign and other branches have doubled, and in some cases, trebled their membership. (Letter from Walter White [July 29, 1942].) A great proportion of the members in some branches as in Norfolk, Virginia, and Mobile, Alabama, are workers. (Roy Wilkins in memorandum [August 11, 1942].)

[39] One of the officers of the National Office is Branch Director, one is Field Secretary, one Branch Coordinator, and one, Youth Director. The National Secretary and the other national officers frequently visit the branches.

⁴⁰ Bunche, *op. cit.*, Vol. 1, pp. 45-47.

⁴¹ *Program Book for N.A.A.C.P. Branches* (1939), p. 1. Quoted in *ibid.*, p. 45. A main tactic, for the branches as well as for the National Office, is legal redress. The great majority of the cases handled by the Association originate in the branches. The branches are advised to carry the financial and legal responsibility for local cases themselves as far as possible. When they cannot be so handled, the branches appeal to the National Office and its Legal Committee for assistance. If the National Office enters a case, it works in collaboration with the branches. (See *ibid.*, p. 38.) It is held that neither the National Office nor the branches should function, or could function, as a legal aid society:

"It [the Association] only handles cases where it seems great injustice has been or is about to be done because of race or color prejudice, or cases where its entry will clearly establish a precedent affecting the rights of colored people in general." (E. Frederic Morrow, *An Outline of Branch Functions*; cited in *ibid.*, p. 39.)

Thus, even if the individual sufferings cannot be disregarded as a motive for action, the main consideration must be its importance as a test case. Bunch summarizes:

"In the selection of the issues on which fights are to be waged, the branches are told to select 'live issues,' in which discriminations are glaring, 'where the correction of the injustices will benefit a large number of Negroes,' and where there is a chance to win. Publicizing the fight is regarded as an important element in the struggle, and the branches are advised never to 'start on a big campaign without telling the folks that count . . . what it is the branch is about to do,' and enlisting their support. The aid of the other organizations, such as interracial, civic, religious, and labor union groups, is also to be solicited in the campaigns, in efforts to bring maximum pressure to bear on officials, and to mold a favorable public opinion." (*Ibid.*, pp. 49-59.)

Publicity should be a vital part of the work of the branches, they are told. They are advised to build up a "contact list" of prominent people of both races, "who could assist in sending telegrams and letters of protest to officials when impending legislation is detrimental to the best interest of the group, or letters and telegrams urging enactment of impending legislation that will protect or enhance the best interests of colored people." (E. Frederic Morrow, *An Outline of Branch Functions*, p. 1; cited in *ibid.*, pp. 49-50.)

⁴² The Association has been unable, for financial reasons, to carry out its old plan to employ regional secretaries to supervise and stimulate the activity of the branches. (Information from Roy Wilkins in memorandum [March 12, 1941].)

⁴³ An account of the observations made of N.A.A.C.P. branches by interviewers for this study is given in Bunche, *op. cit.*, Vol. 1, pp. 108 ff. See also White's and Wilkins' critiques. The present writer himself visited, in the years 1938-1940, a great many N.A.A.C.P. branches in all parts of the country.

⁴⁴ Bunche, *op. cit.*, Vol. 1, p. 117.

⁴⁵ *Ibid.*, Vol. 1, p. 118.

⁴⁶ *Ibid.*, Vol. 1, pp. 128-129.

⁴⁷ For a survey of the independent local organizations, see *ibid.*, Vol. 4, pp. 587-667.

⁴⁸ *Ibid.*, Vol. 1, pp. 116-117; compare *ibid.*, Vol. 4, pp. 598 ff.

⁴⁹ Interview (November, 1939); quoted in *ibid.*, Vol. 1, p. 130.

⁵⁰ *N.A.A.C.P. Press Service*, Series No. 22; cited in *ibid.*, Vol. 1, p. 40. (See also *ibid.*, Vol. 1, p. 100.)

[51] *Ibid.*, Vol. 1, pp. 100 ff.

[52] *Ibid.*, Vol. 1, p. 105.

[53] *Program Book for N.A.A.C.P. Branches*, p. 6; cited in *ibid.*, Vol. 1, p. 50.

[54] For a summary of N.A.A.C.P.'s achievements in the legal field, see *ibid.*, Vol. 1, pp. 55 ff.; and the critical memoranda by Walter White and Roy Wilkins.

[55] See Bunche, *op. cit.*, Vol. 1, pp. 69 ff.

[56] *Ibid.*, Vol. 1, pp. 63 ff.

[57] *Ibid.*, Vol. 1, pp. 78 ff.

[58] *Ibid.*, Vol. 1, pp. 98 ff.

[59] See *ibid.*, Vol. 1, pp. 79 ff.

[60] See *ibid.*, Vol. 1, pp. 83 ff.

[61] *Ibid.*, Vol. 1, pp. 83-100.

[62] ". . . instead of waiting until cases arose out of fundamental legal and cultural patterns which were viciously anti-Negro, we began as far as our means would permit to attack the fundamental evils." (Letter from Walter White [March 15, 1941].)

This change is usually not seen or understood by the few social scientists, Negro or white, who have given some attention to the Association. Guy B. Johnson, for example, writes:

"While the organization has carried on a great deal of educational work along the line of stimulating race consciousness and race pride and has taken the offensive in a few legislative ventures, it has for the most part found itself carrying on a defensive legalistic program. That is, it has largely been concerned with specific cases involving disfranchisement, segregation, discriminatory legislation, injustice in the courts, lynching, peonage, etc." ("Negro Racial Movements and Leadership in the United States," in the *American Journal of Sociology* [July, 1937], p. 66.)

[63] E. Frederic Morrow, *An Outline of Branch Functions*, p. 1; cited by Bunche, *op. cit.*, Vol. 1, p. 46.

[64] *Program Book for N.A.A.C.P. Branches*, p. 6; cited in *ibid.*, Vol. 1, p. 50.

[65] Bunche, *op. cit.*, Vol. 1, p. 51.

[66] ". . . the possible influence of reform organizations as well as of individual reformers in the field of race relations is definitely limited to the correction of particular instances of injustice—especially those which are so outrageous as to exceed the limits of popular prejudiced approval—and to campaigns of public enlightenment concerning the basic community of interests among all people in the United States.

"This is our reason for omitting discussion of the hundreds of organizations and movements for the improvement of race relations and the securing of justice for minorities in our country. What have such organizations as the National Urban League, the National Association for the Advancement of Colored People, the Association for the Study of Negro Life and History, the Commission on Interracial Cooperation accomplished to justify their existence? The answer is: Much in the way of fighting particular instances of atrocious injustice, a little in the way of the dissemination of interracial facts, and nothing so far as any general change in racial attitudes is concerned. Shortly after the World War, lynchings of Negroes declined rapidly, and a good share of the credit for this decline was claimed by the Commission on Interracial Cooperation. Seven Negroes were reported to have been lynched in 1929, counting only those who were killed by mobs and not those who were otherwise mistreated, and twenty in 1930. If the Commission was responsible for declines in lynchings, is its negligence also responsible for this increase? Actually, of course, lynchings fluctuate in practical independence of the efforts of such organizations, which have no means of attacking the fundamental causes of lynching. All praise should go to the efforts of the interracial pioneers who are sacrificing much for their ideals and who have fought valiantly for the adjustment of interracial relations. Nothing, however, is to be gained by carrying our confidence in them to the extent of believing that they may do more than battle the symptoms of race prejudice, as a fever may be reduced by the application of ice, affording some relief to the patient but not curing the disease." (Donald Young, *American Minority Peoples* [1932], pp. 589-590; compare *ibid., passim.*)

Young's proof against the claims of the Commission on Interracial Cooperation of a good share in the credit for the decline in lynching is not entirely convincing. No one denies that other factors than the fight of the organizations have influence on the yearly *fluctuations*—and even the trend—of lynchings. But this does not exclude the fact that the organizations also have an influence, primarily on the *trend*, but also on the fluctuations. (See footnote [a] on p. 423.)

[67] "Now, while this legalistic approach has been successful in the sense that it has sometimes served as a goal to the South and that it has won numerous important legal cases—some of the United States Supreme Court decisions involving new precedents—it is doubtful whether it has brought the Negro any nearer his goal. The N.A.A.C.P. has been, from the standpoint of the southern white man, in the same class with abolitionists and carpetbaggers, an outside agency which has tried to impose its ideas upon him. Sociologically the weakness of the movement is inevitable and incurable; it attempts to undo the folkways and mores of the southern caste system by attacking the results and symptoms of the system. Paradoxically, if it leaves the attitudes and folkways of the white man out of its picture, it is doomed to fail; and if it takes those attitudes and folkways into account, it is either forced back to the gradualistic and conciliatory position of Booker Washington or forced forward into revolutionary tactics. One wonders then, whether its chief function, *aside from its value in actually obtaining racial rights* [n.b.], has not been to serve as a catharsis for those discontented, impatient souls who, while they see no hope of normal participation in American life, feel that they must never give in and admit that they are beaten down spiritually." (Guy B. Johnson, "Negro Racial Movements and Leadership in the United States," *op. cit.*; p. 67 [italics ours].) The obtaining of "racial rights" is, of course, the main purpose of the N.A.A.C.P.

[68] ". . . it can scarcely be claimed that these victories [won by resort to court] have materially altered any of the fundamental conditions determining the relations between the races in the country." (Bunche, *op. cit.*, Vol. 1, p. 141; compare *ibid.*, Vol. 1, pp. 143-144; see also Chapter 38, Section 5, of this book.)

[69] *Negro Americans, What Now?* (1934), p. 39.

[70] *Ibid.*, p. 38.

[71] Bertram W. Doyle, *The Etiquette of Race Relations in the South* (1937), p. 162.

[72] "The interracial make-up of the N.A.A.C.P. is also an undoubted source of organizational weakness. There can be no doubt that the Negro leaders in the organization have always kept a weather eye on the reactions of their prominent and influential white sponsors to any innovation in the program of the organization. These white sympathizers are, in the main, either cautious liberals or mawkish, missionary-minded sentimentalists on the race question. Their interest in the Negro problem is

motivated either by a sense of 'fair play' and a desire to see the ideals of the Constitution lived up to, or an 'I love your people' attitude. Both attitudes are far from touching the realities of the problem. But the evident concern for the opinions of the white supporters of the organization, especially on the part of the National Office, has been a powerful factor in keeping the Association thoroughly 'respectable' and has certainly been an influence in the very evident desire of the Association to keep its skirts free of the grimy bitterness and strife encountered in the economic arena. This has also been a responsibility of the Negro members of the Board, who, by and large, have never been distinguished for the advanced nature of their social thinking. At best they have been cautious, racially minded liberals, and not infrequently, forthright reactionaries. In general they have suffered from an intellectual myopia toward all but narrowly racial problems. The liberal, white or black, northern or southern, recoils from the shock of class conflict. Yet the twitchings of liberalism within him seek release; lacking the courage and conviction to face the harsher realities, he seeks to find release and solace in counterfeit substitutes, in political and social *ersatz*. He recognizes and revolts against injustices, but seeks to correct them with palliatives rather than solutions; for the solutions are harsh and forbidding, and are not conducive to optimism and spiritual uplift.

"The N.A.A.C.P. is an interracial organization, and, though to lesser degree than the less militant interracial groups, still leans heavily upon interracial good-will and understanding. Such reliance is a basic weakness in any organization designed to work on behalf of an economically and politically oppressed group, and where 'good-will' and inter-group 'understanding' are only will-o'-the-wisps which confuse the problem and mislead thinking on it." (Bunche, *op. cit.*, Vol. 1, pp. 147-148.)

[73] "It has not been able to become a solid political factor . . . through taking a strong hand for or against a particular party, because of the conflicting political interests of its membership. Thus, its politics is 'Negro' politics; its political interests are measured solely in terms of the attitude of a candidate or a party toward measures directly concerned with Negro welfare." (Bunche, *op. cit.*, Vol. 1, p. 54.)

[74] Winning a greater membership is also important in order to give the Association a solid financial basis. On the other hand, a main impediment to the organization in attempting to recruit a larger membership is its lack of financial resources.

It is, of course, a vital necessity to the Association to keep independent as far as possible from outside support in order to maintain freedom of action. It is a public secret that one of the foundations working in the Negro field, that had earlier contributed to the Association, has tried to convince the N.A.A.C.P. that it should merge, first with the Urban League and, at a later occasion, with both the Urban League and the Commission on Interracial Cooperation. The N.A.A.C.P. refused as it was not greatly dependent on support from foundations and Community Chests and felt that a merger would hamstring the program of the Association and infringe upon its freedom to challenge the interracial *status quo*. As a result, it lost its earlier support from the foundation.

[75] See Bunche, *op. cit.*, Vol. 2, pp. 218 ff.; and Paul E. Baker, *Negro-White Adjustment* (1934), pp. 21 ff.

[76] Information from Lester B. Granger (letter, August 7, 1942). Some of the contributions have the form of membership dues.

[77] Bunche, op. cit., Vol. 2, p. 265.

[78] *Idem.* "It tries to make the most out of the condition of racial separatism and

appeals to the conscience and good will of the white community, especially the employing class. That the Urban League has rendered valuable services for Urban League populations throughout the country is not disputed, but it is equally true that its policy operates within the genteel framework of conciliation and interracial good will. Its efforts have had to be directed at winning the sympathies of white employers, professionals, and intellectual groups, and the top ranks of the hierarchy of organized labor. With its interracial basis, it must rely upon the good will of responsible whites." (*Ibid.*, Vol. 2, pp. 265-266.)

"As an interracial, dependent organization it can never develop a program which will spur the Negro masses and win their confidence. It has not exerted, nor can it, any great influence upon the thinking of Negroes nor upon their course of action. It operates strictly on the periphery of the Negro problem and never comes to grips with the fundamentals in American racial conflict." (*Ibid.*, Vol. 2, pp. 271-272.)

[79] Letter from Eugene Kinckle Jones (August 8, 1940).

[80] Memorandum by Eugene Kinckle Jones (June 17, 1941).

[81] Annual Conference of the Urban League in 1919, held in Detroit, Michigan.

[82] Spero and Harris quote several cases of strike-breaking. (Sterling D. Spero and Abram L. Harris, *The Black Worker* [1931], pp. 140-141.) See also, Bunche, *op. cit.*, Vol. 2, pp. 268-269.

Eugene Kinckle Jones states: "No local League has ever openly engaged in strike-breaking activities. The only case in our records . . . was . . . on a job where we had furnished Negro workers on a project where the racial element was involved and not the question of wages and hours." (Memorandum, June 17, 1941.)

For a complete evaluation of this question, see Horace R. Cayton and George S. Mitchell, *Black Workers and the New Unions* (1939), pp. 398-412.

[83] Bunche writes: "The labor policy of the Urban League has been spotty. The organization's interest in increased economic opportunity for the black worker has led it to exert effort toward the lifting of trade union barriers against the Negro worker, but these efforts to get the Negro into the labor unions have been, for the most part, confined to negotiations with prominent trade union officials. No effective program for carrying the message of organized labor to the rank and file of white and black workers has yet been devised by the League. Moreover, it is doubtful that if a program revolving about labor organization and white and black labor unity were instigated by the Urban League it could be executed through the branches as they are now constituted." (Bunche, *op. cit.*, Vol. 2, p. 267.

". . . basically the policy of the Urban League is not a policy of labor organization or of working class unity. It is a policy thoroughly middle class in its orientation and perspective, which is interested only in getting jobs for Negroes. The interracial and business class structure of the directing boards of the Urban League locals have often made it impossible for the work of the League to be as soundly liberal as the local executive secretaries might often wish it to be." (*Ibid.*, Vol. 2, p. 270.)

"It [the League] apparently has never convinced itself that one Negro worker in a labor union may, in terms of ultimate benefits to the Negro group, weigh more heavily than ten Negroes placed in temporary jobs as marginal workers." (*Ibid.*, Vol. 2, p. 271.)

To this Jones replies: "Doctor Bunche evidently has in his mind the type of organization he would form to correct the problems as he sees them, and he judges the National Urban League on the basis of this conception while the National Urban League has never announced a plan to solve all of the labor problems of the Negro. . . . It has never announced that its programs is to *organize* Negro labor. It has sense enough to know that it could not be successful in this if it tried any more so than any other group, outside of the workers themselves." (Letter, August 8, 1940.)

And: "Such a program [of securing employment for Negroes] demands not only that Negroes be induced to prepare formally for jobs which the League helps to open for them, but also that labor unions be induced to welcome Negroes to membership and Negroes be educated to the value of collective bargaining as a necessary development in progressive society. . . . I think that any student of social problems must confess that the real job of workers' education belongs to the workers themselves and is a part of the program of most well organized labor movements." (Memorandum, June 17, 1941.)

The League also points to its Workers' Councils which have been organized during recent years to educate the Negro workers in the principles of collective bargaining. "The work of these Councils was not simply theoretical education. They actually organized Negroes and got them into unions where union membership was a requisite for obtaining jobs. . . . It was estimated that at least 1,000 Negro workers moved into union ranks within a space of two years as a result of the Workers' Councils' leadership." (Lester B. Granger, letter of August 7, 1942.)

[84] Concerning the effect of the War on the activity of the Urban League, Lester B. Granger informs that it "has been to intensify and emphasize some of its activities rather than to change its program; for instance, in the employment field, attention has been put on war jobs for Negroes on the semi-skilled and skilled levels. Employers have been approached with a new argument—that of the need for all-out 100% use of every available labor resource. As the public employment service became more and more important in filling war job orders, more attention has been given by the League to correcting unsound practices and inadequate policies of state employment services. This concern was increased when first the President federalized all state employment services and merged them into the United States Employment Service, and when the War Manpower Commission, using the U.S.E.S. facilities, was given full authority in registering, classifying, assigning, and possibly drafting labor for war uses. In this situation, the professional placement experience of the Urban League has proven to be invaluable as an aid to educating and otherwise influencing public employment officials.

"The League has given a good deal of attention to war housing of Negroes in such key cities as Buffalo, Detroit, Baltimore, Kansas City, New Orleans, and Atlanta. Work with local housing authorities has been accompanied by work with the National Housing Agency to insure a fair proportion of war housing for Negro workers. Local Urban Leagues have been active in the Civilian Defense program, recruiting and helping to train volunteer workers, assisting in the sale of defense and war bonds, disseminating information for consumers, and carrying on similar activities." (Letter of August 7, 1942.)

[85] Emily H. Clay observes on this point:

"For the past couple of years the Southern Region of the Y.M.C.A., which occupies space on the same floor with us, has had in its office a Negro Student Secretary. Also, for about two years (1924-1926) Mr. David O. Jones served as our General Field Secretary, resigning in 1926 to become president of Bennett College. During that period he spent part time in an office provided for him at our headquarters and part time, for convenience, in an office provided on one of the local campuses [in a Negro university].

Although it has been discussed from time to time, we have not had a Negro on our headquarters staff since 1926." (Letter, August 24, 1942.)

[86] *The Negro: The Southerner's Problem* (1904), p. 16.

[87] Emmett J. Scott and Lyman Beecher Stowe, *Booker T. Washington* (1916), p. 26.

[88] Ray Stannard Baker, *Following the Color Line* (1908), p. 20.

[89] "A week after the Armistice one might have observed a subtle but ominous change. Distrust was awakened. What would be the attitude of the Negro troops when they returned from France? Rumors filled the air, and by the time the soldiers began to return suspicion and fear had taken deep hold upon both races. Mob violence, which had greatly declined during the war, burst out afresh. In city after city race riots flamed up, with casualties on both sides. The tension tightened everywhere, and with dread suspense the Nation awaited the outcome." (*The Interracial Commission Comes of Age*, leaflet [February, 1942].)

[90] *A Practical Approach to the Race Problem*, leaflet published by the Commission on Interracial Cooperation (October, 1939).

[91] Bunche, *op. cit.*, Vol. 3, pp. 449 ff.

[92] Jessie Daniel Ames, *Democratic Processes at Work in the South, Report of Commission on Interracial Cooperation 1939-1941* (October, 1941). On the activity of the state and local committees as of 1939-1940, see Bunche, *op. cit.*, Vol. 3, pp. 461 ff.

[93] "We now have active State Committees in Alabama, Georgia, Kentucky, Mississippi, North Carolina, South Carolina, Texas, and Virginia. . . the ground work is now being laid for the reorganization of active committees in Arkansas and Florida. . . . We have the following active local or county committees: Alabama—Jefferson County; Florida—Ocala; Georgia—Fulton-DeKalb County, Griffin, Macon Area (17 counties), and Savannah; South Carolina—Charleston, Florence, Greenwood County, and Sumter County; Texas—Austin, Dallas, and Houston; Tennessee—Memphis. There are also local committees in North Carolina and Virginia, but I cannot give you a current list of these just now.

"Although the actual membership of our committees is not large, it is representative of a great many organizations through which we are able to extend our program." (Letter from Emily H. Clay, [August 24, 1942].)

The field staff now includes two full-time workers in addition to the white Director of Field Work in the Atlanta Office; of the two field workers, one is a Negro.

[94] *The Interracial Commission Comes of Age*, leaflet (February, 1942).

[95] ". . . the Commission has refused to bind either itself or the state committees, with rigid rules and regulations. It still refuses to dictate a program to any state or community. It does, however, assist in setting up state and local committees and, if they request help, will cooperate in the development of a program upon which the community agrees." (*Ibid.*)

[96] The figure is an average from 1922 to 1942. (Information from Emily H. Clay letter, August 24, 1942.)

[97] Information from Emily H. Clay, letter, August 27, 1942.

[98] Quoted in Paul E. Baker, *op. cit.*, p. 19.

[99] R. B. Eleazer in comment at the Seminar on American Racialism held by the American Missionary Association Division, New York City, January 16, 1942.

[100] Sections 7, 15, and 716 of the Penal Code of Georgia. (See Chapter 11, Section 9.)

[101] Emily H. Clay, memorandum, August, 1942.

[102] "A Practical Approach to the Race Problem," *op. cit.*

[103] Letter, August 13, 1942.

[104] Bunche, *op. cit.*, Vol. 4, p. 551.

[105] *Ibid.*, Vol. 4, pp. 557 ff.

[106] Questionnaire returned by Arthur Raper, formerly Research Secretary of the Commission, February 26, 1940; cited in *ibid.*, Vol. 3, p. 460.

[107] "Six of the eight State Committees . . . have dues paying memberships, as follows: Alabama—61, $2.00; Georgia—191, $2.00; Kentucky—155, $1.00; Texas—135, $5.00; Mississippi—120, $2.00; South Carolina—137, $1.00. Some of the local or county committees also have dues, among these the Fulton-DeKalb and Macon Area Committees, to which the members pay fifty cents annually." (Emily H. Clay, letter, August 24, 1942.)

[108] *The Crisis* (July, 1918), p. 111. (Italics ours.)

[109] *N.A.A.C.P. Press Release* (December 12, 1941).

[110] The story is told by Earl Brown, "American Negroes and the War," *Harper's Magazine* (April, 1942), pp. 545-552.

[111] A. Philip Randolph, National Director, March-on-Washington movement, Madison Square Garden, June 16, 1942, pp. 13-14.

[112] This demand is not only raised by critical Negro intellectuals (see Chapter 38, Section 5), but also by many conciliatory white friends of the Negro cause. Guy B. Johnson, for instance, in a commencement address at a Virginia Negro college (published in the *Virginia State College Gazette* [December, 1939]) pointed out:

"The . . . great need in the strategy of the Negro group is an effective organization. Now I realize that there are many organizations, but there is not one which has the confidence of anything like a majority of the Negro population . . .

"An organization such as I have in mind should be race-wide, drawing support from all segments of the Negro population. It should be militant but not so militant as to scare off the majority of Negroes who have to earn their bread and butter in the South. It should combine the idealism of the N.A.A.C.P. with the patience and opportunism of the Southern Commission on Interracial Cooperation. It should be realistic in its tactics." (*Ibid.*, p. 12.)

And Johnson adds:

"I am aware that all this sounds like the rankest sort of opportunism. That is exactly what it is, and, in my humble opinion, that is exactly what it takes to form a good strategy for a minority group organization. But whether you agree with me or not on this point, I believe you will agree that the Negro's bargaining power would be much stronger if he could consolidate his forces into one organization which would command the respect and the support of many thousands of Negroes in all walks of life." (*Ibid.*, p. 14; compare the discussion in *The Crisis* [July, 1939], p. 209 and [September, 1939] pp. 271-272.)

[113] *Race Adjustment* (1908), p. 24.

[114] *Negro Americans, What Now?* pp. 81 and 87.

[115] *The World Crisis and the Negro People Today*, p. 14.

[116] *Ibid.*, p. 21.

Chapter 40. *The Negro Church*

[1] A few had been slaves in Portugal. Most of these were probably Christians, as were a few who had been converted in Africa and the West Indies. Some others had been converted to Islam in Africa. (Melville J. Herskovits, "Social History of the Negro" in Carl Murchison [editor], *A Handbook of Social Psychology* [1935], pp. 234-240.)

[2] *White and Black* (1879), p. 132.

[3] See Allison Davis, "The Negro Church and Associations in the Lower South," unpublished manuscript prepared for this study (1940), pp. 36-37.

[4] Charles S. Johnson, *Growing Up in the Black Belt* (1941), pp. 135-136.

[5] For an imperfect but reasonable substantiation of these statements, see the manuscripts prepared for this study, already referred to, by J. G. St. Clair Drake, "The Negro Church and Associations in Chicago" (1940); Allison Davis, "The Negro Church and Associations in the Lower South" (1940); and Guion G. Johnson and Guy B. Johnson, "The Church and the Race Problem in the United States" (1940). Also see: Benjamin E. Mays and J. W. Nicholson, *The Negro's Church* (1933); and U. S. Bureau of the Census, *Religious Bodies, 1936* (1941), Vol. 1.

[6] U. S. Bureau of the Census, *Religious Bodies, 1936*, Vol. 1, pp. 86 and 851. The total reported church membership was 55,807,366. The figure for white churches was calculated by subtracting the Negroes from the total, thus ignoring Orientals and Indians.

[7] Population is taken as of 1940. Sources: *Religious Bodies, 1936*, pp. 86 and 851; and *Sixteenth Census of the United States: 1940, Population*. Preliminary Release, Series P-10, No. 1.

[8] Guy B. Johnson, "Some Factors in the Development of Negro Social Institutions in the United States," *American Journal of Sociology* (November, 1934), pp. 329-337. Also see Guion G. Johnson and Guy B. Johnson, *op. cit.*, Vol. 2, p. 292; Hortense Powdermaker, *After Freedom* (1939), pp. 245-246; and Drake, *op. cit.*, pp. 254-255. The Johnsons point out that ". . . almost every Negro religious body listed in the census has its white counterpart in doctrine and policy, except for minor variations." (*Op. cit.*, Vol. 2, p. 292.)

[9] Drake, *op. cit.*, p. 255.

[10] "The majority of Negro youth of all classes believe that God is white. To lower-class youth, He resembles a kindly paternalistic, upper-class white man. They believe that because of His goodness and justice, colored people will not suffer discrimination in the other world." (E. Franklin Frazier, *Negro Youth at the Crossways* [1940], p. 133.)

[11] Drake, *op. cit.*, pp. 426 ff.

[12] Charles S. Johnson, *Growing Up in the Black Belt*, p. 135.

[13] James Weldon Johnson, *Black Manhattan* (1930), pp. 165-166. For further discussion of this point, see Chapter 43, Section 3, of this book.

[14] The Roman Catholic Church, though not state-supported, often gets persons from all social classes in the same congregation. It is my belief that, for this reason, there is a relatively greater feeling of equality among Catholic laymen.

[15] Edwin R. Embree, *Brown America* (1933; first edition, 1931), pp. 208-209.

[16] Thomas P. Bailey, *Race Orthodoxy in the South* (1914), pp. 343-345.

[17] Robert R. Moton, *What the Negro Thinks* (1929), p. 253.

[18] For a discussion of Southern church attitudes, see Virginius Dabney, *Liberalism in the South* (1932), pp. 287-308, and Wilbur J. Cash, *The Mind of the South* (1941), pp. 333-337.

[19] Baker quoted a Southern clergyman's description of the situation up to 1900:

"The Rev. H. S. Bradley, for a long time one of the leading clergymen of Atlanta, now of St. Louis, said in a sermon published in the Atlanta *Constitution*:

" '. . . We have not been wholly lacking in our effort to help. There are a few schools and churches supported by Southern whites for the Negroes. Here and there a man like George Williams Walker, of the aristocracy of South Carolina, and a woman like Miss Belle H. Bennett, of the blue blood of Kentucky, goes as teacher to the Negro youth, and seeks in a Christly spirit of fraternity to bring them to a higher plane of civil and moral manhood, but the number like them can almost be counted on fingers of both hands.

" 'Our Southern churches have spent probably a hundred times as much money since the Civil War in an effort to evangelize the people of China, Japan, India, South America Africa, Mexico, and Cuba, as they have spent to give the Gospel to the Negroes at our doors. It is often true that opportunity is overlooked because it lies at our feet.' " (Ray Stannard Baker, *Following the Color Line* [1908], p. 56.)

Weatherford pointed out in 1912 that: "The Southern Baptist Convention has only been asking from its large membership $15,000 annually, or less than one cent per member . . ." (W. D. Weatherford, *Present Forces in Negro Progress* [1912], pp. 164-165.)

[20] Quoted in Ray Stannard Baker, *op. cit.*, pp. 121-122.

[21] Guion G. Johnson and Guy B. Johnson, *op. cit.*, Vol. 1, pp. 212-213.

[22] A study of 64 ministers in Chicago (pastors of churches either owning or buying their buildings) revealed that:

" '. . . four-fifths of the ministers of the regular sample condemned racial division, the accompanying attitudes or both. Yet only one-third of the regular sample were unwilling to grant that the religious needs of Negroes are best served by separate racial churches. Stated differently, all but one-fifth condemned racial division, but only one-third took the position that the separate Negro church does not serve the religious needs of colored people best . . .' " (Jesse H. Atwood, "The Attitudes of Negro Ministers of the Major Denominations Toward Racial Division in Protestantism," unpublished M.A. thesis, University of Chicago [1930], p. 78. Quoted in Drake, *op. cit.*, pp. 283-284.)

[23] According to the 1936 census of Religious Bodies, the proportion in 1936 was only 3.8 per cent in New Jersey, 1.4 per cent in New York, 2.1 per cent in Illinois, and 2.7 per cent in Pennsylvania. (U. S. Bureau of the Census, *Religious Bodies, 1936*, Vol. 1, pp. 878, 888, and 892.) These proportions do not include a significant number of Negroes who attend mixed Catholic churches, and the census, as we have pointed out, under-enumerates the Negro Catholics. The highest reported proportion of Negro Catholics, irrespective of whether they attended Negro or mixed churches, was 7.4 per cent for Harlem in 1930. (The Greater New York Federation of Churches, *The Negro Churches in Manhattan* [1930], pp. 11-18.)

[24] See Guion G. Johnson and Guy B. Johnson, *op. cit.*, Vol. 1, pp. 198-200.

[25] There is one type of contact between Negro and white churches that usually causes unfriendliness. As Negro districts have expanded in Northern cities, white congregations have felt forced to sell their church edifices to Negro congregations. Not

only this, but the attendant financial difficulties promote ill-will. The whites usually do not realize that their church buildings have deteriorated in value since the time they were built, and the Negroes are often unwise in assuming obligations which they cannot meet. (See Mays and Nicholson, *op. cit.*, pp. 181 ff.)

26 "The Churches have either had nothing to say on the subjects of low wages and long hours in the mills, or have distracted attention from economic wrongs by stressing the calamities of individual sinfulness." (Broadus Mitchell and George S. Mitchell, *The Industrial Revolution in the South* [1930], p. 144.)

27 Booker T. Washington, *The Future of the American Negro* (1899), p. 170.

28 There are plenty of Negro preachers. In 1930, Negroes constituted 9.7 per cent of the total population, but about 16.8 per cent of all clergymen. The actual figure is probably higher than this, since some Negro preachers have other occupations, and the latter may be the ones reported to the census-taker. (*Fifteenth Census of the United States: 1930, Population*, Vol. IV, pp. 32-33.) Many of these preachers—the so-called "jack leg" preachers—have no congregation.

29 See Mays and Nicholson, *op. cit.*, pp. 10 *passim.*

30 On the basis of their sample study of 185 rural Negro churches and 609 urban Negro churches in 1930, Mays and Nicholson (*ibid.*, pp. 171 and 261) report the following percentage distribution of church expenditures:

	185 Rural Churches	*609 Urban Churches*
Salaries	69.9	43.2
Interest and Reduction of Church Debt	2.0	22.9
Benevolence and Miscellaneous Items (including insurance, rent, heat, light)	15.8	21.0
Education, Missions, etc.	5.9	6.6
Repairs and Upkeep	6.4	6.3
	100.0	100.0

Of the urban churches, 71.3 per cent reported that their buildings were under a mortgage.

31 Fry's analysis of the 1926 Census of Religious Bodies indicates that the following percentages of Protestant clergymen reported that they graduated either from college or seminary:

	Negro	*White*
Urban	38	80
Rural	17	47

(C. Luther Fry, *The United States Looks at Its Churches* [1930], pp. 64-66.) These figures are inflated by exaggeration in reporting and by overlooking some of the smaller churches. Mays and Nicholson (*op. cit.*, p. 302) questioned 590 urban Negro ministers and found that only 27.7 per cent claimed to have graduated from college or seminary. They also reported that 57.5 per cent of 134 rural Negro ministers had only a grammar school education or less. (*Ibid.*, p. 238.)

In a study of 1,200 Negro ministers, Woodson found that 70 per cent had no college degree. He also found that those with a degree—either in theology or in liberal arts, or both—were mostly from unaccredited colleges. (Carter G. Woodson, *The Negro Professional Man and the Community* [1934], p. 64.) When we speak of the college-trained Negro clergymen, we must keep in mind that the standards of their colleges and seminaries in the South are pitifully poor in most cases.

[32] In 1930, clergymen still constituted 18.4 per cent of all professionals among Negroes and only 3.4 per cent among native whites. (*Fifteenth Census of the United States: 1930, Population*, Vol. IV, pp. 32-33.)

[33] Davis, *op. cit.*, pp. 120-125. Also see Willis D. Weatherford and Charles S. Johnson, *Race Relations* (1934), p. 497; and the recent studies of The American Youth Commission, especially E. Franklin Frazier, *Negro Youth at the Crossways* (1940), p. 133.

[34] Charles S. Johnson supports, and has some evidence to prove, the position that rural Negro youth are more dissatisfied with the church than urban Negro youth. (*Growing Up in the Black Belt*, pp. 145-164.)

[35] We may cite again Woodson's finding that only seven-tenths of 1 per cent of a sample of high school graduates expressed the intention of entering the ministry. (Woodson, *op. cit.*, p. 80.)

[36] On the basis of a sample study of 5,512 Negro college graduates, who were not quite representative of the total population of Negro college graduates, Charles S. Johnson reports the following percentage distribution suggesting the degree of adherence to the church on the part of this group:

Not a member	5.3
Inactive member	15.1
Active member	48.1
Officer	12.5
Preacher	3.1
Not given	15.9
	100.0

(Charles S. Johnson, *The Negro College Graduate* [1938], p. 347.)

[37] *Op. cit.*, pp. 102 and 139.

Chapter 41. *The Negro School*

[1] Caroline F. Ware, *Greenwich Village* (1935), pp. 455-461.

[2] Cited by Ray Stannard Baker, *Following the Color Line* (1908) p. 247.

[3] John Dewey, "The Determination of Ultimate Values or Aims through Antecedent or A Priori Speculation or through Pragmatic or Empirical Inquiry," in *The Scientific Movement in Education, the Thirty-Seventh Yearbook of the National Society for the Study of Education*, Part 2 (1938), pp. 475-476.

[4] Booker T. Washington, *Up From Slavery* (1901; first edition, 1900), pp. 29-30.

[5] Sir George Campbell, *White and Black* (1879), p. 259.

[6] James Bryce, *The American Commonwealth* (1910; first edition, 1893), Vol. 2, p. 520.

[7] *Op. cit.*, p. 53.

⁸ Bryce, *op. cit.*, Vol. 2, p. 320.

⁹ The Southern pro-slavery theory was expounded upon the principle of equality among the whites just as much as of their superiority over the Negroes (see Chapters 20 and 31). One of the glaring contradictions between philosophy and life in the Old South was, therefore, its aristocratic educational system which left the masses of poor whites altogether uneducated. This was seen by some of the pro-slavery advocates. George Fitzhugh, for instance, wrote:

"We need never have white slaves in the South, because we have black ones. Our citizens, like those of Rome and Athens, are a privileged class. We should train and educate them to deserve the privileges and to perform the duties which society confers on them. Instead, by a low demagoguism depressing their self-respect by discourses on the equality of man, we had better excite their pride by reminding them that they do not fulfill the menial offices which white men do in other countries. Society does not feel the burden of providing for the few helpless paupers in the South. And we should recollect that here we have but half the people to educate, for half are Negroes; whilst at the North they profess to educate all. It is in our power to spike this last gun of the abolitionists. We should educate all the poor." (*Sociology for the South* [1854], p. 93; compare pp. 144, 147 ff., 255 ff., *passim*.)

¹⁰ Before the Civil War many of the Northern states had separate schools for Negroes, but these were not very inferior to those for whites. Most colleges—with the notable exceptions of Oneida Institute, New York Central College, and Oberlin College (whose President was Horace Mann, the greatest leader of public education in the United States)—refused to accept Negroes, but three Negro colleges—Avery College (Pennsylvania, 1849), Ashmun Institute (now Lincoln University, Pennsylvania, 1854), Wilberforce University (Ohio, 1856)—were established there. (See Doxey A. Wilkerson, "The Negro in American Education," unpublished manuscript prepared for this study [1940], Vol. 1, p. 91.)

¹¹ Horace Mann Bond, *The Education of the Negro in the American Social Order* (1934), p. 21. See also Willis D. Weatherford and Charles S. Johnson, *Race Relations* (1934), pp. 350-351. South Carolina and Georgia had such laws in the eighteenth century.

¹² W. E. B. Du Bois, *Black Reconstruction* (1935), p. 638. The Census of 1870 reports that 18.6 per cent of all Negroes 10 years old and over were literate. (U.S. Bureau of the Census, *Negroes In the United States: 1920-1932*, p. 231.) This figure includes the *ante-bellum* free Negro population (who could go to school in the North), and it probably includes many Negroes whose literacy consisted in nothing more than ability to write one's name. Too, it refers to a date five years after the end of the Civil War.

¹³ Du Bois, *Black Reconstruction*, p. 123.

¹⁴ They have been very differently judged. A Southern white liberal in the previous generation, Thomas Nelson Page, wrote:

"But the teachers, at first, devoted as many of them were, by their unwisdom alienated the good-will of the whites and frustrated much of the good which they might have accomplished. They might have been regarded with distrust in any case, for no people look with favor on the missionaries who come to instruct them as to matters of which they feel they know much more than the missionaries, and the South regarded jealously any teaching of the Negroes which looked toward equality. The new missionaries went counter to the deepest prejudice of the Southern people. They lived with the

Negroes, consorting with them, and appearing with them on terms of apparent intimacy, and were believed to teach social equality, a doctrine which was the surest of all to arouse enmity then as now." (*The Negro: the Southerner's Problem* [1904], pp. 38-39.) Modern Southern liberals are much more appreciative. T. J. Woofter, Jr., for instance, writes:

"For some time after the Civil War these boards gave considerable more than money. They sent some of the choicest spirits in their ranks as missionary teachers. Facing discouragement, ostracism, and many other difficulties, these white teachers preserved the link of connection between the white race and the training of Negroes in the higher schools. They have left their indelible imprints upon such institutions as Fisk, Howard, Atlanta, Tougaloo, Talladega, Lincoln, Straight, Hampton, Clark, and Meharry Medical College, as well as upon a number of smaller denominational high schools. The character and devotion of many of the well-trained Negroes of today is due largely to the efforts of these missionaries, and the South and the Negro race owe them much gratitude." (*Basis of Racial Adjustment* [1925], p. 194.)

Negroes have been almost consistently appreciative of the "Yankee teachers." Booker T. Washington said:

"Whenever it is written—and I hope it will be—the part that the Yankee teachers played in the education of the Negroes immediately after the war will make one of the most thrilling parts of the history of this country. The time is not far distant when the whole South will appreciate this service in a way that it has not yet been able to do." (*Op. cit.*, p. 62.)

Du Bois amplifies the praise even more:

". . . which once saintly souls brought to their favored children in the crusade of the sixties, that finest thing in American history, and one of the few things untainted by sordid greed and cheap vainglory. The teachers in these institutions came not to keep the Negroes in their place, but to raise them out of the defilement of the places where slavery had wallowed them. The colleges they founded were social settlements; homes where the best of the sons of the freedmen came in close and sympathetic touch with the best traditions of New England. They lived and ate together, studied and worked, hoped and harkened in the dawning light. In actual formal content their curriculum was doubtless old-fashioned, but in educational power it was supreme, for it was the contact of living souls." (W. E. B. Du Bois, *The Souls of Black Folk* [1903], p. 100.)

[15] Paul H. Buck, *The Road to Reunion 1865-1900* (1937), p. 166.

[16] Du Bois, *Black Reconstruction*, p. 667.

[17] *Op. cit.*, p. 60.

[18] The difference in opinion existed before the Civil War. Free Negroes in the South had hoped the whites there would let them have schools if they were of the "industrial" type. In 1853, Frederick Douglass expressed himself as in favor of "an industrial school" when Harriet Beecher Stowe offered some money either for this or for an "educational institution pure and simple." He wished established ". . . a series of workshops, where colored people could learn some of the handicrafts, learn to work in iron, wood, and leather, and where a plain English education could also be taught." His opinion was ". . . that *want* of money was the root of all evil to the colored people. They were shut out from all lucrative employments and compelled to be merely barbers, waiters, coachmen and the like at wages so low that they could buy up little or nothing."

(See Frederick Douglass, *Life and Times of Frederick Douglass* [1941; first edition, 1893], p. 315.)

[19] Armstrong was one of the few "carpetbaggers" who did not come from New England; rather, he had been a missionary to the natives in Hawaii. This may explain the differences between him and the other leading carpetbaggers with respect to their attitudes toward Negro education. General O. O. Howard, for example, the head of the Freedmen's Bureau, established Howard University in Washington, D. C., as a liberal arts college. Similarly, General Swayne established the liberal arts Talladega College; and E. M. Cravath left the Federal Army to build up Fisk—a liberal arts college.

[20] Most of the facts about the work of the foundations in the educational field have been taken from Weatherford and Johnson (*op. cit.*, pp. 363-364); from a pamphlet by Robert M. Lester, Secretary of the Carnegie Corporation of New York, "Corporation Grants for Education of the Negro" (November, 1941); and from Bond (*op. cit.*, pp. 130-144).

[21] The Peabody Fund was discontinued in 1914 and divided its money between the Slater Fund and the George Peabody College for Teachers, at Nashville. Although only whites are taught at this college, they are given some understanding of Negro needs and abilities.

[22] While everyone agrees that the Jeanes teachers have made a great improvement in Southern Negro education, they have been criticized as overworked, disorganized, and inclined to bow too much to Southern folkways. Regarding the latter point, one white school superintendent in Louisiana stated:

"Somehow they see only the best things in the colored schools in their parish. That's what they talk about—the rosy things. They forget about all the bad things, they just ignore them—never talk about them. Why, I've been to their meetings, and to hear them talk every one of them comes from the best parish in the state. They just see the world through rose-colored glasses. You see, that has the effect of leaving people who *might* do something about colored schools in ignorance." (Interview in Charles S. Johnson, "The Negro Public Schools," *Louisiana Educational Survey*, Section 8 [1942], p. 40.)

When judging the Jeanes teachers and their work—as so much else in Negro education—it should be remembered, however, that they are nothing else than heroic attempts to mitigate in a small way what is actually the result both of the extreme poverty and cultural backwardness in the Southern rural Negro community, and the outright discrimination against the Negro schools, which keeps them on an often incredibly low standard in regard to both equipment and training of teachers. When the Jeanes teacher is viewed in this setting, she becomes a remarkable and pathetic figure in the history of Negro education.

[23] Schrieke describes the activities and problems of the General Education Board supervisors:

"For the most part it was the work of the state agents for the Negro schools, who emphasized the needs and grasped the opportunities. Nobody who has not actually seen them in their work can realize the difficulties they must face almost daily. Although nominally officers of the state departments of education, their salaries are paid by the philanthropic foundations; they are supervisors of Negro education but have no authority whatever. For their success must depend entirely upon the goodwill they manage to create and upon their personal prestige. They live and work in the South with its prejudices. Of course they are Southerners themselves and know how far they can go, but they are restrained in their efforts by the milieu. They have to be extremely careful not to arouse sentiments that would impede the progress of their work. For their success they must depend upon the traditional paternalistic attitude towards the Negro who keeps in his place. They have a definite task, but they are subordinate to the state superintendent of education, who may be an educator and an organizer, but who may also be a politician, playing partisan politics." (B. Schrieke, *Alien Americans* [1936], pp. 163-164.)

The present writer has been equally impressed by the activity of the state agents for Negro education. To Schrieke's evaluation I should like to add a few observations. The independence of the agents, since they drew their salaries not from state funds but from an outside agency which could keep a control over their selection, has given this group of public servants a rare spirit of zeal and devotion which is now upheld as a great tradition. To the outsider, it is striking that this group contains individuals who are extraordinary in their surroundings on account of freedom from prejudice and thorough knowledge and understanding not only of the Negro school but of the whole setting of social and economic problems in which it is enclosed. Their policy could be called "progressive opportunism."

[24] Between 1913 and 1932, some 5,357 Negro school buildings in 15 Southern states were constructed with Rosenwald aid. "The total cost of these buildings was $28,408,520 of which $18,104,155 (64%) came from tax funds, $1,211,975 (4%) from personal contributions of white friends, $4,366,519 (15%) from the Julius Rosenwald Fund . . . and $4,725,871 (17%) in a flood of small contributions from Negroes themselves—striking evidence of the desire of members of this race for schooling for their children." (Edwin R. Embree, *Julius Rosenwald Fund: Review of Two Decades, 1917-1936* [1936], p. 23.)

Doxey Wilkerson makes the following comparison:

"When the number of 'Rosenwald buildings' constructed during this 20-year period is compared with the total number of Negro schools in 12 States for which information is available, it will be seen that the number of buildings constructed with Rosenwald aid is equivalent to about one-fifth (20 per cent) of the total number of Negro school buildings in 1935-36. More than one-fourth of the Negro school buildings in Arkansas, Louisiana, and Maryland, and nearly one-third in North Carolina and Tennessee were constructed with Rosenwald aid. Similarly, in the 10 States for which information is at hand, the amount of money invested in 'Rosenwald buildings' is equivalent to nearly one-third (32 per cent) of the total value of Negro school property in 1935-36. In South Carolina the corresponding proportion is more than one-half, in Arkansas nearly three-fourths, and in Mississippi nearly nine-tenths." (Doxey A. Wilkerson, *Special Problems of Negro Education* [1939], pp. 32-33; Wilkerson's sources are David T. Blose and Ambrose Caliver, *Statistics of the Education of Negroes: 1933-34 and 1935-36*, U.S. Office of Education, Bulletin No. 13 [1938], p. 22, and *Negro Year Book: 1937-38* [1937], p. 185.) See also, U.S. Office of Education, *Biennial Survey of Education in the United States: 1934-36*, Bulletin No. 2 (1938), Vol. 1, pp. 80-89.

[25] For a recent, good impressionistic survey of both white and Negro colleges and universities in the South, see Virginius Dabney, *Below the Potomac* (1942), pp. 139-176 and 226-233.

[26] Charles S. Johnson, *Shadow of the Plantation* (1934), p. 129.

[27] Page, *op. cit.*, pp. 295-297.

[28] Kelly Miller, *Out of the House of Bondage* (1914), pp. 151-152.

[29] The last point, and the entire caste issue, is illustrated by the following quotation from Thomas Nelson Page:

"At this point, the question arises: How shall they [the Negroes] be improved? One element says, Improve them, but only as laborers, for which alone they are fitted; another, with a large charity, says, Enlarge this and give them a chance to become good mechanics, as they have shown themselves capable of improvement in the industrial field; a third class goes further yet, and says, Give them a yet further chance—a chance to develop themselves; enlighten them and teach them the duties of citizenship and they will become measurably good citizens. Yet another says, Give him the opportunity and push him till he is stuffed full of the ideas and the learning that have made the white race what it is.

"The last of these theories appears to the writer as unsound as the first, which is certainly unsound. Keep them ignorant, and the clever and the enterprising will go off and leave to the South the dull, the stupid, and the degraded.

"The question is no longer a choice between the old-time Negro and the 'new issue', but between the 'new issue', made into a fairly good laborer and a fairly enlightened citizen, who in time will learn his proper place, whatever it may be, or the 'new issue', dull, ignorant, brutish, liable to be worked on by the most crafty of those who would use him; a noisome, human hot-bed, in which every form of viciousness will germinate." (*Op. cit.*, pp. 299-300.)

[30] "Student labor is two-fold in its object, instruction and production, knowledge and support. . . . To destroy the industrial system would . . . destroy its best results, and place it beyond the reach of the most needy and deserving class of pupils." (*Report of the Hampton Normal and Agricultural Institute* [1875], pp. 6-7.)

[31] Winfield H. Collins, *The Truth about Lynching and the Negro in the South* (1918), pp. 154-155.

[32] Within the same city, public schools for whites offer different vocational training than do public schools for Negroes:

"In Little Rock, for example, the white schools offer printing, aviation, automobile retail selling, and cosmetology; the Negro schools offer bricklaying, carpentry, automobile mechanics, and sewing. In Pine Bluff four vocations were offered in the white and Negro high schools—carpentry and automobile mechanics in both of them—with bookkeeping and typing making up the third and fourth for the whites and cooking and sewing for the Negroes; in Anniston, Alabama, five for whites and none for Negroes; Phoenix City, two for whites, one for Negroes; Selma, similar number. In a few instances the Negroes had more courses, but in general they had fewer courses and more of the most menial ones." (Arthur Raper, "Race and Class Pressures," unpublished manuscript prepared for this study [1940], p. 230.) Raper bases his information on a questionnaire returned by 88 Negro high school principals of the South.

[33] Charles S. Mangum, Jr., *Legal Status of the Negro* (1940), pp. 132-133.

[34] A vigorous and detailed plea for giving the Negro special training to meet special problems may be found in Carter G. Woodson, *The Mis-Education of the Negro* (1933).

James Weldon Johnson gives a good account of these ideas as they have become common among Negro intellectuals today:

"The old pattern was designed to give us a sound general education, an education to fit us to take our places as intelligent American citizens. That idea of education is fundamental and right; for whatever may be the opinions and attitudes on the matter, the solid fact remains that we are, for good or ill, a part of American civilization. We may be segregated and Jim-Crowed, but there is no way to subtract or extract us from American life; so we must be prepared to keep adjusted to it, to keep pace with it. And that means that our institutions must give Negro youth as good, as broad, and as high an education as is correspondingly given to white youth.

"But we need not only an education that will enable us to meet the general situation as American citizens, we need also an education that will enable us to meet our peculiar situation as Negro Americans.

". . . the teaching of history to Negro youth should not confine itself to the experiences of the race in America, but should explore the achievements that lie in the African background. A study of the African cultural background will give our youth a new and higher sense of racial self-respect, and will disprove entirely the theory of innate race inferiority. . . .

"What I have said about the teaching of American history is to be said also about the teaching of economics, political science, sociology, literature, and other of the arts. It is something pretty close to a waste of time for Negro students to study the laws of economics without being given an interpretation of the effects of those laws on the economic and industrial plight of Negro Americans. In teaching the science of government, what is purely academic should be supplemented by inferences drawn from government as it is constituted, maintained, and enforced in the United States and the various states, and from its operation on Negro Americans as a group. I do not in the least advocate that our colleges become any part of political machinery or touched by partisan politics, but I firmly believe that special political education of Negro youth is a proper and necessary function for them. The political history of the race should be reviewed; independent political thinking should be inculcated; political rights and responsibilities should be explained, and preparation for exercising those rights and assuming those responsibilities should be given." (*Negro Americans, What Now?* [1934], pp. 48-49.)

[35] "The stimulation of race pride demands that colored pupils be taught more of the history and achievements of their own race. The growing body of literature by colored writers should be studied and the accomplishments of colored men of mark held up as inspiring examples." (Woofter, *op. cit.*, p. 183.)

[36] See Part VII. It is remarkable that segregation is upheld even in the institutions for higher learning and even in the graduate schools. This is, of course, related to the fact that colleges in America generally stress the social side of life so much (the so-called extra-curricular activities) and the scholarly side less. In the South this stress is even more apparent. Even the graduate schools in the South do not have much of the spirit of the age-old ideal of the "academic republic" where abstract truth-seeking is supreme and where age, nationality, language, and other individual characteristics are ignored. It is probable, however, that segregation will first break down, if ever, in the graduate institutions.

Wilkerson polled 838 students in a white land-grant college in the Deep South on the issue of mixed education and reports the following reaction:

Questions and Choices Presented Students	Percentage of Total Students (N = 838)

"I. If a few Negroes are admitted by order of court or legislature: 'Should the other students leave in protest?'

(a) Certainly should not	23
(b) Probably should not	17
(c) Can't say; not sure	9
(d) Probably should	16
(e) Certainly should	34

"II. If a student plans to enter, but learns a few Negroes might be enrolled: 'Should he enter the institution anyway?'

(a) Certainly should	21
(b) Probably should	15
(c) Can't say; not sure	7
(d) Probably should not	19
(e) Certainly should not	37

"III. If a few Negroes are admitted by order of court or legislature: 'How should the other students treat them?'

(a) Go out of the way to be friendly to them	0.4
(b) Make no advances but accept their presence in good grace	46
(c) Can't say; not sure	7
(d) Deliberately ignore them so they'll feel they are not wanted	27
(e) Organize to make life miserable for them; try to force them to leave	20

"IV. If court or legislature orders admission of Negroes: 'Out of a class of 100, how many might be Negroes before their presence would create a serious problem?'

0-1	49
2-5	19
6-11	17
16 and over	15"

(Wilkerson, "The Negro in American Education," pp. 183-184.)

[37] See, for instance, Robert R. Moton, *What the Negro Thinks* (1929), p. 114.

[38] W. E. B. Du Bois, "Does the Negro Need Separate Schools?," *Journal of Negro Education* (July, 1935), p. 335.

Booker T. Washington, in reply to an inquiry from whites on how to accomplish segregation in the North, said:

"As a rule, colored people in the Northern States are very much opposed to any plans for separate schools, and I think their feelings in the matter deserve consideration. The real objection to separate schools, from their point of view, is that they do not like to feel that they are compelled to go to one school rather than the other. It seems as if it was taking away part of their freedom. This feeling is likely to be all the stronger where the matter is made a subject of public agitation. On the other hand, my experience is that if this matter is left to the discretion of the school officials it usually settles itself. As the colored people usually live pretty closely together, there will naturally be schools in which colored students are in the majority. In that case, the process of separation takes place naturally and without the necessity of changing the constitution. If you make it a constitutional question, the colored people are going to be opposed to it. If you leave it simply an administrative question, which it really is, the matter will very likely settle itself." (Quoted in Emmett J. Scott and Lyman Beecher Stowe, *Booker T. Washington* [1916], pp. 42-43.) For another similar situation, see Moton, *op. cit.*, pp. 112 ff.

[39] Schrieke, *op. cit.*, pp. 166-167.

[40] The latter type may be exemplified by the following quotation from Schrieke:

". . . the same curriculum is taught in the Negro schools as in the white, and the same books are supposed to be used. The children are grouped in grades, but, as a matter of fact, these grades have only a theoretical value which does not correspond with that which the white schools attach to it. I found pupils in an eighth grade studying commercial geography without maps, and in another place I found them studying the state history. In both cases they understood almost nothing of the subjects, with the result that the geography and history classes simply developed into very poor reading classes— poor because the worst kind of training in reading is the reciting of words and sentences which have no meaning for the reader. I have seen textbooks on literature used when the pupils did not understand one word of what they read. The English was far too difficult. I found seventh- and eighth-grade pupils unable to spell 'April' or 'cotton.' " (*Op. cit.*, pp. 160-161.)

[41] The theory behind it may be exemplified by the following quotation from Willis D. Weatherford:

"Perhaps the weakest point in the Negro school is its maladjusted course of study. Most of the Negro children are located in the rural districts. These children, like the white rural children, are being taught from books made almost entirely by city teachers and adapted to city children. They talk about problems and situations arising in urban communities. The city is glorified and the country neglected. This has a tendency to make the rural child dissatisfied with the rural surrounding, and desirous of getting away to the city . . . but if nine-tenths of the material in their readers and histories relates to things that do not concern their daily life, how can we expect their school work to give them any appreciation of their surroundings? . . . There is a great need that we have two sets of text books, one for the rural children and one for the urban . . . the body of the text for the rural child will deal with the materials at hand. It will teach him the beauty of nature, and it will help him observe the birds and bees, the flowers and plants and trees; it will help him see new beauty in the growing crops and the fallow fields. Who would dare say there was not as much real culture in studying the life about him as in studying the life offered by the city zoo? . . . What the rural child needs—and especially is this true of the Negro child—is a new ability to interpret the life that surrounds him." (Weatherford and Johnson, *op. cit.*, pp. 360-361.)

Chapter 42. *The Negro Press*

[1] Willis D. Weatherford and Charles S. Johnson, *Race Relations* (1934), p. 485.

[2] Frederick G. Detweiler, *The Negro Press in the United States* (1922), p. 79.

[3] "The Negro Press—Today and Tomorrow," *Opportunity* (July, 1939), p. 205.

[4] Florence Murray (editor), *The Negro Handbook* (1942), p. 201. (The figures are taken from a U.S. Bureau of the Census report for 1940.)

[5] *The Negro Handbook*, p. 201.

[6] The U.S. Bureau of the Census reported that there were 210 Negro newspapers in 1940, but only 155 reported their circulation figures. These 155 newspapers reported a combined circulation per issue of 1,276,600. (Cited in *The Negro Handbook*, p. 201.) The eminent Negro journalist, George S. Schuyler, estimates that the total circulation of the weekly Negro newspapers is around 1,600,000 (Pittsburgh *Courier*, May 9, 1942). We feel conservative in speaking of the circulation as around one and a half millions. The Pittsburgh *Courier* has the largest circulation of all Negro newspapers; it sells about 141,500 copies weekly. The Chicago *Defender* is second, with a weekly circulation of about 83,500. (*Ayer's Directory of Newspapers and Periodicals* [1942], pp. 845, 217.)

[7] Estimate based on the assumption that there are one and a half million Negro newspapers sold per week. (See text footnote in this chapter.) Johns estimates that a third of Negro adults in Chicago "regularly read" Negro newspapers. (Elizabeth D. Johns, "The Role of the Negro Newspaper in the Negro Community," unpublished manuscript made available through the courtesy of the author [1940].)

[8] Detweiler, *op. cit.*, pp. 6-7.

[9] In an unpublished study of certain localities in Mississippi, Alabama, and Louisiana, Charles S. Johnson found that more Northern newspapers were read than local ones. Cited by Detweiler, *op. cit.*, pp. 10-11.

[10] The following historical notes are based mainly on G. James Fleming, "The Negro Press," unpublished manuscript prepared for this study (1940); and Detweiler, *op. cit.*

[11] *Op. cit.*, p. 39.

[12] James Weldon Johnson, *Black Manhattan* (1930), p. 15.

[13] Irvine Garland Penn, *Afro-American Press and Its Editors* (1891), pp. 112-114.

[14] Fleming, *op. cit.*, pp. II: 4-5.

[15] *Ibid.*, p. III: 12.

[16] In February, 1919, the town of Somerville, Tennessee, decreed that no "colored newspapers" might be circulated in that town, but that every "darkey" must read a newspaper edited by a Confederate veteran. (Detweiler, *op. cit.*, p. 1.) In February, 1921, an agent for the Philadelphia *American* was lynched in Athens, Georgia. Whites claimed that he had murdered a white woman; Negroes claimed that his only crime was to have tried to build up a Northern Negro newspaper's circulation. (*Ibid.*, p. 20; see also pp. 19-22.)

[17] *PM*, although a daily, does not have complete coverage of the news, and it has a higher price than usual. Its attention to national Negro issues and protests, however, is said to have given it a large circulation among Negroes in New York and Washington, especially those in the upper classes. *PM* does not, however, give the Negro society,

religious and organizational news. It does not, therefore, attempt to substitute for a Negro newspaper. Nevertheless, and in spite of *PM's* pronounced pro-Negro attitude, a New York Negro newspaper was disturbed by the competition and admonished Negroes to stick to the Negro press. Something like *PM* is the Chicago *Sun,* which is a newspaper also owned by Marshall Field.

[18] Fleming, *op. cit.,* p. VII: 11. In a footnote on the same page, Fleming draws the following parallels:

"In New York the Hearst *Evening Journal* (now the *Journal-American*) and the *Amsterdam News* (Negro); in Chicago Hearst's *Herald Examiner* and his *American* (now merged as the *Herald-American*) and the Chicago *Defender* (Negro); in Pittsburgh the Hearst's *Sun-Telegraph* and the Pittsburgh *Courier* (Negro)."

[19] "Gist of numerous interviews with editors and publishers." *Ibid.,* p. VIII: 3.

[20] See Johns, *op. cit.,* pp. 79 ff.

[21] Fleming, *op. cit.,* p. IV: 36.

[22] *Ibid.,* p. IV: 43.

[23] E. Franklin Frazier, *Negro Youth at the Crossways* (1940), p. 289.

[24] Park, *op. cit.,* p. 113.

[25] See Fleming, *op. cit.,* Chapter VI.

[26] Ralph J. Bunche, "The Political Status of the Negro," unpublished manuscript prepared for this study (1940), Vol. 6, p. 1303. Also see *ibid.,* pp. 1251-1252, for a concrete example of attempted corruption of the Negro press.

[27] White neighborhood businesses might, however, have an interest that a Negro newspaper should not preach the advantages of Negro business too much. The duty to favor Negro business is, however, such an important part of the dominant Negro ideology that no Negro newspaper would dare to come out against it. But it is worth noticing that many Negro newspapers have kept cool or critical toward local movements with the slogan "Don't buy where you can't work." For such an attitude there are perfectly honest reasons (see Chapter 38, Section 6), but an additional reason might be the advertising from white businesses in Negro neighborhoods, which is usually much more substantial than the advertising from Negro businesses.

In two cases I have been told by Negro editors that Jewish merchants in Negro neighborhoods have made representations as advertisers against an occasional story with an anti-Semitic tendency. In both cases the editors explained that there was no conflict, as they, themselves, were against any anti-Semitism among Negroes, and that the stories had been slips.

[28] This whole problem of the economy of Negro newspapers and the outside financial controls deserves study. In general terms the problem is often touched upon in Negro public discussion. P. B. Young, the editor of the Norfolk *Journal and Guide,* writes thus:

"How to *advocate* our cause without suffering the prohibitions which modern business places upon *agitation* is a question which every Negro publisher has to answer in defining a business policy that will blend with the ideals for which the Negro press must contend." ("The Negro Press—Today and Tomorrow," p. 205.)

[29] See Fleming, *op. cit.,* Chapter X.

[30] The A.N.P. asks for a small weekly fee. It is frequently accused of acting more as a publicity agent for some institutions and groups than as an impartial news service. The director ". . . denies that ANP ever 'sells out' its news service to any party, although

he makes no secret of the fact that subjects of pictures are generally asked to under-write the cost of cuts and mats." (*Ibid.*, p. X: 4.)

[31] Edwin Mims, *The Advancing South* (1926), p. 268.

Chapter 43. *Institutions*

[1] "Should the Negro Care Who Wins the War?" *The Annals of the American Academy of Political and Social Science* (September, 1942), p. 84.

[2] The reader interested in the controversy may wish to compare the two points of view as expressed in two pieces of research: E. Franklin Frazier, *The Negro Family in the United States* (1939); Melville J. Herskovits, *The Myth of the Negro Past* (1941). See also these authors' reviews of each other's books: Herskovits' review of Frazier: *Nation* (January 27, 1940), pp. 104-105; Frazier's review of Herskovits: *Nation* (February 14, 1942), pp. 195-196.

Herskovits earlier took just the opposite stand from the one he now takes. In 1925, he was even more extreme than Frazier in denying an African tradition: "What there is today in Harlem distinct from the white culture which surrounds it is as far as I am able to see, merely a remnant from the peasant days in the South. Of the African culture, not a trace. Even the spirituals are an expression of the emotion of the Negro playing through the typical religious patterns of white America." ("The Negro's Americanism" in Alain Locke (editor), *The New Negro* [1925], p. 359.)

[3] "In the small upper class, where it [licensed marriage] has been accepted in form and in meaning, it is altered chiefly by the emphasis and symbolism it has acquired. For this class marriage is bound up with the moral and religious ideas of sin and virtue. It carries the stern obligation of continence and fidelity, and is regarded as a solemn contract upon which rest the stability and ultimately the meaning of the family. Since marriage is expected to be permanent and binding, it is entered into with deliberation and formality. To this group the courtship is highly important. Its form resembles that in analogous white circles today, but the emphasis and the somewhat ceremonial flavor are reminiscent of earlier white patterns. . . .

"In such courtships the idea of sexual relations before marriage would be scandalous. It is considered essential that the girl be a virgin when she is married, and that the marriage be legal, usually with a church ceremony. No member of this class in Cotton-ville has had a divorce or separation. Their code requires that a marriage be maintained even if it is not sexually or temperamentally satisfactory. For them divorce carries the stigma it had in most white communities a generation ago, and which it still carries in certain rural white communities today.

"Toward adultery also, this small group maintains an attitude more general among whites of a generation ago, regarding it as an unforgivable sin." (Hortense Powder-maker, *After Freedom* [1939], pp. 149-150.)

[4] We may present some samples of what is available in the way of legal divorce and desertion statistics: In Mississippi, in 1934, the divorce rate for Negroes was 4.4 per 100 marriages, while for whites it was 12.6 per 100 marriages (Frazier, *op. cit.*, p. 379). In Chicago, in 1921, the Court of Domestic Relations reported that official recognition of desertion was given to 414 couples in which the husband was Negro. This was 15.6 per cent of all desertions recognized, and it is to be compared with the

fact that Negroes constituted only 4.1 per cent of Chicago's population in 1920. (Figures on desertion from Ernest R. Mowrer, *Family Disorganization* [1939], p. 95. Population figures are from the *Fourteenth Census of the United States: 1920, Population,* Vol. III, Table 13.)

⁵ Some of the doubling up is due to the presence of collateral relatives in the household. In a study of 612 rural Negro families in Macon County, Alabama, 30 per cent of the families were found to contain 1 to 6 relatives. (Charles S. Johnson, *Shadow of the Plantation* [1934], p. 29.)

⁶ Charles S. Johnson, "Negro Personality Changes in a Southern Community," in E. B. Reuter (editor), *Race and Culture Contacts* (1934), p. 216. Most of the facts in this paragraph are taken from Charles S. Johnson and from E. Franklin Frazier.

⁷ Allison Davis, Burleigh B. Gardner, and Mary R. Gardner, *Deep South* (1941), p. 123.

⁸ As noted in Chapter 40, Section 3, we have calculated this figure simply by taking the total number of members reported by Negro churches (as reported in the census of *Religious Bodies: 1936*) and dividing it by the total Negro population in 1940. The resulting figure is much too low as a measure of the proportion of Negro church members because: (1) the Negro population grew between 1936 and 1940; (2) some of the smaller Negro churches are overlooked in the Census; (3) children are usually not included in the church figures but are included in the population figures. It is also to be noted that the figure cited in the text does not include Negroes who were members of "mixed" churches.

⁹ Richard Wright, *12 Million Black Voices* (1941), p. 131.

¹⁰ B. E. Mays and J. W. Nicholson, *The Negro's Church* (1933), p. 11.

¹¹ J. G. St. Clair Drake, "The Negro Church and Associations in Chicago," unpublished manuscript prepared for this study (1940), pp. 388-395.

¹² For a discussion of the lower class Negro preacher, see Drake, "The Negro Church and Associations in Chicago," pp. 366-371.

¹³ "The Methodists and Baptists look down upon the Sanctified, considering their noise and dancing somewhat heathenish." (Powdermaker, *op. cit.,* p. 234.)

¹⁴ Drake, "The Negro Church and Associations in Chicago," p. 434.

¹⁵ *Op. cit.,* pp. 102, 139, 253.

¹⁶ Guion G. Johnson and Guy B. Johnson, "The Church and the Race Problem in the United States," unpublished manuscript prepared for this study (1940), Vol. 2, pp. 217 ff.

¹⁷ *Ibid.,* pp. 296-298.

¹⁸ *Idem.*

¹⁹ ". . . Negroes regularly attend church whether Christians or sinners. They have not yet accumulated wealth adequate to the construction of clubhouses, amusement parks and theaters, although dance halls have attracted many. Whether they derive any particular joy therefrom or not, the Negroes must go to church, to see their friends, as they are barred from social centers open to whites. They must attend church, moreover, to find out what is going on; for the race has not sufficient interests to maintain in every locality a newspaper of its own, and the white dailies generally mention Negroes only when they happen to commit crimes against white persons. The young Negro must go to church to meet his sweetheart, to impress her with his worth and woo her in marriage, the Negro farmer to find out the developments in the business world,

the Negro mechanic to learn the needs of his community and how he may supply them." (Carter G. Woodson, *The History of the Negro Church* [1921], pp. 267-268.)

[20]

ORGANIZATIONS AND ACTIVITIES OF 609 URBAN CHURCHES

Organizations and Activities	Number of Churches	Per Cent Frequency
Preaching	609	100.0
Union services and interchurch cooperation	609	100.0
Missionary societies	609	100.0
Clubs (Social, Educational, Financial)	609	100.0
Sunday church school	608	99.8
Poor relief	590	96.9
Revivals	561	92.1
Choirs	503	82.6
Young People's work	398	65.4
Prayer Meetings	388	63.7
Recreational work	191	31.4
Pastors' aid boards	77	12.6
Gymnasium classes	30	4.9
Church papers	22	3.6
Extension work in missions	21	3.4
Feeding the unemployed	18	3.0
Junior churches	13	2.1
Daily vacation Bible school	10	1.6
Benevolent societies	6	1.0
Clinic (free)	5	0.8
Motion pictures	5	0.8
Cooperate Y. W. and Y. M. C. A.	5	0.8
Girl Scouts	5	0.8
Boy Scouts	5	0.8
Kindergarten	4	0.7
Nurseries (day)	3	0.5

Source: Benjamin E. Mays and Joseph W. Nicholson, *The Negro's Church* (1933), pp. 122-123.

[21] W. E. B. Du Bois, *The Souls of Black Folk* (1903), p. 190.

[22] Allison Davis, "The Negro Church and Associations in the Lower South," unpublished manuscript prepared for this study (1940), pp. 63-64.

[23] Drake, "The Negro Church and Associations in Chicago," pp. 273-274.

[24] *Ibid.*, pp. 274-277.

[25] The information for this paragraph on the relation of church to politics is taken from *ibid.*, pp. 231-235, and from Harold F. Gosnell, *Negro Politicians* (1935), pp. 94-100.

[26] Gosnell, *op. cit.*, pp. 94-100. We have noted, in Chapter 22, Section 4, that the Northern Negro manifests unusual interest in politics.

[27] Davis, *op. cit.*, p. 85; and Powdermaker, *op. cit.*, p. 238.

[28] The facts in the remainder of this paragraph are taken from Mays and Nicholson, *op. cit.*, pp. 168-197.

[29] *Ibid.*, p. 195.

[30] This can be inferred from Table 4 since practically all Northern Negroes are

urban. It is also directly corroborated by Doxey A. Wilkerson, *Special Problems of Negro Education* (1939), p. 7.

[31] David T. Blose and Ambrose Caliver, *Statistics of the Education of Negroes: 1933-1934 and 1935-1936*, U. S. Office of Education, Bulletin No. 13, (1938), p. 2. Also see other statistics in that study.

[32] *Sixteenth Census of the United States: 1940, Population.* Preliminary Release, Series P-10, No. 8.

[33] Charles S. Johnson, "The Negro Public Schools," *Louisiana Educational Survey*, Section 8 (1942), p. 66.

[34] Wilkerson records some of the other conclusions of such scholastic achievement tests:

"They have demonstrated such facts as these: (1) that the extent of racial differences in scholastic achievement varies markedly among different school systems; (2) that such differences are greater in segregated than in nonsegregated schools; (3) that there is close correspondence between the extent of racial differences in scholastic achievement and racial differences in school environment; (4) that differences between the achievements of white and Negro pupils in Northern school systems are attributable almost entirely to scholastic deficiencies on the part of Negro migrants from impoverished school systems in the South; and (5) that Negro graduates of Northern high schools maintain better scholastic records in Southern Negro colleges than do graduates of Southern Negro high schools." (Wilkerson, *op. cit.*, p. 153.)

One of the best of these investigations was the Rosenwald Survey of 10,023 children in the third and sixth grades in 16 Southern counties. This is reported in Horace Mann Bond, *The Education of the Negro in the American Social Order* (1934), pp. 339-349. Other studies are listed by Wilkerson (*op. cit.*, p. 153):

"Doxey A. Wilkerson, 'Racial Differences in Scholastic Achievement,' Journal of Negro Education III (1934), pp. 453-77, and 'A Racial Index Number of Relative Educational Efficiency for Virginia County and City Systems of Schools,' Virginia Teachers Bulletin IX (1932), pp. 1-5, 8-12; Charles H. Thompson, 'A Study of the Reading Accomplishments of Colored and White Children,' unpublished master's thesis, The University of Chicago, 1920, and 'The Educational Achievements of Negro Children,' Annals of the American Academy of Political and Social Science, CXL (1928), pp. 193-208; J. H. Johnston, 'Graduates of Northern High Schools as Students at a Southern Negro College,' Journal of Negro Education, II, (1933), pp. 484-6; T. E. Davis, 'A Study of Fisk University Freshmen from 1928 to 1930,' Journal of Negro Education, II (1933), pp. 477-83; and Forrester B. Washington, 'The Negro in Detroit' (Detroit: Bureau of Government Research, 1926)."

[35] Ambrose Caliver, *Vocational Education and Guidance of Negroes*, U.S. Office of Education, Bulletin No. 38 (1938), p. 12.

[36] In Nashville, Tennessee, for example, the President of the Board of Education admitted in court (February 23, 1942) that there is a larger percentage of Negro teachers with college degrees in the schools of Nashville, than there is of whites. (N.A.A.C.P. news release [February 27, 1942]).

[37] Negro teachers in the city schools sometimes manifest their upper class status to the detriment of the lower classes of Negroes. Frazier (E. Franklin Frazier, *Negro Youth at the Crossways* [1940], p. 282) records that they sometimes use their teaching positions to advance their own status and cites the case of a school principal who did

not wish to have the correct number of under-nourished pupils reported because she did not want to be known as the principal of a "poorhouse." Frazier and others report that light-skinned upper class Negro teachers sometimes make it hard for dark-skinned lower class pupils. (*Ibid.*, pp. 96-99.) Davis and Dollard, for example, say about the dark-skinned pupil:

"He finds that he is not granted these privileges; instead he is stigmatized by teachers and their favored students on grounds of the 'ignorance' of his parents, the dialect which he speaks, the appearance of his clothes, and, very likely, the darkness of his skin. It does not take him long to discover that something is wrong and that the teacher's 'pets' of high status are the only ones who can make the prestige goal responses. If there is no reward for learning, in terms of privilege and anxiety-reduction, there is no motive for work. The lower-class child soon becomes a 'dummy'. Frequently he is openly aggressive toward the teacher; if not, he plays hookey, and he displaces his aggression from the powerful teacher to the more vulnerable upper-class and upper-middle-class pupils. He becomes like his parents, 'bad' and 'ignorant.' " (Allison Davis and John Dollard, *Children of Bondage* [1940], p. 285.)

[38] Wilkerson, *op. cit.*, pp. 39-40.

[39] *Ibid.*, p. 40. "From another point of view, though Negroes constitute about 24 percent of the total rural population in these 18 States, they had only 7 percent of the rural high schools in 1933-34 and formed 4 percent of the rural high school enrollment. By contrast, whereas Negroes constitute about 21 percent of the urban population, they had 30 percent of the 1933-34 urban high schools and 14 percent of the urban high school enrollment. It is in rural areas, primarily, that Negroes fail to share the benefits of public secondary education." (*Ibid.*, p. 41.)

[40] There were 70 public junior colleges in these states for whites, enrolling 17,695 students. (*Ibid.*, pp. 44-45.)

[41] *Ibid.*, p. 64.

[42] Fred McCuistion, *Graduate Instruction for Negroes in the United States* (1939), p. 39. The five Negro institutions offering graduate work before 1937 are: Howard, Fisk, Hampton, Atlanta and Xavier. By 1939 nine Southern states had no provision for the education of Negroes on the graduate and professional level. Two other states claimed to offer graduate instruction in their public colleges (Texas and Virginia) but the quality of such instruction was very poor, and its range very limited. The remaining six states and Virginia, offered to Negro students scholarships which could be used either in the private universities within the state or in out-of-state universities. These scholarships, however, are not granted freely. The District of Columbia has Howard University.

[43] Alexis de Tocqueville, *Democracy in America* (1900; translated by Henry Reeve; first edition, 1835), pp. 114-118; James Bryce, *The American Commonwealth* (1910; first edition, 1893), p. 294; Max Weber, "Geschäftsbericht," *Verhandlungen des Ersten Deutschen Soziologentages vom 19-22 Oktober, 1910 in Frankfurt a.M.* (1911), translated for private use by E. C. Hughes (1940), pp. 52-60.

[44] Drake, "The Negro Church and Associations in Chicago," p. 438.

[45] Davis, *op. cit.*, p. 139.

[46] Herbert Goldhamer, "Voluntary Associations," unpublished manuscript (1937), pp. 107-112.

[47] J. G. St. Clair Drake, "Churches and Voluntary Associations in the Chicago Negro Community," W.P.A. District 3, Chicago: project under the supervision of Horace R. Cayton (December, 1940), p. 185.

[48] *Op. cit.*, p. 55.

[49] Drake, "Churches and Voluntary Associations in the Chicago Negro Community," pp. 207 and 282. (The latter page has statistical substantiation of the fact that lower class Negroes join fewer associations than do upper class Negroes.)

[50] *Finding a Way Out* (1920), p. 170.

[51] Out of 22 local Urban League secretaries responding to a questionnaire sent out for our study, all but one reported that lodges and fraternal orders were decreasing among Negroes in their respective cities, and that Negro youth were showing less and less interest in them. (T. Arnold Hill, "Churches and Lodges: Digest and Analysis of Questionnaires Submitted by Urban League Secretaries for 'The Negro in America,'" unpublished manuscript prepared for this study [1940], pp. 14-15.) Also see Drake, "The Negro Church and Associations in Chicago," p. 500; and Harry J. Walker, "Negro Benevolent Societies in New Orleans," unpublished manuscript available at Fisk University (Nashville, Tennessee) (1936), p. 305.

[52] Hill, *op. cit.*, p. 13. According to Drake, it was mainly the lower class Negroes who left the lodges within the past ten years, since they were primarily interested in the death benefits given by lodges until the latter became financially unstable during the 1930's. ("The Negro Church and Associations in Chicago," pp. 500-502.)

[53] Criticism of the waste of money by Negro lodges and clubs is made by many Negro leaders. See, for example, James Weldon Johnson, *Negro Americans, What Now?* (1934), pp. 32-34.

[54] As late as the 1930's, there were between 300 and 600 benevolent and mutual aid organizations among Negroes in New Orleans. This was much more than among whites in that city. (See Walker, *op. cit.*, p. 18. This is, by far, the best study of Negro lodges that has come to our attention.)

[55] E. Nelson Palmer, "A Note on the Development of Negro Lodges in the United States," unpublished manuscript prepared for this study, under the direction of Guy B. Johnson (1940), p. 12. Palmer bases this statement on two sources: Howard W. Odum, *Social and Mental Traits of the Negro* (1910), p. 99; and Carter G. Woodson, "Insurance Business among Negroes," *The Journal of Negro History* (April, 1929), pp. 203-204.

[56] W. E. B. Du Bois (editor), *Some Efforts of American Negroes for Their Own Social Betterment* (1898), p. 17.

[57] *The Story of the Negro* (1909), Vol. 2, pp. 168-169. Both the Du Bois and the Washington evaluations are quoted in Palmer, *op. cit.*, pp. 14-15.

[58] Also see Abram L. Harris, *The Negro as Capitalist* (1936), p. 178.

[59] Cited in Hill, *op. cit.*, p. 16. In a few communities in the Deep South, lodges have a few judicial functions.

"On St. Helena Island, for example, a man rarely goes to court before first laying the case before his local lodge, 'praise house,' or church. Few cases even reach the courts, for most of them are settled satisfactorily by these lodge and church 'courts', including some rather serious offenses, such as theft and assault." (T. J. Woofter, Jr., *Black Yeomanry* [1930], pp. 238-242, summarized by Guy B. Johnson, "Some

Factors in the Development of Negro Social Institutions in the United States," *The American Journal of Sociology* [November, 1934], p. 336.)

60 Drake, "The Negro Church and Associations in Chicago," p. 440.

Chapter 44. *Non-institutional Aspects of the Negro Community*

1 Negro spokesmen have glorified the Negro's ability to enjoy life and have found in it a means of group survival. James Weldon Johnson long ago said:

"These people talked and laughed without restraint. In fact, they talked straight from their lungs and laughed from the pits of their stomachs. And this hearty laughter was often justified by the droll humour of some remark. I paused long enough to hear one man say to another: 'W'at's de mattah wid you an' yo' fr'en' Sam?' and the other came back like a flash: 'Ma fr'en'? He ma fr'en'? Man! I'd go to his funeral jes' de same as I'd go to a minstrel show.' I have since learned that this ability to laugh heartily is, in part, the salvation of the American Negro; it does much to keep him from going the way of the Indian." (*The Autobiography of an Ex-Coloured Man* [1927; first edition, 1912], p. 56.)

More recently, W. E. B. Du Bois has claimed:

"This race has the greatest of the gifts of God, laughter. It dances and sings: it is humble; it longs to learn; it loves men; it loves women. It is frankly, baldly, deliciously human in an artificial and hypocritical land. If you will hear men laugh, go to Guinea, 'Black Bottom,' 'Niggertown,' Harlem. If you want to feel humor too exquisite and subtle for translation, sit invisibly among a gang of Negro workers. The white world has its gibes and cruel caricatures; it has its loud guffaws; but to the black world alone belongs the delicious chuckle. . . . We are the supermen who sit idly by and laugh and look at civilization. We, who frankly want the bodies of our mates and conjure no blush to our bronze cheeks when we own it. We, who exalt the Lynched above the Lyncher, and the Worker above the Owner, and the Crucified above Imperial Rome." (*Dusk of Dawn* [1940], pp. 148-149.)

2 "The death of Denmark Vesey and Nat Turner proved long since to the Negro the present hopelessness of physical defense. Political defense is becoming less and less available, and economic defense is still only partly effective. But there is a patent defense at hand,—the defense of deception and flattery, of cajoling and lying. It is the same defense which the Jews of the Middle Age used and which left its stamp on their character for centuries. To-day the young Negro of the South who would succeed cannot be frank and outspoken, honest and self-assertive, but rather he is daily tempted to be silent and wary, politic and sly; he must flatter and be pleasant, endure petty insults with a smile, shut his eyes to wrong; in too many cases he sees positive personal advantage in deception and lying. His real thoughts, his real aspirations must be guarded in whispers; he must not criticize, he must not complain. Patience, humility, and adroitness must, in these growing black youth, replace impulse, manliness, and courage. With this sacrifice there is an economic opening, and perhaps peace and some prosperity. Without this there is riot, migration, or crime. Nor is this situation peculiar to the southern United States,—is it not rather the only method by which undeveloped races have gained the right to share modern culture? The price of culture is a Lie." (W. E. B. Du Bois, *The Souls of Black Folk* [1903], pp. 204-205.)

[3] See, for example, B. Schrieke, *Alien Americans* (1936), pp. 150-151, and James Weldon Johnson, *Negro Americans, What Now?* (1934), pp. 85-86 *passim*. Negro intellectuals, as the group which is rising most rapidly, are especially jealous of each other. That is one reason why they are so critical of Negro leaders. A Negro friend of the author's, shortly after he confided that, in his opinion, certain Negro leaders accomplished absolutely nothing for the race, received an excellent position in a white institution due to the efforts of one of the leaders he so severely criticized.

[4] Allison Davis, Burleigh B. Gardner, and Mary R. Gardner, *Deep South* (1941), p. 244.

[5] "In spite of emancipation Negroes still feel it necessary to conceal their thoughts from white people. In speech and in manner they may convey the impression of concurrence and contentment when at heart they feel quite otherwise. In these recent days the psychologists have come to call this a 'defense mechanism,' and some are sure that it is the only thing that enables the Negro to survive in his contact with the white man. Negroes are sometimes warned, even now, that they dare not manifest any resentment toward mistreatment; that the safest policy to pursue is to acquiesce in the judgment of those white people who have manifested a friendly attitude toward them and appeal to their consciences for the redressing of wrongs and correction of abuses. Small wonder that the Negro is so generally secretive." (Robert R. Moton, *What the Negro Thinks* [1929], pp. 12-13.)

[6] Hortense Powdermaker, *After Freedom* (1939), p. 286.

[7] See Zora Neale Hurston, *Mules and Men* (1935), pp. 229-287, and Newbell N. Puckett, *Folk Beliefs of the Southern Negro* (1926).

[8] In 1930, 58.3 per cent of all Negroes living in the North and West were Southern-born, counting Missouri in the North. With continuing migration, a low birth rate, and a recalculation putting Missouri in the South, the proportion today would no doubt be higher. (U. S. Bureau of the Census, *Negroes in the United States: 1920-1932*, p. 22.)

[9] For an analysis of Negro words that refer to personality types, see Samuel M. Strong, "The Social Type Method: Social Types in the Negro Community of Chicago," unpublished Ph.D. thesis, University of Chicago (1940).

[10] U. S. Bureau of the Census, *Eleventh Census of the United States: 1890*, "Crime, Pauperism, and Benevolence," Vol. 1, p. 126.

[11] See Guy B. Johnson and Louise K. Kiser, "The Negro and Crime," unpublished manuscript prepared for this study (1940), pp. 65 and 291 ff.

[12] *Ibid.*, p. 95. A similar criticism of Negro crime statistics is given by one of the nation's leading students of crime:

"Conclusions have been reached that the Negro is responsible for a 'larger proportionate share of crime'; and that 'the Negro has committed more crime than any other racial group'; and that 'the Negro crime rate as measured by all comparative records is greater than that of the white.' . . . The data hitherto compiled from the sources discussed, permit only one conclusion, namely, that the Negro appears to be arrested, convicted and committed to penal institutions more frequently than the white. Any other conclusion would be based on the assumption that the proportionate number of arrests, convictions or commitments to the total number of offenses actually committed is the same in both groups. This assumption is untenable, for there are specific factors which seriously distort the arrest, conviction and commitment rates for Negroes without affecting these rates for whites in a similar manner. No measurement has as yet been devised for the evaluation of these factors." (Thorsten Sellin, "The Negro and the Problem of Law Observance and Administration in the Light of Social Research," in Charles S. Johnson, *The Negro in American Civilization* [1930], p. 447.)

[13] "Negro Criminality," *Journal of Social Science* (December, 1899), pp. 78-98.

[14] Edwin H. Sutherland, "White-Collar Criminality," *American Sociological Review* (February, 1940), pp. 1-12.

[15] Johnson and Kiser, *op. cit.*, p. 347. There are other ways in which white criminals divert suspicion from themselves to Negroes; see *ibid.*, pp. 345-348.

[16] After making a special analysis of some statistics on homicides in the South collected for this study by George K. Brown, A. J. Jaffe concludes: "It appears statistically significant that a Negro who murders a white man receives a much stiffer penalty than if he murders a Negro. On the other hand, a white man can murder another white man with about the same (or perhaps even more) impunity as one Negro can murder another. Also a white can murder a Negro with relative freedom from punishment." (Unpublished memorandum prepared for this study [August 19, 1940].) Brown's data are in Appendix B of Johnson and Kiser, *op. cit.* Johnson and Kiser also present some data which further corroborate this point; see *ibid.*, pp. 358-362 and Appendix D. Independently, Powdermaker has presented some similar data for Mississippi (*op. cit.*, pp. 395-396).

With respect to parole and probation, the U. S. Bureau of the Census reported: "It is quite apparent . . . that Negroes remain in the institutions to the expiration of their sentence in much greater proportions than do whites." (*Prisoners in State and Federal Prisons and Reformatories: 1939* [1941], p. 43.) With respect to length of prison term, it reported: ". . . among the State prisoners, the Negroes generally served longer periods of time than did the whites. . . . It is quite apparent that whites served less time than Negroes in the Southern States, for murder, manslaughter, burglary, forgery, rape, and other sex offenses. The whites serve a little longer for aggravated assault, and for larceny . . . [and] for auto theft." (*Ibid.*, p. 70.)

The Detroit survey reported similar findings:

"The Detroit survey disclosed that of the number of whites convicted of felonies 13.5 per cent were given the alternative of a fine or a prison sentence while only 7.1 per cent of the Negro felons were so favored. Over 12 per cent of the white defendants were placed on probation as compared with 7.2 per cent Negroes. Similar disproportions were revealed in the number of suspended sentences. The Detroit Survey is typical of situations throughout our state jurisdictions." (Nathaniel Cantor, "Crime and the Negro," *The Journal of Negro History* [January, 1931], p. 63.)

[17] E. Franklin Frazier, "The Pathology of Race Prejudice," *The Forum* (June, 1927), p. 860.

[18] Johnson and Kiser, *op. cit.*, 411-412.

[19] Interview (November 18, 1942).

[20] Johnson and Kiser, *op. cit.*, pp. 258-263.

[21] *Ibid.*, p. 212.

[22] For examples of false accusations of rape for which Negroes have been arrested and punished, see *The Negro Year Book: 1931-1932* (1931), pp. 291-292. Also see Ray Stannard Baker, *Following the Color Line* (1908), pp. 8-9.

[23] R. M. Lightfoot, Jr., *Negro Crime in a Small Urban Community* (1934), pp. 30

and 62; see, also, pp. 24-28. For similar evidence of the high proportion of minor offenses among Negro arrests, see Maurine Boie, "An Analysis of Negro Crime Statistics for Minneapolis for 1923, 1924 and 1925," *Opportunity* (June, 1928), p. 173; H. P. Brinton, "Negroes Who Run Afoul the Law," *Social Forces* (October, 1932), pp. 98-99; B. P. Chamberlain, *The Negro and Crime in Virginia* (1936), p. 107; Ira DeA. Reid, *Social Conditions of the Negro in the Hill District of Pittsburgh* (1930), pp. 59-60; Detroit Bureau of Governmental Research, *The Negro in Detroit* (1926), Section 9, p. 8; and H. L. Andrews, "Racial Distinctions in the Courts of North Carolina," unpublished M.A. thesis, Duke University (1933), p. 50. This footnote and the quotation to which it refers is taken from Johnson and Kiser, *op. cit.*, pp. 201-202.

[24] The Mayor's Commission on Conditions in Harlem, "The Negro in Harlem: A Report on Social and Economic Conditions Responsible for the Outbreak of March 19, 1935," typescript (1936), pp. 97-99.

[25] The study was made by New York City's Welfare Council. It is summarized in the *Report of the Sub-Committee on Crime and Delinquency of the City-Wide Citizens' Committee on Harlem* (1942), p. 5.

[26] Johnson and Kiser, *op. cit.*, p. 216.

[27] "Many colored tenants do not regard the taking of small amounts of stock or cotton from their landlords as stealing but rather as a just compensation for the money stolen from them by their landlords in the reckoning of accounts or for the beatings administered to them by their landlords. Under the systems of economic control and intimidation exercised by the landlord, the colored tenant often justifies his thefts on the grounds that his only means of securing his fair share of the proceeds from his crop is by the use of stealth." (Davis, Gardner, and Gardner, *op. cit.*, pp. 395-396.)

"One of my earliest recollections is that of my mother cooking a chicken late at night, and awakening her children for the purpose of feeding them. How or where she got it I do not know. I presume, however, it was procured from our owner's farm. Some people may call this theft. If such a thing were to happen now, I should condemn it as theft myself. But taking place at the time it did, for the reason that it did, no one could ever make me believe that my mother was guilty of thieving. She was simply a victim of the system of slavery." (Booker T. Washington, *Up From Slavery* [1901; first edition, 1900], pp. 4-5.)

[28] "This system has many bad results. It encourages the Negro in crime. He knows that unless he does something pretty bad, he will not be prosecuted because the landlord doesn't want to lose the work of a single hand; he knows that if he *is* prosecuted the white man will, if possible, 'pay him out.' It disorganises justice and confuses the ignorant Negro mind as to what is a crime and what is not. A Negro will often do things that he would not do if he thought he were really to be punished. He comes to the belief that if the white man wants him arrested, he will be arrested, and if he protects him, he won't suffer, no matter what he does. Thousands of Negroes, ignorant, weak, indolent, to-day work under this system." (Baker, *op. cit.*, p. 97.)

[29] Clifford R. Shaw and Henry D. McKay, *Juvenile Delinquency and Urban Areas* (1942).

[30] Some have claimed that Negroes had less mental disease before Emancipation than afterward, supposedly because they received better care under slavery and did not have to worry about the struggle for existence. See: (1) J. W. Babcock, "The Colored Insane," *Alienist and Neurologist* (1895), pp. 423-447; (2) A. H. Witmer, "Insanity

in the Colored Race in the United States," *Alienist and Neurologist* (January, 1891), pp. 19-30.

[31] The facts in this paragraph have been taken from (1) Benjamin Malzberg, "Mental Disease among American Negroes: A Statistical Analysis," in Otto Klineberg (editor), *Characteristics of the American Negro*, prepared for this study, to be published, manuscript pages 5-6; (2) Solomon P. Rosenthal, "Racial Differences in the Incidence of Mental Disease," *Journal of Negro Education* (July, 1934), pp. 484-493.

[32] Malzberg, *op. cit.*, manuscript pages 7 ff.

[33] Rates standardized to hold age constant: New York City (1929-1931): Negroes—233; Whites—104. (*Ibid.*, manuscript page 21.)

[34] *Ibid.*, manuscript pages 8 ff.

[35] Their poverty and younger average age, in addition to their concentration in cities, would help explain why Negroes have more dementia praecox. (See Rosenthal, *op. cit.*, p. 490.)

[36] "Psychotic Symptoms and Social Backgrounds" in M. Bentley and E. V. Cowdry (editors), *The Problem of Mental Disorder* (1934), pp. 339-345.

[37] U. S. Bureau of the Census, *Vital Statistics—Special Reports, Mortality Summary for U. S. Registration States: Suicide* (September 19, 1942), Table E.

[38] Frank Tannenbaum describes the lack of recreational patterns in the rural South, with special reference to the whites:

"Studies of rural social life in single-crop areas have shown that there are few parties, few picnics, few dances, and fewer public meetings. In one locality over 70 per cent of the people had not attended a party during the year, over 90 per cent had not been to a dance, over 80 per cent had neither participated in nor attended an athletic exhibition, and over 70 per cent had not been to a public meeting.

"And in one county only one family had seen a moving picture show during the year. . . . The weekly visit to the nearest town is the only break in the monotony of life. This monotony is so great that a public hanging has been known to attract mothers with children in their arms, who have come trooping for miles to get some contact with other people." (*Darker Phases of the South* [1924], pp. 139-140.)

[39] "Rural life has its period of intense work and its period of dull and uneventful calm. When the soil is being broken and prepared for crops, all hands strong enough for the plow are engaged from early sunrise to sundown. Again when the crop matures and particularly when the cotton is ready for picking, idleness and leisure are costly. Between seasons the most common answer to the question about how and where the children play is likely to be 'We don't do nothing, mostly just sit and talk.'" (Charles S. Johnson, *Growing Up in the Black Belt* [1941], p. 170.)

[40] There seem to be few caste restrictions on hunting and fishing, partly because they supplement the food supply of meagerly fed plantation tenants, partly because there is an element of "sportsmanship" and "fair play" in hunting and fishing traditions. Negroes sometimes hunt and fish with whites; they are seldom deprived of their game; they are usually left undisturbed in the spots they have chosen to hunt and fish; and there are few segregated fishing and hunting places. (See Arthur Raper, *Preface to Peasantry* [1936], pp. 396-397.)

[41] See Charles S. Johnson, *Growing Up in the Black Belt*, pp. 184-185 and 228; for an excellent picture of this sort of amusement, see Richard Wright's story, "Big Boy

Leaves Home," in *Uncle Tom's Children* (1938), and Zora Neale Hurston, *Their Eyes Were Watching God* (1937), especially pp. 98-109 and 200-202.

[42] James Weldon Johnson tells of this recreation in a small Southern town: "We always went to the railroad station on Saturdays to see the four trains come in and go out. . . . I never saw anybody that I knew getting off, but there was a faint excitement in watching the traffic. At any rate, I got an understanding of why country people love to meet passing trains." (*Along This Way* [1934], p. 114.)

[43] Much of all the recreational life in the rural community is carried on in and around the church, which is the natural meeting place in the community (see Chapter 43, Section 3); in some areas the church tries to provide healthful organized recreation for the young people in the form of social and athletic clubs (see Charles S. Johnson, *Growing Up in the Black Belt*, pp. 175 ff.).

[44] In Charles S. Johnson's study of 916 families in the rural Deep South, only 17.4 per cent of the families had radios (*ibid.*, p. 55). Some of the younger children had never heard a radio (*ibid.*, p. 183). The census figures indicate that only .003 per cent of the Negro families in the rural Deep South had radios as compared to 11.9 per cent of the white families. (*Fifteenth Census of the United States: 1930, Population*, Vol. VI, State Tables 16 and 4.)

[45] In Charles S. Johnson's study 27.6 per cent of the homes had victrolas (*Growing Up in the Black Belt*, p. 56). Unfortunately, certain companies producing records have issued a special series for Negroes, "race records," many of which are vicious and obscene, and these were widely sold in the rural areas. (Donald R. Young, *American Minority Peoples* [1932], pp. 306-307, and Forrester B. Washington, "Recreational Facilities for Negroes," *The Annals of the American Academy of Political and Social Science* [November, 1928], p. 279.)

[46] For a discussion of how rural patterns of recreation are considered normal in the county and delinquent in the city, see Charles S. Johnson, *Growing Up in the Black Belt*, pp. 186-187.

[47] *Black Manhattan* (1930), pp. 162-163.

[48] For a discussion of amateur theatricals among Negroes, see Sterling A. Brown, "The Negro in American Culture: Section D—The Negro on the Stage," unpublished manuscript prepared for this study (1940), pp. 148 ff.

[49] In the past all-day excursions, especially where facilities were available along the Mississippi and Ohio Rivers and along the sea coast, were popular with rural Negroes; they even developed their own excursion steamers. (Washington, *op. cit.*, p. 279.) This form of recreation seems to have disappeared.

[50] Young, *op. cit.*, p. 296.

[51] "In a recent survey of the Negroes of Richmond, Virginia, 698 men and 889 women were asked what they did for amusement. 'Going to church' was placed first by 198 men and 331 women; 'movies and theaters' by 134 men and 254 women; 91 men and 176 women 'played with their children' or 'enjoyed their homes and friends.' Reading was reported by 101 men and 88 women. And 91 men and 93 women had no amusements or recreations whatever. 'Smoking, hunting and fishing' were extremely popular with men. Society or lodge meetings, sewing and fancy work, were favorites of the women. Music, singing, and playing of musical instruments were named repeatedly by both men and women. Almost everything in life was mentioned by a sprinkling of both as an amusement: 'walking,' 'drinking,' 'eating,' 'sleeping,'

'praying,' 'resting,' 'working,' 'gardening,' 'traveling,' 'sitting around,' 'using snuff,' 'helping to make others happy,' 'policy playing,' 'automobile riding,' etc." (*Ibid.*, pp. 269-270.)

[52] Charles S. Johnson, *The Negro College Graduate* (1938), p. 339.

[53] Alain Locke, *Negro Art: Past and Present* (1936), pp. 34-42 and 93-117.

[54] *Time* (May 11, 1942), p. 53.

[55] *Black Manhattan*, p. 87.

[56] Brown, "The Negro in American Culture: Section D—The Negro on the Stage," p. 16.

[57] *Ibid.*, pp. 7 and 12.

[58] James Weldon Johnson gives the following evaluation of the minstrel shows:

"Minstrelsy was, on the whole, a caricature of Negro life, and it fixed a stage tradition which has not yet been entirely broken. It fixed the tradition of the Negro as only an irresponsible, happy-go-lucky, wide-grinning, loud-laughing, shuffling, banjo-playing, singing, dancing sort of being. Nevertheless, these companies did provide stage training and theatrical experience for a large number of coloured men. They provided an essential training and theatrical experience which, at the time, could not have been acquired from any other source. Many of these men, as the vogue of minstrelsy waned, passed on into the second phase, or middle period, of the Negro on the theatrical stage in America; and it was mainly upon the training they had gained that this second phase rested." (*Black Manhattan*, p. 93.)

[59] Alain Locke, *The Negro and His Music* (1936), pp. 57 and 70.

[60] See Vernon Winslow, "Negro Art and the Depression," *Opportunity* (February, 1941), pp. 42 and 62.

[61] Sterling A. Brown, "The Negro in American Culture: Section G—Music," pp. 208-212.

[62] Locke, *The Negro and His Music*, pp. 18-27.

[63] *Ibid.*, p. 30.

[64] "Part of the 'coon-songs' popularity comes from the vicarious enjoyment by white audiences of things forbidden. Goldberg says that 'what the whites were thinking in the gilded Nineties, the blacks were singing.' (Isaac Goldberg, *Tin Pan Alley* [1930], p. 156.) The franker side of sex, the 'gold-digging,' fighting for one's man or one's woman, the various degrees of sexual proficiency, could be mentioned if the actors involved were Negro. But to approach the borderline between the genteel and the gross, to venture into the risqué, to mention the unmentionable, was 'not damaging to one's social or business reputation,' if the songs were about Negroes. Negro life was the fantastic Cockaigne, beckoning to the inhibited, offering escape no less attractive for being droll. Today Hollywood stars, such as Mae West and Marlene Dietrich, in the roles of sirens of the 'nineties, sing as throatily as they are able, the hot numbers of Negro honkytonks as their mating-calls." (Brown, "The Negro in American Culture: Section G—Music," p. 90.)

[65] See, for example, Nick Aaron Ford, *The Contemporary Negro Novel* (1936). *passim*, especially pp. 94-102.

[66] *Time* (August 28, 1933), p. 32.

[67] "The Negro-Art Hokum," *Nation* (June 16, 1926), p. 662.

Chapter 45. *America Again at the Crossroads in the Negro Problem*

[1] A parallel analysis of the relationship between war and improvement in the status of Negroes may be found in Guion G. Johnson, "The Impact of War Upon the Negro," *Journal of Negro Education* (July, 1941), pp. 596-611.

[2] Horace R. Cayton, "The Morale of the Negro in the Defense Crisis," unpublished manuscript of paper read to the 20th Annual Institute of the Society for Social Research, The University of Chicago (August 15, 1941), p. 11.

Cayton reflected pessimistically:

"It is not that any of these men or groups are really interested in changing in any fundamental way, the position of the Negro in the United States. This would prove, in most instances, just as embarrassing to them as it would to those leaders who are interested in an immediate declaration of war. But the Negro presents a 'pat' argument for those who want to say that democracy should be built at home. Nevertheless, the Negro was thrilled to at last have national figures speak about this plight on the radio, from the platform and in the newspapers. Neglected, for the most part, by the pro-war groups, the anti-war crowd has made a deep impression on the Negro public." (*Idem.*)

[3] There is a question whether Negroes have identified themselves with other colored peoples as much as Southern whites have identified American Negroes with Japan. A confidential public opinion poll taken before Pearl Harbor showed that the South, with no Japanese population, was more anti-Japanese than Americans on the West Coast, who had a definite Japanese problem. Also symbolic is the following AP dispatch from Atlanta, Georgia (from the New York *Herald Tribune* [April 5, 1942], p. 3).

"Atlanta children were heard reciting this wartime rhyme:

> 'Eenie, meenie, minie, moe,
> Catch the emperor by the toe,
> If he hollers make him say:
> "I surrender to the U.S.A." ' "

This, of course, is a paraphrase of the doggerel containing an anti-Negro sentiment, known to every American child (in two versions):

> "Eenie, meenie, minie, moe,
> Catch a nigger by the toe
> If he hollers, let him go
> Eenie, meenie, minie, moe."

> "Eenie, meenie, minie, moe,
> Catch a nigger by the toe
> If he hollers, make him pay
> Fifty dollars every day."

[4] Raleigh *News and Observer* (May 3, 1942).

[5] Earl Brown, "American Negroes and the War," in *Harper's Magazine* (April, 1942), p. 546.

[6] Horace R. Cayton, "Fighting for White Folks?," *Nation* (September 26, 1942), p. 268.

[7] "The Negro in the Political Life of the United States," *Journal of Negro Education* (July, 1941), p. 583.

[8] Cayton, "The Morale of the Negro in the Defense Crisis," p. 14.

[9] "Shadows of the Slave Tradition," *Survey Graphic* (November, 1942), p. 467.

[10] New York *Times*, April 3, 1942.

[11] Cited in New York *Times*, July 20, 1942.

[12] W. E. B. Du Bois, *Darkwater* (1920), p. 236.

[13] Guion G. Johnson, *op. cit.*, pp. 609-610.

[14] Letter (August 13, 1942).

[15] Cited from *PM* (August 16, 1942), p. 17.

[16] *Along This Way* (1934), p. 411.

[17] *American Unity and Asia* (1942), p. 29.

[18] *Ibid.*, p. 25.

[19] *Contemporary China. A Reference Digest*, published by Chinese News Service, Inc. (August 10, 1942).

[20] *The Negro Question* (1890), p. 48.

[21] *Following the Color Line* (1908), p. 305.

INDEX TO BOTH VOLUMES

Human inclinations, etiquette in cases involving, 616-617

Humanitarianism, 6-7; of American Creed, 598; in Reconstruction period, 739, 741

Humor, Negro, 959-961, 1431; function of, in race question, 38-39; simulated, 960

Hurd, John C., cited, 531-532

Hurston, Zora Neale, cited, 965

Huxley, Julian S.; on adaptation to environment, 1199; on miscegenation, 1209

Huxley, J. S., and Haddon, A. C., on genetic racial differences, 146

Idealism, American, lxviii, lxx, 712, 810; and behavior, disparity between, 21-23; 745, 755-756, 1008; history of, 6-8; inscribed in laws, 14

Ideals: conflict of, 209; lip-service to, 21-23; unity of, 3-5

Ideology: business, 800-803; defense, 30-32, 56-57, 62, 88, 104-105, 283-284, 441-445, 460, 962n., 1432; equalitarianism, see Equalitarianism; national, see American Creed; Negro, see Popular theories, Negro; Northern, 603, 1375-1376; "pure woman," 1356; Southern (see also Liberalism, Southern), 441-445, 670; working class, 407; of World War II, 517, 745, 755, 790n., 915, 1004, 1006, 1007, 1012, 1016

Ignorance, mutual, of Negroes and whites, 762, 956, 957

Ignorance, Negro, 961, 970; simulated, 961; of whites, 659

Ignorance about social affairs, 1034

Ignorance, white, about Negroes (see also Misinformation about Negroes), 40-42, 279, 339n., 382, 600, 647, 1010, 1143n., 1293, 1370-1371, 1373-1374; convenience of, 40-42, 48; as a factor in social inequality, 656-659; in the North, 383-386, 606, 644; in the South, 394-395

Illegality: pattern of, 558-560, 1346; tradition of (see also Law, lack of respect for, in America), 405, 435, 440, 441, 448-451, 525, 526, 536

Illegitimacy, 177-178, 932, 933, 935

Illinois: death penalty in, 554n.; lynching in, 561; riots in, 567; school segregation in, 633

Immigrants: competition of, with Negroes, 603; exploitation of, 50, 292; inferior schools for, 338; newspapers for, 911, 912; physical changes in, 122, 1202-1203; voting among, 491; voting rights of, 438

Immigration, 17, 50-52, 157-159, 166, 196, 713, 714, 927; decline of, 715; legislation on, 92, 196, 198; of Mexicans and Canadians, 159; Negro, 120, 135, 165, 166; restricted, 998, 1190

Imperialism, American, 1020

Improvement organizations, 744, 800, 812-852, 877

Income: farm, 255, 1283-1285; Southern white, 45n., 297n.

Income, Negro (see also Salaries and Wages), 307, 364-366, 1270, 1283-1285, 1288; of artists 329 330; differential in, 164-165; of doctors, 324-325; and family size, 366-367; of teachers and ministers, 319-320, 321

Inconsistency: between American ideals and practices 21-23, 745, 755-756, 1008; of attitudes in America, lxvii, lxx, 1140-1141; of beliefs, 111, 283-284, 446; intellectual and moral, 39-40; of Negro clergymen, 940; in social orientation, 52-53; of valuations, see Valuations, conflicts of

Independent Labor League of America, 812n.

India, potential revolt in, 1006

Indians, American, assimilability of, 53

Indiana: lynching in, 561; school segregation in, 633

"Indifferent equilibrium": in the North, 392-394; in the South, 394-396

Individual enterprise, decreased sanctity of, 213

Individualism, 709, 710; of immigrants, 714; Negro, 961; Southern, 458-459

Inequality; see Discrimination and "No social equality," doctrine of

Industrial Congress of 1873, 1296

"Industrial" education; see "Vocational" education

Industrial Revolution, effect of, on Negroes and women, 1077

Industrialization: future, of "backward" countries, 1017-1018; impact of, on Negroes, 645; in the South, 44, 199, 263, 398, 463, 515

Industry: Negroes in, 198, 199, 279-303, 380, 424, 1079-1124, 1256-1259, 1295-1296, 1386; exclusion of Negroes from, 389-390; history of Negroes in, 393-394

Infant mortality, 162, 171, 174, 1223, 1224

Inferiority doctrine, 54-55, 97-101, 577-578, 583, 642, 751; applied to women, 1077; deliberate fostering of, 101-106; disproving of, 76; Negro attitude toward, 62-65, 208, 758-759, 760; un-

New Deal, 9, 93, 556, 1183; decreased discrimination under, 335, 463-464, 494, 504, 546, 600; educational benefits of, 343, 465-466; effect of, on administrative standards, 437; and federal jobs for Negroes, 328; importance of, to Negroes, 74, 479n., 1000-1001; a liberal reform party, 511; and Negro social workers, 326; Negro support of, 510, 511, 1332; as popular movement, 465; and social reform, 545; and Southern liberals, 467, 471, 472; and youth assistance, 361

New England, Negro population in, 1309

New Jersey: riots in, 568n.; school segregation in, 633

New Mexico, school segregation in, 633

New Negro Alliance, 816

New Negro movement, 599, 750, 753, 754, 990

New York *Age*, 918n.

New York *Amsterdam News*, 918n.

New York City: Negro Democratic vote in, 492n., 494, 495; Negro population of, 1125-1126

New York State: anti-discrimination legislation in, 408, 418n., 1367; Negro population in, 1309

New York State Employment Service, 418n.

Newbold, N. C., 891

News agencies, Negro, 923

Newspapers; see Negro press *and* Press

Niagara movement, 742-744, 913n.

"No social equality" doctrine, 58, 395, 449, 457, 537, 550, 573, 575, 586-589, 628, 646, 669, 998, 1142; beliefs supporting, 582-586; critical evaluation of, 589-592; gradual breakdown of, 660-663; in the North, 603

Nobility, European, 1375

Nonpartisan elections, 487-488, 500

Nonpolitical Negro institutions; see Church, Negro, Schools, Negro, *and* Negro press

Nonsegregation: in housing, 1276; of Negro criminals and insane, 968-969

"Nordic race," 114n.

Norfolk *Journal and Guide*, 917

Norgren, Paul H.: cited, 1090-1091, 1092, 1095-1096, 1096-1097, 1100-1102, 1104, 1111-1112, 1112-1113, 1119-1120, 1122, 1123, 1302; on abolition of racial discrimination in promotion, 1118; on A.F.L. and color line, 1298; on coal mining, 1112; on laws against discrimination, 1300; on Negro jobs, 1080-1082; on Negro-white social intercourse, 1114-1115; on turpentine production, 1089; on union discrimination, 1299; on

whites and Negroes in auto industry 1119

Norgren, P. H., and Bailer, L. H., on Negro occupations in auto industry, 1120

North: accommodating leadership in, 722-723, 733; attitude in, toward amalgamation, 57-58, 603; attitude in, toward Civil War, 45, 47; caste system in, 46, 693; color line broken in, 678; compared with the South, 44-49; crime rate in, 969, 971, 977; definition of, 1071; depression in, 295; discrimination in, 66-67, 199, 599-604, 609, 610, 612-613, 614, 617-618, 626, 722, 999, 1010-1011, 1367; disfranchisement in, 438; economic opportunities in, 191, 196; educational segregation in, 633, 901, 945-946; equalitarianism in, 383, 384, 526-529, 1014-1015; housing segregation in, 352, 618-622, 623, 624, 626; housing shortage in, 196; ignorance about Negroes in, 383-386, 606, 644, 658-659; interracial sex relations in, 126; literacy requirements for voting in, 1310; measures against discrimination in, 418, 1367; mental situation in, on race problem, 44-49; migration to, 46, 183, 189, 191-197, 295, 329-330, 527, 568, 599, 602, 652, 999; mixed churches in, 869-870; Negro behavior in, 491-492; 530; Negro church in, 860, 862-863, 872; Negro education in, 879, 1421-1422; Negro employment in, 291-296; Negro leaders in, 722-724, 733, 777-779; Negro ministers in, 862-863; Negro police in, 543n.; Negro press in, 910; Negro protest in, 777-779; Negro suffrage in, 437-440, 725, 733; Negro voting in, 200, 491-497, 754-755, 1328, 1329; Negroes in politics in, 491-497; "no social equality" theory in, 603; participation in elections in, 475; poll tax in, 1324; prisons in, 555; racial isolation in, 649-650; race prejudice in, 1142-1143; relative judicial equality in, 526-529; segregation in, 626, 722; social segregation and discrimination in, 577, 599-604, 636, 999; and Southern suffrage problem, 515-518; standards of social welfare in, 355; white and Negro newspapers in, 916

North Central Association, 951n.

North Carolina: birth control program in, 1226; death penalty in, 554n.; education requirement for voting in, 484; liberalism in, 467-468; Negro jurors in, 550; Negro police in, 543n.; poll tax repealed in, 482; primaries in, 486; recreational facilities in, 1275; riots in, 568n.; terror organizations in, 449; voting in, 483, 488n.

North Carolina Mutual Life Insurance Company, 1263

North Dakota, expenditures for education in, 1271

North Star, 913

Northrup, Herbert R.: cited, 408, 1097, 1099, 1101, 1102, 1103-1104, 1106, 1108-1110, 1113, 1118, 1119n.; on discrimination in unions, 1299-1300

Nourse, E. G., Davis, J. S., and Black, J. D., cited, 257

Number of Negroes in America; *see* Quantitative goal for Negro population policy

Numbers game, 330-331, 940, 985, 1267, 1269

Nurses, Negro, 172, 325, 638, 796, 1224

Oberlin College, 1076n., 1415

Occupational mobility, 213

Occupational status of Southern whites, 297

O'Connor, W. B., cited, 393

Odum, Howard W., 96, 844; on criticism of Interracial Commission, 847; description of South by, 1320-1321

Office of Civilian Defense, discrimination in, 1367

Officeholders: Negro, 497, 501-504, 535, 542-543, 723-724, 755; power of, 435, 716, 717n.; publicity afforded, 718

Offord, Carl, cited, 1085

Ogburn, William, 1389; on institutional changes, 1051; on materials of social planning, 1052

Ohio: lynching in, 561; school segregation in, 633

Oklahoma: expenditures for education in, 1271; prohibition in, 457; transportation segregation in, 635; voting in, 483, 488

Old age benefit system, 357, 358, 359, 400, 1280-1281; occupations not covered by, 358, 1280-1281

Old Age and Survivors' Benefit System, 357n.

"Old Americans," 47, 114n., 138

Oliver, King, 988

Olmsted, Frederick, on slave-breeding, 1202

One-party system in the South, 452-455, 474, 475, 519, 1322

Oneida Community, 712

Operative Plasterers' and Cement Finishers' International Association, 1102

Opinion correlation, system of, 72-73

Opinion research; *see* Public opinion polls

Opinions, "personal" and "political," 1139-1141

Opportunism, 208, 471, 600, 774, 796, 830, 834n., 840, 843, 848, 854, 893, 1010, 1139, 1270, 1410

Opportunistic beliefs; *see* Stereotypes about Negroes

Opportunity, equality of, 573, 671-672, 884, 893

Opportunity, 837, 839, 909

Optimism-pessimism, scale of, 1038-1039

Order of Railway Conductors, 1105

Ordnance industry, Negroes in, 413

Organization (*see also* Trade Unions and Unionization): of Negroes to resist attack, 681n.; of plantation tenants, 250, 262, 263, 1250

Organizations: anti-Negro, 812n.; duplication of, 825, 854; left-wing, 812n.; Negro, 812-852, 952-955

Organizers, labor: importance of, 713, 714; terrorization of, 1300

Orientals; *see* Chinese *and* Japanese

Out-patient services, 346

Over-crowding in Negro homes, 376, 377, 378-379, 977, 978, 1127, 1291, 1308, 1426

Over-population in rural South, 205, 231-232, 253, 264, 265, 424

Over-production of cotton, 251

Overtime, payment for, 398

Ovington, Mary White, 819

Owen, Chandler, 749

Owenites, 712

Owens, Jesse, 734

Owens, John R., cited, 1099

Packing House Workers' Industrial Union, 1123

Page, Thomas Nelson, 732; characterization of Negro masses by, 1386-1387; on fight for race purity, 586, 1354-1355; on interracial friendship, 741n.; on interracial work, 843; on Negro education, 888, 896, 1419; on Northern teachers for Southern Negroes, 1415-1416; on retrogression of Negro workmen, 283; on Southern industrial labor, 280-281

Page, Walter Hines, 460

Paige, "Hot Lips," 645n.

Pale Faces, 449

Palmer, Edward Nelson, cited, 871n., 955, 1086

Panunzio, Constantine, cited, 1360

"Parallel civilizations," 578-582, 595, 741, 754, 1358

Parent-Teacher Associations, 948-949, 954n.

Park, Robert E., 1049-1050; on accommodation, 1050; on advertisements in Negro press, 922; on bi-racial organization,

Training: for leadership, 719n.; of policemen, 1342; of teachers, 904-905; vocational, *see* Vocational training

Training courses in war work, Negroes in, 1307

Transportation: discrimination in, 634-635, 1340; of Negro school children, 947, 948; police authority of operators and conductors, 537; segregation in, 537, 576, 581, 588, 628, 634-635, 742, 795, 1351, 1353, 1369

Tross, J. S. Nathaniel, on Negro tension, 1013

Trotter, Monroe, 742

Trowel trades, Negroes in, 286, 412, 1101, 1102

True Inspirationists, 712

Truth, Sojourner, 737

Tuberculosis, incidence of, 142

Tubman, Harriet, 737

Turner, Frederick Jackson, 433n.; on democracy, 5

Turner, Nat, 567, 736, 859

Turpentine farms: Negro workers on, 1089-1090; wages on, 1089-1090

Tuskegee compromise, 739-742, 913n., 1391-1392

Tuskegee Institute, 889, 890, 892, 898, 899, 1308

"Underground railroad," 578, 860

"Understanding" requirement for voting, 446, 484, 489, 514, 1325

Undertakers, Negro, 309-310, 317, 638; and insurance, 1262-1263

Underworld, Negro, 330-332, 655, 733, 1266-1268; class structure of, 704-705; leaders in, 1391; protection for, 498, 499, 501

Unemployment, 211, 301-303, 394, 1256, 1282; of agricultural labor, 252, 264, 266; caused by mechanization, 399; and crime, 1293; post-World War II, 401, 408, 409, 424, 425, 1010-1011; power over, 788

Unemployment, Negro, 206, 207, 299, 301-303, 525, 754, 799, 806, 1001, 1282; in the North, 295; as a result of discrimination, 998; during war boom, 410

Unemployment Check Census of 1937, 1259

Unemployment compensation, 357, 1281

Unemployment risks, 367n.

Union shop, 405, 407

Union Theological Seminary, Negro member of Board of, 1368

Unionization (*see also* Trade unions): effect of, for Negroes, 401-403, 643; and **equal opportunity**, 384; independent

Negro, 1107; law protecting, 399, 713; of longshoremen, 1097, 1098-1099; in lumber industry, 1095-1096; in the South, 463, 515

Unions: *see* Trade unions

United Automobile, Aircraft and Agricultural Implement Workers' Union, 413

United Automobile Workers' Union, 1121

United Brotherhood of Carpenters and Joiners, 1103

United Cannery, Agricultural, Packing and Allied Workers of America, 262, 263, 1250

United Mine Workers' Union, 402, 1113, 1114, 1297

United Service Organizations, discrimination policy of, 1367

United States Employment Service, 400-401, 412, 416-418, 1087, 1303, 1304, 1307; policy of, 1307-1308

United States Housing Authority, 350-351, 352-353, 378n., 400, 503, 678, 755, 1104-1105; and segregation, 625-626, 627

United States Steel Corporation, 1118

United Steel Workers of America, 402, 1117

United Transport Workers of America, 1107

Unity: cultural, lxx, 1029; of ideals, 3-5; of interest, between capital and labor, 222; of mankind, 115-116; of Negro problem, 73-75, 77

Universal Negro Improvement Association, 747, 748, 812-813

Universities, control of, 718-719

Unskilled labor, 296-297, 395, 410, 788, 1257, 1303

Upper class Negro, 645-647, 690, 693, 702-704, 1387-1388; broader basis for, 697; clothing of, 963; criteria for attaining, 694; dilemma of, 794-797, 921; family background and, 695, 697, 702; and family stability, 931-933; growth of, 651; and leadership, 727-728, 730-731, 732, 733, 767, 804-805; and lower classes, friction of, 703, 729-730, 731, 1395; moral standards of, 931-933, 939, 1425; political confusion in, 703-704; reactions of, to discrimination and segregation, 764-766; "shady," 1391; withdrawal of, from leadership, 1388

Upper class, white, 592-597; as allies of Negroes, 786-788; "America's 60 families," 676n.; and leadership, 715; Southern, dilemma of, 1318

Urban League, liv, 793, 803, 835, 837-842, 843, 854, 1406-1408; effect of World War II on, 1408; functions of,

69 70 71 72 73   12 11 10 9 8 7 6 5 4 3 2 1

Selected titles, revised June, 1967

harper ✦ torchbooks

HUMANITIES AND SOCIAL SCIENCES

American Studies: General

HENRY STEELE COMMAGER, Ed.: The Struggle for Racial Equality TB/1300
EDWARD S. CORWIN: American Constitutional History. △ *Essays edited by Alpheus T. Mason and Gerald Garvey* TB/1136
CARL N. DEGLER, Ed.: Pivotal Interpretations of American History TB/1240, TB/1241
A. S. EISENSTADT, Ed.: The Craft of American History: *Recent Essays in American Historical Writing* Vol. I TB/1255; Vol. II TB/1256
CHARLOTTE P. GILMAN: Women and Economics ‡ TB/3073
OSCAR HANDLIN, Ed.: This Was America: *As Recorded by European Travelers in the Eighteenth, Nineteenth and Twentieth Centuries. Illus.* TB/1119
MARCUS LEE HANSEN: The Atlantic Migration: 1607-1860. *Edited by Arthur M. Schlesinger* TB/1052
MARCUS LEE HANSEN: The Immigrant in American History TB/1120
JOHN HIGHAM, Ed.: The Reconstruction of American History △ TB/1068
ROBERT H. JACKSON: The Supreme Court in the American System of Government TB/1106
JOHN F. KENNEDY: A Nation of Immigrants. △ *Illus.* TB/1118
LEONARD W. LEVY, Ed.: American Constitutional Law TB/1285
LEONARD W. LEVY, Ed.: Judicial Review and the Supreme Court TB/1296
LEONARD W. LEVY: The Law of the Commonwealth and Chief Justice Shaw TB/1309
RALPH BARTON PERRY: Puritanism and Democracy TB/1138
ARNOLD ROSE: The Negro in America: *The Condensed Version of Gunnar Myrdal's An American Dilemma* TB/3048
MAURICE R. STEIN: The Eclipse of Community: *An Interpretation of American Studies* TB/1128
W. LLOYD WARNER: Social Class in America: *The Evaluation of Status* TB/1013

American Studies: Colonial

BERNARD BAILYN, Ed.: The Apologia of Robert Keayne: *Self-Portrait of a Puritan Merchant* TB/1201
BERNARD BAILYN: The New England Merchants in the Seventeenth Century TB/1149
CHARLES GIBSON: Spain in America † TB/3077
LAWRENCE HENRY GIPSON: The Coming of the Revolution: 1763-1775. † *Illus.* TB/3007

PERRY MILLER: Errand Into the Wilderness TB/1139
PERRY MILLER & T. H. JOHNSON, Eds.: The Puritans: *A Sourcebook* Vol. I TB/1093; Vol. II TB/1094
EDMUND S. MORGAN, Ed.: The Diary of Michael Wigglesworth, 1653-1657: *The Conscience of a Puritan* TB/1228
EDMUND S. MORGAN: The Puritan Family: *Religion and Domestic Relations in Seventeenth-Century New England* TB/1227
RICHARD B. MORRIS: Government and Labor in Early America TB/1244
KENNETH B. MURDOCK: Literature and Theology in Colonial New England TB/99
JOHN P. ROCHE: Origins of American Political Thought: *Selected Readings* TB/1301
JOHN SMITH: Captain John Smith's America: *Selections from His Writings. Ed. with Intro. by John Lankford* TB/3078
LOUIS B. WRIGHT: The Cultural Life of the American Colonies: 1607-1763. † *Illus.* TB/3005

American Studies: From the Revolution to 1860

JOHN R. ALDEN: The American Revolution: 1775-1783. † *Illus.* TB/3011
RAY A. BILLINGTON: The Far Western Frontier: 1830-1860. † *Illus.* TB/3012
EDMUND BURKE: On the American Revolution. ‡ *Edited by Elliott Robert Barkan* TB/3068
WHITNEY R. CROSS: The Burned-Over District: *The Social and Intellectual History of Enthusiastic Religion in Western New York, 1800-1850* TB/1242
GEORGE DANGERFIELD: The Awakening of American Nationalism: 1815-1828. † *Illus.* TB/3061
CLEMENT EATON: The Freedom-of-Thought Struggle in the Old South. *Revised and Enlarged. Illus.* TB/1150
CLEMENT EATON: The Growth of Southern Civilization: 1790-1860. † *Illus.* TB/3040
LOUIS FILLER: The Crusade Against Slavery: 1830-1860. † *Illus.* TB/3029
WILLIAM W. FREEHLING, Ed.: The Nullification Era: *A Documentary Record* ‡ TB/3079
FELIX GILBERT: The Beginnings of American Foreign Policy: *To the Farewell Address* TB/1200
FRANCIS GRIERSON: The Valley of Shadows: *The Coming of the Civil War in Lincoln's Midwest: A Contemporary Account* TB/1246
ALEXANDER HAMILTON: The Reports of Alexander Hamilton. ‡ *Edited by Jacob E. Cooke* TB/3060
JAMES MADISON: The Forging of American Federalism: *Selected Writings of James Madison. Edited by Saul K. Padover* TB/1126
BERNARD MAYO: Myths and Men: *Patrick Henry, George Washington, Thomas Jefferson* TB/1108

† The New American Nation Series, edited by Henry Steele Commager and Richard B. Morris.
‡ American Perspectives series, edited by Bernard Wishy and William E. Leuchtenburg.
* The Rise of Modern Europe series, edited by William L. Langer.
** History of Europe series, edited by J. H. Plumb.
¶ Researches in the Social, Cultural and Behavioral Sciences, edited by Benjamin Nelson.
§ The Library of Religion and Culture, edited by Benjamin Nelson.
Σ Harper Modern Science Series, edited by James R. Newman.
○ Not for sale in Canada.
△ Not for sale in the U. K.

3

5

Christianity: The Roman and Eastern Traditions

Oriental Religions: Far Eastern, Near Eastern

Philosophy of Religion

Religion, Culture & Society

NATURAL SCIENCES AND MATHEMATICS

Biological Sciences

10